KODANSHA
ENCYCLOPEDIA OF
JAPAN

Distributors
JAPAN: KODANSHA LTD., Tokyo.
OVERSEAS: KODANSHA INTERNATIONAL LTD., Tokyo.
  U.S.A., Mexico, Central America, and South America: KODANSHA INTERNATIONAL/USA LTD.
   through HARPER & ROW, PUBLISHERS, INC., New York.
  Canada: FITZHENRY & WHITESIDE LTD., Ontario.
  U.K., Europe, the Middle East, and Africa: INTERNATIONAL BOOK DISTRIBUTORS LTD.,
   Hemel Hempstead, Herts., England.
  Australia and New Zealand: HARPER & ROW (AUSTRALASIA) PTY. LTD., Artarmon, N.S.W.
  Asia: TOPPAN COMPANY (S) PTE. LTD., Singapore.

Published by Kodansha Ltd., 12-21, Otowa 2-chome, Bunkyo-ku, Tokyo 112 and Kodansha
International/USA Ltd., 10 East 53rd Street, New York, New York 10022.
Copyright © 1983 by Kodansha Ltd.
All rights reserved.
Printed in Japan.
First edition, 1983.

LCC 83-80778
ISBN 0-87011-623-1 (Volume 3)
ISBN 0-87011-620-7 (Set)
ISBN 4-06-144533-2 (0) (in Japan)

Library of Congress Cataloging in Publication Data
Main entry under title:

Kodansha encyclopedia of Japan.

  Includes index.
  1. Japan—Dictionaries and encyclopedias. I. Title:
Encyclopedia of Japan.
DS805.K633 1983   952'.003'21   83-80778
ISBN 0-87011-620-7 (U.S.)

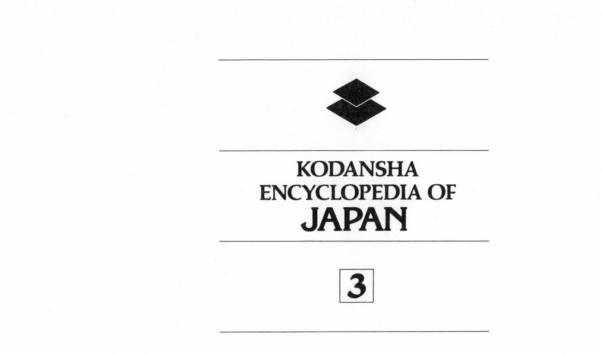

KODANSHA
ENCYCLOPEDIA OF
JAPAN

3

KODANSHA

G

gagaku

Traditional music of the Japanese imperial court. Derived from the Chinese word *yayue (ya-yüeh)*, which denotes ancient ritual music played by a large orchestra of stone chimes, bronze bells, flutes, drums, and numerous other instruments, the term was applied in both Japan and Korea to all of the music of the court.

Repertoire —— *Gagaku* comprises three main bodies of music: *tōgaku*, music said to be in the style of the Tang (T'ang) period (7th–10th centuries) of China; *komagaku*, a music style said to have been introduced from ancient Korea; and finally, all of the many forms of native Japanese music associated with rituals of the Shintō religion.

Tōgaku comprises the largest part of the repertoire and includes well over 100 compositions. These can be performed as instrumental concert pieces, called *kangen* ("winds and strings") or as dance pieces, in which case the performance is referred to as *bugaku* ("dance music"). *Komagaku* includes a smaller number of compositions which are always performed as *bugaku*.

The *tōgaku* and *komagaku* repertoires exist in written Japanese notation, a different method of notation being required for each instrument of the ensemble. According to tradition, *tōgaku* is said to include not only compositions from Tang China, but a number of compositions from India, Southeast Asia, and Central Asia. Today the exact origins of each *tōgaku* composition are not clear, since compositions from many parts of Asia were already combined into the *tōgaku* style at the time of the introduction of this music into Japan from China. Subsequently new compositions in the *tōgaku* style were added by Japanese composers.

Komagaku is thought to include compositions from each of the three Korean kingdoms of ancient times: Silla, Koguryō, and Paekche. Japanese compositions in the *komagaku* genre were even more numerous than in *tōgaku*.

The oldest and most carefully preserved of the various forms of Shintō ritual music and dance used in the imperial court is the KA-GURA, formally called *mikagura* (court *kagura*) in order to distinguish it from the various folk forms of Shintō music which are also called *kagura*. Besides the *mikagura*, this group of Shintō ritual songs and dances includes the Yamato *uta*, Azuma *asobi*, and Kume *uta*. The *mikagura* is central to the style, and the other three forms are in some way modeled on it. All are thought of as sacred ritual offerings of music and dance intended to please and pacify Shintō deities.

Also included in the *gagaku* repertoire are SAIBARA and *rōei*, two forms musically related to *tōgaku*. *Saibara* originated as a body of regional Japanese folk songs which were brought to the capital and reset in an elegant court style during the Heian period (794–1185). *Rōei* lyrics are based on Chinese poetic forms. Today, only a small number of *saibara* and *rōei* compositions continue to be performed by court musicians.

History —— Something akin to the *kagura* songs and dances existed before the beginning of formal diplomatic contacts with the courts of Tang and Korea, when mainland forms of music were introduced into Japan. During the Nara period (710–794), a great number of these styles of music existed, each with its own special musicians, dancers, and types of instruments. The musicians and dancers responsible for the native Japanese rituals were grouped together into the Ōuta-dokoro (Bureau of Music). Sometime during the early part of the Heian period, the various styles of foreign music were combined into the two categories, *tōgaku* and *komagaku*. During the Heian period, *gagaku* was performed both by the court nobles and by hereditary guilds of professional musicians. The TALE OF GENJI *(Genji monogatari)* gives a rich and detailed picture of how this music and dance functioned as an integral part of the life of nobles of the period.

With the fall of the noble classes in the early part of the Kamakura period (1185–1333), the popularity of *gagaku* waned. It was maintained by guilds and the remaining nobles, each in relative isolation from the other. The musicians were divided into three groups and were in service in Kyōto, Nara, and Ōsaka. From this time until the mid-19th century, the *gagaku* tradition continued without the support of regular court rituals, banquets, and other occasions requiring music and dance. The performance method for several compositions was lost forever.

With the Meiji Restoration of 1868 and the subsequent relocation of the Imperial Palace in Tōkyō, the three groups were brought together as the official musicians of the newly established state. Although their numbers had dwindled significantly over the centuries since the end of the Heian period, there now began a period of renewed interest and activity in *gagaku* which has continued to the present day.

The musicians of the Imperial Palace Music Department are still largely the direct descendants of the members of the first guilds that performed this music in Japan during the 8th century. They are trained thoroughly for several years in the performance of the songs and dances of the tradition. Each musician is expected to have learned and memorized the entire repertoire on one of the wind instruments, and in addition, to have learned one of the string instruments, one form of dance, and the entire song and dance repertoire of the sacred Shintō rituals. The musicians perform all the ritual music and dances required by the court and also give regular public *gagaku* concerts.

Bugaku —— The dance repertoire, *bugaku*, is divided into two groups, dance of the left (*sahō no mai*) and dance of the right (*uhō samai no mai* or *umai*), referring to the two sides of the Imperial Presence. The left dance uses music of the *tōgaku* category and the right dance uses *komagaku* along with a few compositions specially adapted from the *tōgaku* repertoire. Cutting across the division into left and right are two different methods of classifying the dances according to form and style. One set of classifications, *bu no mai* (military dance) and *bun no mai* (civil dance), was borrowed from the ancient Chinese ritual dances. The civil dance is also referred to as *hira-mai* (level or even dances), as opposed to *hashiri-mai* (running dances), a term which refers to a group of solo masked dances of strong character making use of relatively rapid movements. In addition, a few dances from all classifications of the repertoire are special variant forms called *dōbu* which are danced by children.

The richly embroidered and complexly woven silk costumes worn by the dancers represent the civil or military dress of the Heian court. The costumes of *sahō no mai* tend to be red while those of *uhō no mai* are generally blue or green, which are the colors appropriate to the court ranks associated with those two traditions. The musicians also wear richly embroidered silk robes of many colors when accompanying the dance. For *kangen*, the chamber music performance, the musicians wear simpler, almost austere silk robes of dark rust brown into which green silk vertical threads have been woven, giving them an iridescent sheen as they move. For the performance of the sacred Shintō ritual most of the musicians wear white robes in the style of Heian courtiers, or may use pure red or blue robes, depending on the particular form of dance being performed. See also THEATRICAL COSTUMES.

Instruments —— The instruments used in performances of *gagaku* are Japanese modifications of those used in the Tang court ensembles. The instrumentation is determined by the type of music being performed: Shintō ritual, *komagaku*, or *tōgaku*, the latter in either *kangen* or *bugaku* form. A small double-reed pipe similar to an oboe or shawm, called the HICHIRIKI, is used in all the instrumental ensembles. Three different types of flute are used, the *kagurabue* generally for the Shintō rituals, the *komabue* for *komagaku*, and the *ryūteki* or dragon flute for *tōgaku*. In addition to these wind instruments, *tōgaku* uses a small mouth organ of 17 bamboo pipes called the SHŌ, which plays tone clusters of five or six notes. Since the reeds vibrate either when the performer inhales or exhales, these rich, sweet harmonies permeate the sound of *tōgaku* performances.

Tōgaku and *komagaku* each use three percussion instruments, two of which are common to both types of music. These are a hanging TAIKO or large drum, which plays the main strong beat in each phrase, often highlighted with a few additional strokes, and the *shōko,* a small bronze gong whose dry metallic tone complements the dark sound of the *taiko.* To stabilize the slow rhythms and widely spaced strokes of the *taiko* and *shōko,* a smaller drum is used to subdivide the patterns. In *komagaku,* this is a small hourglass drum called *san no tsuzumi,* which is played with a single stick (see TSUZUMI). The *kakko,* a small drum played with two sticks and using both single strokes and slow rolls, is used in *tōgaku.* In Shintō vocal music the only percussion instrument is a pair of wooden clappers *(shakubyōshi)* played by the main singer of the group, or each of the main singers when there are the usual two groups of singers.

Stringed instruments are no longer used in the *tōgaku* dance repertoire or in *komagaku.* There are two stringed instruments used in the *kangen,* or chamber music setting of *tōgaku:* the *gakusō,* which is usually called by its common name, KOTO, and the BIWA. The *gakusō* is a 13-stringed zither with individual movable bridges under each string. The strings are plucked with the fingers of the right hand, to which three small leather rings with bamboo plectra have been attached. The *biwa* is a four-string lute, the strings of which are struck with a wooden plectrum. Like the *gakusō,* it was also used in the older Chinese court ensembles. Only one stringed instrument is used in Shintō music. This instrument, the *wagon,* has six strings and is struck with a short plectrum producing a dry sound against the silk strings.

Rōei and *saibara* both use the wind instruments of the *tōgaku* ensemble to accompany the voices. The rhythm is delineated by *shakubyōshi,* similar to those clappers used in the Shintō music. *Saibara* also uses strings, the *koto* and *biwa.*

The *tōgaku kangen* ensemble is the most texturally varied of all the *gagaku* styles. The stringed instruments add another layer of sound to those of the wind instruments and the three percussion instruments. The strings provide an abstracted version of the melody of the winds, but in a fixed pattern which synchronizes with the percussion patterns and thus links together the melodic and rhythmic elements of the ensemble. See MUSICAL INSTRUMENTS.

Theory and Formal Structure —— The main melody of each composition is carried by the winds and the singing voices in the Shintō music. *Gagaku* melodies are generally very slow in tempo, and in longer compositions may have an elaborate phrase structure. The main point of reference for these long, slow melodies lies in the use of regular and fixed percussion patterns which are repeated throughout each composition. The melodies sometimes synchronize with the percussion patterns and at other times, particularly in the longer compositions, may drift away from the rhythmic structure by the use of phrases of irregular length, but they always return to a synchronous relation to the rhythmic pattern at the end of the composition.

In terms of theoretical and formal structure, the Shintō repertoire can be thought of as the simplest of the three *gagaku* categories and *tōgaku* as the most complex, with *komagaku* falling somewhere between the two.

The Shintō ritual music, with the *kagura* songs as the core of its repertoire, is first and foremost a body of pure songs. The texts are of prime importance and thus also the human voice. The instruments are used to set the pitch for the singers, to play short preludes before certain songs, and to accompany the singers and strengthen the melodic line. The melody for the Shintō ritual music is not based on any theoretical scale or system but is instead developed as a natural formalization of a unique and characteristic vocal style and a typical Japanese melodic pattern.

The *komagaku* system combines some elements of the formalized Chinese theoretical modal system with a melody type which in certain respects resembles the type used in the Shintō music. Three mode types, or *chōshi,* are used in *komagaku: koma ichikotsuchō, koma sōjō,* and *koma hyōjō.* Almost the entire *komagaku* repertoire is set in the first two of these.

Tōgaku has the most complex formal structure and theoretical system of the three types of *gagaku,* and retains more of the elements of ancient Chinese musical theory than any other music tradition in Japan. In theory, the Chinese generated sets of tones and scales from the superimposition of a number of consecutive perfect fifths. After twelve such consecutive fifths the thirteenth tone would not be exactly the same as the first, but would begin a new series of twelve pitches. In practice most ensembles were set within one se-

Gagaku

Imperial Palace musicians performing *tōgaku*-style music at the National Theater. Front row (left to right): bronze gong *(shōko),* large drum *(taiko),* and small drum *(kakko).* Middle row: two zithers *(koto)* and two lutes *(biwa).* Back row: three flutes *(ryūteki),* three pipes *(hichiriki),* and three mouth organs *(shō).*

ries of twelve tones. Each pitch within such a twelve-tone system could become the initial pitch for a different seven-note scale. Furthermore, any one series of seven tones could provide different modes, known as *chōshi* in Japanese, by having one of the five main tones of the scale serve as a beginning tone, thus permitting five different possible modes within each seven-tone scale. By then changing to different seven-tone scales within the same twelve-tone system, a new set of five modes could be obtained. Although the full potential of this system seems never to have been put into practice, a rather rich modal system was, in fact, used. The *tōgaku* system as it survives today has been considerably simplified from the original Tang system of 28 modes, and is generally said to include only 6 modes: *ichikotsuchō, hyōjō, sōjō, ōshikichō, banshikichō,* and *taishikichō.* However, it is in reality somewhat more complex, since *ichikotsuchō, ōshikichō, banshikichō,* and *taishikichō* each contain compositions in additional modes. *Saibara* and *rōei* share the *tōgaku* modal system.

The modes are an important element in the full appreciation of *gagaku.* They are not merely scales or transpositions of scales. Each has its own special character and color, the result of a combination of specific ornaments, tunings, and ranges unique to the particular mode. In performance the mode must first be established. In *komagaku* and *tōgaku* there are short preludes in free rhythm called *netori* which are first performed. In the performance of *bugaku* there is frequent use of longer and more complex introductions which are called, like the modes themselves, *chōshi.*

The compositions of the *tōgaku* repertoire are divided by length into three categories, *shōkyoku* or short pieces, *chūkyoku* or medium-length pieces, and *taikyoku* or great pieces, which are in fact suites of several compositions and interludes played consecutively as a unit. In addition, each composition can belong to a specific rhythmic type, either free rhythm, or a metered four beats to a rhythmic unit, eight beats to a rhythmic unit, or a combination of two plus four beats or two plus three beats. They are then combined into different types of rhythmic phrases of cycles, usually with four or eight rhythmic units to a cycle. In each of these combinations there are a number of specific percussion patterns which are required for the particular composition being played. Over these rhythm structures floats the melody of the piece, with all of the inherent definitions of the *chōshi,* creating an elegant, rich, and complex texture. The entire repertoire is played at tempos which, although varied, all seem very slow when compared to Western music or even to other forms of Japanese music. The intricacies of form in *gagaku* therefore remain elusive to all but the experienced or the very patient.

■——Robert Garfias, "The Sacred Mikagura of the Japanese Imperial Court," *Selected Reports,* Institute of Ethnomusicology, University of California at Los Angeles 1.2 (1975). Robert Garfias, *The Music of a Thousand Autumns* (1976). Eta Harich-Schneider, *The Rhythmic Pattern in Gagaku and Bugaku* (1954). Eta Harich-Schneider, *A History of Japanese Music* (1973). Carl Wolz, *Bugaku, Japanese Court Dance* (1971). *Robert* GARFIAS

Gagen shūran

A classical Japanese-language dictionary compiled toward the close of the Edo period (1600–1868) by ISHIKAWA MASAMOCHI, a learned KOKUGAKU (National Learning) scholar and KYŌKA ("mad verse") poet. A typical example of an early dictionary, the *Gagen shūran* consists of 50 fascicles in 21 volumes. It mainly contains the vocabulary of Heian-period (794–1185) classical literature arranged in traditional *iroha* alphabet order along with abundant examples of word usage and the sources quoted. It was compiled as a standard reference for use in writing classical-style Japanese and remains a valuable research tool for the study of ancient Japanese. Publication began in 1826 but was discontinued halfway through; the unpublished remainder has been handed down in manuscript form. Copies presently in circulation are of the enlarged 1887 edition with a supplement by Nakajima Hirotari (1792–1864).　　*Uwano Zendō*

gaijin → foreigners in Japan

gaikoku bugyō

(commissioner of foreign affairs). A short-lived (1858–68) government post created by the Tokugawa shogunate to oversee diplomatic relations. Forced in 1858 to sign the ANSEI COMMERCIAL TREATIES with the United States, the Netherlands, Russia, Britain, and France, the shogunate replaced its coastal defense officers (*kaibōgakari*), whose duties were mainly military, with the *gaikoku bugyō*, who received diplomatic missions and performed related functions. Initially, five direct shogunal vassals (HATAMOTO) were selected to serve on a monthly rotating basis; later the number varied. The commissioners were responsible to the senior councillors (*rōjū*) and maintained a bureaucratic staff that included translators and other specialists. After 1862 their subordinates also included assistant commissioners of foreign affairs (*gaikoku bugyō nami*). The commissioners' responsibilities were reduced to mere paperwork, however, when the *rōjū* themselves took direct control of diplomacy in 1867, creating the new posts of director of foreign affairs (*gaikoku jimu sōsai*) and the subordinate commissioner-general of foreign affairs (*gaikoku sōbugyō*). All of these posts were abolished the following year after the fall of the shogunate.

gaikoku hōjin

(foreign juristic person). A juristic person (HŌJIN) established under the provisions of the law of a foreign country. Only the existence of states, administrative divisions of states, and trading companies as foreign juristic persons is recognized under the Japanese CIVIL CODE. However, the code does provide that other foreign juristic persons can be recognized, provided that they have been established under the provisions of Japanese laws or treaties. The code also provides that foreign juristic persons enjoy the same rights as those of the same classes of Japanese juristic persons, provided that they are not rights which aliens, as individuals, cannot enjoy and that there are no provisions to the contrary in laws or treaties. In addition to the provisions in the Civil Code, which are basic, the COMMERCIAL CODE contains a chapter relating to foreign companies and their operations in Japan as juristic persons (Civil Code, art. 36).　　*John M. Maki*

gaikokujin gakkō

(schools for foreigners). A term used in Japanese educational circles to refer to two types of schools, both of which are outside the regular school system and both of which are classified legally as MISCELLANEOUS SCHOOLS (*kakushu gakkō*). One type is the schools on the primary and secondary level set up by foreigners in Japan to educate their children in their own languages and cultures. A certain number of Japanese students also attend these schools. The other type consists of schools on various levels established by Japanese to teach the Japanese language to foreigners. Nationwide there are over 100 *gaikokujin gakkō*.　　*Takakura Shō*

Gaikokusen Uchiharai Rei

(Order for the Repelling of Foreign Ships). Also known as Ikokusen Uchiharai Rei. Order issued in 1825 embodying the policy of the Tokugawa shogunate toward foreign ships. The shogunate had maintained a NATIONAL SECLUSION policy since 1639, but toward the end of the 18th century an increasing number of foreign ships began to appear in Japanese waters. In particular, Russian ships appeared with alarming frequency near Ezo (now Hokkaidō), demanding trade. There ensued a major political debate centering on the seclusion policy, and in 1791 the shogunate issued a new order ruling that whenever a foreign ship drifted ashore or approached the coast, the circumstances should be investigated and the ship and crew detained and readied for eventual passage to Nagasaki, pending shogunal instructions. In 1806, however, as a result of negotiations with the Russian envoy Nikolai Petrovich REZANOV, who came to Japan in 1804, the 1791 order was revised to provide that foreign ships entering Japanese waters would be peacefully made to leave and that those that drifted ashore or were damaged would be given firewood, water, and food and then be requested to leave. The 1806 order was maintained in spite of the PHAETON INCIDENT of 1808, as well as the violence inflicted by Rezanov's crew on the Japanese residents of Sakhalin and Etorofu between 1806 and 1807.

At the beginning of the 19th century English and American whaling ships began to appear in coastal waters. When an English whaler in search of firewood, water, and food entered the port of Uraga near Edo (now Tōkyō) in 1822, troops from several nearby domains were mobilized by the commissioner (*bugyō*) of Uraga, and the ship was made to leave after being supplied with provisions. This and similar events necessitating mobilization of armies imposed heavy burdens on the financially hard-pressed domains. The shogunate had just begun to review its policy when in 1824 another incidence of violence, by an English whaling ship, occurred in Satsuma (now part of Kagoshima Prefecture). Chastened, the shogunate issued a new order in the following year, the Gaikokusen Uchiharai Rei, prescribing that all foreign ships were to be repelled at once. The shogunate seems not to have worried about the practical consequences of such an order but issued it merely to prevent domestic turmoil; if the danger of international conflict became real enough, it could revoke the order. This danger arose in 1837, when the *Morrison*, an American merchant ship attempting to enter Uraga, was bombarded and forced to withdraw. The MORRISON INCIDENT, as well as the news of China's defeat in the Opium War (1839–42), prompted the shogunate to reassess its seclusion policy. In 1842 the shogunate revoked the *uchiharai* order and replaced it with the SHINSUI KYŌYO REI (Order for the Provision of Firewood and Water).　　*Numata Satoshi*

Gaimushō → Ministry of Foreign Affairs

Gakken Co, Ltd

(Gakushū Kenkyūsha). The largest general and educational publishing company in Japan. Established by Furuoka Hideto in April 1946. When its first publication of an educational magazine was rejected by wholesale distributors, Furuoka organized his own sales network and expanded the business. Today, in addition to educational magazines, Gakken publishes 27 other types of magazines, as well as general books and dictionaries. It also produces and sells educational films, toys, and other teaching aids.　　*Kobayashi Kazuhiro*

gakkōrei → school orders

gakubatsu

(academic clique or alumni clique). A mutual support group formed of graduates of the same school. *Gakubatsu*, like other BATSU or cliques in Japan, are characterized by mutual aid and strong "in-group" feelings. They are particularly common in Japanese corporations and government bureaucracies.

Most universities and colleges have alumni associations (*dōsōkai*) to which all graduates automatically belong. These associations serve to bring alumni together and facilitate the formation of *gakubatsu* within large corporations and government bureaus. When employment openings occur or opportunities for advancement arise, members of the same alumni group will receive preferential treatment; as the clique grows, its influence within the work organization is extended.

The development of *gakubatsu* is closely linked to the history of Japanese modernization. During the Meiji period (1868–1912), the government placed great importance on the school system as a modernizing institution. Tōkyō University and a network of higher educational facilties were established to produce high-level bureaucrats and scholars and to develop business, educational, and military leaders. Great numbers of graduates from these institutions took posts in government or large enterprises, where they received protection and special privileges and were guaranteed a rapid climb up the social ladder. Graduates of a particular school tended to monopolize positions in a certain field, leading to competition with graduates of the private universities established in the ensuing years. This competition spurred the formation of new gakubatsu.

Modernization was accompanied by the development of bureaucracy and by specialization in certain fields. Since bureaucracy is characterized by formalistic fairness, the system tended to evaluate its members by educational background. Emphasis was placed on seniority and academic background more than on ability, and in some fields graduation from a certain top-level school became a basic qualification for employment. This led to the marked development of cliques within government and industry.

In order to strengthen harmony and cooperation within the group, standards recognized by all members, such as the year of graduation, become important in determining the social ranking of members. From this arise the important distinctions of SEMPAI-KŌHAI (senior-junior), teacher and disciple, and school classmate. The gakubatsu also contains elements of GIRI AND NINJŌ relations, with their complex of favors and indebtedness. Such relations exhibit characteristics of what some scholars consider the rational gesellschaft-type of social group, in that mutual aid and the acquiescence of juniors can be unconditionally expected and that members calculate the risks and rewards of their participation in the group. However, the characteristics of the affective gemeinschaft-type of social group predominate, in that the clique functions on solidaristic and nonrational linkages.

Some have contended that the prevalence of gakubatsu have transformed Japanese society into a "degree-ocracy" (GAKUREKI SHAKAI), where a person's worth is measured by academic degree and school. This conceptualization has both a vertical and horizontal axis. The vertical axis has as its standard the level of schooling an individual has completed; the person with the highest education will receive unconditional, favored treatment. On the horizontal axis, individuals have completed the same level of schooling, but those graduating from the most prestigious and influential schools will receive preferential treatment. In a social framework based on this system, those in favorable positions join together to preserve and expand their privileges, while those less favored join in opposition.

The gakubatsu tends to foster feelings of superiority among members of the group while ignoring the abilities of those not belonging to a leading academic clique. It provides emotional support to members of the group, but it also breeds factionalism and inefficiency through exclusiveness. There are some indications that ability is beginning to take precedence over background in Japanese society, but the gakubatsu still exert a powerful influence.
📖 ——Shimbori Michiya, Nihon no daigaku kyōju shijō: Gakubatsu no kenkyū (1965).   SHIMBORI Michiya

Gakumon no susume

(An Encouragement of Learning). A series of pamphlets intended as an elementary-school text and reader for the general public by FUKUZAWA YUKICHI, the preeminent thinker of the so-called Meiji Enlightenment, the movement to modernize Japan on the Western model. The series developed from an address given at the opening of a school in Fukuzawa's native domain, Nakatsu (now part of Ōita Prefecture), in 1871. After the speech was published in February 1872, it enjoyed such brisk sales that over 200,000 copies of the first pamphlet had been sold by 1880. This reception led the author to issue other tracts on loosely related issues under the same general title until there were 17 in all, the last appearing in November 1876. The later pamphlets were not as popular as the first, which enjoyed wide usage as an ethics text; nevertheless, the total circulation was over 1 million by 1890, making the series one of the best selling and most influential works of the early Meiji period (1868–1912).

The first pamphlet began with Fukuzawa's famous assertion that "heaven never created a man above another man nor a man below another man." By this Fukuzawa meant his readers to understand that in Meiji society, where hereditary rank no longer prevailed, wealth and honor would result only from diligence and study. In discussing the proper objects of this effort, Fukuzawa argued that traditional education and customs were inadequate for the task of strengthening Japan against the West, and that Western learning and

an independent spirit of rationality were appropriate for the new age.

Another major concern of Gakumon no susume was the threat to political stability raised by those who felt wronged by the changes of the Meiji period. Fukuzawa met this issue in the first pamphlet by arguing that those who felt hurt had only themselves to blame for their poverty and low rank. Individual study and hard work were the answers, not political action or violence.

Against a background of samurai resentment, rebellion, and political agitation, largely stemming from reductions in samurai privileges and income, Fukuzawa raised this same issue in subsequent pamphlets. He articulated a "social contract" theory of government, which argued that because of the "contractual" relation between people and government, the people must uphold their part of the "contract" even if they are inconvenienced by government actions. This argument drew heavily upon the writings of Francis Wayland (1796–1865), president of Brown University and author of a popular textbook, The Elements of Moral Science (1835). To this assertion ideologues of the FREEDOM AND PEOPLE'S RIGHTS MOVEMENT raised the objection that a nonrepresentative government was tyrannical and ought to be opposed. Fukuzawa countered by contending that the way to achieve change was through martyrdom, not ineffective individual action or morally unjustifiable rebellion. This, too, he took virtually verbatim from Wayland.

Despite its conservative emphasis, Gakumon no susume was banned as a textbook in 1881 as part of a government reaction to the people's rights movement and to Western influence in general. After 1890 publication of Gakumon no susume ceased.
📖 ——Fukuzawa Yukichi, Gakumon no susume (1872–76), tr David A. Dilworth and Umeyo Hirano as An Encouragement of Learning (1969). Fukuzawa Yukichi, Fukuō jiden (1899), tr Eiichi Kiyooka as The Autobiography of Fukuzawa Yukichi (1934, repr 1960). Itō Masao, Fukuzawa Yukichi ronkō (1969). Earl H. Kinmonth, "Fukuzawa Reconsidered: Gakumon no susume and its Audience," Journal of Asian Studies 37.4 (1978).

Gakuō Zōkyū (fl ca 1482–ca 1514)

Zen monk-painter identified in a contemporary monk's diary as a disciple of SHŪBUN, the influential master painter of the SHŌKOKUJI Zen temple in Kyōto. Associated with Ise Province (now part of Mie Prefecture), where many of his paintings were preserved, Gakuō was the most faithful follower of Shūbun's style of ink landscape painting. Gakuō's assimilation of typical compositional formulae from Shūbun led many later historians to confuse his paintings with those of his teacher. Although few details are known concerning Gakuō's biography, his paintings survive in relatively large numbers and record his artistic career more completely than those of many of his contemporaries. His close association with Ryōan Keigo (1425–1514), an abbot of the Tōfukuji Zen temple in Kyōto, is documented by numerous inscriptions by this eminent monk on Gakuō's paintings from the 1480s to 1514 (some of the inscriptions are dated).

Included among Gakuō's extant paintings are a few figure subjects such as the bodhisattva KANNON in a bamboo grove and Ling Zhao (Ling Chao), the Chinese paragon of filial piety. The majority of his paintings are, however, landscapes. Notable among these are several depicting the Eight Views of Xiao (Hsiao) and Xiang (Hsiang), a Chinese subject, called SHŌSHŌ HAKKEI in Japanese, that became a prominent theme of Japanese ink landscape painting during the late 15th century. Gakuō's Xiao–Xiang paintings survive in greater numbers than works on this theme by other 15th-century artists, and they clearly reveal his close study of model paintings in the style of the Song (Sung) dynasty (960–1279) Chinese painter, Xia Gui (Hsia Kuei; fl ca 1195–1224).

The evolution of Gakuō's own painting style demonstrates his gradual assimilation and integration of ideas from both Shūbun and Chinese model paintings. From the example of Xia Gui he evolved a typical method of defining mountains and rocks with sharp textural strokes utilizing contrasting tones of ink. He shared with his late-15th-century contemporaries an interest in more unified articulation of solid forms, but throughout his career he maintained a concern for the suggestive, spiritual quality of space that was the hallmark of the mid-15th-century masterpieces attributed to Shūbun. Gakuō's painting presents a striking contrast to the contemporary work of SESSHŪ TŌYŌ, who introduced to Japanese painting a highly rational approach to the definition of space in landscape, sacrificing evocative atmosphere to a structurally logical articulation of solid forms. See also INK PAINTING.

——Richard Stanley-Baker, "Gakuo's Eight Views of Hsiao and Hsiang," *Oriental Art* 20.3 (Autumn 1974). Tanaka Ichimatsu, "Gakuō Zōkyō no shiteki tachiba," in *Nihon kaigaishi ronshū* (1966).

Ann YONEMURA

gakureki shakai

("education-record society"). Term used in Japan from the 1960s to refer to the great emphasis the Japanese place on a person's educational background. In Japan an individual's social and occupational status is generally considered to be determined not only by the level of education completed, but also by the rank and prestige of the particular universities attended. Factors such as class, race, religion, and personal wealth, which are important determinants of social status in other societies, are not quite as significant in Japan because of the country's high level of homogeneity and lack of extreme inequalities in the distribution of wealth. A person's educational career, on the other hand, provides a convenient determinant of status. Since the 1970s, with more than 90 percent of the students who complete their nine years of compulsory education going on to high school, and almost 40 percent of those of college age attending institutions of higher learning, the status distinctions among schools have become increasingly pronounced. As a result, the competition to gain entrance to the most prestigious schools has intensified markedly. See ENTRANCE EXAMINATIONS; CRAM SCHOOLS.

USHIOGI Morikazu

Gakuren Incident → Kyōto University Incident

Gakusei → Education Order of 1872

Gakushūin University

(Gakushūin Daigaku). A private university located in Toshima Ward, Tōkyō. A forerunner of the present institution was the Gakushūjo, an academy for the children of court nobles established in Kyōto in 1847, but its immediate predecessor was the Gakushūin, opened in 1877 in Tōkyō under the auspices of the Kazoku Kaikan (Peers' Hall). In 1884 the school was put under the direct jurisdiction of the Ministry of the Imperial Household (Kunaishō), acquiring the status of a government institution. The school remained an educational institution for children of the imperial family and the nobility and was known as the Peers' School until after World War II, when the peerage system was abolished. In 1947 it became a private school open to the general public. It maintains faculties of law, economics, letters, and science, and is known for its Institute of Oriental Studies. Enrollment was 6,125 in 1980.

Gamagōri

City in southeastern Aichi Prefecture, central Honshū, on Atsumi Bay. Long known for its cotton cloth (Mikawa *momen*) and hemp nets, Gamagōri has a port with facilities for freighters. Mandarin oranges are cultivated on nearby mountain slopes. The city is situated within the Mikawa Bay Quasi-National Park; Miya and Nishiura Hot Spring and Takeshima, an island connected to the mainland, are favorite tourist sites. Pop: 85,294.

gambaru

(to persist, to hang on, to do one's best). An important word in Japanese interpersonal relationships. Probably derived from *ga o haru* (to be self-willed), the word originally had the negative connotation of asserting oneself against group decisions and norms. Since the 1930s, however, *gambaru* has become a positive word, commonly used to exhort enthusiasm and hard work, usually toward a group objective. For example, when a village youth, on leaving for a new job in the city, promises to his friends, parents, and teachers that he will *gambaru*, the implication is that he will try not to disappoint them. The word is also used among members of a group to encourage each other in cooperative activities, often in the imperative form *gambare*. The term connotes high achievement motivation and orientation to group harmony.

——Tada Michitarō, *Shigusa no Nihon bunka* (1972).

Hiroshi WAGATSUMA

gambling

(*tobaku* or *bakuchi*). Today, all forms of gambling other than those specifically recognized by law, such as horse, bicycle, or powerboat racing, and certain lotteries (*takarakuji*), are prohibited in Japan.

Among the many importations from China in the 6th century was a board game resembling backgammon called *sugoroku*. In this game, pieces were advanced by rolls of a die. Often, items like food were wagered. When Japan started to mint copper coins in the early 8th century, people found it more interesting to bet money on the outcome of the game. Soon, *sugoroku* and other dice games, as well as simpler forms of gambling like flipping coins, gained great popularity in the Nara capital and spread to other areas of Japan. At times, the central government issued edicts prohibiting *sugoroku* and other dice games, but the spread of gambling continued to parallel the developing money economy.

In the 16th century, when Europeans began arriving in Japan, the Japanese became familiar with various aspects of Western culture, including Christianity, through the Dutch and the Portuguese. At this time, many words of Portuguese origin such as *tabako* (tobacco) and *birōdo* (velvet) became part of the Japanese language. *Carta*, the Portuguese word for "playing card," was adopted as *karuta* and card games became popular in the large cities.

Early Japanese playing cards consisted of 48 illustrated cards divided into four suits. Various games were developed using all the possible combinations of numbers, elements of the Japanese KANA syllabary, and pictures. As card playing grew in popularity, so did gambling. Gambling was often prohibited by law, but as each type of game was banned, another replaced it. Thus, when the Tenshō *karuta* game (in which cards were matched according to the 12 months of the year) was prohibited, a game called *kabufuda* (played like the Western twenty-one) took its place. When it too was banned, such games as *garafuda* (with cards matched to numbers, letters, or pictures on pieces shaken out of a bamboo tube) developed.

At the end of the 18th century, a card game called *hanakaruta* (flower cards) made its appearance. In this game the cards were divided into suits for each season of the year, marked with the number of each month, and illustrated with seasonal pictures of flowers, animals, and insects. By this time, although gambling was still prohibited, card games were no longer routinely banned, and *hanakaruta* continued to be played throughout the remainder of the Edo period (1600–1868). *Hanakaruta* (now called HANAFUDA) survived the transition period of the late 19th century and is still played today. It remains the most popular form of card gambling in Japan. See PLAYING CARDS.

From the end of the 18th century professional gamblers called YAKUZA (or *bakuchi uchi* or *bakuto*) provided places for farmers, merchants, craftsmen, and cargo transport workers to engage in gambling. They extracted a service fee from the players and offered protection from arrest or harassment. In southwestern Japan, around Ōsaka, and in parts of Kyūshū, they also managed gambling dens for *hanafuda* card players.

The emergence of professional gamblers spurred the development of sophisticated cheating techniques, including loaded dice and marked cards. Nowadays, electromagnetically controlled dice are said to be used. Since World War II, dice games have declined in popularity and *hanafuda* gambling has become predominant.

Europeans living in Yokohama first instituted a system of buying pari-mutuel tickets for betting on horses in 1880. This practice was soon picked up by the Japanese in Tōkyō. By the early 20th century, the government was officially permitting horse racing, and racetracks were built all over the country. These courses were sponsored either by the central or local government, and none of them was privately owned. Thus, horse racing marked the beginning of "public" (government-sponsored) gambling. The expression "public gambling," however, was not used in this sense until 1950. From around that time bicycle, motor boat, and motorcycle racing (also government sponsored) became more popular than horse and dog racing. There are at present more than 150 race courses of different kinds in Japan, most of them located in large cities. The government taxes these enterprises at 25 percent and donates the revenue to various local enterprises. In the past few years, government taxes on public gambling have totaled about one trillion yen (about US $4.5 billion) annually.

Betting on animal contests such as BULLFIGHTING and DOG-FIGHTING is very popular in Japan. This, together with "public gambling" and private establishments where one can play *hanafuda*, dice *(saikoro)*, MAH-JONGG, or PACHINKO (pinball), makes Japan a haven for gamblers. For example, there are more Mah-Jongg and *pachinko* parlors than elementary and secondary schools in Japan. Although *pachinko* parlors do not award money prizes, and there are always notices prohibiting cash wagering in Mah-Jongg parlors, in reality there are no parlors in which gambling does not occur. In spite of the fact that gambling has been prohibited by various laws and edicts since the 5th century, gamblers and proprietors of such facilities are rarely prosecuted.   KATA Kōji

games

The Japanese have, from ancient times, indulged in all kinds of games ranging from "matching games," board games, word games, and cards, to a great variety of outdoor, parlor, and children's games.

Matching games or "comparisons" *(awase)* have a long history in Japan: two of the earliest games, of which there are records in Heian period (794–1185) literature, are *e-awase* (picture-comparing contests), where contestants carefully compared their paintings for beauty and quality of style, and UTA-AWASE (poetry contests), where teams of poets vied with each other in composing poems on preannounced topics. Similar games involved comparing flowers, roots, incense (see INCENSE CEREMONY), birds, and insects. KAI-AWASE, the shell-matching game, involved the delicate task of matching the two halves of clam shells that had been separated and mixed with others.

Many board games were imported from China. The best known are GO; SHŌGI, a form of chess; and SUGOROKU, a type of backgammon. These were first played among aristocrats and gradually spread among the common people. A popular children's board game was JŪROKU MUSASHI, which resembled pachisi.

Writing, picture, and WORD GAMES are abundant in Japan because of the great number of homonyms in the language and the wonderful versatility possible in calligraphy, using pictorial sweeps of the brush.

Games using PLAYING CARDS (referred to as *karuta*) were influenced by foreign games introduced in the 16th century and afterwards. Many of these were matching games, in which players matched a card containing one part of a plant, animal, Chinese character, and so forth, with a card containing the other. Among the most popular today are HANAFUDA, a flower-card game, and HYA-KUNIN ISSHU, in which one must match the first and last halves of one hundred 31-syllable *waka* poems.

Important traditional children's games are OHAJIKI, a game resembling marbles; BEANBAG *(otedama)*; cat's cradle *(ayatori)*; TOPS, including the BEIGOMA, a top spun with a whipcord; MENKO, a game in which players attempt to flip over their opponents' cardboard pieces with a skillful tossing of their own; hide-and-seek *(kaku-rembo)*; tag *(onigokko)*; KAGOME KAGOME, a guessing game; NEKKI, a game of tossing skill; *tōsenkyō*, a game in which players throw folding fans at a target; *takeuma asobi* (stilts or hobby horse); and *temari* (handball). KEN are games of forfeit involving hand signals and are still played today. Two pastimes enjoyed by both children and adults are a game played with Japanese PAPER BALLOONS *(kami fūsen)*, and the art of Japanese paper folding (ORIGAMI).

New Year's is not only the most important holiday of the year but the time of greatest leisure; thus many games are particularly associated with the holiday. Among these are kite flying *(takoage; see* KITES) and the *Hyakunin isshu* card game. Others are FUKU WARAI, a game in which the blindfolded player must place the features within the outline of a face on a piece of paper, and battledore and shuttlecock (see HANETSUKI).   SAITŌ Ryōsuke

Gamō Kumpei (1768–1813)

Japanese classical scholar of the Edo period (1600–1868). Born into a merchant family in the castle town of Utsunomiya (now in Tochigi Prefecture), he studied the Japanese classics from an early age. His frequent visits to the Mito domain (now part of Ibaraki Prefecture) and association with FUJITA YŪKOKU and other members of the MITO SCHOOL of historical studies further inspired his interest in the past. In particular, his studies on the question of the "true relations between sovereign and subject" *(taigi meibun)* awakened in him a deep concern for the imperial family and its decline in power and prestige. In 1796 and 1799 he toured the country inspecting imperial tombs and found many of them in disrepair. He published a report, *Sanryōshi* (History of Imperial Tombs), in 1808. For his proimperial ideas Kumpei is considered a precursor of the movement to over-throw the shogunate and restore direct imperial rule in the late Edo period.

Gamō Ujisato (1556–1595)

(Gamō Masuhide; Christian name, Leão). *Daimyō* of the Azuchi-Momoyama period (1568–1600); son of Gamō Katahide (1534–84), lord of Hino Castle in Ōmi (now Shiga Prefecture), the scion of a baronial family prominent in that province since the 12th century. The Gamō sided with ODA NOBUNAGA when that emergent hegemon marched on Kyōto in 1568; Ujisato was married to Nobunaga's daughter and served Nobunaga in various campaigns from his expulsion of the shōgun ASHIKAGA YOSHIAKI (1537–97) from Kyōto in 1573 to the conquest of the TAKEDA FAMILY in 1582. After Nobunaga's assassination later that year, Ujisato passed into the service of the national unifier TOYOTOMI HIDEYOSHI, distinguished himself in the invasion of Ise Province (now part of Mie Prefecture) in 1583, and was the next year granted a domain assessed at 120,000 *koku* (see KOKUDAKA) at Matsugashima (now Matsusaka) in that province; he won further distinction in Hideyoshi's Kyūshū campaign in 1587 and, after participating in the ODAWARA CAMPAIGN of 1590, was rewarded with a 420,000-*koku* domain (in effect comprising present Fukushima Prefecture) at what is now the city of Aizu Wakamatsu in northern Honshū. In 1591 Ujisato took part in the sweep through northernmost Honshū that completed Hideyoshi's unification of Japan; his domain was more than doubled to an assessed yield of 919,320 *koku,* and he thereby became one of Japan's five greatest daimyō. Ujisato fell ill while in Nagoya (now in Saga Prefecture), the Kyūshū headquarters for Hideyoshi's invasions of Korea, and died in Kyōto on his way home; the story that he was poisoned is unfounded. A cultivated man, Ujisato was an amateur of poetry and the tea ceremony, and studied Buddhism and Confucianism with the celebrated Zen monk and scholar Nange Genkō (1538–1604). He was converted to Christianity in 1585 through the efforts of TAKAYAMA UKON, a fellow disciple of the great tea master SEN NO RIKYŪ; the Jesuit missionaries rightly rejoiced over the baptism of "one of the most important and influential persons yet to become Christian," but Ujisato lost his zeal for the faith after Hideyoshi issued his ANTI-CHRISTIAN EDICTS in 1587.   *George* ELISON

Gangōji

Also known as Shin Gangōji. Temple of the KEGON SECT of Buddhism. Located in the city of Nara. Founded by SOGA NO UMAKO in 588, the temple originally was located in Asuka, where it was known by both its formal title Hōkōji and the popular name ASUKADERA.

When the imperial court moved to Nara (HEIJŌKYŌ) from Asuka, this temple was one of the first to reestablish itself there in 718 and was called Shin (New) Gangōji. The new plan featured a single large golden hall enclosed in a rectangular courtyard, flanked by a pair of separately enclosed 5-story pagodas. By 749 it was considered second only to TŌDAIJI among all temples. Formally classified as a SANRON SCHOOL temple during the Nara period (710–794), Gangōji is mentioned as having played a part in many important state ceremonies of the Nara and Heian (794–1185) periods. The priests Chikō (b 709) and Raikō (died after 729) lectured here on the Sanron (Three Treatises centered on Mādhyamika), and Shōgo (732–811), Shin'ei (d 737), Gomyō (750–834), and Myōsen (789–868) were renowned masters of the *Hossō* doctrine (Skt: Vijñā-navāda, see HOSSŌ SECT). Since Gangōji was south of Kōfukuji—also a Hossō center—these two temples were called the southern and northern branches of Hossō. Gangōji prospered and was numbered among the so-called "Seven Temples of Nara" including Tōdaiji, KŌFUKUJI, DAIANJI, YAKUSHIJI, SAIDAIJI, and HŌRYŪJI. From the middle of the Heian period (794–1185), however, Gangōji fell into disrepair. It barely continued as a center of worship of the bodhisattva Kannon (Avalokiteśvara) and of the Pure Land faith, which centered on the Pure Land mandala attributed to Chikō, an early devotee of the Pure Land. Nothing remains now of the original buildings except the stone pagoda base, excavated in modern times after its final destruction by fire in 1859.

Today, the main hall, known as Gokurakudō, together with an attached *zenshitsu* (meditation hall), originally a Nara-period monks' quarters rebuilt in the Kamakura period (1185–1333), is all that remains on the site. Both these buildings have been designated National Treasures. Other treasures housed here include a 9th-century wooden icon of Yakushi Nyorai (Skt: Bhaisajyaguru; the Buddha of Healing) and a 5.5 meter (18 m) model of a five-storied pagoda from

Ganjin

This image of the blind monk in meditation is thought to have been produced shortly before his death in 763. Hollow dry lacquer, painted. Height 79.7 cm. Portrait chapel (mieidō), Tōshōdaiji, Nara Prefecture. National Treasure.

the 8th century. The temple also houses statues of AMIDA Buddha (from the mid-Heian period), Prince SHŌTOKU (from the 13th century), and KŪKAI (from the 14th century), all of which have been designated Important Cultural Properties, and two mandalas, known as copies of the original mandala by Chikō, one painted on wooden boards from the 13th century, the other a 15th-century copy on silk, both of which have been designated Important Cultural Properties (see MANDALA).

■——Gorai Shigeru, ed, Gangōji gokurakudō chūsei shomin shinkō shiryō no kenkyū (1964). Iwaki Takatoshi, ed, Gangōji hennen shiryō, 3 vols (1963, 1965, 1966). Minoru Ōoka, Temples of Nara and their Art, vol 7 (1973). Ōta Hirotarō et al, Yamato koji taikan, vol 3 (1977). Tsuji Taihan et al, Gangōji, vol 6 of Koji junrei: Nara (1979).   Jane T. GRIFFIN

Ganjin (688–763)

Chinese Buddhist monk who introduced the RITSU SECT of Buddhism to Japan and founded the temple TŌSHŌDAIJI in Nara. Ganjin is the Japanese pronunciation of the Chinese name Jianzhen (Chien-chen). Born in Yangzhou (Yang-chou), China. In 701, at the age of 13, he became a monk at a local temple. He received the bodhisattva precepts (J: bosatsukai) in 705 and studied monastic discipline under the famed master Daoan (Tao-an) at the Longxing (Lung-hsing) monastery in Yuezhou (Yüeh-chou). At the age of 20 he became a full-fledged Buddhist monk when he received the complete precepts (J: gusokukai) in the capital city of Chang'an (Ch'ang-an). He preached the importance of Buddhist conduct and discipline in and around Luoyang (Lo-yang) and Chang'an, the two main centers of Chinese society of the time. He pursued further studies in the vinaya (Buddhist precepts) and Tiantai (T'ien-t'ai; J: Tendai; see TENDAI SECT) doctrine and gave lectures and helped to establish numerous temples. He copied volumes of Buddhist scriptures and built homes for the sick and poor.

In 732 the Japanese government decided to resume dispatching envoys to Tang (T'ang; 618–907) China (see SUI AND TANG CHINA, EMBASSIES TO). It also hoped to invite to Japan Chinese monks who were not only well-versed in Buddhist teaching and discipline but who would firmly establish the precepts necessary to regulate monastic life and establish in the capital an authentic ordination platform which the Buddhist clergy had lacked. For 10 years the Japanese monks Yōei and Fushō had no success in persuading any

Chinese monk to sail across the China Sea to Japan. They had nearly given up and were preparing to return home in 742 when they had an audience with Ganjin at Yangzhou. Already a widely known and highly venerated monk throughout China, Ganjin readily accepted their offer, notwithstanding the formidable perils of sailing to a far-off country. Between 743 and 748, Ganjin made five attempts to cross but was turned back each time either by pirates or storms at sea. These abortive attempts to reach Japan resulted in the death of a number of disciples, and Ganjin himself was suffering from cataracts.

In 752 the Japanese government dispatched another group of envoys to China to urge Ganjin to come to Japan. Thus in 753, Ganjin left Yangzhou on his sixth voyage, and at the age of 66, he finally reached the southern shores of Kyūshū. By this time Ganjin was totally blind. Three months later, in the spring of 754, he arrived in Nara and immediately established an ordination platform at TŌDAIJI. He was given by imperial order the authority to ordain priests and to give instruction on Buddhist precepts. Many monks came to be ordained by him or to receive Ganjin's instruction on Buddhist morality and discipline. From him the empress KŌKEN and the retired emperor SHŌMU received the bodhisattva precepts. In 758 he was granted the honorary title daiwajō (great preceptor) by the emperor. In 759 he established Tōshōdaiji, where he resided and continued to instruct his students. Henceforth Tōshōdaiji became the headquarters of the Ritsu sect. Four years later Ganjin, who had given up a brilliant career and fame in his homeland to dedicate himself to the propagation of Buddhist dharma in Japan, died, reportedly while in the full lotus position of meditation.

■——Andō Kōsei, Ganjin wajō (1967). Ishida Mizumaro, Ganjin, sono kairitsu shisō (1973). Ishida Mizumaro, Ganjin, sono shisō to shōgai (1958).   T. James KODERA

gankake

Also termed gandate; prayers or petitions to a Shintō or Buddhist deity to obtain a specific request. Gankake are accompanied by offerings or promises to fulfill certain acts or penances and may be made either by groups or individuals. In the former case gankake often involve an entire village or community in prayers for the rain or sun necessary for a good harvest, for protection from the ravages of war or epidemic, or for a villager who is gravely ill. Individual petitions, generally for personal health or marital happiness, may involve the entire family; they have remained the more prevalent form of gankake in modern times and are still made at temples or shrines noted for their miraculous powers.

PILGRIMAGES to shrines and temples are considered a form of gankake, one common type of which is the 100-visit pilgrimage, or hyakudo mairi, to a local shrine. The pilgrimage might be conducted under conditions of self-mortification (e.g., without shoes or adequate clothing in winter) and might involve fixed periods of retreat (komori); the performance of a set number of ritual ablutions; and specific abstinences (e.g., salt, tea, sake, or fire; see TACHI-MONO).

Offerings made to the deity may include food or goods (e.g., rice cakes, wine, or cloth). One popular practice, for example, is to offer a votive tablet (EMA) inscribed with an appropriate picture (for example, an eye or ear in the case of afflictions of these organs) to Yakushi NYORAI, the Buddha of healing. Some gankake involve sympathetic magic, for example, presenting a bowl, stone, or sea shell with a hole strung with thread (a pun on gan ga yoku tōru, "one's request comes through"), or an attempt to coerce the deity, as in the practice of binding an image of the deity JIZŌ with rope and promising to untie it when one's petition is answered. The process of gankake is concluded by a special visit of thanks to the shrine or temple in question upon fulfillment of the petitioner's request.

ŌTŌ Tokihiko

Ganku (1756–1838)

Painter and founder of the Kishi school of painting. Surname Kishi; given name Koma. Born in Kanazawa (now in Ishikawa Prefecture). He served in Kyōto in the household of the princely family of Arisugawa from 1784; he later served at the imperial court and toward the end of his life was given the honorary title of Echizen no Kami (Governor of Echizen). A self-taught artist, Ganku seems to have studied KANŌ SCHOOL techniques, and he acknowledged a debt to the Chinese painter SHEN NANPIN (Shen Nan-p'in); the influence of the MARUYAMA-SHIJŌ SCHOOL is also present. Ganku's style, however eclectic and rooted in other schools of painting, is bold and vigorous. In addition to Ganku's son Gantai (1782–1865) and his son-in-law Ganryō (1797–1852), the Kishi-school painters include Renzan (1804–59), who was adopted by Ganku, Yokoyama Kazan, and Shirai Kayō (fl ca 1840–60). These artists all specialized in BIRD-AND-FLOWER PAINTING themes and animals. Ganku is especially well known for his paintings of tigers.

garabō

(*gara* spinning). A process for spinning cotton thread, onomatopoetically named for the clattering noise made by the water-driven throstles. The *garabō* spinning frame, invented by a Buddhist monk named Gaun Tatsumune (1842–1900) in 1876, was capable of mass-producing cotton yarn from almost any kind of waste fiber. A simple and efficient process because it did not require carding before spinning, it spread rapidly throughout the country and played an important part in the early development of Japan's modern spinning industry. The *garabō* process especially thrived in the Mikawa area of Aichi Prefecture, where boats were fitted out as spinning mills and equipped with water wheels to supply power; by 1897 there were 1,000 such boats on the river Yahagigawa, each operating as many as 300 spindles. With the increased importation of modern Western machinery after 1900, the *garabō* process virtually disappeared. The Mikawa area, however, has remained a center of *garabō* spinning, producing such specialized goods as cotton blankets, rugs, and the soles for TABI (a kind of Japanese sock) with electrically powered *garabō* machinery.

gardenia

(*kuchinashi*). *Gardenia jasminoides* f. *grandiflora*. Also known as cape jasmine. The *kuchinashi* is the most common species of gardenia found in Japan. An evergreen shrub of the family Rubiaceae, it reaches a height of about 2 meters (6.6 ft). The leaves are opposite, oblong, and glossy. In summer it produces fragrant white flowers 6–7 centimeters (2.5 in) across. The fruit is obovate and turns yellowish red when ripe. The plant grows wild in Honshū westward from the Kantō region as well as in Shikoku and Kyūshū. It has long been cultivated in gardens and for cut flowers, and numerous varieties, such as those with variegated leaves or with double flowers, have been developed.

The fruit of the *kuchinashi* has long been valued as a source of yellow dye for clothes, but nowadays the dye is limited to use in foodstuffs and as a stain for wooden utensils. In traditional medicine, tea made of the dried fruit was used to treat jaundice and a plaster made of the powdered dried fruit mixed with flour and water was used as a folk remedy for bruises or cuts. Japanese gardenias have been exported and crossed with other species. Some of these horticultural varieties have larger double flowers and roundish leaves.   Matsuda Osamu

gardens

Japanese gardens possess a unique beauty derived from the combination and synthesis of various elements. There are no sculptured fountains, dynamic watercourses, or profusion of flowers in bloom. Rather, together with the functional beauty of the garden's purpose, there is a compositional beauty derived from a blending of various manifestations of material beauty provided by natural plantings, sand, water, and rock. This compositional beauty is made unique by the natural beauty of Japan's landscape, which undergoes considerable seasonal change, and a symbolic beauty arising from the expression of SHINTŌ beliefs and Buddhist intellectual conventions. Factors in the creation of the Japanese gardens are the land and the climate, the beliefs and the spirit of the people, and the social and economic basis upon which the gardens are realized. The interrelationship of these elements establishes the form of the garden. For this reason Japanese garden styles are referred to by the names of ancient provinces, historical periods, and the men for whom or by whom they were designed.

History —— It has been said that the use of groupings of rocks is a distinguishing feature of the Japanese garden and provides its basic framework. Rock groupings are well balanced and are made up of a few stones whose natural form has been retained. The ancestors of the modern Japanese referred to places surrounded by natural rock as *amatsu iwasaka* ("heavenly barrier") or *amatsu iwakura* ("heav-

Gardens

Pond of the garden at Mōtsuji. *Funa asobi* type. Typical of the gardens built for *shinden-zukuri* mansions. Hiraizumi, Iwate Prefecture.

Gardens

The famous rock and sand *(kare sansui)* garden at the Zen temple Ryōanji in Kyōto.

enly seat"), believing that gods dwelled there. Dense clusters of trees were also thought to be the dwelling places of gods and were called *himorogi* ("divine hedge"). Moats or streams which enclosed sacred ground were called *mizugaki* ("water fences"). The creative origin of the Japanese garden can be seen in the ancient people's use of stone, water, trees and in the beliefs that supported such use. Even today, the Japanese feel that naturally formed rocks possess a quality of sacred spirituality. Other ancient practices that may have contributed structural elements to the Japanese garden include the planting of windbreaks to the rear of dwellings and the digging of moats for protection from enemies and wild beasts.

The story of Japanese gardens begins with the establishment of a Japanese state in the YAMATO area (now Nara Prefecture) during the 6th and 7th centuries AD and the establishment of the capital at Nara in the 8th century. One theory holds that when the ancestors of the Japanese passed through the Inland Sea area on their way to settle the Yamato area they were impressed by the seascape studded with islands. It was perhaps for this reason that when they first made gardens amidst the mountains of Yamato they imitated ocean scenes by making large ponds with wild "sea shores" and islands. During this period Buddhism was transmitted to Japan and immigrants from PAEKCHE on the Korean peninsula contributed continental influences to the Japanese garden, incorporating the theme of Shumisen (Skt: Sumeru), one of the Buddhist paradises, and adding stone fountains and bridges of Chinese origin. It was at this time that there arrived from China and Korea a court recreation *(kyokusui no utage)* enjoyed by emperors and courtiers, in which poems were composed and the participants floated cups of rice wine to one another along a winding garden stream.

In 794 the capital was moved to Kyōto. Here there was much marshland and it became necessary to engineer the control of water

Gardens

This garden at Jōjuin, a subtemple of Kiyomizudera, makes use of a "borrowed view" (shakkei) of the hill behind it. Kiyomizudera, Kyōto.

Gardens

Pond-side view at Kenrokuen, a kaiyū-style garden and one of the most noted gardens in Japan. Kanazawa, Ishikawa Prefecture.

Gardens

View of the kaiyū-style garden of the Katsura Detached Palace in Kyōto from the Old Shoin (Ko Shoin) section of the main house.

flow, reinforce riverbanks, and solidify the rims of ponds. In order to provide a sense of relief from the heat of summer, waterfalls, ponds, and narrow streams (yarimizu) were made, which, passing between the buildings of the SHINDEN-ZUKURI mansions, also flowed through the gardens. The ponds were of simple shape yet large enough for boating, and at their edges, jutting out over the water, were erected fishing pavilions (tsuri dono) connected by roofed corridors to the other structures of the mansion. The large area between the main buildings and the pond was covered with white sand and used for formal ceremonies. This type of garden, called the shinden style, was modeled after the Buddhist paradise described in the scriptures as the Pure Land (Jōdo) of Amida Buddha. A good example of this is the garden of the BYŌDŌIN, a temple at Uji. Before the amidadō (Amida hall), popularly known as the Hōōdō (Phoenix Hall), was constructed a pond in the shape of the first letter of the Sanskrit alphabet. Chinese Taoist belief in the importance of the attainment of immortality, expressed in Japan through the symbolism of the crane and the tortoise (tsuru and kame) merged with the Buddhist JŌDO SECT tradition and subsequently this combined theme became the central motif of Japanese gardens. Because of the interest in gardens among aristocrats, there appeared many excellent critical works on the subject, the oldest of which was Tachibana Toshitsuna's Sakuteiki (Records on Garden Making) written in the early part of the Kamakura period (1185–1333).

By the Kamakura and Nambokuchō (1336–92) periods, temples had gradually been moved from cities to the mountains. Their restricted views, enhanced by construction on sloping ground, were designed to provide an environment more appropriate to the practice of various Buddhist disciplines. During this period priestly garden designers were called "rock-placing monks" (ishitate sō), the

placement of rocks implying the creation of a garden. The greatest of these "rock-placing monks" was MUSŌ SOSEKI (1275–1351). At the temple SAIHŌJI he constructed a garden with ten views based upon the Chinese compositional method known as shijing (shih-ching; J: jukkyō) or "ten realms."

The Muromachi period (1333–1568) has been called the golden age of Japanese gardens. Skilled groups of craftsmen known as senzui kawaramono ("mountain, stream, and riverbed people") were active, and there appeared the new kare sansui ("dry mountain stream") style of garden. The warrior class had replaced the aristocracy and was securely entrenched in government administration. The concepts of ZEN Buddhism which had earlier been introduced from China were also well established. It is customary to speak of the origin of waterless rock and sand gardens (kare sansui) as deriving from a combination of such traditions as Zen doctrine, shoin-style architecture (SHOIN-ZUKURI), Chinese ink painting, potted dwarf trees (BONSAI), and tray landscapes, the basic idea being the symbolic expression of a whole universe within a limited space. Though kare sansui is a garden form found nowhere else in the world, its development was probably influenced by the methods and perspective employed in the Chinese ink paintings known as can-shan shengshui (ts'an-shan sheng-shui; J: zanzan jōsui), landscapes of barren mountains and dry riverbeds. Shoin-style structures were small and faced onto gardens whose view was designed to be seen from within. In this way was developed a garden possessing an almost pictorial delicacy of composition which could endure long and studied observation.

The confidence of the parvenu samurai who had managed to remain unscathed during the Sengoku period (Age of Warring States; 1467–1568) was expressed in their gardens. They composed groupings of boulders of unique shape and striking color and used exotic foreign plants such as the sotetsu, a variety of sago palm, in the gardens. Standing in opposition to such superficial splendor was the TEA CEREMONY or Way of tea (sadō) as taught by SEN NO RIKYŪ, who emphasized a quiescent spirituality. The tea spirit represented an attempt to achieve inner peace, harmonious intercourse among men, and self-forgetfulness through the drinking of tea. The approach to a teahouse was through a tea garden (roji niwa) the ideal of which Rikyū sought in the desolate tranquility of a mountain trail. Among the contributions of the tea garden to the contemporary Japanese garden are stepping-stones, stone lanterns, groves of trees, as well as stone washbasins and simply constructed gazebos for guests being served tea.

Gardens——Table 1

Elements of Japanese Garden Design

A. Design in terms of function

Function	Compositional unit
Enclosure: Closing off the perimeter. The most basic device for creating space.	Bamboo fences such as the *ajiro* (wickerwork) and *yotsume* (lattice). Fences may also be made of wooden slats, stone, clay, or other materials. Other enclosing elements include moats, gateways, and a variety of hedges differing in type of plant, height, and manner of trimming.
Division: Spatial division and distinction according to use or atmosphere.	Hedges and other plantings provide complete visual and physical separation. *Yotsume* fences and *shiorido* (a wicket made from the bent branches of saplings) achieve visual connection but physical separation. *Sekimori ishi* ("barrier stone"; a smooth, round stone with a rope tied around it) are used as direction-indicating barriers at forks in tea garden paths.
Connection: Direct or visual connection between different spaces or objects.	Stepping-stones and rectilinear stone walkways provide horizontal connection; these should exhibit rhythmic variation. Stepping-stone stairs give vertical connection. Bridges connect near and opposite shores and suggest the Buddhist metaphor for existential travail and the distant realm of enlightenment. They may be constructed of natural or finished stone, wood, or earth and may be flat or gently or fully arched.
Concealment: Unsightly things may be concealed or the front portion of something may be hidden in order to provide a sense of anticipation.	High hedges create a sense of anticipation for that portion of the garden yet unseen. *Sodegaki* (low fences) are used for concealment.
Covering: Ground cover used to provide a sense of broad space and to facilitate the entrance of visitors.	Flagstones (cut stones, joined stones, large rectilinear stones, rounded stones from streambeds, or a combination of cut and rounded stones) are used for pavement or, on occasion, to suggest the shape of a riverine sand island. In the *kare sansui* style of garden, sand is spread and patterns may be drawn in it symbolizing the rippling surface of a pond or the sea. Sand prevents the growth of grass and functions as a ground cover. Moss and grass are also used as ground cover.

B. Design in terms of effect

Effect	Compositional unit
Decoration: Objects placed in gardens to emphasize symbolic composition add accent to the garden and aid the viewer in establishing points of focus.	Groupings of rocks, such as those in the form of a triad of Buddhist images (*sanzon ishigumi*) or a waterfall (*taki ishigumi*), are especially effective as symbolic or decorative points, particularly when placed before a tree or shrubbery. Stone lanterns come in a variety of shapes and sizes and are placed in strategic locations throughout the garden. Usually purely decorative or used as landmarks, lanterns sometimes serve a practical purpose in illuminating certain sections of the garden.
Breadth and depth: Allows the composition within a small piece of land of a scene suggesting vast distance and a broad expanse.	This effect is created by a three-dimensional mass of plantings set against a flat plane of spread sand or moss, and by the difference in heights of a fence and trees. Trees with spreading branches planted before a pond and trees that partially obstruct the view of a waterfall or lantern also heighten the sense of distance. Low groupings of rocks emphasize a horizontal line, giving a sense of breadth and serenity.
Movement: Water, wind, and animals add movement to a garden; movement acts as a counterpoint to, and thus heightens the atmosphere of quiet.	Impressions of movement, breadth, quiet, and coolness arise from a cascading waterfall, a flowing stream, a rippling pond, or the upswell of water in a spring. According to the manner in which the water descends, waterfalls are given such names as *sandan ochi* (three-stage fall) or *nuno taki* (cloth waterfall). Varieties of streams are *yarimizu* (a narrow flow drawn from a nearby river) and *kyokusui* (winding stream). *Sōzu* (also called *shishi odoshi*) is a length of bamboo that, while at rest at an acute angle, is filled by running water until it tips, spilling out the water. The bamboo swings back to its original position, the lower end striking a rock and producing a sound. The process is then repeated. Other components involving movement include *kakehi* (a bamboo pipe from which water trickles); *suisha* (waterwheel); and carp, which bestow movement and color to the still surface of a pond.

During the Edo period (1600–1868) a synthesis of preceding forms took place. The garden of the KATSURA DETACHED PALACE, which achieved considerable renown through the writings of the German architect Bruno Taut (1880–1938), is made up of a number of tea gardens. This is an example of the *kaiyū,* or "many-pleasure" style, which became fully established midway in the Edo period, succeeding the *kare sansui* and *shoin* garden styles. The Katsura garden was built by an aristocrat but the majority of *kaiyū* gardens belonged to *daimyō* (feudal lords). In the Edo period, an age of synthesis in all cultural spheres, compositional details developed in the gardens of previous eras were used to create a synthetic whole. Around a large pond there might be scattered miniature scenes from the 53 stages of the TŌKAIDŌ highway, views of Mt. Fuji (Fujisan), the three famous views of Japan (see NIHON SANKEI) or the many places sung of in classical Japanese WAKA poetry; there might be a winding stream *(kyokusui),* a pond in the shape of the Chinese character for heart *(kokoro)* accented by the extreme convolution of its shoreline, a representation of the island of Hōrai (a fantastic island in Chinese mythology inhabited by immortal ascetics), *sanzonseki* (groupings of stones symbolizing three Buddhas, usually Yakushi, Amida, and Shaka, each accompanied by two attendants), Chinese-style embankments and bridges, Confucian-style towers, representations of ancient Chinese-style rice paddies, teahouses, and gardens where daimyō and their advisers entertained themselves, practice grounds for archery and horse riding, and "yin and yang stones," symbolizing the male and female. All such elements were merged in harmonious unity with natural scenes—reduced in scale—of mountains, rivers, and valleys. The use of a large number of motifs was a natural development of the application of garden planning to the large grounds upon which daimyō built their mansions. As the grounds were customarily on low-lying flat land marked by little topographical variation, the builders dug ponds, raised hills, employed the technique known as "borrowed views" (J: shakkei), in which distant hills in the background were integrated into the perspective of the garden, and introduced numerous other motifs into the design. In an age when the art of printing flourished, many noted garden texts were widely distributed, effecting a general popularization of the garden. A representative garden designer of this period was KOBORI ENSHŪ, whose work included the gardens of the Sentō Palace in Kyōto.

Technique and Composition of the Japanese Garden——It has been said that the soul of the Japanese garden lies in its symbolic significance. However, this is true only when the original function of topiary composition has been fulfilled. In order for a garden to be usable as a garden certain elements of its design must be purely functional; at the same time, in order to impress viewers with its beauty, certain elements must be designed for effect. These conditions are of course not unique to Japanese gardens. What is particularly Japanese about Japanese gardens is that design elements of both types of detail are essentially independent units which, for the most part, adhere to traditional Japanese forms. These units are made up of natural rock, trees, and bamboo. Garden planning consists of selecting, according to terrain, a number of compositional units and placing them so that they form an organic whole. Skill in the making of a Japanese garden is based on an understanding of conventions concerning form, type, and implementation of compositional units. These units of compositional detail have been given names taken from the gardens in which they were originally employed.

The Use of Space——Methods of dividing the surface plane of a Japanese garden may be classified into four groups. The *funa asobi* ("pleasure boat") style (centered on an oval-shaped pond where courtiers went boating) was a popular type of garden in the Heian period for mansions on the outskirts of the capital. The *shūyū* ("stroll") style (a garden whose chief feature is a path leading from vantage point to vantage point from which changing scenes could be viewed) was often employed in gardens of temples and of mansions of the wealthy and powerful during the Heian, Kamakura, and Muromachi periods. The *kanshō* or *zakan* ("contemplation") style (in which the garden is viewed from within a central structure, emphasis being placed on the creation of a carefully composed scene suggestive of a picture and suitable for long and studied viewing) was designed to be seen from a *shoin,* a room in a type of building known as *shoin-zukuri,* which was often built by men of the samurai class during the Muromachi and Azuchi–Momoyama (1568–1600) periods. The *kaiyū* ("many pleasure") style (in which various gardens, usually tea gardens, were constructed around a central pond, displaying striking changes of scene to viewers) was often employed

Gardens——Table 2

Major Japanese Gardens

Garden	Location	Style	Period	Area (sq meters)	Features
Mōtsuji	Hiraizumi, Iwate Prefecture	*funa asobi*	Heian (794–1185)	145,616	oldest existing garden
Kōrakuen	Tōkyō	*kaiyū*	Edo (1600–1868)	58,337	daimyō garden
Hama Detached Palace	Tōkyō	*kaiyū*	Edo	249,015	daimyō garden
Kenrokuen	Kanazawa, Ishikawa Prefecture	*kaiyū*	Edo	100,462	daimyō garden; oldest fountain
Asakuratei Yakata Ato	Fukui, Fukui Prefecture	*kanshō*	Muromachi (1333–1568)	13,715	daimyō garden
Byōdōin	Uji, Kyōto Prefecture	*funa asobi (shinden)*	Heian	20,714	Jōdo symbolism; garden of the *amidadō*
Saihōji	Kyōto	*shūyū*	Nambokuchō (1336–92)	16,883	*jukkyō* compositional method; designed by Musō Soseki
Tenryūji	Kyōto	*kanshō*	Nambokuchō	12,065	designed by Musō Soseki
Katsura Detached Palace	Kyōto	*kaiyū*	Edo	42,900	garden belonging to the imperial household resort house; contains seven teahouses
Ryōanji	Kyōto	*kanshō (kare sansui)*	Muromachi	38,488	noted for its rock garden
Kinkakuji	Kyōto	*shūyū*	Muromachi	93,077	noted for beautiful pine trees on the shore of its pond
Ginkakuji	Kyōto	*shūyū*	Muromachi	22,338	oldest tea ceremony room; garden designed in imitation of Saihōji
Daisen'in	Kyōto	*kanshō (kare sansui)*	Muromachi	1,363	reduced-scale scenes; symbolization of mountains and water
Daigoji Sambōin	Kyōto	*kanshō*	Azuchi-Momoyama (1568–1600)	15,454	noted for large size of design elements
Nijō Castle	Kyōto	*kaiyū*	Azuchi-Momoyama	1,589	noted for large, stirring components
Konchiin	Kyōto	*kanshō (kare sansui)*	Edo	3,792	crane-tortoise symbolization
Shūgakuin Detached Palace	Kyōto	*kaiyū*	Edo	47,320	*shakkei;* designed by the retired emperor Go-Mizunoo
Sentō Gosho	Kyōto	*kaiyū*	Edo	30,000	designed by Kobori Enshū
Nishi Honganji	Kyōto	*kanshō (kare sansui)*	Azuchi-Momoyama	760	sago palm garden
Kōrakuen	Okayama, Okayama Prefecture	*kaiyū*	Edo	114,365	daimyō garden
Shukkeien	Hiroshima, Hiroshima Prefecture	*kaiyū*	Edo	46,286	daimyō garden
Ritsurin Park	Takamatsu, Kagawa Prefecture	*kaiyū*	Edo	750,875	*shakkei* of mountain in rear; daimyō garden
Jōeiji	Yamaguchi, Yamaguchi Prefecture	*kanshō*	Muromachi	394,469	reduced-scale scenes
Tsuki no Katsura no Niwa	Hōfu, Yamaguchi Prefecture	*kanshō (kare sansui)*	Edo	70	a noted rock garden
Kohōan	Kyōto	tea garden *(roji niwa)*	Edo	1,554	designed by Kobori Enshū

in the gardens of daimyō during the Azuchi–Momoyama and Edo periods. In other words the *funa asobi* style is a garden for amusement, the *shūyū* for walking about, the *kanshō* for quiet contemplation, and the *kaiyū* for strikingly varied scenes. Various adaptations of these four styles are also used. (Note: Both the *shūyū* and *kaiyū* styles, which have much in common, are referred to as "stroll" gardens in English. The word *funa asobi* [literally, "boat pleasure"] is written with Chinese characters that can also be, and often are, pronounced *shūyū* in referring to gardens; the word *shūyū* meaning "stroll" is written with different characters.)

Methods of Scenic Composition —— There are three basic principles of scenic composition: reduced scale, symbolization, and "borrowed views." Reduction in scale refers particularly to the *kaiyū* style garden, which brings together in a confined area adaptations of famous scenes and places of historical interest through miniaturization of natural views of mountains and rivers, and as in tea gardens, the creation, even within a city, of idealized scenes from a mountain village. Themes of Buddhist paradise such as Shumisen or Jōdo (the Pure Land), which derive from the Buddhist cosmology and are inappropriate for expression by means of scenic reduction, are represented through symbolization. Methods of symbolization are abstraction, as in the use of white sand to suggest the ocean, and inference, as in a grouping of stones or an island signifying the felicitous crane and tortoise. Use of a portion of a mountain or river

to suggest the whole is a powerful symbolic device employed in Chinese paintings. The term "borrowed view" *(shakkei)* describes the use of background views outside and beyond the garden, such as a beautiful mountain, a broad plain, or the sea. These are used in such a way that they become part of the interior scenic composition. It is for this reason that the surrounding view is an important factor in the selection of a garden site.

■ ——Masao Hayakawa, *The Garden Arts of Japan* (1973). Teiji Itoh, *Space and Illusion in the Japanese Garden* (1973). Loraine Kuck, *The World of the Japanese Garden* (1968). SHINJI ISOYA

GARIOA-EROA

(Government and Relief in Occupied Areas–Economic Rehabilitation in Occupied Areas). Two US legislative programs in the post-World War II period (EROA was later included in GARIOA) authorizing funds for economic relief and reconstruction in occupied countries. Contributions to Japan under these programs from 1947 to 1951 totaled about $2.1 billion. Major items were food, fertilizer, petroleum, medical supplies, and nonindustrial raw materials; some civilian personnel costs were also paid from GARIOA funds. Soybeans, among the first commodities shipped to Japan, later became a major export item for the United States. In 1962 the United States and Japan agreed on the figure of $1.8 billion as Japan's total

GARIOA debt to the United States for postwar assistance and on the sum of $490 million as what Japan would pay over 15 years in settlement. The United States agreed to use $25 million of this money for educational and cultural exchange between the two countries. It used about half of this amount for various cultural and educational purposes in Japan, including the Fulbright educational exchange program, and in 1976 appropriated the remainder for use by the US–Japan Friendship Commission.

■ ——Jerome B. Cohen, *Japan's Economy in War and Reconstruction* (1949). US, Department of State, *Bulletin,* 29 January 1962.

Richard B. FINN

garment industry

Total sales in the Japanese ready-made garment industry amounted to ¥5 trillion (US $16.8 billion) in 1976. The industry had experienced an average annual growth of 25 percent in the four preceding years. This dramatic growth was largely a consequence of two factors: first, the steady increase in personal income in recent decades enabled Japanese consumers to spend more on clothing; and second, a rapid drop in homemade and custom-made attire left ready-made garments with the unchallenged leadership of the clothing industry.

The major companies in the industry are RENOWN, INC (ready-made garments), GUNZE, LTD (underwear), WACOAL CORPORATION (ladies' underwear), and KASHIYAMA & CO, LTD (ready-made garments). Their combined sales equal that of the 10 leading garment producers in the United States. The major companies concentrate their activities on design and sales while contracting production out to numerous small manufacturers, which generally employ about 10 people each.

Ōsaka, Tōkyō, and Okayama are the garment production centers, contributing about 30 percent of the nation's total production. Since wage rates are high in Tōkyō and Ōsaka, production in those cities is limited to quality goods, with mass production taking place in the less urbanized areas. In recent years, mass-produced garments have been imported in large quantities from South Korea and Taiwan. Imports now account for 20 to 30 percent of annual garment sales.

TOMISAWA Konomi

Gassan

Shield volcano in central Yamagata Prefecture, northern Honshū. Along with the neighboring Hagurosan and Yudonosan, Gassan is one of the Dewa Sanzan (Three Mountains of Dewa Province), a center for the religious exercises of the SHUGENDŌ sect (see DEWA SANZAN SHRINES). Gassan Shrine is on the summit. Alpine flora abound, particularly large tracts of Japanese black fritillary *(kuroyuri)*. There is summer skiing and mountain climbing. Height: 1,980 m (6,494 ft).

gates

(mon). The gate or gateway in Japan is a major architectural feature of temples and shrines, palaces, castles, and domestic architecture; its various forms range from imposing edifices symbolizing sacred or secular authority to simple bamboo or thatch gates of teahouse gardens. The gate provides potent visual definition of character, role, status, sanctity, and security. Gates have been so highly regarded by the Japanese that the word *mon* came to be used frequently in a figurative sense. For example, *mikado* ("honorable gateway"); *kado* is an alternate pronunciation of the Chinese character for *mon*) refers to the emperor; *kemmon* ("gate of power") to a powerful or influential person; *shūmon* ("gate of religion" or "sect gate") to a religious sect or denomination; and *ichimon* ("one gate") to a family or household.

Temple gateways establish hierarchic divisions between different parts of the Buddhist temple and give eloquent testimony to the power and authority of Buddhism in Japan. The *nandaimon,* or "south great gate," is the main exterior gateway of the temple, located on its major north-south axis. The *chūmon,* or "inner gate," provides access to the inner precinct of the temple and is usually aligned with the *nandaimon* on the north-south axis.

The *chūmon* of the Nara temple HŌRYŪJI is the oldest extant gateway in Japan, built in the early 8th century. It has two stories with a simple hip roof above the first and an elegant hip-gable roof above the second. Cloud-shaped bracket-arms *(kumo hijiki)* support the wide eaves, a feature typical of other early Hōryūji buildings such as the main hall *(kondō).*

Gates——Chūmon ("inner gate"), Hōryūji

The oldest extant gateway in Japan, dating from the early 8th century. Height (excluding stone base) 14.44 m. Nara. National Treasure.

Gates——Karamon, Toyokuni Shrine

This *karamon,* with front and rear cusped gables, once stood at Nijō Castle. Height 10.5 m. Late 16th century. Kyōto. National Treasure.

The *nandaimon* of the temple TŌDAIJI, Nara, was built in the mid-8th century under Emperor Shōmu as part of an ambitious program to symbolize the grandeur of central power with material accomplishments. Destroyed during battles between the Taira and Minamoto families in the 1180s, it was rebuilt at the end of the 12th century by the Kamakura shogunate. It is one of the largest gateways in Japan, over 27 meters (88.6 ft) in height, and a rare surviving example of *tenjikuyō,* a monumental but structurally unsophisticated building style adopted from Southern Song (Southern Sung; 1127-1279) China at this time. The enormous but stark bracket sets are an important characteristic. They are corbeled out from the columns six steps and braced laterally by tie-beams running the length of the building, not by further bracket arms as in *wayō* (Japanese-style) architecture. See also BUDDHIST ARCHITECTURE.

The open TORII gateway is a distinctive feature of native SHINTŌ ARCHITECTURE. It consists primarily of two principal columns and bridging architrave and its absence of doors symbolizes permanent openness. Placement of *torii* at intervals along the approaches to sacred sites was borrowed from Buddhist practice. Early Shintō shrines, or those preserving ancient forms such as ISE SHRINE, have gates identical to Buddhist temple gateways.

The ancient Japanese capitals of HEIJŌKYŌ (Nara) and HEIANKYŌ (Kyōto) were modeled on Chinese cities and had many gateways on their main avenues, at city entrances, and leading to government buildings and palaces in accordance with Chinese practice. The most spectacular of the Nara and Kyōto gateways were the *rajōmon* (or *rashōmon*), the main southern entrance to the city, and the *suzakumon,* at the south central entry to the Imperial Palace complex. These gates were large, two-storied, brilliantly painted, and heavily tiled. The Kyōto *rajōmon* was over 32 meters (105 ft) in width, according to excavations, or approximately 4 meters (13.1 ft) wider than the Tōdaiji *nandaimon.*

Gates are also an important feature of domestic architecture. They were integral to the SHINDEN–ZUKURI mansions of the aristocracy during the Heian period (794–1185). Although no example of these Heian gates remains, picture scrolls (EMAKIMONO) furnish information about their appearance. They show three common gate types. The *agetsuchimon*, or "raised earth gate," is a simple two-pillared gate set into and supported by the outer wall of the mansion. It is roofed with wooden slats and covered with clay for weather-proofing and decoration. The *munamon*, or "ridged gate," is incorporated into the mansion wall, but has a more elaborate gabled roof of wood shingle or tile. The *yotsuashimon*, or "four-legged gate," was usually larger than the *agetsuchimon* and *munamon* and was free-standing by virtue of two pillars at front and two central pillars bracing the rear. Mansion gateways such as these were important status symbols and objects of government regulations, which ensured close correlation between architectural style and the social status of the family for which they were constructed. Gateways onto the main avenues of Nara and Kyōto were restricted to higher-ranking aristocratic families under a law issued in 731.

New gate types developed in response to changing political and social circumstances in the Kamakura period (1185–1333). Gate style became a virtual badge of rank within the *samurai* class. The *yakuimon* became a common gate form, a stylistic hybrid of the *munamon* and *yotsuashimon* built with two principal and two support pillars. The roof is spread over all four and may be large and impressive, while the support system remains structurally simple.

The *karamon* developed in the Muromachi period (1333–1568) as a stylistic synthesis of gateways associated with the *shinden* mansion, especially the *yotsuashimon*, and Buddhist architecture, particularly the curvilinear emphasis of *zenshūyō* ("Zen style"). The *karamon* has large cusped gables at front and rear or at each side. During the Azuchi–Momoyama period (1568–1600) and the early part of the Edo period (1600–1868), it was heavily encrusted with sculpture and other ornament in keeping with the decorative exuberance of the age. It was used as a ceremonial entrance to the great *daimyō* mansions of Edo (now Tōkyō) and to official temples and shrines such as the TŌSHŌGŪ at Nikkō, before the Tokugawa shogunate curbed these architectural extravagances.

Nagayamon, or gate rowhouses, were used as outer walls to daimyō mansions and as housing for lower-ranking retainers. Edo laws insisting upon frugality in gate construction later restricted main daimyō-mansion entrances to *nagayamon*, rather than more elaborate gate types. Higher status was indicated by fine detailing of sentry windows and guard houses. There were exceptions to the *nagayamon* rule. The Maeda family was permitted to build a large *munamon* with flanking guard houses to commemorate intermarriage with the Tokugawa family in 1827. This is now the famed Akamon, or Red Gateway, at the entrance to Tōkyō University.

Gates were a vital aspect of the fortifications of CASTLES of the Azuchi–Momoyama and Edo periods. Gateways were constructed at critical points of entry and had to be effectively defended to maintain the security of the castle. They were often incorporated into ingenious maze-like entrances and cunningly constructed to maximize their defensive advantage. The *masugatamon*, for example, was a commonly used barbican gateway of great size and strength. A small outer gate affords limited access to, and therefore hinders ready escape from, a courtyard surrounded by high walls and a heavily guarded tower gate. Attackers could easily be dealt with in the confined space of the courtyard from the numerous fire positions overlooking it. EDO CASTLE was protected by a ring of these *masugatamon*, which also provided articulate expression of the shogunate's power.

━━ Kishi Kumakichi, *Nihon monshō shiwa* (1946).

William H. COALDRAKE

GATT

(General Agreement on Tariffs and Trade). GATT was established in 1947 to bring about the standardization and reduction of TARIFFS. The organization operates through the extension of most-favored-nation status to member nations, whereby tariff reductions granted to one trade partner are extended automatically to all GATT members.

Japan joined GATT in 1955, after the nation's economy had recovered from war damage and was on the threshold of rapid economic growth. When Japan joined, 14 member nations invoked the agreement's article 35, which allows members to withhold most-favored-nation treatment to new members at the time of their accession. This was done out of fear that Japan would continue its rapid recovery and utilize its supply of cheap labor to conduct "export raids" on the economies of the industrialized countries. Most GATT members relinquished these discriminatory import restrictions during the 1960s.

The second problem Japan faced upon joining GATT was the requirement of trade liberalization, i.e., the lifting of import restrictions. It was only during the 1960s, when it moved toward an open economy in response to the demands of the Organization for Economic Cooperation and Development (OECD), that Japan seriously confronted the question of liberalization. The liberalization rate was extremely low in the early 1960s (only 43 percent of all imports had been decontrolled), but it increased to 90 percent by 1963. The remaining restrictions were treated as residuals. By 1964 it was felt that Japan had completed its postwar reconstruction and should join the other industrialized nations in the International Monetary Fund (IMF) as an "article 8" nation. Because of this change in status, Japan was no longer allowed to enforce trade restrictions; instead, it was required to fulfill the liberalization principles of article 11 of GATT, which prohibit all quantitative import restrictions. By the late 1970s, the liberalization rate was said to have reached 97 percent, with residual restrictions on 27 import items, a rate equal to the average for major countries.

The third problem Japan confronted in joining GATT was the reduction of tariffs. Tariffs were lowered substantially in 1955, and reduced further in 1967 as a result of the Kennedy Round negotiations. Also in 1967, Japan granted preferential duties to developing countries. In the early 1970s, in an effort to reduce the surplus in its international BALANCE OF PAYMENTS, Japan unilaterally reduced tariffs even further. As a result of the compromise settlement at the Tōkyō Round talks in 1979, Japan is working to eliminate nontariff trade barriers as well.

Japan is a trade-dependent country, largely because of its severe shortage of natural resources. In addition, unlike the countries of the European Community, Japan does not have natural trade partners with which to enter into an economic alliance. Given this position, it appears likely that Japan will continue to support GATT's principles of nondiscrimination and trade liberalization.

TSUCHIYA Rokurō

Gaun nikkenroku

Diary of the Zen priest Zuikei Shūhō (1391–1473) of the temple Shōkokuji in Kyōto. Noted for his erudition in the Chinese classics, Zuikei (pen name Gaun) was a confidant of the shōgun ASHIKAGA YOSHIMASA. The diary extends from 1446 to 1473 and is an important source of information on Zen Buddhism, scholarship, the arts, and to a lesser extent the social conditions and political history of Zuikei's time. The original text, in 74 fascicles, survives only in a partial copy made by Koretaka Myōan in 1562.

geese

(*gan* or *kari*). Large water birds of the family Anatidae, measuring 61–87 centimeters (24–34 in) in length. The bodies of most geese, both male and female, are grayish brown. Nine varieties have been recorded in Japan, all as winter visitors. They frequent areas safe from predators such as broad paddies and fields, salt marshes, and coastal waters, but in recent years they have become rare except in wildlife refuges. Among the geese found in Japan, the *kokugan* (brant; *Branta bernicla*) and *magan* (white-fronted goose; *Anser albifrons*) are also found in both Europe and North America; the *haiirogan* (greylag goose; *A. anser*), *karigane* (lesser white-fronted goose; *A. erythropus*), and *hishikui* (bean goose; *A. fabalis*) are found in Europe; and the *shijūkaragan* (Canada goose; *B. canadensis*), *hakugan* (snow goose; *A. caerulescens*), and *mikadogan* (emperor goose; *A. canagicus*) are found in North America. The only species found in Asia alone is the *sakatsuragan* (swan goose; *A. cygnoides*), which in recent years has become rare.

TAKANO Shinji

In the account of the reign of the legendary emperor Nintoku in the KOJIKI (712), there is an anecdote in which the laying of an egg by a goose was taken as an auspicious sign of the emperor's enduring rule. (Geese normally do not lay eggs during the season of their stay in Japan.) A similar account appears in the NIHON SHOKI (720). Poets of the MAN'YŌSHŪ (latter half of the 8th century) and later generations have portrayed geese realistically but have also used their arrival as a symbol of the coming of autumn, a poetic convention borrowed from China.

SAITŌ Shōji

Geiami (1431–1485)

Also known as Shingei. The successor of NŌAMI in many, if not all, of the roles required of the leading painter-connoisseur-curator of the Ashikaga shōguns' collection. He appears to have worked for the shōguns from at least 1458 on, and like Nōami and his own son and successor, SŌAMI, he gave evaluations of paintings and was charged with the care of the collection. In 1478, when painter-priest Kenkō SHŌKEI came from Kamakura to study with him, Geiami provided him with works from the shōguns' collection to copy; when Shōkei returned to Kamakura in 1480, Geiami presented him with his painting of *Viewing a Waterfall (Kambakuzu)* as a form of graduation certificate. From this work, and from a detailed record by painter Shōjū Ryūtō (1428–98) describing Geiami at work on a pair of sixfold screens, using as models screens from the shogunal collection by Xia Gui (Hsia Kuei), it is apparent that his major landscape mode was based on Southern Song (Sung; 1127–1279) academy model styles, notably that of Xia Gui. Moreover, his artistic heritage, reflected in works of the Shōkei school in Kamakura, further suggest that he paid little attention to the wash-oriented landscape styles of Muqi (Mu-ch'i; J: MOKKEI) and Yujian (Yü-chien); he does appear, however, to have transmitted, like so many contemporaries, a Muqi-oriented style in figure paintings. See also AMI SCHOOL; INK PAINTING.   *Richard STANLEY-BAKER*

Geibikei

Gorge in the town of Higashiyama, southern Iwate Prefecture, northern Honshū. Created when the Satetsugawa, a tributary of the Kitakamigawa, eroded limestone for a distance of approximately 4 km (2.5 mi). Designated a Natural Monument, it abounds in steep cliffs and strangely shaped rocks on both sides.

geisha

Also called *geigi* and *geiko*. Women entertainers of a traditional type, who provide singing, dancing, conversation, games, and companionship to customers in certain restaurants. The *geisha* world in general is referred to as the *karyūkai* ("flower and willow world").

The total number in the 1920s was roughly 80,000, but geisha became fewer as Japan mobilized for war in the 1930s. By the early 1940s, geisha entertainment was forbidden for all but the military, and most of the women were pressed into factory work for the war effort. In the late 1970s geisha numbered around 17,000.

One reason for their current decline in number is the encroachment by Western-style bar hostesses on what was once the exclusive preserve of the geisha. Many modern Japanese, unfamiliar with the proper etiquette of geisha entertainment, find the bar girls much more in keeping with the tempo of the times. From the women's point of view, it is much easier to become a hostess than a geisha, since the long training, discipline, and expense of maintaining a *kimono* wardrobe are not necessary. It is also true, however, that hostesses do not have the professional pride and career consciousness of geisha.

A love for the traditional arts seems to be the most important motivating factor for women who choose to become geisha, and, while some social prejudice against them exists, they are respected as preservers of traditional art and culture.

The Profession —— The profession of geisha is rather unusual in the Japanese entertainment business in that women can make it a lifelong career. Since the premium is on artistic skills and conversational abilities rather than just youth and good looks, geisha may continue to work to an advanced age. If they cease working as geisha, many go into related occupations like operating a restaurant, bar, or shop, where they can use their geisha background and connections to advantage. Occasionally they become the mistresses or even wives of their customers. In one possible pattern, a geisha who has been a man's mistress may marry him if his first wife dies; thus ex-geisha have sometimes become the second wives of very wealthy or powerful men.

When geisha marry they quit their profession, but while they are working, their relations with men may be of several types. It is generally considered desirable to have a patron (*danna*), with whom the geisha is involved emotionally, sexually, and economically. In addition to the patron, every geisha tries to build up a clientele of dependable favorite customers (*gohiiki*), whom she can count on to call her when they give parties and to contribute to the expenses involved in her public performances of dancing or other arts.

Before World War II, a geisha generally had to have a patron to help support her and often had little say in deciding who he would be. Furthermore, every apprentice had to undergo the "deflowering ceremony" (*mizuage*) with some important customer before she could attain full geisha status. But now it is quite possible to make a living from wages and tips alone, so the matter of whether or not to accept a man as one's patron can be decided more freely.

There can be great differences in the status and behavior of geisha, largely depending on where they work. The high-class urban geisha are very discriminating in their choice of a patron, and their relationships tend to be long-term, but geisha at hot-springs resorts or other tourist spots generally have a transient clientele, and many of them engage in prostitution on the side.

Training —— No matter where they work, aspiring geisha must take lessons in various traditional arts. Some arts that do not directly concern their skills as entertainers are optional (such as tea ceremony, flower arranging, calligraphy, and painting); but lessons in classical dancing, playing the SHAMISEN (a stringed instrument), and several styles of singing are required. Even if a woman has no background in the arts when she enters the geisha life, her lessons begin immediately during the trial period, called *minarai*, after which she must pass an examination at the local geisha registry office, presided over by senior members of the geisha union. The lessons become part of her life as a geisha and she continues them as long as she works.

Traditionally, children were often adopted into geisha houses (*okiya*) for training. Such girls (called *shikomi*) were assigned much of the hard drudgery of housework as part of their discipline and treated like maids or servants. Sometimes girls were indentured by their parents, especially in times of famine when a family could not support all its children. The father would receive a lump sum in exchange for which his daughter would be trained at the geisha house, and its owner would later turn over to the father a specified percentage of her income. Actually, the young girls sent to geisha houses were at least able to learn some skills and refined manners, with a good chance of later finding a patron to pay for their freedom.

From the ages of about 13 to 18, would-be geisha used to serve as "apprentices," generically termed *oshaku* and called *hangyoku* ("half-jewel") in the Kantō area around Tōkyō or *maiko* (dance child) in the Kansai area around Kyōto and Ōsaka. Such apprentices wore a distinctive kimono and hairstyle while they underwent their initial training period. At present, the apprentice stage has all but vanished in Tōkyō, and while the *maiko* have managed to continue in Kyōto, their numbers are dwindling. One reason for this is the compulsory education law requiring everyone to complete middle school, with the usual age of graduation at 15. This means a modern-day *maiko* starts out at the age when traditionally she would be getting ready to assume full-fledged geisha status. It is much more common now for girls to start their careers in their early 20s and skip the apprentice stage altogether.

Organization —— The geisha are divided into discrete groups called *hanamachi* ("flower towns"), each organized around its own registry office (*kemban*). These communities provide the focus for the geisha's private and professional life. The *hanamachi* are highly systematized from the viewpoint of guest and geisha. Every geisha must be registered in her particular area and receive her assignments through the *kemban* to attend those establishments that are members of the "restaurant union" (*ryōtei kumiai*) of the area. *Ryōtei* is a generic term for this kind of restaurant, although, in Kyōto, establishments where geisha entertain are generally called *ochaya*. Meals are not prepared in the *ochaya* but are brought in by catering shops called *ryōriya*. The Tōkyō equivalent of the *ochaya* was known as *machiai-jaya* or simply *machiai* ("waiting and meeting house"). Because of its connotation of behind-the-scenes prostitution, the term *machiai* fell into disuse during the postwar Occupation, and legitimate places labeled themselves *ryōtei* or *kashi zashiki* ("rental banquet room").

The guest makes arrangements for geisha entertainment through these restaurants, and must abide by the rules of the geisha union (*geigi kumiai*) regarding times of attendance and fees for the geisha. The local *kemban* is the central organizing office that coordinates geisha schedules, and it is also the location of the "three unions" (*sangyō kumiai*), which are the working elements of each *hanamachi*. In addition to the restaurant union and geisha union, there is the geisha house union (*geigiya kumiai*), consisting of those establishments with a license (*kamban*). The geisha houses (*okiya* or *geigiya*), with which every geisha must be affiliated, pay fees to the *kemban* for these licenses.

Most geisha begin their careers by actually living in the *okiya,* and though eventually they may take apartments, they still set out for their evening's work from the geisha house, which they use as a home base. In fact, the *okiya* resembles a family or home for the geisha associated with it. At present, the majority of *okiya* are managed by women (often older ex-geisha) who are called "mother." Customers are never entertained in the *okiya,* since it is considered the private domain of the geisha off duty.

A customer contacts one of the restaurants to reserve a room *(ozashiki)* and requests a certain number of geisha. The manager of the restaurant then contacts the *kemban,* and the *kemban* contacts the various *okiya.* The *kemban* keeps records of where geisha are working at any time in order to coordinate the supply of geisha with the demand for their services.

After the first party *(enkai)* of the evening, the guests may break up into smaller groups, which proceed elsewhere with a few of the geisha for "after parties" *(atokuchi).* Although these are spontaneous, the geisha must keep her *okiya* informed of where she goes so that she can be contacted if there is a call for her to appear at other parties.

Fees —— A geisha's fees are paid through the same system. The customer receives a bill from the restaurant itemizing the food, drink, room rental, and geisha. He pays the restaurant, which separates the geisha fee and sends a voucher for that amount to the *kemban.* The *kemban* in turn calculates the amount for each woman, figures the tax (usually 10 percent), takes a small percentage (3 percent) for operating expenses, and turns over the remainder to the geisha, who picks it up in the form of a salary once or twice a month.

The geisha fee (called *hanadai, senkōdai,* or *gyokudai)* applies equally to all geisha in a given area. Rather than being calculated by the hour, it is referred to in units of "sticks," since the fee was formerly figured by the length of time it took a stick of incense to burn down. One hour generally consists of "four sticks," which is the minimum amount of payment. The practice of calling a full-fledged geisha *"ippon"* ("one stick") is etymologically related, because she received the full wage. The apprentice geisha *(oshaku)* used to receive half the set wages, and although they now get the full amount, the old terminology persists.

Besides this taxable income, geisha also receive substantial tips directly from the customer. The tips, which are not taxed, may amount to as much as regular wages. While there is great variation, a geisha's average monthly income compares favorably with a salaried man's wage, and is quite good compared to that of other working women. Even though the rate of payment is fixed equally, popular geisha have more occasions to work. The amount of the tip, which is left to the discretion of the guest, also varies.

History —— The geisha system emerged around the middle of the Edo period (1600–1868). The very first geisha were male entertainers (also called *hōkan* or *taikomochi)* and thus the first such women were designated *onna* (female) *geisha.* Gradually such entertaining came to be primarily a feminine occupation; "geisha" came to be considered a female term and *otoko* (male) *geisha* was used to refer to the men. The first recorded usage of the term geisha occurred in 1751 in Kyōto and 1762 in Edo (now Tōkyō). Their antecedents included the SHIRABYŌSHI, who were dancers and sometimes mistresses of the warrior class and nobility in the court from around the 12th century.

By the 1700s the profession of geisha was related to the government-licensed brothel quarters, or *yūkaku* (see YOSHIWARA). There were various ranks of courtesans and prostitutes in these quarters, but the geisha were a separate group called in to entertain the courtesans and their guests with singing and dancing. Geisha were explicitly told not to compete with the courtesans who provided sexual services, although apparently the distinction was often blurred, since the government promulgated new orders of this type every 20 years or so. The government also attempted to limit the luxuriousness of the geisha's dress, and often plain or older women were purposely recruited as geisha.

Besides the geisha who were connected with the licensed quarters, there were also "free-lance" geisha in other areas of the city. These areas *(okabasho)* gradually came into their own as centers of sophisticated urban culture, and their geisha were often the leading arbiters of contemporary fashion. In Kyōto the present high-class *hanamachi* named Gion was one of the first such areas, and in Tōkyō the districts of Fukagawa and Yanagibashi were famous. (But since the vicissitudes of political patronage are more pronounced in

Tōkyō, these two areas have now been overshadowed by such others as Akasaka.)

In the early 19th century the *haori geisha* of Fukagawa (so called because of their habit of wearing an outer coat or *haori* over their kimono) were known as proud exponents of the cultural aesthetic of *iki* (see IKI AND SUI), emphasizing an understated elegance and a studied nonchalance. Much of the literature, music, and graphic arts of this period drew inspiration from the geisha, who were often depicted with their guests, refined men-about-town, in the teahouses or the small roofed boats *(yakata-bune),* which plied the network of rivers in Edo.

From the end of the Edo period to the present, geisha have had considerable connection with politics. The *samurai* from the outer provinces who provided the impetus for the Meiji Restoration of 1868 found the teahouses of Kyōto convenient gathering places for their meetings. There they could discuss political plans under the cover of revelry, so as to minimize governmental suspicion of their activities. With the establishment of the Meiji government in Tōkyō, some of these new leaders continued liaisons with geisha from Kyōto and elsewhere; for example, Kido Matsuko (1843–86) was a Kyōto geisha with the name Ikumatsu before her marriage to KIDO TAKAYOSHI.

Since then, however, the Tōkyō geisha have been most involved with politicians. Each faction of the government has its favorite entertainment districts, where, often with the help of *sake* and a relaxed atmosphere, much behind-the-scenes political negotiation is accomplished. The fortunes of the various *hanamachi* tend to rise and fall according to the state of the political faction which patronizes them. At present, the area called Akasaka is in the ascendancy, being closely associated with the Liberal Democratic Party (LDP). Occasionally the press condemns the so-called *machiai seiji,* or "waiting-house politics." Geisha find it professionally in their interest to be close-mouthed about what goes on at these gatherings, but even so, opposing factions seldom patronize the same geisha.

■ —— Liza Crihfield, "The Institution of the Geisha in Modern Japanese Society," PhD dissertation, Stanford University (1977). Kishii Yoshie, *Onna geisha no jidai* (1974). Nakano Eizō, *Sei fūzoku jiten* (1958). A. C. Scott, *The Flower and Willow World* (1960).

Liza CRIHFIELD

Geiyo Islands

(Geiyo Shotō). Group of islands in the central Inland Sea, between Hiroshima Prefecture, southwestern Honshū, and Ehime Prefecture, Shikoku. The group includes Mukaishima, INNOSHIMA, ŌMISHIMA, and Ikuchishima. They are hilly islands with an average elevation of 400 m (1,312 ft). Principal activities are the cultivation of citrus fruit and shipbuilding. The islands have many scenic spots as well as historic remains of the piracy active in the Inland Sea in ancient times. The Ōyamazumi Shrine (on Ōmishima) and other noted spots are here. In the early 1980s work was underway on a planned series of bridges to connect Honshū and Shikoku via the Geiyo Islands; expected completion: 1987.

gejijō

A form of old document *(komonjo),* also known as *gechijō.* A modification of the KUDASHIBUMI style of document and second only to it in importance, *gejijō* were used to transmit orders to subordinates. They were named for the words *geji kudan no gotoshi* ("the above is herewith ordered"), written at the conclusion. It was customary to write the name of the issuing authority next to the date of a *gejijō;* the name of the addressee was usually omitted. During the Kamakura period (1185–1333) *gejijō* were issued by shogunate officials to hand down decisions in lawsuits, confirm landholdings (ANDO), and order prohibitions. *Gejijō* were used less frequently in the Edo period (1600–1868), although such shogunate officials as the Kyōto deputies (KYŌTO SHOSHIDAI) are known to have issued them to merchants to grant them commercial privileges or to prohibit them from engaging in certain practices. See also DIPLOMATICS.

gekokujō

(literally, "those below overcoming those above"). A term applied to conditions of political or social upheaval when large numbers of persons of inferior status are seen to displace their superiors: when vassals usurp the place of their lords or junior officers reject the authority of their commanders. The first occurrence of the term in

Japanese literature is probably in the GEMPEI SEISUIKI, an anonymous 13th-century military romance. It appears most frequently in the diaries of court nobles and the military chronicles of the 14th through 16th centuries. These were times when, for those who enjoyed wealth and high social status, the world was being turned upside down. They witnessed the bloody destruction of the KAMAKURA SHOGUNATE (1333), the failed attempt of Emperor GO-DAIGO to restore imperial rule (1333–38), the treachery of ASHIKAGA TAKAUJI who established the MUROMACHI SHOGUNATE (1338), the lengthy war between the NORTHERN AND SOUTHERN COURTS (1336–92), the devastating ŌNIN WAR (1466–77), and the century of warfare among the provincial *daimyō* that followed. In the course of these events, the court nobility lost first their political power and then their landed estates to the warrior aristocracy, while each generation of military lords was threatened by the ambitions of their vassals. And below them all, the agrarian populace resorted to mass violence to gain debt relief or to obtain rights of village self-government. A frequently cited example of the complaint of those who were losing out during these years is the passage in the TAIHEIKI, a military romance of the mid-14th century, that reads, "Now is a time when vassal kills lord and child kills father. Only naked strength prevails. Indeed it is the extremity of *gekokujō*."

Since the medieval period (13th–16th centuries) writers have used the term, often quite loosely, to describe a variety of situations in which established authority was being challenged from below. Modern Japanese historians also have employed the term as an explanatory concept. They suggest either that there are certain times in Japanese history when the spirit of *gekokujō* was the dominant force behind social change or that the Japanese political process is particularly susceptible to *gekokujō* action. Illustrative of the first usage is the Marxist interpretation exemplified by Suzuki Ryōichi, who sees the changes in Japanese society during the 14th to 16th centuries as being generated by the struggle of the peasantry to liberate themselves from feudal bondage. The most visible signs of this struggle were the uprisings (TSUCHI IKKI) that shook the country during the 15th century. An example of the second usage is found in MARUYAMA MASAO's analysis of the insubordinate behavior of young military officers during the 1930s (see FEBRUARY 26TH INCIDENT; MAY 15TH INCIDENT; MILITARISM). Defining *gekokujō* as "an irrational explosion of irresponsible, anonymous power, which can occur only in a society in which power from below is not officially recognized," he suggests that the established leaders of the time were particularly vulnerable to the *gekokujō* phenomenon because of both their authoritarianism and their indecisiveness.

■ ——Maruyama Masao, *Thought and Behavior in Modern Japanese Politics*, ed, Ivan Morris (1963). Suzuki Ryōichi, *Gekokujō no shakai* (1949). *Taiheiki* (14th century), tr Helen Craig McCullough as *The Taiheiki: A Chronicle of Medieval Japan* (1959).

John W. HALL

Gembikei

Gorge in the city of Ichinoseki, southern Iwate Prefecture, northern Honshū. Created when the Iwaigawa, a tributary of the Kitakamigawa, carved through veins of liparite for a distance of about 2 km (1.2 mi). Designated a Natural Monument, it abounds in waterfalls and strangely shaped rocks.

Gembō (?–746)

Buddhist priest and court official of the Nara period (710–794). In 717, with the scholar KIBI NO MAKIBI, he accompanied an embassy to Tang China (see SUI AND TANG [T'ANG] CHINA, EMBASSIES TO), where he remained to study the doctrines of the HOSSŌ SECT. Gembō returned to Japan in 735 with some 5,000 scrolls and many Buddhist images. In 737 he was rewarded with the high ecclesiastical title *sōjō* (primate) and the favor of Emperor SHŌMU; he and Kibi no Makibi soon became influential in government under the patronage of the powerful minister TACHIBANA NO MOROE. In 740 Fujiwara no Hirotsugu raised a rebellion in northern Kyūshū in an attempt to overthrow these men and return his own family to power (see FUJIWARA NO HIROTSUGU, REBELLION OF); he failed, but Gembō's position was no longer secure. Gembō's influence in Nara declined with the rise to power of FUJIWARA NO NAKAMARO, the favorite of Shōmu's consort, Empress KŌMYŌ. In 745 Nakamaro banished him to Kyūshū, ostensibly to supervise construction of the temple Kanzeonji at Dazaifu, where he died the following year.

Gembudō

Basaltic cave in the city of Toyooka, northern Hyōgo Prefecture, western Honshū. Located on a mountain slope on the east bank of the river Maruyamagawa, it is composed of hexagonal and other types of columnar joints, and has been designated as a Natural Monument. Gembudō is flanked by similar basaltic caves called Seiryūdō and Suzakudō. Kinosaki Hot Spring, located nearby, attracts numerous visitors.

gembun itchi

(unification of the spoken and written language). Process through which the classical styles of the written language (*bungo*) used in the Meiji period (1868–1912) were replaced by colloquial styles (*kōgo*).

The written language of the latter part of the Edo period (1600–1868) comprised an almost continuous chain of styles ranging from pure classical Chinese, through its adaptations and mixed forms, to pure classical Japanese. After the Meiji Restoration of 1868 some of these styles continued to be used, but in addition a new modernized classical style, the Classical Standard, developed on their basis. Neither the traditional styles nor the Classical Standard were close to the spoken language and were incomprehensible without concentrated study. At the same time as the Classical Standard emerged, a different style of language, both written and spoken, started to develop on the basis of the spoken language of the Tōkyō area. This Colloquial Standard penetrated gradually into the domains of the classical styles and it is this process, accompanied by lively discussions, that has been given the name *gembun itchi*.

The idea of *gembun itchi* goes back to the beginning of the Meiji period, but the term was used first by KANDA TAKAHIRA in 1885. The number and quality of attempts to employ a colloquial style in writing was increasing gradually. The first great achievement was FUTABATEI SHIMEI's novel *Ukigumo* (1887–89, Drifting Clouds). Other writers followed suit, and by 1908 all novels were in the Colloquial Standard. Primary school textbooks completed the switch by 1903, and the transition of the newspapers to the Colloquial Standard was completed in the 1920s. However, the administration and the law continued to use the Classical Standard until 1946. In contemporary Japan the Classical Standard only survives in practical communication as the language of the legal codes promulgated before 1946. (When individual articles of such codes, e.g., the Commercial Code, are amended, they are still drafted in a simplified version of the Classical Standard.)

The contemporary Colloquial Standard (Standard Japanese) uses basically the same grammar as the contemporary spoken language, but many of its written styles are considerably distant from the spoken language, both in their complicated syntax and in their vocabulary. This fact has led some Japanese educators (e.g., Nishio Minoru) to the slogan of the "second *gembun itchi*." However, this movement has had little success and even today most written styles of the Colloquial Standard are widely distant from the spoken language.

■ ——Yamamoto Masahide, *Gembun itchi no hassei*, Kokugo Shirīzu 65 (1969).

J. V. NEUSTUPNÝ

Gempei jōsuiki → Gempei seisuiki

Gempei no Sōran → Taira-Minamoto War

Gempei seisuiki

(The Rise and Fall of the Genji and Heike). Also known as *Gempei jōsuiki*. A military chronicle (GUNKI MONOGATARI) of unknown authorship dating from the Kamakura period (1185–1333), it recounts the shifting fortunes of the MINAMOTO FAMILY (or Genji) and TAIRA FAMILY (or Heike) at the close of the Heian period (794–1185). It is generally considered to be a variant of another famous military chronicle, the HEIKE MONOGATARI, but presents greater historical detail and breadth than that work, especially in its descriptions of the Minamoto. It also boasts a large number of incidental legends, religious fables, and tales from Chinese antiquity not included in the *Heike monogatari*. The style features a mixture of Japanese and Sino-Japanese vocabulary (*wakan konkōbun*) and seems to have been intended for reading, unlike the *Heike monogatari*, which was generally recited by professional entertainers or bards. There are numerous variations and irregularities in the text. See also TAIRA-MINAMOTO WAR.

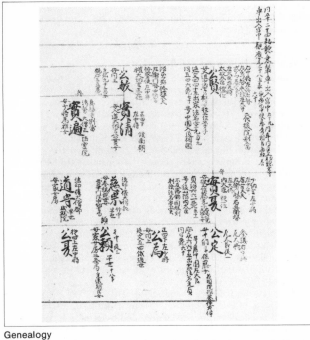

Genealogy

A page from a 16th-century copy of the *Sompi bummyaku* showing the Tōin family genealogy. The names of male family members are written in large characters with posts and ranks to the right of the name. Other personal data appear to the left of the name. 28.3 × 22.5 cm. Imperial Household Agency.

Gempei War → Taira-Minamoto War

gempuku

A coming-of-age ceremony, observed from at least the 7th century through the Edo period (1600–1868), in which a boy assumed adult clothing, hairstyle, and name. The term itself means "basic clothing." There was no precise age for the ceremony (in early times it was performed when a boy reached the height of about 136 cm or 4.5 ft), but it generally fell between the ages of 10 and 16, depending on family convenience. After the ceremony the boy was considered eligible to take on adult responsibilities, participate in religious ceremonies, and marry.

Among the court nobility the event was known as *kanrei* or "cap ceremony," because it was then that the young man began to wear the kind of cap called a *kammuri* (see HEADGEAR). A *samurai* youth began to wear the *eboshi* cap, and later, from about the 16th century, he had the front of his head shaved (see HAIRSTYLES). A boy of the lower classes might receive a loincloth (FUNDOSHI), in which case the event was called *heko-iwai* ("loincloth celebration"). In all such ceremonies the boy usually received gifts of adult clothing from either his father or a respected man who was thenceforward considered his patron. In fact, the boy's adult name often incorporated part of the name of the patron, who was called *kakan* ("he who bestows the cap"), *hikiire* ("guide"), or *eboshioya* ("cap parent"). Girls had a similar ceremony between the ages of 12 and 16, involving a patroness and changes in hairstyle and clothing; it was most often called *mogi* or "putting on the skirt."

Even today the concept of a formal coming-of-age ceremony survives in the national holiday Adulthood Day (Seijin no Hi), observed each 15 January, when young people who have reached their legal majority (20 years) in the past year are encouraged to visit shrines and attend receptions held by local governments. Often the young people receive gifts of business suits and formal *kimono* from relatives. See also LIFE CYCLE.   *David W. PLATH*

Genda Minoru (1904–   )

Naval officer and politician. Born in Hiroshima Prefecture. Upon graduating from the Naval Academy in 1924, he became a fighter pilot. He was appointed a staff officer in 1941, and was entrusted by Admiral YAMAMOTO ISOROKU to draft the details of the plan for the attack on PEARL HARBOR. He ended the war as a captain. After the war he joined the Air Self Defense Force and became its chief of staff from 1959. He retired in 1962 and was elected to the House of Councillors. He plays an active role as a senior member of the National Defense Committee of the Liberal Democratic Party.
HATA Ikuhiko

Gen'e (1279–1350)

Buddhist priest and Confucian scholar of the latter part of the Kamakura period (1185–1333) and early part of the Muromachi period (1333–1568). He is thought to have been an adherent of the Tendai sect who later converted to Zen. Gen'e tutored Emperor GO-DAIGO in the Confucian classics and was involved in his unsuccessful attempts to overthrow the Kamakura shogunate (see KEMMU RESTORATION). After Go-Daigo was himself overthrown by ASHIKAGA TAKAUJI in 1336, Takauji employed Gen'e to help him formulate the KEMMU SHIKIMOKU, the basic code of the Muromachi shogunate. TEIKIN ŌRAI, a manual of letter writing, is also attributed to Gen'e.

genealogy

(keifugaku). Since ancient Japanese society was based on the family or clan (UJI) system and appointment to public office was hereditary, it is reasonable to suppose that there was keen interest in genealogy from the earliest times. It is known that an attempt was made in 761 to draw up simple genealogies of certain families for presentation to the throne, but the project was never finished. In 815, however, the compilation of genealogical records known as SHINSEN SHŌJIROKU was completed, listing more than 1,100 families of the capital region and describing their historical background. More detailed genealogies (called *ujibumi*) like the *Takahashi no ujibumi* of the early years of the Heian period (794–1185) and the *Ōnakatomi honkeichō* (906), as well as family histories like the *Muchimaro den* and *Taishokukan den* (ca 1000, known collectively as the TŌSHI KADEN), give accounts of the origins, history, and government posts of a family and invariably supply dates and places of birth of family members.

Most scholars date the use of genealogical charts from the Heian period. These charts show family relationships, inheritance of certain landholdings, or the transmission of Buddhist teachings from master to disciple (the last being known as *kechimyaku*, or "blood vessels"). Their obvious usefulness prompted wide-scale compilation of such charts by the end of the period.

The Japanese words *keifu* and *keizu* are used interchangeably to mean genealogical records, but strictly speaking, *keizu* are graphic representations of *keifu*, or genealogical relations. The charts known as *kakeizu* usually recorded the line of male descent and gave only cursory treatment to female relatives. Such charts were originally written from top to bottom on sheets of paper vertically attached. A famous example of a vertical chart (*tatekeizu*) is the Wake family genealogy preserved in the temple Onjōji in Shiga Prefecture. Later charts were written from right to left on sheets horizontally attached (*yokokeizu*); they included the childhood name, bureaucratic positions, Buddhist name, marital connections, and accomplishments of each family member.

In the Kamakura (1185–1333) and Muromachi (1333–1568) periods lineage and family tradition were closely connected with rights to family landholdings and other property, and, not suprisingly, a great many counterfeit genealogies appeared. The SOMPI BUMMYAKU, compiled by Tōin Kinsada (1340–99) and others, however, is fairly reliable. The collection of ancient literary works GUNSHO RUIJŪ includes a genealogical table of the imperial family (*Honchō kōin shōun roku*, 1416) as well as tables for 15 families, including the Sugawara and the Ōe. The sequel to *Gunsho ruijū* contains more than 70 additional genealogical tables, including a chart for the MUSASHI SHICHITŌ line, and so we have an almost complete record of warrior families up to and including the Sengoku period (1467–1568), although the information is not always accurate.

The principal genealogical works of the Edo period (1600–1868) include the officially sponsored KAN'EI SHOKA KEIZU DEN (1643) and the KANSEI CHŌSHŪ SHOKA FU (1812). These have great historical value, for they were carefully checked by scholars after they were presented to the Tokugawa shogunate by the *daimyō* and *hatamoto* (bannermen). The *Fuchō yoroku* (1684–88) is a similar compilation. All of these records have been published either in typeset editions or in photolithographic copies of the originals. The court nobility also had genealogical charts drawn up during the Edo period. They are included in such collections as the *Shoka den* (1670) and the more succinct *Shoka chifu sekki* (1692).

📖 —— Ōta Akira, *Seishi kakei daijiten* (1934–36). Ōta Akira, *Kakei keizu no nyūmon* (1967). YAMAMOTO Takeo

general clause

(*ippan jōkō*). A legal term referring to a provision that abstractly and generally determines legal conditions; also called a summary provision. Most such instances arise in private law; examples are provisions that determine public order and good morals (see KŌJO RYŌZOKU), ABUSE OF RIGHT, suitable reasons for cancellation of land leases and house leases (Leased Land Law, art. 4; Leased House Law, art. 1, para. 2), and major reasons making the continuation of a marriage relationship difficult (CIVIL CODE, art. 770).

Such matters as what types of JURISTIC ACT contravene public order and good morals and what kinds of activity constitute an abuse of rights are left to the judge's individual judgment. Since the general clause can be applied to complicated and diverse social conditions, it has often been incorporated in legislation in recent years. This has given rise to the concern that, since there are many cases where the judge has wide discretion, it is difficult for the disputants to make any prediction about the outcome of many cases. The result is a loss of legal stability. Efforts have been made to counter these effects by making interpretations on the basis of other legal principles and by systematizing precedents, and some have advocated the addition of special systems to the examination procedures (for example, requiring the attendance of expert witnesses or the conducting of official examinations by examiners with knowledge and experience).

In public law provisions regarding determinations for which there are no concrete standards, such as "when it is recognized to be necessary for the public good" (Local Railway Law, art. 22) or "when it is necessary for the public good" (Railway Operation Law, art. 9), are also called general clauses. *ENDŌ Hiroshi*

General Corporation

(Zeneraru). Company engaged in the production of household electric appliances, television sets, acoustic equipment, and office machines. Its forerunner was Yao Shōten Co, Ltd, established in 1936 by Yao Keijirō. It started manufacturing radio sets, gramophones, and loudspeaker equipment in 1942. In the latter half of the 1950s it diversified its operations to include the manufacture of televisions, refrigerators, washing machines, and other household electrical appliances, as well as communications equipment, thus becoming one of Japan's major electric equipment makers. It took its current name, which is used as its brand name, in 1966. In 1968 it began production of calculators to strengthen its electronics division. It has a special contract with the National Federation of Agricultural Cooperatives for the sale of its products, thus capturing a stable market among the farmers of Japan. It has sales companies in the United States, West Germany, Australia, and the United Kingdom. Sales for the fiscal year ending March 1982 totaled ¥98.9 billion (US $410.9 million), and the company was capitalized at ¥2.7 billion (US $11.2 million). Corporate headquarters are located in Kawasaki, Kanagawa Prefecture.

General Council of Trade Unions of Japan → Sōhyō

General Sekiyu

(Zeneraru Sekiyu). A company selling various types of petroleum products, General Sekiyu was established in 1947. It took on its present name in 1967 and is affiliated with Exxon. It is one of the principal members of the General Sekiyu group, which is engaged in the refining, transportation, and sale of oil and liquified petroleum gas (LPG). It has strengthened its affiliation with Exxon since 1979. Future plans call for establishing a system to ensure a long-term stable supply of crude oil, increasing refining capacity, and developing into a comprehensive oil enterprise utilizing Exxon's technology and information. General Sekiyu is also planning to develop alternate energy sources by participating in Exxon's coal liquification project. Sales for the fiscal year ending March 1982 totaled ¥835.8 billion (US $3.5 billion), of which gasoline accounted for 29 percent, naphtha 12 percent, light oil 15 percent, heavy oil 35 percent, and other products 9 percent. The company was capitalized at ¥4.7 billion (US $19.5 million) in the same year. Corporate headquarters are located in Tōkyō.

General Strike of 1947

Commonly known as the Niichi Suto (February First Strike). A general strike scheduled for 1 February 1947 but prohibited on 31 January by General Douglas A. MACARTHUR, Supreme Commander for the Allied Powers. It marked a turning point in the postwar Japanese labor movement and was the first confrontation between labor and the OCCUPATION, which until then had not only officially encouraged unionization but remained neutral in labor disputes.

The strike promised a rare show of labor unity, led by the government workers' joint struggle committee, which spoke for 2.6 million government workers and teachers, with later pledges of participation by millions of workers in the private sector. Much, but not all, of the initiative and leadership came from communist or procommunist organizers and the radical labor federation, SAMBETSU KAIGI. The demands of the strike were both economic and political: higher wages and the ensurance of minimum wages to counter the spiraling inflation amid general worsening economic conditions, and the resignation of the YOSHIDA SHIGERU cabinet and its replacement by a leftist coalition.

Many see the banning of the strike as the start of the so-called reverse course of the Occupation, in which emphasis on democratic social and political reform was superseded by economic reconstruction. Whether the ban was necessary to prevent social chaos, as MacArthur claimed, or was the denial of democratic ideals for cold war aims is still a topic for political debate.

In the aftermath of the ban, labor unity was shattered, and the communists lost most of their influence in the labor movement to the more moderate socialists. To this day Japanese labor has been plagued by lack of unity and political divisions. See also HISTORY OF JAPAN: postwar history. *Paul HENRIQUES*

general trading companies

(*sōgō shōsha*). The very large, highly diversified Japanese commercial houses which structure and facilitate the flow of goods, services, and money among client firms, operating both within Japan and globally. The nine firms listed in the table are considered to constitute the ranks of the general trading companies, or *sōgō shōsha*, although some smaller and less diverse trading houses are also sometimes called by the same designation. The total sales of the nine firms equal almost 25 percent of Japan's gross national product, and the imports and exports handled by them account for about half of the nation's foreign trade.

Origins of the Sōgō Shōsha —— The *sōgō shōsha* have their roots in Japan's Meiji period (1868–1912), when the development of industry and foreign trade became national priorities. After two-and-a-half centuries of commercial isolation under the Tokugawa shogunate (1603–1867), Japan found itself critically short of the skills necessary to conduct foreign commerce and build a modern economy. The foreign merchant houses, which initially handled Japan's external commerce, were perceived as not having Japanese national interests among their foremost priorities, and so it became a matter of governmental and commercial concern to find ways of having larger portions of Japan's trade handled by Japanese firms.

The forerunners of today's *sōgō shōsha* can be considered an institutional response to this need. With knowledge of shipping, insurance, foreign markets, and even foreign languages in short supply among Japanese businesses, there were obvious advantages in having trading houses emerge as repositories of these scarce resources, to be drawn upon by firms which had need of them.

A basic distinction can be made between firms such as MITSUI & CO, LTD, and the MITSUBISHI CORPORATION, which grew as the trading arms of emerging ZAIBATSU groups of enterprises, and firms which grew as specialized traders in newly developing industries, especially textiles and metals. The former had the obvious advantage of close relations with their sister *zaibatsu* companies and could relatively easily utilize economies of scale and bargaining power in representing them in overseas transactions.

The non-*zaibatsu* firms originally performed a different kind of economic function. In both metals and textiles, the industrial structure came to be composed of large-scale, mass production, "modern" firms at certain stages of production (spinning and production of pig iron, for example), and small-scale "traditional" firms at other stages. It was necessary to coordinate product flows, finance inventories, and otherwise manage these complex production processes, creating opportunities for skillful traders. As the metal and textile industries grew, they became dependent on foreign trade for raw materials and markets, creating a need for internationalization of the trading companies in these sectors.

The *zaibatsu* firms dominated Japan's pre–World War II trade, with Mitsui alone handling almost 20 percent of all imports and exports in the early war years. The other firms were important in their own sectors but lacked the same scale or diversity. *Zaibatsu* dominance proved costly, however, as it led to the dissolution of both Mitsui and Mitsubishi *sōgō shōsha* during the Allied OCCUPATION, providing major opportunities for the smaller firms to diversify and gain market share. In time Mitsui and Mitsubishi were reconstituted but only after the growth of their non-*zaibatsu* rivals into formidable competitors. See ZAIBATSU DISSOLUTION.

Functions and Characteristics——Each of the *sōgō shōsha* maintains a system of domestic offices connected to a worldwide network of overseas offices by a sophisticated telex network. Managers working in these offices maintain close contact with local corporations, markets, business environments, and governments. When opportunities to engage in profitable business transactions appear, these global information networks are mobilized to initiate and carry through deals. A *sōgō shōsha* earns either a commission or a trading profit on such transactions.

Although it is difficult to separate domestic and international transactions of the *sōgō shōsha*, their business appears to be split equally between the two spheres. The overwhelming portion of international trade consists of exports from and imports to Japan, but a growing portion of international business, roughly 10 percent, consists of "third-country trade," that is, trade not involving Japan.

The products handled by a *sōgō shōsha* are highly diverse. Each buys and sells at least 10,000 different products. A popular catchphrase says the firms will deal in anything "from noodles to guided missiles." However, most of the trade volume consists of such commodities as ferrous and nonferrous metals, chemicals and petrochemicals, foodstuffs, fuels, textiles, and lumber. Involvement with highly differentiated or brand name products is relatively limited.

The functions of a *sōgō shōsha* include both financing and conducting trade. A firm may offer its clients a wide assortment of financing, including trade credit, inventory financing, factoring, loan guarantees, and even equity participation, as well as financial services such as foreign-exchange risk management. In Japan, the *sōgō shōsha* are a very important source of funds for business borrowing.

The *sōgō shōsha* are themselves also enormous borrowers of money, especially from the city banks of Japan. About 95 percent of the liabilities of a *sōgō shōsha* consists of debt; only 5 percent is equity. In a sense, the *sōgō shōsha* borrow money from the banks at "wholesale" and lend it out to client firms at "retail," earning the interest differential as income. One major reason they are able to perform this function is that they have access to very good information on the financial situations of their clients, derived from their extensive business dealings with them.

Sōgō shōsha also manage the logistics of the flows of goods and services involved in their trading activity. Arranging for shipping, insurance, delivery, inventory management, and other complex details is among their important functions. Because of its scale, a *sōgō shōsha* can often achieve substantial savings in performing these functions.

The trading companies also play an important role in the establishment of large-scale projects by consortia of firms, especially overseas. Iron mining in Australia, petrochemical complexes in the Middle East, and aluminum smelting in the United States are major projects in which these companies play important multiple roles as coordinators, suppliers, customers, financiers, and part owners. In Japan and overseas, they are able to act as corporate intermediaries in arranging important and complicated business deals.

Each of the *sōgō shōsha* is staffed by a managerial cadre of several thousand lifetime employees, recruited at graduation from leading Japanese universities. These traders typically begin their careers in Japan, working in one or more related product areas. Over time, they may be posted to a variety of locations throughout Japan and the world. The *sōgō shōsha* makes a very heavy investment in developing the expertise of these managers over a period of many years. The accumulated knowledge, skills, and relationships of these traders must be considered the primary business asset of the companies. Many non-Japanese nationals as well are employed in overseas offices.

Sōgō shōsha also maintain scores of subsidiaries and affiliates, both in Japan and overseas. These firms, which may or may not be majority owned, generally perform functions related to the primary trading mission. Examples would be the operation of a coal dock or downstream manufacturing in the textile industry.

Each of the six largest *sōgō shōsha* is a member of one of the six major ENTERPRISE GROUPS, and the three smaller firms maintain looser relations with one or more of the groups. However, none of them enjoys an exclusive hold on the trading business of group member companies. Large Japanese firms prefer to have at least two *sōgō shōsha* competing for their business, while the trading firms often have close business relationships with members of rival groups.

Strategy and Competition——Because *sōgō shōsha* borrow so much of their capital, fixed costs for interest are extremely high. Operating a global network of offices is also largely a fixed cost. As a consequence, the trading firms compete vigorously with each other to maximize trading volume, while cutting their margins very thin, typically to 1 or 2 percent. The average pretax profit on sales of the nine firms was one quarter of 1 percent in 1978. Nonetheless, since they deal in huge quantities, revenues are substantial. Even more than on price, *sōgō shōsha* compete on service, endeavoring to make themselves into "eyes and ears" for their clients, bringing opportunities to their attention.

Particularly with Japanese clients, the emphasis is on longstanding business relationships governed by trust and long-term reciprocity. Although a firm may occasionally speculate on commodities, the real essence of its strategy lies in building long-term, high-volume business for its clients and itself.

With its size, diversity, and excellent human resources, a *sōgō shōsha* is often able to take a broader and longer-term perspective of complex global business systems, such as the ferrous metals industry, than its clients can. As a consequence, it is able to discover opportunities for synergistic benefits. For example, if the firm coordinates the logistics of product flow among clients, it may be possible to reduce the in-process inventories of coal, pig iron, steel, rolled steel, and fabricated steel within the total system. The *sōgō shōsha* is able to coordinate such a system and can share the savings among the members of that system and itself.

Future of the Sōgō Shōsha——The *sōgō shōsha* have seen many changes and adaptations as Japan's status and role in the world economy have changed. The necessity for change and adaptation continues. The evolution of the Japanese economy away from resource-processing industries toward higher value-added manufacturing and service sectors is one challenge. The bulk of *sōgō shōsha* business volume lies in serving the basic resource-processing industries, which are in relative decline.

Another competitive threat is the growing internationalization and sophistication of the managerial organizations of many client firms. As these firms become more capable of dealing with international trade, one of the original motives for using the services of a trading company becomes weaker. As clients face the need to cut costs, there is considerable pressure to perform internally the services supplied by a *sōgō shōsha*.

Another threat to the *sōgō shōsha* lies in the possibility of an increasingly hostile business environment. In Japan, *sōgō shōsha* have been linked to scandals involving aircraft sales, commodities speculation, and allegations of other harmful activities. Because of their enormous size and their secrecy, *sōgō shōsha* have been viewed with suspicion by segments of the Japanese public.

Overseas governments may also be suspicious of *sōgō shōsha*. Particularly in countries where Japanese business presence is itself controversial, the *sōgō shōsha* may be singled out for special scrutiny owing to their size and secrecy. The fact that managerial staffs are dominated by Japanese nationals, with relatively few significant positions for indigenous managers, may be another source of suspicion or hostility.

Competition among the *sōgō shōsha* is intensifying, and the benefits of scale appear to be growing in importance. Smaller firms in the sector are increasingly vulnerable to the risks inherent in such a high fixed-cost business. In 1977 Ataka & Co, then the 10th largest *sōgō shōsha*, was liquidated as a result of accumulated bad debts and other problems. Parts of it were absorbed by C. ITOH & CO, LTD. For the smaller *sōgō shōsha*, the future appears threatening indeed.

To surmount these challenges, the *sōgō shōsha* will once again have to adapt its institutional role. The extent to which this can be done will vary from firm to firm. However, to the extent that the world needs to coordinate access to raw materials, markets, information, money, and talented managers, there will remain a potential role for the *sōgō shōsha*. See also KANEMATSU-GŌSHŌ, LTD; MARU-BENI CORPORATION; NICHIMEN CO, LTD; NISSHŌ-IWAI CO, LTD; SUMITOMO CORPORATION; TŌYŌ MENKA KAISHA, LTD.

Thomas B. LIFSON

Geneva Naval Conference of 1927

(Junēbu Kaigun Gunshuku Kaigi). Naval conference held from June to August 1927 in Geneva, Switzerland, and attended by representatives of Great Britain, the United States, and Japan to discuss the limitation of auxiliary ships (cruisers, destroyers, and submarines). This conference followed the WASHINGTON CONFERENCE of 1921–22, which had set limits on the size of each country's fleet of battleships. The Japanese delegates at Geneva were Admiral SAITŌ MAKOTO, former navy minister, and ISHII KIKUJIRŌ, Japanese ambassador to France. The discussions were inconclusive, largely because of substantial disagreements among the participating nations, and the issue remained unresolved until the LONDON NAVAL CONFERENCES.

genin

(literally, "inferior people"). A term applied to certain members of the lower class from the early part of the Heian period (794–1185) through the Edo (1600–1868) period; its use varied according to time and place. At first the term was applied to peasants in general, but with the rise of private landed estates (SHŌEN) in late Heian times, it came to mean peasants who worked the soil for the proprietors and officials of *shōen*. By the Kamakura period (1185–1333) *genin* were virtually serfs or slaves, owned by aristocrats, religious institutions, *samurai*, or independent cultivators (MYŌSHU) and formed a majority of the agricultural labor force. They lived in their masters' households, had no economic rights, marital choice, or freedom of movement, and could be sold, transferred, or bequeathed as property. From the latter part of the Muromachi period (1333–1568) onward, the status of *genin* gradually improved; they were no longer serfs but tenant farmers with some degree of independence and rights to the land. By the Edo period, the term *genin* referred to annually contracted tenant farmers and to servants in general. See also NAGO; FUDAI.

Genji → Minamoto family

Genji Keita (1912–)

Novelist. Real name Tanaka Tomio. Born in Toyama Prefecture. He had worked for more than 15 years as a white-collar worker before he made his literary debut with the short story "Tabako musume" (1947, Cigarette Girl), after which he continued working as a company employee for nine more years. The joys and sorrows of white-collar workers are described with humor and pathos in *Santō jūyaku* (1951–52, A Third-rate Executive). His "Eigoyasan" (1951, tr *The English Interpreter*, 1972) received the Naoki Literary Prize.

Genji monogatari → Tale of Genji

Genji monogatari emaki

General term for illustrated handscrolls (EMAKIMONO) portraying scenes from the 11th-century novel TALE OF GENJI (*Genji monogatari*). Elaborate and richly colored as a rule, *Genji* illustrations have formed one of the main themes of YAMATO-E (native-style Japanese painting) since the 12th century.

The oldest and finest examples of *Genji* handscrolls now exist only in sections and are found in the Tokugawa Art Museum, Nagoya, and the Gotō Art Museum, Tōkyō, with a few additional fragments in other collections. All date from the early 12th century, slightly more than a hundred years after the novel was written. Only 20 of the 54 chapters of the *Tale of Genji* are represented among the surviving portions of these handscrolls (13 of them illustrations). Originally there must have been one to three illustrations for each chapter, with a descriptive text preceding each illustration. The complete set would probably have comprised 10 scrolls.

The illustrations that have survived intact, with their accompanying texts, include the following; two from "Suzumushi" (chap. 38) and one each from "Yūgiri" (chap. 39) and "Minori" (chap. 40), in the Gotō Art Museum; one each from "Yomogiu" (chap. 15) and "Sekiya" (chap. 16), three from "Kashiwagi" (chap. 36), one from "Yokobue" (chap. 37), two from "Takekawa" (chap. 44), one each from "Hashihime" (chap. 45) and "Sawarabi" (chap. 48), three from "Yadorigi" (chap. 49), and two from "Azumaya" (chap. 50), plus one complete text section from "E-awase" (chap. 17), all in the Tokugawa Art Museum. Nine additional fragments of text are scattered among various other collections. A heavily retouched painting in the Tōkyō National Museum has recently been identified, with the help of X-ray photographs, as part of this set, illustrating "Wakamurasaki" (chap. 5). Since the set was obviously broken up at an early date, more text fragments or paintings may yet be discovered.

The paintings are relatively uniform in size: 21 to 22 centimeters (8.3 to 8.7 in) wide and either 39 or 48 centimeters (15.4 or 18.9 in) long. The scenes selected for illustration tend to be relatively static, depicting not major events but the moments just before or after them, when the characters pause to contemplate their interlocking lives and perhaps to compose poems expressing their feelings. This lyrical quality, further enhanced by the stylistic characteristics of the paintings, is very much in keeping with the spirit of the novel and with the artistic sensibilities of Heian-period (794–1185) courtly society.

Perhaps the most striking peculiarity of the style employed for these paintings is the technique of drawing faces known as *hikime kagibana*, "line-for-an-eye, hook-for-a nose." Both male and female figures have round, fat-cheeked faces, usually shown in three-quarter view, with the same highly conventional features: thick eyebrows, eyes that appear at first to be a single line, a simple hook shape for the nose, and a small red dot for the mouth. Paradoxically, it is the most important and high-ranking characters who show the greatest anonymity of facial features. This deceptively simple technique was probably used in order to encourage the viewer's identification with the characters and vicarious participation in their emotions. A careful comparison of the faces shows that, despite their lack of individuality, there are appropriate differences in facial expression, producing subtle variations in emotional effect.

Further clues to the emotional tenor of each scene are provided by the architectural setting. The interior views utilize a strongly diagonal perspective combined with the FUKINUKI YATAI, or "blown-off roof" technique, whereby roofs of buildings are omitted to produce clear overhead views of the inhabitants. This device is common to much of Japanese narrative painting, but it is especially well used in the *Genji* scrolls. A clear example of the expressive powers of this type of composition is the first illustration of "Kashiwagi," in which the retired emperor visits his daughter, Genji's wife, who, despite her youth and beauty, has decided to become a nun. The steep diagonal lines of the architecture, crossed at many different angles by the screens set up around the lady, echo the conflicting emotions of the characters.

The single most important factor in the artistic impact of the *Genji monogatari emaki* is the lavish use of thick colors, carefully selected to enhance the mood of each scene. Mineral pigments such as bright red, green, and blue were used together with gold and silver for a gorgeous effect, and the costumes and furnishings were decorated with delicate patterns. Production of the paintings was clearly a group project. The supervising artist first made an underdrawing in ink. The colors were filled in by assistants, following notations such as those now visible in some areas where the pigment has worn off. Finally, the outlines were retraced and the fine lines of the faces redrawn by the master artist. The solid black areas, such as ladies' hair and men's hats, were finished with ink mixed with resin, forming black accents that set off the bright colors. This elaborate method of constructing a painting is referred to in Heian documents as *tsukuri-e*, "manufactured painting."

Another descriptive term found in Heian literature, a somewhat puzzling one, is *onna-e*, or "women's painting." The word seems to indicate paintings illustrating romantic literature, featuring brilliant colors and faces drawn in the *hikime kagibana* style. It implies that such paintings, like the literary works that they illustrated, were enjoyed primarily, although not exclusively, by women; it may also indicate that this painting style originated in amateur paintings by court ladies. It has even been suggested that the *Genji* scrolls were based on sketches supplied by aristocratic patrons, though the finished product is clearly the work of professionals.

The exquisite decorative quality of this *emaki* is apparent not only in the pictures but in the text sections as well. The texts are written in a running style on sheets of fine paper made of fibers of the shrub called *gampi (Wikstroemia sikokiana)*, each differently decorated. The decorations of the paper include brown, red, and yellow colors; delicate underpaintings of grasses, flowers, and bamboo; and gold and silver leaf in the form of small squares and triangles, hair-like threads, or tiny dots (*kirihaku, noge,* and *sunago,* respectively). Five different calligraphic styles have been recognized.

The paintings have been traditionally attributed, at least since the Edo period (1600–1868), to Fujiwara no Takachika (fl mid-12th century) or his father, Takayoshi (1127–74); the calligraphy, to Fujiwara no Korefusa (1030–96), JAKUREN (ca 1139–1202), Fujiwara no Masatsune (1170–1221), and Takachika. All of these attributions are plausible, but there is no proof for any of them. Furthermore, it is now clear that the paintings, as well as the calligraphy, are in several distinct hands. The divisions of paintings and calligraphy correspond exactly, suggesting that the entire project was divided into separate sections, each probably under the supervision of a court noble. A set of *Genji* pictures is known to have been commissioned by the emperor in 1119, but it is unlikely that these are the same ones. However, a comparison with dated works in the *tsukuri-e* style, such as the *Kunōji kyō* of 1141 and the *Heike nōkyō* of 1164, shows that the *Genji* scrolls represent an earlier version of the style. A date of circa 1110–20 for the *Genji* scrolls seems likely.

■——Akiyama Terukazu, *Genji-e* (vol 1 of *Nihon no bijutsu;* 1958). Akiyama Terukazu, *Genji monogatari emaki,* vol 2 of *Nihon emakimono zenshū* (Kadokawa Shoten; rev ed 1975). Ivan Morris, *The Tale of Genji Scroll* (1971).   *Sarah* THOMPSON

Genkai Sea

(Genkai Nada). Arm of the East China Sea off the northern coast of Fukuoka and Saga prefectures, Kyūshū. The East China Sea is on the west, and the Hibiki Sea leads to the Sea of Japan on the east. The Genkai Sea has long been important as a transportation link between Japan and the continent. The Tsushima Current flows through these waters, making them a rich fishing ground for sea bream, squid, mackerel, and yellowtail. The Genkai Sea forms the Genkai Quasi-National Park. Average depth: 50–60 m (164–197 ft); deepest point: approximately 100 m (328 ft).

Genkō Incident

(Genkō no Hen). The civil strife from 1331 to 1333 (Genkō 1–3) that led to the fall of the Kamakura shogunate. Emperor GO-DAIGO, determined to rule in his own right and to keep the succession in his line of the imperial family, had been enlisting supporters against the HŌJŌ FAMILY regents and the shogunate since his unsuccessful coup of 1324 (see SHŌCHŪ CONSPIRACY). In 1331 he was pressed by the shogunate to abdicate; he refused and fled to Nara, whereupon the shogunate set up Emperor KŌGON of the rival line in his place. The following year Kamakura forces captured Go-Daigo, exiled him to the Oki Islands (now part of Shimane Prefecture), and formally enthroned Kōgon. Go-Daigo's son Prince MORINAGA, however, continued resistance with the aid of KUSUNOKI MASASHIGE and other local warriors. When Go-Daigo escaped from Oki in 1333, the whole country was thrown into civil war. ASHIKAGA TAKAUJI, the Kamakura general sent to suppress the rebellion, saw an opportunity to become shōgun himself and suddenly changed sides, capturing Kyōto in Go-Daigo's name. Shortly thereafter the general NITTA YOSHISADA marched on Kamakura and destroyed the Hōjō and the shogunate. Go-Daigo then returned to Kyōto to inaugurate the KEMMU RESTORATION (1333–36).

Genkō shakusho

The earliest comprehensive history of Japanese Buddhism. The first word of the title refers to the year when the book was completed and presented to the throne, Genkō 2 (1322); *shakusho* might be translated as monks' history, or history of the line of Shakyamuni (Śākyamuni), the historical Buddha. The author, KOKAN SHIREN, is reckoned one of the founders of GOZAN LITERATURE, Chinese secular learning cultivated in the Zen monasteries; the work is therefore written entirely in Chinese. The models for the arrangement of its contents were likewise Chinese, including not only works by Buddhist historians but the most venerable works of Confucian historiography. There are three major divisions: biographies *(den),* annals, and essays. The first is by far the largest, and also the most widely read; a Japanese rendering of it, together with portions of the essays, was printed in 1690 for a popular audience. It recounts the lives of over 400 persons, predominantly monks but also a few women and

pious laymen, and even some native deities who the author believed had shown special favor toward Buddhism. Since the purpose of biography was to provide moral exempla as well as to reward the memory of the virtuous, many of the biographies are followed by eulogies *(san)* or discourses *(ron)* that praise (or in some cases censure) the behavior of their subjects.

Like the contemporaneous history of the monarchy, JINNŌ SHŌTŌ KI, *Genkō shakusho* expresses an awareness of history as process that was new to its century. The work is best appreciated, however, if the reader accepts the fact that many of its fundamental ideas are not those of the modern historian. These include the conviction that supernatural experience is proof of holiness and a preoccupation with questions of religious genealogy. Investigating whether a doctrine had been transmitted in an orthodox manner through generations of masters and disciples was one of the first concerns of the historian. Kokan was convinced that Zen was the highest form of Buddhism and that it was his duty to honor the patriarchs of his own lineage within Zen. He nevertheless attempted to give a balanced account of all the schools of Buddhism. Intensely proud of being Japanese, he believed that the Shintō *kami* (deities) welcomed Buddhism and that Japan was the destined home of Buddhism, after it had failed in India and undergone persecution in China.   *Marian* URY

genre painting → fūzokuga

genrō

(elder statesmen; literally, "the original elders"). The unofficial designation given to the "founding fathers" of the modern state of Japan who survived into the middle of the Meiji period (1868–1912) to become the chief advisers to the emperor with the right to select and recommend prime ministers to the emperor for appointment. Most authorities agree that there were nine, including two added in 1912. The *genrō* undoubtedly originated in the traditional councils of elders (RŌJŪ) so common in the Edo period (1600–1868), but the term seems to have been first used by a newspaper in 1892. The term is often linked with the GENRŌIN, the legislative Chamber of Elders that functioned (or rather malfunctioned) from 1875 to 1890, but the establishment of the *genrō* was not related to that body or its abolition. Experienced leaders were singled out for meritorious service, honored by the emperor as *genkun* (veteran or elder statesmen), and asked to act as imperial advisers. The institution was extraconstitutional and informal, and members exercised, collectively and individually, a crucial, though eventually declining, influence on high government policy.

The Meiji leadership was essentially a collective one, and the *genrō*'s importance was greatest when they functioned as a group, as when resolving leadership crises. With the exception of SAIONJI KIMMOCHI, the last of the *genrō*, who came from an imperial court family, all the *genrō* were *samurai* of medium or lower rank, four each from Chōshū (now Yamaguchi Prefecture) and Satsuma (now Kagoshima Prefecture), the domains that had played the most prominent roles in the MEIJI RESTORATION of 1868.

The first two Meiji leaders to be given the title of *genkun,* in 1889, were ITŌ HIROBUMI and KURODA KIYOTAKA. Five others were similarly honored later, constituting the original seven Meiji *genrō.* They were MATSUKATA MASAYOSHI, ŌYAMA IWAO, SAIGŌ TSUGUMICHI, YAMAGATA ARITOMO, and INOUE KAORU. These seven men were the SANGI (imperial councillors) from Satsuma and Chōshū who remained in this office when the title, established in 1869, was abolished in 1885. Besides their advisory duties as *genrō,* these "original seven" dominated the ministries of the mid-Meiji years. For most of the years from 1885 to 1900, Chōshū and Satsuma *genrō* alternated as prime minister; Itō was prime minister three times, Yamagata and Matsukata twice, and Kuroda once. Almost all were ministers in more than one ministry or served in important court offices.

Kuroda and Saigō died in 1900 and 1902, respectively. The five remaining *genrō* exercised power indirectly, through their followers. Between 1901 and 1913 KATSURA TARŌ and Saionji, the protégés of the most powerful *genrō,* Yamagata and Itō, alternated as prime minister. Katsura adhered to Yamagata's opposition in principle to party government, and Saionji continued Itō's alliance between bureaucrats and his own party, the RIKKEN SEIYŪKAI.

Katsura and Saionji became *genrō* in 1912, but Itō had died in 1909, and the institution began to decline in number and effectiveness. Yamagata died in 1922 and Matsukata in 1924, leaving Saionji as the last *genrō*. He continued to influence the choice of prime ministers until 1937, dying in 1940 at the age of 91.

Much hostility was expressed against the Chōshū–Satsuma monopoly of power that the *genrō* represented (see HAMBATSU), but at least until the beginning of the Taishō period (1912–26), the *genrō* served as a stabilizing force in the developing nation and facilitated the peaceful transition from cabinet to cabinet. In 1913 Katsura died, the Katsura–Saionji alternation ended, and the party leaders HARA TAKASHI and KATŌ TAKAAKI, more independent of the *genrō*, took the center of the political stage. One quality that distinguished the *genrō* from later leaders was a broad view and ambition for Japan that prevented them from equating Japan's interests with the narrow interests of whatever institution they served, as did most of their successors. However, once Japan's new government institutions had passed their earlier tests, under *genrō* stewardship, and Japan had achieved confidence and status in the world, ambitious younger leaders began to resent the *genrō* as elderly and out-of-date, overcautious, and ill-informed. From 1914 to 1916, the *genrō* clashed with Foreign Minister Katō Takaaki, forcing him to adopt more conciliatory policies toward China and Russia, but the days of such influence on crucial issues were numbered. In Saionji's last years, his warnings against overaggressive policies were largely overlooked.

■ ——Roger Hackett, "Political Modernization and the Meiji *Genrō*," in Robert Ward, ed, *Political Development in Modern Japan* (1968). *Charles D. SHELDON*

Genrōin

(Chamber of Elders, or Senate). A quasi-legislative body of the early Meiji period (1868–1912). Established in April 1875 as part of an administrative reform of the DAJŌKAN system following the ŌSAKA CONFERENCE OF 1875, the Genrōin replaced the Sain (Chamber of the Left) and was responsible for reviewing legislation. Its members, who were theoretically nominated by the emperor, were chosen from the ranks of the peerage, upper-grade bureaucrats, and legal scholars. The minister of the left *(sadaijin)* and the minister of the right *(udaijin)* served as chairmen. In fact the Genrōin had no power to initiate legislation, since bills were delivered to it by the executive section of the Dajōkan (this was called the *naikaku* or cabinet) in the form of imperial ordinances; moreover, in emergencies the executive section could itself issue decrees subject only to retroactive examination by the Genrōin. In 1876 the Genrōin was commissioned to draw up a constitution. The draft, the Nihon Kokken An, completed in July 1880, was rejected by the government leaders ITŌ HIROBUMI and IWAKURA TOMOMI as too liberal. The Genrōin was dissolved in October 1890 with the formation of the IMPERIAL DIET. Although it was short-lived, the Genrōin, together with the Daishin'in (GREAT COURT OF CASSATION), represented an early attempt by the Meiji government to establish a separation of powers. *TANAKA Akira*

Genroku era

Genroku, the era name (NENGŌ) for the years 1688–1704, is commonly used to refer to the entire rule of the fifth Tokugawa shōgun, TOKUGAWA TSUNAYOSHI, from 1680 to 1709. As the name for a cultural period, it is sometimes used even more broadly to include the flowering of culture, especially among the townsmen (CHŌNIN), from the middle of the 17th to the middle of the 18th centuries. The present article discusses cultural developments in both the *chōnin* and *samurai* classes from approximately 1650 to 1725. See also HISTORY OF JAPAN: Edo history.

During the first half of the 17th century, the TOKUGAWA SHOGUNATE established a strict ordering of all groups in the society. It disciplined the *daimyō* and tightened the class order that separated samurai, farmers, and townspeople (SHI-NŌ-KŌ-SHŌ). By the time of the death of the third shōgun, TOKUGAWA IEMITSU, in 1651, and the succession of his child TOKUGAWA IETSUNA, the security of the regime had been clearly demonstrated and the policy of strict controls gradually moderated. Education of samurai had been encouraged from the early 17th century in order to direct them toward peacetime employment in administrative functions rather than in military roles. The use of textbooks based on Confucian classics, the opportunity to read literary texts and poetry, and the leisure to pursue cultural pastimes, effected a gradual change in the samurai that made them more bureaucrats and gentlemen than military men. Although this trend continued throughout the Edo period (1600–1868), it was given special encouragement by Tsunayoshi, who played the

role of Confucian pedant and neglected the cultivation of military skills. He also set an example of extravagance and self-indulgence that reflected the spirit of his prosperous times.

Attention to the education of samurai was followed by an increase in literacy among the other social groups, especially merchants, but also other urban residents and prosperous farmers. The rapid increase in agricultural productivity and the quickening of commerce in the 17th century were accompanied by the rapid growth of cities, in particular the great urban centers of Kyōto, Edo (now Tōkyō), and Ōsaka. As unprecedented affluence came to a larger number of merchants and artisans of the cities, their demand for goods and services stimulated the development of new styles of clothing, entertainment, and arts tailored to their tastes. Their distance from samurai in social status and education also reflected a difference in values. While samurai were disciplined by a moral obligation to perform military and administrative service, urban commoners were free to follow their self-interest in making money and spending it. Hence they were considered morally as well as socially inferior. Their pastimes were less restrained and their tastes less informed by tradition and education.

While NŌ was considered the form of drama appropriate to the samurai class, KABUKI and the PUPPET THEATER, which developed from the early 17th century, were shaped increasingly to *chōnin* audiences. Both types of drama underwent remarkable development during the late 17th century. The most famous names in the history of these theaters are from this period, and the Genroku is celebrated as the golden age of both types of theater. This is more a tribute to the creativity of the performers and writers than to the maturity of their art, for both dramatic forms underwent considerable refinement during the following century. Nonetheless, SAKATA TŌJŪRŌ I is remembered as the founder in Kyōto and Ōsaka kabuki of the acting style of the great lover, and Yoshizawa Ayame (1673–1729) for his manner of playing female roles. In Edo, Ichikawa Danjūrō I (see ICHIKAWA DANJŪRŌ) established the *aragoto* ("rough business") style of the brawny hero. The conventions of type roles, facial makeup, and costuming were largely formulated in their time and are preserved in early woodblock prints and book illustrations. The range of subject matter and the structure of plots, as well as a variety of conventional episodes of later kabuki, owe a great debt to this classical period.

The most famous of Japanese playwrights, CHIKAMATSU MONZAEMON, wrote for both the kabuki and puppet theaters, but his preference turned increasingly to JŌRURI texts for the latter. Since *jōruri* were partly recited and partly sung by a narrator, and since the texts were published and sold, the playwright had the opportunity to write in a rich literary style. He could construct the plot and shape his style free of the demands actors placed on kabuki playwrights to include material that showed their talents to best advantage. Chikamatsu wrote approximately 100 *jidaimono* (period pieces) for the puppet theater, dealing with heroes of Japanese history, but he is best remembered for his development of the *sewamono*, domestic plays that dealt with incidents and scandals in the lives of the commoners of his time. The first of these 24 plays, *Sonezaki shinjū* (1703, The Love Suicide at Sonezaki), treated a double suicide of thwarted lovers that had occurred recently in Ōsaka. So popular were the many plays by Chikamatsu and others that sensationalized these death pacts, and so frequently did such suicides occur, that plays and stories on this theme were banned in 1722. Chikamatsu's first important *jōruri* were written for the reciter Takemoto Gidayū (1651–1714), whose contribution to the art was so important that the style of most of *jōruri* recitations is called *gidayū*.

The introduction of improved printing techniques from Korea at the end of the 16th century and the encouragement of education spurred a rapid increase of publication by woodblock printing. In addition to the printing of Japanese literary classics and Confucian works, small booklets (KANA-ZŌSHI) written in simple language for popular consumption became numerous. Among these, storybooks, guidebooks, textbooks, and other manuals were the most common, and illustrations were frequently included. As the readership became larger and more sophisticated, the variety of storybooks broadened, and there appeared more urbane stories about contemporary urban society in illustrated books called UKIYO-ZŌSHI (booklets of the floating world). The most famous writer of such works, Ihara SAIKAKU, took first as his subject stories of sexual love *(kōshoku-mono)*, beginning with *Kōshoku ichidai otoko* (tr *The Life of an Amorous Man*, 1964) in 1682. He also wrote stories of how merchants made and lost money *(chōnin-mono)* and stories about samurai *(buke-mono)* and homosexual love. A detached observer of his society, he depicted, with spare, incisive comments, the personalities of people of different ages and professions. His training as a *haikai* (see HAIKU) poet contributed to a style that employed economy of phrase, unexpected twists and turns in sentences, and a sharp wit to bring his fast-paced stories to their ironic conclusion. Saikaku was at his best when he captured the esprit of the Genroku townsman who lived for the moment, absorbed in making money and spending it in the pursuit of pleasure as a sophisticated rake. Saikaku was emulated by EJIMA KISEKI and Andō Jishō (d 1745) in their HACHI-MONJIYA-BON and was a forerunner of the popular GESAKU writing in Edo of a century later.

Saikaku's stories of sexual love, like Chikamatsu's love-suicide plays, usually involved the pleasure quarters of the cities, where there were establishments with well-appointed rooms for drinking, dining, and the enjoyment of the company of male and female entertainers and prostitutes. These licensed quarters were moved to the edges of the major cities in the middle of the 17th century, the Shimabara quarter of Kyōto in 1640, the Shimmachi of Ōsaka in 1629, and the New Yoshiwara (see YOSHIWARA) of Edo in 1657. The prosperity of the 17th century brought an aura of glamor to the brothel quarters and its courtesans of the highest rank *(tayū)*, whose legendary beauty, wit, and cultural accomplishments made them as well-known throughout the cities as the stars of the kabuki stage.

The fame of the leading actors and prostitutes was spread not only by critical booklets and stories in the *ukiyo-zōshi* but also by their portraits in woodblock prints and book illustrations. They became increasingly the favorite subject of paintings and prints known as UKIYO-E. The *ukiyo-e* style, a clean, direct reduction of Japanese-style painting in the tradition of the TOSA SCHOOL and the SUMIYO-SHI SCHOOL was shaped by Hishikawa MORONOBU and others in painted handscrolls and in book illustrations and prints. From the second and third decades of the 18th century color began to be added to the prints by the use of additional woodblocks, and the art of the multiple-block Japanese print was born.

During the Genroku era there was also a resurgence of the Tosa style of painting, which had long been in the shadow of the Chinese-inspired KANŌ SCHOOL. From a melding of the two traditions grew the RIMPA style of Ogata KŌRIN with its rich colors, strong patterns, and precise draftsmanship. A similar boldness of design was also found in new textile patterns in YŪZEN dyeing and NISHIJIN-ORI, in lacquer and metal work, and in other crafts. While the finest of these works were only for the wealthy, patrons included merchants as well as the samurai and court elite.

A major development in poetry, which found practitioners in all classes, was the evolution of Matsuo BASHŌ's style of *haikai renga* (linked verse) and *haiku* (17-syllable poems) composition, known as Shōfū or Shōmon. Moving beyond the Teimon style of MATSU-NAGA TEITOKU and the DANRIN SCHOOL style of NISHIYAMA SŌIN with a greater seriousness of purpose, Bashō expressed a sensitivity to nature and an understanding of human emotions that made him the most celebrated haiku poet.

The decades that bracketed the turn of the century brought a flowering of scholarship to the samurai class, especially in the study of Confucianism. Among the well-known scholars of Chinese studies of this time were YAMAZAKI ANSAI, KUMAZAWA BANZAN, KINOSHITA JUN'AN, YAMAGA SOKŌ, the commoner ITŌ JINSAI, KAI-BARA EKIKEN, ARAI HAKUSEKI, and OGYŪ SORAI, who made original contributions in adapting Confucian ideas to Japanese society. These years saw the beginning of serious scholarship in classical Japanese literature (KOKUGAKU) and the writing of the first important commentaries, as exemplified in the works of KITAMURA KIGIN, KEICHŪ, and KADA NO AZUMAMARO.

The image popularly invoked by the name Genroku, however, is of a time of prosperity, extravagance, and indulgence, with only the vendetta of the Forty-Seven Rōnin (see FORTY-SEVEN RŌNIN INCI-DENT) to remind people of honor, loyalty, and sacrifice. It is in this sense that the mass media in Japan called the 1960s, when the recovery of the economy after the war years permitted the enjoyment of affluence, the Shōwa Genroku (Genroku of the Shōwa era).

Donald H. SHIVELY

Gensen

A dictionary of the Japanese language in five volumes plus index. Edited under the supervision of HAGA YAICHI (1867–1927) until his death in 1927 and published 1921–29, it is a revision and enlargement of an earlier dictionary, OCHIAI NAOBUMI's *Kotoba no izumi* (5 vols; 1898–99). It has some 300,000 entries, including not only modern standard Japanese, but also classical Japanese, dialect items, and argot. As it also contains many proper nouns, the dictionary is encyclopedic in nature.

YAMAZAKI Yukio

Genshin (942–1017)

Scholar monk of the TENDAI SECT of Buddhism. Popularly known as Eshin Sōzu. Author of the ŌJŌYŌSHŪ (985, Essentials of Pure Land Rebirth) and considered the founder of the Eshin school of Tendai oral transmission. His scholarship had a great influence on the later development of PURE LAND BUDDHISM in Japan.

Genshin was born in Yamato Province (now Nara Prefecture) into a family of provincial gentry named Urabe. Very little is known of his childhood, but it is said that he left home in 950 and entered the Tendai center on Mt. Hiei (HIEIZAN) near Kyōto. He is thought to have formally entered the Tendai order in his teens and to have become the disciple of the noted Tendai reformer, RYŌGEN (912–985). Genshin first gained fame in 974 (Ten'en 2) when he was appointed to serve in the prestigious and demanding role of respondent in an official debate at one of the Tendai sect's most important ceremonies. He later retired to the Shuryōgon'in, a small temple in a secluded area of the Tendai precinct known as Yokawa, where he devoted himself to scholarship and writing.

Genshin's study of the LOTUS SUTRA convinced him that there must be a way to achieve salvation that was open to all people at all times. His solution was trust in the saving powers of the Buddha AMIDA (Skt: Amitābha). He felt that enlightenment begins with an aversion to the realms of transmigration (Skt: *saṃsāra*), the major battleground of selfishness, greed, and suffering. As man refrains from these evil acts, he is drawn to a realm of peace through devotion to Amida. The essence of the religious life is thus a disgust for the suffering of karmic bondage and a longing for the Pure Land of Amida.

Genshin presents this view in his *Ōjōyōshū*. He describes in graphic terms the terrors of transmigration, the bliss of the Pure Land and the devotion to Amida necessary to achieve rebirth in the Pure Land. Genshin wrote several other works, including the *Ichijō yōketsu* (1006, a defense of the Tendai "One Vehicle" of Buddhahood for all) and the *Kanjin ryakuyō shū* (997, an exposition of the importance and benefits of Tendai "insight meditation"). Though none of his artistic works remain, he also gained fame as an artist and sculptor, and he inspired a major style of Buddhist art (RAI-GŌZU) which depicts such scenes as the torments of hell, the wonders of the Pure Land, and the compassionate Amida welcoming the faithful.

In Japanese Buddhist circles there has been a long controversy as to whether Genshin was primarily a Tendai or Pure Land thinker, whether his essential message was Tendai enlightenment or Pure Land rebirth. This controversy is the product of an age which has come to understand these two positions as mutually exclusive. Genshin's age and mind were more inclusive. For him Pure Land faith was totally consistent with the Tendai teaching that all beings are destined to ride the One Vehicle *(ichijō)* to Buddhahood by following seemingly different paths. Pure Land faith was for Genshin such a different path, one especially appropriate for beings of diminished capacity in the decadent age of the dharma (*mappō*; see ESCHATOLOGY). For Genshin, NEMBUTSU was the fundamental practice for rebirth and his concept of *nembutsu* was founded on the Tendai scripture *Maka shikan* (Ch: *Mohe zhiguan* or *Mo-ho chih-kuan*) expounded by Zhiyi (Chih-i) in 594. Thus it included *rikan* (abstract meditation upon the absolute Buddha-nature), *jikan* (contemplation of the physical characteristics of a Buddha), and *shōnen* (invocation of Amida Buddha with the phrase *Namu Amida Butsu*) in aspiration for rebirth into his Pure Land, what later ages came to understand as the only form of *nembutsu*. *Rikan* was for Genshin the superior practice because it could achieve *samādhi* (concentration of mind) and immediate enlightenment, but *shōnen* was the more practical form of cultivation because it could be utilized by anyone in any circumstance to achieve rebirth. Genshin never ceased to believe in the ultimate truth of Tendai teachings, yet was himself a fervent cultivator of vocal *nembutsu*.

Thus Genshin greatly stimulated the Japanese Pure Land movement. The vivid descriptions of the sufferings of this world and the beatitudes of the Pure Land in his *Ōjōyōshū* and in the artworks of his school have been an enduring inspiration to popular Pure Land faith, and his summaries of Pure Land doctrine and practice served as a point of departure for the Pure Land reformers of the Kamakura period (1185–1333).

Allan A. ANDREWS

Gensuikin → atomic weapons, movement to ban

Gensuikyō → atomic weapons, movement to ban

gentians

(rindō). The best known of the various species of the gentian family (Gentianaceae) found in Japan is the *rindō* (*Gentiana scabra* var. *buergeri*), a perennial herb which grows wild in fields and forests of Honshū, Shikoku, and Kyūshū. Its flower has long been a beloved symbol of autumn. The stem grows vertically or at an angle and may reach a height of 60 centimeters (24 in). The opposite leaves have no leaf stalks and are lanceolate in shape. Three veins run parallel along each leaf. In autumn violet bell-shaped flowers bloom on top of the stem or in the upper leaf axils. Each flower is split into five lobes. There is also a variety with white flowers, called the *sasarindō*. The roots of the *rindō* are used as a stomach medicine.

The *oyama rindō* (*G. makinoi*) grows wild in alpine areas northward from central Honshū, reaching a height of 20–60 centimeters (8–24 in), with one to seven violet flowers blooming in autumn. Along with the similar species Ezo *rindō* (*G. triflora* var. *japonica*) it is also cultivated for cut flowers. The *tōyaku rindō* (*G. algida*) also grows wild in high mountains northward from central Honshū and is 10–25 centimeters (4–10 in) in height. The flowers, pale yellow with fine green spots, bloom in summer. This species is known as a medicinal herb. Other species include the Asama *rindō* (*G. sikokiana*), which grows in Shikoku and western Honshū; the *miyama rindō* (*G. nipponica*), which grows in alpine areas of central Honshū and points north, and the Yakushima *rindō* (*G. yakushimemsis*) which grows on Yakushima, an island south of Kyūshū. The *haru-rindō* (*G. thunbergii*), *kokerindō* (*G. squarrosa*), and *fuderindō* (*G. zollingeri*) are all spring-blooming species, with flowers and leaves smaller than the others.   MATSUDA Osamu

Gentlemen's Agreement

(Nichibei Shinshi Kyōyaku). An executive agreement between the United States and Japan in 1907–08 by which the United States limited the number of Japanese immigrants while Japan avoided the embarrassment of having its nationals barred by the act of another government. Its immediate cause was anti-Japanese agitation in California and elsewhere on the American Pacific coast, which, having begun in the early 1890s, became intense in early 1905. Later that year there was an outbreak of hooliganism directed at Japanese in San Francisco, and 11 October 1906 the school board ordered all Japanese pupils—there were 93 of them attending 23 different schools—to attend the already existing schools for Chinese, who had been segregated for decades (see SEGREGATION OF JAPANESE SCHOOLCHILDREN IN THE UNITED STATES). When garbled versions of what had occurred were printed in Tōkyō newspapers nine days later, the whole matter of discrimination against Japanese residents in the United States became a major issue between the two powers. In his annual message to Congress in December 1906, President Theodore Roosevelt lashed out at the "wicked absurdity" of "shutting [Japanese] children out of the common schools." Roosevelt, confusing segregation with exclusion, proposed an act of Congress providing for the naturalization of Japanese, who, along with other Asians, had been denied that right by an 1870 federal statute which limited naturalization to white persons and persons of African descent. Had such a bill been enacted, the entire history of Japanese Americans would have been different, but there is no evidence that the president and his supporters ever intended to fight for such a measure, the passage of which was dubious at best. But Roosevelt did want to settle the immigration question with Japan, and, from the fall of 1906 to the spring of 1908, Washington and Tōkyō discussed the matter.

Although he had no direct authority over a local school board, Roosevelt was most adept at using the moral authority of his office. In February 1907 he invited the San Francisco school board to the White House and persuaded its members to rescind their order. Later that month Congress passed an act, drafted by Secretary of State Elihu Root, enabling the president by executive order to forbid the entry of laborers whose passports had been issued for entry to another place. Although the obvious targets of this legislation were Japanese residents of the Territory of Hawaii, most of whom had passports issued by the Japanese government specifically for that place, no real offense was given because the legislation did not single

out Japanese, and it could be argued that the United States was merely enforcing restrictions set by the Japanese government.

With these preliminaries out of the way, the negotiations that led to the Gentleman's Agreement could begin. The agreement is not a single document; its substance is found in six notes exchanged between the governments in late 1907 and early 1908. Its essence was that Tōkyō agreed not to issue passports valid for the continental United States to laborers, either skilled or unskilled, and that Washington agreed not to object to the issuance of passports to "laborers who have already been in America and to the parents, wives, and children of laborers already resident there." This agreement endured until its unilateral abrogation by the United States in the 1924 immigration act which, in effect, excluded Japanese. See also UNITED STATES IMMIGRATION ACTS OF 1924, 1952, AND 1965.

Intended as a tension-reducing device, in the final analysis the Gentlemen's Agreement probably exacerbated trans-Pacific relations. Roosevelt and Root represented the Gentlemen's Agreement to Californians and other Westerners as tantamount to exclusion. When, under its provisions, thousands of Japanese men resident in America sent for wives—many of whom were so-called picture brides, married by proxy to men they had never seen—and these wives began to have children, the Californians and their supporters felt that they had been tricked. Similarly, Tōkyō represented the Gentlemen's Agreement as a permanent solution that maintained the honor of the Japanese nation. When, in 1924, that honor was besmirched by an act of Congress, the Japanese were outraged. Had American statesmen understood the demographic facts of Japanese-American life, they might have been able to prepare Western public opinion for the brief spurt in the birth rate that was bound to come. Had Japanese statesmen listened more closely to their West Coast consuls, they too might have been better able to prepare public opinion for the shocks that were bound to come. On the other hand, the Gentlemen's Agreement did calm tensions for a while, and, although the welfare of the small Japanese-American community was not of real concern to either set of statesmen, the Gentlemen's Agreement did, unintentionally, provide a firm demographic basis for the establishment of second-generation JAPANESE AMERICANS *(nisei)* who, by virtue of their American birth, were citizens.

■——Roger Daniels, *The Politics of Prejudice: The Anti-Japanese Movement in California and the Struggle for Japanese Exclusion* (2nd ed, 1978). US Department of State, *Foreign Relations of the United States, 1924* (1939).   Roger DANIELS

Gen'yōsha

(Black Ocean Society). Pioneer ultranationalist group founded in 1881 by Hiraoka Kōtarō (1851–1906), TŌYAMA MITSURU, and other former *samurai* of the Fukuoka domain (now part of Fukuoka Prefecture). Until its disbandment after World War II, the society promoted Japanese expansion in Asia and conservative values in Japan.

The former samurai of Fukuoka had felt left out of the new government formed after the MEIJI RESTORATION of 1868. They had taken up the cry that the Meiji government was not sufficiently nationalistic or aggressive in revising the Unequal Treaties with the Western powers (see UNEQUAL TREATIES, REVISION OF). They had participated in the uprisings of former samurai dissatisfied with the government's abolition of their feudal privileges, but after the government suppressed the SATSUMA REBELLION in 1877, they had moved toward a more peaceful form of opposition, joining the FREEDOM AND PEOPLE'S RIGHTS MOVEMENT and forming a political organization called the Kōyōsha to agitate for the establishment of a national parliament. When the government promised a national assembly in 1881, the group began to argue that the rights of the people could best be served by Japanese expansion on the Asian mainland, and to mark this change of purpose the Kōyōsha was in 1881 renamed the Gen'yōsha. The new name referred to the Genkai Sea, the strait that separates Kyūshū from the Korean peninsula, and thus signified the members' determination to push for an aggressive policy of continental expansion. The group chose reverence toward the emperor, love of country, and the defense of people's rights as their guiding principles; their professed aim was to keep watch over the government's foreign policy and to protect the national honor.

In 1889 the Gen'yōsha criticized the treaty revision plan of ŌKUMA SHIGENOBU as imperiling Japan's sovereignty. When its attempts to block the negotiations faltered, a society member named Kurushima Tsuneki threw a bomb at Ōkuma, leaving him seriously wounded. Although the Gen'yōsha used terrorist tactics to influence the government, it also intimidated members of opposition parties who were against military expansion and assisted the government in the election interference (see SENKYO KANSHŌ) of 1892. As the SINO-JAPANESE WAR OF 1894–1895 approached, members of the group engaged in undercover activities in Korea, taking secret orders from the Imperial Army Staff Office. They plotted to bring about the war and also engaged in intelligence gathering.

Before the RUSSO-JAPANESE WAR of 1904–05, the Gen'yōsha co-operated with the military in calling for a hard-line policy toward Russia. After the war's outbreak, society members mustered the support of bandit groups in various parts of Manchuria to put together a guerrilla band. There too, they engaged in covert intelligence-gathering activities. After the war the Gen'yōsha supported various Asian revolutionary groups under the slogan of PAN-ASIANISM and cooperated in the annexation of Korea in 1910. Gen'-yōsha leader Tōyama Mitsuru, an influential behind-the-scenes figure in Japanese government circles, pulled strings on behalf of Japanese right-wing activists at large on the Asian mainland (see TAIRIKU RŌNIN). At the same time, Tōyama supplied aid to such Asian revolutionaries as KIM OK-KYUN, SUN YAT-SEN, and Emilio AGUINALDO.

The Gen'yōsha also worked against the currents of TAISHŌ DE-MOCRACY. It joined the RŌNINKAI, an offshoot organization, in challenging their critic YOSHINO SAKUZŌ to an open debate. In other instances, it suppressed its opponents by violent means. In response to the rise of the labor movement, it called for an emperor-centered reconstruction of the state and formed the Greater Japan Production Party (Dai Nippon Seisantō) to work against the spread of socialism in the labor unions. The Gen'yōsha also gave birth to a number of other right-wing organizations, the most famous of which is the AMUR RIVER SOCIETY.

In its later years the Gen'yōsha became the educational and cultural organ of the emperor cult and of pan-Asianism, producing such important political figures as NAKANO SEIGŌ and HIROTA KŌKI and exerting considerable influence on the politics, diplomacy, and thought of pre-World War II Japan.

As a result of this influence, the Gen'yōsha came to be feared abroad, perhaps more than the reality justified. After World War II it was ordered disbanded by the OCCUPATION authorities, and at the WAR CRIMES TRIALS Hirota Kōki, on the basis of his connection with the Gen'yōsha, received the class-A war criminal classification and was sentenced to death.

——Gen'yōsha Shashi Henshū Iinkai, *Gen'yōsha shashi* (1917).
FUJIMURA Michio

Genzammi Yorimasa → Minamoto no Yorimasa

Geographic Survey Institute

(Kokudo Chiriin). Government bureau under the Ministry of Construction that conducts geological and topographical surveying and mapmaking. The major functions of the institute involve the collation of statistical information concerning triangulation, water levels, power resources, and geological structure; aerial photographic surveys; the preparation of standard topographical maps; and the compilation of maps and tables concerning land utilization, which are used in drawing up land development and disaster prevention programs. It also carries out research in earthquake forecasting, administers the national examinations for licensed land surveyors, and offers assistance in map preparation to developing countries. Established in 1888, the parent body of the present organization was first attached to the land survey section of the General Staff Office of the Japanese Imperial Army. From the end of World War II until 1948, it belonged to the Ministry of Interior, and since then has been under the Ministry of Construction. It was reorganized as the Geographic Survey Institute (GSI) in 1960. Institute headquarters are located in TSUKUBA ACADEMIC NEW TOWN, and it maintains nine regional survey offices around the country. The GSI currently employs some 1,000 workers. *SHIKI Masahide*

geography

Development of Geographical Studies

—— Descriptive regional geography in Japan has a long history, dating back to the beginning of the 8th century when regional gazetteers known as FUDOKI were compiled in accordance with government edict. It was not, however, until after the 17th century that modern geographical concepts

emerged. The factors that accelerated the growth of modern geography as a discipline in Japan were the rational thinking contained in the Zhu Xi (Chu Hsi; see SHUSHIGAKU) and Wang Yangming (see YŌMEIGAKU) schools of Confucianism as well as scientific technology and new knowledge about the world introduced to Japan by Christian missionaries and Dutch traders. An early example of a concerted attempt to compare and describe the geographical characteristics of Japan in relationship to the cartography and geography of the then known world is found in the *Nihon suidokō* written by the mid-Edo period (1600–1868) astronomer and geographer NISHIKAWA JOKEN. Other works by Nishikawa emphasized the importance of the science of geography as well as the author's predominant interest in regional geographic differences together with attempts toward explaining the natural features and climate of Japan. His work, however, as represented by *Kai tsūshōkō* (1695), said to be Japan's first world geography, is limited to simple geographical descriptions and is a far cry from the more elaborate *Sairan igen* (1713) compiled by the scholar-statesman ARAI HAKUSEKI.

From that time on, a number of Dutch books on astronomy and geography were translated into Japanese and, as the number of foreign ships in Japanese waters grew, geographical studies necessary for Japan's defense and trade were increasingly made. Starting with a detailed coastal survey of Hokkaidō in 1800 by the noted Edo cartographer INŌ TADATAKA, various projects involving the systematic exploration and surveying of the coastline of Japan culminated in Inō's comprehensive geographic survey DAI NIHON ENKAI JIS-SOKU ZENZU (popularly known as the "Inō Maps") in 1821. *Shintei bankoku zenzu*, a world geography compiled in 1810 by TAKAHASHI KAGEYASU, an astronomer of the Tokugawa shogunate, was noted for its high standards. Several other detailed world geographies appeared during the closing days of the Tokugawa shogunate, including Mitsukuri Shōgo's (1821–46) *Kon'yo zushiki* (1845) and MI-TSUKURI GEMPO's *Hakkō zushiki* (1851).

Tokumei zenken taishi: Beiō kairan jikki, the official account of the 1871 IWAKURA MISSION to Europe and the United States by KUME KUNITAKE, was a monumental undertaking. It was UCHI-MURA KANZŌ who first introduced to Japan some of the ideas of the geographers Alexander von Humboldt and Karl Ritter. Uchimura's book *Chirigaku kō* (first published in 1894; republished in 1896 as *Chijinron*), along with SHIGA SHIGETAKA's *Nihon fūkei ron* (1894) and MAKIGUCHI TSUNESABURŌ's *Jinsei chirigaku* (1903), played a valuable role in enlightening the people about geography at a time when formal courses in geography were not offered in Japanese universities.

Geography in School Education

—— Geography came to be included in the curriculum for elementary and middle schools from the early years of the Meiji period (1868–1912). Although there were various changes in school curriculum with the reformation of the Japanese educational system following World War II, Japanese geography and world geography are currently taught for two years at the junior high school level. Senior high schools offer (as part of social studies) an elective course in systematic geography that emphasizes a human geography approach. This course is almost always optional, however, and studies in foreign geography tend to be neglected.

The first university in Japan to teach a course in geography was Kyōto University in 1907. OGAWA TAKUJI became the principal lecturer in 1908. Tōkyō University was next, offering in 1911 a geography course under the auspices of the geology department. In 1919 a department of geography was established in the School of Science with YAMAZAKI NAOMASA as department head. Tōkyō Bunrika Daigaku (later Tōkyō University of Education) established a similar department in 1929. Higher normal schools also offered courses in geography, while commercial colleges offered lectures on economic geography. Since World War II, courses in human geography have generally been included in the general education course work for the first two years. An increasing number of schools have begun adding upper-level courses on geography. However, only some 20 universities offer graduate study programs in geography.

Organizations

—— The oldest geographical society in Japan is the TŌKYŌ GEOGRAPHICAL SOCIETY, established in 1879. The most representative society today, however, is the ASSOCIATION OF JAPANESE GEOGRAPHERS, formed in 1925. Other nationwide societies are the Human Geographical Society of Japan (1948), the Tōhoku Geographical Association (1948), the Association of Economic Geographers (1954), the Association of Historical Geographers in Japan (1958), and the Japan Cartographers Association (1962). English language résumés of papers on geography are published by Tōkyō University, Tōkyō Metropolitan University, and Tsukuba University. The GEOGRAPHIC SURVEY INSTITUTE under the Ministry of Construction also plays an important role in the application of geography and cartography. The International Geographic Congress was held for the first time in Japan in 1980.　　　*Nishikawa Osamu*

Geography in Japan

A collection of academic papers by Japanese geographers in the English language published in 1976 by the Association of Japanese Geographers. Edited by KIUCHI SHINZŌ, this special collection, the third in a series begun in 1966, was published in commemoration of the association's 50th anniversary. Papers cover all aspects of geography, including the history of geography, topography, and natural and human geography.　　　*Nishikawa Osamu*

geography, regional → regional geographies

geological structure → Japan

Geological Survey of Japan

(Chishitsu Chōsajo). Government institute that undertakes the drawing of basic geological maps in Japan, as well as the survey and research of Japanese natural resources, geotechnics, and hydraulics. Located in the town of Yatabe, Ibaraki Prefecture. The institute is subordinate to the AGENCY OF INDUSTRIAL SCIENCE AND TECHNOLOGY of the MINISTRY OF INTERNATIONAL TRADE AND INDUSTRY (MITI). It publishes the *Bulletin of the Geological Survey of Japan* (monthly), *Report: Geological Survey of Japan,* and *Geology Monthly.*

Germany and Japan

German-Japanese relations date back to the 17th century. Diplomatic relations were established with Prussia in 1861, and mutual economic, scientific, and other relations followed soon afterwards. During World War I diplomatic relations were suspended. A second interruption followed the defeat in 1945, but relations between Japan and the Federal Republic of Germany were reestablished in 1952; relations with the German Democratic Republic were established in 1973.

Early Relations in the Edo Period (1600–1868) —— In 1611 the second shōgun, TOKUGAWA HIDETADA, ordered that all "German ships" coming to Japan should be given help and shelter. At that time the term "German ships" already referred only to Dutch ships, but as the Dutch belonged to the Holy Roman Empire until 1648, the broader term "German" was used. In 1639 a certain gunner, Hans Wolfgang Braun from Ulm (today a Bavarian city), in the Dutch service was ordered by the third shōgun, TOKUGAWA IEMITSU, to cast mortars in the Dutch factory at Hirado (in what is now Nagasaki Prefecture). From 1690 to 1692 Engelbert KAEMPFER, a German physician attached to the Dutch East India Company, lived in Japan. He published two scientific books on Japan and helped shape the European image of Japan. Philipp Franz von SIEBOLD, another German physician, was also in the Dutch service and, like Kaempfer earlier, had to be presented to the Japanese as a "mountain-Dutch" because the Japanese quickly noticed his German accent. He arrived at Nagasaki in August 1823, traveled to Edo (now Tōkyō) in 1826 and obtained permission to stay in Dejima, where the Dutch were quartered, in order to give lessons in medicine and surgery. Later he was allowed to leave Dejima, take up residence in Nagasaki, and travel throughout the country. By teaching medicine and Dutch to Japanese students, he used language exercises to make them describe their living conditions and surroundings, and thereby obtained a remarkable insight into the Japanese society of the 1800s. After illegally obtaining maps of Japan, Siebold was expelled from the country in 1829. He returned once more in 1859 but could not get a diplomatic post because the Japanese remained suspicious of him.

Neither Kaempfer nor Siebold were scientific explorers of foreign countries. They both were well educated and possessed the necessary skills to gather knowledge about the history of this foreign land, its people, culture, folklore, and nature, and then were able to transmit all this to Europe. The best example is Siebold's book entitled *Nippon, Archiv zur Beschreibung von Japan,* which contains valuable information about 19th-century Japan.

The first German trader to reach Japan was August Luedorf, supercargo of the brig *Greta,* who arrived in Shimoda in 1855, just a few months before the American envoy Townsend HARRIS settled there. His request to the Japanese authorities to grant the Germans the same rights as had been given to the Americans, Russians, and British had to be refused because the *Greta* had come to Japan under the American flag. The letter of rejection, which was published in Bremen soon afterwards, however, contained a clause stating that Japan would be ready for negotiations following an official mission. This might have been one reason that prompted the government of Prussia to send a diplomatic mission to Japan.

Relations from the Late 1860s to World War I —— The opening of Yokohama to foreign trade encouraged several German merchants to establish offices there, mostly under Dutch, French, or American flags. But their situation soon changed. On 4 September 1860 the Prussian ships *Arcona* and *Thetis* anchored in Edo Bay. The leader of this mission was Ambassador Graf Fritz zu Eulenburg (1815–81), who had been ordered by the Prussian king Wilhelm I to conclude a treaty with Japan. Besides five Prussian diplomats and a party of Prussian scientists, physicians, artists, and merchants, many of whom became famous later on, there was also a diplomat from Saxony who accompanied the mission. After four months of difficult negotiations, a treaty of friendship, trade, and shipping was signed in January 1861 which came into force in January 1863. It was not possible, however, for Ambassador Eulenburg, representing Prussia and the Northern German Confederation (the word "Germany" still being a geographical term without national significance at that time) to carry out his plan to include the other German states besides Prussia in this treaty. Only after the establishment of the first consulate under the Prussian consul Max von BRANDT (1835–1920) in 1862 did it become possible to enlarge the number of states covered by the treaty. Max von Brandt then became the consul general of the Northern German Confederation. During his consulship he appointed resident German merchants in Japan as honorary consuls in Kōbe (or Hyōgo as it was known then), Nagasaki, and Niigata. When Kōbe was opened to foreign trade in January 1868, there were about 25 Germans among the foreigners who arrived there to set up business in this new treaty port. Most of them had come from Yokohama, Nagasaki, and Chinese ports. During 1869, 24 German ships called at Kōbe, but during the following year the number had grown to 41, the third largest number among the treaty powers. The years between 1868 and 1880 were very difficult for the merchants because of the rapid political and economic changes taking place in Japan. A few German merchants liquidated their businesses during this time, but some of them overcame the difficulties, and from 1881 until World War I an increasing number of German merchants established themselves throughout Japan.

One event raised Germany's interest in East Asia. The German ship *R. J. Robertson* sank off the coast of the island called Typinsan (today known as Miyako in the southern Ryūkyū chain) during a typhoon in July 1873. The crew, saved by the isle's inhabitants, were fortunate and able to return to Germany that same year. To commemorate this event and to thank the islanders, the German emperor presented a stone monument to the island which was shipped to Miyako in 1876 on the gunboat *Cyclop.* The crew of the *Cyclop* initiated naval investigations and surveys which are believed to have been an attempt at colonial expansion by Germany in East Asia. The attempt obviously failed when Japan incorporated all of the Ryūkyū Islands in 1879. Germany afterwards turned to the south and occupied various islands there.

Max von Brandt, ambassador of the German Empire in Japan from 1871 to 1875, used his diplomatic skills to introduce a growing number of German scientists to the Japanese government and so secured their employment. Figures for the number of Germans employed by the Japanese government or private firms differ widely. In 1872 there were eight Prussians working in government employ or so-called *oyatoi gaikokujin* (see FOREIGN EMPLOYEES OF THE MEIJI PERIOD), and nine Saxons are reported to have been employed by other Japanese institutions. In the following years a growing number of German experts were employed by the Japanese government, reaching a peak in 1888 of 48 persons. The number of Germans employed in Japan from about 1870 to 1890 ranked fourth after the British, Americans, and French.

One of the first German scientists in Japan was Gottfried WAGENER (1831–92), a chemist, who was employed in 1868 by an American firm in Nagasaki. He was subsequently invited to Arita (Saga Prefecture), where he introduced new methods of manufacturing porcelain still in use today. From 1870 to 1892 he taught chemistry and physics in Kyōto and Tōkyō. Rudolf Lehmann (1842–1914), an engineer and chemist who came to Japan as a merchant, was engaged to build the first ship made of steel in Japan. He also concentrated his efforts on paper manufacturing and taught at various schools in Tōkyō and Kyōto. A mining engineer from Saxony, Curt Netto (1847–1909), was employed by the Ministry of Industry in 1873. He worked at the Kosaka mine in Akita Prefecture where he introduced new mining techniques that were simple enough to be used by unskilled workers. He also rendered a valuable service by improving Japanese knowledge of metallurgy. In 1877 he lectured at Tōkyō University on mining and metallurgy and published several books and articles.

The newly established experimental agriculture station in Komaba (today the College of Agriculture at Tōkyō University) was led in its early years by the German agricultural chemist Oskar KELLNER (1851–1911). He was not only in charge of classrooms, lectures, and experiments, but also contributed much to the analytical study of Japan's soil, rice cultivation, improvement of sericulture, and research on fertilizers. Another famous teacher at the Komaba school was Max FESCA (1846–1917), who investigated Japan's geography, climate, and land prices and paid special attention to Japanese agriculture. Japanese printing techniques, too, owe much to the Germans. Karl Anton Brueck and Bruno Liebers are said to have contributed greatly to the progress of relief printing.

Paul Mayet (1846–1920), a political economist, was first employed in 1874 to assist in the inauguration of a postal savings system; four years later he was concurrently employed by the Ministry of Finance and the Ministry of Agriculture and Commerce. His contributions during his term of employment include advice and assistance in the establishment of a system for redemption of public debentures, an audit board, emergency relief funds, fire insurance, and a number of other institutions inaugurated by the Japanese government.

The Japanese government employed several law experts from Germany. Hermann ROESLER (1834–94) and Albert MOSSE (1846–1925) worked for the government to assist in the projected law reforms, and Roesler served as special adviser to ITŌ HIROBUMI in the drafting of a new commercial law. Otto Rudorff was employed by the Ministry of Justice, and Heinrich Weipert lectured on German Law at Tōkyō University.

The most striking influence of Germans in the scientific field is seen in medicine. The first physicians who came to Japan in 1871 were Leopold Mueller and Theodor Hoffmann. After these two pioneers, the famous Julius Scriba (1848–1905) and Erwin von BÄLZ (1849–1913) both lectured and worked in Japan from 1876 to 1905. Bälz, who married a Japanese, even became court physician in 1890.

Despite the decrease in the number of Germans employed by the government in the 1890s, German-Japanese relations expanded rapidly through a growing import-export trade, the center of which gradually shifted from Nagasaki to Yokohama, and then to Tōkyō. The growing number of Germans in Japan led to the establishment of schools (in Yokohama and Kōbe) and a university. With financial aid from Germany, Sophia University (Jōchi Daigaku) was founded in 1913 by German Jesuits in Tōkyō. Besides the Jesuits, German missionaries from the Steyl Missionary Society (SVD) started work in 1907 and opened several schools. Protestant missionaries from Germany had already arrived in Japan in 1885.

German-Japanese relations were suspended after 23 August 1914, when the declaration of war was given to Ambassador Graf von Rex. The German colonial territory of QINGDAO (Tsingtao) on the Chinese mainland was attacked by the Japanese and fell on 7 November 1914. German prisoners of war were held in custody in several camps in Japan, later concentrated in Tokushima Prefecture. German residents in Japan were left unharmed, and only merchants were forced to suspend their business activities.

Relations in the Interwar Period—— It took six years before the next German ambassador came to Japan. He was the former minister of colonial affairs and minister of foreign affairs, Wilhelm Solf (1862–1936), who reestablished normal relations between Germany and Japan during his eight-year stay in Japan. Japan handed back 70 percent of confiscated German property and accounts, but for many German business concerns the situation deteriorated. A number of old companies went bankrupt, but others became stronger because of the lack of competition and opened up different branches. Intensive cooperation between German and Japanese industry began. Several German companies, which had already established business ties before World War I (like Siemens & Schuckert and Siemens & Halske), established subsidiaries in Japan in cooperation with Japanese companies. During these years a remarkable change took place. Inasmuch as economic activities were now centered in the Ōsaka area, since most of Yokohama had been destroyed as a result of the great Tōkyō Earthquake in 1923, many German merchants tried to make a new start in the area around Ōsaka and Kōbe. A culminating point of these economic activities was the signing of a German-Japanese trade treaty in 1927; however, because of the depression that followed, this had practically no significant effect.

A mutual understanding of both nations was promoted by German teachers in the Japanese higher school system. Most of them had been influenced by the older teachers like Rudolf Lange, who resided in Japan between 1874 and 1882 and later taught Japanese in Berlin and also published language textbooks, and Karl Florenz (1865–1939), a philologist, who translated and annotated several of the Japanese classics and taught from 1889 to 1914 at Tōkyō University. He became the first professor of Japanese studies at the University of Hamburg. Among the German high-school teachers, Herman Bohner, Horst Hammitzsch, Herbert Zachert, Walter Donat, Dietrich Seckel, and Wilhelm Gundert should be mentioned. They were to become responsible for the spread of Japanese studies in Germany after World War II. The establishment of a number of institutes, the Japan-Institut in Berlin in 1926, the Japanisch-Deutsches Kulturinstitut in Tōkyō in 1927, and another Japanisch-Deutsches Forschungsinstitut in Kyōto in 1934 strengthened the cultural exchange between both countries. German-Japanese cultural relations have also been greatly influenced by several societies, among which the Deutsche Gesellschaft für Natur und Völkerkunde Ostasiens (OAG), founded in 1873, was (and still is) the most active.

With the rise of fascism both countries began a closer political cooperation. The Anti-Comintern Pact was signed on 25 November 1936, and a treaty for cultural exchange followed two years later. From 1938 onward the ambassadors of both countries were chosen from the military service. In September 1940 the treaty among the three powers of Germany, Italy, and Japan, the so-called Dreimächte-Pakt (TRIPARTITE PACT), was signed, but the significance of this treaty for Japan was practically nil as neither of the two European powers was willing to fulfill the close political or military cooperation called for in the treaty. During the war, exchange between the two countries nearly ceased, consisting only of special transport submarines carrying military equipment from Germany to Japan and returning to Germany with raw materials like tungsten. Only after the German defeat and the announcement that the provisional German government had stopped its activities on 23 May 1945 did the German ambassador Heinrich Stahmer and Japan's minister of foreign affairs Tōgō Shigenori come to an agreement to suspend all official activities of the German embassy in Tōkyō and the consulates general in Kōbe and Yokohama.

Relations from World War II to the Present—— Both Germany and Japan were suspended from international diplomatic activities after their defeats. German property in Japan was expropriated by an agency of the Occupation government, and nearly all Germans were repatriated in 1947 and 1948. Japan got back its full sovereignty in 1952, but the Federal Republic of Germany was only allowed to establish limited diplomatic relations entrusted to a chargé d'affaires. It was not until 8 May 1955, with a mutual exchange at the ambassador level, that full diplomatic relations between the two countries were reestablished. After the conclusion of the treaty between the two German states, the German Democratic Republic established diplomatic relations with Japan in 1973. The mutual exchange of ambassadors took place in 1974.

German activities in Japan started up again in 1951. Two years before, German Catholic missionaries from the Steyl Missionary Society had opened a new university in Nagoya, the present-day Nanzan University, founded as a high school in 1931. Other property was released by the Occupation authorities, and after the San Francisco Peace Treaty the return of repatriated Germans became possible, but only a few returned to Japan. There were only 1,100 Germans living in Japan in 1960, and and 2,743 in 1981 (compared to 13,991 Japanese nationals in the Federal Republic of Germany).

Present-day diplomatic relations with the Federal Republic of Germany are friendly. Consultations between ministers of foreign affairs are held regularly. Economic relations became especially important after World War II, from the Japanese point of view, and the Federal Republic of Germany sets an example for Japan with its policy of social market economy (Soziale Marktwirtschaft). Economic relations were reestablished on 23 August 1951 after both countries agreed on the reapplication of the German trading and shipping treaty of 1927. A mutual trade agreement was extended until December 1977, according to a decision by the European Community (EC). Other economic relations were based on an air route treaty of 1961, the establishment of a German chamber of commerce in 1964, the conclusion of a report on German restriction of imports in 1964, a treaty of alternative taxation in 1966, and on shipping agreements in 1967. The Federal Republic of Germany is Japan's most important customer and supplier in Europe, as Japan is Germany's most important trading partner in Asia.

In 1980 exports from the Federal Republic of Germany to Japan came to US $2.2 billion (1.1 percent of its total exports, Japan thus ranking 17th among the export targets). Main export items were chemicals, machinery, and cars. The imports from Japan to the Federal Republic of Germany reached $5.75 billion (3.1 percent of total imports, which ranks Japan 8th among all importing countries). The main import articles were electro-technical equipment of all kinds, cars, bikes, and fine-mechanical items (cameras, watches). German capital investment in Japan up to 1980 reached nearly $230 million in value (mainly in banking and the machinery industry) compared with the Japanese capital investment in the Federal Republic of Germany which amounted to $800 million (mainly in the chemical and machinery industries). Since January 1970 German-Japanese economic relations have been subject to the joint trading policy of the EC. Consultations between the EC Commission and Japan take place every six months, and bilateral consultations between Japan and the Federal Republic of Germany have been fixed as well. Talks on economic and trading policies are also held regularly.

German cultural activities in Japan have been supported by a treaty signed on 14 December 1957. The German Goethe Institute with offices in Tōkyō, Ōsaka, and Kyōto, aims at promoting the German language and culture in Japan. A mutual exchange of students and teachers is organized under the Deutscher Akademischer Austauschdienst (DAAD) or German Academic Exchange Service. Scientific exchanges were strengthened by a treaty signed in October 1974 and are also supported by the DAAD and the Humboldt Foundation. Both organizations eagerly invite Japanese students and scholars to study at German universities.

Japan's diplomatic activities in the Federal Republic of Germany are represented by the embassy in Bonn and four consulates general in Düsseldorf, Hamburg, Berlin, and Munich. Japanese economic activities formerly concentrated at the port of Hamburg and in Frankfurt, the financial center of Germany, were moved in the late 1960s when Düsseldorf became the most important center for German-Japanese economic relations. Japanese organizations such as JETRO (Japan External Trade Organization) and others have their main offices here. Japanese cultural activities in Germany center around the Japanisches Kulturinstitut at Cologne, founded in 1969.

■ ——Toku Baelz, *Erwin Baelz* (1930). Generalkonsulat der Bundesrepublik Deutschland, ed, *1874–1974 Hundert Jahre Deutsches Konsulat Kōbe* (1974). Hayashi Keisuke, *Bandō furyo shūyōjo*, Awa bunko 6 (1978). Engelbert Kaempfer, *Geschichte und Beschreibung von Japan* (1777). Kurt Meissner, *Deutsche in Japan 1639–1960*, Mitteilungen der Deutschen Gesellschaft für Natur und Völkerkunde Ostasiens, supp 26 (1961). Kurt Meissner, *100 Jahre Deutsch-Japanische Beziehungen*. Martin Ramming, *Japan Handbuch* (1940). Otto Schmiedel, *Die Deutschen in Japan* (1920). Hans Schwalbe and Heinrich Seemann, *Deutsche Botschafter in Japan, 1860–1973* (1974). Philipp Franz von Siebold, *Nippon: Archiv zur Beschreibung von Japan* (1897). Erich PAUER

Gero

Town in central Gifu Prefecture, central Honshū, on the river Mashitagawa. A part of the Hida–Kisogawa Quasi-National Park, Gero has been famous for more than a thousand years for its hot springs. NAKAYAMA SHICHIRI, a 23 km (14 mi) long gorge on the river Mashitagawa, is noted for its beauty. Tourists are also attracted to the historical houses in the nearby Hida–Takayama region. Forestry and lumber industries flourish in the area. Pop: 15,554.

gesaku

(also pronounced *kisaku, gisaku,* and *kesaku*). The generic term for all popular fiction written between the middle of the 18th century and the close of the Edo period (1600–1868), and for literature of the early part of the Meiji period (1868–1912) that continued this tradition. The term originally meant "written for fun"; appropriately enough, the genre is characterized by the flippant attitude of the author, or *gesakusha,* toward his work and a certain inimitable style combining facetiousness of tone with elaborate structure. The history of *gesaku* literature may be divided into early *gesaku* (up to about 1800), late *gesaku* (ca 1800 to ca 1868) and Meiji *gesaku* (ca 1868 into the 1880s).

The Rise of Gesaku —— The rise of the *gesaku* spirit in literature can be understood as a reaction to the impasse that Tokugawa feudalism had reached at the outset of the 18th century. The vigorous development of 17th-century society and culture had been arrested; the energies that had generated in it a kind of renaissance spirit were lapsing into a state of enforced stagnancy. The emergence of the *bunjin* (dilettantist men of letters) epitomizes these conditions. Some of these *bunjin,* who originally cultivated in their art a lofty style reflecting a more general detachment from their environment, began from about the middle of the 18th century to concern themselves—purely for their own diversion—with so-called vulgar literature, particularly with fiction. This new interest was partly due to their study of Chinese popular literature. Fiction not being classified as literature, the *bunjin* kept it distinct from their "serious" work, either passing it off as a joke or disowning it altogether. However, steeped as they were in Chinese scholarship, it was inevitable that their own attempts at vulgar literature could not conceal their erudition. It is in this synthesis of the demotic and the erudite that the origins of *gesaku* literature are to be found. The intellectually sophisticated, somewhat tongue-in-cheek attitude set the new literature off from the fiction of the first half of the Edo period, which was much more concerned with straightforward storytelling designed to edify and entertain the reader (see LITERATURE: Edo literature).

Early Gesaku —— Later generations, looking back on the development of *gesaku,* viewed HIRAGA GENNAI as the founding father of the tradition. Gennai, with his witty, at times, vehement satirical prose, was indisputably the first great author of *gesaku;* it was his work that heralded the golden age of early *gesaku* in the 1770s and 1780s. Besides the rather heterogeneous groups of books classified today as early KOKKEIBON and early YOMIHON (including translations and adaptations of Chinese fiction), the main *gesaku* genres of this period were KIBYŌSHI and SHAREBON. Representative authors of early *gesaku* besides Hiraga Gennai include ŌTA NAMPO and SANTŌ KYŌDEN. Early *gesaku* was essentially the literature of the urban intelligentsia of *samurai* stock, although Santō Kyōden belonged to the merchant class.

With regard to style, early *gesaku* is characterized by wordplay, parody of earlier works, and intricate formal construction at the expense of the story itself; with regard to content, life in the fashionable circles, the gossip and the goings-on, especially at the theater and in the pleasure quarters, provides the main subject-matter. Behind the jocular facade there can at times be detected a sense of passive opposition to the values of feudal society. Transcending the limits of fiction, these features of *gesaku* style are to be found across a broad spectrum of the contemporary popular arts, for example in KYŌKA ("mad verse") and UKIYO-E prints. It sometimes happened that the same artist was active in these stylistically similar, though otherwise distinct art forms. Besides writing *gesaku,* Santō Kyōden was respectively a *kyōka* poet and *ukiyo-e* artist in his own right. Woodblock illustrations played some part in most *gesaku* genres, and in *kibyōshi* they were indispensable, forming one organic whole with the text they accompanied.

Late Gesaku —— The KANSEI REFORMS (1787–93) were a watershed in the history of *gesaku.* Designed to reinforce the crumbling structure of feudalism, they effectively silenced some writers and admonished others to mend their ways. More significantly, the expansion of the reading public was to fundamentally affect the relationship between authors and their readers. The dilettanti of early *gesaku,* who wrote to amuse themselves and a like-minded coterie, were outstripped by professional writers supplying an anonymous public (with growing emphasis on women readers) on a nationwide scale. Booksellers and lending libraries became the driving force behind *gesaku* production. From about 1800, *kokkeibon* and NINJŌBON (both to some extent developments of the *sharebon*), GŌKAN (which can be traced back to the *kibyōshi*) and *yomihon* gradually crystallized as the main genres of late *gesaku,* represented by the work of JIPPENSHA IKKU, SHIKITEI SAMBA, TAMENAGA SHUNSUI, RYŪTEI TANEHIKO, BAKIN, and Santō Kyōden (the only leading writer active in both early and late *gesaku*). The above writers are known collectively as the Gesaku Rokkasen, the Six Poetic Sages of Gesaku.

Typical of late *gesaku* is the disappearance of the earlier intellectual sophistication, and the blatant moralizing (often merely perfunctory) in obedience to official Confucianist ethics. But, in symbiosis with the performing arts (JŌRURI, KABUKI, RAKUGO, etc) and book illustration, it did achieve immense popularity, thus creating for the first time in Japan a broad reading public for fiction. However, the commercialization of literature also produced enormous quantities of mere "pulp."

In linguistic skill and technical virtuosity these professional writers sometimes matched the achievements of early *gesaku*, but their virtuosity was marred by a dearth of provocative ideas. In late *gesaku* there are virtually no references to the progressive intellectual currents of the age, namely National Learning (KOKUGAKU) or WESTERN LEARNING (Yōgaku). In the wake of the TEMPŌ REFORMS (1841–43), which were the last desperate attempt to save feudalism, another generation of writers was again suppressed and *gesaku* writing completely lost its vigor and creative force.

Gesaku Tradition and Modern Literature —— The far-reaching political changes of the MEIJI RESTORATION of 1868 left the *gesaku* writers in a state of total disorientation. Some authors like the *kokkeibon* writer KANAGAKI ROBUN and the *ninjōbon* writer Sansantei Arindo (also known as Jōno Saigiku, 1832–1902) began writing for the new popular press and managed to adjust to the new age. There were very few writers like Mantei Ōga (1818?–90) who were prepared to keep their traditional role by poking fun at the new "civilization." Despite a brief revival after the initial shock was over, the production of *gesaku* proper (absorbed by the rising tide of journalism) had ceased at the end of the 1880s.

Late *gesaku* did, however, remain popular reading throughout the early Meiji period, notably the works of Bakin and Tamenaga Shunsui, and it was indeed the literary grounding of some of the champions of the new literature who emerged in the late 1880s. Elements of *gesaku*, though gradually receding, are to be found in the style of TSUBOUCHI SHŌYŌ and FUTABATEI SHIMEI.

In the 1890s, the young romantics fought relentlessly to extinguish all traces of the *gesaku* spirit; the modern reader's neglect of *gesaku*, particularly late *gesaku*, is a measure of their influence. For all his skill, the *gesaku* writer was just an entertainer: there could never be any question of his competing against the charisma of the romantic poet, to whom literature was the most sublime and serious activity of life.

The history of mainstream modern Japanese literature is remarkable for having eradicated all traces of the *gesaku* spirit. Though excluded from "pure literature," the tradition did, however, live on in commercial literature, popular journalism, and other forms of modern mass culture. Even in "pure literature" it is sometimes irrepressible: in the relaxed, witty style of NATSUME SŌSEKI's early works or the sensuousness of NAGAI KAFŪ unmistakable echoes of *gesaku* can be heard.

——Mizuno Minoru, *Edo shōsetsu ronsō* (1974). Nakamura Yukihiko, *Kinsei shōsetsu shi no kenkyū* (1961). Nakamura Yukihiko, *Kinsei sakka kenkyū* (1961). Nakamura Yukihiko, *Gesakuron* (1966). Okitsu Kaname, *Meiji kaikaki bungaku no kenkyū* (1968).

Wolfgang SCHAMONI

Gesshō (1813–1858)

Buddhist priest associated with the late Edo-period (1600–1868) movement to overthrow the Tokugawa shogunate and restore imperial rule. Born in Ōsaka. In 1854 he relinquished his post as abbot of a subtemple of Kiyomizudera in Kyōto to devote himself to the proimperial movement. He became friends with such activists as UMEDA UMPIN and SAIGŌ TAKAMORI. To escape shogunate suppression of loyalists in 1858 (see ANSEI PURGE), Gesshō and Saigō fled to the domain of Satsuma (now Kagoshima Prefecture). When they were refused asylum by the domain authorities, they threw themselves into Kagoshima Bay. Saigō survived, but Gesshō drowned.

gestures

The Japanese have an innate preference for communication by means other than direct verbalization, and this preference is often manifested by gestures, which in Japan are characterized by their abundance, their variety, and their tact.

Foreign visitors to Japan may observe gestures, called *temane* or *teburi* in Japanese, even more frequently than might be otherwise expected inasmuch as some Japanese will utilize gestures more than

words in their efforts to communicate with foreigners who do not speak Japanese. This belief in the universality of gesture meanings is not always justified. Although some gestures carry approximately the same meaning in Japan as in the West, there are others that do not, and these should be noted.

Forming a circle with the right thumb and index finger is a reference to money, whereas a tightly clenched fist means tight-fisted. If one hooks his forefinger, he is saying that the person under discussion has the unfortunate habit of taking things not his. The little finger pointing up into the air originally had the meaning of baby, but nowadays it is more commonly used to mean girlfriend, mistress, or wife. The thumb held straight up may mean boyfriend, father, or master. When one wishes to call a person to him, he extends his right arm straight out, bends his hand downward, and flutters his hand several times. By raising those fingers only a few inches, he could convert that motion into the Western gesture for goodbye. The rapid crossing of the index fingers tells the viewer of a fight or bad feelings between two persons. The thumb rubbed against the side of the nose indicates a card game called HANAFUDA, the name deriving from the pictures of flowers on the backs of the playing cards. *Hana* is the word for nose as well as for flower.

If one brings his hands to his forehead and points the forefingers up and outward like horns, he is suggesting jealousy, whereas the Western connotation would be the cuckolding of a husband. Moving the thumb back and forth indicates the upright pinball game of PACHINKO, which has been popular in Japan throughout most of the postwar years. The thumb is used in that manner to operate the lever on the machine. If one hits the heel of his open hand lightly against his forehead, he is telling the viewer of his consternation at having forgotten something or having made a mistake. If one puts his hand on the top of his head and rubs or scratches it briefly, he is informing the viewer that he is in a predicament. The cupping of the left hand just below the level of the mouth with the right hand going through the motions of using chopsticks is a readily understood reference to food or to eating.

Gestures are used in the underworld for not only the same reasons that other Japanese utilize them but also because the users of such gestures may not want to be overheard. Striking the forehead with the thumb-side of a fist is a message that the forces of the law are approaching and that all malefactors should resort to immediate flight. The right forefinger drawn across the cheek in a slashing movement is a reference to a gangster.

Whereas Westerners will point to their hearts when indicating themselves, Japanese will often point to their noses. If one holds his stiff right hand in front of his face with the thumb nearest the nose and the palm facing to the left, he is making the gesture used to ask indulgence when crossing the path of another or when passing between two persons. If the right arm is bent at the elbow and raised, then jerked spasmodically once, it becomes an informal gesture of greeting, favored particularly by boys and younger men.

What gives gestures in Japan particular significance is that they are a manifestation of the Japanese fondness for communication without words. Another facet of this preference is called *ishin denshin* or mental telepathy. For many Japanese, the truth is to be found in what is implied rather than in what is stated. ZEN Buddhism itself is based on a wordless tradition in which enlightenment is achieved by intuitive understanding rather than by a study of the words of scriptures. It can also be seen in the poetic form HAIKU, where so much can be transmitted by so few words, in Zen gardens, where a few small rocks surrounded by raked sand can depict mountains rising from an ocean, and in *sumie*, in which blank space can be the heart of the ink drawing (see INK PAINTING).

A partial explanation for the Japanese avoidance of direct expression is the high degree of homogeneity of the Japanese people, whose social history for hundreds of years was little influenced by exotic forces. Leading similar lifestyles in close proximity, they became acutely sensitive to the feelings, reactions, and desires of others, as in a large but closely knit family where intuitive understanding can replace specific verbalization.

Japanese attitudes toward intuitive understanding and communication by means other than words can be suggested by the following quotations of the statements of prominent Japanese:

"Vagueness is often a virtue. . . . " (NOGUCHI YONEJIRŌ)

"We simply do not think it civilized to be too direct in expression." (Akashi Yasushi)

"A strong distrust develops between Japanese if they try to express everything through words." (Katō Shūichi)

"To give in so many words one's deepest thoughts and feelings is taken by us as an unmistakable sign that they are neither profound nor very sincere." (NITOBE INAZŌ)

Americans, conditioned to admire eloquence and deft persuasion through apt words, might be puzzled to learn that in Japan the best salesman may be an awkward speaker who is reticent in his dealings with potential customers. If he were a smoothly persuasive speaker, his listeners might entertain doubts about his sincerity. See also NONVERBAL COMMUNICATION.   Jack SEWARD

geta

Outdoor footwear consisting of a thong attached to a wooden platform with two crosswise supports; called *ashida* in the Heian period (794–1185) and *bokuri* in the Muromachi period (1333–1568). TA-GETA (snowshoelike footwear used for working in paddies) have been excavated at KARAKO SITE and TORO SITE, both belonging to the Yayoi period (ca 300 BC–ca AD 300). The word *geta* as distinct from *ashida* came into use during the Edo period (1600–1868). The word *takageta* refers to *geta* with especially high supports. The *geta* platform is usually made of paulownia or cryptomeria wood; the supports (called *ha*, "teeth") of oak or magnolia; and the thong of cloth or leather.   MIYAMOTO Mizuo

ghosts

The term for ghost in Japanese is *yūrei*, which generally means the spirit or soul of a dead person. In popular parlance, the term *yūrei* is often confused with *yōkai*, a related yet different phenomenon. Japanese folklorists make a clear distinction between *yūrei* and *yō-kai*. A *yūrei* is the departed soul of a person, which appears as a shadowy likeness of the deceased. A *yūrei* is said to have a specific purpose for returning to the world of the living and to reveal itself only to certain persons, most often surviving relatives but occasionally other intimate acquaintances. By contrast, a *yōkai* is a fantastic or grotesque apparition whose appearance is connected with a specific time or place rather than a specific individual. A *yōkai* may manifest itself to anyone unfortunate enough to trespass on its particular abode. See BAKEMONO.

The spirits of those who died natural deaths and are given proper rites are thought to lose their individual identities after the memorial service marking the 33rd anniversary of their death, at which time they join their ancestral spirits. The spirits of those who died violently or unnaturally—whether by accident, murder, suicide, or in battle—are believed to be unable to make their final passage into the world of the dead; they appear before their relatives and acquaintances and express their reluctance to depart this world.

From the late years of the Muromachi period (1333–1568) to the early years of the Meiji period (1868–1912), ghosts were frequent subjects of literary treatment. Since the middle part of the Edo period (1600–1868), in such ghost stories as TŌKAIDŌ YOTSUYA KAI-DAN (The Ghost Story of Tōkaidō Yotsuya) and *Botan-dōrō* (Peony Lantern), *yūrei* have been depicted as having disheveled hair, elongated dangling arms, and no feet. See also MONONOKE.
                                    INOKUCHI Shōji

GHQ

(General Headquarters). Term used in post–World War II Japan to refer to the combined military headquarters in Tōkyō of the Supreme Commander for the Allied Powers (SCAP) and the US FAR EAST COMMAND (FEC). SCAP was responsible for the Allied administration of occupied Japan, and FEC for administering US military forces throughout the Far East.   Richard B. FINN

gidayū-bushi

Type of JŌRURI narrative chant originated by Takemoto Gidayū I (1651–1714) for his Takemotoza, a puppet theater in Ōsaka (founded 1684). His most important collaborator at this theater was the playwright CHIKAMATSU MONZAEMON (1653–1724) and the style and repertoire created by these two men and their successors are partially preserved today by the Bunrakuza theater in Ōsaka. *Gidayū-bushi* also had a profound influence on all later styles of KABUKI music, and on regional styles of puppetry and of SHAMISEN chant.

Nothing of Gidayū I's own recitation style has survived directly. In 1703 one of his pupils, Toyotake Wakatayū I (1681–1764), founded a rival theater, the Toyotakeza; this represented what came to be known as the "Eastern" school, and used the brighter *yō* scale,

as opposed to the "Western" Takemoto school, which used the more astringent *in* scale. During the 18th century various other subschools developed, but after a celebrated performance of *Chūshingura* in 1748, the Eastern and Western schools began to reconcile their differences, even though the two styles of chanting can still be distinguished.

In general *gidayū-bushi* is powerful and expressive music. The chanting is forceful and declamatory, and the single *shamisen* which accompanies it is a large, deep-toned instrument. Chikamatsu had introduced a new type of puppet play, the *sewa-mono*, which treats domestic themes, as opposed to the longer historical plays, *jidai-mono*. The former consist of three sections *(dan)*, the latter of five; there are further subsections; and the music for each subsection is largely made up of named, stereotyped melodic fragments. This type of construction antedates the development of *gidayū-bushi*, and the repertoire of such melodic fragments is very large. The three main categories are *chi, fushi*, and *kotoba*, two others are *sanjū* and *okuri*, and there are subtypes of each. They vary greatly in melodic and emotional character, and their origins are quite diverse. Many come from Buddhist chant, HEIKYOKU, NŌ chant, and older *jōruri* singing; others are taken from folk song, folk religious chant, and so on.

📖 ——Geinōshi Kenkyūkai, ed, *Jōruri: Katari to ayatsuri*, in *Nihon no koten geinō*, vol 7 (Heibonsha, 1970). Gunji Masakatsu, ed, *Gidayū*, in *Hōgaku taikei*, vol 5 (Chikuma Shobō and Japan Victor 1971).   David B. WATERHOUSE

Gidō Shūshin (1325–1388)

Zen monk of the Rinzai sect and an important figure in GOZAN LITERATURE (Chinese learning in the medieval Japanese Zen monasteries). Born in Tosa Province (now Kōchi Prefecture), Gidō was a disciple of MUSŌ SOSEKI and became leader of his lineage after Musō's death in 1351. After residing at Engakuji in Kamakura and other temples in the Kantō area for about 20 years, he was invited in 1380 (Tenju 6) to Kyōto to reside at Nanzenji, the head temple of the Gozan. He became a Confucian tutor to the young shōgun ASHI-KAGA YOSHIMITSU. Gidō's journal, entitled *Kūge nichiyō kufūshū* (also known as *Kūge nikkushū)*, is an invaluable source for the history of this period. Gidō was passionately fond of Chinese poetry; his works include an anthology of poems by Chinese Zen monks, and he himself is considered one of the greatest poets of the Gozan monasteries. His numerous poems, reflecting his warm, gentle, pious temperament, are collected in the anthology *Kūgeshū*. Unlike other major Gozan poets, Gidō never visited China.   *Marian URY*

gift giving

Gift giving in Japan involves elaborate rules and is part of a larger system of social exchange. Gifts may be brought each time a visit is made and are usually exchanged on other specified occasions. An average Japanese family probably gives or receives a gift at least once a week, and the money spent on these gifts constitutes a substantial portion of the family budget. Usually gifts are presented to a family as a unit and rarely exchanged within the family.

There are several major gift-giving seasons during the year: the New Year (OTOSHIDAMA given to children), the end of the year (SEIBO gifts), and the midyear (CHŪGEN gifts). Significant stages in human life such as birth, coming of age *(seijin)*, and marriage, as well as funerals and partings (see FAREWELL GIFTS) require gifts. Gifts are given to the sick or victims of fire or other disasters as encouragement (MIMAI), or are given as souvenirs for friends, relatives, and others after even the shortest trip (see MIYAGE), and for happy celebrations (see SHŪGI). On formal occasions gifts are wrapped in heavy white paper decorated with a special tie (MIZU-HIKI), and on joyous occasions they are wrapped with a symbolic ornament (NOSHI). When money is given as a gift, as it often is, the bills must be clean and crisp and enclosed in a special money envelope *(noshibukuro)*, sold at stationery stores. On inauspicious occasions, such as funerals, the tie is gray and white or black and white, while on happy occasions the tie is usually red and white.

Traditionally gifts in Japan had religious or magical significance. Foods and liquor were offered to the gods on the altar and then eaten in a banquet called NAORAI, so that by sharing the god's food, one acquired some of the god's spirit and power. Edible gifts given by a healthy person to the sick were believed to have, upon being consumed, the magical power of helping to restore health. These religious and magical qualities are seldom remembered or appreciated

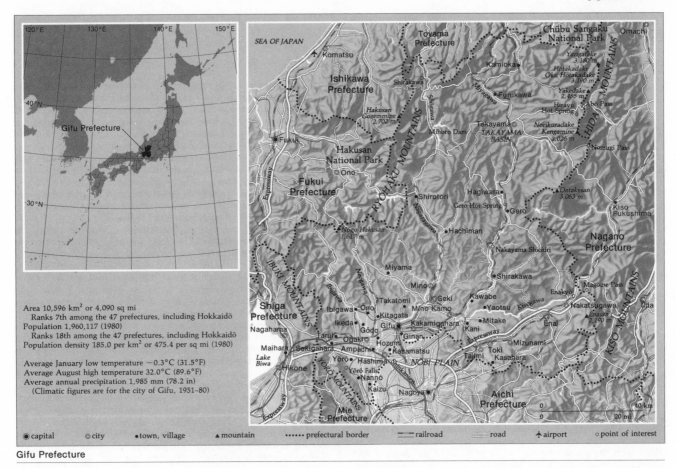

Area 10,596 km² or 4,090 sq mi
  Ranks 7th among the 47 prefectures, including Hokkaidō
Population 1,960,117 (1980)
  Ranks 18th among the 47 prefectures, including Hokkaidō
Population density 185.0 per km² or 475.4 per sq mi (1980)

Average January low temperature −0.3°C (31.5°F)
Average August high temperature 32.0°C (89.6°F)
Average annual precipitation 1,985 mm (78.2 in)
  (Climatic figures are for the city of Gifu, 1951–80)

◉ capital ◎ city ● town, village ▲ mountain ⋯⋯ prefectural border ══ railroad ══ road ✈ airport ○ point of interest

Gifu Prefecture

now. Gifts are often given out of a sense of obligation and in turn require a return gift (KAESHI). It is not unusual for people to keep lists of gifts received in order to be able to give a return gift of the exact value. Gifts given to a superior, such as *seibo, chūgen,* or to a teacher or a person to whom one is indebted, do not require a return gift.

Gifts given before services are rendered *(hizatsuki)* are an advance expression of thanks, brought for example when one begins lessons in traditional arts like the tea ceremony. When asking for an unusual or substantial favor of a person one has not been formerly acquainted with, an advance gift *(meishigawari;* literally, "in place of name card"), often of considerable value, is given. Only a thin and tenuous line separates gifts expressing genuine thanks from those with ulterior motives, better classed as "bribes." Actually most gifts simultaneously express one's gratitude or respect, serve material ends, and fulfill important social obligations.

◾ ——Harumi Befu, "Gift-Giving in a Modernizing Japan," *Monumenta Nipponica* 23 (1968).   Harumi BEFU

Gifu

Capital of Gifu Prefecture, central Honshū, on the river NAGARA-GAWA. A castle town of the Toki family during the Muromachi period (1333–1568) and known as Inokuchi, in the late 1500s it came under the rule of the warlord ODA NOBUNAGA, who changed its name to Gifu. It prospered during the Edo period (1600–1868) as a post-station town on the highway Nakasendō. Traditionally known for its umbrellas, lanterns, and fans, it now has a flourishing textile industry and an emerging machinery industry. Tourist attractions are Gifu Castle (completely rebuilt in 1956), on the summit of Kinkazan, the temple Entokuji, associated with the Oda family, and CORMORANT FISHING *(ukai)* on the Nagaragawa. Pop: 410,368.

Gifu Prefecture

(Gifu Ken). Located in central Honshū and bounded by Toyama Prefecture to the north, Nagano Prefecture to the east, Aichi and Mie prefectures to the south, and Shiga, Fukui, and Ishikawa prefectures to the west. The terrain is almost totally mountainous, and major ranges include the Hida and Ryōhaku mountain ranges in the north, with some peaks measuring over 3,000 m (9,840 ft) in height. The southern section is composed of lower mountains and the NŌBI PLAIN around the city of Gifu, which is the prefecture's major economic and population center. Major rivers are the KISOGAWA, IBI-GAWA and NAGARAGAWA. The climate is mild in the southern section, but cooler in the mountainous north. Precipitation is heavy in both areas. Almost all major cities are located in the south and form an integral part of the CHŪKYŌ INDUSTRIAL ZONE centering on NAGOYA.

Modern Gifu Prefecture was created in 1876 through the merger of Hida and Mino provinces, which correspond roughly to the northern and southern portions of the prefecture. The area has long been of strategic importance as a link between eastern and western Honshū as well as between the Pacific and the Sea of Japan coasts. It was the site of several major battles, including the Battle of SEKIGAHARA (1600), which established the hegemony of the Tokugawa shogunate.

Industrial activity, centered in the south, is led by such manufactures as textiles, clothing, ceramics, transportation equipment, pulp, and paper. Gifu is also a leading producer of lumber.

The mountain scenery and historic villages and towns of the Hida region, notably TAKAYAMA, constitute Gifu's outstanding tourist attractions. CORMORANT FISHING *(ukai),* also a major attraction, is carried out on the Nagaragawa. Part of the CHŪBU SANGAKU NATIONAL PARK is within the prefecture. Other parks include the Hida–Kisogawa Quasi-National Park and the Ibi–Sekigahara–Yorō Quasi-National Park. Area: 10,596 sq km (4,090 sq mi); pop: 1,960,-117; capital: Gifu. Other major cities include ŌGAKI, TAJIMI, KAKA-MIGAHARA, and Takayama.

gigaku

Ancient masked dance drama introduced into Japan during the Nara period (710–794). *Gigaku* was one of many forms of foreign music and dance which were adopted from mainland Asia. Although the performance tradition for this genre died out during the Edo period (1600–1868), there are a number of historical documents as well as artifacts which tell us something about *gigaku.*

It was said to have been introduced into Japan in the early 7th century by a certain Mimashi, a native of Paekche, one of the three kingdoms of Korea. Mimashi had apparently traveled widely and had learned the dances in the region of Wu in China. Subsequently, *gigaku* played an important role in court ceremonies and entertainments of the Nara period as well as in those associated with the larger Buddhist temples.

From surviving evidence, it appears that *gigaku* may have been a mime performance or a processional combined with dance and music. As such, it may have resembled a mystery play or a masked dance drama in which the actors or dancers took the roles of stereotyped stock characters. An excellent set of Nara period MASKS, carved of camphor wood, is preserved in the SHŌSŌIN repository in Nara. In style and character, these masks bear only a slight resemblance to those used in the later *bugaku* (see GAGAKU) dances of the court. The *gigaku* masks, portraying Indian-style figures such as Baramon (Brāhmana), Karura (Garuda), and Kongō Rikishi (Vajradhara), seem to come from an earlier stage of mainland Asian Buddhist culture, and do not appear in *bugaku* dances.

The music for the *gigaku* performances made use of a group of singers and an ensemble of flutes, hourglass-shaped drums, and cymbals. Examples of the music survive in a manuscript containing notation for the flute, which gives only the basic melodic contour and the placing of the main drum strokes. Since notation for Japanese music of this period seems to have been used primarily as a mnemonic aid, with the filling out of melodic ornaments and style left to the player's knowledge of the tradition, the surviving notation tells us very little about the manner in which *gigaku* might have actually been performed.

The numerous historical references to *gigaku* indicate an ensemble of one or two transverse flutes and as many as nine drums, called TSUZUMI, with bodies carved of wood in an hourglass form. The drumheads were attached by means of laces, which could be tightened by hand to tune the drums to different pitches. These drums are similar to the *tsuzumi* used in the NŌ theater. A number of different types of *tsuzumi* have been preserved in the Shōsōin, along with the *gigaku* masks. Some portions of the dancers' and musicians' costumes have also been preserved in the Shōsōin collection.

Two important pictorial sources on *gigaku* are *Shinzei kogakuzu* (Shinzei's Illustrations of Ancient Music), a 12th-century scroll which depicts musicians, dancers, and acrobats of the Nara period, and the minute drawings depicting similar figures painted along the narrow surface of a hunting bow *(dankyū)* in the Shōsōin. Although these sources do not specifically indicate *gigaku* performances, together they give an excellent view of the theatrical and dance style of the period during which *gigaku* flourished.

■ ——Hayashi Kenzō, *Shōsōin gakki no kenkyū* (1964). Shōsōin Office, ed, *Musical Instruments in the Shōsōin* (1967).

Robert GARFIAS

gijutsu dōnyū

(technology importation). The importation of technologies into Japan after World War II was led by basic industries, such as steel, petrochemicals, and synthetic fibers, and the machinery assembly industries, such as automobiles and home electrical appliances. The imported technologies of these industries, combined with vigorous plant and equipment investment, brought about high productivity, which in turn helped Japan to become less dependent upon imports. Eventually these became export industries, leading Japan's postwar economic growth.

The importation of technology caused Japan's balance of technology trade to run a deficit: for 1960–70, payments for importation of technology amounted to US $2.3 billion, while receipts from exportation of technology came to a mere $0.2 billion. The balance has since improved, with a technology importation figure of $1.3 billion and a technology exportation figure of $0.3 billion in 1979.

The causes of this vigorous importation of technology during the postwar period of rapid economic growth were several: (1) the enlarged technology gap owing to the lack of technological exchanges during World War II; (2) the ease of technology importation under the Foreign Investment Law of 1949; (3) the adaptability of technologies developed for American and European consumption patterns to the urbanized, modern life of Japan; (4) the worldwide explosion of such new technologies as electronics; (5) the intense rivalry among firms which led to competitive introduction of foreign technologies.

The high average level of education in Japan has also facilitated the application and improvement of imported foreign technologies. See also TECHNOLOGY TRANSFER.

KATŌ Masashi

Gikeiki

Popular account of the life of MINAMOTO NO YOSHITSUNE (1159–89); written around 1400 to 1450; translated as *Yoshitsune*, 1966. The anonymous author drew selectively on a large body of popular legends concerning Yoshitsune which developed during the centuries following his death. The author gives little weight to the public career of Yoshitsune as a Minamoto warrior, the image developed in such warrior tales as HEIKE MONOGATARI and GEMPEI SEISUIKI. Similarly *Gikeiki* largely avoids the more supernatural elements found in other Yoshitsune legends and presents a relatively naturalistic fictional biography of Yoshitsune with sympathetic depiction of his mistress Shizuka and several of his loyal retainers. One of these, Saitō Musashibō BENKEI, emerges as a figure of interest equal to Yoshitsune himself. Particularly in the latter half of the work, Yoshitsune is depicted as a passive character in contrast to the powerfully assertive Benkei who remains devotedly loyal to Yoshitsune.

Among the most memorable episodes in *Gikeiki* are the following. After childhood training in a temple at Kurama in Kyōto, the teenage Yoshitsune journeys toward Ōshū (northeastern Japan) to seek the support of Fujiwara no Hidehira in his plan to rebel against the Taira family, who then controlled Japan. En route, traveling in disguise in the company of a gold merchant, Kichiji, Yoshitsune kills several robbers who have failed to take him seriously because his looks and costume are so beautiful he is thought to be a girl.

Yoshitsune gains access to a secret Chinese martial-arts treatise. Its owner, angry at Yoshitsune's act, sends Yoshitsune to murder an awesome ruffian, Tankai, certain that he is thereby consigning Yoshitsune to death. Instead Yoshitsune succeeds in his mission.

Yoshitsune meets Benkei, a monster of a man who has been stealing swords in the capital. His attempt to steal the sword of the young, apparently delicate, Yoshitsune fails, and Benkei swears to serve Yoshitsune. The latter puts on Benkei's armor over his own, symbolically taking on Benkei's strength and protection.

The narrative tells of the enmity of Yoshitsune's elder half-brother MINAMOTO NO YORITOMO which accounts for Yoshitsune's eventual death and for the popular sympathy toward Yoshitsune which developed subsequently. In his flight from Yoritomo's men, Yoshitsune parts from his mistress Shizuka; she is captured and taken before Yoritomo. She gives birth to Yoshitsune's son, who is murdered on Yoritomo's command. Later, while dancing observed by Yoritomo, Shizuka bravely sings a song that expresses her continuing love for Yoshitsune.

Yoshitsune flees northward, frequently aided by Benkei's resourcefulness. For example, Benkei beats Yoshitsune, who is disguised as a lowly member of the traveling party, to avoid suspicion. Benkei's flogging of his master and his subsequent apology provide one of the most stirring scenes of the entire work.

Finally the loyal Benkei withstands the onslaught of a large band in the last attack on Yoshitsune. While giving Yoshitsune, for whom there is no possibility of escape, sufficient time to commit suicide calmly, Benkei dies standing, his eyes glaring, his body riddled with arrows, the very picture of defiance and force.

■ ——*Gikeiki*, tr Helen Craig McCullough as *Yoshitsune* (1966). Okami Masao, ed, *Gikeiki*, in *Nihon koten bungaku taikei*, vol 37 (Iwanami Shoten, 1959). Shimazu Hisamoto, *Yoshitsune densetsu to bungaku* (1935).

Susan MATISOFF

giko monogatari

(literally, "tales copied after the old"). Tales of the Kamakura period (1185–1333) imitating the style and themes of Heian-period (794–1185) classical fiction. In a broader sense the term includes Edo-period (1600–1868) works such as *Temakura* (The Pillowing Arm) by the KOKUGAKU (National Learning) scholar MOTOORI NORINAGA. Written by aristocrats for an aristocratic audience and concerned with the lives of the nobility, *giko monogatari* such as *Sumiyoshi monogatari* (The Tale of Sumiyoshi) and *Koke no koromo* (The Moss-Covered Robe) were most strongly influenced by the *Genji monogatari* (TALE OF GENJI), but manifested a greater sense of Buddhist millenarian fatalism, focusing on themes of ascetic reclusion, dreams, and death. As a genre, they are derivative and generally unimaginative and in the Muromachi period (1333–1568)

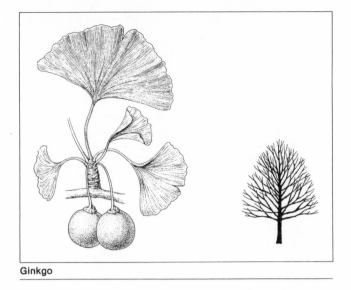

Ginkgo

room in which Yoshimasa practiced meditation. The upper story holds a gilt image of Kannon. The Tōgudō, which served as the residence and private chapel of Yoshimasa, contains altars enshrining images of Amida Buddha and Yoshimasa as well as the memorial tablets of the Ashikaga shōguns. In the northeast corner of the building is a famous tearoom (chashitsu) designed by Yoshimasa, reputedly the oldest tearoom in Japan. Between the Tōgudō and Ginkaku is a splendid garden, originally modeled upon that of the temple SAIHŌJI but redesigned during the Kan'ei era (1624–44). The Ginkakuji is referred to as the epitome of the HIGASHIYAMA CULTURE.
Stanley WEINSTEIN

ginkgo

(ichō). Ginkgo biloba. A deciduous tree, and the only surviving member, of the family Ginkgoaceae, grown in China and Japan. The ripe fruit has a fleshy, foul-smelling outer covering, but its kernel, called *ginnan,* is edible. The gingko grows fast and is resistant to cold weather, fire, diseases, and urban atmospheric conditions; it often is planted as a roadside tree or firebreak. The tree attains a height of up to 30 meters (98 ft) with a diameter of 2 meters (7 ft); some huge trees have aerial roots called *chichi* ("breasts") growing from the base of the branch. The leaves are fan-shaped and turn yellow in autumn. The ginkgo bears flowers around April. The male flowers grow on separate trees from the female, with pollen of male flowers being carried by the wind to female flowers in early autumn. The fact that the pollen produces motile sperm cells at this time was first discovered in 1896 by HIRASE SAKUGORŌ, who also clarified the ginkgo's taxonomic position, previously unknown, as a single-species genus.

The genus *Ginkgo* is said to have thrived worldwide in the prehistoric period but now grows abundantly only in Japan, China, and Korea. The ginkgo was first introduced to Europe in an 18th-century book by Engelbert KAEMPFER, a German naturalist who had visited Japan.
MATSUDA Osamu

Ginowan

City on the island of Okinawa, Okinawa Prefecture. Situated north of Naha, Ginowan was heavily damaged during World War II. After the war about half the city was allocated for American military use. The city's economy is largely dependent on the American military. Pop: 62,550.

ginza → kinza, ginza, and zeniza

Ginzan Hot Spring

(Ginzan Onsen). Located in the city of Obanazawa, central Yamagata Prefecture, northern Honshū. A hydrogen sulfide spring containing salt; water temperature 63°C (145°F). Said to have been discovered when an abandoned Edo-period (1600–1868) silver mine was being remined. This spa, situated along the Ginzan Gorge east of the center of the city, has been designated as a National Health Resort Hot Spring. Snowfall is heavy in this area.

Gioji

Convent in Ukyō Ward, Kyōto, affiliated with the DAIKAKUJI branch of the SHINGON SECT of Buddhism. Gioji, which was first known as Ōjōin, was originally a minor hermitage in Kyōto of uncertain origin. Its fame is based on the story from the HEIKE MONOGATARI (The Tale of Heike) of Giō, a great beauty, who, after losing the favor of the great Taira family (Heike) chieftain TAIRA NO KIYOMORI, renounced the world at the age of 21 along with her sister and mother to take up residence here and devote herself to the Buddha AMIDA and rebirth in his Pure Land. The convent, long in a state of disrepair, was rebuilt and given its present name in honor of Giō in 1895. On the convent grounds is a tombstone said to mark her grave. Among its treasures are wooden images of Giō and her sister, with eyes made of crystal, which date from the 14th century. The convent is now dedicated to the Buddha DAINICHI (Skt: Mahāvairocana).
Stanley WEINSTEIN

Gion Festival

(Gion Matsuri). Gion festivals are conducted throughout Japan, but the best known is that sponsored by the YASAKA SHRINE in Kyōto.

---

generally unimaginative and in the Muromachi period (1333–1568) were superseded by OTOGI-ZŌSHI, brief tales designed to reach a broader readership.

Gila River Relocation Center

A wartime relocation facility for Japanese Americans located on the Gila River Indian Reservation, Arizona, in operation from 20 July 1942 until 10 November 1945. It held a maximum of 13,348 persons at any one time; a total of 16,655 persons were confined there. Internees came from central and southern California. It was one of two camps located on Indian reservations. See JAPANESE AMERICANS, WARTIME RELOCATION OF; WAR RELOCATION AUTHORITY.
▬——Samuel T. Caruso, "After Pearl Harbor: Arizona's Response to the Gila River Relocation Center," *Journal of Arizona History* 14 (1973).
Roger DANIELS

Ginkakuji

(Temple of the Silver Pavilion). Formally known as Jishōji. Temple in Sakyō Ward, Kyōto, belonging to the SHŌKOKUJI branch of the Rinzai sect of Zen Buddhism. The Ginkakuji stands on the site of an abandoned Tendai monastery, the Jōdoji, in a scenic area of Kyōto that was favored by ASHIKAGA YOSHIMASA, the eighth Muromachi shōgun (r 1449–74). In 1465 Yoshimasa announced his intention of building a retreat here and ordered that a search be made throughout the provinces to find materials of the highest quality for his new residence. Yoshimasa formally moved here in 1483, the year the construction of his new residence was completed. Two years later he took holy orders under a monk of the temple Shōkokuji. On his death in 1490, Yoshimasa's elegant residence was converted into a temple in accordance with his last wishes and given the name Jishōji, which was taken from his posthumous religious title, Jishōin. The eminent Zen monk, Musō Soseki (1275–1351), who had been chosen as the honorary first abbot of the Shōkokuji, was designated the honorary first abbot of this temple as well. Hōsho Shūzai, a tonsured adopted son of Yoshimasa, was chosen as the second (actually the first functioning) abbot. Thereafter, most of the abbots of the Ginkakuji were selected from such aristocratic families as the Konoe.

According to temple records, the Ginkakuji originally consisted of 12 buildings. Influenced by the example of the gilded KINKAKUJI built in 1397, Yoshimasa planned to cover one of the buildings, the Kannon Hall, with silver leaf, but died before this could be done. Although the silver leafing was in fact never accomplished, the Kannon Hall is traditionally referred to as the Silver Pavilion (Ginkaku). Only two buildings, the Ginkaku and the Tōgudō, survived the disastrous fire that occurred in the Tembun era (1532–55). By the advent of the Meiji period (1868–1912), the Ginkakuji had fallen into disrepair but was eventually restored through a combination of private donations and municipal support.

The Ginkaku building is a two-story structure. The lower story, which is laid out in the *shoin* style (SHOIN-ZUKURI), contains the

The deity honored is Gavagriva (J: Gozu Tennō), a god of good health and the guardian deity of the Jetavana monastery (J: Gion Shōja) in India. The festival is also called Gion Goryōe (goryōe meaning "service for souls"), often abbreviated to Gion'e. It had its origins in 869 when, to counter an epidemic that had swept the city, 66 tall spears (hoko) representing the provinces of Japan were erected in the Imperial Park (Shinsen'en) and prayers were offered. After Gozu Tennō was enshrined at Yasaka, the festival became the responsibility of that shrine, and it had become well established by the late 10th century. Discontinued in the confusion following the ŌNIN WAR of 1467–77, the festival was revived in the 16th century by an organization of merchants and reached its present form during the Edo period (1600–1868). Conducted throughout the month of July, it reaches its high point on the 17th with a parade of floats (yamaboko; see DASHI). The original hoko (spears) were replaced by giant, wheeled floats of the same name: topped by a tall spearlike pole, they carry groups of musicians playing music known as gion-bayashi. The smaller floats, termed yama ("mountains") are largely shoulder-borne, although a few are wheeled; these bear life-size figures of famous historical or mythical personages. Both yama and hoko are decorated with valuable art works, including medieval European tapestries.

As the floats increased in splendor over the years, similar festivities sprang up throughout the country, including the Gion Yamagasa in Hakata, the Sannō Festival in Edo (now Tōkyō), and the Takayama Festival in Gifu Prefecture. *Ōtō Tokihiko*

Gion Nankai (1677–1751)

A poet, calligrapher, and one of the pioneers of BUNJINGA painting. Real name Gion Yu. Born the eldest son of a Confucian scholar and physician to the Kii domain (now Wakayama Prefecture). As a young boy he accompanied his father to Edo (now Tōkyō), where he studied Confucianism and Chinese poetry with the scholar KINOSHITA JUN'AN. He quickly established himself as a Chinese-language poet and a fine calligrapher. In 1697 he returned to Kii to serve as official Confucian scholar to the domain. In 1700, however, he was placed under confinement in a small village for some unspecified offense. Upon his pardon 10 years later, Nankai was asked to participate in a reception for a Korean mission, and in 1713 he was appointed a professor at the newly opened domainal school.

It seems that Nankai had no particular teacher of painting but was self-taught through woodblock manuals, especially the *Bazhong huapu* (Pa-chung hua-p'u; J: Hasshu gafu; Eight Albums of Painting). Although it is not clear when and how he became interested in the so-called bunjinga, it is quite probable that because of his father's conversion to the ŌBAKU SECT of Zen Buddhism, Nankai was exposed early in his life to Chinese paintings and calligraphy introduced by Chinese Ōbaku monks. Most of his extant paintings and calligraphy date from his later days. His models, he said, were Zhao Mengfu (Chao Meng-fu; 1254–1322) in calligraphy and Tang Yin (T'ang Yin; 1470–1523) in painting. In actuality, however, the style reflected in his paintings varies from Yuan (Yüan) to 17th-century styles and shows no consistent stylistic development. *Stephen ADDISS*

Girard case

(Jirādo Jiken). Also called the Sōmagahara Incident. A case involving legal jurisdiction over American military personnel on duty at US bases in post-Occupation Japan. On 30 January 1957 William S. Girard, an American soldier guarding the Sōmagahara rifle range in Gumma Prefecture, shot and killed a Japanese farm woman, Nakai Saka, who, despite his warnings, was scavenging for empty shell cases on the range. There was great public outcry in Japan, and after lengthy consideration the United States decided that it would not claim that Girard had been acting in the line of duty and would not assert its right to try him under the status-of-forces agreement with Japan. Girard appealed the decision to surrender him to the Japanese authorities, and his case reached the US Supreme Court, which upheld the government's action on 11 July 1957. Girard was tried for causing bodily injury resulting in death, under article 205, paragraph 1, of the Japanese Criminal Code, and was found guilty; on 19 November 1957 he was sentenced to three years' imprisonment, but the sentence was suspended. The Girard case was significant in several ways: legally, the decision of the highest US court established that criminal jurisdiction arrangements under status-of-forces agree-

ments were valid; diplomatically, it showed restraint by both governments in handling a complex and emotional issue; and politically, it served to reduce Japanese concerns over possible abuse of military-base rights accorded to the United States. See also UNITED STATES MILITARY BASES, DISPUTES OVER. *Richard B. FINN*

giri and ninjō

Social obligation (giri) and human feelings (ninjō). Giri refers to the obligation to act according to the dictates of society in relation to other persons. It applies, however, only to particular persons with whom one has certain social relations and is therefore a particularistic rather than a universalistic norm. Ninjō broadly refers to universal human feelings of love, affection, pity, sympathy, sorrow, and the like, which one "naturally" feels toward others, as in relations between parent and child or between lovers.

Giri is a norm that obliges the observance of reciprocal relations—to help those who have helped one, to do favors for those from whom one has received favors, and so forth. The concept implies a moral force that compels members of society to engage in socially expected reciprocal activities even when their natural inclination (ninjō) may be to do otherwise. In Japan, to be observant of giri is an indication of high moral worth. To neglect the obligation to reciprocate is to lose the trust of others expecting reciprocation, and eventually to lose their support.

To warriors of feudal days, giri referred foremost to their obligation to serve their lord, even at the cost of their lives, and to repay the ON (favor) received from the lord, such as land or stipend. To nonwarriors, it referred not only to obligations between superiors and inferiors—master–servant, employer–employees, and so forth—but between equals as well. In rural Japan, even now, various labor exchanges in farm work are often referred to as giri. Whether in the city or country, attending funeral services and helping at these occasions are also giri-bound obligations.

Ninjō-banashi, a popular genre in the latter half of the Edo period (1600–1868), were tales told by professional storytellers that treated human feelings as a central theme. NINJŌBON, also in vogue about the same time, were books dealing more specifically with romantic relations, often featuring extramarital escapades and describing erotic scenes in graphic detail.

Generally human feelings do not conflict with social norms, and observance of giri does not contradict ninjō. However, in this imperfect world, occasions arise where one is caught between social obligation and natural inclination. Stories from the feudal period of a warrior sacrificing his son's life to deflect assassins from murdering his lord's son, or of lovers committing double suicide because marriage is forbidden by social norms, illustrate the conflict between giri and ninjō. That in almost all such cases social norm was preserved at the expense of human feeling is an indication of the extent to which society maintained its normative order.

Though giri and ninjō as terms have outmoded connotations in modern Japan, the concepts are still important in guiding the conduct of Japanese. Younger Japanese are inclined to value ninjō over giri, but as they enter the adult world, where human relations depend so much on reciprocal obligations, they learn to conform to social norms and become more observant of giri obligations, onerous though they may be. In neglecting these obligations, a Japanese will find it difficult to get along with others, let alone advance in a career.

—— Harumi Befu, *Japan, an Anthropological Introduction* (1971). Hamaguchi Eshun, *Nihonrashisa no hakken* (1977). Minamoto Ryōen, *Giri to ninjō—Nihonteki shinjō no ichi kōsatsu* (1969). Sakurai Shōtarō, *On to giri—shakaigaku-teki kenkyū* (1961). *Harumi BEFU*

Girl Scouts

The first Girl Scouts organization in Japan was formed in 1920. Girl Scout activities were prohibited during World War II but reappeared in 1949 with the formation of the Girl Scouts of Japan. In 1966 the world conference of Girl Scouts was held in Tōkyō, and in 1974 the Asian Pacific Camp took place in Japan. Summer camp activities are held annually, and international exchanges are also conducted. As of 1979, there were 1,268 Girl Scout groups with a total membership of approximately 78,000. *SHIBANUMA Susumu*

Gissha

A *gissha* as portrayed in the early 14th century handscroll *Kasuga gongen genki*. Colors on silk. Imperial Household Agency.

Glass ───── Satsuma cut glass

A *sake* server produced at the Shūseikan in Kagoshima. Clear glass overlaid with purple. Height 15.8 cm. Mid-19th century. Suntory Museum of Art, Tōkyō.

Girls' Festival → Doll Festival

Gishi wajinden → Wei zhi (Wei chih)

gissha

A two-wheeled, single-ox-drawn, enclosed carriage used by the nobility in the Heian period (794–1185). Although transportation by horseback was common in ancient Japan, horse-drawn vehicles were never used. The average *gissha* had a capacity of four passengers. There was considerable variation in the size, style of construction, and decorative embellishment depending on the rank or title of the owner, and strict rules determined which social strata were entitled to use them. In addition, there was a detailed code of etiquette on how one should board or alight from the carriage compartment and how these vehicles should be lined up when in procession or on review. The loud creaking of these broad-wheeled carts was a characteristic sound in the streets of the Kyōto capital, and many instances of the vehicle's use are described in the TALE OF GENJI. In the Kamakura period (1185–1333), the *gissha* declined in popularity as a means of conveyance, being replaced by the palanquin. It continued to be used, however, for the transportation of freight up until the modern period.   *Inagaki Shisei*

glass

At first an esteemed treasure suitable for the most sacred uses, glass in Japan eventually, under Western influence, became more utilitarian and appreciated for its functionalism as well as its beauty. The earliest Japanese words for glass were *hari* (colorless glass) and *ruri* (colored glass), with some later confusion between these terms; during the Edo period (1600–1868) the terms *bīdoro* and *giyaman* were used. Today, glass is known simply as *garasu*. From the first, both soda-lime glass and lead glass were produced in Japan, with lead content generally ranging from 60 to 70 percent.

Yayoi Period (ca 300 BC–ca AD 300) —— The earliest glass pieces were all found in northern Kyūshū. In the past, scholars have repeatedly stated that primitive Japan could not have produced this glass, that examples excavated in Kyūshū must have originated in the more advanced Chinese culture. At least one whole glass *bi* (*pi*; J: *heki*; the open-centered disc made of glass or jade and generally found in ancient Chinese tombs) and a few *bi* fragments have been discovered in Kyūshū burial sites, but the *bi* was foreign to Japanese burial customs and, unlike imported bronze mirrors and ritual weapons, was not imitated. Analyses of these *bi* fragments and a few beads have revealed the presence of barium, which is present in some ancient Chinese glass. Thus, it might seem that these beads as well as *bi* were imports. However, more likely the *bi* fragments were leftovers after the melting down of whole *bi* to provide material for forming beads. Glass *magatama* ("curved jewel"; see BEADS, ANCIENT) from this period, beads, and several other items, as well as half a sandstone mold for making glass *magatama*, have also been found, and these appear to be the earliest glass products produced in Japan. How long it took to develop mixing of local ingredients, melting, and forming techniques is not known, but by the close of the period these had been mastered.

Kofun Period (ca 300–710) —— Increasing use of glass and expanding technology mark this period. Survival in various place names of the term *tamatsukuri* (beadmaking) confirms that there was widespread production of beads. Glass *magatama* and vast quantities of glass *marudama* (round beads), *kodama* (small beads), *kudatama* (tubular beads), and several natural forms have all been excavated from burial mounds of this period. Sculptural representation in figures of clay *(haniwa)* of strings of beads and *magatama* are frequent.

When the color range expanded, drops of molten colored glass or bits of cooled glass were sometimes added to a molten body to make a new form of glass, the *tombodama* (dragonfly bead). Another innovation was the attachment by wires of glass beads for decorative purposes, as in a ceremonial gilt-bronze crown and shoes from a burial mound in Mie Prefecture.

Several glass vessels, probably imports, remain from this period: a cut-glass bowl from Emperor Ankan's tomb, a similar and obviously contemporaneous one and five other items in the SHŌSŌIN (the 8th-century imperial art repository in Nara), and a cut-glass bowl and a plate from the Niizawa excavations, Nara Prefecture.

After the introduction of Buddhism to Japan in 538, glass was used for making reliquaries for Buddhist relics *(shari)*. Later on small pellets, often of glass, were sometimes substitutes for the necessarily limited number of actual relics. In 7th-century Japan, temple authorities placed the relics in small glass jars within a series of gold, silver, and gilt-bronze containers and elaborately installed them beneath the foundation stone of the temple's pagoda. The most superb example is at the Nara temple HŌRYŪJI and consists of a small green jar enclosed in a hinged oval case of openwork gold, a similar, slightly larger case of silver, a small gilt-bronze chest, and finally a lidded metal jar secured by a chain of heavy silver links. This was held by an open metal bowl, surrounded by masses of glass beads and other items. Uncovered during modern repairs of Hōryūji's pagoda, these ritual objects were later reinterred with solemn ceremonies.

A new treatment of beads is evident in this period. The "jewel pillow" in the Abusan tomb near Kyōto consists of hundreds of large and small glass beads in a decorative repeat pattern strung on silver wire, then wrapped in a special covering as a secret and protective amulet to safeguard the deceased in his tomb. Official records note the existence at this time of a government casting bureau, the Imono no Tsukasa, which among other things produced glass and was possibly the source of the urn of transparent green glass interred in 707 in the grave of the nobleman Fumi no Nemaro.

Nara Period (710–794) —— Under the aegis of Buddhist zeal, glassmaking advanced technologically and artistically. Many temples had construction bureaus of their own. A document in the Shōsōin from one such bureau, the *Zōbutsusho sakumotsuchō* (Record of Products of the Buddhist Construction Office), lists the requisites for manufacturing various glass beads. Other records itemize deliveries of beads, often several hundred thousand at a time, and of *jikutan*, the fingerholds for the rods of scrolls of Buddhist scriptures and official records. Large stores of unused glass beads and chests of broken fragments are preserved in the Shōsōin, with sash accessories including five glass fish-form tallies, four small glass measuring scales, and a handsome silver mirror ornamented on the reverse with brilliant CLOISONNÉ *(shippō)*, which marks the beginning of this craft in Japan.

Beads continued to have symbolic as well as decorative significance, adding solemnity to imperial costumes and temple implements, while glass insets were used in Buddhist ritual objects. Bead techniques included casting, coiling, and blowing to produce a variety of forms, often with an added crosswise bore for intricate decorative stringing. Nara glass beads, although often filled with unfused particles, are strikingly beautiful. Except for a few dark blue soda-lime glass beads, Nara glass has a high lead content, ranging from 70 to 79 percent.

Heian Period (794–1185) —— Glassmaking declined after the demise of imperial and temple construction bureaus, and extant examples from this period are rare. However, the increasing use of wood instead of bronze for Buddhist images stimulated the addition of *yōraku*, or suspended decorations, often made of glass, replacing those formerly a part of the bronze casting.

Beads in this period show greater variety, some having larger bores and some larger examples appearing hollow and fragile. An ingenious new technique incorporated inlaid bits of colored glass in mother-of-pearl, in turn inlaid in lacquer, as in a sword sheath at Kasuga Shrine depicting cats catching sparrows in a bamboo grove.

Medieval Period (1185–1600) —— Glass beads were still cherished, but local glassmaking clearly declined by the Kamakura period (1185–1333). Nevertheless, zealous parishioners continued to festoon Buddhist images and their pedestals with glass *yōraku*. Glass inlays were also used, but when glass vessels appear in contemporary paintings, they are always in characteristic Chinese forms, suggesting imports. The decline continued through the Muromachi period (1333–1568), almost to the point of extinction; even bead usage shrank under the influence of Zen Buddhism, which eschewed image worship. Small frames enclosing *shari* appeared, but whether their small transparent fronts are of glass or crystal is undetermined; if glass, they may be fragments of older broken items, or perhaps imported. By the period's end, the use of glass, except in a few symbolic beads, was apparently unknown.

Although glass was not being made in the Azuchi-Momoyama period (1568–1600), cloisonné appeared as a decorative enhancement of metal *kugikakushi* ("nailhead concealers") and other small items. So forgotten was glass that the first blown-glass vessels brought by traders and Jesuit missionaries in the latter part of the 16th century were greeted as an entirely new, exotic substance.

Edo Period (1600–1868) —— The earliest glass imports from Portugal and Spain were of soda-lime glass, called *bīdoro*, a transliteration of the Portuguese *vidro*. Later, the Dutch brought lead glass called *giyaman* (or *giaman*: "diamond") because it was often diamond-point engraved. These glass objects were utensils for everyday use or ornament and did not have the symbolic power that had been associated with glass earlier. Admiration and curiosity, however, led to attempts at imitation. Progress was hindered by Japan's policy of isolation, which at first deprived artisans of any practical knowledge of Western techniques. Nevertheless, by persistent trial and error, success was slowly achieved. Techniques spread to Ōsaka and Edo (now Tōkyō), where glassmaking techniques developed and advanced. The first quarter of the 19th century was noted for its fine glass products.

By the mid-19th century, certain feudal lords, notably of Saga (now Saga Prefecture), Satsuma (now Kagoshima Prefecture), Fukuoka (now part of Fukuoka Prefecture), and Chōshū (now Yamaguchi Prefecture), were experimenting with glass in their own domains. Particularly outstanding was the Satsuma workshop, the Shūseikan, at Kagoshima, which in the 1850s, with a number of kilns and over a hundred workers, produced the famed Satsuma glass, including cut glass (*kiriko*).

Glass manufacturing was disrupted as pressure from foreign shipping for entry into Japanese ports increased, and skills and funding were needed for national defense to meet this threat. Only in

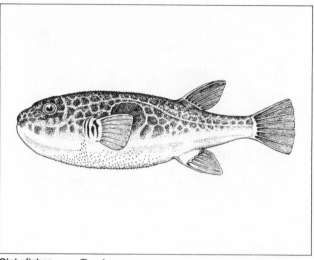

Globefishes —— Torafugu

Kagoshima did it continue to flourish, with production helping to defray defense expenditures. In Edo private glass shops continued as usual, though some also supplied defense-related items such as ships' signal lights. Numerous Edo-period glass items survive, manifesting skill and often a fascinating ingenuity.

Meiji Period (1868–1912) to Present —— Under the impetus of Western influence there were new needs for glass from the Meiji period (1868–1912) onward. Foreign-style buildings required glass windows and lamps; railways and ships needed window panes and glass protection for signal lights; street lighting called for glass. Initially, imports were necessary until the Japanese could master unfamiliar mechanized equipment and techniques. Foreign experts provided tutelage, and there were government-sponsored efforts to solve problems of industrial management, financing, and the initial insufficient demand not consistent with rapid manufacture. As a result, industrial glass has advanced phenomenally. In addition, individual 20th-century pioneers like Iwaki Tokijirō, Iwata Tōshichi, and Kagami Kōzō initiated an era of high-quality artistic production and good design.

📖 —— Dorothy Blair, *A History of Glass in Japan* (1973).

Dorothy BLAIR

glass industry

Japan today is one of the world's largest producers of glass, ranking third after the United States and the Soviet Union in the production of sheet glass. Of the total 1978 sheet glass production of just under 1.7 million metric tons (about 1.9 million short tons), 80 percent was supplied to the construction industry, with the automobile industry purchasing a large share of the remainder. The oligopolistic industry is dominated by three firms: ASAHI GLASS CO, LTD, NIPPON SHEET GLASS CO, LTD, and CENTRAL GLASS CO, LTD. Spurred by the rapid growth of construction, the industry experienced an 8 percent annual growth rate in the decade preceding the OIL CRISIS OF 1973. Production peaked that year at 1.7 million metric tons, after which the industry entered a period of stagnation. Underutilized capacity has also caused a decline in profits. In response, the industry has attempted to diversify its product lines, increase exports, and manufacture high-quality products. The market for glass fiber appears to be a potential growth area because of increasing demand for energy conservation materials, and production is expected to rise beyond the 1977 level of 170,000 metric tons (187,400 short tons). Glassware production in the same year was 2.5 million metric tons (2.8 million short tons). MURAKAMI *Yumi*

globefishes

(fugu). In Japanese the word *fugu* is a general name for fish of the family Tetraodontidae, class Osteichthyes, order Tetraodontiformes, but it is also used more broadly, like the English word globefish, to indicate other fish which can swell their bellies or have a solid square shape. It is also used more narrowly as the name of the genus *Fugu* of the family Tetraodontidae living only in waters sur-

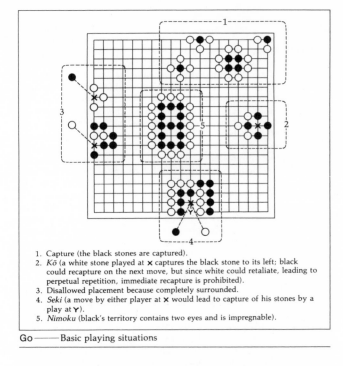

1. Capture (the black stones are captured).
2. Kō (a white stone played at **x** captures the black stone to its left; black could recapture on the next move, but since white could retaliate, leading to perpetual repetition, immediate recapture is prohibited).
3. Disallowed placement because completely surrounded.
4. Seki (a move by either player at **x** would lead to capture of his stones by a play at **Y**).
5. Nimoku (black's territory contains two eyes and is impregnable).

Go——Basic playing situations

rounding Japan and the rivers emptying into them. Several species including the *torafugu (Fugu rubripes)* are used for food.

ABE Tokiharu

While the *fugu* has long been praised in Japan as the most delicious of all fishes, it has also been dreaded, as improper preparation may cause fatal poisoning. Even in the Meiji period (1868–1912) the sale of *fugu* was prohibited in some districts. Recently the poisonous parts such as the ovary and the liver have been identified and strict supervision has been exercised by health authorities. This development has served to decrease the number of accidents, but, nonetheless, *fugu* caused the death of a famous *kabuki* actor in 1975. At present, *fugu* dishes are enjoyed as a delicacy, and lanterns made of *torafugu* skins, originally children's toys, are sold to tourists as folk art in Kanazawa, Shimonoseki, Moji, and other cities.

SAITŌ Shōji

Glover, Thomas Blake (1838–1911)

English trader active in Japan during the last years of the Tokugawa shogunate (1603–1867) and early in the Meiji period (1868–1912). Born in Scotland, the son of a naval officer, he traveled to Shanghai in 1858 and the following year founded the firm of Glover and Co in Nagasaki. In this turbulent period, soon after Japan's abandonment of its 200-year NATIONAL SECLUSION policy, Glover exported gold, silver, and marine products to the West and imported ships and arms. The latter, which he supplied to the domains of Satsuma (now Kagoshima Prefecture) and Chōshū (now part of Yamaguchi Prefecture), centers of activity against the shogunate, proved especially profitable. Glover is believed to have assisted several Japanese, including ITŌ HIROBUMI, INOUE KAORU, and GODAI TOMOATSU, to go abroad secretly.

The offices of Glover and Co were located on the Ōura Coast Road in Nagasaki. In 1865 the firm imported a steam locomotive from Shanghai, set up temporary tracks along the Ōura shoreline, and made trial runs. Beginning in 1868 it cooperated with the Saga domain (now part of Saga Prefecture) in developing the TAKASHIMA COAL MINE, introducing new types of mining equipment from England. It also participated in the construction in 1868 of the Kosuge shipyards, the forerunner of the Mitsubishi shipyards. Glover and Co opened new offices in Ōsaka and Kōbe but went bankrupt in 1870 as a result of the drastic reduction in orders for arms following the Meiji Restoration (1868). Glover himself remained active, and when the Takashima mines became the property of Mitsubishi in 1881, he became an adviser to the company in its dealings with foreigners.

In his later years he is reported to have said that he had been one of the foremost rebels against the Tokugawa shogunate. In 1908 the

Meiji government, on the recommendation of Itō Hirobumi and Inoue Kaoru, awarded him the Order of the Rising Sun, second class, an honor rarely conferred upon foreigners. He died in Tōkyō on 16 December 1911. The wood-frame, Western-style Glover mansion still stands today in Minami Yamate Machi and is a major tourist attraction in Nagasaki.

TANAKA Akira

Gneist, Rudolf von (1816–1895)

German legal scholar and politician. Law professor at the University of Berlin; representative to the Prussian national assembly from 1858 to 1893 and to the German national assembly from 1868 to 1884; German supreme court judge from 1875. In 1882, when the Meiji politician ITŌ HIROBUMI and his party traveled to Europe to learn first-hand about European constitutions, Gneist instructed them privately in German constitutional law for six months. The Meiji CONSTITUTION of 1889 reflects the German conservatism of Gneist, who believed in limiting the power of the parliament (especially over the budget, diplomatic affairs, and the military) and strengthening that of the ministers of state. Although the Meiji government extended an invitation to Gneist to come to Japan as legal adviser, he declined because of his age and sent his student Albert MOSSE in his stead.

go

Also called *igo*. A game for two players, in which black and white stones are alternately placed at the intersections of lines on a board with the object of capturing the opponent's stones and securing control over open spaces on the board.

Some historical accounts place the origin of *go* in ancient China, while others trace the game to India, where early forms of chess were also played over 4,000 years ago. Whereas chess spread widely throughout the West and the East (it is called SHŌGI and played by somewhat different rules in Japan), *go* was until recently only played in China (where it is known as *weiqi* or *wei-ch'i*), Korea *(patuk)*, and Japan. It is somewhat hard to understand why the game did not spread further in early times, for it is among the most complex and exciting games in the world. Some have called it the most intellectual game in the world, and many aficionados in Japan consider it a true art. Its rules are simple and few, yet the number of possible play sequences is staggering; it is calculated to be 10^{750} or 1 followed by 750 zeros.

Basic Rules——Modern *go* is played on a wooden board, the surface of which is engraved with 19 vertical and 19 horizontal lines, thus producing 361 intersections. Nine of the intersections are specially marked with a small dot and called *hoshi* (star); these serve to orient the players and are also used as positions for handicap stones in official matches (see diagram).

Only four basic rules are necessary to describe *go*, the second of which contains the central premise of the game: (1) Two players (Black and White) alternate in placing their stones on unoccupied intersections of the board, Black being the first to play. A stone cannot be moved once it is played, except when it is captured. (2) If a stone or a group of stones is completely surrounded by the opponent's stones with no empty points within the surrounding area (Example 1), they are captured and removed from the board. Captured stones are retained by the opponent. (3) Each captured stone and each surrounded intersection counts as one point. (In China the stones on the board are also counted.) (4) If a move would result in the reversal of the previous move by the opponent (Example 2), the player is required to abstain from that move until other plays have been made; this is called *kō* and is meant to prevent stalemates through perpetual repetition.

Roughly speaking, this is all the information that is required in order to play *go*. Additional rules that derive from the above four disallow the placement of a stone in territory completely surrounded by enemy stones (Example 3) unless enemy stones are captured by the play. When an impasse *(seki)* is reached in which a move by either player at certain points would result in the subsequent capture of several of his stones by the other (and thus neither player will initiate play on the points in question; see Example 4), the stones in the interlocking formation are left as is until the end of the game, when they are discarded. Points that are completely surrounded by one player's stones are called eyes (*me* or *moku*), and territory that contains two eyes *(nimoku)* is impregnable (Example 5). The game ends when all stones have been placed or the possibilities for gaining territory or capturing the opponent's stones have been exhausted. At this point, all captured stones are placed in the opponent's vacant spaces, and the player with the most remaining vacant spaces under his control wins.

A high-quality set of go equipment includes a board (goban) of kaya (Japanese nutmeg, *Torreya nucifera*) wood, 181 black stones (goishi) traditionally made from slate found near Nachi Falls in Wakayama Prefecture, 180 white stones made from old shells found in Kyūshū, and bowls (goke) for the stones made from chestnut wood. Wood imported from Canada or California and newer shells from Mexico are now often used for expensive sets, while plastic or glass stones and cheaper woods are used for inexpensive sets.

History ——— Legend attributes the invention of go to a vassal named Wu in ancient China, perhaps 4,000 years ago. By other accounts, it developed in India about the same time. Confucius mentions the game in writings of the 5th century BC. From China, go was brought to Korea and later to Japan by Chinese missionaries sometime in the 5th or 6th century AD. The oldest go board in Japan is displayed at the SHŌSŌIN in Nara. The game also appears in a famous scene in the TALE OF GENJI, written in the 11th century. The rules of the game and the number of lines on the board changed somewhat over the years, but the character of the game remained consistent.

Modern go history begins in 1612 when the Tokugawa shogunate set up four go schools, which received annual allowances from the government. The four schools were called HON'IMBŌ, Hayashi, Inoue, and Yasui. Intense competitions were held to determine the best player of the game, who was installed in the position of godokoro. Annual official games were held in the presence of the shōgun at his castle in Edo (now Tōkyō); these were called oshirogo. Dōsaku, Hon'imbō IV (1645–1702), was the most outstanding player of the medieval period and is referred to as the "saint of go."

Professional go players met hard times after the Meiji Restoration (1868) when their stipends were discontinued by the government. Top professionals formed a study group called Hōensha in the Meiji period (1868–1912), and the NIHON KIIN (Japan Go Association) was formed in 1924 with the assistance of ŌKURA KIHACHIRŌ. At this time Shūsai, Hon'imbō XXI (1874–1940) gave the title Hon'imbō to the association to be awarded in regular competition thereafter. Kitani Minoru and Go Seigen invented a new type of fuseki (opening theory) in the 1930s. Takagawa Kaku and Sakata Eio were the outstanding players of the post–World War II period. Younger players active in the 1980s included Rin Kaihō, Ishida Yoshio, Katō Masao, Takemiya Masaki, and Ōtake Hideo.

Professional and International Go ——— There are millions of go fans in Japan, but only about 400 professionals. Amateurs are ranked from the ninth kyū or degree, the lowest, to the first kyū; from there the rankings advance to shodan (first grade), with rokudan (sixth grade) usually the highest amateur ranking. A small number of nanadan (seventh grade) amateurs are as strong as professionals of the professional first grade (shodan); the top of the professional rankings is kudan (ninth grade). The ranks are used to decide handicaps for official matches; each rank represents a one-stone handicap for amateurs and a one-third stone handicap for professionals. Promotions are granted on the basis of official games (ōteai). Professional organizations include the Nihon Kiin and the Kansai Kiin. Newspapers sponsor regular competitions under such names as Hon'imbō, Meijin, Kisei, Ōza, and Jūdan; professionals make their living through prize money offered in these matches.

Go is slowly but steadily spreading in the Western world. Iwamoto Kaoru, a former Hon'imbō, contributed much to the internationalization of the game. There are now go associations in the United States and in Europe. The first annual World Amateur Go Championship was held in Tōkyō in 1979, and the International Go Federation, based in Tōkyō, was organized in 1982.

Go is a lunchtime hobby for some amateurs and an intellectual competition for others. For professionals it is an art, to be compared with superior music, painting, or literature. It can become a way of life, and philosophies have been built on go principles. Go found its way into modern literature in Kawabata Yasunari's *Meijin* (1942–54; tr *The Master of Go*, 1972); in this novel old and modern Japan confront each other in a fictionalized account of an actual go match played between Hon'imbō Shūsai and Kitani Minoru, a young challenger who is called Ōtake in the novel. The challenger wins the hotly contested match, and the old master dies shortly after the game.

■ ———Iwamoto Kaoru, *Go for Beginners* (1972). Nihon Kiin, *Go! The Most Fascinating Game in the World* (1974). Sakata Eio, *Modern Jōseki and Fuseki* (1970). Manfred Wimmer, *The Way to "Go"* (1977). Manfred WIMMER

gō

(township or village). A unit of local administration from the Nara (710–794) through the Muromachi (1333–1568) periods. Under the RITSURYŌ SYSTEM of government established at the end of the 7th century, local administrative divisions were the kuni (or koku, province), the gun (district; see KOKUGUN SYSTEM), and the RI (village). In 715, with the enactment of the GŌRI SYSTEM, a fourth layer was added. The preexisting ri were renamed gō, and each gō was subdivided into two or three new ri (hamlets), each of which in turn comprised 50 households. The gōri system was never fully established, however, and in 740 the new ri were abolished, leaving the gō as the smallest administrative units. By the middle of the 11th century, the gō no longer functioned as subdivisions of the gun but were directly controlled by the central government. The township or village headmen (gōji), through the authority vested in them, became the nucleus of the emergent local landholding class (RYŌSHU). The gō remained as a directly governed local unit until the last vestiges of ritsuryō administration were abolished at the time of the nationwide land survey (KENCHI) in the 1580s. *HARUHARA Akihiko*

gobies

(haze). Salt, fresh, or brackish water fish of the order Perciformes, family Gobiidae. Over 200 species are found in Japan; most are small and live along sea or river bottoms. The best known of these is the mahaze (*Acanthogobius flavimanus*), often simply called haze, an edible species caught in bays and mouths of rivers. It grows to about 25 centimeters (10 in) in length. It is also found in Korea and China. One of the most popular sport fish in Japan, it is used in TEMPURA and other traditional dishes. Haze fishing was a favorite autumn recreation of the people of Edo (now Tōkyō).
ABE Tokiharu and SAITŌ Shōji

Gobō

City in central Wakayama Prefecture, central Honshū, at the mouth of the river Hidakagawa. Gobō developed as a temple town (MONZEN MACHI) of a branch of the temple NISHI HONGANJI, the headquarters of the Jōdo Shin sect, and as a collection center for lumber transported down the Hidakagawa. Greenhouse cultivation of vegetables is widespread. Scenic attractions are the cape Hinomisaki and the coast of Enjugahama. It is the site of the temple Dōjōji, celebrated in NŌ and KABUKI plays. Pop: 30,400.

Gobō no Keiji

(Five Public Notices). Ordinances issued by the government immediately following the MEIJI RESTORATION (1868). Promulgated together with the CHARTER OATH, which set down the broad outlines of government, the Five Public Notices were the first formal statements made by the new Meiji government regarding its policies for the people at large. The first two, besides exhorting the traditional Confucian virtues, prohibited homicide, arson, robbery, the formation of factions, and desertion of the home (CHŌSAN) in order to escape taxes. The third notice proscribed Christianity and other "heterodox" sects, the fourth forbade any injury to foreigners, and the fifth prohibited travel out of Japan. Apart from the fourth, they did not differ from ordinances issued by the Tokugawa shogunate, and were on the whole ignored.

Gobusho

(The Five Books of Shintō). Also called *Shintō gobusho*. The basic canon of the Watarai school of Shintō (see WATARAI SHINTŌ). The works were attributed to such persons as the semilegendary Yamatohime no Mikoto (who is reputed to have established the Grand Shrine of Ise at its present location in 4 BC), and the popular Buddhist monk Gyōgi (668–749). Scholars now generally agree, however, that the Gobusho were produced around the 13th century by members or associates of the Watarai family, hereditary priests of the Outer Shrine (Gekū) of Ise, in order to enhance the status of the Outer Shrine (see ISE SHRINE). The Gobusho assert that the deity of the Outer Shrine, Toyuke no Ōkami, is none other than Kuninotokotachi no Mikoto, a deity who preceded the Imperial Ancestress, Amaterasu Ōmikami, and hence should be ranked above her.

The Gobusho borrowed heavily from Buddhism, Taoist philosophy, yin-yang thought, and Confucianism. The texts were regarded as secret, not to be taken beyond the shrine precincts or to be shown to anyone under the age of 60. The loyalist KITABATAKE CHIKAFUSA (1293–1354), and the aristocratic scholar ICHIJŌ KANEYOSHI (1402–81) were strongly influenced by the *Gobusho*. The spurious origin of the *Gobusho* was first established by the scholar Yoshimi Yukikazu (1673–1761) in his critique, *Shintō gobusho setsuben*.

Stanley WEINSTEIN

Go-Daigo, Emperor (1288–1339)

The 96th sovereign *(tennō)* in the traditional count (which includes several nonhistorical emperors); reigned 1318–39. The second son of Emperor GO-UDA, Go-Daigo was responsible for the brief restoration of direct imperial rule known as the KEMMU RESTORATION. Because of the practice of designating emperors alternately from the Daikakuji and Jimyōin lines of the imperial family, Go-Daigo (who represented the Daikakuji line) was already 30 when he ascended the throne. Go-Daigo resented the usurpation of political power by the KAMAKURA SHOGUNATE and secretly planned to overthrow it. Undaunted when a plot was discovered by the shogunate in 1324 (see SHŌCHŪ CONSPIRACY), he planned a second attempt. This, too, was uncovered, and the emperor was arrested and banished to the Oki Islands (see GENKŌ INCIDENT).

Go-Daigo escaped in 1333 and enlisted the support of military figures in western Japan, most notably KUSUNOKI MASASHIGE. The turning point in the conflict came later that year, when ASHIKAGA TAKAUJI, commander of a shogunal army sent against him, changed his allegiance and destroyed the shogunate. This allowed Go-Daigo to establish personal rule in Kyōto, which he exercised through new institutions like the ZASSO KETSUDANSHO.

His rule alienated many of his former supporters, however, particularly on the question of rewards, and in 1335 Ashikaga Takauji abandoned the emperor's cause and rose in revolt against him. Go-Daigo's forces were quickly defeated, and he fled to a remote stronghold in the mountains of Yoshino in Yamato Province (now Nara Prefecture). Although Takauji soon placed a new ruler, Emperor Kōmyō (1322–80; r 1336–48), on the throne, Go-Daigo stoutly maintained his claim to be the legitimate sovereign, establishing what is known as the Southern Court at Yoshino. The existence of two emperors resulted in a succession dispute and civil war that lasted until 1392 (see NORTHERN AND SOUTHERN COURTS). Go-Daigo abdicated in 1339 in favor of his son Emperor Go-Murakami (1328–68; r 1339–68) and died at his palace in Yoshino the next day.

Godaiō ki → Godai teiō monogatari

Godai teiō monogatari

(Tale of Five Imperial Reigns; also known as *Godaiō ki*). A historical tale of unknown authorship, composed probably near the end of the Kamakura period (1185–1333). It describes the various events of the reigns of the emperors Go-Horikawa (r 1221–32), Shijō (r 1232–42), GO-SAGA (r 1242–46), GO-FUKAKUSA (r 1246–60), and KAMEYAMA (r 1260–74), concluding with the death of Go-Saga in retirement in 1272. It appears to have been drawn from the observations of the courtiers of the day and is a valuable source of information on the events leading to the decision to have members of the two rival branches of the imperial house—the Jimyōin line (descendants of Go-Fukakusa) and the Daikakuji line (descendants of Kameyama)—succeed to the throne in alternation. This policy eventually resulted in the schism between the NORTHERN AND SOUTHERN COURTS.

G. Cameron HURST III

Godai Tomoatsu (1835–1885)

An entrepreneur active early in the Meiji period (1868–1912). Born in the Satsuma domain (now Kagoshima Prefecture), Godai, the son of a Confucian scholar and local *samurai* official, received a traditional education but supplemented it with study at the Nagasaki Naval Training Center (KAIGUN DENSHŪJO) from 1857 to 1859 and a visit to Shanghai. After personal involvement in the military skirmish between Satsuma and Britain (1863; see KAGOSHIMA BOMBARDMENT) he went to Europe for a year with several other Satsuma samurai. During his trip he negotiated with the Comte des Cantons de MONTBLANC about joint business ventures. As a minor official and a leading theoretician of Satsuma's reforms, he persuaded the

daimyō to build steamships, to develop the spinning industry, and to send promising students abroad. At the same time, Godai used his European contacts to purchase weapons and supplies for the struggle against the Tokugawa shogunate (1603–1867). He assisted in bringing together Satsuma and Chōshū (now Yamaguchi Prefecture), the other leading anti-Tokugawa domain, in a joint economic venture, and he worked to smooth relations with the British during this critical period.

Soon after the MEIJI RESTORATION (1868), Godai, now a junior councillor *(san'yo)* and a staff officer of the precursor of the Ministry of Foreign Affairs, used his diplomatic skills in handling several incidents of antiforeign violence on the part of samurai. He also helped to lay the groundwork for contact between foreigners and the people of Ōsaka when that city was opened in 1868.

Resigning from government office in 1869, Godai turned his full attention to the economic development of Japan. He organized, operated, or promoted no fewer than 10 major companies in the fields of mining, indigo production, copper refining, and transportation. Godai's entrepreneurship was distinguished by an emphasis on international trade, the systematic organization of economic plans, and reliance on Western technology and the joint-stock company system of organization. Convinced of the need for cohesion, guidance, and stimulation in the Ōsaka business world, he took the lead in establishing the Ōsaka Shōhō Kaigisho (1878; now Ōsaka Chamber of Commerce), the Ōsaka Stock Exchange (1878), and the Ōsaka Commercial Training School (1880; now Ōsaka City University). As president of the Chamber of Commerce he worked to coordinate and stimulate commercial enterprise in the Ōsaka–Kōbe area and counseled both local and national government officials on economic issues. Godai, who was often compared with the financier-entrepreneur SHIBUSAWA EIICHI, had close political ties, which he used both in his own interest and for the advancement of the country. His name was linked to the HOKKAIDŌ COLONIZATION OFFICE SCANDAL OF 1881 when one of his companies tried to obtain timber, mining, and other concessions from the government at a very low price.

William D. HOOVER

gods → kami

gofu

A protective amulet commonly termed *omamori* or *ofuda*, distributed or sold at Shintō shrines and Buddhist temples and believed to bring good health, household safety, financial success, and so forth. These rectangular-shaped slips of paper (or occasionally wood) are generally placed in the *kamidana* (SHINTŌ FAMILY ALTARS), affixed to a doorway, or carried on one's person. They usually bear the name of a deity; those issued by Buddhist temples may display a Buddhist image as well. The *gofu* issued by the Mitsumine Shrine in Chichibu (Saitama Prefecture) carries the image of a wolf who is the familiar of the god: it is said to prevent burglary when affixed to doorways and to prevent rat damage if displayed in rooms where silkworms are tended. Amulets from the Haruna Shrine (Gumma Prefecture) are often displayed in the fields, attached to a bamboo pole, in order to prevent damage by birds and insects.

Ōtō Tokihiko

Go-Fukakusa, Emperor (1243–1304)

The 89th sovereign *(tennō)* in the traditional count (which includes several nonhistorical emperors); reigned 1246–60; a son of Emperor GO-SAGA. During his childhood his father continued to rule from retirement (see INSEI) and in 1260 forced Go-Fukakusa to abdicate in favor of his younger son Emperor KAMEYAMA, at the same time making Kameyama's son (later Emperor GO-UDA) crown prince. To Go-Fukakusa's further frustration, Kameyama went on to dominate the court as retired sovereign. Go-Fukakusa appealed to the KAMAKURA SHOGUNATE and was subsequently (in 1275) able to have his own son, the future Emperor FUSHIMI (r 1287–98), named Go-Uda's successor; during his son's reign, Go-Fukakusa finally came to control state affairs. Thereafter, succession to the throne alternated between the senior Jimyōin line (descended from Go-Fukakusa) and the junior Daikakuji line (descended from Kameyama), a practice that was later made official by the shogunate. The autobiography TOWAZUGATARI (ca 1307; tr *The Confessions of Lady Nijō*, 1973) deals extensively and sympathetically with Go-Fukakusa's character.

G. Cameron HURST III

gōgai

"Extra" editions put out by newspapers. The first such "extra" in Japan was a special issue put out by the *Chūgai shimbun* on 5 July 1868 reporting on the Battle of Ueno, a short-lived revolt by diehard retainers of the Tokugawa shogunate in opposition to the Meiji Restoration of 1868. Japanese newspaper readers started to expect rapid news reporting from around the time of the Sino-Japanese War of 1894–95 when hawkers first began selling extra editions in the streets of Tōkyō by ringing bells to attract attention. For several decades, Japanese newspapers competed with one another in publishing extra editions at times of major news events, but with radio and television becoming widespread after World War II, only a few newspaper extras now appear each year.　　*Haruhara Akihiko*

gōgaku

(literally, "village schools"). Educational institutions set up during the Edo period (1600–1868). Known also as *gōkō, gōgakkō,* or *gōgakusho,* many of them lasted until the beginning of the Meiji period (1868–1912), when they were incorporated into the public primary and middle school system under the Education Order of 1872. *Gōgaku* were mainly of two types. The first, like the *hankō* (domainal schools), was for the education of domainal retainers and their children and under the control of domainal authorities, but was located in outlying areas. The second type was under the control of commoners, but unlike the TERAKOYA, received domainal or shogunate guidance. In both cases, the curriculum centered on reading and writing and arithmetic. Among the better-known *gōgaku* were the Shizutani Gakkō, founded by IKEDA MITSUMASA, the *daimyō* of Okayama, in 1668, and the KAITOKUDŌ, founded by Ōsaka merchants in 1724.　　*Etō Kyōji*

Go-Hanazono, Emperor (1419–1471)

The 102nd sovereign *(tennō)* in the traditional count (which includes several nonhistorical emperors); reigned 1428–64. Great-grandson of Emperor Sukō (1334–98; r 1348–51) of the Northern Court and eldest son of Prince Fushimi no Miya Sadafusa. In 1428 Emperor Shōkō (1401–28; r 1412–28), who had no heir, became seriously ill. Although the Muromachi shogunate had healed the schism between the NORTHERN AND SOUTHERN COURTS in 1392, as a long-time supporter of the Northern Court it disapproved of a descendant of the Southern Court succeeding to the throne. As a compromise, Go-Hanazono was adopted by the retired emperor GO-KOMATSU (of the Northern Court) and enthroned as emperor without being officially invested as crown prince. He relinquished the throne to his son Emperor Go-Tsuchimikado (1442–1500; r 1464–1500) in 1464. The latter's reign saw the devastation of the ŌNIN WAR (1467–77) and a decline in the power of the imperial court. Go-Hanazono was a patron of scholarship and the arts and an accomplished poet.

gohei

Also called *shide, nigite, nusa,* or *mitegura.* A wand decorated with paper or cloth streamers that is used by shrine priests or MIKO (female attendants, usually young girls, at Shintō shrines) in performing Shintō rituals. The streamers, though usually white, are occasionally gold, silver, or of several different colors. Zigzag paper streamers, also called *gohei,* are often attached to the straw ropes (called *shimenawa*) that are used to mark sacred precincts or are affixed, for example, to the ridgepole during a house-raising ceremony (see KENCHIKU GIREI). The *gohei* serves to attract and house the gods in Shintō ceremonies or may be waved over the heads of worshipers as a gesture of purification.　　*Ōtō Tokihiko*

Goichigo Jiken → May 15th Incident

Go-Ichijō, Emperor (1008–1036)

The 68th sovereign *(tennō)* in the traditional count (which includes several nonhistorical emperors); reigned 1016–36. Son of Emperor ICHIJŌ (r 986–1011) and JŌTŌ MON'IN, eldest daughter of FUJIWARA NO MICHINAGA. He succeeded Emperor SANJŌ (r 1011–16), whose designated heir had been Prince Atsuakira, later known as KOICHIJŌ IN. Michinaga forced both men to abdicate their positions and installed Go-Ichijō on the throne. The young emperor married Michinaga's third daughter, Ishi (999–1036), who was his mother's sister.

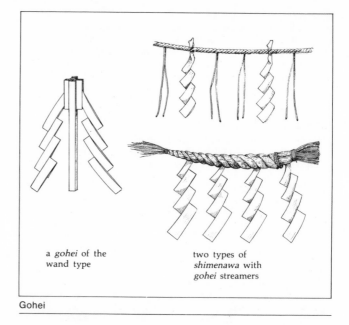

a *gohei* of the wand type

two types of *shimenawa* with *gohei* streamers

Gohei

Michinaga became regent (*sesshō;* see REGENCY GOVERNMENT) and, although he soon resigned the post, continued to dominate the court during most of Go-Ichijō's reign.　　*G. Cameron Hurst III*

Gojō

City in west central Nara Prefecture, central Honshū, on the river Yoshinogawa. Its importance as a transportation center dates from ancient times. It is a market center for lumber and woodworking; pears and persimmons are cultivated. Gojō was the site of an anti-Tokugawa uprising, the TENCHŪGUMI REBELLION, in 1863. Eizanji, an 8th-century temple associated with the FUJIWARA FAMILY, is in the area. Pop: 33,825.

gojūon zu

(literally, "chart of the 50 sounds"). A table of the 48 syllables in the Japanese phonetic writing system (KANA), arranged in intersecting vertical columns *(gyō)* and horizontal rows *(dan)* in such a way that each horizontal row brings together all syllables that end in the same vowel and each vertical column brings together all syllables that begin with the same consonant.

The accompanying table shows the syllables in roman letters in the traditional arrangement (for the *kana* characters themselves, see the table in KANA). The table can be reversed so that the horizontal rows read from right to left rather than, as here, from left to right; however, the order of the vowels and the consonant-vowel combinations remains the same. The syllables *chi* and *fu* belong to the "t" and "h" columns, respectively, an anomaly that disappears when *kana* or a slightly different system of romanization is used. The "(e)" and "(i)" in the "w" column stand for older *kana* characters no longer in general use. Both these and the "o" in the same column have now lost a former initial "w" in pronunciation. The "n" in the last column is syllable-final "n."

Such syllabic charts were once known as *go onzu* or "five-sound charts," referring only to the vowel sounds; in some of the older charts the order of the vowels varied. While the exact origin of such charts is unknown, they may have been influenced by the Chinese system (called *hanzetsu* in Japanese), which uses two Chinese characters to indicate the Chinese pronunciation of a third (the initial sound of the first character indicating the initial sound of the third, and the final sound of the second character indicating the final sound of the third). A more obvious influence is the traditional order of vowels and consonants in the Sanskrit alphabet known as SIDDHAM (or Siddhamatrka; J: Shittan), which came into Japan along with Buddhist textual study; this order markedly resembles that of the *kana* charts. The earliest surviving example of such a chart in Japan dates from the beginning of the 11th century, in the *Kujakukyō ongi,* a kind of concordance to the *Kujakukyō* or Peacock Sutra now at the temple Daigoji in Kyōto.

Gojūon zu

a	ka	sa	ta	na	ha	ma	ya	ra	wa	n
i	ki	shi	chi	ni	hi	mi	i	ri	(i)	
u	ku	su	tsu	nu	fu	mu	yu	ru	(u)	
e	ke	se	te	ne	he	me	e	re	(e)	
o	ko	so	to	no	ho	mo	yo	ro	(o)	

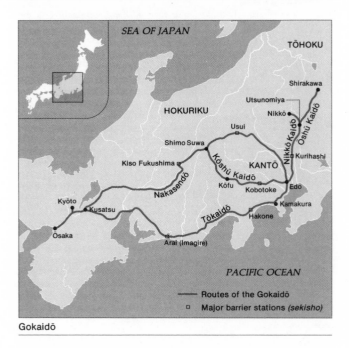

Gokaidō

The chart of 50 sounds came to be used in the traditional Japanese grammar that developed particularly in the Edo period (1600–1868). Verb stems were classified according to which column or *gyō* their final syllables fell into, and the verb conjugations were named according to which or how many rows or *dan* were represented in them, as *yodan, shimonidan,* etc (see CLASSICAL JAPANESE). The order of syllables in the chart also came to be used, along with the *iroha* system (see IROHA POEM) for classifications and dictionary listings, and now this standard order of syllables (a-i-u-e-o, ka-ki-ku-ke-ko, etc) is used in Japan just as alphabetical order is used in the West. YAMADA Toshio

Gokaidō

(The Five Highways). Collective name for a network of centrally administered highways crossing central Japan and converging at Nihombashi in Edo (now Tōkyō) during the Edo period (1600–1868). These roads were the TŌKAIDŌ, NAKASENDŌ, Kōshū Kaidō, Nikkō Kaidō, and Ōshū Kaidō.

During the Edo period Japanese rulers established a finely balanced pattern of local autonomy (see BAKUHAN SYSTEM) strategically controlled by various levers of centralization. Among the most crucial of these levers wielded by the shogunate was the system of road management over the major access routes to the national administrative center in Edo. The Gokaidō radiated like spokes from Edo, serving as arteries in the circulation of people across Japan. Special controls ensured tight regulation of travel along these roadways.

Of the five roads the Tōkaidō was by far the busiest. Traffic along this thoroughfare followed fairly close to the coastline from the suburban post station of Shinagawa as far southwest as Kyōto. Immortalized in the woodprints of HIROSHIGE, the 53 POST-STATION TOWNS spaced along this 500-kilometer road connected a densely populated corridor, in modern times referred to as the TŌKAIDŌ MEGALOPOLIS. The function of this corridor as the major link to

western Japan persists today. The Nakasendō took a slightly longer and more mountainous inland course to Kyōto, offering travelers some 67 post stations en route. It represented the alternative east-west roadway as well as a bridge to the northern domains in the Hokuriku region along the Sea of Japan. Bisecting these two major highways, the Kōshū Kaidō quickly tapered off into a quiet country road as it wound through the mountains to Kōfu. The fact that only three of Japan's more than 250 DAIMYŌ traversed the Kōshū Kaidō as the approved route for fulfilling their SANKIN KŌTAI (alternate attendance) service obligations in Edo indicates its insignificance. Nonetheless, in the immediate vicinity of Edo, traffic along this road brought supplies from the garden belt of western Kantō and contributed to the bustle of the post station at Shinjuku. North and northeast of Edo, the Nikkō and Ōshū Kaidō roads shared 17 post stations, including Edo's third major suburban post station at Senju, before bifurcating. While the Nikkō road assumed special significance at the time of the annual expedition to the Tokugawa family shrine, the Ōshū Kaidō continued north from Utsunomiya to Shirakawa, offering facilities to many daimyō based in the Tōhoku region.

Of course, the Edo government did not create these roads. A developed road system long preceded the Edo period; when Kamakura served as the national administrative center (1185–1333), the task of linking the northeast with the more developed southwest had already assumed critical proportions. During the first decade of Tokugawa rule, the Gokaidō system established a new degree of centralization. The five roads were divided into sections, with post stations and nearby villages assigned responsibility for bridge construction, road maintenance, and planting trees as well as for regular assessments of men and horses to keep the traffic moving (see SUKEGŌ). In 1659 a new official post, commissioner of roads (dōchū bugyō), was created to enhance central control over the hundreds of sections along these roads.

The Gokaidō system symbolized the supremacy of central government in three respects: communications, military deployment, and the controlled movement of the population—especially of the daimyō and their retinues. Through direct administration of these five roads, the shogunate controlled essential internal communications; the flow of information through messengers on horseback centered in Edo. The authority of the Tokugawa shogunate reached its peak with regard to the movement of troops or individuals who threatened the public order. Officials checked identifications at a number of barriers (SEKISHO), most carefully at the mountain pass of Hakone, the 10th station from Edo on the Tōkaidō. Here travelers were searched to verify that no guns or other unauthorized weapons would be carried into Edo and, for those headed in the opposite direction, to establish that women from daimyō households would remain confined to Edo as hostages against rebellious activity. The long reign of peace and order testifies to the effectiveness of this system of controls.

Above all, the Gokaidō are known as the mechanism for the *sankin kōtai* system requiring residence in Edo, normally in alternate years, for the daimyō of Japan and their large retinues. The accommodations (HONJIN) and provisions for these DAIMYŌ PROCESSIONS of hundreds or even thousands of samurai did not come cheaply. Undoubtedly the extraordinary land transportation network represented by the Gokaidō would not have been possible without the vast expenses that went into these centrally orchestrated travels. The Gokaidō controls smoothed the operation of the *sankin kōtai* system, which in turn served as a vital force for national integration. Along with the primarily water-based commercial routes that integrated the Japanese economy, the Gokaidō as the core of the road system for official and personal travel integrated the Japanese polity.

── Tamura Eitarō, *Edo jidai no kōtsū* (1970). Toshio G. Tsukahira, *Feudal Control in Tokugawa Japan: The Sankin Kōtai System* (1966). Gilbert ROZMAN

Gokajō no Goseimon → Charter Oath

Go-Kameyama, Emperor (?–1424)

The 99th sovereign (*tennō*) in the traditional count (which includes several nonhistorical emperors); reigned 1383–92 as the fourth and last emperor of the Southern Court. Through the intercession of the shōgun ASHIKAGA YOSHIMITSU, in 1392 he effected the reconciliation and reunification of the NORTHERN AND SOUTHERN COURTS after 56 years of schism. It was agreed that members of the two rival branches of the imperial family would thenceforth occupy the throne in alternation, and Go-Kameyama surrendered the imperial regalia to Emperor GO-KOMATSU of the Northern Court. After Yoshimitsu's death (1408), when it became clear that the Northern Court was not going to observe the conditions for reconciliation, Go-Kameyama in 1410 fled to Yoshino and tried to revive the Southern Court; but the next year he gave up and returned to Kyōto.

G. Cameron HURST III

gōkan

(literally, "bound-together volumes"). A format for illustrated fiction that was popular from the first decade of the 19th century forward, but suggests also the kind of fiction usually published in that format. Physically, the gōkan derives from the KIBYŌSHI ("yellow covers"), the dominant medium for illustrated fiction in the late 18th century. By 1800, individual kibyōshi titles were being published as sets consisting of as many as five or more separately bound fascicles or volumes, each with its own illustrated cover. Sometime around 1805, publishers began the practice of binding these separate fascicles into one or two larger volumes, thus saving themselves the expense of printing individual covers for each fascicle. SHIKITEI SAMBA (1776–1822) claimed to have introduced the form with his Ikazuchi Tarō gōaku monogatari of 1806, and the success of this work may have helped to ensure the subsequent popularity of the gōkan format, but most scholars now agree that the format came into existence, if not general use, a few years earlier.

The appearance of the gōkan coincided with and in fact fostered a new vogue in illustrated fiction for intricately plotted historical romances and adventures of considerably greater length than the stories previously presented in the kibyōshi format. One staple plot type in early gōkan fiction was that of the vendetta, in which the protagonists are propelled through a series of often highly romantic, not to say fantastic adventures as they seek to avenge wrongs perpetrated against a parent or overlord. Another popular plot revolved around the exploits of bandits and their final apprehension. Most gōkan stories are set in the past, most often a vaguely defined medieval era, both as a matter of literary convention and in accordance with censorship laws that prohibited stories that in any way could be construed as dealing with or commenting upon recent or contemporary political events or conflicts within the samurai class.

From the beginning the gōkan showed a strong influence from the KABUKI theater. A great many gōkan, if not indeed the majority, borrow their plots explicitly from popular kabuki plays and may, in fact, have sometimes been written to publicize new kabuki offerings. Gōkan illustrations, many of which were produced by the UTAGAWA SCHOOL of UKIYO-E artists who otherwise specialized in theatrical prints, were very much in the kabuki style, and SANTŌ KYŌDEN (1761–1816) is credited with popularizing the use of nigao-e, illustrations in which characters in the stories are made to resemble famous actors. The relationship between gōkan and the theater was made clearer still in Shōhonjitate by RYŪTEI TANEHIKO (1783–1842) and many subsequent imitations. This lengthy work, which appeared in 12 parts between 1815 and 1831, was written in the style of a kabuki script and not only was illustrated with nigao-e but remarked upon "stage properties" and costuming as if it were describing an actual kabuki performance.

Ryūtei Tanehiko is the name most closely identified with the gōkan in its heyday, and his Nise Murasaki inaka Genji (The False Murasaki and the Rustic Genji), which appeared between 1829 and 1842, is regarded as the masterpiece of the genre. This work, in a manner typical of kabuki, combines several different historical and spiritual "worlds" in a single, complicated plot. The main story line is that of the early 11th-century TALE OF GENJI, but the events and characters of the original are superimposed upon the 15th-century court of the Ashikaga shōguns while the value system and plot devices are those of the 19th century.

Gōkan continued to be produced in vast numbers down to the end of the Edo period (1600–1868) and even after the Meiji Restoration of 1868 until their place was taken by newspaper serials. In the days of their greatest popularity, gōkan were turned out by most of the major popular writers of the time, Santō Kyōden, JIPPENSHA IKKU (1765–1831), Shikitei Samba, and even Takizawa BAKIN (1767–1848) among them. The gōkan appeared in numbers larger by far than any other of the fictional forms of the late Edo period; as many as 20,000 or more copies of the most popular works are said to have been printed. Many gōkan, however, if not most, seem to have

been intended for a juvenile audience, and only a very few works of gōkan fiction can be said to have enduring literary value. See also GESAKU.

Robert W. LEUTNER

Gokanoshō

Hamlet in the mountain recesses of eastern Kumamoto Prefecture, Kyūshū. According to local tradition, Gokanoshō was settled in the 12th century by remnants of the defeated TAIRA FAMILY. Principal products are lumber, rice, wheat, tea, and shiitake (Japanese mushrooms). The area is known for its traditional dance and songs.

Gokasegawa

River in northern Miyazaki Prefecture, Kyūshū, originating in the Kyūshū Mountains and flowing east to empty into the Hyūga Sea at the city of Nobeoka. Numerous electric power plants are located along the river. The Takachihokyō, the gorges in its upper reaches, are the supposed site of the legend of the descent of the Shintō gods from heaven (see MYTHOLOGY). Length: 103 km (64 mi); area of drainage basin: 1,804 sq km (696 sq mi).

gokasho shōnin

(literally, "merchants of the five places"). Merchants of the Edo period (1600–1868) who monopolized the trade in raw silk imported from China. Merchants from the cities of Sakai, Nagasaki, and Kyōto were authorized to buy, allocate, and set the price of this silk under the ITOWAPPU system, established by the Tokugawa shogunate in 1604. They were joined by merchants from Edo (now Tōkyō) and Ōsaka in 1631, and thereafter they were called gokasho shōnin. See also SAKAI MERCHANTS; NAGASAKI KAISHO.

Gokayama

Hamlet in southwestern Toyama Prefecture, central Honshū. Located in the mountainous recesses of the upper reaches of the river Shōgawa, Gokayama was secluded from the outside world for centuries and retained a medieval way of life until comparatively recently. Its old houses, made in the gasshō-zukuri style (see MINKA) attract visitors.

gokenin

(housemen). Direct vassals of the shogunate in the Kamakura (1185–1333) through Edo (1600–1868) periods. With the founding of the Kamakura shogunate, some 2,000 warriors of MINAMOTO NO YORITOMO, mostly from eastern Japan, became hereditary vassals of his house. He gave them land grants or confirmation (ANDO) of their ancestral holdings, appointments as estate stewards (JITŌ) or military governors (SHUGO), and special status before the law, in proportion to their services. In return, these gokenin fought for the shogunate in wartime, served as guards at Kyōto and Kamakura in peacetime, and contributed funds to the shōgun. Thus they formed the military and economic base of the shogunate, which strove to control and protect them. To strengthen control of the gokenin in western Japan who had taken part in the JŌKYŪ DISTURBANCE of 1221, shogunal deputies (ROKUHARA TANDAI) were stationed at Kyōto. To protect gokenin from destitution, partly because of the rise of a money economy and of usury (KASHIAGE) in the 13th century, the shogunate repeatedly issued edicts of debt cancellation (TOKUSEI) forbidding the mortgage or sale of gokenin estates and repossessing those already sold. This protection policy failed, however, and gokenin discontent with the Kamakura shogunate eventually caused its downfall. In the Muromachi period there were two types of gokenin; those who were direct vassals of the shogunate (these were called hōkōshū) and those who were under the control of shugo (these were called jitō gokenin). In the Edo period, gokenin were the lowest-ranking direct vassals of the Tokugawa shogunate. They held minor bureaucratic and military posts and, unlike the bannermen (HATAMOTO) above them, did not enjoy the right of audience with the shōgun. By 1800 there were some 20,000 gokenin. Their stipends ranged from 260 KOKU (1 koku = about 180 liters or 5 US bushels) of rice to a mere 4 RYŌ in cash; most gokenin received less than 100 koku, however. Economic hardship forced many of these marginal samurai to eke out their living as craftsmen or to sell their status by adopting the sons of commoners in return for money.

Goken Sampa Naikaku

(literally, "Cabinet of Three Groups Supporting the Constitution"). A coalition cabinet headed by KATŌ TAKAAKI from June 1924 to July 1925. It was a product of the second MOVEMENT TO PROTECT CONSTITUTIONAL GOVERNMENT, in which three major political parties joined forces to reassert party control of the government. They were the KENSEIKAI, led by Katō; the RIKKEN SEIYŪKAI, led by TAKAHASHI KOREKIYO, who became minister of agriculture and commerce in the new cabinet; and the KAKUSHIN KURABU, led by INUKAI TSUYOSHI, who was appointed minister of transportation. Major acts passed under this cabinet in 1925 included the Universal Manhood Suffrage Law, the elimination of four army divisions, the establishment of diplomatic relations with the Soviet Union, and the repressive PEACE PRESERVATION LAW (Chian Iji Hō). In July 1925, internal dissension over taxation policy broke out between the Kenseikai members of the cabinet and those from the Seiyūkai, which had absorbed the Kakushin Kurabu in May. The cabinet resigned en masse, and Katō formed a new Kenseikai cabinet the following month. *Matsuo Takayoshi*

Goken Undō → Movement to Protect Constitutional Government

Gōke shidai

Also known as *Gōshidai*. An encyclopedia of court ceremonial completed in 1111 by the scholar-official ŌE NO MASAFUSA. *Gōke* refers to the Ōe family, who had served the court for generations as literary scholars. Masafusa undertook the work at the request of the regent (KAMPAKU) Fujiwara no Moromichi (1062–99). The surviving 19 chapters (out of 21) include extensive information about the various annual observances of the court, the duties of officials, the order of appointments, and other matters to serve as precedents in the conduct of court affairs. *G. Cameron Hurst III*

Goki Shichidō

(Five Home Provinces and Seven Circuits). A general term for the administrative units of Japan under the RITSURYŌ SYSTEM, which was instituted in the late 7th century. Goki refers to the five provinces around the old capitals of Nara and Kyōto (see KINAI): Yamato, Yamashiro, Settsu, Kawachi, and Izumi. Shichidō refers to the seven regions or circuits (dō; literally, "roads") into which the remaining 60-or-so provinces were grouped: Tōkaidō, Tōsandō, Hokurikudō, San'indō, San'yōdō, Nankaidō, and Saikaidō. See also map at PROVINCES.

gokō gomin

(literally, "five for the lord; five for the commoner"). A term of the Edo period (1600–1868) indicating that half of a crop yield was to be paid as tax (nengu) to one's lord while half was to be retained by the producer for his family's sustenance. The term derived from shogunate tax regulations and was reiterated in agronomic literature (jikatasho) of the period. It expressed a goal rather than actuality; in practice the percentage of yield paid as tax varied widely from domain to domain and year to year, rarely exceeding the 50 percent level and in shogunate domains (tenryō) commonly falling into the 30 to 35 percent range. See also JŌMEN. *Conrad Totman*

Gokokuji

Large temple in Bunkyō Ward, Tōkyō, center of the Buzan branch (see HASEDERA) of the SHINGON SECT of Buddhism in eastern Japan. The Gokokuji was founded in 1681 by the monk Ryōken (1611–87) at the request of the fifth Tokugawa shōgun, Tsunayoshi (1646–1709), and his mother Keishō In (1627–1705), who together served as its lay patrons. The main hall of the temple, now designated an Important Cultural Property, was constructed in 1698. Its cemetery contains the graves of more than 40 Confucian scholars of the Edo period (1600–1868). Because of its close connection with the Tokugawa family, prayers were regularly offered here at the behest of the shogunate. The temple is dedicated to the bodhisattva Nyoirin Kannon. *Stanley Weinstein*

Go-Komatsu, Emperor (1377–1433)

The 100th sovereign (tennō) in the traditional count (which includes several nonhistorical emperors); reigned 1382–1412. Eldest son of Emperor Go-En'yū (1359–93; r 1371–82) and like him a ruler of the Northern Court at the time of the succession dispute between the NORTHERN AND SOUTHERN COURTS. In 1392 the schism in the imperial house ended when the Muromachi shogunate persuaded Emperor GO-KAMEYAMA of the Southern Court to abdicate in favor of Go-Komatsu and turn over to him the IMPERIAL REGALIA, the symbols of imperial legitimacy. Although Go-Komatsu thereby became the sole legitimate ruler of Japan, he was in fact always under the firm control of the shōgun ASHIKAGA YOSHIMITSU. Go-Komatsu abdicated in 1412 and entered the Buddhist priesthood in 1431.

gold beetle

(koganemushi). *Mimela splendens.* A beetle of the order Coleoptera, family Scarabaeidae, whose distribution ranges over all Japan as well as Korea, Taiwan, China, and India. Its body is oval, usually glossy golden green, and widest in the posterior section, with a rounded back. About 20 millimeters (0.8 in) long, it appears in June and July and feeds on young leaves of *kunugi* (a kind of oak) and cherry. The larva is a grub which lives in the soil and feeds on tree roots. The insect takes from one to two years to develop from an egg into an adult. *Nakane Takehiko*

goldfish

(kingyo). *Carassius auratus.* A freshwater fish of class Osteichthyes, order Cypriniformes, family Cyprinidae. The goldfish is thought to have been artificially bred from the crucian carp in China. At present more than 20 varieties are raised in Japan, some of which were originally imported and some of which were developed domestically. *Abe Tokiharu*

It is presumed to be around the 11th century that goldfish breeding was conducted actively in China, and goldfish seem to have been imported to Japan on several occasions during the 16th and the 17th centuries. During the Genroku era (1688–1704), a "goldfish boom" came about in Edo (now Tōkyō). Goldfish reached a high degree of popularity during the Bunka and Bunsei eras (1804–30) when they were frequently kept in garden ponds, and ukiyo-e artists such as Kitagawa Utamaro and Utagawa Kunisada portrayed them in their woodblock prints. Street vendors carrying goldfish in a well-polished oval tub—long a familiar and poetic sight of the Japanese summer—seem to have first appeared during these years and were common until the outbreak of World War II. Goldfish are thought to have been imported to Europe for the first time by the Portuguese, who brought them from China via the East Indies. Exports to the United States from Japan began in the 1890s, with a large-scale trade starting around 1907 but declined after 1933 when the United States succeeded in mass goldfish breeding. *Saitō Shōji*

golf

Golf was introduced to Japan by Arthur H. Groom, an English merchant, who opened Japan's first golf course in the Rokkō Hills of Kōbe in 1901 and founded the Kōbe Golf Club in 1903. Since World War II the popularity of golf has increased greatly; at the same time it has become one of Japan's most costly sports and hence chiefly a leisure activity of the white-collar class. The number of professional golfers has also increased and is now well over 1,000. There are approximately 930 golf courses, which are used by approximately 40 million players a year. *Watanabe Tōru*

Golovnin, Vasilii Mikhailovich (1776–1831)

Russian naval officer and explorer, famous for his book *Memoirs of a Captivity in Japan, during the Years 1811, 1812, and 1813.* Born into a noble family of Ryazanskaya Province in central European Russia, Golovnin was orphaned at the age of 9. In 1788 he entered the Naval School. Although his normal course of studies ended in 1792, he was held back for another year because of his youth—he had not yet turned 17—and received additional instruction in the English language, history, geography, and physics. He became particularly interested in the literature of exploration and, following his graduation and commission as a naval officer, obtained assignments on vessels traveling abroad. From 1798 to 1800 he served as adjutant and interpreter of Vice Admiral M. K. Makarov, the commander of the Russian squadron operating jointly with the English fleet in the North Sea. In 1802 Golovnin was attached to the British navy for further training. He served for over three years on English men-of-war and earned the praise of Admiral Horatio Nelson and Admiral Cuthbed Collingwood. Given command of his own vessel, the Russian frigate *Diana,* in 1806 Golovnin was sent on an around-the-world expedition from Kronstadt to Kamchatka and thence to the little-known islands between northeastern Asia and northwestern America. It was his account of his capture by the Japanese while charting the Kuril (Chishima) archipelago that brought him world fame.

The events leading to Golovnin's capture were as follows: in 1792–93 another Russian naval officer, Lieutenant Adam Erikovich LAXMAN, fruitlessly negotiated with Japanese officials on Ezo (now Hokkaidō) to establish commercial relations between their countries. He was turned away with a permit to discuss the question in Nagasaki. In 1804 Nikolai Petrovich REZANOV sailed to Nagasaki in the belief that the document was a permit to conclude a trade agreement. When the Japanese persisted in their refusal, he induced two young Russian naval officers in the employ of the Russian-American Company to raid Japanese settlements on the Kuril Islands in an effort to intimidate Japan into trading with Russia. It was in retaliation for these attacks that Lieutenant Commander Golovnin and several subordinates were lured ashore on Kunashiri Island and taken prisoner in July 1811. Lieutenant Commander Petr Ivanovich Rikord, who had stayed aboard the *Diana,* captured an influential Hokkaidō merchant, TAKATAYA KAHEI, and with his help eventually negotiated the release of the Russians, the commandant of Okhotsk having given written assurance that the raids on the Japanese settlements had been carried on without the authorization or knowledge of the tsarist government.

The memoirs of Golovnin's three-year-long captivity, published in 1816 and translated and reprinted widely, were the most significant first-hand portrayal of the Japanese available in Russia until the opening of Japan, if not until the beginning of the 20th century. Remarkably objective and sympathetic, Golovnin praised the high level of Japanese education, the concern of the Japanese government for its subjects, the sensibility, astuteness, honesty, hospitality, and cleanliness of the Japanese people. He portrayed the Japanese as fiery patriots, conscious not only of the harm that foreign actions had brought in years past, but confident of their own superiority. He felt that the Japanese lagged behind Europe in many respects, but he noted that their capabilities were tremendous and predicted that they would catch up with the Europeans and become potential rivals in the future.

To the Japanese, Golovnin was a mine of information. Scholars and officials interrogated him at length. The explorer and astronomer MAMIYA RINZŌ inquired about Russian methods of land surveying and astronomical observation; the academician Adachi Sannai (1769–1845) queried him about mathematics; the young Dutch interpreter Baba Sajūrō (1787–1822) revised a Russo-Japanese dictionary with Golovnin's help. Not all the information provided by Golovnin was accurate, however. To encourage his release and that of his comrades, Golovnin deliberately exaggerated Russian might in the Far East, thereby unwittingly contributing to Japanese fears of Russian expansion.

Golovnin returned to St. Petersburg in mid-1814, seven years after having left there. In addition to his memoirs, which he published privately, Golovnin wrote scientific accounts of his voyages, brought out by the Admiralty. Continuing his voyages of exploration and his writings, Golovnin rose in rank and influence. In 1821 he became assistant director of the Naval School from which he had graduated; in 1829 he was appointed quartermaster general of the fleet, in which capacity he contributed to the growth of the Russian navy. One of the bays in the Bering Sea, a strait between the Kuril Islands, and a cape and a mountain on Novaya Zemlya in the Arctic Ocean bear his name.

■──V. M. Golovnin, *Zapiski flota kapitana Golovnina o prikliucheniiakh ego v plenu u iapontsev v 1811, 12, i 13 godakh i pr.* (1816), tr *Memoirs of a Captivity in Japan, During the Years 1811, 1812, and 1813; With Observations of the Country and the People.* George Alexander Lensen, *The Russian Push toward Japan: Russo-Japanese Relations, 1697–1875* (1959). George Alexander Lensen, *Report from Hokkaido: The Remains of Russian Culture in Northern Japan* (1954). Takano Akira, *Nihon to Roshia* (1971).

George Alexander LENSEN

Gomi Yasusuke (1921–1980)

Novelist. Born in Ōsaka. Writer of popular historical fiction. Attended Waseda University. In the late 1940s and 1950s he created a fad with his stories of *kengō,* or skilled swordsmen, and contributed to the popularity of stories about *ninja,* or spies with magical powers (see NINJUTSU). Recipient of the Akutagawa Prize in 1953 for his short story "Sōshin" (1952); other works include the short story "Yagyū Ren'yasai" (1955) and *Futari no Musashi* (1956–57).

Go-Mizunoo, Emperor (1596–1680)

The 108th soverign *(tennō)* in the traditional count (which includes several nonhistorical emperors); reigned 1611–29. The third son of Emperor Go-Yōzei (1572–1617; r 1586–1611), in 1620 he married TOKUGAWA KAZUKO, daughter of the shōgun TOKUGAWA HIDETADA; she became his official empress in 1624. Unhappy with his forced marriage and other shogunal interference in court affairs (see SHIE INCIDENT), he abdicated in 1629 in favor of his five-year-old daughter Empress Meishō (1624–96; r 1629–43), the first reigning empress since the 8th century. For the next 51 years, until his death, Go-Mizunoo dominated the court from retirement. In northeastern Kyōto he built the SHUGAKUIN DETACHED PALACE, one of the most famous and beautiful imperial villas in Japan. A devout Buddhist and amateur scholar, he was also a notable *waka* poet; his verses are collected under the title *Ōsōshū* (A Seagull's Nest).

gomoku narabe → renju

gonaisho

Personal letters from the shōguns. They were used from the mid-1300s through the Edo period (1600–1868) to convey holiday congratulations, messages about gifts or private matters, and even requests for military aid. Less formal than the official orders (KUDASHIBUMI) or "instructions" *(migyōsho),* they began to replace these forms as a means of transmitting shogunal policy during the rule (1369–95) of ASHIKAGA YOSHIMITSU. They were usually dictated but sometimes written by the shōgun himself, and they bore his monogram (KAŌ) or, in the Edo period, his personal seal *(inshō).*

Goncharov, Ivan Aleksandrovich (1812–1891)

Russian novelist whose description of mid-19th-century Japan influenced generations of Russian readers. Born into a prominent merchant family in Simbirsk (now Ul'ianovsk), Goncharov inherited an interest in the sea and in foreign travel from his godfather, a retired naval officer who was in charge of his early education. Upon graduation from Moscow University as a philologist in 1834, and after a brief stint as secretary in the office of the governor of Simbirsk, Goncharov worked as a translator in the Department of Finance in St. Petersburg (now Leningrad). He supplemented his salary by tutoring the children of the artist Nikolai Apollonovich Maikov and his wife, the poetess Evgen'ia Petrovna Maikova. He became a member of the Maikovs' literary salon and met many leading writers.

In August 1852 Maikov was invited to accompany Vice Admiral Evfimii Vasil'evich PUTIATIN as his secretary on a round-the-world expedition via the Cape of Good Hope to Japan, China, the Philippines, and the Russian colonies in North America. When Maikov refused the offer, Goncharov applied in his stead and was accepted because of his literary reputation. He stayed with Putiatin until the outbreak of the Crimean War in 1854. Back in St. Petersburg, Goncharov published his account of the voyage of the frigate *Pallada,* Putiatin's flagship, in serialized form. In December 1855 Goncharov was transferred to the Ministry of Education, where he worked as a senior censor. He was made a state councillor in reward for his services to Putiatin. After serving in several government posts, he retired in 1868, because of failing eyesight.

Goncharov is best known for his novel, *Oblomov,* begun before his voyage to Japan but completed upon his return and published in 1859. Critical of Russian society, notably the "superfluous men" of intellect who were too impractical and lazy to accomplish anything, the work strongly influenced FUTABATEI SHIMEI and other writers of Meiji (1868–1912) Japan. Although all his novels contained an autobiographical strain, Goncharov's account of the voyage of the *Pallada* most clearly revealed his own temperament. He had an eye for the smallest details of daily life and custom as well as a knack for phrasing his observations in an entertaining and realistic fashion.

As Goncharov's fame as a novelist spread, so did the popularity of *Fregat Pallada,* published in book form in 1858. Generations of Russian students were raised on this work, because it was a fine adventure story, at once wholesome, educational, and written in simple, effective prose. Its amusing characterization of the Japanese left a lasting imprint on the minds of its impressionable young readers. Unfortunately the effect of Goncharov's masterful portraits was often achieved through mockery and ridicule. Asserting that "it was difficult to look without laughter at these skirt-clad figures with their little topknots and their bare little knees," Goncharov depicted the Japanese military as "diametrically opposed" to what Russians would call soldiers. His description of the Japanese as ludicrous and effeminate contributed to the fatal failure of the Russian government and public to take the Japanese sufficiently seriously at the turn of the century.

■ ——I. A. Goncharov, *Fregat Pallada,* abridged but annotated version, ed S. D. Muraveitskii (1949), ed and tr N. W. Wilson as *The Voyage of the Frigate Pallada* (1965). William E. Harkins, *Dictionary of Russian Literature* (1959). George Alexander Lensen, "The Historicity of *Fregat Pallada,*" *Modern Language Notes* (1953). George Alexander Lensen, *Russia's Japan Expedition of 1852 to 1855* (1955). *George Alexander* LENSEN

Gondō Seikyō (1868–1937)

Rightist thinker and writer; also known as Gondō Nariaki. Born in Fukuoka Prefecture. An extended trip to Korea and China in 1886 made Gondō a proponent of Japanese expansion on the Asian continent. Joining the AMUR RIVER SOCIETY as editor of one of its periodicals, *Tōa geppō* (East Asia Monthly News), he made several more trips to the continent. In 1900 he moved to Tōkyō, where he became acquainted with KITA IKKI, ŌKAWA SHŪMEI, and other rightist thinkers. He joined the Rōsōkai, a study group concerned with national problems, and in 1920 he founded his own school, the Jichi Gakkai (Self-Rule School), through which he sought to spread his beliefs. A proponent of agrarian nationalism (NŌHON SHUGI), Gondō envisioned a state composed of self-governing village communities directly ruled by the emperor and free of bureaucracy and monopolistic capitalism. Although he personally eschewed revolutionary terrorism, his teachings had a great influence on the radical nationalist movements of the early 1930s. Suspected of involvement in two ultra-right-wing plots of 1932, the LEAGUE OF BLOOD INCIDENT and the MAY 15TH INCIDENT, he was detained by the government but later released. Gondō's writings include *Kōmin jichi hongi* (1920, Basic Principles of Self-Rule by the Emperor's Subjects) and the influential *Jichi mimpan* (1927, People's Guide to Self-Rule).

gongen → avatar

goningumi

(literally, "five-man groups"). Mutual-responsibility units of local political organization during the Edo period (1600–1868). Promoted by rulers in the early 17th century as a mechanism of social control, they gradually evolved into devices for local self-help and self-governance. Other forms of mutual responsibility have been used in other periods of Japanese history; TONARIGUMI (neighborhood groups) were established by the government during the 1930s and 1940s to mobilize and control the population.

The model for *goningumi* was a system of group organization employed in Tang (T'ang) dynasty (618–907) China. It was introduced to Japan shortly after the Taika Reform of 645, and was at that time called *goho.* In subsequent centuries it gave way to other forms of village organization and control. Much later, in late-16th-century Japan, several types of group responsibility appeared. Local groups of citizens formed self-defense units, often 10-household groups (*jūningumi*) to regulate their affairs or protect their communities from marauding bands of soldiers and other outsiders. Military leaders began organizing their forces into small combat units of 5 to 10 men when they began using firearms in the final decades of the century. In orders of 1596 TOYOTOMI HIDEYOSHI applied analogous patterns of group responsibility to his vassal forces and commoners, evidently to reduce lawlessness and stabilize social relationships in the Kyōto area.

TOKUGAWA IEYASU employed similar techniques once he established hegemony over Japan. In 1603 he promoted local *jūningumi* to reduce outlawry in Kyōto. In 1612 he set up similar 10-household units in Edo (now Tōkyō) to thwart free movement of unemployed

samurai (RŌNIN) and any others who might be promoting Christian doctrine or engaging in other illicit activity. Gradually the system was employed elsewhere, and during the rule (1623–51) of the shōgun TOKUGAWA IEMITSU, *goningumi* became a part of the formally codified local administration in both shogunal and *daimyō* domains.

The "five-man groups" did not consist of five men. Optimally they consisted of five households, but in fact, depending upon the particulars of local terrain and village or town settlement patterns, a group might be composed of one to more than a dozen households. The groups provided members with communal defense against outsiders and an organized system for mutual aid, resolution of internal disputes, and allocation of such tasks as road and waterway maintenance and corvée labor service. They provided rulers with identifiable groups that could be held collectively responsible for tax obligations and other forms of financial liability. The groups also supervised members' behavior and maintained statistics on births, deaths, marriages, and adoptions of group members. Each group had a leader (often called *goningumi-gashira),* who might be appointed or elected. Most often the leader was the head of one of the most wealthy and influential households in the group. The leader would then represent his group's interests in the town or village, thus constituting one segment of the local political leadership.

The procedures of *goningumi* varied greatly from place to place. Their members assembled periodically in gatherings known as *goningumi yoriai.* These meetings might occur regularly once or several times a year, or they might be called as need arose or for local ceremonial affairs. They might be called by the members, by their leader, or by higher local or district authorities to deal with such local issues as settling disagreements or preparing petitions for submission to higher officials.

Goningumi chō (also known as *goningumi tegata, gohatto-gaki,* and *gouke-gaki*) were compilations of regulations and prohibitions to guide *goningumi* members in their daily lives. The registers usually had a preface consisting of hortatory admonitions and Confucian precepts explaining the general purpose of the *goningumi.* The register proper might consist of only a few articles or as many as 150, but they usually numbered about 50 articles concerning such matters as licentious behavior, the use of personal and communal property, local judicial procedures, tax and status considerations, ways of dealing with outsiders, and means of preventing fires, floods, or other disasters. In some localities the registers were read and discussed at *goningumi yoriai* or were used as instructional material in local schools for village youngsters. To some extent they constituted effective guides for local behavior, and to some extent they were formalistic devices used by villagers and townsmen to meet the requirements of higher authority. But they did help *goningumi* evolve from instruments of the government into forms of local social organization.

■ ——Hozumi Nobushige, *Goningumi hōki shū* (1921). Nomura Kentarō, *Goningumi chō no kenkyū* (1944). John H. Wigmore, "Notes on Land Tenure and Local Institutions in Old Japan," *Transactions of the Asiatic Society of Japan* 19 (1890). *Conrad* TOTMAN

Gonki

Also called *Yukinari Kyō ki.* Diary of the Heian-period (794–1185) courtier and calligrapher FUJIWARA NO YUKINARI (also known as Fujiwara no Kōzei, 972–1027; see CALLIGRAPHY). Its name derives from one of Yukinari's official posts, *gon dainagon* (provisional great counselor). The diary runs to 50 chapters covering the years 991–1011. Like Fujiwara no Sanesuke's SHŌYŪKI and the MIDŌ KAMPAKU KI of FUJIWARA NO MICHINAGA, *Gonki* is an important source of information on politics and court life during the heyday of Fujiwara rule. *G. Cameron* HURST III

gōnō

(literally, "rich farmers"). General term for farmers who had extensive landholdings or managed large-scale operations; more particularly, in the writings of modern historians concerning the latter part of the Edo period (1600–1868) and early part of the Meiji period (1868–1912), it refers to local farmers and wealthy merchants who acted as the economic and administrative leaders of their communities.

Having participated in domain and shogunate politics as village officials, *gōnō* became even more politically conscious as Japan was swept up in the events that eventually led to the MEIJI RESTORATION (1868). Many of them took part in the movement to overthrow the Tokugawa shogunate (1603–1867), acting as the leaders of the movement in their villages. Again, after the restoration, as the FREEDOM AND PEOPLE'S RIGHTS MOVEMENT in opposition to the "tyranny" of the new government gained momentum throughout the country, *gōnō* acted as the leaders and representatives of the farming populace.

The question of the exact role of the *gōnō* in bringing about the Meiji Restoration, first discussed by the Marxist scholar HATTORI SHISŌ before World War II, was taken up anew by Fujita Gorō after the war. Fujita saw the *gōnō* as a Japanese-type bourgeoisie, and in contrast to domainal lords and privileged merchants who pushed modernization from "above," he saw them as a force which propelled society forward from "below." A scholarly debate over the *gōnō* ensued, which has continued to the present. Scholars seem to agree, however, on two points: that both as conservative landlords and as progressive antifeudal merchants, *gōnō* were "two-faced"; and that, with the LAND TAX REFORM OF 1873–1881, the *gōnō* as a class either disintegrated or were absorbed into the new landlord class. See also NIHON SHIHON SHUGI RONSŌ.

——Denda Isao, *Gōnō* (1978). Fujita Gorō, *Fujita Gorō chosakushū*, vols 3 and 4 (1969; 1971). Hattori Shisō, *Hattori Shisō chosakushū*, vol 1 (1955). Ōishi Kaichirō, *Nihon chihō zaigyōsei shi josetsu* (1962). Sasaki Junnosuke, *Bakumatsu shakai ron* (1969).

UNNO Fukuju

Gōnokawa

Also known as Gōgawa and Gōkawa. River in Hiroshima and Shimane prefectures, western Honshū, originating in the Mikasa Pass and flowing through the Chūgoku Mountains to empty into the Sea of Japan at the city of Gōtsu. Numerous multipurpose dams have been constructed on the upper and middle reaches. The water is used for electric power generation, as well as for drinking and industrial purposes by the Inland Sea Industrial Region. Length: 200 km (120 mi); area of drainage basin: 3,810 sq km (1,470 sq mi).

go on

(the Wu pronunciation). One of the several varieties of *on* readings of Chinese characters (KANJI) as used in Japan. *On* readings are Japanese approximations of the way the characters were pronounced in Chinese, and the fact that for any one character there may be two or three possible *on* readings (reflecting the Chinese pronunciations of different periods and different regions) is one of the causes of the complexity of the Japanese writing system. *Go on* consist of pronunciations that had been introduced into Japan in the 6th century and before. In the 7th century a new variety of pronunciations called *kan on* (markedly different from *go on* and a closer approximation of the contemporary pronunciations of the Tang [T'ang] dynasty capital) were introduced, and there was an attempt to have these supersede the old pronunciations (*kan on* were declared official in 793). However, *go on* persisted alongside the new pronunciations, particularly in words related to Buddhism and also in many common words that had become deeply entrenched in Japanese. Wu (J: Go), originally the name of an ancient kingdom, referred to a region in the lower Yangzi (Yangtze) River area, and it is usually explained that the older Japanese pronunciations came from the Chinese of this area; however, Wu as used by Chinese of the capital area was equivalent to "nonstandard," and could have referred to the out-of-date as well as the dialectal. See ON READINGS.

YAMADA Toshio

gorintō

(literally, "five-wheel pagoda"). A kind of small stupa that came into use in Japan about the middle of the Heian period (794–1185) as a Buddhist memorial, grave marker, or sutra mound monument. Usually constructed of stone, a *gorintō* is composed of five distinct tiers of different shapes, each representing one of the five elements believed in ESOTERIC BUDDHISM to make up the universe. From bottom to top, they are square (earth), globular (water), pyramidal (fire), hemispherical (wind), and tear-drop (emptiness). A Sanskrit character is often inscribed on each. See also SUTRA MOUNDS.

KITAMURA Bunji

gōri system

(*gōrisei*). Refers to the two smallest units—village (*gō*) and hamlet (*ri*)—in the four-tier structure of local administration that was briefly incorporated into the RITSURYŌ SYSTEM in the 8th century. The TAIKA REFORM of 645 had established a three-tier structure—province (*kuni*), district (*gun*), and village (*ri*)—with each village

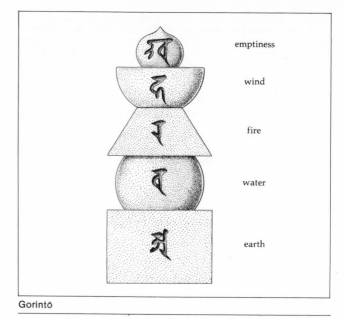

emptiness

wind

fire

water

earth

Gorintō

nominally comprising 50 households. The *gōri* system, initiated in 715, subdivided the smallest unit in order to improve government control of the expanding rural population and particularly to facilitate tax collection. The former villages (*ri*) were now designated *gō*, and each village was to contain two or three new and smaller hamlets (*ri*). Each village and hamlet was to have its own headman responsible for a specified number of households. The household system was to be changed as well. The villages (*gō*) were meant to organize extended families or groups of related families, called *gōko*; the new hamlets (*ri*) were meant to organize smaller family units, called *bōko*. Because of the social and political instability of the times, however, such a sweeping program could not be implemented. The attempt was abandoned in about 740, and the local administration reverted to the three-tier structure of province, district, and village (now called *gō*).

goroku

("recorded sayings"). A term which strictly speaking refers to records of the oral teachings of masters of the ZEN sect of Buddhism taken down by their disciples but which is also used loosely to refer to collections of the teachings of other religious leaders or even tracts written by the teachers themselves. One of the basic ideas of Zen, expressed in the phrase FURYŪ MONJI ("not standing on words or letters"), was that enlightenment cannot be communicated by writing or even by words, but can only be initiated directly from heart to heart. As a result, Zen masters were not in the habit of putting down their teachings in writing, and *goroku* came into being through the desire of disciples to make records of their masters' words and deeds. The tradition originated in Tang (T'ang) dynasty (618–907) China, and was transmitted to Japan, where most examples are from the Kamakura period (1185–1333). *Goroku* were classified in various categories, such as *kōroku* (those that were particularly inclusive and detailed), *goyō* (those that were devoted to the words and deeds of only one master) and *tsūshū* (those devoted to a number of masters). In the strict sense, the term *goroku* referred only to such records written in classical Chinese (KAMBUN). Similar collections written in Japanese (*wabun*) and particularly intended for the masses were called *hōgo*. However, in the loose sense referred to above, the term *goroku* is used to refer to any such collections of sayings or teachings, regardless of sect or language, and regardless of whether written by a disciple or by the master himself. Some of the best-known *goroku* (in the broad sense) include TANNISHŌ by SHINRAN, *Ippen Shōnin goroku* by IPPEN, *SHŌBŌ GENZŌ* by DŌGEN, and *Minobusan gosho* by NICHIREN (persons cited as authors are the masters whose words are recorded).

goryō

Also called *onryō*. Malevolent spirits of persons of high rank or great influence who died unnaturally or in a state of anger or resentment. It was generally believed that spirits of the dead influenced the living, and that the spirits of those who lived extraordinary lives or died unusual deaths were to be particularly feared and placated lest they cause harm, bring diseases, or haunt their enemies. Buddhist monks and ascetics were solicited to perform religious services on behalf of such vengeful spirits, who were in some cases deified to appease and avert their wrath. The fear of vengeful spirits and the ensuing *goryō* cult became prominent with the political troubles at the end of the Nara period (710–794) and played a significant role in the court intrigues of the Heian period (794–1185). Warriors in feudal times were also sensitive to the need to appease the spirits of enemies slain in battle.

Generally speaking, the festivals or *matsuri* of such deified spirits take place in summer, while those of traditional deities (KAMI) such as the god of fertility are observed in spring and autumn. The former overwhelm the latter in scale and dynamism (for example, the GION FESTIVAL and the Tenjin Festival in honor of SUGAWARA NO MICHIZANE are largely urban phenomena), while the latter are rural in origin.

Kyōko NAKAMURA

Goryōkaku, Battle of

(Goryōkaku no Tatakai). Battle that marked the end of the BOSHIN CIVIL WAR that accompanied the MEIJI RESTORATION; also known as the Battle of Hakodate. In October 1868, ENOMOTO TAKEAKI, vice commander-in-chief of the naval forces of the recently overthrown Tokugawa shogunate, assembled more than 2,000 troops still loyal to the shogunate, sailed with eight warships to Ezo (now Hokkaidō), and in December established his headquarters in a Western-style fortress called Goryōkaku at the port city of Hakodate. In January of the following year Enomoto declared Ezo a republic. Late in May 1869 an imperial force under KURODA KIYOTAKA arrived in Ezo, quickly gained control of the hinterland of Hakodate, and entered the harbor. They began their assault on the city on 20 June and, on 27 June 1869 (Meiji 2.5.18), forced the surrender of Goryōkaku in the last armed conflict between imperial forces and intransigent supporters of the Tokugawa regime.

Go-Saga, Emperor (1220–1272)

The 88th sovereign (*tennō*) in the traditional count (which includes several nonhistorical emperors); reigned 1242–46; eldest son of Emperor TSUCHIMIKADO. His accession set an important precedent, for the Kamakura shogunate intervened in his behalf when a court faction wished to enthrone instead Prince Tadanari, a son of the retired emperor JUNTOKU, who had been exiled for his part in the JŌKYŪ DISTURBANCE. Go-Saga had already taken Buddhist vows before his accession, and he abdicated after a reign of only 4 years but continued to dominate the court from retirement for the next 26 years. In 1260 he forced his son and successor Emperor GO-FUKAKUSA to relinquish the throne to his younger and favorite son, Emperor KAMEYAMA. The ensuing rivalry between the two brothers eventually led to the practice (beginning with the reign of Emperor FUSHIMI [r 1287–98]) of alternating the succession between the senior Jimyōin line (descended from Go-Fukakusa) and the junior Daikakuji line (descended from Kameyama) of the imperial house. This practice was later made official by the KAMAKURA SHOGUNATE. The anthology *Zoku kokinshū*, sequel to the KOKINSHŪ, was compiled at the order of Go-Saga, who was himself an accomplished poet.

G. Cameron HURST III

Go-Sanjō, Emperor (1034–1073)

The 71st sovereign (*tennō*) in the traditional count (which includes several nonhistorical emperors); reigned 1068–73. Son of Emperor Go-Suzaku (r 1036–45) and Yōmei Mon'in (Princess Teishi), he succeeded his half-brother Emperor Go-Reizei (1025–68; r 1045–68). Because he was not directly related to the Fujiwara regents' house (see REGENCY GOVERNMENT), he was able in his brief reign to exercise considerable power and largely restore the authority of the throne. Having surrounded himself with non-Fujiwara officials, Go-Sanjō established a manorial Records Office (KIROKU SHŌEN KENKEIJO) to check the proliferation of tax-exempt private estates (SHŌEN). Determined to free the imperial succession from manipulation by the regents, he abdicated in favor of his son Emperor SHIRAKAWA (r 1073–87) and arranged for his two sons by a consort from the MINAMOTO FAMILY to succeed in turn. Some historians credit him with establishing the system of government by retired emperors (see INSEI), but that innovation dates from Shirakawa's time. Go-Sanjō died six months after his abdication.

G. Cameron HURST III

Gosanke

(The Three Successor Houses). The three *daimyō* families at the domains of Mito (now part of Ibaraki Prefecture), Owari (now part of Aichi Prefecture), and Kii (now Wakayama Prefecture); the most highly ranked SHIMPAN daimyō and the most honored branches of the Tokugawa family. They traced their ancestry from the three youngest sons of TOKUGAWA IEYASU, the dynastic founder: the Owari branch (with a domain assessed at 619,000 *koku*; see KOKUDAKA) from Yoshinao (1600–1650), the Kii branch (550,000 *koku*) from Yorinobu (1602–71), and the Mito branch (350,000 *koku*) from Yorifusa (1603–61). The Gosanke were expected to support the shōgun against any daimyō challengers and to supply successors in the event that he died without male issue. They were frequently involved in Tokugawa family politics, but they were in fact great autonomous lords themselves, and much of their enduring influence in state affairs derived not from their ancestry and high status but from their large and vigorous domains and warrior forces. The Gosanke, like all daimyō, were dispossessed after the Meiji Restoration of 1868. See also GOSANKYŌ; genealogical chart in TOKUGAWA FAMILY.

Conrad TOTMAN

Gosankyō

("The Three Lords"). The three junior collateral houses of the Tokugawa family. The three senior collateral houses of Owari, Kii, and Mito (see GOSANKE) had been established by the Tokugawa dynastic founder TOKUGAWA IEYASU to fill any vacancy in the shogunal succession, but as the blood relationship between the shōgun and the three houses became more distant, it became necessary to look elsewhere for a successor. Three new houses were set up from sons born to shōguns by secondary wives: the Tayasu from the 8th shōgun TOKUGAWA YOSHIMUNE's second son, Munetake (1715–71) was set up in 1730; the Hitotsubashi from Yoshimune's fourth son Munetada (1721–64) in 1740; and the Shimizu from the 9th shōgun TOKUGAWA IESHIGE's second son, Shigeyoshi (1745–95) in 1759. The names were taken from their place of residence. Each was granted a yearly stipend of 100,000 *koku* (see KOKUDAKA) but no domain. The 11th shōgun TOKUGAWA IENARI and the 15th and last shōgun TOKUGAWA YOSHINOBU were from the house of Hitotsubashi. See also genealogical chart in TOKUGAWA FAMILY.

Gosannen no Eki → Later Three Years' War

Gose

City in west central Nara Prefecture, central Honshū. Gose was a castle town during the Edo period (1600–1868). Traditionally known for its *yamatogasuri* (ikat weave) and traditional medicines that were sold by itinerant peddlers, it now specializes in cotton goods, footwear, and fountain pens. The area also produces persimmons. There is a keyhole-shaped tumulus (KOFUN) here. Gose is a part of the Kongō–Ikoma Quasi-National Park. Pop: 37,388.

gosechi no mai

A form of *bugaku* dance (see GAGAKU) performed by women from ancient times as part of court ceremonies; it is said to have originated in the late 7th century during the reign of Emperor Temmu (r 672–686), having been modeled on dances of Tang (T'ang) China. During the Nara period (710–794) the dance was customarily performed in the imperial presence on major holidays and special occasions. But in the Heian period (794–1185) performance was limited to the two feasts known as DAIJŌSAI (Great Food Offering Ritual), an enthronement ceremony, and NIINAMESAI (Festival for the New Tasting), an annual harvest rite. Dancing maidens (five for the former festival and four for the latter) were selected from among the imperial family and nobility. Although the dance was discontinued during the Sengoku period (1467–1568), it was revived with new music and dances on the occasion of the formal enthronement of Emperor Taishō in 1915. The *gosechi no mai* was also performed during the enthronement ceremonies for Emperor Hirohito in 1928.

INAGAKI Shisei

Goseibai Shikimoku

(The Formulary of Adjudications). One of the best-known and most important law codes in Japanese history; established by the KAMAKURA SHOGUNATE for its vassals (GOKENIN) in the eighth month of 1232 (Jōei 1); also known as Jōei Shikimoku and by several other titles. The original of this code is no longer extant, and controversies persist as to its exact format and wording. According to later copies the code consisted of a short preamble, 51 articles, and an oath attested to by 13 high-ranking shogunate officials.

The Goseibai Shikimoku was the first codification and the cornerstone of what is known in legal history as warrior house law, or BUKEHŌ, which remained dominant in Japan from the 13th through the mid-19th centuries. Originally warrior law was a synthesis of the laws of other, older insititutions such as the imperial government in Kyōto, provincial governments, private estates (SHŌEN), ecclesiastic orders, and so forth, within whose jurisdictions warrior society had emerged and gradually gained prominence in the 12th century. Unlike the generally dogmatic and inflexible codes of the RITSURYŌ SYSTEM of the Kyōto authorities, warrior law as exemplified in the Goseibai Shikimoku was basically pragmatic, dictated by common sense, precedent, and rule by consensus of the shogunate leadership.

The Goseibai Shikimoku owed its birth to the JŌKYŪ DISTURBANCE of 1221, which tilted the balance of power greatly in favor of the shogunate vis-à-vis other traditional authorities. By establishing this code the shogunate aimed to clarify on broad principles the extent of its newly expanded jurisdiction against that of the Kyōto authorities in particular, and to strengthen and formalize its relationship with its own vassals. However, the Goseibai Shikimoku was not a code of law in the traditional sense. Rather, it was a compilation of the most common and important types of court cases heard by the shogunate during the unsettled post-Jōkyū Disturbance years. Although the nature of the cases varied greatly, they were predominantly what might be termed civil cases—in particular, property disputes.

Supplementary articles (tsuika) to the Goseibai Shikimoku were issued from time to time. Many of these were also based on actual court cases, and to this day over 700 supplementary articles have been accounted for. It was primarily through these officially reported judgments in the form of "articles" that Kamakura vassals learned the broad outlines of both the substantive and procedural rules being formulated and enforced by the shogunate. Of even more significance to the vassals was the fairness, so clearly stipulated in the oath to the code, with which the shogunate settled or tried to settle various types of disputes involving its adherents. Consequently, the Goseibai Shikimoku soon came to be regarded as the symbol of fair and equitable law, and the settlements attained through the shogunate court were long honored as the sources of legitimacy, not only by the people of the time but also by those of later periods. The subsequent MUROMACHI SHOGUNATE regarded its laws as supplements to the Goseibai Shikimoku.

James KANDA

Gō Seinosuke (1865–1942)

Businessman. Born in what is now Gifu Prefecture. After studying at Dōshisha Eigakkō (now Dōshisha University), he went on to Tōkyō University. In 1884 he went to Germany for further education. On his return, he worked for the Ministry of Agriculture and Commerce. He became president of Nippon Un'yu in 1895 and later served as an executive in a variety of large corporations, including Nippon Meriyasu, Iriyama Saitan, and Ōji Paper. Skilled in rebuilding and merging corporations, he played a leading role in pre–World War II business and industrial circles despite his lack of *zaibatsu* affiliations.

Asajima Shōichi

Gosekke

(Five Regents' Houses). The five major branches of the FUJIWARA FAMILY, from which the regents (sesshō and kampaku) and the empresses were chosen; specifically the KONOE, KUJŌ, Nijō, Ichijō, and Takatsukasa families, which were established early in the Kamakura period (1185–1333). They were all descended from FUJIWARA NO MICHINAGA of the powerful Northern Branch (Hokke) of the Fujiwara, and more specifically from Michinaga's fifth-generation descendant Fujiwara no Tadamichi (1097–1164). The first division occurred when Tadamichi's eldest son, Motozane (1143–66), adopted the name Konoe and his third son, KUJŌ KANEZANE (1149–1207), took the name Kujō. Later, two younger sons of Kanezane's grandson Kujō Michiie (1193–1252) branched off to form the Nijō and Ichijō houses. In 1252 the Takatsukasa house branched off from the Konoe in a similar fashion. The five houses thus formed stood at the apex of courtier society until the Meiji Restoration (1868) and beyond. Although some scholars believe that these divi-

sions were encouraged by the Kamakura shogunate to weaken Fujiwara power, such splits were in fact common in other large families in both courtier and warrior society of the time and reflected a general breakdown of the patrimonial system. See SŌRYŌ SYSTEM.

G. Cameron HURST III

Gosen

City in central Niigata Prefecture, central Honshū, on the river Aganogawa. During the 19th century Gosen was noted for its *gosenhira*, a silk fabric used for making the pleated *hakama* skirt. Since World War II, it has been one of the largest producers of knitted goods in Japan. Pop: 39,937.

Gosen wakashū

(Later Collection of Japanese Poetry; the full title is commonly abbreviated to *Gosenshū* or often simply to *Gosen*). The second imperial anthology (chokusenshū) of classical Japanese poetry; ordered in 951 by Emperor Murakami (926–967; r 946–967); compiled by the so-called Five Men of the Pear Chamber (Nashitsubo no Gonin): ŌNAKATOMI NO YOSHINOBU, Kiyohara no Motosuke, MINAMOTO NO SHITAGAU, Ki no Tokibumi, and Sakanoue no Mochiki; 20 books; 1,426 poems in the most authoritative text; date of completion unknown, but conjectured as sometime between 955 and 966. Some medieval authorities, including the great FUJIWARA NO SADAIE (Teika), believed that the anthology never proceeded beyond the draft stage.

As its title, "Later Collection," suggests, the anthology stands in the shadow of the KOKINSHŪ (ca 905, Collection of Ancient and Modern Times), the intent being primarily to provide a supplement to the earlier work rather than a collection of new poetry. Thus, no poems by the compilers are included, and the 219 poets represented belong chiefly to the age of the *Kokinshū,* the late 9th and early 10th centuries. Poets having the largest number of poems included are: KI NO TSURAYUKI, 77; Lady ISE, 70; ŌSHIKŌCHI NO MITSUNE, 23; and FUJIWARA NO KANESUKE, 22. The arrangement of the 20 books follows the *Kokinshū* model, but differs in several details. A distinctive feature, said to reflect the growing interest of the period in narrative and dramatic fiction, is the lengthy headnotes (kotobagaki) preceding many poems. These provide detailed prose accounts of the circumstances of composition, real or imagined, in the manner of such collections of lyrical tales (uta monogatari) as ISE MONOGATARI (Tales of Ise) and YAMATO MONOGATARI (Tales of Yamato). The *Gosenshū* also has the unusually large number of 180 sets of poetic exchanges between individuals. Such verse dialogues—as, for instance, between a lover and his coy mistress—also often have the dramatic quality and "story interest" esteemed by the age. In overall quality, the *Gosenshū* is inferior to the *Kokinshū,* but it nonetheless contains many famous poems. As one of the first three imperial anthologies, the so-called Collections of Three Eras (Sandaishū), it was venerated as an authoritative source of elegant diction and poetic precedent.

■——Robert H. Brower and Earl Miner, *Japanese Court Poetry* (1961).

Robert H. BROWER

gōshi

(rural *samurai*). Prior to the 16th century the term *gōshi* was probably applicable to the majority of retainers, who were expected to support themselves, and maintain a horse and equipment in readiness for a call to war, from the income of land, whether granted in fief (ryōchi) or not (musoku, a term designating part-time warriors, dates from the Kamakura period, 1185–1333). With the separation of status groups and disarmament of the peasants in the 1590s (heinō bunri), samurai were expected to be on call for full-time service, and in the Edo period (1600–1868) their residences were gathered around the lord's residence in the castle town.

In the Edo period the term *gōshi* had both narrow and inclusive meanings ranging from a distinct status group whose members sometimes lived in the castle town to regular samurai permitted to reside in the countryside. In its proper sense it signified low-ranking members of the retainer band resident outside the walls of the castle town who supported themselves from holdings that they oversaw personally. Relative rank and status privileges varied by region but were uniformly below those of their superiors who resided in the castle town. *Gōshi* classifications were part of the social structure of the southwestern domains of Tosa, Satsuma, and Higo (now Kōchi,

Kagoshima, and Kumamoto prefectures, respectively), and functionally equivalent groups were to be found in the domains of Chōshū, Kii, Sendai, Yonezawa, and Sōma (now Yamaguchi, Wakayama, and Miyagi prefectures respectively and the latter two part of Yamagata Prefecture, and part of Fukushima Prefecture respectively); thus they were more commonly found in less developed TOZAMA ("outside" vassal) domains than in the Kinai and Kantō plains.

Gōshi could serve a military and administrative function. In Tosa the first patents of rank were granted retainers of the dispossessed CHŌSOKABE FAMILY to supplement the new Yamanouchi lords (see YAMANOUCHI KAZUTOYO). In Satsuma, where gōshi were concentrated in rural communities of their peers, they were in charge of every village, fishing community, and rural town as well as serving at frontier and highway checkpoints. In Tosa the rank came to be used as an incentive to reward reclamation of land producing at least 30 KOKU of rice (1 koku = about 180 liters or 5 US bushels) annually, with further promotion possible for those particularly successful; gōshi came to number close to one thousand. Thus, even in its narrow meaning, a status designation that signified the recently defeated or least honored ranks of the retainer corps came to serve the broader purpose of upward mobility for a rural elite whose holdings might be scattered and whose residence might become urban.

In its most inclusive sense the term gōshi designated men as different as "regular" castle-town samurai who received permission to live in the countryside, and non-samurai village heads who were given permission to assume surnames and carry swords. By the early 19th century this diverse rural elite had developed considerable awareness of its shared interests and social importance and occasionally demonstrated an irritable resistance to the status pretensions and privileges of castle-town samurai and administrators. Gōshi provided significant numbers of late-Edo and early-Meiji participants in local and national politics. Loyalist groups in Tosa and Chōshū and "peasant" military formations everywhere owed much to these "semi-samurai."

In 1872 the Grand Council of State (DAJŌKAN) classified most gōshi as SHIZOKU (former samurai), thus erasing the disadvantages they had known in the Edo period. Since they retained their lands, in contrast to the urban samurai, who lost their stipends in the reforms of the 1870s (see CHITSUROKU SHOBUN), it was to independent, strong-willed, and responsible social leaders of this sort, "country gentlemen" (inaka no shinshi), that TOKUTOMI SOHŌ and others like him looked for leadership in early Meiji Japan.

📖 ——Irimajiri Yoshinaga, Tokugawa bakuhansei kaitai katei no kenkyū (1957). Marius B. Jansen, Sakamoto Ryōma and the Meiji Restoration (1961). Marius B. Jansen, "Tosa in the Seventeenth Century: The Establishment of Yamauchi Rule," in John W. Hall and Marius B. Jansen, ed, Studies in the Institutional History of Early Modern Japan (1968). Robert K. Sakai, "Feudal Society and Modern Leadership in Satsuma-han," Journal of Asian Studies 16 (May 1957). Robert K. Sakai, ed, The Status System and Social Organization of Satsuma (1975). Marius B. JANSEN

Gōshidai → Gōke shidai

Goshikinuma

Marshes in the Ura Bandai Plateau, northern Fukushima Prefecture, northern Honshū. The group includes such marshes as Akanuma and Aonuma. The name Goshikinuma ("five-colored marshes") refers to the coloration of the waters by minerals and microorganisms.

goshintai

(literally, "body of the divine"). A sacred object in Shintō, regarded as the "support" of the divine, evidencing its presence. Also called shintai, mitama no mikata, mitamashiro, mishōtai. The origins of this phenomenon are obscure, and it appears that not all Shintō divinities were worshiped through a concrete symbol. As shrines were gradually established, certain practices became common, one of which was the choice of a particular object, either natural or manmade, as the "support" of divinities. Natural objects include trees or branches, stones, bodies of water, and mountains; man-made objects include mirrors, swords, polished comma-shaped stones (tama), bells, clothes, dishes, and later, statues or paintings. At the time of religious ceremonies, it is believed that a divinity that is called upon descends and locates itself in the object in question, which then becomes a focus for ritual activity. In general, this object, which is

regarded at all times as sacred, is not visible, for it is kept in the main sanctuary within a box (shirushi no hako; at Ise Shrine mihishiro). When it is paraded, it is installed by the priests in a portable shrine (mikoshi), which is also closed.

Within the tradition of SHRINE SHINTŌ, the divine character of the functions held by the emperor is symbolized by three goshintai, known as the IMPERIAL REGALIA: the mirror, the sword, and the magatama or curved jewels.

It is under the influence of continental culture that the anthropomorphic divinities of Shintō came to be represented in sculpture or painting, and treated as goshintai. This was also the case in the Shintō-Buddhist syncretism, where, for instance, practitioners envisioned the presence of the bodhisattva of compassion (KANNON) in a sacred waterfall, or in a sacred tree or stone. The Shintō deity HACHIMAN was often visualized in Buddhist iconography. What is worshiped is, however, beyond the "form" of the sculpture, the anthropomorphic character of which serves ultimately to suggest the presence of the divine within the human, and a certain combination of elements within the dynamics of nature and culture. See also MISHŌTAI. Allan G. GRAPARD

Go-Shirakawa, Emperor (1127–1192)

The 77th sovereign (tennō) in the traditional count (which includes several nonhistorical emperors); reigned 1155–58. After his abdication he controlled state affairs for 34 turbulent years, which saw the rise and fall of the TAIRA FAMILY and the establishment of the KAMAKURA SHOGUNATE. The fourth son of Emperor TOBA, Go-Shirakawa came to the throne in the face of opposition from the retired emperor SUTOKU; this led to the HŌGEN DISTURBANCE of 1156, after which Go-Shirakawa reaffirmed his authority with Taira support. In his retirement Go-Shirakawa established numerous imperial estates, most notably the CHŌKŌDŌ RYŌ, and strove to maintain the power of the imperial house by unscrupulously playing off factions against one another. In the so-called Shishigatani Conspiracy of 1177 he attempted to dispose of the Taira with the aid of the monk SHUNKAN; in the HEIJI DISTURBANCE of 1160 he cunningly exploited the rivalry between the Taira and the MINAMOTO FAMILY; and finally, in the face of rising Minamoto power, he turned MINAMOTO NO YORITOMO against his younger brother MINAMOTO NO YOSHITSUNE. According to a contemporary, KUJŌ KANEZANE, Go-Shirakawa "could not tell black from white," and even the redoubtable Yoritomo called him the "number-one scoundrel (tengu) in Japan." Yet at the same time, the former sovereign was a fervent Buddhist and an accomplished musician; he was responsible for the compilation of contemporary songs (imayō) called RYŌJIN HISHŌ. G. Cameron HURST III

Goshkevich, Iosif Antonovich (?–1875)

Russian linguist and diplomat in Japan. The son of a village priest, Goshkevich was educated at the seminary in Minsk, Belorussia. In January 1840 (December 1839 according to the old Russian calendar) he set out for Beijing (Peking) by way of the so-called Tea Road through Tibet and Xikang (Hsi-K'ang) as a member of the Russian Orthodox Mission. During almost 10 years of residence in the Chinese capital, Goshkevich became well versed in Chinese language, history, and thought. He also engaged in astronomical observations and studied Chinese agricultural plants. Upon his return to Russia, he became a member of the Asiatic Department of the Russian Foreign Ministry. He served as Chinese language interpreter for the Russian expeditions to Japan from 1852 to 1855 under Vice Admiral Evfimii Vasil'evich PUTIATIN. Tachibana Kōsai (later christened Vladimir Iosifovich Yamatov), a Japanese who was smuggled out by the Russians, became Goshkevich's tutor in the Japanese language. Together they compiled a Japanese-Russian dictionary, published by the Russian Foreign Ministry in 1857 under the dual titles Iaponsko-Russkii slovar' and Wa-Ro tsūgen hikō.

Turning down a professorship in Japanese language at Kazan University, Goshkevich headed back for Japan in 1858 to serve as Russia's first consular representative. In Hakodate, where he lived with his wife Elizaveta Stepanovna and their son Vladimir from 1858 to 1865, Goshkevich continued his Japanese studies. At the same time he acquainted local townspeople with various aspects of Western life and science. In 1865 his wife died in Hakodate after a prolonged illness. The same year a fire which began in the neighboring house of the British consul engulfed Goshkevich's residence and destroyed the library, notes, and assorted materials that he had compiled over the years. Goshkevich returned to Russia and the following year was separated from the foreign service. Settling down near Vilna with his second wife, Ekaterina Semenovna, Goshkevich continued to write until his death in October 1875. His book on the roots of the Japanese language, *O korniakh iaponskogo iazyka,* was published posthumously in Vilna in 1899.

📖 —— V. Guzanov, *Odissei s Beloi Rusi* (1969). George Alexander Lensen, *Report from Hokkaido: The Remains of Russian Culture in Northern Japan* (1954). George Alexander Lensen, *The Russian Push Toward Japan: Russo-Japanese Relations, 1697–1875* (1959). Watanabe Shintarō, comp, *Nichi-Ro kōshō i ho* (1896).

George Alexander LENSEN

Goshogawara

City in western Aomori Prefecture, northern Honshū. Located on an alluvial plain formed by the river Iwakigawa and its tributaries, its principal products are rice and apples. It is also a distribution center for the agricultural produce of the surrounding area. Pop: 50,631.

Gosho Heinosuke (1902–1981)

Film director. Noted for his human interest stories of contemporary life. He made the first successful Japanese sound film, *Madamu to nyōbō* (1931, The Neighbor's Wife and Mine). It was successful because Gosho avoided using sound for its own sake in the rush of technological development. He incorporated the need for sound into the picture's plot: a harried writer is bothered by a jazz band playing next door and complications develop. Gosho's films are almost invariably based on contemporary life, taking as their subject events that disrupt ordinary lives. He found both humor and pathos in equal measure in these lives and though he tended toward sentimentality, his characters are believable and likable. The most notable technical device he employed is the painstaking editing of hundreds of separate shots to create the proper atmosphere for his story and characters. This is in contrast to others who use fewer, longer shots and a less complicated editing scheme.

Among Gosho's finest films are *Entotsu no mieru basho* (1953, Where Chimneys Are Seen), about a childless couple who find an abandoned baby; *Ōsaka no yado* (1954, An Inn at Ōsaka), about the financial difficulties of several women who work at a small hotel; and *Takekurabe* (1955, Growing Up), about the destinies of several adolescents living in a crowded Tōkyō neighborhood at the turn of the century.

David OWENS

Goshun → Matsumura Goshun

gōso

(forceful appeals). A form of protest or appeal made by groups of people to high authorities. During the Heian period (794–1185) deputations of WARRIOR-MONKS *(sōhei)* from the temples ENRYAKUJI and KŌFUKUJI marched into the capital from time to time to protest government policy or, more often, to make unreasonable demands. They usually bore portable shrines or other sacred objects to intimidate the court. These demonstrations proved so effective that Emperor SHIRAKAWA lamented that he could no more control them than he could the river Kamogawa or the roll of the dice. In the Kamakura (1185–1333) and early Muromachi (1333–1568) periods *gōso* referred to peasant demands that the proprietors of landed estates (SHŌEN) lower the land tax (NENGU) and corvée labor (BUYAKU) requirements; aside from collective absconding (CHŌSAN), it was their principal means of protest. Both priestly and peasant protests of this nature disappeared by the end of the 14th century. During the Edo period (1600–1868), and especially from the 1700s onward, *gōso* was used synonymously with HYAKUSHŌ IKKI, armed uprisings by peasants.

gōson system

A rural community system based on the *gōson,* semiautonomous villages that developed from *sō,* local self-governing bodies dating from the 14th century. These villages served as the basic administrative units of the BAKUHAN SYSTEM (shogunate-domain system) of the Tokugawa shogunate (1603–1867).

From the end of the 13th century to the 14th century great economic and political developments took place in the KINAI, the

"capital provinces" centering on Kyōto and Nara, and the surrounding areas. With the disintegration of the *myōden* system—the landholding pattern under the *kōryō* (imperial or public domain) and SHŌEN (private estate) systems—class stratification began to develop among the MYŌSHU (local landholders). The more powerful among them created self-governing organizations called *sō, sōshō,* or *sōjū,* with *gō* and *mura* (villages) as the units of area. Bearing such titles as OTONA, *toshiyori,* and *satanin,* they represented the *sō,* took over the water and IRIAI (commonage) rights that had hitherto been held by *shōen* proprietors, and also assessed and collected NENGU (land taxes) from the villagers. (Tax collection by such local landholders was called *hyakushōuke* or *jigeuke.*) By exclusively holding these collective functions among themselves, they effectively controlled the smaller cultivators.

During the Muromachi period (1333–1568) the *sō* held meetings called *yoriai,* at which they decided on rules regulating the *sō* (called *sō okite),* the administration and operation of irrigation and commonage, as well as punishment for those who violated the *sō* regulations. They also controlled other aspects of village life by taking over the MIYAZA, the local shrine association. At the same time, they organized villagers against exploitation by *shōen* proprietors, SHUGO DAIMYŌ, and KOKUJIN (local gentry) by resorting to group petitions *(gōso),* CHŌSAN (desertion of farmland), and TSUCHI IKKI (peasant uprisings).

In the Sengoku (Warring States) period (1467–1568) the territorial warlords (SENGOKU DAIMYŌ) ruled their domains through the *gōson* as a unit and accelerated the disintegration of the estate system. In the Kinai region, peasant uprisings were extensive. As the coalition of *gōson,* the moving force of the peasant uprisings, spread throughout the domain, some of the influential local landowners *(myōshu)* who headed the *gōson* became armed provincial barons themselves. This phenomenon of GEKOKUJŌ (overturning of those on top by those below) hampered the consolidation of territorial rule by Sengoku daimyō. In parallel with this movement, small farmers, who had grown more independent, also actively resisted their *gōson* overlords. The Sengoku daimyō took advantage of this conflict and, by incorporating *gōson* leaders into their own vassal groups, tried to gain control of the *gōson.*

At the end of the 16th century, by enacting land surveys (KENCHI), *katanagari* (see SWORD HUNT), and laws controlling social classes, the hegemons ODA NOBUNAGA and TOYOTOMI HIDEYOSHI were able to separate the cultivating class from the warrior class. As a result some of the *gōson ryōshu* and influential *myōshu* became vassals of the DAIMYŌ and were forced to live in CASTLE TOWNS. The rest of the farmers were classified into various smaller groupings such as HOMBYAKUSHŌ (propertied farmers), *kobyakushō* (petty farmers), MIZUNOMI-BYAKUSHŌ (landless agricultural laborers), and GENIN (menials, servants). By the method called *muragiri* (village division) village boundaries were redrawn and such administrative divisions as *gō* and *shō,* dating from the *shōen* system, disappeared. Thus did the village evolve into the new administrative unit of the Tokugawa *bakuhan* system.

Social differences existed among the *hombyakushō* (who owned a fixed amount of arable land and were responsible for paying annual taxes) between those who owned more than 10 *chō* (10 hectares or 24.5 acres) of fields and rice paddies and those—the majority—who had less than 5 *tan* (0.5 hectare or 1.2 acres). Besides the *hombyakushō* there were cultivators who did not own land but worked the land owned by influential *hombyakushō* or rented land from others. In addition there were NAGO and *genin,* workers and servants who were indentured to the *hombyakushō.*

The more powerful of the *hombyakushō* or those from older established families became village headmen (called *shōya, nanushi,* or *kimoiri,* depending on the district) and took care of overall village administration; they were assisted by *kumigashira* (group leaders). Later, in the Edo period (1600–1868), *hyakushōdai* (peasant spokesmen), who represented farmers' interests, were appointed. Sometimes several villages were put together into *gō* (districts) or *kumi* (groups), and village leaders variously known as *ōjōya, ōkimoiri,* and *tomura* were appointed.

Each *gōson* was allocated responsibility for a certain amount of taxes based on estimates of the gross production of rice each year. The *hombyakushō* were made collectively responsible for payments, as well as for establishing village regulations pertaining to lawsuits, contracts, and loans within the village, the internal policing of the village, and the proper exercise of commonage and water rights. Neighborhood associations known as GONINGUMI (five-man groups) were set up to enforce joint responsibility and assure mutual surveillance against abuses. These also served as mutual aid associations for production and daily living (called *yui* and *maki*). *Miyaza* or shrine associations were set up to take charge of community ceremonies.

The last years of the Tokugawa shogunate saw such economic and social changes as the crumbling of status distinctions among *hombyakushō* and shifts in the traditional landlord-tenant farmer relationship, for example, merchants became landlords by reclaiming land. The *gōson* system itself was shaken, as cultivators resisted village authorities, villages rebelled (see HYAKUSHŌ IKKI), and peasants participated in millenarian movements (YONAOSHI REBELLIONS). However, even after the fall of the Tokugawa shogunate the new Meiji government retained the *gōson* as an administrative unit. Soon after the establishment of the prefectural system the government enforced the large and small census district *(daiku, shōku)* system in 1872 in order to strengthen centralization, combined towns and villages, and tried in general to crush the autonomy of the villages. In response to opposition from the FREEDOM AND PEOPLE'S RIGHTS MOVEMENT and other groups, a law to organize districts *(gun)*, wards, towns, and villages (Gunkuchōson Hensei Hō) was put into effect in 1878, and the old town and village system was revived. However, in accordance with a revision in 1884, towns and villages were again merged and mayors of the new towns and villages were appointed by the government. Under the *shisei chōsonsei* (municipal organization system) of 1888–90, a nationwide merger of towns and villages was carried out. New villages were organized through a merger of four or five old villages, or from 300 to 500 family units, and the old villages remained as community units under the name of *ōaza*, but the *gōson* system as an administrative unit was dissolved. See also LOCAL GOVERNMENT.　　　　　　　　　　　*SHIMADA Jirō*

Gotemba

City in northeastern Shizuoka Prefecture, central Honshū, at the base of Mt. Fuji (Fujisan) and the Hakone mountains. Gotemba developed as a POST-STATION TOWN and as a base camp for Mt. Fuji. With the opening of the Tōmei Expressway in 1969, acoustic and automobile-related industries have developed. Tourist attractions are the Otome Pass, Komakado Lava Tunnel, and a botanical garden. Pop: 69,221.

Gotō Art Museum

(Gotō Bijutsukan). Located in Tōkyō. A collection of Chinese and Japanese paintings, calligraphy, sutras, ceramics; Chinese mirrors and early jades; Japanese tea-ceremony, lacquer, and archaeological objects; and a few Korean ceramics built around the private collection of the late GOTŌ KEITA. The museum is perhaps best known for its sections of the GENJI MONOGATARI EMAKI, a well-known picture scroll (EMAKIMONO) of the Heian period (794–1185). It also owns *emakimono* from the Kamakura period (1185–1333), Heian and Kamakura religious paintings and decorated sutras, and examples of RIMPA painting. The large collection of Japanese CALLIGRAPHY includes fragments of anthologies copied in the Heian period and attributed to FUJIWARA NO KINTŌ, ONO NO TŌFU, Fujiwara no Sukemasa (944–998), KI NO TSURAYUKI, and FUJIWARA NO YUKINARI. Chinese paintings of the Song dynasty (Sung; 960–1297) include a bird attributed to Muqi (Mu-ch'i; J: MOKKEI) and a duck attributed to the emperor Huizong (Hui-tsung). Among the objects connected with the TEA CEREMONY are well-known Raku teabowls (see RAKU WARE) created by CHŌJIRŌ, Nonkō (1599–1656), and HON'AMI KŌETSU. Japanese archaeology is represented by a group of gilt-bronze harness trappings excavated at the Kofun-period (ca 300–710) SAITOBARU TOMB CLUSTER in Miyazaki Prefecture. The Dai Tōkyū Memorial Library of Chinese and Japanese books adjoins the museum.　　　　　　　　　　　*Laurance ROBERTS*

Go-Toba, Emperor (1180–1239)

The 82nd sovereign *(tennō)* in the traditional count (which includes several nonhistorical emperors); reigned 1183–98; his given name was Takahito and his Buddhist name after taking orders in 1221 was Ryōzen. After his death he was first called Kentoku and later Go-Toba, by which name he is known to history. He was also called the Oki ex-emperor from the place of exile in which he spent the last years of his life. The fourth son of Emperor Takakura (1161–81; r 1168–80) and a Fujiwara court lady, Go-Toba was placed on the throne at the age of three. He remained titular sovereign for 15 years, abdicating at the age of eighteen. Thenceforth for 23 years he

exercised as ex-emperor such actual imperial power as existed, placing his sons TSUCHIMIKADO (1195–1231; r 1198–1210) and JUNTOKU (1197–1242; r 1210–21) and then Juntoku's son Chūkyō (1218–34; r 1221) in turn upon the throne.

Go-Toba was one of the most intelligent and gifted of Japan's many emperors, and one of the most active. He was the foremost patron of literature and the arts of his time, and a talented poet in the courtly tradition of the noble dilettante. His intention was to rule as well as reign, and both culturally and politically to make his age equal in brilliance to those of Emperors DAIGO (885–930; r 897–930) and Murakami (926–967; r 946–967), which he idealized. But his attempt to concentrate the real power in his own hands led eventually to disaster. Determined even before his abdication to bring down the "illegitimate" Minamoto–Hōjō shogunal regime at Kamakura and "restore" authority to the Kyōto court, Go-Toba and his close adherents began military preparations on the death of the first Minamoto shogun, MINAMOTO NO YORITOMO, in 1199. The blow was finally struck in 1221, when in the brief JŌKYŪ DISTURBANCE, Go-Toba forced Juntoku to abdicate in favor of his son Chūkyō and issued an edict for the destruction of HŌJŌ YOSHITOKI who was the power behind the infant shogun Kujō Yoritsune. The ex-sovereign's forces attacked the shogunal warden in Kyōto, who committed suicide; but they were swiftly and utterly defeated by a large force from Kamakura which marched on the capital, deposed Chūkyō after a reign of only 70-odd days, and set up yet another new emperor of their own choosing, Go-Horikawa (1212–34; r 1221–32). The three ex-emperors went into exile: Go-Toba to the island of Oki, Tsuchimikado to the province of Tosa (now Kōchi Prefecture) in Shikoku, and Juntoku to the island of Sado. Go-Toba was destined never to return to Kyōto, spending all 18 of his remaining years on the inhospitable island of Oki in the Sea of Japan.

A man of great energy and many talents, but willful and capricious, Go-Toba took a lively interest in military and athletic pursuits and in the arts, especially after his abdication freed him from the extremely confined, ritualized life of a reigning sovereign. Possessing several country estates ("detached palaces") in different places around the capital, he used his newfound freedom as ex-sovereign to move restlessly from one to the other and back to the capital again, staging cockfights, wrestling matches, archery contests, equestrian races, singing performances by female entertainers, and most important, poetry meetings and contests. He also made frequent pilgrimages to the important Shintō-Buddhist cult center of Kumano, his hapless courtiers struggling over rugged mountain roads with stops along the way at branch shrines, where the ex-sovereign convened poetry gatherings and entertainments to honor the local deities and offered ostentatious prayers for the overthrow of the Kamakura regime. He practiced swordsmanship and is said to have tempered swords with his own hands and given them to his courtiers to wear; he went out to Uji between Kyōto and Nara to swim in the river; he played kickball (KEMARI) and wrote a treatise on the subject known as *Ommari no ki* (Chronicle of Ball Playing), of which only a fragment survives. He also took a great interest in music, especially the lute (BIWA), about which he wrote a work entitled *Ombiwa-awase* (Contest of Royal Lutes). Only a fragment of his personal diary, *Shinki* (Royal Chronicle), is extant.

It was as a poet and patron of the native poetry, however, that Go-Toba stands out in Japanese cultural history. He began to take a serious interest in WAKA, or Japanese poetry, immediately after his abdication. Officially his teacher was the great Fujiwara no Shunzei (FUJIWARA NO TOSHINARI) and although the actual contact between them was probably minimal, Shunzei being 84 years old to Go-Toba's 18, the ex-sovereign always treated the master with marked respect, and his poetic taste was shaped in large measure by Shunzei's ideals. Go-Toba threw himself into the writing of poetry and the sponsorship of poetry meetings, contests, and the like with characteristic gusto. Immediately after his abdication it became common knowledge that he intended to commission a new imperial anthology, and many of the poetic events he sponsored were for the purpose of creating a fresh stock of poems from the most talented poets of the day to be considered for inclusion in this eighth imperial collection. And because the writing of poetry had by this time come to be regarded by dedicated poets as a quasi-religious way of life, competition was intense, particularly between the Mikohidari family and the school of Shunzei and his son Fujiwara no Teika (FUJIWARA NO SADAIE) on the one hand and the more conservative and less brilliant Rokujō school of Fujiwara no Suetsune (1131–1221), KENSHŌ, and their supporters on the other. Each group was backed by great nobles, whose political rivalries were matched by their patronage of competing poetic factions.

Go-Toba himself, though raised above all partisan dispute in his exalted station, was in a way caught between the rival groups. Shunzei (himself placed above politics by his prestige as the great arbiter and grand old man of Japanese poetry) was Go-Toba's revered teacher; at the same time, Go-Toba's father-in-law, Minamoto no Michichika (1149–1202), had a good deal of influence over him and was the foremost patron of the Rokujō school while politically the enemy of the Kujō family, the patrons of Shunzei's Mikohidari faction.

The political and poetic rivalries came to the fore in the so-called Hundred-Poem Sequences of the Shōji Era, two successive poetic events of 1200, of which the earlier was the first important poetic occasion commissioned by Go-Toba after his abdication. Suetsune contrived through his influence with Michichika to have Teika and several other important Mikohidari partisans omitted from the participants, and it was only because of a direct plea from Shunzei that Go-Toba commanded that Teika be added to the list. Thereafter Go-Toba continued to favor the Mikohidari school as well as the Rokujō, and his relative impartiality and general enthusiasm played a major part in making the late 12th and early 13th centuries a brilliant epoch for court poetry.

Another of Go-Toba's important poetic acts was the establishment in 1201 of a Bureau of Poetry (Wakadokoro) at his Nijō palace, and the appointment of 11 fellows (yoriudo) from the most prominent and promising literati of both conservative and innovating factions. The Bureau of Poetry immediately became the scene of numerous poetry gatherings, and more important, it provided the base for work on the new imperial anthology, the ex-sovereign in 1201 designating a committee of 6 of the 11 fellows as official compilers. The eighth such imperial anthology, the new collection was given the name SHIN KOKINSHŪ (New Collection of Ancient and Modern Times), thus proclaiming that it was to be a worthy successor to the first and most honored of the imperial anthologies, the KOKINSHŪ of 905. Although the committee did the ground work of selecting poems and determining their place in the collection, Go-Toba retained veto power, taking an unusually lively interest in the enterprise, and his final decisions were often at variance with the compilers', especially the stubborn and acerbic Teika. The resulting anthology, containing both old and new poems and constructed so as to invite comparison with its illustrious ancestor the Kokinshū, was a brilliant product of a brilliant poetic age. The intricate and ingenious structure of the anthology, the succession of poems within its 20 books determined by complex and subtle principles of association and progression, was probably due at least as much to the former emperor's taste as to any of the compilers. Not surprisingly, although the anthology was celebrated as complete in 1205, deletions and substitutions continued to be made at Go-Toba's command long afterward.

While work on the Shin kokinshū was progressing, Go-Toba continued to stage poetic events of many kinds. The single most important was the epoch-making Sengohyakuban uta-awase, or Poetry Contest in 1,500 Rounds, commissioned in 1201 and probably completed in late 1202. This was a poetry contest put together from sequences of 100 poems written by the ex-emperor and 29 other poets, the 3,000 resulting poems being paired into 1,500 rounds, with Go-Toba and nine other major participants acting as judges of different segments of the whole. Go-Toba's enthusiasm was largely diverted into other interests after the Shin kokinshū was officially completed in 1205, but he continued to fuss over the collection, revising it over and over by adding and deleting poems. He resumed this work during his years in exile, having little else to occupy him, and the resulting text (no longer extant as such) is known as the Oki text.

The best of Go-Toba's own poetry is of excellent quality, if not quite up to the standard of such "professional" poets as Shunzei or Teika. It is of a prevailingly conservative stamp in the great tradition of courtly elegance inherited from the Kokinshū, and for this reason the ex-sovereign may be described as one of the middle-of-the-road "rhetoricians" of the age. At the same time, his style is tempered by certain personal preferences and modified in accordance with the new ideals of his time. He greatly admired Shunzei and Saigyō among the older poets of the period, and he accepted the aesthetic ideals of Shunzei and his school: tonal depth and resonance, purity of poetic diction, elegance and grace of phrasing and cadence. He particularly favored the "lofty style" (taketakaki yō) of noble and elevated forthrightness often conveyed in simple declaration or panoramic description of nature. Some 2,364 of his poems survive in variant texts of his personal collection and in other sources. During his exile he communicated with a few of his former courtiers in the capital, with whom he exchanged poems. In 1236 he even conducted, with the help of the faithful FUJIWARA NO IETAKA, a modest poetry contest known as the "Poetry Contest from the Distant Isles" (Entō Uta-awase). For this the ex-emperor had Ietaka send him sets of 10 poems composed for the occasion by some of his former associates in the capital, which he then paired (including 10 of his own) into 80 rounds and judged, writing out his decisions for each round. Many of Go-Toba's poems written in exile deal with his loneliness and unhappiness in quite direct terms, and their insistent demands for sympathy can seem rather overdone to the Western reader. However, they have been greatly admired by many Japanese, who have responded to the plight of the ex-sovereign himself as much as to his poems.

During his exile, Go-Toba also wrote a poetic treatise commonly known as Go-Toba no In gokuden (Ex-Emperor Go-Toba's Secret Teachings) which despite its brevity is one of the important poetic documents of the age. Ostensibly written as a kind of primer, the treatise gives the ex-sovereign's evaluation of a number of poets, past and present, together with a few guidelines and words of advice to the aspiring poet; but nearly half of the treatise is given over to sharp criticism of Teika, with whom Go-Toba had been on increasingly cold terms ever since differences of opinion over the Shin kokinshū had begun to divide them many years before. Besides the traditional court poetry in the 31-syllable form, Go-Toba also wrote poetry in Chinese, and he was an enthusiast of renga, or linked verse, a relatively new poetic genre that was beginning to come into popularity in his day. The TSUKUBASHŪ (1356), the first anthology of superior renga stanzas, contains 18 of the ex-sovereign's verses. Thirty-four of Go-Toba's poems were included in the Shin kokinshū, and some 219 more in later imperial anthologies.

■——Robert H. Brower, "Ex-Emperor Go-Toba's Secret Teachings: Go-Toba no In gokuden," Harvard Journal of Asiatic Studies 32 (1972). Robert H. Brower and Earl Miner, Japanese Court Poetry (1961).   Robert H. BROWER

Gotō Chūgai (1866–1938)

Novelist. Born in Akita Prefecture. Real name Gotō Toranosuke. Graduate of Tōkyō Semmon Gakkō (now Waseda University). Adept at psychological description, he played an active part in the literary world of the middle Meiji period (1868–1912). Gotō edited Shinshōsetsu, a prominent literary magazine, from 1900 on and made it successful with the help of writers belonging to the KEN'YŪSHA (Friends of the Inkstone), an influential circle in the literary world. He criticized Japanese NATURALISM (shizen shugi), which began to flourish at that time. His writings include Funikudan (1899), a collection of short stories, Hi shizen shugi (1908), an essay collection, and Meiji bundan kaikoroku (1936), a reminiscence about the Meiji literary establishment.   ASAI Kiyoshi

Gotō Fumio (1884–1980)

Bureaucrat and politician. Born in Ōita Prefecture; graduate of Tōkyō University. Gotō held high positions in the Home Ministry, served as director of administration in the Government-General of Taiwan, and in 1930 was appointed to the House of Peers. A leader of the so-called new bureaucrats (shinkanryō), who after the MANCHURIAN INCIDENT (1931) were sympathetic with the militarists and favored military expansion, he served in turn as minister of agriculture in the SAITŌ MAKOTO cabinet, home minister and acting prime minister in the OKADA KEISUKE cabinet, and finally minister of state in the TŌJŌ HIDEKI cabinet. Barred from public office by the OCCUPATION authorities after World War II, he later returned to politics and in 1953 was elected to the House of Councillors.

Gotō Islands

(Gotō Rettō). Group of islands in the East China Sea, west of the Nishi Sonogi Peninsula, Nagasaki Prefecture, Kyūshū. The group includes Nakadōrishima, Wakamatsujima, Narushima, Hisakajima, and Fukuejima. These islands are rich in heavily indented coastlines created by the sinking of horst mountains. Fishing is the chief industry with abundant catches of horse mackerel, mackerel, and sardines. Sweet potatoes are cultivated on terraced land. Located near the Chinese mainland, the islands have played a historic role as a stopping place for priests dispatched to China and as a base for pirates. The islands have been the site of numerous Christian hamlets since the Edo period (1600–1868) and are part of the Saikai National Park. Area: 632 sq km (244 sq mi).

Gotō Katsu (1863–1889)

Early spokesman for the Japanese community in Hawaii. Born in 1863 in what is now Kanagawa Prefecture, he was recruited at the age of 22 for a three-year contract as sugar plantation laborer in Hawaii. After the expiration of his contract, he opened a general store in Honokaa and served other plantation workers as an interpreter and adviser in the endless labor disputes resulting from their harsh working conditions. During one such dispute he was killed by agents of the planter R. M. Overend in the first lynching of a Japanese living outside of Japan. A jury in Hilo found four of the seven lynchers guilty after three became state witnesses.

Karl G. YONEDA

Gotō Keita (1882–1959)

Entrepreneur. Founder of the TŌKYŪ CORPORATION, a major conglomerate comprising electric railways, tourism, department stores, and real estate, based in the Tōkyō–Yokohama area. Gotō was born in Nagano Prefecture, and graduated from Tōkyō University. After serving in the government (including the Railway Agency) for 10 years, Gotō became very successful in railroad construction in the Tōkyō suburbs. He later successively amalgamated other railroad companies in the suburban Tōkyō area, becoming the most powerful man in the Japanese private railway industry. He moved into bus transportation, department stores, and motion pictures during World War II. When the Excessive Economic Power Decentralization Law was passed after World War II, he was forced to relinquish control of five railroad companies which had been amalgamated during the war. Although purged by the Occupation authorities after the war, Gotō later returned to active business life, once again gaining control of a majority of railroad and bus companies in the southern part of Tōkyō. He also made investments in housing land development and tourist facilities. Enthusiastic about cultural affairs, he created the network of schools and colleges known as the Gotō Ikueikai and the GOTŌ ART MUSEUM. *YUI Tsunehiko*

Gotō Konzan (1659–1733)

Doctor of the Edo period (1600–1868). Classicist school *(koihō)*. Also called Gotō Saichirō. Born in Edo (now Tōkyō). Gotō studied medicine on his own after being turned down by NAGOYA GEN'I, a teacher of *koihō*. He subsequently achieved fame as a physician. Gotō regarded the cause of all diseases as being the stagnancy of *ki* (Ch: *qi* or *ch'i*), the vital energy that existed in the universe. He defined health *(genki)* as that condition in which the body is filled with this energy, and advocated that medical treatment be based on *junki*, i.e., correcting the imbalance of *ki*. He frequently used MOXA TREATMENT and recommended hot spring therapy and such medicines as dried bear gall. See also MEDICINE: history of medicine. *YAMADA Terutane*

Gotō Mitsutsugu (1571–1625)

Also known as Gotō Shōzaburō. Metalworker and minter; probably born in Ōmi Province (now Shiga Prefecture). In Kyōto he became a disciple of the master metalworker Gotō Tokujō (1547–1631), who allowed him to adopt the Gotō name, and through this connection entered the service of the future shōgun TOKUGAWA IEYASU. While still a *daimyō* in Suruga (now part of Shizuoka Prefecture), Ieyasu employed Mitsutsugu to mint gold coins (see ŌBAN; KOBAN). In 1601, having gained control of the country, he appointed Mitsutsugu head of the *kinza*, the official gold mint (see KINZA, GINZA, AND ZENIZA). In that capacity, Mitsutsugu was instrumental in establishing a standardized national currency and served also as an adviser to the Tokugawa shogunate in matters of finance, trade, and diplomacy. His heirs and successors, all of whom retained the name Shōzaburō, served as directors of the *kinza* until the dissolution of that institution in 1869. The ōban coins minted by the Gotō all bore their distinctive family mark.

Gotō Ryūnosuke (1889–   )

Political figure of the decade preceding World War II; close adviser to KONOE FUMIMARO, who served twice as prime minister (1937–39 and 1940–41).

Gotō and Konoe were longtime friends; they were classmates at the First Higher School in Tōkyō and at Kyōto University. Later, Gotō secured a position in the Japan Youth Hall (Nihon Seinenkan), in which Konoe served as an executive director. Gotō soon became active in the national Youth Association (Seinendan) and later helped to form the Young Adult Association (Sōnendan) movement to study Japan's agricultural problems and to build a mass base for a new political party.

Perceiving a national crisis in 1933, Gotō created a study group of intellectuals and government officials to devise policies for a future Konoe cabinet. This group, under Gotō's direction, evolved into the Shōwa Research Association (SHŌWA KENKYŪKAI), which the media labeled as Konoe's "brain trust." In 1940 Gotō's influence on Premier Konoe was particularly evident during the latter's NEW ORDER MOVEMENT (Shin Taisei Undō), planned by the association as an attempt to replace the established political parties with a new "national organization." Gotō assumed a top post in the resulting IMPERIAL RULE ASSISTANCE ASSOCIATION (Taisei Yokusankai) in the fall of 1940 but was forced to resign within six months because of allegations that he was a communist.

After 1945 Gotō was active in the Shōwa Brotherhood (Shōwa Dōjinkai), an organization led by former Shōwa Research Association members who promoted public discussion of important issues facing Japan.

🔳——Sakai Saburō, *Shōwa kenkyūkai: Aru chishikijin shūdan no kiseki* (1979). *Wm. Miles* FLETCHER III

Gotō Shimpei (1857–1929)

Bureaucrat of the Meiji (1868–1912) and Taishō (1912–26) periods; he established his reputation as a brilliant administrator through service in various medical institutes and in government positions in Taiwan, Manchuria, and Tōkyō. Born in the Mizusawa domain (in what is now Iwate Prefecture) as the son of a *samurai* of the Sendai domain (now Miyagi Prefecture). Shortly after the Meiji Restoration (1868), Gotō began to study medicine at the Sukagawa Igakkō in Fukushima Prefecture and graduated in 1876. He continued his studies at the Nagoya Medical School and also worked at the Aichi Prefectural Hospital. In 1877 Gotō served as a physician for the government during the SATSUMA REBELLION. A few years later Gotō, then only 25, was appointed president of the Nagoya Medical School. In this capacity he gained fame for his outspoken views on hospital management, social welfare, and health education. In 1890 Gotō was sent to Germany to study, and upon his return he was appointed chief of the medical bureau of the Home Ministry. An appointment in 1895 as director of the Army Quarantine Office further added to his prestige as a medical administrator. In 1898 Gotō became civilian governor of Taiwan (under the governor-general) and was put in charge of all governmental affairs on that island. Gotō sought to establish a constructive and evenhanded civil rule. He created monopolies in camphor and salt, built railways, encouraged industries in general, and founded educational and health facilities. His constructive administration brought him an appointment in 1903 to the House of Peers and in 1906 to the presidency of the newly created SOUTH MANCHURIA RAILWAY Company. In 1908 Gotō was appointed minister of communications and director-general of the Railway Agency (Tetsudōin) and the Colonization Bureau (Takushokukyoku) in the second KATSURA TARŌ cabinet. He continued to oversee the affairs of the South Manchurian Railway through these agencies. In 1912 Gotō again served as minister of communications in the third Katsura cabinet. Following the TAISHŌ POLITICAL CRISIS of 1912–13, he assisted Katsura in organizing a political party, the RIKKEN DŌSHIKAI, which brought together groups opposed to HARA TAKASHI and his RIKKEN SEIYŪKAI.

In 1916 Gotō was appointed home minister and then in 1918 minister of foreign affairs in the TERAUCHI MASATAKE cabinet. As a leader of the Provisional Foreign Affairs Research Committee, he advocated an aggressive and expansionist diplomacy. An avid pan-Asianist, he promoted the establishment, with government funds, of an East Asian Economic League that would rely on Japanese capital and Chinese labor. Funds earmarked for this project, however, were used for corrupt adventures abroad, as in the NISHIHARA LOANS, leading to severe criticism of Gotō. He also endorsed the plan to send Japanese troops to Siberia during the Russian Revolution, a project that turned into a fiasco and stirred further criticism (see SIBERIAN INTERVENTION).

After the Russian Revolution, Gotō turned his attention to establishing formal diplomatic ties with the new regime through discussions with Soviet representatives. During this same period Gotō, who had been appointed mayor of Tōkyō in 1920 and home minister in 1923, contributed enormously to the reconstruction of the capital following the devastation of the TŌKYŌ EARTHQUAKE OF 1923.

Although Gotō was known primarily for his administrative skills, he was also described as a man of many talents, one who could do almost anything. Besides promoting a number of grandiose imperialist schemes, he was an organizer and president of the Boy Scouts of Japan, head of the Japan-Russia Society, president of Takushoku University, an active member of the Association of East Asian Societies, and a vigorous promoter of a movement for ethical government. He also wrote numerous articles on a wide variety of subjects, including the effective use of ocean water, problems of public health, political ethics, and the Swiss system of workmen's compensation.

📖 —— Tsurumi Yūsuke, Gotō Shimpei den, 10 vols (1944).

Tetsuo Najita

Gotō Shōjirō (1838–1897)

Politician of the latter part of the Edo period (1600–1868) and early part of the Meiji period (1868–1912). Born in the domain of Tosa (now Kōchi Prefecture). Recognized by the reformist *daimyō* YAMANOUCHI TOYOSHIGE, Gotō played an influential role in formulating the military and economic policies of the domain. Eventually, under the influence of his fellow Tosa *samurai* SAKAMOTO RYŌMA, Gotō was drawn to the proimperial (SONNŌ JŌI) cause, which was then gaining momentum. Hoping to counter the growing influence of the more belligerent domains, Chōshū (now Yamaguchi Prefecture) and Satsuma (now Kagoshima Prefecture), through Toyoshige he called on the shōgun TOKUGAWA YOSHINOBU to return rule peaceably to the emperor (see TAISEI HŌKAN). After the MEIJI RESTORATION (1868) he was appointed to high posts, among them *san'yo* (junior councillor), governor of Ōsaka Prefecture, and vice-minister of public works *(kōbu tayū)*. In 1873 he was appointed *sangi* (councillor) but resigned in opposition to the government's decision not to invade Korea (see SEIKANRON). Together with ITAGAKI TAISUKE, who had also resigned, Gotō formed the AIKOKU KŌTŌ, the predecessor of the JIYŪTŌ (Liberal Party), and petitioned the government for a representative assembly. After the ŌSAKA CONFERENCE OF 1875 he rejoined the government as a member of the GENRŌIN (Senate) but resigned soon after. He managed the TAKASHIMA COAL MINE in Kyūshū for a time, but failing to realize profits, he sold his interests to IWASAKI YATARŌ, the founder of the Mitsubishi industrial combine. In 1881 he joined Itagaki in forming the Jiyūtō and criticized the government for its domination by the Satsuma and Chōshū cliques (HAMBATSU). The following year, however, he and Itagaki were persuaded by the government to travel to Europe, with funds from MITSUI, to study political institutions, an act that was seen as a betrayal by members of the FREEDOM AND PEOPLE'S RIGHTS MOVEMENT. After his return to Japan, he tried unsuccessfully to help KIM OK-KYUN establish a reform government in Korea. In 1887 he organized the DAIDŌ DANKETSU MOVEMENT to press the government for revision of the so-called unequal treaties (see UNEQUAL TREATIES, REVISION OF). However, in the face of growing government repression, he deserted the movement and joined the KURODA KIYOTAKA cabinet as communications minister. He held the same post in the YAMAGATA ARITOMO and MATSUKATA MASAYOSHI cabinets and was named agriculture and commerce minister in the second ITŌ HIROBUMI cabinet but he resigned when he was implicated in a scandal concerning the establishment of a stock exchange.

Gotō Shuichi (1888–1960)

Archaeologist. Born in Shizuoka Prefecture. After graduating from Tōkyō Higher Normal School (later Tōkyō University of Education) in 1913, he taught at a middle school in Shizuoka and became interested in archaeology. In 1921 he joined the staff of the Tōkyō Imperial Household Museum (now the Tōkyō National Museum) and in 1927 traveled to Europe and the United States to study museum facilities. He subsequently became a professor at Meiji University

and served as a specialist adviser to the National Commission for the Protection of Cultural Properties.

Gotō had broad interests in Japanese prehistory and early history, directing excavations at the TORO SITE and ŌYU STONE CIRCLES and acting as secretary for the Archaeological Society of Nippon. His specialty, however, was the mounded tombs (KOFUN) and culture of the Kofun period (ca 300–710). His major works include *Nihon kōkogaku* (1927, Japanese Archaeology) and *Nihon rekishi kōkogaku* (1937, Japanese Historical Archaeology). *Abe Gihei*

Gōtsu

City in central Shimane Prefecture, western Honshū, at the mouth of the river Gōnokawa. Gōtsu developed in the Edo period (1600–1868) as a port town on the Sea of Japan. Its main industry is ceramics (Gōtsu rust-colored tiles are known for their endurance); pulp and textile industries are also well established. The *tōro nagashi* (casting lanterns on the water as offerings to the departed), an event held every August during the Bon Festival, is well known. Pop: 28,264.

Go-Uda, Emperor (1267–1324)

The 91st sovereign *(tennō)* in the traditional count (which includes several nonhistorical emperors); reigned 1274–87. Son and successor of Emperor KAMEYAMA, the founder of the Daikakuji line of the imperial family, he lived in an era of intense rivalry over the succession to the throne. Go-Uda was succeeded on his abdication by the emperors FUSHIMI (1265–1317; r 1287–98) and Go-Fushimi (1288–1336; r 1298–1301), both of the rival Jimyōin line; he later induced the Kamakura shogunate to recognize officially the tradition that had already developed of alternating succession from the two lines, and as a result he was able to exercise political control from retirement during the reigns of his sons, the emperors Go-Nijō (1285–1308; r 1301–08) and GO-DAIGO (1288–1339; r 1318–39). From 1322 onward, however, Go-Daigo was determined to rule in his own right, and Go-Uda's influence came to an end. Thereafter he devoted himself almost exclusively to scholarship and the practice of ESOTERIC BUDDHISM. *G. Cameron Hurst III*

government agricultural policy → agriculture

government bonds

(kokusai). The Public Finance Law, the fundamental law governing the management of public finance in Japan, stipulates that the central government operate on a balanced budget, but it also authorizes the issuance of government bonds for government investment projects. The law provides that these bonds be sold on the open market to banks, corporations, and individuals, but it prohibits their sale to the BANK OF JAPAN.

The general account budget of the central government remained in balance between 1947 and 1964, the first period of a balanced budget since the Meiji period (1868–1912). This was made possible by Japan's rapid economic growth during this period; even with annual tax cuts through the revision of tax laws, tax revenues rose faster than the gross national product, thus assuring a balanced budget.

Since 1965, when the government increased its expenditures to provide recession relief and issued bonds to cover the cost, the government has issued bonds each year. During the 1970s the bond issue exceeded investment expenditures. The continuing issue of bonds is in part a response to the worldwide recession that followed the oil crisis early in the decade, and in part the result of government policy to stimulate domestic demand in order to reduce the surplus in the international balance of payments. In addition to central government bonds, PUBLIC CORPORATIONS finance their operations through bond issues, which are made in the same manner as those of private enterprises. Government bonds issued in fiscal 1979 amounted to ¥15.3 trillion (US $69.5 billion), equivalent to 39.9 percent of the total revenue. The national debt at the end of 1978 stood at ¥43 trillion (US $203.7 billion). *Udagawa Akihito*

government compensation

(kokka baishō). Compensation for damages paid by a government or a public body when it illegally invades the rights of a citizen. This legal responsibility is called both state tort liability and state liability.

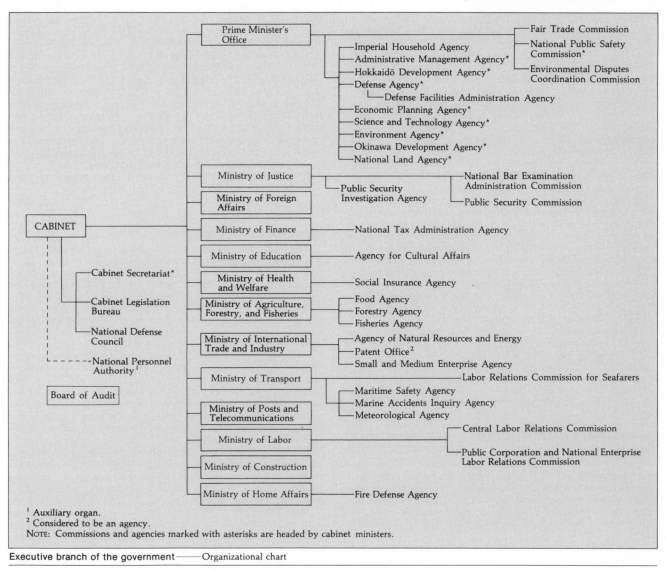

Executive branch of the government ——— Organizational chart

Inside chart:

Prime Minister's Office

- Fair Trade Commission
- National Public Safety Commission*
- Environmental Disputes Coordination Commission

- Imperial Household Agency
- Administrative Management Agency*
- Hokkaidō Development Agency*
- Defense Agency*
  - Defense Facilities Administration Agency
- Economic Planning Agency*
- Science and Technology Agency*
- Environment Agency*
- Okinawa Development Agency*
- National Land Agency*

CABINET

- Cabinet Secretariat*
- Cabinet Legislation Bureau
- National Defense Council
- National Personnel Authority[1]

Board of Audit

Ministry of Justice — Public Security Investigation Agency — National Bar Examination Administration Commission / Public Security Commission

Ministry of Foreign Affairs

Ministry of Finance — National Tax Administration Agency

Ministry of Education — Agency for Cultural Affairs

Ministry of Health and Welfare — Social Insurance Agency

Ministry of Agriculture, Forestry, and Fisheries — Food Agency / Forestry Agency / Fisheries Agency

Ministry of International Trade and Industry — Agency of Natural Resources and Energy / Patent Office[2] / Small and Medium Enterprise Agency

Ministry of Transport — Labor Relations Commission for Seafarers / Maritime Safety Agency / Marine Accidents Inquiry Agency / Meteorological Agency

Ministry of Posts and Telecommunications

Ministry of Labor — Central Labor Relations Commission / Public Corporation and National Enterprise Labor Relations Commission

Ministry of Construction

Ministry of Home Affairs — Fire Defense Agency

[1] Auxiliary organ.
[2] Considered to be an agency.
NOTE: Commissions and agencies marked with asterisks are headed by cabinet ministers.

Under the Meiji Constitution there was not always compensatory liability for the TORTS of the government and public bodies. In other words, the basic premise with respect to the activities of the government and public bodies was that, under the principle of sovereign immunity, the national government would not bear any compensatory responsibility for torts caused by the use of powers such as the police or the taxing power. Since 1915, however, it has been recognized that there is government liability for harm caused by defects in the administration of structures such as roads, rivers, and harbors. Moreover, under the CIVIL CODE, government compensatory liability was recognized for torts caused by the government's operation and administration of profitable enterprises.

The 1947 constitution, recognizing basic human rights, guarantees the right of the people to seek compensation for damages (art. 17). Based upon this principle, the State Compensation Law and various special laws were enacted. The substance of those laws is as follows: First, with respect to injuries caused by an exercise of the authority of the government or a public body, the government or public body bears liability for compensation when a public official, in the exercise of his duties, uses his public authority and, intentionally or negligently, illegally injures another person. Second, when a person is injured by the defective administration or establishment of a public enterprise, such as a road or river, the government or public body will bear compensatory liability. Third, compensatory liability will be imposed by the Civil Code for injuries caused by those types of activities not covered under the State Compensation Law.

Compensatory liability is also governed by separate individual laws, such as article 68 of the Postal Law, article 27 of the Postal Savings Law, article 15 of the Postal Exchange Law, article 109 of the

Public Telecommunications Law, and the Law regarding Compensation for Special Damages Caused by Acts of the United States Armed Forces, etc, stationed in Japan. NARITA Yoriaki

government educational policy → education

government, executive branch

(gyōseifu). The central administrative section of the Japanese government. It consists of the cabinet and the organizations under its control and jurisdiction: the PRIME MINISTER'S OFFICE and 12 ministries, as well as 24 agencies and 8 commissions.

According to the 1947 CONSTITUTION of Japan, the executive power is vested in the cabinet (art. 65). The cabinet (naikaku) consists of the prime minister and 20 ministers of state and is collectively responsible to the DIET, the highest organ of the state.

The prime minister (naikaku sōri daijin) is designated by the Diet from among its members and nominally appointed by the emperor. As the head of the cabinet, he appoints or dismisses the ministers of state (kokumu daijin). More than half of these ministers must be Diet members. The prime minister, representing the cabinet, submits bills to the Diet, supervises and controls the administrative branch, and reports on national and foreign affairs to the Diet. The cabinet is charged with the formulation of national policy, the preparation of the annual budget, the conduct of foreign relations and the conclusion of treaties, the administration of the civil service, and the administration of government programs and laws. See also PRIME MINISTER AND CABINET.

The responsibility for national administration is initially assigned to the 12 ministries and the Prime Minister's Office (Sōrifu), the latter performing the functions that do not fall to any of the ministries. Agencies are set up as independent organs of the ministries and the Prime Minister's Office, to take on part of their responsibilities with substantial independence. Commissions are also set up as independent panels to perform mainly adjudicatory functions on matters requiring impartiality in judgments. Several agencies of the Prime Minister's Office are headed by ministers of state and enjoy cabinet status. The chairman of the NATIONAL PUBLIC SAFETY COMMISSION and the chief cabinet secretary (naikaku kambō chōkan) are also ministers of state.

The cabinet is assisted by the Cabinet Secretariat (Naikaku Kambō), the Cabinet Legislation Bureau (Hōseikyoku), the NATIONAL DEFENSE COUNCIL, and the NATIONAL PERSONNEL AUTHORITY. The Cabinet Secretariat, besides providing numerous staff services for the cabinet, coordinates and integrates the administrative measures of government offices in order to maintain a general uniformity and consistency of government measures. The Cabinet Legislation Bureau reviews draft legislation proposed by the ministries and agencies before its submission to the Diet. The National Defense Council deliberates on matters concerning national defense.

The BOARD OF AUDIT is guaranteed independence from the cabinet. It audits the final accounts of state expenditures and revenues and investigates the financial procedures of all public offices. Its annual statement of audit is submitted to the Diet.

In addition, a fairly large amount of the activities of the state are delegated to the heads of local governments, in accordance with the Local Autonomy Law (Chihō Jichi Hō, art. 150). Governors and mayors are called "state agencies" when they carry out delegated state business. Further, in order to perform state business more efficiently, special PUBLIC CORPORATIONS have been established; these totaled 106 as of 1982.

government grants-in-aid

(hojokin). Government subsidies, primarily from the central government of Japan to local governments. In principle, prefectural and municipal governments are totally responsible for the expenses of their administration, but the national government assists in the payment of social welfare, public works projects, disaster relief, and other major government expenses. The assistance comes in the form of treasury grants, which totaled ¥7.8 trillion (US $29.1 billion) in 1977.

Such grants-in-aid are considered an effective means of ensuring local execution of national policies and provision of governmental services. The assistance also enables local governments to provide disaster relief and undertake large-scale construction projects that would otherwise exceed the scope of their ordinary revenue. Aid is granted on the basis of need, and serves to standardize the quality of government services throughout the nation. At the same time, central government assistance has been criticized for leading to excessive dependence and opening the door for national government intervention in local affairs. Inadequate provision of aid has also placed severe constraints on local governments.

In addition to aiding local governments, subsidies are extended to individuals and private enterprises that cooperate in national projects. In fiscal 1979, grants totaled ¥12.9 trillion (US $58.6 billion), of which some 85 percent was extended to local governments. See also FINANCE, LOCAL GOVERNMENT.   UDAGAWA Akihito

government-operated factories, Meiji period

(kan'ei kōjō). Factories operated by the Japanese government in a variety of fields, mainly in the first half of the Meiji period (1868–1912) as part of the official policy to import advanced Western technology and facilitate Japan's industrialization. The factories consisted of plants inherited from the Tokugawa shogunate and various domains, such as the NAGASAKI SHIPYARDS, and the SAKAI SPINNING MILL as well as enterprises set up by the Meiji government, such as the TOMIOKA SILK-REELING MILL and the SENJU WOOLEN MILL. The experiment in state enterprise centered in the Ministry of Public Works (Kōbushō) and the Home Ministry (Naimushō), though most other departments were also directly involved in the management of factories. Reflecting changes in the government's SHOKUSAN KŌGYŌ (Increase Production and Promote Industry) policy, the emphasis varied from enhancement of national power, as in the case of the strategic industries under the Ministry of Public

Works and the service ministries, to import substitution and promotion of private enterprise, as in the case of the model factories under the Home Ministry and the Hokkaidō Colonization Office (KAITAKUSHI). From the outset, most of the factories were caught in a dilemma between profit making and profit-blind encouragement of private industry. The majority proved to be a drain on state finances and were sold off to private interests in the 1880s as part of the program of financial retrenchment and deflation under Finance Minister Matsukata Masayoshi (see KAN'EI JIGYŌ HARAISAGE; MATSUKATA FISCAL POLICY). The bulk of the strategic industries, however, remained in government hands, to be joined later by the YAWATA IRON AND STEEL WORKS, the largest of Meiji government enterprises, founded in 1896. Despite their shortcomings from a managerial standpoint, the government factories played a pioneering role in the introduction and diffusion of modern technology.

Steven J. ERICSON

governors and mayors

In Japanese, governors of prefectures are chiji and mayors of cities, towns and villages are shichō, chōchō, and sonchō, respectively. As chief executives, these officials initiate local policies, present the budget and draft bills for enactment by the local assemblies, and coordinate and supervise the enforcement by local officials. They represent their local entities, e.g., in securing subsidies, grants, and loan permits from the national government. As agents of the national or prefectural governments, they also carry out certain assigned tasks under direction from above.

According to the CONSTITUTION, local chief executives are directly elected. In contrast to the parliamentary type of democracy at the national level, Japan has a presidential system at the local level. However, local chief executives may lose their office by a vote of nonconfidence of their assemblies or by a successful recall. It is an indication of the preeminent position of the chief executives that bills and budgets are usually approved by the assembly and that nonconfidence votes are rare.

For many years local government was considered a "conservative paradise." Even today most local assemblies have conservative majorities, and the mayors of towns, villages, and smaller cities are usually conservatives who run as independents in the elections. However, since the 1960s, the system of direct election of chief executives has made it possible for progressive candidates (who are running as independents but are supported by parties in opposition to the conservative government at the national level) to get elected as governors of urbanized prefectures or as mayors of larger cities. In 1975 nine prefectures, including those of Tōkyō, Kyōto, and Ōsaka, had progressive governors. Of the 643 cities more than 130—including 16 prefectural capitals and 6 of the 9 "designated cities" (which exercise some prefectural functions)—had progressive mayors. A National Association of Progressive Mayors was founded in 1964. In more recent elections this progressive trend has abated. However, the elections of chief executives in urban areas are now highly politicized and competitive.

■——Katō Kazuaki, Katō Yoshitarō and Watanabe Yasuo, *Gendai no chihō jichi* (1975). Terry Edward MacDougall, *Localism and Political Opposition in Japan* (1981). Kurt Steiner, *Local Government in Japan* (1965). Kurt Steiner, Scott Flanagan, and Ellis Krauss, ed, *Political Opposition and Local Politics in Japan* (1980).

Kurt STEINER

goyōkin

Forced loans levied during the Edo period (1600–1868) by the shogunate on GOYŌ SHŌNIN (chartered merchants, i.e., official merchants to the shogunate) and others. The funds were initially used to regulate the price of rice but were later used for repairs to the shogunal castle, coastal defense, and other emergency needs. These periodic demands for cash were not taxes as such and were in theory intended to be returned with interest. The domain governments also issued orders for goyōkin from time to time.

The first of some 18 known instances of goyōkin was demanded of the fourth SUMITOMO KICHIZAEMON (real name Sumitomo Tomonori) and 33 other merchants in the mid-1700s. Levies of goyōkin became more frequent toward the end of the period as the worsening of shogunate finances was compounded by the need for military preparedness against foreign encroachment and domestic unrest. The largest demand was made in 1866, when the shogunate called for 7 million ryō (1 ryō could buy 1 koku or about 5 US bushels [180 liters] of rice) to support the second of its punitive expeditions against the Chōshū domain (now Yamaguchi Prefecture; see CHŌSHŪ EXPEDITIONS). At the time of the MEIJI RESTORATION (1868) the government levied goyōkin, mostly on Tōkyō, Ōsaka, and Kyōto merchants, to help consolidate its finances, but the following year it abandoned the practice in favor of government bonds.

goyō shōnin

(chartered merchants). General term for merchants and traders who were regular purveyors to the Tokugawa shogunate and the daimyō domains during the Edo period (1600–1868). Many goyō shōnin also acted as financial agents and advisers for samurai officials who disdained to concern themselves with money matters. Such officials often became totally dependent on the financial expertise of these townsmen, especially because their stipends were paid in rice (KURAMAI) and had to be converted to cash. The merchants profited greatly from the association, although they were periodically obliged to supply large loans (GOYŌKIN) to the government. Many of these privileged merchants, despite their commoner status, assumed positions of power and responsibility within the administrations of the shogunate and the domains. Because of this mutual dependency, few goyō shōnin survived the demise of the shogunate in 1867–68. Notable exceptions included the MITSUI family, who went on to become leading entrepreneurs in the Meiji (1868–1912) and later periods. See also KAKEYA; FUDASASHI.

Gozan

(The Five Temples; literally, "five mountains," the word mountain being synonymous with temple or monastery). Also pronounced Gosan. A ranking system of officially sponsored Zen Buddhist monasteries organized in the 14th and 15th centuries by the Kamakura (1192–1333) and Muromachi (1338–1573) shogunates. In the narrow sense the term referred to five monasteries in Kamakura and five in Kyōto; in a broader sense it included a system of temples of lesser ranks that numbered about 300.

During the 14th and 15th centuries the major RINZAI SECT Zen monasteries in Kamakura and Kyōto, together with their provincial satellites, were integrated by the HŌJŌ FAMILY regents and ASHIKAGA FAMILY shōguns into a three-tiered hierarchy of officially sponsored monasteries modeled after the network of official Zen monasteries established in China during the Song (Sung) dynasty (960–1279). In official Japanese monasteries abbots were appointed, monks promoted, and monastic life regulated by the secular authorities. This control, however, was accompanied by patronage, and the official monasteries enjoyed a privileged position in the Buddhist circles of their day.

Formation of the Gozan —— In China some 50 Zen monasteries had been ranked as official monasteries. In Japan by the mid-15th century, when the system reached its apogee, some 300 monasteries had been included. The hierarchy of official monasteries was headed by the great metropolitan monasteries known as the "Five Mountains" or Gozan. In China, there had been only five monasteries in this category as the name implies. In Japan, the Gozan system originally included three monasteries in Kyōto and two in Kamakura, but it was soon expanded to comprise five in each city. In 1380 the Kamakura Gozan in order of seniority were: KENCHŌJI, ENGAKUJI, Jufukuji, Jōchiji, and Jōmyōji. The corresponding Kyōto monasteries were: NANZENJI, TENRYŪJI, KENNINJI, TŌFUKUJI, and Manjuji. In 1386 Nanzenji was raised to a special position at the head of the Gozan in order to allow for the inclusion of the newly built SHŌKOKUJI as the second-ranking Kyōto monastery, making a total of six Gozan monasteries in Kyōto. The 1386 ranking remained unchanged.

Beneath the 11 full Gozan was a tier made up of major provincial monasteries referred to as the "10 temples" or jissatsu. In China, and originally in Japan, this category had been restricted to 10 monasteries. In Japan, however, by the 15th century 60 monasteries had been given the rank of jissatsu. The lowest tier in the system of official Zen monasteries consisted of smaller provincial monasteries known as the "various mountains" or shozan. This category included 230 monasteries in Japan, compared with 35 in China.

This whole nationwide network was centralized and tightly integrated in Japan. A talented monk might be promoted from abbot of a provincial shozan to abbot of a jissatsu and, eventually, to abbot of one of the major Kyōto Gozan. The rapid growth of the Gozan system in Japan, the coexistence of Kamakura and Kyōto Gozan and

the dramatic inflation of the other two tiers of the hierarchy can be attributed to cultural, political, and economic as well as religious factors unique to medieval Japan.

Religious and Cultural Factors —— In terms of religious development, the phenomenon is a dramatic indication of the hold that Zen, as developed by Chinese in the Song dynasty, had achieved in Japanese society—especially warrior society—by the 14th century. From hesitant beginnings after its formal introduction by the priests EISAI and ENNI in the 12th and 13th centuries, the new branch of Chinese Buddhism had grown in little more than a century to be one of the most vital branches of Japanese Buddhism. Even in the remotest parts of Japan, local warrior leaders were eager to build Zen monasteries and install Zen abbots.

Culturally, the spectacular growth of the Gozan network reflects the surge of popularity of Chinese literature and arts that marked the late Kamakura and Muromachi periods. The metropolitan Zen monasteries served as conduits through which the cultural interests and values of the Chinese gentry, with whom Chinese Zen monks consorted, poured into Japan, to be imbibed by warriors and courtiers alike. Chinese monks like ISSAN ICHINEI, who came to Japan in the late 13th century, not only taught Zen meditation and KŌAN study but also lectured on the Chinese classics, poetry, ink painting, calligraphy, and even political thought. Gozan monasteries were centers for the development of the literary and cultural movement known as GOZAN LITERATURE, which involved the writing of poetry, diaries, and criticism in literary Chinese (KAMBUN) by Japanese monks. Zen monasteries also set the pace for the major changes in Japanese aesthetic sensibility and appreciation of nature, as in architecture, garden design, cuisine, tea ceremony, and so on. As for the Hōjō regents and Ashikaga shōguns, patronage of Zen monks provided them with cultural credentials appropriate to their newfound political authority that were as impressive as those of the imperial court and nobility. Moreover, the nationwide extension of the Gozan system carried these new ideas and values throughout Japan.

Political and Economic Background —— Politically the Gozan network was very much the creation of the Hōjō and Ashikaga rulers. In beginning to build up the Gozan system in Kamakura, the Hōjō seem to have conceived of it as a counterweight to the power and influence of the older Buddhist monasteries in Kyōto and Nara that were closely connected with the imperial court and Kyōto nobility. Likewise, it was no accident that in moving from the Kantō area to Kyōto the Ashikaga should have begun to increase the number of the Kyōto Gozan. Like the Hōjō, they used Zen monasteries to counter the influence of the powerful temple ENRYAKUJI over the city and to display the glory, beneficence, and culture of the shogunate to the nobility and commoners of Kyōto. The articulation of the Gozan, in practice, involved both a nationwide extension of central influence over warrior leaders and the expansion of those Zen schools (sects), especially the one derived from MUSŌ SOSEKI, that had the closest links with the Ashikaga. The promotion of a provincial monastery to the rank of shozan or jissatsu not only conferred favor on its local patron, it also tied him more closely to the shogunate. The coming and going of Zen monks between Kyōto and the provinces provided a valuable source of communication and information. Gozan Zen monks were used as shogunate agents in delicate domestic negotiations and as leaders of trading embassies to China, where their knowledge of the country and the language was invaluable.

On the one hand, Gozan monasteries were economically dependent on their warrior patrons for grants of land, buildings, tax rights, and immunities. On the other hand, the Ashikaga shōguns squeezed money out of the official monasteries for loans and levies and obtained other income from the Gozan system in a variety of ways. A regular income was derived from the sale of certificates of appointment. Each time an abbot was appointed to one of the official monasteries he paid a fee to the shogunate in proportion to the importance of the appointment. With abbots in the 300 monasteries being reappointed every three years, this represented a substantial income. To increase its revenues from this source the shogunate, from the early 15th century, began to shorten the duration of appointments and to sell certificates of absentee (i.e., honorary) appointment to monks who were prepared to pay for them. In Kyōto, Gozan monasteries were involved in moneylending, and some of their monk-administrators built up private fortunes as overseers of monastic estates. The shogunate also imposed frequent levies on these monasteries and their bursars.

Decline —— Not all medieval Zen monasteries were included in the official Gozan system. The several thousand SŌTŌ SECT temples as well as the Kyōto Rinzai sect monasteries DAITOKUJI and MYŌ-SHINJI and their branches were excluded. The Gozan dominated the religious world of Muromachi Japan, but Gozan monasteries were hard hit by the disturbances in the mid-15th century that culminated in the ŌNIN WAR (1467–77). The moneylending activities of the Kyōto Gozan monasteries exposed them to sporadic bouts of mob violence. Moreover, as the political authority of the Ashikaga and their ability to protect the Gozan declined, scattered Gozan domains began to suffer intrusion and alienation by local warriors. By the end of the century the Gozan had lost most of their landholdings. The decline of the Gozan was paralleled by the growth of the Daito-kuji and Myōshinji schools in the Sengoku period (1467–1568) under the patronage of SENGOKU DAIMYŌ and merchants from Kyōto and Sakai. It is from these schools, via the priest HAKUIN (1686–1769), rather than from the Gozan schools, that the modern Japanese Rinzai Zen sect traces its ancestry.

■ ——Martin Collcutt, *Five Mountains: The Zen Monastic Institution in Medieval Japan* (1981). Heinrich Dumoulin, *A History of Zen Buddhism* (1963). Imaeda Aishin, *Chūsei zenshū shi no kenkyū* (1970). Tamamura Takeji, *Gozan bungaku* (1955).

Martin C. COLLCUTT

Gozan literature

A term which, in its broadest sense, refers to the whole tradition of Chinese learning as cultivated in the GOZAN monasteries of Kyōto and Kamakura and in the affiliated smaller monasteries (*jissatsu* and *shozan*) from about the second half of the 13th century through the end of the 17th. The writings of the monks, exclusively in the Chinese language, included religious and secular compositions both in poetry and in prose: diaries, biographies, prefaces, commentaries, congratulatory pieces, treatises of all kinds, records of the teachings of eminent monks, poems, and poetic anthologies. In the narrow sense it denotes, within this literature, a large corpus of Chinese poetry on preponderantly secular subjects.

ZEN teaching distrusts reliance on scripture and often claims to scorn the written word. It may therefore seem paradoxical that the practice of literature, and particularly of secular literature, should flourish in Zen monasteries. But the history of Zen itself provides ample reason why it should do so. Almost from the beginning, Zen teaching used biographies and anecdotes of its patriarchs to provide exempla for disciples; Zen monks expressed their spiritual intuition in a kind of verse called *gāthā* (a Sanskrit word; Ch: *ji* or *chi*; J: *ge*). During the Song (Sung) and Yuan (Yüan) dynasties in China, Zen (Ch: Chan or Ch'an) had a special attraction for members of the educated class; monks were often men who had originally studied for the civil service examination and retained their interest in secular learning after entering the monastery. There they had ample opportunity to make use of literary skills. Poems in the standard secular verse form, the *shi* (*shih*), and compositions in parallel prose were used in the celebration of religious anniversaries; they were presented to new abbots and to others who retired from their posts and in general were used to smooth social intercourse among the monks. Japanese pilgrims to China brought back not only their masters' teachings in the abstract but also the organization and daily-life routine of the monasteries in which they had learned them. For the Japanese monks, moreover, Chinese secular learning had a special utility. Early Zen in Japan was threatened by the jealousy of the older Buddhist sects and needed the favor of powerful patrons. The glamour that Chinese learning lent them helped Zen monks gain entree to both the imperial court and the shogunate. It might be mentioned also that many Zen monks, especially during the 13th and early 14th centuries, began as students of Tendai and Shingon doctrines, which have no prejudice against the written word, and never entirely abandoned their loyalty to them. Some Gozan monks, such as the renowned MUSŌ SOSEKI, vehemently disapproved of the craze for literature, but in many of the Gozan monasteries, from the 15th century on, such admonitions came to be entirely forgotten. The monks became no more than tonsured literati.

Whatever its effect on the practice of religion, seen under the aspect of the history of Chinese literature in Japan, Gozan literature may well be described as a golden age. The reason lies not just in the quantity but in the quality of the work. Gozan monks on the whole possessed greater facility in the Chinese language than did the *kambun* and *kanshi* (see POETRY AND PROSE IN CHINESE) writers of earlier times, if only because significant numbers of them had actually lived and studied in China; some indeed managed to remain in touch with their Chinese mentors even after returning home. Though the subject matter of their poems might have been highly conventional by Chinese standards, it was nevertheless far broader than that of Nara (710–794) and Heian (794–1185) period poets who wrote in Chinese. Their tastes were also broader and more sophisticated: where before Chinese poetry in Japan had meant almost exclusively the poems of Bo Juyi (Po Chü-i; 772–846)—and among Bo Juyi's poems those that most resembled Six Dynasties verse—the Gozan monks now prized most highly the work of the poets of the high Tang (T'ang), particularly Li Bo (Li Po; 701–762) and Du Fu (Tu Fu; 712–770), and along with them such Song poets as Su Shi (Su Shih; 1037–1101). Models for verse composition were provided by an anthology called *Santi shi* (*San-t'i shih*; J: *Santaishi*; Poems in Three Forms), compiled in China in the mid-13th century and introduced to Japan not long after. After about 1390 the poetic doctrines of Huang Tingjian (Huang T'ing-chien; 1045–1105) and the so-called Jiangxi (Kiangsi) school which espoused them became highly influential; the creative use of allusion that this school teaches, however, can easily lead to mechanical displays of learning, and it contributed to the ultimate decline of Gozan poetry.

Gozan scholars also interested themselves in philosophy and were responsible for the importation of many Song Neo-Confucian works. Their own studies as a rule centered on questions of the relationship between Buddhism and Confucianism or among Buddhism, Confucianism, and Taoism, many writers arguing that these doctrines could be shown to be fundamentally one (*nikyō itchi*, *sankyō itchi*). It was not until the Edo period (1600–1868) that Japanese, in or out of the monastery, would make new departures in Neo-Confucianism itself.

Development and Change —— A number of different ways of periodization have been suggested for Gozan literature. One authority divides it into three periods, the first lasting until the end of the Nambokuchō period (1336–92), the second until the beginning of the Ōnin War (1467), and the third to the beginning of the Edo period. A recent author on Gozan poetry, Kageki Hideo, treats his subject under four periods: growth to 1330; full artistic maturity, to 1386 (the year the Gozan system itself reached its mature institutional form); overripeness, to 1467; and decay, to 1615. All authorities agree that the best years of Gozan poetry lie toward the latter part of the 14th century. Although religious subject matter was not uncommon in the first half of the century, as time passed the subject matter became more and more secularized. The deterioration of Gozan poetry in the 15th and 16th centuries accompanied a general deterioration of the spiritual life of the monasteries and the aristocratization of the Ashikaga shogunate, whose members the literati served. But with the decline of the quality of the original verse that was produced came increasing interest in scholarship, poetic criticism, and composition of parallel prose.

Outstanding Figures —— Gozan literature received impetus not only from Japanese pilgrims returning from China but from Chinese missionaries who came to Japan in considerable numbers in the 13th and early 14th centuries, many of them refugees from the Yuan. The most important, an emissary not a refugee, was ISSAN ICHINEI (Ch: Yishan Yining or I-shan I-ning; 1244–1317), who arrived in 1299. To a far greater extent than any previous Zen master, Issan provided his pupils with secular as well as religious instruction; for this reason he is often described as the founder of Gozan literature. Among the disciples who flocked to him were KOKAN SHIREN and SESSON YŪBAI. Kokan is perhaps better known as a historian than as a poet; he was the author of the monumental GENKŌ SHAKUSHO, the earliest comprehensive history of Japanese Buddhism, composed, according to one account, because of questions put to him by Issan. Other major 14th-century figures are BETSUGEN ENSHI, unusual in that he belonged to a Sōtō rather than a Rinzai lineage, and CHŪGAN ENGETSU. Like Sesson, Chūgan was a man of prickly temperament and an independent cast of mind, qualities which are expressed in his verse. Paradoxically, it might seem, the two poets generally considered the best were both dharma-disciples of Musō: GIDŌ SHŪSHIN, a gentle, pious man who suffered pangs of conscience over his love for poetry and who was adviser to the young shōgun Ashikaga Yoshimitsu, and ZEKKAI CHŪSHIN, a virtuoso whose verse is replete with learned allusions. Among the many later Gozan masters praised for their accomplishments were Taihaku Shingen (d 1415), who excelled at parallel prose, and the poet Shinden Seihan (1375–1447).

Scholarship —— Of all the fields within Japanese literature, Gozan literature is one of the most difficult to study. Even in Japan, it is only comparatively recently that it has begun to attract a few dedi-

Graffiti

A comic sketch, known as the *Daidairon*, found on an 8th-century scroll in the Shōsōin in Nara.

cated students. The scholar must contend not only with the voluminousness of this literature but with the fact that, since so many of the productions had the express purpose of displaying their authors' learning, they are in their very nature extremely recondite. As yet, commentaries are virtually nonexistent. The interested scholar, however, can sample a selection of Gozan poems, with meticulous annotation and translation into Japanese, thanks to an excellent volume edited by Yamagishi Tokuhei in the Iwanami series of Japanese classics.

■——Kageki Hideo, *Gozan shishi no kenkyū* (1977). Kamimura Kankō, ed, *Gozan bungaku zenshū* (1936). Tamamura Takeji, *Gozan bungaku* (1966). Tamamura Takeji, ed, *Gozan bungaku shinshū* (1967–72). Marian Ury, *Poems of the Five Mountains* (1977). Burton Watson, *Japanese Literature in Chinese*, vol 2, *Poetry and Prose in Chinese by Japanese Writers of the Later Period* (1976). Yamagishi Tokuhei, *Gozan bungaku shū—Edo kanshi shū*, in *Nihon koten bungaku taikei*, vol 89 (Iwanami Shoten, 1966). Marian URY

goze

Blind women who traveled about Japan singing and playing the SHAMISEN. First appearing in the 16th century, the *goze* spread throughout Japan during the Edo period (1600–1868). Their numbers have gradually dwindled in the 20th century, and few now remain; the best known are in Jōetsu, Niigata Prefecture.

The *goze* lived in tightly organized groups, each based in a communal house, usually established in a castle town under the protection of the local *daimyō*. In a time when entertainment was scarce in the countryside, they were welcomed warmly. The *goze* played an important part in the spread and development of Japanese folk song. Their repertoire included not only folk and popular ballads but also sequences of song mixed with formalized recitation several hours long, based on Shintō or Buddhist teachings.

Wanderers, the handicapped, and performing artists were often thought to have supernatural powers, and many *goze* served as healers and casters of agricultural fertility spells. In most parts of Japan blind women tended to become *goze;* in the northeast, however, they often became MIKO, or shamans. The term *goze* may derive from the old word *gozen*, a respectful form of address. See also ZATŌ; BIWA HŌSHI. MISUMI Haruo

gozen kaigi

(imperial conferences). Conferences on matters of grave national importance convened in the presence of the emperor from time to time between 1894 and 1945. These conferences, which were extraconstitutional, usually sought final imperial approval of and authority for courses of action already decided upon by the other participants, usually elder statesmen (GENRŌ), the prime minister, important cabinet officials, and representatives of the armed forces. The first *gozen kaigi* was convened on the eve of the SINO-JAPANESE WAR OF 1894–1895; others were held to deliberate on such events as the TRIPARTITE INTERVENTION of 1895 and the RUSSO-JAPANESE WAR of 1904–05. No further conferences took place until 1938, during the SINO-JAPANESE WAR OF 1937–1945. More than a dozen

were held thereafter, to deliberate such matters as the signing of the TRIPARTITE PACT in 1940, the attack on PEARL HARBOR in 1941, and the acceptance of the POTSDAM DECLARATION surrender terms in August 1945. At this last *gozen kaigi*, which was convened when the Supreme War Council was unable to reach a decision, the emperor, who usually remained silent, broke the deadlock by personally advocating unconditional surrender. TANAKA Akira

graduate schools

(daigakuin). Japanese graduate schools were reorganized along American lines in 1947. The usual program is five years, two for the master's degree and three for the doctorate. Exceptions are medical and dental schools, which have a four-year doctoral program only. Since 1974 it has been possible for a school to offer a graduate program for which it has no corresponding undergraduate program.

The first Japanese graduate school was at Tōkyō University, where postgraduate courses in various faculties were instituted in 1880. Such postgraduate courses at this and other universities were eventually organized into graduate schools. Before World War II graduate schools had no exclusive facilities or teaching staff, and the number of students was very small. Even after the war not all universities had graduate schools; in 1978 the number was 242 or 56 percent of the nation's universities. Of these, 160 schools had doctoral programs. Fewer than 30 universities had graduate programs in all faculties. Approximately 5 percent of college graduates went on for master's degrees; of these 63 percent attended national universities. Forty-five percent of the master's candidates were in engineering. About 25 percent of master's degree holders proceeded into doctoral programs, of which science and engineering fields accounted for 30 percent and medical studies 32 percent. As of 1980 the total number of graduate students was 37,000 in master's and 16,000 in doctoral programs. AMANO Ikuo

graffiti

(rakugaki). The word *rakugaki* corresponds closely to the casual use of the English word "graffiti"; *rakusho*, another reading for the same characters, has a broader range of meaning, often with an emphasis on the elements of social and political criticism. In this article "graffiti" is used in the broadest sense of *rakusho*.

Most Japanese graffiti are anonymous, although a few are signed. They are found in every sort of setting from public rest rooms to historical monuments. Their contents may be sexual or political, commemorative or informative. Such writings are also put on paper and dropped along public roads, thrown into someone's garden, pasted or scribbled on walls or gates, etc.

From the mid-13th century through the Muromachi period (1333–1568), there even existed a type of public trial sometimes known as *rakugaki kishō* ("graffiti confession"): people with knowledge of a crime would be encouraged to inform on the perpetrator through one of the above-mentioned types of graffiti. In the middle of the Edo period (1600–1868), the literary scholar MOTOORI NORINAGA discussed graffiti, mentioning also *rakushu*, or graffiti in the style of WAKA poetry in his collection of essays *Tamakatsuma*. He also includes in the graffiti category the *wazauta*, an ancient type of anonymous popular song that lampooned public figures or criticized political policy, often taking the form of an oracular revelation.

Japanese graffiti carry on the tradition of satire found in ancient Chinese graffiti; such graffiti provided the Japanese with one avenue of political participation. Perhaps for this reason, such graffiti were usually left in public places—shrine or temple precincts, bustling crossroads or gateways, and bridge approaches; although often couched in metaphor, they were not timid or sneaking.

In 1945 an enormous number of graffiti were discovered on the ceiling boards of the main hall of the temple HŌRYŪJI, which dates from the 7th century. Later, graffiti from the Tempyō era (729–748) were found in numerous locations. These graffiti are thought to be the work of lower-class laborers who expressed their discontent during a boom period in the erection of government temples and Buddhist images. They include references to poor living conditions and low wages as well as to sex; some are extremely angry in tone. On the platform of a statue of Buddha at the TŌSHŌDAIJI are images of human faces, horses, rabbits, frogs, etc. In one corner of a scroll in the SHŌSŌIN is a drawing of a pop-eyed, bearded man with shoulders hunched angrily—perhaps a young priest in the heat of a doctrinal debate.

The satirical songs called *wazauta* are also frequently encountered. *Waza* here means a boy who serves as an oracle or a mouthpiece for a divine spirit. These oracles are the forerunners of the Kyō *warawabe* who strolled through the streets of Kyōto singing about living conditions and current events. One of their songs was the NIJŌGAWARA NO RAKUSHO; beginning with the line, "The current fads in the capital are night attacks, robberies, and false imperial orders," it lampoons the confusion following the KEMMU RESTORATION. According to the KEMMU NENKAN KI, this long, lively, and elegantly turned ballad was displayed in writing along the river flats of the Kamogawa in 1334 and was sung by the Kyō *warawabe*. Satirical songs of this type are also numerous in the war chronicle TAIHEIKI and among the *imayō* songs in the RYŌJIN HISHŌ. The river flats provided an area for the dissemination of information through these songs. Their role became even more important during the unrest following the period of the NORTHERN AND SOUTHERN COURTS (1336–92), and again as an outlet for protest against the attempts at hegemony during the SENGOKU PERIOD (1467–1568). TOYOTOMI HIDEYOSHI's plans to invade Korea evoked particularly biting sarcasm. Satirical songs occurred in many forms; one of the more common was the "counting song" form, which was particularly popular during the heavy wave of protest against the despotic rule of TOKUGAWA TSUNAYOSHI (r 1680–1709). Later, cheap books in the style of graffiti appeared, such as *Hōei rakusho* in the Hōei era (1704–10).

Graffiti criticizing government policies began to flourish during the rule of TOKUGAWA YOSHIMUNE (1716–45). Subsequently, because of their political content, graffiti were banned by the Tokugawa shogunate and repeated warnings were issued against writing them; yet they continued to appear. Criticism was leveled not only at the government but at temples and other institutions.

Near the end of the Edo period graffiti assumed a still greater role as an information conduit, a trend accelerated by the arrival of Commodore Matthew PERRY's ships in 1853. Around this time their informational content increased, but at the same time the elements of satire and wordplay waned as graffiti became a deadly serious political weapon. Following the MEIJI RESTORATION, graffiti satirized or praised modernization and Western customs, but they yielded their role of political criticism to cartoons.

During the Meiji period (1868–1912) the role of graffiti was partly taken over by newspapers, and the appearance of "letters to the editor" columns in the Taishō period (1912–1926) further absorbed the functions of graffiti. However, newspapers could not serve all the traditional functions of graffiti; for example, walls of public rest rooms continue to provide a venue for sexual writings. Japanese student activists of the late 1960s, influenced by the Paris student uprisings, adopted the slogan "white walls belong to me" and conducted what amounted to public trials by criticizing the "establishment" through graffiti. Their writings, however, were confined to the walls of public rest rooms and certain university walls. In this respect they lacked the public effectiveness of the modern Chinese wall posters and the graffiti on the walls of public buildings throughout Europe in this same period.

▬ ——Kida Jun'ichirō, *Rakugaki nihonshi* (1967). Rinoie Masabumi, *Rakugaki shi* (1960). Rinoie Masabumi, *Rakugaki shōwa shi* (1956). HAGA Noboru

grain embargo controversy

Known in Japan as Bōkokurei Jiken (Grain Protection Order Incident). Dispute between Japan and Korea over an embargo on rice and soybeans in 1889. Following the acquisition of commercial privileges in Korea with the signing of the Treaty of KANGHWA (1876), Japan had advanced its political and economic penetration of that country, which was still technically a protectorate of China. In the fall of 1889, because of a poor harvest, a Korean provincial governor issued a decree prohibiting the export of rice and soybeans. Japanese brokers in Korea, who had cornered the Korean market in those staples, claimed that they had incurred huge losses and demanded that the Japanese government put pressure on the Korean government to revoke the order and give them monetary compensation. The order was rescinded in January of the following year. Further negotiations, during which Korea insisted that the embargo was in principle allowed under the terms of the treaty, resulted in the payment of ¥110,000 in 1893. Japan's handling of the incident, which included military threats, further fanned anti-Japanese sentiment in Korea; Japan's relations with China were also strained, as the Japanese suspected that the Korean government's conduct had been instigated by the Chinese government. See also KOREA AND JAPAN: early modern relations.

Grant, Ulysses Simpson (1822–1885)

American general and 18th president of the United States. He was born in Ohio and was a graduate of West Point. He distinguished himself in the Civil War as commander of the Union Army and was elected president in 1868. Early in 1872 he greeted the IWAKURA MISSION that was exploring the possibilities of revising the so-called Unequal Treaties imposed on Japan by the United States and other Western powers during the 1850s (see UNEQUAL TREATIES, REVISION OF). After his retirement Grant set out on a 28-month tour of the world, stopping in Japan in 1879; here he met with Emperor Meiji and government leaders. During the trip he also acted as mediator, albeit unsuccessfully, between China and Japan to settle the problem of suzerainty over the Ryūkyū Islands. See RYŪKYŪ KIZOKU MONDAI.

grapes

(budō). Several species of grape are found growing wild in Japan; the principal cultivated species are the wine grape (*Vitis vinifera*) and the fox grape (*V. labrusca*). The native Kōshū variety of wine grape has been grown in the Kōfu Basin of Yamanashi Prefecture since early times, but Campbell Early and Delaware grapes, which were introduced from the United States in 1872–73, are now the main varieties grown throughout the country. The fox grape is suited to the Japanese climate with its rainy summers, but wine grapes such as Muscat of Alexandria are grown in greenhouses to avoid diseases. Wine grape varieties such as Neo Muscat and Kyoho have been especially developed for the Japanese climate and are grown both in fields and under cover. Most of the grapes grown in Japan are consumed as table fruit, but about 10 percent of the harvest, consisting principally of Kōshū and Delaware, is devoted to wine production. NAGASAWA Katsuo

Great Court of Cassation

(Daishin'in; sometimes called Taishin'in). The highest judicial tribunal in Japan under the Meiji CONSTITUTION of 1889. Although the leaders of the Meiji Restoration had vaguely envisioned a separation of powers, there was no distinction made between administrative and judicial affairs, most cases being decided by the court attached to the Gyōbushō (Ministry of Punishments, merged with the Danjōdai, or Board of Censors, in 1871 to form the Shihōshō, or Ministry of Justice). In May 1875, as a result of the ŌSAKA CONFERENCE, it was decided to establish a separate judicial organ that would act as a final court of appeal for both civil and criminal cases, deal with crimes against the state or the imperial family, and decide cases affecting diplomatic relations. The position of the Daishin'in as the highest court of appeal was formalized in article 57 of the Meiji Constitution. However, all inferior courts remained under the jurisdiction of the minister of justice, as did the administration and personnel of the Great Court of Cassation itself, although the minister was forbidden to interfere in its procedures and decisions. Thus it was only with the creation of the SUPREME COURT after World War II that a truly independent judiciary was realized in Japan.

Greater East Asia Coprosperity Sphere

(Dai Tōa Kyōeiken). A slogan used by the Japanese government during World War II to express the idea of a politically and economically integrated Asia free from Western domination and under Japanese leadership but also used to rationalize its expansionist ambitions on the continent. Members of the sphere initially included Japan, China, Manchukuo (the puppet state in Manchuria), French Indochina, and the Dutch East Indies. There were many variations of the sphere over the years but no precise consensus on its geographic boundaries or, indeed, its political function.

Background: The New Order in East Asia —— The direct predecessor of the Greater East Asia Coprosperity Sphere was the "New Order in East Asia" (Tōa Shinchitsujo), a concept of the Asian political order enunciated by KONOE FUMIMARO's government on 3 November 1938. Although the 16-month-old SINO-JAPANESE WAR OF 1937–1945 had been marked by an almost uninterrupted series of tactical successes, there were some farsighted statesmen and soldiers who were aware that Japan was becoming mired in what threatened to become an endlessly protracted war. If the Chinese could not defeat Japan in such a war, it seemed very possible that Japan could not win either. The result for Japan could be stalemate and exhaustion that would leave the Japanese Empire vulnerable, it was feared, to pressures from either the Soviet Union or the Western imperialist nations. There was every reason, then, for the government of Japan to make at least some conciliatory gestures toward China in the hope that the Chinese will to resist would diminish or that a Chinese collaboration movement might emerge and become viable.

It was in this context that Konoe proposed the New Order. Striking a relatively accommodating pose, Premier Konoe assured China that Japan, far from desiring territory or special privileges in China, looked forward to cooperating with China against both communism and the imperialistic ambitions of the occidental powers. Out of this cooperation would emerge the New Order in East Asia, an equal partnership between Japan and China. While CHIANG KAI-SHEK, skeptical of how equal any partnership with Japan might be in practice, rejected Konoe's demarche, Chiang's longtime rival WANG JINGWEI (Wang Ching-Wei) did defect from Chongqing (Chungking) in December 1938 and began the long, tedious task of negotiating terms of Chinese participation in the New Order that would culminate in the creation of a collaborationist regime, the so-called REORGANIZED NATIONAL GOVERNMENT OF THE REPUBLIC OF CHINA, in March 1940.

The New Order was flawed but it was nonetheless far from an empty slogan. It reflected Japanese—and Chinese—bitterness about the "Old Order," a system of international relations erected by the Western imperialists during the century that had passed since the Opium War (1839–42), in which Britain inflicted a humiliating defeat on China. During that time, the Western powers had accumulated in China a host of economic and political rights, guaranteed by a network of interlocking treaties that were sanctioned by international law and backed by the presence of foreign gunboats and marines stationed in privileged enclaves throughout China. As a result, although China could not be formally described as a colony of the Western imperialists, many Japanese felt that it was exploited by the West in exactly the same fashion that colonies were exploited. The old diplomatic order made this possible, but so also did China's long history of disorder and backwardness, which invited foreign encroachment. In contrast, Japan saw itself as the one example of an Asian nation that had been able to strengthen and modernize itself so as to withstand the aggression of the Western imperialist bloc—and fend off communism as well. In proclaiming the New Order in East Asia, Japan was offering to share with China its strength and successful experience in meeting the twin challenges of imperialism and communism. What bothered the Chinese, however, was the conviction that Japan's own record in East Asia was at least as self-aggrandizing as that of the Western imperialists. Japan's seizure of Taiwan, Korea, and Manchuria—and its more recent efforts to promote an autonomous North China—constituted evidence to support the conviction that Japan was an untrustworthy partner.

The passage of the next two years, from 1938 to 1940, resulted in little change in the strategic position of Japanese forces in China; battle lines moved only slightly; the predictions of a protracted war of attrition were proving correct. The world situation, however, had changed dramatically. The Germans overran Denmark, Norway, the Low Countries, and France in the spring of 1940, and a cross-channel invasion to take Britain out of the war by the end of the year was widely expected. The apparent invincibility of the Reich allowed pro-Axis spokesmen like Foreign Minister MATSUOKA YŌSUKE the opportunity to press for full-scale participation by Japan in the TRIPARTITE PACT. Opposition by those who feared that the pact would propel Japan into a war with the Allied Powers was overcome, and the pact was signed in September 1940. At the same time, Japan moved to widen the scope of the New Order in East Asia; increasingly, the phrase "Greater East Asia" appeared in the rhetoric of the expansionists.

Greater East Asia Coprosperity Sphere ——— For some time, one wing of the Japanese expansionist movement had stressed the necessity of a Japanese drive southward to gain control of the resource-rich and strategically important European colonial possessions in Southeast Asia. Until 1940 these ambitions were seen as too hazardous, involving as they did the near certainty of a clash with the colonial mother countries, France, the Netherlands, Great Britain, and perhaps the United States. Now, however, with the defeat of France and the Netherlands, and the precarious position of Britain, it could be argued that the time was ripe for the drive south (see SOUTHERN EXPANSION DOCTRINE). In September 1940 Japan made the first move by demanding of French authorities the right to sta-

tion troops, use airfields, transport supplies, etc, in the northern part of French Indochina; the French had no choice but to yield. In August Matsuoka had proclaimed that the New Order had been expanded into a "Greater East Asia Coprosperity Sphere." In addition to the countries embraced by the New Order (Japan, China, and Manchukuo), "Greater East Asia" would include French Indochina and the Dutch East Indies, he announced, adding that for the time being Japan would refrain from using force against the Indies.

In December 1941, the China war expanded to become World War II, the Pacific phase of which was officially designated as the "Greater East Asia War" (Dai Tōa Sensō) by Japan shortly after the Pearl Harbor attack. While there were many variations of the Coprosperity Sphere, it was generally seen as including the mandated islands of the Pacific, all of Southeast Asia, and the core countries of Japan, China, and Manchukuo. In the more wildly ambitious versions of the sphere, India, Australia, and New Zealand were also included.

The Greater East Asia Ministry ——— In about May 1942 the government of Premier TŌJŌ HIDEKI began to make plans for the creation of a Greater East Asia Ministry (Dai Tōa Shō) that was to be responsible for coordinating relations between Tōkyō and the various nations and territories of the sphere. Although the proposal ran into opposition from professional diplomats who were disgruntled to learn that Tōjō intended to leave the Foreign Ministry with no more than purely ceremonial functions in its relations with the sphere, the ministry was created on 1 November 1943. In actual practice, however, the ministry did not live up to its mission. There was little centralized direction or planning in Tōkyō. The constituent parts of the sphere were directed through a great variety of administrations. In Indochina, for example, Japan made no attempt to replace the French authorities until the closing days of the war. The Dutch East Indies, on the other hand, were ruled under direct military administration—in fact, several military administrations: one army command ruled Sumatra and British Malaya as as unit; Java was administered by a separate Japanese army; Borneo, Celebes, and the Moluccas were under the jurisdiction of the Imperial Navy, and so on. In China, Burma, and the Philippines, although Japan assisted in the creation of supposedly independent, national governments, the activities of these regimes were kept under the close scrutiny of "advisers" dispatched from Tōkyō and from local military headquarters.

The Greater East Asia Conference ——— In November 1943 the leaders of five major nations of the Coprosperity Sphere assembled in the Imperial Diet Building in Tōkyō for the Greater East Asia Conference (Dai Tōa Kaigi), the only meeting of its kind held during the existence of the Coprosperity Sphere. The leaders attending the Tōkyō conference were: Wang Jingwei (Wang Ching-wei), the ranking official of the Reform Government of the Republic of China; Zhang Zhunghui (Chang Chung-hui), prime minister of Manchukuo; Prince Wan Waithayakon of Thailand (which had formally declared war on the Allies in January 1942); José Paciano LAUREL, president of the Republic of the Philippines (which had been established by Japan just three weeks before the conference met); and BA MAW, the leader of a Burmese regime that had gained its "independence" in August 1943. Also attending as an "observer" from the recently proclaimed Azad Hind (Free India) was the fiery Indian nationalist, Subhas Chandra BOSE, who with Japanese aid had organized the INDIAN NATIONAL ARMY from Indian troops captured by Japan in Malaya in the opening weeks of the war.

The conference addressed few substantive problems; it was really an occasion for ringing oratorical pledges of solidarity, condemnation of Western imperialism, and visions of a resurgent Greater East Asia. Ba Maw undoubtedly spoke for many of those present when he declared that Asians had for centuries lost sight of the fact that East Asia was a world in itself. As a result, he said, Asians had paid dearly: they had lost Asia. Now, however, thanks to Japan, Asians had begun to recapture the truth of their common brotherhood and were destined to recover Asia for the Asiatics.

Many years after the end of the war, Ba Maw reflected on the shortcomings and the successes of the Coprosperity Sphere in his memoirs Breakthrough in Burma: Memoirs of a Revolution, 1939–1946 (1969). On the one hand, he condemned Japanese policymakers for the harsh exactions they made on the peoples of the sphere and deplored the brutal and arrogant behavior often displayed by Japanese soldiers throughout Asia. He conceded that Burmese notions of liberty and nationalism were altogether different from the official Japanese aims of the Coprosperity Sphere. On the other hand, he said, Burmese too often "saw what the Japanese were taking from them to carry on the combat, but not what they were getting back from the Japanese in return." He concluded with a moving statement of the debt that he felt Burma—and all independent Asia—owed to Japan. "Nothing can ever obliterate the role Japan has played in bringing liberation to countless colonial peoples. The phenomenal Japanese victories in the Pacific and in Southeast Asia, which really marked the beginning of the end of all imperialism and colonialism; the national armies Japan helped to create during the war, which in their turn created a new spirit and will in a large part of Asia; the independent states she set up in several Southeast Asian countries as well as her recognition of the provisional government of Free India at a time when not a single other belligerent power permitted even the talk of independence within its own dominions . . . , these will outlive all the passing wartime strains and passions and betrayals in the final summing-up of history."

📖——Joyce C. Lebra, ed, *Japan's Greater East Asia Co-Prosperity Sphere in World War II: Selected Readings and Documents* (1975).

John H. BOYLE

Grew, Joseph Clark (1880–1965)

United States ambassador to Japan from 1932 until the attack on Pearl Harbor in 1941. The leading American career diplomat of his generation, he believed that war could be averted and strove until the end, though with declining hope, to keep the peace.

Born 27 May 1880 of a wealthy Boston family, he graduated from Harvard College in 1902. He married Alice Perry, great-grandniece of Commodore Matthew PERRY. Entering diplomacy in 1904, he served briefly at various posts before settling down to almost 10 years as secretary of the embassy in Berlin. During the submarine crises that led to American entry into World War I, he was principal assistant to the ambassador. Conscientious, tactful, and skilled in diplomatic methods, Grew advanced rapidly to higher positions. He became minister to Denmark in 1920, then minister to Switzerland, under-secretary of state, and from 1928 to 1932 ambassador to Turkey. During the 1920s he played an important part in establishing American diplomacy as a professional career.

Grew arrived in Japan toward the end of the MANCHURIAN INCIDENT of 1931–33. He worked to calm Japanese-American relations and hoped to rebuild friendship. As Japanese expansion on the Asian continent persisted he came to expect less of diplomacy, but from time to time he believed that the forces of moderation in Japan were gaining influence and might restrain the military. He urged step-by-step settlement of differences to halt the drift toward confrontation between Japan and the United States. Japan could not be expelled from China except by force, he argued, and American interests in East Asia were insufficient to justify war. Therefore the United States should acquiesce in Japanese control of parts of China. Respect for the territorial intregrity of nations was fine in theory, he believed, but difficult to apply in practice. Japan in particular reacted adversely to stern American lectures on the principles of international conduct. He also felt that nations could avoid the devastation of war by reconciling differences patiently, practically, and quietly. Grew proved over optimistic in his hopes and assessments. Even so, the road to Pearl Harbor was full of twists and turns, and a more conciliatory American policy might have avoided war. Never complacent, Grew warned the Japanese that Americans were easily provoked and urged Washington to build up the American navy.

In 1940 Japan's advance into Indochina and alliance with Germany convinced Grew that sterner measures were necessary. He advised Washington to begin applying economic pressure to restrain Japan. By the following summer Japan seemed anxious to negotiate and Grew urged a meeting between President Roosevelt and Prime Minister KONOE FUMIMARO. He saw a chance to keep peace in the Pacific while the United States confronted the graver menace of Germany. But Washington preferred deterrence to diplomacy. As war neared Grew warned of a possible Japanese surprise attack. After Pearl Harbor he and his staff returned to the United States in exchange for Japanese diplomats. Near the end of the war, as under-secretary of state, Grew advised President Truman to inform the Japanese that after defeat they would be permitted to retain the emperor. He recognized that such an assurance would be critical in a decision to surrender. Truman failed to give explicit assurance before using atomic weapons. The final surrender terms, however, gave the Japanese just enough hope on this crucial issue for them to submit and end the war (see POTSDAM DECLARATION). In the spring of 1945 Grew, who was strongly anticommunist, pressed for resistance to Soviet expansion in Eastern Europe. He retired at the end of the war.

📖——Joseph C. Grew, *Ten Years in Japan* (1944). Joseph C. Grew, *Turbulent Era: A Diplomatic Record of Forty Years, 1904–1945*, ed Walter Johnson (1952). Edward M. Bennett, "Joseph C. Grew: The Diplomacy of Pacification," in Richard Dean Burns and Edward M. Bennett, ed, *Diplomats in Crisis* (1974). Waldo H. Heinrichs Jr, *American Ambassador: Joseph C. Grew and the Development of the United States Diplomatic Tradition, 1880–1945* (1966).

Waldo HEINRICHS

grievance procedure

(*kujō shori tetsuzuki*). A system for resolving alleged violations of employee rights specified in COLLECTIVE LABOR AGREEMENTS. Prototypical grievance procedures appear in local union contracts in the United States. These contracts detail the conditions of employment, rights, and responsibilities of workers in each job category, along with a procedure for obtaining relief if an employee feels these conditions are violated. A typical procedure directs a grievance through a number of stages of negotiations between labor and management representatives, after which it is turned over to a neutral third party for final ARBITRATION.

In Japan, just under 40 percent of all labor agreements contain grievance procedures, but their substance and function differ greatly from those in the United States. First, because Japanese labor agreements do not specify the conditions of employment in great detail, grievances are often ill-defined and reflect a vague sense of unease an employee may feel toward the employment relationship. In other words, the standard for resolving grievances is not clearly spelled out. Second, the procedures do not include arbitration as their final step but rather specify only various stages of negotiation between labor and management; thus, an employee is not guaranteed a neutral hearing for a grievance. Finally, the most important difference is that grievance procedures are not widely utilized even where they exist perhaps because the Japanese as a people do not like to formalize their disputes. See also LAW, ATTITUDES TOWARD; LABOR LAWS.

SUGENO Kazuo

Griffis, William Elliot (1843–1928)

American educator, clergyman, and author of numerous books and articles on Meiji-period (1868–1912) Japan. Born in Philadelphia. While a student at Rutgers University, from 1865 to 1869, Griffis tutored several Japanese students who were among the first to study in the United States. In 1870 he accepted an offer to teach science in the provincial capital of Fukui in Echizen (now Fukui Prefecture), but after less than a year he resigned to teach at one of the schools that was later to form part of Tōkyō University. Among his students were future prime ministers, ambassadors, businessmen, and scholars. Perhaps Griffis' greatest contribution was his voluminous writing on Japan, including 18 books, several hundred articles, and hundreds of public lectures. Griffis left Japan in 1874 and in 1876 published *The Mikado's Empire*, an early firsthand account of things Japanese. By 1912 this book had gone through 12 editions. Throughout his life he kept up with Japanese affairs and toward the end of his life visited Japan once more. He was twice recipient of the Order of the Rising Sun.

📖——Edward R. Beauchamp, *An American Teacher in Early Meiji Japan* (1976).

Edward R. BEAUCHAMP

group hiring

(*shūdan shūshoku*). The practice of hiring middle-school and high-school graduates from rural areas in groups, rather than as individuals. The first instance of group hiring is believed to have been in 1954, when an association of stores in Setagaya Ward in Tōkyō hired a group of middle-school graduates from Niigata Prefecture. Its success is attributed to the employers' provision of good working conditions, including wage regulations and retirement benefits, which had not previously existed in small and medium enterprises. In 1955 group hiring was carried out jointly by the Tōkyō Metropolitan Labor Bureau and PUBLIC EMPLOYMENT SECURITY OFFICES. The practice spread so quickly that by 1958 about 12,000 middle-school and high-school graduates had been placed in jobs through this method. However, the number of those who quit their new jobs soon after arriving also increased.

In the 1960s, a period of rapid economic growth, a severe shortage of labor occurred, and from 1963 on, the MINISTRY OF LABOR, metropolitan and prefectural governments, and the JAPAN TRAVEL BUREAU, INC, pooled resources to transport trainloads of high-school graduates to metropolitan areas. There was also a tendency for larger enterprises to hire young job seekers in the countryside before the ministries or local governments could find them. More recently, group hiring has declined. By 1976 group hiring under the auspices of the Ministry of Labor was confined to Okinawa Prefecture, and the following year the practice was abandoned altogether.

Tsuchida Mitsufumi

groups

In Japanese society, group consciousness is learned from an early age in the family, which is the most important primary group for the individual. The family is important, not only because it provides the context in which socialization takes place, but also because patterns of interaction learned in that context are applied in other, secondary groups to which a person later belongs, such as school and neighborhood cliques, clubs in and out of school, and groups at one's place of employment. This article deals with the structure and function of nonfamily groups. For a discussion of the family itself, see FAMILY.

A word of caution. The following generalizations apply in varying degrees of imperfection to actual groups since these generalizations describe only ideals. Of course such ideals do help to orient the behavior of members, but actual behavior itself is affected not only by group ideals but by multitudes of other factors as well. Failure to realize this distinction between the ideal to which individuals orient their behavior and the behavior itself, which is always only an imperfect reflection of the ideals, would create a danger of stereotyping the Japanese as though they were mindless robots, all acting the same way.

The Japanese are highly rank-conscious, and Japanese groups have fairly clear-cut ranking among members. Higher ranking persons expect respect, deference, and obedience from those below. Each person is linked to a particular individual above him. The person above takes those below him under his wing, accepting personal responsibility for socializing them when newly inducted into the group, and in general providing material and psychological support as well as moral and social guidance. The person above may be linked to another member still above him in a similar fashion. At the top of the group is one individual to whom all others are related through subordinate linkages.

Whatever is imparted or provided by a senior to his subordinate is considered a favor, and is in some contexts called ON, an especially profound debt. Whether *on* or not, the favor must be repaid in the form of respect, service, and loyalty to one's superior. The obligation to repay one's debt is often called *giri* (see GIRI AND NINJŌ). The relationship among group members is "functionally diffuse," that is, it is not circumscribed in terms of specific roles, but tends to encompass almost all aspects of one's life.

Ideally, within the group, harmony and cooperation among members prevail, and competition is eschewed. In reality, however, competition for approval or recognition by superiors is extremely keen among those of equal rank. Furthermore, loyalty to the group and service to the leader are not entirely selfless. There is often a calculation of self-interest, in that loyalty and service to the group are perceived as linked to self-interest. Hard work is likely to be recognized by the leader and bring about the advancement of one's career within the group. If loyal service makes the group stronger, individual members also stand to benefit. For example, if the devoted work of employees increases a company's profits, they are likely to gain through higher wages or other benefits.

Looked at in this way, Japanese group motivation may not seem very different from that of American workers. However, there is a genuine difference, in that the realization is much stronger among Japanese workers that the fate of the company is affected by the workers' output and their cooperative endeavor than among American workers, who are more likely to think of their personal interest first and think of it as being pitted against that of the company.

Dedicated service to one's group, sometimes requiring hard work and self-sacrifice, comes from self-discipline achieved through a type of character building that the Japanese value called *seishin shūyō*. This self-discipline includes deferment of gratification, physical hardship, and the like, in combination with a cognitive orientation that values inner strength and peace through outward physical experience. *Seishin shūyō* is so important that some companies incorporate it into their new employee orientation programs.

Japanese groups are "particularistic"—meaning that warm, intimate relationships are maintained only among group members and that the group closes its doors to outsiders. This form of group relations exists, for example, within the context of a large bureaucracy, such as a business firm or a government office. In such a context, a section or a department of the organization tends to be the basic functioning group; heads of these units and executive officers of the organization form another, overarching group. A group's internal cohesion is often heightened by recognizing a rival group with which it competes in obtaining certain resources. Branches of a bank, for instance, may be pitted against one another for increasing deposits. Factions (HABATSU) of a political party compete for such political resources as the presidency of the party or ministerial posts.

——Takie S. Lebra, *Japanese Patterns of Behavior* (1976). Nakane Chie, *Japanese Society* (1970). Edwin O. Reischauer, *The Japanese* (1977). Thomas P. Rohlen, *For Harmony and Strength* (1974).

Harumi Befu

group travel

Most Japanese prefer to travel in groups, both within Japan and abroad. Aside from such practical considerations as reducing expenses and the trouble of travel arrangements, the Japanese derive a strong satisfaction from doing things with friends or fellow workers. Group travel has a long history in Japan; PILGRIMAGES became popular late in the Heian period (794–1185) among city people, for religious reasons as well as to escape the drudgery of daily life. Even today, groups of pilgrims dressed in white, perhaps following one of the many set routes to a number of temples, can be seen throughout Japan. School excursions *(shūgaku ryokō)*, particularly during high school, are important milestones in Japanese life. Japanese take advantage of various associations to plan trips: neighborhood organizations, companies, agriculture cooperatives, or old people's groups. The travel industry caters to the demand by offering numerous package tours both domestically and abroad. See also GROUPS.

Naitō Kinju

growth industries

Each period of economic development in Japan has had its leading growth industries. Prior to World War II, light industries such as the TEXTILE INDUSTRY and SUNDRY GOODS INDUSTRY experienced strong growth, while heavy industry and the CHEMICAL INDUSTRY were the growth industries of the 1950s and 1960s.

The first stage of postwar development began in the 1950s, when the government nurtured such basic industries as COAL, electric power, and shipbuilding (see SHIPBUILDING INDUSTRY) to provide a foundation for the future development of heavy industry (see INDUSTRIAL POLICY). In the 1960s the IRON AND STEEL INDUSTRY, PETROCHEMICAL INDUSTRY, and transportation equipment, electric machinery, and synthetic fibers industries led growth, as both human and financial resources went to them. By the 1970s these industries were capable of competing on the international market. Their growth rates declined after 1975, however, because of restrictions imposed by importing countries and competition from developing nations.

The new growth industries of the 1970s were the service, distribution, and advanced processing industries. After 1976, capital and human resources moved into retailing, restaurants, medical services, education, and hotels; managerial innovations were introduced in many service industries. "Knowledge-intensive" industries such as the COMPUTER INDUSTRY, office machine industry, MACHINE TOOL INDUSTRY, and PRECISION MACHINERY INDUSTRY have not encountered strong competition from developing nations. Although resistance from importing countries may develop, they appear likely to continue as growth industries. See also INDUSTRIAL STRUCTURE; DECLINING INDUSTRIES.

Machida Yōji

Guadalcanal

A volcanic island in the Solomon Islands, southwestern Pacific Ocean; area, 6,475 square kilometers (2,500 sq mi). Occupied early in 1942 by Japanese forces, it was the site of the first Allied invasion (August 1942) to retake Japanese-held territory in World War II. In February 1943, after heavy fighting in which more than 17,000 men died, the Japanese abandoned the island to the Allies.

Guam

An island belonging to the Mariana group in the western Pacific. Area: 549 square kilometers (212 sq mi); population: 116,000 (1979). Now an unincorporated territory of the United States. Guam was discovered by Magellan in 1521, and from 1668 it was governed by

Spain. Following the Spanish–American War of 1898 it became the property of the United States. The Japanese invaded Guam on 9 December 1941, two days after the attack on PEARL HARBOR, and, by 1944, 18,500 Japanese soldiers were stationed there. In July 1944 three and a half American divisions landed in Guam, defeating the Japanese in August. The island was used as a base for air raids on the Japanese mainland. Since World War II Guam has been the site of an American air base. It has become a very popular Japanese tourist resort. In January 1972 Yokoi Shōichi, a Japanese Imperial Army sergeant who had not realized that World War II was over, was discovered after remaining in hiding on Guam for 27 years.

Guandong (Kwantung) Army

(J: Kantōgun). Unit of the Imperial Japanese Army that was originally assigned to guard areas in southern Manchuria leased by Japan from China after the RUSSO-JAPANESE WAR of 1904–05, but in the 1930s seized all of Manchuria, expanded into Inner Mongolia, and prepared for war against the Soviet Union.

Created on 1 August 1906 from Japanese forces occupying southern Manchuria after the Russo-Japanese War, the Guandong Army was assigned responsibility for defending the Guandong Leased Territory and the railway zone between PORT ARTHUR (Ch: Lüshun; J: Ryojun; now part of Lüda) and Changchun (Ch'ang-ch'un). It consisted at first of one division (about 10,000 men), supplemented in 1907 by a detachment of railway guards. For over a decade it was administered as a department within the Guandong Government-General, with the governors-general serving concurrently as commanders of the Guandong Army. Among the commanders during this period was Lieutenant General FUKUSHIMA YASUMASA, who had achieved popular fame in 1893 for a solo equestrian odyssey across Siberia.

On 12 April 1919 the Guandong Government-General was replaced by separate civilian and military administrations, the Guandong Government and the Guandong Army Command, respectively. Based in Port Arthur, the latter consisted of one division, an independent railway garrison of six battalions, an artillery battalion, and military police (kempeitai). Accountable to the emperor through the army high command, the Guandong Army soon showed its operational independence from civilian control.

Faced with a rising tide of Chinese nationalism and anti-Japanese sentiment spilling over into Manchuria during the 1920s, Guandong Army officers came to favor strong measures to protect Japanese interests. A few activist staff officers resorted to unauthorized initiatives, but not without a degree of tacit sympathy from superiors in Port Arthur and Tōkyō. One of the more sensational of such actions was the assassination of the Manchurian warlord ZHANG ZUOLIN (Chang Tso-lin) on 4 June 1928, directed by Colonel Kōmoto Daisaku. On 18 September 1931 colonels ISHIWARA KANJI and ITAGAKI SEISHIRŌ staged an explosion on the tracks outside of Mukden (now Shenyang) that led to fighting between Guandong Army railway guards and local Chinese forces. Accepted as a fait accompli by the Guandong Army commander, General HONJŌ SHIGERU, the MANCHURIAN INCIDENT (sometimes called the Mukden Incident) precipitated the occupation of all of Manchuria, notwithstanding reservations among civilian and military leaders in Tōkyō.

In October 1932 Guandong Army headquarters were moved to Xinjing (Hsinking; formerly Changchun), capital of the newly created puppet state of MANCHUKUO. With its commanders acting concurrently as ambassadors-extraordinary to Manchukuo and as directors of the Guandong Government, the Guandong Army came close to monopolizing political power in Manchuria. In the economic sphere, the Guandong Army wielded strong influence over the SOUTH MANCHURIA RAILWAY Company, the major vehicle for Japanese investment and development. By the end of the 1930s, Manchuria had become a testing ground for Japanese notions of military management as well as a base for further expansion into North China, Outer Mongolia, and the Soviet Far East.

After 1931 Guandong Army strategists regarded the Soviet Union as their chief enemy. As both sides built up their forces, border clashes along the Amur and Ussuri rivers erupted with increasing frequency and severity. The Guandong Army did not play a direct part in the 1938 pocket war at Changgufeng (Ch'ang-ku-feng; see CHANGGUFENG [CH'ANG-KU-FENG] INCIDENT) on the Soviet-Manchurian frontier near Korea, but in 1939 it lost close to 18,000 men in a series of battles with the Red Army at Nomonhan over a disputed section of the Outer Mongolia–Manchukuo border (see NOMONHAN INCIDENT). After the German invasion of the

USSR on 22 June 1941, the Guandong Army held maneuvers involving 700,000 troops in anticipation of operations against the Soviet Far East. Tōkyō's decision in the summer of 1941 to give priority to a southern advance (see SOUTHERN EXPANSION DOCTRINE) left the Guandong Army with a defensive role in Manchuria. While manpower levels remained stable, the Guandong Army turned into a shell of its former self after 1943 as crack units were transferred to Pacific battlegrounds. Within two weeks of a Soviet Red Army strike into Manchuria on 9 August 1945, the Guandong Army lay shattered. About 80,000 of its 787,000 soldiers were killed. Most of the survivors were sent to labor camps in the USSR and Outer Mongolia. Just over 500,000 were repatriated between 1947 and 1950. General Yamada Otozō (1881–1965), last commander of the Guandong Army, returned to Japan from Soviet imprisonment in 1956 and died in 1965.

📖 ——Bōei Kenshūjo, ed, Kantōgun, vol 1 (1969), vol 2 (1974).

John J. STEPHAN

Guandong (Kwantung) Territory

(J: Kantōshū). A Japanese leasehold from 1905 until 1945, located on the tip of the Liaodong (Liaotung) Peninsula in southern Manchuria. With an area of 3,463 square kilometers (1,337 sq mi), the Guandong Territory comprised land south of a line running along the 39°20″ north latitude and included the adjacent Changshan Islands, Port Arthur (Ch: Lüshun; J: Ryojun; now part of Lüda) and Dairen (Ch: Dalian or Ta-lien; J: Dairen; Russ: Dalny). The Chinese name Guandong, literally "East of the Pass," traditionally referred to Manchuria, the area east of the Shanhaikwan (Shanhaiguan; "Mountain-Sea Pass") composed of the three present-day provinces of Liaoning, Jilin (Kirin), and Heilongjiang (Heilungkiang). The Japanese applied the name to their holding on the tip of the Liaodong Peninsula, only a small portion of the area originally encompassed by Guandong.

Japan seized the Liaodong Peninsula during the SINO-JAPANESE WAR OF 1894–1895 and forced China to cede it in the Treaty of SHIMONOSEKI on 17 April 1895, but within two weeks was compelled to return it to China in return for an increased indemnity under diplomatic pressure from Russia, Germany, and France (see TRIPARTITE INTERVENTION). In 1898 Russia obtained from China a 25-year lease to Port Arthur and Dairen. Two years later Russia occupied the entire Guandong region during the BOXER REBELLION, only to lose the whole area to Japan during the RUSSO-JAPANESE WAR of 1904–05. The Treaty of PORTSMOUTH (5 September 1905) awarded Japan all of Russia's rights to the Guandong region. Three months later, Japan secured China's approval for this transfer.

In October 1905, to administer the Guandong Territory and the railway zone between Port Arthur and Changchun, the Guandong Government-General (Kantō Sōtoku Fu, soon renamed Kantō Totoku Fu) was established in Liaoyang under General Ōshima Yoshimasa (1850–1926). Moved to Port Arthur in May 1906, the government-general consisted of military and civil departments. Defense matters fell to the military department, better known as the GUANDONG (KWANTUNG) ARMY. Civil administration was conducted only in part by the civil department, which delegated responsibility for public works, health, and education to the SOUTH MANCHURIA RAILWAY. Civil law was administered by consular courts, which remained under the jurisdiction of the Ministry of Foreign Affairs in Tōkyō. Successive governors-general, invariably army officers, claimed authority over the Guandong Territory's civil as well as military affairs, an attitude that caused a certain amount of local friction, particularly among police agencies, and required negotiations between the army and the Ministry of Foreign Affairs. Meanwhile, in May 1915, after Japan presented China with the TWENTY-ONE DEMANDS, the Guandong Territory lease was extended from 25 to 99 years (until 1997).

On 12 April 1919, in order to resolve bureaucratic rivalries, the Guandong Government-General was abolished and replaced by separate military and civil agencies: the Guandong Army Command and the Guandong Government (Kantōchō) respectively. The reorganization enhanced civilian authority in the Guandong Territory, for until 1919 every governor-general had been an army officer. Hayashi Gonsuke (1860–1939), first director of the Guandong Government, was a diplomat directly responsible to the Japanese prime minister.

Under increasingly unstable conditions in Manchuria culminating in the MANCHURIAN INCIDENT in 1931, the Guandong Army gradually reasserted control over the Guandong Territory. In August 1932, five months after the creation of a puppet state called

MANCHUKUO, the Guandong Army commander, General Mutō Nobuyoshi (1868–1933), became director of the Guandong Government and concurrently ambassador-extraordinary to Manchukuo. As the Guandong Army deployed throughout Manchuria and Inner Mongolia, the governance of the Guandong Territory came to play a comparatively subsidiary role in its operations. Consequently, the Guandong Government lapsed in 1934 and was succeeded by a two-tiered structure: (1) the Guandong District Government (Kantōshū Chō), based in Port Arthur and after 1937 in Dairen, which handled the territory's civil administration and was presided over by (2) the Guandong Bureau (Kantōkyoku) in Xinjing (Hsinking; formerly Changchun), headed by the commander of the Guandong Army, who in turn reported to the president of the Manchurian Affairs Bureau in Tōkyō, a post held by the army minister.

Although under military rule after 1932, the Guandong Territory enjoyed a more tolerant political climate than other Japanese colonies, namely Korea and Taiwan. Port Arthur and Dairen remained self-governing cities; approximately half of their municipal assemblies were popularly elected by Japanese residents, the remainder (generally Chinese) being appointed by the civil administrators. Dairen grew into a modern commercial port, with a population in 1934 of 198,912 Chinese and 127,654 Japanese. In the Guandong Territory as a whole, however, Japanese did not number more than 15 percent of the population, which stood at 1,453,491 in 1941.

Occupied by Soviet forces in August 1945, the Guandong Territory reverted to China, except for Port Arthur, where the Russians maintained a naval base until 1955.

——Carl Walter Young, *Japan's Jurisdiction and International Legal Position in Manchuria* (1931). John J. STEPHAN

Guan Yu (Kuan Yü) → Kan U

Gukanshō

("Notes on Foolish Views"). A secular history of Japan written by the high-ranking Buddhist priest JIEN (1155–1225) just before the JŌKYŪ DISTURBANCE of 1221. The author, who meant to show how a single course of events was moving directly and inevitably from the past into the future, argued that human affairs are always driven along that course by continuous interaction between divine imperatives called *dōri* (principles).

The work is colored by Jien's preoccupation with the interdependent functions of three institutions: the imperial household, with which he had close familial ties; the TENDAI SECT of Buddhism, which he had served four times as chief abbot; and the Kujō branch of the Fujiwara family, of which he was probably the most influential member (see KUJŌ FAMILY). Jien's concern for the imperial household is reflected in the first two chapters, which contain the imperial chronology, in the expressions of pride in Japan's unbroken line of rulers descended from the sun goddess (AMATERASU ŌMIKAMI), and in the way the seven-part periodization of Japanese history is linked to the reigns of emperors. His Buddhist concern is revealed in his claim that improvements in early Japanese history were due to the introduction and spread of Buddhism, in his identification of four great historical figures as incarnations of Buddha, and above all in his tendency to use Buddhist doctrines and ideas in interpreting historical change. Finally, the author's detailed treatment of the events of his own lifetime, in which he admits a special interest and to which he devotes half the book, leaves the impression that the work is mainly a history of the Kujō house. We are told that the breakdown of order late in the Heian period (794–1185) was reversed only when KUJŌ KANEZANE (1149–1207), Jien's brother, became imperial regent (*sesshō* and *kampaku*) and worked closely with the Kamakura shogunate's founder, MINAMOTO NO YORITOMO (1147–99), and that future improvement would be possible only if another member of the Kujō family rose to become both imperial regent and shōgun.

Although the *Gukanshō* is deeply colored by the author's secular concerns, its main interest lies in its view of history as propelled by divine principles. The book's theological character, in fact, led early readers to call it a "tale of principles" (*dōri no monogatari*). Jien believed in the existence and power of destructive principles, derived from the ancient Hindu conception of kalpic cycles that were driving secular affairs toward ultimate ruin. He also believed in constructive principles (some Buddhist and some Shintō), which, when followed by enlightened leaders, produced temporary improvement. Destructive principles underlay his assumption of inevitable deterioration that would allow Japan only 100 reigns.

Nevertheless, the author was more interested in periods of substantial improvement. Indeed, the primary focus of the *Gukanshō* is on the possibilities of a better future, when the principle, created by the sun goddess and other ancestral gods, would be realized by which imperial rule would be supported through both aristocratic learning and military might.

Recently discovered letters written before and after the completion of the *Gukanshō* suggest that Jien's belief in a divinely created plan for the future was reinforced by dreams in which that plan had been revealed to him. The *Gukanshō* does not mention such dreams. Although the author bases his case on the direction in which Japan's single course of history is moving and not on prophetic revelations, dreams may well have strengthened his conviction that the Shintō gods had a plan for the future of Japan, a conviction that is central to the interpretation of the past of the *Gukanshō*. See also HISTORIOGRAPHY.

——Jien, *The Future and the Past: A Translation of the Gukanshō*, Delmer M. Brown and Ichirō Ishida, ed (1979).
Delmer M. BROWN

gulls

There are several species of gull (medium-sized birds of the family Laridae) in Japan, known collectively by the name *kamome*, but the name is also used to refer in particular to one of the most common species, the mew gull (*Larus canus*). The mew gull measures roughly 45 centimeters (about 18 in) in length. Its back is gray and the rest of its body is white except for black wing tips with white spots and yellow bill and feet. Widely distributed in the northern portion of the northern hemisphere, it is a winter visitor to Japan where it inhabits seacoasts and harbors. It is not as common as the *umineko* (black-tailed gull; *L. crassirostris*) or the *yurikamome* (black-headed gull; *L. ridibundus*). In the broader usage of the term there are a variety of *kamome*, among which the *ōseguro kamome* (slaty-backed gull; *L. schistisagus*), *zuguro kamome* (Saunders's gull; *L. saundersi*), and *umineko* are found only in Asia.
TAKANO Shinji

From ancient times the gull has been an indispensable indicator of conditions at sea. The *miyakodori*, a bird whose name appears in the 8th-century poetry anthology MAN'YŌSHŪ and in the ISE MONOGATARI, is in fact the *yurikamome*. Because the birds gather in flocks over schools of fish they are useful to fishermen.
SANEYOSHI Tatsuo

gumbatsu

(military faction). In modern Japanese history this term refers either to the military in general, when it vied with nonmilitary factions for control of the government's domestic and foreign policy, or to a group of army or navy officers, linked by common regional origin, social background, or expertise, that competed with similar military groups for control of its services policy and, by extension, of government military and civil policy as a whole. The term first entered common Japanese parlance in the Taishō period (1912–26).

From the establishment of the Imperial Japanese Armed Forces (see ARMED FORCES, IMPERIAL JAPANESE) following the Meiji Restoration of 1868 to their abolition following Japan's defeat in World War II, it is evident that the army and navy played a crucial role in Japanese politics, for between 1885 and 1945 generals and admirals held 15 of the 30 premierships and 115 of the 404 civilian cabinet portfolios. The military's ability to act as a political faction was based on the common *samurai* heritage and concern for the development of national power of both civilian and military leaders during the Meiji period (1868–1912); the military power and prestige of the armed forces; broad popular support mobilized through the IMPERIAL MILITARY RESERVISTS' ASSOCIATION and other mass organizations; the independence from civilian control of the Army and Naval General Staff Offices; and the appointment of only active-duty officers to the posts of service ministers in the cabinet (see GUMBU DAIJIN GEN'EKI BUKAN SEI). The political influence of the military increased substantially in the 1930s, reaching its apex in World War II, but it was completely eliminated with Japan's defeat in 1945 (see MILITARISM).

Until the Taishō period the dominant factions within the military were the Satsuma faction of the navy and the Chōshū faction of the army. The Satsuma faction, whose leaders included Admirals SAIGŌ TSUGUMICHI and YAMAMOTO GONNOHYŌE, was composed mostly of former samurai from the Satsuma domain (now Kagoshima Prefecture), as was the Chōshū clique of former samurai from the Chōshū domain (now Yamaguchi Prefecture). Both domains had played a leading role in the Meiji Restoration (see HAMBATSU). It is evident that the Satsuma faction dominated the navy, for of the 16 officers promoted to the rank of admiral during the Meiji period, 13 were natives of Satsuma. By the Taishō period, however, the Satsuma faction had given way to cliques consisting of NAVAL ACADEMY and Naval Staff College graduates, who by then had taken over the positions of naval leadership. Most scholars have explained the factionalism among these graduates as a conflict between supporters and opponents of the naval limitation treaties resulting from the WASHINGTON CONFERENCE of 1921–22 and the London Naval Conference of 1930. By 1934 the prolimitation "treaty faction," including such moderate admirals as SAITŌ MAKOTO, OKADA KEISUKE, and TAKARABE TAKESHI, had lost control of naval policy to the "fleet faction," led by Admirals KATŌ HIROHARU and Suetsugu Nobumasa (1880–1944), who opposed the treaty system and called for naval expansion. Other scholars have viewed the same basic division as a clash between an internationalist "administrative group" in the Navy Ministry and a hawkish "command group" in the Naval General Staff or, especially from the mid-1930s, as a struggle between a pro-Anglo-American faction and a pro-German faction.

The Chōshū faction not only controlled the army but also exercised a major influence on civil government well into the 1920s. Its ability to do so largely rested on the power of its leader, Field Marshall YAMAGATA ARITOMO, the founder of the modern Japanese army and a dominating force in Meiji and Taishō politics. During his long and prominent career, Yamagata handpicked army ministers and helped to select prime ministers. Four of his followers, KATSURA TARŌ, KODAMA GENTARŌ, TERAUCHI MASATAKE, and TANAKA GIICHI, served as army minister between 1898 and 1924, and three of these—Katsura, Terauchi, and Tanaka—served as prime minister between 1901 and 1928, thereby promoting Yamagata's goals after his retirement from active service at the turn of the century and even after his death in 1922. Furthermore, Yamagata ensured that before World War I advancement in the army's highest circles went mostly to Chōshū faction officers; only after 1912 did graduation from the Army Staff College begin to supplant affiliation with the Chōshū clique as the principal criterion for promotion to army leadership positions.

After Yamagata's death the Chōshū faction's power dissolved, as leaders of other factions competed with his successors for supremacy. Tanaka Giichi, the last of his protégés, coveted Yamagata's influence in the army, particularly his power to choose army ministers. But his attempts to assume Yamagata's mantle met fierce army resistance. A group of officers led by UEHARA YŪSAKU, the chief of the General Staff Office, and including such important generals as ARAKI SADAO and MAZAKI JINZABURŌ, resisted the continuation of Chōshū power and Tanaka's efforts to appoint UGAKI KAZUSHIGE his successor as army minister in 1924. Although Tanaka eventually pushed through this appointment, his premiership in 1927–28 marked the end of the Chōshū faction's domination of the army.

This collapse of Chōshū power in the 1920s ironically ushered in an era of even more intense army factionalism in the 1930s. As the focus of military loyalty and as one of the few foci of civilian loyalty, Yamagata could claim to speak for the emperor in a constitutional system that directed all loyalty to the emperor. With the demise of Yamagata, nearly the last survivor of the original elder statesmen (GENRŌ), no one person or group held such power. The political vacuum was intensified by the fact that neither Emperor TAISHŌ nor Emperor HIROHITO was trained to make governmental decisions. Thus, after 1922 a variety of cliques inside and outside the services claimed to speak for the emperor. This contention led to unrestrained factionalism within the army during the 1930s, the very time the army as a whole was increasing its influence in the government.

The rampant army factionalism of the wartime years, from the MANCHURIAN INCIDENT of September 1931 to Japan's surrender in August 1945, has been interpreted variously. Some have pointed to the seeds of factionalism within the very institutions set up in the Meiji period to assure military independence and strength. For instance, the independence given the Army and Naval General Staff Offices encouraged the growth of highly disruptive rivalries within and between the services before and during World War II. Also, the high status of graduates of the Army Staff College aroused great resentment among many line officers, the bulk of the officer corps, who had not attended the college. Intense feuds arose between

planners of the Army Staff College clique (rikudaibatsu) and troop leaders of the nongraduate group (mutengumi). Even among the Army Staff College graduates, factionalism developed along the lines of the countries in which they specialized. Some scholars have noted the existence of a German faction, which advocated, as in Germany, the integrated development of the industrial economy, natural resources, and new weaponry; a Russian clique, which urged spiritual training over modernization and rational economic planning and sought a preemptive war against the Soviet Union; and a China faction, which involved itself in intrigues on the mainland and urged war there.

Other scholars have viewed army factionalism in the 1930s as a clash between two primary cliques. The Imperial Way faction (KŌDŌHA) comprised of anti-Chōshū generals and young activist officers, emphasized Japanese spirituality centered on the emperor cult and preventive war against the Soviet Union, while the Control faction (TŌSEIHA) comprised of strategic planners, urged army discipline and rational economic planning before the commencement of war. The Control faction's victory in 1936 then led to war with China in 1937 and with the United States in 1941. Yet others consider this factionalism a battle between bureaucratic military managers and hot-headed young officers. And some prefer to interpret it as an almost infinitely complex combination of all these and other factors. Finally, some scholars view it as a red herring, a phenomenon overemphasized by outside observers; there was no more factionalism in the army or navy than in any other Japanese organization.

The complexity of the factionalism of the 1930s, and the difficulty of using an analysis of cliques as a tool for understanding the "road to war," becomes clear if one looks at the factional affiliations of officers who participated in certain incidents in the thirties. In September 1931 two field-grade army officers, ITAGAKI SEISHIRŌ and ISHIWARA KANJI, neither of whom could be considered a "young officer," both of whom were elite-track, Army Staff College graduates associated with the Control faction, engineered an incident that led to the Japanese seizure of Manchuria. Although the incident seems to have been Tōseiha-inspired, everyone in the military applauded its success, and General Araki Sadao, reputed to be the leader of the rival Imperial Way faction, was appointed army minister to clean up loose ends during the immediate postincident period. On 26 February 1936, officers of the First Division, often called the "Imperial Way Faction Young Officers," attempted a coup d'etat (see FEBRUARY 26TH INCIDENT), hoping to place one of their Imperial Way heroes, General Araki or General Mazaki Jinzaburō, in control of the government. Interpretations vary over the degree of the generals' complicity. However, recent scholarship not only absolves Araki of involvement but also indicates that he was in favor of maintaining army discipline by suppressing the uprising. What the complex politics of these and other incidents of the 1930s suggest is that an orderly interpretation of the prewar period in terms of factional conflict, or of the victory of one clique over another—say, of the Control faction over the Imperial Way faction—is hard to sustain.

However one views military factionalism between 1931 and 1945, three incontestable points can be made. First, when one considers the whole military as a single faction, one cannot doubt its impact on the political life of modern Japan, particularly during the years 1937–45, when over half of the cabinet ministers were drawn from among army and navy officers. Second, although military factions based on common regional origin or social background were important in the Meiji and early Taishō periods, they had disappeared almost entirely by the 1930s. Former samurai from Chōshū and Satsuma dominated the army and navy before World War I, but in the 1920s the retirement and death of the last of the ex-samurai, Yamagata Aritomo, Tanaka Giichi, and Uehara Yūsaku, and the ascendance of the graduates of the modern military educational system, led to the downfall of geographically or class-based factions. Third, the powerful Chōshū and Satsuma factions, headed by such prestigious leaders as Yamagata and Saigō Tsugumichi, had given way by the 1930s to smaller and more fragmented factions based on the type of training officers received rather than on who they were or where they were born. The factions of the 1930s consisted, for example, of German experts who tended to favor rational strategic planning; Russian specialists who tended to be the most anti-Soviet in an officer corps of anti-communists; or officers without the cosmopolitan training received at the staff colleges who tended to downgrade economic and strategic planning. Without respected leaders like Yamagata and Saigō to integrate the army and navy, each faction went its own way, vying for power.

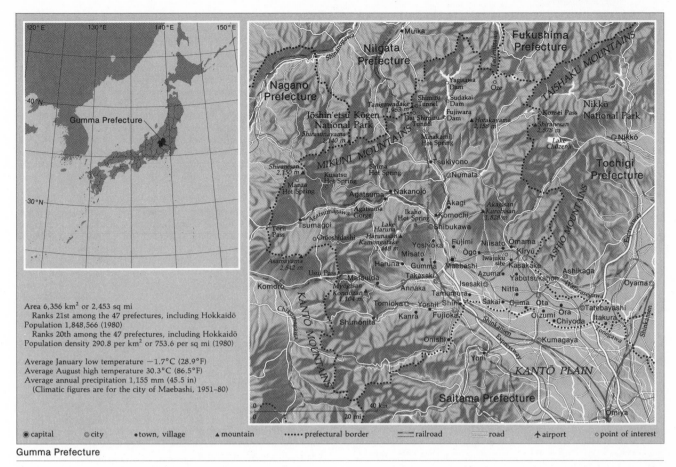

Area 6,356 km² or 2,453 sq mi
  Ranks 21st among the 47 prefectures, including Hokkaidō
Population 1,848,566 (1980)
  Ranks 20th among the 47 prefectures, including Hokkaidō
Population density 290.8 per km² or 753.6 per sq mi (1980)

Average January low temperature −1.7°C (28.9°F)
Average August high temperature 30.3°C (86.5°F)
Average annual precipitation 1,155 mm (45.5 in)
  (Climatic figures are for the city of Maebashi, 1951–80)

◉ capital   ◎ city   ● town, village   ▲ mountain   ⋯⋯ prefectural border   ═══ railroad   ══ road   ✈ airport   ○ point of interest

Gumma Prefecture

It has been said that military factionalism helped the army and navy to increase their power within the government in the 1930s, but the extent to which it did this is unclear. True, government leaders tended to give the armed forces more and more political power in the thirties because of the civilians' forlorn hope that only the military could control its insubordinate factions. For example, in 1936 the cabinet reinstated the legal requirement that the army and navy ministers be active-duty officers not to satisfy military demands for independence from civilian control but rather to enable the army and navy better to control their dissidents. However, what seems to have allowed the armed forces to dominate the government after 1937 was not so much factional activity as a belief, widespread among the public and official civilian circles, that the military could best solve Japan's problems. Most likely the army and navy would have increased their power even if military factions had not existed; or to go one step further, the armed forces might have increased their power faster and more systematically, and in the end have attained even more power, if the various army and navy cliques, and the divisiveness they engendered, had not arisen at all.

📖 ——Asada Sadao, "The Japanese Navy and the United States," in Dorothy Borg and Shumpei Okamoto, ed, *Pearl Harbor as History* (1973). James B. Crowley, *Japan's Quest for Autonomy* (1966). Fujiwara Akira, *Gunji shi* (1961). Matsushita Yoshi, *Nihon gumbatsu no kōbō* (1975).   *Richard* SMETHURST

gumbu

("military component"). Broadly, *gumbu* signifies the pre-1945 military arm of the government and more narrowly the army and navy when, by taking advantage of the right of supreme command (TŌSUIKEN) of the emperor as defined in the 1889 Meiji CONSTITUTION, they asserted their independence from the civil government (in this connection, often referred to as the *gyōseibu*, or "administrative component") and increased their political power in the years before World War II. More specifically, *gumbu* refers to the military leadership centering on the army and navy general staff headquarters, but also including the two service ministries, military counselors (*gunji sangikan*), and field marshals.

The historian Inoue Kiyoshi (b 1913) has found the first use of the term *gumbu* in the narrower sense in a letter of 2 February 1913 addressed by Major General TANAKA GIICHI to General TERAUCHI MASATAKE, the governor-general of Korea. Inoue also notes that by that time the military had succeeded in asserting its independence from the government and that by the early 1930s the term *gumbu* had entered common usage. See also MILITARISM; GUMBATSU; ARMED FORCES, IMPERIAL JAPANESE.

📖 ——Inoue Kiyoshi, *Shimpan: Nihon no gunkoku shugi*, vol 3 (1975).   *TANAKA Akira*

gumbu daijin gen'eki bukan sei

(active-duty officers as service ministers). Pre–World War II rule whereby only military men on active duty could serve as ministers of the army and navy. It originated in 1871, when the Ministry of Military Affairs (Hyōbushō) required that its head minister hold the rank of major general (or rear admiral) or above, and it continued after that ministry was supplanted by the separate Army and Navy ministries in 1872. In order to check the growing power of political parties, the YAMAGATA ARITOMO cabinet strengthened the rule in 1900 with the added provision that the service ministers must be a full general and a full admiral on active duty. In keeping with the trends of TAISHŌ DEMOCRACY, this provision was abolished by the first YAMAMOTO GONNOHYŌE cabinet in 1913, although in fact the cabinet posts continued to be held by officers on active duty. The rule was formally revived in 1936 by the HIROTA KŌKI cabinet following the FEBRUARY 26TH INCIDENT, an attempted coup by young army officers. It was used by the military to enlarge their role in politics, and by refusing to nominate service ministers they often prevented the parties from forming cabinets (see GUMBATSU).

Gumma Incident

(Gumma Jiken). Riot in May 1884 by indebted farmers in the southern part of Gumma Prefecture. Hard pressed by the deflationary impact of the fiscal policy of Finance Minister MATSUKATA MASAYOSHI (see MATSUKATA FISCAL POLICY), farmers in the district rallied under the leadership of local JIYŪTŌ (Liberal Party) members who hoped to use this opportunity to increase party membership. Frustrated after repeatedly unsuccessful attempts to petition the Meiji government for reduction of interest rates, they planned to attack government officials scheduled to be present at Emperor Meiji's opening of a new railway station at Takasaki; but the ceremony was postponed by the authorities, who had been alerted to the danger. However, the more than 3,000 farmers, who had already gathered at the foot of the mountain Myōgisan, attacked the house of a money-lender and took over a police station in nearby Matsuida. The rioters planned next to attack the garrison at Takasaki, 30 miles to the east, but they were overcome by hunger and exhaustion and were dispersed by police before reaching the garrison. The leaders were arrested shortly afterward and imprisoned in 1887.

Gumma Prefecture

(Gumma Ken). Located in central Honshū and bounded by Niigata and Fukushima prefectures on the north, Tochigi Prefecture on the east, Saitama Prefecture on the south, and Nagano Prefecture on the west. The terrain is largely mountainous, except for the southeastern corner, which constitutes part of the KANTŌ PLAIN. The TONE-GAWA, Japan's second longest river, originates in the extreme north of the prefecture and flows through it in a southerly direction. Most of the major cities are concentrated in the southern plains area. The mountain areas are noted for heavy snowfalls, and the southern plains area has summer thunderstorms and strong, dry winter winds.

The area was settled early on, as evidenced by IWAJUKU and numerous other archaeological sites. It was known as Kōzuke Province under the ancient provincial system (KOKUGUN SYSTEM). During the medieval period (13th–16th centuries) it was divided among various local warlords; some areas were controlled directly by the Tokugawa shogunate in the Edo period (1600–1868). Gumma took its present form in 1876 after the abolition of feudal domains.

Long a center of raw silk and cereal production, Gumma has recently shifted to vegetable farming to supply the Tōkyō market. The textile industry is still dominant in cities such as KIRYŪ, ISESAKI, and TATEBAYASHI, but in recent decades other major cities, notably TAKASAKI and SHIBUKAWA, have become centers for chemical, electrical, and machine industries, reflecting the northward expansion of the KEIHIN INDUSTRIAL ZONE. Its proximity to Tōkyō and excellent transportation links provide a basis for further expansion.

Although Gumma is gradually taking on many of the characteristics of a suburb of Tōkyō, its mountains in the north, including part of NIKKŌ NATIONAL PARK and JŌSHIN'ETSU KŌGEN NATIONAL PARK, continue to be popular with climbers, skiers, and vacationers. Hot spring resorts such as Minakami, Ikaho, and Kusatsu also attract numerous visitors. Area: 6,356 sq km (2,453 sq mi); pop: 1,848,566; capital: Maebashi. See map on previous page.

gun → kokugun system

gunchūjō

Reports drawn up by warriors in the 14th and 15th centuries in which they recounted their successful military exploits; these were submitted after battle to the commander, who endorsed them with his monogram (KAŌ). The reports were influential in determining subsequent promotions and awards of land and were preserved by the warriors' families. The earliest gunchūjō date from the GENKŌ INCIDENT of 1331–33. They provide valuable information not only on such matters as logistics, but also on warrior ethics.

gundai

District deputies or regional intendants. Major provincial officials of the shōguns began to hold this title in the 14th century. Under the Tokugawa shogunate (1603–1867), gundai were generally assigned to shogunal land (TENRYŌ) assessed at over 100,000 koku (see KOKUDAKA), while the more numerous DAIKAN (intendants) had charge of smaller shogunal territories. Both types of official were in charge of tax collection, census registration, law and order, and other administrative functions. In 1590 TOKUGAWA IEYASU appointed INA TADATSUGU as his first gundai of the Kantō region, which would become the heartland of his shogunate. In the latter half of the Edo period (1600–1868), the number of gundai decreased to four, assigned to Kantō, Mino, Hida, and Saigoku. On a smaller scale, the daimyō also appointed gundai in their own domains.

gundan

(war stories). Popular Edo-period (1600–1868) tales about famous battles and the lives of illustrious warrior generals that circulated both as small handwritten books and as oral narratives recited by professional storytellers. They were generally in the form of fictionalized biography or embellished accounts of the rise and fall of well-known warrior families—for example, the Hōjō godai ki (incomplete), a history of five generations of HŌJŌ FAMILY rule; the Nobunaga Kō ki (1600), heroic episodes from the life of ODA NOBUNAGA; and the Taikōki (1625), a romanticized retelling of the exploits of TOYOTOMI HIDEYOSHI. The oral form of these hero stories originated with the professional reciters of the TAIHEIKI, an earlier historical romance; by the 1600s gundan were appearing in handwritten copies at commercial book lenders, where they reached a large audience. They were adapted for the stage by writers for KABUKI troupes and the JŌRURI puppet theater. In the 18th century, when there was an increased Japanese interest in Confucian studies and Chinese literature, Japanese versions of Chinese colloquial fiction enjoyed popularity among gundan readers. Toward the end of the Edo period, accounts of happenings in China like the Opium War (1839–42) and the Taiping (T'ai-p'ing) Rebellion (1850–64) were transformed into gundan almost as soon as the news reached Japan.

David DUTCHER

gunji

Local officials charged with the administration of the gun (districts), administrative subdivisions of the kuni (provinces) under the RITSU-RYŌ SYSTEM of government, which had evolved after the TAIKA REFORM of 645. They were put under the jurisdiction of the KOKU-SHI (provincial officials). Divided into four ranks, the gunji performed such local government functions as law enforcement and land registration. In contrast to the kokushi, who came from the ranks of the central administration, the gunji came from influential local families (KUNI NO MIYATSUKO). They were appointed for life, and the office was virtually hereditary. Strong local ties provided their political power base, and when the central government began to weaken and local uprisings occurred, the gunji often sided with the peasants against the kokushi. With the decline of the ritsuryō system and the rise of the SHŌEN (private estate) system, the post of gunji disappeared, and former office holders became leaders of warrior bands (BUSHIDAN).

Gunjin Chokuyu → Imperial Rescript to Soldiers and Sailors

Gunji Shigetada (1860–1924)

Naval strategist, colonist, adventurer, and entrepreneur in northeast Asia. Born in Edo (now Tōkyō), the second son of Kōda Shigenobu, a minor shogunal official, and adopted into the Gunji family, he entered a naval preparatory school in 1873, graduated as a midshipman in 1879, and reached the rank of first lieutenant by 1890. Regarding as vital to Japan's defense the sparsely inhabited northern Kuril Islands, acquired from Russia in 1875 by the Treaty of ST. PETERSBURG, Gunji called for their colonization. When the government remained unresponsive, he resigned his naval commission and in 1892 founded the Chishima Hōkō Gikai (Kuril Service Society), following the example of another "northern activist," OKAMOTO KANSUKE. On 20 March 1893, amid much popular fanfare, he embarked from Tōkyō's Sumida River (Sumidagawa) with 60 volunteers (mostly naval reservists) and five boats for Shimushu, the Kuril island closest to Kamchatka. Harsh weather and inadequate provisions decimated the expedition, but by 1901 the Shimushu colony was raising its own crops and developing local fisheries. On 6 June 1904, during the RUSSO–JAPANESE WAR, Gunji launched on his own initiative an attack on Kamchatka but was captured and imprisoned. After his release, he wrote on naval strategy and in 1907 headed a fisheries consortium in the Russian Maritime Province. Starting in 1914 he undertook a series of confidential government assignments in Siberia until 1920, when illness forced him to return to Japan and retire in Odawara, Kanagawa Prefecture, southwest of Yokohama. Gunji's younger brother, KŌDA ROHAN, was a novelist and dramatist.

■——John J. Stephan, The Kuril Islands: Russo-Japanese Frontier in the Pacific (1974).

John J. STEPHAN

gunka

Military songs; especially a genre of Westernized music originating in the late 19th century. The history of Japanese military songs can be traced back to the Kume *uta* supposedly sung by Emperor Jimmu's soldiers in the 7th century BC, and still preserved in the court music repertoire, to certain songs in the MAN'YŌSHŪ (completed AD 759), and to various genres of music for BIWA, including HEIKYOKU.

Biwa music was especially popular among the clans in southern Japan, who were the first to show interest in Western military music. At the Meiji Restoration in 1868 the victorious soldiers sang a marching song in Western style, "Miya san, Miya san," later borrowed by Gilbert and Sullivan for *The Mikado* (1885): this was the first true *gunka*. The foreign bandmasters who taught in Japan in the 1870s and 1880s, the educational songs of the 1880s, and the Westernized verses in *Shintaishi shō* (1882, New Style Poetry Collection) all helped to develop the style further. One song taken from the last source was "Battōtai" (1885), composed by the Frenchman Charles Leroux. Another influence was Japanese folk song. Other well-known early *gunka* are: "Kitare ya kitare" (1893), "Teki wa ikuman" (1891), and "Michi wa roppyakuhachijū ri" (1891).

The Sino-Japanese War (1894–95) and the Russo-Japanese War (1904–05) stimulated the composition of many *gunka*. The most famous is "Gunkan kōshinkyoku" (1900, The Battleship March), a celebration of Japan's new naval might, but almost all the rest have been forgotten. One exception is "Sen'yū" (1905), a gloomy lament for fallen comrades overseas. During the 1930s and World War II many more *gunka* were composed. The genre later fell into disfavor, but has enjoyed a strong revival in recent years.

■——Horiuchi Keizō, *Teihon Nihon no gunka* (1969). Irikata Hiroshi, ed, *Nihon no uta: Gunka hen* (1968). Kata Kōji, *Gunka to nihonjin* (1965). Osada Gyōji, *Nihon gunka zenshū* (1976). Yamaki Akihiko and Fukuda Shinji, ed, *Gunka to senji kayō dai zenshū* (1972).   David B. WATERHOUSE

gunki monogatari

(war tales). A category of prose literature which developed in the Kamakura (1185–1333) and Muromachi (1333–1568) periods, and which deals not with those subjects (principally the love affairs of courtiers) standard in Heian-period (794–1185) court romances and later imitations thereof, but with warfare, above all with the cataclysmic civil wars of the period 1156–1221 and those that ushered in the Muromachi period.

The story of the political succession struggles of 1156 and 1159–60 that led to the eclipse of the Fujiwara and to Taira supremacy is told in two works bearing the names of the eras in which the events occurred, HŌGEN MONOGATARI and HEIJI MONOGATARI (see also HŌGEN DISTURBANCE and HEIJI DISTURBANCE). The subsequent arrogant behavior of the Taira leader, Kiyomori, and the events leading up to and during the TAIRA–MINAMOTO WAR of 1180–85 (Gempei no Sōran), when the Taira were overthrown by MINAMOTO NO YORITOMO (assisted by, among others, his younger brother MINAMOTO NO YOSHITSUNE, the supreme hero figure in Japanese history) form the subject matter of the finest war tale, HEIKE MONOGATARI (13th century), as well as of a parallel work, GEMPEI SEISUIKI. The events of the Jōkyū (or Shōkyū) era (1219–22), when Emperor GO-TOBA attempted to reassert imperial authority against the Hōjō family (see JŌKYŪ DISTURBANCE), figure in a minor work called the *Jōkyūki* (or *Shōkyūki*). The final attempt to reassert imperial authority, by Emperor GO-DAIGO in the first half of the 14th century, and the resultant long-drawn-out wars against the ASHIKAGA FAMILY, are recounted in another major work, TAIHEIKI (14th century). Two other notable Muromachi war tales differ from the rest in centering on individual lives—the at first heroic but later pathetic career of Yoshitsune in GIKEIKI and the short lives of the Soga brothers in an archetypal revenge story, SOGA MONOGATARI (14th century).

Precedents for war tales in earlier literature were few—the 10th-century SHŌMONKI and the 11th-century *Mutsu waki*, both in a form of classical Chinese (KAMBUN), and a few tales of warriors in Book 25 of the early-12th-century KONJAKU MONOGATARI. These latter anticipate the language of *Heike monogatari* and other war tales, a Japanese very different from that of Heian romances. Grammatically simpler and containing numerous Chinese words, these tales are set down in a vigorous style suited to the portrayal of action and heroic deeds rather than to the expression of fine shades of romantic feeling. Certainly the audiences for *gunki* were quite different from that for the TALE OF GENJI (ca 1000). Whatever the

original form of *Heike monogatari*, for instance, and despite the development of texts for silent reading culminating in *Gempei seisuiki*, it developed principally, as early as the mid-13th century, as a text for chanting. This text was in the 7- and 5-syllable rhythm of poetry, and it was used by itinerant blind priests for the entertainment and religious edification of the public at large. There is evidence that *Hōgen* and *Heiji* were performed in the same way. *Taiheiki*, though not "chanted," was propagated by *monogatari sō* (storyteller priests). The spread and development of *Soga monogatari* owes much not only to itinerant priests but also to quasi-religious female entertainers.

The wide propagation of *gunki* is important in several respects. It greatly influenced the language, content, and form of the texts, which tended to be highly episodic and were constantly modified and amplified. Again, though they reflected national attitudes and ideals of conduct now regarded as quintessentially Japanese, for example, unflinching bravery and self-sacrificing loyalty, *gunki* may actually also have fostered those concepts. Many characters and events in *gunki* became the stuff of national legend, figuring prominently in numerous NŌ, KABUKI, and JŌRURI dramas, as well as in prose. In some *gunki*, e.g., *Soga monogatari*, a pronounced element of religious propaganda is present. Certainly the tone of the *Heike* as we now know it developed out of its propagation by itinerant "lute-priests" (BIWA HŌSHI), who made the tale not only stirring entertainment but also a deeply moving vehicle for the Buddhist doctrine that all human activity is ephemeral and illusory.

Although having a definite historical basis, *gunki* are romanticized, not accurate, history. To some extent they have epic qualities; the *Heike* in particular has sometimes been called "Japan's national epic." Yet for all its grand sweep, this finest of the *gunki monogatari* contains many episodes, especially tragic love episodes, whose lyrical atmosphere is redolent of the MONO NO AWARE of Heian court literature.

■——Helen Craig McCullough, "A Tale of Mutsu," *Harvard Journal of Asiatic Studies* 25 (1964–65). William C. McCullough, "An Account of the Shōkyū War of 1221," *Monumenta Nipponica* 19.1–2, 3–4 (1964). William Ritchie Wilson, "The Way of the Bow and Arrow: The Japanese Warrior in *Konjaku monogatari*," *Monumenta Nipponica* 28.2 (1973).   Douglas E. MILLS

Gunreibu → Naval General Staff Office

Gunsho ruijū

(Classified Collection of Japanese Classics). A monumental collection of Japanese classics and old documents compiled by HANAWA HOKIICHI (1746–1821). The first series, consisting of some 1,270 documents in 530 fascicles, was completed in 1819; the second, known as *Zoku gunsho ruijū* and consisting of 2,103 documents in 1,150 fascicles, was completed in 1822. The documents, which date from the ancient past to the beginning of the Edo period (1600–1868), were divided into 25 categories by Hanawa.

The project was begun in 1779. Beginning with the printing of the *Ima monogatari* in 1786, other materials were published on a fairly regular basis. After the establishment in 1793 of the Wagaku Kōdansho, a research bureau, at the request of Hanawa, the work of collation and editing variant manuscripts became much easier. Hanawa was also given access to the best extant manuscripts, not only in the collections under direct shogunate control, but those owned by temples, court nobles, and *daimyō*. Moreover, he obtained the help of such capable scholars as YASHIRO HIROKATA and Nakayama Nobuna (1787–1836). After the compilation of the first series in 1819, it was decided to put out another series, *Zoku gunsho ruijū*. The sequel was completed in 1822, the year after Hanawa's death.

The *Gunsho ruijū* set the highest standards for bibliographical and philological scholarship. Even after the Meiji Restoration (1868) it remained an important reference. The set of wooden printing blocks—17,244 in all—are preserved at the Onko Gakkai Historical Society. Even for its time, the expense of making the printing blocks was considerable, and Hanawa had to labor to procure the necessary monies, calling on the shogunate and the KŌNOIKE FAMILY. The series has been reissued using modern type.   YAMAMOTO Takeo

gun'yaku

Military levies that warrior lords required of their vassals. During the Kamakura period (1185–1333) the shogunate expected vassal family heads (*sōryō*; see SŌRYŌ SYSTEM) to mobilize their kinsmen for military service upon call. The territorial lords (SHUGO DAIMYŌ) of the Muromachi period (1333–1568) exacted similar service from warriors in their domains. By the end of the 16th century the magnitude of a vassal's obligation was determined by the assessed productivity of the lands assigned him in fief (CHIGYŌ) and specified in terms of so much manpower per *koku* (see KOKUDAKA).

Throughout the Edo period (1600–1868) the Tokugawa shogunate adhered to this policy, issuing *gun'yaku* regulations for all *daimyō* and lesser direct vassals (HATAMOTO and GOKENIN) in 1616, 1633, and 1649. Those regulations specified precisely the number of men and the number and type of weapons that each vassal was to provide upon command. For example, a *samurai* with a 200-*koku* fief was expected to equip five men in specified ways, while a daimyō with 100,000 *koku* was expected to provide 2,155 men, including 170 cavalry, 350 musketeers, 150 pikemen, and 60 archers. The regulations of 1649 remained unchanged for 200 years, but in fact daimyō and lesser vassals rapidly lost the capacity to provide the men and weaponry required as they shifted income to peacetime uses. Accordingly, in 1862 and 1866, when the shogunate attempted to modernize its military system in the face of dangers both external and internal, it issued regulations that greatly reduced the service requirements of its vassals. The *gun'yaku* system was abandoned by the shogunate in 1867, and after the MEIJI RESTORATION (1868) the new government adopted the principle of universal military conscription.

Conrad TOTMAN

Gunze, Ltd

Manufacturer of textile goods, including knitted goods, stockings, and reeled silk. It is a leading enterprise in Japan's silk industry, as well as the foremost maker of knitted underwear. Established in 1896 in Kyōto, it soon became a major silk manufacturer, organizing a nationwide network of plants and exporting its products from an early period. After World War II, with the decline of the silk industry, it switched to the production of synthetic fabrics and then to secondary textile products. Since the 1960s it has held the largest shares in Japan's knitted goods and stocking markets. It is currently diversifying its lines of business by entering new fields such as plastic films and fashion apparel. Gunze has subsidiary manufacturing firms in Korea, Hong Kong, and Brazil and sales subsidiaries in the United States and West Germany. Sales for the fiscal year ending November 1981 totaled ¥152 billion (US $679.4 million), and the company was capitalized at ¥7.1 billion (US $31.7 million) in the same year. Corporate headquarters are located in Ōsaka.

Guo Moruo (Kuo Mo-jo) (1892–1978)

(J: Kaku Matsujaku). A major Chinese writer and historian, Guo Moruo spent many years in Japan as a student and later as a political exile. He was a leader of the Creation Society (Chuangzao She or Ch'uang-tsao She), which was a formative force in modern Chinese literature and which, in its transition from romanticism to Marxism, reflected the evolution of many young Chinese intellectuals. Guo was influenced by modern Japanese fiction as well as by Western works and set many of his stories in Japan. He remained an important figure in China after the establishment of the People's Republic of China in 1949, holding the positions of chairman of the All-China Federation of Writers and Artists and president of the Chinese Academy of Sciences.

In 1914 Guo Moruo enrolled in a preparatory class for Chinese students at the First Higher School in Tōkyō, and between 1915 and 1918 he studied at the Sixth Higher School at Okayama. It was during this time that Guo met YU DAFU (Yü Ta-fu) and ZHANG ZIPING (Chang Tzu-p'ing), his future companions in the Creation Society, and Satō Tomiko, his future wife.

Guo Moruo studied medicine at Kyūshū University in Fukuoka from 1918 until 1923. He combined medical studies with literary activities, traveling between Fukuoka and Shanghai, where he helped found the Creation Society in 1921 to promote romantic literature. In 1924 Guo announced his conversion to Marxism after translating writings of the noted Japanese Marxist KAWAKAMI HAJIME. In 1924 he also wrote his most famous novel, *Lo ye* (Lo yeh; 1933, Fallen Leaves), an autobiographical account of his love affair with Satō Tomiko. At the end of 1924 Guo moved to Shanghai. After the MAY 30TH INCIDENT in 1925, he devoted himself to leftist propaganda work. The Creation Society also became more radical, advocating "revolutionary" and "proletarian" literature.

In 1928 Guo was sent to Japan to escape arrest by the Guomindang (Kuomintang; Nationalist Party) government. For the next 10 years he lived in Ichikawa, a suburb of Tōkyō, translating and writing. Guo returned to China in 1937 where he participated in patriotic literary efforts during the Sino-Japanese War of 1937–1945.

■——Guo Moruo, *Moruo Zizhuan* (Mo-jo tzu-chuan; 1956). Guo Moruo, *Moruo wenji* (Mo-jo wen-chi; 1957–63). David Tod Roy, *Kuo Mo-jo: The Early Years* (1971).

Guo Songling (Kuo Sung-ling) (1883–1925)

(J: Kaku Shōrei). A leading commander in the army of ZHANG ZUOLIN (Chang Tso-lin), the Chinese warlord based in Manchuria, Guo revolted against Zhang in 1925 and nearly drove him from power but failed when the Japanese GUANDONG (KWANTUNG) ARMY supported Zhang. Guo may have felt that he had not received sufficient reward for his services in Zhang's war against the Zhili (Chihli) warlords in 1924. Rivalry between officer factions in the Fengtian (Fengtien) clique also played a role. Moreover, it was rumored that Guo's wife encouraged him to accept liberal political values at odds with Zhang's conservatism; the rumors seemed confirmed when Guo declared alliance with Feng Yuxiang (Feng Yü-hsiang; 1880–1948), the "Christian warlord," who was thought to be leftist and pro-Russian. Guo launched the revolt with a public denunciation of Zhang Zuolin on 22 November 1925, and during the following two weeks won a series of victories that seemed to make Zhang's position hopeless. But Guo had begun his rebellion without sufficient preparation, and his troops suffered from inadequate supplies. Li Jinglin (Li Ching-lin), the military governor of Zhili, did not give the cooperation that Guo had expected, and Feng's assistance was too little and too late. Most important, Japanese leaders concluded that Zhang's continued rule in Manchuria served Japan better than would a change to Guo's control. Japan therefore gave crucial support to Zhang, notably by forbidding military operations in areas of strong Japanese interests, which included Zhang's capital of Mukden (now Shenyang) and other key areas. Guo therefore could not swiftly follow up his early victories, and his forces were decisively defeated on 23 December. Zhang's men captured Guo and his wife the following day and shot them.

James E. SHERIDAN

Gurin → Chūyūki

Gusai (1281?–1375?)

Renga (linked verse) poet and Buddhist priest. Of humble origins, he was taught linked verse from an early age by the master Zenna. It was not until his late fifties, however, that he began to emerge as the most important *renga* poet of the age. He formed close associations with members of both the court and military aristocracies, and became the teacher of such masters as Shūa (dates unknown), ASAYAMA BONTŌ, and the high court noble NIJŌ YOSHIMOTO. With Yoshimoto he compiled the *Tsukubashū* (Tsukuba Collection), the first anthology of choice *renga* verses, which in 1357, by Yoshimoto's influence with the sovereign, was granted official status and respectability equivalent to an imperial anthology of classical poetry. Gusai also aided Yoshimoto in his efforts, extending over nearly 30 years, to codify the rules of linked verse composition, which had long existed in a very confused state. He also wrote several poetic treatises, mostly no longer extant. One hundred and twenty-six of his *renga* verses are included in the *Tsukubashū*. See also RENGA AND HAIKAI.

Robert H. BROWER

Gushikawa

City on the island of Okinawa, Okinawa Prefecture. Known early on for its sugarcane. Cattle and hogs have been raised since World War II. The majority of residents, however, are engaged in service-related business and commercial activities. Spinning and paper industries have also been introduced. Pop: 46,634.

gymnastics

Western-style gymnastics began in Japan with the introduction of German gymnastic exercises from the United States in 1877. During the Taishō period (1912–26), Swedish gymnastic exercises were introduced and widely practiced in most schools. In recent years there has been increasing public interest in gymnastic exercises, usually calisthenics, to compensate for the stress and lack of exercise in modern city life. Radio fitness exercises are particularly popular. The public NHK (Japan Broadcasting Corporation) has been broadcasting such exercises since 1928.

In 1930 the All-Japan Gymnastic Association was founded, and around the same time, the first organized gymnastic competition was begun, including such events as floor exercises, parallel bars, and horizontal bars. The first Japanese participation in international competition was that of a men's team in the Olympic Games of 1932 at Los Angeles, where the team finished in last place. Since World War II, however, the level of Japanese gymnastics has improved rapidly, and Japan has compiled excellent records in many international championships. In particular, since 1960, the men's team has taken first place 10 times successively in both the Olympic Games and International Championships. Currently, the Japan Gymnastic Association is a controlling organization for gymnasts and as of the late 1970s had 18,500 members.　　　　　　　　　*WATANABE Tōru*

Gyōda

City in northern Saitama Prefecture, central Honshū, between the rivers Tonegawa and Arakawa. With the construction of Oshi Castle in the late 15th century, it developed as a castle town. Long known for its TABI (socks worn with *kimono*) during the Edo period (1600–1868), after World War II textile industries became prevalent. Rubber and machinery industries are also well developed. Pop: 73,205.

Gyōgi (668–749)

Also known as Gyōki. Monk of the HOSSŌ SECT of Buddhism (Ch: Faxiang or Fa-hsiang). Born in Izumi Province (now part of Ōsaka Prefecture). He studied Hossō teachings at the temple Yakushiji. Following the death of his mother, he traveled widely with his disciples, devoting himself to many social welfare activities and the building of temples. His contributions toward the construction of the temple TŌDAIJI are particularly noteworthy. He also undertook numerous social welfare projects for the people, such as dam and bridge building, land clearing, and construction of irrigation systems. During his later years, the emperor SHŌMU bestowed on him the name Daibosatsu ("Great Bodhisattva") and raised him to the rank of Daisōjō (great bishop or primate). Because of his outstanding virtue, he was often known as Gyōgi Bosatsu (Bodhisattva Gyōgi) and was popularly taken to be a manifestation of Mañjuśrī Bodhisattva. He was long remembered as an ascetic with great charisma and many temples are attributed to him.

MATSUNAMI Yoshihiro

Gyōki → Gyōgi

Gyokudō → Uragami Gyokudō

Gyokudō Art Museum

(Gyokudō Bijutsukan). Located at Ōme in the suburbs of Tōkyō. One of the most attractive of the museums devoted to the work of an individual artist, it consists of a Japanese-style building designed in 1961 by YOSHIDA ISOYA and houses a collection of paintings and sketches by KAWAI GYOKUDŌ (1873–1957). There is also a room set up as a reproduction of the artist's studio, which contains his painting equipment and some of his furniture.　　　*Laurance ROBERTS*

Gyokuen Bompō (1348–ca 1420)

Zen monk-scholar who specialized in subdued, monochrome ink paintings of orchids. A poet, calligrapher, and painter as well as a monk, he attained the elevated status of abbot of two major Zen monasteries in Kyōto, first the Kenninji and then the Nanzenji. Bompō's colophons appear on many well-known ink paintings executed by his friends in the Zen cultural milieu in Kyōto. His earliest dated colophon is the preface to the painting *New Moon over the Brushwood Gate (Saimon shingetsu)* dated 1405. At least 30 of his paintings of orchids, the traditional emblem of moral virtue, are recorded in Japanese and American collections. The compositions generally include long, swaying blades of orchid leaves grouped like a still life with thorns and a sprig of young bamboo, all emerging from the soft folds of a moss-dotted rock. His style has been traced to the work of the mid-14th century Chinese priest-painter Xuechuang (Hsüeh-ch'uang) and to that of Bompō's older contemporary, the Japanese priest-painter TESSHŪ TOKUSAI.

■——Kanazawa Hiroshi, *Japanese Ink Painting: Early Zen Masterpieces,* tr Barbara Ford (1979). Tanaka Ichimatsu, *Kaō, Mokuan, Minchō,* vol 5 in *Suiboku bijutsu taikei* (Kōdansha, 1974). Yoshiaki Shimizu and Carolyn Wheelwright, ed, *Japanese Ink Painting* (1976).

Julia MEECH-PEKARIK

gyokugan

A technique of inlaying crystal balls as the eyes of a Buddhist sculpture. The pupils were either painted directly on the back of the transparent crystals or on a piece of silk cloth which was attached thereto. In either case, the pupils were seen from the backs of the crystal balls, producing a more realistic effect than the conventional technique of carving and painting eyeballs directly on the sculpture's surface. The technique of *gyokugan*, which was applied from the mid-12th century, was one expression of the general tendency towards realism in BUDDHIST SCULPTURE of the Kamakura period (1185–1333), most notably that of the master UNKEI. One of the earliest surviving examples of the technique is the Amida trinity of the Chōgakuji temple in Nara Prefecture.

Gyokukai → Gyokuyō

Gyokuyō

(Leaves of Jade; also called *Gyokukai*). Diary of the court official KUJŌ KANEZANE; its 66 chapters, written in KAMBUN (classical Chinese prose), describe in great detail the events of the years 1164–1200. Because Kanezane not only served as regent (*sesshō* and *kampaku;* see REGENCY GOVERNMENT) in the imperial court, but was also an important liaison between the court and the newly founded KAMAKURA SHOGUNATE (1192–1333), his diary is, with the later chronicle AZUMA KAGAMI, one of the two most valuable sources of information on the tumultuous events of the last three or four decades of the 12th century.　　　*G. Cameron HURST III*

Gyokuyō wakashū

(Collection of Jeweled Leaves; the full title is abbreviated to *Gyokuyōshū*). The 14th imperial anthology (*chokusenshū*) of classical Japanese poetry; ordered in 1311 by the retired emperor FUSHIMI; completed between 1312 and 1314; compiled by KYŌGOKU TAMEKANE; 20 books; 2,796 poems.

In 1293, Emperor Fushimi commanded Tamekane and several other leading poets to compile a new imperial anthology, but the project dragged on inconclusively and was eventually abandoned. However, when Emperor Hanazono gained the succession in 1308, his father Fushimi had a second opportunity to sponsor an anthology. This time he designated Tamekane as sole compiler. Despite numerous strong protests from Tamekane's poetic and political arch-rival, NIJŌ TAMEYO, Fushimi stood firm, and finally, in 1311, Tamekane was officially appointed. He completed the task with dispatch barely six months later. There is some doubt as to the date of completion of the final version, but it was surely no later than 1314.

Owing to the domination of court poetry by the conservative Nijō faction, of the last 10 imperial anthologies compiled between 1275 and 1439, Nijō family members and supporters compiled 8, the dissident Kyōgoku and Reizei factions only 2: the *Gyokuyōshū* and the *Fūgashū* (ca 1346, Collection of Elegance; the 17th). These collections are, therefore, virtually the sole repositories of what the innovating poets of the age considered their own best work. It is probably no accident that Tamekane made the *Gyokuyōshū*, with its nearly 2,800 poems, the bulkiest of the 21 imperial anthologies; he no doubt feared that this might be the only opportunity to publish the work of the Kyōgoku–Reizei poets. Ironically, the collection contains not only the most typical poems by the innovators, but also, by Tamekane's deliberate choice, those poems by the conservatives which were closest to the innovating styles and therefore surely regarded by their authors as among their least distinguished works. Thus, the collection is of unusual value as a record of what the innovators considered best and their opponents considered worst in contemporary poetic practice.

The structure of the anthology also shows a disregard for the norm established by the first imperial anthology, the KOKINSHŪ (905, Collection of Ancient and Modern Times). Tamekane made a radical departure by beginning the section of love poems with Book 9 instead of the normal Book 11; by including more books of miscellaneous *(zō)* poems than was customary, and the like. Even such seemingly minor differences were fraught with significances in this basically conservative age and helped to underscore Tamekane's break with the traditional authority and poetic precedent dogmatized by his opponents.

As in all imperial anthologies, the individual poems in the *Gyokuyōshū* are arranged in such a way as to provide smooth, natural transitions from one to the next by associations and contrasts of common or related imagery, progressions of time or spatial movement, and the like. Poems juxtaposed in the *Gyokuyōshū,* however, sometimes appear to have no association with each other whatsoever, apart from a loose topical connection (both poems are on autumn or love, for instance), and the relationship can only be discovered by recognizing that the imagery or phraseology of the two verses together may provide an allusion to an older poem, which then forms a link in the reader's mind between the two. Such distantly related verses, called *soku,* were a relatively new ideal among the Kyōgoku–Reizei poets, and they were opposed by the conservatives, who accepted only the traditional *shinku* (closely related verses).

Apart from poets of earlier periods (FUJIWARA NO SADAIE, for example, is represented by 68 poems), the principal figures in terms of number of poems are: the retired emperor Fushimi, 76; Lady Jusammi Tameko (Tamekane's sister), 59; Saionji Sanekane, 57; Fushimi's consort, EIFUKU MON'IN, 43; and Tamekane, 36. These and other accomplished poets belonging to the Kyōgoku faction represent what is new in the poetry of the age.

The *Gyokuyōshū* was scorned and rejected in its day by the conservative majority. Such an attitude to the collection and the work of the Kyōgoku–Reizei poets became traditional with the consolidation of the Nijō hegemony from the 15th century onward. No good modern editions have yet been produced, and only in recent times have the collection and its distinctive poetry begun to receive the serious attention they deserve, either in Japan or in the West.
■ ——Robert H. Brower and Earl Miner, *Japanese Court Poetry* (1961).
                              Robert H. BROWER

Gyōnen (1240–1321)

Scholar-monk of the KEGON SECT, renowned for his erudition. Born in Iyo Province (now Ehime Prefecture). He was long the abbot of the Kaidan'in of the Nara temple Tōdaiji. His writing, said to include more than 120 works, encompasses the whole range of Buddhist learning. In particular, his *Hasshū kōyō* (1268), an outline of the eight sects of Japanese Buddhism, has been esteemed as an excellent introductory textbook to Buddhism.   Robert RHODES

Gyōsai → Kawanabe Gyōsai

gyōzui

(sponge bath). The term *gyōzui* was originally applied to ritual bathing by worshipers in streams, pools, or waterfalls in or near a religious precinct. In the Edo period (1600–1868), families who did not have a regular bath chamber would take sponge baths, using a wooden tub in the yard, and such scenes were a frequent theme in Edo art and literature.   MIYAMOTO Mizuo

H

habatsu

(factional clique). A group or faction resulting from a struggle for leadership within a larger group. Although this term is essentially a synonym for the BATSU (cliques) found in many large organizations, it is most often used to refer to factions within political parties, business corporations, and trade unions. For example, there are several factions within the Liberal Democratic Party (LDP), named for each person who can potentially become prime minister. By supporting a certain man, faction members hope to receive political rewards, the greatest plum being a ministerial appointment when the faction leader becomes prime minister. *Habatsu* generate internal power struggles for the leading position within the organization. Often the struggle hinges on monetary considerations. See also GROUPS.   *IWAI Hiroaki*

Habeas Corpus Law

(Jinshin Hogo Hō). Judicial inquiry into lawfulness of physical detention, patterned on Anglo-American habeas corpus. Japan's 1947 CONSTITUTION (art. 34) prohibits detention without lawful cause and allows detained persons to demand a showing in open court, while represented by counsel, of reasons for detention. Procedure to effectuate the constitutional right is provided by the Habeas Corpus Law (Law No. 199, 1948, as amended).

Persons in confinement, their counsel, or persons acting on their behalf may apply to a district or high court for an immediate hearing on lawfulness of detention. Although in Anglo-American practice imprisoned criminal defendants make extensive use of the writ and the Japanese law contemplates redress in both civil and criminal matters, Japanese convicts rarely seek, and are never granted, statutory redress. Instead, the legality or constitutionality of court-ordered imprisonment, whether before or after adjudication, may be challenged only through procedures established in the Criminal Procedure Law. Habeas corpus proceedings must be in open court and counsel must be supplied for a detained person unable to retain counsel. If lawful grounds for detention exist the application is denied; if they are wanting the person is ordered released immediately. Appeal lies against either ruling.

▪ ——George M. Koshi, *Japanese Legal Advisor: Crimes and Punishments* (1970). Tanaka Hideo and Malcolm D. H. Smith, *The Japanese Legal System: Introductory Cases and Materials* (1976).
                                                                                    B. J. GEORGE, Jr.

Habikino

City in southeastern Ōsaka Prefecture, central Honshū. Situated on a highway that connected the ancient capitals of NANIWAKYŌ and ASUKA, Habikino developed as a market town. There are several imperial tombs, including the ŌJIN MAUSOLEUM, and temples of historical interest. The city is now a residential suburb of Ōsaka. Vineyards are located on the slopes of Nijōsan in the eastern part of the city. Winemaking is the principal industry. The city is part of the Kongō–Ikoma Quasi-National Park. Pop: 103,147.

Habōhō → Subversive Activities Prevention Law

haboku

(Ch: *po mo* or *p'o mo*; literally, "break ink"). A technique of INK PAINTING based on vivid tonal contrasts of spontaneously applied ink. Darker washes or lines or dots "break" lighter tonalities of ink or ground to suggest rather than explicate landscape forms, which appear saturated in moist atmosphere.

The first reference to *haboku* in Chinese art texts occurs in the *Lidai minghua ji (Li-tai ming-hua chi)* of 847, where Zhang Yanyuan

(Chang Yen-yüan) associates the method with the poet-painter Wang Wei (ca 699–ca 759). Later, a second term pronounced the same *(po mo)*, but written with characters meaning "splash ink," was used to describe the development of the technique by the 9th-century artist Wang Xia (Wang Hsia). The Japanese did not attempt to differentiate the two terms, nor did they observe the Chinese evolution of *po mo* by Mi Fei (1051–1107) and his followers during the Song (Sung; 960–1279) and Yuan (Yüan; 1279–1368) dynasties. From the time the *haboku* mode first appeared in Japan in the 14th century through the period of its popularity at the end of the 15th century and its establishment as a type style during the 16th century, the Japanese linked it almost exclusively with the Yuan priest-painter Yujian (Yü-chien). The paintings they endorsed as the works of this master feature vivid splashes of saturated ink against a background of diluted washes.

From the Yujian prototype, Japanese painters interpreted the *haboku* manner according to their own inclinations. In the late 15th and early 16th centuries, SESSHŪ TŌYŌ and his followers clearly structured these abbreviated motifs. In the late 16th century, KAIHŌ YŪSHŌ used this technique to exploit contrasts in the plasticity of surfaces and the momentum of incisive lines. And in the 17th century, KANŌ TAN'YŪ further economized, reducing forms to spurts of ink in spacious, airy compositions.   *Carolyn WHEELWRIGHT*

Habomai Islands

(Habomai Shotō). A small group of islands northeast of Nemuro Peninsula, eastern Hokkaidō. It includes Tarakujima, Shibotsujima, and Suishōjima. The Habomai Islands have been under occupation by the Soviet Union since the end of World War II, when the Japanese population was forced to move to the main islands of Japan. (See also TERRITORY OF JAPAN.) The waters abound in crab, scallops, and kelp. Area: 102 sq km (39.4 sq mi).

Hachigyaku

(Eight Outrages). The eight most serious crimes as defined by the TAIHŌ CODE (701) and the YŌRŌ CODE (effective 757). They were: (1) rebellion against the emperor, (2) damage of imperial palaces or tombs, (3) treason against the state, (4) murder of one's kin, (5) murder of one's wife or more than three members of a family, (6) theft or damage of imperial or religious property, (7) unfilial acts toward one's parents or senior kin, and (8) murder of one's superior or teacher. The first three were always punished by death, the offender's family often being exterminated as well. The other crimes were punishable by death or by various terms of hard labor or banishment. Sentences for these crimes could not be commuted under any circumstances, even by general amnesty. See also RITSURYŌ SYSTEM.

Hachihachi Kantai

(Eight Eight Fleet). Refers to the plan of building a Japanese fleet that would consist of eight battleships and eight battlecruisers as its first-line units; decided upon as a part of the 1907 Imperial National Defense Policy, which posited the United States as the hypothetical enemy. Because of financial constraints, it was decided to implement the plan in stages, first eight four and then eight six. Funds for an eight eight fleet were finally approved in 1920 by the HARA TAKASHI cabinet, with completion scheduled for 1927, but the plan was interrupted because of the limits on capital ship tonnage imposed by the WASHINGTON NAVAL TREATY OF 1922. In the end, only four ships were built in accordance with this plan, the battleships *Nagato*, *Mutsu*, *Akagi*, and *Kaga*, the latter two of which were later converted to aircraft carriers.   *ICHIKI Toshio*

Hachimaki

A man wearing a *hachimaki* while selling morning glories at a morning glory fair at a Buddhist temple in Tōkyō.

Hachijōjima

Island approximately 180 km (112 mi) southeast of the Izu Peninsula, central Honshū; one of the IZU ISLANDS, under the administration of the Tōkyō prefectural government. It is part of the Fuji-Hakone-Izu National Park. Tourism, fishing, and farming are carried on. The local silk fabric known as *kihachijō* has been designated an Intangible Cultural Property. During the Edo period (1600–1868) the island was a place of exile for convicts. Area: 69 sq km (27 sq mi).

hachimaki

A thin towel (TENUGUI) or strip of cloth tied around the crown of the head; also, the custom of wearing a *hachimaki*. Originally worn during religious acts, *hachimaki* are still commonly worn by men performing heavy physical labor and for such strenuous activities as carrying MIKOSHI (portable shrines) at festivals. The custom is mentioned in early Chinese accounts of Japan and depicted in the early clay figures known as HANIWA. Prior to the Kamakura period (1185–1333) it was called *makkō*.

Hachimaki came to be worn in battle, apparently because they were felt to strengthen the spirit. They were also believed to repel evil spirits; for this reason boys wore *hachimaki* made of iris leaves on Boys' Day (see CHILDREN'S DAY), and sick people or women giving birth often donned *hachimaki*.

📖 —— Abe Masamichi, *Nihonjin to hachimaki* (1975).

MIYAMOTO Mizuo

Hachiman

A popular Shintō deity who protects warriors and generally looks after the well-being of the community. Since the Heian period (794–1185) identified as the deified spirit of the legendary emperor Ōjin, he is worshiped as the central deity in a shrine known as a Hachimangū, where he is usually flanked by two other deities, Okinagaōtarashihime no Mikoto (the spirit of Ōjin's mother, the legendary empress Jingū) and Hime Ōkami, Ōjin's spouse deified. The three deities together are sometimes collectively referred to as Hachiman.

The origins of Hachiman are unknown. The Chinese characters for the name, which can also be read Yahata, literally mean "eight banners," which has been interpreted as referring to the legend that eight banners appeared from heaven at the birth of Emperor Ōjin, who is associated with a legend concerning a successful campaign of conquest in Korea. More likely, however, is the theory that Yahata was merely the name of the region in the Usa district, Kyūshū, where the cult of this deity first arose. Although the *Fusō ryakki* (12th century, Abridged Annals of Japan) states that the Usa Jingū, the earliest and foremost Hachiman shrine, was built in 571, the oldest attested reference to the shrine occurs in a chronicle *(Shoku nihongi)* under the year 737, which suggests a relatively late origin. After an oracle declared that Hachiman would provide protection for the construction of the Great Buddha image (DAIBUTSU) in Nara (749), he began to be viewed as a protector of Buddhism and was given the Buddhist title Daibosatsu (Great Bodhisattva). His cult became firmly established in Kyōto after the IWASHIMIZU HACHIMAN SHRINE, a derivative shrine of the Usa Jingū, was built there in accordance with a petition in 859 by the Buddhist monk Gyōkyō.

Being identified with military prowess, Hachiman was adopted as the patron deity of the MINAMOTO FAMILY and subsequent other warrior clans. The main shrine to this deity in eastern Japan is the TSURUGAOKA HACHIMAN SHRINE in Kamakura, established there in 1191 by MINAMOTO NO YORITOMO, the founder of the Kamakura shogunate. The popularity of the Hachiman cult has grown steadily, as is clearly evidenced by some 25,000 Hachiman shrines throughout Japan today. See also HAKOZAKI SHRINE. Stanley WEINSTEIN

Hachimantai

A highland area in the Nasu Volcanic Zone, on the border between Akita and Iwate prefectures, northern Honshū. The area includes the highland called Hachimantai Kōgen, and the mountains Yakeyama and Chausudake. Alpine flora, forests, and swamp plants abound. Swamps such as Hachimannuma and Gamanuma have been created by volcanic gas explosions. The foothills have numerous hot springs and skiing grounds. Principal part of Towada-Hachimantai National Park. Height: 1,614 m (5,294 ft).

hachimonjiya-bon

Books of the genre UKIYO-ZŌSHI (tales of the floating world) produced in the first half of the 18th century by the Kyōto publisher and bookseller Hachimonjiya Jishō (d 1745). The term is also used in a broader sense to refer to other *ukiyo-zōshi,* mainly of the Kyōhō era (1716–36) and later, which, like Hachimonjiya's publications, are character studies of denizens of the floating world or tales about courtesans and the disowned sons of wealthy merchants and feudal lords, were adapted from JŌRURI and KABUKI plays. Although these works derive from the oeuvre of Ihara SAIKAKU, to which they are uniformly inferior, they mark a distinct literary-historical period, which is customarily subdivided to distinguish between works contemporary with the foremost Hachimonjiya writer, EJIMA KISEKI, and those which appeared after his death. Moreover, *hachimonjiya-bon* influenced the development of subsequent literature: many YO-MIHON, more truly novelistic works written in a style partly borrowed from the tradition of the Chinese vernacular novel, adopted the theme of the disowned son.

Hachinohe

City in southeastern Aomori Prefecture, northern Honshū. Situated on the Pacific Ocean, Hachinohe developed during the Edo period (1600–1868) as a castle town of the Nambu domain. The city is noted for its chemical, paper, and steel industries, as well as mackerel and cuttlefish fishing and the processing of marine products. Each year from 17 to 20 February an agricultural festival called the Emburi Matsuri is held to ensure success in the coming rice-growing year; the Hachinohe Festival (20–23 August) at Shinra Shrine is also a tourist attraction. Pop: 238,208.

Hachiōji

City in southwestern Tōkyō Prefecture. Hachiōji developed during the Edo period (1600–1868) as a POST-STATION TOWN on the highway Kōshū Kaidō and as a market center for raw silk. At present Hachiōji produces over 80 percent of the neckties made in Japan. The electrical appliance industry is growing in importance. In recent years it has become a residential suburb for commuters to Tōkyō as well as an educational center, a number of universities having moved here from central Tōkyō. Pop: 387,162.

Hachirōgata

Also called Kotonoumi. Lagoon in the eastern part of the Oga Peninsula, northwestern Akita Prefecture, northern Honshū. It was the second largest lake in Japan (after Lake Biwa) before land reclamation projects (1957–66) converted practically all the lagoon area into land. Before land reclamation the lagoon provided abundant catches of a variety of fish. It is now one of Akita Prefecture's most important agricultural districts, with large-scale group farming utilizing modern machinery. Total acreage of land reclaimed: 172 sq km (66 sq mi); area of lagoon before land reclamation: about 220 sq km (85 sq mi); current area: 48.1 sq km (18.6 sq mi); circumference: 78 km (48 mi); depth: 4.7 m (15.4 ft).

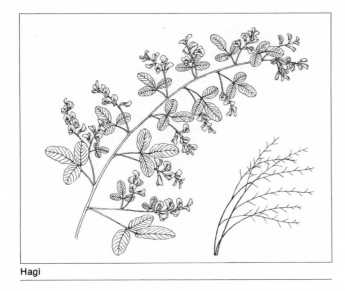
Hagi

wife, between antagonists, and between fellow samurai. While *Hagakure* once served as a handbook for young warrior vassals of the Hizen domain, its chief value today is as a documentary source in the history of *bushidō*. There was, however, one ardent modern follower of its ideals, the writer MISHIMA YUKIO. Translated as *Hagakure: The Book of the Samurai* (1979).

Haga Yaichi (1867–1927)

Scholar of Japanese literature. Born in Echizen Province (now Fukui Prefecture). Graduate of Tōkyō University, where he later became a professor. Haga applied the methods of German philology to the study of traditional Japanese classical works. His principal books include *Kokubungaku shi jikkō* (1899), a history of Japanese classical literature, *Kokuminsei jūron* (1907), an exploration of the Japanese national character through an analysis of Japanese literature, and *Meiji bunten* (1904), a forerunner of modern concepts of Japanese orthography and grammar.

Hagerty Incident

A demonstration that took place in Tōkyō on 10 June 1960, when James C. Hagerty, press secretary to President Eisenhower, arrived to make final preparations for the president's visit. The visit was scheduled to begin on 19 June, the day after the Diet was to complete its approval of the newly revised United States–Japan Security Treaty. The automobile taking Hagerty and two other officials, including American Ambassador Douglas MacArthur II, from Haneda Airport to the United States Embassy was surrounded by 8,000 to 10,000 demonstrators, mostly labor union members and students who opposed the treaty. After over an hour a United States military helicopter was finally able to land, pick up the officials, and take them to downtown Tōkyō. Further demonstrations followed, and on 16 June the Eisenhower visit was cancelled. On 23 June Prime Minister KISHI NOBUSUKE announced his decision to resign. The demonstration against Hagerty and the disorders that followed were the most serious manifestations of public opposition to government policy in the postwar period and were marked by anti-American overtones. See also UNITED STATES–JAPAN SECURITY TREATIES.

──George R. Packard III, *Protest in Tokyo: The Security Treaty Crisis of 1960* (1966). Richard B. FINN

Hagi

City in northern Yamaguchi Prefecture, western Honshū. Situated on the Sea of Japan, Hagi was the castle town of the MŌRI FAMILY during the Edo period (1600–1868). The city is also known as the birthplace of KIDO TAKAYOSHI, ITŌ HIROBUMI, and several others who were the leaders of the MEIJI RESTORATION (1868). Principal products are *natsumikan* (summer oranges) and marine products. The city is one of the better preserved of premodern castle towns; the ruins of Hagi Castle (in Shizuki Park), a district containing former *samurai* homes, and the Shōka Sonjuku, a school directed by the proimperial ideologue YOSHIDA SHŌIN, are chief tourist attractions. The production of HAGI WARE dates from the early 1600s. Pop: 53,692.

hagi

(Japanese bush clover). *Lespedeza bicolor* var. *japonica*. Also known as *yamahagi*. A deciduous shrub of the pea family (Leguminosae), growing wild in fields and mountains throughout Japan. It has long been celebrated in Japanese culture as the first of the "seven plants of autumn" *(aki no nanakusa)*. Hagi reaches about 2 meters (7 ft) in height and has many thin branches. The compound leaves are composed of three wide oval leaflets. In autumn, it produces long reddish-purple flowers in long clusters (raceme) at the tips of the branches.

The *hagi* has been a well-known plant in Japan since early times. Its stems and leaves were used as feed for livestock, and the stems were also trimmed and used in making fences and thatching roofs, or peeled and used for rope. It is said that in ancient times the seeds were ground and mixed with rice gruel and the leaves were used as a substitute for tea. In the MAN'YŌSHŪ, Japan's oldest poetic anthology, the *hagi* is one of the most frequently mentioned plants, appearing in 141 poems.

Several other types of *hagi* are also found in Japan, including the *marubahagi (L. cyrtobotrya),* which has round leaves; the *miyagino-*

Hadaka no shima

(Naked Island; shown abroad as *The Island*). A 1960 semi-autobiographical black-and-white film written and directed by SHINDŌ KANETO. Toiling for survival with their two sons on a tiny, barren island in the Inland Sea, a middle-aged farmer (played by Tonoyama Taiji) and his wife (played by OTOWA NOBUKO) experience simple pleasures and great sorrow. With minimal dramatic incident and no dialogue, this elegy to peasant life relies primarily on a highly pictorial style, natural sounds, and background music. In making this film, Shindō pioneered the extremely low budget ($14,000), independent feature produced communally by a small group. It won first prize at the 1961 Moscow Film Festival.

J. L. ANDERSON

Hadano

City in eastern Kanagawa Prefecture, central Honshū. Formerly a production center for tobacco and peanuts, in recent years it has become a residential district. There is a growing automobile industry here. Many tourists visit Tanzawasan, the mountain that was the epicenter of the TŌKYŌ EARTHQUAKE OF 1923, and Lake Shinsei, which was created by the earthquake. Pop: 123,130.

Hagakure

("In the Shadow of Leaves"). Properly titled *Hagakure kikigaki* ("Notes of What Was Heard in the Shadow of Leaves"). An 11-fascicle manual for SAMURAI; consisting of some 1,300 short anecdotes and reflections and completed in 1716. It is considered one of the classics on BUSHIDŌ (the way of the samurai). *Hagakure* is believed to have been dictated by Yamamoto Tsunetomo (1659–1719), a middle-ranking retainer of Nabeshima Mitsushige (1632–1700), *daimyō* of Hizen Province (now Saga Prefecture), to Tashiro Tsuramoto (1687–1748). At the time of his lord's death, Yamamoto was thwarted in his desire to follow Mitsushige in death by committing *seppuku* because this practice (JUNSHI) had been outlawed. Instead he entered the priesthood to spend the remainder of his life in prayer for the repose of Mitsushige's soul. The compilation of *Hagakure*, which reflects Yamamoto's personal convictions on the proper attitude and duties of a samurai, was begun about 10 years after he took the tonsure and was completed 7 years later.

The work's often quoted first line, "Bushidō is a way of dying," expresses the theme that is elaborated upon throughout the work: only a samurai prepared and willing to die at any moment can devote himself fully to his lord. Moreover, this devotion is conceived of as an emotional bond. The desire to serve one's lord, Yamamoto declares, should be like the desire to please a lover—a homosexual lover. Indeed, the proper conduct of a homosexual relationship is given detailed attention, as well as conduct between husband and *hagi (L. thunbergii)*, whose drooping branches and elegant flowers make it a highly popular ornamental shrub; the *shirahagi* or *shirobanahagi (L. japonica)*, which has white flowers and is also widely planted in gardens; and the *kihagi (L. buergeri)*, which grows to over 2 meters (7 ft) in height. All these species are shrubs with woody stems; other species, including the *makiehagi (L. virgata)*, the *inuhagi (L. tomentosa)*, and the white-flowered *nekohagi (L. pilosa)*, are perennial herbs. Their flowers bloom in the axils from late summer through autumn and are a common sight in autumn fields.

MATSUDA Osamu

Hagi Rebellion

(Hagi no Ran). Rebellion in October 1876 by former *samurai* at Hagi, Yamaguchi Prefecture. Disturbed by the modernizing policies of the new government and outraged by recent decrees stripping them of their traditional privileges (see SHIZOKU), dispossessed samurai rose in arms almost simultaneously in several parts of southwestern Japan (see also JIMPŪREN REBELLION and AKIZUKI REBELLION OF 1876). A large group of ex-samurai of the former Chōshū domain (now Yamaguchi Prefecture) led by MAEBARA ISSEI, a onetime high official of the Meiji government, planned to attack the prefectural office at Hagi on 26 October. When government troops arrived from the Hiroshima garrison, Maebara and his men attempted to flee but were captured on 6 November. Maebara and 8 others were put to death, and 60 were imprisoned.

Hagiwara Kyōjirō (1899–1938)

Poet. Born in Gumma Prefecture. After graduating from middle school he worked briefly for the Japanese Red Cross Society and as a bank employee. In 1923, together with the poets TSUBOI SHIGEJI and Okamoto Jun (b 1901), he founded the anarchist poetry magazine *Aka to kuro* (Red and Black). Hagiwara was an early champion of dadaism, futurism, and nihilism. One of his best poems, "Morokuzukin" (1932, Hood of Senility), deals with the dismal life of a farm village. Major collections are *Shikei senkoku* (1925, Death Sentence) and *Dampen* (1931, Fragments).

Hagiwara Sakutarō (1886–1942)

Poet. Acclaimed as a major poet for his extraordinarily brilliant free-style poems, Hagiwara is generally considered to have established modern colloquial poetry in Japan. He also wrote poems in the classical style, and in either colloquial or classical language, the quality of his works has scarcely been surpassed. Born the eldest son of a Maebashi physician in Gumma Prefecture, north of Tōkyō, he wrote TANKA (31-syllable traditional WAKA poetry) against his parents' wishes and contributed his works to various magazines. Doubtful about what direction to take in choosing a career or the desirability of a regimented life, he withdrew from two different national higher schools and spent seemingly idle years in Maebashi and Tōkyō, practicing the mandolin and frequenting the theater, but, in fact, writing poetry. In 1913 a leading poet of the day, KITAHARA HAKUSHŪ, published five of Hagiwara's free-style poems in his journal *Zamboa* (Shaddock). Hagiwara met and became fast friends with MUROO SAISEI through *Zamboa* and collaborated with him in launching a little magazine called *Takujō funsui* (1915, Tabletop Fountain) in which both published their poems. In 1916 he and Muroo founded another journal, *Kanjō* (Feeling), which, opposed to the current naturalist literature, served as an important medium for young lyricists until its demise in 1919.

Hagiwara's first collection of poems, *Tsuki ni hoeru* (1917; tr *Howling at the Moon*, 1978), published with an introduction by Hakushū, marked an epoch in the world of Japanese poetry. It did not share Hakushū's and other contemporary poets' "symbolism" which, relying on unusual words and difficult expressions in literary language, presented a colorful but ambiguous world. For Hagiwara, poetry was neither merely symbolic nor mystic. He maintained that poetry, more fundamental and closer to himself, was "a lonesome consolation for his wounded soul" expressed in the precise language that appealed to his unique musical sense. He saw himself as a forlorn dog "howling at the moon" and found inherent sadness in such traditionally praised flora as the bamboo, the cherry, and the chrysanthemum. In *Aoneko* (1923; tr *Blue Cat*, 1978) he further displayed his mastery of diction and his deepened skepticism and pessimistic visions of life. The sharp sensuousness of the earlier poems was subdued, replaced by a faltering sense of inescapable melancholy which came to dominate his works.

It has often been pointed out that he was influenced by Edgar Allan Poe and, therefore, the French symbolists. Hagiwara himself quoted Baudelaire often. But he also learned from the ancient classical Japanese poets who, singing of ordinary phenomena, exposed in a most suggestive way the solitary depth of their hearts. His critical study *Ren'ai meika shū* (1931, A Collection of Best-loved Love Poems) was a manifestation of Hagiwara's appreciation and devotion to classical Japanese poetry, while his *Kyōshū no shijin Yosa Buson* (1936, Nostalgic Poet Yosa Buson) was an expression of his love for the 18th-century HAIKU poet BUSON who advocated a return to the poetics of BASHŌ, the 17th-century master haiku poet. In 1934 Hagiwara wrote, and in 1938, published, an essay entitled *Nihon e no kaiki* (Return to What Is Japanese). All these were in opposition to the contemporary movements by proletarian and realist writers in Japan. By the time he published *Hyōtō* (1934, Frozen Island), Hagiwara was divorced and living in Tōkyō with his children. He posed as a wanderer and expressed his longing for an eternal homeland in poems couched in heavy classical style.

Hagiwara managed his own journals, cultivated the genre of aphorism, wrote essays on poetic theory, edited works by other poets, and lectured on literature. He taught briefly at Meiji University in Tōkyō. His major work of criticism, *Shi no genri* (1928, Principles of Poetics), was a detailed delineation of his beliefs and practices in poetry. *Shukumei* (1939, Fate) was a collection of his prose poems, one of the earliest of a rather rare genre in the history of Japanese verse. He was said to have been clumsy and absentminded by nature and a trifle neurotic, and yet he developed an interest in juggling and magic and continued to play the mandolin. He died of pneumonia, leaving a rich legacy to the modernist practice of poetry in Japan. See also LITERATURE: modern poetry.

—— Hagiwara Sakutarō, *Hagiwara Sakutarō zenshū*, 15 vols (Chikuma Shobō, 1975–78). Hagiwara Sakutarō, *Face at the Bottom of the World and Other Poems*, tr Graeme Wilson and Ikuko Atsumi (1969). Hagiwara Sakutarō, *Howling at the Moon: Poems of Hagiwara Sakutarō*, tr Hiroaki Sato (1978). Itō Shinkichi, ed, *Hagiwara Sakutarō kenkyū* (1972). Naka Tarō, ed, *Hagiwara Sakutarō kenkyū* (1974). Nihon Bungaku Kenkyū Shiryō Kankōkai, ed, *Hagiwara Sakutarō* (1971). Takada Mizuho, *Hagiwara Sakutarō kenkyū* (1973).

James R. MORITA

Hagiwara Yūsuke (1897–1979)

Astronomer. Known for his work in celestial mechanics, particularly on the behavior of planets and planetoids. Born in Ōsaka, Hagiwara graduated from Tōkyō University in 1921. He served as professor there from 1935 to 1957, and was also director of Tōkyō Astronomical Observatory from 1946 to 1957. He received the Order of Culture in 1954. His publications include *Temmongaku* (1956, Astronomy) and *Celestial Mechanics*, 2 vols (1970, 1972).

Hagi ware

(hagi-yaki). Glazed, high-fired ceramics made in the castle towns of Hagi (now a city) and Fukawa (now part of the city of Nagato) in Nagato Province (now Yamaguchi Prefecture) from the late 1500s to the present.

Although originally production consisted primarily of tableware, *hibachi*, and small storage vessels, Hagi became renowned for TEA CEREMONY wares. Hagi teabowls are classified by shape, color, surface embellishment, and number of "nicks" cut in the foot. Typical Hagi-ware decoration includes *hakeme*, or light-colored slip brushed over the surface of the darker clay body and *mishima*, or slip inlaid in a darker clay. The two basic glazes are "loquat," a thin, yellowish glaze composed of feldspar and mixed hardwood ash, and "straw white," a thin, milky glaze made by adding straw ash, an opacifier, to the loquat glaze. Celadon, red, and brown glazes are also used. Pinkish spots in the glaze, dark blotches under the glaze, and scars left from stacking pots inside the kiln are considered attractive byproducts of the firing process.

Early Hagi potters were Koreans who came or were brought to Japan around the time of warlord Toyotomi Hideyoshi's invasions of Korea in 1592 and 1597. The earliest known Hagi kiln, which was excavated in the mid-1970s, had 14 chambers. Local iron-bearing clay was originally used to make the hard, heavy "Old Hagi ware." Bluish white, sandy clay with little iron, suitable for making soft, lightweight teabowls, was discovered 50 kilometers (31 mi) to the east, possibly around the early 1700s.

The Hagi kilns were run by the Saka and Miwa families, who served the Mōri *daimyō* in Hagi until the Meiji Restoration (1868). Generations of potters from these two families used the professional names Kōraizaemon and Kyūsetsu, respectively (see MIWA KYŪWA). In the Meiji period (1868–1912), they produced colorfully decorated household wares which were fired in smaller kilns. In 1887 the Saka family built a four-chamber kiln, 10.89 meters (35.7 ft) long by 3.45 meters (11.3 ft) wide.

The Fukawa potters, whose kilns were located farther from the daimyō's castle, were less dependent on daimyō patronage. These potters formed three guilds with communal linked-chamber climbing kilns *(noborigama)*. One 11-chamber kiln, built in 1763, was 37.6 meters (123.4 ft) long and 3.5 meters (11.5 ft) wide. In the Meiji period many Fukawa potters turned to other occupations to support their families.

Today Hagi has over 100 potters. Traditional tea wares and the more artistic innovative shapes are fired for approximately 30 hours in *noborigama* that reach temperatures of 1,200°–1,300°C (2,192°–2,372°F). Souvenir wares are mass-produced in electric kilns.

Hagi-ware collections can be seen in three museums in Hagi. Kumaya Art Museum displays the Hagi-ware collection of the Kumaya family; the Ishii Teabowl Art Museum displays Ishii Kigensai's collection of 130 Hagi, Raku, and Korean teabowls; and the Hagi-yaki Tōgei Kaikan has a collection of over 400 pieces, principally Old Hagi ware.

◾ ———Kawano Ryōsuke, *Hagi,* vol 17 of *Nihon no yakimono* (1975). Yoshiga Daibi, *Hagi,* vol 6 of *Karā Nihon no yakimono* (1974). *Jeanne* CARREAU

hagoita

A wooden paddle used in *hanetsuki,* a game played during the New Year's holidays; commonly translated as battledore. Auspicious symbols such as pine, bamboo, or plum trees, or portraits of beautiful women are portrayed on one or both sides of the paddle. The first recorded mention of the game occurs in 1432, when it was played at the imperial court. During the Edo period (1600–1868), the decorations on the *hagoita* became increasingly elaborate, the figures—often of popular *kabuki* actors—being made of silk collage. In December *hagoita* fairs (HAGOITA ICHI) are held throughout Japan. *YAMADA Tokubei*

hagoita ichi

A traditional fair at which HAGOITA (decorated battledores) are sold; held at the end of the year in major cities. In Tōkyō the fair is held on 15 December at the Fukagawa Fudō Shrine, on 17 and 18 December at the Asakusa Shrine, and on various dates at other shrines. Small *hagoita ichi* are also held in the streets. In Kyōto the fair is held in the Shijō and Shin Kyōgoku districts. *INOKUCHI Shōji*

Hagoromo legend

("The Feather Robe"). Legend found throughout Japan, particularly well known for its adaptation in the Nō play *Hagoromo.* While a celestial nymph *(tennyo)* is bathing in the sea, a man steals her garment made of feathers. She then has no choice but to become his wife and bear his child. Later she recovers her garment and returns to heaven. Other supernatural women who marry mortals in Japanese legend include Kaguyahime (see TAKETORI MONOGATARI) and Uguisuhime (Princess Nightingale). *SUCHI Tokuhei*

Hagurosan

Mountain in northwestern Yamagata Prefecture, northern Honshū; along with neighboring GASSAN and YUDONOSAN, Hagurosan is one of the Dewa Sanzan (Three Mountains of Dewa Province), a center for religious exercises of the SHUGENDŌ sect. The shrine Ideha Jinja is on the summit. Tall cedar trees designated as natural monuments border the road leading to the shrine. Height: 436 m (1,430 ft).

haibun

Brief, informal essays, usually light in tone and commonplace in theme, which flourished during the Edo period (1600–1868).
Characteristics——— The typical *haibun* begins with a short title, followed by a prose text of from four to five lines to several pages,

and generally ends with a HAIKU which derives from or recapitulates the sense of the prose. Compared to earlier prose genres, *haibun* displayed greater freedom in its use of vocabulary, and its range of subject matter included everyday objects and occurrences which had traditionally been shunned in Japanese literature.

Since it is essentially a medium of the haiku poet, *haibun* shares certain haiku characteristics: ellipsis, suggestion, and the use of classical allusion. For the same reason, it also shares with haiku such devices as the associate word *(engo)* and the pun. However, it should be noted that *haibun* differs from haiku in several important ways, in addition to the obvious one of form. Allusions to Chinese literature and history are relatively uncommon elements in haiku, but indispensible components of *haibun,* as are proverbial allusions, both Chinese and Japanese. Personification is another staple. There are, for example, a number of *haibun* that personify and describe the lives and loves of the kitchen mortar and pestle. Such pieces also illustrate another characteristic of *haibun* somewhat less common in haiku, a thematic concern with everyday experiences and material things—a fan, the joys of sleeping late, the pitfalls of borrowing money.

Despite the fact that many of its topics were commonplace, *haibun* was enjoyed by a relatively narrow, elite audience, unlike most of the literature of the Edo period. While literacy increased greatly during this period and a sizable reading public had come into being, *haibun,* because of its pseudoclassical diction, its endless punning, and its many recondite historical and literary allusions, was too difficult for all but the most highly educated to enjoy. Much of this writing may offend modern literary sensibilities with its studied artifice and frequent sacrifice of cogency for rhetorical flourish, but at its best, *haibun* is a felicitous wedding of brevity of form and profundity of content, offering a view of life that is both fresh and reflective.

Early Haibun——— The Japanese have shown enduring preference for attenuated continuity and the episodic in literature, as manifested in the popularity of older genres such as the poem-tale *(uta monogatari),* the diary (NIKKI BUNGAKU), and the random essay (ZUIHITSU). Both the poem-tale and the random essay are spiritual ancestors of *haibun,* although a direct paternity is not provable, or even plausible. The poem-tale is a collection of loosely related episodes, each composed of a brief narrative preface in prose followed by a poem or an exchange of poems. The prose sections, however, are little more than explanatory headnotes for the poems, which is a reversal of the *haibun* prose-poetry relationship. Without their haiku, the *haibun* pieces of the Edo period structurally bear more than a passing resemblance to the *zuihitsu* prose of SEI SHŌNAGON's 10th-century *Makura no sōshi* (tr *The Pillow Book,* 1967) and the *Tsurezuregusa* (tr *Essays in Idleness,* 1967) of YOSHIDA KENKŌ (ca 1283–ca 1352).

The first collection of what later came to be known as *haibun* is *Takaragura* (A Storehouse of Treasures) by Yamaoka Genrin (1631–72), published in 1671. It consists of short, unrelated prose segments, which record with flair and imagination the author's observations on everyday articles of living such as paper, pillows, and cooking pots. This subject range is narrower than that of later *haibun,* and allusions, puns, and associative words are less common. Genrin ended each of his pieces with two poems, a haiku and a *kyōshi,* or comic verse written in Chinese.

Roughly during the lifetime of Matsuo BASHŌ (1644–94) *haibun* evolved into a recognized and practiced literary genre, as a result both of Bashō's own writing and of his influence on the writing of others. The style of Bashō's *haibun* has been traditionally characterized as tranquil, elegant, and free. More concretely, we can say of his diction that he tended to use Chinese characters where the Japanese syllabary would have been adequate, due, in part, to his frequent use of Chinese allusions. This gives his pieces the appearance, if not the reality, of brevity. The subjects of Bashō's *haibun* generally involve nature and the bucolic. He was less interested in writing about the homely commonplaces of life that intrigued *haibun* writers before and after him, and in this sense he and his so-called Pristine school (Junseiha) constitute a deviation from the thematic norm.

Anthologies———Some years after Bashō's death the first of the *haibun* anthologies was published, the *Fūzoku monzen* (1706), and throughout the Edo period the anthology continued to be the usual vehicle for the publication of *haibun.* The *Fūzoku monzen* is significant in Japanese literary history not only because of its high quality, but also because as a pioneering work it helped set standards for the genre. Most of its contributors belonged to the Bashō school of haiku. The *monzen* in the title suggests that the compiler, Bashō's disciple MORIKAWA KYOROKU (1656–1715), took the 6th-century Chinese literary anthology *Wen xuan* (*Wen hsüan*; J: *Monzen*) as his model, but in terms of topic classification it follows a later Chinese pattern of the Song (Sung) or Yuan (Yüan) dynasty.

Under the anthology format, *haibun* are grouped into categories on the basis of the last word of the title, which supposedly indicates the nature of the piece. Thus *Tōfu no ben*, a discourse (*ben*) on bean curd, is classified as a discourse and grouped together with other *ben* pieces. In contrast to the Chinese anthologies, however, the categorization scheme is more elaborate than meaningful.

The art of *haibun* flourished with special vigor during roughly the latter half of the 18th century through the brushes of many writers, but two are particularly important: Yosa BUSON (1716–84) and YOKOI YAYŪ (1702–83). Buson's reputation today rests largely on his haiku and painting, but he is also remembered for his *haibun*. They perhaps lack the economy and elegance associated with Bashō's *haibun*, and they are certainly not as elaborate as many of Yayū's pieces.

Yokoi Yayū's *haibun* collection *Uzuragoromo* (1788–1823, Quail Cloak) is considered the best representative of the genre because of its erudition, gentle humor, and adept exploitation of the various prosodic devices of haiku poetry. Japanese literary scholars have traditionally divided *haibun* into two categories, Bashō's elegant Pristine school and the more whimsical Farcical school (*Yūbunha*). The *Uzuragoromo*, however, is a kind of synthesis of elements ascribed to each school, a confluence of the solemn elegance of the Pristines and the frothy wit of the Farcicals.

Decline of Haibun——*Haibun* continued to be written throughout the Edo period and into the modern Meiji period (1868–1912), but most of the later works have been assailed by Japanese literary historians as mediocre and unlearned. The genre has survived changes in literary tastes and interests less successfully than haiku. The novelist KAWAKAMI BIZAN (1869–1908) also wrote *haibun*, and, in fact, was known in the early years of his career as a modern Yayū. Today, *haibun* is not published in any significant quantity and has ceased to exist as a viable literary form although it is still read and remains the object of vigorous scholarship.

■——*Kinsei haiku haibun shū*, Nihon koten bungaku zenshū, vol 42 (Shōgakukan, 1972). Noda Sempei, *Kōhonkei Uzuragoromo: Hombun to kenkyū* (1980). Lawrence Rogers, "Rags and Tatters: The *Uzuragoromo* of Yokoi Yayū," *Monumenta Nipponica* 34.3 (Autumn 1979). Ueda Makoto, *Matsuo Bashō* (1970).

Lawrence W. ROGERS

haibutsu kishaku

(literally, "abolish the Buddha and destroy Śākyamuni"). Refers to the government repression of Buddhism during the early part of the Meiji period (1868–1912). The policy of the early Meiji government was to promote SHINTŌ as the state religion, and in 1868 the complete removal of Buddhist influence from Shintō shrines was decreed (see SHINTŌ AND BUDDHISM, SEPARATION OF). In some areas official antagonism soon developed into a full-scale movement to abolish the Buddhist religion, resulting in the destruction of many temples, statues, and implements before the movement declined around 1871. This crisis was instrumental in precipitating the subsequent reform movement within Buddhism. *Robert RHODES*

haihan chiken → prefectural system, establishment of

Haikai shichibushū

(Seven-Volume *Haikai* Collection). Compiled by Sakuma Ryūkyo (1695–1748) in the early 18th century. Popularly known as *Bashō shichibushū*, it brings together, in a chronological arrangement that reflects the development of Matsuo BASHŌ's style of *haikai* (prototype of HAIKU), the seven most representative anthologies of linked verse (*renku;* see RENGA AND HAIKAI) and haiku (*hokku*) of the Bashō school, namely *Fuyu no hi, Haru no hi, Arano, Hisago, Sarumino, Sumidawara,* and *Zoku sarumino.* It established a seven-volume format that was employed by many later *haikai* collections.

haiku

A 17-syllable verse form consisting of three metrical units of 5, 7, and 5 syllables respectively. One of the most important forms of traditional Japanese poetry, *haiku* remains popular in modern Japan, and in recent years its popularity has also spread to other countries.

The Terms Haiku, Hokku, and Haikai——Loose usage by students, translators, and even poets themselves has led to much confusion about the distinction between the three related terms *haiku, hokku,* and *haikai.* For example, the following verse by NOZAWA BONCHŌ (d 1714), which might at the present day be casually referred to as a haiku, was in Bonchō's day called a *hokku:*

ichinaka wa (5 syllables)	in streets and alleyways
mono no nioi ya (7 syllables)	the smells of the city:
natsu no tsuki (5 syllables)	the summer moon

The term *hokku* literally means "starting verse." This refers to the fact that a *hokku* was not itself an autonomous, complete poem, but rather the first or "starting" link of a much longer chain of verses known as a *haikai no renga,* or simply, *haikai.* In this particular *haikai* from the famed anthology *Sarumino* (1691; tr *Monkey's Raincoat,* 1973), the poetic suggestion introduced by Bonchō's *hokku* of 5-7-5 syllables is followed up by Matsuo BASHŌ's (1644–94) second link of two 7-syllable units:

| atsushi atsushi to (7 syllables) | "how hot! how hot!"— |
| kado kado no koe (7 syllables) | voices at the doors |

The third link in this *haikai,* written by MUKAI KYORAI (1651–1704), is again a verse of 5-7-5; the fourth, composed by Bonchō, returns to the 7-7 pattern, and the poem goes on thus for 36 links. In this manner, the three poets gradually articulate the *haikai,* beginning with the *hokku* and linking together alternating sections of 5-7-5 syllables and 7-7 syllables into an extended chain of poetic associations. This is a typical example of how *haikai* was composed—though of course the number of poets and links could vary. (For details, see RENGA AND HAIKAI.) To summarize then, a *hokku* was the starting link in a chain of verses known as a *haikai.*

Because the *hokku* set the tone for the rest of the poetic chain, it enjoyed a privileged position in *haikai* poetry, and it was not uncommon for a poet to compose a *hokku* by itself without following up with the rest of the chain. Though in principle all *hokku* were destined to be integrated into longer *haikai,* a long tradition of anthologies devoted exclusively to *hokku,* beginning with SŌGI's (1421–1502) posthumous *Jinensai hokku* (1506) and running through the *Kokin meika kusen* (1776) of the Bashō school, indicates the natural tendency of *hokku* to take on the character of independent poems.

Largely through the efforts of MASAOKA SHIKI (1867–1902), this independence was formally established in the 1890s through the creation of the term "haiku." As Shiki conceived of the term, haiku designated a new type of verse, in form quite similar to the traditional *hokku,* but different in that it was to be written, read, and understood as an independent poem, complete in itself, rather than part of a longer chain. Haiku for Shiki were essentially *hokku* liberated from the *haikai* chain. After Shiki the form that haiku should take became a subject of much debate, but all proposals for new haiku forms had in common the notion of a haiku as an autonomous poem.

Strictly speaking, then, the history of haiku begins only in the last years of the 19th century. The famous verses of such Edo-period (1600–1868) masters as Bashō, Yosa BUSON (1716–84), and Kobayashi ISSA (1763–1827) are properly referred to as *hokku* and must be placed in the perspective of the history of *haikai* even though they are now generally read as independent haiku.

Development of Haikai——*Renga,* or linked verse, which began to be written in the Heian period (794–1185), was originally considered a diversion by which poets could relax from the serious business of composing WAKA poetry. By the time of *renga* master Sōgi, however, it had become a serious art with complex rules and high aesthetic standards. *Haikai no renga,* or simply *haikai,* was conceived as a light-hearted amusement in which poets could indulge after the solemn refinements of serious *renga.*

When *haikai* began to emerge as a serious poetic genre in the early 16th century, two characteristics distinguished it from serious *renga,* its humorous intent and its free use of *haigon* (colloquialisms, compounds borrowed from Chinese, and other expressions which had previously been banned from the poetic vocabulary), but the erudite MATSUNAGA TEITOKU (1571–1653) succeeded in establishing a more conservative and formalistic approach to haikai. For Teitoku, humor implied a sort of intellectual wit, and the distinction between haikai and renga lay ultimately only in the use or nonuse of haigon. He established strict rules concerning the composition of haikai and sought to endow the form with the elegance and aesthetic elevation of waka and serious renga.

Teitoku contributed greatly to the popularization and propagation of haikai, and while he was alive he dominated the haikai world. After his death, however, his formalistic approach was challenged by the more free-wheeling DANRIN SCHOOL of haikai led by NISHIYAMA SŌIN (1605–82). Sōin emphasized the comic aspects of haikai. He sought to separate haikai as much as possible from the stuffy formalities of renga, and by doing so, to restore to it the full play of the creative imagination.

Characteristic of the Danrin style of poetry was the practice of yakazu haikai in which a single poet would reel off verse after verse as quickly as possible in a sort of exercise in free association. The most renowned example of this is the legendary performance by Ihara SAIKAKU (1642–93) in 1684 at the Sumiyoshi Shrine in Ōsaka, where he composed 23,500 verses in a single day and night. Obviously, such practices were hardly conducive to the crafting of fine poetry, and the movement led by Sōin failed to develop beyond the stage of mere amusement. But in opening up the creative sphere of haikai and broadening its scope, the Danrin school played an important part in haikai history. As Bashō would remark later, "Were it not for Sōin we would still be licking the slobber of old Teitoku."

Bashō was not only the greatest of haikai poets, he was also the poet who was primarily responsible for establishing haikai as a true art form. Having received instruction in both the Teitoku and Danrin styles of haikai, he gradually developed in the late years of the 17th century a new style which through its artistic sincerity transcended the conflict between serious renga and comic haikai, and could express humor, humanity, and profound religious insight all within the space of a single hokku. A man for whom artistic discipline was intimately associated with spiritual discipline, Bashō set the artistic standard for haikai. During the two centuries between his death and the appearance of Masaoka Shiki, major poetic reforms were essentially Bashō revivals; good poetry meant a return to the style of Bashō.

It would be a mistake, however, to think that Bashō transformed haikai into an art by himself. UEJIMA ONITSURA (1661–1738), if not quite the poetic giant that Bashō was, nevertheless wrote haikai of exceptional quality, and his notion of makoto or "sincerity" represents one of the high points of Japanese poetic theory (see LITERARY CRITICISM, PREMODERN). Other notable poets of the time include KONISHI RAIZAN, IKENISHI GONSUI, and YAMAGUCHI SODŌ. Bashō also had a great number of disciples. Of these, the so-called Ten Philosophers are particularly well known. They are NAITŌ JŌSŌ, Mukai Kyorai, SUGIYAMA SAMPŪ, MORIKAWA KYOROKU, HATTORI RANSETSU, KAGAMI SHIKŌ, OCHI ETSUJIN, Enomoto Kikaku, Shida Yaba, and Tachibana Hokushi. The haikai of Jōsō, though somewhat limited in scope, most faithfully capture the spirit of Bashō both in their humor and their spiritual tranquillity. Shikō and Kyoroku are well known as theoreticians and transmitters of Bashō's teachings. The rather objective verse of Nozawa Bonchō, another of Bashō's disciples, is also worthy of mention.

After Bashō's death many of his disciples followed their personal whims and set up their own schools of haikai, sacrificing much artistic integrity in the process. In general these poets sought special effects, with some writing enigmatic, puzzle-like verse and others satisfying themselves with witty wordplay, and at times their haikai became virtually indistinguishable from ZAPPAI AND SENRYŪ, popular comic verse forms which had come into vogue in the Genroku period (1688–1704). In the latter half of the 18th century, however, there arose a movement of poets who lamented this decline in the haikai art and sought to restore its high aesthetic standards. The principal figure in this haikai reform was the talented painter-poet Buson, and the main cry of the movement was "Return to Bashō!" Though not as deeply spiritual as Bashō, Buson possessed great imagination and culture, and a painter's eye for vivid pictorial scenes. He is usually ranked after Bashō as the second greatest of haikai poets. Other important haikai poets of the period include TAN TAIGI, who excelled in poems about human affairs, KATŌ KYŌTAI, whose commentaries on Bashō and sense of aesthetic elegance reflected the general trend of the times, and ŌSHIMA RYŌTA, who

probably contributed most to the propagation of haikai in this period.

The number of composers of haikai grew rapidly at the beginning of the 19th century. This popularization, however, was accompanied by a general decline in quality, and few poets produced poetry of lasting depth. The most notable exceptions were Iwama Otsuni (1756–1823) and Kobayashi Issa. Otsuni was a religious man who spent much of his life traveling, seeking to deepen his understanding of the haikai discipline. Issa wrote prolifically in a very personal, simple style. His poems about his poverty and about his love for small animals and insects are particularly memorable, and today he ranks with Bashō and Buson as one of the most beloved haikai poets.

The history of haikai up until the 1890s may be summarized as a pendulum movement between serious artistic discipline and free imaginative creativity. On the one hand, the original inspiration of haikai led it away from the solemn refinements and narrow aestheticism of the more formal waka and renga toward daily life, laughter, and freedom of the imagination. On the other hand, as popularity induced banality, humor became crudity, and freedom led to absence of discipline, poets were led to formalize haikai, restrain its wildness, and elevate its aesthetic standards. When, in turn, this serious-minded formalism stifled the creative impulse and excluded the humor which is such an essential part of life, the demands for comic verse again came into the foreground. In the hands of poetic masters, however, haikai reconciled and transcended this conflict and became one of the great forms of Japanese literary art.

KURIYAMA Shigehisa

Modern Haiku——The history of modern haiku dates from MASAOKA SHIKI's reform, begun in 1892, which established haiku as a new independent poetic form. It is a history that features constant experimentation and the confluence of various literary trends such as naturalism, romanticism, symbolism, and proletarianism. It is thus a history that is rich in diversity. Though the demise of haiku is periodically predicted, the form continues to flourish, as the many hundreds of amateur haiku clubs and periodicals attest.

Basic to the modernization of haiku was Shiki's most important concept, shasei, or sketching from life—a term borrowed from the critical vocabulary of Western painting. Though in the beginning this implied a simplistic literalness, Shiki later incorporated many particulars, such as selectivity, composition, and internal harmony. In the work of the poet-painter Buson he found painterly elements of descriptive realism to mitigate the unpoetic modern world: vivid color, clarity of impression, and imagination. The magazine that Shiki began in 1897, HOTOTOGISU, became the haiku world's most important publication.

Shiki's reform did not change two traditional elements of haiku: the division of 17 syllables into three groups of 5, 7, and 5 syllables, and the inclusion of a seasonal theme. KAWAHIGASHI HEKIGOTŌ (1873–1937), a talented poet who succeeded his mentor Shiki as haiku editor of the newspaper Nihon, carried Shiki's reform further with two proposals. The first was an extension of Shiki's shasei: haiku would be truer to reality if there were no center of interest in it. The logical extension of this idea was free-verse haiku, since the traditional patterning was seen as another artificial manipulation of reality. Hekigotō also urged the importance of the poet's first impression, just as it was (sono mama), of subjects taken from daily life, and of local color to create freshness. He was recognized for a time as the leading figure in the haiku world. Other poets associated with Hekigotō's Shinkeikō (New Trend) movement were Anzai Ōkaishi, ŌSUGA OTSUJI, and OGIWARA SEISENSUI.

Protesting against the prosaic flatness characteristic of much of the works of Hekigotō's school, Seisensui maintained in 1912 that free-verse haiku must also discard the seasonal theme, which he declared was only another burden from the feudalistic past. Rejecting Shiki's concept of a harmonious whole and Hekigotō's objective naturalism, Seisensui maintained that haiku must capture in its rhythms not the object perceived but the poet's perception. In spite of the usual problems of an unintelligible private symbolism inherent in such a position, his insistence on the need for the inclusion of the ineffable and evanescent in haiku attracted many able poets, whose works appeared in his magazine Sōun. Notably successful among them were TANEDA SANTŌKA and OZAKI HŌSAI, who both led wandering lives of poverty, like the beggar priests of the past. In their free verse, the cadence of perception and a musicality beyond mere repetition captured the "light and power" which Seisensui valued.

In 1912, TAKAHAMA KYOSHI began in the pages of *Hototogisu* (which he had edited since 1898) his lifelong defense of the traditional 17-syllable form, the seasonal theme, and the descriptive realism of Shiki. He outlined his views in a collection of essays published under the title *Susumubeki haiku no michi* (1915–17, The Path Which Haiku Must Take). Kyoshi's position as a giant among modern haiku poets is considered unassailable by the Japanese. The first flowering of the traditional school was in the Taishō period (1912–26) and featured such gifted poets as IIDA DAKOTSU, admired for his classic dignity and depth, Kawabata Bōsha, known for his religious verse, MURAKAMI KIJŌ, a deaf poet with a sensibility reminiscent of Kobayashi Issa, and Watanabe Suiha, distinguished for verses of austere purity.

By 1920 Kyoshi's position as the foremost haiku figure was established, and a second generation of poets clustered about *Hototogisu,* including MIZUHARA SHŪOSHI, AWANO SEIHŌ, YAMAGUCHI SEISHI, and TAKANO SUJŪ. Sujū, although he wrote several admired verses, exemplifies a weakness inherent in the *Hototogisu* school: myopic minuteness for its own sake, with consequent triviality. The first Shōwa-period (1926–) poet to break away into subjects heretofore avoided was Hino Sōjō, who wrote verses on romantic and sensuous love. Though other important poets also broke away from *Hototogisu,* it continues to represent the central position in haiku to the present day.

Mizuhara Shūoshi broke away from *Hototogisu* in 1931, two years after having assumed the editorship of the magazine *Ashibi.* His rejection of Kyoshi's attitude of detached realism, because of its exclusion of romantic imagination and overt sentiment, stems in part from his early *tanka* experience under KUBOTA UTSUBO, once a member of the romantic *Myōjō* group. Shūoshi's talent for making imaginative use of the historical past shines in his collection *Katsushika* (1930), which echoes the 8th-century WAKA anthology, the *Man'yōshū.* *Ashibi* was an important outlet for such poets as Yamaguchi Seishi, ISHIDA HAKYŌ, and Hashimoto Takako, the foremost woman haiku poet.

In the early Shōwa period, the term *shinkō haiku* (new haiku) loosely identified all groups that deviated in one way or another from the traditional *Hototogisu* school. In addition to the *Ashibi* poets and the modernistic school of Hino Sōjō's magazine *Kikan,* the term also included the so-called proletarian school, headed by Kuribayashi Issekiro, originally of Seisensui's group. Other prominent proletarian poets were Hashimoto Mudō, Shimada Seihō, and Yoshioka Zenjidō. Another politicizing group centered around the liberal publication *Kyōdai haiku,* which appeared during the period 1933–40 and accepted both conventional and free verse haiku.

Joining *Hototogisu* in 1933, NAKAMURA KUSATAO deplored the *shinkō* haiku movement for its emphasis on technique and methodology. For him the central haiku question was not what or how to write, but how to live. Haiku was a measure of the man—of his will and convictions—and an instrument for probing into the essence of humanity. By 1939 he was identified along with Ishida Hakyō, KATŌ SHŪSON, Shinohara Bon, Ishizuka Tomoji, and Nishijima Bakunan as a member of the Ningen Tankyū Ha ("Humanness" school). Much of Kusatao's verse, as well as that of Hakyō and Shūson, is known for its difficult imagery.

In the late 1930s Japan prepared for war beyond the on-going Sino–Japanese conflict. The government demanded that haiku poets actively support the war effort, and, in 1940, 12 members of the politically liberal Kyōto University haiku association were arrested for their refusal to cooperate. The following year, 13 persons associated with the proletarian haiku magazines *Haiku seikatsu* and *Dojō* were jailed, including Hashimoto Mudō, Kuribayashi Issekiro, and Shimada Seihō. Nihon Haiku Sakka Kyōkai, an umbrella group covering all haiku factions, was formed by the government in 1940 and headed by Takahama Kyoshi. Two years later it was incorporated into a government-mandated general literary organization. No criticism was tolerated, and censorship and control were severe, effectively restricting developments in new directions.

The immediate postwar period saw an effort by the leftist union Shin Haikujin Remmei, led by Kuribayashi Issekiro and Ishibashi Tatsunosuke, to "break the hold of feudalism in haiku and to expose war collaborators," a pronouncement aimed at *Hototogisu* and other traditional schools. In 1947, many leading poets withdrew from this union. Through the cooperative efforts of Ishida Hakyō and Saitō Sanki, the Modern Haiku Association (Gendai Haiku Kyōkai) was formed in July 1947 to "enhance modern haiku" with the inclusion of all groups from the political left to the literary traditionalists.

The effort to unite all factions was stimulated by a widely discussed 1946 article entitled "Daini geijutsuron" (On a Second-Class Art), in which the critic KUWABARA TAKEO maintained that modern haiku was not a serious literary genre but only a pleasant pastime. Major poets like Seishi, Shūoshi, Sōjō, and Sanki attacked the validity not only of Kuwabara's selection of supposedly representative modern haiku but also of his comparison of haiku to the novel as a vehicle of expression. A number of efforts to "modernize haiku"— to make it relevant to contemporary experience—were stimulated by the publicity given Kuwabara's article.

One such effort is found in *Tenrō,* a magazine begun in 1948 under Yamaguchi Seishi's editorship and supported by the prewar liberal Kyōto University group together with some former *Ashibi* poets. A prominent contributor was Saitō Sanki, generally characterized as a nihilist for whom haiku was a monologue. *Tenrō* and the prewar *Ashibi,* which continues to appear, are the two most important vehicles of the nontraditional haiku. Other prewar magazines which continue to appear are Iida Dakotsu's *Ummo,* Ishida Hakyō's *Tsuru,* and Katō Shūson's *Kanrai.* The extreme haiku fringe of symbolism and surrealism is found in such magazines as *Taiyōkei,* founded in 1946 by Mizutani Saiko (1903–67) and Tomizawa Kakio (1902–62), and *Bara,* started in 1952 by Tomizawa Kakio and Takayanagi Shigenobu (b 1929).

YAMAMOTO KENKICHI, perhaps the foremost haiku analyst, states that with the death of the old leaders—Takahama Kyoshi, Matsumoto Takashi, Iida Dakotsu, Saitō Sanki, and Ishida Hakyō— and, it should be added, with the hiatus due to wartime censorship, a vacuum of leadership exists at present. Poets formerly associated with the three dynamic impulses of the Taishō and Shōwa periods— the traditionalists, the new haiku poets who abandoned the seasonal theme and the strict objectivity of *shasei* or espoused free verse, and the members of the Ningen Tankyū Ha—are now scattered among new groupings. Future directions are difficult to foresee, while constant and energetic experimentation continues. *Kenneth* YASUDA

Haiku Abroad —— The West's first introduction to haiku came in B. H. Chamberlain's pioneer work, *Japanese Poetry* (1910), in a chapter entitled "Bashō and the Japanese Epigram." The term epigram is indicative of how haiku was first interpreted abroad. William Porter's early anthology of translations was also entitled *A Year of Japanese Epigrams* (1911). Haiku was first introduced to France by Paul-Louis Couchoud, the philosopher-doctor who took an interest in haiku during his stay in Japan at the time of the Russo–Japanese War. The title of his introduction to haiku was *Les Epigrammes Lyriques du Japon.* It was this misinterpretation of haiku as epigrams which led the poet John Gould Fletcher to remark as late as 1945 that the relationship between Chinese classical poets and Japanese *tanka* and *hokku* poets was like that of "full grown and mature human figures to a group of rather small and temporarily attractive children," and that the *hokku* was "nothing more than a sketch."

More astute poets, however, realized haiku's potential as a full-fledged poetic form and began to experiment with it at an early date. Ezra Pound, for example, quickly noticed the technique of cutting up the poem into two independent yet associated images (see "The Technique of Cutting" below) and gave it the name of superposition. In France, Paul Eluard wrote poems in the haiku style. Haiku has rapidly become naturalized both in Europe and the United States, and magazines of original haiku are published. Haiku magazines in America include *Modern Haiku, byways, Tweed,* and *New World Haiku.*

On Writing Haiku in English —— Poets desiring to compose haiku in English are confronted immediately by one major problem: there exists at present no consensus on either the subject matter that English haiku should treat or the form that it should take. There does exist, however, an invaluable guiding principle concerning the composition of all haiku, which helps reduce this problem to manageable dimensions. That principle is this: a haiku in any language, if it is to be called a haiku at all, must take into consideration the features of haiku in Japanese and incorporate at least some of these features to at least some degree. Here we will study the more fundamental characteristics of Japanese haiku, and try to use them to compose a haiku in English.

The first question is, of course, what to write about. That is, what subjects are suitable for treatment in haiku? To this, the history of *haikai* responds: virtually anything. Certainly, famous haiku poets have written about the grandiose and the elegant, about the

Milky Way stretching over a stormy sea, for example, or about svelte herons standing in the evening breeze. At the same time, however, a look at the great haiku over the ages reveals that the most seemingly trivial things—a scarecrow in the rain, a clock's ticking in summer heat, a frog jumping into a pond—can also become subjects for haiku, and that the haiku sensibility is extremely versatile. It treasures the graceless as well as the graceful, the modern as well as the traditional, the sharp crunch of beer cans crushed by destitute men as well as the mellow echoes of a temple bell in the mountains. To repeat, virtually anything can become the subject of haiku.

Of course, within this "virtually anything" there are limitations imposed by considerations of form. The brevity of haiku makes it ill-suited for subjects so complex or so removed from common experience or culture that they require extensive explanations. Thus, haiku necessarily tends to concentrate on images, sounds, smells, and situations from everyday life, on simple experiences which the imagination can evoke with the aid of just a few verbal hints. This is both a weakness—because haiku easily becomes trite, prosaic, and stereotyped—and a virtue, because when a haiku is successful, it endows our lives with freshness and new wonder and reveals the charm and profundity of all truly simple things.

The above observations suggest that perhaps one good way for the beginner to orient his efforts at composing haiku is to conceive of a relatively commonplace happening or experience and to try to present it in such a way that it seems not quite so common, that, indeed, makes it quite interesting. Consider the following event: you are taking a stroll, and you run into someone you know. The two of you engage for a while in casual conversation and then go on your separate ways. Common and simple enough. Let us make it the subject of a haiku.

Having thus decided on *what* to write about, we must now consider the next important problem, namely, *how* to write about it. Traditional Japanese haiku are based on three principal elements: the form of 5-7-5 syllables, the technique of cutting, and the principle of the seasonal theme. Let us take them up one by one.

The metrical pattern of haiku. The first thing that students normally learn when beginning the study of haiku is that it is a 17-syllable form in 3 units of 5-7-5 syllables respectively. This metrical pattern is the most basic rule of Japanese haiku. For starters, then, we might express our roadside encounter thus:

> meeting on the road,
> we chat leisurely awhile
> and go on our ways

In applying the 5-7-5 pattern here, however, it is important to keep in mind that at the present moment its use in English represents a somewhat artificial convention. Behind the 5-7-5 rhythm of the Japanese haiku is a long literary tradition in which all major poetic forms are constructed out of units of 5 and 7 syllables. The great bulk of English poetry, on the other hand, is written in meters which count accents as well as syllables. This historical difference has linguistic roots. Japanese is a minimally accented language with little variation in syllable length. Therefore, pure syllable count serves as a natural measure for poetic rhythm in Japanese, but not in English, which is an accented language with great variation in the length of syllables.

In the absence of a consensus on the ideal English haiku form, however, imitation of the Japanese pattern is not without its merits. Most important, it furnishes us with a set standard form with simple rules. This is crucial if haiku is to be distinguished from short free verse. Moreover, it avoids the dangers of putting haiku in forms that are more traditional and natural to English poetry, such as in rhymed couplets, which by their very "Englishness" tend to detract from the freshness of the Japanese haiku form as a new mode of organizing words, which is to say, a different way of looking at the world. In our present effort to compose a haiku, then, we shall adopt the 5-7-5 pattern from the Japanese.

But as our effort above shows, the 5-7-5 pattern by itself does not make a haiku. The problem with this verse is that it tells us something but evokes nothing. It is flat and one-dimensional and offers no challenge or invitation to the imagination. Let us examine other aspects of haiku and see if we can't infuse this verse with a little more thought-provoking tension.

The technique of cutting. From the point of view of formal technique, the most vital element (after brevity) in the creation of haiku-like expression is the technique of cutting. What this involves is the introduction of a caesura after either the first or second metrical unit so that the poem is cut into sections of 5 and 12 syllables (5/-7-5) or 12 and 5 syllables (5-7/-5). In Japanese this break may be effected in a variety of ways, the most notable method being the use of *kireji* (cutting words) such as *ya* or *kana*. In English the effect is roughly equivalent to a line break punctuated by a colon, long dash, or ellipsis.

Cutting is vital to haiku expression because the cut divides the poem into two parts and forces the reader's imagination to somehow relate or reconcile these two parts. This struggle to intuit or grasp the poetic association between two images or ideas represents the heart of haiku complexity. Let us apply this technique to our verse and see if it improves our haiku:

> a roadside meeting:
> we chat leisurely awhile
> and go on our ways

The improvement here is minimal. The main problem is that the contents of the two sections are too closely related to each other. The last two lines are merely an explanation of what happened in the event announced by the first line. In order for cutting to be effective, there must be a certain imaginative distance between the two sections, and the two sections must remain, to a degree, independent of each other.

> a baby's crying:
> we chat leisurely awhile
> and go on our ways

This is more interesting than the previous attempt because the distance between the poetic ideas suggested by the first and second sections is much greater. Unfortunately, it is too great. The reader is left at a loss as to how to relate the two sections. Despite the fact that a baby is crying, we converse at leisure and then go on our ways. It this a sign of cruelty? Deafness? Ignorance? Though each is intriguing in its own way, the two images fail to call and respond to each other in the way that the parts of a good haiku should.

> a peaceful country:
> we chat leisurely awhile
> and go on our ways

Here we finally have two images which are independent and yet cooperate in such a way that each image enriches the understanding of the other. The notion of a peaceful country expands the scale of the haiku and places this banal encounter of two acquaintances against the panoramic backdrop of all the other imaginable people and activities of a nation enjoying peace. At the same time this one experience shared by just two people crystallizes the abstract notion of a peaceful country.

It is thus apparent that the successful use of cutting involves three conditions. First, the two sections must be sufficiently distinct and disassociated from each other; i.e., in terms of imaginative distance they must not be too near each other. Second, these sections must be related to each other in a manner that precludes total mystification; i.e., they must not be too far apart. Third, the relationship between the two sections must be two-sided; in other words, the first section must enhance the appreciation of the second, and the second section must enhance the appreciation of the first. The internal comparison must be reciprocal.

We now have a verse which incorporates the 5-7-5 metric and the technique of cutting. It may now be further improved by including the third indispensable element of traditional Japanese haiku: the seasonal theme.

The principle of the seasonal theme. Historically, the critical importance of the *kidai*, or "seasonal theme," was recognized in Japanese poetry even before the birth of *haikai*, and its function has continued to be a subject of central interest to poets through modern times. The earliest full discussion of the seasonal theme appears in *Renri hishō* (1349), a treatise by the *renga master* NIJŌ YOSHIMOTO. In the 20th century the need for *kidai* in haiku has been defended by such leading haiku critics as Takahama Kyoshi and Ōsuga Otsuji.

What the principle of the seasonal theme requires is that each haiku contain a *kigo*, or "season word," which indicates the season in which the haiku is set. In the haiku world view, then, all people, things, and events can be fully appreciated and take on their proper meanings only in the context of temporal flow and the rhythms of nature. In Japan there exist voluminous dictionaries of *kigo* explaining which words refer to which seasons (see SAIJIKI). To take some obvious examples, cherry blossoms indicate that the season is spring, mosquitoes refer to summer, chrysanthemums to autumn, and snow to winter. In English, of course, there are no formal compilations of season words, but that need not concern us. What is important is that the haiku contains an expression or image which clearly indicates the season.

But when *did* this encounter take place? From the perspective of practical possibility, anytime. Poetic possibility, however, is much more restrictive, and precise matching of scene and season is imperative if the seasonal theme is to be more than a mechanical convention. Winter, for example, is too cold for lingering outside. With spring we would rather associate the fresh encounters of the young than the leisurely chats of old acquaintances. Autumn is too suggestive of reflective maturity and eventual partings. Only summer suits the relaxed, commonplace nature of our encounter, neither exciting nor sentimental but pleasant in its daily familiarity. Thus:

> another hot day:
> we chat leisurely awhile
> and go on our ways

Almost, but not quite. The problem is that the word "leisurely" does not quite match the notion of a hot day. It suggests that the slow pace of things is more or less voluntary, a reflection of a relaxed state of mind; one would rather associate it with summer evenings and after-dinner strolls. The peacefulness of a hot day, on the other hand, is more consonant with involuntary lethargy, with afternoon naps and the nuisance of flies. In a poem where the seasonal theme fulfills its true evocative function, there must be reciprocity between the season which expands the scope of the haiku and creates the atmospheric background of associations for the specific scene, and the specific scene which points out a characteristic yet often forgotten aspect of the season and thus enriches our understanding of it. Let us make a final corrective effort then:

> another hot day:
> yawning "good-bye" and "take care"
> we go on our ways

Not a haiku masterpiece, but not discreditable for a first try. In any case, our original intention was not so much to write a haiku of great quality as to study some of the formal characteristics and artistic techniques which go into composing haiku. Equipped now with an understanding of the major principles of haiku composition, the aspiring poet should be able to apply his or her personal genius and go on to create verses of far superior quality.

KURIYAMA Shigehisa

📖 —— Asō Isoji, *Haishumi no hattatsu* (1944). R. H. Blyth, *Haiku*, 4 vols (1949–52). R. H. Blyth, *A History of Haiku*, 2 vols (1963). Ebara Taizō, *Haikaishi no kenkyū* (1949). Joan Giroux, *The Haiku Form* (1974). Harold Henderson, *The Bamboo Broom* (1934). Harold Henderson, *An Introduction to Haiku* (1958). Harold Henderson, *Haiku in English* (1967). Kaneko Kinjirō et al, ed, *Renga haikai shū* (1974). Kuriyama Riichi et al, ed, *Kinsei haiku haibun shū* (1972). Makoto Ueda, *Modern Japanese Haiku* (1976). Matsui Toshiko, *Kindai hairon shū* (1973). Matsui Toshihiko, *Kindai hairon shi* (1973). Matsune Tōyōjō, ed, *Gendai haiku shū* (1958). Earl Miner, *Japanese Linked Poetry* (1979). Nakajima Takeo, *Gendai haikai zenkō* (1976). Ōsuga Seki, *Otsuji hairon shū* (1947). Yamamoto Kenkichi, *Junsui haiku* (1952). Yamamoto Kenkichi et al, ed, *Nihon no shiika*, vols 3 and 9 (1971). Kenneth Yasuda, *The Japanese Haiku* (1957). Yokozawa Saburō et al, ed, *Haiku hairon* (1959).

hairstyles

(*kamigata*). In Japan, as in other cultures, hairstyles and dress closely parallel the course of social history. The changing fashions in Japanese hairstyles reflect the formation of an aristocratic class, the subsequent rise to power of a warrior class, rigid social stratification under the Tokugawa shogunate (1603–1867), and the later modernization of Japan.

The hairstyles of the 4th and 5th centuries can be seen on the HANIWA (clay burial mound figures) of that era. Men wore their hair in the *mizura* style, parted in the middle and pulled together in loops over the ears. The women pulled their hair up into a loose

Hairstyles —— Japanese traditional hairstyles over the centuries

loop resting on the top of the head and fastened in the middle. This latter style is now called *shimadamage*, after the 18th-century hairstyle which it resembles.

The heavy influence of Chinese and Korean culture from the 5th to the 8th century included the borrowing of Chinese dress. In 604 an order (see KAN'I JŪNIKAI) was issued for all courtiers in Japan to wear a *kammuri* (formal headdress) in accordance with the Chinese custom of the Sui dynasty (589–618). As a result, the *kanka no ikkei* replaced the *mizura* hairstyle. In this new style the hair was pulled into a topknot at the back of the head; it is also known as the *chommage* or topknot style. Women also followed the Sui Chinese hairstyles. When in ceremonial dress, the women of the aristocracy wore their hair in the *hōkei* or *kōkei* styles, which called for a fancy knot piled high on the head with a flower-shaped ornament (*saishi*) at its base. Another common hairstyle was one in which the hair was arranged in one or two topknots, as seen in several statues of Buddha and GIGAKU masks housed among the treasures of the temple Hōryūji.

Hairstyles which varied according to age and social rank appeared between the 5th and 8th centuries. In the late 7th century Emperor TEMMU ordered all men and women to do up their hair, a possible indication that many people had previously worn their hair long and straight.

In contrast to the aristocratic culture of the early part of the Heian period (794–1185) with its elaborate costumes and hairstyles, the warrior class (*samurai*), which came into power after the 13th century, maintained its own distinct and more functional hairstyles. Men continued to wear the *kanka no ikkei* style. However, to reduce the heat under their helmets, samurai had their heads shaved from the forehead back in a circular pattern before going into battle. They let the remaining hair under the helmet fall straight down. When not wearing helmets, they pulled the side and back hair into a topknot at the back of the head. This style, known as *sakayaki*, appeared in several varieties, including *ōsakayaki*, *hondamage*, and *chasemmage*. In the 16th century the style became so established that it was worn by samurai in peacetime as well. Merchants and commoners also adopted it, but the shapes of the topknots clearly distinguished townsmen (CHŌNIN) from the military class.

The majority of women wore their hair long and straight, though women of the lower classes tied their hair in the back for convenience. This style changed gradually, and by the late 16th century, some women of the merchant class were wearing their hair up. One such style, the *karawamage*, was an imitation of the men's topknot. The women of the aristocracy and military class were more conservative and continued to wear their hair long and straight.

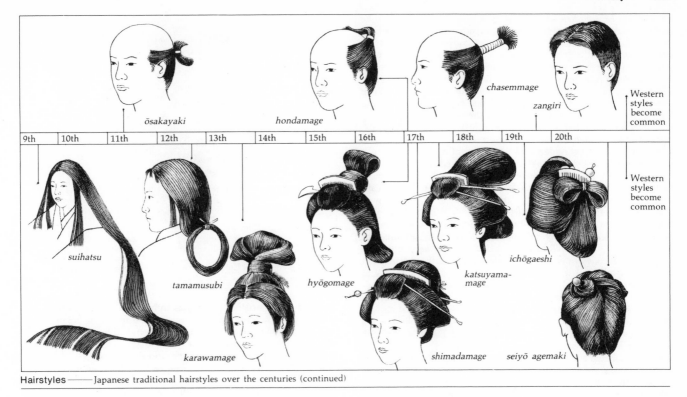

ōsakayaki   *hondamage*   *chasemmage*   *zangiri*   Western styles become common

9th | 10th | 11th | 12th | 13th | 14th | 15th | 16th | 17th | 18th | 19th | 20th

Western styles become common

suihatsu   *tamamusubi*   *hyōgomage*   *katsuyamamage*   *ichōgaeshi*

karawamage   *shimadamage*   *seiyō agemaki*

Hairstyles —— Japanese traditional hairstyles over the centuries (continued)

During the long period of peace under the Tokugawa shogunate, men's hairstyles remained basically the same, although a large variety of new hairstyles for women appeared. In the early part of this period women's hairstyles were rather crude in form, copied from men's styles, and designed for both practicality and beauty. During the middle part of this period, hairstyles became more artistic, with the hair being separated into five sections—forelocks, *bin* (right and left sidelocks), *mage* (bun), and *tabo* (rounded puffed-out back hair). Much use was made of colorful hair ornaments such as the *kushi* (see COMBS), KANZASHI, and KŌGAI to help keep the rolled or knotted hair in place.

Many traditional Japanese hairstyles were created in this period, the most popular of which were the *katsuyamamage* and the *shimadamage*. Hairstyles emphasizing a beautiful rounded curve of the back hair *(tabo)* were most popular. Shapes resembling birds were given such names as wagtail *tabo* and seagull *tabo*. The hair was arranged around special forms in order to achieve the different shapes of *tabo*. In the latter part of the era, the right and left sidelocks were emphasized instead of the *tabo*. One such style, called the *tōrōbin* because its shape was like that of a lantern *(tōrō)*, utilized a form made by pasting black rice paper onto flexible copper wires.

During this period women's hairstyles—as well as overall dress—varied according to social class, age, and marital status. Courtesans and GEISHA paid particular attention to their hairdos and had their own characteristic styles. Men's hairstyles also differed according to their social class and occupation.

Hashimoto Sumiko

After a government order in 1871 encouraging all males to cut off their topknots (DAMPATSUREI), men's hairstyles in Japan differed little from those in the West. The most popular women's hairstyle during the late 19th and early 20th centuries was the butterfly style *(ichōgaeshi)*, but women's hairstyles also were soon influenced by those of the West. Among women of the middle and upper classes, Western influence was seen in the popular *obako* and *seiyō agemaki* hairstyles. In 1885 a Women's Western Hairstyle Association was organized, and wearing the hair in various types of buns became fashionable. During the Taishō period (1912–26), the hair iron was introduced from France and waved hair became popular. By this time most young women wore their hair in Western styles; middle-aged and older women tended to favor the traditional Japanese hairstyles. Permanent waves were introduced from Europe early in the Shōwa period (1926-). During World War II permanent waves were prohibited by the military, but after the war hairstyles once again followed international patterns. The traditional Japanese hairstyles

continued to be worn until early in the Shōwa period, but after World War II they were simplified to eliminate the necessary paraphernalia. Traditional Japanese hairstyles are seen today only at New Year's and on other special occasions. See also CLOTHING; COSMETICS; HEADGEAR.

Yamano Aiko

Haitōrei

Edict prohibiting the wearing of swords; handed down by the Meiji government in March 1876, not long after the abolition of the *samurai* class (see SHIZOKU). Exceptions were made for formal-dress occasions and for members of the military and the police force. Earlier, in 1871, the government had discouraged the wearing of topknots (see DAMPATSUREI) as part of an overall policy to do away with old customs of dress related to status. The prohibition of the former samurai privilege of wearing swords, together with the universal CONSCRIPTION ORDINANCE OF 1873 and the termination of hereditary stipends for samurai (CHITSUROKU SHOBUN), were major causes of discontent among former samurai, some of whom rose in rebellion in the late 1870s (see HAGI REBELLION; JIMPŪREN REBELLION; SATSUMA REBELLION).

haji

(shame). In classifying cultures into "guilt cultures" and "shame cultures," the anthropologist Ruth BENEDICT described Japanese culture as a typical shame culture. According to her definition, a guilt culture inculcates absolute standards of morality and relies on the development of a personal conscience, while in a shame culture people feel bad only when caught in the act, rather than feeling guilty in an absolute sense. In other words, a shame culture relies on external sanctions for good behavior, not on an internalized conviction of sin. Accordingly, as long as an individual's bad behavior is not exposed to public scrutiny, he need not feel ashamed.

Benedict's understanding of shame consists of an oversimplistic dichotomy: in her judgment members of a guilt culture develop a conscience and blame themselves for bad conduct, whereas members of a shame culture act only to avoid criticism, ridicule, or rejection. The implication of this dichotomy is that people from a shame culture are incapable of internalizing behavioral standards, and will do anything as long as there is little likelihood of their bad conduct being discovered. In actuality, however, Japanese culture depends heavily upon individual internalization of behavioral standards and on a deep sense of conscience with regard to personal conduct, whether exposed to public scrutiny or not. Although there is an expression, *Tabi no haji wa kakisute* (While on a trip shame can be thrown away, that is, a traveler away from home can do as he likes), and some Japanese tend to act less scrupulously when away from their community, the same notion exists in Western societies as well. A more accurate sense of the Japanese notion of shame is reflected in the expression from the Confucian classic *Zhong yong (Chung yung; Doctrine of the Mean), Kunshi wa hitori o tsutsushimu* (When alone, the superior man is watchful of himself). The Japanese try to live up to an internalized ideal image of themselves and when they fail, they feel ashamed of themselves in their own eyes and in the eyes of others. Shame is not so much a reaction to other people's criticism—as Benedict understood it—or fear of ostracism, as it is a reaction to the realization that one has tarnished one's ideal self-image (or ego-ideal in Freudian terms, the formation of which owes much to the internalization of other people's expectations, ideals, and sanctions). Again, Benedict's classification of shame and guilt cultures creates a false dichotomy, since Western individuals, presumably belonging to a guilt culture, in fact experience shame as well as guilt, and people of so-called shame cultures, including the Japanese, feel guilt as well as shame. Cultures may vary in the degree to which codes emphasize the importance of guilt or shame, but it does not follow that shame and guilt are mutually exclusive in determining behavior. Definitions of these two concepts are imprecise in Western psychological literature. When one inflicts hurt on another, guilt is what one feels when one's attention is focused on the person who has been hurt, and shame is what one feels when one's attention is focused on one's ego-ideal (ideal self-image), which has been tarnished by one's misconduct.

■——Ruth Benedict, *The Chrysanthemum and the Sword: Patterns of Japanese Culture* (1946). George DeVos, "Relation of Guilt toward Parents to Achievement and Arranged Marriage among the Japanese," *Psychiatry* 23 (1960). Takeo Doi, *The Anatomy of Dependence,* tr John Bester (1973). Mori Mikisaburō, *Na to haji no bunka* (1971). Edward Norbeck, *Religion and Society in Modern Japan: Continuity and Change* (1970). Sagara Toru, *Bushido* (1968).

Hiroshi WAGATSUMA

Haji Seiji (1893–1977)

Novelist. Real name Akamatsu Shizuta. Born in Okayama Prefecture. After distinguishing himself for a number of years as a reporter and as a literary and drama critic in Ōsaka, Haji established his reputation as an outstanding writer of popular fiction with *Suna-e shibari* (1927, Curse of the Sand Picture), serialized in the newspaper *Asahi shimbun,* a historical novel whose chief character was a nihilistic swordsman. He subsequently devoted his energies to serialized fiction, producing a number of period works prized for their excellent style and skillful construction. Other works include the novels *Abare noshi* (1951) and *Fūsetsu no hito* (1957–58).

haji ware

(hajiki). A plain, unglazed, reddish earthenware manufactured from the 4th through the 10th centuries. *Haji* ware of the Kofun period (ca 300–710) grew out of the preceding native YAYOI POTTERY, the transition being marked by the gradual disappearance of surface decoration and the standardization of shapes.

During the early Kofun period, *haji* ware served both ritual and utilitarian functions: sets of small jars with stands and pedestaled bowls were used during ceremonial festivities, while jars, pots, and various bowls were used for food preparation and everyday needs. In the early 5th century, SUE WARE—a gray stoneware—was introduced from the southern part of the Korean peninsula, and from then on *haji* and *sue* wares were used together for ceremonial and household purposes.

Beginning in the Nara period (710–794), some *haji* vessels were burnished and smoke-blackened and came to be known popularly as *kokushoku doki* ("black-colored pottery"). From this practice developed the *gaki* ("tile vessels"), bowls fired in an atmosphere of reduced oxygen but at low temperatures. The manufacture of *haji* ware as a cohesive tradition came to an end with the development of glazes and the rise of the medieval pottery traditions (see CERAMICS: medieval ceramics). But some reddish earthenware articles, such as oilwick saucers for lanterns and flanged rice kettles, continued to be made as late as the 13th and 14th centuries. The pottery of the

Haji ware

A 5th-century jar from a site in Komae, Tōkyō Prefecture. Earthenware. Height 31.8 cm. Meiji University Archeological Collection, Tōkyō.

northern SATSUMON CULTURE was influenced by *haji* pottery, and remnants of the *haji* tradition can still be found in Japan today.

Little is known of *haji* craft organization, and few kilns or manufacturing sites have been found. It is assumed that the ware was produced in specialized workshops, and during the late Kofun period, at least some *haji* ware is said to have been produced by BE (production groups) for the exclusive use of the YAMATO COURT. *Hajibe,* as these groups were called, may also have been connected with the production of the HANIWA funerary sculptures that decorated the mounded tombs of the Kofun period.

Haji ware was coil- or ring-built rather than thrown on a potter's wheel; its exterior and often interior surface was finished by scraping with a piece of wood. Jar and pot interiors were often shaved down to make them thin; shaving was also used selectively on bowl pedestals and some bowl bases. Globular bodies and round bases are characteristic of *haji* ware, but flat bases as well as some body decorations—mainly combing and comb or cylindrical punctates—remained in early *haji* ware from the Yayoi tradition. Burnished motifs *(ammon)* were also retained from the Yayoi tradition of polishing some vessel surfaces.

Haji ware forms the basis for dating many archaeological sites. Despite the ware's uniformity in shape, scholars working in each region of Japan have found it necessary to construct separate schemes for naming the successive phases of *haji* development in their areas. The Kantō region *haji* chronology is the most detailed and well-known, comprising the following phase names from the 4th to 9th centuries: Goryō, Izumi, Onitaka, Mama, and Kokubu (some scholars include a Yakuradai phase between Izumi and Onitaka and an Ochiai phase between Mama and Kokubu). Some attempts have been made to integrate the different phase names throughout Japan into a comprehensive chronology, but most regional schemes are incomplete and still in the process of being defined. Newly excavated materials belonging to the transitional period from Yayoi to *haji* pottery are contributing to the revision of the chronologies and reassessment of the beginning of the Kofun period.

■——Sugihara Sōsuke and Ōtsuka Hatsushige, ed, *Hajishiki doki shūsei,* 4 vols (1971–74).

Gina Lee BARNES

hakase

(doctor or teacher). Official post in the RITSURYŌ SYSTEM of government. The *hakase* instructed and examined students at the DAIGAKURYŌ, the centrally located university for training government officials, and at the *kokugaku,* the provincial schools for training provincial officials. There were also *hakase* at the ON'YŌRYŌ (Bureau of Yin and Yang), the Ten'yakuryō (Medical Bureau), and other bureaus. On occasion they were sent as instructors to such places as DAZAIFU, the government outpost in Kyūshū. The post became hereditary in the middle of the Heian period (794–1185). The term is currently used to refer to those holding a doctorate, who are more commonly called *hakushi.*

ETŌ Kyōji

Hakodate——Goryōkaku

The first Western-style fort in Japan, the Goryōkaku was completed in 1864 under the supervision of Takeda Ayasaburō, a scholar of Western Learning. It was the scene of the last battle of the civil war that accompanied the Meiji Restoration of 1868.

Hakata → Fukuoka

Hakata Dontaku

A festival held in the Hakata district of the city of Fukuoka in Kyūshū on 3–5 May. It had its origins as a NEW YEAR celebration of the Muromachi period (1333–1568) in which local citizens dressed up as the SEVEN DEITIES OF GOOD FORTUNE (Shichifukujin) or as CHIGO (child shrine and temple attendants) and performed before their feudal lord in the style of the *matsubayashi* processional then popular in Kyōto. Doll-decorated platforms and elaborate floats (DASHI) were added during the Edo period (1600–1868), when the current name was adopted (apparently from the Dutch word *zondag*, "Sunday," which was taken to mean "holiday"). After World War II the festival was revived and amalgamated with the Harbor Festival in May, and to the Seven Deities of Good Fortune procession were added various other musical and dance performances.

MISUMI Haruo

Hakata merchants

Wealthy merchants of the Muromachi period (1333–1568) and early part of the Edo period (1600–1868) who were active in the seaport city of Hakata (now part of Fukuoka). Down through the 16th century Hakata prospered as the principal base for trade with China and Korea. Among its merchants were the Koizumi and Sōkin houses, who engaged in the TALLY TRADE with the Ming dynasty (1368–1644) of China during the Muromachi period, and SHIMAI SŌSHITSU and KAMIYA SŌTAN, who were both active in the late 16th century under the patronage of the national unifier TOYOTOMI HIDEYOSHI. These powerful merchants also conducted the affairs of the city. In the early 17th century Hakata lost its preeminence in overseas trade to Hirado and Nagasaki; many Hakata traders moved to those places and became ITOWAPPU merchants, members of the official silk-importing guild.

Hakata Station film decision

A Supreme Court decision defining protections of and limitations on news-gathering operations of the press. The case involved a January 1968 clash at the Hakata Station in Fukuoka Prefecture, Kyūshū, between local police and student demonstrators opposed to the calling of the American nuclear-powered aircraft carrier USS *Enterprise* at a Japanese port. A request for a quasi-judicial hearing on the incident was filed on the grounds of police abuse of authority and brutality. The plaintiffs, the Japan Socialist Party and the National League for the Protection of the Constitution, requested the subpoena (as evidence) of television film that had been taken at the scene of the incident by four television stations, and the lower court issued the subpoena. The television stations, asserting that use of the films for any purpose other than news reporting jeopardized the freedom to engage in news gathering, refused the court order and filed a special appeal with the Supreme Court. The high court rejected the appeal; acknowledging the usefulness of the press in maintaining the "people's right to know" and recognizing the constitutional protection of the freedom of news gathering, the court ruled that there are limitations on this protection when balanced against a constitutional request such as one involving the fair conduct of a criminal trial (23 Keishū 1490). The case was a landmark in the interpretation of the constitution, since it clarified the constitutional guarantee of the right to gather news and established the legal concept of the people's right to know. The fact that a balancing test was used in this case is also notable. In a later case, the 1978 Ministry of Foreign Affairs Cable Leak case (Gaimushō Kōden Rōei Jiken), the Supreme Court upheld the freedom to gather news even where national secrets are concerned.

SHIMIZU Hideo

Hakkōdasan

Volcano group in the Nasu Volcanic Zone, central Aomori Prefecture, northern Honshū, on the northern fringe of the Ōu Mountains, north of Lake Towada. The highest peak is Ōdake (1,585 m, 5,199 ft). The group is divided into north and south Hakkōdasan; north Hakkōdasan is generally referred to alone as Hakkōdasan. It has numerous hot springs such as Sukayu, Tsuta, and Sarukura. A principal part of Towada–Hachimantai National Park.

hakkō ichiu

(literally "eight cords, one roof"). Political slogan, widely used by the Japanese government from 1940 to the end of World War II. The eight cords indicate the "eight directions," and thus symbolize the world. The phrase was adapted from a quotation in the 8th-century chronicle *Nihon shoki*, where it was attributed to the legendary first emperor, JIMMU. Two years before his enthronement in 662 BC, Jimmu is said to have commanded the construction of a capital, adding cryptically that "thereafter, the capital may be extended so as to embrace all the six cardinal points, and the eight cords may be covered so as to form a roof." On 1 August 1940 the second KONOE FUMIMARO cabinet announced a "Fundamental National Policy" that opened with these words: "The basic aim of Japan's national policy lies in the firm establishment of world peace in accordance with the lofty spirit of *hakkō ichiu* in which the country was founded, and in the construction, as the first step, of a new order in Greater East Asia." The four characters for *hakkō ichiu* were carved in the calligraphy of Prince CHICHIBU, younger brother of Emperor HIROHITO, on a monument erected at the city of Miyazaki in Kyūshū to commemorate the 2,600th anniversary (1940) of the legendary founding of Japan. This is now called Heiwa no Tō (Peace Tower), but during Japan's 1941–45 conquest of "Greater East Asia," the slogan *hakkō ichiu* seemed to imply Japanese control (*ichiu*) over the whole world (*hakkō*), rather than universal brotherhood or peace.

Robert M. SPAULDING

Hakodate

City in southwestern Hokkaidō located on the southeastern tip of the Oshima Peninsula jutting out into the Tsugaru Strait. A flourishing fishing port since 1741, it was one of the first ports opened to foreign trade under the KANAGAWA TREATY (1854). It was the largest city in Hokkaidō up through the 1930s, but in 1934 two-thirds of the city was destroyed by a fire; it again incurred heavy damage during World War II. With the resumption of north sea fishing in 1952, the city has gradually regained its former prosperity. The processing of seafood and other foodstuffs, shipbuilding, and transport machinery manufacturing are major industries. Its chief agricultural products are rice, Irish potatoes, and vegetables grown on the Hakodate Plain. A ferry connects the city with Aomori on Honshū. Hakodate Airport is in the eastern part of the city. The fort of Goryōkaku, the scene of the last military conflict accompanying the Meiji Restoration (see GORYŌKAKU, BATTLE OF); the Trappist convent; the Holy Resurrection Church in Hakodate (locally known as the Harisutosu Seikyōkai); and the mountain Hakodateyama attract many tourists. Pop: 320,152.

Hakodate bugyō

(commissioner of Hakodate). An office of the Tokugawa shogunate, established in Hakodate in the early 19th century when government leaders became alarmed at Russian expansionism north of Japan (see LAXMAN, Adam Erikovich). In 1799 the shogunate took charge of part of the island of EZO (now Hokkaidō) and dispatched officials to supervise affairs there, designating them Ezo *bugyō* and later Hakodate *bugyō*, after the port of Hakodate at the southern tip of the island. In 1807 the shogunate took over from the Matsumae domain (situated in southern Hokkaidō) control of all of Ezo, but in 1821, after the foreign danger had receded, returned it to Matsumae and abolished the commissioner's office. In 1855, as foreign problems escalated, the shogunate again took charge of the Hakodate area, and then all of Ezo, and reestablished the office, which survived until the Meiji Restoration (1868). In its final form the post of commissioner was under the authority of the senior councillors (RŌJŪ) and had an office stipend of 2,000 *koku* (*see* KOKUDAKA), an assigned force of 100 patrolmen (YORIKI AND DŌSHIN), and responsibility for administering the island, preparing defenses, and conducting foreign affairs on the island and in the trading port of Hakodate.

Conrad TOTMAN

Hakodate Dock Co, Ltd

Medium-scale shipbuilder whose specialty is the building of small- and medium-sized ships such as mini-bulk carriers. It was established in Hakodate, Hokkaidō, in 1896 by SHIBUSAWA EIICHI and ŌKURA KIHACHIRŌ. Following the OIL CRISIS OF 1973, the company attempted to cope with the depression in the shipbuilding industry by going into the fields of salvage ship and work vessel construction, ship repairs, machinery, bridge and road construction, and other activities. It is assisted financially by the MARUBENI CORPORATION, FUJI BANK, LTD, and other members of the Fuyō group. Sales for the fiscal year ending March 1982 totaled ¥32.2 billion (US $133.8 million), with an export ratio of 57 percent; the company was capitalized at ¥1.8 billion (US $7.5 million) in the same year. Corporate headquarters are located in Tōkyō.

Hakone

Town in southwestern Kanagawa Prefecture, central Honshū, located on the lake ASHINOKO. Hakone developed as a POST-STATION TOWN on the Tōkaidō, the major highway during the Edo period (1600–1868). A barrier station, HAKONE NO SEKI, was established here by the Tokugawa shogunate in 1618. The town is the official center of the Fuji–Hakone–Izu National Park, serving as a tourist base for the lake Ashinoko and the mountain HAKONEYAMA. The city affords a magnificent view of Mt. Fuji (Fujisan). There are several hot springs in the area. The remains of the barrier station, the cedar-lined Tōkaidō, a cluster of stone Buddha images dating from the 12th century, and the HAKONE OPEN-AIR MUSEUM are other attractions. A parade, reminiscent of Edo-period *daimyō* processions, is held on 3 November. Pop: 19,879.

Hakone Canal

(Hakone Yōsui). Irrigation canal in eastern Shizuoka Prefecture, central Honshū. The water source is the lake Ashinoko. A tunnel bored under the crater of the mountain Hakoneyama carries the lake water to irrigate approximately 1,000 hectares (2,470 acres) of farmland surrounding the city of Susono. Construction was completed in 1670 during the Edo period (1600–1868). Three small power-generating stations are located on the canal.

Hakone Museum of Art

(Hakone Bijutsukan). Located in Hakone, Kanagawa Prefecture; formerly known as the Kyūsei Hakone Art Museum. This museum, opened in 1952, and its sister museum, the MOA MUSEUM OF ART in Atami, belong to the SEKAI KYŪSEI KYŌ (The Religion for the Salvation of the World). The two museums share the collections, assembled by the late founder of the church OKADA MOKICHI. The Hakone Museum of Art exhibits Japanese pottery and porcelains in the larger of two buildings set in a garden. Included are Jōmon, Yayoi, and Kofun period objects as well as wares from nearly every well-known Japanese kiln of the Azuchi-Momoyama period

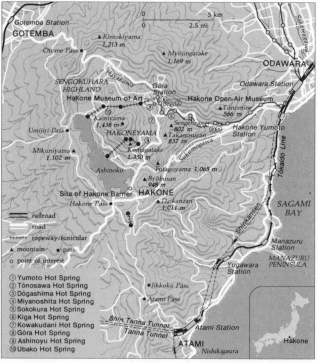

Hakone

Hakone

The scenic crater lake Ashinoko, a popular Hakone tourist spot. Mt. Fuji (Fujisan) can be seen in the background.

(1568–1600) through the Edo period (1600–1868). The smaller building houses an exhibition of Japanese ceramic techniques.

Laurance ROBERTS

Hakone no Seki

(Hakone Barrier). A checkpoint maintained at the Hakone Pass (now in Kanagawa Prefecture) on the TŌKAIDŌ highway during the Edo period (1600–1868). The 32-kilometer (20-mi) pass between Mishima and Odawara was considered the most arduous stretch of the Tōkaidō. To secure the defense of Edo (now Tōkyō), the Tokugawa shogunate set up a barrier and post station there in 1618, after the fall of Ōsaka Castle (see ŌSAKA CASTLE, SIEGES OF). Traffic through this strategic nexus was tightly controlled. Since the wives and daughters of *daimyō* were required by the shogunate to remain in Edo as part of the SANKIN KŌTAI system, especially stringent checks were made on women leaving the city. People were also carefully checked for weapons. The barrier station remained under the authority of the daimyō of the Odawara domain (now part of Kanagawa Prefecture) until it was removed in 1869, a year after the MEIJI RESTORATION. See also SEKISHO.

Hakone Open-Air Museum

(Chōkoku no Mori Bijutsukan). Located in Hakone, Kanagawa Prefecture. The museum, established in 1969 by the Fuji–Sankei group of companies in the media industry, owns a collection of 19th- and 20th-century Western and Japanese sculpture, almost all of it shown out-of-doors in a park. The Western section has works by Archipenko, Arp, Bourdelle, Calder, Despiau, Giacometti, Maillol, Marini, Moore, Isamu NOGUCHI, Picasso, and Rodin. One room is devoted to the studies made by Manzu for the doors of St. Peter's in Rome; Emilio Greco's figures are displayed in a garden by themselves. Japanese artists of the older generation featured in this collection are Amenomiya Jirō (b 1889), Nakahara Teijirō (1888–1921), OGIWARA MORIE, Shimizu Takashi (1897–1981), TAKAMURA KŌTARŌ, and Tobari Kogan (1882–1927). Nearly every younger Japanese sculptor is represented. The museum is also noted for its active publication program. *Laurance ROBERTS*

Hakone Pass

(Hakone Tōge). Located on the border of southwestern Kanagawa Prefecture and eastern Shizuoka Prefecture, central Honshū. It was considered one of the most difficult passes of the highway Tōkaidō during the Edo period (1600–1868). A national highway runs through the pass. Hakone Pass is the area in Fuji–Hakone–Izu National Park from which roads leading to tourist areas such as HAKONE, the lake ASHINOKO, and Izu Peninsula regions branch off. Altitude: 849 m (2,785 ft).

Hakoneyama

Composite volcano on the border between southwestern Kanagawa and eastern Shizuoka prefectures, central Honshū. The highest peak is Kamiyama (1,438 m; 4,717 ft). It has two crater rims, one old and one new, and seven central domes including Kamiyama and Komagatake (1,350 m; 4,428 ft). Tōnomine, Myōjingatake, Kintokiyama, Hakone Pass, and Daikanzan line the old crater rim. Sengenzan, Takanosuzan, and Byōbusan line the new crater rim. The crater lake ASHINOKO is on the southwestern part of the mountain. Hakoneyama is the center of the Hakone area of the Fuji–Hakone–Izu National Park and includes such scenic spots as Ashinoko, Komagatake, the Sengokuhara highland, and numerous hot spring spas such as Gōra and Yumoto.

hakoniwa

Miniature Japanese gardens created in shallow boxes using sand, stones, ceramic figurines, houses, and bridges, as well as miniature trees (BONSAI) and such plants as azalea, goyōmatsu pine, and zelkova. Miniature gardens first became popular during the middle of the Edo period (1600–1868), when the art of landscaping Japanese gardens had been perfected. See also BONKEI AND BONSEKI.

Hakozaki Shrine

(Hakozakigū). Shintō shrine in the Hakozaki section of the city of Fukuoka, Kyūshū, dedicated to Emperor ŌJIN and Empress JINGŪ (both legendary) as well as the deity Tamayorihime no Mikoto. This shrine is one of the three great HACHIMAN shrines of Japan, the other two being the USA HACHIMAN SHRINE and the IWASHIMIZU HACHIMAN SHRINE. According to one tradition, the Hakozaki shrine was established in the early 10th century as an offshoot of the Usa Shrine to afford protection from incursions from the Korean kingdom of Silla. The Engi Shiki (927, Procedures of the Engi Era) ranked Hakozaki as an eminent shrine (myōjin taisha). Its annual festival is held on 15 September. *Stanley WEINSTEIN*

Hakuba

Village in northwestern Nagano Prefecture, central Honshū, situated on the eastern slopes of SHIROUMADAKE. Once a rice and silkworm cultivation area, its ideal location has transformed it into a popular ski resort. Pop: 7,131.

Hakubakai

(White Horse Society). An association of Western-style painters and sculptors active in the later part of the Meiji period (1868–1912). It was founded in 1896 when KURODA SEIKI, Kume Keiichirō, and other liberals broke away from the Meiji Bijutsukai (Meiji Fine Arts Society) to be free of its bureaucratic organization and to practice the brighter, more colorful plein-air style. Membership included many major artists of the day, and the association became the leading group in Western-style painting circles. Both Kuroda and Kume were appointed to professorships at the Tōkyō Bijutsu Gakkō (now Tōkyō University of Fine Arts and Music); this cemented the association's position as the academic mainstream of Western-style painting. It sponsored exhibitions, supported research, and trained many young painters before it dissolved in 1911.

Hakubunkan

Publishing company; one of Japan's largest and most influential publishing houses in the late 19th and early 20th centuries. Founded in 1887 by ŌHASHI SAHEI and his son Ōhashi Shintarō (1863–1944). Beginning with Nihon taika ronshū (1887), a collection of major articles from various magazines which became a record-breaking best seller, Hakubunkan went on to publish a large number of magazines totaling 77 by the mid-1920s. Several of them, such as Taiyō, Bungei kurabu, and Shōnen sekai, dominated the field of popular magazines. Operating on the guiding principle of its founder, who believed in mass production with little regard for profits, Hakubunkan also published a variety of other books. The encyclopedia Teikoku hyakka zensho (200 vols), which took over 20 years to compile, and the Teikoku bunko, inexpensive editions of 100 selected works from Japanese literature, also helped establish the house. About 1920, however, Hakubunkan began to be eclipsed by newly emerging competitors like Jitsugyō no Nihonsha and KŌDANSHA, LTD. The firm was dissolved in 1947 and reorganized as Hakubun Shinsha in 1950, specializing in diary notebooks. Magazine and book publication was taken over by Hakuyūsha in 1949. *FUKUDA Kizō*

hakubyōga

("white drawing picture"). A type of monochrome ink line painting often used to illustrate scenes from Japanese courtly romances, dating from the latter part of the Heian period (794–1185) onward. Conservative and classical in both subject matter and style, hakubyō paintings make use of light and precise lines in combination with rhythmic patterns of solid black created through the rendering of men's black caps, women's long black hair, interior architectural details, and so on. Occasionally, touches of red or gold pigment are added. Among the earliest and finest hakubyōga is a 13th-century album with text and illustrations of the TALE OF GENJI now in the Tokugawa Art Museum, Nagoya, and the Yamato Bunkakan, Nara.

In a broad sense, hakubyōga may refer to any ink line painting that does not employ areas of wash; it may also refer to preliminary monochrome underpainting or ink drawings used as models. In this sense, hakubyōga can be traced as far back as the 9th century, when Buddhist clergy in Japan were copying religious images in simple line drawings (zuzō) to serve as iconographic models. Satirical ink sketches by monk-painters for their own amusement were also produced, notably at the Kōzanji temple in the northeastern section of Kyōto, best known for the 12th-century handscrolls of frolicking animals, CHŌJŪ GIGA. There is also a Chinese precedent for a monochrome style from at least the Tang dynasty (T'ang; 618–907); courtly paintings by the artist Li Longian (Li Lung-mien; 1049–1106) are perhaps the earliest surviving examples.

The most immediate source for illustrations of courtly romances in the hakubyō style may have been the final, thin, and unfluctuating ink outline drawing that was applied over the thick color pigments in 12th-century picture scrolls such as the GENJI MONOGATARI EMAKI. ■———Shimbo Tōru, Hakubyō emaki, no. 48 of Nihon no bijutsu (May 1970). *Julia MEECH-PEKARIK*

Hakuhō culture

The culture of the Hakuhō period, a period in Japanese art history extending from the latter half of the 7th century to the beginning of the 8th century; so called after the Hakuhō era (672–686), an unofficial reign name (nengō) associated with Emperor· TEMMU (r 672–686), who had his palace in Asuka (in what is now Nara Prefecture). Politically, it was a time of vigor when, under the impetus of the TAIKA REFORM (645), the authority of the emperor was built up. Artistically, it was a continuation of the ASUKA CULTURE, though with stronger Tang (T'ang; 618–907) dynasty Chinese influences. The latter half of the period showed the influence of the Gupta court in India transmitted via Tang China. Outstanding examples are the east pagoda of the temple YAKUSHIJI, the seated statue of the Bodhisattva Miroku (Maitreya) at the temple TAIMADERA, and the Amida (Amitābha) Triad, housed in the Lady Tachibana Shrine at HŌRYŪJI. Hakuhō culture was succeeded by TEMPYŌ CULTURE, in which Buddhist art under continental influence reached its peak. See also BUDDHIST ART; PAINTING; BUDDHIST SCULPTURE.

Hakuhōdō, Inc

Advertising firm; Japan's second largest after DENTSŪ, INC. Hakuhōdō was founded in 1895 by SEKI HIRONAO as an agency specializing in advertisements for the line of magazines put out by the publishing house HAKUBUNKAN. Today it controls a major share of advertising in Japan's mass media involving commercial television, radio, newspapers, and magazines. It is also active in international advertising markets. Hakuhōdō was the first in the Japanese advertising industry to employ an on-line computer system.

HAYAKAWA Zenjirō

Hakui

City in central Ishikawa Prefecture, central Honshū, located on the western coast of the Noto Peninsula. Hakui has a flourishing silk and rayon fabric industry. Agricultural products include rice, vegetables, and fruit. A part of Noto Peninsula Quasi-National Park, the drive along the Chirihama coast is known for its beauty. The city has several famous temples and shrines, among them Hakui Shrine, where a keyhole-shaped mounded tomb (KOFUN) dating to the 5th century can be seen. The area is also noted for its many sumō wrestlers. Pop: 28,782.

Hakuin (1686–1769)

Also known as Hakuin Ekaku. RINZAI SECT Zen master, painter, and calligrapher. Hakuin was born in Hara (in what is now Shizuoka Prefecture). A frail but intellectually gifted child, he early turned to Buddhism. He describes in his writings how he decided to become a monk after he heard a sermon on the tortures of hell when he was 7 or 8 years old. In his 15th year he entered the Zen temple of Shōinji in his native village. He experienced a religious crisis in his 19th year and decided to take up the life of a wandering monk. It was in his 24th year, while he was a pupil of Shōju Rōjin (Dōkyō Etan, 1642–1721), a Zen master of the Ō–Tō–Kan line of transmission, that he had his first experience of enlightenment. Hakuin writes that he was assailed by a "great doubt," but after feeling as though he were frozen in a sheet of ice, he suddenly heard the sound of the temple bell and was transformed, "as though the sheet of ice had been smashed." This was the first of a series of metaphysical experiences he had as he wandered from temple to temple. In 1716 he returned to the temple Shōinji in Hara, where he began to instruct a growing number of followers. He reformed the traditions of Zen teachings, insisting that each pupil undergo training with an overriding faith and dogged perseverance. He said that a student must first see into his own nature, and then "break his conceptual thought" by meditating upon the unsolvable questions called KŌAN. Most of these kōan were taken from early Chinese Zen masters, but Hakuin also used a kōan of his own, "What is the sound of one hand clapping?" Hakuin's success in revamping Rinzai training was so decisive that the principles he established are still followed in Rinzai temples.

Hakuin's writings are voluminous and cover a wide range of styles and purposes. He wrote long letters to officials and daimyō, composed sermons, poems, and stories in colloquial style for laymen, and authored Zen texts for his followers. He also produced various autobiographical writings. He frequently traveled, and the money he received for his preaching was used to support his pupils and to print his works.

Although Hakuin was a Zen master, he did not believe in the exclusivity of Zen truths and encouraged his parishioners to follow whatever form of Buddhism they found most meaningful. Nevertheless, he taught his Zen followers a combined program of formal meditation and active work, insisting upon the importance of caring for the temple grounds, growing grains and vegetables, and becoming as self-sustaining as possible. He wrote that to find one's own self-nature, "Nothing can surpass meditation in the midst of ac-

tivity." Hakuin thus took pains that monks should not become leeches upon the general public nor lose touch with everyday life.

Unlike many of the Zen masters of his day, Hakuin did not aspire to the temporal glory of leading one of the great temples in Kyōto or Edo (now Tōkyō). By remaining in the country, Hakuin also avoided conflicts with the Tokugawa shogunate, which took an active role in determining temple succession. Instead, Hakuin devoted much of his time to the common people and farmers, insisting that "men are all living Buddhas" if they could but see their true nature.

In his sixties, Hakuin turned to brushwork to express his Zen enlightenment. He painted a number of works, usually using ink on paper, with a gentle humor and wry wit. His subject matter was varied but often consisted of figures such as Hotei that were popular in folk mythology. At this time Hakuin's use of line was thin and rather sinuous, and his ink tones were primarily grey rather than deep black. In his next decade, Hakuin's brushwork took on a new power and strength. By his eighties, Hakuin's subject matter was severely limited; his portrayals of Daruma (Bodhidharma) are especially notable for their profound impact: the eyes of the first patriarch of Zen are rendered with great intensity; brushlines are thick, with strong tonal variation. All extraneous detail is omitted, and we are given a portrait of Daruma that fully expresses Hakuin's vision of meditation and enlightenment.

Hakuin's calligraphy in his last years has a fullness, an almost childlike blocky simplicity unique in the Zen tradition of art. From the large number of scrolls that survive from Hakuin's final decades, it is clear that he found brushwork important not only for its artistic value but even more for its power to awaken the mind of the beholder. In his epistolary treatise Orategama (1749), he wrote: "Look at painting or calligraphy, or at genius in music . . . if we ask where that genius lies, nobody will be able to understand . . . the mysterious nature of the mind, with which all people are endowed, is like this." See also ZEN.

📖 ——Hakuin Ekaku, Orategama, tr R. D. M. Shaw as The Embossed Tea Kettle (1963). Rikukawa Taiun, Kōshō Hakuin oshō shōden (1963). Takeuchi Shōji, Hakuin (1964). Philip B. Yampolsky, The Zen Master Hakuin (1971). Stephen ADDISS

hakurai

("arrived from abroad"). A word in use until the early 1940s to refer to imported products. The terms hakurai and hakuraihin ("imported goods") were used from the Nara period (710–794) to refer to imported goods primarily from China and Korea. During the wave of Western culture after the Meiji Restoration (1868), however, hakurai came to mean anything made in Europe or the United States. The Japanese considered these imported products (especially cameras, razors, fountain pens, watches, and automobiles) superior to and therefore more prestigious than domestic products. The word hakurai and the phrase jōtō hakurai ("first class imported from abroad") were synonymous with "good" or "of the highest quality." Japan's war efforts during World War II and the more recent trade competition with Western nations should be understood with reference to these past feelings of inferiority toward Western products. See also FOREIGNERS, ATTITUDES TOWARD.

📖 ——H. Wagatsuma, "Problems of Cultural Identity in Modern Japan," in George DeVos and Lola Romanucci-Ross, ed, Ethnic Identity: Cultural Continuities and Change (1975).

Hiroshi WAGATSUMA

Hakusan

Volcano on the border between Ishikawa and Gifu prefectures, central Honshū; the highest peak in the Hakusan Volcanic Zone. Along with FUJISAN (Mt. Fuji) and TATEYAMA, Hakusan is one of the three most popular mountains in Japan as objects of religious worship and for climbing. On the summit are three central domes, Gozemmine (2,702 m; 8,863 ft), Ōnanjimine (2,685 m; 8,807 ft), and Kengamine (2,656 m; 8,712 ft), and a crater lake, Senjagaike. Alpine flora and wild birds abound. Hakusan is the center of Hakusan National Park.

Hakusan National Park

(Hakusan Kokuritsu Kōen). Situated in central Honshū, in Toyama, Ishikawa, Fukui, and Gifu prefectures. The park's desolate mountain terrain features numerous caldera lakes, rivers, and spectacular gorges. In the center of the park is HAKUSAN (meaning "White

Mountain" from the snow that covers it all year round), an extinct volcano with caldera lakes. Together with Mt. Fuji (FUJISAN) and TATEYAMA, Hakusan is one of Japan's three sacred mountains. Its highest peaks are Gozemmine (2,702 m; 8,863 ft), Ōnanjimine (2,685 m; 8,807 ft), and Kengamine (2,656 m; 8,712 ft). To the north of these peaks lie the hot spring resorts of Chūgū and Iwama, closed during the winter months because of the heavy snow. The mountain is open to climbers only in the summer. Hakusan is rich in virgin forests of creeping pine, Japanese beech (buna), Japanese oak (nara), as well as colorful alpine flora, and is noted for the 100 or more species of wild bird, including a rare golden eagle (inuwashi). Area: 474 sq km (183 sq mi).

Hakusan Volcanic Zone

(Hakusan Kazantai). Volcanic zone, extending from HAKUSAN, on the border of Ishikawa and Gifu prefectures, central Honshū, to UN-ZENDAKE, Nagasaki Prefecture, northern Kyūshū. The major volcanoes in the zone are Hakusan, DAISEN, SAMBESAN, HIKOSAN, Yufudake, KUJŪSAN, and Unzendake. Hot springs and scenic spots abound.

Hakusukinoe, Battle of

(Hakusukinoe no Tatakai). Naval battle fought in 663 near the mouth of the river Hakusukinoe (or Hakusonkō; Kor: Paek-kang, now Kŭm-kang) on the southwestern coast of the Korean peninsula (near present-day Kunsan), in which a Tang (T'ang) Chinese naval force destroyed a Japanese expedition sent to restore the kingdom of PAEKCHE. Paekche, with which Japan had had close ties for some two hundred years, was occupied in 660 by the Tang in alliance with the kingdom of SILLA. The Paekche king (King Ŭija) surrendered to the Tang forces and was taken to China, where he died that year. Paekche remnants elevated to the throne P'ung Chang (Puyŏ Pung), a younger son of Ŭija who had been in Japan as a "hostage" since 631. He returned to Paekche with a Japanese supporting force of 5,000 men in 661. In 663 Emperor TENJI dispatched this relief force under the command of ABE NO HIRAFU to aid P'ung Chang's loyalist army, but it was decisively defeated in a naval engagement by a superior Tang fleet. As a result, the effort to restore the kingdom of Paekche collapsed, and Japan, convinced of the strength of the Tang and Silla, resolved to strengthen its government administration (see TAIKA REFORM).

Hamada

City in western Shimane Prefecture, western Honshū. Situated on the Sea of Japan, Hamada developed during the Edo period (1600–1868) as a port and castle town. Today it is the administrative, commercial, and industrial center of the Iwami region of Shimane. As one of the largest fishing ports in western Japan, it has a thriving marine-products-processing industry. Shipments of foreign lumber have led to a growing woodwork industry. The ruins of Hamada Castle, dating from the 17th century, may be seen. Pop: 50,800.

Hamada Hikozō (1837–1897)

Also known as Joseph Heco or Amerika Hikozō. The first Japanese to become an American citizen. Hamada was born the son of a ship captain in Harima (now Hyōgo Prefecture). In 1850 on his way back from Edo (now Tōkyō) his ship was wrecked, and after drifting on the open sea for 52 days, he and 16 other survivors were rescued by the American ship Oakland. The ship arrived in San Francisco in February 1851. The American government of that time was preparing an expedition under Commodore Matthew PERRY to force the OPENING OF JAPAN, and arranged to have the 17 castaways sent back with Perry. The squadron sailed for Japan in 1852. Reaching Hong Kong, however, Hamada was asked by Americans on the ship to return to the United States. He therefore parted with his companions and went back to San Francisco. There he made the acquaintance of a customs officer, B. C. Sanders, who took him to Baltimore in August 1852. During the journey he rode on a train for the first time and was much impressed by the telegraph. In October 1854 he was baptized a Catholic and was known thereafter as Joseph Heco; he obtained American citizenship in June 1858.

Hamada missed Japan, however, and after several attempts to return, in September of 1858 he was given permission by a friend, Captain John Mercer BROOKE, to travel on his surveying ship, which

would be passing in the vicinity of Japan. In Shanghai on his way back to Japan he met Townsend HARRIS, the first American minister to Japan, who appointed him interpreter for the American consulate in Kanagawa. Hamada arrived in Yokohama in June 1859. When the ship KANRIN MARU was commissioned in 1860 to sail to the United States (see UNITED STATES, MISSION OF 1860 TO), it was through Hamada that Captain Brooke was named as technical adviser.

Hamada left the consulate in 1860 and opened a trading company in Yokohama. He visited the United States again in 1861 and met Abraham Lincoln in March 1862. After his return, Hamada began publishing Kaigai shimbun (Overseas News), the first modern Japanese newspaper, with KISHIDA GINKŌ and others in June 1864. The newspaper covered mainly foreign events, but with its 18th issue it began a series on American history and a translation of Genesis. The latter was quite a bold undertaking, for Christianity was still officially proscribed in Japan. The paper ceased publication after 26 issues when Hamada decided to devote his talents to business. During the early years of the Meiji period (1868–1912) he served for a while in the Ministry of Finance. Hamada wrote two autobiographies, Hyōryūki (1863, Record of a Castaway) in Japanese and The Narrative of a Japanese (1895) in English.

YAMAGUCHI Osamu

Hamada Kōsaku (1881–1938)

Archaeologist. Born in Ōsaka. Pen name, Hamada Seiryō. Hamada graduated in 1905 from Tōkyō University, where he majored in art history. In 1909 he became a lecturer at Kyōto University in Japanese art history and archaeology. After studying in Europe, mainly Britain, from 1913 to 1916, he was appointed professor at Kyōto University in 1917, the first in Japan to hold a university chair in archaeology. He served as president of Kyōto University from 1937 until his death the following year.

Hamada was the first to introduce scientific methods of archaeology to Japan, and his research group published a total of 14 volumes of research work from 1917 to 1937, many of which concerned reports of his excavations in Japan, Korea, and China. In 1925 Hamada formed the Far Eastern Archaeological Society with Professor HARADA YOSHITO of Tōkyō University and Professor Ma Heng of Beijing (Peking) University to engage in archaeological studies in East Asia and disseminate the results.

Hamada is known for his work in a wide range of fields, including Chinese and Buddhist art history. Shina komeiki deishō zusetsu (1927) contains the results of his studies in Chinese archaeological remains and Tenshō ken'ō shisetsu ki (1931) is a study of a mission sent by Christian daimyō to Europe in 1582 (see MISSION TO EUROPE OF 1582). His best-known works are Tsūron kōkogaku (1922), which is based on his lectures at Kyōto University, and Kōkogaku nyūmon (1930).

Hamada Shōji (1894–1978)

Japan's most renowned potter and a major figure in the Japanese FOLK CRAFTS (mingei) movement. Born in Kawasaki, Kanagawa Prefecture, he studied ceramics at Tōkyō Industrial College (now Tōkyō Institute of Technology). He joined fellow potter KAWAI KANJIRŌ as an employee at the Kyōto Ceramic Testing Institute. In 1920 he accompanied Bernard H. LEACH to England and helped establish The Leach Pottery in St. Ives, Cornwall. He returned to Japan in 1924 and settled in Mashiko, Tochigi Prefecture, a pottery center since the latter part of the Edo period (1600–1868). He also worked in Okinawa and Aizu Wakamatsu, traveled extensively in Korea and China, and assembled a large collection of folkcraft products, which is now open to the public in Mashiko. He was designated a Living National Treasure in 1955 and awarded the Order of Culture in 1968. Though his technical education was highly advanced, Hamada used only traditional Mashiko glazes made of local clay, stone, and various types of ash, as well as underglaze pigments, overglaze enamels, and salt glaze. He achieved a great range of effects by free combination of this limited glaze palette.

——Bernard Leach, Hamada, Potter (1975). Susan Peterson, Shoji Hamada: A Potter's Way and Work (1974).

Hamada Yahyōe (fl 1620s)

The captain of a vermilion seal ship (see VERMILION SEAL SHIP TRADE) sent to Taiwan in 1626 by the Nagasaki merchant SUETSUGU

HEIZŌ. Frustrated in his trading efforts by the Dutch colonists on that island, Yahyōe returned to Japan but sailed back to Taiwan in 1628 with a band of armed men to seek restitution. When the Dutch tried to detain him, Yahyōe held their chief factor, Pieter Nuijts, at swordpoint in his own chamber until he obtained free passage home, hostages, and reparations. As a result of this incident, the Tokugawa shogunate (1603–1867) undertook reprisals against the Dutch in Japan; the Dutch were forced to surrender Nuijts to the Japanese; and friendly relations were not fully restored until 1636, when Shōgun TOKUGAWA IEMITSU accepted the apologies of a Dutch mission to Edo (now Tōkyō).   *George* ELISON

Hama Detached Palace Garden

(Hamarikyū Kōen). Municipal park in Chūō Ward, Tōkyō. The site of a former villa of the Matsudaira family of Kōshū Province (now Yamanashi Prefecture) the garden later came into the possession of the Tokugawa shogunate (1603–1867). It was donated to the city of Tōkyō and opened to the public after World War II. Area: 25 hectares (62 acres).

Hamaguchi Osachi (1870–1931)

Also known as Hamaguchi Yūkō. Politician, prime minister (1929–31). Born in Kōchi Prefecture. Hamaguchi entered the Ministry of Finance after graduation from Tōkyō University. Elected to the House of Representatives in 1915, he joined the KENSEIKAI party. He served as finance minister in the first and second KATŌ TAKAAKI cabinets (1924, 1925) and as home minister in the WAKATSUKI REIJIRŌ cabinet of 1926. In 1927, with the merger of two political parties, the Kenseikai and SEIYŪ HONTŌ, into the RIKKEN MINSEITŌ, he became its president. When the TANAKA GIICHI cabinet collapsed as a result of the 1928 assassination of ZHANG ZUOLIN (Chang Tsolin), he became prime minister and formed a Minseitō cabinet in 1929. In his efforts to strengthen the national economy, he adopted a policy of austerity while lifting the gold embargo to stimulate exports. In foreign policy, he worked to improve relations with the United States and Great Britain. In 1930, despite opposition from the Naval General Staff Office, he pushed through ratification of the treaty resulting from the LONDON NAVAL CONFERENCES. This treaty assigned Japan to a naval position inferior to that of the United States and Britain. As a result, Hamaguchi was accused by the military, the Privy Council, and the political party RIKKEN SEIYŪKAI of having encroached on the emperor's prerogative of supreme command (see TŌSUIKEN). He died in August 1931 from gunshot wounds inflicted by a right-wing youth at Tōkyō Station the previous November.

Hamaguchi Yūkō → Hamaguchi Osachi

Hamaguri Gomon Incident

A military encounter in August 1864 in which forces from the Chōshū domain (now Yamaguchi Prefecture) were prevented from reentering Kyōto; also known as the Kimmon or Palace Gate Incident. In the COUP D'ETAT OF 30 SEPTEMBER 1863, antiforeign, antishogunate Chōshū *samurai* had been expelled from Kyōto by forces from the domains of Satsuma (now Kagoshima Prefecture) and Aizu (now part of Fukushima Prefecture). In 1864 MAKI IZUMI and other radicals proposed a counterattack. After the IKEDAYA INCIDENT on 8 July 1864 (Genji 1.6.5), in which many Chōshū activists were killed by shogunal agents, Maki's plan received official Chōshū approval. Chōshū squads advanced on Kyōto to press for permission to enter the city and to seek pardon for pro-Chōshū imperial nobles who had been forced to flee during the 30 September coup (see SHICHIKYŌ OCHI). Shogunal leaders, with the support of Satsuma and Aizu, persuaded the court to deny these requests. When Maki Izumi and KUSAKA GENZUI, another Chōshū extremist, attempted to force their way into the city on 20 August (Genji 7.19), they were turned back by Satsuma, Aizu, and Kuwana domain (now part of Mie Prefecture) troops. Kusaka was wounded in the hostilities and Maki captured; both later committed suicide. (The battle ignited a fire which destroyed nearly 30,000 buildings in Kyōto.) As a result of the incident, Chōshū was immediately declared an "enemy of the court," and the shogunate was ordered by the court to dispatch a punitive force, the first of the CHŌSHŪ EXPEDITIONS.

Hamamatsu

Grand pianos being manufactured at Nippon Gakki's Hamamatsu plant, one of the largest piano factories in the world.

Hamakita

City in western Shizuoka Prefecture, central Honshū. Hamakita is the site of numerous automobile and textile industries. Agricultural products include mandarin oranges, saplings, gourds, stud pigs, and chickens. Many of the residents commute to the city of HAMAMATSU. Tourists are drawn to the Prefectural Forest Park and to the nearby town of Arai, where the original structure of a toll barrier (SEKISHO) may be seen. Pop: 72,472.

Hamamatsu

City in western Shizuoka Prefecture, central Honshū. Situated on the western bank of the river Tenryūgawa. Hamamatsu developed as a castle town and POST-STATION TOWN on the Tōkaidō, the major highway in premodern times. Today it is best known for its motorcycles and its musical instruments (both NIPPON GAKKI CO, LTD, better known by its trade name Yamaha, and KAWAI MUSICAL INSTRUMENT MFG CO, LTD, are located here). There is also a cotton textile industry. Melons, tea, and mandarin oranges are grown on the plateau MIKATAHARA; eels and edible seaweed *(nori)* are raised in Lake HAMANA. Tourist attractions include the ruins of Hamamatsu Castle, the site of the Battle of Mikatahara (1572), in which TOKUGAWA IEYASU was defeated by TAKEDA SHINGEN, the IBA SITE (an archaeological site), the temple KANZANJI, and the Nakatajima sand dunes. On 3–5 May a kite-flying competition is held. Pop: 490,827.

Hamamatsu Chūnagon monogatari

(The Tale of the Hamamatsu Middle Counselor). An 11th-century tale often ascribed to SUGAWARA NO TAKASUE NO MUSUME, the author of the SARASHINA NIKKI. Evidence from the MUMYŌ-ZŌSHI, an early 13th-century work of criticism, suggests that *Hamamatsu Chūnagon monogatari* was highly regarded well into the Kamakura period (1185–1333). Thereafter, the work seems to have been largely ignored, and by the middle of the 16th century both the first and last chapters had disappeared. The rediscovery of two copies of the last chapter in the 1930s (the first chapter remains missing) has once again brought the work to the attention of scholars and critics.

  The story concerns the romantic entanglements of the "Hamamatsu Counselor," a Japanese nobleman, in China and Japan. While in China for a visit to a young Chinese prince (actually the reincarnated soul of his father) the counselor has a fateful affair with the prince's mother, a half-Japanese consort of the Chinese emperor. Upon his return to Japan the counselor attempts to serve as guardian for the consort's half sister, a timid young maiden living in the secluded hills of Yoshino. The girl, however, is abducted by a philandering prince, and the story ends with the counselor's realization that the child born of this incident is to be none other than the reincarnated soul of the Chinese consort. In describing the above events and a secondary plot involving the counselor's strained relationship with a former lover, the author portrays in detail the psychological suffering incurred in ill-fated love affairs—a major theme in literature of the latter part of the Heian period (794–1185). The major figures in this tale resemble characters found in the TALE OF

GENJI, though the extensive use of dreams, karma, and transmigration of souls to control plot and characterization indicates a more intense concern with fantasy and religion than is found in earlier *monogatari* literature.

——Endō Yoshimoto and Matsuo Satoshi, ed, *Takamura monogatari, Heichū monogatari, Hamamatsu Chūnagon monogatari,* in *Nihon koten bungaku taikei,* vol 77 (Iwanami Shoten, 1964).

Thomas ROHLICH

Hamana, Lake

(Hamanako). In southwestern Shizuoka Prefecture, central Honshū. A popular tourist spot also known for its eels. The coastline is irregular because the lake is a flooded valley. In 1498 an earthquake broke the sandbars separating the lake from the sea, resulting in seawater entering the lake. Oyster, *nori* (a type of seaweed), and prawn culture flourish. The southern bank forms an industrial district, while mandarin oranges and flowers are cultivated on the lake's other banks. Tourist attractions are the island Bentenjima and the hot spring of Kanzanji. Area: 68.9 sq km (26.6 sq mi); circumference: 103 km (64 mi); depth: 16.1 m (52.8 ft).

Hamao Arata (1849–1925)

Educational administrator and president of Tōkyō University. Hamao was born in Edo (now Tōkyō), the son of a *samurai* retainer of the Toyooka domain (now part of Hyōgo Prefecture). His early education included English and French studies. He got his start in educational administration in 1872 when he was employed briefly at the Daigaku Nankō (a forerunner of Tōkyō University). The following year he went to study in the United States. After his return to Japan, Hamao served as acting and assistant head of Tōkyō Kaisei Gakkō (successor to Daigaku Nankō) and played a leading role in the consolidation of the newly established Tōkyō University in 1877. In 1880 he joined the Ministry of Education, where he worked for administrative reorganization and systemization of higher education. He became minister of education in 1897. Hamao twice served as president of Tōkyō University, from 1893 to 1897 and again from 1905 to 1912, and made important contributions to its growth. During his administration he instituted the lecture system and was instrumental in establishing separate facilities for individual fields of study. In his later years he held important posts as councillor to and president of the Privy Council.

TERASAKI Masao

hamaya and hamayumi

Good-luck charms sold at Shintō shrines in early January when Japanese make their first shrine visit of the year *(hatsumōde)*. *Hama* is now written with characters meaning "to repel evil spirits," although it originally meant "target"; *yumi* and *ya* mean "bow" and "arrow" respectively. It is still fairly common for a mother's family to send these two items to her male child on the occasion of his first NEW YEAR or CHILDREN'S DAY festival. Today the bows and arrows are merely symbolic, but according to the 1830 work KIYŪ SHŌRAN, in former times they were meant to be used. Until recently, in certain areas, young boys held archery competitions at New Year's to predict the next fall's harvest.

ŌTŌ Tokihiko

hamayū

Crinum asiaticum var. *japonicum.* Also known as *hamaomoto.* A large evergreen perennial herb of the family Amaryllidaceae, found in sandy coastal areas of Okinawa, Kyūshū, Shikoku, and central and western Honshū. The cylindrical stem, which grows to 50 centimeters (20 in) in height, with a circumference of 5 to 10 centimeters (2–4 in), is actually a false stem made up of multiple layers of fleshy leaf stalks. Large green leaves sprout from the tip of the stem. In summer, flower stalks measuring about 70 centimeters (28 in) in height appear from between the leaves, bearing clusters of fragrant white blossoms. Like many other Japanese plants, the *hamayū* grows only in areas where the mean annual temperature exceeds 15° C (59° F). The northernmost limit of its range, called the *hamayū* line by botanists, is an important frontier in the distribution of Japanese flora. A related species originating in India, the *indo hamayū* (*C. latifolium*), is also grown in Japan; its flowers have a pale red stripe in the middle of the outer petals.

MATSUDA Osamu

hamba seido

(labor-boss system). A system of labor recruitment and management in which a foreman or labor boss, called the *hamba-gashira* or *naya-gashira,* under contract to a company, hired, supervised, and provided food and lodging for workers. The *hamba-gashira*'s responsibilities also included arbitrating quarrels and tending the workers in sickness. Based on the traditional *oyakata-kokata* (parent figure–child figure) personal relationship (see OYABUN-KOBUN), the labor-boss system was characteristic of the Edo period (1600–1868), but survived into Meiji times (1868–1912), particularly in the mining and building industries. The word *hamba* (literally, "a place to eat") generally referred to the lodge where the workers ate and slept while working at a construction or mining site. The lodge was also called *naya* (shed), *kangokubeya* (slave pen), or *takobeya* (bond-laborers' shack), all of which reflected the miserable conditions under which the workers were forced to live. The *hamba-gashira* received from the company the money for the wages of all his workers and, before doling out their pay, he was allowed to deduct the expenses for services provided as well as a commission, thus making the system subject to frequent abuses. The ASHIO COPPER MINE LABOR DISPUTE of 1907, for example, was staged by the miners to protest their exploitation by *hamba-gashira.* The system was outlawed with the passage of the Labor Standards Law of 1947 (see LABOR LAWS), but traces of it still remain today in some of Japan's mining industries.

hambatsu

(domain clique). A term referring to the close-knit group of men—often referred to as the Meiji oligarchs—who dominated the Japanese government from the beginning of the Meiji period (1868–1912) until the middle of the Taishō period (1912–26). These men came from the domains (HAN) that had played a leading role in the MEIJI RESTORATION of 1868: Satsuma, Chōshū, Tosa, and Hizen (now Kagoshima, Yamaguchi, Kōchi, and Saga prefectures, respectively). Power became increasingly concentrated in the hands of the so-called Satchō (Satsuma and Chōshū) *hambatsu* with the departure of Tosa and Hizen men following the 1873 debate over sending a military expedition to Korea (SEIKANRON) and the expulsion from the government of the Hizen native ŌKUMA SHIGENOBU and his followers in the POLITICAL CRISIS OF 1881. With the exception of Ōkuma and SAIONJI KIMMOCHI, a court noble, every prime minister from 1885 to 1918 was from Satsuma or Chōshū. Members of the "Satchō *hambatsu*" not only monopolized important government posts but also controlled the army and navy (see GUMBATSU) and extended their influence into the bureaucracy through the appointment and promotion of protégés. After the fourth ITŌ HIROBUMI cabinet (1900–1901), the original *hambatsu* leaders no longer served as prime ministers but continued to exercise political influence as elder statesmen (GENRŌ). The term *hambatsu* was used loosely and pejoratively by those excluded from the center of political power in the Meiji and early Taishō periods to describe the arbitrary rule of these government leaders and their followers. For this reason English-speaking scholars prefer to translate *hambatsu* as Meiji oligarchs or oligarchy.

The Tokugawa shogunate was overthrown in 1867 by the combined military forces of Satsuma, Chōshū, and Tosa. Moreover, one of the most urgent tasks facing the new Meiji government—the abolition of the feudal domains and the establishment of a centralized PREFECTURAL SYSTEM—was accomplished in 1871 largely through the coercive power of those domains. For these reasons men from Satsuma, Chōshū, and Tosa, such as ŌKUBO TOSHIMICHI, SAIGŌ TAKAMORI, and KIDO TAKAYOSHI, had an overwhelming influence within the government. To these were added Ōkuma Shigenobu and ETŌ SHIMPEI from Hizen, which had played a supporting role in the Restoration. Initially the monopoly of political power by the coalition of these four domains (the so-called Sat-Chō-Do-Hi clique) was not brought into question, mainly because the coalition managed to control intragroup rivalry by outwardly acting in unison.

But in 1873 the clique split over the issue of whether Japan should send a punitive expedition to Korea. Those like Saigō and ITAGAKI TAISUKE who insisted on sending an expedition resigned from the government and became outspoken in their criticism of it. Because the nascent opposition movement they headed was still closely identified with the leading domains, however, the term they generally used to criticize the government at this time was not *hambatsu,* but *yūshi sensei* or "tyranny by officials." In their famous 1874 memorial calling for a representative assembly, Itagaki and his

Tosa compatriots charged that "political power resided neither in the throne nor in the people but solely in government officials *(yūshi)."*

In 1875 Itagaki and his followers decided to launch a nationwide movement for the establishment of a national assembly. Two years later Saigō Takamori and his army of former *samurai* were defeated in the SATSUMA REBELLION. At this point, having lost much of its association with the four leading domains, the opposition began to use the term *hambatsu* to criticize the government. At a public meeting held in January 1881 by members of the FREEDOM AND PEOPLE'S RIGHTS MOVEMENT, Suehiro Tetchō (1849–96) of the newspaper *Chōya shimbun* asserted that government posts, from the highest to the lowest, were filled with men from either Satsuma, Chōshū, or Hizen. Suehiro's opening statement to the audience included the words "Perhaps you are aware of the existence of so-called *hambatsu* in Japan," which would seem to indicate that the term had only recently come into circulation.

With the expulsion of Ōkuma and his followers in 1881, power came to rest exclusively in the hands of men from Satsuma and Chōshū, and *hambatsu* thus came to mean government by the Satsuma and Chōshū cliques. Upon resigning from the regime with Ōkuma, KŌNO TOGAMA (from Tosa) presented a memorial to the government in which he attacked the "evils of *hambatsu."*

Thereafter, the term *hambatsu* was used as a synonym for the Meiji government, and from about 1890 it was used interchangeably with a new term, *chōzen naikaku* ("TRANSCENDENTAL" CABINETS). No conscious distinction was made between the two terms, although the older term more often referred to the personnel of the government and the newer one to its supraparty nature. An article on the *hambatsu* leadership in the 6 May 1888 issue of the newspaper *Tōkyō nichinichi shimbun* traced the provenance of those who had held either ministerial or vice-ministerial posts in the government during the previous 21 years. Eighteen were found to be from Satsuma, 19 from Chōshū, 9 from Tosa, and 7 from Hizen. Even if these figures are not altogether reliable, the article does make clear that the term *hambatsu* referred more to the composition of government personnel than to the nature of government policy. Again, when the JIYŪTŌ and SHIMPOTŌ merged to form the KENSEITŌ political party in June 1898 and subsequently formed Japan's first party cabinet under Ōkuma, party members, in demanding the appointment of Kenseitō men to positions in the bureaucracy, called for the elimination of "*hambatsu* elements" rather than "transcendental bureaucrats" *(chōzen shugi teki kanryō).*

By the time of the TAISHŌ POLITICAL CRISIS of 1912–13 the slogan used by the antigovernment movement was not "Down with *hambatsu*" but "Down with *batsuzoku* (cliquists)." Although in his diary the opposition leader HARA TAKASHI used the term *hambatsu* more frequently than *batsuzoku*, more often than not he referred specifically to the "Yamagata faction," i.e., the faction led by YAMAGATA ARITOMO (from Chōshū). This decline in use of the term *hambatsu* reflected several changes in the political scene. First, for a period of 16 years following the resignation of the second MATSUKATA MASAYOSHI (from Satsuma) cabinet in 1897, not one Satsuma man had been chosen to head the government; six out of the nine cabinets since then had been headed by Chōshū men. Second, when Itō Hirobumi (from Chōshū) decided to form his own political party, the RIKKEN SEIYŪKAI, in 1900, Chōshū men themselves were divided into bureaucrats who belonged to the Yamagata faction and those who joined the new party. Third, from the time of the first KATSURA TARŌ (from Chōshū) cabinet in 1901, restoration leaders were no longer named prime ministers, and rather than the term *hambatsu*, with its close identification with the achievements of the restoration, the term *batsuzoku*, with its connotation of bureaucratic factionalism, more accurately described the political reality. Thus, in a party resolution of July 1903, the antigovernment KENSEI HONTŌ called for the "expunging of *batsuzoku* and the upholding of constitutional government."

In the Taishō period, as bureaucrats split into cliques representing the army, navy, and House of Peers, the term *batsuzoku* came to be replaced by such phrases as *gumbatsu naikaku* (military faction cabinet) and *tokken naikaku* (special privilege cabinet). See also POLITICAL PARTIES.

■ ——George Akita, *Foundations of Constitutional Government in Modern Japan, 1868–1900* (1967). Banno Junji, *Meiji kempō taisei no kakuritsu* (1971). Itō Takashi and Fukuchi Atsushi, *Hambatsu to mintō*, in Iwanami kōza: *Nihon rekishi*, vol 15 (1976). Tetsuo Najita, *Hara Kei in the Politics of Compromise, 1905–1915* (1967).

BANNO Junji

han

(domain). The basic unit of provincial government under the BAKUHAN SYSTEM during the Edo period (1600–1868). Although often translated as "domain" or "*daimyō* domain," the term *han* refers not only to the particular area of land entrusted to a DAIMYŌ by the TOKUGAWA SHOGUNATE but also to its military, administrative, and fiscal superstructure. Apparently first used in China during the Zhou (Chou) dynasty (ca 1027 BC–256 BC) to denote the fiefs of feudal magnates, it came into popular use in Japan only during the 18th century and into official use at the beginning of the Meiji period (1868–1912).

Early in the 17th century TOKUGAWA IEYASU acknowledged the existence of 185 *ryōbun* (as domains were then called), having received pledges of allegiance from that number of territorial magnates. By the end of the century the number of domains had grown to 243 and stabilized during the 18th century at around 260. This numerical stability is somewhat misleading, for although most domains enjoyed continuity in location and proprietorship, it is possible to distinguish more than 540 individual domains, most of which existed only briefly, during the years of Tokugawa rule.

All domains had certain features in common. Each was in the charge of a daimyō, and so, by definition, had an assessed annual productivity of at least 10,000 *koku* of rice (see KOKUDAKA). Each, too, had been assigned directly by the Tokugawa shōgun, unlike fiefs of the same or greater productivity that were assigned by the larger daimyō to their senior vassals. Each daimyō was expected to meet the expenses of local administration and of service to the head of the Tokugawa house. The nature of the service differed for each daimyō and from period to period, but it always included the obligation of SANKIN KŌTAI, or alternate-year attendance at the shogunal capital and the maintenance of an army of *samurai* ready to respond when the shōgun required them. These obligations represented the major expense of each domain.

Such similarities apart, the domains were remarkable for their many dissimilarities. There were, for example, tremendous differences in size. Some of the larger domains encompassed whole provinces, others a few acres. Their official productivity (OMOTEDAKA) ranged from the minimum 10,000 *koku* to the Kanazawa domain's enormous figure of more than a million. Most were below 50,000 *koku*, and fewer than one-tenth were above 200,000. Variations in real productivity *(uchidaka)* were even wider. The domains differed from one another also in geographical configuration, for while some were self-contained units, others derived a substantial portion of their income from widely scattered pockets of land. Some domains were situated in areas offering little opportunity for commercial exploitation, but more than 20 percent developed official monopolies (HAN'EI SEMBAI) of local products like wax, paper, or sugar. Their political structures were as varied as their economies; some daimyō governed in person, while others were supplanted by relatives, senior vassals, or ambitious junior vassals. In 83 percent of the domains, the samurai had been gathered into CASTLE TOWNS and put on salaries; in large parts of the country, however, they continued to live and work in the villages.

In the context of national political life, too, there were enormous variations. Some domains were too small, or too overshadowed by powerful neighbors, or too close to the seat of shogunal government in Edo (now Tōkyō) to attain significant independence. Others, larger and usually far from Edo, could discreetly but firmly resist attempts to integrate them completely into the *bakuhan* system. For those who lived in the latter, the domain, not the shogunate, marked the boundaries of political awareness; their interests, too, were most immediately centered there, rather than upon the nation as a whole. While the domains and loyalties based upon them remained paramount, Japan could not achieve true national unification. That was to require a political and social revolution—the MEIJI RESTORATION—in which both shogunate and domains were destroyed; and even then the domains, more durable then the shogunate, did not give up without a struggle.

■ ——John W. Hall, *Government and Local Power in Japan* (1966). Kanai Madoka, *Hansei* (1962).

Harold BOLITHO

han, abolition of → prefectural system, establishment of

Hanabusa Itchō (1652–1724)

Painter. Real name Taga Shinkō. Born in Kyōto, the son of a physician. At the age of 15 he moved to Edo (now Tōkyō) with his

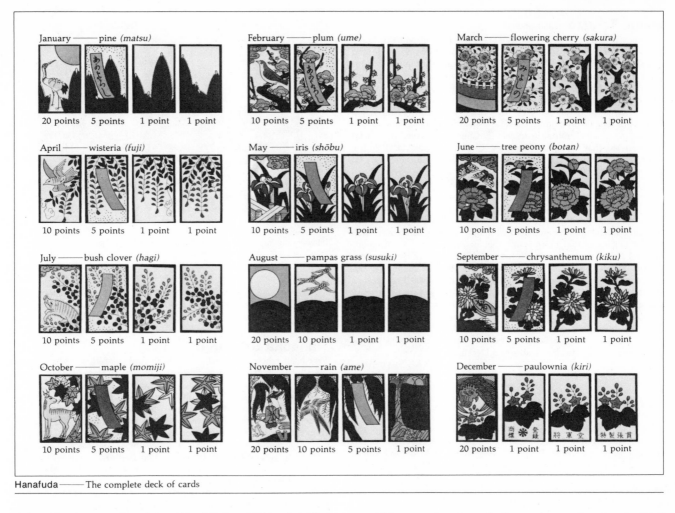

Hanafuda——The complete deck of cards

father. He was a member of the cultural circles of Edo and studied HAIKU with Matsuo BASHŌ, calligraphy with Genryū Bunzan, and, purportedly, painting with Kanō Yasunobu, eventually establishing himself as a painter. In 1698 for reasons unknown he was exiled by the shogunate government to Miyakejima, an island south of Edo, where he remained until his pardon in 1709. He returned to Edo, changing his name to Hanabusa Itchō. Many of his paintings, basically of the KANŌ SCHOOL style, are sophisticated depictions of city life.

Hanada Kiyoteru (1909–1974)

Literary critic, novelist, playwright. Born in Fukuoka Prefecture, he studied at Kyōto University. During World War II, he published many essays criticizing militarists in the magazine *Bunka soshiki,* which he founded in 1939. After the war he became an important contributor to KINDAI BUNGAKU, a progressive literary magazine founded in 1946. It was at this time that he gained recognition as a critic for his book *Fukkōki no seishin* (1946), a collection of essays he wrote during the war on such writers as Dante and Cervantes. These essays display the unbending spirit of his opposition to fascism. He was a Marxist and advocated the dialectical fusion of art and politics. Hanada played a leading role in the postwar avant-garde movement for an integrated audiovisual art form. Most of his writings are in *Hanada Kiyoteru chosakushū* (1963–66).

hanafuda

Also known as *hanakaruta* (literally, "flower cards"). A gambling game played with a 48-card deck divided into twelve 4-card suits which are represented by trees, shrubs, or flowers, each corresponding to a particular month of the year (i.e., pine for January, wisteria for April, iris for May, etc). Each of the 12 suits also has one card depicting a bird, animal, or stylized figure appropriate to the suit sign and 2 suits have two such cards. Three suits have one "poem card" showing a red strip of Japanese poem-writing paper (*tanzaku*)

on which a poem is written alluding to the month and to the floral symbol of the suit, while 4 other suits have one card with a red *tanzaku* on which no poem is written. In addition, 3 suits have one card with a blue *tanzaku.*

Hanafuda, which became popular as a gambling game in the early 19th century, is the evolutionary product of Western-style playing cards introduced by the Dutch during the Tenshō era (1573–91) and a court pastime dating from the Heian period (794–1185) called *kachō-awase* (literally, "matching birds and flowers"). Although details of the rules of play and scoring vary widely on a regional basis, the fundamentals are the same everywhere.

Actual play is simple and luck is more important than skill. The object of the game is to collect as many cards as possible by matching suits. All cards have an assigned value of 20, 10, 5, or 1 points, and if scoring involved merely adding up face values, *hanafuda* would be little more than a child's game. However, much of the excitement and fun lies in the many exotic extra-score combinations and the special names and symbolism of the cards themselves because of their poetic connections with the changing seasonal phenomena. August's suit sign, for example, is *susuki* (pampas grass). The highest card—worth 20 points—pictures a full moon over a field of *susuki,* the traditional symbol of the Festival of the August Moon. The drawing of the field has been stylized to a round, smooth shape which gives the suit its nickname, *bōzu,* or "priest," because it resembles a Buddhist priest's shaven head. If the cards collected during a game include the full-moon *bōzu,* the crane and pine (January), a red-banded screen and cherry blossoms (March), and a demon mask and paulownia leaves (December) play immediately halts and the holder receives 80 points each from the totals of the other players. Minus scores for some players are thus inevitable. The combination (*shikō;* four brilliances) described above is one of several winning combinations (*ageyaku),* in the absence of which scores are determined by card value. *Hanafuda* is still played and remains a gambling game more at home in the backrooms of the underworld than the parlors of polite society. See also GAMBLING; PLAYING CARDS.   John E. THAYER III

Hanai Takuzō (1868–1931)

Attorney and legal scholar. Born 11 August 1868 in Mihara, Hiroshima Prefecture, the fourth son of Tachihara Shiroemon; adopted as heir to the Hanai family in 1888. He graduated at the head of his law class in what is now Chūō University; he then placed first among 1,668 candidates in the 1890 bar examinations and quickly became one of Japan's best-known attorneys. He was elected president of the Tōkyō Bar Association, received a doctorate in law (1909), wrote numerous books on criminal law and justice, taught criminal law and the Code of Criminal Procedure at Chūō, and served on official committees that drafted Criminal Code revisions (1907), the courts–martial law (1921), and the seldom-used law authorizing trial by jury (1923). But he was most famous as a defense attorney in many of Japan's most sensational criminal trials from 1892 until his retirement in 1926. Among these were the Viscount Sōma poisoning and libel case (1893), the HOSHI TŌRU assassination (1901), the KŌTOKU SHŪSUI high treason trial (1910), the RICE RIOTS trials (1918), and several corruption cases involving high-ranking politicians, such as the sugar scandal (1909) and the Siemens naval procurement scandal (1914; see SIEMENS INCIDENT). Noted for subtle legal reasoning and skill as an orator, Hanai was elected seven times to the House of Representatives (serving 1898–1903 and 1914–1920, and as deputy speaker of the House in 1915) and was a leader in unsuccessful efforts to enact universal manhood suffrage (see UNIVERSAL MANHOOD SUFFRAGE MOVEMENT) and abolish discrimination against private university graduates in the judicial and bar examinations. He was an imperially appointed member of the House of Peers from 1922 until his death on 3 December 1931.

Robert M. SPAULDING

Hanamaki

City in central Iwate Prefecture, northern Honshū. Situated on the river Kitakamigawa, Hanamaki developed as a castle town of the Nambu domain and as a POST-STATION TOWN on the Ōshū Kaidō, a major highway of the Edo period (1600–1868). The town produces electrical appliances, farm implements, rice, and dairy products. A complex of hot springs in the suburbs and SHISHI ODORI (deer dance) performances attract tourists. Hanamaki is also known as the birthplace of the poet MIYAZAWA KENJI. Pop: 68,875.

Hana Matsuri

(Flower Festival). The name of several different annual festivals. One is the Buddhist celebration of the birth of Śākyamuni, held on 8 April, in which flowers are used; also called Kambutsue (see BUDDHIST RITES). Another is the folk festival held in the Kita Shitara district of Aichi Prefecture at the end of the year. The main event centers around the boiling of water to offer to the deities, while the townspeople perform various dances (see KAGURA). Various other festivals held during April at Shintō shrines are also referred to as Hana Matsuri.

INOKUCHI Shōji

hanami

(literally, "flower viewing"; generally, cherry-blossom viewing). Excursions and picnics for enjoying flowers, particularly cherry blossoms; one of the most popular events of the spring. In some places flower-viewing parties are held on traditionally fixed dates according to the old lunar calendar. The custom probably derives from the ancient agricultural practice of picnicking in the fields and hills during the religious festivals that marked the beginning of spring farm activity. The subject of flower viewing has long held an important place in literature, dance, and the fine arts. In the Heian period (794–1185), flower-viewing parties were popular among the aristocracy, and in the Azuchi-Momoyama period (1568–1600) they reached extravagant proportions in the public cherry-blossom-viewing parties of the hegemon TOYOTOMI HIDEYOSHI at the temple Daigoji. By the Edo period (1600–1868), the custom had spread to the common people: sitting under the blossoming trees, they ate, drank sake, sang, and danced, not only in the daytime but occasionally well into the evening. Today picnics beneath the blossoms with family, friends, and fellow workers are still popular. The importance of this custom is underscored by the fact that, in early April, radio and television stations broadcast hourly reports on the blossoming of local cherry trees. Popular flower viewing spots include

Hanami

Flower viewing parties in Ueno Park, Tōkyō.

YOSHINOYAMA in Nara Prefecture, ARASHIYAMA in Kyōto, and Ueno, the river SUMIDAGAWA, KOGANEI, and Asukayama in Tōkyō.

INOKUCHI Shōji

Hanaoka Seishū (1760–1835)

Physician who performed the first surgical operation under general anesthesia. Personal name Shin; also known as Hanaoka Zuiken. A native of Kii Province (now Wakayama Prefecture), he studied medicine of the classicist school (koihō, see MEDICINE: traditional medicine) with Yoshimasu Nangai, the son of YOSHIMASU TŌDŌ, in Kyōto. He also studied Western surgery under Yamato Kenryū. He then returned to his native area to practice.

After some 20 years of experimenting, Hanaoka succeeded in preparing an anesthetic substance called mafutsusan. It was a mixture of six crude drugs, including datura and aconite, from the traditional Chinese pharmacopoeia. He used it successfully in a surgical operation for breast cancer in 1805, about 40 years before the first use of ether at Massachusetts General Hospital, Boston. He subsequently used it for various kinds of operation, including those for malignant tumors, gangrene, tuberculous lymphadenitis of the neck, hemorrhoids, and anal prolapse. Hanaoka's motto was Katsubutsu kyūri, naigai gōitsu (Elucidate the principles of life, unite internal medicine with surgery). Students from all over the country came to study under him, and his surgical techniques came to be known as the Hanaoka method. He published many books, but only manuscript copies survive.

YAMADA Terutane

Hanasaka jijii

(The Old Man Who Made the Trees Bloom). Folktale. An honest old man finds gold with the help of his wondrous dog. A greedy old man who lives next door imitates him without success and kills the dog in anger. The good man buries the dog and plants on its grave a tree from which he later makes a mortar. When he pounds rice in the mortar, the rice is immediately transformed into gold pieces, but when the greedy man borrows the mortar, he pounds in vain and burns it. The honest man scatters the ashes on lifeless trees, which burst into bloom. It is believed that the story was originally known in many areas as The Old Ash Spreader or The Old Goose Hunter (in which versions the old man spreads ashes and catches geese), and that it was combined with stories of wondrous dogs (see MOMOTARŌ) to reach its present form. For another version of this tale, see FOLKTALES.

SUCHI Tokuhei

Hanasanjin (1790–1858)

Popular writer of the late Edo period. Real name Hosokawa Namijirō; other pen name Tōri Sanjin. Originally a police officer, he became a disciple of SANTŌ KYŌDEN and began producing works in many of the genres of Edo popular literature (see GESAKU). Hanasanjin is often mentioned along with TAMENAGA SHUNSUI as an early writer of the NINJŌBON (a genre of popular fiction); however, after an initial success he was unable to adapt himself to the new themes of the genre and was eclipsed in popularity by Shunsui. He ended his days in poverty as a seller of books on magic tricks. Principal works include *Satokagami* (1822, Mirror of Flowertown), a SHAREBON, and *Kuruwa zōdan* (1825, Tales of the Pleasure Districts), a *ninjōbon*.

hanashōbu → irises

Hanawa Hokiichi (1746–1821)

A KOKUGAKU (National Learning) scholar and textual editor of the latter part of the Edo period (1600–1868). Born in Musashi Province (now Saitama Prefecture) into a farming family. Although blind from the age of 5, at 13 he went to Edo (now Tōkyō) to learn acupuncture. He was fond of studying, however, and he decided to study the Japanese classics under KAMO NO MABUCHI and other Kokugaku scholars. Relying on his extraordinary memory, he was able to master the Chinese and Japanese classics. In 1793, with help from the shogunate he established the Wagaku Kōdansho, a center for the study of Japanese classics. He devoted his life to the editing and publication of classical texts, compiling with the assistance of YASHIRO HIROKATA the monumental 530-volume GUNSHO RUIJŪ (1779–1819).

Hanayagi Shōtarō (1894–1965)

Stage and film actor. ONNAGATA (female impersonator). Real name Aoyama Shōtarō. Born in Tōkyō, he studied acting under KITAMURA ROKURŌ and first appeared on stage in *Yukiko fujin* at the Hongō Theater. Hoping to revitalize the SHIMPA school of drama which was in decline, he participated in the founding of the Shingekiza (New Drama Theater) in 1921 and the theatrical troupe Shōchiku Gekidan in 1927. He produced "new *shimpa*" works such as *Futasujimichi* (1931), and dramatizations of works such as MORI ŌGAI's *Gan*.

In 1939 he starred in MIZOGUCHI KENJI's *Zangiku monogatari* (The Story of the Last Chrysanthemum). Its good reception launched him on a successful movie career. He appeared in NARUSE MIKIO's *Uta andon* (1943, The Song Lantern) and Mizoguchi's *Meitō bijomaru* (1945, The Famous Sword Bijomaru).

He was awarded numerous prizes, such as the Japan Art Academy Prize (1954), and the Asahi Bunka Prize (1962). He was designated one of the Living National Treasures (*ningen kokuhō*, 1960) and a Person of Cultural Merits (1964). He also wrote several books, among them *Kimono* (1941). ·*ITASAKA Tsuyoshi*

Hanazono Tennō shinki

Diary of the emperor Hanazono (1297–1348), who reigned from 1308 to 1318 in the confusing period when succession to the throne alternated between the rival Daikakuji and Jimyōin branches of the imperial house. Hanazono was himself of the Jimyōin line but remained aloof from the schemes and struggles. He was conversant with both Chinese and Japanese scholarship, a considerable poet, and a firm believer in Zen Buddhism. His diary covers the years 1310–32 and is an important source for the study of relations between the court and the shogunate at the end of the Kamakura period (1185–1333). *G. Cameron HURST III*

Handa

City in Aichi Prefecture, central Honshū, on the eastern coast of the Chita Peninsula. In the Edo period (1600–1868) it was a prosperous port of call for cargo ships (KAISEN) plying between Ōsaka and Edo (Tōkyō). Today it is the largest producer of vinegar in Japan. Other industries include *sake* and soy sauce brewing, textiles (the area has long been known for its Chita *sarashi*, a cotton cloth), steel, rolling stock, and machinery. Horticulture in the hills relies on water from the AICHI CANAL. The temple Jōrakuji has associations with TOKUGAWA IEYASU, the founder of the Tokugawa shogunate. Pop: 89,328.

handen shūju system

(land allotment system). A system for state distribution of land among the peasant population; instituted in late-7th-century Japan and most widely applied during the 8th century. Although it was modeled on contemporary Chinese practice, the Japanese system differed in the frequency with which land grants were made, in the qualifications for receiving land, and in the kind and amount of land

allotted. In Japan, every six years local officials granted small parcels of paddy land to all commoners and menials aged six years and older. The subsistence grant enabled the local and central governments to draw frequently on peasant labor services, the most important economic resource in a sparsely populated land with a rural economy. The *handen shūju* system gradually deteriorated in the late 8th and 9th centuries as a result of growing population pressure on limited land resources and ecclesiastical and aristocratic encroachment on government lands.

In the late 5th century AD, which was an age of great social upheaval, the Northern Wei dynasty (386–535) of China began to distribute state land to peasants on a systematic basis. The principal reason for this new system, called the *jun tian (chün t'ien)* or "equal field" system, was the need to collect taxes and enlist labor from the floating peasant population of northern China. A parcel of land was given to a peasant couple to farm during their working lives. As long as they worked the land, they were under obligation to pay taxes in the form of cloth and grain. When they grew too old to farm, the land reverted to the state, which then granted it to another couple. Careful census and land records were kept by the central and provincial governments to operate this system successfully.

The Tang (T'ang) dynasty (618–907), which ruled a unified China, brought the institution of *jun tian* to its highest development. The laws provided that every male between the ages of 18 and 60 should receive 5.32 hectares (13.3 acres) of fields and mulberry groves. From the ages of 21 to 59 the recipient was required to pay taxes on his land in the form of cloth and grain. Census and tax documents contained all relevant information, enabling local officials and household heads to redistribute land annually to those who were eligible. The sale and rental of land was severely restricted. It is uncertain how widely the system was applied in China, and in any case, it collapsed in the 8th century.

The JINSHIN DISTURBANCE of 672 brought new rulers to power in Japan. The new government, to strengthen its control over the population, took the Chinese land distribution and tax collection system as their model. Imperial court annals from the last quarter of the 7th century reveal that the central government was establishing a legal basis for the new system, expanding arable land area by building up a checkerboard pattern of paddy cultivation known as the JŌRI SYSTEM, and registering more and more of the population as it came under its political jurisdiction. The first certifiable record of a registration of the population was the Kōin Nenjaku of 690. The first distribution of state lands took place in 692. The *handen shūju* system remained in effect throughout Japan, except in the southern third of Kyūshū and the northern third of Honshū, until 800.

The regulations governing the operation of state land distribution can be found in two official documents from the 8th century, the TAIHŌ CODE of 701 and the YŌRŌ CODE of 718 (effective 757). Land legally defined as "personal-share land" (KUBUNDEN) was central to the allocation process. Provincial officials granted personal-share land to all commoners and menials when they reached the age of six. The basic grant was two *tan* (1 *tan* = 0.1 hectare or 0.25 acre) of paddy land for a free male and two-thirds of that amount for a woman. Members of the lowest classes usually received one-third of this amount of land. Everyone who received a *kubunden* grant was automatically responsible for paying a light tax of 1.5 sheaves of rice per *tan*, or about 3 percent of the total annual yield. Recipients were also obliged to contribute labor and military service (see SO, YŌ, AND CHŌ). Permanent transfer of personal-share land was strictly forbidden by law. In the first year of state land distribution after a recipient's death, the household head returned the vacant parcel of land to state control.

The complex process of allocating land took place every six years. The first step was to prepare the HOUSEHOLD REGISTERS, a process that began in the 11th month of a registration year and ended six months later. Household registers recorded the name, age, sex, and tax status of each individual in every household. After local officials had completed this task they notified the central government at Heijōkyō (now Nara) that they were ready to distribute land. Six months after that, the central government sent emissaries to consult with the provincial officers and household heads on local land allocation. Thus the actual allocation was completed about a year and a half after household registration was begun. If there was any personal-share land available after land grants were awarded, the provincial governor (KOKUSHI) was permitted to rent this land to any grantee who wanted it.

The *handen shūju* system began to break down after the middle of the 8th century for two interrelated reasons. First, an increase in population during the 8th century placed pressure on the small rice-paddy resources of early Japan. Administrative documents from the time reveal clearly that this was a growing problem. One household register from northern Kyūshū shows an abundance of land in 702. A local record from Tōtōmi Province (now part of Shizuoka Prefecture) in central Honshū reveals an even balance of land and population in 740. But in 766 a governor's report from Echizen Province (now part of Fukui Prefecture) on the Sea of Japan suggests that peasants were migrating to other parts of the country because of insufficient land for allotments.

Second, court aristocrats and Buddhist monks began to accumulate large holdings now subject to the government allotment and tax systems. By clearing forests and constructing new rice paddies, these two classes took advantage of the imperial court's inability to remedy the problem of land scarcity. The court recognized its own growing dependence in 743, when it allowed anyone who reclaimed land to pass it along to his heirs (see KONDEN EISEI SHIZAI HŌ). First Buddhist temples, such as Tōdaiji in Heijōkyō, began to accumulate large holdings for themselves. Court nobles soon joined in the rush to clear land. Their landed estates, called SHŌEN, became even more prevalent in the 9th century. The mainstay of the labor force, the peasants, began to work in large numbers for the shōen to escape the onerous forced labor and military duties imposed on those who received land from the central government.

The last nationwide state allocation of land took place in 800. Although the imperial court, now located at Heiankyō (now Kyōto), made various attempts at reviving the handen shūju system through the reign (897–930) of Emperor Daigo, the land grant system worked only infrequently and unevenly. See also RITSURYŌ SYSTEM.

📖——John W. Hall, *Government and Local Power in Japan, 500 to 1700* (1966). Imamiya Shin, *Jōdai no tochi seido* (1957). Iyanaga Teizō, "Ritsuryōseiteki tochi shoyū," in *Iwanami kōza: Nihon rekishi*, vol 3 (Iwanami Shoten, 1962). Miyamoto Tasuku, "Ritsuryōteki tochi seido," in *Taikei nihonshi sōsho*, vol 6 (Yamakawa Shuppansha, 1973). Torao Toshiya, *Handen shūju hō no kenkyū* (1961). D. C. Twitchett, *Financial Administration under the T'ang Dynasty* (2nd ed, 1970). Kozo Yamamura, "The Decline of the Ritsuryō System: Hypotheses on Economic and Institutional Change," *Journal of Japanese Studies* 1.1 (1974).   Wayne FARRIS

han'ei sembai

(domainal monopolies). Commercial operations that were supervised or operated as monopoly enterprises by domainal (HAN) governments during the latter part of the Edo period (1600–1868). The purpose of most of these monopolies was to improve the condition of the domainal fisc, and accordingly they were formed in whatever field of production seemed most advantageous considering the resources and location of a particular domain.

Domainal monopolies began to appear in the 1760s, notably the Higo domain's (now Kumamoto Prefecture) monopoly of silk-thread spinning, the Saga domain's (now Saga Prefecture) monopoly of ceramic production, and the Tottori domain's (now part of Tottori Prefecture) monopoly of iron smelting. In the following decades monopolies were established over local production of such commodities as salt, paper, wax, and medicines. The early monopolies involved little more than the appointment of some domain officials to supervise existing production operations and assure that a portion of the proceeds went into the domainal treasury. During the 19th century, however, domains established offices (KOKUSAN KAISHO) to gain more complete control of operations, from production to marketing, either because private enterprises were proving difficult to control or because more complex technological processes were being introduced. After the 1840s, in particular, as the threat of foreign aggression became more pronounced, several domains set up monopoly defense industries: notably the reverberatory furnaces (HAN-SHARO) of Mito (now part of Ibaraki Prefecture) and Saga, the shipyards of Saga and Chōshū (now Yamaguchi Prefecture), and the military industries of Satsuma (now Kagoshima Prefecture) and the shogunate itself.

The development of domainal monopolies in the late Edo period reflected the general recognition that government was rooted in the economy and the growing realization of the importance of money income to government finance. Thus, scholars such as SATŌ NOBU-HIRO advocated governmental management of industry as crucial to the solution of problems facing the rulers. Awareness of the importance of industrial production to national stability and growth was equally evident in the commercial policies of the new government

that emerged following the Meiji Restoration of 1868 (see SHOKU-SAN KŌGYŌ).

📖——Horie Yasuzō, "Clan Monopoly Policy in the Tokugawa Period," *Kyōto University Economic Review* 17.1 (1942). Horie Yasuzō, *Waga kuni kinsei no sembai seido* (1933).   Conrad TOTMAN

hanetsuki

Traditional girls' game for New Year's played by one or two persons. A wooden paddle called a HAGOITA is used with a shuttlecock (*hane*) made of soapberry seed and feathers. When one person plays, the object of the game is simply to keep the shuttlecock in the air. When two people play, the game resembles badminton without a net. In either case, the score depends on the number of times the shuttlecock falls to the ground. The game has existed since the 15th century and is still played today.   SAITŌ Ryōsuke

han'gŭl

The modern Korean term for Korea's phonetic alphabet, traditionally called ŏnmun. Developed during the Yi-dynasty reign of King Sejong (1418–50) and promulgated in 1446. Last standardized in 1933, it consists of 19 consonants, 10 simple vowels, and 11 compound vowels. Only after 1910 (the year of Korea's annexation by Japan) did Koreans cease using Chinese as the standard written language. North Korea now uses only this native alphabet, while a mixed Chinese-Korean script is used in South Korea. See also KOREAN LANGUAGE.   C. Kenneth QUINONES

Hani Gorō (1901–1983)

Historian and critic. Born in Gumma Prefecture; married to Hani Setsuko, daughter of the educator HANI MOTOKO, and adopted into the Hani family. He studied history at Tōkyō University and philosophy at Heidelberg University, after which he taught at Japan University and at Jiyū Gakuen, the school founded by Hani Motoko. In the 1930s, together with NORO EITARŌ, a fellow Marxist, he was a prominent contributor to the series NIHON SHIHON SHUGI HATTATSU SHI KŌZA (Studies on the History of the Development of Capitalism in Japan). He also published studies on the period immediately preceding the Meiji Restoration (1868) and the Restoration itself. Hani was imprisoned briefly during World War II for his political opinions. In 1947 he was elected to the House of Councillors as an independent and worked for the establishment of the National Diet Library. His works, especially his study of cities, *Toshi no ronri* (1968), had a profound influence on the radical student movement of the 1960s and the 1970s. The film director HANI SUSUMU is his son. See also NIHON SHIHON SHUGI RONSŌ.

Hani Motoko (1873–1957)

Japan's first woman newspaper reporter, publisher of magazines for women and children, and founder of the private school Jiyū Gakuen. Born in Hachinohe, Aomori Prefecture, into a former *samurai* family; original name, Matsuoka Moto. In 1891, she was in the first graduating class of the Tōkyō First Higher Girls' School (Daiichi Kōtō Jogakkō). Baptized a Christian around 1890, she went on to study at Meiji Girls' School (Meiji Jogakkō), where she was influenced by the educator IWAMOTO YOSHIHARU and worked for his magazine JOGAKU ZASSHI. She taught for a while in Aomori but then, after a brief, unhappy marriage, returned to Tōkyō. There she was employed at the home of the renowned woman doctor YOSHIOKA YAYOI. With her encouragement, Motoko secured a position with the newspaper *Hōchi shimbun*. Initially a copy editor, in 1897 she became the first woman advanced to the rank of reporter, and was given assignments covering women, education, and religion. In 1901 she married a colleague, Hani Yoshikazu (1880–1955), who was to become her partner in journalistic and educational ventures. After editing the magazine *Katei no tomo* (Friend of the Home), from its beginning in 1903, Motoko and her husband took it over in 1906 as their own journal, calling it *Katei jogaku kōgi* (Home Study for Women), and two years later renamed it FUJIN NO TOMO (Woman's Friend). Other publications by this husband-and-wife team included the periodicals *Kodomo no tomo* (1914–29, · Children's Friend), *Shin shōjo* (1915–20, New Girls), and *Manabi no tomo* (1920, Learning Companion, 9 issues). Of these, *Fujin no tomo* alone has survived Japan's drastic changes in political structure, social mores, and journalistic vogues. The couple's vision of educating women to be self-reliant members of society was sustained over the years by the Tomo no Kai (Friends' Association), a nationwide association of loyal readers of this magazine. Founded in 1930, the group is still active, with over 30,000 members.

In 1921 Motoko and her husband founded the school Jiyū Gakuen, with a philosophy of liberal education combining both Protestant and Confucian ethics. Starting out with an enrollment of 26 girls about age 13, it later added an elementary division in 1927, a boys' middle school in 1935, a men's higher education division in 1949, and a women's higher education division in 1950. In 1981 it had 1,173 students and 104 teachers.

The school remained largely independent of the increasingly restrictive orders from the Ministry of Education during World War II, pursuing educational goals that emphasized the students' ability to reason, to make their own decisions, and to master basic skills. As part of their curriculum, students have been required to perform all necessary tasks such as cooking and cleaning. They have also built Japan's smallest hydroelectric plant to serve their campus, and they have run child care centers in six prefectures, maintained a farm to provision their kitchens, and published original scientific research.

Until the end of her long life, Motoko, supported by her husband, was the mainstay of Jiyū Gakuen and Fujin no tomo. They had two daughters, the social critic Hani Setsuko (b 1903; wife of the social critic HANI GORŌ and mother of the film director HANI SUSUMU) and the educator Hani Keiko (b 1908), who succeeded her mother as principal of Jiyū Gakuen.

📖———Hani Motoko, *Hani Motoko chosakushū*, 20 vols (Fujin no Tomo Sha, 1974). Akinaga Yoshirō, *Hani Motoko: Jiyū kyōiku no haha* (1969). Hani Keiko, *Jiyū Gakuen no kyōiku* (1961). Chieko Mulhern, "Hani Motoko: Japan's First Newspaperwoman," *The Japan Interpreter* 12.3–4 (1978). Chieko Mulhern, "Memoirs of a Successful Woman," in Aoki and Dardess, ed, *As the Japanese See It: Past and Present (1981)*.   Chieko MULHERN

Hani Susumu (1928–   )

Film director and theorist of the postwar era. Hani began his film career as a maker of documentaries, and his concern for truth in the aesthetics of film emerges in the techniques of his later dramatic films as well as in his writings on the subject. His ethnographic interests have carried him as far afield as Africa and Latin America, but whether filming the life of Peruvian Indians or Japanese juvenile delinquents or women, he has consistently sought out the culturally disadvantaged as his subjects. His work attempts to be nonjudgmental, his narratives sometimes ending in highly unconventional ambiguities and making provocative artistic statements.

Born in Tōkyō, Hani descends from an illustrious and controversial family. His mother, Setsuko, was a noted social critic who married leftist scholar HANI GORŌ. Susumu's grandmother, HANI MOTOKO, was Japan's first newspaperwoman and cofounder, with her husband, of one of Japan's first progressive schools in 1921. Susumu graduated from this school, the Jiyū Gakuen, in 1947.

In the distaff family tradition, Hani took his first job as a reporter for the Japanese wire service Kyōdō News Service. But in 1952 he left to join the new film and photography division of Iwanami Shoten Publishers. He began as an editor of photograph anthologies, through which experience he learned about photography as a communication medium.

Without any previous film experience, Hani directed his first film for Iwanami in 1952, a documentary sponsored by the Welfare Ministry called *Seikatsu to mizu* (Water and Life). Learning as he went, Hani continued to make educational and industrial films for Iwanami until 1960. Among his most influential early works are *Kyōshitsu no kodomotachi* (1955, Children in the Classroom) and *E o kaku kodomotachi* (1956, Children Who Draw), which introduced a revolutionary camera technique to documentary filmmaking. Instead of employing the conventional hidden camera, Hani set up his apparatus in the middle of the classroom and allowed the school children to become accustomed to its presence. The results are works of surprising candor and sympathy, leading directly, according to film historian Satō Tadao (b 1930), to the documentary-style techniques of the 1960s New Wave, or *Nouvelle Vague*, in commercial cinema. Hani's films also inspired his 1958 theoretical writings *Engi shinai shuyakutachi* (Protagonists Who Do Not Act) and 1960 *Kamera to maiku* (Camera and Microphone).

In 1961 Hani's first feature, *Furyō shōnen* (Bad Boys), incorporated his documentary techniques and won the top national awards for the year. Using all amateur actors who had been through reform

school, he put their language, street sense, and "inside" experiences into the film, a work of authenticity that remains striking to this day.

During the political and social upheaval of the early 1960s Hani made two open-ended, very sensitive, feminist films, *Mitasareta seikatsu* (1962, A Full Life) and *Kanojo to kare* (1963, She and He). The first examines the feelings of a stage actress who finds the courage to divorce a worthless husband, resuming her career and establishing a new political and emotional life. *Kanojo to kare*, starring actress-director HIDARI SACHIKO, then Hani's wife, portrays the alienation of a young housewife in one of the huge exurban apartment complexes called *danchi*. Her involvement with ragpickers from a nearby shantytown and her husband's complete failure to understand her emotional needs provide a disturbing indictment of the Japanese *sararīman* (literally, "salary man"), or white-collar worker.

In the mid-1960s Hani embarked on unusual and stirring portraits of Japanese abroad. *Buwana Toshi no uta* (1965, Bwana Toshi) uses only one Japanese actor, the brilliant ATSUMI KIYOSHI, to teach African natives—all nonactors—how to put up prefabricated housing. Hani's first film with his own production company, *Andesu no hanayome* (1966, Bride of the Andes) again stars Hidari Sachiko, as the mail-order bride of a Japanese anthropologist among the Peruvian Indians.

Hani later returned to the turmoil of Japanese urban life in 1968 with *Hatsukoi jigoku hen* (Nanami: Inferno of First Love), where alienated teenagers try to make their way in a hostile environment. The script by poet-playwright-film director TERAYAMA SHŪJI did not conclude with Hani's melodramatic ending. Hani continued to use nonactors, natural settings, and contemporary subject matter into the 1970s, even having the actresses participate in the filming with super-8 cameras in his 1972 *Gozenchū no jikanwari* (Morning Schedule), but the results have not matched the quality of his earlier work.

Since 1975 Hani has produced no feature films, but he has made commercials and documentaries on African animals for television. He has also continued writing, on youth: *Hōnin shugi* (1972, Permissiveness); on education: *Ni tasu ni wa yon ja nai* (1975, $2 + 2 \neq 4$); and on film: *Ningenteki eizō ron* (1972, A Theory of a Human Film Image). In 1978 he resumed script collaboration with Terayama Shūji in the coproduction of *Afurika monogatari* (1980, Africa Story), which was filmed on location in Africa.   Audie BOCK

haniwa

A collective term for the unglazed earthenware cylinders and hollow sculptures that decorated the surface of the great mounded tombs (KOFUN) built for the Japanese elite during the 4th to 7th centuries. *Haniwa* sculptures were as tall as 1.5 meters (4.9 ft) and were made in a variety of forms: houses, human figures, animals, and a multitude of military, ceremonial, and household objects. But the basic and most common shape was the simple cylinder, averaging 40–50 centimeters (16–20 in) in diameter and 1 meter (3.3 ft) in height. *Haniwa* literally means clay *(hani)* ring *(wa)*.

Unlike tomb figurines from other parts of the world, *haniwa* were erected on the exterior surface of the tomb mound rather than buried in the chamber with the deceased. Half-embedded in the earth for stability, the cylinders stood in rows on or around the mound; they may have been joined together by rope or wooden poles threaded through holes in their upper walls. *Haniwa* sculptures, stabilized upright on similarly embedded cylindrical bases, highlighted the patterns made by the rows of cylinders, occupying the corners or interiors of the rectangles or dotting the tomb mound, which was marked off at the edges by the rows of cylinders.

The coil and slab building techniques used to create *haniwa*, as well as the scraped surface finish, occurred in common with HAJI WARE. The tomb sculptures were manufactured from the same iron-bearing clay as utilitarian pottery and fired in the same reduced-oxygen atmosphere at low temperatures, producing a warm buff color. Appliqués were used for such features as noses, ears, clothing, and ornaments, but the eyes and mouths of human and animal figures were characteristically cut through to the hollow interior. Details of form or costume together with decorative motifs of zigzag, diamond, herringbone, or CHOKKOMON ("straight-curved pattern") were incised on the clay surface. Pigments of red, blue, or white highlighted these patterns, and the faces of many *haniwa* figures were painted in iron red pigment with enigmatic designs possibly representing tattoos or special ritual makeup.

Archaeologists now recognize two principal patterns of *haniwa* placement on the tombs, each associated with a different kind of burial facility. The first was prominent during the 4th and 5th centuries and accompanied pit-style graves dug into the summit of the tomb mound. *Haniwa* cylinders and sculptures of houses, pieces of military equipment like shields and quivers, and ceremonial parasols were grouped in rectangular patterns around the graves. This placement pattern has been found mainly in and around the Kinai (Ōsaka-Kyōto-Nara) region, the center of the early Kofun culture. The second pattern was associated with a corridor-type stone burial chamber that was introduced from the continent in the late 5th or early 6th century. At the same time as this introduction, *haniwa* production ceased in the Kinai and blossomed in the Kantō region of eastern Japan; thus the second placement pattern is mainly known from the Kantō tombs and consists of the cylinders and sculptures lined up on the slopes of the tomb or outlining the contours of the tomb mound.

The Kinai ceremonial and military *haniwa* appear to have performed the ritual function of defining the sacred precincts of the burial and providing protection for its occupant. These *haniwa* are stately in appearance and very large. The uniformity of subject matter and surface treatment suggests that the *haniwa* manufacturers operated under prescribed rules or customs that allowed for little individuality of expression. In contrast, Kantō *haniwa* are lively and expressive, reflecting the frontier blend of military and common folk. Soldiers in full military dress, their mounts decorated with lavish horse trappings (see HORSE TRAPPINGS, ANCIENT), contrast with dancing farmers and women balancing jugs on their heads or carrying babies on their backs. The simple symbolic house of Kinai *haniwa* developed into entire estates in the Kantō, including granaries, storehouses, and even barnyard animals.

Haniwa Origins —— According to a legendary account in the chronicle NIHON SHOKI (720), *haniwa* originated as substitutes for sacrificial victims—attendants of the deceased who were buried alive in the tomb mound. Historians have since recognized this as a fiction; despite the modern archaeological excavation of thousands of mounded tombs, there is no evidence of an ancient practice of burying sacrificial victims alive or dead. It has also been demonstrated that the earliest *haniwa* were not human figures but cylinders, followed later by *haniwa* houses and military and ceremonial objects.

The cylinders developed from an hourglass-shaped jar stand that was popular during the preceding Yayoi period (ca 300 BC–ca AD 300). The jar stand appears to have played a role in the burial ceremonies of Yayoi society, possibly holding vessels filled with ritual offerings. As the jar stand became a permanent fixture of the tomb mound, it lengthened and filled out into a cylindrical shape, finally losing its function of providing a stable base for jars. Sculptural *haniwa* may have originated in the Chinese custom of lining up large stone statues of men and animals along "spirit paths" leading to important tombs. However, great differences between Chinese tomb figures and *haniwa* in materials, manufacturing techniques, placement on the tombs, and historical development of subject matter all argue against direct transmission of customs or skills from China to Japan. At most, Chinese tomb figures may have played a limited conceptual role in stimulating the production of *haniwa* sculptures.

▬——J. Edward Kidder, Jr, "Haniwa: The Origin and Meaning of Tomb Sculptures," *Transactions of the Asiatic Society of Japan,* 3rd Series, No. 9 (1966). Kondō Yoshirō and Harunari Shūji, "Haniwa no kigen," *Kōkogaku kenkyū* 13.3 (1967). Miki Fumio, *Haniwa: The Clay Sculpture of Protohistoric Japan,* tr Roy Andrew Miller (1960). Miki Fumio, *Haniwa,* tr Gina Lee Barnes (1974).

Gina Lee BARNES

Haniya Yutaka (1910–   )

Novelist, literary critic. Real name Hannya Yutaka. Born in Taiwan. Studied at Nihon University. He joined the Japan Communist Party in 1927, but abandoned his Marxist activities after being imprisoned (1932–33) during the government crackdown on communists. After World War II he helped found the magazine KINDAI BUNGAKU (1946–64), which serialized the first three and a half chapters of his monumental and still unfinished novel *Shirei* (Dead Soul) from 1946 to 1949. After a period of protracted inactivity due to poor health, he resumed work around 1955 and began to publish critical essays on literature and politics. His vehemently anti-Stalinist stance and unusual existentialist theory of eternal revolution significantly influenced the new left intellectuals of the late 1950s and 1960s. In 1976 he finally published *Shirei* in book form after completing the fourth chapter and adding a fifth, and a sixth was published as a separate

Haniwa——House

Excavated from the Saitobaru tomb cluster, Miyazaki Prefecture. Earthenware. Height 52.1 cm. 5th century. Tōkyō National Museum.

Haniwa——Falconer

This 6th-century *haniwa* sculpture was excavated in Gumma Prefecture. Typical of *haniwa* produced in the Kantō region, the figure has a lively appearance, the falcon perched on the falconer's raised arm. Earthenware. Height 76 cm. Yamato Bunkakan, Nara Prefecture.

volume in 1981. The novel, which won the 1976 Japan Literary Prize, explores in a highly abstract style the protagonist's metaphysical quest for meaning in existence. Other works include *Yami no naka no kuroi uma* (1970, Black Horse in Darkness), a collection of short stories, and *Genshi no naka no seiji* (1960, The Politics of Illusion), a collection of essays about politics.

Hankanfu

A 13-volume historical work of the Edo period (1600–1868), compiled by the scholar-statesman ARAI HAKUSEKI at the order of TOKUGAWA IENOBU, *daimyō* of the Kōfu domain (now part of Yamanashi Prefecture), who later became the sixth Tokugawa shōgun. Completed in 1702, the *Hankanfu* (meaning "genealogy of those who protect the shogunate") records the enfeoffment and later development of 337 daimyō families with domains over 10,000 *koku* (1 *koku* = about 180 liters or 5 US bushels; see KOKUDAKA), from 1600 to 1680. The work, which also includes biographies and genea-

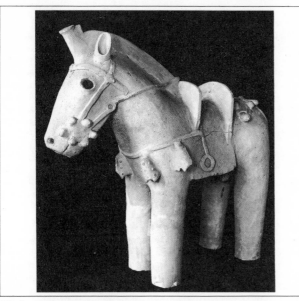

Haniwa——Horse

Excavated from the Kami Chūjō site, Kumagaya, Saitama Prefecture. Height 85.2 cm. Earthenware. 6th century. Tōkyō National Museum.

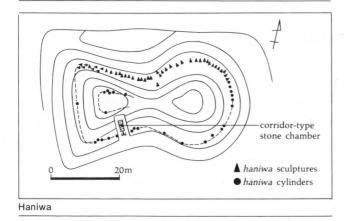

corridor-type stone chamber

▲ *haniwa* sculptures
● *haniwa* cylinders

Haniwa

The diagram shows the distribution of *haniwa* at the Himezuka tomb in Chiba Prefecture. The sculptural *haniwa* lined the slope on the side of the mound opposite the stone chamber and included a pack-horse driver, horses, military figures, and male and female figures.

logical tables, is generally considered an objective account of the daimyō families' relationship with the house of Tokugawa. A supplement was written by Okada Kansen (1740–1816) and others at the order of the shogunate in 1806.

hanko → seals

Hankyū Corporation

(Hankyū Dentetsu). Private railway company whose principal line of business is the transport of passengers in the Kinki (Kyōto-Ōsaka-Kōbe) area. Founded in 1906 as Minoo Arima Railway by KOBAYASHI ICHIZŌ and others. Some of the ideas he implemented were housing developments along the railway lines to induce greater use of the railway, the purchase and sale of real estate, the construction of a station building at the line's terminus to be used as a department store, and other enterprises to supplement the railway business. Other private railway companies sought to emulate Kobayashi's management policies.

In 1913 he organized the famous Takarazuka Girls' Opera Company in an effort to attract more passengers to the Takarazuka Hot Spring Spa. The company expanded its network of railway lines in the Kinki region supported by the flourishing economy of that district. In the fiscal year ending March 1982 revenue was ¥101.7 billion (US $422.5 million), of which railway lines earned 67 percent and real estate 33 percent. The company's profit ratio was the highest among large private railway companies. Its total trackage was 141 kilometers (87.6 mi). In the fiscal year ending March 1982 the company was capitalized at ¥30.8 billion (US $127.9 million). The head office is in Ōsaka. See also HANKYŪ DEPARTMENT STORES, INC.

Hankyū Department Stores, Inc

(Hankyū Hyakkaten). Leading "railway terminal" department store chain with its main store in Ōsaka. Established by the HANKYŪ CORPORATION in 1929, it became independent in 1947, but remains a core member of the Hankyū group of transportation, distribution, real estate, and leisure industry companies. The company has worked to systematize management and modernize retail operations, including strengthening of foreign activities through its London and other international buying offices. It has six stores in Tōkyō, Ōsaka, Kyōto, and Kōbe, and overseas stores in Los Angeles, London, Paris, and Milan. Sales for the fiscal year ending March 1982 totaled ¥245.3 billion (US $1 billion); the Ōsaka store boasts the largest sales of any single store in Japan. Hankyū's strength has been in soft goods and foodstuffs; clothing accounted for 36 percent of its total sales volume, foods 31 percent, sundries 8 percent, household goods and furniture 10 percent, and other merchandise 15 percent. The company was capitalized at ¥6.6 billion (US $31.2 million) in the same year.

Hannō

City in southwestern Saitama Prefecture, central Honshū, on the river Irumagawa. Situated at the junction of several railways, Hannō is the distribution center for agricultural products from neighboring villages. Long a textile center—according to local tradition the area was settled by Korean immigrants (KIKAJIN) in the 8th century—there are also lumber and electrical appliance industries. More recently it has become a residential area for commuters to Tōkyō. The city is part of the Oku Musashi Prefectural Park. Pop: 61,178.

hansatsu

(domainal paper money). Paper currency *(satsu)* issued during the Edo period (1600–1868) by various *daimyō* domains *(han)* and fiefs held by senior vassals *(hatamoto)* of the Tokugawa shogunate; *hansatsu* was used mainly to pay for the daimyō's expenses and those of the domain monopolies. Valid only in the domain in which it was issued, *hansatsu* was in theory convertible into the coinage issued by the shogunate. The first of its kind was issued by the Fukui domain (now part of Fukui Prefecture) in 1661 with shogunate permission; other domains quickly followed suit. In spite of repeated injunctions by the shogunate, *hansatsu* continued to be issued in large amounts throughout the period, causing its rapid devaluation, rampant inflation, and general confusion in domainal finances. *Hansatsu* continued to circulate after the Meiji Restoration of 1868. Between 1871 and 1879 the new government assumed responsibility for converting all *hansatsu* to the new national currency at a cost of ¥25 million.

Hanshan (Han-shan) and Shide (Shih-te) → Kanzan and Jittoku

hansharo

(reverberatory furnace). Introduced into Japan on a practical basis in the 1840s (an experimental furnace was built in 1842), the reverberatory furnace enabled the Japanese to build large iron artillery pieces, something that the existing crucible furnaces could not accomplish. In 1850, the Saga domain (in what is now Saga Prefecture) built the first working reverberatory furnace in Japan, using a description in a translation of a Dutch work. The Tokugawa shogunate's huge furnace, built under the direction of EGAWA TARŌZAEMON at Nirayama, Izu Province (now part of Shizuoka Prefecture), began partial operation in 1855 and was completed in 1857. By the mid-1860s several other domains also had reverberatories.

Hanshin Industrial Zone

(Hanshin Kōgyō Chitai). Extends along the northeastern shore of Ōsaka Bay with Ōsaka and Kōbe as the principal cities. It is the second largest industrial zone in Japan after the KEIHIN INDUSTRIAL ZONE. Before World War II, it ranked first in the value of industrial goods produced. As a result of recent expansion west to Himeji, northeast to Kyōto and Ōtsu, and south to Wakayama and Arida, the zone is also called the Keihanshin Industrial Zone or Kinki Industrial Zone. The major industrial products are metals, iron and steel, electric machinery and equipment, general machinery and equipment, textiles, chemicals, and foodstuffs.

Hanwa Co, Ltd

(Hanwa Kōgyō). Firm chiefly engaged in the export, import, and domestic sale of steel, but also handling oil, synthetic goods, specialty steel, machinery, food products, and lumber. Founded in 1947, it was the first in the industry to erect a modern, large-scale center on the seacoast for the storage of mass-produced steel. The center also serves as an outlet for efficient delivery of merchandise to customers. The company has opened numerous overseas offices and controls four subsidiary corporations in foreign countries. Sales for the fiscal year ending March 1982 totaled ¥641.3 billion (US $2.7 billion) and capitalization stood at ¥5.1 billion (US $21.2 million). Corporate headquarters are located in Ōsaka.

Hanyū

City in northeastern Saitama Prefecture, central Honshū, on the southern bank of the river Tonegawa. Hanyū has been known as a clothing manufacturing town since the Edo period (1600–1868). There is an emerging automobile industry. The town provided the setting for *Inaka kyōshi* (1909, Country Teacher), a story by TAYAMA KATAI. Pop: 48,488.

hanzei

(literally, "half payment"). A tax system whereby the Muromachi shogunate (1338–1573) assigned to its vassals, for one-year terms, one-half of the land tax (NENGU) collected from private landed estates (SHŌEN), the proprietors retaining the other half. These grants, which were ostensibly for the support of troops in the field, were calculated to win support for the shogunate. Conferral documents, usually authorized by provincial military governors (SHUGO), survive from the 1330s. It was difficult, however, to withdraw these temporary grants, once conferred, and in 1352 the shogunate issued a law standardizing the area, length of tenure, and proportion of yield for *hanzei* grants in the provinces of Owari (now Aichi Prefecture), Ōmi (now Shiga Prefecture), and Mino (now Gifu Prefecture). The enforcement of these guidelines was left to the *shugo*, who increasingly abused their power, especially during the ŌNIN WAR of 1467–77 (see SHUGO DAIMYŌ). *Hanzei*, together with earlier practices of WAYO and SHITAJI CHŪBUN, contributed to the final disappearance of *shōen*. *SHIMADA Jirō*

hara

(abdomen, stomach, belly, viscera, womb). An important concept in Japanese traditional popular psychology and in interpersonal relationships. In addition to referring to actual body parts, the word *hara* is also used in a number of Japanese idioms having to do with emotions, thoughts, intentions, or character. For example, when a person is angry, it is said that his "*hara* stands up" (*hara ga tatsu*). Similarly, when a person's anger is vented or when he takes vengeance, he may say that his "*hara* is cured" (*hara ga osamaru*). When one tries to probe another's plans, intentions, or thoughts without verbal communication, one "gropes around," "reads" or "gauges" the other's *hara* (*hara o saguru*). An individual with evil in mind or an ulterior motive "has something in his *hara*" (*hara ni ichimotsu ga aru*). A person having a frank talk with another "cuts his *hara* open" (*hara o waru*). A wicked man's *hara* is "dirty" or "black" (*hara ga kitanai/kuroi*). A generous person's *hara* is "broad" (*hara ga futoi*); a resolute person's *hara* is "sitting down" (*hara ga suwaru*). When two individuals "put their *hara* together" (*hara o awaseru*), they either cooperate or have reached a secret understanding. *Haragei*, or "belly play," favored by politicians in Japan, is a way of reaching mutual understanding without direct

verbal communication. Only those with strong personalities are believed to be capable of it.

These and other expressions using the word *hara* indicate that the abdominal region has traditionally been considered the focus of emotions, thoughts, and intentions. In the practice of Zen meditation and the martial arts, the student is told to concentrate his energies on the center of the abdominal region (*seika tanden*) to become at the same time relaxed and alert. The ritual suicide by disembowelment developed by Japanese warriors (*seppuku* or HARAKIRI) testified to their belief that *hara* is the locus of life and character. See also KI; MUSHI; NONVERBAL COMMUNICATION.

——John Condon, *Patterns of Communication In and Out of Japan* (1974). Karlfried Graf von Dürckheim, *Hara—The Vital Centre of Man*, tr Sylvia-Monica von Kospoth and Estelle R. Healy (1962). Fukasaku Mitsusada, *Nihon bunka oyobi nihonjin ron* (1972). *Hiroshi WAGATSUMA*

Harada Magoshichirō (fl late 16th century)

Overseas trader of the Azuchi–Momoyama period (1568–1600). Born in Higo Province (now Kumamoto Prefecture). As an agent for the Nagasaki trader Harada Kiemon, Magoshichirō made frequent voyages to Luzon and became both fluent in Spanish and well informed about the Philippines. He and his master encouraged the national unifier TOYOTOMI HIDEYOSHI to annex the islands of the southern seas, and in 1592 Magoshichirō was sent by Hideyoshi to Manila with a letter urging the Spanish viceroy to pay tribute to Japan. The next year he went to Taiwan for the same purpose. Both missions failed in their aims.

Harada Naojirō (1863–1899)

Western-style painter of the Meiji period (1868–1912). Born in Edo (now Tōkyō). He graduated from the Tōkyō School of Foreign Languages (Tōkyō Gaikokugo Gakkō) in 1881 and began studying oil painting with TAKAHASHI YUICHI. From 1884 to 1887 he studied painting in Munich, where he specialized in genre and history painting in the style of the German realists. During this time Harada became acquainted with MORI ŌGAI, who was also abroad. When he returned to Japan he helped to found the Meiji Bijutsukai (Meiji Fine Arts Society) in 1889. He established a private art school, the Shōbikan, in Hongō, Tōkyō; among his students was WADA EISAKU. At the time of his death, Harada was involved in the creation of a modern style of Japanese painting in which techniques of Western realism were combined with Japanese elements.

Harada Yoshito (1885–1974)

Archaeologist. Born in Tōkyō. Harada earned a degree in Asian history from Tōkyō University and then joined the faculty there. After participating in the excavation of the SAITOBARU TOMB CLUSTER, he pursued his archaeological studies in Europe and the United States from 1921 to 1923.

Harada's many contributions to the study of cultural history and the development of archaeology in East Asia include his founding of the Far Eastern Archaeological Society, together with HAMADA KŌSAKU, in 1925. He is also known for his studies of clothing and accessories in Central Asia and Han (206 BC–AD 220) and Tang (T'ang; 618–907) China, based on both archaeological remains and literary records, as well as for his excavations of fortress sites such as Muyang of the Han dynasty, the eastern capital of the BOHAI (Pohai) state, and the Chinese Luolang (Lo-lang) commandery on the Korean peninsula. Among his works are *Kan rikuchō no fukushoku* (1937, Clothes and Accessories of the Han and the Six Dynasties) and *Tōa kobunka kenkyū* (1940, Studies on East Asian Culture). *ABE Gihei*

harae

Shintō rite of purification or act of atonement; the word is the nominal form of the verb *harau* (to cleanse). *Harae* has, since the distant past, possessed two complementary aspects. It is first a ceremonial purification which prepares participants in Shintō observances for visitations from and union with gods, and has been traditionally accomplished by means of ritual ablution (*misogi*); hence the expression *misogi harae*. The antiquity of this practice is indicated by the myth related in the historical chronicles KOJIKI (712) and NIHON SHOKI (720) of the deity Izanagi no Mikoto's journey to the land of the dead *(yomi)* in order to see his spouse Izanami no Mikoto. Immediately on his return he performs *misogi* in order to cleanse himself of defilement (KEGARE) wrought by contact with cadavers. Casting away his staff, cap, wrist bindings, and clothes he immerses himself in water, thus bringing about the births of the deities Amaterasu Ōmikami, Tsukuyomi no Mikoto, and Takehaya Susanoo no Mikoto from his left and right eyes and his nose (see MYTHOLOGY: Birth of Amaterasu and Susanoo). In the *Izumo* FUDOKI (733) it is recorded that local officials (KUNI NO MIYATSUKO) of Izumo Province (now part of Shimane Prefecture) performed *misogi* in a nearby river before entering the capital of the emperor, who was thought to be divine (i.e., an *arahitogami* or "man-god"). Although ceremonial bathing is still performed by the chief celebrants before Shintō observances following a ritual of purification and abstention *(imi),* ordinarily devotees merely wash their hands and mouths *(temizu)* under the direction of shrine officials.

Harae is also an act of atonement which is represented in the *Kojiki* and *Nihon shoki* cycles of myth by accounts of Susanoo's offences against Amaterasu and the penance *(harae)* exacted from him by the other gods of the High Plain of Heaven (Takamagahara). Susanoo breaks the embankments between celestial rice paddies, desposits excrement in his sister's palace, and commits other atrocities, and the horrified Amaterasu hides herself in a cave (Ama no Iwayato). After luring her out, the eight million gods *(yaoyorozu no kami)* demand as signs of contrition that Susanoo cut off his beard and the nails of his fingers and toes (see MYTHOLOGY: The feuding of Amaterasu and Susanoo). Offenders against the sacred were in ancient times made to atone for their sacrileges by banishment or by the submission of material articles *(agamono;* now *harae no gu* or *haraetsu mono);* the chronicle of the legendary empress Jingū in the *Nihon shoki* mentions such imposts on groups of people as well as individuals. Criminal defilements (TSUMI)—a body of taboos which preceded the development of secular legal convention—are categorized as either *amatsu tsumi* (heavenly *tsumi)* or *kunitsu tsumi* (earthly *tsumi). Amatsu tsumi,* the transgressions described in the *Kojiki* and *Nihon shoki* as having been committed by Susanoo, are of three types: actions deleterious to agriculture; wanton ruthlessness; and desecration of sacred places. Earthly *tsumi* include the letting of blood; hereditary abnormalities; sickness; incest and bestiality; various natural calamities; and witchcraft. It can be seen from this list that passive afflictions as well as willful actions result in a burden of *tsumi;* hence, the affliction of *tsumi* inevitably touches everyone, necessitating recurrent purification.

In 802 an earlier division between malevolent *harae (ashi no harae)* and benevolent *harae (yoshi no harae)* was discarded and a four-grade system, led by *ōharae* (grand *harae),* was adopted, establishing standards for both the penitential and purificatory aspects of *harae. Ōharae* was performed on the last day of the 6th month (see NAGOSHI) and the 12th month, and before the imperial rite of thanksgiving (DAIJŌSAI) celebrated after a new emperor's formal enthronement. In the ENGI SHIKI (927; tr *Procedures of the Engi Era,* 1970–72) are listed offerings which were to be given at the yearly observance of the 6th month *ōharae,* among which are iron human figures, thread, strips of paper made from the bark of the paper mulberry *(kōzo),* hemp, articles of clothing, plows, rice, *sake,* seaweed, dried fish, and salt. At ordinary observances items such as the following were given: paper or straw human figures (see KATASHIRO), sedge (from which hats were woven), hemp (from which most clothing was once made), rice stalks, rice, *tokinawa* (unravelled cord; one end of a two-strand cord was held in the mouth and unravelled, a strand in each hand), and *harae-gushi* (sacred mulberry paper called *nusa,* attached to sticks). Today strips of mulberry paper *(yū,* from which *nusa* are fashioned) and hemp cloth are offered at *ōharae* observances, and at ordinary rites, salted hot water and *harae-gushi,* which were waved to dispel defilement. It is also thought that the stick, made of the SAKAKI tree or bamboo, to which strips of sacred paper were attached, functioned as a *shimboku* ("god-tree"), which attracted and gave habitation *(yorishiro)* to benevolent deities.

Among variant forms of *harae* were *nanase no harae,* a monthly imperial observance of ancient provenance, in which the emperor rubbed paper dolls called *katashiro* against his body and breathed on them, thus transferring defilements, before sending them with seven emissaries to seven river shallows where they were cast in the water; and *yudachi* (boiling water), still performed today, in which a Shintō priestess (MIKO) dips a leafy bamboo branch in boiling water and shakes it over herself and devotees. The influence of *harae* is also apparent in the annual cycle of FESTIVALS called *nenchū gyōji,* particularly in such observances as: Tango no Sekku (see CHIL-DREN'S DAY), the original purpose of which was to protect participants from epidemic disease; SETSUBUN, a ceremonial driving-out of evil influences performed in early February; and the BON FESTIVAL, a Buddhist rite which has adopted a number of Shintō practices related to *nagoshi.* See also SHINTŌ RITES.

Hara Kei → Hara Takashi

harakiri

Japanese ritual suicide by self-disembowelment. Written with the two Chinese characters for abdomen and cutting, the word *harakiri* is better known in the Western world than the more formal term *seppuku,* which consists of the same two Chinese characters written in reverse order. The latter term is more commonly used in Japan.

The abdomen was chosen as the target of the suicidal knife inasmuch as ancient Japanese regarded it as the place where the soul resides and the source of action-derived tension. Additionally, the abdomen, at the physical center of the body, came to be regarded as the cradle of the individual's will, boldness, spirit, anger, and generosity. Many proverbs and idiomatic expressions in Japanese illustrate this belief: *hara ga tatsu* ("the abdomen stands up") meaning the person is angry, *hara ga futoi* ("the abdomen is broad") meaning the person is generous, among other possible meanings (see HARA).

One of the first legendary instances of *seppuku* was that of the bandit Hakamadare Yasusuke who, when faced with capture by the police in 988, disemboweled himself, leaning against a pillar in his own home. He did not die until the following day.

According to an apocryphal account in the military romance *Heike monogatari* (The Tale of the Heike), Minamoto no Yorimasa, defeated in battle and wounded, sought refuge in the Byōdōin, a temple south of Kyōto. Leaving behind a farewell poem, he sat on his fan and pressed the point of a long sword to his abdomen, then leaning forward, forced the blade into his body. This style of *seppuku* or *harakiri* became widely accepted shortly thereafter.

Another early and dramatic example of *seppuku* was that of Murakami Yoshiteru in 1333, a *samurai* who, with his master Prince MORINAGA, was trapped in a house by his foes. To distract the attention of the enemy so that his master might escape, Murakami took a torch in hand and made his way to the roof of the house. Using the torch to set fire to the thatch of the roof, Murakami shouted taunts at the enemy samurai waiting in the garden below. Telling them that he himself was Morinaga, he invited them to watch how a true warrior dies. Removing his outer robe, he made a long, deep slash across his abdomen, just below the navel. In spite of the pain and the heat, he was able to keep his face impassive, steeling himself with the knowledge that his master had by that time doubtless escaped. Seizing a handful of intestines from his open wound, he cut a length free and tossed it down into the faces of the enemy below. Then with one last effort he withdrew his long sword, placed the point of it in his mouth, and fell forward onto the burning thatch of the roof.

During Japan's early feudal period, suicide by self-disembowelment gradually became more ritualized and by the time of the Edo period (1600–1868), it had become one of the five grades of punishment for wrongdoers among the samurai class. It was, in short, a way of death with honor.

All aspects of the *seppuku* ritual were prescribed with precision: apparel, site, time, witnesses, inspector, and assistant. When the site had been readied and the witnesses, guards, and inspectors assembled, the doomed man would open his *kimono* and stretch out his right hand to grasp his knife and without hesitation cut into his abdomen from left to right. Often this wound was neither deep nor intended to bring on death. Having arranged beforehand with his *kaishakunin* (assistant), he would make a signal, whereupon the *kaishakunin's* sword slashed down, severing his head. The *kaishakunin* was chosen for his skill in leaving the head connected to the body by only a small strip of flesh so that it would not roll away from the body.

A famous instance of mass *seppuku* is that of the 47 *rōnin* (masterless samurai), who were ordered to commit *seppuku* after they had murdered KIRA YOSHINAKA whom they regarded as responsible for the death of their master, Asano Naganori. Since their act of vengeance had been praised by many, the authorities determined that the *rōnin* should die with as little suffering as possible. Accordingly, as soon as one of the *rōnin* stretched out his hand to take the knife, his *kaishakunin* decapitated him with one clean cut (see FORTY-SEVEN RŌNIN INCIDENT).

One of the most famous instances of *seppuku* to be witnessed and recorded by a Westerner took place in February 1868, when a number of Japanese soldiers from the province of Bizen (now Okayama Prefecture) fired on the foreign settlement in Kōbe. The samurai responsible for giving the order to open fire was Taki Zenzaburō, and for this act he was ordered to commit *seppuku*. The ceremony took place at night in a temple, and seven foreign consular officials, including the author of the account, Algernon MITFORD, were present as witnesses. After being led into the main hall of the temple, Taki Zenzaburō took his place in the middle of a raised platform, accepted the ceremonial knife with a bow, and then confessed to the alleged crime and announced his intention to commit *seppuku* in atonement. Opening his kimono, he stabbed himself deeply in the lower left side of his abdomen, pulled the blade across to the right side and then finished the cut with a slight upward turn on the blade. Next he withdrew the blade and, leaning forward, stretched out his neck as a signal to the *kaishakunin,* who instantly severed his head. Making a low bow, the *kaishakunin* wiped his blade with a piece of paper and withdrew. The ceremony ended as the two representatives of the shogunate called upon the seven foreign witnesses to attest to the fact that the sentence had been faithfully carried out.

Seppuku was not mentioned in the revised criminal code promulgated in 1873, but the nationalism of the Meiji period (1868–1912) and the partial reversion to traditional values combined to keep the practice alive, if not as an official punishment than as a courageous method to bring about one's own demise.

Periodic instances of *seppuku* continued to dot the pages of the modern history of Japan, the most famous being that of General NOGI MARESUKE who, in 1912, chose to follow the emperor Meiji in death. A considerable number of persons committed *seppuku* on the grounds in front of the Imperial Palace in Tōkyō shortly after the emperor broadcast the announcement of Japan's surrender to the Allied Forces in 1945. And in November 1970, novelist MISHIMA YUKIO committed *seppuku* in a sensational and theatrical manner: with several of his followers he forced his way into the headquarters of the Japanese Self Defense Forces in Ichigaya in Tōkyō and exhorted a crowd of soldiers to reject the "pernicious progress" of modern times and return to Japan's traditional values and ways. Immediately thereafter, he cut open his stomach with a short dagger. Using a famous old sword called Seki no Magoroku, his *kaishakunin* needed three strokes to decapitate Mishima.

■ ——Inazō Nitobe, *Bushidō: The Soul of Japan* (1900). Mishima Yukio, *The Way of the Samurai: Yukio Mishima on 'Hagakure' in Modern Life,* tr Kathryn Sparling (1977). Jack Seward, *Hara-kiri* (1968). *Jack* SEWARD

Haramachi

City in northeastern Fukushima Prefecture, northern Honshū, on the Pacific coast. Haramachi developed as a POST-STATION TOWN on the highway Hamakaidō. Principal industries are electrical equipment, paper, and machine manufacturing. The city is known for its Nomaoi (wild horse chase) Festival, held each July at Ōta Shrine. Pop: 46,057.

Hara Martinho (ca 1570–1629)

One of the young envoys sent by the CHRISTIAN DAIMYŌ of Kyūshū on the MISSION TO EUROPE OF 1582. Born in Hasami in the Ōmura domain (now part of Nagasaki Prefecture), he studied at the Jesuit seminary in Arima. The mission visited Spain, Portugal, and Italy, had a papal audience in 1585, and returned to Japan in 1590. Hara's eulogy in praise of Valignano was published in Goa under the title *Oratio Habita A Fara D. Martino* (1588). He entered the Society of Jesus in 1591 and was ordained in 1608; when the Tokugawa shogunate intensified its persecution of Christianity, he went to Macao in 1614. There he assisted Fr. Rodrigues Tçuzzu with his *História de Japam* (1620–34) and taught Japanese at the Jesuit college. He died in Macao on 23 October 1629. *Adriana* BOSCARO

Hara Setsuko (1920–   )

Film actress. Real name Aida Masae. Born in Yokohama. Known in the Japanese film world as the "eternal virgin." She joined NIKKATSU CORPORATION in 1935, and that same year made her motion-picture debut appearing in Taguchi Tetsu's *Tamerau nakare wakō-doyo* from which she went on to become a major box-office attraction. She gained further popularity as the Japanese heroine in Arnold Fanck and ITAMI MANSAKU's joint German-Japanese film *Atarashiki tsuchi* (1937, The New Earth). Her quiet beauty and talent were featured in such favorite OZU YASUJIRŌ films as *Banshun* (1949, Late Spring), *Bakushū* (1951, Early Summer), *Tōkyō monogatari* (1953, Tōkyō Story), and *Akibiyori* (1960, Late Autumn). Her brother-in-law, Kumagai Hisatora, a movie director, is said to have encouraged both her entry into Nikkatsu and her later move to TŌHŌ CO, LTD. She retired from the film world in 1963. *ITASAKA Tsuyoshi*

Hara Takashi (1856–1921)

Also known as Hara Kei or Hara Satoshi. Influential party politician of the early 20th century; home minister from 1906 to 1908, 1911 to 1912, and 1913 to 1914, and prime minister from 1918 to 1921, he is recognized as one of the principal architects of party government in modern Japan. Although as a party leader he was known as a "commoner," he was born on 9 February 1856 into a *samurai* family, the second son of Hara Naoji, in the domain of Morioka (now part of Iwate Prefecture) in north-central Japan. Since Morioka remained loyal to the faltering Tokugawa shogunate (1603–1867) to the very end, Hara acquired at an early age a sense of being an outsider vis-à-vis the new MEIJI RESTORATION government, an attitude that sustained him through a variety of careers that culminated in his becoming a party politician.

Hara's education began in the domain school. In 1871, like many others of his generation, he went to Tōkyō to study and acquire new skills appropriate to the new era. He studied English and French and was baptized into the Catholic faith as David. In 1875 he entered the law school of the Ministry of Justice. Before graduating, however, he assumed responsibility for a student protest against the room-and-board system and left the school.

Hara's career continued in this uncertain pattern. In 1879 he joined the newspaper *Yūbin hōchi shimbun* as a reporter, only to leave it three years later after a disagreement with other reporters, including YANO RYŪKEI and INUKAI TSUYOSHI, who sought to make the paper an organ of the RIKKEN KAISHINTŌ, the political party of ŌKUMA SHIGENOBU. He became editor of the newspaper *Daitō nippō* in Ōsaka in April 1882 but left in October 1882 to take a position in the Ministry of Foreign Affairs on the recommendation of Foreign Minister INOUE KAORU. Inoue had been impressed by Hara's views on the future of Japanese politics, expressed during a trip both men took to Korea in 1884 to consult with ministerial representatives from China, and he quickly elevated Hara to consul-general in Tianjin (Tientsin) and then to first secretary in the embassy in Paris. Through Inoue's sponsorship, Hara was brought to the attention of MUTSU MUNEMITSU and ITŌ HIROBUMI, two of the most important government leaders of the time. Hara served as Mutsu's personal secretary during his term as minister of agriculture and commerce in 1890–91 and later as vice-minister to Mutsu during his term as minister of foreign affairs. In 1896, through Mutsu, Hara was appointed ambassador to Korea. Within a year, however, Hara resigned from government service to become editor-in-chief of the newspaper *Ōsaka mainichi shimbun.*

Hara's relationship with Inoue, Mutsu, and Itō was complex. Although he owed his bureaucratic career to Inoue, their relationship ended in bitter misunderstanding when later, as a party politician, Hara pursued policies aimed at weakening the position of the bureaucracy. Mutsu, who had risen in government with support from Inoue and Itō, advised Hara to leave the government to serve the country in another capacity. In 1900 Hara joined Itō's party, the RIKKEN SEIYŪKAI, as secretary-general. Hara had great admiration for Itō as the chief creator of the Meiji constitutional order, but as he did not see Itō as an effective party leader, he seized the opportunity to gain a position of preeminence in the party. Ironically, it was Inoue who had encouraged Itō to invite Hara into the party as a key officer, a factor that added to growing estrangement between Inoue and Hara.

Hara's career as a party leader in the Rikken Seiyūkai for over 20 years secured him a lasting place in the political history of modern Japan. He ran the party with Matsuda Masahisa (1845–1914) and SAIONJI KIMMOCHI (the party president from 1903) from 1901 until 1914, and from then until his death he took sole charge as successor to Saionji. In 1900, during Itō's fourth cabinet, Hara succeeded HOSHI TŌRU as minister of communications. Later that year he ran successfully for a seat in the lower house of the Diet as a representative from Iwate Prefecture, and was reelected eight times. In the lower house he served as chairman of the budget committee and floor leader. In 1906, during Saionji's first cabinet, Hara served as home minister, a powerful post equivalent to that of vice-prime minister. He served in the same post in 1911 in the second Saionji cabinet, and again in 1913 in the YAMAMOTO GONNOHYŌE cabinet. Following the resignation of the TERAUCHI MASATAKE cabinet because of its mishandling of the nationwide RICE RIOTS OF 1918, Hara formed the first party cabinet in which the head of the majority party in the lower house became prime minister.

In any assessment of his historical significance, Hara must be seen as a master political strategist. During his editorship of the Ōsaka mainichi, Hara became convinced that the corrective to a government dominated by narrow bureaucratic cliques, especially the faction that clustered around YAMAGATA ARITOMO, was the systematic strengthening of political parties and the establishment of party government within the constitution. Hara shaped this vision into a strategy; he set out to build a powerful political party by integrating agricultural and industrial interests throughout Japan. His party dominated the lower house, undermined the power of the Yamagata faction, and imposed its influence on the various ministries of the government (to bring about a change in the allocation of national resources). During his terms as home minister, Hara appointed governors sympathetic to his party and promoted regional economic development plans, including the building of railways, schools, roads, and dams, all of which were clearly intended to satisfy regional party interests.

Hara's impact on the political structure and process was extensive. He established the political party as a permanent institution within the constitutional order. He defined the fundamental political tension within that order as being between the lower house and the bureaucracy and maintained that, to overcome the strength of the bureaucracy, there should be a one-party domination of the lower house rather than a two-party system that would vitiate the strength of the lower house at the expense of the bureaucracy. And finally, Hara perceived that the maintenance of party power must involve a long-term economic policy, the coordination and satisfaction of regional interests, and the pursuit, in general, of an investment policy that emphasized domestic economic needs. That approach to politics often placed him at serious odds with the military, which had its own ideas about investing according to logistical requirements.

The severest challenge to Hara's strategy came from KATSURA TARŌ. Hara had maintained with Katsura a compromise relationship, sometimes referred to as the politics of "mutual understanding." Hara supported Katsura's budget in the lower house, while Katsura in return agreed to have Saionji, president of the Seiyūkai, appointed to the next prime ministership. It was in accord with this arrangement that Hara gained the post of home minister, through which he promoted his policies of party expansion. As this political relationship clearly favored Hara over the long run, Katsura decided to challenge Hara by organizing a party of his own, the RIKKEN DŌSHIKAI, during the TAISHŌ POLITICAL CRISIS of 1912–13. Backed by the MOVEMENT TO PROTECT CONSTITUTIONAL GOVERNMENT, Hara survived the challenge, while Katsura went down in utter defeat. A rival anti-Seiyūkai coalition, however, had come into existence to contest the powerful claims of Hara's party in the Diet.

Hara's popularity with the public declined during his prime ministership. He did not use the absolute majority he controlled in the lower house to endorse the UNIVERSAL MANHOOD SUFFRAGE MOVEMENT. He believed manhood suffrage to be inevitable, but wished it to be achieved gradually, by means such as lowering the tax requirement, a measure that he implemented to double the electorate. The public, however, expected more from a "commoner" prime minister. Liberals and socialists, as well as traditional moralists and nationalists, accused him of being concerned only with power. As his detailed 10-volume diary reveals, Hara was aware of these criticisms but believed firmly that he would be vindicated in the end for promoting the growth of the Seiyūkai into an undeniable force within the constitutional order.

Hara's dedication to his party was unusual among Japanese politicians. He traveled to every region in the country to attend party rallies and give encouragement. He cemented the relationship between party headquarters and branches with concrete rewards. He was generous in providing campaign funds. He took little for himself, living in humble surroundings and avoiding ostentatious display.

On 4 November 1921, while on his way to a regional party rally in western Japan, Hara was fatally stabbed by a young ultrarightist in Tōkyō Station.

■——Hara Takashi, Hara Takashi nikki, 10 vols (1951). Masumi Junnosuke, Nihon seitō shi ron, 4 vols (1966). Mitani Taichirō, Nihon seitō seiji no keisei: Hara Takashi no seiji shidō no tenkai (1967). Tetsuo Najita, Hara Kei in the Politics of Compromise (1967).   Tetsuo NAJITA

Hara Tamiki (1905–1951)

Poet, novelist. Born in Hiroshima Prefecture. Graduate of Keiō University. He began writing poems and short stories as a student. His works are characterized by a delicate sensibility and a pessimistic view of life and reflect the influence of dadaism and art modes of the 1930s. In the summer of 1945, he was living with his brother in Hiroshima when the atomic bomb was dropped. This experience moved him to write a series of short stories, published as Natsu no hana (1947, Summer Flowers), the title story of which is an ominous account of a family dispute on a summer day just prior to the fateful explosion. It is considered not only his best work but one of the best on the subject. In 1951 he committed suicide.

Hara Yasusaburō (1884–   )

Businessman. Born in Tokushima Prefecture and graduated from Waseda University, Hara entered the business world in 1910 and assisted in the revitalization of some 70 faltering corporations. He became president of Chūgai Mining in 1932 and, in 1935, president of NIPPON KAYAKU CO, LTD, of which he became the chairman. An expert in tax systems, Hara participated in a variety of the government's advisory organs, serving as chairman of the National Railways Council and the Customs Tariff Council.
                                                TANAKA Yōnosuke

Harbin

(Ch: Haerbin or Ha-erh-pin). A once cosmopolitan city on the right bank of the Sungari River in Heilongjiang (Heilungkiang) Province, northeastern China. Founded by Russians in 1897 as a railway construction settlement at the junction of the CHINESE EASTERN RAILWAY trunk lines to Vladivostok and Dalny (J: Dairen; Ch: Dalian or Ta-lien), Harbin developed into the economic hub of northern Manchuria with a 1922 population of 485,000, including 80,000 Russians and fewer numbers of Ukrainians, Poles, Baltic Germans, and Jews, many of them refugees from the Bolshevik Revolution. The Japanese presence in Harbin, largely commercial during the 1920s, became predominant following Japan's seizure of Manchuria in 1931–33 (see MANCHURIAN INCIDENT) and was further strengthened by Tōkyō's purchase of the Chinese Eastern Railway from the Soviet Union in 1935. From 1932 until 1945 the GUANDONG (KWANTUNG) ARMY, a semiautonomous Japanese military unit in Manchuria, used Harbin as field headquarters for intelligence operations against the USSR. The Russian army occupied Harbin on 19 August 1945 and handed the city over to the Chinese communists in April 1946. Harbin is currently a food-processing and industrial center with a population of 1,670,000, but only a few dozen members of the old Russian community remain, the rest having returned to the USSR or emigrated to North and South America, Australia, and Hong Kong.
                                                John J. STEPHAN

hares → rabbits

haribako

(sewing box; literally, "needle box"). Traditional box or basket used for sewing equipment. Considered essential belongings for Japanese women, haribako were traditionally included in dowries. Some were simply made of lacquered paper or bamboo; others were of lacquered wood with several drawers and sometimes gold or silver decoration. As haribako became more elaborate, they were equipped with a collapsible arm with a pin cushion for hemming, special slots for rulers, and so forth. Since World War II, the traditional sewing boxes have been largely replaced by more easily portable baskets with top-mounted handles, much like Western sewing baskets.

hari kuyō

(literally, "needle memorial service"). An annual event originating in the Edo period (1600–1868). On 8 February or 8 December, or both days in some districts, women take a day off from their sewing chores and collect all their old needles. Sticking them into cakes of *tōfu* (bean curd) or of *konnyaku* (a paste made from the root of a plant called devil's tongue), they pray for the repose of the needles, improvement in their sewing skills, and safety from injury while sewing. The details of the ceremony differ according to region, and recently the majority of the participants have been tailors or those learning Japanese-style dressmaking.

Harima Sea

(Harima Nada). Part of the INLAND SEA. Bounded by western Honshū (Hyōgo Prefecture) on the north, northeastern Shikoku (Tokushima and Kagawa prefectures) on the south, and the islands of Awajishima on the east and Shōdoshima on the west. Formerly a fine fishing ground, these waters have become polluted in recent years due to land reclamation and industrial development in the area. The sea forms part of the INLAND SEA NATIONAL PARK. Length: approximately 60 km (37 mi); width: approximately 40 km (25 mi); average depth: 40 m (131 ft); area: approximately 2,500 sq km (965 sq mi).

Harinoki Pass

(Harinoki Tōge). Located on the border of Nagano and Toyama prefectures, central Honshū. It is on a trans-Northern Alps route, from Ōmachi in Nagano Prefecture to the Kurobe and Toyama regions in Toyama Prefecture. In former days, salt and other commodities were transported over the pass. Altitude: 2,541 m (8,334 ft).

Harris, Merriman Colbert (1846–1921)

American Methodist missionary to Japan and Korea. Born in Beallsville, Ohio, and a graduate of Allegheny College, in 1873 he became American Consul to Hakodate while serving as the first Protestant missionary to Hokkaidō. There he baptized a number of students at the Sapporo Agricultural College, including NITOBE INAZŌ and UCHIMURA KANZŌ, and began what matured into a lifelong acquaintance with another Christian student, Chinda Sutemi (1856–1929), a diplomat. Harris returned to America in 1898 to work with Japanese immigrants in San Francisco until he became a bishop, first in Japan and then Korea, from 1904 to 1916. His acceptance of Japan's colonial policies helped him become, for his time, the foreigner most decorated by the Japanese government. Although they considered both Harris and his wife Flora Best (1850–1909) mistaken in their attitude toward government policies, men like UEMURA MASAHISA and Uchimura respected them. Uchimura wrote that "probably no missionary to Japan . . . is remembered by Japanese with greater respect or affection." Harris wrote three books on Japan and its Christianity, and his wife did the first translation of the *Tosa nikki* (Tosa Diary) of KI NO TSURAYUKI into English. *John F. HOWES*

Harris, Thomas Lake (1823–1906)

American poet, socialist, and spiritualist. As "primate" of the Brotherhood of the New Life, Harris dominated this organization based on his own social and religious principles. Born in Fenny Stratford, England, he emigrated in 1828 with his parents to Utica, New York. After educating himself, Harris began an unorthodox Christian ministry. The death of his mother, two tragic marriages, belief in revelation, and friendship with Horace Greeley (1811–72), William H. Channing (1810–84), and George Ripley (1802–80) led him to formulate a blend of transcendentalism, universalism, and Swedenborgian theology. Beginning in 1854, Harris expounded his theories in verse in 40 volumes, proposing that man in his original state of grace had contained both sexes, and that man had once possessed a yoga-like ability to attune himself to the cosmos. To recapture their lost physical and spiritual perfection, Harris's followers engaged in sexual communion and breathing exercises in a socialist utopia.

Harris established the brotherhood in New York State, first at Wassaic in 1861, then at Amenia in 1863, and at Brocton in 1867. Journeys to Great Britain in 1859 and 1865 attracted wealthy followers, principally Laurence OLIPHANT, a former diplomat to Japan. Because of Oliphant, who promoted Harris as a "living Confucius," some 20 Japanese entered the brotherhood, although most eventually returned to Japan. Among them the five most notable were Hatakeyama Yoshinari (1843–76), later president of Tōkyō Kaisei Gakkō (a predecessor of Tōkyō University); Ichiki Kanjūrō, commonly known as Mitsumura Junzō (1842–1919) later an admiral in the Japanese navy; and MORI ARINORI, Samejima Hisanobu (1846–80), and Yoshida Kiyonari (1845–91), all future ambassadors. A sixth member, ARAI ŌSUI, transmitted Harris's ideas to Japan, and a seventh, NAGASAWA KANAYE, became Harris's lieutenant and heir.

In 1875 Harris moved with selected followers to Santa Rosa, California, where he established a new colony named Fountain Grove. There the utopians prospered by making wine, but scandal drove Harris into retirement in 1892, although the brotherhood survived under Nagasawa until 1934. Despite his belief that he was immortal, Harris died on 23 March 1906. *Joseph W. SLADE*

Harris, Townsend (1804–1878)

New York merchant and first United States consul general in Japan. Active in public service and local Democratic Party politics in New York, Harris had helped to found the Free Academy, a predecessor of the City College of New York, while serving as president of the Board of Education. In 1849, following a quarrel with his older brother over their business partnership, he left home to explore trading possibilities in the Pacific and eastern Asia. Between 1849 and 1855 Harris lived in or visited several of the Chinese treaty ports and coastal cities of Southeast Asia, acquiring extensive knowledge of the region and becoming widely acquainted with diplomats, merchants, and missionaries.

Disappointed in his quest for an important consular post in China in 1854, he successfully lobbied the Democratic administration of Franklin Pierce for appointment as the first consul general at Shimoda, a post established as a result of the KANAGAWA TREATY. He arrived in Japan in August 1856 after a short mission to Siam (now Thailand). Under instructions from the president and secretary of state to secure a full commercial treaty with Japan, Harris and his secretary-interpreter Henry HEUSKEN, a young immigrant from the Netherlands, spent 14 frustrating months in their temple headquarters in Shimoda, closely watched by Japanese guards and able to negotiate only a convention with lesser officials. They were joined in June 1857 by two Japanese women, recruited ostensibly as servants. Whatever the truth, the legend of TŌJIN OKICHI, the beautiful courtesan forced into liaison with the "barbarian" envoy for the sake of her country, was born and became in Japan as much a part of the Harris story as diplomacy.

In December 1857, the Tokugawa shogunate, wary of commercial ties and caught in the throes of a succession crisis, reluctantly granted Harris a shogunal audience at Edo Castle, where he presented his credentials and delivered the president's letter. By exploiting the concurrent efforts of the Dutch to acquire commercial concessions and the Anglo-French punitive expedition against China (the so-called *Arrow* War), Harris secured a draft treaty the following February. When the senior councillor HOTTA MASAYOSHI was unable to win prior approval from the imperial court in Kyōto—an increasingly significant force in national politics—II NAOSUKE, a wealthy and powerful *daimyō*, was given the title of *tairō* (great elder), reserved for times of emergency, and arranged for the formal signing of the Japanese-American Treaty of Amity and Commerce (HARRIS TREATY) at Edo (now Tōkyō) on 29 July 1858. Taking effect in July 1859, the treaty set the pattern for commercial agreements (see ANSEI COMMERCIAL TREATIES) with other Western nations and helped intensify agitation against the shogunate.

Promoted to minister resident in June 1859, Harris promptly set up the United States legation at a temple in Edo but yielded to Japanese officials when they insisted on substituting the village of Yokohama for Kanagawa as one of the open ports. Although this change was motivated by a desire to keep the foreigners at a safer distance, Yokohama had the greater potential as a harbor and had rapidly developed into an important trading center. Remaining in Japan until 1862, he encouraged the shogunate's plans to send an embassy to Washington (see UNITED STATES, MISSION OF 1860 TO) and assisted local authorities in framing the regulations necessary for the establishment of foreign residence and facilitation of international trade. These were years of violence, including Ii's assassination, the burning of legations and other foreign property, assaults on foreigners and their Japanese employees, and the murder of Heusken in January 1861. Having become increasingly knowledgeable about Japan's political problems and appreciative of its culture, Harris stayed in Edo while other diplomats fled to safety in Yokohama; he later supported a request by the shogunate to delay the opening of Edo and Ōsaka, but only after it had paid a substantial indemnity to Heusken's mother. In ill health and unhappy with the ascendancy of the Republican Party back home, Harris resigned his post and left Japan in May 1862 for New York, where he retired from public life and only occasionally commented on Japanese-American relations.

——— Townsend Harris, *The Complete Journal of Townsend Harris, First American Consul and Minister to Japan,* ed Mario Cosenza (1930, rev ed 1959). John McMaster, "Alcock and Harris, Foreign Diplomacy in Bakumatsu Japan," *Monumenta Nipponica* 22 (1967). Oliver Statler, *Shimoda Story* (1969). *Marlene J. Mayo*

Harris Treaty

First commercial treaty between Japan and the United States, signed on 29 July 1858. Also known as the Nichibei Shūkō Tsūshō Jōyaku (United States–Japan Treaty of Amity and Commerce). The American consul general, Townsend HARRIS, arrived in Shimoda in August 1856 with the purpose of securing provisions for free trade, which the KANAGAWA TREATY, signed in 1854, lacked. On the grounds that the earlier treaty did not authorize his visit, the Tokugawa authorities met Harris with hostility. He persisted, however, and finally, in early December 1857, Harris had an audience with the shōgun in Edo (now Tōkyō). Thereafter, with a skillful blend of cogent reasoning, conciliation, and veiled threats, he negotiated with shogunal representatives HOTTA MASAYOSHI, INOUE KIYONAO, and IWASE TADANARI, and by 25 February 1858 he had secured a draft treaty.

Before signing the treaty, Hotta wished to obtain imperial approval in order to silence anticipated opposition to the shogunate's decision, but the emperor would not give it. Uncertain how to proceed, and beset by internal problems as well, the shogunate in early June appointed II NAOSUKE as *tairō* (great elder) in full control of the government. Harris now reminded the shogunate of the Anglo-French defeat of China in the so-called *Arrow* War earlier in 1858 and suggested that, unless Japan signed the American draft treaty, the European powers would soon impose far less favorable terms. Ii reluctantly conceded, and the treaty was signed without imperial sanction on 29 July aboard an American warship in Edo Bay (now Tōkyō Bay).

The 14-article treaty stipulated, *inter alia:* the exchange of diplomatic agents and consuls at each capital and at all the treaty ports, with freedom of interior travel; the opening of the ports of Nagasaki, Kanagawa (later changed to nearby Yokohama), Niigata, and Hyōgo (now Kōbe) in addition to Shimoda and Hakodate; the right of American citizens to reside in those ports, to trade without interference, to practice their religion, and to enjoy extraterritorial privileges; the opening of Edo and Ōsaka for trade on 1 January 1862 and 1 January 1863, respectively; and a moderate, fixed scale of import and export duties. In addition, the treaty provided for friendly mediation by the American president in the event of a dispute between Japan and any European power; the Japanese government's right to procure warships, steamers, and arms from the United States, and to employ American scientific advisers, military men, and artisans; and the prohibition of opium importation to Japan.

Within the next several weeks, the Netherlands, Russia, Great Britain, and France concluded similar treaties (see ANSEI COMMERCIAL TREATIES). The Harris Treaty was an unequal treaty in that extraterritoriality, conventional tariff, and the most-favored-nation provision benefited only the United States. For the next 10 years, the Harris Treaty, as well as the other treaties, proved to be a constant source of difficulties and embarrassment for the shogunate in both domestic and foreign affairs. Even after the MEIJI RESTORATION (1868), despite the original stipulation of 1872 as the earliest possible date for its revision, the treaty remained unchanged until 1899, when a new commercial treaty, concluded with the United States in 1894, went into effect (see UNEQUAL TREATIES, REVISION OF).

——— Townsend Harris, *The Complete Journal of Townsend Harris, First American Consul General and Minister to Japan,* ed Mario Cosenza (1930, rev ed 1959). W. G. Beasley, *Select Documents on Japanese Foreign Policy 1853–1868* (1955). *Shumpei Okamoto*

Hartmann, Carl Sadakichi (1867–1944)

Poet, writer, and art critic; an eccentric Bohemian once described by his friend John Barrymore as "presumably sired by Mephistopheles

out of Madame Butterfly." He was born on Dejima, in Nagasaki, the second son of Oskar Hartmann, a German trader and member of the German consulate. His mother, Osada, who was Japanese, died soon after his birth, and he was sent with his brother, Hidetaru, to his father's hometown of Hamburg, Germany, where he received his early education under the care of wealthy relatives. His rebellious temperament, however, caused alienation from his father, who had returned to Germany and remarried. After dropping out of a naval academy in Kiel, he was disinherited and shipped to the United States to the care of his great-uncle in Philadelphia.

Fending for himself during his teen years, he educated himself through extensive reading and started writing on his own. He established a curious friendship with the aging Walt Whitman, to whom he introduced himself in 1884. By the early 1890s he had wandered several times through Europe, where he associated with a variety of *fin-de-siècle* literary celebrities, most notably Stéphane Mallarmé and other French symbolists. His early efforts were largely devoted to introducing European literary movements to American audiences as well as to writing symbolist plays and short stories of his own. It was in Greenwich Village during the two decades before World War I, however, that his manifold talents and interests as an avant-garde artist developed most colorfully. He was a pioneer advocate of photography as an art, an enthusiastic promoter of new American art movements, particularly the imagists, and a connoisseur of traditional Japanese art and poetry, although it is doubtful if he was able to read Japanese. He was an anarchist sympathizer, joining in Emma Goldman's protest against the execution of the Japanese radical KŌTOKU SHŪSUI. Above all, he was a true eccentric, well deserving his assigned title of "King of Bohemia."

Until the mid-1920s, when he settled in California, he spent most of his life wandering about the country, giving numerous lectures on literature and the arts. In his final years he lived on the Morongo Indian reservation near Riverside, California, entertained as mascot by a Hollywood coterie and suffering from chronic asthma and deterioration from alcoholic excesses and from harassment by FBI officials, who suspected him of being a Japanese spy. He died on 21 November 1944 in St. Petersburg, Florida, while visiting one of his 13 children. His work and even his name had long been forgotten, but his contribution to modern American art is now being rediscovered by a small group of scholars. His major works include *Christ* (play, 1893), *Conversations with Walt Whitman* (1895), *Buddha* (play, 1897), *Shakespeare in Art* (1900), *A History of American Art* (1902, rev 1932), *Japanese Art* (1904), *The Whistler Book* (1910), *My Rubaiyat* (poetry, 1913), *Tanka and Haikai* (1915), and *The Last Thirty Days of Christ* (novel, 1920).

——— Gene Fowler, *Minutes of the Last Meeting* (1954). George Knox and Harry W. Lawton, ed, *Sadakichi Hartmann: Chrysanthemums* (1971). Ōta Saburō, *Hangyaku no geijutsuka* (1972). *Kokubo Takeshi*

Haruma wage

(Halma Translated). The first Dutch-Japanese dictionary published in Japan. Based on François Halma's (1653–1722) Dutch-French dictionary *Woordenboek der Nederduitsche en Fransche Taalen* (1708), it was compiled by INAMURA SAMPAKU and several other scholars of Rangaku (Dutch Learning), as WESTERN LEARNING was then known. The 27-volume work, with its more than 80,000 entries, took over 13 years to complete. It was printed at Edo (now Tōkyō) in 1796 in an edition of 30 copies. In 1810 an abridged and amended edition, *Yakuken* (Key to Translation), was put out by Fujibayashi Fuzan (1781–1836), a disciple of Sampaku. Another Dutch-Japanese dictionary, similarly based on the Halma work, was completed in 1815–16 under the editorship of Hendrik DOEFF, head of the Dutch trading post at Nagasaki. In distinction to the earlier "Edo Haruma," this work is known as the "Nagasaki Haruma." Both contributed greatly to the advance of Western studies in Japan.

Haruna, Lake

(Harunako). Crater lake in central Gumma Prefecture, central Honshū. Located on the summit of Mt. Haruna (HARUNASAN), this lake attracts tourists throughout the year. Ice skating is possible in winter. Area: 1.2 sq km (0.5 sq mi); circumference: 5 km (3 mi); depth: 13.3 m (43.6 ft); altitude: 1,084 m (3,556 ft)

Harunasan

Composite stratovolcano in central Gumma Prefecture, central Honshū. On the summit are Haruna Fuji (1,391 m; 4,562 ft), the central cone, and Lake Haruna, a crater lake to the west. On the crater rim is Kamongadake (1,448 m; 4,749 ft), the highest point. On the northeastern slope is the Ikaho Hot Spring resort. Harunasan forms Haruna Prefectural Park.

Harunobu (1725?–1770)

Full name Suzuki Harunobu. UKIYO-E artist. Harunobu's life, like that of many Japanese artists, is shrouded in uncertainty, but his place in the history of Japanese art is assured by his delicate and exquisitely designed color prints of women and other subjects. He was also the first major Japanese print artist to produce full-color woodcuts (nishiki-e); his work in this technique, using 4 to 10 pigments in addition to the black key-block outline, rendered obsolete the old two- and three-color prints.

Despite assertions to the contrary, there is no evidence that Harunobu originally came from Kyōto: his early works, datable to the early 1760s (one perhaps to 1757), are in the style of Edo (now Tōkyō), and most depict KABUKI actors in character for particular performances. There may be something to the old tradition that Harunobu was a pupil of Nishimura Shigenaga (1697?–1756), though Japanese scholars commonly question this. Most of the early prints, in the old two- or three-color technique, are in the small, narrow *hosoban* format. Harunobu made a group of prints in *mizu-e* technique (using a color outline), probably in 1764. In 1765 and 1766 he was the principal artist selected to design pictorial calendars (*egoyomi*) that were privately printed for groups of Edo connoisseurs, whose names frequently appear on the print together with or instead of that of the artist. The best of these calendars, and other prints commissioned by the same men, were in the new full-color technique and in the larger *chūban* format, and they led directly to the commercial production of *nishiki-e*.

Pictorial calendars earlier than 1765 are not unknown but are very rare. New research indicates that the sudden appearance of so many *egoyomi* in 1765 is connected with the opening of the shogunate observatory in Edo in the sixth month of that year and furthermore that Harunobu's patrons and friends included men who were close to the shōgun, Tokugawa Ieharu (1737–86). Many, if not most, of the 1765 calendars were apparently made between the fifth and eighth months for exchange at parties in the Ushigome district of Edo. Harunobu's best-known patron, Kikurensha Kyosen, was probably known personally to the shōgun, and his friend and neighbor HIRAGA GENNAI was an intimate of the shōgun's adviser TANUMA OKITSUGU. A youthful acquaintance of both Gennai and Harunobu was the scholar ŌTA NAMPO; other literary men whom Harunobu must have known can be identified. A host of small details corroborate this general picture, and it is clear that Harunobu's art was addressed partly to a *samurai* clientele, even if it cannot be shown that he himself was of samurai origin.

Between 1765 and his early death in 1770, Harunobu produced hundreds of single-sheet color prints, about 20 illustrated books (from a total of about 26), and a number of paintings. The single-sheet prints are mainly in the *chūban* or *hashira-e* (pillar-print) formats, are on a superior *hōsho* paper, and may use embossing, size, mica dusting, and other special techniques. They cover a wide variety of subjects: very many of them are whimsical illustrations of classical or sometimes contemporary poems; others depict courtesans or beauties of the day, notably the tea-stall girl Osen and the toothpick seller Ofuji; others are parodies of mythical and literary subjects; others show scenes of domestic life; and as with all *ukiyo-e* artists, there is also a group of erotic prints (SHUNGA).

Many of the prints belong to sets, some of which may have been issued originally as portfolios or albums. Thus there is a set of the Thirty-Six Poetic Geniuses (SANJŪROKKASEN), of which 32 designs survive; an incomplete series of the Hundred Poems (HYAKUNIN ISSHU), of which only 16 (possibly 19) designs can be distinguished; and smaller sets on such themes as the Eight Views of Ōmi (ŌMI HAKKEI) and parodies thereof; the Six Crystal (*tama*) Rivers (Mutamagawa); the SEVEN DEITIES OF GOOD FORTUNE (Shichifukujin); NŌ plays; the Three Evening Poems (Sanseki no Waka); the Seven Aspects of ONO NO KOMACHI (Nanakomachi); flowers of the four seasons; the Five Constancies (Gojō); the 12 months and their festivals; HAIKU poems from the *Goshikizumi* collection; and so on. Sometimes we find several versions of the same theme in more than one format. Harunobu often borrowed ideas for his designs from other print artists: from ISHIKAWA TOYONOBU, TORII KIYOHIRO, OKUMURA MASANOBU, and above all, the Kyōto book illustrator NISHIKAWA SUKENOBU. However, the final result usually bears the mark of his own personality, style and technique.

Harunobu's illustrated books, with two exceptions, are in black and white, and nearly all were published in Edo by Yamazaki Kimbei. Nine of them have a text or preface by someone who signed himself Tokusōshi, who also wrote or edited 17 other books, mostly educational works. Harunobu's own works include: *Ehon kagamigusa* (1761); *Ehon kokinran* (1763); *Ehon shogei no nishiki* (1763); *Ehon hanakazura* (1764); *Ehon sazareishi* (1766); *Ehon kotowazagusa* (1767); *Ehon misaogusa* (1767); *Ehon warabe no mato* (1767); *Ehon chiyo no matsu* (1767); *Ehon nishiki no tamoto* (1767); *Ehon haru no yuki* (1767); *Ehon yachiyogusa* (1768); *Ehon haru no tomo* (1768); *Ameuri Dohei den* (1769); *Ehon ukiyobukuro* (1770); *Yoshiwara bijin awase* (1770; 5 vols, in color); *Ehon haru no nishiki* (1771; in color); and *Kyōkun iroha no uta* (1775).

It is possible to date most of Harunobu's work quite finely, either on stylistic grounds or on external evidence. In the last year of his life his style changed somewhat, and the general effect is coarser. After his death imitations with his signature were made for a few years by SHIBA KŌKAN; reprints also appeared, using original blocks that had survived the Edo fire of 1772. Further reprints were made during the 19th century, and reproductions were also produced, especially from the Meiji period (1868–1912). All these have greatly magnified the difficulties of connoisseurship. Today prints and books by Harunobu are scattered throughout the world, and much comparative study of them remains to be done.

📖——Gakushū Kenkyūsha, ed, *Zaigai hihō: Suzuki Harunobu* (1972). Hayashi Yoshikazu, *Empon kenkyū: Harunobu* (1964). Jack Hillier, *Suzuki Harunobu* (1970). Kobayashi Tadashi, *Harunobu* (1970). David Waterhouse, *Harunobu and His Age* (1964). David Waterhouse, *The Harunobu Decade: A Catalogue of Woodcuts by Suzuki Harunobu and His Followers in the Museum of Fine Arts, Boston* (forthcoming). Yoshida Teruji, *Harunobu zenshū* (1942).

David B. WATERHOUSE

harvest rites → agricultural rites

Hase

Also known as Hatsuse. District in the eastern part of the city of Sakurai, northern Nara Prefecture, central Honshū. It developed as one of the POST-STATION TOWNS on the Ise Road (Ise Kaidō) and as a temple town around HASEDERA. It was a favorite resort of court nobles in the Heian period (794–1185). The temple is noted for cherry trees and tree peonies.

Hasebe Kotondo (1882–1969)

Anthropologist. Born in Tōkyō, Hasebe graduated from the Tōkyō University School of Medicine in 1906. After graduation he continued his study of anthropology and anatomy under the noted anthropologist ADACHI BUNTARŌ and lectured on anatomy at Kyōto and Tōhoku universities. He studied in Europe from 1921 to 1922, principally at Munich University in Germany. In 1939 he established the first full-scale department of anthropology in Japan within the Faculty of Science at Tōkyō University and concentrated on the study and teaching of comprehensive anthropology centered on morphological studies. He excavated shell mounds and carried out extensive anthropological studies on the human skeletal remains from burial mounds. Hasebe held that Jōmon-period (ca 10,000 BC–ca 300 BC) man was a direct ancestor of modern Japanese man and opposed the theory that the AINU were the direct ancestors of the Japanese. His research covered a wide range of subjects, including study of the human bones found near the city of Akashi (see JAPANESE PEOPLE, ORIGIN OF), islanders of Micronesia, and Peking man excavated at Zhoukoudian (Chou-k'ou-tien) in the suburbs of Beijing (Peking).

Hasedera

Head temple of the Buzan branch of the SHINGON SECT of Buddhism, located in the city of Sakurai, Nara Prefecture. According to tradition, the Hasedera, also called Chōkokuji, was founded by the monk Dōmyō on the order of Emperor Temmu (r 672–686). In 747, under the patronage of the emperor Shōmu (r 724–749), the cleric

GYŌGI is said to have consecrated the image of the Eleven-headed KANNON (Jūichimen Kannon), the bodhisattva who became the main object of worship at the temple. It originally belonged to the HOSSŌ SECT but in 1587 it was converted to a center of the Shingi (New) Shingon sect by the monk Sen'yo (1530–1604). During the Edo period (1600–1868) the temple thrived as a center of Buddhology. Over the centuries Hasedera suffered damage from numerous fires. The present image of Kannon dates from 1536, and the main hall from 1650. Hasedera is the 8th stopping place for pilgrims making the tour of the 33 Kannon temples in western Japan. The Buzan branch included 2,459 temples, including MURŌJI and GOKOKUJI, in 1977. *Stanley WEINSTEIN*

Hasegawa Kazuo (1908–　)

Actor. Born in Kyōto. Hasegawa joined Shōchiku Productions in 1927. He won recognition for his performance in the highly successful *Yukinojō henge* (1935, Yukinojō's Disguise; refilmed in 1963). As the sensuously handsome hero Yukinojō, he fascinated both male and female audiences. After World War II he appeared in *Jigokumon* (1953, Gate of Hell), which won the Grand Prix at the Cannes Film Festival. Altogether he has appeared in more than 300 films. His acting skills, however, have not won much acclaim. More recently he has turned to directing; *Berusaiyu no bara* (1974, The Rose of Versailles), which he directed for the all-female TAKARA-ZUKA KAGEKIDAN, was a great success. *Itasaka Tsuyoshi*

Hasegawa Kiyoshi (1891–1980)

Print designer; born in Yokohama. He studied line drawing with KURODA SEIKI and oil painting with OKADA SABURŌSUKE and FUJI-SHIMA TAKEJI. About 1912 he also began experimenting with woodcuts and copperplates. In 1918 he visited the United States and went on to Paris the following year, where he revived the art of *manière noire*, a kind of mezzotint. He was accepted as a member of the Salon d'Automne, was awarded the Légion d'Honneur in 1935, and received the French Order of Merit in 1966. Hasegawa is identified with the School of Paris style.

Hasegawa Nyozekan (1875–1969)

Social critic and journalist. Real name Hasegawa Manjirō. Born in Tōkyō. Hasegawa studied criminal law at Tōkyō Hōgakuin (now Chūō University) and graduated in 1898. He joined the staff of KUGA KATSUNAN's newspaper *Nihon* in 1903. In 1907 he moved to the periodical *Nihon oyobi nihonjin*, headed by MIYAKE SETSUREI. He then joined the newspaper *Ōsaka asahi shimbun* and established a reputation as a political liberal. In 1918, together with ŌYAMA IKUO, TORII SOSEN, and other staff members, he resigned his position in the wake of the ŌSAKA ASAHI HIKKA INCIDENT, in which the newspaper was censured by the government for printing a purportedly subversive article. The following year he and Ōyama began a periodical *Warera* (We), which was renamed *Hihan* (Critique) in 1930 and continued until 1934. Through his writings, which included novels and dramas, Hasegawa sought to provide a theoretical underpinning for political and social democracy and to combat the growing fanaticism of militarist cliques. He remained true to his principles throughout World War II, and in 1948 he was awarded the Order of Culture. His writings are collected in *Hasegawa Nyozekan senshū*, 8 vols, 1969–70. His *Nihonteki seikaku* has been translated as *The Japanese Character: A Cultural Profile* (1966, tr John Bester). *YAMARYŌ Kenji*

Hasegawa Roka (1897–1967)

Painter. Real name Hasegawa Ryūzō. Born in Kanagawa Prefecture. In 1921 after graduating from the Tōkyō Bijutsu Gakkō (now Tōkyō University of Fine Arts and Music), he went to France and studied the technique of fresco. He returned to Japan in 1927 and showed works in the exhibitions of the Imperial Academy and the Japan Art Institute. After World War II he produced, in addition to Japanese-style paintings, fresco and mosaic wall-paintings. In 1949 he executed a wall-painting for the St. Francis Xavier Memorial Church in the city of Kagoshima, Kyūshū. In 1950 he went to Italy and in 1955 completed a fresco wall-painting for a hall in the town of Civitavecchia commemorating 16th-century Japanese Christian martyrs (see TWENTY-SIX MARTYRS), for which he was named an honorary citizen of Rome. In 1964 he completed a three-part wall-painting entitled *Chikara, bi, yūkyū* (Strength, Beauty, and Eternity) for the National Athletic Stadium in Tōkyō. He also painted a number of wall-paintings in other parts of the country. He died in 1967 while visiting Italy at the invitation of Pope Paul VI.

Hasegawa school

A school of painters founded by HASEGAWA TŌHAKU (1539–1610). Short-lived and with few adherents, the Hasegawa school survived the death of its founder by only a generation. Judging from documentary evidence and works attributed to Tōhaku and his disciples, it is clear that Tōhaku and his followers were in competition with KANŌ SCHOOL artists and with UNKOKU TŌGAN and KAIHŌ YŪSHŌ as well, for they all specialized in the Chinese academic style of painting *(kanga)*.

The Hasegawa school was probably located in Kyōto in or near Hompōji, a Nichiren sect temple affiliated with Tōhaku's family temple in Sakai, near Ōsaka. Tōhaku, Tōgan, and Yūshō all studied painting under Kanō masters, but rather than take the Kanō name they sought and received commissions as independent artists specializing in Chinese themes and styles. Large-scale works involving many rooms of sliding-wall paintings *(fusuma-e)* required group effort. Tōhaku, his son Kyūzō (1568–93), and perhaps other disciples are thought to have collaborated on such paintings, including those at the CHISHAKUIN in Kyōto, which were executed in 1592 for the Toyotomi family.

Records indicate that Tōhaku had at least four artist sons: Kyūzō, Sōtaku and Sakon (both active before 1650), and Sōya (d 1667). The school appears to have disappeared by the end of the 17th century, although some later artists in the Kanō ranks had the Hasegawa surname, like Hasegawa Yōshin (d 1726), and may have been related. *Glenn T. WEBB*

Hasegawa Shin (1884–1963)

Writer of POPULAR FICTION and drama; known for his historical novels and plays dealing with *samurai* and gamblers. Born Hasegawa Shinjirō in Yokohama, Kanagawa Prefecture (he later took his pen name Shin as his legal name), he was only three when his father, a building contractor, went bankrupt, necessitating the dispersal of the entire household. He was separated from his mother, and his subsequent longing for her was to be a basic theme of many of his works. As a youth he was forced to take a variety of menial jobs, but always found time to study on his own. Fond of the theater, Hasegawa started writing reviews, and as a consequence he was invited to join the staff of the newspapers *Japan Gazette* and MIYAKO SHIMBUN. He also began to write fiction at about this time, and the recognition he won with his first published work, the story "Yomo-sugara kengyō" (1924), enabled him to devote himself to writing as a full-time occupation.

In 1928 Hasegawa's play *Kutsukake Tokijirō* brought a new approach to the *matatabi-mono*, a popular literary genre portraying the world of gamblers and gangsters. An important Hasegawa character is the loner who cuts loose from the traditional OYABUN-KOBUN (boss-follower) ties to make his own way, and to the traditional codes and norms of the Japanese underworld Hasegawa adds the new elements of wanderlust and individual feelings.

His most famous *matatabi-mono* work, the play *Mabuta no haha* (1930, Mother in My Dreams) centers on the outlaw Bamba no Chū-tarō. Separated from his mother at 5 and losing his father at 12, Chūtarō goes to Edo (now Tōkyō) and makes a living as a henchman for gambling bosses. Sustaining him throughout his solitary wanderings is the image of his mother; he always carries money with him so that he may help her in the event of a chance meeting. Many years later, he is finally reunited with his mother and younger sister, who now own a large restaurant, but the mother is cold and aloof. Suspecting that her gangster son has come to seize her money, she rejects him. The deeply hurt Chūtarō leaves, but resolves to continue cherishing the image of the mother that he has held up to now. Meanwhile his sister appeals to her mother to change her mind. Full of remorse, the mother runs after Chūtarō. The curtain falls as we see Chūtarō turn his back to his mother, who is calling him from a distance. This play revealed the author's own longing for his mother, and as a result of its performance, Hasegawa was reunited with her in 1933. The play was later given a second ending, with a reconciliation between mother and son. *Matatabi-mono* soon became popular material for movies and popular songs.

Another *matatabi-mono* drama by Hasegawa, *Ippon-gatana dohyōiri* (1931, A One-Sworded Outlaw Enters the Ring) celebrates the beauty of *ninjō* (human feeling; see GIRI AND NINJŌ) in a world of Robin Hood-like outlaws. The protagonist, an orphan named Komagata Mohei, aspires to a career as a *sumō* wrestler, but fails. Feeling sorry for the penniless and hungry Mohei, Otsuta, a prostitute, offers him money. Ten years later Mohei, who is now a professional gambler, meets Otsuta, impoverished and at the mercy of gangsters. He gives her a large sum of money, explaining that it is "a small token of gratitude from someone who once hoped to be a champion *sumō* wrestler." Popular from the start, the play is still widely performed.

Hasegawa also dealt with revenge, an important theme in popular literature. A representative work is *Araki Mataemon* (1936–37). In writing about the vendetta at Iga Ueno, Mie Prefecture, a favorite topic of traditional storytellers, Hasegawa did extensive research on the feudal code of revenge and on the antagonism between *hatamoto* (direct vassals of the Tokugawa shogunate) and *daimyō*. His *Nihon katakiuchi isō* (1961, Different Faces of Revenge in Japan) is also notable.

In contrast to many writers of popular fiction who cater to changing public tastes, Hasegawa consistently took critical and at times defiant stands. In his *Sagara Sōzō to sono dōshi* (1940, Sagara Sōzō and His Comrades), he depicted the unsavory underside of the MEIJI RESTORATION of 1868, going against the accepted view of that event. After World War II, when Japan's treatment of prisoners of war was being criticized throughout the world, Hasegawa painstakingly researched Japan's military history from the 7th century to 1945, at the same time attempting to define the concept of *ninjō*. The result of this labor was his monumental *Nihon horyo shi* (1949–50, A Study of Japan's Prisoners of War), in which he sought to explain the Japanese attitude toward war captives in its historical context.

Aside from giving a fresh impetus to popular literature with his focus on *giri* (duty) and *ninjō* from the viewpoint of the common people, Hasegawa also served as a mentor for many popular writers, including YAMATE KIICHIRŌ, MURAKAMI GENZŌ, YAMAOKA SŌHACHI, Togawa Yukio (b 1912), and Hiraiwa Yumie (b 1932). Following his death, the Shin'yōkai, an organization to promote literature and its advancement, was established in his memory. The Hasegawa Shin Prize was also established.

📖——Satō Tadao, *Hasegawa Shin ron* (1975). Asai Kiyoshi

Hasegawa Shirō (1909–　)

Novelist, poet. Born in Hakodate, Hokkaidō. Brother of the novelist HAYASHI FUBŌ (a pen name). Graduate of Hōsei University, where he taught German literature after World War II. He was taken prisoner in Manchuria at the end of World War II by the Soviet army and sentenced to five years at hard labor in a Siberian prisoner-of-war camp. Drawing from these experiences, he wrote *Shiberiya monogatari* (1951–52), which is remarkable for its emotional restraint and intellectual style. He is also known for his poetry and translations of such Western authors as Samuel Beckett, Bertolt Brecht, and Franz Kafka.

Hasegawa Tai (1842–1912)

Medical educator and administrator. Born in Echigo Province (now part of Niigata Prefecture). Hasegawa studied Western medical science under Tsuboi Hōshū and Satō Shōchū (1827–82). He was responsible for founding Daigaku Tōkō, a predecessor of the present Faculty of Medicine of Tōkyō University. In 1876 he established the Saisei Gakusha, a private medical school, in Hongō, Tōkyō, which trained many physicians. In 1878 Hasegawa entered the Home Ministry and worked under NAGAYO SENSAI, the first director of its Bureau of Public Health; he was appointed director of the bureau in 1898. He became a member of the House of Representatives in the first general election of 1890. Sōda Hajime

Hasegawa Tenkei (1876–1940)

Literary critic and scholar. Real name Hasegawa Seiya. Born in Niigata Prefecture. Graduate of Tōkyō Semmon Gakkō (now Waseda University). A writer for the journal *Taiyō*, he translated and introduced to Japan many Western works. Although his criticism lacks consistency, he is remembered as one of the earliest theoreticians of Japanese literary NATURALISM. In an article entitled "Genjitsu bakuro no hiai" (1908, The Pain of Exposing Reality), he wrote

Hasegawa Tōhaku

Detail from *Pine Trees*, a pair of six-panel folding screens painted around 1600. Ink on paper. Each screen 155.7 × 346.9 cm. Seals of artist. Tōkyō National Museum. National Treasure.

that the true purpose of literature is to lay bare reality in all its darkness and ugliness. The title of this essay became the motto for the naturalist movement, which reached its zenith around 1910.

Hasegawa Tōhaku (1539–1610)

Painter. Founder of the HASEGAWA SCHOOL of painting. Records suggest that his original family name was Okumura, but that he was adopted by the Hasegawa, a family of dyers in Noto Province (now part of Ishikawa Prefecture). He is said to have studied KANŌ SCHOOL painting in Kyōto under Kanō Shōei (1519–92) or KANŌ EITOKU. The earliest extant dated painting bearing Tōhaku's signature is an ink painting of a dragon at the Kyōto temple Daitokuji, done in 1589. Not much is known about Tōhaku's life and work before this time, and scholars are not in agreement concerning the works sometimes attributed to the "young Tōhaku."

Tōhaku considered himself the successor of SESSHŪ TŌYŌ, a claim that is reputed to have been challenged by a rival, UNKOKU TŌGAN. Tōhaku received many commissions from Daitokuji, as well as from the Toyotomi, Tokugawa, and other powerful military families, and was awarded the priestly title *hōgen*. Until the present century, Tōhaku was known mainly for his INK PAINTING, often depicting monkeys or gibbons, of the sort done by Zen priests since the 13th century. He is credited with the pair of six-fold *Pine Trees*, screens now in the Tōkyō National Museum. Tōhaku's views on Chinese ink painting appear in the *Tōhaku gasetsu*, a document written around 1592 by the priest Nittsū, the abbot of Hompōji in Kyōto, Tōhaku's ancestral temple.

In the early 1930s, art historians added a sizable body of large-scale polychrome works to Tōhaku's known oeuvre, usually by transferring the attributions from Eitoku or KANŌ SANRAKU, the two great Kanō-school masters of Tōhaku's day. All of these works are decorative sliding-wall paintings in Kyōto temples. The famous group of paintings in color and gold leaf at Chishakuin had been attributed to Tōhaku in the late 18th century but was later claimed as the work of the better-known Sanraku; the Tōhaku attribution is generally accepted today. Stylistic analysis of the Chishakuin paintings has focused on the unique way that Tōhaku and his sons Kyūzō and Sōya painted rock formations. On that basis, the rooms of paintings at Sambōin and Myōrenji have likewise been assigned Hasegawa authorship.

As for important monochromatic ink paintings, scholars have attributed a large number to Tōhaku. The earliest may be the one now housed in the Shōden'in Shoin, formerly a building within the temple Kenninji in Kyōto but now located at Urakuen, a park near Nagoya. Among others, the ink paintings at Entokuin, Kōdaiji; a room of landscape paintings at Rinkain, Myōshinji; and the wall paintings at Tenjuan, Nanzenji, are thought to be by Tōhaku, as are the illustrations of famous anecdotes concerning four Chinese Zen priests on the sliding walls of two rooms in the Shinjuan, Daitokuji, dated to 1601.

Hasekura Tsunenaga —— Portrait

Believed to have been painted in Madrid or Rome. Detail. Oil on canvas. 80.8 × 64.5 cm. 1615 or 1616. Sendai City Museum.

—— Doi Tsugiyoshi, *Hasegawa Tōhaku/Nobuharu dōjin setsu* (1964). Doi Tsugiyoshi, *Hasegawa Tōhaku*, no. 87 of *Nihon no bijutsu* (August, 1973). Takeda Tsuneo, *Tōhaku; Yūshō*, vol 9 of *Suiboku bijutsu taikei* (Kōdansha, 1973).　　　　Glenn T. WEBB

Hasekura Tsunenaga (1571–1622)

Retainer of DATE MASAMUNE; also known as Hasekura Rokuemon. From 1613 to 1620 Hasekura led an embassy to Mexico City, Madrid, and Rome; he was the first official Japanese envoy to visit the American continent. In July 1611 an embassy under Sebastian VIS-CAINO brought back from New Spain (Mexico) the Japanese merchants who had traveled there with Rodrigo VIVERO DE VELASCO in the previous year. This inspired Date Masamune, the *daimyō* of Sendai (now Miyagi Prefecture), to send an exploratory embassy to seek trade with Mexico and southern Europe. Encouraged by the Franciscan Luis Sotelo, whom he had rescued from shogunal persecution, Date named Hasekura, a veteran of the INVASIONS OF KO-REA IN 1592 AND 1597, as his representative.

Under Spanish supervision, Japanese shipwrights built a galleon at the small fishing village of Tsukinoura, north of Sendai; on 27 October 1613 (Keichō 18.9.14) Hasekura, at the head of a party of 180 Japanese, set out for Acapulco, accompanied by Sotelo and what was left of the Mexican mission. Ahead lay audiences with the Mexican viceroy in March 1614, with the Spanish monarch Philip III the following January, and with Pope Paul V in October 1615. Although he was baptized as Felipe Francisco in Madrid, Hasekura seems to have savored more the secular aspects of his mission. He received Roman citizenship, toured the Italian city republics, attempted to obtain fiscal exemptions for Japanese goods imported into Spanish territory, and negotiated the sale of his ship to the authorities in Mexico. During his absence of almost seven years, the Tokugawa shogunate (1603–1867) had consolidated its control over the outlying daimyō, and Spain had closed the Mexican Pacific coast to foreign shipping; thus, his mission failed of its aims. After two years in the Philippines, Hasekura returned to Japan in September 1620 (Genna 6.8). His arrival coincided with the prohibition of Christianity in the Date domain, but he was given special dispensation from renouncing his faith.

—— Lothar Knauth, *Confrontación Transpacífica* (1972).
　　　　Lothar G. KNAUTH

Hashiguchi Goyō (1880–1921)

Painter and printmaker. Born in Kagoshima Prefecture, he studied NIHONGA (Japanese-style painting) with HASHIMOTO GAHŌ. In

1905 Goyō graduated at the top of his class from the Western-style painting division of the Tōkyō Bijutsu Gakkō (now Tōkyō University of Fine Arts and Music). He entered the first Bunten exhibition in 1907. He achieved overnight success in 1911 by winning a poster contest; he subsequently abandoned oil painting and threw himself wholeheartedly into a study of woodblock prints (see UKIYO-E; MODERN PRINTS). By 1915 he was the central figure in the Taishō-period (1912–26) revival of printmaking, although his prints are relatively few and are mainly *bijinga*, or pictures of beautiful women. Goyō was closely associated with the literary world and achieved further distinction as a designer of dust jackets and magazine covers, including the covers for NATSUME SŌSEKI's *Wagahai wa neko de aru* (1905, I Am a Cat) and TANIZAKI JUN'ICHIRŌ's *Atsumono* (1912).

Hashikuiiwa

Group of rocks in southern Wakayama Prefecture, central Honshū. These huge pillar-like rocks extend in a line from a point off the coast of the town of Kushimoto to the island of Ōshima opposite. The pillars were formed by the erosion of dolerite by the sea. They are a natural monument and one of the scenic spots in Yoshino–Kumano National Park.

Hashima

City in southern Gifu Prefecture, central Honshū, between the rivers Kisogawa and Nagaragawa. Hashima is known for its woolen cloth cottage industry. It is also a grain-producing area. Pop: 56,975.

Hashima

Small mining island west of Nagasaki Peninsula, Nagasaki Prefecture, northwestern Kyūshū. In 1890 the Mitsubishi Mining Company (now Mitsubishi Mining and Cement Co, Ltd) started mining coal approximately 1,000 m (3,280 ft) under the sea here. The mine once reached an annual output of 250,000 metric tons (275,600 short tons) and the population density climbed to 50,000 per sq km, but the mine closed in 1974 and the island is now uninhabited. Area: 0.1 sq km (0.04 sq mi).

Hashimoto

City in northeastern Wakayama Prefecture, central Honshū, on the river Kinokawa. At the intersection of the highways Yamato and Kōya Kaidō, Hashimoto developed as a regional transportation center. It is known for its bamboo ware, and particularly its fishing rods. Because of its proximity to Ōsaka, it has recently become a residential suburb for commuters. Pop: 35,922.

Hashimoto Gahō (1835–1908)

One of the last KANŌ SCHOOL painters. Born in Edo (now Tōkyō), he was the son of the painter Hashimoto Seien Yōhō, who served the Matsudaira family (see TOKUGAWA FAMILY). Gahō studied under Kanō Shōsen'in. After mastering Kanō-school techniques, he set up his own studio in 1860. In the difficult years just before and after the Meiji Restoration (1868), he was barely able to support himself and earned what income he could by painting on fans and by drawing maps for the Naval Academy. In the early 1880s, in the first and second Domestic Painting Competitive Exhibitions (Naikoku Kaiga Kyōshinkai), he won silver medals. In 1884, on OKAKURA KAKUZŌ's recommendation, Gahō became the chief professor of painting at the Tōkyō Bijutsu Gakkō (now Tōkyō University of Fine Arts and Music) at its inception in 1889. In 1898 when the school's director, Okakura, left to found the JAPAN FINE ARTS ACADEMY (Nihon Bijutsuin), Gahō accompanied him to become the principal teacher at the academy. He taught there until his death. In 1890 he was among the first to be named an artist for the imperial household (*teishitsu gigeiin*). He competed successfully in many exhibitions and was a judge at some major fine arts exhibitions.

Gahō's style owes much to the work of KANŌ HŌGAI. Although Gahō was basically a traditionalist, Western-derived spatial depth and atmospheric qualities, as well as considerable attention to shading and color, are apparent in his paintings. His best-known works are *White Clouds and Autumn Leaves* (1890), *Dragon and Tiger* (1895), and *Rinzai Admonishing a Pupil* (1897). He had many important pupils, including HISHIDA SHUNSŌ, SHIMOMURA KANZAN, KAWAI GYOKUDŌ, and YOKOYAMA TAIKAN.

　　　　Frederick BAEKELAND

Hashimoto Kansetsu (1883–1945)

Japanese-style painter. Born in Kōbe, the son of the Confucian scholar and literati painter Hashimoto Kaikan. He first studied the MARUYAMA–SHIJŌ SCHOOL of painting and in 1903 became a disciple of the Kyōto literati painter TAKEUCHI SEIHŌ. Kansetsu developed an eclectic style, a blend of traditional literati painting (BUNJINGA), Maruyama–Shijō school realism, and elements of European impressionism, that was heralded by critics as the "new literati style." Among his most often depicted subjects are monkeys and Chinese historical themes. Although he was interested in Western-style painting (YŌGA) and visited Europe in 1921, he carried on his father's primary interest in China and classical Chinese literature and traveled to China more than 30 times. He was appointed a member of the Teikoku Bijutsuin (Imperial Fine Arts Academy) in 1935. His former residence in Kyōto, the Hakusa Sonsō, is now a museum open to the public.

Hashimoto Kingorō (1890–1957)

Army officer. Born in Okayama Prefecture. Graduated from the Army Academy in 1911 and the Army War College in 1920. An outspoken advocate of military expansion, he organized middle-echelon army officers of the Army General Staff Office and Army Ministry into a secret society called the SAKURAKAI in 1930, and is generally believed to have masterminded the abortive coups in March and October of the following year (see MARCH INCIDENT and OCTOBER INCIDENT, respectively). In the wave of personnel reassignments following the failed coup d'etat by army officers on 26 February 1936 (see FEBRUARY 26TH INCIDENT), he was put on reserve status. That same year he founded the profascist Dai Nippon Seinentō (Great Japan Youth Party). Upon the outbreak of the Sino-Japanese War in 1937, he was recalled to active duty to command an artillery regiment but was again retired for his part in firing on and capturing the British gunboat *Ladybird* (see LADYBIRD INCIDENT). In 1944 he was elected to the Diet as a candidate of the Dai Nippon Sekiseikai (Great Japan Loyalty Society), of which he was a founder. Tried as a class A war criminal by the Allied Powers after World War II (see WAR CRIMES TRIALS), he was sentenced to life imprisonment but released in 1955.

Hashimoto Sanai (1834–1859)

Physician and political reformer of the latter part of the Edo period (1600–1868). Born in the castle town of the Fukui or Echizen domain (now part of Fukui Prefecture); son of the domainal physician. By turns a doctor, educator, and political activist, he left a legacy little understood by his many adulators. Executed during the ANSEI PURGE, he was, by some, erroneously esteemed as a martyr of the campaign to topple the Tokugawa shogunate. On the contrary, he supported the shogunal system, advocating only limited reform.

At the age of 15 Hashimoto went to Ōsaka to study at a school of Western medicine run by OGATA KŌAN (1810–63). Early in 1852 he returned to Fukui, where he helped his father administer smallpox vaccinations and worked for the introduction of other European medical practices. Following his father's death late that year he became head of the Hashimoto family and in 1854 entered under the tutelage of Sugita Seikei (1817–59) and other Edo scholars for the study of European languages and the basic sciences, as well as medicine. He also studied the Chinese classics under the eminent sinologist Shionoya Tōin (1809–67) and met with FUJITA TŌKO (1806–55), the leading scholar of the MITO SCHOOL, and other intellectuals, from whom he gained insight into the contemporary political situation. Highly regarded by MATSUDAIRA YOSHINAGA (1828–90), the daimyō of Echizen, he was granted *samurai* status and in 1856 returned from Edo to head the domainal school, Meidōkan. He instituted reforms in the traditional Confucian education by emphasizing Western studies (*yōgaku*) and pragmatic studies (*jitsugaku*). Nevertheless, his chief concern was not the introduction of a system of thought based upon a European paradigm but the use of positivist methods in order to strengthen the shogunal system. In 1857 he was summoned to Edo (now Tōkyō) by Yoshinaga to help him promote reform of the shogunate. In 1858 Hashimoto was sent to Kyōto to seek backing among the court aristocracy for a movement urging the selection as shōgun of Hitotsubashi Yoshinobu (TOKUGAWA YOSHINOBU; 1837–1913), who planned to institute reforms. In June of the same year II NAOSUKE (1815–60), representative of the conservative element in the shogunate, was made great elder (*tairō*), and two months later the daimyō of the Kii domain (now Wakayama

Prefecture), Tokugawa Yoshitomi (TOKUGAWA IEMOCHI; 1846–66), was chosen to succeed the shōgun Tokugawa Iesada (1824–58). In July, pressed by the American diplomat Townsend HARRIS and without obtaining the perfunctory imperial permission, Naosuke signed the HARRIS TREATY, establishing diplomatic and commercial relations between the two countries. Supporters of Hitotsubashi Yoshinobu, though desirous of opening Japan, joined forces with the Kyōto aristocrats in decrying the development as a means of attacking Ii's faction. However, in an attempt to suppress opposition and to strengthen the dictatorial powers of the shogunate, Naosuke responded by instituting the Ansei Purge. Hitotsubashi Yoshinobu, Matsudaira Yoshinaga, and Hashimoto, among some hundred others who received varying punishments, were placed under house arrest. In November 1859 Hashimoto, an eloquent but relatively minor figure in the reform movement, was decapitated. In his thought Hashimoto combined two powerful intellectual traditions, Western studies and the nationalism of the Mito School, which were to supply theoretical support for the imperial restoration in 1868 and the sweeping reforms of the Meiji period (1868–1912).

📖 ——*Hashimoto Keigaku zenshū*, 2 vols (1943). George M. Wilson, "The Bakumatsu Intellectual in Action: Hashimoto Sanai in the Political Crisis of 1858," in A. M. Craig and D. H. Shively, ed, *Personality in Japanese History* (1970). Yamaguchi Muneyuki, *Hashimoto Sanai* (1962).   George M. WILSON

Hashimoto Shinkichi (1882–1945)

Linguist and Japanese grammarian. Born in Fukui Prefecture, graduated from Tōkyō University, majoring in linguistics, in 1906. He served as assistant to UEDA KAZUTOSHI (1867–1937) from 1909 until 1927, when he succeeded Ueda as professor of Japanese at Tōkyō University.

Hashimoto worked in the phonology, grammar, and historical development of Japanese. His most noted research was perhaps his account of Old Japanese vowels, based on the earliest systems of KANA. Though scholars like KEICHŪ (1640–1701), MOTOORI NORINAGA (1730–1801), and ISHIZUKA TATSUMARO (1764–1823) had anticipated the major discoveries, Hashimoto elaborated the framework for modern research in Old Japanese phonology. His investigation of the Christian literature of the 16th and 17th centuries similarly shaped the study of the Japanese at that period.

Hashimoto's grammatical system is based on the *bunsetsu* (phonological phrase), an attempt to substitute the approach of Ueda or SHIMMURA IZURU (1876–1967) for the more traditional grammar of YAMADA YOSHIO (1873–1958) or MATSUSHITA DAISABURŌ (1878–1935). He was responsible for the *Shin bunten bekki* (1931, 1936, 1938, 1939, Supplement to the New Grammar), the official school reference grammar established by the Ministry of Education. Thus his grammatical ideas enjoyed the widest possible distribution and remain influential to the present time. As professor at Tōkyō University, Hashimoto trained and inspired many of the linguists and grammarians who became prominent after World War II. See JAPANESE LANGUAGE STUDIES, HISTORY OF.   George BEDELL

Hashimoto Shinobu (1918–   )

Screenwriter. Born in Hyōgo Prefecture. He studied scenario writing with ITAMI MANSAKU. His first screenplay to be made into a movie was the celebrated RASHOMON (1950), written with and directed by KUROSAWA AKIRA. Following this Hashimoto collaborated on the team production of scripts for a number of other Kurosawa films, including IKIRU (1952, To Live), *Shichinin no samurai* (1954, SEVEN SAMURAI), *Kumonosujō* (1957, Throne of Blood), and *Kakushi toride no san akunin* (1958, The Hidden Fortress). The intensity with which Kurosawa's film characters come to life on the screen owes much to Hashimoto's screenplays. Deserving of special mention is his script for the acclaimed television drama *Watashi wa kai ni naritai* (A Clam Is What I Want to Be), whose dramatic impact turns on this single line spoken by the leading character, a soldier who is to be hanged for war crimes. Other films for which Hashimoto wrote the screenplays include SEPPUKU (1962), directed by KOBAYASHI MASAKI; *Shiroi kyotō* (1966, The White Tower), directed by YAMAMOTO SATSUO; *Nihon no ichiban nagai hi* (1967, Japan's Longest Day), directed by Okamoto Kihachi; and *Nihon chimbotsu* (1974, Japan Sinks), directed by Moritani Shirō.

ITASAKA Tsuyoshi

Hasuda

City in eastern Saitama Prefecture, central Honshū. The rivers Moto Arakawa and Ayasegawa and the Minumadai Canal flow through the district, making it an area ideal for rice and fruit. About 40 km (25 mi) from Tōkyō, it is rapidly being urbanized. Pop: 45,594.

hata → flags and banners

Hata family

Influential family or clan (UJI) of ancient Japan, descended from continental immigrants (KIKAJIN). According to family legend, its more important members were descendants of YUZUKI NO KIMI, who arrived from the Korean state of PAEKCHE around AD 400. He brought with him a large number of people, whose descendants became known as *hatahito*. The Hata are associated in early historical accounts with silkworm culture, weaving, and metallurgy (techniques they may have helped to introduce to Japan), as well as land development, supervision of government storehouses, and diplomatic service. By the end of the 5th century, members of the Hata family held the status title (KABANE) of *miyatsuko*, changed in the 7th century to *imiki*. Although branches of the Hata spread to many parts of Japan, their principal settlement was in the Kyōto basin, especially the Kadono area. Hata no Kawakatsu, a friend of the regent Prince SHŌTOKU, founded the temple KŌRYŪJI in the early 7th century; other family members are said to have founded the Matsunoo Taisha, the FUSHIMI INARI SHRINE, and the Hirano Jinja, all Shintō shrines in the Kyōto area. At the end of the 8th century the Hata provided financial assistance for the building of the new capital city HEIANKYŌ.

The name Hata is written with the character for the Qin (Ch'in) dynasty (221 BC–206 BC) of China, and some scholars believe that the Hata were, as they claimed, descendants of Chinese who had lived for many generations in Korea. The reason for the pronunciation *hata*, however, is unclear. Some ascribe it to the family's early association with textiles and, presumably, looms *(hata)*; others suggest an association with the Korean word meaning "ocean."

■ ———Hirano Kunio, "Hata no kenkyū," *Shigaku zasshi* 70.3-4 (1961). *William R.* CARTER

Hatakeyama family

Warrior family of Musashi Province (now Saitama', Tōkyō, and part of Kanagawa prefectures) in the Kamakura period (1185–1333). Although descended from the Kammu Heishi branch of the TAIRA FAMILY, HATAKEYAMA SHIGETADA helped MINAMOTO NO YORITOMO to destroy the Taira and became a powerful retainer (GOKENIN) of the Kamakura shogunate. In 1205 Shigetada's son was killed by the shogunal regent HŌJŌ TOKIMASA; Shigetada rose in rebellion but was killed, and his line was extinguished. His widow, however, who was a daughter of Tokimasa, married Ashikaga Yoshizumi, a descendant of the Seiwa Genji branch of the MINAMOTO FAMILY; he succeeded to the Hatakeyama domains and adopted their family name. In the following century the Hatakeyama helped ASHIKAGA TAKAUJI to found the Muromachi shogunate (1338–1573) and as shogunal kinsmen were made military governors (SHUGO) of several provinces. In 1398 Hatakeyama Motokuni became the first of his line to serve as shogunal deputy (KANREI). Violent conflicts over the family headship were one cause of the disastrous ŌNIN WAR (1467–77), after which the Hatakeyama never regained their power. Descendants fought under the national unifiers TOYOTOMI HIDEYOSHI and TOKUGAWA IEYASU and during the Edo period (1600–1868) served as masters of court ceremony (KŌKE).

Hatakeyama Museum

(Hatakeyama Kinenkan). Located in Tōkyō. The collection of the late Hatakeyama Issei, a descendant of the HATAKEYAMA FAMILY; housed in a handsome, contemporary Japanese-style building, opened in 1964. It includes Chinese and Japanese paintings, calligraphy, sculpture, metalwork, and ceramics; Japanese lacquer, tea-ceremony objects, and costumes; and Korean ceramics. The Japanese paintings range from those of the Muromachi period (1333–1568) to those in the RIMPA style; the ceramics, largely pieces for the tea ceremony, include Old SETO WARE, Shino and Oribe wares (see MINO WARE), and items by CHŌJIRŌ, HON'AMI KŌETSU,

KENZAN, and NONOMURA NINSEI. The Chinese section ranges from a Shang dynasty (2nd millennium BC) bronze to paintings attributed to Muqi (Mu-ch'i; J: MOKKEI), Zhao Chang (Chao Ch'ang), Liang Kai (Liang K'ai), and Yin Tuoluo (Yin T'o-lo). The museum publishes small but excellent catalogs for its quarterly exhibitions.

Laurance ROBERTS

Hatakeyama Shigetada (1164–1205)

Warrior of the early part of the Kamakura period (1185–1333); son of an estate *(shōen)* official of Hatakeyama in northern Musashi Province (now Saitama, Tōkyō, and part of Kanagawa prefectures). The HATAKEYAMA FAMILY were descended from a branch of the TAIRA FAMILY, and Shigetada initially fought against MINAMOTO NO YORITOMO; he soon submitted to him, however, and took a prominent part in Yoritomo's struggle against the Taira. He distinguished himself in the Battle of DANNOURA (1185), in which the Taira were finally destroyed, and served in the 1189 campaign against the ŌSHŪ FUJIWARA FAMILY, gaining Yoritomo's trust and respect. In 1205 his son was killed by the shogunal regent HŌJŌ TOKIMASA after a dispute with Hiraga Tomomasa (d 1205), a son-in-law of Tokimasa's second wife. Shigetada took up arms against the Hōjō and was killed in battle later that year. His exploits have been celebrated in popular literature; one story relates that while descending a precipitous slope during the Battle of Ichinotani (1184), Shigetada became concerned for the safety of his horse and threw the animal across his shoulders and carried it to the bottom.

hatamoto

(bannermen). Direct *samurai* retainers of the TOKUGAWA SHOGUNATE (1603–1867); about 5,000 in number, they occupied positions analogous to the officer corps in a standing army or the bureaucracy of a central government. Nearly all of the *hatamoto* were descendants of warriors who had helped TOKUGAWA IEYASU in establishing the shogunate. The *hatamoto* received from the shogunate annual stipends of at least 100 *koku* (1 *koku* = about 180 liters or 5 US bushels; see KOKUDAKA), the type of payment depending on rank (high-ranking *hatamoto* received their payment in the form of a fief, whereas low-ranking ones were paid directly in rice); if the stipend exceeded 10,000 *koku*, the recipient became a DAIMYŌ. GOKENIN or housemen outnumbered the *hatamoto* 3.5 to 1. These *gokenin*, who occupied various low-level military and bureaucratic positions, often under the *hatamoto*, were for the most part recipients of less than 100 *koku*.

Though the status of *hatamoto* could be revoked for such reasons as flagrant incompetence, commission of a serious crime, immorality, or habitual drinking, the status was in principle hereditary, as were the specific positions that the *hatamoto* held within the military or bureaucratic branches of the shogunal government. The military positions ranged from captain of the Great Guard (Ōban), which was usually occupied by a *hatamoto* of the 5,000-*koku* class, to unranked member of a less prestigious unit, assigned to guard various gates and ordnance depots. The civil positions ranged from grand chamberlain (SOBAYŌNIN), who worked directly under the RŌJŪ (senior councillors), often as their deputy, and held at least 5,000 *koku* in stipend, to financial or record clerk in charge of *gokenin* and other office personnel. A large majority of *hatamoto* held positions in the shogunal capital of Edo (now Tōkyō), but scores of others were assigned duties elsewhere, for example, as intendants (DAIKAN) or as guards at Sumpu Castle, the original headquarters of the Tokugawa family.

We can fairly say that the *hatamoto*, who remained loyal to the Tokugawa to the end, served the shogunate well and, in general, competently. An important reason was that, despite the practice of primogeniture, the *hatamoto*, in selecting heirs to their stipends, often designated a younger son to lead the lineage if he proved more capable than the eldest. At times an able son of another *hatamoto* or of a high-ranking samurai of another domain was chosen. From genealogical records of the second half of the Edo period (1600–1868) it has been established that in about 20 percent of the cases a younger son inherited his father's position and that in as many as 40 percent of the cases an adopted son succeeded a *hatamoto* who lacked male issue or had only unsuitable sons.

As was true for all samurai, the lives of the *hatamoto* grew increasingly difficult during the second half of the Edo period. One of the major problems facing the *hatamoto* was a decline in income relative to that of many merchants and even some peasants. Though their incomes in absolute terms remained higher than that of most commoners, they were forced to incur increasingly larger debts to employ subordinate assistants and servants in accordance with their station and to maintain their standards of living. The shogunate, facing increasing financial difficulties of its own, was in no position to increase *hatamoto* income. A second major problem was the difficulty of maintaining the morale of the *hatamoto,* who spent their days either practicing martial arts and performing ceremonial functions, or performing routine and increasingly circumscribed bureaucratic functions that they shared with a few other *hatamoto.* After the collapse of the shogunate in the MEIJI RESTORATION (1868), most *hatamoto* were reduced to living on inadequate stipends provided by the new government. Few of them rose to any position of significance in the Meiji government, ENOMOTO TAKEAKI, KATSU KAISHŪ, and a handful of others being exceptions.

Future research on the *hatamoto* must address two questions: Why did the *hatamoto,* despite the economic and morale problems just described, remain loyal to the shogunate to the end? And what were the social consequences of the increasing number of *hatamoto* children who were unable to succeed to their fathers' lineages?

📖——John W. Hall, *Tanuma Okitsugu* (1955). Kozo Yamamura, *A Study of Samurai Income and Entrepreneurship* (1974).

Kōzō YAMAMURA

hatamoto yakko

A type of *samurai* ruffian of the early part of the Edo period (1600–1868). YAKKO was a term for footmen and other attendants *(hōkōnin)* of samurai families, some of whom strove to compensate for their low rank by affecting extravagant costumes and coiffures, long facial hair, outsized swords, and swaggering behavior, after the manner of *kabukimono* (a word current since the last years of the 16th century and denoting "outlandish person," with some of the connotations of "swinger"). Some HATAMOTO (direct retainers of the Tokugawa shōgun) imitated this swaggering fashion and became known as *hatamoto yakko.* One reason for the phenomenon may have been the lack of opportunity, in the Tokugawa realm of peace, to demonstrate manliness by military valor; flaunting irregular behavior in order to show that one had "style" and a devil-may-care spirit became an alternative way of proving that one was a "real man" *(otoko o tateru;* hence *otokodate* is another term for this general type). Not content with this virile pose, *hatamoto yakko* organized gangs *(kumi)* and engaged in violence in the streets of Edo (now Tōkyō), on occasion coming into conflict with their townsman equivalents, the MACHI YAKKO. This brought down on them the wrath of the Tokugawa shogunate, which consistently sought to curb *kabukimono* as deviants who flouted its rules of social behavior. Among the best-known *hatamoto yakko,* Yamanaka Genzaemon (a member of the shogunal Great Guard, Ōban, with a stipend of 500 *koku*) was in 1645 ordered to disembowel himself for absence without leave and unruly behavior; Miura Kojirō (a notorious swaggerer nicknamed Yoshiya for "anything goes") was in 1663 put in confinement for causing a disturbance at the Sannō Festival; and the most celebrated of all, Mizuno Jūrōzaemon (a major *hatamoto* with a fief assessed at 3,000 *koku*) was the following year condemned to commit suicide for continued lawlessness and the temerity of appearing before the shogunal tribunal (Hyōjōshū) in improper attire. The shogunate thereby eliminated the *hatamoto yakko* phenomenon, and in 1686 there followed a general crackdown on *machi yakko,* but the various kinds of *otokodate* were immortalized in the popular theater. For instance, Mizuno Jūrōzaemon's murder of his *machi yakko* rival Banzuiin Chōbei, a historical incident that occurred in 1657, became the subject of the famous *kabuki* play *Kiwametsuki Banzui Chōbei* (1881) by Kawatake MOKUAMI. *George* ELISON

Hatano Kanji (1905–)

Psychologist. Born in Tōkyō, Hatano graduated from Tōkyō University. After teaching at various institutions, including Hōsei University, he became a professor at the Tōkyō Women's Higher School (now Ochanomizu Women's University) in 1947. He was president of the university from 1969 to 1971. Since the 1930s he has conducted a wide range of research in such areas as child development, written and visual communication, and audiovisual education. He has actively promoted the use of broadcasting for educational purposes and the idea of continuing education. His use of the theories of psychologists such as Jean Piaget has opened up new paths in the study of child development in Japan. *TAKAKUWA Yasuo*

Hatano Seiichi (1877–1950)

Scholar and specialist in the history of philosophy and the philosophy of religion. Hatano studied the history of Western philosophy with Raphael Koeber (1848–1923) at Tōkyō University, where he first concentrated on Spinoza and then turned to reading the Greek philosophers in the original. During a period of study in Germany he attended the lectures of C. G. A. von Harnack (1851–1930) and E. Troeltsch (1865–1923) and was deeply influenced by their ideas on Christianity and Christian theology. He embarked upon a historical study of the Bible and ultimately came to establish his own philosophy of religion. Instead of attempting to study religion through an objective philosophical inquiry into the object of faith (God), Hatano sought to explain the religious experience—the highest experience attained by man—as it related organically and psychologically to other life experiences. The idea of eternity was first introduced academically to Japan in his book *Toki to eien* (1943, Time and Eternity). After a long tenure as professor at Kyōto University, he became president of Tamagawa University. *TANIKAWA Atsushi*

Hata Sahachirō (1873–1938)

Bacteriologist. Born in Shimane Prefecture, Hata completed a full medical course at the Third Higher School in Kyōto. He studied epidemic diseases under KITAZATO SHIBASABURŌ at the Institute for Infectious Diseases in Tōkyō. He studied immunology at the Koch Institute, Berlin, and chemotherapy at the National Institute for Experimental Therapeutics in Frankfurt am Main, Germany. He then studied chemotherapeutics under Paul Ehrlich, and in 1909 he described the chemotherapeutic effects of Ehrlich's 606 (salvarsan or arsphenamine) on syphilis. Hata and Ehrlich thus opened up a new avenue of chemotherapy. After returning to Japan, he took part in establishing the Kitazato Institute and was subsequently appointed one of the directors and vice-president of the institute and professor at Keiō University. *SŌDA Hajime*

Hata Toyokichi (1892–1956)

Producer, translator, writer. Born in Tōkyō. Hata studied German literature at Tōkyō University. He is remembered for his translations of Goethe's *Die Leiden des jungen Werthers* (1774, *The Sorrows of Young Werther*) and Remarque's *Im Western nichts Neues* (1929, *All Quiet on the Western Front*). In 1934 he joined Tōhō Productions, establishing himself as a producer. Taking the pen name Maruki Sado, a play on "Marquis de Sade," he wrote variously on humorous and erotic subjects. His list of credits includes musical productions and the founding of the Nichigeki Dancing Troupe (similar to the Rockettes of Radio City Music Hall in New York City).

Hatogaya

City in southeastern Saitama Prefecture, central Honshū. During the Edo period (1600–1868) Hatogaya was a prosperous POST-STATION TOWN on the highway Nikkō Kaidō. It is noted for its nurseries. In recent years many housing complexes have been built. Pop: 55,952.

Hatoyama Haruko (1861–1938)

Educator. Born into a *samurai* family in Matsumoto (now in Nagano Prefecture); maiden name, Taga. Graduated in 1881 from the Women's Normal School (now Ochanomizu Women's University), where she later taught. She was married in 1881 to HATOYAMA KAZUO, a politician and lawyer; their eldest son, HATOYAMA ICHIRŌ, later became prime minister, and their second son, HATOYAMA HIDEO, became a prominent legal scholar. In 1886 she helped Miyagawa Hozen (1852–1922) to found the women's vocational school Kyōritsu Joshi Shokugyō Gakkō (now Kyōritsu Women's University), and she served as its president from 1922 until her death. She was also active in the patriotic women's society AIKOKU FUJINKAI. Her works include *Waga jijoden* (1930, My Autobiography).

Hatoyama Hideo (1884–1946)

Scholar of law and politician. Born in Tōkyō. After graduating from Tōkyō University in 1908, he was appointed assistant professor there in 1910 and the following year went to study in France and

Germany. On his return in 1916 he was appointed professor and taught civil law at Tōkyō University until 1926. After his retirement he became a lawyer and was elected to the House of Representatives in 1932. His elder brother was the politician HATOYAMA ICHIRŌ. His interpretation of civil law in the Germanic tradition was highly influential during the Taishō period (1912–26). Among his principal works were *Nihon saiken hō sōron* (1918, Introduction to the Law of Obligations in Japan) and *Nihon mimpō sōron* (1923, Introduction to the Civil Code in Japan). His *Saikenhō ni okeru shingi seijitsu no gensoku* (Trust and Sincerity and the Law of Obligations, an article written in 1924 and published in book form in 1955) was an attempt to break away from Germanic interpretations of law.

KATŌ Ichirō

Hatoyama Ichirō (1883–1959)

Prime minister from December 1954 to December 1956. Born in Tōkyō, the eldest son of the politician HATOYAMA KAZUO and his wife, the educator HATOYAMA HARUKO. After graduation from Tōkyō University in 1907, Hatoyama followed a political career. He was first elected to the Diet in 1915 and eventually became secretary-general of his party, the RIKKEN SEIYŪKAI. From 1927 to 1929 he was director of the Cabinet Secretariat in the TANAKA GIICHI cabinet. From 1931 to 1934 he served as minister of education under prime ministers INUKAI TSUYOSHI and SAITŌ MAKOTO. In the era of intolerance for unorthodox thinking that followed the MANCHURIAN INCIDENT (1931), Hatoyama contributed to the trend by dismissing liberal teachers from the universities (see KYŌTO UNIVERSITY INCIDENT).

After World War II Hatoyama organized the Japan Liberal Party (Nihon Jiyūtō) and became its president. In May 1946, when he was ready to form a cabinet after an election victory, he was purged by the Occupation authorities (see OCCUPATION PURGE). He gave the Japan Liberal Party presidency to YOSHIDA SHIGERU and did not participate in politics until his rehabilitation in July 1951. In November 1954 Hatoyama aligned with the Kaishintō (Reform Party) to form a new party, the NIHON MINSHUTŌ (Japan Democratic Party). As its president and leader of the opposition, he successfully challenged Prime Minister Yoshida's coalition and became prime minister in December 1954.

As prime minister, Hatoyama broadly hinted that the 1947 constitution, including article 9 (RENUNCIATION OF WAR), might be amended. Revision of the constitution was one of the hotly debated issues in the general election of February 1955, and a law establishing the COMMISSION ON THE CONSTITUTION was passed in June 1956. (Attached to the cabinet and composed of 30 Diet members, 20 scholars, and former office holders, the commission continued its deliberations until June 1964; it was abolished in 1965.) In October 1956 Hatoyama concluded a treaty with the Soviet Union to end the state of war that had existed between the two nations since August 1945. The treaty also removed the Soviet threat to veto Japan's entry into the United Nations.

Elected to the Diet 15 times in the prewar and postwar eras, Hatoyama was a major political figure in periods of transition. But for the purge he would have been prime minister in 1946. It was during his term as prime minister that the LIBERAL DEMOCRATIC PARTY was formed, combining all the conservative parties. Yet the political benefits of the merger went not to Hatoyama but to KISHI NOBUSUKE and other politicians.

David J. Lu

Hatoyama Kazuo (1856–1911)

Politician and lawyer. Born in Edo (now Tōkyō). He attended Kaisei Gakkō (now Tōkyō University) and studied law at Columbia and Yale universities. Upon returning to Japan, he taught at Tōkyō University but left teaching to practice law. In 1885 he entered the Ministry of Foreign Affairs to help in the revision of the so-called Unequal Treaties with Western nations (see UNEQUAL TREATIES, REVISION OF). He returned to teaching at the university but again resigned to practice law. In 1892 he was elected to the House of Representatives as a member of the RIKKEN KAISHINTŌ party, and became speaker of the House in 1896. He also served as president of Waseda University. His wife, HATOYAMA HARUKO, was a well-known educator; the politician and prime minister HATOYAMA ICHIRŌ was his eldest son, the legal scholar HATOYAMA HIDEO was his second son, and the politician SUZUKI KISABURŌ was his son-in-law.

Hatsukaichi

Town in southwestern Hiroshima Prefecture, western Honshū, on Hiroshima Bay. Hatsukaichi developed early as a market (the name means twentieth-day market) and POST-STATION TOWN. Its main occupations are farming and the manufacture of wood products. The town is fast becoming a satellite town of Hiroshima. Pop: 42,315.

Hatsushima

Small island in Sagami Bay, 10 km (6 mi) southeast of the city of Atami, Shizuoka Prefecture, central Honshū. It is composed of a basalt plateau, averaging about 40 m (131 ft) in elevation. Some 40 households have been carrying out communal fishing here since the early part of the Edo period (1600–1868). It has developed in recent years as a vacation area. Area: 0.4 sq km (0.2 sq mi).

Hatsuuma

The first "day of the horse" in February as determined by Chinese and Japanese zodiacal traditions (see JIKKAN JŪNISHI); also, the event held on that day. It is connected with the belief in INARI (the deity of cereals). Since the 8th century many Inari shrines have held festivities on Hatsuuma. At the FUSHIMI INARI SHRINE in Kyōto, it was the custom for worshipers to break off branches of cedars growing in the precincts to take home. Today, shrines give worshipers cedar leaves with consecrated paper streamers and sell seeds, fox statues (the fox is one of the forms of Inari), and insect-shaped bells. In eastern Japan Hatsuuma is a festival of the silkworm deity, and people make offerings of cocoon-shaped dumplings. Many regions celebrate a horse or ox festival on Hatsuuma. INOKUCHI Shōji

Hatta, Mohammad (1902–1980)

The first vice-president (1945–56) and later prime minister (1948–50) of the Republic of Indonesia. Born in West Sumatra, Hatta studied for 10 years in the Netherlands and was active in an anticolonial organization of Indonesian students. After returning to the Dutch East Indies, he was arrested and imprisoned from 1934 until 1942, when he was released by the Japanese. During the Japanese occupation, he served as an adviser to the military administration and as vice-director of the Japanese-sponsored nationalist organization, Putera. When a petition for organizing the PETA ARMY (national defense forces) was submitted to the Japanese military authorities by Indonesian youths, strong support by both SUKARNO and Hatta proved decisive. After Japanese Premier KOISO KUNIAKI indicated in September 1944 that independence would be granted the East Indies, Hatta served as a member of a number of preparatory and investigatory committees. Two days after the Japanese surrender on 15 August 1945, Sukarno and Hatta declared an independent republic. During the struggle with the Dutch for independence, he shared responsibility with Sukarno as vice-president and as prime minister. He led the Indonesian delegation to the Hague peace conference in August 1949. Dissenting from Sukarno's view on the unsuitability of Western-style democracy in Indonesia, he resigned the vice-presidency in 1956, three years before the beginning of Sukarno's "guided democracy" system. See also INDONESIA AND JAPAN.

NAGAZUMI Akira

Hattori Kintarō (1860–1934)

Entrepreneur. Founder of K. HATTORI & CO, LTD, and Seikōsha Co, Ltd, the maker of Seikō-brand products. Born in Edo (now Tōkyō), Hattori became an apprentice at a watch dealer's in 1874. In 1881 he established K. Hattori & Co and engaged in the repairing, importing, wholesaling, and retailing of timepieces. He established Seikōsha in 1892 and became a leading producer of wall clocks and watches. He won first prizes for his timepieces at the Second Tōkyō Industrial Exposition of 1912. In 1913, he succeeded in manufacturing wristwatches domestically and started exporting timepieces to Western countries as well as to China. Hattori established a measuring instrument plant in 1929 and started production of various measuring instruments and fuses for military use. MORI Masumi

Hattori Nankaku (1683–1759)

Confucian scholar of the Edo period (1600–1868); also regarded as a poet and painter of distinction. Born in Kyōto, as a youth he went to

Edo (now Tōkyō) to serve under YANAGISAWA YOSHIYASU, one of the senior councillors (rōjū) of the Tokugawa shogunate (1603–1867). He also studied under OGYŪ SORAI, founder of the KOBUNJIGAKU school of Confucianism, which emphasized philological studies of the original Confucian classics. When Nankaku opened his own school in 1716, students, drawn by his reputation as a warm and unassuming scholar, came from as far as Kyūshū.

Hattori Ransetsu (1654–1707)

HAIKU poet of the early part of the Edo period (1600–1868); founder of the Setsumon school of haiku. Born in Edo (now Tōkyō). Real name Hattori Harusuke. A leading and devoted disciple of BASHŌ, he carried on the master's tradition in his own verses and also trained many young poets. Ransetsu's haiku are earlier characterized by a graceful lyricism that reflects his warm personality and later by a quiet, contemplative tone that conveys a sense of inner peace and enlightenment. Main collections: Sono fukuro (1690) and Ransetsu bunshū (1774).

Hattori Shirō (1908–   )

Linguist. Born in Mie Prefecture, Hattori was educated at Tōkyō University, where he became professor, and then later professor emeritus, of linguistics. He was awarded the title Contributor to Culture and became a member of the Japan Academy. His research, which concentrated on Altaic languages, also included studies on several non-Altaic Asian languages. He made many significant contributions toward advancing methods of language research and clarifying general rules operating in the structure of language. Although he often employed modern Western (especially American) linguistic research methods in his work, he also endeavored to establish a Japanese tradition of systematic linguistic study. His published works include: Onseigaku (1951, Phonology), Nihongo no keitō (1959, The Genealogy of the Japanese Language), Gengogaku no hōhō (1960, Methods in Linguistics), and Eigo kiso goi no kenkyū (1968, Research into the Basic Vocabulary of English). See also JAPANESE LANGUAGE STUDIES, HISTORY OF.   Uwano Zendō

Hattori Shisō (1901–1956)

Historian. Born in Shimane Prefecture; graduate of Tōkyō University. While a student, Hattori joined the progressive study group SHINJINKAI and became interested in Marxism. In 1928 he published Meiji ishin shi, considered at the time a groundbreaking study of the MEIJI RESTORATION from a dialectical-materialist viewpoint. Together with HANI GORŌ he was an important contributor to the series NIHON SHIHON SHUGI HATTATSU SHI KŌZA (7 vols, 1932–33; Studies on the History of the Development of Capitalism in Japan), but with the growing suppression of radical thought in the late 1930s he decided to abandon writing. After World War II he published works on the FREEDOM AND PEOPLE'S RIGHTS MOVEMENT and the thought of the 13th-century religious figure SHINRAN. See also NIHON SHIHON SHUGI RONSŌ.

■——Hattori Shisō zenshū, 24 vols (Fukumura Shuppan, 1973–76).

Hattori Tohō (1657–1730)

Also known as Hattori Dohō. Real name Hattori Yasuhide. HAIKU poet of the early part of the Edo period (1600–1868). Born in Ueno, Iga Province (now part of Mie Prefecture), which was also the haiku master BASHŌ's hometown. He is best known for the Sanzōshi (1702), his faithful recording of the master's later teachings about haiku. This work, along with the Kyoraishō by MUKAI KYORAI, is considered to be the most authoritative source on Bashō's poetics. In particular, it deals with the important concepts of fūga no makoto, "the truth of haiku," and fueki ryūkō, the dialectic of "permanence and change" in haiku. Minomushian shū, compiled by Tohō between 1688 and 1729, is a valuable record of his own verses and those of the other members of the Iga haiku circles.

Hausknecht, Emile (1853–1927)

German educator who brought the educational theories of Johann Friedrich Herbart (1776–1841) to Japan. Hausknecht studied languages and history at Berlin's Friedrich-Wilhelm University and became a teacher after graduation. He came to Japan in 1887 at the invitation of the Ministry of Education and lectured on education and the German language at Tōkyō University. In 1889 the curriculum for secondary-school teacher training was established in accordance with his proposals and under his guidance. Among his students were many leading educators of the Meiji (1868–1912) and Taishō (1912–26) periods, such as TANIMOTO TOMERI. He left Japan in 1890.   Kurauchi Shirō

hawks and eagles

(taka and washi). Some 28 species of birds of prey belonging to the order Falconiformes are found in Japan, including 22 of the family Accipitridae and 6 of the family Falconidae; of these, 7 of the larger species are called washi (eagles) by the Japanese, and the other 21, taka (hawks). Since the distinction between hawks and eagles is based mainly on size, with different standards employed in Japan and the West, some species known as eagles in English are classified as taka by the Japanese. Sixteen taka species are also common to Europe, including 7 which are also common to America; the following 5 are peculiar to Asia: the tsumi (Japanese lesser sparrow hawk; Accipiter gularis) breeds in mountain forests throughout Japan; the sashiba (gray-faced buzzard eagle; Butastur indicus) summers in forests south of Honshū; the kumataka (Hodgson's hawk eagle; Spizaetus nipalensis), a resident bird, breeds in mountain forests north of Kyūshū; the akaharadaka (Chinese sparrow hawk; A. soloensis) and madarachūhi (pied harrier; Circus melanoleucos) are both migrants seen infrequently in Japan.

Other species generally called taka in Japan include the nosuri (Japanese buzzard; Buteo buteo); the hayabusa (Siberian peregrine falcon; Falco peregrinus); the chōgembō (Japanese kestrel; F. tinnunculus); and the chūhi (marsh harrier; Circus aeruginosus). Species generally called washi in Japan include the inuwashi (Japanese golden eagle; Aquila chrysaetos); the ōwashi (Steller's sea eagle; Haliaeëtus pelagicus); and the ojirowashi (white-tailed sea eagle; H. albicilla). See also KITE, BLACK.   Takano Shinji

The earliest record of hawks used for hunting in Japan is found in the KOJIKI (712), which states that hawking for pheasants took place in the Yamato area (now Nara Prefecture) during the reign of Emperor Nintoku (first half of the 5th century). The practice has undergone periodic rises and declines in popularity and continues on a small scale at present. The ōtaka (northern goshawk) and hayabusa were the birds most frequently used, along with the haitaka (sparrow hawk), the tsumi, and occasionally the kumataka. See also FALCONRY.   Saneyoshi Tatsuo

Hayabusa

("Falcon"). Japanese army fighter plane in World War II; officially designated Nakajima Isshiki Sentōki (Nakajima Mark I Fighter). Construction of the first test model began in 1937 and was completed the following year. The model was officially adopted in April 1941 and was used that summer in China for the first time. With the outbreak of World War II, the Hayabusa was used as the army's principal fighter aircraft. As a result of several remodeling efforts and improvements, it finally attained speeds of up to 550 kilometers per hour (342 mph). The plane was equipped with two 12.7-mm (0.5-in) machine guns. The Hayabusa was renowned for its agility, stability, and dependability; a total of 5,751 were manufactured before the conclusion of the war.   Kondō Shinji

Hayachinesan

Mountain in central Iwate Prefecture, northern Honshū. It is the highest peak in the Kitakami Mountains, a monadnock composed of basic rocks such as serpentine. The alpine flora belt above the mountain's sixth station is designated a natural monument. Hayachine Shrine is on the summit. Hayachinesan forms a prefectural natural park. Height: 1,914 m (6,278 ft).

Hayaishi Osamu (1920–   )

Biochemist. Born in Kyōto. A graduate of Ōsaka University, he later taught at Kyōto University and Tōkyō University. He discovered oxygenase while conducting research in the United States and has continued to explore new areas of biochemical research. He was awarded the Order of Culture in 1972.   Suzuki Zenji

Hayakawa Sesshū (1886–1973)

Film actor. Known abroad as Sessue Hayakawa. Born in Chiba Prefecture, his real name was Hayakawa Kintarō. In 1906 he went to America to attend the University of Chicago. He later joined an amateur theater group and through a chance encounter with director Thomas Ince made his movie debut in *Typhoon* (1914). Hayakawa was the most successful Japanese actor in Hollywood, making a total of 40 films there. However, his roles were invariably portrayals of Japanese as seen through Western eyes. He gained critical acclaim for his performance in Max Ophuls's *Yoshiwara* (1936) and was much praised for his portrayal of the shrewd, iron-willed Japanese army officer in *Bridge over the River Kwai* (1957) directed by David Lean. He returned to Japan in 1949. Although he appeared in many Japanese films, he was never as successful in his native country.

Itasaka Tsuyoshi

Hayama

Town in southern Kanagawa Prefecture, central Honshū, on the western coast of the Miura Peninsula. Because of its mild climate Hayama early developed as a resort for the well-to-do. A marina is located here. Pop: 28,360.

Hayama Yoshiki (1894–1945)

Novelist and short-story writer; one of the leading writers of the PROLETARIAN LITERATURE MOVEMENT of the 1920s and early 1930s; known for his vivid accounts of the hard-pressed lives and working conditions of the laboring classes, written in spare, compact prose and largely devoid of sentimentalism.

Hayama was born in 1894 in the village of Toyotsu in Fukuoka Prefecture in northern Kyūshū. His father was a petty official in the local county (*gun*) government, and he spent his childhood in genteel poverty. Graduated from Toyotsu Middle School, Hayama was admitted to Waseda University in 1913, but was eventually dismissed for irregular attendance and failure to pay tuition. He signed on as an apprentice seaman on a freighter bound for Calcutta and then worked as a seaman third-class on a collier.

Abandoning the seafaring life because of injury, Hayama drifted from one job to another. Usually employed as a temporary office clerk, he worked, among other places, for a railway firm, a small private technical school, and a cement factory. During this time he began reading avidly the works of Dostoevsky and Gorky. His conscious imitation of the latter's style is said to be manifest in his early works, though his absorption of literary influence is not so obvious to modern readers.

In June 1920 Hayama secured a job as a reporter with the *Nagoya shimbun*. By now he was becoming progressively more involved in local labor movement activities, having already lost one job for trying to unionize workers at a cement factory. When a strike broke out at the Aichi Tokei Denki Co, Ltd, in October of that year, he quit his newspaper job and joined the strikers. He was subsequently arrested, charged with breach of the public peace, and sentenced to two months in jail. For the next several years Hayama was in and out of prison. Granted access to pen and paper, in prison he wrote the half-dozen stories and long novel that are regarded as his most representative works.

In between jail terms he was busily engaged in various socialist and labor organizing campaigns until the early 1930s, when the movement was finally suppressed by the government. From the mid-1930s to the early 1940s he moved about with his family from village to village in the mountains of Gifu and Nagano prefectures, never settling in any place for long. Though continuing to write and hoping to try his hand at farming, Hayama found himself ill suited to life in the mountains. He longed, he wrote, for the peaceful expanse of the open sea. In June 1945 he moved with his eldest daughter to a farming settlement in Manchuria, but the move proved injurious to his health. He died from a stroke in October of that year while on his way home to be repatriated.

Work —— Hayama's first important work was "Imbaifu" (The Prostitute), a short story published in the journal *Bungei sensen* (Literary Front) in November 1925. Written from prison, "Imbaifu" is a starkly moving account of the narrator's encounter with a prostitute on the verge of death and of his efforts to aid her. Praised for its hauntingly beautiful style, it won Hayama the recognition of such establishment writers as HIROTSU KAZUO and UNO KŌJI and marked a high point in proletarian literary output. It was followed in the next six months by a stream of stories in a similar vein, including "Semento daru no naka no tegami" (1926; tr "Letter Found in a Cement Barrel," 1962), "Rōdōsha no inai fune" (1926, A Boat with No Workers), "Dare ga koroshita ka" (1926, Who Was It That Killed?), and "Puroretaria no chichi" (1926, Proletarian Milk).

But it was the long novel *Umi ni ikuru hitobito*, published by Kaizōsha in 1926, that firmly established Hayama's reputation. Hailed as Japan's first true proletarian novel because of its cast of revolutionary characters, it broke new ground in both scale and style as proletarian-school writing. The novel describes a group of seamen on a coal-carrier plying the icy waters between Muroran in Hokkaidō and Yokohama and the inhuman conditions under which they are forced to labor. Though each sees the class struggle in different terms, together they organize, press the captain for improved working conditions, and force him to capitulate. Their victory is short-lived, for once back in port at Yokohama the captain has the ringleaders arrested by the naval authorities. Though the story has a number of stylistic faults, Hayama manages to transform the potentially gloomy subject matter into a gripping narrative of oppressed workers who realize that they must organize to protect themselves. There are many passages of high lyric intensity. Hayama does not sentimentalize his victims, and he holds the reader's interest despite an obviously contrived plot and a heavily colored message. The novel exerted considerable influence on later proletarian works.

Hayama's literary potential was never fully developed. Though he carefully avoided letting his work become too politicized or dogmatic as happened to much proletarian literature of the time, he never went beyond these early achievements. His later writings merely echoed what he had done before. A number of his early works were translated into Russian and other Eastern European languages, but like most of the other proletarian literature, his works have yet to be seriously studied by Western scholars of Japanese literature.

—— Hayama Yoshiki, *Hayama Yoshiki zenshū*, 6 vols (Chikuma Shobō, 1975–76). *Dennis M. Spackman*

Hayami Gyoshū (1894–1935)

Japanese-style painter. Born in Tōkyō, Gyoshū began the study of traditional Japanese painting at the age of 15 under Matsumoto Fūko (1840–1923). Two years later his talent was recognized by IMAMURA SHIKŌ and he became a member of the Kōjikai, a group that Shikō had organized composed of leading young artists. He also joined the revived Nihon Bijutsuin (Japan Fine Arts Academy). He lost his left leg in a streetcar accident in 1919 but continued to pursue his artistic career with considerable success until his death from typhoid fever. He practiced many styles of painting, including YAMATO-E, RIMPA, and BUNJINGA. His style gradually moved toward detailed realism, especially after his study of Chinese painting of the Song (Sung; 960–1126) and Yuan (Yüan; 1279–1368) dynasties. Later his style changed again, to a fantasy-rich symbolism more decorative and intellectually structured than his earlier work.

hayashi

A broad term covering different types of musical accompaniment or vocal "encouragement" for dancers, singers, actors, and other kinds of performers; it may also indicate the performers themselves. The term derives from the Japanese verb *hayasu*, meaning "to encourage" or "spur on." In folk singing (see FOLK SONG), *hayashi* may refer to accompaniment provided by handclaps or instruments; most commonly, however, it indicates the unison vocal response to the lead singer (which is also called *hayashi-kotoba*) or a rhythmically spoken section of the song. In the traditional FOLK PERFORMING ARTS (*minzoku geinō*) it refers to the instrumental accompaniment, generally drums and flutes. In the music of the KANDA FESTIVAL, GION FESTIVAL, and other similar festivals, the *hayashi* itself constitutes the performance (often called *matsuri-bayashi*, or "festival hayashi"). In the case of the *taiko odori* (drum dance), the dancers provide their own drum and vocal *hayashi*. Usually, however, dancers and musicians are separate persons.

In the NŌ drama, the *hayashi* instrumental group consists of one flute plus two or three TAIKO and TSUZUMI drums. In KABUKI MUSIC, the *hayashi* is provided by the same contingent as in the Nō. These, with the singers and SHAMISEN players, form the onstage orchestra (*debayashi*). Offstage music (*geza ongaku*) is provided by a varied group of musicians and noisemakers referred to as the *kage-bayashi*. *Kojima Tomiko*

Hayashi Akira → Hayashi Fukusai

Hayashi Fubō (1900–1935)

Novelist. Real name Hasegawa Umitarō. Other pen names are Tani Jōji and Maki Itsuma. Born on the island of Sado in Niigata Prefecture. Brother of novelist HASEGAWA SHIRŌ. After he left middle school he traveled to the United States, where he lived for six years. After his return to Japan in 1924, he began writing, under the pen name Tani Jōji, about the Japanese community in America in a popular series known by the general title *Meriken jappu*. He also wrote mystery stories and stories of family life under the pen name Maki Itsuma. Under his third pen name, Hayashi Fubō, he is known for a number of pseudohistorical romances, including *Shimpan Ōoka seidan* (1927–28), whose hero is Tange Sazen, a one-eyed, one-armed super swordsman. A prolific popular writer despite his short life, he was referred to by members of Japan's literary establishment as a "monster" (partly in the sense of "prodigy"). His principal works include the novel *Chijō no seiza* (1932–34, The Terrestial Constellation) and *Tekisasu mushuku* (1928, Homeless in Texas), a collection of his *Meriken Jappu* stories.

Hayashi Fukusai (1800–1859)

Confucian scholar of the latter part of the Edo period (1600–1868). Born into the Hayashi family, hereditary scholars to the Tokugawa shogunate; sixth son of HAYASHI JUSSAI. Fukusai was appointed head of the shogunate academy for Confucian studies (SHŌHEIKŌ) in 1853. The following year he represented the shogunate in the signing of the KANAGAWA TREATY, which opened the country after 200 years of NATIONAL SECLUSION.

Hayashi Fumiko (1903–1951)

Novelist. Born in Yamaguchi Prefecture, the fourth illegitimate child of Hayashi Kiku, fathered by Miyata Asatarō, a peddler 14 years younger than Kiku. Her parents later sold secondhand goods in the city of Wakamatsu (now Kita Kyūshū, Fukuoka Prefecture), but when Fumiko was around 7 years old, Kiku ran off with her husband's store manager, over 20 years her junior, taking her daughter along as they traveled to peddle goods in various places.

When they briefly settled in Onomichi, Hiroshima Prefecture, Fumiko at last graduated from elementary school; her teacher and literary mentor Kobayashi Masao assisted her entry into Onomichi Higher Girls' School, although she had to work to pay her own fees; she also began to publish poetry in local newspapers. After graduation she went to Tōkyō to join a Meiji University student whom she had known in Onomichi. When he broke their engagement, she began a rootless life employed as a maid, factory worker, saleswoman, barmaid, and café waitress while continuing to write poetry. The diary she began around the time her lover left became the basis of her first novel, *Hōrōki* (1928–30; tr *Journal of a Vagabond*, 1951).

In 1924 she met Tanabe Wakao (1889–1966), leader of the theater group Shiminza, and through him she became acquainted with a circle of anarchist poets and other avant-garde writers. She lived briefly with Tanabe, and later, again briefly, with the poet Nomura Yoshiya (b 1903), who often beat her. During this period she became friends with the poet TSUBOI SHIGEJI and his wife the novelist TSUBOI SAKAE, as well as the novelist HIRABAYASHI TAIKO. She married the painter Tezuka Ryokubin (b 1902) in late 1926 and at last found some peace and security.

In 1929 she published the first of her poetry anthologies, *Aouma o mitari* (I Saw a Pale Horse). In October the same year, the first portion of her autobiographical novel *Hōrōki* began to appear in the magazine *Nyonin geijutsu* (Women's Arts). While this novel was still being serialized, its first portions were published in book form in 1930. This proved a best seller, enabling Fumiko to afford a first-class trip to Manchuria and China. Part two was published as *Zoku hōrōki* in 1930; part three, written along with the two previously published parts but delayed for fear of censorship, was published in 1947. Such autobiographical outpourings later matured into a third-person novel, *Ukigumo* (1949–51; tr *The Floating Clouds*, 1965), concerning the desolate journey of a woman who works in Southeast Asia and then roams war-shattered Tōkyō trying to find her former lover.

A wanderer since her childhood, even after her marriage to Ryokubin, she continually traveled inside and outside Japan, with visits to Europe (1931–32) and China, Manchuria, and Southeast Asia as a reporter. She also was one of the authors sent on group trips to comfort soldiers. After the war, in a burst of creativity, she steadily contributed many works to newspapers and magazines. In all, she left approximately 25 novels, 20 collections of short stories, two poetry anthologies, three children's tales, and numerous essays, diaries, and travelogues. Although sometimes criticized for melodramatic tendencies, she maintained the popularity she earned with *Hōrōki* throughout her life by repeatedly and compassionately capturing the poverty, darkness, and misery of war, of rootless women, or of couples tortured by stale marriages.

While such earlier stories as "Fūkin to sakana no machi" (1931, Town of the Accordion and Fish) and "Seihin no sho" (1931, Record of Clean Poverty) are autobiographical, her later outstanding short stories are masterful works of pure fiction; for example, "Kaki" (1935, Oyster) details how a humble pouch maker married to a boardinghouse maid gradually goes mad, and "Bangiku" (1948; tr "Late Chrysanthemum," 1956) depicts an older woman's disillusioning reunion with her former lover. "Dauntaun" (1949; tr "Downtown," 1961) and "Hone" (1949; tr "Bones," 1966) are also among her most highly regarded short stories.

▪——*Hayashi Fumiko zenshū*, 23 vols (Shinchōsha, 1951–53). Hirabayashi Taiko, *Hayashi Fumiko* (1969). Itagaki Naoko, *Hayashi Fumiko no shōgai* (1968). *Kyōko Iriye* SELDEN

Hayashi Fusao (1903–1975)

Novelist and literary critic. Real name Gotō Toshio. Also known as Shirai Akira. Born in Ōita Prefecture. Attracted to Marxism while a student at Tōkyō University, he joined the PROLETARIAN LITERATURE MOVEMENT with the publication of his short story "Ringo" in 1926. After he was jailed twice in the 1930s for political activities, however, his views shifted profoundly to the right, and he became an outspoken champion of ultranationalism. After World War II he established himself as a writer of apolitical family novels, such as *Musuko no seishun* (1950). However, in the 1960s he reemerged as a polemicist against left-wing pacifism with *Daitōa sensō kōtei ron* (1963), an apologia for Japan's actions in World War II. His principal works include the novels *Seinen* (1932, Youth) and *Musuko no endan* (1954).

Hayashi Gahō (1618–1680)

Confucianist of the early part of the Edo period (1600–1868). Son of HAYASHI RAZAN, a Confucian scholar and adviser to the Tokugawa shogunate. A native of Kyōto, he went to live in Edo (now Tōkyō), where he instructed the shōgun TOKUGAWA IEMITSU in the Confucian classics. Known for his prodigious memory and erudition in history and genealogy, he wrote, with his father, *Kan'ei shoka keizu den*, a genealogy of warrior families, and *Honchō tsugan*, a history of Japan; his own works are collected under the title *Gahō bunshū*. Upon his father's death Gahō became official adviser to the shōgun.

Hayashi Hōkō (1644–1732)

Confucian scholar of the Edo period (1600–1868). Born in Edo (now Tōkyō); grandson of HAYASHI RAZAN and son of HAYASHI GAHŌ, both Confucian scholars to the Tokugawa shogunate (1603–1867). He lectured at Edo Castle to the shōgun TOKUGAWA TSUNAYOSHI and shogunal retainers. When the private academy of the Hayashi family was designated as the official shogunate school (see SHŌHEIKŌ) in 1691, Hōkō became its first head. The post (*daigaku no kami*) thereafter became a hereditary prerogative of the Hayashi family. It was at Hōkō's suggestion that Confucian scholars were permitted to discard their priestlike robes and to be entered in *samurai* registers. After Tsunayoshi's death, Hōkō continued to serve as lecturer and adviser to the succeeding shōguns. Although he lacked the incisiveness or creativity of his contemporary ARAI HAKUSEKI, many of his disciples became important officials in the shogunate and local domain administrations.

Hayashi Jussai (1768–1841)

Confucian scholar of the late Edo period. The third son of Matsudaira Norimori, *daimyō* of Iwamura (now part of Gifu Prefecture), he was chosen by MATSUDAIRA SADANOBU to become head of the Hayashi family, hereditary Confucian advisers to the Tokugawa shogunate, when Hayashi Nobutaka died without an heir in 1793. Jussai thus became head of the Hayashi family school, which Sadanobu had designated as the official shogunal academy (see SHŌHEIKŌ) in 1790 as part of his program to establish the Zhu Xi (Chu Hsi) school of Neo-Confucianism (SHUSHIGAKU) as the shogunate's official doctrine (see also KANSEI REFORMS). With the help of such scholars as Koga Seiri (1750–1817), BITŌ NISHŪ, and SHIBANO RITSUZAN, Jussai thoroughly reorganized the curriculum of the school, which during his 45-year tenure became the most important center of learning in Japan. A skillful administrator rather than an original thinker, Jussai supervised the compilation of the TOKUGAWA JIKKI, a history of the Tokugawa family, and other important works.

Hayashi Razan (1583–1657)

An important Neo-Confucian scholar of the early part of the Edo period (1600–1868). In his long and conspicuous career as adviser to the Tokugawa shogunate, propagandist, historiographer, and educator, he promoted Zhu Xi (Chu Hsi) Neo-Confucianism (see SHUSHIGAKU) as the shogunate's favored school of Confucian learning and contributed to its diffusion in the society of his day.

Razan, born in Kyōto, son of Hayashi Nobutoki, was adopted by his father's elder brother Yoshikatsu. The family claimed samurai ancestry but had declined during the second half of the 16th century, and Razan's adoptive father was a dealer in rice. In 1595 Razan entered the Rinzai sect Zen temple of Kenninji in Kyōto. He resisted pressure to take the tonsure and in 1597 returned home. In 1600 he read Zhu Xi's edition of the Confucian classics and in 1603 began lectures on the Lun yu (Lun yü; Analects) using Zhu's interpretations. The following year he was introduced to FUJIWARA SEIKA (1561–1619), whom he regarded as his mentor, though there remained openly declared differences between them. Razan's Neo-Confucianism, more exclusively loyal to Zhu Xi than Seika's, may have been influenced by the similarly orthodox style of Korean Confucianism. In 1605 Razan first appeared before the retired shōgun TOKUGAWA IEYASU (1543–1616). Probably the same year Ieyasu rejected an appeal by a court Confucian scholar, Kiyowara Hidekata, to have Razan's lectures stopped on the grounds that such lectures required court sanction. This judgment was the final landmark in the establishment of Neo-Confucianism as an independent school of learning in the Edo period. In 1607 Razan was summoned to Ieyasu's castle at Sumpu, where he was ordered against his own inclination to take the tonsure in the manner of the Zen-Confucian advisers of the Muromachi (1333–1568) period and to assume the name Dōshun. Thus began Razan's long service with the shogunate. He was employed chiefly for his erudition and command of Chinese. Though Ieyasu may have had a general appreciation of the ideological value of Confucianism, there is no evidence that he had much understanding of or interest in the Zhu Xi school; rather, he and his immediate successors were Buddhists and inclined to favor Buddhist advisers such as Tenkai (1536–1643) and Sūden (1569–1633). Razan was useful, however, in handling international correspondence, drafting documents, and providing ideological support for shogunal actions.

Following Ieyasu's death in 1616, Razan was temporarily eclipsed by his younger brother Nobuzumi (1585–1683). Under the third shōgun, TOKUGAWA IEMITSU (1604–51), Razan's position was restored, and in 1629 both brothers were awarded the honorary Buddhist rank of hōin. In 1630, as recognition for his long service to the shogunate, Razan was given money and land with which to build a school in Edo (now Tōkyō). This institution, the private academy of the Hayashi family rather than an official school, probably accommodated between 20 and 30 pupils at any one time.

Following the death of Sūden in 1633, Razan moved closer to the center of shogunal counsels. In 1635 he and Nobuzumi drafted the second BUKE SHOHATTO (Laws for the Military Houses) and the Hatamoto Shohatto (Laws for the Shōgun's Vassals). For the remainder of his life, Razan continued active in shogunal service, drafting official documents, participating in diplomacy with Korea, advising on shogunal ceremonial, helping formulate the anti-Christian program, and participating in historiographical projects. He died in early 1657.

Though Razan thus participated in the shogunate during its early years, he did not influence the formation of its institutions significantly in the direction of Confucianism. Rather, he is important as an ideologue and propagandist. A man of great energy, prodigious erudition, and, in the judgment of some historians, a certain shallowness, he was well suited for this role. His achievement was to consolidate the independence of Zhu Xi Confucianism from the

Buddhist institutions and the Kyōto court aristocracy and, through his long association with the shogunate, to endow it with the status of a semiofficial government orthodoxy. He used his position to disseminate Neo-Confucianism, editing and publishing a large number of Confucian texts. In popular works such as Shunkanshō (1629, Spring Mirror Notes) and Santokushō (probably about the same date, Notes on the Three Virtues) Razan set out in simple Japanese the basic concepts of Zhu Xi Neo-Confucian thought. These works show how the principles of a hierarchical but harmonious and stable society are based on the natural order and how each person is endowed with a moral nature that, if realized, enables him to play his part in such a society. Razan's officially sponsored national history, begun in 1644 and completed by his son in 1670, later known as the Honchō tsugan (Comprehensive Mirror of Our Nation's Dynasty), was designed to explain and legitimate the political ascendancy of the warrior (samurai) class. Razan also attempted to apply Confucian rationality to Japanese history, reinterpreting the mythical accounts of the early history of the imperial family in rational, humanistic terms.

Razan's desire to promote Zhu Xi Neo-Confucianism made him an outspoken polemicist against other traditions, particularly Christianity. His anti-Christian arguments, at first based on rational refutation, assumed a political character as the shogunate's suppression of Christianity intensified. He also attempted to suppress the Wang Yangming school of Confucianism (see YŌMEIGAKU) in Japan and attacked Buddhism from a moral and social point of view for its denial of the reality of human relationships and for the economic burden it imposed on the country. It was perhaps partly a sense of powerlessness in the face of the pervasive influence of Buddhism in his time that encouraged Razan, like many Tokugawa Confucians, to look to SHINTŌ as an ally. He proclaimed the identity of Confucianism and Shintō and attempted to reinterpret the cosmogony of the NIHON SHOKI (720), the second oldest extant history of Japan, in Neo-Confucian terms, equating the Shintō deities (KAMI) with basic categories of Neo-Confucian thought.

After Razan's death, the office of shogunal Confucian adviser became hereditary in the Hayashi family. During the lifetime of his son HAYASHI GAHŌ (1618–80) and, more particularly, of his grandson HAYASHI HŌKŌ (1644–1732), who enjoyed the favor of the fifth shōgun, TOKUGAWA TSUNAYOSHI (1646–1709), the Hayashi family and its school prospered, but from the fourth generation their intellectual quality declined. In the seventh and eighth generations the family was perpetuated by adoption. In 1790, Zhu Xi Confucianism was finally adopted as the official government orthodoxy, and in 1797 the Hayashi academy was radically reorganized into the official shogunal college known as SHŌHEIKO.

—— Hayashi Razan bunshū, 2 vols (Kyōto Shisekikai, 1918–19). Hayashi Razan shishū, 2 vols (Kyōto Shisekikai, 1920–21). Hori Isao, Hayashi Razan, vol 18 of Jimbutsu sōsho (Yoshikawa Kōbun Kan, 1964). Ishida Ichirō and Kanaya Osamu, ed, Fujiwara Seika; Hayashi Razan, vol 28 of Nihon shisō taikei (Iwanami Shoten, 1975). Ryūsaku Tsunoda, Wm. Theodore de Bary, and Donald Keene, ed, Sources of Japanese Tradition, vol 1 (1958). James McMULLEN

Hayashi Senjūrō (1876–1943)

Army general and prime minister, briefly, in 1937. Born in Ishikawa Prefecture; a graduate of the Army War College. After serving as head of the Army War College and the Konoe (Imperial Guard) Division, he was sent to command the Japanese army stationed in Korea, then a Japanese colony. During the MANCHURIAN INCIDENT (1931), Hayashi dispatched his troops to support the Guandong (Kwantung) Army, the Japanese field army stationed in Manchuria, without authorization from the Tōkyō government. When the army gained control of Manchuria, however, this action won him official approbation as a man of initiative. He was appointed army minister in the SAITŌ MAKOTO cabinet in 1934. Later, as army minister in the OKADA KEISUKE cabinet in 1935, he dismissed the extremist general MAZAKI JINZABURŌ from his post as inspector-general of military education. His action aggravated the rivalry between the KŌDŌHA and TŌSEIHA factions in the army and contributed indirectly to the FEBRUARY 26TH INCIDENT, an attempted coup d'etat by Kōdōha officers sympathetic to Mazaki's position. After the attempt was quashed, Hayashi retired from active military service. In 1937 he became prime minister, and after trying unsuccessfully to convince party leaders to unite behind him, he formed a cabinet without party representation. He then dissolved the Diet. But the two major parties, the RIKKEN SEIYŪKAI and the RIKKEN MINSEITŌ, won overwhelmingly in the April election, and Hayashi was forced to resign after barely four months in office.

Hayashi Shihei (1738–1793)

Edo-period (1600–1868) expert on administrative and military affairs. Born in Edo (now Tōkyō), in 1757 Hayashi moved to the Sendai domain (now part of Miyagi Prefecture), where his elder brother was in service to the DATE FAMILY. From 1767 on, he went several times to Edo to study, and he presented memorials to his domainal government on educational reforms and methods of increasing productivity. Beginning in 1775, he made three trips to Nagasaki, then the only port open to the outside world. Learning from the resident Dutch traders of the Russian move southward toward Japan, he became convinced of the need to strengthen national defenses and immersed himself in the study of geography and military science. In Edo, his contacts with ŌTSUKI GENTAKU and KATSURAGAWA HOSHŪ, both eminent scholars of WESTERN LEARNING, deepened his knowledge of world conditions. In 1785 Hayashi wrote Sangoku tsūran zusetsu (Illustrated Survey of Three Countries), a geographical treatise on Korea, the Ryūkyū Islands, and Ezo (now Hokkaidō) in which he advocated the development of Japan's northern frontiers to forestall Russian encroachment.

Hayashi is best known for his treatise on naval defense, Kaikoku heidan (Discussion of the Military Problems of a Maritime Nation). Writing in response to the consternation stirred by a Russian adventurer named Benyowsky, who had briefly visited Japan in 1771 and subsequently written letters to Dutch officials at Nagasaki intimating a future Russian attack, Hayashi completed the book in 1786 and, after great difficulty in securing funds, published in 1791. In it he stressed the need to prepare for naval warfare to defend the nation. He also praised European legal systems and military techniques and called for the reeducation of the warrior samurai class, who had been too long accustomed to peace. Eight months after the publication of his book, Hayashi was arrested by the Tokugawa shogunate for disseminating false information and criticizing official policies. Not only printed copies of the book but the printing blocks themselves were confiscated. Hayashi was placed in domiciliary confinement, where he wrote a famous poem lamenting his lot: "I have no parents, no wife, no children, no printing blocks, no money, no desire to die." His book was well timed, however, for a few months after Hayashi's arrest, the Russians arrived in Ezo. Further events confirmed the significance of the work, and between 1848 and 1853 several editions appeared.   KATAGIRI Kazuo

Hayashi Tadasu (1850–1913)

Diplomat. Born in Shimōsa Province (now part of Chiba Prefecture); adopted into a family of hereditary physicians to the Tokugawa shogunate. Under shogunate orders he studied in England from 1866 to 1868. After the MEIJI RESTORATION (1868) he joined the group of die-hard Tokugawa loyalists led by ENOMOTO TAKEAKI and fled to Hokkaidō but was captured at the Battle of GORYŌKAKU. Released in 1870, he joined the new government and accompanied the IWAKURA MISSION to Europe and the United States. He later served in the Ministry of Public Works (Kōbushō) and held governorships in Kagawa and Hyōgo prefectures, as well as diplomatic posts in China, Russia, and Great Britain. As minister to Britain from 1900, he worked to bring about the ANGLO-JAPANESE ALLIANCE of 1902. On becoming foreign minister in the first SAIONJI KIMMOCHI cabinet (1906), he concluded agreements with France (see FRANCO-JAPANESE AGREEMENT OF 1907) and with Russia (see RUSSO-JAPANESE AGREEMENTS OF 1907–1916). He served as minister of communications in the second Saionji cabinet (1911–12).

Hayashi Yūzō (1842–1921)

Politician. Born in the Tosa domain (now Kōchi Prefecture), he was active in the movement to overthrow the Tokugawa shogunate. After the Meiji Restoration (1868) he joined the Ministry of Foreign Affairs, but resigned along with ITAGAKI TAISUKE and others in 1873 following the defeat of the group which was in favor of invading Korea (see SEIKANRON). He joined the RISSHISHA (the group formed by Itagaki at Kōchi) and helped to form the AIKOKU KŌTŌ (Public Party of Patriots). He was jailed briefly for procuring weapons during the SATSUMA REBELLION (1877), but was released under a general amnesty. He was purged the following year under the newly passed Peace Preservation Law (Hoan Jōrei) of 1887 for antigovern-

ment activities. In 1890 Hayashi helped Itagaki to organize anew the Aikoku Kōtō, which had been dissolved soon after its formation in 1874, and was elected to the Diet in the first general election held the same year. He served as minister of communications in the first Ōkuma Shigenobu cabinet and, after helping to form the RIKKEN SEIYŪKAI (Friends of Constitutional Government Party), was appointed minister of commerce and agriculture in the fourth Itō Hirobumi cabinet. He withdrew over party differences and retired from politics in 1908.

Hayato

Tribal people who lived in southern Kyūshū, mainly on the Ōsumi and Satsuma peninsulas (now Kagoshima Prefecture) in ancient times. Like the name EZO, which referred to the aboriginal peoples of northeastern Honshū, Hayato was used pejoratively of those in the south who strongly resisted subjugation by the YAMATO COURT. The accounts of the submission of Hoderi no Mikoto to Hikohohodemi no Mikoto in the mythological sections of the Kojiki (712) and the Nihon shoki (720)—see the section on the Luck of the Sea and The Luck of the Mountains in MYTHOLOGY—are believed to reflect the submission of the Hayato to the rulers of Yamato, although there is some doubt whether this could have taken place at so early a date. It is thought, however, that by the 8th century the government was able to implement its land allotment system (see HANDEN SHŪJU SYSTEM) in the area and that any resistance to the program was promptly crushed by the government-appointed general, ŌTOMO NO TABITO. A central office, the Hayato no Tsukasa, was established under the RITSURYŌ SYSTEM of administration to supervise the Hayato in the service of the court.   KITAMURA Bunji

Hayatozuka

(Hayato tomb). A square tomb mound measuring about 15 meters (49 ft) in length and 3 meters (9.8 ft) in height, located in a rice paddy in Hayato Chō, Kagoshima Prefecture. Tradition holds that it is one of the mounds, mentioned in the chronicles Kojiki (712) and Nihon shoki (720), on which pagoda-like stone memorials and images of the Shitennō (Four Heavenly Kings) were erected during the 8th century to placate the spirits of the indigenous HAYATO and KUMASO peoples, who had been conquered by the YAMATO COURT. It is not certain, however, that the tomb was built at that time; the stone images and memorials that occupy the mound today are known to date from the medieval period (13th–16th centuries).
                              ABE Gihei

Hazama–Gumi, Ltd

Major international contractor specializing in large dams and power stations. Founded in 1889, the company launched overseas activities in 1903 with the Seoul–Pusan railroad project in Korea. It proposes to increase overseas contracts to 20 percent of its total annual business, and has established branches throughout the world. Sales for the fiscal year ending September 1981 totaled ¥334.6 billion (US $1.5 billion), and the company was capitalized at ¥11 billion (US $47.8 million) in the same year. Corporate headquarters are located in Tōkyō.

haze → gobies

headgear

Traditional Japanese headgear can be broadly classified into three categories: kammuri (literally, "crown"), kasa, and headcloths (TENUGUI and zukin). Kammuri include highly ornate crowns decorated with gold and strings of beads as well as simpler caps of lacquered or soft fabric. In 604 noblemen were ordered to wear kammuri as part of their ceremonial or court dress following the customs of Sui (589–618) China (see KAN'I JŪNIKAI). The 12 ranks of court nobles were differentiated by, among other things, the shape and color of the kammuri. For less formal occasions and for those without rank, a plain kammuri such as a keikan or a tokin made of soft, thin, black silk was worn.

Kammuri were gradually replaced by the lower-ranking eboshi, a soft or hard roundish hat of silk or gauze, later made of paper covered with lacquer. Etiquette prescribed the wearing of a head covering when greeting another person, and eboshi, like kammuri,

| kammuri | tate eboshi | kazaore eboshi | ichimegasa | tsunokakushi |

| jingasa | ayaigasa | okoso zukin | maruzukin | anesan kamuri |

Headgear

were such an integral part of a nobleman's dress that, despite their lack of function, they were often worn indoors, sometimes even while sleeping. During the Muromachi period (1333–1568), when the *chommage* hairstyle (see HAIRSTYLES) came into use, the popularity of the *eboshi* declined, and it was worn thereafter only in ceremonies or rituals of the court or shrines.

The *kasa*, in contrast to the *kammuri*, was a functional hat, providing protection from rain and sun, and often from the curiosity of other people. Woven of rush, sedge, straw, or bamboo, *kasa* came in a variety of shapes. *Sugegasa* (sedge *kasa*) were worn when working outdoors; women wore sedge *ichimegasa* for traveling or outings. Of the variety of mesh-woven *kasa* called *amigasa*, the *ayaigasa* was worn by warriors in medieval times for hunting or horseback archery, the cone-shaped *kumagaigasa* was also worn by warriors, and the crescent-shaped *oriamigasa* by ordinary people. Wandering SHAKUHACHI-playing priests called *komusō* wore a large cylindrical *tengai* which concealed the entire head, and this costume became a favorite disguise for spies in popular drama and in period movies. During the Edo period (1600–1868), express messengers called HIKYAKU, who made three round trips each month between Edo (now Tōkyō) and Ōsaka, wore a dome-shaped *sandogasa*, a popular accoutrement for *samurai* in modern television series. Some *kasa* were papered or lacquered, like the *jingasa* worn in battle. In the Edo period one could tell people's occupations by the type of *kasa* they wore.

Tenugui are long rectangular pieces of cotton gauze (expensive ones are silk), still made today as towels and sometimes used for head coverings. In the Edo period there were many fashionable styles such as the *anesan kamuri* ("elder sister covering") or *hoo kamuri* ("cheek covering"). Some areas still maintain the old custom of keeping the *tenugui* on the head when greeting a guest. *Tenugui* or any other long cloths may be rolled and tied as headbands called *hachimaki*, a style still common among laborers and participants at festivals.

The cloth *zukin* was most popular during the Edo period, when there were 50 or so different types, such as the circular *maruzukin*, square *sumizukin*, or sleeve-shaped *sodezukin*. The most popular type of *zukin* worn by women during the Meiji (1868–1912) and Taishō (1912–26) periods was the *okoso zukin*, which covered the entire head except for the eyes and nose. Besides *zukin*, a heavy scarf called *kakumaki* was used as a shawl in cold weather.

Traditional Japanese weddings today still require a *tsunokakushi* (literally, "horn covering") for the bride. An oblong white silk cloth lined with red silk, it covers the forehead and fastens at the back.

With the opening of Japan to Western commerce in the Meiji period, Western-style hats and caps were introduced. In 1878 the straw *mugiwara-bōshi* was introduced, an imitation of the Western straw boater. Derbies, felt hats, and caps were soon adopted. Stu-

dents in elementary and middle schools wore military-style uniforms and caps with emblems, apparel still seen throughout the country.   ISHIYAMA Akira

health care system

(iryō seido). The modern medical care system in Japan originated with the promulgation of the Medical Order (Isei) in 1874, which called for a comprehensive system, covering the spectrum of medical affairs and including medical education, pharmaceutical affairs, public health, and health administration. The order was based on medical care systems in Western European countries, in particular, Germany.

In Japan the medical care service system has developed with particular emphasis on physicians with private practices. Community medical care owes much to the activities of local medical associations that have organized physicians in private clinics and hospitals. Training, research, and other professional functions, however, are carried out by public general hospitals.

In recent years a program to consolidate medical facilities for emergency medical care, rural health care, cancer treatment, cerebro-cardiovascular disease control, and so on has been under way. The concept of primary care as a new health care system is now under consideration.

Until recently medical care had mainly focused on curative medicine in the hands of private physicians, and relatively little attention had been given to preventive measures. A new medical system is now being developed, with emphasis on community health. In an effort to relieve hardship caused by medical care expenses, a comprehensive medical care insurance system for the entire population was put into operation in 1961 (see MEDICAL AND HEALTH INSURANCE).

National Health Administration—— The Japanese national health administration is built on a pyramidal system, with the state (MINISTRY OF HEALTH AND WELFARE) at the apex, followed by prefectural departments of health, health centers, and then local (cities, towns, and villages) departments of health. In the case of 10 designated cities and the Tōkyō Metropolitan special wards, the prefectural level of offices is bypassed.

The Ministry of Health and Welfare is the vital center of national health administration, with responsibility for the planning and implementation of the National Health Plan. In addition to a secretariat, the ministry consists of nine bureaus (public health, environmental sanitation, medical affairs, pharmaceutical affairs, social affairs, children and families, health insurance, pension, and war victims' relief); a Social Insurance Agency; and a number of affiliated institutions and committees (Institute of Population Problems, Institute of Public Health, National Institute of Mental Health, National

Institute of Nutrition, National Institute of Health, Port Quarantine Stations, National Hospitals, National Sanatoriums, National Institute of Hospital Administration, National Institute of Leprosy Research, National Cancer Center, National Cardiovascular Disease Center, National Institute of Hygienic Science, and seven other institutes).

Medical Service —— In Japan everyone is covered by one of the various types of insurance under the NATIONAL HEALTH INSURANCE program. A person can go directly to a private clinic or the hospital of his choice. For the insured person, the entire cost of the medical services, including clinical examination, treatment, and medicine, is reimbursed. A family member of the insured is required to pay 30 percent of the medical cost, but when the payment exceeds a specific sum (¥39,000, or about US $132, per person monthly in 1976), the amount in excess is reimbursed from the fund. Drugs for personal use are available at any drugstore. Those for clinical treatment are usually given to patients at the clinic or hospital (see MEDICINE: drugs).

In-patient care is available at both general clinics and hospitals. General clinics, most of which are private, have beds for 19 patients or fewer. The average hospitalization period per bed in 1976 was 35 days for general diseases and 308 days for tuberculosis. Unlike the United States, Japan has no nursing homes for hospitalized persons, and no introduction by a practitioner is required for admission to a general hospital.

Health Care Activity —— Health centers are the primary organizations responsible for health education and public health measures, including preventive medicine and health promotion. All public institutions, they numbered 858 in 1978. Each center has a staff with physicians, dentists, pharmacists, veterinarians, radiologists, laboratory technicians, nutritionists, public health nurses, midwives, and nurses.

The main services of these centers are health counseling, maternal and child health care, health education, dental health care, nutrition advice, environmental health care, food sanitation, laboratory examination, and public health facilities. These centers carry out mass health screening for local residents and give them advice, collectively or individually, but they do not usually provide medical treatment, since their main activities are concentrated on prevention.

Health Care Personnel —— The main health care personnel consist of physicians, dentists, pharmacists, and certified nurses. The number of registered physicians at the end of 1977 was 138,316, a ratio of 121.2 physicians per 100,000 population. Comparative figures for the United States, Canada, and France were 165, 158, and 141, respectively. To cope with the shortage of physicians in Japan, new medical colleges were being created.

The number of registered dentists at the end of 1977 was 45,715, or 40.0 per 100,000 population. The number of pharmacists was 100,897, or 88.4 per 100,000 population, for the same period. The number of public health nurses, midwives, and clinical nurses working at the end of 1977 was 16,590; 26,618; and 404,156 respectively.

Medical Education System —— Medical education consists of two years of premedical courses and four years of professional medical courses. Applicants are required to pass the entrance examination for the faculty of medicine of a university or a medical college. In the premedical curriculum they undertake general studies, including philosophy, psychology, mathematics, biology, chemistry, and physics. At the faculty of medicine they study medical science (anatomy, physiology, biochemistry, pathology, and so forth), social medicine (public health, forensic medicine, and so forth), and clinical medicine (internal medicine, surgery, gynecology, and so forth). They take the national medical examination immediately after graduating from the university or medical college; each successful candidate is awarded a license. The majority of newly qualified doctors go on to a training hospital, such as a university or national hospital, for a clinical training period of two years.

Medical Facilities —— *Hospitals.* A hospital is defined as a place where physicians or dentists practice medicine or dental surgery and where there is accommodation for more than 20 patients. Requirements for a general hospital include accommodation for more than 100 patients and facilities for special treatment in the areas of internal medicine, surgery, gynecology, ophthalmology, and otolaryngology. The number of hospitals at the end of 1977 was 8,470, with a total of 1,207,003 beds, or 105.7 beds per 10,000 persons.

If classified according to founders, in 1977 national hospitals totaled 446 (5 percent), public hospitals 1,368 (16 percent), and private hospitals established by medical corporations, other corporations, or individuals, 6,514 (77 percent). National and public hospitals providing major facilities accounted for 13.6 percent of available beds, while private ones with minor facilities accounted for 56.8 percent. Hospital beds were divided into 773,739 (60.9 percent) for general diseases, 290,121 (24.7 percent) for psychosis, 109,671 (12.1 percent) for tuberculosis, 20,084 for contagious diseases, and 13,388 for leprosy.

General clinics. A clinic is defined as a medical facility with either no in-patient accommodation, or, if accommodation is provided, beds for fewer than 20 patients; some 65 percent of the clinics are equipped with fluoroscopes. According to a survey made in 1976, the number of general clinics totaled 73,915 (an increase of 801 or 1.1 percent from the previous year), with 65.4 per 10,000 population, or a ratio of 1,530 population per unit. Of these, 90.2 percent were private. The clinics are divided into ones with accommodation, totaling 29,107 (39.4 percent), and the others, with no beds, 44,808 (60.6 percent). In the same year there was an increase of 798 facilities (1.8 percent) in the nonaccommodation clinic category compared with 1975. The number of beds provided by general clinics was 266,954. A classification of private clinics by main specialty was as follows: 66.0 percent for internal medicine, 39.3 percent for pediatrics, 21.1 percent for surgery, and 14.6 percent for gastro-intestinal diseases.

Present Conditions and Priorities for the Future —— The level of the Japanese medical care is generally considered on a par with that of advanced European countries. The noteworthy progress made in recent years in medical care and the development of chemotherapy have been achieved through new technology in fields such as electronic engineering and biochemistry.

At the same time changes in the population structure and social environment of Japan have resulted in a number of new problems in the areas of degenerative diseases, geriatrics, mental diseases, and traffic accident injuries. Many feel that it is essential for the medical administration authorities to establish a comprehensive community health service, although individual measures already operate in connection with emergency medical care and degenerative disease control. It is also important to note that improvements in both the quality and quantity of medical care have led to higher costs. See also MEDICINE: public health.

📖 ——International Medical Foundation of Japan, *One Hundred Years of Health Progress in Japan* (1971). Ministry of Health and Welfare, *Guide to Health and Welfare Services in Japan* (1979). Ministry of Health and Welfare, *Health and Welfare Services in Japan* (1977). Social Insurance Agency, Ministry of Health and Welfare, *Guide to the Social Insurance System in Japan* (1978).

NOSE Takayuki

Hearn, Lafcadio (1850–1904)

(Japanese name Koizumi Yakumo). Author, translator, educator; his books, with their exotic, romantic view of Japanese people, customs, and folklore, were widely read and influential in shaping Western views on Japan from the late 19th century.

Hearn was born on the Greek island of Lefkas, son of an Anglo-Irish surgeon major in the British army and a Greek mother. After the breakup of his parents' marriage when he was seven, he was brought up by an affluent great-aunt in Dublin. He experienced a difficult childhood, attending boarding schools in England and France. When he was at school he suffered a serious accident that left him permanently blind in his left eye, a disfigurement that remained a psychological as well as a physical burden for the rest of his life. In 1869 Hearn was given a small sum of money and sent to live with a distant relative in Cincinnati, Ohio. He suffered hardships at first, holding numerous menial jobs before he became a newspaper reporter and acquired a local reputation for his vivid writing and predilection for the macabre. An avid reader and aspiring writer, he also translated some French stories and novels into English. Hearn subsequently worked as a reporter in New Orleans, New York, and Martinique.

In 1889 he decided to go to Japan, and upon his arrival in Tōkyō in 1890 was befriended by the great linguist and professor at Tōkyō University, Basil Hall CHAMBERLAIN. Chamberlain helped Hearn secure a position teaching English at a middle school (roughly equivalent to the present high school) at Matsue in Shimane Prefecture, where he fell in love with a Japan that was rapidly passing into history. In 1891 Hearn married Koizumi Setsuko, daughter of a respected local *samurai*. Just before the birth of their first son, Hearn transferred to a government college at Kumamoto where he continued his teaching and completed his book, *Glimpses of an Un-*

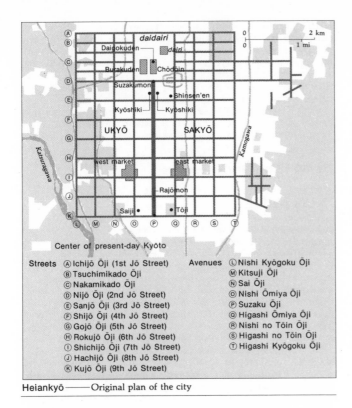

Streets Ⓐ Ichijō Ōji (1st Jō Street)
Ⓑ Tsuchimikado Ōji
Ⓒ Nakamikado Ōji
Ⓓ Nijō Ōji (2nd Jō Street)
Ⓔ Sanjō Ōji (3rd Jō Street)
Ⓕ Shijō Ōji (4th Jō Street)
Ⓖ Gojō Ōji (5th Jō Street)
Ⓗ Rokujō Ōji (6th Jō Street)
Ⓘ Shichijō Ōji (7th Jō Street)
Ⓙ Hachijō Ōji (8th Jō Street)
Ⓚ Kujō Ōji (9th Jō Street)

Avenues Ⓛ Nishi Kyōgoku Ōji
Ⓜ Kitsuji Ōji
Ⓝ Sai Ōji
Ⓞ Nishi Ōmiya Ōji
Ⓟ Suzaku Ōji
Ⓠ Higashi Ōmiya Ōji
Ⓡ Nishi no Tōin Ōji
Ⓢ Higashi no Tōin Ōji
Ⓣ Higashi Kyōgoku Ōji

Heiankyō —— Original plan of the city

familiar Japan (1894), which established his reputation as an interpreter of Japan to the West.

In his initial enthusiasm for Japan and the Japanese, Hearn took on a Japanese lifestyle and, indeed, became a Japanese citizen, taking the name Koizumi Yakumo. In 1894 he accepted a position with the English-language Kobe Chronicle, but soon Chamberlain again helped Hearn by arranging for him to teach English literature at Tōkyō University, a post Hearn held until 1903. However, Hearn disliked the pace of Japanese modernization and became increasingly disillusioned with his adopted country.

Hearn's most famous work, Japan: An Attempt at Interpretation (1904), resulted from a request from Cornell University in 1903 for Hearn to deliver a series of lectures on Japan in return for a handsome sum of money. When the offer was suddenly withdrawn, Hearn arranged for publication of the lectures himself, but died on 26 September 1904 before they could be published. Hearn's writings on Japan are large in number and are noted for their prose style. His works were extremely popular in the United States, particularly before World War II, and are currently regaining popularity. His other books on Japan include Exotics and Retrospective (1898), In Ghostly Japan (1899), Shadowings (1900), A Japanese Miscellany (1901), and Kwaidan (1904).

📖——Henry Goodman, ed, The Selected Writings of Lafcadio Hearn (1949). Nina H. Kennard, Lafcadio Hearn (1967). Koizumi Setsuko, Reminiscences of Lafcadio Hearn (1918). Arthur E. Kunst, Lafcadio Hearn (1969). Elizabeth Stevenson, Lafcadio Hearn (1961).
Edward R. Beauchamp

Heart Mountain Relocation Center

A wartime relocation facility for Japanese Americans, located near Cody, Park County, Wyoming; in operation from 12 August 1942 until 10 November 1945. It held a maximum of 10,767 persons at any one time; a total of 14,025 persons were confined there. Internees came from southern and central California and central Washington. It was the focal point of draft resistance in the camps. See also JAPANESE AMERICANS, WARTIME RELOCATION OF; WAR RELOCATION AUTHORITY.

📖——Estelle Ishigo, Lone Heart Mountain (1972). Douglas W. Nelson, Heart Mountain: The Story of an American Concentration Camp (1976).
Roger DANIELS

heaven

(ten). In Japanese mythology, as recorded in the KOJIKI (712), heaven or the High Celestial Plain (TAKAMAGAHARA) is depicted as the abode of the deities. One of them, Ame no Minakanushi no Mikoto, was later seen as personifying heaven's transcendent, infinite, and immutable quality, but no significant cult developed around this deity. It was the sun goddess, AMATERASU ŌMIKAMI, who was given the highest place in the Shintō pantheon and is described as the progenitor of the imperial line in the mythology.

In Mahāyāna BUDDHISM, introduced to Japan in the 6th century, heaven is conceived of as the future dwelling place of the virtuous. In the popular mind it was understood to mean the Pure Land (Jōdo) or Paradise (Gokuraku) to which one went through the saving power of the Buddha. The Chinese concept of heaven (tian or t'ien) as the ultimate principle of the moral and physical universe, though accepted by Confucianists, never gained wide acceptance in Japan. The Christian heaven is translated as ten or tengoku.
FUJITA Tomio

Hebei–Chahar (Hopeh–Chahar) Political Council → Ji-Cha (Chi-Ch'a) Autonomous Political Council

Heco, Joseph → Hamada Hikozō

Hegurajima

Also known as Hekurajima. Volcanic island in the Sea of Japan, 47 km (29 mi) north of the Noto Peninsula, Ishikawa Prefecture, off central Honshū. It is composed of andesite and lava; no trees grow on the island. Women divers from the city of Wajima on the mainland travel to the island in the summer and dive for abalone and turbo in the nearby reefs, returning home in the fall. Area: 0.6 km (0.2 sq mi); circumference: 6 km (4 mi).

Heian history → history of Japan

Heiankyō

(literally "Capital of Peace and Ease"). Original name of KYŌTO; capital of Japan from 794 to 1868 when Tōkyō was made the capital. Heiankyō was situated between the rivers Kamogawa and Katsuragawa in the Kadono District of Yamashiro Province (now Kyōto Prefecture), with its original center a little to the west of what is today the central part of Kyōto. The only gap in this span of over a thousand years was a period of six months in 1180 when TAIRA NO KIYOMORI (1118–81) removed the capital to FUKUHARAKYŌ in Settsu Province (now part of Ōsaka and Hyōgo prefectures).

The word kyōto (capital, or site of the imperial palace) had been used earlier as an informal name for the capital at Nara (HEIJŌKYŌ), and it was also applied to Heiankyō. By the latter part of the 11th century, Kyōto had for practical purposes become the name of the city, both informally and formally.

In 784 Emperor KAMMU (r 781–806), with the support of the FUJIWARA FAMILY of government bureaucrats and aided by the economic power of the HATA FAMILY of earlier immigrants (KIKAJIN) from the Korean peninsula, moved the seat of government from Nara to NAGAOKAKYŌ in order to eliminate the excessive political power of the Nara Buddhist sects (see DŌKYŌ) and to bring new vigor to the RITSURYŌ SYSTEM of government. However, the assassination in 785 of Fujiwara no Tanetsugu, the leading advocate of the transfer, and the implication in the crime and subsequent banishment and death of Kammu's brother Crown Prince Sawara (d 785) were followed by a series of natural disasters which were attributed to Sawara's angry spirit, and construction of the capital slowed, eventually coming to a halt. In 793, on the advice of WAKE NO KIYOMARO, the emperor ordered Fujiwara no Oguromaro (733–794) to build a new capital in the village of Uda (now Ukyō Ward, Kyōto), which, like Nagaokakyō, was in Yamashiro Province, an area that had long been inhabited by the Hata family.

Although both cities were patterned after Chang'an (Ch'ang-an), the capital of Tang (T'ang) China, Heiankyō was larger than Heijōkyō. It was also more conveniently situated for transportation by land and blessed with an abundance of water. The course of the Kamogawa was shifted to flow around the city and canals were dug parallel to the major north-south avenues. The new capital measured approximately 4.5 kilometers (2.8 mi) east to west and 5.2 kilometers (3.2 mi) north to south. With the exception of the state-sponsored TŌJI and Saiji, constructed near the gate Rajōmon, no temples were to be allowed within the precincts of Heiankyō. The residence of the emperor and imperial government offices were located in an area called *daidairi* (outer palace grounds) in the northernmost part of the city. Also located there was the hall called DAIGOKUDEN, from which, initially, the emperor governed the country. The Daigokuden, approximately 53 meters (174 ft) long and 17 meters (56 ft) wide, and the Burakuden, 52 meters (171 ft) long and 20 meters (66 ft) wide, were raised off the ground on high stone pediments and their roofs, covered with green tiles, were supported on crimson pillars in imitation of the Chinese style. In contrast, the palace of the emperor, which stood at the right center of the *daidairi* within the *dairi* (inner palace grounds), was a simple affair; roofed with cryptomeria bark and constructed of straight-grained wood left unpainted, it was strikingly different from the splendid Daigokuden and Burakuden. Directly south of the *daidairi* was a large park, Shinsen'en, for the exclusive use of the emperor and his courtiers. Also conceived after a Chinese model, there was a pond with a fishing pavilion, a hall for entertainment (the Kenrinden), and a tower from which one could survey the capital.

Heiankyō was divided by the broad avenue Suzaku Ōji (84 m or 276 ft wide)—running from the gate Suzakumon of the *daidairi* south to Rajōmon, the main entrance to the city—into two districts, Sakyō to the east and Ukyō to the west. In each of these districts was an office called Kyōshiki; these together administered the affairs of the capital. The two main districts were each further divided into large square sectors called *bō* by streets running east to west and avenues running north to south. One *bō* sector was composed of 4 *hō* and 1 *hō* of 4 *chō*. A *chō* had an area of 1,450 square meters (1,734 sq yds) and was divided into 4 parts east to west and 8 parts north to south, forming 32 lots 8.3 meters (27.2 ft) wide and 16.6 meters (54.4 ft) long. These lots, called *henushi*, were the basic unit of land measure for residential plots. The east-to-west rows of *bō* sectors were called *jō* and were numbered north to south. The east-to-west cross streets were named after them, e.g., Ichijō Ōji (First Jō Street), Nijō Ōji (Second Jō Street), and so on.

The ordinary inhabitants of Heiankyō were the aristocracy, government workers, and the common people *(kyōko)*. They were augmented by various people such as *eji* (see EFU), who came from outlying provinces to serve as guardsmen and in other minor capacities for a period of one year (later three years). Heiankyō, like Heijōkyō before it, originally functioned solely as a government center and had no private sector, but as the *ritsuryō* system slowly eroded, various independent enterprises appeared. A transport industry developed to carry tax tributes (see SO, YŌ, AND CHŌ) to government storehouses and stipends in kind (see FUKO) to the establishments of aristocrats or to shrines and temples. Eventually a merchant class arose as well and shops began to appear, their goods displayed along the streets, forcing the government-operated markets in the east and west districts into decline. Craftsmen who had served at court, in the mansions of aristocrats, and at shrines and temples gradually became independent and built workshops of their own.

The residences of aristocrats were concentrated in the north around the first three cross streets; the district south of the fourth cross street, Shijō Ōji, was the center of industry and commerce. The Ukyō quarter, located near the river Katsuragawa, was a damp lowland which failed to prosper, and the city developed toward the east, straddling the Kamogawa with its population center near the west bank of the river. Houses of the common people were concentrated in the Sakyō quarter near the Kamogawa, but south of the fifth cross street, Gojō Ōji, there was much vacant land. During the INSEI period of rule by retired emperors (latter part of the 11th to the mid-12th century), Shirakawa, a suburb of the capital east of the Kamogawa, flourished as the locus of political authority, and when Taira no Kiyomori wrested power from the retired emperors, Rokuhara, area east of the Kamogawa, prospered.

In the latter half of the Heian period (794–1185) crime in the city increased dramatically. The mansions of the aristocracy were plundered and put to the torch, street thugs roamed freely, and robberies occurred in broad daylight. The Burakuden burned in 1063 and was never rebuilt, nor were the Daigokuden and others of the main government buildings after fire swept through them in 1177. Fires broke out in the emperor's quarters in the *dairi* 16 times between 960 and 1227, after which restoration was no longer attempted.

In the Kamakura period (1185–1333), with the shift of political power from the emperor to the shogunate in Kamakura, Heiankyō changed from a political to an economic center. Under the Muro-machi shogunate (1338–1573) the city again became the seat of power, but during the ŌNIN WAR (1467–77) more than half of it was destroyed. However, its broad streets were repaired and the city and the imperial palace gradually rebuilt by ODA NOBUNAGA (1534–82) and TOYOTOMI HIDEYOSHI (1537–98) in the 16th century. Most of what remains today of the old city dates from this period. The palace was moved to its present site in the north central section of modern Kyōto in the 18th century, but the present buildings, now known as the Kyōto Imperial Palace, date from the 19th century. See also HISTORY OF JAPAN: Heian history; KYŌTO. *ABE Takeshi*

Heian literature → literature

Heian period

As defined in this encyclopedia, the Heian period is a span of nearly 400 years extending from 794, when Emperor KAMMU established HEIANKYŌ (now Kyōto) as the imperial capital of Japan, to 1185, when MINAMOTO NO YORITOMO's forces defeated those of the TAIRA FAMILY, thus setting the stage for the establishment of the KAMAKURA SHOGUNATE. The name of the period is taken from that of the capital and means "peace and tranquility." Some classifications begin the period in 781, the year of Kammu's accession to the throne, or in 784, when the capital was removed from HEIJŌKYŌ (now Nara) to NAGAOKAKYŌ; some end it in 1180, when Yoritomo took up arms and established his headquarters at Kamakura, or in 1183, when the Taira family fled Heiankyō before the advancing army of MINAMOTO NO YOSHINAKA. The period may be conceived as one of transition from the decaying RITSURYŌ SYSTEM of government to a feudal society in which the warrior class dominated. It is notable also as the period of the greatest flowering of the aristocratic culture centered on the imperial court. See also HISTORY OF JAPAN: Heian history; PERIODIZATION.

Heian Shrine

(Heian Jingū). Shintō shrine in Sakyō Ward, Kyōto, dedicated to the spirits of Emperor Kammu (r 781–806), in whose reign Heiankyō (now Kyōto) was established as the capital of Japan, and of Emperor Kōmei (r 1846–1867), the last emperor to sit on the throne in Kyōto before the capital was moved to Tōkyō in 1868. The shrine was built in 1895 to commemorate the eleven hundredth anniversary of the founding of the capital. The oratory *(haiden)* and main gate are replicas of the original buildings of the Kyōto palace. The shrine is also noted for its superb gardens. Festivals are held annually on 3 April in honor of Emperor Kammu, and on 30 January in honor of Emperor Kōmei. In addition, the shrine sponsors a spectacular procession, the JIDAI FESTIVAL (Festival of the Ages), celebrated on 22 October, which draws huge numbers of visitors to Kyōto.

Stanley WEINSTEIN

Heibonsha, Ltd, Publishers

A publisher, mainly of encyclopedias, dictionaries, and books in the fields of science and philosophy. Heibonsha was established in 1914 by SHIMONAKA YASABURŌ, following the success of a one-volume home reference work that he had edited entitled *Ya! Kore wa benri da.* Heibonsha published its *Gendai taishū bungaku zenshū* (Modern Popular Literature Series) in 60 volumes in the mid-1920s and a large general encyclopedia entitled *Dai hyakka jiten*, which became a model for later modern Japanese encyclopedias, in 28 volumes between 1931 and 1935. Since World War II Heibonsha has published not only encyclopedias, such as its *Sekai dai hyakka jiten*, but also books on art and literature, including the series Tōyō Bunko (Library of Eastern Literature). *KOBAYASHI Kazuhiro*

Heichū monogatari

A work of the *uta monogatari* (poem tale) genre, made up of 39 episodes and containing 152 WAKA and 1 *chōka*. The anecdotes in this work are united by the central hero, Heichū, who is identified as Taira no Sadabumi (ca 871–923; also known as Taira no Sadabun or Sadafun). The author is unknown, and the work is generally believed to have been compiled some time between 959 and 965. In both *Heichū monogatari* and another poem tale, YAMATO MONOGATARI, Heichū emerges as a dismal failure as a lover, a striking contrast to ARIWARA NO NARIHIRA, whose exploits are featured in the poem tale ISE MONOGATARI. It is believed that stories about celebrated lovers continued to be transmitted up to the time of Lady Murasaki, who described the ideal Heian lover in the TALE OF GENJI.

Taira no Yoshikaze, Heichū's father, was the nephew of Princess Hanshi (833–900), the mother of Emperor Uda (867–931; r 887–897). Yoshikaze was known to have been an amorous man, and in time his son acquired the same reputation.

In *Heichū monogatari* the hero emerges as a pathetic figure. In one episode, Heichū woos a woman for two long years but is never given an opportunity to be intimate with her. In another episode, Heichū becomes intimate with a young lady-in-waiting in the Imperial Palace; however, he fails to send her a morning-after letter, or even communicate with her, and so the distraught woman becomes a nun. These and other stories show that Heichū was far from being an all-conquering lover.

In later works, such as the *Tale of Genji* and KONJAKU MONOGATARI, Heichū is described as being comical. One story known in Lady Murasaki's time relates how he splashed his face with water, pretending to weep at a lady's unkindness. To expose him, the lady mixed some ink with water so that when next he played his little trick, his face was blackened. *Mildred TAHARA*

Heiji Disturbance

(Heiji no Ran). A clash between MINAMOTO NO YOSHITOMO and TAIRA NO KIYOMORI in January 1160 (Heiji 1.12). The two men had shared the victory in the HŌGEN DISTURBANCE of 1156, but Kiyomori had received greater rewards and, with FUJIWARA NO MICHINORI, exerted great influence over the powerful retired emperor GO-SHIRAKAWA. Taking advantage of Kiyomori's absence from Kyōto on a pilgrimage, Yoshitomo seized power with the aid of Michinori's rival Fujiwara no Nobuyori (1133–60) and other disgruntled courtiers. He imprisoned Go-Shirakawa and Emperor Nijō (1143–65), killed Michinori, and made new official appointments before Kiyomori returned to crush the uprising. Yoshitomo and Nobuyori were captured and killed while fleeing to the east, and Minamoto influence was swept from the court, leaving the Taira firmly in control. The war tale HEIJI MONOGATARI is based on this incident, and the events are vividly depicted in the scrolls known as the HEIJI MONOGATARI EMAKI. *G. Cameron HURST III*

Heiji monogatari

One of a pair of war tales, GUNKI MONOGATARI, which together tell the story of the succession struggles of the mid-12th century that resulted in the eclipse of Fujiwara power and the rise to supremacy of the former provincial warrior clan, the TAIRA FAMILY, more commonly known as the Heike. The first phase of the struggles, in 1156, is treated in HŌGEN MONOGATARI, the second and decisive phase in 1160 in *Heiji monogatari*, the titles coming from the respective era names (see HEIJI DISTURBANCE). A significant difference between them, perhaps simply reflecting historical fact, is that in *Hōgen* the warriors supporting the court factions are not known (despite the depiction of MINAMOTO NO TAMETOMO as an almost superhuman hero) as dominating or directing events to the same extent as in *Heiji*. Partly because by 1159 the supporters of the rival court factions had become largely polarized into Minamoto on the one side and Taira on the other, the incidents of the Heiji Disturbance are depicted mainly as struggles between these two families, at least after the first few sections of the first of the three books, in which following a moralizing introduction with a strongly Chinese flavor, the facts of the dispute are set out.

The Taira leader was of course TAIRA NO KIYOMORI. The Minamoto leader was Minamoto Yoshitomo, killer in the *Hōgen monogatari* of his own father Tameyoshi, while another prominent figure is Yoshitomo's doughty eldest son Akugenta Yoshihira. In many of the 33 different extant texts, the work ends after the rout of the Minamoto with the murder of Yoshitomo by one of his retainers, the capture and execution of Akugenta, the capture of Yoshitomo's third son, MINAMOTO NO YORITOMO, the sparing of his life at the request of Kiyomori's stepmother and his subsequent exile to Izu, and the humiliation of Yoshitomo's beautiful young wife Tokiwa Gozen, who has to yield to the advances of Kiyomori in order to save her three young children, including Ushiwakamura, later known as MINAMOTO NO YOSHITSUNE. Some texts, however, go on to events of later years, with Yoshitsune's flight to northeast Japan, Yoritomo's revolt, the defeat of the Taira and even Yoritomo's death in 1199.

Even in those texts which omit mention of the final victory of the Minamoto, the work's sympathies are clearly with them, and it can hardly have been written before that victory. Some evidence suggests that an early version may date from the first decade or so of the 13th century. However, *Heiji monogatari* (and for that matter *Hōgen monogatari*) underwent a century or more of textual evolution, in the same way as HEIKE MONOGATARI. We find them mentioned at the end of the 13th century as chanted texts. Thus to speak of one date of composition is meaningless. In many ways *Hōgen* and *Heiji* form a pair, and may even have been originally composed by the same person. Both treat their material chronologically and in three books, in very similar, clear, and direct styles. Both are swift-moving narratives full of vivid description and adventurous episodes. Neither exhibits much of the lyrical pathos so prominent in *Heike monogatari*, nor do they have such a strong Buddhist flavor.

There are in existence three superb scrolls (see HEIJI MONOGATARI EMAKI) illustrating in YAMATO-E style sections of book one of the Heiji story (one, depicting the burning of the Sanjō Palace, is in the Boston Museum of Fine Arts). Thought to date from about a century after the Heiji Disturbance, they were probably originally part of a larger set. The basis for the text accompanying the picture is unknown; this is briefer than and varies significantly from the corresponding passages in the standard texts of *Heiji monogatari*, but could perhaps be based on some early form of the work.

📖 ——Partial translation in E. O. Reischauer and J. K. Yamagiwa, *Translations from Early Japanese Literature* (1951); includes references to articles on Heiji Scrolls. *Douglas E. MILLS*

Heiji monogatari emaki

Handscrolls illustrating the HEIJI MONOGATARI (Tale of Heiji), a chronicle of the brief war between the Taira and Minamoto clans that occurred in the winter of the first year of the Heiji era (1160). There are four complete scrolls and fragments of a fifth, all polychrome; however, these belong to different sets, suggesting that originally there were many more scrolls. All these handscrolls date from the Kamakura period (1185–1333), when handscrolls illustrating the recent bloody warfare were popular.

Three of the extant *Heiji* scrolls illustrate episodes from the first part of the tale, in which the background for the war is set and early skirmishes described. *The Burning of the Sanjō Palace*, in the Boston Museum of Fine Arts, illustrates an attack on the palace of the retired emperor GO-SHIRAKAWA. *Shinzei*, in the Seikadō Collection, Tōkyō, deals with the fate of a rival courtier, FUJIWARA NO MICHINORI (also called Shinzei), who was forced by the Minamoto to flee Kyōto and was subsequently captured and decapitated. *The Flight to Rokuhara*, in the Tōkyō National Museum, describes the removal of the emperor from the Nijō palace to Rokuhara.

The Battle of Rokuhara shows TAIRA NO KIYOMORI leading his troops to victory over the Minamoto forces. This was the key battle of the war, and the climactic episode in the second part of the tale. The scroll is preserved in 14 fragments mounted on hanging scrolls in scattered collections, and there is no text. The sections can be easily identified, however, since an Edo-period (1600–1868) copy of this scroll is preserved in the Tōkyō National Museum.

The last of the group, in a private collection in Japan, covers three separate episodes from the final part of the story. These are: *The Flight of the Lady Tokiwa and Her Return to Rokuhara, The Exile of Tsunemune and Korekata,* and *The Exile of Yoritomo*. All of these deal with the commutation of death sentences to sentences of exile for Minamoto family members and their retainers.

The five scrolls date from the late 13th century. They can be divided stylistically into four groups. The earliest seem to be *The Burning of the Sanjō Palace* and *Shinzei. The Flight to Rokuhara* and *The Battle of Rokuhara* are usually attributed to the same school. *Lady Tokiwa* is stylistically different from the other scrolls. It is also smaller than the other three complete scrolls. It is apparently the work of a different school and may be later than the other scrolls.

Despite slight differences in style and date, all of these scrolls are remarkable examples of war pictures, executed with a strong sense of drama. This, combined with an acute observation of details, such as the arms and armor, makes the scrolls a rich source for study. See also EMAKIMONO.

📖 ——Tanaka Ichimatsu, ed, *Heiji monogatari emaki; Mōko shūrai ekotoba*, vol 9 of *Nihon emakimono zenshū* (Kadokawa Shoten, 1964). *M. YOCHUM*

Heiji no Ran → Heiji Disturbance

Heijōkyō

City and pair of imperial palaces in the Nara Basin in use from 710 to 784 AD as the capital of Japan; i.e., the capital usually referred to as NARA. Located 18 kilometers (11.2 mi) almost due north from the preceding capital, FUJIWARAKYŌ, in the western sector of the present city of Nara, the city was built on a plain crossed by the rivers Sahogawa and Akishinogawa, where there had been some villages and mounded tombs (KOFUN). After two years of construction, Empress Gemmei (661–721; r 707–715) moved her court in the fourth month of 710, and Heijō remained the seat of government for eight successive rulers until NAGAOKAKYŌ was built by Emperor KAMMU in 784. Several rulers kept palaces elsewhere and periodically used them, and during the period 741–745 Emperor SHŌMU moved the capital to three different places (KUNI NO MIYA, NANIWAKYŌ, and SHIGARAKI NO MIYA) until he realized he had antagonized the spirits of nature and returned to Heijōkyō.

The city was laid out on a square grid pattern modeled on that of the Chinese Tang (T'ang) dynasty (618–907) capital at Chang'an (Ch'ang-an). Nine major streets running north to south intersected with ten running east to west so as to form 72 large blocks which were called bō—9 rows (jō) consisting of 8 blocks each. To these were later added 12 additional blocks on the northeast side of the city and partial blocks in the northwest to form the sections known as Gekyō and Hokuhen, respectively.

Each large block was 1,800 shaku (553 m or 1,814 ft) square. The entire city, not including its outer additions, measured perhaps slightly more than 4.8 by 4.3 kilometers (3.0 mi by 2.7 mi). The grounds containing the palaces occupied 4 blocks in the center of the north end of the city. The wide Suzaku Ōji, the main street, led from the southern edge of the city to the palace grounds, where it ran perpendicular into a large street stretching the width of the city. Rajōmon was the main gate at the southern edge of the city; and Suzakumon was the entrance gate to the palace complex. The east market was located toward the south in the eighth jō and third bō and the west market, also toward the south in the eighth jō and second bō (counting jō from north to south and counting bō out from Suzaku Ōji in both cases). Besides this there was a kind of symmetrical arrangement of the six major temples within the city: SAIDAIJI, TŌSHŌDAIJI, and YAKUSHIJI on the west side in Ukyō, and KŌFUKUJI, Gangōji, and DAIANJI on the east side in Sakyō. The temple TŌDAIJI lay in the northeast outside the designated limits of the Gekyō, and the temple SHIN YAKUSHIJI was even farther out. Several scattered family temples occupied smaller blocks. The city's population is thought to have reached 200,000 by the end of the 8th century.

After Heijōkyō was abandoned, the temples remained the object of pilgrimages. The city drifted eastward toward the hills and most of the western part reverted to villages and rice fields. Large areas have been available for excavation and the site of the east palace in the north of the city has been fully exposed, revealing the location of the main buildings, several wells, and, to the northwest, a garden.

A remarkable cross-section of objects of daily use and court products has been recovered. Among the ceramic finds are three-color ware, ornamented roof tiles, inkstones, SUE WARE, and HAJI WARE, some of the last decorated with curiously painted faces. Unearthed metal objects include tools and examples of many of the so-called twelve coinages of the imperial court (KŌCHŌ JŪNISEN); wooden objects include implements, shield parts, combs, looms, clogs, human effigies, and wooden tablets (MOKKAN).

The inscribed mokkan, almost 20,000 of which have been unearthed, are especially instructive on business transactions and taxes submitted to the palace. Dating from between 709 and 782, these tablets provide a detailed record of the sources of raw materials and the kinds and quantities of goods known in Heijō during its prime.

📖 Satō Kōji, "Heijōkyō to Heijōkyū," in Ueda Masaaki, ed, Tojō (1976). Tsuboi Kiyotari and Suzuki Kakichi, ed, Rekishi jidai 1: Umoreta kyūden to tera, in Kodaishi hakkutsu, vol 9 (Kōdansha, 1974). Tsuboi Kiyotari, Heijōkyū seki, no. 115 of Nihon no bijutsu (December 1975).   J. Edward KIDDER, Jr.

Heike monogatari

(The Tale of the Heike). The most important of the Kamakura (1185–1333) and Muromachi (1333–1568) period prose tales known

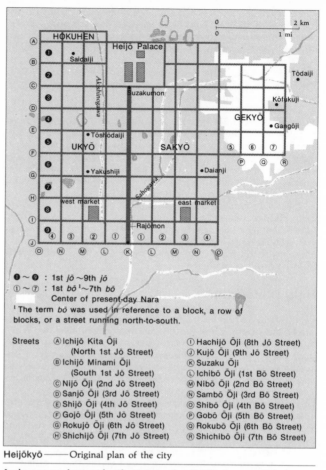

Heijōkyō —— Original plan of the city

● ~ ❾ : 1st jō ~9th jō
① ~ ⑦ : 1st bō[1] ~7th bō
      Center of present-day Nara
[1] The term bō was used in reference to a block, a row of blocks, or a street running north-to-south.

Streets		
Ⓐ Ichijō Kita Ōji (North 1st Jō Street)	Ⓘ Hachijō Ōji (8th Jō Street)
Ⓑ Ichijō Minami Ōji (South 1st Jō Street)	Ⓙ Kujō Ōji (9th Jō Street)
Ⓒ Nijō Ōji (2nd Jō Street)	Ⓚ Suzaku Ōji
Ⓓ Sanjō Ōji (3rd Jō Street)	Ⓛ Ichibō Ōji (1st Bō Street)
Ⓔ Shijō Ōji (4th Jō Street)	Ⓜ Nibō Ōji (2nd Bō Street)
Ⓕ Gojō Ōji (5th Jō Street)	Ⓝ Sambō Ōji (3rd Bō Street)
Ⓖ Rokujō Ōji (6th Jō Street)	Ⓞ Shibō Ōji (4th Bō Street)
Ⓗ Shichijō Ōji (7th Jō Street)	Ⓟ Gobō Ōji (5th Bō Street)
	Ⓠ Rokubō Ōji (6th Bō Street)
	Ⓡ Shichibō Ōji (7th Bō Street)

In the system of street identifications used at Heijōkyō, rows of blocks running north-to-south were called bō and those running east-to-west were called jō. Streets were named after these rows, using the same bō or jō nomenclature. Bō were counted outward from Suzaku Ōji; jō were counted from north to south.

as GUNKI MONOGATARI, or "war tales." It deals with the short heyday of the TAIRA FAMILY (the 20 years following the HŌGEN DISTURBANCE [1156] and HEIJI DISTURBANCE [1160], when they not only defeated their rivals, the MINAMOTO FAMILY, but also ousted the FUJIWARA FAMILY from their dominant position at court), and the five years of the TAIRA-MINAMOTO WAR that began with the Minamoto rising again in 1180 and ended with the crushing defeat of the Taira in 1185. The tale divides into roughly three parts. The central figure in the first is TAIRA NO KIYOMORI. Arrogant, evil, and ruthless, he is above all so consumed by the fires of hatred for the Minamoto that he dies in agony, his feverish body beyond all cooling, even when he is immersed in water. The main figures of the second and third parts are generals on the Minamoto side, first MINAMOTO NO YOSHINAKA and then after his death, the heroic MINAMOTO NO YOSHITSUNE, a youthful military genius wrongly suspected of treachery by his elder brother MINAMOTO NO YORITOMO.

Heike monogatari abounds in stirring scenes of battle, recounting brave deeds by warriors proud of their lineage and military prowess and prizing loyalty above life. In its exhaustive enumerations of warriors participating in the battles and its detailed descriptions of their conduct and even of their dress, the work resembles many Western epics. Dealing with the cataclysmic upheavals of this time of Taira and Minamoto rivalry, it undoubtedly has a grand sweep about it that can be described as "epic." Whether it may truly be termed an epic is debatable for various reasons, but principally because of its lyrical and emotional content. Several episodes about tragic lovers or love affairs have an atmosphere redolent of the MONO NO AWARE of Heian court literature. Also, the emphasis throughout is very much on the pathos of the situation of the Taira, a warrior family risen to importance at court, only to be forced out by uncouth rivals from eastern Japan. The atmosphere of the whole work is permeated by the Buddhist doctrine that all human activity is ephemeral and illusory, that the mighty are soon cast down, and that nothing avails but faith in the grace of Amida Buddha.

Such Buddhist sentiments are not uncommon in the literature of the time, but the reason for their prominence in *Heike monogatari* is that those responsible for the development of this work were chanters (BIWA HŌSHI), lute-playing priests who traveled the country reciting this and other chronicles. They were blind men who used no fixed text, but rather recreated the work at each performance on the basis of oral formulae. The original *Heike* text was probably written by a court noble of the early 13th century, in Chinese (KAMBUN). He incorporated material from various sources, including oral tales about the wars, some of which may have been first told as religious rituals for the benefit of the dead warriors. From the mid-13th century, two traditions developed. One was a line of texts for silent reading, culminating in GEMPEI SEISUIKI, and the other was a line of texts for oral chanters, which contained many passages in the 7-5 syllable rhythm of classical poetry. The chanted tradition continued well into the Muromachi period, but of all the approximately 100 texts of the *Heike,* the accepted standard is the version dictated by a master *Heike* performer, Akashi Kakuichi, just before his death in 1371. *Heike* texts vary not only in wording but also in content, revealing the development of social attitudes and ideals of conduct.

Heike monogatari contains so much of varied human interest that it has been almost as popular a source for later Japanese writers as has *Genji monogatari* (TALE OF GENJI). It has, for instance, provided material for a number of NŌ plays. Some of these, such as *Atsumori,* are "warrior pieces," but several are based on more lyrical episodes about tragic lovers, particularly women, such as *Giō, Senju,* and *Kogō.*

■———*Heike monogatari,* tr Hiroshi Kitagawa and Bruce T. Tsuchida as *The Tale of the Heike* (1975), and tr A. L. Sadler as *The Heike Monogatari* in *Transactions of the Asiatic Society of Japan* 46.2 (1918), 49.1 (1921–22); abridged in A. L. Sadler, *The Ten Foot Square Hut and Tales of the Heike* (1928, repr 1972). K. D. Butler, "The Textual Evolution of the Heike Monogatari," *Harvard Journal of Asiatic Studies* 26 (1966). K. D. Butler, "The Heike Monogatari and the Japanese Warrior Epic," *Harvard Journal of Asiatic Studies* 29 (1969). T. Hasegawa, "The Early Stages of the Heike Monogatari," *Monumenta Nipponica* 22 (1967). Jacqueline Pigeot, "Histoire de Yokobue," *Bulletin de la Maison Franco-Japonaise,* Nouvelle Série, 9.2 (1972).   *Douglas E.* MILLS

heikyoku

Episodes from HEIKE MONOGATARI (The Tale of the Heike), chanted to the accompaniment of the BIWA (lute). Yoshida Kenkō (1281–1350), in his *Tsurezuregusa,* section 226, ascribes *Heike monogatari* to one Yukinaga, a former official and courtier of the cloistered emperor Go-Toba, and later a Tendai monk at the monastery Enryakuji on Mt. Hiei. Yukinaga collaborated with a blind monk, Shōbutsu, who was the first to chant the text. This probably all occurred before 1220. The *heikyoku* style of biwa music (also called Heike *biwa*) incorporated elements of court music, Buddhist chant, and *mōsō biwa* (blind monks' lute). At the same time, other military tales were being set to music, but by the 13th century they had been eclipsed by *heikyoku.*

Shōbutsu's disciples split into two schools known as the Ichikataryū and Yasakaryū. In the early part of the Muromachi period (1333–1568), guilds of blind musicians were formed under government protection. Consequently *heikyoku* schools proliferated further; and in the 16th century blind *biwa* players were recruited as secret agents. In the Edo period (1600–1868) the *biwa* was gradually overtaken in popularity by the SHAMISEN, on whose technique and repertoire it had a considerable influence. The two main schools were now Hatanoryū, in Kyōto, and Maedaryū, in Edo (now Tōkyō). In the Meiji period (1868–1912) a revival was led by Tateyama Zennoshin (1845–1916) and his family; there has been a further revival in recent years.

The *heikyoku* repertoire contains 200 pieces, of which 176 are *hira-mono* (ordinary items), 19 are *hikyoku* (secret pieces), and 5— the most weighty—are *hiji* (secret material). Another classification is: *fushi-mono* (melodic, lyrical pieces), *hiroi-mono* (narrative pieces, often about battles) and *yomi-mono* (recitative pieces). *Heikyoku,* like *shōmyō* and *yōkyoku,* is composed of stereotyped melodic fragments built on a structure of fourths. The *biwa* generally alternates with the voice.

■———Fujii Seishin, *Heikyoku* (1966). Hasegawa Tadashi, "The Early Stages of the *Heike monogatari*," *Monumenta Nipponica* 22.

1–2 (1967). Nakayama Tarō, *Nihon mōjin shi* (1934). Tateyama Zennoshin, *Heike ongaku shi* (1910).   *David B.* WATERHOUSE

heimin

(commoners). One of the three classes of society in a system adopted by the Meiji government in 1869. The other two classes were the *kazoku* (court nobles and former *daimyō;* see PEERAGE) and the SHIZOKU (former *samurai*). The word *heimin* had been used loosely since ancient times to refer to the common people as opposed to the court nobility or, later, the samurai, but it was not until the Meiji period (1868–1912) that it became part of an official class that included the three lowest categories of the Edo-period (1600–1868) division of society (SHI-NŌ-KŌ-SHŌ). In 1870 *heimin* were permitted for the first time to have surnames, and in 1871 certain outcast groups that had at first been excluded from the tripartite classification were included as *heimin.* The class status of each family was duly noted in the HOUSEHOLD REGISTERS. Marriage and adoption between classes also became legal, and theoretically all three classes were now equal, but the custom of social ranking persisted until the spread of education and the rise of political and economic power among commoners led to greater class equality. During World War II official use of the terms *kazoku, shizoku,* and *heimin* was discontinued.

Heiminsha

(Society of Commoners). A socialist organization founded in October 1903 by KŌTOKU SHŪSUI and SAKAI TOSHIHIKO soon after their departure from the newspaper YOROZU CHŌHŌ in protest over its prowar stance on the eve of the Russo-Japanese War of 1904–05; the center of socialist activities during the first decade of the 20th century. Besides Kōtoku and Sakai, who were materialist socialists, the group included a number of Christian socialists, most notably ISHIKAWA SANSHIRŌ and KINOSHITA NAOE. The society published a newspaper, *Heimin shimbun* (weekly from 15 November 1903 to 29 January 1905 and daily from 15 January 1907 to 14 April 1907), which served as a vehicle for pacifist as well as socialist thought and enlisted the contributions of such writers as UCHIMURA KANZŌ and TAOKA REIUN. It also published tracts written by its members. The newspaper was discontinued in 1905 because of government repression and a lack of resources. Another weekly, *Chokugen* (Straight Talk), took its place, but after eight months this, too, was prohibited. A short time later the Heiminsha itself was forced to close down because of internal dissension and financial difficulties. In January 1907 both the society and the *Heimin shimbun* were revived (the latter also served as a party organ for the Japan Socialist Party, which had been formed in 1906 and whose membership overlapped with that of the Heiminsha), but in April of the same year the Heiminsha was forced to disband, again because of internal disunity and government prohibition, and the newspaper also ceased to exist.

Heimin shimbun

("Commoner's News"). Socialist weekly newspaper launched in Tōkyō in November 1903 by KŌTOKU SHŪSUI and SAKAI TOSHIHIKO. Proclaiming the cause of democracy, socialism, and pacifism, it advocated peace and social reform. As the official voice of its parent organization, the HEIMINSHA, the paper quickly became the country's foremost leftist news publication. Regular contributors included well-known socialist thinkers like ISHIKAWA SANSHIRŌ. Kōtoku and Sakai were as openly radical in their editorializing as press laws permitted but never promoted open violence. Readership reached a peak early in 1904 but fell off rapidly as government authorities mounted a campaign to halt publication and popular sentiment grew in favor of war with Russia. Two damaging editorials, one by Kōtoku protesting higher taxes to support the war effort and another by Ishikawa recommending that elementary school teachers embrace socialism, resulted in the arrest and indictment of the editors. When the *Heimin shimbun* carried the first Japanese translation of the *Communist Manifesto* in November 1904, the government suspended publication. The paper struggled briefly to survive but was forced to close down on 29 January 1905, printing a final "red ink" edition after the example of Marx's *Neue Rheinische Zeitung.* It was revived as a daily in January 1907, partly as a party organ of the Japan Socialist Party but ceased publication in April because of police pressure and ideological differences among editorial board members.   HARUHARA Akihiko

heimon

(house arrest; literally, "closed gate"). A form of punishment established by the Tokugawa shogunate (1603–1867) as part of an elaborately codified body of civil and criminal law (see KUJIKATA OSADAMEGAKI). Like enryo and hissoku (two other forms of domiciliary confinement), it was imposed on samurai and priests. The analogous punishment for commoners was known as tojime ("door-shutting"). The degree and duration of the punishment varied with the gravity of the offense. Heimon was the most onerous of the four and was imposed for the most serious infractions. When sentenced to tojime, enryo, or hissoku, one's front gate was nailed shut and one was confined during the day but permitted to leave from a side entrance at night if one went discreetly. In the case of heimon one was forbidden to go out even at night, and entry of others was circumscribed. Thus if someone in the house became ill, the doctor could call only at night, or if someone died, the body could be removed to the temple only at night. If a fire erupted, one could leave only when in imminent danger. These forms of punishment were abolished after the Meiji Restoration of 1868.　　Conrad TOTMAN

Heishi → Taira family

Heizei, Emperor → Kusuko Incident

Hekinan

City in south central Aichi Prefecture, central Honshū, at the mouth of the river Yahagigawa. A port town during the Edo period (1600–1868), Hekinan has traditionally been known for tile making, brewing, and spinning, and more recently for its emerging metal, machinery, and food-processing industries. Its chief agricultural product is carrots. Many residents commute to Nagoya and Toyoda. Pop: 62,022.

hekisho → kabegaki

Hekizan nichiroku

Diary of Daikyoku (1421–86?), a priest of the Rinzai sect of Zen Buddhism who lived in the temple TŌFUKUJI in Kyōto. The surviving sections of the diary cover the period 1459–63 and 1465–68. Daikyoku, whose pen name was Hekizan, was a skilled poet and quite learned in Chinese Song (Sung) dynasty literature and historiography, having studied with such notable figures as ICHIJŌ KANE-YOSHI. His diary is an important source for study of the social unrest that characterized the years leading up to the outbreak of the ŌNIN WAR (1467–77).　　G. Cameron HURST III

hell

(jigoku). Although ancient Japanese myths mention Yomi no Kuni, an underworld of the dead much like the Greek Hades, the concept of hell (jigoku) as a place of punishment for the damned was introduced with BUDDHISM. The Buddhist hell itself was of Hindu origin (Skt: naraka). Hindu sacred texts usually refer to many distinct hells, which include Avīci (J: Abi Jigoku or Mugen Jigoku; "Interminable Hell") and Raurava (J: Kyōkan Jigoku; "Hell of Sorrowful Crying"). Sinners are hurled into Abi Jigoku, where they are torn apart, then reborn, only to experience new suffering. In Kyōkan Jigoku, inhabitants cry and weep in their endless torment. The ruler of hell is known as EMMA (Skt: Yama), popularly believed to be a fearful judge, who, after reviewing a person's past deeds, consigns him to the appropriate hell.

The concept of hell became increasingly widespread from the latter part of the Heian period (794–1185), as Pure Land Buddhists (see PURE LAND BUDDHISM) preached salvation in the Pure Land in contrast to punishment in hell. Many JIGOKU-ZŌSHI (Scrolls of Hells) produced in this period depict the torments of hell. See also NIHON RYŌIKI; ŌJŌYŌSHŪ.　　MATSUNAMI Yoshihiro

Henderson, Harold G. (1889–1974)

American scholar of Japanese language and literature. Born in New York City; graduate of Columbia University, where he received a degree in chemical engineering. Henderson developed an interest in Japan through his father's collection of Japanese paintings. In 1929 he was appointed the curator of Far Eastern art at the Metropolitan Museum of Art, and the following year he went to Japan to study the language and compile material for his first book, Bamboo Broom, a collection of translations of haiku. From 1935 to 1945 he taught Japanese language and art history at Columbia. After World War II he returned to Japan as head of the Education, Religion, Arts, and Monument section of SCAP (the headquarters of the Allied Occupation of Japan). Later he resumed his teaching duties at Columbia. He also wrote Handbook of Japanese Grammar (1948) and An Introduction to Haiku (1958).

Henjō (816–890)

Classical (WAKA) poet, Buddhist prelate. His lay name was Yoshimine no Munesada. A favorite of Emperor Nimmyō (810–850; r 833–850), he took Buddhist orders on the sovereign's death in 850. Thenceforth he rose rapidly in ecclesiastical ranks, becoming abbot of the important Tendai (now Shingon) temple Gangyōji (or Kazanji), which he founded in Kyōto on the birth of Emperor Yōzei (868–949; r 876–884) in 868. Henjō enjoyed the confidence of Emperor Kōkō (830–887; r 884–887) and was accorded numerous honors at court, advancing to the rank of bishop (sōjō) in 885.

Henjō is one of the so-called Six Poetic Geniuses (ROKKASEN). His poetry, though fashionable in the witty, subjective style esteemed by his age, often seems excessively mannered and overwrought. Some 36 of his poems are included in imperial anthologies beginning with the Kokinshū. His personal collection, Henjōshū, contains a mere 34 or 36 poems, depending on the text, most of them identical with those appearing in the imperial anthologies. Despite their small number, the poems are provided with lengthy prose headnotes, and the work is arranged like a collection of lyrical tales (uta monogatari) similar to YAMATO MONOGATARI (Tales of Yamato), from which several passages appear to have been borrowed.
📖——Robert H. Brower and Earl Miner, Japanese Court Poetry (1961).　　Robert H. BROWER

hentai kambun

(literally, "variant Chinese"). A now defunct hybrid form of literary Japanese combining both Chinese and native Japanese elements. It is often called kirokutai, meaning "Japanese used in documents," because it was used for the writing of court and shogunate records. This language was also used in the private diaries of male courtiers, clerics, and military men.

The Japanese learned to write Chinese (KAMBUN) from immigrant Korean teachers in the 5th century, some two centuries before a system for writing their own language was developed. By the 7th century, Chinese was being used as the official language of legal documents and formal correspondence. Chinese studies in Japan and the ability of the bureaucrats to write Chinese reached their height in the early 9th century, only to decline with the termination of official missions to China in 894. Thereafter, Chinese written in Japan became increasingly corrupted by Japanese words and constructions and a hybrid language emerged as a separate entity. Before the end of the Heian period (794–1185) "variant Chinese" had become the dominant mode of written expression in the conduct of day-to-day business.

The term hentai kambun refers to a spectrum of Chinese styles ranging from the slightly ungrammatical to a style that has a heavy admixture of Japanese words and grammatical forms. The latter end of the spectrum contains distinctive vocabulary not found in either orthodox Chinese or other kinds of Japanese prose and is regarded as a special form of literary Japanese. Two examples of that hentai kambun which most resembles orthodox Chinese are the NIHON RYŌIKI, a collection of early Buddhist tales (ca 822), and the SHŌ-MONKI, a 10th-century military epic (ca 940). The bulk of historical materials surviving from the premodern period are recorded in the more corrupt style of hentai kambun.

In the Heian period hentai kambun achieved a degree of uniformity of vocabulary and phraseology and reached maturity as a style of writing. It was more practical and easier to use than pure Chinese, yet retained much of the latter's value as an indication of status compared to Japanese, which was written in the KANA syllabary. For this reason, hentai kambun was the style of writing most used by male elites. One finds stylistic differences from writer to writer, but on the whole, brief and direct expression was valued. There are some hentai kambun writings of exceptional expressive beauty; one need only read parts of the *Meigetsuki*, a personal journal of the poet FUJIWARA NO SADAIE (1162–1241), to conclude that the literary value of some *hentai kambun* deserves to be further explored. The language of the AZUMA KAGAMI, a record of the political achievements of the Kamakura shogunate (1192–1333), is considered to be archetypal of the mature form. Thus, the term *Azuma kagami tai* (the *Azuma kagami* style) is often used synonymously with the term *hentai kambun*.

The following characteristics distinguish mature *hentai kambun* from orthodox literary Chinese:

1. Difference in meaning in the Japanese use of Chinese words, such as the word *annai*, which commonly means "the actual situation" in *hentai kambun* usage but means "in the (legal) case" in Chinese.

annai　　案内

2. Use of compound-character expressions coined in Japan:

shutsubutsu　　出物　　"forward, pushy"

3. High incidence of words constructed by *ateji* (rebus characters). Two examples of *ateji* usage are the words:

ame　　　　　　下米　　　"rain"
tsumabiraka (ni)　一　二　"in detail, closely"

4. Common use of variant ideographs and .substitution of homophonous but semantically unrelated characters. An example of the latter is the characters for *nyokan*, "lady-in-waiting":

nyokan　　如官　　instead of　　女官

5. Frequent occurrence of Japanese honorific expressions such as:

-shimu　　～令
-makaru　　～罷
-tamau　　～給
-sōrō　　～候

6. Nonadherence to Chinese syntax and grammar.
7. Infiltration of *man'yōgana*, *katakana*, and *hiragana*, especially in post–Heian-period texts.
8. Repetitious use of certain formulaic expressions such as *(to) unnun* meaning *to iu koto de aru*, namely, "end of quote" and *-owannu*, equivalent to *-nu*, a suffix of completion.

to unnun　　云云
-owannu　　～了

Hentai kambun continued to be used with some variation throughout the Edo period (1600–1868) and was still being used in the SŌRŌBUN epistolary form in the early decades of the 20th century. Despite the lengthy duration and broad extent of its use in Japan, *hentai kambun* has been the object of little linguistic research.

📖——Kokugo Gakkai, *Kokugogaku jiten* (Tōkyōdō, 1974); rev ed, *Kokugogaku daijiten* (1980). Matsushita Teizō, "Kirokutai no seikaku: *Azuma kagami* o chūshin to shite," *Kokugo kokubun* (December 1951). Minegishi Akira, "Kirokutai," in Ōno Susumu and Shibata Takeshi, ed, *Iwanami Kōza: Nihongo*, vol 10: *Buntai* (1977). Tsukishima Hiroshi, "Hentai kambun kenkyū no kōsō," *Tōkyō daigaku jinbun kagaku ka kiyō* (August 1957).

Judith N. RABINOVITCH

Hepburn, James Curtis (1815–1911)

Physician. Popularizer of the "Hepburn" system of romanizing Japanese. Born in Milton, Pennsylvania, he earned his BA at the College of New Jersey (now Princeton University) in 1832 and his MD at the University of Pennsylvania in 1836. Hepburn served as a Presbyterian medical missionary in Singapore and Xiamen (Amoy) between 1841 and 1845. In 1845 he returned to New York City, where he practiced medicine before going to Japan in 1859. He operated a thriving dispensary in Kanagawa (now part of Yokohama) and trained young men in Western medicine. Hepburn was one of the founders of MEIJI GAKUIN UNIVERSITY and served as its first president in addition to teaching physiology and hygiene. Probably his greatest contributions, however, were his *A Japanese and English Dictionary* (1867, *Waei gorin shūsei*), the first Japanese-English dictionary, and his adoption of a system of ROMANIZATION OF JAPANESE that is still widely used. He also played a major role in translating the Bible into Japanese (see BIBLE, TRANSLATIONS OF). He returned to the United States in 1892.

📖——William Elliot Griffis, *Hepburn of Japan and His Wife and Helpmates: A Life Story of Toil for Christ* (1913).

Edward R. BEAUCHAMP

herbs and spices

Japanese cuisine has traditionally used very few herbs and spices, probably as a result of the reliance from early times on rice, fish, and vegetables rather than on fats, meat, and dairy products. The techniques of preserving fish and vegetables by salting and drying and of making SOY SAUCE (*shōyu*) and MISO also date from early times. The strongly flavored *miso* was used to season *iwashi* (sardines), *saba* (mackerel), and other fish considered low-grade, and ginger has been in use since at least the 8th century. Until the Meiji Restoration (1868), the herbs and spices used in Europe were known in Japan by their Chinese names and considered part of the pharmacopoeia of traditional Chinese medicine. With the opening of Japan to foreign influences in the Meiji period (1868–1912), curry powder and Worcestershire sauce were introduced. Since World War II, the eating habits of the Japanese have changed considerably, and a wide variety of herbs and spices is now used. The following are some of the more commonly used herbs and spices in Japanese cooking:

bōfū or *hamabōfū* (*Glehnia littoralis*; family Umbelliferae): fresh leaves used as a garnish for SASHIMI (raw fish).

goma (sesame; *Sesamum orientale*): roasted or ground sesame seeds used to season various sauces; mixed with roasted salt to make *gomashio*; used to flavor boiled rice.

mitsuba (honewort, wild chervil; *Crytotaenia japonica*): fresh leaves and stems minced and used as a garnish for *sashimi* or cooked as a vegetable.

myōga (*Zingiber mioga*): raw roots used as a garnish for *sashimi* or TŌFU; also marinated in rice vinegar or pickled in salt.

negi (Welsh onion): minced and used as a garnish for *yudōfu* (see TŌFU) or noodles; also cooked as a vegetable.

nira (leek-scallion; *Allium odorum*): minced and used as a garnish for *misoshiru* (bean paste soup); also cooked as a vegetable.

sanshō (Japanese peppertree, *Zanthoxylum piperitum*): young leaves (called *kinome*) used in soups and various side dishes; the dried and pulverized seeds may be sprinkled on broiled eel (*unagi*) or *teriyaki* dishes.

shichimi tōgarashi: a mixture of *tōgarashi* (cayenne pepper), *sanshō*, *aonori* (a kind of seaweed), poppy seed, sesame seed, dried orange peel, and *shiso* seed; used to season various side dishes, soups, and noodles.

shiso (beefsteak plant, *Perilla frutescens*): aromatic leaves pickled in salt; leaves and tiny buds are used as a garnish for *sashimi*.

shōga (ginger): grated or minced ginger root is used as a garnish for *sashimi* and pickles; is also marinated in rice vinegar for a garnish; found in Japanese cooking since at least the 8th century.

tōgarashi (cayenne pepper): dried and ground seeds used for making pickles; also used with broiled meat.

wasabi (*Eutrema wasabi*): a kind of horseradish whose grated raw roots are used for making SUSHI; also mixed with soy sauce as a dip for *sashimi*.

yuzu (citron): minced peel used for *yudōfu*, various side dishes, and as a garnish for soups.

ŌTSUKA Shigeru

herons

(*sagi*). In Japanese, *sagi* is the common name for wading birds of the family Ardeidae, distinguished by long legs, necks, and bills. Approximately 37–95 centimeters (15–37 in) in length. Some 18 species are found in Japan. Small numbers of the *sankanogoi* (Eurasian bittern; *Botaurus stellaris*) breed in the reed plains of northern Hokkaidō. There are also three species of the *yoshigoi* (little bitterns; *Ixobrychus* spp.), one of them breeding only in the Ryūkyūs. Colonies of *shirasagi* (egrets) and *goisagi* (night heron; *Nycticorax nycticorax*) are found from Honshū southwards but their numbers are diminishing. The *mizogoi* (Japanese night heron; *Gorsakius goisagi*) lives in mountain woodlands.

TAKANO Shinji

White herons such as the *daisagi* (large egret) and *kosagi* (little egret), which stand gracefully on one leg, have long been a favorite subject for Japanese artists. Herons also figure as a theme in folk dances such as the *sagi-mai* performed at Yasaka Shrine in Yamaguchi Prefecture and in the "Sagi musume," a dance performed in NAGAUTA and in the NŌ play *Sagi*. Before they were designated a protected species, the plumes, or aigrettes, of herons were used to decorate hats, and their flesh was eaten in soups or roasted.

SANEYOSHI Tatsuo

hero worship

In Japan beliefs and cults centering on heroes are a common phenomenon, especially since the line of demarcation between KAMI, or god, and man is not easily drawn. One may say that in most cultures hero worship is based on the belief that the spirits of the dead coexist with and influence the living, and that the spirits of those who led extraordinary lives and/or died under remarkable circumstances are particularly influential. The heroes' spirits, then, may function as guardian spirits.

There are certain features which characterize Japanese heroes. They are often of noble birth and endowed with charismatic qualities, they contribute to the general good of the nation or society, they often incur official disfavor, they meet death with calm resignation for the sake of glory, and they often leave behind farewell poems. A typical example is found in the mythical figure Prince YAMATOTAKERU. According to the KOJIKI (712), he was the son of Emperor KEIKŌ, who, jealous of his son's courage and strength, sent him away to conquer aboriginal tribes on the frontier. With wit and bravery, as well as divine protection, the prince carried out his mission successfully but his wife, who accompanied him, sacrificed herself so that her husband could vanquish the dragon king of the seas. On his way home he died as a result of a curse by a local deity. It is said that after his death at age 30, a white bird flew up from his grave to heaven. His poems lamenting the death of his wife or expressing his longing for his homeland are also recorded in the *Kojiki*. Yamatotakeru is enshrined at ATSUTA SHRINE in Nagoya.

SUGAWARA NO MICHIZANE (845–903) offers a contrasting example. A man of letters and a minister at the court, Michizane was slandered by his rival, Fujiwara no Tokihira (871–909), and was banished to Kyūshū, where he died. Soon after his death, a number of untoward events took place in the capital. These were attributed to his angry spirit and the KITANO SHRINE was set up to appease him. As Michizane was well versed in the Chinese classics and noted for his poetry and calligraphy, in time he came to be regarded as the patron deity of learning, and shrines dedicated to him (TEMMANGŪ) became popular with young people anxious for academic success.

In modern times, cults surrounding war heroes such as TŌGŌ HEIHACHIRŌ and NOGI MARESUKE were officially encouraged in order to help foster patriotism. Shrines have also been dedicated to folk heroes like NINOMIYA SONTOKU. In the Japanese religious tradition, however, the spirits of the dead easily lose their individual characteristics and veneration is accorded more often to the collective ancestral spirit rather than to a specific hero or deity.

■ —— Hori Ichirō, *Folk Religion in Japan* (1968).

Kyōko NAKAMURA

herring

(nishin). In Japanese, *nishin* is the common name of the Pacific herring *(Clupea pallasi)*, a migratory fish of class Osteichthyes, order Clupeiformes, family Clupeidae. It grows to 30 centimeters (12 in) long. It is distributed in the temperate and subarctic zones of the northern Pacific Ocean and the adjoining seas and approaches the coast for spawning. It feeds mainly on plankton. The annual catch in Japan fluctuates from about 1 million metric tons (1.1 million short tons) to between 20,000 and 30,000 metric tons (22,000–33,000 short tons).

ABE Tokiharu

Herring roe was commonly used for New Year's dishes and wedding feasts until the outbreak of World War II, but sharp declines in the size of the catch have made it expensive in recent years; foods such as dried, smoked herring and herring pickled in *sake* lees are also expensive delicacies. Up to the Meiji period (1868–1912) herring was used as a fertilizer in paddy fields, especially in western Japan.

SAITŌ Shōji

He-Umezu (Ho-Umezu) Agreement

(Umezu-Ka Ōkin Kyōtei). An agreement concluded on 10 June 1935 between General He Yingqin (Ho Ying-ch'in), acting as CHIANG KAI-SHEK's military deputy, and Lieutenant General Umezu Yoshijirō, commander of the Japanese army's Tianjin (Tientsin) garrison. China agreed to transfer all armies of the central government and all organs of the Guomindang (Kuomintang; Nationalist Party) out of the province of Hebei (Hopeh), which included the cities of Beiping (Peiping; now Beijing or Peking) and Tianjin. China also agreed to suppress the activities of the Lanyi She (Lan-i She; "Blue Shirts"; an elite organization established by Chiang in 1932 on European fascist models) in that province and to prohibit anti-Japanese movements throughout China. In dictating the terms of the agreement, it was Japan's intention to exclude the Nationalist government from Hebei and to dominate the province by manipulating the local warlords who would hold sway there in the absence of the Nationalists. Although these provisions were humiliating to Chiang Kai-shek, they did at least foreclose for the moment more aggressive measures by expansionist elements in Japan and allow him to proceed with his campaign to exterminate the communists, his highest priority. For the time being, Chiang was willing to appease Japan and postpone the goal of national unification in order to check growing communist strength. Although the He-Umezu Agreement was made in secret, the Chinese public soon became aware of its general nature. As a result, there was an outburst of patriotic indignation directed at both Japan and at the timidity of the Nationalists' appeasement policy. See also SINO-JAPANESE WAR OF 1937–1945. *John H. BOYLE*

Heusken, Henry C. J. (1832–1861)

Given name Hendrik C. J. Heusken. Secretary and translator to Townsend HARRIS, the first American resident consul in Japan. Born in the Netherlands, he was fluent in Dutch, English, and French. Arriving in Japan in 1856 with Harris, he acted as a Dutch-English interpreter during negotiations surrounding the ANSEI COMMERCIAL TREATIES, Dutch being the official diplomatic language because of Japan's long association with the Netherlands. In January 1861 Heusken was murdered by an antiforeign extremist from the Satsuma domain (now Kagoshima Prefecture). The British and French ministers temporarily withdrew to Yokohama as a result of this incident; Harris remained in Edo (now Tōkyō) and negotiated an indemnity of 10,000 Mexican dollars to be paid to Heusken's mother.

He Yingqin (Ho Ying-ch'in) (1889–   )

(J: Ka Ōkin). Nationalist China's minister of war from 1930 to 1944 and army chief of staff from 1938 to 1944.

Like many leaders of republican China, He received his professional education in Japan; he was a graduate of the Rikugun Shikan Gakkō (Army Academy) in Tōkyō. He's long association with CHIANG KAI-SHEK began in 1924, when he was placed in charge of military training at the Huangpu (Whampoa) Military Academy by its commandant, Chiang. In 1935, at a time when Japanese expansionists were endeavoring to exclude the Nationalists from North China, Chiang assigned He the task of negotiating an understanding with the local Japanese commander in North China, Lieutenant General UMEZU YOSHIJIRŌ. The resulting HE–UMEZU (HO–UMEZU) AGREEMENT represented a capitulation by the Nationalist government to Japanese demands for a withdrawal of Nationalist troops and party organs from the province of Hebei (Hopei). For his role in the He-Umezu Agreement, General He became the focus of widespread resentment over the Nationalist government's policy of appeasing Japan.

Following the Sino-Japanese War of 1937–45, General He took an active interest in establishing friendly Sino-Japanese relations. He visited Japan on numerous occasions, either privately or in his capacity as president of the Sino-Japanese Cultural and Economic Association, an organization headed by He since its inception in 1952. From 1951 to 1973 he also occupied the largely honorific post of chairman of the Strategy Advisory Committee to the President.

John H. BOYLE

hibachi

A type of charcoal burner used as a source of heat. In ancient days the *hibachi* was also called *hioke* and *hibitsu*. Several copper and

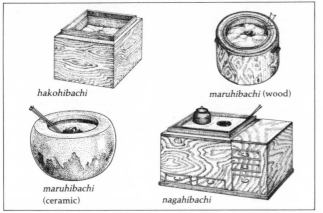

hakohibachi

maruhibachi (wood)

maruhibachi (ceramic)

nagahibachi

Hibachi

Four types of *hibachi*. The drawers in the *nagahibachi* are for pipes, tobacco, and other small articles. Visible atop it are a small teakettle and metal chopsticks *(tetsubashi)* for handling charcoal.

nickel *hibachi* made during the Nara period (710–794) are at the SHŌSŌIN repository in Nara. Until the middle of the Edo period (1600–1868) *hibachi* were mainly for the use of the ruling class. There are several types of *hibachi,* the *maruhibachi,* made by hollowing out a log; the boxlike *hakohibachi* and *nagahibachi,* made by fitting together boards of hardwood; and those made of ceramic. The *hibachi* is filled with ash and pieces of charcoal are arranged in the center. A trivet is sometimes placed over the burning charcoal to hold a kettle. Today the *hibachi* has been largely replaced by more efficient and safer heating appliances. It should be noted that what is known in the West as a *hibachi* (i.e., a charcoal grill for cooking) is quite different from the Japanese *hibachi,* which was used essentially for warmth and only incidentally for heating water or food.

Hibara, Lake

(Hibarako). On the Ura Bandai highland, northern Fukushima Prefecture, northern Honshū. Located within Bandai–Asahi National Park. In 1888 Mt. Bandai (Bandaisan) erupted, damming a river of the Nagasegawa system and creating this lake. Popular resort with many recreational facilities. Area: 10.4 sq km (4 sq mi); circumference: 38 km (24 mi); depth: 31 m (102 ft); altitude: 822 m (2,696 ft).

Hibi Ōsuke (1860–1931)

Businessman. Born in what is now Fukuoka Prefecture; graduated from Keiō Gijuku (now Keiō University) in 1884. Hibi worked for Mosurin (Muslin) Shōkai, then joined MITSUI BANK, LTD, in 1895, and became the manager of Mitsui Gofukuten (Mitsui Dry Goods Store) in 1898. He participated in the modernization of Mitsui Gofukuten (now MITSUKOSHI, LTD) and became its executive director. Based on the policy of "small profits and quick returns," Hibi's management turned Mitsukoshi into the first modern department store in Japan.   *MAEDA Kazutoshi*

Hibiya Incendiary Incident

(Hibiya Yakiuchi Jiken). A city-wide riot in Tōkyō arising from a mass rally held at Hibiya Park on 5 September 1905 to protest the Treaty of PORTSMOUTH, which concluded the RUSSO-JAPANESE WAR (1904–05). The Japanese public, ignorant of the actual war situation, attacked the government for signing what it considered a humiliating peace with Russia. Prime Minister KATSURA TARŌ and the oligarchs *(genrō)* ignored the public clamor, and through a secret bargain secured the RIKKEN SEIYŪKAI party leaders' pledge not to join in the popular attack on the government. It was in this charged atmosphere that the Kōwa Mondai Dōshi Rengōkai ("Joint Council of Fellow Activists on the Peace Question"), formed chiefly by members of minor political parties, such as KŌNO HIRONAKA, the sometime leader of the FREEDOM AND PEOPLE'S RIGHTS MOVEMENT, lawyers, and journalists, in defiance of the government ban held a mass rally at Hibiya Park on the day of the signing of the treaty.

The participants appealed to the emperor to reject the treaty ratification and urged the Japanese army in Manchuria to continue to fight. After the rally, a crowd of 2,000 with black mourning flags marched to the Imperial Palace grounds, where they clashed with police. Skirmishes between the crowd and the police quickly spread to other parts of the city. The Imperial Guards and the Army First Division were called out to suppress the riot. On 6 September the government declared martial law in the city and its vicinity, restricting the movements of citizens and banning the antigovernment press. A heavy rain fell the following day, and the riot finally subsided.

More than 350 buildings, including the official residence of the home minister, the office of the *Kokumin shimbun,* TOKUTOMI SOHŌ's progovernment newspaper, 9 police stations and more than 70 percent of police boxes, 13 Christian churches, and 53 private homes, were either smashed or burned down. Fifteen streetcars were destroyed by fire. The recorded casualties exceeded one thousand: 450 policemen, 48 firemen and soldiers, and more than 500 of the crowd, including 17 dead.

Similar antipeace demonstrations were held throughout the nation. As for the historical significance of the riot, opinions are divided; some have seen it as a sign of a growing mass political consciousness and as a precursor of the so-called TAISHŌ DEMOCRACY, while others have regarded it as fundamentally a manifestation of chauvinism.

📖——Shumpei Okamoto, *The Japanese Oligarchy and the Russo-Japanese War* (1970).   *Shumpei OKAMOTO*

Hibiya Park

(Hibiya Kōen). In Chiyoda Ward, Tōkyō, next to the Imperial Palace. Formerly the site of a *daimyō*'s mansion, it later became a drill ground for the army and was opened as a public park in 1903. It is laid out partly in Western and partly in Japanese style. Tōkyō Metropolitan Hibiya Library and Hibiya Public Hall are located here. Area: 16 hectares (40 acres).

Hibiya Yakiuchi Jiken → Hibiya Incendiary Incident

Hiburishima

Island in the Uwa Sea, west of Ehime Prefecture, western Shikoku. FUJIWARA NO SUMITOMO (d 941) gathered together warships and led a revolt from this island in 939. Stone walls from his castle can still be seen on top of a hill here. It was used as a place of exile during the Edo period (1600–1868). Fishing is now the chief activity. Area: 5 sq km (2 sq mi).

hichiriki

A short cylindrical-bore oboe, used as a melody instrument in GAGAKU music. Its body, 18 centimeters (7 in) long, is of bamboo bound with birch cord, lacquered brown on the outside and red inside; it has seven elliptical finger holes on top, and two thumbholes underneath; and an integral double reed fitted with a bridle (and cover, when not in use). The sound is heavy but not strident. The *hichiriki* is generically related to other cylindrical-bore oboes found widely on the Eurasian mainland, and directly to the old Chinese *bili (pili),* which was probably introduced to China from Kučā in Central Asia in the 6th century. This instrument was used in Tang (T'ang) court music, found its way to Japan in the 7th century, and is played for both the *tōgaku* and the *komagaku* repertoires of *gagaku.*
               David B. WATERHOUSE

Hida Folklore Village

(Hida Minzoku Mura). Located in Takayama, Gifu Prefecture. A collection of buildings—farmhouses and their accompanying structures, priests' residences, the house of a village headman—brought from villages in the region as well as from Takayama. This architectural group provides an excellent sample of the rural architecture for which the Hida region is noted. A number of private houses in Takayama have also been converted into museums.
               Laurance ROBERTS

Hidaka Mountains

(Hidaka Sammyaku). Mountain range running 130 km (81 mi) north to south, south central Hokkaidō. Part of the Ezo Mountains, its highest peak is Poroshiridake (2,052 m; 6,731 ft). This watershed between the Ishikari and Tokachi plains consists of many peaks in the 1,500–2,000 m (4,920–6,560 ft) range. Near the summit is a cirque, and the foothills are covered with subarctic coniferous forests.

Hida Mountains

(Hida Sammyaku). Mountain range running north to south through Niigata, Toyama, Nagano, and Gifu prefectures, central Honshū. It is the northernmost of the three ranges forming the JAPANESE ALPS and is often called the Northern Alps. There are numerous peaks in the 3,000 m (9,840 ft) range including YARIGATAKE, HOTAKADAKE, TATEYAMA, TSURUGIDAKE and NORIKURADAKE. Near the summits of the mountains, the remnants of cirques and moraines can be seen. Alpine flora abounds at higher altitudes. The snow grouse (raichō) and the Japanese serow (KAMOSHIKA) living here have been designated as protected species. The range is known as the birthplace of modern mountain climbing in Japan. Most of the peaks in the Hida Mountains are included in the Chūbu Sangaku National Park.

Hidari Jingorō (fl late 16th–early 17th century)

Carpenter and sculptor. Born in Akashi (now part of Hyōgo Prefecture). Son of a retainer of Ashikaga Yoshiteru, the 13th shōgun of the Muromachi shogunate, his real name was Itami Toshikatsu. As a disciple of a master carpenter of the imperial court in Kyōto from whom he derived his name, he assisted in the reconstruction of the temple Negoroji in Kii Province (now Wakayama Prefecture) and in the construction of the bell tower of the temple Hōkōji in Kyōto. Later he went to Edo (now Tōkyō), where he married the daughter of Kōra Munehiro, master carpenter for the Tokugawa family. He has been credited with many famous works from early in the Edo period (1600–1868), including the nemurineko or "sleeping cat" of the shrine TŌSHŌGŪ in Nikkō and the so-called nightingale floors of the temple CHION'IN in Kyōto, which "sing" loudly when walked on. Although information about his life is scant, he has become known as an artist of prodigious skill, and stories of his genius abound in popular literature. The Hidari family has continued to produce fine craftsmen up to the present day.

Hidari Sachiko (1930–   )

Japanese actress and film director. Born in Toyama Prefecture, Hidari Sachiko was a high-school music and gymnastics teacher before becoming a film actress in 1952. Discovered by director GOSHO HEINOSUKE, she had her first significant roles in two of his films, Ōsaka no yado (1954, An Inn at Ōsaka) and Niwatori wa futatabi naku (1954, The Cock Crows Again). Hidari achieved international recognition in 1957 when she received the award for best actress at the Cork Film Festival in Ireland for her role in Kamisaka Shirō no hanzai (1956, The Crime of Shiro Kamisaka), directed by Hisamatsu Seiji.

An outspoken woman who lives by what she believes, Hidari displayed great personal courage in 1956 when she left Nikkatsu (see NIKKATSU CORPORATION), one of the major studios, to become an independent film performer. Hidari came into her own as an actress in the 1960s, developing her distinctive screen persona as an earthy, independent-minded woman who awakens from the passive social role assigned to Japanese women by tradition.

In director IMAMURA SHŌHEI's Nippon konchū ki (1963, The Insect Woman), Hidari gave her most significant performance as an actress, portraying Tome, a rural woman who moves from the country to the city, unskilled and unprotected. Her quest for survival takes her to a variety of jobs: from factory worker to maid and, later, ruthless brothel madam—a pilgrim's progress which fails to crush her indomitable spirit.

In HANI SUSUMU's Kanojo to kare (1963, She and He), Hidari won the award for best actress at the Berlin Film Festival, portraying a middle-class wife who rejects the role of child-wife imposed on her by her husband, a well-meaning but unaware SARARĪMAN, or white-collar worker. One of Hidari's finest portrayals was as the "picture bride" in Hani's Andesu no hanayome (1966, Bride of the Andes).

In 1977, after directing several short films in Paris, Hidari made her debut as both a producer and director of a major feature film, Tōi ippon no michi (Far Road). Discussions held with over 300 housewives in the course of her frequent lecturing throughout Japan led Hidari to make this film about the harsh living conditions of Japan's railway workers, people who, Hidari has said, "have been sacrificed in the name of 'rationalization,' or the streamlining of the work force." Although financed by the Japanese National Railway Workers' Union, the film is not a "union picture"; it is an examination by Hidari of larger questions, including her conviction that "it is 'civilization' that causes distress, despite the fact that 'civilization' in the sense of economic progress has been advocated for the well-being it promises." Tōi ippon no michi was chosen as part of the 1978 New Directors series jointly sponsored by the Museum of Modern Art and the Film Society of Lincoln Center in New York. It was screened as well at the Berlin Film Festival in 1978 and marked the emergence of Hidari as a director. Hidari Sachiko thus becomes, with another actress, TANAKA KINUYO, one of the few women to have succeeded in breaking into the commercial Japanese cinema.

Joan MELLEN

hiden'in

Also known as hiden-dokoro. Refuges for the poor and orphaned; sponsored by both the government and Buddhist temples from the 8th century. Both the hiden'in and the SEYAKUIN for the sick are said to have been started by Prince SHŌTOKU (574–622), who was inspired by Buddhist examples of charity in China; but the first clear records date from 723, when such institutions were established at the temple KŌFUKUJI in the capital city of Nara. In 730 both types of refuge came under the sponsorship of the empress KŌMYŌ. Soon refuges for the poor opened in many other areas, usually under temple management, and functioned until at least the 10th century. The hiden'in in the temple Sennyūji in Kyōto endured into the 15th century and was revived under the Tokugawa shogunate (1603–1867).

Hieda no Are (650?–?)

Attendant (TONERI) in the service of Emperor TEMMU; commissioned by the court to recite from memory the imperial genealogy and ancient legends so that Ō NO YASUMARO could record them in what came to be Japan's first written history, the KOJIKI. It is not known whether Hieda no Are was a man or a woman. See also KATARIBE.

Hieizan

(Mt. Hiei). Mountain on the border between Kyōto and Shiga prefectures, central Honshū; a horst mountain made up mainly of paleozoic strata, extending north to south. On the eastern slope is the temple ENRYAKUJI, an important center of the Tendai sect of Buddhism founded by the priest SAICHŌ in 788. (The name Hieizan is often synonymous with Enryakuji.) On the same slope is HIE SHRINE enshrining the guardian deity of Enryakuji. Height: 848 m (2,781 ft).

Hie Shrine

1. (Hie Taisha; also known as Hiyoshi Taisha). A Shintō shrine in the city of Ōtsu, Shiga Prefecture. The shrine is divided into two parts: the East Shrine, dedicated to Ōyamakui no Kami (the deity of Mt. Hiei; see HIEIZAN), and the West Shrine, dedicated to Ōnamuchi no Mikoto (the deity of the mountain Miwayama in Nara Prefecture). According to tradition, the former shrine was established in 91 BC. After Emperor TENJI (r 661–672) moved his capital to Ōtsu in 668, he built the West Shrine to house Ōnamuchi no Mikoto, who as the god of ŌMIWA SHRINE had protected the imperial family and the YAMATO COURT. After SAICHŌ, the founder of the Tendai sect of Buddhism, established the temple ENRYAKUJI on Mt. Hiei in 788, this shrine was regarded as the guardian (known by the Buddhist name Sannō Gongen) of the temple and hence came to be closely associated with it (see SANNŌ ICHIJITSU SHINTŌ). The Hie Shrine developed other subsidiary shrines, and the 21 larger shrines, including the two main shrines mentioned above, were collectively called Sannō Nijūissha (21 shrines of the Sannō). Throughout the Medieval period (13th–16th centuries) the Hie Shrine was very powerful and its militant acolytes, along with the WARRIOR-MONKS of Hieizan, constituted a politically powerful group. The Hie Taisha is

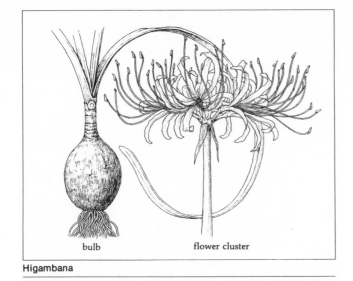

bulb   flower cluster

Higambana

regarded as the central shrine for the more than 3,800 Hie Sannō shrines throughout Japan. The two main shrines, known for their unique architectural style (*hiyoshi-zukuri,* or *shōtai-zukuri*), were rebuilt by the warlord Toyotomi Hideyoshi (1537–98) and are designated National Treasures. Its annual festival is celebrated on 12–15 April.

2. (Hie Jinja). A Shintō shrine in Chiyoda Ward, Tōkyō, dedicated to Ōyamakui no Kami (the deity who presides over Mt. Hiei) and three other deities. Ōta Dōkan (1432–86), who built his castle in Edo (now Tōkyō) in 1457, ordered that a shrine dedicated to Sannō Gongen (the Buddhist name for Ōyamakui no Kami) be transferred from nearby Kawagoe to the precincts of his castle. Later removed to its present site outside the castle grounds, the shrine was venerated by the Tokugawa shōguns (1603–1867), who regarded its central deity as the protector of Edo. Moreover, the shrine, located in the busiest downtown area of the capital, grew into one of the most popular shrines in Edo. The shrine festival, the SANNŌ FESTIVAL held on 10–16 June, is one of the two major shrine celebrations in Tōkyō, the other being the festival of the KANDA SHRINE. (The two festivals are held in alternate years.) Until the official separation of Buddhism and Shintō in 1868, the Hie Shrine was known as the Sannō Gongen. *Stanley WEINSTEIN*

higaki kaisen → kaisen

higambana

Lycoris radiata. Also known as *manjushage.* A perennial herb of the family Amaryllidaceae; widely found from Honshū to Kyūshū, in fields, along roadsides, and on ridges between rice paddies. Thriving on sunlight, in early September it sends out a shoot of about 30 centimeters (12 in) from its bulb. Toward the end of the month, corresponding with the autumnal equinox *(higan),* clusters of red flowers appear on the tip of the stem. The six petals face directly outward from the stalk and are wrinkled at the edges. The pistil and stamen are prominent. After flowering, the plant sends out shiny dark leaves, which wither the following spring. Although the bulb is poisonous, it is said that in times of famine its starch was consumed after the bulb was thoroughly washed. It is also said that the bulb was crushed and plastered on walls to ward off mice and rats. This hardy plant is also found along the Yangzi (Yangtze) River in China and was most likely introduced to Japan from there. In contrast to the Japanese variety, the Chinese plant frequently bears fruit. *MATSUDA Osamu*

higan

(literally, "the other shore"). A seven-day Buddhist memorial service held twice a year, centering on the vernal and autumnal equinoxes. More formally called *higan'e,* it is common to all Japanese Buddhist sects. This custom is not found in India, China, or other Buddhist countries. The word *higan* is derived from the Chinese equivalent of the Sanskrit word *pāramitā,* which refers to the eternal paradise awaiting those who achieve enlightenment (SATORI), as opposed to "this shore" *(shigan),* that is, this world in which one wanders through the pain of living. The *higan'e* rites are intended to help souls pass from the world of confusion to the world of enlightenment. The earliest reference to *higan'e* is a passage in the *Nihon kōki* (see RIKKOKUSHI), which mentions that such services were held in 806.

In a rite formerly conducted at the temple SHITENNŌJI in Ōsaka, believers worshiped the sunset from the west gate while praying for rebirth into paradise. A major sutra of the JŌDO SECT, the *Kammuryōjukyō,* espouses the practice of watching the sunset while meditating on the Western Paradise of the Pure Land. The equinoxes were most likely chosen as the middle days of *higan'e* observances because on those two days the sun rises due east and sets due west.

Higan is an important event even today. At temples throughout Japan, sutras are read and services are conducted for lost souls. It is a time for family gatherings, for visiting family graves and offering "*higan* dumplings." A proverb associates this occasion with the change of seasons: "Winter cold and summer heat end at *higan.*" *ŌUCHI Eishin*

Higashi Ajia bunkaken → East Asia cultural sphere

Higashi Hiroshima

City in central Hiroshima Prefecture, western Honshū, contiguous with the city of Hiroshima. Formerly a major rice-growing area, it is fast being urbanized. Its Saijō district has long been known for its *sake.* Principal industries are automobiles, electric equipment, and machinery. Pop: 75,810.

Higashi Honganji

The head temple of the Shinshū Ōtani branch of the Buddhist True Pure Land sect (Jōdo Shinshū; see JŌDO SHIN SECT), located at Shichijō and Karasuma Avenue in Shimogyō Ward, Kyōto. The temple was founded in 1603 as the result of a succession dispute which split the great religious organization of the HONGANJI into two rival branches. (The year 1602 is usually given as the foundation date but on the basis of suspect sources.)

After the death in 1592 of the Honganji's 11th pontiff *(hossu),* Kennyo Kōsa, his eldest son, Kyōnyo Kōju (1558–1614), assumed the abbacy. Kyōnyo, however, had once been disowned by his father (see ISHIYAMA HONGANJI), making plausible the claims of a party supporting his younger brother Junnyo Kōshō (1577–1631), which produced Kennyo's will in favor of their candidate. When the national hegemon TOYOTOMI HIDEYOSHI (1537–98) recognized Junnyo as the temple's abbot in 1593, Kyōnyo was forced into retirement, but he retained strong support among the Honganji's branch temples. Moreover, he succeeded in establishing ties with the future shōgun TOKUGAWA IEYASU (1543–1616), whom he attended on the eve of the climactic Battle of SEKIGAHARA in 1600. The nature of Kyōnyo's relationship with Ieyasu remains unclear, although it is undoubtedly a legend that the two made a compact enabling Ieyasu to use, divide, and thereby ultimately subjugate the True Pure Land sect's adherents *(monto);* it is, however, possible that Kyōnyo had Ieyasu's support when he left his retirement quarters at Junnyo's Honganji for his own new temple in 1603. Eventually, that temple came to be called Higashi (eastern) Honganji to distinguish it from its rival Nishi (western) Honganji, located a few city blocks to the west on Horikawa Avenue, which remained in the possession of Junnyo and his successors. Junnyo and Kyōnyo are each listed as the 12th *hossu* of the Honganji in the pontifical lineages of their respective temples.

The Tokugawa shogunate did not officially recognize the establishment founded by Kyōnyo as an independent branch of the Jōdo Shinshū until 1619. Thereafter the two Honganji enjoyed equal status, dividing between them the major portion of the True Pure Land sect's adherents.

An *amidadō* (Amida hall) was dedicated at the Higashi Honganji in 1603, and a *goeidō* (portrait hall; enshrining a statue of the True Pure Land sect's first patriarch, SHINRAN) the following year. These halls of worship underwent a fundamental reconstruction between 1652 and 1670 but were destroyed in the great Kyōto fire of 1788 and were rebuilt only to be burned down again in 1823, once more in 1858, and yet again in 1864. As a result, the Higashi Honganji lacks the architectural monuments and artistic masterpieces boasted by the NISHI HONGANJI. The large scale of its present temple buildings is, however, impressive. For instance, the present *goeidō* (portrait hall; also known as *soshidō* and *taishidō,* founder's hall), which was built between 1880 and 1895, has horizontal dimensions of 76 by 58 meters (249 by 190 ft) and a height of 38 meters (125 ft), thereby ranking with the *daibutsuden* (great Buddha hall) of the TŌDAIJI in Nara as one of the world's largest wooden buildings.

In 1978 the Higashi Honganji had 6,150,141 members and 9,188 branch temples.

Higashikuni Naruhiko (1887–)

Imperial prince, prime minister (1945), and army general. Born in Kyōto, the ninth son of Prince Kuni no Miya Asahiko (1824–91), he married one of the daughters of Emperor MEIJI. He was given the name Higashikuni in 1906. He graduated from the Army Academy and the Army War College and studied in France for several years. Upon returning to Japan, he held several military posts, becoming general commander of defense during World War II. Following the decision to surrender in August 1945, he was appointed prime minister in the hope that his prestige as an imperial prince would enable him to unite a defeated and demoralized country and see to the peaceful disbanding of the military forces. It was the only time that a member of the imperial family headed a cabinet. He presided over the formal signing of the surrender on 2 September 1945 and the liquidation of the armed forces but resigned in October 1945 in opposition to an order from the Occupation authorities to abolish the PEACE PRESERVATION LAW OF 1925 and the SPECIAL HIGHER POLICE. In 1947 he formally renounced membership in the imperial family.

Higashi Kurume

City in north central Tōkyō Prefecture. Situated on the Musashino plateau, the city developed as an agricultural district in the Edo period (1600–1868). It is now a residential area for commuters to Tōkyō. Pop: 106,521.

Higashi Matsuura Peninsula

(Higashi Matsuura Hantō). Located in northwestern Saga Prefecture, northwestern Kyūshū. Extending into the Genkai Sea, its heavily indented coastline has numerous promontories as well as hundreds of inlets. Several good harbors such as Karatsu, Yobuko, and Imari are found here. The peninsula is part of Genkai Quasi-National Park.

Higashi Matsuyama

City in central Saitama Prefecture, central Honshū. Primarily an agricultural town, with silkworm cultivation, dairy farming, and fruit orchards, it has become rapidly urbanized. Tourist attractions are the Yoshimi no Hyakketsu (ancient graves dug into the hillside), the Iwadono Kannon, a statue of the bodhisattva at the temple Shōhōji, and the Yakyū Shrine. Pop: 63,889.

Higashi Murayama

City in north central Tōkyō Prefecture. Once an agricultural district, since 1965 it has become a residential suburb of Tōkyō. There are several hospitals and convalescence homes, and a famous reservoir to the southwest. Pop: 119,382.

Higashine

City in central Yamagata Prefecture, northern Honshū, situated in the delta of the river Midaregawa. In its layout Higashine retains its character as a medieval castle town. Principal agricultural products are rice, tobacco, and fruit, particularly apples and cherries. It is the site of Yamagata Airport. Higashine Hot Spring is located in the northwestern part of the city. Pop: 40,560.

Higashi Ōsaka

City in Ōsaka Prefecture; contiguous with the city of Ōsaka to the west. Established in 1967 with the merger of the three cities of Fuse, Kawachi, and Hiraoka; it is now a satellite city of Ōsaka. Industry and commerce flourish in the Fuse district (principal products are rubber, celluloid, toys, sewing machines, rolling stock, machinery,

and metal products); the electric appliance, textiles, wire and cable industries in the Kawachi district; and machinery manufacturing in the Hiraoka district. Numerous tumuli (KOFUN) and other sites of historical interest are located on the slopes of the mountain Ikomayama to the east. Pop: 521,635.

Higashiyama culture

(Higashiyama *bunka*). The culture that flourished during the rule and retirement of the eighth Muromachi shōgun ASHIKAGA YOSHI-MASA (1436–90), who spent his last years at his villa in the Higashi-yama section of Kyōto. It was distinguished by its blend of the aristocratic traditions of the Heian court nobility, the religious influences of Zen Buddhism, and the tastes and ethos of the dominant warrior society. The personality of Yoshimasa was central to the culture. His reign as shōgun was marked by grave political unrest, largely stemming from his own negligence and mismanagement. At the start of his rule in 1443, he had had every intention of wielding governmental power, but on realizing that he was too weak-willed to combat more astute political rivals, he quickly gave himself over to sensual and artistic pleasures. It was said that his wife HINO TO-MIKO and his concubines, among others, made most of the important decisions. During Yoshimasa's rule, the government was in such chaos that it was forced to cancel all debts 13 times in order to avoid public uprisings (see TOKUSEI). At the age of 29, Yoshimasa decided to retire. He named his brother Yoshimi (1439–91) as successor, but Tomiko wished to designate their newborn son Yoshihisa (1465–89) as heir. The succession dispute was to be one of the major causes of the ŌNIN WAR (1467–77), which decimated Kyōto and destroyed Ashikaga political power.

While Kyōto burned, Yoshimasa pursued his interests in poetry, painting, and the TEA CEREMONY. In 1474 Yoshimasa handed the shogunate over to Yoshihisa and in 1483, he retired to his newly built villa (popularly known as GINKAKUJI) at Higashiyama. His retreat soon became the center for the arts, attracting *daimyō* and townspeople alike. Yoshimasa's patronage of the tea ceremony awakened a new interest in implements, MAKI-E lacquer work, architecture, garden design, and flower arrangement. Inspired by Chinese Ming paintings, the genre of the *suibokuga* (INK PAINT-ING) was perfected by SHŪBUN and SESSHŪ TŌYŌ. There were also technical refinements in NŌ drama by KOMPARU ZENCHIKU and in linked-verse poetry by SŌGI. Studies on the classics by such scholars as ICHIJŌ KANEYOSHI and SANJŌNISHI SANETAKA were encouraged as well.

The aesthetic canons of Higashiyama culture—YŪGEN and WABI—have come to typify Japanese art. An aura of mystery and ineffability rather than descriptive realism, a stress on sparseness, understatement, and rusticity rather than artifice represent to this day the highest ideal of aesthetics in Japan.

Higashi Yamato

City in north central Tōkyō Prefecture. Formerly a farming village, it has developed as a new residential area since 1955 with the construction of large housing complexes. The city has numerous factories for manufacturing electric machinery and appliances as well as for processing foodstuffs. Lake Tama is located in the northern part of the city. Pop: 65,415.

Higeki kigeki

(Tragedy, Comedy). Influential theater journal. Originally founded by a drama study group headed by KISHIDA KUNIO, the journal was in its third revival in the early 1980s. Series one was short-lived, appearing from October 1928 to July 1929. It introduced Western drama while publishing original works by Japanese playwrights and critics including KUBOTA MANTARŌ, YAMAMOTO YŪZŌ, KOBAYA-SHI HIDEO, KINOSHITA MOKUTARŌ, and FUNAHASHI SEIICHI. Series two was published from October 1947 to June 1964. In late 1950 it changed from a quarterly to a monthly. This postwar series included special issues on contemporary and historical drama and encouraged the development of amateur and school dramatic programs. Contributors during this period included TANAKA CHI-KAO, HINO ASHIHEI, TERAYAMA SHŪJI, and YAMAZAKI MASAKAZU. Series three began in January 1966.   *Theodore W. GOOSSEN*

High Energy Physics, National Laboratory for

Government research center under the administration of the Ministry of Education. Located at the TSUKUBA ACADEMIC NEW TOWN in Ibaraki Prefecture. Opened in 1976, it is the largest research center for high-energy physics in Japan and carries out studies of elementary particles with such equipment as a 12-giga electron-volt proton accelerator.

higher education

Japan has a large, highly developed system of higher education. In 1980 approximately 2.3 million students were enrolled in universities and colleges. Moreover, the proportion of youth aged 18–21 attending higher education institutions in Japan was 43.4 percent, among the highest in the world.

The Development of the System——Higher education institutions were established in Japan as early as the 8th century AD, but most existing institutions have a more recent history. During the Edo period (1600–1868), the shogunal government established several Confucian institutions for the education of the elite and scholars as well as for research. However, it was only following the MEIJI RESTORATION (1868) that higher education began to assume its present form and placed primary emphasis on Western knowledge. In 1877 the new government established Tōkyō University by consolidating and restructuring several of the old Tokugawa institutions. The university had departments of jurisprudence, liberal arts, natural science, and medicine, with a faculty composed of Europeans and Americans, who taught in their own languages. A long preparation, mainly in foreign languages, was required prior to entrance. In addition, the government established a normal school, an engineering school, and several other higher education and research institutions; several hundred foreigners were invited for short periods to teach in these new institutions (see FOREIGN EMPLOYEES OF THE MEIJI PERIOD).

Apart from government institutions, various scholars and religious groups had also established small schools in the Edo period, and following the Restoration some of these expanded to become full-fledged higher education institutions; for example, FUKUZAWA YUKICHI's Keiō Gijuku (later Keiō University) and INOUE ENRYŌ's Tetsugakukan (later Tōyō University). Also during the Meiji period (1868–1912), several leading statesmen founded higher education institutions, including ŌKUMA SHIGENOBU's Waseda University, MORI ARINORI's Shōhō Kōshūjo (later to become Hitotsubashi University), and several law schools (which ultimately became universities such as Hōsei, Chūō, and Meiji). Finally, Western Christian groups supported the establishment of several universities, including Dōshisha, Meiji Gakuin, Aoyama Gakuin, and Kansei Gakuin.

From the mid-1880s, the central government began to take firm steps to systematize higher education. As a result, the Imperial University was established in 1886 through a reorganization of Tōkyō University (see IMPERIAL UNIVERSITIES). As preparatory institutes for this university, five higher middle schools (later HIGHER SCHOOLS) were established in various parts of the country. During the 20th century, the Imperial University was to become the center for academic research and the training of civil servants and scholars. It enjoyed considerable autonomy in finance, selection of personnel, and the organization of curriculum. At the same time, from the beginning there were limits on academic freedom, as indicated in the law authorizing the establishment of the Imperial University, which stipulated that its functions were to be "in accordance with the needs of the state." The university comprised six schools: law, medicine, technology, liberal arts, natural science, and agriculture; a graduate school and courses were set up in each school. Students had many privileges, including exemption from the national examinations demanded for bureaucratic and professional careers.

By the latter half of the 1890s the Imperial University was ready to employ Japanese instructors and teach classes in Japanese and to gradually raise the level of instruction and research. Until the second imperial university was established in Kyōto in 1897, there was only one university. By the 1930s seven had been established in various parts of the Japanese empire. Renamed national universities after World War II in accordance with the National School Establishment Law of 1949, they still occupy a central position in Japanese higher education.

Subordinate in status to the imperial universities, and under much closer supervision by the MINISTRY OF EDUCATION, were several other types of higher education institutions: higher schools (kōtō gakkō) to prepare students for the university, higher normal schools (kōtō shihan gakkō) to train advanced teachers, ordinary normal schools (shihan gakkō), and single-faculty institutions in medicine and certain other specialized areas (SEMMON GAKKŌ). All of these schools were attended by middle-school graduates.

For some time, private institutions were not allowed to claim university status. However, from 1918, private institutions that maintained prescribed standards were permitted official university charters. Moreover, public and private semmon gakkō were also allowed to receive charters. These reforms led to a rapid expansion of higher education, and by 1937 there were 45 universities (25 of them private) and a total of 356 institutions of higher education. These enrolled 5.4 percent of all males and 0.6 percent of all females aged 17 to 22. This was Japan's first step toward developing a mass higher education system oriented to the various social demands being generated by rapid industrialization.

Following World War II, the Allied Occupation authorities proposed as part of the complete reform of Japan's educational system that the various existing institutions of higher learning, such as universities, higher schools, semmon gakkō and normal schools, be consolidated into a smaller number of four-year universities offering both general and specialized education. These proposals were embodied in the SCHOOL EDUCATION LAW OF 1947. Unlike the privileged educational organs of the prewar period, postwar universities opened their doors to all people with the mission of providing general and technical education to train leaders for a democratic society.

The greatest change was seen in the national institutions. Those institutions within the same prefecture were combined into one university, except in a few areas such as Tōkyō. Private universities were carried over as they were, and most of the semmon gakkō were elevated to university status. However, some semmon gakkō lacked proper facilities and teaching staff to qualify as universities and, as a relief measure, they were temporarily recognized as two-year JUNIOR COLLEGES, for which permanent recognition came only in 1964. Public semmon gakkō and most of the public universities were reorganized into four-year universities, and some of them became new national universities. In addition, provisions were made for qualified institutions to establish GRADUATE SCHOOLS with two-year master's and three-year doctor's programs. By 1952 some 220 universities (with 399,513 students) and 205 junior colleges (with 53,230 students) had been recognized. Since 1962 a new category of technical colleges (kōtō semmon gakkō), which accept middle-school graduates for a five-year course, has been recognized. Table 1 provides statistics for 1980 on the number of institutions and student enrollments.

A Heterogeneous Multitiered System——There is considerable diversity in the types of institutions. The system is centered on the universities, which enroll over 80 percent of all students in higher education. The universities are mostly coeducational and vary from several mammoth private institutions with enrollments in excess of 30,000 to numerous small liberal arts and specialized colleges. Graduates of the most prestigious schools are welcomed by many employers and tend to rise rapidly in organizational hierarchies; hence, competition for admission to these institutions is especially fierce.

Beneath the universities are the junior colleges, attended largely by women, and the technical colleges, attended primarily by young men. The vast majority of the entrants to these institutions come directly from secondary schools, but in response to current education trends, many institutions have established public lecture series, and some institutions admit small numbers of adults as auditors. Apart from degree-granting institutions, in 1980 over 720,000 people were enrolled in MISCELLANEOUS SCHOOLS (kakushu gakkō) and 430,000 in special training schools (senshū gakkō), schools that represent a rapidly expanding layer of the education structure, where courses are available in areas such as foreign languages, computer and other technical skills, accounting, the arts, and home economics.

An important dimension of the system's diversity is the existence of a hierarchy according to the quality of institutions, ranging from the most prestigious universities to the least prestigious proprietary institutions. This is predominantly demonstrated in the differences between the private sector and the public sector, the latter consisting of institutions established by the national government or prefectural or local governments. Thanks to government assistance, the public sector has always been more generously funded, maintained higher standards, and enjoyed higher prestige than the private sector. In contrast, the private sector, through intensive utilization of limited human and capital resources, has been more responsive to the popular demand for higher education. As can be seen in Table 1, in 1980, 80 percent of all students were enrolled in the private sector. Likewise, within each sector, there have always been remarkable differences in institutional quality. The national universities have set the example for the public sector, while certain ambitious private universities have always made special efforts to maintain quality programs, even in the face of severe financial difficulties.

Finance——Japanese higher educational institutions obtain revenues from diverse sources. National universities are totally dependent on the national government, and other public institutions rely heavily on prefectural or local governments. Private universities, in contrast, have until recently depended primarily on student tuition for their revenues. Supplemental sources were loans, income from attached businesses, and gifts. In the prewar period, private universities were expected to have endowments, but in most cases these were depleted by the extreme inflation of the postwar years. Thus private institutions in the immediate postwar period were financially distressed. The Occupation authorities urged the central government to provide assistance, but it ultimately declined, claiming that article 89 of the constitution prohibited such measures. While short on revenues, most private institutions survived through increasing the size of their student bodies and raising student tuitions at a faster rate than they increased staff or educational facilities.

By the mid-1960s these strategies had reached the limit of popular tolerance. Some private institutions were reported to be asking in excess of $100,000 in "contributions" of parents whose children were accepted into their medical schools. Student-teacher ratios were also alarmingly high. Whereas at the national universities the ratio varied between 8 to 1 and 17 to 1, at several private institutions there were over 100 students per full-time staff member. Some 55 percent of all staff at private institutions were part-time lecturers. At the largest private universities, it was not uncommon for 500 or more students to be enrolled in a class. Professors would use microphones to address their students, and there was virtually no possibility for student questioning of lecturers or for private consultations.

Dissatisfaction with these conditions was one of the main themes of the STUDENT MOVEMENTS that troubled higher education between 1965 and 1970. In 1970 the government finally acted to relieve the financial plight of private universities by establishing a promotion foundation. By 1976 this foundation was providing approximately 22 percent of the operating funds of all private institutions, and the role of the minister of education in appointing the trustees of this foundation has enabled the government to increase its influence on private university decision making. Subsequently, tuitions at national universities were raised to bring them more in line with private university tuitions.

Higher Education and Culture——Common to all Japan's major institutions for higher learning over the centuries is their focus on foreign cultures—Buddhist, Confucian, or Western. Currently the Japanese are discussing further "internationalization" of their universities, but virtually no provision is made in these universities for the study of what foreigners, at least, think of as Japanese culture. Traditional music, art, and crafts are best studied outside the university. Even Japanese history and literature are slighted. Less than 3 percent of all higher education faculty specialize in these fields.

But perhaps Japanese culture is better thought of as all those cultural elements, whatever their origin, Japanese people are interested in. With this broader definition, it may be claimed that higher education in Japan, in comparison to elsewhere, has developed an exceptionally efficient formula for cultural transmission. For regardless of the national source of a cultural element, Japanese higher education (with the exception of the early Meiji period) has insisted on teaching it in the Japanese language. This practice has enabled Japanese universities to convey a broad range of cultures with a minimum of reliance on foreign languages. The use of translations is efficient in terms of the number of years students have to spend in preparation before entering universities and effective in terms of students' comprehension of the foreign cultural material; it also helps explain how Japan could rapidly expand its higher education system without a serious degeneration of standards.

Concentration by field of study varies considerably by sector and layer. Proprietary schools cover everything from foreign languages to technical subjects, whereas junior colleges tend to emphasize home economics and the humanities. As indicated in Table 2, two-fifths of all students enrolled in four-year universities specialize in the social sciences (especially law and economics) while only one-

Higher education——Table 1

Types of Institutions and Enrollment, 1980

Type of institution	National	Prefectural and local	Private	Total
	Number of institutions			
Technical colleges	54	4	4	62
Junior colleges	35	50	432	517
Four-year universities	93	34	319	446
Graduate schools[1]	(77)	(21)	(159)	(257)
Total	182	88	755	1,025
	Number of students			
Technical colleges	39,211	4,018	3,119	46,348
Junior colleges ·	14,685	19,002	337,437	371,124
Four-year universities[2]	406,644	52,082	1,376,586	1,835,312
Graduate schools	(32,728)	(2,386)	(18,878)	(53,992)
Total	460,540	75,102	1,717,142	2,252,784

[1] Graduate schools are attached to four-year universities; figures indicate the number of universities that offer graduate study programs.
[2] Includes graduate students, non-degree advanced-course students, and registered course auditors.
SOURCE: Mombushō (Ministry of Education), *Mombu tōkei yōran* (annual): 1982. Numbers of graduate students are based on unpublished Ministry of Education statistics.

Higher education——Table 2

University Enrollment in Japan by Discipline, 1980

Discipline	Public institutions[1]		Private institutions		Total	
	Numbers of students and percentages					
Humanities	31,759	7.9%	208,231	15.5%	239,990	13.8%
Social sciences (including law)	67,078	16.8	637,659	47.5	704,737	40.5
Physical sciences	23,601	5.9	30,978	2.3	54,579	3.1
Engineering	99,547	24.9	238,220	17.8	337,767	19.4
Agriculture	29,443	7.4	30,115	2.2	59,558	3.4
Health	39,728	9.9	72,330	5.4	112,058	6.4
Merchant marine	1,595	0.4	–	–	1,595	0.1
Home economics	3,578	0.9	28,352	2.1	31,930	1.8
Education	86,525	21.6	46,686	3.5	133,211	7.7
Arts	4,072	1.0	40,086	3.0	44,158	2.5
Other	13,098	3.3	8,823	0.7	21,921	1.3
Total	400,024	100.0%	1,341,480	100.0%	1,741,504	100.0%

[1] Includes national, prefectural, and local universities.
SOURCE: Mombushō (Ministry of Education), *Mombu tōkei yōran* (annual): 1982.

fifth specialize in engineering. However, whereas the private sector universities place greater emphasis on the social sciences and humanities, the public sector emphasizes engineering, agriculture, and the health and physical sciences. In recent years, the number of graduate schools and universities has rapidly expanded; over half of all master's course students and a little over a quarter of those in the doctor's program specialize in science or engineering. See also UNIVERSITIES AND COLLEGES; EDUCATION.

——Makoto Asō and Ikuo Amano, *Education and Japan's Modernization* (1972). William K. Cummings, Ikuo Amano, and Kazuyuki Kitamura, ed, *Changes in the Japanese University* (1979). William K. Cummings and Ikuo Amano, "Japanese Higher Education," in Philip G. Altlack, ed, *Comparative Higher Education: Bibliography and Analysis* (1976). Kokusai Bunka Shinkōkai, ed, *Higher Education and the Student Problem in Japan* (1972). Michio

Nagai, *Higher Education in Japan: Its Take-off and Crash* (1971).
OECD, *Reviews of National Policies for Education: Japan* (1971).

William K. CUMMINGS

higher schools

(*kōtō gakkō;* now referred to as *kyūsei kōtō gakkō,* or "old-system high schools"). Three-year institutions of learning which existed before the EDUCATIONAL REFORMS OF 1947; they prepared students for imperial universities. Five higher schools were set up at the same time as the establishment of the imperial university system in 1886. (At the time of their inception, they were called "higher middle schools" *[kōtō chūgakkō]* but came to be called higher schools from 1894.) The number of higher schools increased, and by 1935 there were 32: 25 state-run, 3 public, and 4 private higher schools. All were abolished in 1947. Middle school students had to pass an arduous entrance examination, and the acceptance ratio was frequently one out of seven to eight applicants. Foreign languages such as English, German, and French dominated the curriculum. Unlike universities, students lived in dormitories, which were noted for their free atmosphere. Graduates were virtually assured of entrance into imperial or other government universities.

AMANO Ikuo

high schools → elementary and secondary education

High Treason Incident of 1910

(Taigyaku Jiken). Also known as the Kōtoku Incident. An anarchist plot to assassinate Emperor Meiji that led to mass arrests of left-wing activists in 1910 and culminated in the execution of KŌTOKU SHŪSUI and 11 alleged coconspirators in 1911.

On 20 May 1910 Nagano prefectural police searched the room of a young lumber-mill employee named Miyashita Takichi as a result of a local investigation into conduct deemed suspicious, and uncovered a number of metal canisters as well as a supply of chemicals that could be used for the construction of bombs. Within five days the police had amassed sufficient evidence to arrest Miyashita, Nitta Tōru (a local accomplice) and in quick succession, Niimura Tadao, Niimura Zembei, and Furukawa Rikisaku. Kōtoku Shūsui and KANNO SUGA, his common-law wife, were apprehended soon afterward. Questioning of these people and further investigation by the police soon uncovered what the prosecutor general's office regarded as a nationwide conspiracy against the throne.

After a preliminary investigation conducted by government prosecutors, in which hundreds of left-wing activists and sympathizers were interrogated, 25 men and 1 woman were brought to trial on charges of violating article 73 of the Criminal Code. This article stated that "any person inflicting harm against the Emperor, the Empress, the Queen Mother, the Crown Prince, or the Emperor's eldest direct line grandson, or anyone who contemplates such an act against the same persons shall be condemned to death."

In closed extraordinary sessions before the GREAT COURT OF CASSATION, the government prosecutors, headed by HIRANUMA KIICHIRŌ, presented what was fundamentally a threefold case. Concentrating on the central figure of the incident, Kōtoku Shūsui, the government argued that after his return from the United States in 1906 Kōtoku had become an avowed anarchist; that he was in close contact with Western anarchists such as Peter Kropotkin; that while in the United States he had organized a Social Revolutionary Party to work in concert with revolutionaries in Japan; and that after the RED FLAG INCIDENT OF 1908, in which several socialists were imprisoned for parading with flags inscribed with revolutionary slogans, he had become increasingly attracted to violence and toured the country speaking of a need for revenge against the government.

With Kōtoku as their ideological leader, the prosecution maintained, a group of young radicals headed by Miyashita Takichi, Kanno Suga, Niimura Tadao, and Furukawa Rikisaku had organized a conspiracy to assassinate the emperor. Finally, it was argued, this conspiracy was not limited to radicals active in the Tōkyō area, but was nationwide in scope, with particularly strong connections in Ōsaka, Shingū (a city in Wakayama Prefecture), and Kumamoto.

Much of the controversy surrounding the High Treason Incident and trial involves the final portion of the prosecution's case. Even defense attorneys such as Imamura Rikisaburō conceded that the government could present a well-documented case against Kōtoku, Miyashita, Kanno, Niimura, and Furukawa. Evidence clearly

showed that Kōtoku had been deeply disturbed by the Red Flag Incident, had vowed to avenge the arrest of his followers, and had spoken in Ōsaka of the need for a "spirit of rebellion." Further evidence indicated that he had visited Ōishi Seinosuke, a physician in Shingū, and inquired of him how to make bombs, and that he had told Uchiyama Gudō, a Zen priest in Hakone, that the time was no longer one for "talk." Moreover, the prosecution could show quite clearly that Miyashita Takichi had informed Kōtoku early in 1909 of his belief that the imperial myth was the chief impediment to the propagation of socialism in Japan, and that to destroy that myth the emperor would have to be killed. Miyashita had also said that the best way to do this was to make bombs and throw them at the imperial carriage.

Although evidence indicated that Kōtoku had not been prepared to join Miyashita at this juncture, it also revealed that he had recommended Niimura and Furukawa to Miyashita as men who could be thoroughly trusted. Government prosecutors, moreover, showed convincingly that by the autumn of 1909 Kōtoku's attitude towards Miyashita's scheme had changed. Under government pressure that resulted in the demise of his journal, *Jiyū shisō* (Free Thought), and heavy fines for violations of the press laws, Kōtoku had actively joined Kanno and Niimura in a discussion of tactics that Niimura described in the preliminary interrogation as follows: "First of all we discussed the matter of bombing the imperial procession in the autumn of 1910, and then we conferred about simultaneously assembling 20 or 30 comrades, each armed with his own bomb, and setting out to start riots, destroy prisons, release prisoners, kill ministers, and attack government offices." Kōtoku was further implicated in the conspiracy when it was shown that he had provided Miyashita with a formula (acquired from OKUMIYA TAKEYUKI) for the construction of bombs, which allowed Miyashita to explode a working model on 3 November 1909.

If there were any extenuating circumstances in Kōtoku's case, they were his apparent withdrawal from the conspiracy in the closing months of 1909 after Miyashita's successful experiments. Government prosecutors, for their part, glossed over this change of attitude (which quite possibly involved an accommodation with the Home Ministry), arguing that Kōtoku's ideas were responsible for the conspiracy.

Evidence against Miyashita, Kanno, Niimura, and Furukawa furthermore showed that they had practiced throwing the bombs in January 1910, and on 17 May had drawn lots to see who would be the first to make an attempt on the life of the emperor. Kanno had won the drawing, but as she was about to enter prison for a three-and-a-half month term for not having paid fines for a previous offense, further actions had to be postponed until her release in August.

Although evidence against the 5 principal conspirators seemed conclusive, the dealing with the other 21 defendants was often less than adequate. Many of the minor figures in the case appear to have become entangled in the incident more through "angry talk" than through any concerted plan to destroy the emperor. Despite such circumstances, the court found all of the defendants guilty as charged on 18 January 1911. Twenty-four were sentenced to death by hanging for violations of article 73; the remaining two were sentenced to 8 and 11 years respectively for violations of the laws governing the manufacture and possession of explosives. On 19 January 1911 an imperial rescript commuted the sentences of 12 of those condemned to life imprisonment. Five days later, on 24 January, Kōtoku Shūsui, Miyashita Takichi, Niimura Tadao, Furukawa Rikisaku, Ōishi Seinosuke, Uchiyama Gudō, Okumiya Takeyuki, Morichika Umpei, Matsuo Uichita, Nariishi Heishirō, and Niimi Uichirō were executed. Kanno, the only female involved, was executed the following day.

The impact of the High Treason Incident on the Japanese intelligentsia of the time was immense. Aware that the issues of the case involved the defendants' ideas as much as their will to act, intellectuals such as TOKUTOMI ROKA, MORI ŌGAI, and NAGAI KAFŪ were rightly concerned that the case underscored a shift from the open intellectual environment of the early Meiji years to increased censorship and government control in the area of thought. To socialists the incident spelled a virtual end to their movement. Those few who avoided implication in the case were forced to recant, to go underground, or, as in the instance of KATAYAMA SEN, to leave Japan for exile abroad. With the conclusion of the High Treason Incident, the Japanese socialist movement entered what has often been described as the "winter years" *(fuyu no jidai)* from which it was not to emerge until the stimulus of the Russian Revolution and the more liberal environment of the so-called TAISHŌ DEMOCRACY permitted a second start.

📖——Itoya Toshio, *Taigyaku jiken* (1960). Kanzaki Kiyoshi, *Kakumei densetsu* (1960). Kanzaki Kiyoshi, *Taigyaku jiken kiroku*, 3 vols (1964). Kanzaki Kiyoshi, *Taigyaku jiken* (1964). Miyatake Gaikotsu, *Kōtoku ippa taigyaku jiken temmatsu* (1946). F. G. Notehelfer, *Kōtoku Shūsui: Portrait of a Japanese Radical* (1971). Ira Lev Plotkin, "A Question of Treason: The Great Treason Conspiracy of 1911," PhD dissertation, University of Michigan (1975).

F. G. NOTEHELFER

Higuchi Ichiyō (1872–1896)

The most prominent female writer of the Meiji period (1868–1912), Higuchi Ichiyō was the author of 20-odd short and medium-length stories treating primarily the unhappy and circumscribed lives of young women of her day. She also composed some 3,800 TANKA (31-syllable poems in the classical WAKA genre), several essays, and a highly regarded diary. The lyricism and sensitivity of her stories and diary, together with the tragic circumstances of her brief life, have combined to endear her to subsequent generations of Japanese readers. Her role as the first important woman writer of the modern period is also significant.

Childhood and Youthful Literary Interests——Ichiyō was the pen name of Higuchi Natsu, born the daughter of a minor official in the Tōkyō city government. Her earliest years were ones of relative comfort, enabling her to study the *koto* (a 13-stringed zither) and flower arrangement. In late 1883, she completed her formal education at the end of the fourth year of elementary school at the head of her class. Both she and her father would have liked to have seen her continue her education, but her mother opposed it on the grounds that too much learning was not good for a woman.

Ichiyō showed an interest in literature from a very early age. Hiding from her mother in the family godown, she immersed herself in romances and adventure stories. She had already begun to write *tanka* while in primary school, but it was only after 1886, when she entered a poetry academy, the Haginoya, directed by the woman poet Nakajima Utako (1842–1903), that she developed her poetic talents. Since almost all the other students were young women of the upper class, Ichiyō felt out of place as the daughter of a minor official. Yet her economic inferiority undoubtedly spurred her to excel in the area of poetry. This determination to overcome all obstacles characterized Ichiyō for the remainder of her life.

Poverty and Early Writing Career——With the death of Ichiyō's eldest brother in 1887, followed by the business failure, illness, and death of her father in 1889, the Higuchi family fell into dire poverty. For a time Ichiyō, her mother, and her younger sister were reduced to taking in laundry and sewing to maintain themselves. Furthermore, after her father's death the Shibuya family broke off the engagement between their son Saburō and Ichiyō, a bitter blow since she and Saburō had been childhood sweethearts. This broken engagement is surely responsible for the fact that many of her stories treat the unfulfillment of young love. Virtually the only bright spot in those years was the stimulus Ichiyō received from the publication of a novel by a fellow Haginoya student, who thereby earned a considerable sum. This inspired Ichiyō to begin writing fiction herself in 1890, and in the following year she became the pupil in fiction-writing of a handsome young widower, Nakarai Tōsui (1861–1926), a writer for the *Asahi shimbun*, a Tōkyō daily newspaper. Under his tutelage, she published her first story, "Yamizakura" (1892, Cherry Blossoms in the Dark) in the first issue of *Musashino*, a magazine Tōsui was editing. This story, treating the unhappy love of a boy and a girl, dealt with a theme common to many of her later works.

More important than the training which Tōsui provided was the fact that Ichiyō fell deeply in love with him. Yet she was forced to sever relations because she believed, mistakenly, that he was the father of a child born to a young woman boarding at his home and also because rumors of Ichiyō's involvement with Tōsui had spread to the Haginoya. This rupture with Tōsui and her consequent suffering, following upon her broken engagement with Shibuya Saburō, reinforced Ichiyō's belief that she would not find fulfillment in love, and she poured forth her unhappiness in the pages of her diary.

Although she continued publishing stories in various magazines, including the influential *Bungakukai*, and in newspapers, she received so little financial compensation that she decided to give up writing and moved in July 1893, with her mother and sister, to Ryū-

senji near the Yoshiwara prostitution quarter of Tōkyō. There they opened a store selling kitchenware and cheap candy. Although this venture was a business failure, her 10-month stay at Ryūsenji provided her with the material for her best-known and most highly praised story, "Takekurabe" (1895–96, Comparing Heights; tr "Growing Up," 1956), which treated the lives of young people growing up in a licensed prostitution quarter and focused on the heroine Midori, destined to follow her older sister into prostitution.

Literary Flowering and Early Death——In May 1894 Ichiyō moved to the Hongō district of Tōkyō where she resumed her writing and also began to teach at the Haginoya. During this period she developed close relations with many of the prominent writers associated with *Bungakukai* who admired her literary talents. In rapid succession she produced her best stories, on which her fame is securely based. "Ōtsugomori" (1894, The Last Day of the Year) is a superbly crafted story dealing with the plight of a maid who steals money from her employer to aid her uncle. She escapes punishment because, shortly thereafter, her employer's wastrel son takes an unspecified sum of money from the family safe, thereby concealing her theft. While "Takekurabe" was still being serialized, Ichiyō wrote "Nigorie" (1895; tr "Muddy Bay," 1958), a compelling portrait of the bar-girl and semiprostitute Oriki who, though she loves an affluent man, one of her customers, becomes involved with a married man, Genshichi. The latter expels his wife and young son from their home in order to continue his relationship with Oriki. Ultimately Genshichi and Oriki die together, but it is not clear whether Oriki dies willingly. "Jūsan'ya" (1895; tr "The Thirteenth Night," 1960–61) treats the unhappy marriage of Oseki, who wishes to leave her cruel husband but is persuaded by her parents to return to him. On her way back from her parents' home she discovers that the rickshaw-puller is Rokunosuke, the youth who had loved her prior to her marriage. Once again, young lovers have been forced apart by cruel circumstances.

Overwork and economic hardship contributed to Ichiyō's final illness, tuberculosis. From July 1896 her condition worsened, and she died, much lamented by her family and friends, on 23 November of the same year.

📖——Higuchi Ichiyō, *Higuchi Ichiyō zenshū*, 7 vols (Chikuma Shobō, 1953–56). "Takekurabe" (1896), tr Edward Seidensticker as "Growing Up," in Donald Keene, ed, *Modern Japanese Literature* (1956). Shiota Ryōhei, *Higuchi Ichiyō* (1960).

Valdo H. VIGLIELMO

Hiikawa

River in eastern Shimane Prefecture, western Honshū, originating in the mountain Mikuniyama, flowing into the Izumo Plain at the city of Izumi, and emptying into Lake Shinji. The river figures in the legend of "Yamata no Orochi" (Eight-headed Dragon). Length: 153 km (95 mi); area of drainage basin: 2,164 sq km (835 sq mi).

Hijikawa

River in Ehime Prefecture, Shikoku, originating in the Uwa Mountains and flowing northwest to the town of Nagahama and into the Iyo Sea. The Kanogawa Dam is located midstream. Length: 90 km (56 mi); area of drainage basin: 1,210 sq km (467 sq mi).

hijiki

Hizikia fusiformis. A brown alga of the family Sargassaceae that grows attached to rocks in coastal waters of the sea. It is a perennial and grows profusely from winter to early spring. When fully grown, it is yellow brown in color and reaches lengths of up to 1 meter (3 ft). It has a narrow tubular stem with several branches; its leaves are 3–10 centimeters (1–3 in) long, thick, pointed, and flat in shape. The plant turns a blackish brown color when dried. Young plants are suitable for human consumption and are rich in vitamins A, B, and C as well as such minerals as calcium and iron. *Hijiki* has traditionally been used in East Asia not only as food, but also as a remedy for hardening of the arteries, asthma, hernias, and other ailments. See also SEAWEED.

Michio KUSHI

hijiri

A holy man. Although the term dates from pre-Buddhist times and was even an appellation of the emperor, it came to mean by the middle of the Heian period (794–1185) Buddhist holy men who led

Hikeshi———Edo machi hikeshi

Detail of a copy of an Edo-period illustrated handscroll entitled *Kaji emaki* (The Fire Scroll), showing firemen engaged in extinguishing a fire. The differently shaped standards identify various units of firemen. Colors on paper. Height of scroll 28.9 cm. Mitsui Collection, Tōkyō.

lives of itineracy or ascetic retreat. Some were ordained, others were not. Initially, they were independent of, and occasionally in opposition to, the official Buddhist institutions. Notable among these early *hijiri* was KŪYA (also Kōya, 903–972), the "*hijiri* of the market," who urged the common people to chant the name of the Buddha Amida. Many other *hijiri* were devoted to the Lotus Sutra.

In the 11th and 12th centuries, *hijiri* were organized into formal groups chartered by the great Buddhist temples for purposes of fund-raising. Chief among these groups were several based at Mt. Kōya (Kōyasan). The *hijiri* of Mt. Kōya were responsible for the spread of legends about KŪKAI, the founder of the temple complex on the mountain. Perhaps the most prestigious *hijiri* organization, however, was that founded by Chōgen (1121–1206), who was appointed in 1181 (Yōwa 1) to rebuild TŌDAIJI after it had burned in the warfare of the period. So successful were his *hijiri* in raising funds that other temples organized similar groups.

Hijiri thus became a permanent feature of medieval Japanese Buddhism and a major factor in the spread of Buddhism to the Japanese masses. From institutions usually called *bessho* (literally, "separate places"), which enjoyed a franchise granted by a parent temple, they traveled throughout the country preaching and raising funds. Their fund-raising, called *kanjin*, consisted of distributing talismans *(fuda)*, having a Buddhist icon printed in the name of a believer, or having some other devotional act performed at the temple, all these in exchange for a contribution. Contributors' names would then be enrolled in a register, which was kept at the temple or even placed within images built by such funds. In their preaching, the *hijiri* drew from legends of the temple they represented, often illustrating their talks with picture scrolls, as well as relying on dramatic and musical techniques. They were thus a major force in the establishment of popular literary and performing arts. These *hijiri* are also called *bessho hijiri, kanjin hijiri,* and *yugyō* (wayfaring) *hijiri.* Two Pure Land Buddhist groups, the JI SECT and the YŪZŪ NEMBUTSU SECT drew heavily on the traditions and techniques of *hijiri.*

In the 16th and 17th centuries, many *hijiri* settled in villages to minister to local congregations, and some *hijiri* groups evolved into craft or performance guilds.

📖———Gorai Shigeru, *Kōya hijiri* (1965). Ichirō Hori, "On the Concept of Hijiri (Holy Man)," *Numen* (1958). Hori Ichirō, *Wagakuni minkan shinkō shi no kenkyū,* 2 vols (1953–1955).

James H. FOARD

Hikaku Sangensoku

(Three Nonnuclear Principles). Japan's nuclear policy that specifies that "Japan will not produce, possess, or let others bring in" nuclear weapons. Declared as a national policy by Prime Minister SATŌ EISAKU in January 1968 and adopted by the ruling Liberal Democratic Party as part of its party platform, the three principles were unanimously adopted as a resolution by the Diet in 1972. The Nobel Peace Prize was awarded in 1974 to Satō largely because of his non-

nuclear policy. Today there are two schools of thought on these principles. One seeks to legislate them while the other proposes to delete the phrase "let others bring in" to accommodate the requirements for national defense under the United States–Japan Security Treaty. See also NUCLEAR POLICY; ATOMIC BOMB.

IWASHIMA Hisao

hikan ➞ oyakata and hikan

Hikari

City in southeastern Yamaguchi Prefecture, western Honshū, on the Inland Sea. Originally a farming village, Hikari was the site of a naval arsenal before World War II. The site of the arsenal is now the center of a pharmaceutical and steel industry. The beach at scenic Nijigahama and Mishima Hot Spring, with its curative waters, draw tourists. Pop: 48,992.

Hikawa Shrine

(Hikawa Jinja). A Shintō shrine in the city of Ōmiya, Saitama Prefecture, dedicated to SUSANOO NO MIKOTO (the younger brother of the sun goddess and so-called imperial ancestress, Amaterasu Ōmikami) and two other deities. The shrine has enjoyed great popularity because of the close association Susanoo no Mikoto has had with both agriculture and military prowess. In Saitama Prefecture 162 offshoot shrines bear this name; in Tōkyō there are 59 such shrines. Despite their popularity in the prefectures around Tōkyō, Hikawa shrines are virtually unknown in other areas of Japan. An imperial emissary was customarily dispatched to make an offering at the annual festival on 1 August. Although the origins of the shrine are shrouded in obscurity, it was ranked by the Engi Shiki (927; tr *Procedures of the Engi Era,* 1970–72) as an eminent shrine (*myōjin taisha*).

Stanley WEINSTEIN

hikeshi

Fire fighters during the Edo period (1600–1868). The scores of cities in Japan, consisting of wooden buildings built cheek by jowl, were repeatedly ravaged by fire. To meet this worst of urban menaces, fire-fighting brigades were formed, and like most groups in Tokugawa society, they were organized according to major status categories. In the great cities of Edo (now Tōkyō), Kyōto, and Ōsaka units were organized by the shogunate. *Daimyō* and HATAMOTO formed *hikeshi* units both in Edo and in their own castle towns (*jōka machi*) and fief headquarters (*jin'ya*), while urban commoners set up their own fire-fighting units to protect their neighborhoods. The best-known fire brigades were those of Edo: the shogunate's fire brigades (*jōbikeshi* or *jōhikeshi*) and those of daimyō (*daimyō hikeshi*) and townsmen (*machi hikeshi*).

The *jōbikeshi* (also called *yoriai hikeshi* or *jūnin hikeshi*) were first established as 4 units (*kumi*) in 1650, expanded after the disastrous MEIREKI FIRE of 1657, and stabilized at 10 units in 1704. These were treated as regular shogunate offices under the authority of the junior councillors (WAKADOSHIYORI). The force was commanded by *hatamoto*, and each unit consisted of 36 stipended *samurai*. These units were initially expected to fight fires or respond to other emergencies throughout the city, taking command of *daimyō hikeshi* and *machi hikeshi* when doing so. As Edo grew, however, they became less and less adequate and their relationship with the other firemen became increasingly abrasive. Cooperation was poor by the 1760s, and after 1792, at the request of townsmen, *jōbikeshi* were forbidden to fight fires in commoners' districts of the city except in the event of a major conflagration. After 1819 they were further restricted to the area bounded by the outer moat (*gaikaku*) of Edo Castle.

From 1629 the shogunate had begun ordering daimyō to furnish *daimyō hikeshi* in Edo at the rate of 30 men per 10,000 *koku* of official domainal size (OMOTEDAKA). It subsequently expanded and reorganized the brigades of fire fighters and fire lookouts (*hinoban*), working out an elaborate system for their development. Lookouts were placed at strategic points throughout the city, and fire fighters were in essence assigned four types of duty. Some were under orders to proceed immediately upon call to the site of the fire. Some were assigned to posts near certain designated structures (Edo Castle, the temples Kan'eiji and Zōjōji, and the rice warehouses at Asakusa and Honjo). Some were under orders to remain on guard in their own immediate residential areas. Other emergency recruits were subject to whatever special duty the shogunate might require in the event of a major conflagration.

The *machi hikeshi* of Edo were first established in 1718 to protect commercial establishments; five years later, they were reorganized and expanded to 47 units *(kumi)* of firemen and eventually numbered 48. Placed under the authority of the city commissioners (EDO MACHI BUGYŌ), each unit included a commander and his assistants, standard bearers, ladder carriers, plain firemen, and coolies *(ninsoku)*. *Machi hikeshi* were often assisted by local volunteers (called *tobi ninsoku*), especially when wrecking buildings to create firebreaks or clearing wreckage. These volunteers, whose spirit of rough generosity contributed to the image of the devil-may-care *edokko* ("son of Edo"), were sometimes more interested in betting on the outcome of fires in progress than in fighting them and often became rowdy public nuisances when not otherwise occupied. Perhaps because of the dubious reputation that the volunteers helped give to *machi hikeshi* and perhaps for reasons of class prejudice or economic rivalry, *machi hikeshi* were not authorized to function in samurai districts of the city, these being left to the *jōbikeshi* and *daimyō hikeshi.*   Conrad TOTMAN

hikidemono

Commemorative souvenir given to guests at banquets for special occasions. The most frequent occasions for giving *hikidemono* are wedding banquets, but those observing someone's 60th or the 77th birthday or celebrating receipt of special awards such as commendation for a long teaching career also require *hikidemono*. Elegant utensils, such as decorative dishes, silver spoons, or flower vases, as well as sweets and other delicacies, are common souvenirs for such occasions. The initials or the name of the person or persons honored and the occasion commemorated are inscribed on the gift. See also GIFT GIVING; SHŪGI.   Harumi BEFU

hikiita → naruko

hikimawashi

(literally, "dragging around"). An extra penalty imposed in the Edo period (1600–1868) upon a criminal whose offense was considered to deserve something more than the death penalty. As an example to others, the criminal was led on horseback through the city to the execution grounds. The criminal was accompanied by a parade of HININ (members of the lowest class of society) holding flags and wooden plaques with the nature of the offense written on them. Although there were two different fixed routes for such parades in Edo (now Tōkyō), sometimes it was specially arranged to pass by the site of the offense or the criminal's home.

Hikitsuke

(High Court). An organ of both the Kamakura (1192–1333) and Muromachi (1338–1573) shogunates for the adjudication of lawsuits. It was first established in 1249 by the fifth shogunal regent *(shikken)*, HŌJŌ TOKIYORI, in order to aid the Hyōjōshū (Council of State) by expediting and clarifying decisions. It was composed of a president *(tōnin)* and several coadjutors *(hikitsukeshū)*, all selected from the Hyōjōshū, who were assisted by several secretaries *(bugyōnin)*. There were three, later five, such tribunals, which divided up the month and served in rotation. Hikitsuke were established both at Kamakura and in the office of the Rokuhara deputies in Kyōto. Although they were originally intended to hear only suits involving vassals of the shogunate, their jurisdiction was later extended to include more general matters of landholding and taxation.
                                           G. Cameron HURST III

Hiki Yoshikazu (?–1203)

Military general of the early part of the Kamakura period (1185–1333); member of a powerful family of the Hiki district in Musashi Province (now Saitama and Tōkyō prefectures). The adopted son of the nurse of MINAMOTO NO YORITOMO, the founder of the Kamakura shogunate, Yoshikazu served Yoritomo from an early age. Rendering distinguished service in various battles, he won Yoritomo's confidence, and his daughter was married to Yoritomo's son, MINAMOTO NO YORIIE, the second shōgun. After his daughter

bore a son, Yoshikazu was able to exercise strong influence as Yoriie's father-in-law and held important posts in the shogunate. When Yoriie became seriously ill in 1203, HŌJŌ TOKIMASA, the shogunal regent, whose authority had been challenged by Yoshikazu, planned to reduce by half the administrative power to be inherited by Yoriie's son by transferring the other half to Yoriie's brother MINAMOTO NO SANETOMO. This infuriated Yoshikazu and led him to plot the overthrow of the Hōjō family. The plan was discovered and Yoshikazu was assassinated by the Hōjō, Yoriie's son was killed, and he himself was removed from office to be replaced by his brother Sanetomo.

Hikone

City in eastern Shiga Prefecture, central Honshū, on the eastern shore of Lake Biwa. A castle town under the powerful Ii family during the Edo period (1600–1868), Hikone retains intact its castle as well as many merchant and *samurai* houses. Besides traditional goods such as Buddhist altars and textiles, the town produces pulp, machinery, and tires. The site of the castle has been made into a park, with several lovely gardens. Pop: 89,698.

Hikosan

Mountain on the border of Fukuoka and Ōita prefectures, Kyūshū. Known from ancient times as a center for religious exercises of the SHUGENDŌ sect. Hikosan Shrine is divided between the summit and slopes. There are strange rock formations, beech forests, and numerous cultural properties. Hikosan is known for its rare insects and is a center of interest in Yaba–Hita–Hikosan Quasi-National Park. Height: 1,200 m (3,936 ft).

Hikoshima

Island in the western mouth of the Kammon Strait, city of Shimonoseki, Yamaguchi Prefecture, western Honshū. The site of numerous metal, shipbuilding, chemical, and fishery plants, Hikoshima is an important zone of heavy industry in Shimonoseki. Truck farming and the hothouse cultivation of flowers and cabbages are also carried out here. Area: 8.6 sq km (3.3 sq mi).

hikyaku

(literally, "flying feet"). Couriers or runners who carried messages and small packages on foot along established routes. Known by a variety of names, such runners date from the Kamakura period (1185–1333); they are known to have made the 483-kilometer (300–mi) trip between Kamakura and Kyōto in seven days in 1185, shortening it to four days a half-century later. Runners also linked Kamakura with Dazaifu, the government headquarters in northern Kyūshū. During the Edo period (1600–1868), the *hikyaku* system developed into an orderly postal system linking the three major cities of Edo (now Tōkyō), Kyōto, and Ōsaka. TOKUGAWA IEYASU requisitioned runners and pack horses from POST-STATION TOWNS along the TŌKAIDŌ for official use. By the Genroku era (1688–1703) improved roads and a pacified countryside had reduced the Edo-to-Kyōto running time of shogunate couriers to 82 hours, and by the Hōreki era (1751–64) to 68 hours.

Major *daimyō* also set up courier services early in the Edo period to link Edo with their own castle towns, stationing men at rest stops on the route. Another courier service was established in 1615, when members of a shogunate guard unit in Ōsaka, perhaps wishing news from home, arranged with post-station operators on the Tōkaidō to have some of their retainers serve as runners. These runners made three regular trips monthly, and the service proved so useful that merchants in Ōsaka subsequently established a similar scheduled courier service of their own, arming their runners with swords for protection against highwaymen.

In 1663 merchants in Ōsaka, Kyōto, and Edo jointly established a courier service between the three cities and, the times being more peaceful, dispensed with the swords. Known as *machi·hikyaku* or "common couriers," these runners made the trip between Ōsaka and Edo daily, covering the distance in six days. At Nihombashi in Edo, and at comparable places in Ōsaka and Kyōto, a person could deposit a letter together with postage coins at collection points during the day, and in the evening the courier would pick up the mail pouch and depart. The regularity, reliability, and economy of the service enabled *machi hikyaku* to displace the other services, except for emergency deliveries by shogunate couriers. The *machi hikyaku* system flourished for another two centuries, finally collapsing in the disorder of the 1860s to be replaced by ship, vehicular, and telegraph communications. *Conrad TOTMAN*

Hill, James Jerome (1838–1916)

American railroad magnate. Born in Ontario, Canada, he built up a railroad empire stretching from the Great Lakes to the Pacific and consolidated his properties into the Great Northern Railway Company in 1890. He held a strong interest in China, Japan, and India, and in 1896, together with a Japanese shipping line, the NIPPON YŪSEN, formed a short-lived steamship company to promote trade between the United States and the Far East.

himachi and tsukimachi

(literally, "waiting for the sun" and "waiting for the moon"). Traditional social gatherings, held on predetermined nights, at which neighbors talked and feasted while awaiting dawn or moonrise. Such parties originally had some religious significance, and they were often held by the various types of religious groups called KŌ. The duty of hosting the parties rotated among the members of the group. The parties frequently coincided with major annual events, such as the end of harvest or the "Little New Year" (Koshōgatsu; see NEW YEAR). Some gatherings were for women only and were held on nights when it was considered unlucky to become pregnant. Common dates for *himachi* were the 15th or 23rd day of the 1st, 5th, and 9th lunar months; *tsukimachi* parties were often held on the 13th, 15th, 17th, or 23rd day of the 1st, 5th, 9th, and 11th months. The dates varied widely from place to place, and they were sometimes determined by the traditional sexagenary calendar cycle (JIKKAN JŪNISHI). Groups that held such parties often set up commemorative stone tablets by the roadside or in temple or shrine precincts, where some can still be found today. *Ōtō Tokihiko*

Himeji

City in southern Hyōgo Prefecture, western Honshū, on the river Ichikawa. A castle town since the 14th century, Himeji is most noted for HIMEJI CASTLE, completed by IKEDA TERUMASA in 1610. It is the principal city of the Harima region and now a part of the Harima Industrial Zone; major industries are textiles, food processing, steel, and oil refining. Besides the castle, tourists are drawn to the temple Enkyōji on the outskirts of the city. Pop: 446,255.

Himeji Castle

A castle located in the city of Himeji, Hyōgo Prefecture. The castle is also known as Shirasagi (Egret) Castle, because of an alleged resemblance to an egret in its tall, white elegance. The castle changed hands through centuries of war and was enlarged by successive nobles into its present form. First constructed during the mid-14th century by the AKAMATSU FAMILY, the castle soon came under the ownership of the Kodera family and then, after further fighting, was in 1580 eventually ceded to TOYOTOMI HIDEYOSHI, who added 30 turrets. A later lord of the castle, IKEDA TERUMASA, took 9 years (1601–09) to add 20 more turrets. The main compound is located on a hill 45 meters (approximately 150 ft) high; the main and the adjoining west compounds are surrounded by three rings of outer compounds. The main donjon, 5 stories high on the outside and 7 on the inside, is connected with 3 minor donjons in an arrangement that combines beauty of design with security against attack. The Himeji Castle ranked second to ŌSAKA CASTLE in size. Most of the original structures survive; the grounds have been designated a Historic Site and the castle a National Treasure. See photo and illustrations at CASTLES.

Himeji Plain

(Himeji Heiya). Also known as Harima Plain or Banshū Plain. Located in southern Hyōgo Prefecture, western Honshū, bordering the Inland Sea. It consists of the deltas of the rivers Kakogawa and Ibogawa, flowing parallel north to south. Despite the low precipitation, numerous ponds and reservoirs allow the cultivation of rice. Industries have developed along the coastal region, including the iron industry. The major city is Himeji. Length: 10 km (6 mi); width: 40 km (25 mi).

Himeyuri Butai

(Star Lily Corps). A corps of 223 field hospital nurses from Okinawa; composed of female high school and normal school students and their teachers. The Himeyuri Butai was organized on 23 March 1945 in response to the American invasion of Okinawa. On 1 April, in the face of Japanese defeat, many of its members committed suicide. The unit's total dead from war casualties and suicides numbered 167. The Himeyuri Butai is particularly remembered by the Japanese because of the novel *Himeyuri no tō* (1950) by Ishino Keiichirō and its movie version (1953), telling the girls' tragic tale, symbolic of the Okinawans' futile but valiant attempt to battle the Americans. A monument to them is located at the site of the mass suicide in the city of Itoman on Okinawa.

Himi

City in northwestern Toyama Prefecture, central Honshū, on Toyama Bay at the base of the Noto Peninsula. Himi is a flourishing fishing port (yellowtail, sardines, and cuttlefish) with a marine food-processing industry. It is a part of the Noto Peninsula Quasi-National Park. Pop: 62,413.

Himiko (fl ca 3rd century AD)

Also known as Pimiko. Female ruler of the early Japanese political federation known as YAMATAI, as described in the WEI ZHI *(Wei chih)*, a Chinese chronicle of the 3rd century.

Yamatai, the location of which has long been debated as being either northern Kyūshū or the Yamato (Nara) region, was at one time controlled by male rulers. According to what the Japanese refer to as the "Wajinden" (the section in the *Wei zhi* dealing with Japan, or the "Land of Wa") warfare erupted among the various countries inhabited by the Wa people around AD 170–180. Himiko, a young female, possibly still in her teens, eventually emerged victorious, and was "jointly established" as sovereign by the chieftains of the various political entities.

Himiko enjoyed a great following among her subjects, largely because of her mastery of *kidō* ("the Way of the demons"), probably a form of SHAMANISM. Her rule was doubtless invested with a strongly religious character. After she became queen, very few persons were allowed to see her. She is said to have had 1,000 female slaves in her service, and only one male was allowed to enter her living quarters, in order to bring food, drink, and messages. Her private quarters and their palisadelike outer enclosure were strictly guarded at all times by soldiers.

Because Himiko was sequestered by a set of taboos, someone else presumably had to take charge of actual affairs of state. According to the account in the *Wei zhi*, "she had a younger brother who assisted her in ruling the country," and we may suppose that this brother was in fact a second sovereign, a nonspiritual ruler who could show himself to the populace and who looked after the concrete details of politics. This dual exercise of authority suggests that Himiko may have reigned during a period of transition from a "religious" to an "actuality-oriented" type of politics.

Relations with Wei China—— At the time Himiko became queen, the northern half of the Korean peninsula was under the strong influence of the Chinese Gongsun (Kung-sun) family. The southern half of the peninsula was also within the orbit of Gongsun influence, but ethnic groups known in Korean history by the names Han and Wae (J: Kan, Wai) were moving toward greater independence and, like the Wa people in Japan, were experiencing warfare among themselves. The Chinese Wei government took note of these movements and in 237 commenced activities aimed at destroying the Gongsun.

Gongsun Yuan (Kung-sun Yüan), who became chief of the Gongsun in 228, was defeated and killed the following year. It is in the summer of 239, 10 months after the fall of the Gongsun, that we have the first record of envoys being sent by Himiko to Wei China. The Wei emperor Ming granted Himiko the title *qinwei Wo wang* (ch'in-wei Wo wang; J: shingi waō; "Wa ruler friendly to Wei"), as well as a gold seal with a purple cord. He also made a gift of exquisite textiles, a large number of bronze mirrors, and other items. A Chinese mission accompanied the returning Wa envoys, and later a second mission was sent to Wa.

In 245 the Wei court sent yellow military banners to a person named Nanshōmai (Japanese pronunciation), who, as Yamatai's chief envoy six years earlier, had been given a military title by the

Chinese. This seems to suggest that fighting had already commenced between Yamatai and an unfriendly country in Japan called Kona (or Kunu). Two years later news of actual fighting was communicated by envoys to the Chinese commandery at Daifang (Taifang). More yellow banners were sent to Nanshōmai, along with an official message from the Wei emperor to Himiko.

It is likely that the war between Yamatai and Kona was proceeding to the former's disadvantage, and that Himiko's missions to Wei China were to request aid. In any event, the *Wei zhi* suddenly announces Himiko's death without recording the outcome of the fighting. It reports that a huge earthen mound was built on her grave site and that over 100 male and female servants followed her in death. Given Himiko's position as a religious ruler, it is possible that she was killed at the hands of subordinate chieftains who thought that the unfavorable course of the war with Kona was due to a waning of her magical powers.

🔲 ——Saeki Arikiyo, *Yamataikoku to Himiko* (1975). Yamao Yukihisa, *Gishi wajinden: Tōyōshi jō no kodai Nihon* (1972).

Saeki Arikiyo

Hina Matsuri → Doll Festival

Hinatsu Kōnosuke (1890–1971)

Poet and scholar of English literature. Real name Higuchi Kunito. Born in Nagano Prefecture. Graduate of and later professor of English literature at Waseda University. Active as a poet from his student days, he became known for the self-described "gothic romanticism" of his poetry. The arcane symbolism of his first poetry collection, *Tenshin no shō* (1917), stood in direct opposition to the simple "people's poetry" *(minshūshi)* then in fashion. His 1929 study, *Meiji Taishō shi shi,* is prized as the first systematic history of modern Japanese poetry and received the 1950 Yomiuri Literary Prize. His numerous translations of romantic and gothic poetry include poems by Edgar Allen Poe and Oscar Wilde. His works are collected in *Hinatsu Kōnosuke zenshū,* 8 vols (Kawade Shobō Shinsha, 1972–73).

hinawajū

The name given to the European harquebus or matchlock musket first introduced to Japan in 1543 by the Portuguese at the island of Tanegashima (now part of Kagoshima Prefecture) near Kyūshū; hence it is sometimes also called *tanegashima.* The harquebus had a bore size of 22 millimeters (0.9 inches), a length of 1.3 meters (4.3 feet), and an effective firing range of 60 to 75 meters (200 to 250 ft). The use of firearms spread quickly throughout Japan during the latter part of the Sengoku period (1467–1568) as domains were eager to use them in warfare. The use of firearm units in the armies of military leaders like ODA NOBUNAGA (1534–82) and TAKEDA SHINGEN (1521–73) brought about a great revolution in military strategy. More than 100 schools teaching the military art of firearms use sprang up, each with its own secret instruction manual. The harquebus continued to be used until about the middle of the 19th century. See also FIREARMS, INTRODUCTION OF. *Tomiki Kenji*

hinin

(literally, "non-humans"). People who belonged to the lowest social class—along with the outcast group now known as *eta* (see BURAKUMIN)—in the Edo period (1600–1868). In premodern Japan, the word *hinin* was used in a broad sense to designate a variety of people who were not accepted by society in general. Under the Tokugawa shogunate (1603–1867), *hinin* were prohibited from making a living by any other means than begging. Subject to compulsory labor, they were assigned to various disagreeable jobs, such as caring for victims of contagious diseases and taking criminals to execution grounds. They lived together, secluded in the poorer sections of the cities. They were also discriminated against in terms of social practices: they were not allowed to tie their hair nor to put anything on their heads; the length of their clothes had to be above the knee; women had to leave their eyebrows unshaved and their teeth undyed. Legally, there were two different divisions in the *hinin* class; those who were born into the class and those who were demoted to that status because of crime or poverty. The latter could move back up to their original class under certain conditions. The class was legally abolished in 1871.

Hino

City in southwestern Tōkyō Prefecture, at the confluence of the rivers Tamagawa and Asakawa. An industrial city since the 1920s, Hino is noted for its automobile, electrical appliance, film, and watch industries. It is fast becoming a residential area for commuters to nearby Tōkyō. Tourist attractions include Tama Zoo, where lions roam freely, the temple Takahata Fudōson, and the Mogusaen Botanical Garden. Pop: 145,417.

Hino Ashihei (1907–1960)

Novelist. Real name Tamai Katsunori. Born in Fukuoka Prefecture. While a student at Waseda University, he was drafted into the army in 1928. Discharged for reading the works of Lenin, he went to work as a stevedore for his father's company in northern Kyūshū, and organized a longshoremen's union. In 1932, he was arrested as a leftist sympathizer, but was released after recanting his beliefs (see TENKŌ). His short story about a city sanitation worker, "Funnyō tan" (1937), won the sixth Akutagawa Prize, which was awarded to him after he had left for military service in China in the SINO-JAPANESE WAR OF 1937–1945. He became known as a war novelist with his popular trilogy about military life, which included *Mugi to heitai* (1938; tr *Barley and Soldiers,* 1939), a realistic account of the war in China. Among his postwar works, *Hana to ryū* (1953, The Flowers and the Dragon), a novel that describes the lives of his parents, is noted for its combination of warmth and keen observation. His works are characteristically colored with humor and satire. After completing the autobiographical novel *Kakumei zengo* (1960, Before and After the Revolution), which dealt with his early involvement in leftist causes, Hino committed suicide.

Hino family

Courtier family descended from the powerful northern branch of the FUJIWARA FAMILY. Their name derived from a place in the Uji district of Yamashiro Province (now part of Kyōto Prefecture) where Fujiwara no Iemune, grandson of Fujiwara no Uchimaro (756–812), founded the temple Hōkaiji in 822 to house a Buddhist image given him by the priest SAICHŌ. In 1051 Iemune's 5th-generation descendant Sukenari (990–1070) took holy orders, retired to the Hōkaiji, which he enlarged, and adopted the name Hino. The family produced generations of poets and Confucian scholars who served as court officials; one of them, Hino Suketomo (1290–1332), was involved in Emperor GO-DAIGO's plot to overthrow the Kamakura shogunate (see SHŌCHŪ CONSPIRACY). After Nariko (1352–1405), daughter of Hino Tokimitsu (1328–67), married the 3rd Muromachi shōgun, ASHIKAGA YOSHIMITSU, the Hino family became especially close to the shogunal house. Perhaps its most famous member was Hino Katsumitsu (1429–76), who, in order to enhance his political power, persuaded the 8th shōgun, ASHIKAGA YOSHIMASA, to marry his sister HINO TOMIKO, who became a powerful figure in her own right. *G. Cameron Hurst III*

hinoki → cypresses

Hinomaru → national flag

Hinomisaki

Cape on western Shimane Peninsula, northern Shimane Prefecture, western Honshū. Located on the Sea of Japan, it is the site of the ancient Hinomisaki Shrine, with the Izumo Shrine nearby. There are bathing beaches and a lighthouse. Hinomisaki is part of Daisen-Oki National Park.

Hino Motors, Ltd

(Hino Jidōsha Kōgyō). Manufacturer of diesel- and gasoline-engine vehicles sold under the Hino brand name. The company was established in 1910 and in 1966 became affiliated with the TOYOTA MOTOR CORPORATION. A world leader in the production of diesel vehicles, Hino is also in annual sales the largest Japanese company handling commercial vehicles with gross vehicle weights of over 8.4 tons. It is known for its diesel engines featuring the Hino micro-mixing system (HMMS), a highly efficient fuel-air mixing and combustion method. Hino has 2 subsidiaries, 6 associated companies, and 78 distributors overseas. The percentage of its production devoted to exports is expected to increase in the future. Currently, efforts are being made to develop products with new safety, energy-saving, and antipollution features. Sales for the fiscal year ending March 1982 totaled ¥420 billion (US $1.7 billion), with diesel trucks and buses accounting for 56 percent, passenger cars and pickup trucks 26 percent, two-ton trucks 1 percent, and engine components 17 percent. The company was capitalized at ¥15.4 billion (US $64 million) in the same year. Corporate headquarters are located in the city of Hino, Tōkyō Prefecture.

Hino Tomiko (1440–1496)

Wife of ASHIKAGA YOSHIMASA, eighth shōgun of the Muromachi shogunate (1338–1573). Born into the aristocratic HINO FAMILY, which had traditionally provided wives for the Ashikaga shōguns, she married Yoshimasa in 1455. In the first 10 years of their marriage she bore two daughters. Lacking a male heir, Yoshimasa named his younger brother Yoshimi (1439–91) as his successor. Tomiko then unexpectedly bore him a son, Yoshihisa (1465–89), and gained for her child the right of succession by forming an alliance with the powerful military leader YAMANA SŌZEN. The succession dispute was a major cause of the ŌNIN WAR (1467–77). In contrast to Yoshimasa, who became increasingly reclusive, Tomiko was adept at financial dealings such as rice speculation and usury, and she amassed an enormous fortune. An image of Tomiko can be seen at the temple Hōkyōji in Kyōto.

Hinuma

Lagoon in eastern Ibaraki Prefecture, central Honshū, located on the Pacific coast. Hinuma was once a valley of the river Hinumagawa and became an inlet which later formed the lagoon. It is a good fishing ground for freshwater and ocean fish. Area: 11 sq km (4.2 sq mi); circumference: 22 km (14 mi); depth: 3.1 m (10.2 ft).

Hirabayashi Hatsunosuke (1892–1931)

Literary critic. Born in Kyōto Prefecture. Graduate of Waseda University. While working as a translator for a news agency, he became a contributor to TANE MAKU HITO (The Sower), the pioneering proletarian magazine founded in 1921, and established his name as an important theoretical spokesman for the PROLETARIAN LITERATURE MOVEMENT with his collection of criticism *Musan kaikyū no bunka* (1923). It was the first expression in Japan of a literary theory based on dialectical materialism. Later, in "Seijiteki kachi to geijutsuteki kachi" (1929), he advocated the equal importance of artistic and political values. This article met strong criticism from those in the movement who considered art as subordinate to political activity. He died in Paris while attending an international writers' convention.

Hirabayashi Taiko (1905–1972)

Novelist, known for stories on the lives of the poor and on her own hardships as a left-wing activist. Born the third daughter in a respected rural family in Nagano Prefecture. Her grandfather had started a silk factory and been active in politics but then lost the family fortune in poor investments. When her father went alone to work in Korea, she helped her mother operate a small store to support the household. She early became an avid reader, especially of translations from Russian literature. Despite her mother's objections, she attended Suwa Girls' High School, where she was encouraged to begin writing by its principal, the poet TSUCHIYA BUMMEI.

Impressed by socialist essays she had read in the leftist magazine TANE MAKU HITO (The Sower), Hirabayashi went to Tōkyō in 1922 to meet those responsible, especially SAKAI TOSHIHIKO. She worked first as a telephone operator, then as a salesgirl, and later as a cafe waitress while she became acquainted with members of various leftist political and cultural groups. In the general police roundup of radicals after the Tōkyō Earthquake of 1923, she and her lover, the anarchist Yamamoto Toshio, were arrested and banished from Tōkyō. They traveled to Dalian (Ta-lien; J: Dairen) in Manchuria, where Yamamoto was arrested again and Hirabayashi gave birth to a baby girl who soon starved to death; this tragedy later became the basis for one of her best known stories, "Seryōshitsu nite" (1927, At the Charity Clinic).

Returning alone to Tōkyō in 1924, she resumed her ties with underground groups and began living with an anarchist named Iida Tokutarō. She described the poverty and disillusion of their life together in another early story, "Azakeru" (1927, To Mock), published in the newspaper *Ōsaka asahi shimbun*. Around this time she became friends with other socially conscious writers such as TSUBOI SHIGEJI, his wife TSUBOI SAKAE, and especially HAYASHI FUMIKO. In 1927 Hirabayashi married Kobori Jinji (1901–59), a leader of the group producing the radical magazine *Bungei sensen* (Literary Battlefront). In this and other publications, her many stories and essays about the impact of urban and rural poverty, especially on women, made her a major figure in the PROLETARIAN LITERATURE MOVEMENT, although she remained unsympathetic with the Communist Party.

Struggling to support her ailing husband, she briefly tried to run a boarding house while she continued her writing. Her stories from this time, such as "Sakura" (1935, Cherry Blossoms), show her hatred of Japan's growing militarism. Although they had been living separately, she and her husband were both arrested after the 1937 POPULAR FRONT INCIDENT. Her health damaged by her imprisonment, she published nothing more until after the end of World War II.

Then, in the newly encouraging atmosphere, she began to produce a flood of works covering a broad range of subjects. She wrote of her wartime hardships in stories such as "Hitori yuku" (1946, To Go Alone), "Kō iu onna" (1946, This Kind of Woman), and "Watakushi wa ikiru" (1947; tr "I Mean to Live," 1963). She described her complex feelings toward her young adopted daughter in "Kishimojin" (1946; tr "The Goddess of Children," 1952) and "Kiyoko-zō" (1948, Portrait of Kiyoko). She portrayed the lives of other leftist writers in *Kuro no jidai* (1950, Age of Blackness). She also produced a number of stories on the lives of criminals (labeled *yakuza-mono*), such as "Chitei no uta" (1948, Song of the Underworld) and "Hito no inochi" (1950; tr "A Man's Life," 1962). Her autobiographical novels *Aijō ryokō* (1953, Love Travels) and *Sabaku no hana* (1955–57, Flowers in a Desert) attracted wide attention.

Although saddened by a final break with Kobori in 1955 and plagued by severe illnesses, Hirabayashi traveled abroad several times and remained a prolific writer and prominent social commentator until her death. Among her notable later works are the stories "Kuroi nenrei" (1963; tr "The Black Age," 1963) and "Himitsu" (1967, Secrets), as well as books on two other women writers, *Hayashi Fumiko* (1969) and *Miyamoto Yuriko* (1972).

Although often identified with proletarian literature, her works showed—rather than political dogmatism—a broad and sensitive concern for basic social problems.

▬——Hirabayashi Taiko, *Hirabayashi Taiko zenshū*, 12 vols (Ushio Shuppansha, 1976–79).   Nancy ANDREW

Hirado

City in northwestern Nagasaki Prefecture, Kyūshū, composed of the islands of Hiradoshima and Takushima. A former castle town of the Matsura family, Hirado flourished as a trading port from 1550, when Portuguese ships cast anchor, until 1641, when the Dutch trading post was transferred to DEJIMA in Nagasaki. Historical sites include the remains of Hirado Castle, the former Dutch trading post, Orandabashi ("Holland Bridge"), and the Hirado Kankō Historical Hall. The city's scenic beauty also attracts tourists. Its principal industries, apart from tourism, are farming and fishing. Pop: 29,924.

Hiradoshima

Island off the Kita Matsuura Peninsula, northwestern Nagasaki Prefecture, northwestern Kyūshū. The city of Hirado covers the entire island, which is connected with the mainland by a bridge. Principal activities are the raising of cattle and the growing of rice, vegetables, and mandarin oranges. It was formerly an important castle town and trading port. Many historical traces remain from the 16th and 17th centuries when Dutch merchants and secret Christians (KAKURE KIRISHITAN) lived here. Area: 165 sq km (63.7 sq mi).

Hirafuku Hyakusui (1877–1933)

Japanese-style painter. Born in Akita Prefecture, he was the son of the painter Hirafuku Suian (1844–90). In 1894 he went to Tōkyō and studied with KAWABATA GYOKUSHŌ. Three years later he entered the Japanese-style painting (NIHONGA) division of the Tōkyō Bijutsu

Gakkō (now Tōkyō University of Fine Arts and Music) and graduated in 1899. The following year, along with Yūki Somei (1875–1957) and other artists interested in advancing the cause of naturalism in painting, he formed the Museikai group in opposition to the romantic idealism of the Nihon Bijutsuin (JAPAN FINE ARTS ACADEMY) headed by OKAKURA KAKUZŌ. Hyakusui worked as an illustrator for several newspapers in Tōkyō and in 1907 joined the staff of the KOKUMIN SHIMBUN, becoming well known for lively sketches of subjects ranging from the Diet in session to sumō wrestling matches. At this time he was studying drawing at the Western-style painting (yōga) division of the Tōkyō Bijutsu Gakkō and at the Taiheiyō Gakai (Pacific Painting Society) research institute. He was represented at the Ministry of Education–sponsored annual Bunten exhibition from 1909. In 1917, along with KABURAGI KIYOKATA and others, he formed the Kinreisha society of artists. He was appointed to the Teikoku Bijutsuin (Imperial Fine Arts Academy) in 1930, and two years later to a professorship at the Tōkyō Bijutsu Gakkō. Earlier he had abandoned his naturalistic styles and began to experiment with the decorative styles of the RIMPA school, although the paintings of his last years were done in the traditional scholarly style of BUNJINGA.

Hiraga Gennai (1728–1780)

Naturalist and writer of the Edo period (1600–1868). Gennai was born in the Takamatsu domain in Sanuki Province (now Kagawa Prefecture), the son of Shiroishi Mozaemon, a low-ranking samurai; he later changed his family name to Hiraga upon becoming family head. Gennai showed imaginative talent from an early age and gained a position working in the herbal garden of the domainal lord, Matsudaira Yoritaka. In 1752, he was sent by the domain to study in Nagasaki for a year. His exposure to new ideas there led to his decision to leave his official post and transfer the headship of the family to his younger sister's husband upon returning to Takamatsu in 1754. He subsequently took up the study of herbal medicine (honzōgaku) with Toda Kyokuzan (1696–1769) in Ōsaka.

Around 1757 Gennai went to Edo (now Tōkyō) and became a student of the herbalist and government physician Tamura Gen'yū (or Ransui; 1718–76). NAKAGAWA JUN'AN was in the same school, and it was through him that Gennai became acquainted with SUGITA GEMPAKU, a scholar of WESTERN LEARNING. Gennai prevailed upon Tamura to join with them in sponsoring a yakuhin'e, a kind of symposium of naturalists, to evaluate new and unusual products (see BUSSANGAKU). By the time the fifth such meeting opened in 1762 under Gennai's direction, it had become an exhibition where herbalists and other specialists from around Japan presented some 1,300 animal, plant, and mineral specimens. From these, Gennai selected about 360 products and wrote detailed explanations, with illustrations, in what is considered his magnum opus, the Butsurui hinshitsu (1763, Classification of Various Materials). By this time Gennai had cut his ties with the Takamatsu domain and become a rōnin or masterless samurai.

In the same year that he published Butsurui hinshitsu, Gennai also produced two satirical novels, Nenashi-gusa (Rootless Weeds) and Fūryū Shidōken den (Gallant History of Shidōken), works that marked the start of his career as a successful writer of the genre of Edo comic literature known as KOKKEIBON. His activities to promote experimentation and improve production won the approval of the senior councillor (rōjū) TANUMA OKITSUGU, who was actively encouraging industry, and under Tanuma's patronage Gennai made a second trip to Nagasaki (1770–72). Around this time he experimented in making asbestos cloth (kakanfu), thermometers, and Dutch-style pottery in addition to conducting surveys for ore deposits. He also tried his hand at wool manufacturing as well as Western oil painting. It was also during this period that Gennai produced several JŌRURI (puppet-play texts), including Shinrei Yaguchi no watashi (Miracle at Yaguchi Ferry), first staged in 1770.

An attempt in 1773 to reopen a copper mine in the Akita domain ended with poor results (although his acquaintance there with the samurai artist ODANO NAOTAKE led to the first flowering of the AKITA SCHOOL of painting). A similar disappointment the following year in exploring the Chichibu iron mine added to his growing feeling that the rank-conscious society of his time was too rigid to recognize his individuality and special genius. His frustration gave way to rage and despair; even his successful experiments with electricity could not ward off his psychological deterioration. In 1777 he finished his Hōhiron (Treatise on Breaking Wind), a self-satirical mem-

oir. Two years later, in a fit of madness, he killed one of his disciples with a sword. He died in prison early in 1780.

Gennai used various pseudonyms. In the areas of natural history and oil painting, he used the name Kyūkei (Dove Valley), while Fūrai Sanjin (Wind Rider) and Tenjiku Rōnin (Wanderer from Abroad) were his pen names for satirical literary works. He signed his creations in jōruri with the name Fukuuchi Kigai (In-with-Fortune, Out-with-Demons). Other whimsical aliases included Kuwazu Hinraku (Enjoying-Poverty-with-Nothing-to-Eat) and Hinka Zeninai (Poor-House, No-Money). This array of names in itself gives some feeling for the multitalented versatility of this man whom contemporaries hailed as a prodigy. We see also signs of the particular stance he took toward society—a mixture of self-praise and mockery, carefree abandon and stubbornness.

📖 ——Hiraga Gennai, Hiraga Gennai zenshū (Ogiwara Seibunkan, 1935). Haga Tōru, Sugita Gempaku, Hiraga Gennai, Shiba Kōkan (1971). Jōfuku Isamu, Hiraga Gennai (1971). Jōfuku Isamu, Hiraga Gennai no kenkyū (1976). HAGA Tōru

Hiraga Motoyoshi (1800–1865)

WAKA poet of the Edo period (1600–1868). Originally a samurai of the Okayama domain (now part of Okayama Prefecture), he gave up his domain affiliation and traveled through western Honshū studying martial arts, history, Shintō, and waka on his own resources. A devotee of the 8th-century anthology MAN'YŌSHŪ, he wrote virile, passionate waka filled with recondite allusions and archaic expressions reminiscent of the anthology, but also with martial and patriotic themes that point to his samurai background. His poetry was admired and rescued from obscurity by the Meiji poet MASAOKA SHIKI. Main collection: Hiraga Motoyoshi kashū (1908).

hiragana → kana

Hiraga Renkichi (1902–   )

Leading figure in the Japanese immigrant community in Brazil. Hiraga was born in Tōkyō and graduated from Tōkyō University's Forestry Department. He settled in Brazil's Pará state in 1931 as a member of the Nambei Takushoku Kabushiki Kaisha (South America Colonization Co, Ltd). A trusted leader and hard-working researcher in tropical agriculture, he has provided a model for farmers in the Amazon Basin and won great respect not only among Japanese settlers but also from the government and people of Brazil. His wife Kiyoko became known as "the angel of the Amazon" because of her tireless efforts on behalf of people in need. SAITŌ Hiroshi

Hiraga Yuzuru (1878–1943)

Vice admiral in charge of shipbuilding for the Imperial Japanese Navy and president of Tōkyō University. Born in Hiroshima Prefecture. Upon graduating in 1901 from Tōkyō University, where he had studied naval architecture, he entered the navy. He served in the Russo-Japanese War of 1904–05 and then studied at the Greenwich School of Naval Shipbuilding and Engineering in England. From the end of the Meiji period (1868–1912) Hiraga was responsible for planning the buildup of the so-called Eight Eight Fleet (HACHIHACHI KANTAI) and later in the Shōwa period (1926–) for the construction of the battleship Yamato and other ships. His warships were known for their innovative designs and he came to be regarded as a world authority on naval engineering. He became a professor at Tōkyō University after retiring from the navy in 1931 and served as its president from 1938 to 1943. In the latter capacity he carried out the so-called Hiraga Purge in 1939, suspending two professors, Hijikata Seibi (1890–1975) and KAWAI EIJIRŌ, to resolve conflicts within the Economics Department. His action led to the resignations of many professors, who protested that university autonomy had been destroyed. ICHIKI Toshio

Hiragushi Denchū (1872–1979)

Sculptor. Born in Okayama Prefecture, he first studied in Ōsaka to become a doll craftsman. In 1898 he moved to Tōkyō, where he learned traditional wood sculpture techniques from TAKAMURA KŌUN. From 1899 he participated in the Nihon Bijutsu Kyōkai exhibitions, and from 1907 in the annual Ministry of Education exhibitions (BUNTEN). With the support of OKAKURA KAKUZŌ, in 1907 he and a group of sculptors, including Yonehara Unkai (1869–1925) and Yamazaki Chōun (1867–1954), founded the Nihon Chōkoku Kai (Japan Sculpture Association), which held exhibitions from 1908. He was also active in the reorganized Nihon Bijutsuin (JAPAN FINE ARTS ACADEMY). In 1937, he was elected to the Teikoku Geijutsuin (Imperial Art Academy). He taught for eight years at what is now Tō-kyō University of Fine Arts and Music and was awarded the Order of Culture in 1962. Denchū's sculpture of Okakura is representative of the realistic, colorful portraits in wood for which he is most well known.

Hiraide site

(Hiraide *iseki*). An ancient settlement site in the city of Shiojiri, Nagano Prefecture, occupied from the Middle Jōmon period (ca 3500 BC–ca 2000 BC) to the Kofun period (ca 300–710). First discovered in 1947, the site was excavated by an interdisciplinary team in 1950–51, yielding 17 round or oval PIT HOUSES belonging to the Middle Jōmon period, 49 square or rectangular pit houses belonging to the Kofun period, 1 oval-shaped stone formation centering on a stone-lined fireplace, and 3 groups of postholes thought to be raised store-houses. Three levels of change can be seen in the pit houses of the Kofun period. First the dwellings existed in spotty distribution and were equipped only with simple fireplaces; later they became larger, more densely clustered, and equipped with enclosed clay hearths that were constructed on an interior wall; in the final stage, the dwellings shrank in size, were irregularly shaped, and had stone masonry hearths.

Artifacts recovered from the site include JŌMON POTTERY, STONE TOOLS such as axes, adzes, and projectile points, and JŌMON FIGURINES; from the latter occupation, HAJI WARE and SUE WARE, a green-glazed pitcher, and iron arrowheads were discovered in abundance. These materials are displayed at the nearby Hiraide Site Archaeological Museum. A pit house has been reconstructed at the site. See also JŌMON CULTURE.

──Hiraide Iseki Chōsakai, *Hiraide* (1955).　　KITAMURA Bunji

Hiraizumi

Seat of the ŌSHŪ FUJIWARA FAMILY and cultural center of northern Japan during the 11th and 12th centuries; now the town of Hiraizumi in southern Iwate Prefecture. Since the 8th century Hiraizumi, situated on the Kitakami River (Kitakamigawa), had been an important military stronghold, and it was there that in 1094 Fujiwara no Kiyohira (1056–1128) settled with his followers. The area was rich in gold, and with the wealth it brought him Kiyohira built the temple CHŪSONJI and established Hiraizumi as a semiindependent provincial metropolis, the first to rival Kyōto in the opulence of its architecture. Kiyohira's son Motohira (d 1157) rebuilt the temple MŌTSUJI, and his grandson Hidehira (1096?–1187), the Muryōkōin. Although Hiraizumi remained an important religious center, the prosperity of the Ōshū Fujiwara came to an end early in 1189, when the forces of MINAMOTO NO YORITOMO annihilated them for having given refuge to his brother MINAMOTO NO YOSHITSUNE. Today there remain only the garden of the Mōtsuji and the Golden Hall (Konjikidō) of the Chūsonji, in which the mummified bodies of the first three generations of the Ōshū Fujiwara are kept.

Hirakata

City in northeastern Ōsaka Prefecture, central Honshū, on the eastern bank of the river Yodogawa. The city developed as a POST–STATION TOWN and port town during the Edo period (1600–1868). It is now a satellite city of Ōsaka. Its principal products are noodles (Kawachi *sōmen*), bamboo products, clothes, furniture, dairy products, and fruit. Of historic interest are several tumuli (KOFUN). Pop: 353,360.

Hira Mountains

(Hira Sanchi). Mountain range running north to south along the west bank of Lake Biwa between Shiga and Kyōto prefectures, central Honshū. It has three main peaks: Hōraisan (1,174 m; 3,851 ft), Bunagadake (1,214 m; 3,982 ft), and Uchimiyama (1,103 m; 3,618 ft). "Evening Snow on Mount Hira" is one of the famous "Eight Views of Ōmi" (see ŌMI HAKKEI). The slopes and surrounding area are popular with hikers, mountain climbers, and skiers. The range is part of Lake Biwa Quasi-National Park.

Hirano Ken (1907–1978)

Literary critic. Real name Hirano Akira. Born in Kyōto Prefecture. Graduate of Tōkyō University. During his student years, he participated in the PROLETARIAN LITERATURE MOVEMENT, and in the post–World War II period he contributed many articles on political and literary issues to KINDAI BUNGAKU, a progressive literary periodical established in 1946. As a monthly literary reviewer for a newspaper, he contributed to the discovery and encouragement of new writers. His principal critical works are *Shimazaki Tōson* (1947), a biography of SHIMAZAKI TŌSON; *Seiji to bungaku no aida* (1956), on the relationship between literature and politics; and *Geijutsu to jisseikatsu* (1958), on fiction and writers' private lives.

Hirano Kuniomi (1828–1864)

Proimperial activist of the latter part of the Edo period (1600–1868). In 1858 he abandoned his domain (Fukuoka; now part of Fukuoka Prefecture) to participate in the antiforeign, antishogunate movement in Kyōto led by *samurai* from the Chōshū domain (now Yamaguchi Prefecture). With other like-minded activists from Kyūshū, he planned to raise an anti-Tokugawa army on the occasion of a visit to Kyōto in 1862 by SHIMAZU HISAMITSU, the father of Shimazu Yoshitada, *daimyō* of the Satsuma domain (now Kagoshima Prefecture). He was arrested after the TERADAYA INCIDENT, in which several of the activists were killed for refusing Hisamitsu's order to abandon their plan. After his release from prison in 1863, Hirano returned to Kyōto, only to be driven out again in the COUP D'ETAT OF 30 SEPTEMBER 1863, which expelled the extremist Chōshū forces from the city. He then went to the Ikuno district of Tajima (now in Hyōgo Prefecture) to organize a peasant army. He was able to mobilize some 2,000 peasants, but they were easily suppressed by troops from neighboring domains (see IKUNO DISTURBANCE), and Hirano was captured and executed.

Hirano Yoshitarō (1897–1980)

Marxist scholar and writer. Born in Tōkyō, he graduated from Tōkyō University, where he became an assistant professor in 1921. During studies in Germany from 1927 to 1930, he deepened his knowledge of Marxism, became acquainted with Comintern agents, and participated in pacifist activities. After returning to Japan, Hirano was arrested in 1930 as an alleged communist sympathizer and consequently resigned his teaching post. He collaborated with NORO EITARŌ, YAMADA MORITARŌ, and Ōtsuka Kinnosuke in writing and editing the seven-volume NIHON SHIHON SHUGI HATTATSU SHI KŌZA (1932–33, Lectures on the History of the Development of Japanese Capitalism), thus establishing himself as a prominent spokesman for the KŌZAHA group of Marxist theorists (see also NIHON SHIHON SHUGI RONSŌ). During World War II, Hirano was engaged in studies of China and Southeast Asia at the Institute of the Pacific (Taiheiyō Kyōkai). After the war he served as a member of the SCIENCE COUNCIL OF JAPAN (Nihon Gakujutsu Kaigi) and as honorary chairman of the Japan Peace Committee (Nihon Heiwa Iinkai). He was also active in movements to improve Japan's relations with China, Southeast Asia, and Africa. Hirano collected and published his articles from the *Kōza* under the title *Nihon shihon shugi shakai no kikō* (1933, Structure of Capitalist Society in Japan). His writings compared the absolutist nature of Japan's imperial institution with the modern political history of European countries.

SUGIHARA Shirō

Hiranuma Kiichirō (1867–1952)

Ministry of Justice official and prime minister who became the doyen of the prewar RIGHT WING and one of the most powerful political leaders of the 1920s and 1930s. The son of a low-ranking *samurai* retainer of the Tsuyama domain (now part of Okayama Prefecture), Hiranuma graduated in 1888 from Tōkyō University with a degree in English law. The 1880s were a period of sharp reaction against Western thought and civilization, a time when Japanese sought new definitions of their own traditions that would provide them with a sense of national pride and uniqueness; and the ideas formed by Hiranuma at that time served as enduring guidelines for his political thought and behavior. Schooled in the writings of early-19th-century MITO SCHOOL and Neo-Confucian philosophers, he held that Japan was blessed with a uniquely moral and sacred political essence (KOKUTAI). The fount of that morality was the innately sacred imperial throne, and the function of the emperor's ministers and officials was to clarify and reify the moral relationship between ruler and subject. For Hiranuma, this moral idealization of the official's role led to a career-long crusade against the intrusion of partisan interests or foreign thought into the process of imperial rule.

Hiranuma entered the Ministry of Justice immediately after graduation. As a personally honest, austere and totally devoted public official, he early became an active opponent of the influence external political cliques (hambatsu) and political parties exercised over the ministry. He promoted the independence of the prosecutor's office to pursue or drop any case solely in accordance with its own judgment and as leader of the prosecution team in 1909, he secured the convictions of 25 current and former members of the Diet for receiving bribes from the Japan Sugar Company. In 1915 he forced ŌURA KANETAKE, home minister in the Rikken Dōshikai (see ŌKUMA SHIGENOBU) cabinet to retire from public life because of suspected bribery, although a year earlier he had been reluctant as prosecutor-general to press charges against suspected miscreants in the navy involved in the SIEMENS INCIDENT. In Hiranuma's view, the navy served the emperor and therefore deserved special consideration, but party politicians and their backers were the tools of partisan and private interests whose influence on the government and imperial rule must be rigorously checked.

Despite the resistance of men like Hiranuma, the parties controlled the cabinet from 1924 to 1932. Hiranuma's attacks on party "venality" and "immorality" nonetheless persisted and indeed increased over time. He also objected vigorously to the "internationalist" tendencies of Japan's party governments, opposing the penetration of foreign ideologies such as liberalism, democracy, and socialism into the Japanese body politic. Concluding his bureaucratic career as vice-minister of justice in 1923, Hiranuma served as justice minister from September 1923 to January 1924 and was then appointed to the PRIVY COUNCIL. In 1924 he created the KOKUHONSHA and developed the organization into a nationwide movement for the accomplishment of his ideological and political goals. Through his residual bureaucratic influence, Hiranuma also actively promoted the development of Japan's "thought police" as a more coercive check on the spread of liberal and left-wing ideas.

In April 1926 he became vice-president of the Privy Council, a position he held for the next 10 years. During this period he led Privy Council opposition to the WAKATSUKI REIJIRŌ cabinet's plan for rescuing the Bank of Taiwan in 1927 (an issue that led to the government's resignation); spearheaded a futile Privy Council drive to block ratification of the London Naval Conference Treaty limiting naval armaments in 1930 (see LONDON NAVAL CONFERENCES); organized support in 1932 and 1933 for new government regulations restricting the freedom of future party cabinets to appoint and dismiss officials in accordance with their political preferences; mobilized support for Japan's seizure of Manchuria (1931) and the creation of Manchukuo; and directed from behind the scenes the prosecution, by the Ministry of Justice, of the Banchōkai in the TEIJIN INCIDENT of 1934, a maneuver calculated to topple the government and replace it with a Hiranuma cabinet. But despite Hiranuma's popularity among right-wing politicians, his activities earned him powerful enemies, including SAIONJI KIMMOCHI, who was able to slow Hiranuma's rise to prominence during the early thirties even as party governments and cooperative diplomacy were becoming a thing of the past. When it became clear to Hiranuma that his career was stalling at precisely the moment when his policy objectives were gaining widespread support, he assumed a less strident political posture and in 1936 dissolved the Kokuhonsha. In turn, Saionji permitted his appointment as the president of the Privy Council the same year, and Hiranuma held that position until becoming prime minister in January 1939.

Hiranuma's tenure as prime minister lasted only eight months. Under his leadership, the cabinet debated at length whether to form a military alliance with Nazi Germany in order to neutralize the Soviet Union. The navy feared that such a move would commit Japan to supporting Germany against the Anglo-American powers as well. Upon the conclusion of the German-Soviet Non-Aggression Pact in August, the futility of the cabinet's European policy was exposed, and Hiranuma resigned.

He was appointed to the KONOE FUMIMARO cabinet in December 1940. As home minister he opposed the establishment of a new mass political party during the NEW ORDER MOVEMENT and pro-

vided the second and third Konoe cabinets with the political weight needed to change the partisan nature of the IMPERIAL RULE ASSISTANCE ASSOCIATION. He withdrew from the government with Konoe's resignation in October 1941 and served during the Pacific War as one of the JŪSHIN, unofficial senior advisers to the emperor, by virtue of having served as prime minister. In late 1944 he and other jūshin successfully maneuvered General TŌJŌ HIDEKI from power, fearing that a prolonged war would lead to communist revolution at home. In April 1945 he was reappointed president of the Privy Council. After the war he was arrested as a class "A" war criminal by the Occupation authorities and sentenced to life imprisonment. He died in prison.

Hiranuma's virulent antiliberalism and anti-internationalism not only won him the support of many conservative and right-wing political activists during the 1920s, it also earned him the title of Japan's leading fascist. He himself repeatedly repudiated fascism and Nazism as foreign ideologies inappropriate for Japan's polity and inconsistent with his own emphasis on the centrality of the "Japanese spirit." Indeed, as a consequence of Japan's swift repudiation of liberalism and internationalism in the early 1930s, Hiranuma's own political ambitions, and his advancing years, he made it increasingly clear after 1936 that his interest in future political reform was limited to restricting party influence and securing the independence of the bureaucracy as a political force. Consequently he lost the political support of the most ardent Japanese admirers of Hitler and Mussolini and was even the target of assassination attempts by "reformist" right-wing activists.

——Hiranuma Kiichirō, Hiranuma Kiichirō kaikoroku (1955). Hiranuma Kiichirō Sensei Itsuwa Shū Kankō Kai, ed, Hiranuma Kiichirō sensei itsuwa shū (1958). Gordon Mark Berger, Parties Out of Power in Japan, 1930–1941 (1977). Itō Takashi, Shōwa shoki seiji shi kenkyū (1969). Richard H. Mitchell, Thought Control in Prewar Japan (1976). G. Richard Storry, The Double Patriots: A Study of Japanese Nationalism (1957). Richard Yasko, "Hiranuma Kiichirō and Conservative Politics in Pre-War Japan," PhD dissertation, University of Chicago (1973). Gordon M. BERGER

Hiranuma Ryōzō (1879–1959)

Leading figure in amateur sports organizations. Born in Yokohama; graduated from Keiō University. Hiranuma served as a member of the House of Peers (1932) and mayor of Yokohama (1951). He led the Japanese delegation to the 1936 Olympic Games in Berlin. He headed numerous sports organizations, including the Japan Amateur Sports Association and the Japan Amateur Athletic Federation. In 1946 he founded the National Sports Festival. He was awarded the Order of Culture in 1955, the first time it was given to a sports figure. TAKEDA Fumio

Hiraodai

Limestone plateau. Southeastern Kokura Minami Ward, city of Kita Kyūshū, Fukuoka Prefecture, Kyūshū. The southern half is covered with terra rossa while the northern half has a well-developed lapies field (Karrenfeld) with 330 dolines, big and small, as well as limestone caves. It was an army maneuvering ground up to World War II but is currently a resort. Vegetables are cultivated and limestone quarried. One of the points of interest of Kita Kyūshū Quasi-National Park. Elevation: 360–680 m (1,181–2,230 ft); length: approximately 7 km (4.4 mi); width: approximately 2 km (1.2 mi).

Hirara

City on Miyakojima, an island belonging to the Miyakojima Islands, Okinawa Prefecture. The principal city of these islands, it is the site of government agencies and company branch offices. Sugarcane cultivation and bonito fishing are Hirara's main activities; other occupations are the making of coral and shell crafts and the shipment of tropical fish to Honshū. Pop: 32,921.

Hirase Sakugorō (1856–1925)

Botanist. Born in Fukui Prefecture. After working as a drawing teacher in Gifu Prefecture, he became botanical illustrator at Tōkyō University and engaged in the production of scientific drawings and microscope specimens. During that time he became interested in botany and, under the guidance of IKENO SEIICHIRŌ, studied the growth of gymnospermous plants. He discovered ginkgo spermatozoa in 1896 and greatly influenced the study of plant systematics.

Suzuki Zenji

Hirashimizu ware

(hirashimizu-yaki). Glazed ceramics, sometimes with underglaze or overglaze decoration, made in Hirashimizu, Uzen Province (now the city of Yamagata, Yamagata Prefecture) from the early 1800s to the present. Sometimes called Chitose ware, after the nearby mountain that provides the source of clay. Products have varied widely, a reflection of the fact that techniques have been drawn from various wares, including ARITA WARE and KUTANI WARE.

Stoneware storage vessels, kitchen utensils, and toilet fixtures have been produced; porcelain tableware and inkwells were made from time to time. Porcelain was not made until 1847 when three experienced porcelain potters were hired to initiate production. By the turn of the century, there were 20 porcelain kilns and 10 stoneware kilns. Eventually, however, because of high costs and an unsteady economy, all the porcelain kilns and some of the stoneware kilns were closed.

Typical decoration includes porcelain slip, matt-white glaze streaked with muted green and brown (called *zansetsu* or "lingering snow"), and a crisp, pale-green glaze with dark spots (called *nashi seiji* or "pear celadon"). In addition, copper red, *temmoku*, "oil spot," and the bright blue green Oribe glaze are widely used. Unglazed surfaces are also utilized.

Five kilns operate today: Seiryū (Niwa family), Heikichi (Abe family), Bun'emon, Shichiemon, and Tentaku. The Seiryū kiln specializes in traditional wares fired in Hirashimizu's only woodburning climbing kiln *(noborigama).* The Yamagata Museum contains a collection of Hirashimizu ware along with other artifacts of the Tōhoku region.

Jeanne CARREAU

Hirata

City in eastern Shimane Prefecture, western Honshū, on the northern shore of Lake Shinji. Hirata prospered during the Edo period (1600–1868) as a market town dealing in cotton cloth. The main activity today is rice cultivation, although the town has several emerging industries. The Wanibuchi gypsum mine in the northwestern part of the city boasts the highest level of production in Japan. Pop: 31,067.

Hirata Atsutane (1776–1843)

KOKUGAKU (National Learning) scholar; Shintō theologian. Literary name Ibukinoya. Hirata was the leader of the RESTORATION SHINTŌ movement known as Fukko Shintō, a movement to revive Shintō by freeing it of what Hirata called debilitating Buddhist and Confucian influences. Known for his xenophobic espousal of the ancient Japanese way, which upheld belief in the divine nature of the emperor, his nationalist thought strongly influenced the *shishi*, loyalist *samurai* who sought the restoration of direct imperial rule in the latter half of the 19th century.

Hirata was born the fourth son of Ōwada Toshitane, a low-ranking samurai of the Akita domain (now part of Akita Prefecture). He began receiving training in the branch of Confucianism begun by YAMAZAKI ANSAI (1619–82) at an early age, but at about age 20, he ran away to Edo (now Tōkyō), where his interest turned to the Chinese philosopher Zhuangzi (Chuang-tzu) and Taoism. Little is known of his early years in Edo, but he was subsequently adopted by Hirata Atsuyasu, a samurai retainer of the Matsuyama domain in Bitchū Province (now part of Okayama Prefecture). It was not until 1801 that Hirata first read the works of the renowned classical scholar MOTOORI NORINAGA (1730–1801), one of the founders of the National Learning movement. He was so impressed by Motoori's brilliance as a scholar that he decided to take up the study of ancient Shintō learning as his lifelong pursuit. Regrettably, Motoori died in October of that same year before Hirata could enroll in his school. He nonetheless styled himself thereafter as Motoori's disciple.

Not as literary as Motoori nor given to the detailed philological studies which had characterized National Learning since the days of KEICHŪ (1640–1701) and which had played a major role in Motoori's studies, Hirata brought a philosophical, even somewhat mystical, approach to the study of Shintō theology. He rejected Confucianism and Buddhism, advocating, instead, a revival of the "ancient way"

and reverence for the emperor. He was disliked by the orthodox school of National Learning, but won a following among Shintoists and farmers and village officials. Hirata's writings were colored by an extreme ethnocentricity: in comparison to Japan, he viewed all other nations as base and contemptible, and held a particularly low opinion of Westerners. Yet he maintained an avid interest in many aspects of WESTERN LEARNING, which he was not above using in attacks on Buddhism and Confucianism. Though his scholarship was not without its faults, his encyclopedic knowledge and missionary-like enthusiasm imbued National Learning with a new purposiveness.

One of his first publications was *Kamōsho,* written in 1803, in which he criticized the Confucian thinker DAZAI SHUNDAI's (1680–1747) treatise on Buddhism titled *Bendōsho.* He made several lecture tours of Shintō shrines around the country at the behest of the Shirakawa family, hereditary heads of the Office of Shintō Worship (Jingihaku), and was invited by the Yoshida family, the head family of YOSHIDA SHINTŌ, to become a teacher. But because of his increasingly bitter criticism of Confucianism and Buddhism and advocacy of reverence for the imperial institution, he incurred the censure of the Tokugawa shogunal authorities and was permanently confined to his home domain in 1841. He died two years later. Hirata's pupils are said to have numbered over 500 at the time of his death and included ŌKUNI TAKAMASA and SUZUKI SHIGETANE. A man of wide interests, which included cosmology and Western science and thought, Hirata was a prolific writer, publishing more than 100 books and tracts. His representative works are *Kodō taii* (1811), *Koshichō* (1811), *Tama no mihashira* (1812), *Tamadasuki* (1824), and *Koshiden* (1825).

━━━ *Hirata Atsutane zenshū,* 15 vols (Hakubunkan, 1911–18). Tahara Tsuguo, *Hirata Atsutane* (1963). Watanabe Kinzō, *Hirata Atsutane kenkyū* (1942). Yamada Yoshio, *Hirata Atsutane (1940).*

ŌTA Yoshimaro

Hirata Gōyō (1903–1981)

Puppet maker. Real name Hirata Tsuneo. Born in Tōkyō. His father, who trained him from an early age, was Gōyō I, a puppeteer best known for his realistic puppets. In 1936 he became the first puppet maker chosen to participate in the Imperial Academy's annual art exhibition. He was designated as one of the LIVING NATIONAL TREASURES in 1955. Gōyō founded an organization of puppet makers known as the Yōmonkai and instructed a talented group of followers in the art of puppet making. Incorporating techniques used in the age-old art of clothed dollmaking, he was considered Japan's foremost realistic puppet maker. In 1974 he was awarded the Fourth Class Order of the Rising Sun.

YAMADA Tokubei

Hirata Tokuboku (1873–1943)

Scholar of English literature. Real name Hirata Kiichirō. Born in Tōkyō. Graduate of Tōkyō Higher Normal School (now Tsukuba University). While still a student at the First Higher School, Hirata joined the influential literary magazine *Bungakukai* and introduced the works of Pater, Keats, and Dante. He is remembered for his translations of Dickens and Lamb. He also translated NŌ drama texts into English for Ernest F. FENOLLOSA. Hirata's work was later used as a draft for *The Classical Noh Theatre of Japan,* jointly authored by Fenollosa and Ezra Pound.

ASAI Kiyoshi

Hirata Tōsuke (1849–1925)

Bureaucrat and politician. Born in the Yonezawa domain (now part of Yamagata Prefecture), he studied at Daigaku Nankō (now Tōkyō University). In 1871 he accompanied the IWAKURA MISSION to the United States and Europe and remained in Germany to study government and law. Upon his return in 1876, he joined the government and worked mainly on the legal system. He was named to the House of Peers in 1890 and served for more than 30 years. As a member of the Saiwai Kurabu, a political club of members of the House of Peers, he was an active supporter of YAMAGATA ARITOMO. He served as minister of commerce and agriculture and later as home minister in the first and second KATSURA TARŌ cabinets (1901–05; 1908–11) and in 1922 was appointed lord keeper of the privy seal, a post he retained until his death.

Hiratsuka

City in south central Kanagawa Prefecture, central Honshū, at the mouth of the river Sagamigawa. A POST-STATION TOWN at the intersection of several highways in the Edo period (1600–1868), the city now produces vehicles, tires, and foodstuffs. Every July people flock to see the TANABATA FESTIVAL. Pop: 214,299.

Hiratsuka Raichō (1886–1971)

Feminist. Born in Tōkyō; original name Hiratsuka Haruko. Daughter of a government official who had studied constitutional law in Europe, she was influenced in her youth by Western culture. Studying English and reading books on Western philosophy, she was at the same time greatly influenced by Zen Buddhism, and practiced Zen meditation throughout her life.

She first aroused public criticism in 1908 when she allegedly planned to commit suicide together with the writer MORITA SŌHEI. This affair is known as the Baien Incident, after the novel *Baien* (Smoke) that Morita wrote about it. Together with other young unmarried women who also came from the upper-middle class and were interested in literature, Raichō in 1911 founded the SEITŌSHA (Bluestocking Society) and, aiming at the "development of women's talent," published the magazine *Seitō* (Bluestocking) by women and for women only. She introduced the first number with the famous manifesto entitled *Genshi josei wa taiyō de atta* (In the Beginning Woman Was the Sun), expressing the feeling of young women who, in the liberal climate of the Taishō period (1912–26), pressed for a better position in society.

In 1914 Raichō left her parents' home to live with the painter Okumura Hiroshi (1891–1964); she gave birth to a daughter and son and faced severe economic hardships. Greatly influenced by the thinking of the Swedish feminist Ellen Key (1849–1926), she now stressed the protection of motherhood, and in 1918 started a published debate on the subject with the famous woman poet YOSANO AKIKO. Together with ICHIKAWA FUSAE and OKU MUMEO, in 1920 she founded the SHIN FUJIN KYŌKAI (New Woman's Association), and engaged in a battle to reform the social and legal position of Japanese women. The group achieved the first political success of the women's movement with the amendment of the Public Order and Police Law (Chian Keisatsu Hō) in 1922, thus making it legal for women to participate to some degree in political activities. However, Raichō generally withdrew from the women's movement until 1930, when she was asked to contribute articles to the radical magazine *Fujin sensen* (Women's Battlefront), published by TAKAMURE ITSUE, an outstanding researcher of the history of Japanese women. At the same time she took part in women's consumer associations.

After World War II Raichō maintained her concern with broad social issues, but this time in the context of pacifism and democracy. She strongly opposed the unilateral SAN FRANCISCO PEACE TREATY and twice appealed personally to the US Secretary of State John Foster Dulles. She continued her campaign for peace as president and later honorary president of the Nihon Fujin Dantai Rengōkai (Federation of Japanese Women's Societies) and as a member of several other national and international organizations until her death.

——Hiratsuka Raichō, *Watakushi no aruita michi* (1955). Hiratsuka Raichō, *Genshi josei wa taiyō de atta*, 4 vols (1971–73). Margret Neuss, "Die Seitōsha—Der Ausgangspunkt der japanischen Frauenbewegung in seinen zeitgeschichtlichen und sozialen Bedingungen," *Oriens Extremus* 18.1–2 (1971).   Margret NEUSS

Hiratsuka Tsunejirō (1881–1974)

Businessman and politician. Born in Hokkaidō; studied at a Russian language school in Sapporo. Hiratsuka established a fishing company, NICHIRO GYOGYŌ KAISHA, LTD, in 1907, soon after Japan obtained fishing rights on the Russian coast in a Russo-Japanese fishery agreement. After introducing modern fishing techniques, he became a leading figure in fishing operations in the Okhotsk Sea. After World War II he was elected to the House of Representatives and joined the first YOSHIDA SHIGERU cabinet as minister of transportation. He was subsequently purged by Allied Occupation authorities but returned to the business world in 1955 when he became president of Nichiro Gyogyō. In his later years, as chairman of the Dai Nippon Suisankai (Japan Fisheries Association) and member of the House of Representatives, he played an important role in Russo-Japanese fishery negotiations.   YUI Tsunehiko

Hiratsuka Raichō

Photo taken in 1911, the year of the establishment of the Bluestocking Society.

Hiratsuka Un'ichi (1895–   )

Print artist. Born and raised in Matsue, Shimane Prefecture. When the Western-style painter and printmaker Ishii Hakutei (1882–1958) came to the city in 1913 to give a painting course, Hiratsuka studied with him. This began a relationship that was to have a profound effect on his future, because Hakutei was part of the *sōsaku hanga* (creative print) movement. Hiratsuka later studied oil painting in Tōkyō at the Hongō Gakai Kenkyūjō under UMEHARA RYŪZABURŌ. His interest in printmaking led him to study the technique of block carving from the traditional craftsman Igami Bonkotsu (1875–1933). With Yamamoto Kanae (1882–1946), ONCHI KŌSHIRŌ, and others, he formed the Nihon Sōsaku Hanga Kyōkai (Japanese Creative Print Association) in 1918 for the purpose of establishing prints as accepted original works of art and ensuring representation in official art exhibitions. He published *Hanga no gihō* (Technique in Picture Printing) in 1927 to explain the technique of the new creative print movement. In 1930 he was invited to join the Kokugakai (formerly the Kokuga Sōsaku Kyōkai; National Creative Painting Association) and became head of its print section, which was organized the following year. When the Tōkyō Bijutsu Gakkō (now Tōkyō University of Fine Arts and Music) finally established a department of printmaking in 1935, he was appointed professor of woodblock printing.

Although his early prints are closely related to Western watercolors, Hiratsuka is best known for his distinctive black-and-white prints of traditional Buddhist and architectural subjects. He is an extremely prolific and popular printmaker and one of the first of the *sōsaku hanga* artists to support himself through his art. Although his work draws on the Japanese tradition in subject matter, his viewpoint and technique put him squarely in the tradition of modern art. He has lived in the United States for a number of years and his work is represented in numerous American collections.

——Fujikake Shizuya, *Japanese Wood-block Prints* (1959). Ono Tadashige, *Kindai Nihon no hanga* (1975).

Elizabeth de Sabato SWINTON

Hirayu Hot Spring

(Hirayu Onsen). Located on the northern slope of Norikuradake at an altitude of 1,230 m (4,034 ft), northeastern Gifu Prefecture, central Honshū. A bicarbonate spring; water temperature 46–96°C (115–205°F). Located within Chūbu Sangaku National Park, it has been designated as a National Health Resort Hot Spring. Utilized since the Edo period (1600–1868) by travelers crossing the mountain, it is presently the base for climbing Norikuradake.

Hirohata

District of the city of Himeji, Hyōgo Prefecture, western Honshū, facing the Inland Sea. After the establishment of a giant steel mill here in 1937 and the completion of a large-scale planning project, it became a center of the Harima Industrial Area.

Emperor Hirohito

Emperor Hirohito opening the 84th session of the Diet in 1977.

Hirohito, Emperor (1901–   )

The present emperor of Japan; the 124th sovereign *(tennō)* in the traditional count (which includes several nonhistorical emperors), Michi no Miya Hirohito has reigned longer than any other Japanese emperor in historical times.

On the death of Emperor MEIJI and the accession of Emperor TAISHŌ in 1912, Hirohito became crown prince. In 1921 he became regent in order to perform imperial duties on behalf of his ailing father. In the same year he traveled to England, becoming the first Japanese crown prince to go abroad. In January 1924 he married Princess Nagako (b 1903), eldest daughter of Prince Kuni no Miya Kunihiko; and on 25 December 1926 he ascended the throne, adopting the era name Shōwa ("enlightenment and harmony") for his reign.

Although the Meiji CONSTITUTION of 1889 vested all rights of sovereignty in the emperor, in practice he was not expected to exercise power directly. Indeed Hirohito's advisers endeavored to isolate and protect him from all political conflict and controversy; hence, although state policies were proclaimed in his name, for the most part he merely approved decisions made by his advisers and officials.

The emperor's chief political adviser during the tumultuous years of the 1920s and 1930s was SAIONJI KIMMOCHI, a liberally inclined elder statesman (GENRŌ) who sought to foster constitutional government at home and peaceful relations abroad. The emperor himself was a political liberal and moderate, but he was restrained from expressing his opinions publicly or even mentioning them in private to political and military leaders. On rare occasions, however, he deviated from the role delineated for him and asserted his views forcefully. For example, he took a strong stand against the young military officers in the FEBRUARY 26TH INCIDENT of 1936; his resolution was chiefly responsible for the swift suppression of the attempted coup. He also personally made the decision to accept the surrender terms of the POTSDAM DECLARATION at the end of World War II. He has been criticized for not having taken an equally strong position against the declaration of war, but he has pointed out that the decision to go to war had already been made and that he had merely been asked for formal approval, which, according to his understanding of the constitution, he was obliged to give, regardless of his personal views. In ending the war, he had been specifically asked by a deadlocked government and military leaders to make a decision. In fact, he has consistently accepted the consensus of the duly constituted authorities. In the February 26th Incident he took the initiative because the prime minister was presumed to have been assassinated.

In the postwar constitution the emperor has been removed completely from the political realm and is retained only as a symbol of the state. This has enabled him to pursue his personal interests, including marine biology. The first reigning emperor to go abroad, in 1972 he visited Europe and in 1975 toured the United States. Although unpleasant demonstrations marred the European visit, the American tour was an unqualified success, a symbolic capstone to the close relationship between the United States and Japan in the postwar period. See also EMPEROR.

——Honjō Shigeru, *Honjō nikki* (1967). Inoue Kiyoshi, *Tennō no sensō sekinin* (1975). Kojima Noboru, *Tennō*, 5 vols (1974). Leonard Mosley, *Hirohito, Emperor of Japan* (1966). Nakamura Kikuo, *Arashi ni taete* (1972). Osanaga Kanroji, *Hirohito: An Intimate Portrait of the Japanese Emperor* (1975).   *Mikiso* HANE

Hiroi Isamu (1862–1928)

Civil engineer who led the early development of bridge and harbor design in Japan. Born in the Tosa domain (now Kōchi Prefecture), he graduated from Sapporo Agricultural School (now Hokkaidō University) and entered the Department of Public Works (Kōbushō) to supervise the construction of railroads. In 1883 Hiroi went to the United States, where he worked on several bridge construction projects. He then studied in Germany, and upon his return to Japan in 1889, became a professor at his alma mater. In 1899 he was named to the faculty of Tōkyō University. Hiroi was responsible for designing Hakodate, Otaru, and several other harbors.

Hironaka Heisuke (1931–   )

Mathematician. Born in Yamaguchi Prefecture. A graduate of Kyōto University, he continued his studies at Harvard University. He now teaches at Harvard and concurrently holds a post at Kyōto University. Hironaka was awarded the Fields Prize in 1970 for his research on algebraic manifolds and the resolution of singularities in analytic spaces. He received the Order of Culture in 1975.

Hiro, Prince (1960–   )

(Hiro no Miya Naruhito). Title of the eldest son of Crown Prince AKIHITO. In 1978 he enrolled in the history department of Gakushūin University, where he was active in the orchestra of the music club. On 23 February 1980 a formal ceremony was held to mark his coming-of-age.

Hirosaki

City in western Aomori Prefecture, northern Honshū. A castle town during the Edo period (1600–1868), it is now the political, economic, and cultural center of the Tsugaru region. Hirosaki is noted for its rice, apples, *sake*, and *tsugaru-nuri*, a local lacquer ware. The remains of the Hirosaki Castle, built in 1611, are in Hirosaki Park, which is also famous for its cherry blossoms. The city is known for the NEBUTA FESTIVAL in early August, and for its colorful kites and other folk crafts. Pop: 175,330.

Hirose Saihei (1828–1914)

Businessman; leader of the SUMITOMO *zaibatsu* (a financial and industrial combine) in the late 19th century. Born in what is now Shiga Prefecture, Hirose started working at the age of 11 at the Sumitomo family's important Besshi Copper Mine in Shikoku, and was later made general manager. After the Meiji Restoration of 1868, he made great contributions to the modernization of the mine and to the formation and development of the Sumitomo *zaibatsu* while serving as "prime minister" for the Sumitomo family. Along with GODAI TOMOATSU, Hirose established the Ōsaka Shōhō Kaigisho (the forerunner of the Ōsaka Chamber of Commerce) and the Ōsaka Stock Exchange.   *Asajima* Shōichi

Hirose Shrine

(Hirose Jinja). Shintō shrine in the Kita Katsuragi District, Nara Prefecture, dedicated to the goddess of cereals, Wakaukanome no Mikoto, and two other deities. First mentioned in 676, the shrine was ranked by the Engi Shiki (927, Procedures of the Engi Era) as an eminent shrine *(myōjin taisha)*; it is often associated with the TATSUTA SHRINE. Because of its reputation for protecting crops, the shrine has had a wide following and has enjoyed the support of the imperial court. Its annual festival is celebrated on 4 April.

Stanley WEINSTEIN

Hirose Takeo (1868–1904)

Naval officer. Born in what is now Ōita Prefecture. A graduate of the Naval Academy in 1889, from 1897 to 1902 Hirose studied in Russia and become fond of Russian literature. He participated in the RUSSO-JAPANESE WAR of 1904–05 as torpedo officer on the *Asahi.* He commanded the *Hōkoku maru* in the first attempt to seal the entrance to the harbor of PORT ARTHUR and in the second try, as commander of the *Fukui maru,* he was killed while searching for one of his men. He was posthumously appointed to the rank of commander and until Japan's defeat in 1945 was revered as a *gunshin* ("war god"), together with Lt. Col. TACHIBANA SHŪTA. It is said that he was personally opposed to the Russo-Japanese War from a humanitarian point of view.

IWASHIMA Hisao

Hirose Tansō (1782–1856)

Confucian scholar and educator of the late Edo period. Born in Bungo Province (now Ōita Prefecture). Learned in the Chinese and Japanese classics, in 1813 he founded in his hometown of Hita the Kangien, a Confucian-oriented school. Over 4,000 students from throughout Japan studied there, including such notables as the Dutch-studies scholar TAKANO CHŌEI and the military strategist ŌMURA MASUJIRŌ. Tansō counted among his friends and associates the well-known literary figures RAI SAN'YŌ and YANAGAWA SEIGAN, as well as the Confucian scholar HOASHI BANRI and the painter TANOMURA CHIKUDEN. His works are collected in the 3-volume *Tansō zenshū* (1925–27).

Hiroshige (1797–1858)

Full name, Andō Hiroshige. UKIYO-E print designer, illustrator, and painter, best known for his many tranquil landscapes which succeeded in infusing the woodblock print with certain techniques and poetry of brush painting.

Hiroshige's lineage sheds some light on social mobility in the Edo period (1600–1868). His paternal great-grandfather, Tanaka Tokuemon, was a steward in the service of the lord of the Tsugaru clan. Tokuemon's third son, Kōemon, was an archery instructor in Edo (now Tōkyō). His son Gen'emon, Hiroshige's father, was adopted into the Andō family, a common practice to insure the succession of a family name, and earned a livelihood as a fireman, perhaps as a brigade supervisor. He lodged at firemen's barracks in the Yayosugashi district (now Yaesu) of Edo and it was there that his three daughters and his son Tokutarō, the future artist, were born.

When Tokutarō was 12 years old, his father and mother died. He had already shown interest in drawing and had taken lessons with Okajima Rinsai, a neighboring fireman who was an amateur painter. Soon after his parents' death, he expressed a wish to study *ukiyo-e* formally and tried unsuccessfully to enter the already crowded studio of the popular print designer UTAGAWA TOYOKUNI. Tokutarō then approached UTAGAWA TOYOHIRO, a more restrained and less popular artist than Toyokuni, whose interest in classical painting and connections with many poets later proved important and useful to his pupil. Tokutarō entered Toyohiro's studio around 1811 and sometime afterwards was given the name Hiroshige and the right to use the Utagawa name (see UTAGAWA SCHOOL).

It is one thing to be honored by a teacher, and another to earn a living by one's work. In the decade beginning in 1810 Hiroshige continued to receive a stipend as a fireman and is said to have distinguished himself in a fire at Kojimachō in 1818. During this period he married a woman of the *samurai* class. The couple either bore or adopted a son, Nakajirō, to whom Hiroshige at his earliest opportunity seems to have relinquished his stipend and responsibilities as a fireman in order to devote himself entirely to art.

Like so many other *ukiyo-e* artists, Hiroshige's first signed works seem to have been book illustrations, the earliest, perhaps, being pictures for a book of comic verse, *Kyōka murasaki no maki* (Book of Purple Kyōka), published in the spring of 1818. His first single-sheet woodblock prints, full-length portraits of actors and beauties, began to appear late the same year. Compared to works by his contemporaries KEISAI EISEN and UTAGAWA KUNISADA, Hiroshige's early figure prints are stiff, awkward, and uninspired. But like HOKUSAI, TORII KIYONAGA, and Suzuki HARUNOBU before him, Hiro-

Hiroshige——Shōno (Rain at Shōno)

Print from the series *Fifty-three Stations of the Tōkaidō.* Woodblock print. 24.3 × 37.4 cm. Early 19th century. Tōkyō National Museum.

shige needed to explore the conventions that were available to him and learn from experience that they could not accommodate his vision of the world and art.

Until the 1820s, most Japanese prints had been pictures of women or actors, and their hallmark was an eloquent outline that created stark separation between individual figures and their surroundings. Hiroshige learned that in modern painting this separation was less distinct, since forms could be suggested by mass and shading instead of outline alone. Block-printed manuals for painting had reproduced many of the effects of brushwork, and sketches of the modern MARUYAMA-SHIJŌ SCHOOL of painting were already being reproduced in privately commissioned books. Hiroshige saw that these new techniques of engraving and printing could infuse new life into the rather stagnant conventions of *ukiyo-e,* and it is perhaps with this in mind that he began to design his first *kachōga* prints (see BIRD-AND-FLOWER PAINTING): painterly subjects, in the narrow upright format of paintings with calligraphic inscriptions and seals, printed with a full range of color. These prints seemed to be made for use: genre pictures of the period often show them pasted on screens and walls. They seem to have been spectacularly successful. Very late impressions are common, showing that hundreds, if not thousands, of impressions of individual subjects were printed. During his career Hiroshige designed nearly 1,000 bird-and-flower subjects, some of them known in two or even three contemporary versions, another indication of their extraordinary popularity.

Around 1830 the publisher Kawaguchi Shōzō invited Hiroshige to design a set of 10 views of the city of Edo. The views were to be printed in a limited range of colors: blue and pink with touches of russet and light green, with decorative printed borders. The prints were the first full expression of Hiroshige's brilliant ability to combine startling designs with a sense of atmosphere and poetry that made the pictures familiar and accessible, not forbidding, in spite of their striking novelty. This set established Hiroshige's reputation and also staked a claim. For the next 20 years he designed thousands of horizontal landscape prints, over 1,000 of them views of his beloved city of Edo.

In 1832 Hiroshige finally relinquished to his son his duties as a fireman and in the same year traveled from Edo to Kyōto and back in the retinue of a government official. This event prompted the set of woodblock prints for which he is best known both in Japan and in the West, *Tōkaidō gojūsantsugi* (Fifty-three Stations of the Tōkaidō Road), which was issued in parts by the publisher Takeuchi Hoeidō. The set was so popular that even before it was completed the earliest views were used as backgrounds for a series of prints of beauties by Kunisada. Before his death, Hiroshige designed 20 sets of views of the TŌKAIDŌ. The Hoeidō set is often called the Great Tōkaidō, to distinguish it from the Reisho Marusei Tōkaidō, also in large horizontal format; the Upright or Vertical Tōkaidō of 1853; the Gyōsho Tōkaidō, published in a slightly smaller horizontal format in the early 1840s; and the many smaller sets.

It was perhaps as a result of this journey to Kyōto that Hiroshige designed the Eight Views of Ōmi, and sets of 10 views each of famous places in Kyōto and Ōsaka. Around 1835 Hiroshige took over from Eisen the responsibility of completing a set of 70 horizontal views of another more mountainous route from Edo to Kyōto, the

Hiroshima

The cenotaph for victims of the atomic bomb in Peace Memorial Park. The Atomic Bomb Dome is visible in the distance.

Kiso Kaidō. To this set he contributed 46 designs, including views of Seba, Nagakubo, and Miyanokoshi, which are among his masterpieces.

Hiroshige's first wife died in 1839 and he remarried a woman named Oyasu, 20 years his junior. His son Nakajirō died in 1845, but by his second wife he had a daughter, Tatsu, who married his pupil Shigenobu.

In the mid-1840s, while print publication languished in the aftermath of the restrictive laws of the TEMPŌ REFORMS, Hiroshige renewed his acquaintance with members of literary circles and illustrated many albums and booklets of comic KYŌKA poetry. In the early 1850s he chose a new, vertical format for his landscape sets, including *Rokujūyoshū meisho zue* (Views of Over Sixty Famous Places), a set of 69 views of the provinces; the celebrated set *Meisho Edo hyakkei* (One Hundred Views of Edo), which included 118 prints; and *Fuji sanjūrokkei* (Thirty-six Views of Mt. Fuji), which was published posthumously. In his later prints he used a more intense and brilliant range of colors, freely using special effects like embossing and overprinting.

Hiroshige died in the cholera epidemic that swept Edo in the middle of 1858. He was buried in the Tōgakuji, a Sōtō Zen sect temple in the Asakusa district of Edo. A memorial portrait by Kunisada shows him kneeling in the robes of a lay priest and holding a rosary. Besides the prints mentioned, Hiroshige designed numerous other landscapes and pictures of comic, historical, and decorative subjects. His designs probably total more than 10,000, aside from his book illustrations and paintings. He was survived by his second wife who lived until 1879, and by his daughter, who soon separated from her husband Shigenobu to marry another of her father's pupils, Shigemasa. Hiroshige had few pupils and few rivals. His immediate work was continued for a few years by Hiroshige II, but his spiritual heirs were the Meiji period (1868–1912) artist KOBAYASHI KIYOCHIKA and the 20th-century print designers Kawase Hasui (1883–1957) and YOSHIDA HIROSHI (1876–1950).

Hiroshige II (1826–1869) —— Like Hiroshige from a family of firemen, Suzuki Chimpei was accepted as one of Hiroshige's new pupils and was given the name Shigenobu. Early in 1859, after the death of Hiroshige, he married his master's daughter Tatsu and took the name of Ichiryūsai Hiroshige II. In the next few years he designed vertical landscapes of the provinces and Edo, several prints of foreigners, and views of Yokohama. In the mid-1860s he abandoned his wife, remarried, and changed his name from Hiroshige to Risshō. He was one of the *ukiyo-e* artists whose paintings were chosen by the Japanese government for exhibition in Paris in 1867. This honor did not increase his standing, however, and he had to eke out a living painting lanterns and tea boxes before he died in poverty.

Hiroshige III (1841–1894) —— A pupil of Hiroshige whose early work was signed Shigemasa and who married Hiroshige's daughter Tatsu on her separation from Shigenobu in the mid-1860s. He adopted the name Hiroshige III, probably after Shigenobu's death in 1869, and designed many garish triptychs of Western buildings, trains, and ships in Yokohama and Tōkyō.

Hiroshige IV (dates unknown) —— Kikuchi Kiichirō, an artist who had used the name Risshō II, took the name Hiroshige IV in 1911 with the permission of the heirs of Hiroshige III.

—— Edward F. Strange, *The Colour-Prints of Hiroshige* (1925).
Roger KEYES

Hiroshima

Capital of Hiroshima Prefecture, western Honshū; located on the Inland Sea coast at the delta of the river Ōtagawa, whose six channels flow through the city. Originally a fishing village, Hiroshima developed as a castle town of the Asano family during the Edo period (1600–1868). In 1889 it was made into a municipality, one of the earliest in Japan, along with Tōkyō. The construction of the port of Ujina was completed in 1889, and the San'yō Railway Line, which runs through Hiroshima, was completed in 1894. During the SINO-JAPANESE WAR OF 1894–1895, imperial headquarters were established there. Hiroshima expanded into the seventh largest city in Japan and flourished until World War II as a military center. On 6 August 1945 the world's first atomic bomb was dropped on Hiroshima, destroying 90 percent of the city and ultimately killing about 200,000 people (see ATOMIC BOMB). Now completely rebuilt, it is one of the most important cities in western Honshū. Major industries are shipbuilding, machinery, and automobiles. Hiroshima is also well known for its oysters and persimmons.

At what was the epicenter of the bomb there are located the Peace Memorial Park (with the Peace Memorial Hall, Peace Memorial Museum, a memorial cenotaph for victims of the bomb, and the Municipal Auditorium), the Atomic Bomb Dome (the only building left unreconstructed), and the World Peace Memorial Cathedral. A commemorative ceremony on 6 August has become Hiroshima's most important annual event. Other sites of interest are Shukkeien, a garden made in 1620 for the Asano family; Hiroshima Castle, rebuilt in 1958; Hijiyama Park, famous for cherry blossoms; and the home of the scholar RAI SAN'YŌ. Area: 613.3 sq km (236.7 sq mi); pop: 899,394.

Hiroshima Bay

(Hiroshima Wan). Inlet of the western Inland Sea, on the coast of southwestern Hiroshima and southeastern Yamaguchi prefectures, western Honshū. Bounded by the islands of Kurahashijima on the east and Ōshima on the south and by Honshū on the west and north. Provides harbors for the cities of Hiroshima, Ōtake, Kure, and Iwakuni. There are numerous islands in the bay; on many of them mandarin oranges and other fruits are grown. The bay is known for its oysters, but these have been endangered in recent years by increasing industrialization. The bay was also the site of a major naval base until the end of World War II.

Hiroshima Plain

(Hiroshima Heiya). This low-lying plain bordering the Inland Sea consists of the delta of the river ŌTAGAWA with its six branches. The industrialized southern part comprises land that has been reclaimed beginning in the Edo period (1600–1868). The major city is Hiroshima, which covers much of the plain. Area: approximately 30 sq km (12 sq mi).

Hiroshima Prefecture

(Hiroshima Ken). Located in western Honshū and bounded by Shimane and Tottori prefectures to the north, Okayama Prefecture to the east, the Inland Sea to the south, and Yamaguchi Prefecture to the west. The northern portion of the prefecture is occupied by the CHŪGOKU MOUNTAINS and is relatively thinly populated. Its climate tends to be cool and humid. The southern area, composed of highlands and coastal plains, has a milder, drier climate. Most of the population is concentrated in urban areas along the Inland Sea coast.

Under the ancient provincial system (KOKUGUN SYSTEM) the area was divided into the provinces of Aki and Bingo. It developed as a center for Inland Sea shipping. Toward the end of the Heian period (794–1185), when the TAIRA FAMILY was in power, TAIRA NO KIYOMORI lavished support on the ITSUKUSHIMA SHRINE and established HIROSHIMA BAY as a base for commercial activities. During the Edo period (1600–1868), the cities of HIROSHIMA and Fukuyama developed as castle towns. The present prefectural boundaries were established in 1876. In 1945 Hiroshima became the first city in the world to suffer an atomic bomb attack.

While agriculture, forestry, and fishing have declined steadily in recent years, industrial growth has been rapid in the coastal cities.

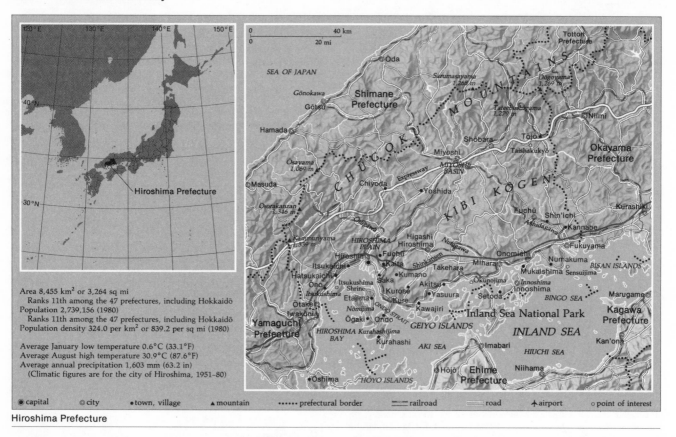

capital ● city ● town, village ▲ mountain ⋯⋯ prefectural border ══ railroad ═══ road ✈ airport ○ point of interest

Hiroshima Prefecture

Area 8,455 km² or 3,264 sq mi
  Ranks 11th among the 47 prefectures, including Hokkaidō
Population 2,739,156 (1980)
  Ranks 11th among the 47 prefectures, including Hokkaidō
Population density 324.0 per km² or 839.2 per sq mi (1980)

Average January low temperature 0.6°C (33.1°F)
Average August high temperature 30.9°C (87.6°F)
Average annual precipitation 1,603 mm (63.2 in)
  (Climatic figures are for the city of Hiroshima, 1951–80)

Major industries include shipbuilding, automobiles, steel, machinery, textiles, petrochemicals, and food processing. Traditional industries such as weaving, *sake* brewing, and the manufacture of *tatami* mats also continue to exist.

Parts of the coast are included in the INLAND SEA NATIONAL PARK. The atomic bomb memorial and Peace Park in Hiroshima bring visitors from around the world. Area: 8,455 sq km (3,264 sq mi); pop: 2,739,156; capital: Hiroshima. Other major cities include KURE, ONOMICHI, and FUKUYAMA.

Hiroshima University

(Hiroshima Daigaku). A national university located in the city of Hiroshima. The university is made up of eight former independent universities, including the Hiroshima Kōtō Shihan Gakkō (Hiroshima Higher Normal School), the Hiroshima Bunrika Daigaku (Hiroshima University of Arts and Sciences), the Hiroshima Kōgyō Semmon Gakkō (Hiroshima Higher School of Technology) and the Hiroshima Kōtō Gakkō (Hiroshima Higher School). It assumed its present name in 1949. In 1953 Hiroshima Prefectural Medical College became part of the university. Hiroshima University maintains faculties of integrated arts and sciences, letters, education, economics, science, medicine, dentistry, engineering, and fisheries and animal husbandry The university is known for its Institute for Peace Science, Research Institute for Theoretical Physics, and Research Institute for Medicine and Biology.

Hirota Kōki (1878–1948)

Diplomat and prime minister (1936–37). Born in Fukuoka Prefecture, from his youth he had close associations with the ultranationalist GEN'YŌSHA. After graduating from Tōkyō University, he entered the Ministry of Foreign Affairs and was appointed to posts in China, Britain, the United States, and the Netherlands. While ambassador to the Soviet Union he negotiated the Hirota–Karakhan fishing agreements in 1932. As foreign minister in the SAITŌ MAKOTO (1933–34) and OKADA KEISUKE (1934–36) cabinets, he negotiated the purchase of the strategic CHINESE EASTERN RAILWAY in Manchuria, and on 28 October 1935 he announced his "three principles" (Hirota *sangensoku*), i.e., the establishment of a Japan–China–Manchukuo bloc, the suppression of anti-Japanese ac-

tivities in China, and the organization of a Sino-Japanese front against communism. He became prime minister in March 1936 after the downfall of the Okada cabinet as a result of the FEBRUARY 26TH INCIDENT, and reinstituted the system of appointing only generals and admirals on active duty as army and navy ministers (GUMBU DAIJIN GEN'EKI BUKAN SEI); he greatly increased the military budget and pushed for the development of war-related heavy industry. Hirota also signed the Japanese-German-Italian ANTI-COMINTERN PACT as a prelude to stronger ties with the Axis powers. His cabinet was obliged to resign in January 1937, however, following a confrontation in the Diet between his army minister, General TERAUCHI HISAICHI, and a Diet member (Hamada Kunimatsu, 1868–1939) who criticized military interference in politics. He was named foreign minister in the KONOE FUMIMARO cabinet (1937–39) in June, and when hostilities broke out between Japanese and Chinese troops (MARCO POLO BRIDGE INCIDENT) in July, he did not attempt to check the military's plan for all-out war. He continued to be active during World War II as a JŪSHIN ("senior statesman") and with the deterioration of Japan's military position he sought peace through the intercession of the Soviet ambassador, I. A. Malik (b 1906), but failed. After the war he was tried as a class-A war criminal at the Tōkyō WAR CRIMES TRIALS and was executed on 23 December 1948. He was the only civilian to be so sentenced.

Hirota Shrine

(Hirota Jinja). A Shintō shrine in the city of Nishinomiya, Hyōgo Prefecture, dedicated to the "rough spirit" (*aramitama;* see TAMA) of the sun goddess and so-called imperial ancestress, AMATERASU ŌMIKAMI. According to shrine tradition, after the legendary empress JINGŪ successfully completed her campaign in Korea and returned to Japan (this story, related in the NIHON SHOKI of 720, has been discounted by modern historians), she received an oracle instructing her to establish a shrine in an area distant from the imperial residence to house the "rough spirit" of Amaterasu Ōmikami. The Hirota Jinja, in addition to the main shrine, contains four subordinate shrines honoring deities associated with Empress Jingū's Korean campaign. The shrine is also believed to afford encouragement and protection to those who write traditional Japanese verse (WAKA). The annual festival is observed on 16 March.

Stanley WEINSTEIN

Hirotsu Kazuo (1891–1968)

Novelist and literary critic. Born in Tōkyō. Second son of novelist HIROTSU RYŪRŌ. Graduate of Waseda University. He started writing critical articles for various literary magazines beginning around 1910. Achieving prominence with his short story "Shinkeibyō jidai" (1917, The Neurotic Age), he became known for his depictions of the nihilism and decadence of modern intellectuals. In the early 1930s he was sympathetic to the PROLETARIAN LITERATURE MOVEMENT but later expressed his displeasure at the movement's inefficacy and fragmentation in such works as Rekishi to rekishi no aida (1941). He devoted much of his work between 1953 and 1963 to the defense of the accused saboteurs in the MATSUKAWA INCIDENT whose plight was the subject of Izumi e no michi (1953–54, The Road to Izumi) and Matsukawa saiban (1954–58, The Matsukawa Trial). His autobiography, Nengetsu no ashioto (The Footsteps of Time), serialized from 1961 to 1963 in the magazine Gunzō, won the 1963 Noma Literary Prize. He became a member of the Japan Art Academy in 1950.

Hirotsu Ryūrō (1861–1928)

Novelist. Creator of the "tragic novel" (hisan shōsetsu) and father of the novelist and critic HIROTSU KAZUO. Born Hirotsu Naoto in what is now Nagasaki Prefecture, he moved to Tōkyō in 1874 and graduated from school in 1877. After trying his hand at business in Ōsaka, he returned to Tōkyō and became an official in the Agriculture and Commerce Ministry from 1881 to 1885. In 1889 Ryūrō met OZAKI KŌYŌ and joined the KEN'YŪSHA, though he largely developed apart from that literary group. He published two novels during 1895 which brought him wide literary fame: Hemeden and Kurotokage. These were the first of his numerous hisan shōsetsu, the most famous of which is Imado shinjū (1896, Suicide at Imado). His creativity then began to decline, and after 1908 he retired from writing.

Ryūrō's "tragic novels" were never entirely free of influence from the Edo-period (1600–1868) GESAKU tradition. They were filled with exaggeration and extremes, improbable or incredible events, rampant romanticism, melodramatic emotion, and wooden posturing. Plot focus was on a relentless progression through a series of pathetic circumstances and wretched experiences toward a destructive finale governed by hostile fate. Although he aimed at penetrating psychological analysis, Ryūrō's standard practice was to stock his characters with stereotyped feelings and behavior paralleling their obligatory agonies. Dominated by events, the characters reacted with perfect predictability.

Ryūrō's works are the carnival sideshow of Meiji fiction. He created gloomy landscapes through which trooped a morbid parade of midgets, dwarfs, beggars, thieves, murderers, prostitutes, imbeciles, and lunatics. Perhaps in reaction to the idealized characters of the other Ken'yūsha writers, Ryūrō favored the blind, deaf, dumb, lame, deformed, disfigured, diseased, and deranged. However grotesque his characters are externally, Ryūrō usually depicted them as internally pure, kind, honest, and sincere. This romantic inversion also extends to the outwardly normal characters, who frequently display brutality, betrayal, dishonesty, and hatred. Normal or abnormal, most of his major characters are subjected to unbearable disasters and an implacable fate leading to death. About half of Ryūrō's works end with suicide. But whatever the vehicle of their demise, Ryūrō's suffering victims are certain to be annihilated.

Thomas E. SWANN

hirugao

(bindweed). *Calystegia japonica*. A twining perennial of the Convolvulaceae family that grows wild in grassy fields and mountains throughout Japan. It is also found in Korea and China. Long twining stems grow from white creeping underground stems and leaves are alternate and arrow-shaped. In summer, pink funnel-shaped flowers about 5 centimeters (2 in) in diameter bloom during the day. These handsome flowers have been appreciated by poets since the time of the 8th-century poetry anthology Man'yōshū. Similar species include kohirugao (C. hederacea), with smaller flowers and leaves, and hamahirugao (C. soldanella), which grows wild in sandy coastal areas and has kidney-shaped leaves. See also MORNING GLORIES.

MATSUDA Osamu

Hiruzen Kōgen

Highland in northern Okayama Prefecture, western Honshū. It has good skiing and camping grounds. Noted for its classical Ōmiya odori (folk dance), giant salamanders, and alpine flora. Part of Daisen–Oki National Park. Average elevation: approximately 500 m (1,640 ft); length: 6 km (3.7 mi); width: 14 km (8.7 mi).

hisago

(also called hyōtan). Dried and hollowed-out bottle gourd traditionally used as a container. Large hisago containing wine or tea were hung at the waist for picnics and when traveling. Small ones were, and are, used for spices or pills. Hisago halved lengthwise were used as ladles.

INOKUCHI Shōji

Hisai

City in central Mie Prefecture, central Honshū. Although Hisai is fast becoming a residential area, pears and rice are all still grown along the river Kumozugawa; there is mixed farming and silkworm cultivation in the foothills of nearby mountains. Sakakibara Hot Spring has drawn visitors since medieval times. Pop: 37,057.

Hisaita Eijirō (1898–1976)

Playwright. Born in Miyagi Prefecture. Graduate of Tōkyō University. He was one of the central figures of the so-called proletarian movement in drama in the 1920s. Later, in Hokutō no kaze (1937, The Northeast Wind), perhaps his best-known play, he described the life and thought of the manager of a textile factory. The work won fame as a masterpiece of realistic drama. After World War II, Hisaita wrote scenarios for movies, including Ōsoneke no asa (1946, Morning for the Ōsone Family), in collaboration with its director KINOSHITA KEISUKE, and Waga seishun ni kui nashi (1946, No Regrets for Our Youth), directed by KUROSAWA AKIRA.

ASAI Kiyoshi

Hisamatsu Shin'ichi (1889–1980)

Philosopher of religion. Born in Gifu Prefecture, Hisamatsu was a student of the philosopher NISHIDA KITARŌ at Kyōto University and later a professor at the same university (1946–49) and others. Concentrating on the philosophical investigation of Zen, he undertook a comparison of Eastern and Western culture from a religio-philosophical point of view. He also concerned himself with a creative design for the "postmodern world." He led a Zen-oriented group called the FAS Association, its name taken from its motto, "To awake to Formless self, to stand for the standpoint of All mankind, to create Superhistorical history." A collection of his works, Hisamatsu Shin'ichi chosakushū (1969–80), includes Tōyōteki mu (1939, Eastern Nothingness) and Zen to bijutsu (1946; tr Zen and the Fine Arts, 1971).

MURAKAMI Shigeyoshi

Hisao Jūran (1902–1957)

Novelist. Real name Abe Masao. Born in Hokkaidō. After participating in the modern theater movement of the 1920s led by KISHIDA KUNIO, he went to France to study theater. Upon his return to Japan, he started writing fiction. Hisao wrote many mystery stories, historical novels, and works of popular fiction in a refined style. His short story "Suzuki Mondo" (1951) won the Naoki Literary Prize, and the story "Boshizō" (1954, The Mother) won first prize in the New York Herald Tribune International Short Story Contest in 1954. Other works include Usuyuki shō (1952) and Hadairo no tsuki (1957, Flesh-colored Moon).

Hishida Shunsō (1874–1911)

Japanese-style painter. Born in Iida, Nagano Prefecture. In 1889 he went to Tōkyō, where he began to study painting in the KANŌ SCHOOL style with Yūki Masaaki (1834–1904). He attended the Tōkyō Bijutsu Gakkō (now Tōkyō University of Fine Arts and Music) from 1890 to 1895. There he studied with the painter HASHIMOTO GAHŌ and was much influenced by the ideas of the art critics and theorists Ernest F. FENOLLOSA and OKAKURA KAKUZŌ, who believed that traditional subject matter and techniques were compatible with a judicious infusion of Western elements. After graduation he worked at copying old religious paintings in Kyōto and Nara for the Imperial Household Museum (now Tōkyō National Museum) and taught at the Tōkyō Bijutsu Gakkō. In 1898, when Okakura left the art school to establish the JAPAN FINE ARTS ACADEMY (Nihon Bijutsuin), Shunsō followed him. With another member, YOKOYAMA TAIKAN, Shunsō rejected the tradition of portraying objects with distinct outlines or contours and experimented by rendering forms through tonal modulation. Using soft and lyrical, though realistic, colors Shunsō depicted idealized natural and historical subjects. Notable examples of this style are his *Parting of Su Wu and Li Ling* (1901), and *Ōshōkun* (1902; Ch: *Wangzhaojun* or *Wang-chao-chün*). From 1903 to 1905 Shunsō traveled and exhibited his works in India, America, and Europe. In his final years he experimented with the RIMPA style. In response to criticism of earlier works, Shunsō finally reintroduced the use of fine bounding lines, but he always kept outline secondary to color.

Shunsō successfully competed in many exhibitions, including the government-sponsored BUNTEN. At these exhibits he first showed some of his most famous paintings: *The Bodhisattva Xianshou* (Hsien-shou; 1907); *Fallen Leaves* (1909); and *Black Cat* (1910).

Frederick BAEKELAND

Hishikawa Moronobu → Moronobu

Historiographical Institute, Tōkyō University

(Tōkyō Daigaku Shiryō Hensanjo; often abbreviated as Shiryō Hensanjo). Research institute devoted to the gathering, study, and publication of historical materials on Japan. Established in 1869, it had a variety of names under several government organizations before receiving its present name in 1929. It became a part of Tōkyō University in 1888. Originally charged with compiling a "great history of Japan," it has since 1895 taken on the broader task of collecting data and documents for historical research. In 1950 it became independent of the university's department of literature. Today it is widely known as the central institution and principal library for the study of Japanese history. Among its continuing projects are the collections DAI NIHON SHIRYŌ and DAI NIHON KOMONJO (both since 1901) and *Dai Nihon kokiroku* (since 1952, Old Records of Great Japan). Another, more recent undertaking was the publication of *Historical Documents Relating to Japan in Foreign Countries* (14 vols, 1964–69), a catalog of the institute's extensive collection of microfilms of mostly Western-language sources. *Theodore F.* WELCH

historiography

(shigakushi). Historical writing in Japan is believed to have originated during the early 6th century, when oral traditions had developed, especially in the imperial house, and intellectuals had mastered the art of Chinese writing to the extent that they were able to express themselves with relative ease. In addition, the century-long struggle of the imperial house to consolidate its power had no doubt led to reflection upon history and to recognition of the need to record and manipulate information.

Early attempts to record the oral tradition resulted in two works, the TEIKI and the KYŪJI. Although neither is extant today, portions of each were incorporated into later works that have survived, and so it is possible to make conjectures about their nature. The *Teiki* was in essence a genealogical record of the imperial line; the *Kyūji* contained myths of the ancient gods and semihistorical figures and drew from legends of heroes and emperors, tales of love, and folksongs. Although the *Teiki* and the *Kyūji* were probably composed by members of the court circle, copies came into the hands of the various UJI (kin groups), who embellished them, often with the express aim of glorifying their own past, and in this way many versions were produced.

The Aristocratic Age —— *Official histories.* To bring order out of the events confused in these many versions of the *Teiki* and the *Kyūji*, in 620 Prince SHŌTOKU collaborated with SOGA NO UMAKO to compile the TENNŌKI AND KOKKI (Record of the Emperors; Record of the Nation) and many family records. All of these were destroyed by fire in 645, but on the basis of the other political and cultural programs Shōtoku espoused, it is believed that these works were compiled with the aim of producing more authoritative chronicles of the emperors and a stronger sense of the Japanese nation as an entity.

Decades later, Emperor TEMMU further strengthened the foundations of imperial rule, completing a process that had begun with the TAIKA REFORM of 645. He turned to history for clarification of the legitimacy of power and the basis of imperial authority and set up a historical commission in 681 to continue the work initiated by Prince Shōtoku.

The work of the historical commission took two directions: the compilation of a history centered on the imperial family through the reordering of the earlier *Teiki* and *Kyūji*, and a new, more systematically organized history of the Japanese nation. Temmu did not live to see the project completed, but it eventually resulted in two works: the KOJIKI, in three volumes, appeared in 712, and the NIHON SHOKI, a much larger work in 30 volumes, in 720; they are the earliest extant Japanese historical records. Produced by the same authority, they resemble each other superficially; each begins with a mythological portion that describes the founding of Japan and the descent of the imperial clan from the ancient gods, and each places the emperor at the center of the nation and at the top of the social hierarchy. The two works are quite different, however, in other respects.

The *Kojiki* was compiled by Ō NO YASUMARO on the basis of materials recited to him by HIEDA NO ARE, who had memorized the traditions of the *Teiki* and *Kyūji*. The purpose of the *Kojiki* was to provide a national history that sanctified the emperor as head of state: it begins with the mythology of the early Japanese, reworked and reorganized to place the emperor at stage center. The *Kojiki* presents a genealogy of the imperial line from the appearance of the legendary first emperor, JIMMU, through the reign (593–628) of Empress SUIKO, based upon the *Teiki* and describing the outstanding events of each sovereign's reign. Woven into this narrative are myths, legends, and folksongs selected from the *Kyūji*; thus, it may be viewed as an epic of the Japanese people. The language of the *Kojiki* varies according to the material being presented: early traditions are recorded as much as possible in the early vernacular, employing Chinese characters solely for their phonetic value; elsewhere pure classical Chinese is used or sometimes a mixture of the two languages.

The *Nihon shoki* covers the period from the mythological founding of the nation through the reign (686–697) of Empress JITŌ. It draws on a number of sources other than the *Teiki* and *Kyūji*, including records of the central and local governments and of the various clans, and even Korean materials. Compilation of the work was undertaken by leading scholars of the day under the supervision of Prince TONERI, a son of Temmu and a respected elder of the imperial household. Following Chinese models, the *Nihon shoki* is in chronicle form and is written in classical Chinese. Its compilers sought to produce a dignified and authoritative history to equal the official histories of China, and they paid considerable attention to the history of Japan's relations with its continental neighbors. It was their desire to emphasize the greatness of Japanese history that caused the editors to set the date of Emperor Jimmu's ascension to the throne at 660 BC, many centuries before any plausible date.

The *Nihon shoki* was the first of six official histories compiled by the imperial government. These histories cover the period of Japan's history up until the year 887 and are known collectively as the RIKKOKUSHI, or "Six National Histories." The other five are the *Shoku nihongi* (797), in 40 volumes; *Nihon kōki* (842), in 40 volumes; *Shoku Nihon kōki* (869), in 20 volumes; *Nihon Montoku Tennō jitsuroku* (879), in 10 volumes; and *Nihon sandai jitsuroku* (901), in 50 volumes. These five national histories were compiled under the direction of a government bureau established for that purpose and headed by high government officials; the actual work was done by leading scholars of the time, who relied chiefly upon government records for their information. The format was similar to that of the latter half of the *Nihon shoki*. The only deviations from a strict chronological order are the biographical obituary sketches added to the death-date entries of high-ranking officials, monks, and members of the nobility.

The more than 200 years during which the Six National Histories were compiled was an age of unparalleled imperial prestige and power. There was intense interest in Chinese and Japanese history among members of the court aristocracy; lectures on Chinese history were offered at the Confucian-oriented court university (DAIGAKURYŌ), and lectures on the *Nihon shoki* were given at fixed times at the court. It was an age that produced a stream of scholars well versed in Chinese and Japanese history: ŌMI NO MIFUNE is representative of historians of the first half of the period, while SUGA-

WARA NO MICHIZANE, the compiler of the monumental RUIJŪ KOKUSHI (205 volumes), a topically classified national history, stands out among those of the second half.

The imperial government continued to sponsor the compilation of histories following the *Nihon sandai jitsuroku,* and the draft of a seventh work, the SHINKOKUSHI, was completed about the middle of the 10th century. The work was never given final form, however, and the draft is no longer extant. The reasons for this failure are unclear, but it did coincide with a serious weakening of imperial authority.

Nonofficial histories. Government involvement in the recording of history came to an end, but private individuals continued, and three types of historical writing appeared that would continue in later centuries.

One of these was much in the tradition of the official histories. It includes works like the NIHON KIRYAKU and the HONCHŌ SEIKI, both composed in classical Chinese by members of the court aristocracy, who drew upon such sources as the *Shinkokushi* and court records. The two works begin where the official histories leave off and cover the period until 1153. Similar in format and style, but differing somewhat in purpose, is the *Fusō ryakki* of Kōen (1112?–69), a scholar-monk of Mt. Hiei. The *Fusō ryakki* begins with Emperor Jimmu and closes with 1094; but Kōen drew from temple records, biographies of monks, and Buddhist tale literature in addition to the usual sources, and the work is close to being a history of Japanese Buddhism. Because of his inclusion of early traditions and Buddhist tales, it was widely read, but the historical accuracy of some of Kōen's work is questionable.

The second type of nonofficial history, that in a narrative style, was based upon historical fact but used the techniques of tale (*monogatari*) literature (see MONOGATARI BUNGAKU) and inaugurated sweeping changes in the entire concept of historical writing. Written in the vernacular, these works portrayed human psychology and gave a fresh, vivid view of the society, something not possible in traditional histories.

The first of the narrative histories was the EIGA MONOGATARI, which begins with 887, the year the *Nihon sandai jitsuroku* left off, and covers nearly 200 years in chronological order. It is concerned with the rise and splendor of the FUJIWARA FAMILY, who gradually took over the reins of government from the emperors, and especially with their most illustrious member, FUJIWARA NO MICHINAGA. The work is in two parts, possibly of different authorship. The first, written around 1030, is believed to be the work of the poet AKAZOME EMON, a woman attendant to the wife of Michinaga said to have been on friendly terms with the novelist MURASAKI SHIKIBU. The bulk of the work is devoted to the age in which the author lived and is written with such vividness and accuracy as to suggest an eyewitness report.

The truly great work of narrative historical literature, however, is the ŌKAGAMI, a work that covers the years from 850 to 1025, the heyday of the Fujiwara. It takes the form of a dialogue between two men, each at least 150 years old, during a pilgrimage to a temple. They are occasionally interrupted by the critical questioning of a young companion, and their great age allows them to recount history as they experienced it. Unlike the traditional chronicle, the work is multidimensional. Use of dialogue allows the presentation of more than one point of view, making the *Ōkagami* comparatively objective. The work was probably written during the period of rule by cloistered emperors (INSEI), the century after the time covered by the book.

Although the *Eiga monogatari* and the *Ōkagami* differ in manner of presentation and in critical attitude, they have much in common. Both works sing the praises of the Fujiwara and avoid any sort of direct criticism, but they view the direct imperial rule before the rise of the Fujiwara—especially the first half of the 10th century (see ENGI TENRYAKU NO CHI)—as a kind of golden age and see the Fujiwara period as fallen and degenerate. Both works glorify the Fujiwara, but they indirectly describe the decline of imperial fortunes and tacitly suggest the rightfulness and superiority of direct rule by the emperors. There is also a Buddhist dimension, for the belief that the world had entered the cycle of decay held immense sway at the time, and in that context Michinaga's glory is little more than an ephemeral bubble on the stream of history, just one more profane phenomenon in a world that has lost sight of the real meaning of human life.

The *Ōkagami* was followed by the imitative IMAKAGAMI and *Mizukagami,* a line later continued by the MASUKAGAMI. *Imaka-*

gami takes up where the *Ōkagami* leaves off, covering the years from 1025 to 1170, while *Mizukagami* deals with the age preceding that of the *Ōkagami.*

The third type of historical writing that appeared about this time was the military chronicle, such as the SHŌMONKI, a mid-10th-century account of the ill-fated rebellion of TAIRA NO MASAKADO, and the *Mutsu waki,* a mid-11th-century narrative of the EARLIER NINE YEARS' WAR in northern Honshū. They are both substantially accurate accounts based upon authentic records, but their compelling literary style and flowery expressions foreshadow the popular historical literature of the later period.

The Feudal Age—— *The critical approach.* Rule by the military aristocracy was established at the end of the 12th century (see WARRIOR GOVERNMENT), and Japanese society passed from the aristocratic age to the feudal. Loss of power and prestige was a traumatic experience for the courtiers, and it was inevitable that some of the intellectuals among them should look to the past for explanations of the collapse of the old order and reflect deeply upon the essence and nature of history. From such a background appeared the GUKANSHŌ, Japan's first philosophical discussion of history.

The *Gukanshō* was written around 1220 by the eminent Buddhist monk JIEN, a direct descendant of the Fujiwara regents, who rose to the highest rank in the Buddhist hierarchy of his day and was also a poet and a scholar of great learning. In this work Jien sought out the historical principles or laws that govern Japanese history. He discovered four that he felt accounted for all movement and change in Japanese society. First is the natural law of inevitability, based upon the Buddhist view of the cyclical movement of history through stages. At work within this greater framework is the law of karma, of cause and effect: each action evokes a reaction; good actions bring reward; evil actions bring punishment. Jien discovered his third principle in the actions of man as a free agent, participating in events and determining their outcome. Finally, Jien discovered a law that controls historical periods within the constantly evolving time process governed by natural law. Within each period, he felt, a certain force, an irreversible *Zeitgeist,* was at work.

Jien analyzed Japanese history from the mythical age to his own time according to these four laws, dividing it into seven periods in descending order and explaining the characteristics of each. He defined his own age as the lowest point of Japanese history, an age without reason, and recounted from its beginnings the rise of provincial warriors, through the struggle of the TAIRA FAMILY and the MINAMOTO FAMILY and the ensuing rule by the military class. However, he did not give way to a totally fatalistic determinism. His third principle, man's involvement in history as a free agent, still allowed for change: to overcome the dangers facing it, the courtly class, Jien argued, must cooperate and come to terms with the military government.

A work like the *Gukanshō* would normally have been written in classical Chinese, and Jien was certainly capable of doing so. Instead, he chose to write in simple Japanese, using the *katakana* syllabary so that people might more readily understand history as he interpreted it.

A second analysis of history was the JINNŌ SHŌTŌ KI written by KITABATAKE CHIKAFUSA, a scholar-statesman who sided with the Southern Court during the schism between the NORTHERN AND SOUTHERN COURTS (1336–92). Kitabatake intended his work as a kind of textbook for the youthful emperor Go-Murakami (1328–68), who had just ascended the throne in 1339. Because of the nature of his intended audience, Kitabatake wrote very clearly and simply, in a mixture of Chinese characters and the native *hiragana* syllabary.

The *Jinnō shōtō ki* begins with a discussion of the uniqueness of Japan's origins and its national polity and continues with a narrative of Japanese history, recounted emperor-by-emperor from the age of the gods to the present. The thread that runs through the work, uniting all its parts, is that Japan is the land of the gods, ruled by divine agreement by an unbroken line of god-descended emperors; this, Kitabatake argues, is the eternal principle that unifies all of Japanese history. Based upon native religious tradition, the *Jinnō shōtō ki* owes nothing to Buddhism. There is no trace of the Buddhist view of continuing decline: on the contrary, Kitabatake discusses the idea of imperial rule with an almost optimistic enthusiasm.

Popular historical literature. The decline of the courtly class and their gradual fall from power around the end of the 12th century and the beginning of the 13th provoked scholars like Jien to question and examine the forces at work in Japanese history. At the other end of the spectrum, the violence and civil strife that heralded the feudal age were the inspiration for a series of popular historical narratives in the tradition of the earlier *Shōmonki* and *Mutsu waki*. Such works as the HŌGEN MONOGATARI, HEIJI MONOGATARI, and HEIKE MONOGATARI, epic tales based on fact, originally oral narratives often accompanied by music, were widely read and recited by the men of the age that produced them and have remained favorites of the Japanese people down to the present. The immediate settings of these narratives are the dramatic HŌGEN DISTURBANCE (1156) and HEIJI DISTURBANCE (1160) and the bloody TAIRA–MINAMOTO WAR (1180–85), respectively, but they dramatically and graphically portray the broader picture of the decline and fall of the old order and the rise of the new. The widely circulated popular editions of these works employ all the devices and embellishments of literature, including many fictional elements. Although they are not historical in the strict sense, their original intent was to relate historical fact as faithfully and accurately as possible (see GUNKI MONOGATARI).

The outstanding representative of this genre is the *Heike monogatari*, which gives an exciting overview of the entire society during one of Japan's most turbulent periods. The old and the new stand in contrast, and the archetypal historical figures who people its pages demonstrate the changes at work in society. Buddhist thought pervades the work and ties the whole together: in the midst of pathos and despair are moments of triumph and exaltation, of awakening to faith, of release from suffering and rebirth in the Buddhist paradise.

Paralleling these popular historical narratives are the *setsuwa* (tales; see SETSUWA BUNGAKU), collections of which were produced in rapid succession. These tales deal with every class of society and were collected and retold as though they were fact. They have the newspaperlike quality of providing an eyewitness account of historical change, and they faithfully describe the society of their age and the consciousness of the men who lived then.

Traditional historical writing. Several traditional histories in the manner of the *Rikkokushi* of the 8th and 9th centuries were also composed during the feudal period. The most representative of these is the AZUMA KAGAMI, edited by officials of the Kamakura shogunate during the latter half of the 13th century as the official version of its history. Written in *kirokutai*, a hybrid of Chinese and Japanese, the work details in chronological order the evolution of military rule from 1180 to 1266. Standing in contrast to the *Azuma kagami* are the *Rokudai shōjiki*, and GODAI TEIŌ MONOGATARI, works that cover the same period of history but were written from the viewpoint of the court nobility. Of unknown authorship, they were almost certainly written by intellectuals of the courtly class. Because they are based on court diaries and on the personal experience of the authors, the information they provide is comparatively accurate, making them interesting and informative balances to the *Azuma kagami*.

Writings on contemporary affairs. With the single exception of the *Jinnō shōtō ki*, all of the historical works discussed thus far belong to the first part of the feudal age, the Kamakura period (1185–1333). During the Muromachi period (1333–1568) that followed, the *Masukagami* and a few other works in the tradition of the *Ōkagami* sought to provide a comprehensive history of the Kamakura period from the standpoint of opposition to military rule, but for the most part, men's thoughts and concerns were not with the past but with the present. The Muromachi period was one of confusion, society was in a constant state of flux, and the focus of historical writings was on contemporary affairs.

Two representative historical pieces of the early part of the Muromachi period are the TAIHEIKI and the BAISHŌRON. The *Taiheiki* is a military chronicle based on the *Heike monogatari*, covering the first 50 years of the struggle between the Northern and Southern Courts, from 1318 to 1367. Authorship has been attributed to a monk named Kojima Hōshi (d 1374), but as with the *Heike*, the original work was edited and added to numerous times, finally arriving at its present form around 1386. The style of the *Taiheiki* set the pattern for all the Muromachi historical literature to follow. The *Baishōron* also covers the struggle between the rival courts, but it was written sometime after 1350 by a samurai in the service of the Ashikaga, who supported the Northern Court.

Relative stability followed the unification of the two courts in 1392, when the Muromachi shogunate extended its rule throughout the country; but the government never undertook the compilation of an official history in the manner of the *Azuma kagami*. Of course, some histories, like KAEI SANDAI KI, which covers the reigns of three Ashikaga shōguns, did appear, but their descriptions are very brief. Again, a number of historical works like KAMAKURA ŌZŌSHI were

written but are limited to the events in the Kantō region. In addition, numerous other historical works such as *Meitokuki* (see MEITOKU REBELLION) and *Ōeiki* (see ŌEI REBELLION) were written in the style of *Taiheiki*, but they are all relatively short pieces focused upon single historical incidents. From the beginning of the ŌNIN WAR in 1467, the Muromachi period was marked by constant civil strife, and men could little afford the luxury of leisurely observing history being made or musing upon its meaning. The historical writings of this period concern localized struggles or relate the rise and fall of single *daimyō*. Almost countless in number, the best known of these concern the Ōnin War.

The first histories devoted to a particular topic or subject appeared in the feudal age. The first of these, a history of Japanese Buddhism completed in 1322, was the GENKŌ SHAKUSHO by the Zen monk KOKAN SHIREN. Another Zen monk, Zuikei Shūhō (1391–1473), completed in 1470 the compilation of ZENRINKOKU HŌKI, a history of Japan's foreign relations with its continental neighbors from ancient times to the present.

The Edo Period —— *New national histories.* After a century of civil war Japan was finally unified by three successive military leaders: ODA NOBUNAGA, TOYOTOMI HIDEYOSHI, and TOKUGAWA IEYASU. During the unification Japan also had its first encounter with the Western world. The appearance of foreigners in Japan and the overseas travels of some Japanese during the 16th century widened the perspectives of the Japanese people and at the same time aroused in their leaders a new sense of national consciousness. These conditions set the stage for the growth and development of Edo-period (1600–1868) historical writings.

The Tokugawa shogunate had no sooner established itself than it set its historians to producing such works as the *Butoku taiseiki* and the *Tōbu jitsuroku*, records of the first and second shōguns that were designed to establish the legitimacy of Tokugawa rule and to assert its power and authority. There was also the compilation of a national history that was begun in 1644 by HAYASHI RAZAN, the father of Tokugawa historical scholarship. Razan did not live to see the project to its end, but his son HAYASHI GAHŌ completed *Honchō tsugan* in 1670. This monumental history, in 310 chapters, begins with the mythological period and continues through the early Edo period.

Both Razan and Gahō were scholars of stature, well versed in the history and classics of China and Japan and preeminently qualified to edit a national history. Razan was the founder of the official school of Neo-Confucianism (SHUSHIGAKU) in Japan, and Gahō was instrumental in spreading its teachings, which formed the ideological foundation of Tokugawa society. In principle, Neo-Confucianism ranked history second to the study of the Confucian canon. The role of the historian was to serve as a kind of moral adviser to the government, to record historical events and the deeds of historical figures, and to evaluate those events and deeds according to Confucian ethical standards. The editors of *Honchō tsugan* sought simply to record history as it occurred, without making ethical judgments, but their Confucian morality was very much at work throughout. The format of the *Honchō tsugan*, moreover, is patterned after that of the *Zizhi tongjian* (Tzu-chih t'ung-chien, 1086), admired as one of the highest achievements of Chinese Confucian historiography, and follows its chronicle style.

The shogunate's histories were an encouragement for many daimyō to undertake their own historical projects. Of those who did so, TOKUGAWA MITSUKUNI, lord of the Mito domain (now part of Ibaraki Prefecture), stands out above the others. He ordered his Confucian scholars to compile their own version of a national history. It was a tremendous undertaking, beginning in 1657 and requiring two and a half centuries for completion; the result was the DAI NIHON SHI, a national history of 397 volumes. Modeled after the official Chinese dynastic histories, it is composed of four independent sections: annals, biographies, monographs and treatises, and tables and charts. The annals and biographies were completed in 1709, but it was not until 1906 that the other two sections were added.

The *Honchō tsugan* and the *Dai Nihon shi*, the outstanding histories produced during the Edo period, have much in common. Both are based upon a Confucian view of history, and they share a negative attitude toward Buddhism. Both are critical of the decadence and decay of the former aristocratic government and emphasize the legitimacy and moral correctness of the military governments that followed. They differ fundamentally, however, in their interpretation of history. *Honchō tsugan*, for example, includes the legendary empress JINGŪ in the line of imperial succession; the *Dai Nihon shi* does not. *Honchō tsugan* treats the Northern Court as the legitimate line during the period of schism; the *Dai Nihon shi* champions the Southern Court. Of the two histories, *Dai Nihon shi* is considered the monument of Tokugawa historiography, and its influence upon later historical scholarship has been tremendous.

The beginnings of modern historiography. The Neo-Confucian view of history that began with Hayashi Razan was continued by Confucian scholars of later generations, but there were some who rejected Razan's approach. Men like YAMAGA SOKŌ and OGYŪ SORAI insisted that the fundamental responsibility of the historian is to investigate fact and establish its significance; they rebelled against the Confucian purpose of writing history to encourage good and punish evil.

It was ARAI HAKUSEKI who made the most significant contribution to Edo-period historical scholarship. A Confucianist, Hakuseki combined a critical spirit with a logical and positive outlook. Hakuseki was born the son of an obscure samurai official who eventually lost his position. Despite poverty and hardship Hakuseki devoted himself to learning and in 1693 was employed as a Confucian scholar by TOKUGAWA IENOBU. When Ienobu became shōgun in 1709, Hakuseki served also as his political adviser. After Ienobu's death, Hakuseki devoted himself to writings on history, government, economics, and linguistics. One of his major achievements in the field of history was his *Tokushi yoron.*

The *Tokushi yoron* was based on notes from lectures on Japanese history given by Hakuseki to Ienobu in 1712; these were later copied by some of his disciples and widely circulated. In his lectures Hakuseki sought to clarify the forces and events that had given shape to the present time, when Ienobu found himself de facto ruler of the Japanese nation. *Tokushi yoron* begins with a discussion of the rise and decline of rule by court aristocrats. This is followed by an analysis of the establishment of rule by the military class, where Hakuseki used the terms "early" and "medieval" to designate different stages in the process. His "medieval" period was subdivided into five stages: the three generations of Minamoto rule (1185–1219); the period of the Hōjō regency (1219–1333); the Muromachi period (1333–1568); the age of Oda Nobunaga and Toyotomi Hideyoshi (1568–98); and the Edo period.

Hakuseki's concept of periodization in Japanese history was new. He tried to uncover the causes of change, and he dissected and analyzed the psychology of the principal participants, writing in a rhythmical, flowing style of Japanese. There were, however, limits to what Hakuseki was able to accomplish. Because the purpose of his work was to guide Ienobu in the administration of government, Hakuseki was limited to a discussion of political history, and his work was colored by a promilitary bias.

Koshitsū and its supplement, *Koshitsū wakumon,* written by Hakuseki in 1716 after the death of Ienobu, more clearly show him as the rational and critical historian. His careful, critical approach to the Japanese classics and to Chinese historical records led him to new interpretations of early history, paving the way for a modern scientific study of the ancient period. In 1716 Hakuseki also wrote the famous *Oritaku shiba no ki,* often called the first Japanese autobiography. Containing Hakuseki's thoughts and reflections about his own life, it is also a revealing history that describes nearly all aspects of the age in which the author lived. Hakuseki is also credited with having written books on historical geography, economic history, monetary history, the history of transportation and of Japan's foreign relations, and even a dictionary of early Japanese. He was truly a giant of a scholar who almost singlehandedly laid the foundations of modern historical studies in Japan.

Japanese classicists. The study of history was largely the province of Confucian scholars during the first half of the Edo period, but in the latter half a new rival group of scholars appeared. Followers of KOKUGAKU, or National Learning, sought to discover the true meaning of Japan's past through a careful examination of classical texts. The man who originated the movement was a Buddhist monk, KEICHŪ, known for his pioneering studies of the 8th-century poetry anthology, the MAN'YŌSHŪ. The influence of Keichū and his work liberated the study of Japanese classics from the esoteric interpretations of the past and heralded the rise of free and independent scholarship. The tradition initiated by Keichū was further developed by such men as KADA NO AZUMAMARO, KAMO NO MABUCHI, and MOTOORI NORINAGA. Like Keichū, none of these men was of the ruling samurai class: Azumamaro and Mabuchi were Shintō priests and Norinaga a physician. Thus they maintained a critical attitude toward the Confucian scholasticism supported by the samurai class. Kokugaku grew out of and developed against the social and intellectual background that had fostered Confucian scholasticism.

Kokugaku began with the study of Japanese literary classics but gradually turned to early Japanese history, and especially to the life and thought of early Japan. Motoori Norinaga brought Kokugaku to maturity as a many-faceted study of the ancient period. From around 1764, Motoori directed all his energies to a study of the *Kojiki* and completed his monumental study *Kojiki den* in 1798. This work is far more than a critical commentary on the *Kojiki;* it is also an examination of the life and thought of the ancient Japanese based upon an exacting analysis of language, and, unlike the works of the Confucian school, it contains no moralistic interpretations.

At about the same time that Norinaga was busy with the *Kojiki,* a friend of his from the same area, also a physician, was at work on a study of the *Nihon shoki.* TANIGAWA KOTOSUGA completed his *Nihon shoki tsūshō* in 1748. *Shoki* studies were further advanced with the *Shoki shikkai* of Kawamura Hidene (1723–92).

Kokugaku scholars were extremely critical of the contemporary society, which was guided by Neo-Confucian ideology. Norinaga, like his predecessors, called for a return to earlier values, concluding from his studies of early literature that the life and thought of the Japanese before the introduction of Buddhism and Confucianism had been simple, uncluttered, straightforward, and highly preferable to that of his own time. After the death of Norinaga in 1801, the Kokugaku school split into two branches: HIRATA ATSUTANE and his followers, who sought to strengthen and spread the idea of a restoration of direct imperial rule, and an academic group led by BAN NOBUTOMO, whose achievements ranged from collation of many ancient texts and commentaries to critical examination of historical events.

The great post-Norinaga contribution in the area of history was made by another Kokugaku scholar, however, Date Chihiro (1802–77), who wrote his *Taisei santenkō* in 1848. *Taisei santenkō* is a history of Japanese political development that examines the social and economic substructures that supported and influenced historical events. His observations and subsequent conclusions led him to divide Japanese history into three periods: the "early period" (pre-645), the "middle period" (645–1185), and the "later period" (1185 to the author's time). Date's division of history corresponds very closely to the clan (UJI), aristocratic, and feudal periods recognized by modern historians.

The rise of critical historical scholarship. Another group of men that contributed greatly to the advancement of Edo-period historiography was the Kōshōgaku (Textual Criticism) school. Kōshōgaku aimed at objective interpretation and evaluation of historical and literary works based on reliable texts established by a process of thoroughgoing textual analysis. The school arose in the latter half of the 18th century and gradually spread among the townsmen of Edo (now Tōkyō), especially among wealthy intellectuals. Its great appeal was that it was a fresh, new academic approach, based upon a rational, scientific spirit unfettered by Neo-Confucianism.

Kōshōgaku developed rapidly, and around the beginning of the 19th century a number of outstanding scholars appeared. HANAWA HOKIICHI, YASHIRO HIROKATA, and Kariya Ekisai (1775–1835), to name only three, undertook textual criticism of a variety of writings and produced a great number of collated texts and commentaries. Ban Nobutomo and others of the Kokugaku school cooperated in the effort, and later even some of the Neo-Confucianists joined in. Kariya Ekisai promoted Kōshōgaku more than any other with his many expertly collated texts and detailed commentaries, but it was Hanawa Hokiichi who made the greatest contribution.

Hokiichi firmly believed that historical writings should faithfully reproduce the shape of past societies and that the ideal history would consist of all the basic primary sources arranged in some meaningful order. As a first step toward the realization of that ideal history, Hokiichi began the compilation of the GUNSHO RUIJŪ in 1779 with the financial backing of the shogunate. He selected more than 3,000 important works on Japanese society and culture, collected available manuscripts, and sought to establish reliable texts for each of the works selected for inclusion. The *Gunsho ruijū* was completed in 1822 after Hokiichi's death, and it remains one of the greatest collections of historical and literary source materials in Japan. During the course of his labors on the *Gunsho ruijū,* Hokiichi established the Wagaku Kōdansho (Institute for Japanese Studies), again with the support of the shogunate. The institute further strengthened activities in investigation, collection, and collation of basic sources. Now Hokiichi was ready to begin his life work. In 1806 he began the compilation of the *Hanawa shiryō,* a chronologically ordered collection of primary historical materials covering 700 years of Japanese history from 887, where the last of the *Rikkokushi* ends, through 1586. The work was not completed during Hokiichi's lifetime, but his disciples carried on until 1861. They were able to complete the collection only up to the year 1024, but the *Hanawa shiryō* was the inspiration and original model for the later DAI NIHON SHIRYŌ. Hokiichi's ideal of assembling reliable historical source materials without actually writing history was far removed from the thinking of traditional Confucian historians, and his efforts mark the turning point toward critical historical scholarship.

At the end of the Edo period the advocates of Kōshōgaku joined with scholars of Kokugaku and Neo-Confucianism, paving the way for the development of modern historical studies in the Meiji period (1868–1912).

The Modern Period——*Toward modern historical scholarship.* Following the Meiji Restoration (1868), significant changes took place both in the concept of history and in historical writing. The modernization program of the new government stimulated in intellectuals an intense desire for knowledge of the West, and countless books were imported and translated into Japanese. Among those books were *Histoire générale de la civilisation en Europe,* by François Guizot (1787–1874), and *History of Civilization in England,* by H. T. Buckle (1821–62). After reading such books, the intellectuals of the time turned to Japan's own past and set about rewriting Japanese history, using Western histories of civilization as their models. A steady stream of books devoted to the history of Japanese civilization appeared in the 1870s and 1880s; the pioneers in this new trend were FUKUZAWA YUKICHI and TAGUCHI UKICHI.

In 1875 Fukuzawa wrote his BUMMEIRON NO GAIRYAKU (An Outline of a Theory of Civilization), in which he directly opposed the Confucian view, arguing that history should be understood in terms of the development of civilization rather than through wars and the achievements of those in power. Taguchi took up this view of history and expanded it in his *Nihon kaika shōshi* (A Short History of the Enlightenment of Japan), written during the period 1877–82. Moreover, he recognized the importance of economic factors in historical development, although he was not altogether successful in presenting Japanese history from an economic perspective. Other books purporting to be histories of civilization followed one after another. Their authors were not professional historians, however, and so despite their fresh approaches, they were not able to back up their ideas with facts and in the end accomplished very little. The "history of civilization" approach was already in decline by the end of the 1880s.

Modern historical scholarship in Japan took an entirely different course. The Meiji government, established under the banner of return to imperial rule, decided in 1869 to sponsor an official compilation of history. After years of preparation, the work was finally begun in 1877 by scholars of the Kōshōgaku school, including SHIGENO YASUTSUGU, KUME KUNITAKE, and Hoshino Hisashi (1839–1917). The original plan was to start from the year 887, where the *Rikkokushi* left off, but because the *Dai Nihon shi,* highly respected at the time, already detailed events of that period, it was decided to begin with the year 1318. The work was to be called *Dai Nippon hennenshi* (Chronological History of Japan).

Once work was under way, however, the editors discovered an increasing number of points of questionable accuracy within the *Dai Nihon shi,* and a thorough review of it became the first order of the day. Using reliable new source materials, these historians, trained in the Kōshōgaku method, examined the accuracy of the *Dai Nihon shi* and eliminated from the text all points raising even the slightest doubt.

Establishment of a new academic tradition. In 1886 the department of history was set up at Tōkyō University, and two years later Shigeno, Kume, and Hoshino were appointed professors. They took their project with them. A year after their arrival, the department of Japanese history was established. Around the same time, the Shigakukai (Historical Society of Japan) was founded and began the publication of *Shigaku zasshi* (Historical Journal).

During these years, links were forged with modern German historical scholarship. In 1887 Ludwig RIESS, a German historian and student of Leopold von Ranke, was invited to Tōkyō University as professor of history. It was Riess who introduced to the Japanese Ranke's historical method, whose primary emphasis was on the importance of scientific study of historical data through rigorous source criticism. Riess advised Japanese historians to avoid making value judgments on historical events. The Ranke method was readily accepted by those Japanese historians who had maintained the Kōshōgaku tradition; Riess's arguments further convinced them of the

validity of their approach, and they redoubled their efforts to establish a modern, critical approach to history at Tōkyō University.

Shigeno and his colleagues, in the meantime, had continued their critical dissection of the *Dai Nihon shi* and struggled to eliminate the Confucian viewpoint that permeated that work. The further they progressed with their work, the closer they came to a direct confrontation with the authority of the *Dai Nihon shi.* The *Dai Nihon shi* was considered by the nationalists at that time to be the absolute authority on Japanese history, and conflict was inevitable. Kume Kunitake lit the fuse in 1891 when he published an article describing Shintō as an ancient practice of heaven worship. The nationalists' anger and indignation toward historians at Tōkyō University exploded when the article was reprinted in 1892, and Kume was forced to resign his post. In 1893 work on the *Dai Nippon hennenshi* was discontinued, and Shigeno, too, was forced to resign.

The departure of Kume and Shigeno was a tremendous blow. Not only did it signal the loss of academic freedom, but it also held grave implications for the future of Japanese historical studies. After this incident the academic historians became discouraged and lapsed into silence, fearing possible government repercussions. In 1895, however, compilation of history was resumed under quite a different concept at what is now known as the HISTORIOGRAPHICAL INSTITUTE (the institute, founded in 1869, had become a part of Tōkyō University in 1888): the institute would undertake collection, source criticism, and compilation of primary historical materials that would result in two companion publications, DAI NIHON SHIRYŌ and DAI NIHON KOMONJO, which began to appear in 1901. *Dai Nihon shiryō* is a monumental collection of primary materials chronologically arranged from the year 887 until 1867. *Dai Nihon komonjo* is a vast collection of old documents divided into three types: documents of the 8th century, documents of single institutions or famous families, and documents of the later Edo period concerning foreign relations. The *Shiryō* involved some editorial trimming and arrangement, but the *Komonjo* reproduced the primary sources in their entirety without change. These two publications laid the foundation for all Japanese historical research on the premodern period and have contributed incalculably to its development. Far from complete even now, publication is expected to continue over many more decades.

By the beginning of the 20th century the Historiographical Institute at Tōkyō University had already achieved its present preeminence in historical study and research. Maintaining a close relationship with the university's department of Japanese history, the institute became the center of the mainstream of Japanese historical scholarship and exerted a great influence upon the future course of historiography. Valuing accuracy, objectivity, and thoroughness, and rejecting metahistorical speculation, the institute found it impossible to apply its approach to certain subjects after the Kume incident. In particular, matters that touched upon the imperial house were avoided altogether.

In the broader and noncontroversial field of Asian history, however, men like SHIRATORI KURAKICHI, unfettered by government pressure, started to bring out pioneering works on the histories of various nations. In European history, men like TSUBOI KUMEZŌ, after study in Germany, returned to Japan and engaged actively in introducing European and specifically German techniques of historical investigation and research. The Nihon Rekishi Chiri Gakkai (Japan Historical Geography Society), a newly organized and energetic group, began to publish its journal *Rekishi chiri* (Historical Geography). Talented young historians in the field of Japanese history appeared from among Tōkyō University graduates, including KUROITA KATSUMI, UCHIDA GINZŌ, Hara Katsurō (1871–1924), and MIURA HIROYUKI. Kuroita produced his *Nihon komonjo yōshiki ron* in 1903, a work that laid the foundations of *komonjogaku,* or the study of old documents (see DIPLOMATICS). This was followed in 1908 by his *Kokushi no kenkyū,* a standard text on historical method and on the political history of Japan. Uchida and Hara, men well versed in European history, attempted new interpretations of Japanese history, Uchida with his study of the early modern period, *Nihon kinsei shi* (1903), and Hara with a study of the medieval period, *Nihon chūsei shi* (1906). Miura explored the new field of legal history. In 1907 a department of Japanese history was established at Kyōto University, and Uchida, Hara, and Miura were appointed as professors. Although the three men carried with them the academic traditions of Tōkyō University, in Kyōto they established a tradition that was to remain relatively independent from that of their alma mater.

The broadening of perspectives and interests. From about 1910, historical research became increasingly specialized: historians focused upon specific periods while exploring various fields, including legal, economic, religious, and literary history. New attempts were made to synthesize the various areas and to grasp the total picture of Japanese history from a viewpoint entirely different from those employed before. The historical writings that resulted are known as cultural histories *(bunkashi)*, but they went far beyond cultural history in its narrow sense. They aimed at a new approach that drew on political, economic, and other fields of history as well as cultural history, a break from earlier works, which had focused mainly on political history. Cultural histories of this type appeared one after another from the time of World War I. Representative of this trend is the *Nihon bunka shi*, a 12-volume set published by Daitōkaku in 1922. Two particularly wide-ranging works of this type were *Nihon bunka shi josetsu* (1932; An Introduction to the History of Japanese Culture) by Nishida Naojirō (1886–1964), presented first as a series of lectures in 1924, and *Nihon seishin shi kenkyū* (1926; Studies on the History of Japanese Thought) by WATSUJI TETSURŌ.

At the same time that these cultural histories were coming out, a school of socioeconomic history appeared on the scene. The economic panic that followed World War I and the resultant social instability aroused widespread interest in social problems, an interest that resulted in the scholarly examination of social problems in Japan's past. Particularly notable were *Kokushijō no shakai mondai* (1920; Social Problems in Japanese History) by Miura Hiroyuki, and *Nihon shakai shi* (1924; History of Japanese Society) by his colleague Honjō Eijirō (1888–1973). The issues addressed by these scholars included the economic relations among social classes; the link was forged between social and economic history very early. Somewhat later, a group of scholars that included Kokushō Iwao (1895–1949), Tsuchiya Takao (b 1896), and Ono Takeo (1883–1949) focused upon the economic elements that underlay social problems, leading them to specialized research in all branches of economic history, including agriculture, fishing, industry, business, trade, transportation, and so on. They planned to write a history of Japan through a systematic approach that drew on all fields of history—political, legal, social, intellectual, etc—but that centered on economic history. In 1930 the Shakai Keizai Shi Gakkai (The Social and Economic History Society) was formed, beginning a period of fruitful research that has continued to the present.

Academic historians after World War I were active in cultural and socioeconomic history, but they avoided any research that might possibly provoke confrontation with government authorities. One historian, however, TSUDA SŌKICHI, a man who made great contributions to the development of historical studies of the ancient period, dared to take up subjects that for scholars at government schools were taboo. In 1913 Tsuda published his *Jindaishi no atarashii kenkyū* (New Studies on the History of the Age of the Gods) and in 1919 *Kojiki oyobi Nihon shoki no shin kenkyū* (New Studies of the *Kojiki* and *Nihon shoki*); these two books were followed by a series of scrupulously objective analytical studies of the Japanese classics. Tsuda was able to show that the opening mythological sections and the following sections on the earliest emperors in both the *Kojiki* and the *Nihon shoki* were fabrications motivated by political purposes and that the first 14 emperors, at least from Jimmu through Chūai, were either fictitious or of questionable historicity. Tsuda was also a pioneer in intellectual history; his book *Bungaku ni arawaretaru waga kokumin shisō no kenkyū* (1916–21; Studies on the Thought of Our People as Expressed in Literature) was the first attempt to explore the historical evolution of Japanese thought. In spite of all his achievements, Tsuda's reward from the government came in 1940 in the form of indictment and conviction for lese majesty.

Another man who, like Tsuda, stood outside the pale of the academic historians but contributed greatly to modern Japanese historiography was YANAGITA KUNIO. Yanagita devoted his life to establishing Japanese folklore as a subject of academic study and devising new approaches and methods for the study of folk life and culture. He sought to shed light on the history of the Japanese masses through fieldwork exploring oral traditions, folk customs, and other ethnological materials in all parts of the country. His method and approach supplemented and strengthened the research of academic historians who relied solely upon written sources.

The trends described above continued through the 1920s; toward the end of that decade writings based on historical materialism were introduced by men like HANI GORŌ and HATTORI SHISŌ, whose ideas were very quickly taken up by younger scholars. Historians who agreed with their historical views formed the Rekishigaku Kenkyūkai (Historical Science Society) in 1932, and began publication of the journal *Rekishigaku kenkyū* (Journal of Historical Studies). His-

torical materialism was born from the straitened circumstances that accompanied the SHŌWA DEPRESSION. Some historians and social scientists who were attracted by Marxism attempted to use it to explain the development of Japanese capitalism and its social structure. This resulted in Hattori Shisō's *Meiji ishin shi* (1928; History of the Meiji Restoration) and NORO EITARŌ's *Nihon shihon shugi hattatsu shi* (1930; Lectures on the History of the Development of Japanese Capitalism). These were followed by a cooperative work, *Nihon shihon shugi hattatsu shi kōza* (1932–33; Studies on the Development of Japanese Capitalism), an archetypal application of Marxist theory to the Japanese situation. These studies focused upon the Meiji Restoration in an attempt to apply a Marxist theoretical framework to explain the events of Japan's history. These historians' activities were short-lived, however; they disappeared around 1935 almost as rapidly as they had appeared, stifled by the government's suppression of Marxism.

From around 1935 until the end of World War II nationalist historians were preeminent in Japan. The Japanese government early on recognized the importance of Japanese history courses in the schools to foster a spirit of nationalism based upon reverence for the emperor; all history textbooks since the Meiji period had been edited with that purpose in mind. In the 1930s this tendency became more pronounced, with Japanese history treated as the history of an empire ruled by divine emperors. During this difficult period some academic historians cooperated with the government and helped in the rewriting of history for political ends.

Recent Trends in Historiography——After Japan's defeat in 1945, the histories written by the ultranationalists totally disappeared. Ancient history was emancipated from myth, and for the first time an objective approach to history became possible; all fetters on historical research were removed.

The first to dominate in the liberated atmosphere following the war were those who had held to the materialistic view of history. Works like *Chūseiteki sekai no keisei* (Formation of the Medieval World) by Ishimoda Shō (b 1912) and *Nihon kodai kokka* (The Ancient Japanese State) by Tōma Seita (b 1913), both published in 1946, were refreshing to the scholarly world in the years immediately following the war. *Rekishigaku kenkyū* replaced *Shigaku zasshi* as the leading historical journal, and for more than 10 years the writings of Marxist-oriented historians held sway. However, the inflexible Marxist theoretical framework that informed their work eventually caused a split between them and members of the traditional academic school of historiography who insisted upon objectivity.

This antagonism, however, gradually diminished around 1960, and a new situation developed in which Japanese historical studies could be advanced through the cooperative efforts of both sides. This rapprochement was not the result of compromise; the two sides drew together naturally as their respective scholarly efforts progressed. Marxist historians came to recognize the importance of strict objectivity and critical examination of historical data. Some men from the traditional school were able to go beyond their previous preoccupation with factual knowledge and attempt to understand Japanese history in theoretical terms, grasping historical developments structurally and dynamically. Inoue Mitsusada (1917–83), for example, in his *Nihon kodai shi no shomondai* (1949; Problems in the Study of Ancient Japanese History), and his later work *Nihon kodai kokka no kenkyū* (1965; Studies on the Ancient Japanese State), attempted a new interpretation of ancient history from a non-Marxist standpoint. The gradual union of these once-opposed groups within the Japanese historical world has led to the present dignified and active state of research.

Among the various fields of research since World War II, those that have made the most significant strides are probably social and economic history, local history, and the history of the Japanese masses. The most notable advances in work on specific periods of history have been in the once tabooed ancient period and in the early modern and modern periods, all areas that were largely ignored by the mainstream of academic historians prior to the war. Recently, there has been increasing cooperation between Japanese historians and scholars in other related fields. The concerns and activities of Japanese historians are growing broader, while at the same time research within the various fields of history is becoming more specialized.

■——W. G. Beasley and E. G. Pulleyblank, ed, *Historians of China and Japan* (1961). Ienaga Saburō, *Nihon no kindai shigaku* (1957). Izu Kimio, *Shimpan Nihon shigakushi* (1972). Kiyohara Sadao, *Nihon shigakushi* (1928). Nihon Shisōshi Kenkyūkai, ed, *Nihon ni okeru rekishi shisō no tenkai* (1965). Ōkubo Toshiaki, *Nihon kindai shigakushi* (1940). Ozawa Eiichi, *Kindai Nihon shigakushi no kenkyū*, 2 vols (1966–68). Ozawa Eiichi, *Kinsei shigaku shisō shi kenkyū* (1974). Rekishigaku Kenkyūkai and Nihonshi Kenkyūkai, ed, *Nihon shigakushi*, vol 8 of *Nihon rekishi kōza* (Tōkyō Daigaku Shuppankai, 1957). Sakamoto Tarō, *Nihon no shūshi to shigaku* (1958). *Sengo Nihon shigaku no tenkai*, vol 24 of *Iwanami kōza: Nihon rekishi* (Iwanami Shoten, 1977). Shigakukai, ed, *Hompō shigakushi ronsō*, 2 vols (1939). Noburu HIRAGA

history of Japan

prehistory
protohistory
Asuka history (mid-6th century to 710)
Nara history (710–794)
Heian history (794–1185)
Kamakura history (1185–1333)
Muromachi history (1333–1568)
Azuchi-Momoyama history (1568–1600)
Edo history (1600–1868)
Meiji history (1868–1912)
Taishō and early Shōwa history (1912–1945)
postwar history (from 1945)

PREHISTORY

(senshi jidai). That portion of the human past which predates written records and can be known only through archaeological investigation (see ARCHAEOLOGY for the development of the discipline in Japan). The prehistoric era in Japan opened during the Pleistocene epoch (Ice Age), when human groups from the continent first occupied the archipelago, and lasted until the first few centuries AD, when activities in Japan began to be recorded in the Chinese dynastic histories. The periods archaeologists traditionally use to study Japanese prehistory are recognized to be fairly arbitrary subdivisions of the country's past, and the boundaries between them are currently being challenged by new discoveries and research.

The paleolithic period (*kyūsekki jidai*, also called the preceramic period) is characterized by cultural remains, mainly chipped stone tools, that predate 10,000 BC. There is great debate over when this period began, that is, when the first peoples occupied the Japanese islands, but the end of the period is marked by the initiation of neolithic pottery manufacture.

The Jōmon period (ca 10,000 BC–ca 300 BC) is generally identified with hunting and gathering ways of life, especially the intense utilization of marine resources in shellfish collecting and deep-sea fishing. The name of this period derives from the *jōmon* (cordmarkings) that decorate much of the pottery made during this time (see JŌMON POTTERY).

The Yayoi period (ca 300 BC–ca AD 300) designates the time of establishment and elaboration of agricultural life, culminating in complex regional political development. The period was named after the place in Tōkyō where the first Yayoi pottery was discovered (see MUKŌGAOKA SHELL MOUND).

The Yayoi period was succeeded by the Kofun or Yamato period (ca 300–710), for which see the following section on protohistory.

Paleolithic Period (pre-10,000 BC)——Geological and environmental factors form an important background for the study of the Pleistocene cultures of Japan. First, the chronological ordering of Japanese paleolithic remains rests primarily on stratigraphical information. Second, climatic changes and lowered sea levels dramatically altered the appearance and form of the country at that time, necessitating the interpretation of archaeological remains according to those ancient, and not modern, conditions. Throughout most of the late Pleistocene, Hokkaidō was a continuous part of the cold Siberian plains. Climatic changes were less extreme in southern Japan. Lowered sea levels exposed coastal shelves to form periodic land connections especially between 20,000 and 18,000 years ago between the Korean peninsula and the area of Kyūshū and western Honshū. Their climatic differences and the fact that they were connected with different parts of the Asian mainland caused northern and southern Japan to form separate cultural spheres throughout the paleolithic period.

Paleolithic artifacts were first discovered in Japan by the amateur archaeologist AIZAWA TADAHIRO in 1946. Since then, more than

1,000 sites dating from the Pleistocene have been located throughout the country. The vast majority of these sites offer little more than a thin scatter of stone tools, but recently a few hints of architectural remains have been found. Few sites have yielded bone tools or faunal remains which might aid in cultural reconstruction, thus little is known about the cultures and lifeways of this period. Well stratified paleolithic period sites, like the NOGAWA SITE in the Kantō region, are rare, and it has proved difficult to date a site with radiocarbon analysis. The establishment of a cultural chronology, therefore, has tended to focus on detailed typological analysis of stone artifacts.

The name "early paleolithic" has been given to a small number of generally crude tool assemblages which are more than 30,000 years old, some maybe dating to the last interglacial (between 100,000 and 70,000 years ago). Occurring at such sites as the FUKUI CAVE and Sōzudai in Kyūshū and in the KANTŌ LOAM strata of the IWAJUKU SITE and HOSHINO SITE on the northern margins of the Kantō Plain, these crude choppers and flake tools have been compared to similar assemblages reported from Zhoukoudian (Chouk'ou-tien) and other sites in North China. Land bridges exposed by lowered sea levels would have allowed human contact between China and Japan, but scholarly agreement on the age of the first human occupation of the islands is still to be had. Many Japanese and foreign archaeologists categorically deny the antiquity of the assemblages, which is based primarily on similarities with continental examples, but more often the detractors simply doubt the human origin of the crude objects assigned to the period.

Late paleolithic remains dating between ca 28,000 and ca 10,000 BC are dramatically different from earlier remains. After about 28,000 BC, there was a sudden increase in the number of sites, and eventually stone tools in northern Japan began to be made with a blade technology similar to that used by other upper paleolithic peoples of Eurasia. These tools have been arranged into a sequence of types based on relatively minor technological variations. The meaning of these variations, however, has been interpreted differently by different groups of scholars, resulting in contrasting views of Japan's cultural relations with the continent. One school interprets new tool types as products of internal cultural development through time, thus proposing that Japan formed a separate cultural area even though it was not yet isolated by water. Another school views innovations as infusions from the outside; because of the land connections, there unquestionably were close links between Hokkaidō and Siberia, and artifact similarities suggest that southern Japan was also sharing in general developments of the North China–Manchuria area. Clearly, some developments were independently made in Japan, but the relative dearth of archaeological data for continental regions surrounding Japan makes it difficult to study external affinities of Japanese materials (see PALEOLITHIC CULTURE).

If the cultural affinities of the Japanese paleolithic cultures are unclear, only slightly more can be said about the lifeways during that period. Paleolithic peoples probably occupied the wide expanses of coastal shelves exposed by lowered sea levels during the terminal Pleistocene. However, modern sea levels have inundated these areas, limiting our knowledge to the small sites surviving in the present plain and hilly upland zone. These appear to have been created by small mobile groups performing several kinds of activity in a well-rounded, generalized (rather than highly specialized) hunting and gathering economy. High quality raw materials for stone-tool manufacture were traded over long distances; for example, obsidian from Nagano Prefecture was worked by groups on the outskirts of modern Tōkyō. Cultural uniformity over fairly large areas seems to have been typical of this period.

Jōmon Period (ca 10,000–ca 300 BC)——Because it lasted so long and was marked by considerable cultural diversity, the Jōmon period has presented archaeologists with the knotty problem of sorting out the various Jōmon cultures and arranging them in chronological order. Initial research focused mainly on ceramic remains, and their analysis led to the establishment by YAMANOUCHI SUGAO of five temporal subdivisions of the Jōmon period based on changes in pottery styles; a sixth phase, Incipient Jōmon, has since been recognized. The Jōmon ceramic tradition which remained in the northern Tōhoku region and Hokkaidō even into the early historical periods is often designated as Continuing Jōmon. This is a cultural rather than a phase designation and Continuing Jōmon eventually became the SATSUMON CULTURE in the 8th century.

It might be noted here that there is some disagreement among archaeologists over the dates of the Jōmon phases and the inclusion of the earliest phase in the Jōmon period. The dates employed here

History of Japan

Phases of the Jōmon Period

Phase	Japanese name	Dates
Incipient (Subearliest) Jōmon	Jōmon Sōsōki	ca 10,000 BC–ca 7500 BC
Initial (Earliest) Jōmon	Jōmon Sōki	ca 7500 BC–ca 5000 BC
Early Jōmon	Jōmon Zenki	ca 5000 BC–ca 3500 BC
Middle Jōmon	Jōmon Chūki	ca 3500 BC–ca 2000 BC (ca 3500 BC–ca 2500 BC)
Late Jōmon	Jōmon Kōki	ca 2000 BC–ca 1000 BC (ca 2500 BC–ca 1000 BC)
Final (Latest) Jōmon	Jōmon Banki	ca 1000 BC–ca 300 BC

NOTE: The phase names and dates listed in this table represent those most widely employed and have been adopted for use throughout this encyclopedia. Those provided in parentheses are the variations preferred by some scholars.

for the Jōmon phases are derived from radiocarbon datings of sites throughout Japan. They are given with variations in the table together with the phase names in Japanese and their English equivalents.

The technological innovation which is used to mark the end of the paleolithic period is the appearance of pottery manufacture. It is possible that this was an independent invention made in Japan, although a few archaeologists believe that the pottery technique spread to Japan from the mainland. In any case, the world's oldest known ceramic vessels have been excavated from sites in western Japan such as the Fukui Cave in Nagasaki Prefecture and the Kami Kuroiwa Rock-Shelter in Ehime Prefecture, where sherds have been securely dated between 10,750 and 10,200 BC. Additional early ceramic remains have been found from the Kyūshū to southern Tōhoku regions, most often in caves in hilly parts of the country.

The time of earliest pottery manufacture between ca 10,000 and ca 7500 BC is frequently included in the Jōmon period as its Incipient phase, but some Japanese archaeologists prefer to consider it as a separate transitional or mesolithic era. Indeed, it appears to stand midway between paleolithic and Jōmon-style lifeways. Hunting and gathering in the interior hills continued to be the economic focus of this period as before, pottery being "grafted" on with little apparent impact. There is no evidence of the utilization of coastal areas or resources which characterizes later Jōmon culture. Thus there is no indication that pottery manufacture was caused by or in turn triggered immediate changes in subsistence or settlement patterns.

Initial and Early Jōmon periods. Around 10,000 BC there began a warming trend in worldwide climate, reaching optimum temperatures between ca 8000 and ca 4000 BC. The results in Japan were the severing of land connections with the Asian mainland caused by rising sea levels, the dramatic increase in available shellfish and fish resources accompanying the warming of the ocean waters around Japan, and the creation of new vegetation zones of deciduous forest in the northeast and broad-leaf evergreen forest in the southwest. This new environment formed the context for early Jōmon development, and although the climate did not remain entirely static throughout the Jōmon period, successive adaptations retained the basic cultural patterns established in the Initial Jōmon phase between ca 7500 and ca 5000 BC.

The major innovation of the Initial Jōmon was the utilization of marine and coastal resources, leading to the accumulation of the first SHELL MOUNDS in Japan. However, as the contents of the most famous early shell midden, Natsushima near Tōkyō Bay, illustrate, these resources were integrated into a well-rounded economy: in addition to fish and shellfish collection, deer and wild pig were hunted. The presence of grinding stones, stone axes, and storage pits in these early sites is clear evidence that wild seeds and other plant foods were also used.

In terms of material culture, several characteristic Jōmon artifacts such as clay figurines (see JŌMON FIGURINES) and tanged chipped stone knives appeared at this time. Pottery with true *jōmon* cord-markings, made by rolling a twisted cord or coil over the semi-dry vessel surface, began to be made, and PIT HOUSES came to be used. However, despite the advent of these universal Jōmon features, a clear cultural difference between eastern and western Japan developed during the Initial Jōmon. These cultural spheres roughly correspond to the complementary distribution of northeastern deciduous

forest and southwestern broad-leaf evergreen forest. These differences, which were not apparent during the Incipient Jōmon phase, continued throughout the rest of the Jōmon period once they were established.

Between ca 5000 and ca 3500 BC in Early Jōmon, the worldwide period of warm temperatures and correspondingly high sea levels reached its peak. In Japan, coastal lowlands like the Kantō Plain were turned into broad tidal swamps. Simple coastal gathering seems to have been an effective means of utilizing the resources, so that huge accumulations of seashells and fishbones were made at this time. In western Japan and the Ryūkyūs, deep-sea fishing may have also been undertaken; similarities between the Sōbata incised pottery of Kyūshū and Comb Pattern (or Geometric) pottery of Korea indicate that there was waterborne contact between these areas.

Middle Jōmon period. During the Middle Jōmon period between ca 3500 and ca 2000 BC (also dated as ca 3500 BC–ca 2500 BC), the cultural center of the Jōmon world seems to have shifted from the coasts to interior regions. This phase was marked by a dramatic increase in the number of sites in the area of the northern Kantō and the adjacent Chūbu region. Moreover, coastal portions of the Kantō and Tōhoku regions which had been intensively inhabited in the Initial and Early Jōmon were somewhat depopulated at this time. The population shift may have been caused by receding sea levels which diminished the economic potential of coastal zones, or may have been the result of improved methods of exploiting plant resources available in the interior. A number of archaeologists are even convinced that some Middle Jōmon peoples actually cultivated taro, nuts, and other crops. Whether or not it reached a point that can be considered true agriculture, there is no question that plant utilization was very intense during this period. The flamboyantly encrusted pottery, figurines, and ornaments made by Middle Jōmon peoples are often presented as their major achievements, but the tenor of Middle Jōmon lifestyle is best understood through their semi-sedentary village patterns and the plant-processing equipment—grinding stones and sealable storage jars—that they used.

Late and Final Jōmon periods. After about 2000 BC, a more vigorous marine economy developed along the Pacific coast of eastern Japan. The fishermen of this Late Jōmon phase invented a vast array of tools and techniques which allowed them to undertake true deep-sea fishing. After about 1000 BC in the Final Jōmon period, a cultural florescence in this same area was marked by the spread of a series of ceramic styles known collectively as Kamegaoka pottery (see KAMEGAOKA SITE) from the Tōhoku region and from as far west as Nara Prefecture. The social mechanisms that spread these aesthetically beautiful and technically excellent potteries across such a wide area are unknown, but it is important to note that the Jōmon cultures which produced Kamegaoka pottery were not associated with any changes in the basic Jōmon lifestyle.

Southwestern Japan in the last millenium BC was not part of the Kamegaoka cultural sphere. But ceramic data indicate that Kyūshū and western Honshū were in contact with the Korean peninsula during Final Jōmon. Moreover, it appears that continental techniques of wet rice cultivation were introduced into Kyūshū around 300 BC. The introduction of rice and its immediate impact on Jōmon groups is being intensively studied, though clearly such cultivation represented a major break with preceding Jōmon subsistence patterns. Nevertheless, Jōmon lifeways survived in the far north throughout the protohistoric and early historic periods.

Yayoi Period (ca 300 BC–ca AD 300) —— Although it accounts for a relatively brief part of Japan's prehistoric past, the Yayoi period was critically important. It can be viewed as a transitional phase during which Japan changed from a land of hunting and gathering cultures to one of rice cultivators organized into the petty political units of the succeeding KOFUN PERIOD (ca AD 300–710). It was the time when rice-farming communities became the major integrators of Japanese rural society; the seasonal rounds, social patterns, and spiritual values which regulated the lives of most Japanese until very recently originated in Yayoi agricultural life. The biological and linguistic roots of the modern Japanese can also be traced back to this time. From the time of wet rice introduction around 300 BC, the Yayoi period is divided into three equal phases of 200 years each: Early (ca 300 BC–ca 100 BC), Middle (ca 100 BC–ca AD 100), and Late (ca 100–ca 300).

Early Yayoi agricultural complex. The earliest Yayoi agricultural sites are concentrated in northern Kyūshū, pinpointing the spot of introduction of wet rice agricultural technology from the continent. Once established there, the agricultural way of life spread quickly through the Inland Sea area, reaching Aichi Prefecture by ca 100 BC.

Until recently, the foreign elements in the Early Yayoi cultural assemblage—BRONZE WEAPONS, agricultural tools, and rice technology itself—were thought to reflect a unitary influx of new people and ideas from the continent. However, no known cultural complex from the mainland matches the culture of the Early Yayoi period, and clear continuity from the Jōmon period is now recognized in YAYOI POTTERY and chipped stone tool types. Thus it is now thought that the foreign elements entered Japan singly throughout later Jōmon and early Yayoi times, then mixed together with the traditional Jōmon culture to create a native Yayoi cultural complex.

Early Yayoi peoples practiced a mixed economy in which hunting and gathering were combined with cultivation of wet rice. Shellfish was an important food source as in the Late Jōmon phases, and shell mounds continued to be deposited until Middle Yayoi. Settlements of pit houses were invariably located near low, marshy areas where rice could be sown in simple paddies without complex irrigation facilities. It is possible that Jōmon patterns of hunting and wild plant gathering continued in the surrounding hilly areas, and they certainly formed the main lifeways of the remaining Jōmon peoples in northern Honshū and Hokkaidō.

Agricultural intensification and cultural expansion. The Middle Yayoi period witnessed the development of water control systems and new tools, probably including iron or iron-edged ones. These greatly increased agricultural productivity, resulting in the explosive increase of farming villages in the plains areas of Kyūshū and western Honshū, settlements of up to ten pit houses being especially common in the Kinki region. By ca AD 100, even narrow valleys and upland areas could be cultivated, and the Yayoi cultural complex had penetrated well into northern Honshū. The strong "local color" of the pottery and other tools of this period suggests that there was little political or economic organization above the level of the individual community.

The Late Yayoi period saw the development of relatively complex political units whose earliest manifestations were described by continental travelers in the 3rd-century Chinese WEI ZHI *(Wei chih)*. (See next section on protohistory.) It is doubtful that the authors of these accounts traveled beyond northern Kyūshū, but they describe Japan as a land of small socially stratified "countries" *(kuni)* bound together by trade and economic interdependence. This, of course, exactly parallels the picture derived from the archaeological record. See also YAYOI CULTURE.

——Peter Bleed, "Yayoi Cultures of Japan: An Interpretive Summary," *Arctic Anthropology* 9.2 (1972). Chester S. Chard, *Northeast Asia in Prehistory* (1974). Fumiko Ikawa-Smith, *Early Paleolithic of South and East Asia* (1978). J. Edward Kidder, *Japan Before Buddhism* (rev ed, 1966). *Kodaishi hakkutsu*, 10 vols (Kōdansha, 1973–74). Richard Pearson, "Paleo-environment and Human Settlement in Japan and Korea," *Science*, 197.4310 (1977).

Peter BLEED

PROTOHISTORY

Protohistory refers to the period of transition from the prehistoric period with no written records to the historical period with written records. Opinions differ as to exactly what time should be assigned to the protohistoric period in Japan, and where to draw the boundaries. Some scholars would extend the protohistoric period from the 3rd century BC to the 7th century AD (see ARCHAEOLOGY: protohistoric archaeology); however, the most commonly accepted thinking today considers the protohistoric period to extend from the latter half of the Yayoi period (ca 300 BC–ca AD 300) to the middle of the Kofun or Yamato period (ca AD 300–710), and for the historic period to begin from the ASUKA PERIOD (latter part of 6th century to 710).

The written materials from this period are fragmentary in nature and limited in quantity and consequently, research into this period is heavily dependent on archaeological and ethnological data and the like. Contemporary Chinese written records extant today include the late-1st-century chronicle *Han shu*, the 3rd-century chronicle WEI ZHI *(Wei chih)*, and the 4th–5th-century chronicle *Hou Han shu*. Other materials concerning the protohistoric period were edited in later ages. Although there is more written documentation for the Kofun period than for the earlier Yayoi period, it is impossible to achieve a complete historical understanding of the period through that material alone, and archaeological site and artifact research is the main means of investigating both the Yayoi and Kofun periods.

During the protohistoric period in Japan, Japanese social and political organization evolved from a complex of regional agricultural communities in the Yayoi period to a unified state in the Late Kofun period.

Late Yayoi Period——The development of agricultural society during the Yayoi period has been described in the previous section on prehistory. In addition to village remains and material culture as known through archaeology, historical sources for the period are available in the Chinese dynastic histories.

The earliest written reference to Japan occurs in the *Han shu*, a history of the Former Han dynasty (206 BC–AD 8) which speaks of a land beyond Korea divided into more than 100 small polities that sent tribute missions to the Han court. (The later *Hou Han shu* provides valuable information on conditions in Japan in the 1st and 2nd centuries and also details the tribute missions of 57 and 107. The continental goods found deposited in Middle to Late Yayoi burials in northern Kyūshū—bronze mirrors, bronze weapons, and jade ornaments—are thought to have been obtained in conjunction with these missions, and a gold seal [KAN NO WA NO NA NO KOKUŌ NO IN] discovered in 1784 in modern Fukuoka Prefecture is considered to have been presented to a "king" in a small northern Kyūshū "country" by the Later Han emperor Guangwu [Kuang-wu] in 57.) After the 1st-century *Han shu* the next mention of Japan is in the reports on non-Chinese peoples included in the Wei-dynasty chronicle, the *Wei zhi*. This 3rd-century account is especially valuable for its description of contemporary Japanese culture, and it also refers to small "countries" like YAMATAI ruled by kings and queens.

However, care must be taken in reading these Chinese descriptions, for they exhibit the tendency of any advanced society to interpret simpler social systems in terms of their own sophisticated organizations. Nevertheless, both the archaeological record and the Chinese documents concur on the structure of Japanese society in the 3rd century as a number of polities integrated by trade conducted between economically specialized villages and regulated by common agricultural rites involving the ceremonial use of imported bronze mirrors and locally produced bronze bells (DŌTAKU) and weapons.

The *Wei zhi* also mentions that the people of WA (Japan) traveled to the southern Korean coast to obtain iron. Tools made from Korean iron were in use in Japan from Middle Yayoi, and by Late Yayoi, iron sickles were plentiful enough to entirely replace polished stone reaping knives. Increased agricultural production due to the efficiency of iron over stone tools provided more resources (including people) to be tapped by leaders, and the importance of agricultural production to Late Yayoi social evolution cannot be overstated. Iron was also important in the increasingly militaristic trend of Late Yayoi society. Warfare between the small "countries" of the Japanese islands mentioned in the *Wei zhi* was confirmed by archaeological evidence of bronze arrowhead production and the establishment of hilltop sites, thought by archaeologists to be protective retreats.

References to tomb building also occur in the *Wei zhi*'s account of the woman ruler HIMIKO: a tomb 100 paces in size was supposed to have been erected upon her death around 250, though no known tomb can presently be identified with Himiko. The construction of large KOFUN (tomb mounds) is a clear indication of the stratification of society into two classes of rulers and ruled. Such stratification was probably brought about by the combination of several trends in Late Yayoi society: increased agricultural efficiency resulting in greater population and resources, the need for iron resources to maintain production, competition between groups to control all such resources, and the stimulation of social institutions through renewed contact with the continent.

The building of large tomb mounds with magnificent grave goods is used to define the beginning of the Kofun period and fully stratified society. Although the historical date for the beginning of tomb building is placed at about 250, archaeological estimates favor approximately 300. See also YAYOI CULTURE.

Gina Lee BARNES

Early and Middle Kofun Period——The Kofun period (ca 300–710) was a time of continued transition during which Japan changed from a land of small polities to a unified state with a strong central government and a vital civilization. This was also the time when the art of writing, using China's well-developed system, took root in Japan, though few records from this period remain. Nevertheless, in addition to Chinese documentary sources and some native Japanese INSCRIPTIONS, the events of the Kofun period are recorded in the earliest chronicles of Japan, the KOJIKI and NIHON SHOKI, compiled in the early 8th century. Thus, the Kofun period can be studied both archaeologically and historically.

The Kofun or Tomb period is characterized archaeologically by large tomb mounds (KOFUN). The origin of this burial pattern can probably be traced to the mounded burials of the Late Yayoi period (ca 100–ca 300). A number of different kinds of mounds were raised but the most distinct were the "keyhole tombs," so called because their outlines when viewed from the air resemble old-fashioned keyhole shapes. Many of the tombs were ringed with large ceramic sculptures called HANIWA portraying a wide range of people and objects and presumably representing the entourage of the important person buried in the mound. The mounds were built throughout western Japan until well into the 6th century. After the introduction of Buddhism from the continent in the mid-6th century, the leaders of Japanese society devoted their wealth to creation of temples, and eventually Buddhist burial patterns came to the fore. Changes in the tombs and their contents are used to divide the Kofun period into Early (4th century), Middle (5th century) and Late (6th–7th centuries) phases.

The tomb mounds of the earliest part of the Kofun period were relatively small. Often they made use of a natural hill, which was remodeled to a round or keyhole shape. The body was placed in a simple slab-lined chamber in a log coffin. Funerary goods placed in the early mounds include carved stone and glass ornaments, utilitarian iron implements, and bronze mirrors as well as straight iron swords, armor, and saddlery. The burial mounds raised after the 4th century differ in many ways from the earlier ones. They are often quite large and typically built in clusters on low, flat land. These clusters apparently reflect the graves of the local elite, perhaps the leaders of local political units known historically as UJI. The fact that some of the mounds and mound clusters are bigger than others is thought to reflect status differences within and between regional groups. The largest 5th-century tombs are located on the southern plains in Ōsaka Prefecture (see NINTOKU MAUSOLEUM; ŌJIN MAUSOLEUM); thus, this area is considered to have been the political center of the Japanese islands at that time.

In the Early and Middle Kofun period, it is clear archaeologically as well as historically that the Japanese were in close contact with the continent. Virtually all the grave goods in the early tombs, except for the stone ornaments, have Korean or Chinese prototypes, and many appear to have been imports. The objects deposited as grave treasures in Middle Kofun burials, such as iron weapons, jewelry, armor and horse trappings and SUE WARE, were derived from the Korean peninsula; many were imports or made of imported raw materials. Contemporary Chinese records of the southern Chinese courts make mention of the 5th-century FIVE KINGS OF WA, which may be identifiable with some of the emperors known from the *Nihon shoki*. The inscription on the KWANGGAET'O MONUMENT, erected in Korea in 414, describes several Japanese invasions during the late 4th century, and historians consider the Japanese political power, the colony of Mimana or KAYA, to have been established on the peninsula around this time. Extensive relations with the southern Korean countries of PAEKCHE and SILLA also resulted in the influx of many skilled craftsmen and peninsular peoples to Japan (see KIKAJIN; AYA FAMILY; HATA FAMILY).

The appearance of horse trappings in the 5th century tombs (see HORSE TRAPPINGS, ANCIENT) led one small school of Japanese scholars to postulate an invasion of "mounted warriors" from the Asian mainland, who subsequently formed the imperial Yamato line (see HORSE-RIDER THEORY). This theory is not generally accepted because there is considerable evidence of smooth and continual cultural development in Japan and because the theory does not help to explain the actual societal trends and developments that took place in the historic Japanese state. Nevertheless, weapons found in tombs of the 5th and 6th centuries as well as the military stance of many of the *haniwa* figures leave no question about the militaristic tone of Kofun period society at that time.

Two lines of evidence indicate that warfare decreased in importance in the late 6th century and was replaced by administrative integration as the major basis for the political power of the Late Kofun period leaders. First, toward the end of the 5th century, weapons and military accoutrements are most often found in smaller or attendant mounds rather than in the huge burials of the most important individuals. Presumably, this indicates that military activities were no longer in the sphere of the leaders but delegated to a specialist group. Second, economic links appear to have been important in binding together various regions of Japan during the Early and Middle Kofun periods. Large manufacturing sites for the production of stone beads (see BEADS, ANCIENT), salt, and ceramics have been found in and around the Yamato area; also, distributional

studies have shown that the Yamato area was the center for the production and distribution of bronze mirrors, which were important symbolic articles in the regalia of local leaders. There must also have been extensive trade in bulk materials such as iron, bronze, precious metals, cinnabar, glass, and processed foods. Organization of this trade to provide goods for the YAMATO COURT became a right and responsibility of the Yamato leaders during the Late Kofun period (see BE).

Although the *Kojiki* and *Nihon shoki* describe events for much of the Kofun period in mythological and semilegendary terms and the chronology is not reliable before the year 500, analysis of these 8th-century sources indicates that the political leaders of Yamato (now Nara Prefecture) became the rulers of the whole country during the Late Kofun period. These rulers were the founders of the Japanese imperial line, and it appears that they ruled the country, or at least an ever-growing portion of it (see INARIYAMA TOMB), by aligning themselves with powerful local chieftains. These alliances may have been militarily enforced but they appear to have rested largely on the superior spiritual power of the Yamato leaders who claimed divine ancestry.

■ ——— J. Edward Kidder, Jr., *Japan Before Buddhism* (rev ed 1966). Cornelius J. Kiley, "State and Dynasty in Archaic Yamato," *Journal of Asian Studies* 33 (November 1973). *Kodaishi hakkutsu*, 10 vols (Kōdansha, 1974). *Kojiki* (712), tr Basil H. Chamberlain as *"Ko-ji-ki" or Records of Ancient Matters* (1932). *Kojiki* (712), tr Donald L. Philippi (1968). Gari Ledyard, "Galloping along with the Horseriders: Looking for the Founders of Japan," *Journal of Japanese Studies* 1.2 (Spring 1975). Saitō Tadashi, *Nihon kōkogaku shi* (1974). George Sansom, *A History of Japan to 1334* (1958). "Symposium: Japanese Origins," *Journal of Japanese Studies* 2 (Summer 1976). *Man'yōshū* (mid-8th century), tr Nippon Gakujutsu Shinkōkai as *The Man'yōshū: One Thousand Poems* (1940; repr 1965). *Man'yōshū* (mid-8th century), tr Ian Levy as *The Ten Thousand Leaves: A Translation of the Man'yōshū, Japan's Premier Anthology of Classical Poetry*, vol 1 (1981). *Nihon shoki* (720), tr William G. Aston as *Nihongi: Chronicles of Japan from the Earliest Times to A.D. 697* (1896). Ryusaku Tsunoda, tr, and L. Carrington Goodrich, ed, *Japan in the Chinese Dynastic Histories* (1951). Peter BLEED

ASUKA HISTORY (MID-6TH CENTURY TO 710)

There are various theories as to when the historic period, one with abundant, reliable written records, started in Japan. However, it is most commonly taken as dating from the use of the ASUKA area as a site for the rulers' palaces and the introduction of Buddhism into Japan, both in the mid-6th century. Written materials concerning Japan before that time, both foreign and Japanese, are small in number and not fully trustworthy. From the ASUKA PERIOD, written materials, from the Chinese *Sui shu* (compilation commenced in 629) to the Japanese NIHON SHOKI (720), become more numerous, of better quality, and of greater reliability in their use of dating. Accordingly, the historic age in Japan can be thought of as starting from the Asuka period.

Establishment of the Yamato Court ——— The Japanese imperial line, also known as the Yamato Sun Line, grew out of one of several lineage groups (UJI) probably in existence from the Late Yayoi period (ca 100–ca 300). These lineages competed with each other for land and power in the KINAI region, one finally achieving a position of superiority and ultimately securing for itself a unique relationship to the others by claiming descent from the sun goddess (AMATERASU ŌMIKAMI).

By the 6th century, the Sun Line, which produced "emperors," ranked supreme among a loose coalition of a considerable number of lineages. The subordinate lineage heads presided over communities *(uji)* which consisted of their relatives and subordinates; they acted as the chief priests for their lineage groups, dealt with political affairs, and directed the use of manpower and other resources within the community groupings. The Yamato rulers used the *uji* chiefs in organizing BE, or hereditary occupational groupings that furnished goods and services to the YAMATO COURT. Each *uji* was assigned a different role and task, and they received honorary titles (KABANE) indicating their relative status and function. Most of the top *uji* held the ranks of *omi, muraji*, or *kimi*. (See UJI-KABANE SYSTEM.)

The most powerful *uji* chiefs at the Yamato court in the mid-6th century were the SOGA FAMILY (tax officials), the Imbe family (diviners), the Nakatomi family (priests), the MONONOBE FAMILY (professional soldiers), and the ŌTOMO FAMILY, all with territorial claims in the Yamato Plain. Each *uji* had certain rights and privileges, one of which was to contribute wives to the imperial line. One of these wives enjoyed the position of imperial consort; the right of contributing her initially belonged to the Soga, who were *omi*, and was later extended to the Nakatomi and Mononobe, who were *muraji*. The throne passed down the fraternal line in the imperial family, and the successor—in the early stages of the Yamato Court—was decided by a consensus of the *uji* heads. After the time of Emperor Keitai (first half of the 6th century), the emperor gained a stronger voice in the selection of his successor; the symbols of investiture also became fixed as the IMPERIAL REGALIA: a sword, mirror, and curved jewels (*magatama*).

Court operations were on a modest scale and controls throughout the country were nominal at best (see IWAI, REBELLION OF), but in the central Kinai area, a system of regional administrative units was developed. The palace was located in the Asuka region of southern Yamato (now Nara Prefecture), though the actual site was changed frequently, often to suit the whim of the chief consort. The surrounding territory was divided into *kuni* administered by KUNI NO MIYATSUKO; below them were the AGATANUSHI, who governed the smaller units of *agata*. Unstable court conditions were generated by the Yamato leaders in the 6th and most of the 7th centuries as each built one or more new palaces, but finally in 694, the first permanent palace and capital city of Fujiwara (FUJIWARAKYŌ) was built just north of Asuka. Several of the earlier palaces had also been built on Chinese models: the ASUKA KIYOMIHARA NO MIYA, built in 672, was probably in a regular symmetrical plan, and the NANIWAKYŌ is definitely known to have been constructed in a formal plan following an order in 683. The greatest Chinese-inspired accomplishment was the building of the Fujiwara palace and its grid-plan city nestled among the mountains of Yamato.

Relations with Korea —— Complicated relations with Korea dominated the 6th and 7th centuries to a degree hampering local consolidation. Japan tried to hold its colony of Mimana (see KAYA) in the southern part of the Korean peninsula against SILLA, which was trying to unify the peninsula, by cultivating the southern Korean kingdom of PAEKCHE. Paekche dispatched Buddhist monks, temple architects, sculptors, tilemakers, and painters to Japan toward the end of the 6th century; and in the early 7th century, a Paekche priest brought over books and taught calendar-making, astrology, and magical practices. Continental music and dances were introduced shortly thereafter via Paekche, and the *Yuanjiali* (*Yüan-chia-li*), a Chinese calendar, was in use from about 604 to around 690. These gifts thus doubled Paekche's contributions to Japanese culture since, in the 5th century, it had sent over readers of the Chinese classics (see WANI) and heads of the craftsmen associations (*be*) of potters, saddlers, brocade weavers, and painters.

Nevertheless, it was not exclusively one-way traffic. The arrival of the first Buddhist articles by emissary in either 538 or 552 was accompanied by requests from Paekche for aid against Silla. Japan on occasion sent aid but was unable to comply with any degree of effectiveness as controls over Kyūshū leaders were inadequate for prosecuting a war against Silla. With its deteriorating internal conditions in the late 7th century, Japan was in no position to stand up to an alliance of the Tang (T'ang) dynasty and Silla.

Finally, however, the situation became so critical that it merited full imperial attention, and Empress SAIMEI herself (r 655–661) went down to Kyūshū to direct military activities. But the empress died there in 661, and her successor was unable to prevent the destruction of the Japanese fleet by Silla in the Battle of HAKUSUKINOE off the coast of Korea two years later. To counter an expected attack from Korea, effort was hurriedly put into the construction of local defenses in Kyūshū (see DAZAIFU). The invasion never came, however, and the loss of Mimana on the whole proved to be salutary to Japan, since the country then devoted itself with fresh vigor to internal development and was soon on an emissarial basis with China. Silla turned its back on Japan as it moved toward consolidating its position on the peninsula.

Buddhism and the Soga Family —— The introduction of BUDDHISM is described in the *Nihon shoki* as an event of 552 that pitted the powerful Soga family against the Mononobe and Nakatomi families during the reign of Emperor KIMMEI (traditional reign dates either 531 or 539 to 571). In order to develop a new state religion that would exercise a powerful influence over the people as well as its political rivals, the Soga adopted Buddhist practices, built temples, and sponsored the clergy. The third ruler after Kimmei's receipt of the Buddhist articles, Emperor YŌMEI (r 585–587), was a Buddhist, as were all his successors. During the Soga-dominated decades of the late 6th and early 7th centuries, Koreans were warmly welcomed into Japan and special attention was given to monks

thought to be bearing the latest tidings. These trends were vigorously resisted by the Mononobe and Nakatomi families, but SOGA NO UMAKO successfully destroyed the Mononobe in a 587 battle. Buddhism thereafter made substantial progress under the patronage of Prince SHŌTOKU, the regent under Empress SUIKO (r 593–628).

Shōtoku retained a Korean tutor and read, interpreted, and expounded several sutras, exploring the devotional aspects of the religion and influencing the mode of cloister life through his convictions. He was connected with the construction of several temples, including the SHITENNŌJI, though tradition associates him with many more. Nevertheless, a strong Confucian orientation is also apparent in the so-called SEVENTEEN-ARTICLE CONSTITUTION, which the *Nihon shoki* credits him with writing. Prince Shōtoku's efforts at propagating Buddhism helped to pave the way for the general adoption of the religion even after the patron Soga family was eradicated for their court excesses in 645.

A *Nihon shoki* entry for 594 notes that the ranking nobles, the *omi* and *muraji*, competed with each other in building temples. A census of temples in 624 listed 46 staffed by 816 monks and 569 nuns, but the biggest impetus for temple building came during the interval following the banning of tomb construction in 646 and preceding the imposition of limits on private temple construction after 710. About 483 temples (see MOTOYAKUSHIJI REMAINS) were erected during this period and the clergy expanded phenomenally, creating a new political power, and imperial donations were made in 680 to the 24 temples in the capital. A *Nihon shoki* record for 690 mentions gifts to 3,363 priests manning seven temples and another to 329 priests in three temples.

The Taika Reforms —— In 643 an event occurred which led to a court intrigue against the Soga family. SOGA NO IRUKA, after exhausting all other means of preventing Prince Shōtoku's son, Prince Yamashiro no Ōe, from being appointed emperor, finally caused the death of Yamashiro, his wives, and attendants. A revolt against Soga oppression was led by Prince Naka no Ōe (later Emperor TENJI) and Nakatomi no Kamatari (later named FUJIWARA NO KAMATARI): Iruka was assassinated in 645 at the Itabuki palace in the presence of Empress Kōgyoku (r 642–645; later reigned as Saimei, 655–661) and Korean emissaries; his father, Emishi, committed suicide the next day. To remove the court from the Soga-dominated region of Asuka, the capital was transferred to Naniwa at the edge of Ōsaka Bay. The edicts of the TAIKA REFORM were issued from there a year later, in 646, by Emperor Kōtoku (r 645–654). The new era, which had begun in 645, was given the name Great Change (Taika), thus starting the NENGŌ system.

The Taika Reform brought on a host of new policies and practices, all intended to subordinate land and manpower to imperial authority, diminish the power of the leading families at the court, and provide an economic system of support for the new political structure. The machinery set up to administer the provisions of the reforms consisted of eight ministries supervised by the Grand Council of State (DAJŌKAN), whose chief administrator was the grand minister of state (*dajō daijin*). Following in rank were the ministers of the left and right (*sadaijin* and *udaijin*), with numerous lower officials in charge of departments, bureaus, and offices (see RITSURYŌ SYSTEM). Moreover, the cap rank system (KAN'I JŪNIKAI), established by Prince Shōtoku in 604, was expanded. Emperor Kōtoku increased the initial 12 ranks to 19 in 649, and Emperor Tenji (r 661–672) revised these to 26 ranks in 664. Appointment and promotion to these bureaucratic ranks was based more on individual merit than hereditary status. Tenji also issued a set of civil and penal codes (ŌMI CODE) in 668 from Ōtsu in Ōmi Province (modern Shiga Prefecture), where he had moved his palace from Naniwa.

To implement the reforms, provincial boundaries were redefined and headquarters and local bureaus were established (see KOKUGUN SYSTEM). A census was taken, taxes (SO, YŌ, AND CHŌ) were levied, and official routes for tax collection were determined. Marked out in regular plots known as *jōri*, tax-yielding land allotments were made to families and individuals, and then grouped together as villages of roughly equal size (see JŌRI SYSTEM; HANDEN SHŪJU SYSTEM). The building of *kofun* tomb mounds was forbidden except for those of fixed size for the very highest ranks, and various funeral practices, including horse sacrifice, were outlawed.

The Reign of Temmu (r 672–686) —— At the death of Emperor Tenji, who, as the former Prince Naka no Ōe, had helped engineer the anti-Soga coup and Taika Reform—there occurred a particularly violent succession dispute known as the JINSHIN DISTURBANCE of 672. Tenji's son, the preferred successor, was ousted by his uncle, Tenji's brother, who ascended the throne as Emperor TEMMU in 672.

In a drastic realignment of the political hierarchy, Temmu promoted his allies and demoted his enemies, greatly strengthening the imperial position. Temmu's restructuring of the *uji-kabane* system in 684 compares with the Taika Reform in importance in altering the course of Japanese history.

The results of Temmu's new eight-rank system (YAKUSA NO KABANE) can be seen in the early-9th-century SHINSEN SHŌJIROKU documents, which record the origins of the leading *uji* as deriving from the imperial line, from divine ancestry, or from immigrant ancestry. The two newly instituted top ranks, *mahito* and *asomi*, were composed primarily of the closest kinship groups of the imperial family. The third-ranking *sukune* were the main deity-descended *uji*, apart from the Sun Line, who had rendered valuable service to the throne. The *imiki* and *michinoshi* had no valid claims to imperial connections. With the institution of all these new ranks at the top, the earlier *omi*- and *muraji*-holding *uji* were displaced toward the bottom of the rank scale; in fact neither Temmu nor the Empress Jitō (r 686–697) made any appointments to most of the lower ranks.

Emperor Temmu moved back to Asuka 27 years after that area had been evacuated following the anti-Soga coup. His palace, the Asuka Kiyomihara no Miya, was occupied by himself and Empress Jitō until the building of the Fujiwara capital in 694. From there, Temmu initiated the compilation of the ASUKA KIYOMIHARA CODE, a law code which became the basis for the later TAIHŌ CODE of the early 8th century.

The Fujiwara Capital (694–710) —— Empress Jitō succeeded Temmu and actively worked for her husband's projects. Her most formidable undertaking—and the logical development in the drive for a stable political system—was the building of the palace and capital city at Fujiwara in 694. Jitō abdicated only three years later in favor of her young grandson Mommu (r 697–707), a great-grandson of Tenji and son of Empress Gemmei (r 707–715).

The Asuka-Kiyomihara Code had been completed and promulgated by Empress Jitō in 689. This was largely embodied in the Taihō Code which Mommu drew up in 701 and which seem to have remained in force until 757, despite the writing of the YŌRŌ CODE and its presentation to the court in 718. In general terms, the Japanese followed the Chinese form and principles in their codes—especially in the penal codes—but tried to avoid some of the pitfalls created in the Chinese legal system, in particular the inviolable rights of the bureaucracy.

In the late 7th century, almost all aspects of life came under government control. Clothing regulations in 681 contained 92 articles. Dress (commoners wore yellow, slaves black) was eventually put under the supervision of a Court Dress and Cap-Regulating Office in Emperor Mommu's time. The use of coins was also ordered by the government in 683 to spur the economy and simplify transactions. Coin production in Japan and the systematization of business dealings was heralded by the standardization of weights and measures in 702. The first Japanese coins, WADŌ KAIHŌ, were minted in 708, modeled after the Tang coins minted in 621. Evidence for the swelling of the bureaucracy and written regulations is found in the thousands of wooden tablets (MOKKAN) excavated from several sites of the early historic period.

For several reasons—the growing lack of space, the provincial location of Fujiwara, and the increasing influence of the city's Buddhist temples over the government—Emperor Mommu decided to build a larger capital in a more convenient place. The site chosen was in the northwestern corner of the Yamato basin, and there Empress Gemmei (r 707–715) built the new capital of HEIJŌKYŌ (now the city of Nara). The capital was officially moved in 710, and that event is used to mark the beginning of the Nara period (710–794), in which the infant state reached full maturity.

📖 —— Asakawa Kan'ichi, *The Early Institutional Life of Japan: A Study in the Reform of 645 A.D.* (1903). Hara Hidesaburō, Kitō Kiyoaki, Satō Sōjun, Kanō Hisashi, and Yoshimura Takehiko, *Nihon kokka shi 1 (Kodai)* (1975). J. Edward Kidder, Jr., *Early Buddhist Japan* (1972). *Kojiki* (712), tr Basil H. Chamberlain as "Ko-ji-ki" or *Records of Ancient Matters* (1932). *Kojiki* (712), tr Donald L. Philippi (1968). *Man'yōshū* (mid-8th century), tr Nippon Gakujutsu Shinkōkai as *The Man'yōshū: One Thousand Poems* (1940; repr 1965). *Man'yōshu* (mid-8th century), tr Ian Levy as *The Ten Thousand Leaves: A Translation of the Man'yōshū, Japan's Premier Anthology of Classical Poetry*, vol 1 (1981). Richard J. Miller, *Ancient Japanese Nobility: The Kabane Ranking System* (1974). *Nihon shoki* (720), tr William G. Aston as *Nihongi: Chronicles of Japan from the Earliest Times to A.D. 697* (1896). Robert K. Reischauer, *Early Japanese History*, 2 vols (1937). Sakamoto Tarō, *Nihon kodaishi no kiso-teki kenkyū*, 2 vols (1964). George Sansom, *A History of Japan to 1334* (1958). Tsuboi Kiyotari and Kishi Toshio, ed, *Kodai no Nihon*, vol 5: *Kinki* (1970). Ueda Masaaki, *Yamato chōtei* (1967). Ryusaku Tsunoda, tr, and L. Carrington Goodrich, ed, *Japan in the Chinese Dynastic Histories* (1951). Ueda Masaaki, *Nihon kodai kokka ron kyū* (1968). Yamao Yukihisa, *Nihon kokka no keisei* (1977).

J. Edward KIDDER, Jr.

NARA HISTORY (710–794)

History of the period during which the seat of government was at HEIJŌKYŌ (now the city of Nara) in YAMATO (now Nara Prefecture). Strictly speaking, the Nara period began in 710, when the imperial capital was moved from FUJIWARAKYŌ, and ended in 784 with the transfer of the capital to NAGAOKAKYŌ. More broadly, however, it includes the 10 years during which the capital was in Nagaoka, and the dates for the period are usually given as 710–794. The period was characterized by the full implementation of the RITSURYŌ SYSTEM of government, the establishment of Buddhism as the religion of the court and, by extension, of the state, and a new height in intellectual and cultural achievements as exemplified in the building of the Great Hall of the temple TŌDAIJI. Early in the period, the central administration was able to exercise close control over the country. During the middle period, however, a power struggle broke out among the court nobility. Modifications in the land-tenure system that led to the accumulation of vast tracts of private land (SHŌEN) by nobles and religious institutions vitiated the *ritsuryō* system, and the absconding from state lands of many peasants, who were overburdened by taxes, added further to its breakdown.

Establishment of the Ritsuryō System —— From the perspective of political history, one may say that the Nara period began with the promulgation of the TAIHŌ CODE in 701. Under the code, the centralizing reforms inaugurated by the TAIKA REFORM (645) were pushed forward, and the period saw the firm establishment of the emperor as the head of a Chinese-style *ritsuryō* state. Under the *ritsuryō* system the central government was headed by the DAJŌKAN (Grand Council of State), which presided over eight ministries. The government was staffed by officials appointed by the emperor and bidden to act as his loyal servants. The country was divided into provinces (*kuni* or *koku*), which in turn were divided into districts (*gun*), villages (*gō*), and hamlets (*ri*). An early Nara-period document lists 67 provinces, comprising 555 districts, 4,012 villages, and 12,036 hamlets. The provinces were administered by governors (KOKUSHI), who were sent out from the capital. All the people were considered the emperor's subjects and were expected to obey the officials who acted in his name. (See also KOKUGUN SYSTEM; GŌRI SYSTEM.)

All rice land was declared public domain. Under the HANDEN SHŪJU SYSTEM the land was redistributed every six years to all males and females over six years of age (five in Western reckoning). A male received 2 *tan* (1 *tan* = 0.12 hectare or 0.3 acre), a female two-thirds that amount. In order to ensure proper allocation of rice land, the census register was updated every six years. The authority of the imperial court at the time extended as far south as the islands off the tip of Kyūshū and as far north as AKITAJŌ, in what is now Akita Prefecture. The population falling within this area is estimated to have been about 5 to 6 million and the acreage of rice land about 601,000 *chō* (about 721,200 hectares or 1.8 million acres); it is clear that even after taking into consideration the ratio of males to females, there was not enough land. Judging from historical materials, however, the *handen* system and the census registration seem to have been implemented throughout the country with little resistance. The allotted rice land was called KUBUNDEN. Holders of *kubunden* were liable to corvée (*zōyō*), a rice tax (*so*), a handicraft or local products tax (*chō*). There was also a handicraft or local products tax (*yō*) in lieu of labor. (See SO, YŌ, AND CHŌ.)

In order to strengthen administrative and military communications with the provinces and to facilitate the payment of taxes, the government established a network of post stations (EKISEI) on the public roads connecting the capital and provincial seats of government. The rice and produce taxes that had hitherto been paid to local chieftains were now sent directly to the central government.

A faithful imitation of the Chinese system of government was bound to have negative side-effects, for it was unsuited to Japan's agricultural reality. According to a document of 730, in the province of Awa (now part of Chiba Prefecture), 412 out of 414 households were listed as being at the bare subsistence level. The figures for Echizen Province (now part of Fukui Prefecture) in that year tell the same story: of 1,019 households, 996 were found to be poverty-stricken. The tax burden fell most heavily on the peasants, and the number of those who absconded increased at an alarming rate. Yet at the same time, under the SANZE ISSHIN NO HŌ (723) and the KONDEN EISEI SHIZAI HŌ (743), reclaimed wasteland was recognized as private property for one or three generations, or in perpetuity. Nobles and religious institutions were able to appropriate extensive landholdings, which were exempted from taxes. Vagrant peasants in search of a livelihood converged upon these lands. Herein lay the basic contradiction of the Nara landholding system.

The project to build an imposing capital on the model of the Chinese capital of Chang'an (Ch'ang-an) was another instance of overzealous imitation. Many of the peasants conscripted for labor ran away; the thousands of restless peasants who assembled daily on the outskirts of Heijōkyō posed a continuous threat, necessitating the deployment of armed guardsmen at the palace arsenal and the emperor's residence. It was in order to adjust the Taihō Code to native realities that the minister FUJIWARA NO FUHITO began compiling the YŌRŌ CODE in 718.

Following the death of Fuhito in 720 the most powerful political figure was Prince Nagaya, but in 729 the prince was ordered by the emperor to commit suicide for allegedly fomenting a rebellion (see NAGAYA NO Ō, REBELLION OF). He had, in fact, been falsely accused by members of the FUJIWARA FAMILY, who, it is believed, hoped to take advantage of social unrest to seize political leadership from the imperial house. The death of all four of Fuhito's sons in a smallpox epidemic in 737, however, put an end to the family's imperial aspirations. See also FUJIWARA NO HIROTSUGU, REBELLION OF.

The emperor SHŌMU (r 724–749), who was married to Empress KŌMYŌ, a daughter of Fuhito, was deeply disturbed by the course of events, and, in the hope that the powers of Buddhism would bring an end to epidemic disease and social ills, in 741 he ordered the construction of temples and nunneries (KOKUBUNJI) in every province. This undertaking was completed only after many years. Shōmu also ordered in 743 the construction of a gigantic statue of the Buddha Vairocana so that the blessings of the Buddha would extend over the entire country. Known as the Great Buddha (DAIBUTSU) of Tōdaiji, it was completed in 752 at great expense.

State expenditures thus went mainly for the construction of imposing religious edifices and statues. Buddhist arts and culture, centering on these good works, reached an unequaled richness and brilliance. Scholars were later to call the artistic efflorescence of this period Tempyō culture, after the era name (nengō) for the years 729–749.

Tempyō Culture and Embassies to China —— The ripening of TEMPYŌ CULTURE was owed in no small measure to the resumption of relations with the Tang (T'ang) dynasty (618–907) of China. The sending of official envoys had been halted since the defeat of Japanese forces by the combined armies of Tang China and the Korean state of SILLA in the Battle of HAKUSUKINOE in 663. In 701 it was decided to send an embassy to China, and the envoys set out for the continent the following year. Between 701 and 777 seven missions were dispatched, each comprising as many as 500 or 600 men.

The voyages across the sea were perilous and often fatal; that they were undertaken indicates the eagerness with which the Japanese hoped to learn from China. Many students and scholars accompanied these embassies, a number remaining in China for many years. Some of them brought back foreign monks and new forms of Buddhism; in all, they contributed significantly to the development of Tempyō culture. GEMBŌ, KIBI NO MAKIBI, and ABE NO NAKAMARO are some of the more famous of these students. Gembō returned with more than 5,000 sutras, while Kibi no Makibi, who had studied Confucianism, military science, and ceremonial rites, set up an educational program for future government officials. The Chinese monk GANJIN finally reached Japan in 754 after four unsuccessful attempts. He conveyed the teachings of the RITSU SECT and founded the temple TŌSHŌDAIJI. See SUI AND TANG (T'ANG) CHINA, EMBASSIES TO.

Visitors came also from as far away as Central and West Asia, Indonesia, Vietnam, Malaysia, and India, adding to the vigor and diversity of Tempyō culture. The quintessence of Nara art is represented in the thousands of objects preserved in the SHŌSŌIN in Nara. Contradictory though it may seem, as evocative as it was of foreign lands, the culture of the period remained uniquely Japanese. The Chinese writing system was adopted, but the Japanese language remained intact. Furthermore, by using Chinese characters in a free and imaginative manner, the Japanese added greatly to the richness and subtlety of their language. The poetic anthology MAN'YŌSHŪ is an outstanding masterpiece of the period. Japan's first history, the KOJIKI, was completed in 712; it was followed eight years later by

another chronicle, the NIHON SHOKI, which was written in Chinese (KAMBUN). The FUDOKI, gazetteers that described local customs, topography, and products, were compiled around the same time. All these projects were completed in the midst of the administrative demands of land and tax reform.

End of the Period —— Emperor Shōmu's excessive zeal in spreading Buddhism imposed an intolerable burden on the peasants. In 757, under the pretext of alleviating the lot of the peasantry, Tachibana no Naramaro attempted a coup. Naramaro was the son of TACHIBANA NO MOROE, who had been put in charge of the government after the death of Fujiwara no Fuhito's sons, and the coup was in fact an attempt to remove FUJIWARA NO NAKAMARO, who had usurped Moroe's place. Nakamaro succeeded in foiling the coup and realizing that the plot had profited from peasant distress, he immediately reduced by half the most burdensome of the taxes, the zōyō (see YŌEKI), which called for 60 days of labor a year. He also commuted the interest on all debts accumulated through the previous year. In 758 Nakamaro dispatched officials throughout the country to listen to the peasants' grievances and to give relief to the indigent. Within officialdom he encouraged the observance of filial piety and renamed official ranks and ministries in the Chinese manner. He publicly commended his grandfather Fuhito for his work in drawing up the Taihō and Yōrō codes, and he belatedly enforced the latter in 757. The government, which had been thoroughly dominated by Buddhism, now took on a more Confucian aspect.

However, the reigning empress KŌKEN (r 749–758) was displeased with the new measures; she dismissed Nakamaro and instead relied heavily on the priest DŌKYŌ, who she believed had cured her of an illness. In 764 Nakamaro instigated a rebellion but was captured and killed. Dōkyō was elevated to the rank of dajō daijin zenji (priestly grand minister of state) and given the title of HŌŌ (priestly retired sovereign). With the appointment of his fellow monks as religious councillors (hōsangi), court politics were monopolized by the Buddhist clergy. Previous policies were reversed, and Buddhism once again became supreme. Finally, on the basis of an oracle he claimed to have received at the Usa Hachiman Shrine, Dōkyō tried to have himself enthroned. He was thwarted by Fujiwara no Momokawa, WAKE NO KIYOMARO, and others. The empress Shōtoku (the name taken by Kōken when she reascended the throne in 764) died without issue in 770, and Dōkyō was banished.

After the death of Shōtoku, Fujiwara no Momokawa and his followers successfully countered the attempts of Kibi no Makibi to install the grandson of Emperor TEMMU (r 672–686) and enthroned instead the grandson of Emperor TENJI (r 661–672), 62-year-old Prince Shirakabe. As Emperor Kōnin (r 770–781), he became the last sovereign whose reign fell completely within the Nara period. His rule was distinguished by efforts to reduce national expenditures, discipline officials and monks, and rebuild farm villages. Government offices founded for the construction of religious edifices were either reduced in size or abolished altogether. Sinecures established outside the ritsuryō administrative framework to provide income for officials were eliminated. In 780 the staff of all government offices was reduced, and men conscripted from the provinces to work in the bureaucracy were allowed to return home. In order to encourage the return of dispossessed peasants who had left their homes to escape debts, a limit was set on the interest on borrowed seed rice (SUIKO). Tax payments to the national coffers continued to decrease, however, and as peasants became increasingly drawn into land-reclamation projects undertaken by nobles and temples, they were deprived of any gainful occupation of their own. The decay of the authority of the central government was felt as far away as northeastern Japan, where the EZO tribes rose in rebellion. The rebellion was to spread to other areas and pose a grave problem for years afterward.

The political and social problems then, which had been latent at the beginning of the period, surfaced through the years and by the last decades of the 8th century were so serious that not even Emperor Kōnin's reforms could contain them. Their resolution would have to await a new beginning in the Heian period (794–1185).

◾️——Aoki Kazuo, Nara no miyako, in Nihon no rekishi, vol 3 (Chūō Kōron Sha, 1965). Engi Shiki (905–927), tr Felicia G. Bock as Engi-shiki: Procedures of the Engi Era, 2 vols (1970–72). Iyanaga Teizō, Nara jidai no kizoku to nōmin (1956). Kitayama Shigeo, Nihon kodai seiji shi no kenkyū (1959). Kojiki (712), tr Basil H. Chamberlain as "Ko-ji-ki" or Records of Ancient Matters (1932). Kojiki (712), tr Donald L. Philippi (1968). Man'yōshū (mid-8th century), tr Nippon Gakujutsu Shinkōkai as The Man'yōshū: One Thousand

Poems (1940; repr 1965). *Man'yōshū* (mid-8th century), tr Ian Levy as *The Ten Thousand Leaves: A Translation of the Man'yōshū, Japan's Premier Anthology of Classical Poetry*, vol 1 (1981). Richard J. Miller, *Ancient Japanese Nobility: The Kabane Ranking System* (1974). Mori Katsumi, *Kentōshi* (1955). *Nihon shoki* (720), tr William G. Aston as *Nihongi: Chronicles of Japan from the Earliest Times to A.D. 697* (1896). Robert K. Reischauer, *Early Japanese History*, 2 vols (1937). George Sansom, *A History of Japan to 1334* (1958). *Shoku nihongi* (late 8th century), tr J.B. Snellen as "Shoku Nihongi, Chronicles of Japan, Continued, from 697–791 A.D.," *Transactions of the Asiatic Society of Japan*, ser 2, 11 (1934), 14 (1937). Takeuchi Rizō, *Ritsuryōsei to kizoku seiken* (1958). Takeuchi Rizō, *Kodai kokka no han'ei*, in *Zusetsu Nihon no rekishi*, vol 3 (Shūeisha, 1974). Ryusaku Tsunoda, tr, and L. Carrington Goodrich, ed, *Japan in the Chinese Dynastic Histories* (1951).

TAKEUCHI Rizō

HEIAN HISTORY (794–1185)

The Heian period lasted for nearly four centuries, from 794 to 1185. It commenced with the removal of the capital to the newly constructed imperial city of HEIANKYŌ (now the city of Kyōto) and ended with the establishment of a warrior government in Kamakura. The period is named Heian simply because the political, social, and cultural center of Japan was located in the capital at Heiankyō, seat of the emperor and his court. It is thus a political division of the most general sort and indicates nothing of the social structure, administrative style, economic organization, or cultural activities of the time. In fact, dividing the period in the middle of the 10th century would be more historically useful, since important changes in economic organization and local government at that time transformed the state. Be that as it may, the Heian period has long been an established division of history, seen by the Japanese as the apogee of the nation's aristocratic age, when some of its finest literary works were produced and one of the world's most exquisitely refined cultural styles flourished.

It was during the Heian period that Japan came of age, fully assimilating the cultural, political, and social elements of Chinese society that the architects of the ancient Japanese state had so assiduously imitated for several hundred years. Things Chinese remained in fashion for much of the Heian period and Chinese Confucian principles of governance never lost their philosophical importance, but in practice the Japanese, in economics and politics, literature, and even art, created their own institutions, which bore only a slight resemblance to Chinese prototypes. By absorbing Chinese values, the Japanese of the Heian period produced a truly national culture.

From Nara to Nagaoka to Kyōto —— In 784 Emperor KAMMU moved the capital from HEIJŌKYŌ (now the city of Nara), seat of power for seven previous reigns, northwest to NAGAOKAKYŌ in Yamashiro Province (now part of Kyōto Prefecture). And yet within a decade this capital city too was abandoned for the final move to Heiankyō. A certain amount of uncertainty surrounds the two removals of the capital, but they were both intimately related to political rivalries at the imperial court. Doubtless one major consideration was an attempt to escape the baneful influence of the Buddhist establishment, which over the course of the Nara period (710–794) had come to exercise what was in the minds of many courtiers an undue influence upon the civil government. The recent ascendency of DŌKYŌ and his associates during the reign of Empress Shōtoku (r 764–770; she had ruled previously as Empress KŌKEN, 749–758) was the most blatant example of abuse of priestly power, but not the only one.

There were other political problems at Nara as well. It was the leading Fujiwara family member Momokawa (732–779) who was responsible for the exile of Dōkyō after Shōtoku's death, and it was he also who enthroned the aging emperor Kōnin (709–782; r 770–781) as her successor. Finally, it was Momokawa who made possible the accession of Emperor KAMMU by eliminating Crown Prince Osabe (761–775); the latter died mysteriously with his mother in prison. Not everyone at court approved of the shift of the succession to Kammu, whose mother, of Korean descent, was of lower rank than Osabe's mother, the nonreigning empress Inoe (717–775). An important change in the succession had already occurred when Kōnin, a descendant of Emperor TENJI, succeeded to the throne, marking a shift away from Emperor TEMMU's line. The Temmu line remained powerful in the Yamato area around Nara, and the Tenji line was dominant in the northern area of Yamashiro. Thus it appears that a combination of factors, including a desire to escape Buddhist influence, a fear of the spirits of the deceased Inoe and

Prince Osabe (see GORYŌ), as well as a desire to move into the area of Tenji-line strength motivated Kammu to move from Nara. Another motive may have been to impress upon the population the power of the throne. The official selected to oversee construction was Momokawa's nephew Fujiwara no Tanetsugu (737–785), who began the work in 784 with a huge complement of conscripted labor. By the fifth month the imperial palace was ready, and Kammu moved his court to Nagaokakyō, though the city itself was far from completed.

Although Tanetsugu enjoyed Kammu's favor, he had enemies at court. One was Kammu's younger brother Crown Prince Sawara (d 785), who expected to succeed him; but Tanetsugu favored Kammu's eldest son, Prince Ate. Such struggles between brothers and sons of an emperor were still common despite a general disposition toward direct father-to-son succession provided for in the various codes issued since Temmu's time. At any rate, one evening while Tanetsugu was riding through the streets of Nagaoka, he was set upon and killed. Kammu rushed to the scene, investigations were carried out, and suspects, including Prince Sawara and members of the ŌTOMO FAMILY, were arrested. Sawara was exiled to the island of Awaji, where he died within a few weeks; he is generally believed to have been innocent. He was replaced as crown prince by Prince Ate, later Emperor Heizei (774–824; r 806–809). Thus did the courtiers close to Kammu effect a change in the succession, at the same time dealing a serious blow to their rivals the Ōtomo.

Despite this incident, the workers were urged on to complete the capital at Nagaoka; yet as the project was nearing completion, Kammu decided to move once again, this time just north to an area in the Kadono district of Yamashiro. His chief motive seems to have been fear of the vengeful spirit of Prince Sawara, to which were attributed the deaths of Kammu's mother and his empress, as well as epidemics and other untoward events. Despite the strain on state finances and the obvious duplication of effort, the decision was made to construct Heiankyō.

Heian Institutions —— The political, social, and economic institutions of the Heian period were all shaped by what was called the RITSURYŌ SYSTEM, based upon the penal (*ritsu*) and administrative (*ryō*) codes of the Chinese Tang (T'ang) dynasty (618–907). The process of borrowing the systematized Chinese institutional superstructure had been going on since the time of Prince SHŌTOKU, who in the first two decades of the 7th century attempted to remodel the particularistic amalgam of powerful kin groups (UJI)—which we know as the YAMATO COURT—into a highly articulated imperium like that of the early Tang. Unsuccessful though Shōtoku's efforts were at the time, they were important as the earliest attempt to reform the emerging Japanese state along Chinese lines. These reforms were carried out largely by members of the ruling house and their close associates among the court nobility, who sought to assert their hegemony over the rest of society by relying upon august Chinese symbols of power and authority.

The period from 645 until the founding of the imperial capital at Heijōkyō in 710 was marked by an intense struggle between the forces for centralization on the Chinese model and those for decentralization represented by the independent power of the locally prominent *uji* chieftains. By the early Nara period, especially through the efforts of Emperor Temmu, the process was completed; there was an impressive imperial capital to demonstrate the transcendent magnificence of the emperor, and a detailed administrative and penal code (see TAIHŌ CODE; YŌRŌ CODE).

Although this system worked only imperfectly during the next century, it remained the fountainhead of political and economic ideals in Japan, and even following the move to Heiankyō, the emperor and nobility continued to cling to the ideal forms envisioned in the early codes. During the Heian period there were numerous changes away from the *ritsuryō* provisions economically, socially, and most of all politically, but the ideals of the system never died out. Especially hardy was the basic concept of a peasantry and a land system that was "public" in the sense that it belonged to the emperor, as opposed to a system in which land and people were controlled by "private" interest. This had been the case under the earlier *uji* society and increasingly became that way with the development of private landed estates (SHŌEN) over the course of the Heian period.

What was developing in place of the *ritsuryō* system was a feudal pattern, dominated by a provincial warrior class that rose gradually to prominence during the Heian period and to dominance in the succeeding Kamakura period (1185–1333). The large body of scholarship devoted to the institutional developments of Heian times, however, tends to view them as having caused the breakdown of the *ritsuryō* system, and the shift to a feudal society is also largely viewed negatively. Despite the rise of more modern historiographical views that tend to see history more as "progress" than decline, and despite the popularity of Marxist historiography, in which the feudal system is seen as a more highly developed stage than the despotic ancient state, there appears to be some sort of historical bias in favor of the *ritsuryō* system. Perhaps this bias derives from the residual Confucian mentality of Japanese historians—just as until the last few decades it was common to suppose that the original position of the sovereign was supreme, in the Chinese fashion, and direct rule the norm, and that later patterns of indirect rule by regents, retired emperors, and shōguns were abnormal, when in fact indirect rule has been the norm in Japanese history.

Politics and Government——There are several ways to divide the political history of the Heian period, the simplest being perhaps to consider the period in an early and a latter phase, divided near the mid-10th century. In the first phase various attempts were made to reinvigorate the *ritsuryō* system borrowed from China, in terms of both an emperor-dominated political system and an economic base of nationally controlled rice fields. In the second, the contradictions of the cumbersome continental system caused continuous breakdowns. First the Fujiwara regents, then the retired emperors, and finally the rising warrior class were successively able to exercise control over the emperor and the political process, and economically the private landed estate, or *shōen*, became the principal form of landholding, undermining the state-centered land system.

A more precise division of the period requires a four-phase scheme. The first phase, roughly the 100 years from the moving of the capital to the end of the 9th century, was initially characterized by the attempts of the powerful Emperor Kammu to reinvigorate the *ritsuryō* system through a change in military organization, the subjugation of the aboriginal EZO people, and reform of provincial government. To some extent this attempt to renew the *ritsuryō* system, with the focus still on the Chinese pattern, was carried on by Emperor SAGA and the other early Heian rulers. The legal codifications and the establishment of new offices outside the *ritsuryō* framework (see RYŌGE NO KAN) to improve governmental efficiency, such as the KEBIISHI (imperial police) and the KURŌDO-DOKORO (Bureau of Archivists, or Secretariat), restored a degree of stability to the political system.

But the creation of extrastatutory offices and other changes during this century provided new avenues to power for nonimperial families among the nobility. Of especial significance during this period was the rise of the FUJIWARA FAMILY, which had already been one of the leading courtier families in Nara times, to a position comparable to that of the imperial house itself. A series of incidents, planned or exploited by clever members of this house—the JŌWA CONSPIRACY of 842, the ŌTEMMON CONSPIRACY of 866, and the AKŌ INCIDENT OF 887—had already enabled the Fujiwara to eliminate many rival families at court and draw close to the sovereign as regents (SESSHŌ or KAMPAKU), and to build the base that would later allow them to establish a permanent regency ruling in the name of the monarchy.

In the second phase—late 9th century until 967—the imperial house managed to preserve both its power and authority in the face of the rising Fujiwara. During this phase the emperors UDA, DAIGO, and MURAKAMI reigned without the "assistance" of a Fujiwara regent (see ENGI TENRYAKU NO CHI). Uda promoted the career of SUGAWARA NO MICHIZANE as a counterweight to Fujiwara influence, and Daigo too attempted to avoid Fujiwara domination. But the court at this juncture was faced with a serious decline in revenues due to its inability to carry out the complex land allotment system in the provinces. Daigo made an attempt to regulate the growth of private estates, and a revision of the system of controlling the provinces left matters of local government in the hands of provincial governors (KOKUSHI), requiring only that they meet the tax quotas set for their provinces. This also marked an abandonment of tax based upon people (see SO, YŌ, AND CHŌ) to one based upon the land itself (see NENGU).

Despite the promulgation of a fine legal formulary (the ENGI SHIKI), great accomplishments in historical compilation, and the flourishing of aristocratic cultural activities, this phase saw a further erosion of *ritsuryō* institutions as local landholders, ever more frustrated by the breakdown of the land system, sought private control over their lands by joining with important central nobles and religious institutions in establishing *shōen*. Control of both land and people by the court continued to weaken.

The date 967 is important as the year in which Fujiwara no Saneyori (900–970) became regent after a hiatus of almost 20 years in which the post had been vacant. Under Uda and Daigo there had been no regent from 891 to 930, but Fujiwara no Tadahira (880–949) had been appointed to the post with the accession of Emperor Suzaku (923–952, r 930–946), holding it until his death in 949. Under Murakami (r 946–967) there had been no regent from 949 to the end of his reign. Now (in 967) Saneyori reestablished the tradition, and it was never broken thereafter. With the exile of leading MINAMOTO FAMILY courtier Takaakira in 969, the Fujiwara were able to dominate the court completely.

The third phase, extending from 967 to 1068, is the period of Fujiwara REGENCY GOVERNMENT *(sekkan seiji)*, when one lineage of the northern branch of the Fujiwara family established permanent domination of the polity. The emperors were all born of Fujiwara mothers and were completely dominated by their uncles, fathers-in-law, or grandfathers, in whose households they were normally raised. This was the time of the greatest political figure of the Heian period, FUJIWARA NO MICHINAGA, father of four women married to emperors and grandfather of three emperors. Michinaga's son FUJIWARA NO YORIMICHI, a high-ranking courtier for three-quarters of a century, continued the Fujiwara glory until the accession of Emperor GO-SANJŌ in 1068, when the Fujiwara regency lost its grip on the imperial line.

This third phase is the one most studied and celebrated in Japan, so much so that we normally take the highly refined aristocratic life of this phase as being typical of the whole Heian period. Michinaga has been considered by some as the model for the hero of the TALE OF GENJI, which so brilliantly depicted the aura of court life. The dominance of the Fujiwara was such that many consider the Heian period synonymous with Fujiwara, and in art the Fujiwara epoch (Fujiwara *jidai*) is a division covering the last 300 years of the period.

The succession of Go-Sanjō, the first sovereign in 100 years whose mother was not of the Fujiwara regents' line, initiated the fourth phase, extending until the establishment of the KAMAKURA SHOGUNATE in 1192. This phase is normally referred to as the period of INSEI, or rule by "cloistered emperor." Whether or not Go-Sanjō conceived of a "system" of retired emperors controlling politics is the subject of academic debate, but the period was dominated by three successive powerful former emperors—SHIRAKAWA, TOBA, and GO-SHIRAKAWA—who replaced the reigning emperors of the earlier period and the regents of the mid-Heian period as the supreme figures in the political process.

In fact, it can be seen as a time of imperial revival, during which the ruling house organizing itself politically and economically in the manner of the Fujiwara family in order to compete more effectively for the rewards of power. *Shōen* expansion continued unabated, and the imperial house, under the active headship of retired emperors, became the focus of commendation, replacing the Fujiwara as the greatest landholder in Japan. No longer simply the repository of sovereignty, as it had been under the Fujiwara, the imperial family developed a strong household system including a large number of clients, both aristocratic and military, as well as the largest bloc of estate holdings in the country, by successfully regaining control over the imperial position that the Fujiwara had effectively captured in the earlier phase.

During this phase, however, the *ritsuryō* system all but disappeared, as powerful local individuals, banding together in large military cliques (BUSHIDAN), continued onslaughts on state control of land; the huge Buddhist institutions of the capital region assembled large armies and fought among themselves for both economic and ecclesiastical prizes, terrorizing the court when their demands were not met. Because in 1052 the world had entered the dreaded "latter day of the law" (mappō; see ESCHATOLOGY), the final phase of human decline according to a Buddhist doctrine popular in Japan, the courtiers felt rather helpless in the face of such a threat.

The military class became essential to the maintenance of civil government in the capital, as clearly demonstrated by the outbreak of the HŌGEN DISTURBANCE (1156) and the HEIJI DISTURBANCE (1160) in the capital. From that time on, the warriors were an indispensable part of court politics, and the rise of one warrior-courtier, TAIRA NO KIYOMORI, was so rapid and unusual that some scholars postulate the existence of a fifth phase of the Heian period, or at least a subdivision of the *insei* phase, from 1160 to 1185, the phase of Taira warrior polity.

Landholding System——In the mid-7th century the ruling family in Yamato maintained a shaky hegemony over the confederation of other *uji* at the Yamato court. Military reverses in Korea, the rise of the Tang dynasty in China, and the increasing economic, military, and political power of other *uji* dictated that the Yamato group take decisive action to preserve its position. That action was the TAIKA REFORM (645), which initiated a process of centralization culminating in the *ritsuryō* system modeled on the Chinese experience.

The most revolutionary reform was in the landholding system. The *ritsuryō* system provided for central-government (imperial) control of Japan's rice paddy land and productive human labor. This was in sharp contrast to the existing system whereby the various *uji* controlled private lands (TADOKORO) and the labor groups (BE) on those lands. Although the general principle was accepted, the *ritsuryō* system never functioned as envisioned. The main reason was that the Yamato ruling house did not possess sufficient military superiority to force other *uji* to yield control over their extensive resources. In order to secure cooperation, the Yamato *uji*, or imperial house, appointed members of the largest *uji* to bureaucratic positions (GUNJI) carrying stipends in land and labor. In effect, they became de facto nobles in a newly created imperial system without yielding their economic resources. *Uji* leaders accepted the change, since it appeared to ensure the maintenance, if not the expansion, of their economic interests.

Under the *ritsuryō* system all land belonged to the government, that is to say, the government sought to exercise administrative control and taxation rights over the land. The land allotment system (HANDEN SHŪJU SYSTEM) provided that rice land would be distributed in fixed amounts to free males and females and to slaves of both sexes. Such lands were called KUBUNDEN (allotment lands) and were to be kept as long as the recipient lived. The members of households then pooled their allotment lands for the purpose of cultivation.

In order to record the lands and the people to whom it was alloted, a census was to be compiled every six years; the land would then be redistributed if the composition of a household had changed—new eligible members would receive lands, and lands held by deceased members would revert to the state. Cultivators were allowed to work the lands for their lifetime, provided they paid the taxes the state levied upon them. There were essentially three: a rice tax *(so)*, probably 3 to 5 percent; a tax in kind *(chō)*, paid mostly in cloth); and corvée (YŌEKI), the heaviest burden of all, perhaps as much as 100 days for males aged 21–60 (20–59 in Western reckoning), for which a substitute tax *(yō)* might be paid in lengths of cloth. Military corvée was levied on the population as well.

From the beginning, the system did not function properly because it was necessary to accommodate the interests of powerful *uji* to ensure cooperation. As a result the *uji* nobility came to control large tracts of land and the labor of numerous cultivators, but the cultivators themselves fared very poorly and were eager to accept alternative solutions when available.

Land-hungry nobles and religious institutions had the capital necessary to open new lands, and their political influence was sufficient to allow such activity despite its illegality. What they needed was labor. Since *kubunden* cultivators could not sustain themselves well on their own lands, they were eager for other opportunities. The central government was unable to check these desires because it was faced with an increase in population without a concomitant rise in the amount of paddy land in cultivation.

The government therefore announced its intention in 722 to open 1 million *chō* (1 *chō* = about 2.5 acres [1 hectare] in the 8th century) of land in the northeast, but it could not muster sufficient labor for the project. The next year the government announced a law (SANZE ISSHIN NO HŌ) allowing people or institutions opening new paddy fields proprietary control for either one or three generations. Finally, in 743 the government found it necessary to grant permanent ownership to anyone who reclaimed new rice lands (see KONDEN EISEI SHIZAI HŌ).

This incentive proved successful, and as a result nobles and institutions with capital lured *kubunden* cultivators away from their allotment lands. Thus the way was paved for the acquisition of private landholdings, a trend counter to the spirit of the *ritsuryō* system but supported by the highest officials of the government, for whom it was profitable. This was the first step in the expansion of private estates. In 765 an edict was promulgated attempting to rescind the 743 law, but it was too late.

The situation continued to worsen despite the efforts of Emperor Kammu, who ordered two land redistributions, appointed provincial inspectors to hear cultivators' grievances, and had compiled three land surveys. None of these measures worked; surveys and censuses revealed great discrepancies in the records, and the inspectors were unable to change the illegal practices of many provincial governors who colluded with capital nobles to turn allotment fields into private holdings. Furthermore, Kammu's campaigns against the Ezo increased corvée levies on the peasantry, and his construction of two new capitals further drained their agricultural output as well as their labor. Finally, Kammu decreased the amount of provincial governors' salaries, but this simply encouraged them to exploit the cultivators further.

The *handen shūju* system continued to decline after Kammu's reign. The redistribution of land was accomplished only twice in the 9th century, in 828 and again between 878 and 880. Noble lands—whether in the form of *shōen* or not—expanded in the 9th century through reclamation, purchase, occupation of lands left by absconding cultivators, and commendation by cultivators. In 902 a *shōen* regulation ordinance was promulgated, aimed at limiting the transfer of public lands into private hands, but it seems to have succeeded in curtailing lands only of the imperial family. Noble land acquisition continued unabated.

By the end of the 9th century the difficulties of provincial government due to the unworkability of the *ritsuryō* provisions were of major concern to great ministers and governors alike. Ministers like Sugawara no Michizane, who had served as a provincial governor, railed against the contradictions of the system, and MIYOSHI KIYOYUKI, in his famous opinion in 12 articles of 914, demonstrated the extent of the problem.

The resistance of the cultivators to the onerous *ritsuryō* levies—by absconding, by falsifying census registers both to avoid losing lands and to escape corvée levies, and by colluding with local or capital powerful figures to make their holdings private and escape taxes—had created a crisis for the central government by drastically curtailing its resources. This further exacerbated the relationship between local authorities and the central government. Changes were inevitable, and many were being taken by governors on their own initiative.

Two major changes were introduced in the provincial government and taxation system during the early 10th century. First, it was necessary to change the *ritsuryō* system of levying tax and corvée on individuals, since the complex system allowed for great falsification. People were difficult to count, but land under cultivation was much easier to calculate. Already in most provinces the interest on government-loaned rice (SUIKO) was being levied on lands rather than people. What was needed was a unit for administration. The state decided to form *myō*, which were essentially taxation units based upon the paddy fields calculated in *tan*, upon which both rent and corvée could easily be levied. The second major change was that the central government entrusted the particulars of local administration entirely to governors—or their deputies, since increasingly the former were absentee governors remaining in the capital—in return for the payment of a stipulated amount of tax revenue, calculated for each province.

By this time the *kubunden* fields no longer existed, reallotment no longer being practiced. This did not mean that such lands were now all privatized. Government fields were now lumped together under the general term "public lands" *(kōden)*. Although the allotment was no longer carried out, the registers of provincial land *(kokuzu)* were still in existence and these came to be relied upon as a record of the amount of *kōden*, that is, taxable land, in each province. (It should be borne in mind that these *kōden* had "owners," cultivators of perhaps many generations living on them, but the government claimed ultimate administrative control and tax rights.) Thus from the 10th century the amount of public taxable land in each province was set and divided for exploitative purposes into units called *myō*.

Lands not controlled as *kōden* were mostly *shōen*, and the growth of *shōen* over the course of the 11th and 12th century was tremendous, so that by the end of the Heian period more than half of Japan's paddy fields were within *shōen* units. The growth of *shōen* reduced further the amount of taxable *kōden*, thus forcing the nobility constituting the central government to seek ever more private *shōen* revenues to replace lost public income.

By the end of the Heian period, *shōen* had been established in every province of Japan, seriously undermining the public revenue of the state; and the system of proprietary control of public lands in the provinces by great nobles (see CHIGYŌKOKU) meant that these lands too were being treated as private possessions of the proprietor or his local governor-representative. Japanese historians do not agree on the percentage of land that shifted from public to *shōen* status, but it was certainly large. On the other hand, there is a tendency to underestimate the amount of public land that remained.

We know that much of it survived into Kamakura times; in fact, the majority of the warriors who rose to power emerged out of public lands, in which they served as hereditary local officials. Nonetheless, the ideal of national control of land and people of the *ritsuryō* system was long dead by the end of the 12th century.

Heian Cultural Life—— The dominant view of the political and economic developments away from the *ritsuryō* system is negative, but in the cultural sphere the evaluations are all positive: the experience is seen as one in which the Japanese created a truly native culture for the first time. The absorption of continental Buddhist ideas, the perfection of a native written language that made possible a truly Japanese method of literary expression, and the emergence of a secular artistic tradition that freed Japanese artists and craftsmen from the rigid traditions learned from the Chinese—it is for these cultural achievements that the Heian period is best known by most Japanese.

Religion—— Although one of the reasons for abandoning the capital at Nara was the undue secular influence of the Buddhist establishment, Emperor Kammu and his successors were not hostile to Buddhism. Buddhism flourished in Heian times, and in combination with native SHINTŌ beliefs it dominated the religious and philosophical lives of the nobility in particular. But it was a different kind of Buddhism from its Nara-period predecessor.

Shortly after the move of the capital, two monks returned from China, where, accompanying an official mission, they had gone to seek the truth of the Buddhist message. SAICHŌ who had founded the temple ENRYAKUJI on Mt. Hiei (Hieizan), returned to establish there the TENDAI SECT. He dedicated himself to creating a monastic order that would serve the country in a more positive manner than the older sects in Nara. Situated as it was in the critically dangerous northeast direction (from which it was believed evil spirits invaded), Enryakuji came to be regarded as the protector of the capital.

KŪKAI, better known by his posthumous title Kōbō Daishi, returned to found his temple far from the center of politics, on Mt. Kōya (Kōyasan) in Kii Province (now Wakayama Prefecture). Kūkai introduced the tantric form of Buddhism to Japan in the form of the SHINGON SECT. Because it emphasized rituals, incantations, and magical formulas and stressed visual representation of the Buddhist cosmology in a cosmic diagram called a MANDALA, Shingon Buddhism proved immensely popular with the Japanese court, both as a religion providing personal comfort and as a spur to greater developments in art. Furthermore, Kūkai's own personality and abilities were not unimportant in the spread of esoteric Shingon, which soon eclipsed Tendai as the most important religion in Heian times.

The headquarters of both these new sects were located outside the capital, reflecting Kammu's desire that the new capital be free from the negative influence of priests. Only two temples, the TŌJI and Saiji, to the east and west respectively of the main north-south avenue of the city and far to the south of the imperial enclosure, were included in the original city plan, and other temples grew up in the suburbs of the city. Yet by the end of the period the aristocracy had constructed a large number of private temples in Heiankyō, and monks from the suburban temples were as common a sight in the Heian capital as they had been in Nara. In fact, they were more threatening, for they were usually armed.

These warrior-monks (*sōhei*) had been recruited by major temples to provide "protection" in the bitter doctrinal and political disputes within one temple or between two, and in conflicts over land rights in their provincial estates. They were also effective in opposing the government; for example, to press their demands they would march into the capital with the sacred palanquin bearing the symbol of the Shintō protective deity associated with their temple. The monks were most ferocious in their disputes with one another, however. The prime example of such infighting was the continuing struggle between the headquarters of the Tendai sect at Enryakuji, atop Mt. Hiei, and its branch temple Onjōji (or MIIDERA), at the foot of the mountain near Lake Biwa. There two institutions alternately burned down each other's buildings in ferocious fighting from the late 10th through the 15th century.

Even though these monks sometimes intimidated the court, still, the separation of religion and politics was maintained to the extent that nothing like the influence of a Dōkyō was permitted in Heian times. The court nobles remained devout, however, and frequent pilgrimages to the major Buddhist and Shintō establishments were a common part of the lives of the court from the emperor on down.

Buddhism did not spread widely among the masses in Heian times, but there was at least the beginning of a popularization of the faith through the development of a belief in the saving grace of AMIDA, the Buddha of Boundless Light, into whose Western Paradise weary souls could be reborn. Amida had supposedly made an "original vow" that all who called on his name (see NEMBUTSU) would be welcome in his Western Paradise, or Pure Land. This doctrine of the Pure Land had been introduced by ENNIN and others who had returned from study and travel in China in the 9th century, and it was popularized to some extent by the priest KŪYA (903–972), who preached it in the streets. The most important Pure Land figure of the Heian period was the priest GENSHIN, whose ŌJŌYŌSHŪ (Essentials of Pure Land Rebirth) depicted graphically the horrors of hell and and the delights of the Pure Land.

Amidism, or PURE LAND BUDDHISM, did not become a separate sect until the succeeding Kamakura period, but it achieved great popularity from mid-Heian times on. The key to the popularity of Pure Land tenets at this time was the Mahāyāna Buddhist idea of *mappō*. This concept held that the Buddhist law would develop after the death of the Buddha through three stages: prosperity of 500 years, decline of 1,000 years, and finally disappearance in the latter day. Once *mappō* began, it would not be sufficient to achieve enlightenment through one's own powers, as preached by most Buddhist sects. The only hope was to throw oneself on the saving grace of Amida.

Thus court nobles and ladies chanted the *nembutsu* to attain rebirth in Amida's Western Paradise. Fujiwara no Michinaga (966–1028), for example, wrote that during a five-day period he repeated the *nembutsu*—Namu Amida Butsu ("I put my faith in Amida Buddha")—700,000 times. With the same fervor, Michinaga, like many other courtiers, built an Amida hall in one of his residences for the worship of this Buddha. Perhaps the greatest such private Amida temple was that at Uji, the Phoenix Hall (Hōōdō) of the BYŌDŌIN, built by Michinaga's son Yorimichi (990–1074).

Although Buddhism thus flourished during the Heian period, it would be wrong to suggest that there was a strict sectarian division among devotees. Apart from the religious community itself, religious belief for most Japanese was highly eclectic. Courtiers seemingly made little distinction between different sects of Buddhism, native Shintō ritualistic beliefs, and imported "Confucian" lore centering on such pseudoscientific concepts as *yin* and *yang* and the "five elements" (see OMMYŌDŌ). Thus, for example, Michinaga visited Tendai and Shingon establishments as well as important Shintō shrines, called upon exorcists, chanted the *nembutsu*, and also had great faith in MIROKU, the Buddha of the future, all without any apparent conscious distinction. Some scholars have viewed such practices with cynicism, but it should be remembered that to the Heian courtier the powers of nature, good and evil, were very real.

Literature—— The height of the Heian creative spirit was reached in the fields of literature. As in other spheres, a convenient psychological dividing point in Heian literary development is the year 838, which marks the last of the Japanese missions to the Tang court (see SUI AND TANG [T'ANG] CHINA, EMBASSIES TO). After that the Japanese, while retaining certain Chinese philosophical tendencies and continuing to value Chinese books, pictures, and so forth, turned increasingly to a more truly native means of expression.

What made possible the tremendous surge of creativity in both poetry and prose was the development of the KANA syllabary. In its final form—some 50 phonetic symbols—it made writing much simpler. Although it was thus theoretically possible to write a Japanese sentence using no Chinese characters (*kanji*) at all, the Japanese had by this time borrowed such an immense corpus of Chinese words, including virtually all the important terms from the Confucian and Buddhist philosophies, that in practice both Chinese characters and *kana* were used. Moreover, despite the availability of *kana*, Heian court nobles remained doggedly devoted to the Chinese written language, if only as a symbol of status, and kept diaries in classical Chinese (KAMBUN) using *kana* only in the composition of Japanese poetry. This left the use of *kana* to women, and by and large it was women who produced the towering works of Heian literature.

As direct interest in China waned, courtiers turned increasingly to the cultivation of the 31-syllable *waka* poem. In fact poetry composition was more a part of the world of the Heian courtier than of that of any other society in history. There were poetry competitions, some held at imperial command, lovers exchanged poems, and on occasion even officials communicated with poems. Inability to compose a *waka* or to recognize a poetic allusion could condemn one to social disgrace. None matched the earlier MAN'YŌSHŪ in size or scope, but a number of anthologies of Japanese poetry were compiled in Heian times, the KOKINSHŪ (ca 905) being perhaps the greatest.

The development of the *kana* syllabary also proved to be a stimulus to the creation of a native prose literature, of which there were essentially two types in Heian times, the *monogatari* (tale) and the *nikki* (diary). The former was a narrative tale, reaching unparalleled heights in MURASAKI SHIKIBU's *Genji monogatari* (TALE OF GENJI), and the latter was more a record of private and intimate impressions of daily events, but they shared at least one common feature, the tendency to intersperse poems throughout the narrative. In fact, one type of *monogatari*, the *uta monogatari*, or poem tale, was little more than a large number of verses linked by brief introductory remarks. The favorite of this genre, ISE MONOGATARI (Tales of Ise), is regarded as one of the classics of Japanese literature.

The *Tosa nikki* (Tosa Diary) by KI NO TSURAYUKI is considered to be the first of its type and deals with his trip to the province of Tosa (now Kōchi Prefecture) in Shikoku. Later the genre was completely taken over by women, two of the most representative examples being the diary of the "mother of Fujiwara no Michitsuna" (*Kagerō nikki*, or The Gossamer Years) and that of *Genji*'s author, Murasaki Shikibu. Unlike the *Tosa nikki*, which focuses on a specific journey, *Kagerō nikki* covers a long period of time, chronicling the author's despair over the growing coldness of her husband, FUJIWARA NO KANEIE.

In a slightly different vein from the *nikki* is the *Makura no sōshi* (Pillow Book) of SEI SHŌNAGON. It is a collection of reminiscences, anecdotes, and very outspoken opinions about the world of the court. The tone is light and witty, expressing what the Heian courtiers referred to as *okashi*, and pioneered the popular genre of short essays known as ZUIHITSU.

Far beyond anything else in the period, it is the *Tale of Genji* that remains the classic work of Japanese literature. By comparison with other Heian works it is massive, composed of some 54 chapters dealing with the life of the court and focusing on the hero Hikaru Genji, the "shining prince." Its language is as elegant as its protagonist. A tour de force of psychological narrative, it is considered by many to be the world's first novel. If the *Pillow Book* represents the Heian aesthetic value of *okashi*—something that brought amusement and delight—then *Genji* is the epitome of another Heian ideal, the sense of MONO NO AWARE, or the sadness inherent in the things of this world. See also LITERATURE: Heian literature.

Art —— The Heian period of art is divided into an early and a late phase, turning on the cessation of official relations with China in 838. The first hundred years or so is known by either of two era names, Kōnin (810–824), or Jōgan (859–877), and the last three centuries are called the Fujiwara age. Like the Tempyō (729–749) era of Nara times, Jōgan was an era in which the Chinese influence remained strong; the development of the arts associated with esoteric Buddhism was especially striking. The major art forms were Buddhist sculpture and mandalas.

In Nara times statues had been cast in bronze or modeled in dry lacquer or clay, but beginning in the Jōgan era the Japanese relied largely on wood. The normal technique was to carve the entire statue from one block of wood, left unpainted except for the lips so as not to interfere with the natural aroma of the wood (sandalwood was especially favored). This meant that Jōgan statues were normally smaller than those of the Tempyō. The fact that the court no longer patronized the Buddhist establishment to the degree it had in Nara meant that there was no more need for massive statues like the Great Buddha of TŌDAIJI, whose function seems to have been as much nationalistic as religious. The smaller scale also meant that it was no longer necessary to employ the large group of government artisan workers for such projects, and in fact from the Jōgan epoch the tendency toward individual craftsmen became strong. The two most famous examples of Jōgan sculpture are the Yakushi Nyorai (healing Buddha) at the temple JINGOJI in Kyōto and the Shaka Nyorai (historical Buddha) at MURŌJI, south of Nara. See also BUDDHIST SCULPTURE.

Few examples of early Heian painting survive. Most numerous are the mandalas, which were used as aids in meditation and are usually found in the form of hanging scrolls or wall paintings. Fine examples are found in the Kyōto temples Jingoji and Tōji. The only other Jōgan paintings are the fierce representations of Fudō Myōō. Although a manifestation of the cosmic Buddha, Fudō were depicted as grotesque, muscular guardians who subdued the enemies of the faith with the rope and sword they normally carried. One of the most representative of these is the yellow Fudō of Onjōji temple.

As in the various works of literature, great changes are readily observable in the art of the long period under Fujiwara domination. One of the most important determinants of the new art was the growing popularity of Amida. Images of Amida became popular, the most noteworthy being that sculpted by the Buddhist artisan (busshi) JŌCHŌ in the Phoenix Hall of the Byōdōin. The serene and gentle countenance contrasts with the stiffer and more severe sculpture of the earlier Jōgan period. The representation of Amida coming to lead the believer to the Western Paradise was also a popular theme. There is an excellent example of this *raigō* theme done as a wall painting at the Byōdōin (see RAIGŌZU). There were also sculptural representatives of this theme, as the idea of the saving grace of Amida's original vow came to be widely accepted by the court nobility.

Perhaps the most marked departure of Fujiwara-period painting from the earlier periods is the development of a secular art, known by the general term YAMATO-E or "Japanese (style) pictures," to distinguish it from what was considered "Chinese pictures" (KARA-E). Very little nonreligious art existed in earlier periods. There were a few copies of Chinese-style landscapes, and portraits in the Chinese fashion of great ecclesiastical figures like the Chinese priest GANJIN. Now in the Fujiwara period, however, there was an outburst of secular painting, both landscape and scenes of daily court life, painted on folding screens (*byōbu*) and on paper doors (*fusuma*). These we know only by description since none of the paintings survive.

Perhaps the finest examples of Fujiwara painting in existence today are the EMAKIMONO, or narrative scrolls, which came into vogue in the 11th and 12th centuries. Some deal with famous historical incidents, such as the BAN DAINAGON EKOTOBA, recounting the fate of the wronged courtier Sugawara no Michizane, or the scroll of the Hōgen Disturbance; some are more religious in nature, depicting Buddhist legends, as in the SHIGISAN ENGI EMAKI, and some even depict the gory details of Buddhist hells. Perhaps the most celebrated is the 12th-century GENJI MONOGATARI EMAKI, which depicts in elegant color the world of Murasaki's novel.

Once painting was freed from the constraints of religion, development in many directions was possible, and the *yamato-e* style influenced the development of a singularly Japanese form of decorative art. New Chinese artistic traditions continued to be introduced (INK PAINTING, for example), but by going back to the *yamato-e* style, Japanese continued to produce new forms of quite distinct character.

■ ——G. Cameron Hurst III, *Insei: Abdicated Sovereigns in the Politics of the Late Heian Japan, 1086–1185* (1976). John W. Hall and Jeffrey P. Mass, ed, *Medieval Japan: Essays in Institutional History* (1974). *Iwanami kōza: Nihon rekishi*, vols 3–4 (Iwanami Shoten, 1975 ed). *Iwanami kōza: Nihon rekishi*, vols 3–4 (Iwanami Shoten, 1964 ed). Kitayama Shigeo, *Heiankyō*, in *Nihon no rekishi*, vol 4 (Chūō Kōron Sha, 1965). William H. and Helen Craig McCullough, *A Tale of Flowering Fortunes: Annals of Japanese Aristocratic Life in the Heian Period* (1980), a translation of the *Eiga monogatari*. Ivan Morris, *The World of the Shining Prince: Court Life in Ancient Japan* (1964). Murai Yasuhiko, *Ōchō kizoku*, in *Nihon no rekishi*, vol 8 (Shōgakukan, 1975). *Ōkagami*, tr Helen Craig McCullough as *Ōkagami: The Great Mirror: Fujiwara Michinaga (966–1027) and His Times* (1980). Edwin O. Reischauer, *Ennin's Travels in T'ang China* (1955). Robert K. Reischauer, *Early Japanese History* (1937). Sakamoto Shōzō, *Sekkan jidai*, in *Nihon no rekishi*, vol 6 (Shōgakukan, 1975). George Sansom, *A History of Japan to 1334* (1958). Takeuchi Rizō, *Bushi no tōjō*, in *Nihon no rekishi*, vol 6 (Chūō Kōron Sha, 1965). Tsuchida Naoshige, *Ōchō no kizoku*, in *Nihon no rekishi*, vol 5 (Chūō Kōron Sha, 1965). Yasuda Motohisa, *Insei to Heishi*, in *Nihon no rekishi*, vol 7 (Shōgakukan, 1975).

G. Cameron HURST III

KAMAKURA HISTORY (1185–1333)

The establishment of a de facto military government at Kamakura in 1185 by MINAMOTO NO YORITOMO, following the victory of his forces over the TAIRA FAMILY in the five-year struggle known as the TAIRA–MINAMOTO WAR, marked the beginning of the Kamakura period. There were new and important developments in nearly every aspect of Japanese life. Politically, the period saw the transfer of actual power from the civil aristocracy (*kuge*) of Kyōto to the provincial warrior class (*bushi*) of eastern Japan, which was at the time still a remote frontier. Economically, it saw a great number of private landed estates (SHŌEN) come under the control of the warrior class, thus serving as its economic basis of power. Because of the peaceful and stable conditions that the Minamoto victory made possible, the productivity of the *shōen* improved, as did economic conditions in general throughout the country. The Kamakura period was also a time of great religious fervor and of new vitality in literature and the arts.

Background——The transfer of power from the civilian to the military had begun centuries earlier when the imperial court attempted unsuccessfully to curb the power of certain territorially based families. By the 12th century the warrior families not only controlled the provinces but had even made serious inroads into the authority of the imperial court in Kyōto; TAIRA NO KIYOMORI had seized control of the court and had come to dominate the government by assisting a faction of the imperial clan in a succession dispute, the HŌGEN DISTURBANCE of 1156. Three years later, the MINAMOTO FAMILY and the FUJIWARA FAMILY challenged the Taira in the HEIJI DISTURBANCE but they were defeated, and the Minamoto were driven out of the capital. Twenty-six years later, Minamoto no Yoritomo finally unseated the Taira and established his government in Kamakura, far away from Kyōto.

The administrative machinery of the new government consisted of three boards. The first was the SAMURAI-DOKORO, or Board of Retainers, established in the first year of the war (1180) by Yoritomo to discipline and control his vassals. The second, established in 1184, was the KUMONJO (Public Documents Office), later absorbed into the MANDOKORO, or Administrative Board. The third was the MONCHŪJO, the Board of Inquiry, which was also founded in 1184 for the purpose of hearing and reviewing claims and lawsuits. Thus, all three boards had come into existence during the war and, more significantly, had been functioning as the government for those areas—largely in the east—controlled by the Minamoto before the war had come to an end. With the final defeat of the Taira in the Battle of DANNOURA at the western end of the Inland Sea in 1185, the entire region of western Japan from the Kyōto area to Kyūshū was brought under the aegis of the Kamakura government. In the same year Yoritomo sought and received from the imperial court the authority to appoint certain officials throughout the country, the conferral of which was tantamount to a formal recognition of the Kamakura government. One class of officials, appointed from among Yoritomo's vassals, was the SHUGO, constables or military governors, who were posted in each province to maintain law and order. To help defray the expense of keeping the peace, Yoritomo obtained the additional authority to levy HYŌRŌMAI, a commissariat rice tax. A second class of officials was the JITŌ, or land stewards, who were assigned to both public and private lands to supervise activities and to see that certain obligations, especially taxes, were met. It is due as much to the imperial delegation of such powers to Yoritomo as to his military victory that 1185 is generally designated as the beginning of the Kamakura period.

But while the military government had come into existence by 1185, the imperial court had not yet conferred on Yoritomo the highest military title in the land—that of *seii tai shōgun* (see SHŌGUN), or "barbarian-subduing generalissimo." This was finally done in 1192 but only after Yoritomo had further demonstrated his prowess by conquering northern Honshū, thus bringing all of Japan proper under one rule for the first time in history, and personally leading a huge army into Kyōto in a show of force. See also WARRIOR GOVERNMENT.

Constitution of the Military Class——The *bushi* of eastern Japan formed the nucleus of the warrior class. Although the majority of them were of humble origin, the *bushi* constituted a new military aristocracy, conscious of rank and with marked gradations. Its leadership consisted, for the most part, of the descendants of former district governors, holders of military commissions, and managers of family estates who had been sent down to the provinces from the capital. Many had been younger sons of nobles for whom suitable positions could not be found at court. Some, like Yoritomo's ancestors, had been of imperial lineage. Thus, it was not surprising that the outlook of this society was distinctly aristocratic.

At the top of this military aristocracy were the shōgun's vassals or retainers, the so-called *kenin* or GOKENIN. Comparatively few in number, they were men of proven loyalty. Among them were some whose families had supported the Minamoto for generations. Yoritomo's policy was to strengthen this group: he protected their economic status by recognizing their holdings and by issuing to them letters of confirmation (ANDO); he assigned them special places in processions and at state functions, thus emphasizing their privileged status. At the same time, when anyone failed to live up to the standards expected of a *kenin*, his title was given to someone more deserving.

Below the *kenin* came the SAMURAI. In later periods the term came to stand for any military man, but in the Kamakura period it referred to a definite rank. There is a passage in a chronicle that reflects the strong sense of hierarchy among the warrior class: "If a man is made a samurai, he will then want to be a *kenin*, forgetting his status." Both *kenin* and samurai were mounted warriors, and each commanded his own following of subvassals. But it should be pointed out that both terms in their original meaning denoted servitude, *kenin* meaning "houseman" or "retainer," and samurai meaning a person who "waited on" or "attended" someone else. They had been elevated when the provincial warrior class became the new aristocracy.

At the bottom of the military class were the foot soldiers, or *zusa*, who fought on foot because they lacked the means to own horses or elaborate armor. Hierarchy was strictly observed, for the Kamakura leadership felt that once laxity was admitted, greater laxity would result.

Life of the Warrior——Life in Kamakura contrasted sharply with the life of the courtier in Kyōto. The *bushi* was dedicated to the martial arts, such as swordsmanship, archery, and horsemanship, prepared physically and mentally for any emergency. The courtier eschewed violence and devoted his time to poetry and other gentle activities. Kamakura society exalted loyalty, honor, bravery, and frugality; in fact, it was during this period that the cult of the warrior, later known as BUSHIDŌ, took shape. See also FEUDALISM.

The Hōjō Regency——The power Yoritomo enjoyed did not remain in his family very long. After his death in 1199, even though he had left two young sons, real power passed to the family of his widow, HŌJŌ MASAKO. As shogunal regents (SHIKKEN) the HŌJŌ FAMILY ruled the country during the greater part of the Kamakura period. No other Minamoto of any importance could lay claim to the title of shōgun, for, ironically, Yoritomo, while seeking to defeat the Taira and to reestablish the Minamoto had effectively eliminated all potential rivals, including his youngest brother MINAMOTO NO YOSHITSUNE, who had emerged as the hero of the Taira–Minamoto War.

On the whole, Hōjō rule was firm and efficient. For example, when the retired emperor GO-TOBA declared the regent HŌJŌ YOSHITOKI a rebel and attempted to take back the reins of government from Kamakura in the JŌKYŪ DISTURBANCE of 1221, Yoshitoki moved swiftly. Within a month, the uprising was quelled, Go-Toba and two other former emperors exiled, the reigning emperor summarily deposed and replaced by another of Kamakura's choosing, and the lands of Kyōto nobles who had supported Go-Toba seized and transferred to Hōjō vassals. Moreover, to prevent future incidents of this kind, the Kamakura government stationed in Kyōto two shogunal deputies, called TANDAI, to watch over the court. Thereafter, the Kyōto government could do nothing without the prior approval of the *tandai*.

Yoshitoki was succeeded by his son HŌJŌ YASUTOKI, who during his regency introduced several new measures that further strengthened the Kamakura government. In 1226 he established the HYŌJŌSHŪ, the Council of State, which was made the chief advisory, administrative, and judicial body of the Kamakura government. Its comparatively large membership of 11 (later around 15) men allowed broader participation in the decision-making process than under Minamoto no Yoritomo, who had tended to rule autocratically. The Hyōjōshū drew upon non-Hōjō families as well and contributed to the strengthening of the Kamakura government.

Earlier, at the outset of his regency, the resourceful Yasutoki had created a new office called RENSHO, or cosigner, and had appointed his uncle Tokifusa (1175–1240) to the post. As the title indicates, the *rensho* cosigned with the regent all decrees and important documents and was, in effect, an associate regent. By thus sharing the authority of his office with another prominent Hōjō, Yasutoki helped minimize factionalism and succession disputes within the family.

The most significant accomplishment of his regency—and perhaps of the entire Kamakura period—was the promulgation in 1232 of a legal code for the warrior class, the GOSEIBAI SHIKIMOKU. Drawn up by the Hyōjōshū and consisting of 51 articles, the formulary embodied the precedents of the Kamakura government and the accepted customs and practices of the warrior class. It enunciated the rights of the warrior class, clarified the duties and responsibilities of Kamakura-appointed officials, such as *shugo* and *jitō*, and attempted in general to restrain and discipline the warriors, enjoining them, for example, to respect the rights of shrines and temples and of *shōen* proprietors. It also reflected the practical nature of justice during this period and the reliance of Kamakura officials on *dōri*, or "plain, reasonable common sense," rather than on the laws and regulations of earlier times that had been modeled on Chinese laws and institutions. In fact, with the promulgation of the Goseibai Shikimoku, the entire RITSURYŌ SYSTEM was swept away and replaced by laws that grew out of the social structure and special needs of the warrior class. See BUKEHŌ.

One other important measure of the Hōjō regency was the establishment in 1249 of the HIKITSUKE or High Court to assist the Hyōjōshū in adjudicating lawsuits, especially the increasing number of those pertaining to land. This body served as the highest appellate court of the shogunate.

The Mongol Invasions —— The most dramatic events of the Kamakura period were the MONGOL INVASIONS OF JAPAN during the regency of HŌJŌ TOKIMUNE. The first was launched in 1274 after the Japanese brusquely rejected a Mongol demand that they acknowledge the suzerainty of Khubilai Khan (1215–94). The invading army consisted of about 40,000 men who landed at Hakozaki Bay near Hakata in northern Kyūshū. Fortunately for the defenders, a storm suddenly arose after only a day of fighting, destroying a good part of the invading fleet and causing many of the invaders to drown.

The Japanese were better prepared for the second invasion seven years later, having built a stone wall around the bay. But Khubilai Khan was determined as well, especially since the Japanese had rejected his demands for the second time and beheaded his envoys. He sent a force of between 140,000 and 150,000 men to Hakata Bay, but again, after nearly two months of fighting, a fierce typhoon arose, forcing the invaders to retreat. Anxiety about another attack was not to subside until the end of the century; the Japanese continued to extend the sea wall and a Kyūshū deputy *(tandai)* was established to oversee shogunal vassals in Kyūshū and to direct the defense of that island in the event of a foreign attack.

The repulse of the invasions seemed to have nourished a certain amount of national pride and to have raised the prestige of the Hōjō regency. But in fact domestic strife increased and confidence in the Hōjō declined sharply because the rewards, specifically land, that the shogunate had promised to its warriors were not forthcoming. Moreover, besides those who had fought, Shintō and Buddhist priests who claimed that their prayers had generated the KAMIKAZE, or "divine winds," also pressed for rewards. The shogunate, with neither war booty nor other means to make good its promises, resorted to a number of expediencies. One was to refer the claims to the Hikitsuke, which deliberately prolonged the investigations and postponed decisions. Another was to refuse after a certain date to entertain any further claims. These moves led to an erosion of vassals' confidence in the shogunate's judicial system, and ultimately in the Hōjō regency itself. Even the issuance of decrees to postpone payment of debts, euphemistically called TOKUSEI, or "acts of virtuous government," while pleasing some, alienated the creditors, whose support the shogunate could ill afford to lose.

The Economy of the Kamakura Period —— With the establishment of peace and the unification of the country under the shogunate, economic conditions improved greatly. The *shugo* maintained law and order in the provinces, while the *jitō* saw to it that land dues were collected from the *shōen*. Both offices, however, initially functioned within the existing administrative framework.

Two economic institutions that had appeared earlier and continued to develop during the Kamakura period were the TOIMARU and the ZA. The former was a shipping agent who took rice and other products of the *shōen* on consignment and distributed them over a wide market. The latter was a guild or association that often engaged in monopolistic practices. Like the *toimaru*, the *za* was to see its greatest development during the subsequent Muromachi period (1333–1568).

Popularization of Buddhism —— One of the far-reaching developments of the Kamakura period was the rise of popular forms of Buddhism. Until this period Buddhism had addressed itself almost exclusively to the ruling class, despite its professed doctrine that everyone had the potential for attaining Buddhahood. Now for the first time Japanese Buddhism turned its attention to the lower strata of society. The movement had begun earlier, in the Heian period, when in reaction to the esoteric doctrines of the TENDAI SECT and the SHINGON SECT there developed a strong sentiment for teachings that centered more on personal salvation. Just such a doctrine was the one associated with the worship of AMIDA, who, according to tradition, had vowed in a previous life that he would not become a Buddha unless all others could be reborn in his Pure Land. By merely invoking Amida's name (NEMBUTSU) and by having faith in Amida, one could be received by him in paradise. New leaders like HŌNEN, the founder of the JŌDO SECT, and SHINRAN emerged. Hōnen taught that to be saved it was easier to rely upon the grace of Amida than on one's own efforts; to assure salvation, he encouraged the continuous invocation of Amida's name. His disciple Shinran further simplified his teachings, claiming that if faith, not conduct, were the test of salvation, all that was necessary to be saved was a single, sincere invocation. It was an idea that for simplicity could not be matched by any other religion, and his sect, called the JŌDO SHIN SECT, attracted many converts.

An even more controversial figure was NICHIREN. A man of forceful character, he stressed the importance of personal effort and criticized the Amida sects, which taught reliance on external help. For that matter, he was critical of virtually all other forms of Buddhism for their failure to see that the supreme and final teaching of Buddhism was contained in one text, the LOTUS SUTRA (*Myōhō renge kyō*). He insisted that its name, not that of Amida, should be on everyone's lips. Some of his severest criticisms were aimed at the leaders of the Kamakura government for patronizing the older sects. To their false faith he attributed earthquakes, famines, and other calamities and prophesied further dire consequences for Japan, including foreign invasion, unless they accepted his teachings. The prophesy was made in 1260, 14 years before the first Mongol invasion. Nichiren was also nationalistic, declaring that Japan was the land where the true teaching of the Buddha would be revived and whence it would spread throughout the world. When he died in 1282 he left a vigorous sect behind him. See NICHIREN SECT.

Still another important form of Buddhism to flourish in this period, especially among the warrior class and in artistic and literary circles, was ZEN. Unlike the other three indigenous sects, Zen Buddhism was introduced from China by EISAI, who made two trips to Song (Sung) China, and it developed into a sectarian movement. In 1199, eight years after his return from his second trip to China, Eisai accepted the invitation of the shogunate to become the abbot of a new monastery in Kamakura. Thus began a close relationship between Zen and the military leadership that was to continue throughout the Kamakura and the ensuing Muromachi period. Eisai introduced what was called the RINZAI SECT. Eisai's pupil DŌGEN, who also studied in China, founded the SŌTŌ SECT of Zen and influenced the regent HŌJŌ TOKIYORI and other members of the Hōjō family. Zen's simplicity and directness and its emphasis on self-discipline and meditation as the best way to attain enlightenment were particularly attractive to the warrior class.

The Arts —— Much of the literature of this period fell into the category of GUNKI MONOGATARI. Unlike the *monogatari* of the Heian period, which described the life and loves of courtiers, the *monogatari* of the Kamakura period concerned themselves mainly with war and the exploits of warriors. The most popular of these military epics was the HEIKE MONOGATARI (13th century; tr *Tale of the Heike*, 1975). Recited by ballad singers, the story recounted the rise and fall of the Taira in the context of the Buddhist philosophy of impermanence.

Although deprived of its political role, the court in Kyōto continued to be a cultural center. TOWAZUGATARI (ca 1307; tr *The Confessions of Lady Nijō*, 1973) is the memoirs of a court lady who at age 14 entered the household of a retired emperor and left the court 36 years later to become a wandering nun. She wrote with nostalgic longing for the past. See also MONOGATARI BUNGAKU.

Similarly, but with greater pessimism and bitterness, KAMO NO CHŌMEI, a former court noble turned recluse who had witnessed the transfer of power from the civilian to the military aristocracy, wrote about the wars, fires, and earthquakes that he had experienced in his *Hōjōki* (1212; tr *The Ten Foot Square Hut*, 1928).

Japan's first interpretative history, which also embodied a Buddhist philosophy of history, was a product of this period. It was written by JIEN, a Tendai abbot, and modestly entitled GUKANSHŌ (1220, "Notes on Foolish Views").

A distinguished literary production of the imperial court was the SHIN KOKINSHŪ (New Collection of Ancient and Modern Times). Completed in 1205 it is regarded by many as second only to the 8th-century anthology MAN'YŌSHŪ. Contributors included FUJIWARA NO SADAIE, SAIGYŌ, FUJIWARA NO IETAKA, and FUJIWARA NO YOSHITSUNE. See also LITERATURE: medieval literature.

A library and center of learning was established by Hōjō Sanetoki (1224–76), a nephew of the regent Yasutoki. His collection of

Chinese and Japanese manuscripts and documents became the nucleus of the famous KANAZAWA BUNKO (Kanazawa Library).

In art, the Kamakura period is known for its sculpture. The favorite medium was wood, noted examples being the two huge guardian figures of the temple TŌDAIJI, by UNKEI and KAIKEI. Among the bronzes the best known is the huge image of Amida in Kamakura (see DAIBUTSU), completed in the mid-13th century (see BUDDHIST SCULPTURE). Kamakura painters as well as sculptors showed much interest in portraiture. Among the many likenesses of religious and secular leaders of the time is a famous early portrait of Minamoto no Yoritomo, done in the YAMATO-E stylistic tradition and attributed to FUJIWARA NO TAKANOBU (see PORTRAIT PAINTING). Another popular art form was the horizontal picture scroll (EMAKIMONO). Based on well-known *monogatari*, the settings were often battle scenes. Other outstanding scrolls depicted the lives of Buddhist leaders such as Hōnen and IPPEN. In general, the picture scrolls of this period tended to include more narrative and naturalistic detail than their Heian predecessors. Another type of painting, *suibokuga* (see INK PAINTING) developed within the Zen community. Inspired by Song (Sung) Chinese painting and characterized by the use of ink line, it ranges from realistic portraits of Zen masters (*chinzō*) to edificatory scenes from Zen and Taoist tradition. The *karayō* style of architecture was used to build the newly established Zen sect temples. See ARCHITECTURE, TRADITIONAL DOMESTIC.

Decline and Fall of the Shogunate —— In 1333 the Kamakura shogunate came to a sudden end when two important military commanders turned against their leaders. ASHIKAGA TAKAUJI had been sent to Kyōto to bring into line the retired emperor GO-DAIGO, who had escaped from Oki Island where he had been banished for having defied the shogunate. But Takauji, who had grievances against the Hōjō, chose to support Go-Daigo, enabling him to return to the throne in what is known as the KEMMU RESTORATION. Subsequently, when NITTA YOSHISADA, another Kamakura vassal, was ordered to proceed against Takauji, Yoshisada too turned against his superiors and forced HŌJŌ TAKATOKI and his family to take their own lives. Thus ended the 150-year rule of the country's first military regime, the same government whose founder had sought to instill in the warrior class a sense of loyalty and honor, and which only 50 years earlier had successfully defended the country against the Mongol invaders.

To be sure, there had been signs of impending collapse as early as the 1280s, when many Kamakura vassals openly expressed dissatisfaction over the shogunate's failure to reward those who had contributed to the victory against the Mongols. Another conspicuous sign was the deterioration in the quality of leadership in the government. Takatoki, the last Hōjō regent of importance, had neither the inclination nor the skills to administer the government, spending much of his time dancing and watching dogfights. There was, too, mounting resentment of the virtual monopolization of offices by the Hōjō. Thus, the fall of the Kamakura shogunate in 1333 was not as sudden and as unexpected as it appeared to be. See also KAMAKURA SHOGUNATE.

■ —— Amino Yoshihiko, *Mōko shūrai*, vol 10 of *Nihon no rekishi* (Shōgakukan, 1974). Peter Duus, *Feudalism in Japan* (1969). Louis Frédéric, *Daily Life in Japan at the Time of the Samurai, 1185–1603*, tr Eileen M. Lowe (1972). *Gikeiki*, tr Helen Craig McCullough as *Yoshitsune: A Fifteenth-Century Japanese Chronicle* (1966). John W. Hall and Jeffrey P. Mass, ed, *Medieval Japan: Essays in Institutional History* (1974). *Heike monogatari*, tr Hiroshi Kitagawa and Bruce T. Tsuchida as *The Tale of the Heike* (1975). Ishii Susumu, *Kamakura bakufu*, vol 7 of *Nihon no rekishi* (Chūō Kōron Sha, 1965). Ishii Susumu et al, ed, *Chūsei 1*, vol 5 of *Iwanami kōza: Nihon rekishi*, ser 3 (Iwanami Shoten, 1975). Frédéric Joüon des Longrais, *Age de Kamakura, sources, 1180–1333* (1950). Jeffrey P. Mass, *Warrior Government in Early Medieval Japan* (1974). Jeffrey P. Mass, *The Kamakura Bakufu: A Study in Documents* (1976). Jeffrey P. Mass, *Court and Bakufu in Japanese History* (1982). Miura Hiroyuki, *Kamakura jidai shi* (1982). Ōyama Kōhei, *Kamakura bakufu*, vol 9 of *Nihon no rekishi* (Shōgakukan, 1974). George Samson, *A History of Japan to 1334* (1958). Minoru Shinoda, *The Founding of the Kamakura Shogunate, 1180–1185* (1960).

Minoru SHINODA

MUROMACHI HISTORY (1333–1568)

The Muromachi period embraces two turbulent centuries of Japanese history, from the mid-14th to the mid-16th, when the central WARRIOR GOVERNMENT—the shogunate—was located in the Muromachi district of Kyōto, to the north of the capital city and close to the imperial palace. The holders of the shogunal office during these centuries were leaders of the ASHIKAGA FAMILY, and the age is also commonly referred to as the Ashikaga period.

Attempts to provide a precise periodization for the Muromachi age raise difficulties. This encyclopedia dates the Muromachi period from 1333, when ASHIKAGA TAKAUJI and others destroyed the Kamakura shogunate. Some historians would set the starting point for the MUROMACHI SHOGUNATE and the Muromachi period in the year 1336, when Takauji defeated the supporters of his erstwhile sovereign, Emperor GO-DAIGO, captured Kyōto, and ended Go-Daigo's brief attempt at direct imperial rule known as the KEMMU RESTORATION. Takauji quickly asserted his authority over the city by setting a child emperor, Kōmyō (1322–80; r 1336–48), on the throne and issuing what was to serve as the basic statement of legal and political principles for the Ashikaga regime, the KEMMU SHIKIMOKU. Although Takauji had secured military control over Kyōto in 1336 and embarked upon the creation of a new machinery of government, he had yet to provide himself with rank and office that would lend a cloak of legitimacy to his usurpation of power. Some historians, therefore, prefer to date the inauguration of the Muromachi shogunate from 1338, the year in which Takauji, following the precedent set by MINAMOTO NO YORITOMO, assumed the title of *seii tai shōgun* (SHŌGUN), thus giving formal identity to his military council, the shogunate. However, whereas Yoritomo had exercised his authority from Kamakura in the eastern provinces, the center of his military power, land base, and vassalage system, Takauji chose to remain in Kyōto. The choice of that cultured, commercially active city as the setting for Ashikaga rule was to affect profoundly the character of the Muromachi shogunate and the cultural and social developments of the Muromachi age.

The assumption of the title shōgun did not give Takauji control of the country. When he had entered Kyōto in 1336 and deposed Go-Daigo, Takauji had tried to keep the emperor in leisured captivity. Within months, however, Go-Daigo had escaped from the capital, taking with him the imperial regalia, and established a rival court—to him, of course, it was the legitimate court—in the thickly forested mountain valleys of Yoshino, 60 miles (96 km) south of Kyōto. The emperor and his supporters, who included warriors and temples as well as nobles, did not take their exclusion from power passively. For the next half-century dwindling but determined bands of loyalists to Go-Daigo and the cause of the Southern Court waged sporadic civil war with supporters of Takauji and the Northern Court in Kyōto. Some scholars have viewed this period of civil war in the mid-14th century as a distinct and significant period in Japanese political and social history, the period of the NORTHERN AND SOUTHERN COURTS. They would date the beginning of the Muromachi period from 1392, the year in which ASHIKAGA YOSHIMITSU, the third Ashikaga shōgun, ended the feuding, secured the unification of the rival imperial lines, and extended shogunal authority throughout the country. It was Yoshimitsu who in 1378 had built his palace in the Muromachi sector of the capital; in Takauji's day the headquarters had been located further south, in the Nijō Takakura area.

The termination of the Muromachi period has also given rise to differing views. The Muromachi shogunate survived into the late 16th century, continuing to function as an institution of central government in Kyōto until 1573, when the hegemon ODA NOBUNAGA expelled the 15th shōgun, ASHIKAGA YOSHIAKI, from the capital city, and retaining a legal existence until 1588, when the exiled Yoshiaki finally resigned his office. This encyclopedia nonetheless ends the Muromachi period with Nobunaga's capture of Kyōto in 1568. Many scholars would argue, however, that the authority of the shogunate over the country had so declined after the ŌNIN WAR (1467–77) that the succeeding century, called the Warring States period (SENGOKU PERIOD), should be treated as a separate period. Although some historians emphasize the durability of the Muromachi shogunate and assert that shogunal authority was not at quite such a low ebb in the late 15th century as is commonly suggested, it is difficult to find convincing evidence of decisive action or extensive authority on the part of the shōguns and their self-appointed deputies, who were scrambling for power in Kyōto during the final century of Ashikaga rule. Decentralizing tendencies are most evident, and such political dynamism as existed was demonstrated in the provinces, where local warrior chieftains (SENGOKU DAIMYŌ) were fighting to build up strong, self-contained domains. It was not until the second half of the 16th century that the political pendulum began to swing back in the direction of centralization as the warlords Oda Nobunaga, TOYOTOMI HIDEYOSHI, and TOKUGAWA IEYASU fought to impose a new unity on the country.

Bearing in mind distinctions of periodization, for the purpose of discussion the dates 1333–1568 will be used for the Muromachi period. In discussing political and institutional developments the rule of Takauji and his immediate successor, Yoshiakira (1330–68; r 1359–68), will be treated as early Muromachi, that of the third shōgun, Yoshimitsu, to the sixth shōgun, ASHIKAGA YOSHINORI, as mid- or high-Muromachi, and the period covered by the eighth shōgun, ASHIKAGA YOSHIMASA, and his successors as late Muromachi. These problems of periodization are raised principally by political historians. The distinctions they make are less useful in trying to grasp the movement of social, economic, and cultural history, where the boundaries within the Muromachi period and between Muromachi and preceding or succeeding ages rarely correspond to political watermarks.

Changing Interpretations —— Until quite recently the Muromachi age was one of the least understood periods in Japanese history. Little scholarly attention was devoted to it, and it was commonly dismissed as a time of political confusion and social disintegration. Compared with the regent HŌJŌ FAMILY who preceded them, or the unifiers and Tokugawa shōguns who followed them, the Ashikaga shōguns were viewed as weak rulers, bereft of economic resources and heading unstable institutions of government. Around them, but outside their control, their provincial deputies, the military governors (SHUGO), worked to convert their provinces of administrative assignment into feudal domains, local warriors (KOKUJIN) extended their power by dismembering the estates (SHŌEN) of central proprietors, and peasants and samurai periodically banded together in leagues (IKKI) and rose in insurrection. The Muromachi age held interest and meaning mainly for cultural historians who were impressed by the development of NŌ, KYŌGEN, and renga (linked verse; see RENGA AND HAIKAI) and by the elite, Song (Sung) dynasty-inspired cultural style of Zen monasteries and shogunal salons. Two visions of the age thus persisted side by side and largely unreconciled: on the one hand an epoch of great cultural achievement, on the other a time of social subversion, of inferiors toppling superiors (GEKOKUJŌ).

In the past few decades more attention has been given to all aspects of the Muromachi period. Although some areas remain in shadow, recent research by Japanese and Western scholars has highlighted more positive, enduring aspects of the period, allowing us to see the links between political, economic, cultural, and intellectual developments.

Political Developments: Central Government —— In taking the title shōgun and establishing the Muromachi shogunate, Ashikaga Takauji borrowed personnel, ideas, and institutions from the Kamakura shogunate and the Hōjō regents, whose vassals the Ashikaga had been. Warriors who helped him draft the Kemmu Shikimoku, for instance, had served the Hōjō, and the principles enunciated in it were avowedly a reaffirmation of the ideals of the Kamakura warrior code, the GOSEIBAI SHIKIMOKU (1232). In addition to the office of shōgun, such offices of central and local warrior government as the Board of Retainers (SAMURAI-DOKORO), Administrative Board (MANDOKORO), Board of Inquiry (MONCHŪJO), the provincial military governors (shugo), and military land stewards (JITŌ) had all been developed under the Kamakura shogunate. The Ashikaga rulers had a ready-made administrative framework that they could staff with their own vassals. Like the Hōjō regents, the Ashikaga shōguns gave considerable attention to the imposition of warrior control over the imperial court. The Hōjō had achieved this after the JŌKYŪ DISTURBANCE (1221) by establishing the office of Rokuhara deputy (ROKUHARA TANDAI) in the imperial capital and by regulating the imperial succession. The Ashikaga maintained their influence over the court by locating the shogunate in Kyōto, supporting the Northern Court in the Northern and Southern Courts dispute, and keeping the imperial court indigent after the unification of the courts in 1392.

Although there were important continuities between the Kamakura and Muromachi regimes, there were also significant differences. Many of these differences sprang from the altered relationship between the Ashikaga shōguns and their principal vassals. Whereas Yoritomo and the Hōjō had built up and maintained, at least until the aftermath of the MONGOL INVASIONS OF JAPAN (1274 and 1281), tight personal control over their house vassals (GOKENIN) through a reciprocal bond of service in the form of military levies and guard duty by the vassal in return for confirmation (ANDO) of landholdings by the Kamakura government, Ashikaga control over the vassals whom they appointed as shugo was weak from the outset. The problem of exerting central control was further compounded by several facts. Many shugo were as powerful militarily as the Ashikaga shōguns. Shugo families were well entrenched in the provinces and able to take advantage of the disturbances of the late 13th and 14th centuries to bid for political favor and to extend their local authority. The Ashikaga shōguns' access to land rights was limited and they therefore had little to offer in the way of spoils to hold the allegiance of their vassals. Finally, powerful shugo families like the SHIBA FAMILY, the HOSOKAWA FAMILY, and the HATAKEYAMA FAMILY came to monopolize the important office of shogunal deputy (KANREI) and to dominate the senior councils of the shogunate. The Muromachi shogunate is, therefore, best described as a coalition of shōgun and shugo. The success of central authority and of the shōguns hung on their ability to develop their own reserves of economic, bureaucratic, and military strength and to manipulate the coalition in the interests of peace and political order.

Several of the earlier Ashikaga rulers were resourceful and determined in imposing their authority, via the shogunate, over the shugo. The later Ashikaga shōguns were much less successful in managing the coalition and were frequently at the mercy of events.

The Muromachi shogunate did not get off to a very strong start. Takauji allowed considerable administrative and judicial authority to his younger brother, ASHIKAGA TADAYOSHI, while reserving for himself feudal and military authority over those offices of the shogunate such as the Samurai-dokoro and Onshō-gata (Office of Rewards) that regulated the affairs of vassals and other warriors. This division of authority eventually hardened into a breach within the shogunate marked by enmity between the brothers and their supporters. This cleavage within the Ashikaga leadership naturally hampered the conduct of the campaigns against the Southern Court loyalists and made it more difficult to contain the local aggrandizements of shugo. The death of Emperor Go-Daigo and the assassination of Tadayoshi left Takauji in a stronger position, but Ashikaga control was still far from secure at his death.

Shogunal authority within the shogunate and over the country was pressed ahead by Takauji's successors, the shōguns Yoshiakira and Yoshimitsu, with the support of the general Sasaki Dōyo (1306–73) and the shogunal deputies (kanrei) Hosokawa Yoriyuki (1329–92) and Shiba Yoshimasa (1350–1410). Appointed shōgun in 1369 while still a child, Yoshimitsu, under the secular tutelage of Hosokawa Yoriyuki and the religious and cultural guidance of the Zen monk GIDŌ SHŪSHIN, grew into a vigorous and cultured ruler. As an assertion of shogunal grandeur he had a splendid new palace, the Hana no Gosho or "Palace of Flowers," built in the Muromachi district close to the imperial palace. Throughout his reign he sought to cultivate and control the imperial court and nobility. His lavish entertainments for emperors, nobles, and high-ranking warriors, his acquisition of increasingly high court ranks culminating with that of grand minister of state (dajō daijin) in 1395, and his successful efforts to unite the rival courts were all expressions of Yoshimitsu's desire to live the life of a courtier and to assert shogunal authority over the imperial court as well as warrior society. As far as the imperial house was concerned there are some indications that Yoshimitsu wanted more than association with, and influence over, emperors. In taking the tonsure and building his elegant retreat with its Golden Pavilion (KINKAKUJI) in the northwestern Kitayama district of the capital, Yoshimitsu was overtly adopting the life of the cloistered emperors of the 11th and 12th centuries (see INSEI), many of whom had ostensibly withdrawn from the world and political activity but continued to wield power from the seclusion of their villas. Yoshimitsu seems also to have conceived the ambition of insinuating his progeny into the imperial lineage, although he died with the dream unrealized.

Although Yoshimitsu relished the life of a courtier, he did not neglect his responsibilities as the warrior ruler of the country. He took the lead in organizing vassals in western Japan to crush uprisings by the TOKI and YAMANA shugo families in 1390 and 1391 and by the ŌUCHI FAMILY in 1399–1400, thus tightening shogunate control over the warrior houses. He commanded sufficient authority to be able to oblige most shugo to establish residences in Kyōto and to remain fairly constantly in attendance at his court. The only important area of the country that remained outside the full scope of shogunal control was eastern Japan, where the governor-general of the Kantō region (Kantō kubō, also known as Kamakura kubō; see KUBŌ), a cadet member of the Ashikaga house, exercised autonomous regional control from the site of the first shogunate in Kamakura.

To enhance his supremacy over warrior (bushi) and noble (kuge) society and to satisfy his refined aesthetic tastes Yoshimitsu adopted a lavish cultural style. Surrounding himself with such arbiters of taste and literary style as the Nō actors and dramatists KAN'AMI and ZEAMI, the courtier-poet NIJŌ YOSHIMOTO, and the Zen masters Gidō Shūshin and ZEKKAI CHŪSHIN, Yoshimitsu patronized Nō and the arts of poetry, painting, and garden design. The force of his interest made the Hana no Gosho and the Kitayama villa into the most vital cultural and intellectual centers of the age (see KITAYAMA CULTURE). In his avid patronage of the arts Yoshimitsu encouraged a process that reached its peak under the eighth shōgun, Yoshimasa, of bringing into the elite cultural circles of the court lowborn but talented individuals. Many of these were connected with the JI SECT of PURE LAND BUDDHISM and in their names used the suffix -ami. Among these shogunal "companions" (dōbōshū), as they came to be known, some, like Kan'ami, were specialists in a single art, while others, less well known, were men of more general discrimination. Such advancement of cultural accomplishment was one important avenue of upward social mobility made available in the Muromachi period. The mingling of elite and popular elements, or the transformation of popular interests into elite, drew on the cultural vitality of Kyōto, but the phenomenon was encouraged by the openness of the shogunal court and the sudden and recent elevation of the Ashikaga from provincial warriors to rulers of the country.

To obtain prized Chinese art objects and to help pay for his palace and temple building and his frequent cultural extravaganzas, Yoshimitsu opened up the controversial and potentially lucrative TALLY TRADE with Ming-dynasty China. Although many at the time and since have criticized his acceptance of the tributary title "king of Japan," in his dealings with the Chinese court Yoshimitsu seems to have paid little more than lip-service to this diplomatic formula. He no doubt regarded it as a small price to pay for the works of art and financial rewards the embassies would yield. In the 6 years after 1404, 37 vessels from six embassies completed the round trip. Since a single embassy might have yielded as much as 10,000 kammon (ten million coins) in profits, the Ming trade opened up an important new source of revenue for the Muromachi shogunate and was pursued by Yoshimitsu as a means of offsetting the relative paucity of income-producing shogunate landholdings. See CHINA AND JAPAN: China and Japan to 1911.

The power and prestige of the shogunate, which Yoshimitsu had so skillfully augmented by his manipulation of court titles, military campaigns, and cultural leadership, declined under his immediate successor, his son Yoshimochi (1386–1428; r 1395–1423). Yoshimochi resented the fact that his father had always shown greater favor for his brother Yoshitsugu, and that even in allowing him the shogunal office, Yoshimitsu had continued to exercise real power until his death in 1408. Yoshimochi promptly proceeded to undo what he felt were the excesses of his father's policies. With the encouragement of the kanrei Shiba Yoshimasa he refused an offer by the imperial court to confer posthumously on Yoshimitsu the imperial title "retired priestly sovereign" (dajō hōō) and broke off the diplomatic and commercial relationship with China. Yoshimochi instituted some administrative reforms and enjoyed a military success in putting down a revolt by Uesugi Zenshū (see UESUGI ZENSHŪ, REBELLION OF) in the Kantō in 1417, but his commitment to government was erratic and he lacked the stature and subtlety of his father. Before his death he ceded the shogunal title to his 15-year-old son Yoshikazu (1407–25), but the boy was dead within three years.

Shogunal authority was reasserted briefly by the ruthless and despotic Yoshinori, son of Yoshimitsu and chief abbot (zasu) of the Tendai monastery ENRYAKUJI, who returned to lay life to assume the title of shōgun on Yoshimochi's death. In a series of campaigns Yoshinori broke a revolt by the Kantō kubō Ashikaga Mochiuji (1398–1439), who had challenged shogunal authority in the east. The shōgun thereby eliminated an aspirant to his position and extended his authority into a region where it had hitherto been weak. In the west Yoshinori brought the ŌTOMO FAMILY and the Ōuchi family to heel. In Kyōto he associated with the nobility and laid down moral prescriptions for the imperial court. In his conduct of foreign affairs he reopened the China trade, and in administration he worked to offset the influence of kanrei and shugo by making greater use of the corps of hereditary bureaucrats, the bugyōninshū, and his palace guards, the hōkōshū, both of which groups were drawn from lower-ranking warrior families close to the Ashikaga. Although Yoshinori's policies strengthened the shogunate briefly, his arbitrary, brutal methods antagonized courtiers and shugo, and in the end proved his undoing. In 1441 Yoshinori was assassinated by AKAMATSU MITSUSUKE, a warlord of Harima Province (now part of Hyōgo Prefecture), who acted on a rumor that Yoshinori intended to dispossess him.

The murder of Yoshinori by one of his vassals is generally seen as marking the beginning of the unraveling of the shogunate's authority over the warrior houses, its inability to protect its landed interests, and its gradual exclusion from the Ming trade, which became a source of contention and profit for the Hosokawa and Ōuchi families and the merchants they patronized. Under the eighth shōgun, Yoshimasa, shogunal influence over the country all but disintegrated. Yoshimasa had little of Yoshinori's aggressive ruthlessness. He shared Yoshimitsu's cultural avocations but lacked his talents for sustained political leadership. Most important, the times had changed. Yoshimasa faced political and social problems that would have defied the efforts of his more active predecessors. Shugo family succession disputes festered in Kyōto and the provinces, encouraging warriors to take sides in volatile alliances. In response to demands by indebted warriors and peasants, Yoshimasa issued a stream of "acts of virtuous government" (TOKUSEI) canceling debts owed to moneylenders, merchants, and temples. These debt moratoria threw markets and sources of credit into confusion, but when Yoshimasa tried to revoke them he provoked further outbursts. His vacillating policy brought rioting and pillaging to the streets of the capital. Yoshimasa's determination to rebuild shogunal palaces and to make for himself an elegant retreat, the Silver Pavilion (GINKAKUJI), in the Higashiyama district of Kyōto depleted the already straitened shogunal coffers. He allowed nobles, monks, and palace women, especially his consort HINO TOMIKO, to meddle in politics. His change of mind, at the insistence of Tomiko, over the choice of his successor gave rise to a succession dispute within the shogunal house that served as a vortex into which were drawn rival leagues of shugo and their warriors led by the Hosokawa and Yamana. Yoshimasa's efforts to halt the Ōnin War were futile, and he abandoned his office in the middle of the great conflict. While the rival armies reduced Kyōto to ashes, the retired shōgun devoted himself to patronage of the arts in his quiet hillside retreat.

After Yoshimasa, one looks in vain for powerful shōguns or effective central government. Shōguns came and went, appointed and deposed almost at will by the Hosokawa family, who monopolized the post of kanrei, or their major domos, members of the Miyoshi family. Such authority as the shogunate preserved was limited to the environs of the capital. What administrative continuity remained in the shogunate was provided by the bugyōninshū and the hōkōshū, who had developed some sense of professional esprit. Without shogunal leadership, however, they were no match for the kanrei and quite unable to stem the drift into the provincial wars of the Sengoku period.

Political Developments: Local Rule——The Muromachi period witnessed a complete restructuring of local control in Japan. The system of court-appointed provincial governors (KOKUSHI) that had provided a bureaucratic network of local control in Nara Japan was under strain by the 10th century and suffered a further setback with the appointment of shugo by the Kamakura shogunate. Vestiges of the old imperial forms of rule persisted, however, until the Kemmu Restoration, when Emperor Go-Daigo sought to revive the ancient system. Under the Ashikaga the imperial institutions of local control withered completely. Provinces, with their scattered estates (shōen) held by absentee noble proprietors resident in the capital or by temples and shrines, and with the holdings of resident local warriors (kokujin), were assigned to the administrative and judicial authority of shugo. To understand the drastic shift that took place in local control during the Muromachi period it is necessary to understand the vicissitudes of these military provincial governors.

The shugo's position was inherently ambivalent. As cadet members of the Ashikaga family or leading vassals of the shōguns they were assigned wide-ranging authority over one or more provinces. They were responsible for local order, justice, and tax collection. While the shogunate expected the shugo to act as its loyal administrative agents, in periods of disorder and under weak shōguns it was able to give the shugo little in the way of positive support or confirmation of rights to land. Nor was it able to restrain their natural urge to try to strengthen their grip on their provinces of assignment. For their part, the shugo had to contend with the local representatives of influential temples and shrines and with long-entrenched kokujin families, some of whom controlled as much land and manpower as the shugo and had direct access to the shogunate. During the middle decades of the 14th century shugo were generally able to take advantage of civil war and division within the shogunate to extend their regional control. Making full use of their authority to adjudicate land disputes and grant as prizes lands confiscated as spoils during the wars, to grant rights to half the tax yield (HANZEI) on local estates to their military supporters, and to impose local levies (HYŌRŌMAI) for presumed national emergencies, the *shugo* invaded the private *shōen* within their territories and organized the powerful *kokujin* as their feudal subordinates. This process of local aggrandizement by *shugo* has been described by modern Japanese historians as the creation of a *shugo* "provincial domain system" (*shugo ryōkokusei*). The inflated *shugo* who headed these domains are referred to as SHUGO DAIMYŌ. The degree of *shugo* control over their provinces of assignment varied from family to family. None were able to convert their territories into fully feudalized domains over which they exerted exclusive proprietary control (ICHIEN CHI-GYŌ). Some, however, like the Ōuchi and Hosokawa, came to exert tight control over several provinces. The Yamana enjoyed a looser hold on 11 provinces in western Japan until an army mobilized by Yoshimitsu trimmed them in the MEITOKU REBELLION of 1391–92.

With the consolidation of shogunal authority by Yoshimitsu and his immediate successors the *shugo* were put on a shorter leash and obliged to reside more or less permanently in Kyōto (or, for Kantō *shugo*, in Kamakura). Some naturally feared and resented this enforced absence from their provinces. Most found compensating advantages in direct involvement in central government politics, in participation in the cultural life of the shogunal court, and in enjoyment of the growing commercial wealth of Kyōto. In their absence they entrusted their provinces to warrior deputies (*shugodai*). The results of this separation from the local power base were soon evident. Without firm control by the *shugo*, provinces were racked by struggles between *shugodai* and *kokujin* for local influence, peasant uprisings increased, tax income failed to reach the *shugo*. A few *shugo*, among them the Ōuchi and Ōtomo, were able to hold on to their domains. The majority of *shugo* houses, however, bereft of the support of strong central authority after the mid-15th century, outmaneuvered by their former deputies or *kokujin*, starved of income, and torn by succession disputes, were toppled in the wars of the late 15th century and their regional domains carved up into more compact political and military units under the control of the warlords of the Sengoku period (Sengoku daimyō), most of whom had emerged from the *kokujin*.

The Sengoku daimyō were a very different breed from the *shugo*. Largely indifferent to shogunal authority, they lived in their domains, devoting all their energies to improving their military and economic strength. Law codes (BUNKOKUHŌ) were promulgated; castle towns were built and warriors encouraged to gather in them; military organization was reformed and military technology improved; land was reclaimed, *shōen* broken up, land surveys (KENCHI) conducted, peasant uprisings crushed, and villages brought under close supervision. It was this fragmented political order the Portuguese found upon their arrival in Japan in the 1540s; and skillful use of the guns they introduced was to help Oda Nobunaga in his drive to reunify the country. (See FIREARMS, INTRODUCTION OF.)

Economic and Social Developments —— The warfare and instability of the Muromachi period did not prevent major advances in agriculture, commerce, transportation, village organization, and urban development. If anything, the demands of warrior leaders for arms and provisions, the growth of local power centers, the loosening of the old political order dominated by the nobility and religious institutions of the capital, and the dismemberment of *shōen* all encouraged economic activity and social diversification. The shogunal court and resident *shugo daimyō* placed a heavy consumer demand on the economy of Kyōto and the surrounding Kinai region. Trade with China fed coins as well as Buddhist texts and art objects into the economy. The policies of Sengoku daimyō aimed at fostering local commerce by new groups of merchants and at reducing barriers to trade within their domains. Overall, the Muromachi period experienced a quantum leap forward in economic activity and witnessed the emergence into the limelight of two powerful new social forces, a self-conscious mercantile group and an increasingly restive and market-oriented peasantry.

On the land, double cropping of rice and barley, which had begun in western Japan in the Kamakura period, had spread into eastern Japan by Muromachi. This was accompanied by improvements in fertilizing, including the use of human wastes, in irrigation, and in the more extensive use of draft animals. There was an increasing availability of commercial crops from all parts of Japan: fruits and vegetables around the urban centers, hemp from northern and eastern Japan, indigo from Settsu Province (now part of Ōsaka and Hyōgo prefectures), sesame seed oil from the banks of the Inland

Sea, tea from Yamashiro Province (now part of Kyōto Prefecture) and Suruga Province (now part of Shizuoka Prefecture), and cotton from Mikawa Province (now part of Aichi Prefecture) and the Kinai (Kyōto–Ōsaka–Nara) region. The earth yielded up more of its treasures in the form of gold from the island province of Sado (now part of Niigata Prefecture) and Kai Province (now Yamanashi Prefecture), silver from Iwami Province (now part of Shimane Prefecture) and Tamba Province (now part of Kyōto and Hyōgo prefectures), and copper from Bizen and Bitchū provinces (now part of Okayama Prefecture). Mines were pushed deeper in order to satisfy demands from Sengoku daimyō and the unifiers for weapons, coins, and gilded decoration. The building of massive CASTLES and castle towns by the daimyō stimulated haulage and forestry, and lumber markets in Kyōto and Kamakura operated by specialist merchants handled timber from all parts of Japan.

Handicraft industries were stimulated by greater demand, greater availability of raw materials, and greater independence on the part of the producers. Metal workers enjoyed an unprecedented demand for weapons, cooking utensils, and agricultural items. Silk weavers from Ming China introduced new techniques for the production of high quality brocade (NISHIJIN-ORI) to Nishijin in Kyōto, whence they spread into the provinces. Cotton and cotton cloth production techniques were introduced from Korea. Paper making developed in Mino Province (now part of Gifu Prefecture), Harima Province (now part of Hyōgo Prefecture), Bitchū, Echizen Province (now part of Fukui Prefecture), and Sanuki Province (now Kagawa Prefecture); ceramics in Seto, Owari Province (now part of Aichi Prefecture; see SETO WARE); and *sake* brewing in Settsu Province. Most of the demand was domestic, but Japanese swords, fans, and screens were also prized on the continent. Self-awareness and independence of craft producers was fostered by the decline of the private estates with their closed economies. The gradual erosion of *shōen* released many village craftsmen from their exclusive obligations to nobles and religious institutions and freed them to produce for rising warrior groups, wealthy townsmen, and the spreading market economy. As these craftsmen grew in numbers, specialization, and professional consciousness they formed guild-like associations known as ZA. Although many of the crafts and craft guilds centered on Kyōto and the Kinai region, they gathered their raw materials from, and sent their products to, all parts of Japan.

Increases in agricultural output, the growth of craft activities, the importation and diffusion of coinage, and demands for payment of taxes and levies in cash instead of in rice or cloth all contributed to the spread of local markets, to greater specialization among merchants, to usury and more sophisticated exchange facilities, to the prosperity of the *za*, and to greater self-consciousness in urban and rural society. Copper cash were imported from Song China in small quantities during the Kamakura period (see SŌSEN), and in much larger quantities from Ming China during the Muromachi period (see KŌBUSEN). Before the end of the Kamakura period annual land taxes (NENGU) to central *shōen* proprietors were, in many cases, being paid partly in cash and partly in kind. In warrior society, the indebtedness of its retainers to moneylenders was a major problem for shogunate administrators. During the Muromachi period monetization of the economy increased markedly. Such shogunate and *shugo* levies as *tansen* (see TANSEN AND TAMMAI) and MUNABETSU-SEN were collected in cash. Some Sengoku daimyō, notably the Go-Hōjō family (see HŌJŌ FAMILY) and the TAKEDA FAMILY in the Kantō developed a "cash assessment" system for the administration of their domains, whereby landholdings, grants of fiefs, and military service required of vassals were expressed in cash units (see KANDAKA). The need for peasants to convert at least part of their crops into cash to pay taxes and levies also contributed to the development of markets and commercial activity. MARKETS (*ichi*), which had been held sporadically in the Kamakura period, were being held regularly on six days of the month even in more remote districts of Japan. Some peasants and craftsmen may have marketed their produce themselves. Increasingly, however, produce from the villages was bought by traveling merchants and transported by wholesalers, to be sold at market stalls by retailers.

Merchants, as well as craftsmen, belonged to *za*, which played a major role in medieval commercial activity. Most *za* were based in the Kinai region, the heartland of economic activity, and enjoyed the sponsorship of nobles or religious institutions to whom they paid dues in return for protection of their monopoly privileges and exemption from barrier charges (SEKISEN) and market fees. There were some 40 *za* based in Kyōto and more than 80 in Nara, many of them under the protection of the great temples KŌFUKUJI and TŌDA-

IJI. Although membership in any *za* was restricted, some of them, such as the oil traders' *za* in Ōyamazaki, had as many as 300 members whose activities spread over a dozen provinces. On the positive side, *za* served to maintain high standards among their members, contributed to small-scale accumulation of capital, and brought orderliness to the growing commercial activity. On the negative side, they were restrictive groups that sought to block the participation of provincial merchants and craftsmen in economic enterprise. The decline of *shōen* and the Ōnin War, both of which undercut the remaining influence of central proprietors, also dealt severe blows to the older *za*. Most Sengoku daimyō were eager to keep domain commerce under their personal supervision and preferred to patronize local merchants rather than the centrally based *za*. From the mid-16th century there was a spate of edicts freeing markets and reducing the privileges of the *za* (see RAKUICHI AND RAKUZA).

Although the Japanese economy was more fully monetized in the late Muromachi period than it had been in any previous era, the process was far from complete or trouble free. The quality and quantity of specie were inadequate. The shogunate continued to rely on an irregular supply of Chinese coins, which varied greatly in quality and were circulated together with privately minted coins. Good coins were hoarded, with adverse effects on prices and market stability. The shogunate passed edicts forbidding "coin selection" (ERIZENI), but these did not go to the root of the problem. Shortage of specie contributed, in the late Muromachi period, to a reversion in some areas to payment of taxes in kind. Usury, which contributed to the monetization of the Kinai economy, could also give rise to contention. In return for the payment of dues (UTOKUSEN) to the shogunate, warehouse owners (DOSŌ) and *sake* brewers (SAKAYA) were permitted to engage in usury. Some Zen temples were also sources of loans. Rates varied between 2 percent and 10 percent per month. Even the lowest rate, over the course of a year, could be a source of hardship and grievance to peasants and samurai who had pledged part of their land or their next crop. It was no accident that *dosō*, *sakaya*, and Gozan Zen temples bore the brunt of destruction in the riots that plagued Kyōto from the mid-15th century.

The vitality of commercial activity was sustained by improved means of transportation and reflected in the growth and diversification of urban life. Although the barriers (SEKISHO) sited at key communication nodes remained major obstacles to the transportation of goods, roads were extended, way stations established in towns and villages, and packhorse haulers (BASHAKU) organized. Coastal navigation was improved and regular freight services brought goods from the most distant parts of Japan to Hakata, Sakai, and other ports. The growth of commerce, the China trade, the diffusion of popular Buddhism and a vogue for pilgrimages, and the deliberate policies of the Sengoku daimyō all contributed to urbanization and the growth of entirely new types of towns. The location of the shogunate in Kyōto, the building of Gozan Zen monasteries, and the development of highly skilled craft industries all stimulated the commercial recovery of the capital in the early Muromachi period. And although the Ōnin War subjected the city to fire and devastation, its citizens quickly rebuilt it. The Iberian missionaries and traders who came to Japan in the 16th century found a bustling, populous, wealthy Kyōto. The ancient capital HEIJŌKYŌ also recovered during the medieval period; around its great temples and *za* grew the city of Nara. New towns sprang up at ports, market sites, and transportation nodes. Ōminato, Obama, Tsuruga, Mikuni, Yodo, Sakamoto, and Ōtsu all developed during this period. Sakai, Hakata, and Hyōgo grew rich on overseas trade. Sakai, in particular, increased its prosperity and influence in the 16th century as it became the principal center for the import and production of the guns that were so sought after by the Sengoku daimyō. Old and new religious centers were the sites of markets and urban growth. Sakamoto grew as the supply point for Enryakuji, Uji-Yamada benefited from the influx of pilgrims to Ise, and the towns of Ishiyama (Ōsaka) and Yoshizaki (Echizen) were the commercial centers for the powerful HONGANJI Pure Land communities. But perhaps the most significant new urban development of the Muromachi period was the building of CASTLE TOWNS (*jōka machi*) by the Sengoku daimyō. By the late Muromachi period castles were no longer being built on craggy peaks but were sited on the plains where daimyō could combine defense with control and protection of the peasantry and their rice-producing fields. Outlying castles of potential rivals were demolished, and warriors, merchants, or craftsmen gathered around the principal castle of the domain, which quickly became an urban center, the focus of the economic as well as the political and military life of the domain. Yamaguchi, Funai, Sumpu, Odawara, and Kago-

shima are all examples of early castle towns that developed during this period and played an important role in the subsequent urban history of Japan.

Daimyō exercised autocratic control over their castle towns. In some of the other towns, however, this period saw the emergence of self-governing civic communities. Thirty-six leading citizens of Sakai formed a council, known as the EGŌSHŪ, which governed the city and managed its defenses. A similar council existed in Hakata, and in Kyōto groups of townsmen (MACHISHŪ) resident in the various districts (*machi*) of the city regulated the affairs of their districts. Each *machi*, to express its community spirit and prosperity, sent elaborately decorated floats to the GION FESTIVAL. The *machishū* were dominated by merchants and guild members, but also included samurai and any nobles who lived in the *machi*. The height of *machishū* political influence in Kyōto came in the Lotus (or Hokke) Uprising of 1532–36, during which followers of the Lotus or NICHIREN SECT of Buddhism, many of whom were members of the *machishū*, seized control of the city (see TEMMON HOKKE REBELLION). These examples of civic control and independence were the product of the new-found affluence and community spirit of the late medieval towns. The freedom of action of townsmen was limited, however, and all such self-governing communities, including the militant Honganji communities, were brought under close regulation by Oda Nobunaga and Toyotomi Hideyoshi.

Urban communities were not the only ones to establish a measure of affluence and independence during this period. Many villages, especially those in the Kinai, organized village councils (YORIAI) to regulate common land and irrigation, to enforce village codes, to organize policing and defense, and to resist excessive claims for taxes and dues by estate proprietors or local *kokujin* (see SŌ). Many villages won the right to collect and forward their own annual taxes (HYAKUSHŌUKE) and to mete out justice to local delinquents. This movement toward village independence and self-regulation resulted from the demise of the *shōen* and the weakening of the divisive control by central proprietors. It was probably fostered in some villages by growing prosperity through greater access to markets for special local products and in others by the sporadic uprisings demanding debt cancellation that spread over whole provinces from the mid-15th century (see KUNI IKKI). It was made more urgent by the violence of the age and the inability of central authority to provide effective protection. Villages were brought under tight control by Sengoku daimyō in their domain-strengthening policies. But as long as villages sent in the prescribed taxes on time, many daimyō were happy to allow them to manage their own internal affairs under their headmen and elders, often rural samurai. Thus was laid the basis for the Edo period village system (see GŌSON SYSTEM). One major change was effected by Hideyoshi, who disarmed the villagers (see SWORD HUNT).

Religious and Cultural Life——Until quite recently, medieval, especially Muromachi-period, religion and culture was commonly held to be synonymous with ZEN Buddhism and Zen-related culture. Certainly Zen Buddhism did exert a profound influence on the religious, aesthetic, and cultural sensibilities of the age. Zen had taken root in Kamakura and Kyōto during the 13th century, but the Chinese teaching really flowered during the Muromachi period under the patronage of the Ashikaga shōguns and their vassals. The GOZAN network of the RINZAI SECT, with its head temples in Kyōto and Kamakura, covered Japan and provided training in meditation and cultural accomplishments for the sons of provincial warriors. Monks of the Rinzai Zen monasteries DAITOKUJI and MYŌSHINJI, both of which held aloof from the Gozan system, established close religious and cultural connections with the townsmen of Kyōto and Sakai and with the local *kokujin* who were to thrust themselves into power as Sengoku daimyō. The Zen of the SŌTŌ SECT spread widely in northern Japan under the patronage of rural samurai and prosperous peasants.

Zen offered to the Japanese elite a rigorous spiritual training involving long hours of meditation (ZAZEN) directed at the attainment of enlightenment (SATORI). Zen masters reasserted the ideals of a precisely regulated monastic life and provided access to the learning and culture of China. Chinese Zen masters like Yishan (I-shan; J: ISSAN ICHINEI; 1244–1317) introduced to Japan not only Zen practices and Buddhist texts, but Neo-Confucian political thought (SHUSHIGAKU) and the appreciation of Chinese poetry and painting. Zen monasteries were also centers for the development of new styles of architecture, design of GARDENS, the TEA CEREMONY, and FLOWER ARRANGEMENT, and Zen thought contributed to the deepening of such aesthetic principles as YŪGEN (mysteriousness), WABI (subdued taste), and SABI (elegant simplicity). By the mid-Muromachi period Zen-inspired arts were spreading from the monasteries into secular society and being blended with other Japanese cultural elements. In ink painting Song-dynasty Chinese styles were mastered by the Japanese monk-painters MINCHŌ, JOSETSU, and SHŪBUN. These were transformed and carried outside Zen cloisters by the master painter SESSHŪ. Sesshū trained as a Zen monk at SHŌKOKUJI (Kyōto), where he studied painting under Shūbun, journeyed to China to learn the latest styles of Ming painting, and returned to Japan to develop his own powerful style and to end his life as an independent professional painter. Under the early KANŌ SCHOOL masters KANŌ MASANOBU and KANŌ MOTONOBU the Chinese style of ink painting derived from Shūbun and Sesshū was further secularized and blended with Japanese-style (YAMATO-E) techniques. A similar secularization and diffusion took place in the development of the tea ceremony, in garden design, and in the art of flower arrangement.

But there is much more to Muromachi-period religion and culture than Zen. The great monasteries like Tōdaiji, Kōfukuji, Enryakuji, KŌYASAN, TŌJI, and Negoro belonging to the older schools of Buddhism maintained considerable religious, cultural and economic influence in medieval society, even while their *shōen* holdings were being whittled away. The new, popular schools of Kamakura-period Buddhism, including the Nichiren (Lotus) sect and the various branches of the Pure Land (Amidist) teachings, which had seemed in danger of withering away with the deaths of their founders, all revived and spread widely during the Muromachi period. The Nichiren sect attracted many samurai followers in the Kantō and put down deep roots among the *machishū* of Kyōto. The adherents of SHINRAN's (1173–1263) JŌDO SHIN SECT were divided by doctrinal disputes after his death but were pulled together into a powerful religious organization under the leadership of the temple HONGANJI by RENNYO in the 15th century. The groups of devotees *(monto)* included peasants and samurai. Their religious devotion and militant organization earned them the title of *ikkōshū*, the "single-minded school," and allowed them to mount a fierce challenge to the authority of the Sengoku daimyō and the unifiers in large-scale uprisings (IKKŌ IKKI). Although the Ji (Hourly) sect derived from IPPEN (1239–89) did not achieve such spectacular development, its followers wandered the roads of Muromachi Japan, chanting and dancing the NEMBUTSU, the sacred invocation of Amida. To this varied religious activity CHRISTIANITY was added with the arrival of Francis XAVIER in 1549. Each of these religious teachings gave to Japanese at all levels of society new hope for salvation, new patterns of social organization and association, new iconography, and new cultural interests.

Muromachi culture was an intricate blending of elite and popular elements, of Japanese, Chinese, and, from the 16th century, European features, and of religious and secular strains. For the first time Japan had achieved a truly national culture to which all sectors of society contributed and from which all derived stimulus and enjoyment. At the elite level the imperial court, in spite of its poverty, continued to exert an influence in ceremonial forms and in the study of Japanese classics. Emperors and courtiers shared with high-ranking warriors an interest in Nō and *kyōgen* and in the historical chronicles and war tales of the age, the JINNŌ SHŌTŌ KI, BAISHŌRON, MASUKAGAMI, and TAIHEIKI. The elite shared with commoners a passion for the short tales known as OTOGI-ZŌSHI, dance and mime (DENGAKU), and linked verse *(renga)*. SŌGI and SŌCHŌ, two of the finest *renga* poets of the age, came from lowly social origins and through their mastery of their art were able to mix with the highest in the land. Indeed many of the most characteristic arts of the age, including Nō and *kyōgen*, had their origins among the common people of Japan before they were elevated through the genius of men like ZEAMI into entertainments for the elite. Even the illiterate were free to participate in the religious and cultural life of the age. The devout recitation of the name of Amida or of the title of the LOTUS SUTRA, sufficient, it was believed, to secure salvation, did not require learning. Jongleurs traveled the country, reciting the epic of the struggle between Taira and Minamoto families or "explaining" scroll paintings to their audiences. Motifs springing from the popular imagination could stir the feelings of all segments of society. The coming and going of *shugo* to and from the capital, the wanderings of jongleurs and poets and pilgrims, the dispersion of monks and nobles from Kyōto during the Ōnin War, and the improvements in commerce and transportation all contributed to cultural interaction and diffusion within the country.

📖 ——Peter Judd Arnesen, *The Medieval Japanese Daimyo* (1979). Martin Collcutt, *Five Mountains: The Rinzai Zen Monastic Institution in Medieval Japan* (1981). George Elison and Bardwell L. Smith, ed, *Warlords, Artists, & Commoners: Japan in the Sixteenth Century* (1981). Kenneth A. Grossberg, *Japan's Renaissance: The Politics of the Muromachi Bakufu* (1981). John W. Hall and Jeffrey P. Mass, ed, *Medieval Japan: Essays in Institutional History* (1974). John W. Hall and Toyoda Takeshi, ed, *Japan in the Muromachi Age* (1977). John W. Hall, Nagahara Keiji, and Kōzō Yamamura, ed, *Japan Before Tokugawa* (1981). Donald Keene, *Nō: The Classical Theater of Japan* (1966). Earl Miner, *Japanese Linked Poetry* (1979). Satō Kazuhiko, *Nambokuchō nairan*; Sasaki Gin'ya, *Muromachi bakufu*; and Nagahara Keiji, *Sengoku no dōran*: vols 11, 13, and 14 of *Nihon no rekishi* (Shōgakukan, 1974). Satō Shin'ichi, *Nambokuchō no dōran*; Nagahara Keiji, *Gekokujō no jidai*; and Sugiyama Hiroshi, *Sengoku daimyō*: vols 9, 10, and 11 of *Nihon no rekishi* (Chūō Kōron Sha, 1965). H. Paul Varley, *Imperial Restoration in Medieval Japan* (1971). H. Paul Varley, *Japanese Culture* (1973).

Martin C. COLLCUTT

AZUCHI-MOMOYAMA HISTORY (1568–1600)

The Azuchi-Momoyama period, a short but spectacular epoch, has aptly been called Japan's "Age of Grandeur." During this pivotal period, Japanese society and culture underwent the transition from the middle ages to the early modern era. The political order was transformed, and there occurred an unprecedented efflorescence of the arts. The activities of European traders and Catholic missionaries in Japan, no less than Japanese ventures overseas, caused a vast expansion of Japan's geographical horizon and gave the period a cosmopolitan flavor that is rare in the country's history.

Periodization —— The principal event of Azuchi-Momoyama was Japan's unification after a century of civil war, the Sengoku period (1467–1568), during which the country's old governing order collapsed. The task of national unification was pursued and accomplished by three grandiose hegemons, ODA NOBUNAGA (1534–82), TOYOTOMI HIDEYOSHI (1537–98), and TOKUGAWA IEYASU (1543–1616). The first of these "Three Heroes" founded, and the second developed, the so-called Shokuhō regime (SHOKUHŌ SEIKEN) which reconstructed Japan's body politic. The third, Ieyasu, won the hegemony at the Battle of SEKIGAHARA in 1600 and three years later founded the Tokugawa shogunate (1603–1867), thereby initiating a new regime and a new epoch, the Edo period (1600–1868). This encyclopedia accordingly sets the dates of the Azuchi-Momoyama period from 1568, the year of Nobunaga's emergence as a power in national politics, to 1600, the year of Ieyasu's great victory.

The thrust of Nobunaga's and Hideyoshi's major policies continued, however, under Ieyasu. Moreover, until Ieyasu in 1615 reduced the fortress of Ōsaka and destroyed its lord, Hideyoshi's son Toyotomi Hideyori (1593–1615), there existed vestigially a rival center of attraction which challenged the supremacy of the Tokugawa regime and of Edo (now Tōkyō). Since Hideyoshi was the central personage of Azuchi-Momoyama, some historians consider it appropriate to date the period at least until 1615, when the great citadel he had built in Ōsaka fell to the Tokugawa, who destroyed his family and his heritage. Another definitive sign of the passing of an age was the beginning of the general persecution of Christianity, ordered by the Tokugawa shogunate the previous year, which signaled the contraction of Japan's horizons.

The epoch's radiance continued even after those events, however, and its terminal date is therefore set forward into the Kan'ei year period (1624–44) by cultural historians focusing on artists such as HON'AMI KŌETSU (1558–1637) and Tawaraya SŌTATSU (d 1643?), whose work brought the aesthetic traditions of Azuchi-Momoyama to a brilliant culmination. According to some of those same historians of art, the date that properly marks the beginning of the epoch is 1566, when KANŌ EITOKU (1543–90), deservedly called the greatest painter of his age and indeed the creator of the flamboyant Azuchi-Momoyama style, produced his first masterpieces in decorating the Jukōin, a priory of the great Zen monastery Daitokuji in Kyōto.

Institutional historians prefer to date the Azuchi-Momoyama period either from 1568, when Oda Nobunaga first entered national attention by occupying Kyōto and installing ASHIKAGA YOSHIAKI (1537–97) as shōgun, or from 1573, when Nobunaga expelled Yoshiaki from the capital city, dealing a mortal blow to the Muromachi shogunate (1338–1573) and establishing himself as the main actor on the stage of national politics. The key to understanding the nature of the period, however, is in appreciating the joint use of power and of art which is perhaps the most remarkable feature of Azuchi-Momoyama. It is therefore important to note that the epoch's name derives from the castle which Nobunaga began to build in 1576 at Azuchi in Ōmi Province (now Azuchi Chō, Shiga Prefecture) as a visible sign of his domination over the realm, commissioning Kanō Eitoku to decorate it; hence the period's dating may likewise properly be begun from the year 1576. The other part of the name Azuchi-Momoyama derives from a hill in Fushimi to the south of Kyōto which was the location of the palatial castle where Hideyoshi died in 1598. That hill, however, was not known as Momoyama (Peach-Tree Hill) until well into the 17th century, when Fushimi Castle was abolished and peach trees (momo) were planted on its leveled site, after the Azuchi-Momoyama period had passed.

Castles are the best symbols of this age. Their distinguishing architectural characteristic, the soaring castle keep (donjon; tenshu), was a novel conceit. Their scale, splendor, and sumptuous interior decoration astonished contemporary observers, Europeans as well as Japanese. They were meant not only for the military defense but for the glorification of their builders. They glittered with gold and dazzled the viewer with refined luxury, displaying the lords' wealth and overwhelming the vassals with a pictorial profusion of emblems of authority. Hence it is not surprising to see, on occasion, the term "castle culture" (shiro no bunka) used to describe the culture of the Azuchi-Momoyama period.

Unfortunately, the magnificent residences of Nobunaga and Hideyoshi are also symbols of their age's brevity and the evanescence of their glory. AZUCHI CASTLE was burnt down in 1582, immediately after the tragic death of its maker Nobunaga, who was assassinated in the HONNŌJI INCIDENT; none of the decorative paintings produced for it by Kanō Eitoku survived. Juraku no Tei (or Jurakudai), the pleasure dome Hideyoshi built in Kyōto between 1586 and 1587, was also decorated by Eitoku and his atelier; it was transferred by Hideyoshi to his nephew and adopted son TOYOTOMI HIDETSUGU (1568–95) in 1592 and was dismantled on the hegemon's orders in the aftermath of the disgrace of Hidetsugu in 1595. Hideyoshi's ŌSAKA CASTLE (another instance of the collaboration between the realm's greatest warlord and its premier artist, Kanō Eitoku), begun in 1583, only survived until 1615; the present structure is a ferroconcrete reproduction built in 1931 (Shōwa 6).

FUSHIMI CASTLE, built between 1592 and 1593 as Hideyoshi's riverside pleasance near the confluence of the Ujigawa and the Yamashinagawa, was from 1594 expanded by him into a grandiose, palatial fortress; it was, however, for the most part destroyed by an earthquake in 1596. Immediately rebuilt by Hideyoshi on a hillside at Kohatayama (the site later called Momoyama), Fushimi Castle was occupied by a Tokugawa garrison prior to the outbreak of the great war of 1600, and burned under attack by Tokugawa Ieyasu's enemies in the war's initial phase, six weeks before the Battle of Sekigahara. Rebuilt again by the Tokugawa between 1602 and 1606 as their principal outpost against Toyotomi Hideyori's party and their counterbalance to Ōsaka, Fushimi Castle lost its military significance after Hideyori and his Ōsaka citadel were destroyed in 1615. The Tokugawa shogunate decided to make Ōsaka its major base in western Japan, and from 1619 commenced large-scale work on its own fortress in that city; hence Fushimi Castle was ordered demolished, its buildings transported elsewhere, and its very stones taken away to be used in the shogunate's fortifications at Ōsaka. By the end of 1624 there was nothing left on the Momoyama site. The present Fushimi Momoyama Castle, impressive from a distance, is another modern ferroconcrete structure, erected in 1964 (Shōwa 39) for commercial purposes and scarcely worth the visit. (Indeed, the country's numerous Shōwa-period [1926–] castles serve but to confuse, not to enlighten, the unwary tourist.) Residential ensembles reputed to be the transplanted relics of Juraku no Tei or of Fushimi Momoyama Castle may be viewed at the Buddhist temple Nishi Honganji in Kyōto.

Authentic examples of the superb castle architecture of the Azuchi-Momoyama period are MATSUMOTO CASTLE in Nagano Prefecture, with a central keep (recently determined to be the oldest extant donjon in Japan) built between 1594 and about 1600 by the Ishikawa family, Hideyoshi's vassals, and HIMEJI CASTLE in Hyōgo Prefecture, the most famous of the period's remaining edifices, completed by the daimyō Ikeda Terumasa (1564–1613) in 1609. The donjon of Inuyama Castle in Aichi Prefecture, often called the oldest, postdates that of Matsumoto Castle and was constructed no earlier than 1599; Maruoka Castle in Fukui Prefecture boasts a central keep that was possibly built by Shibata Katsutoyo (d 1583) as early as 1576, col-

lapsed in an earthquake in 1948, and was reerected in 1955. Of Tokugawa Ieyasu's EDO CASTLE, little remains but the moats and their colossal stone embankments (now surrounding the Imperial Palace in Tōkyō); in any event, it could only serve as the symbol of another era.

Institutional Developments of the Period——— The central governmental system that evolved in Japan during the Azuchi-Momoyama period is called the Shokuhō regime or the Oda-Toyotomi regime. Under that regime, Japan was not only reunified militarily; the basic structures of Japanese society were reformed. By their conquests, Oda Nobunaga and Toyotomi Hideyoshi hammered together again a country that had split apart completely during the previous hundred years. Atop the shards of a fragmented and discredited old order, they constructed a new body politic, devising new measures to regulate society on a nationwide basis. At least one eminent historian, John Whitney Hall, has called the changes brought about by them a revolution.

The Shokuhō regime originated with Nobunaga's march on Kyōto and advent to national prominence in 1568. Nobunaga's ostensible purpose was to ensure the succession of the "legitimate" claimant, Ashikaga Yoshiaki, to the Muromachi shogunate, a crippled political organism that had been in shock since the murder of Yoshiaki's brother, the shōgun Ashikaga Yoshiteru (b 1536; r from 1547), three years previously. The restoration of legitimacy in the old governing order was not, however, Nobunaga's true objective; and it was far from his intention to subordinate himself to Yoshiaki, his protégé. Instead, he wanted to enhance his own prestige and power by playing the lead role on the central stage of politics. From the very beginning, Nobunaga sought to dominate Yoshiaki, and dictated policy to the shogunate. In 1569 and again in 1570, he imposed upon Yoshiaki capitulations which deprived the shōgun of the most important prerogatives of a ruler; in a remonstrance issued in 1572, he accused Yoshiaki of a long list of inadequacies and misdeeds, and concluded the indictment by intimating darkly that Yoshiaki with his reputation as an "evil shōgun" merited a fate similar to that of Ashikaga Yoshinori, another "evil shōgun" who ruled from 1429 and was assassinated in 1441. The pressures Nobunaga exerted upon Yoshiaki would have been presumptuous from a shogunal official, and were truly extraordinary in view of the fact that Nobunaga was an outsider who had refused to accept a post under the Muromachi shogunate. Instead, he posited a separate and supravening polity, the tenka or "realm," a common weal over which he himself presided. In documents issued from 1570 onward, he repeatedly identified the idea of action "for the sake of the realm" with the accomplishment of a goal "for the sake of Nobunaga." In short, he claimed the sole right to define and guide the "realm's" interests.

To be sure, Nobunaga did not remain unchallenged. Indeed, between 1570 and 1573 he was threatened with encirclement and destruction by a formidable coalition that included the daimyō ASAI NAGAMASA (1545–73) of Odani in Ōmi Province (now Kohoku Chō, Shiga Prefecture), ASAKURA YOSHIKAGE (1533–73) of Echizen (now part of Fukui Prefecture), the pontiff Kennyo Kōsa (1543–92) of the Buddhist "religious monarchy" of the HONGANJI, and finally also the great eastern warlord TAKEDA SHINGEN (1521–73), master of Kai (now Yamanashi Prefecture) and its neighboring provinces. All of these were major personages of the Sengoku period; they had little strategic acumen, however, and Nobunaga outmatched them with his statecraft. Their ambitions extended to provincial or regional domination; Nobunaga alone had the vision to strive for national hegemony.

Early in 1573, Takeda Shingen died of a disease that had forced him to break off a successful campaign against Nobunaga's ally Tokugawa Ieyasu. The news of that campaign, however, had enticed the shōgun Yoshiaki into opening hostilities against Nobunaga. Nobunaga first intimidated Yoshiaki to surrender by burning the greater part of Kyōto, the shogunal capital; and when Yoshiaki resumed hostilities three months later, Nobunaga on 15 August 1573 (Genki 4.7.18) drove the shōgun away from the central political arena, into exile with whatever provincial daimyō chose to shelter him and foster his pretensions. Yoshiaki would not resign his post until 1588, so that the Muromachi shogunate retained a shadowy legal identity; as a functioning political entity, however, it was finished. The regime of unification led by Nobunaga had replaced it at the central fulcrum of politics. The middle ages of Japanese history were over.

In that same year of 1573, Nobunaga crushed Asakura Yoshikage and Asai Nagamasa. In 1575, he defeated Shingen's son TAKEDA KATSUYORI (1546–82) at the Battle of NAGASHINO, and conquered

Echizen Province from the armed adherents (IKKŌ IKKI) of the Honganji. There remained before him weary campaigns to reduce the ISHIYAMA HONGANJI itself and to counter its various allies, most notably Mōri Terumoto (1553–1625), the lord of vast territories in the Chūgoku region of westernmost Honshū, and UESUGI KENSHIN (1530–78), the daimyō of Echigo Province (now part of Niigata Prefecture). In 1580, however, the Ishiyama Honganji surrendered, and its provincial domain in Kaga (now part of Ishikawa Prefecture) was conquered by Nobunaga's captain SHIBATA KATSUIE (1522?–83). In 1582, Nobunaga sent a huge army against Takeda Katsuyori, destroyed him, and distributed the Takeda domains among his own victorious generals.

As Nobunaga's power and stature increased in the course of these great conquests, his military command structure turned into a public administration and an emergent national governmental system. Nobunaga achieved mastery over his "realm" by ruthlessly eliminating his daimyō opponents and the armed leagues (ikki) of the populace. He maintained it by a new type of command relationship with his daimyō vassals, from whom he demanded total respect and obedience "for the sake of the tenka."

Nobunaga bound his vassals with "regulations" (okite) even as he assigned them their domains, as in the case of Shibata Katsuie, appointed to govern Echizen Province in 1575. He moved them and their subordinate samurai from one provincial fief to another (kunigae) at will; e.g., MAEDA TOSHIIE (1538?–99) and Sassa Narimasa (d 1588) in 1581. He disenfeoffed those he found lacking in fighting zeal and organizational talent; e.g., Sakuma Nobumori (d 1581) in 1580. In order to reduce independent powers in the provinces, Nobunaga's regime instituted province-wide land surveys (KENCHI), for example in Yamato (now Nara Prefecture) in 1580, and destroyed the indigenous gentry's forts (shirowari), for example in Settsu and Kawachi (now comprised in Ōsaka and Hyōgo prefectures) that same year. In 1575–76 the regime followed up the conquest of Echizen from the Ikkō ikki mobilized by armed sectarians of the Honganji by conducting a SWORD HUNT (katanagari; confiscation of weapons from the populace) in that province, ordering peasants to confine themselves to agriculture, and prohibiting them from changing their status. These measures represent an early attempt at the separation of the military from the farming class (heinō bunri), later identified as one of the regime's cardinal policies. In addition, Echizen villagers were forced to abjure their allegiance to the Honganji and affiliate themselves with temples approved by the regime, foreshadowing the religious inquisition (SHŪMON ARATAME) of the Edo period. Nobunaga interfered in various ways with the affairs of religious groups (e.g., in the Azuchi Disputation of 1579), and even encroached upon the prerogatives of the imperial court. Guided by a good sense of raison d'état, he sought and largely attained supreme authority in his tenka.

When Nobunaga was killed in the Honnōji Incident of 1582, the "realm" governed by his regime covered no less than 30 of Japan's 68 provinces, occupying an area that extended continuously from Kōzuke Province (now Gumma Prefecture) to Bizen Province (now part of Okayama Prefecture) and from the Pacific Ocean to the Sea of Japan. Central Japan had been reunited under one political authority. Great areas, however, remained unsubdued. Nobunaga's planned invasion of Shikoku had to be called off at the news of his assassination, although the troops were ready to embark from Sakai and Sumiyoshi harbors; a year later, the upstart daimyō CHŌSOKABE MOTOCHIKA (1539–99) would make himself master of all the four provinces of the island. On Kyūshū, a ferocious struggle for supremacy over that island's nine provinces raged among the Ōtomo, Ryūzōji, and Shimazu families and their assorted allies. The great Mōri family, although weakened in the contest with Nobunaga, retained seven provinces in westernmost Honshū. On the opposite frontier of Nobunaga's "realm," Kenshin's heir UESUGI KAGEKATSU (1555–1623), the powerful lord of Echigo, showed no signs of abandoning the fight for the provinces of Noto (now part of Ishikawa Prefecture) and Etchū (now Toyama Prefecture) against Nobunaga's generals Maeda Toshiie and Sassa Narimasa. The Kantō region remained under the domination of the Later Hōjō family (see HŌJŌ FAMILY) of Odawara. Farther to the northeast, the Ashina, Date, and Satake families—all three of them major Sengoku daimyō houses—competed for the control of an extensive region in southern Mutsu and Dewa provinces (an area that is now part of Fukushima and Yamagata prefectures). Farther yet, the vast territories stretching toward the northernmost tip of Honshū were divided among some two dozen mutually contending baronial families bearing such names as Andō, Kasai, Mutō, Mogami, Nambu, Nikaho, and Ōsaki.

Over the greater part of Japan, Sengoku conditions still prevailed. The task of national unification was far from over.

Nobunaga's hegemony was abruptly terminated by his violent death, but the task of unification was completed by his erstwhile subordinate Toyotomi Hideyoshi. Hideyoshi, who inherited Nobunaga's policies, was to systematize the Shokuhō regime and extend it nationwide. He did not, however, inherit Nobunaga's base of power effortlessly, but had to fight for the hegemony. First he destroyed Nobunaga's assassin AKECHI MITSUHIDE (d 1582) at the Battle of YAMAZAKI, a mere 11 days after the Honnōji Incident. The next year, Hideyoshi defeated Shibata Katsuie, the daimyō of Echizen and Kaga, at the Battle of SHIZUGATAKE; in this campaign, he was helped by Uesugi Kagekatsu, who threatened Shibata's home base from the rear. By 1583, Hideyoshi had also reached an accommodation with Mōri Terumoto; early in 1585, Tokugawa Ieyasu too agreed to subordinate himself to Hideyoshi, after fighting him to a standoff in the KOMAKI NAGAKUTE CAMPAIGN the previous year. In 1585, Hideyoshi mounted three major campaigns in different parts of the country, defeating the warlike priests of the Shingon sect's temple Negoroji and the armed adherents of the Jōdo Shin sect of Saiga in Kii Province (now Wakayama Prefecture), subduing Chōsokabe Motochika and conquering Shikoku, and obtaining the capitulation of Sassa Narimasa of Etchū. In 1587, he overran Kyūshū with a huge force, bringing the Shimazu to heel. Three years later, he led the armies of his vassal daimyō against the Hōjō of Odawara and subjugated the Kantō region. The ODAWARA CAMPAIGN of 1590 concluded with a massive demonstration of the hegemon's power to dispose of the territories even of the greatest daimyō when the future shōgun Tokugawa Ieyasu was transplanted to the Kantō on Hideyoshi's orders and Nobunaga's son Oda Nobukatsu (1558–1630) disenfeoffed for resisting a similar transfer (kunigae).

But that was not yet the end of the process of national unification. After the Odawara Campaign, there remained the problem of the giant northern provinces, Mutsu and Dewa. (Mutsu Province comprised what are now Fukushima, Miyagi, Iwate, and Aomori prefectures and the northeastern district of Kazuno in Akita Prefecture; Dewa Province was made up of the rest of modern-day Akita Prefecture and what is now Yamagata Prefecture.) As early as 1585, Hideyoshi had sent this region's numerous feuding barons repeated messages to submit to his mediation and stop fighting. Their warfare, however, continued unabated until 1589, when the party of Andō Sanesue (later called Akita Sanesue; 1576–1660) emerged victorious in northern Dewa over a rebellion supported by the Nambu family, and when most of southern Mutsu was subjugated by Date Masamune (1567–1636), the daimyō of Yonezawa, who that year conquered the Ashina family, took over their lands, and moved to their castle town, Kurokawa (now the city of Aizu Wakamatsu).

Masamune formally submitted himself to Hideyoshi's suzerainty in July 1590, a month before the hegemon victoriously concluded the Odawara Campaign; but Hideyoshi, annoyed that his orders to keep the peace in Mutsu and Dewa had been flouted, reduced Masamune to his old holdings, depriving him of his newly conquered Aizu domain and turning it over to GAMŌ UJISATO (1556–95), an old companion in arms and trusted vassal. Other trusted vassals were assigned the confiscated domains of the Kasai and Ōsaki families. Those local barons of Mutsu and Dewa whom Hideyoshi confirmed in their domains were ordered to observe three conditions: to send their wives and children to reside in Kyōto, the national hegemon's capital (a measure prefiguring the sankin kōtai system of the Edo period); to destroy all forts (shirowari) in their territories save for the lord's residential castle, and to have their retainers' wives and children move to the castle town (jōka machi); and to undertake a cadastral survey (kenchi) of their fiefs. Those who resisted his orders, Hideyoshi stated, would be "wiped out (nadegiri) to the last man." These conditions ensured that the provincial lords of Mutsu and Dewa would be integrated into Hideyoshi's national regime. Insofar as Hideyoshi recognized their autonomous existence, petty barons who had never been secure in their possessions were transformed into daimyō with full authority over their vassals and the populace of their domains. That authority was delegated to them by the hegemon. The price they paid was the surrender of their independence to him.

Immediately after the capitulation of the Hōjō of Odawara in August 1590, Hideyoshi himself marched to Aizu and sent armies under his principal generals into the remotest reaches of Mutsu and Dewa to enforce the dispositions he had ordered in the area. By the end of October, having supervised the conduct of land surveys, these occupation troops withdrew. No sooner had they done so, however, than violent uprisings against the new regime and its rigorous policies burst out all over the two provinces, most notably in the old Kasai and Ōsaki domains (centered on what are now the city of Furukawa and the town of Toyoma, Miyagi Prefecture). These uprisings were put down, but not before Gamō Ujisato had accused Date Masamune of laxity in their suppression and thereby brought into the open the split between a hard-line faction and a conciliatory group within the Toyotomi regime. When, early in 1591, yet another uprising of local barons (kokujin ikki) burst out in the region, Hideyoshi determined on a massive show of force to settle the affairs of Mutsu and Dewa once and for all. This rebellion was led by Kunohe Masazane, the lord of Kunohe in Mutsu (now the city of Ninohe, Iwate Prefecture), who resented having been reduced by Hideyoshi to a mere vassal of the Nambu family; against him and his four or five thousand supporters, Hideyoshi mobilized not only all of the region's daimyō but also the armies of outsiders. Toyotomi Hidetsugu, Tokugawa Ieyasu, Ishida Mitsunari (1560–1600), and Ōtani Yoshitsugu (1559–1600) led huge forces in a three-pronged sweep through Mutsu and Dewa which by the end of October 1591 had wiped out all trace of rebellion.

Present at the fall of Kunohe Castle was a band of Ainu equipped with poisoned arrows, fighting for Kakizaki Yoshihiro (later known as Matsumae Yoshihiro; 1549–1617), the lord of a territory on Hokkaidō who was recognized as a daimyō by Hideyoshi. Although small, this domain had a special significance, because it was beyond the traditional boundaries of Japan. When Kakizaki entered Hideyoshi's vassalage, his enclave in Hokkaidō came under the domination of Japan's national hegemon. Unfortunately, that did not satisfy Hideyoshi's taste for overseas expansion. Immediately after the suppression of the uprising of Kunohe Masazane—now that all of Japan had been reunified—Hideyoshi ordered his vassals home to mobilize their troops for an invasion of Korea.

The armies that had reoccupied Mutsu and Dewa enforced another round of cadastral surveys, castle demolitions, and sword hunts (katanagari). Date Masamune was put in his place, being demonstratively transferred from his home ground to the old Kasai and Ōsaki domains. The area of northernmost Honshū had been thoroughly subjugated. The two provinces had required a repeated effort, but in 1591, when he finally subjected them, Hideyoshi could for the first time truly claim that he had succeeded in eliminating the last pockets of resistance to his rule, reducing the daimyō to fealty, and extending the scope of his regime nationwide.

Along with military means, the land survey was Hideyoshi's principal device for unification. Japan was transformed by the great wave of cadastral surveys ordained by him and known, after Taikō, the title he assumed in 1592, as Taikō kenchi. Begun in Yamashiro Province (now part of Kyōto Prefecture) in 1582 immediately after Hideyoshi's victory over Akechi, and entering their mature phase in 1584, when Ōmi Province was surveyed on the basis of a new standard measure, the Taikō kenchi had by the time of Hideyoshi's death in 1598 covered the entire country. All the arable land was measured and assessed by these surveys; its putative agricultural yield (KOKUDAKA; called thus because expressed in measures of rice, koku, of about 180 liters or 5 US bushels) was entered on cadastral registers (kenchi chō) prepared village by village for submission to the overlord Hideyoshi and his daimyō vassals. Made possible thereby was a uniform system of taxation, replacing the multiple accretion of taxes and dues characteristic of the SHŌEN form of landholding, which had originated in the 8th century and was finally eliminated by the Taikō kenchi.

That the land surveys brought suffering to the peasants, actually increasing their tax burden, is a commonplace among Japanese historians. Recent Western scholarship, however, maintains that being listed in the cadastral registers gave the villagers an unprecedented security of tenure, which served as an incentive to increase production. There is no doubt that the samurai class was given a new identity by the Shokuhō regime: the military men were removed from the countryside and made to reside in the castle town (jōka machi) of their daimyō, where they were destined to turn into a class of bureaucratic administrators. Hideyoshi's national sword hunt (katanagari) decree of 1588 disarmed the countrymen, thereby in effect eliminating the yeoman (jizamurai; village samurai) stratum that had been so turbulent in the Sengoku period and making the distinction between samurai and farmer final. In 1591, Hideyoshi prohibited the change of status from samurai to farmer or merchant, or from farmer to merchant, and thereby completed laying the foundation for the Japanese class system of the early modern age.

Among the undoubted accomplishments of the Oda-Toyotomi regime were the encouragement of commerce and the expansion of trade networks, achieved in the course of the campaigns of unification through the systematic elimination of medieval barrier stations (SEKISHO)—which impeded the free flow of trade—encouragement of free markets (rakuichi), and abolition of restrictive trade guilds (rakuza; see RAKUICHI AND RAKUZA). Merchants and artisans were attracted to the castle towns by exemptions from land rents and by other privileges, further stimulating urban growth. Advances in mining technology made possible the intensified exploitation of silver and gold mines, such as those at Ikuno in Tajima Province (now Hyōgo Prefecture), Ōmori in Iwami Province (now Shimane Prefecture), and in the island province of Sado (now part of Niigata Prefecture); the hegemons' policy was to keep such areas under their own direct control (chokkatsu), and their resultant accumulation of wealth in bullion is a well-founded legend. These are the developments which, along with the warlords' active patronage of the arts, underlay the period's cultural efflorescence; they contributed the aura of a "golden age" to Azuchi–Momoyama.

The Oda-Toyotomi regime displaced the long-established—if moribund—medieval political order, but it lacked its own, clearly formulated justification in political theory. The solipsist Nobunaga rid himself of the shōgun Yoshiaki's unwanted presence and even tried to pressure Emperor Ōgimachi (1517–93; r 1557–86) into abdication, but he was not granted the time to develop an ideology for his own political creation, the tenka. After his conquest of the Takeda in 1582, the imperial court was ready to appoint him shōgun or, indeed, "to any rank at all"; but Nobunaga was assassinated before he could make an adequate response to this offer.

The parvenu Hideyoshi sought to mystify his obscure origins, to aristocratize himself, and to bind the daimyō to allegiance by identifying himself with the ideal model of political authority in Japanese history, the imperial institution. No matter how powerful he became, he could not hope to obtain the throne itself; but he drew his legitimation from the use of the traditional symbols of authority associated with it. These included most prominently the lofty aristocratic offices of kampaku (imperial regent), with which he had the emperor invest him in 1585, and of dajō daijin (grand minister of state), which he obtained on 27 January 1587 (Tenshō 14.12.19). When his firstborn son Tsurumatsu (1589–91) died, Hideyoshi had the title of kampaku transferred to his nephew and adopted son Toyotomi Hidetsugu (1568–95), with the evident intention of institutionalizing the office (previously the monopoly of the Fujiwara family's "Regency" lineage [sekkanke]) in his self-created house of Toyotomi during his own lifetime. When, against all expectations, Hideyoshi had another son, Toyotomi Hideyori (1593–1615), Hidetsugu became superfluous. In 1595 Hideyoshi ordered Hidetsugu to commit suicide. That same year, Hideyoshi created a new political instrument designed to guarantee the continuity of Toyotomi rule. This highest governing organ of the last years of the Shokuhō regime was a council composed of five of Japan's greatest daimyō, called the "Five Great Elders" (Gotairō) of the Toyotomi house. They were Tokugawa Ieyasu, Maeda Toshiie (1538?–99), Mōri Terumoto (1553–1625), Ukita Hideie (1572–1655), and Kobayakawa Takakage (1533–97; replaced after his death by Uesugi Kagekatsu [1555–1623]). From his deathbed, Hideyoshi sent to the five the message, "Again and again, I beg you to take care of Hideyori."

The perpetuity of the Toyotomi house and regime could not, however, be safeguarded with such pleas. Upon Hideyoshi's death, the regime was rent by the competing ambitions of his paladins, among whom Tokugawa Ieyasu proved to be the most powerful. After the great succession struggle which climaxed with Ieyasu's victory at the Battle of Sekigahara in 1600, the Azuchi–Momoyama period's Shokuhō regime was followed in 1603 by the Tokugawa shogunate, which built upon the framework of its policies. In order to safeguard its own perpetuity, however, the shogunate in 1615 destroyed the Toyotomi family.

The Culture of the Period —— The culture of the Azuchi-Momoyama period manifests a fundamental ambivalence. Opulence and ostentation coexisted with restraint and studied rusticity in the period's dominant modes of artistic expression. The greatest symbol of Azuchi-Momoyama is the castle—a representation of power, built on a grand scale, decorated lavishly, and meant to overawe the viewer. It is possible to juxtapose it with a nearly coequal symbol, the teahouse—an evocation of aestheticism, content with a space nine feet square in which to construct a cultural microcosm, eschewing ornamental decor, and designed to permit the visitor to withdraw into solitude from the world of affairs. In that case, the aggressive "castle culture" (shiro no bunka) of the period stands contrasted with a contemporaneous quietist "culture of the grass hut" (sōan no bunka). Yet the contrast is imperfect. Even if the glorification of Oda Nobunaga was its main purpose, the decorative program of Azuchi Castle was marked by a sumptuous elegance, that is, a richness of design and ornamentation kept under control by a rigorous sense of taste, if not on the part of the warlord who commissioned the project (although there is no reason to assume that Nobunaga lacked polish), then on the part of the great artist charged with its execution, Kanō Eitoku. Teahouses, on the other hand, could be gaudy, and the TEA CEREMONY was often made to serve political purposes. Nobunaga, who appreciated keenly the attraction exercised by art over the rude but ambitious, reserved for himself the right to regulate his vassals' access to the art of tea; he issued licenses to hold the tea ceremony to his captains as marks of his special favor and cachets of their accomplishment in his service. Toyotomi Hideyoshi, a despot putting on a populist act, invited all the world, specifically including "samurai attendants, townsmen, and farmers" to a grand, 10-day tea ceremony he planned in 1587 at the grove of Kitano in Kyōto, where he showed off his treasured tea implements and personally served tea to hundreds of persons. Although Hideyoshi's threat to prohibit the future performance of the tea ceremony or even the use of tea substitutes to those who failed to attend, as well as his calling off the party after only a day, gave an astringent taste to this mass extravaganza, it may nevertheless have been the greatest public spectacle of his career. The daimyō of the Azuchi-Momoyama period also used the tea ceremony as an opportunity to conduct affairs of state in private; for instance, the seeds of the anti-Tokugawa coalition of 1600 were planted at a meeting held in late 1598 between Ishida Mitsunari and Mōri Terumoto in a teahouse in Hakata (now Fukuoka). Moreover, although the teahouse was ideally meant to provide a "hermitage amid the bustle of the marketplace" (shichū no in, or shichū no sankyo), in actuality the cult of tea and the pursuit of commerce were closely related social media.

Nothing illustrates better the simultaneous attraction toward simplicity and ornateness which is at the heart of Azuchi-Momoyama culture than Hideyoshi's two famous tearooms: the Yamazato no Zashiki built in the "Mountain Village Enceinte" (Yamazato Maru) of Ōsaka Castle, a small rustic hut; and the Kigane no Zashiki, his portable "Golden Tearoom," in which every conceivable surface was covered with plates of solid gold and all the utensils, save for the bamboo tea whisk, were golden. SEN NO RIKYŪ (1522–91), a rich merchant often described as the very incarnation of the ideals of wabicha ("poverty tea"; a type of tea ceremony governed by restraint), served the powerful aspirant to cultural accomplishment, Hideyoshi, as his tea master in both these contradictory settings.

The formal artistic developments of the Azuchi-Momoyama period bear an elitist stamp. The newly risen powerholders of the country invested in culture as a means of bolstering their claims to authority. Their purveyors of culture were in large part men who were engaged in commerce and perforce also in politics. For instance, the tea connoisseur Imai Sōkyū (1520–93), a Sakai merchant, in 1568 insinuated himself into Oda Nobunaga's favor with the gift of two famous tea utensils, helped him to subjugate and to govern the city of Sakai, was active on his behalf in the exploitation of the silver mines in Tajima Province, supplied him with munitions, and acted as Nobunaga's tea master and arbiter of taste. Sen no Rikyū, KAMIYA SŌTAN (1551–1635), SHIMAI SŌSHITSU (1539?–1615), and TSUDA SŌGYŪ (d 1591), other representative tea men of the Azuchi-Momoyama age, had similar careers, evidently being able to reconcile their involvement in the mundane spheres of politics and profits with their immersion in the more ethereal world of the cult of tea. It would be difficult to maintain that such men were co-opted against their wills by Nobunaga, Hideyoshi, and the other warlords of the age. Rather, they sought the hegemons' patronage, served their interests, and were in turn given privileges by them. To be sure, serving such masters as Nobunaga and Hideyoshi was not without its perils. Sen no Rikyū was forced by Hideyoshi to commit suicide. The reason, according to one account, was that Rikyū had engaged in sharp practice in the sale of tea implements; more probably, it was because Rikyū had meddled too overtly in politics.

Painting and the Decorative Arts —— The tea ceremony continued to be an important vessel for cultural expression, and its implements remained highly prized objects of art throughout the Azuchi-Momoyama period, as they had been since early in the Muromachi period (1333–1568); the value that was put on tea utensils astounded contemporary European observers. No doubt the most astute of those observers, the Jesuit missionary João Rodrigues Tçuzzu, commented also that it was "quite beyond all belief" how highly room decorations were valued in Japan. Indeed, the decorative arts flourished in Azuchi–Momoyama, and large-scale decorative paintings (shōbyōga [or shōheiga], a category that includes shōhekiga [wall paintings] and byōbu-e [paintings on folding screens]) for the new aristocracy's residences and the religious shrines they patronized were the period's most important artistic commissions. The grand conception and sumptuous execution of the richly colored and gilded decorative paintings (kimpeki) that are the period's representative works of art distinguish the newly blossoming Azuchi-Momoyama culture from the previously dominant aesthetic heritage of the Higashiyama epoch (1449–90), which was characterized by monochromatic plainness, restrained refinement, and the "withered" element said to typify the wabicha tea ceremony.

The most renowned master of the grandiose Azuchi–Momoyama style of painting was Kanō Eitoku. Eitoku and his atelier decorated several palatial residences, including Hideyoshi's Ōsaka Castle and his Juraku no Tei in Kyōto, the In no Gosho (Retirement Palace) that Hideyoshi undertook to build for Emperor Ōgimachi, and the palace of Hideyoshi's adopted son, Prince Hachijō (Hachijō no Miya Toshihito; 1579–1629). Eitoku made his career, however, with the magnificent project he executed for Nobunaga at Azuchi. His decorative program for the donjon of Azuchi Castle, the axial edifice of Nobunaga's "realm," is known in considerable detail from SHINCHŌ KŌ KI (The Chronicle of Nobunaga), which maintains that "from top to bottom, everything in these chambers, wherever there [were] pictures, all [was] gold." The implication is that even the monochrome ink paintings (sumi-e) in the Azuchi donjon—of which there were several—used gold leaf, an innovative technique that must have created striking and elegant contrasts of black and gold. Most of the paintings there, however, were polychrome kimpeki shōhekiga. Their themes progressed from the standard topics of 16th-century painting, such as birds and flowers of the four seasons, to the portrayal of Taoist immortals and solipsist sages who refused political honors, the depiction of images of power, such as dragons and tigers in combat, then to the representation of Buddha preaching his law, and finally, on the top, seventh story of the great tower, the evocation of the ideally governed realm through the depicted examples of a whole array of classical Chinese culture heroes, sage kings, and lawgivers. Here Eitoku's art was made to reinforce Nobunaga's statecraft: the lavish decorative program bore within itself a clear political message.

Unfortunately, none of these paintings survived when Azuchi Castle was burnt on 4 July 1582 (Tenshō 10.6.15), 13 days after Nobunaga was assassinated in the Honnōji Incident. The force of their message may, however, be visualized on the basis of the (all too few) paintings by Eitoku that remain in existence today, such as Chinese Lions (Karajishi; a screen done in color and gold leaf, now in the Imperial Household Collection, Tōkyō). This is an extraordinarily powerful painting, projecting an exaggerated image of imperiousness if not arrogance; it embodies the spirit of the age of unification in its robust portrayal of the two proud beasts. It is clear from this work that Eitoku succeeded in representing in his art the majestic glory which the hegemons who were his patrons sought as the ultimate attribute of power.

Eitoku's direct successors inherited much of his brilliant and intense technique, but they could not match his grandiose imagination and overpowering force. For instance—to select for comparison with Eitoku's Chinese Lions a few Kanō school paintings with similar subjects—Dragon and Tigers (Ryūko; a pair of kimpeki screens owned by the great Zen monastery Myōshinji in Kyōto), a relatively early work by Eitoku's adopted son Kanō Sanraku (1559–1635), is a superb composition, possessing a tremendous intensity of its own, but it does not have Eitoku's robustness; the six Chinese Lions which Sanraku painted in 1621 on the gilded wainscot of the altar in the Buddhist temple Yōgen'in in Kyōto are amusing rather than imposing; and in Tigers in Bamboo (Chikuko; four sliding doors or fusuma, painted in ink and color over gold leaf, in the Tenkyūin priory of the Myōshinji), done about 1631 and frequently attributed to Sanraku but more likely the work of his adopted son KANŌ SANSETSU (1589–1651), the storm and stress that are characteristic of Eitoku are replaced by a lithe grace and gentle humor. In short, there was a direct line of development from Eitoku to Sansetsu, but the Kanō school lost the keen edge of its self-assertive vigor as it entered the Edo period. In the Tokugawa realm of peace, it would appear, aggressiveness ceased to be regarded with favor even in works of art. In the final event, the Kanō school deteriorated into a staid "official" establishment producing stereotyped paintings for its patrons, the Tokugawa shogunate and its daimyō vassals.

In the Azuchi-Momoyama period, however, artists who wanted to compete with the Kanō school had to do so on the Kanō school's terms. Of the period's major painters, only UNKOKU TŌGAN (1547–1618) remained essentially a conservative, rarely infusing color into his work, dealing with his traditional topics in a severe style, and claiming to be the true successor to SESSHŪ TŌYŌ (1420–1506), the medieval master of ink painting. A brilliant exception to Tōgan's usual sober style is his *Crows in Plum Tree (Ume ni karasu)*, a six-panel *fusuma* painting, done in ink wash and light color over gold leaf, which is now owned by the Kyōto National Museum; to be sure, it is so exceptional that its attribution to Tōgan has been questioned. Eitoku's other great contemporaries KAIHŌ YŪSHŌ (1533–1615) and HASEGAWA TŌHAKU (1539–1610), who were specialists in ink painting, adapted themselves more readily than Tōgan to the tastes of the times, on occasion tried their hands at rich, gilded polychrome, and produced undoubted masterpieces.

Yūshō, a prolific artist, is known primarily for the economy of the images and the spare but sure strokes of the brush in his ink paintings, such as *Heron in Reeds (Roro;* four *fusuma* sliding doors in the Daichūin priory of the great Zen monastery Kenninji in Kyōto; late 16th century); but he also created the profusely colorful *Peonies (Botan;* folding screen owned by the Myōshinji, Kyōto; late 16th century), which in its exuberance almost matches Kanō Sanraku's justly famous *kimpeki fusuma* painting on the same topic (owned by the Shingon sect temple Daikakuji in Kyōto). An even better example of the Azuchi-Momoyama period's ambivalent tastes, and of the versatility of its artists, may be the case of Hasegawa Tōhaku. Tōhaku, whose background is unclear, appears to have begun his career under the name of Shinshun (also read Nobuharu) in Noto Province (now part of Ishikawa Prefecture) as a painter of Buddhist subjects associated with the Nichiren or Lotus sect (Hokkeshū). Apart from paintings depicting Nichiren Shōnin (1222–82) and various Buddhas and deities, a splendid portrait of the warlord TAKEDA SHINGEN (1521–73) is attributed to his early period. In the 1570s Tōhaku came to Kyōto, where his Lotus sect connections apparently helped him establish ties with the rich Nichirenist townsmen (MACHISHŪ) of the capital city and of Sakai; their patronage would in turn have helped him gain an entrée in high political and ecclesiastical circles. Tōhaku, too, was a prolific painter, and it is not easy to say which is his *chef d'oeuvre,* but surely that distinction must belong to either one of two works of art. One is *Maple (Kaede;* now owned by the Shingon sect temple Chishakuin in Kyōto), a wall painting which Tōhaku did in 1592 for Shōunji, a temple built in Kyōto by Hideyoshi in memory of his firstborn son, Tsurumatsu (1589–91). Depicting a husky old tree with its leaves turning in autumn and its base surrounded by bush clover, cockscomb, chrysanthemums, and other colorful autumn plants and flowers, *Maple* is possibly the most dazzling of all the period's *kimpeki* paintings. The other masterpiece is *Pine Woods (Shōrin;* a pair of folding screens now owned by the Tōkyō National Museum; late 16th century), a misty scene in which may be perceived the influence of the 13th-century Chinese master Muqi (Mu-ch'i; J: MOKKEI). This landscape, which is at once grand and restrained, majestically quiet and elegantly simple, is widely regarded as the representative ink painting of the Azuchi-Momoyama period.

Another type of versatility was that displayed by HON'AMI KŌETSU (1558–1637), who was a distinguished calligrapher and an accomplished potter, as well as an inspired designer of elegant colored paper *(shikishi)* and of lacquer ware implements embellished with pictorial patterns filled in with metal dust *(maki-e)*. Kōetsu came from a wealthy Kyōto townsman family who had been hereditary appraisers, grinders, and polishers of swords (all three being exacting and valued crafts) for the Muromachi shōgunate, but who were also mentioned among the leaders of the Nichirenist *machishū* in the so-called Lotus Confederation (Hokke Ikki) that ruled the affairs of the capital city between 1532 and 1536. Kōetsu's social position in the high bourgeoisie, no less than his reputation as a creative connoisseur of the arts, made it possible for him to associate with some of the period's most powerful personages, including Hideyoshi, Maeda Toshiie, and Tokugawa Ieyasu; in 1615, Ieyasu gave Kōetsu some land at Takagamine in the north of Kyōto, where Kōetsu established a community of artists and craftsmen bound by a common religious devotion to the Lotus sect. In addition, Kōetsu was on fairly close terms with such Kyōto aristocrats as Prince Hachijō To-

shihito, the provisional middle councillor *(gon dainagon)* Karasumaru Mitsuhiro (1579–1638), and the sometime imperial regent Konoe Nobutada (1565–1614). These were littérateurs interested in reviving the classical culture associated with the golden age of the imperial court in the Heian period (794–1185), and Kōetsu cooperated enthusiastically with their efforts. Accordingly, in his calligraphy as in the splendidly decorated paper on which it was presented, Kōetsu referred consciously to Heian tastes, seeking to evoke the effect of courtliness *(miyabi)* which was the prime aesthetic category of that period.

The integrative nature of Kōetsu's approach to art expressed itself perfectly in the luxury editions of Japanese classical literature which he began to publish in the first decade of the 17th century at Saga to the northwest of Kyōto; these splendid books are known as *sagabon* (Saga editions) after that location. The *sagabon* combined beautifully adorned covers, colored paper with underdesigns in powdered silver and gold or color, print based on Kōetsu's distinctive calligraphy, and classical texts (including *Ise monogatari, Hōjōki, Tsurezuregusa,* and Nō plays of the Kanze school) in a single product suffused with the courtly taste. Perhaps even finer examples of the artistic integration of paper, underdesign, calligraphy, and evocative text are the handscrolls of Japanese court poetry *(wakakan)* that were the results of the collaboration between Kōetsu and Tawaraya SŌTATSU (d 1643?). That collaboration was so close that it is sometimes difficult to say where in these superbly conceived and executed works of art Kōetsu's brush and his imagination leave off and Sōtatsu's take over. In any event, these scrolls of Japanese courtly poetry, inscribed on paper that is decorated in gold and silver wash *(kingindei)* with motifs—such as "Thousand Cranes" (Sembazuru) and "Plants and Flowers of the Four Seasons" (Shiki Sōka)—which had been familiar in the *yamato-e* tradition of Japanese painting since the Heian period but were transformed by Kōetsu and Sōtatsu into stylized if not archetypal patterns, must be ranked among the most elegant products not only of the Azuchi-Momoyama period but of all of Japanese art history.

Unfortunately little is known about the life of Sōtatsu, the last great painter of Azuchi-Momoyama. In view of the splendid integration of materials, design, and technique which he and Kōetsu achieved, it may be significant that Sōtatsu in all likelihood began his career as an independent craftsman and not as a disciple of one or the other of the period's schools of painting; that is, he seems to have progressed from the trade of a maker of decorated folding fans *(ōgi)* to the profession of an artist. His earliest known works are from the first decade of the 17th century, and include a fan adorned with the *yamato-e* theme "Pines by the Seashore" (Hamamatsu) and done sometime before the New Year of Keichō 12 (1607); among the folding screen *(byōbu)* paintings for which he later became famous are several decorated with fan designs (yet another *yamato-e* convention, called *ōgi nagashi)*; indeed, art historians have noted that the fan shape is the basic principle underlying the composition of his paintings. Sōtatsu remained devoted to *yamato-e* themes throughout his career. His best-known works are depictions of courtly scenes, such as the two *byōbu* paintings of episodes from the *Tale of Genji (Genji monogatari: Sekiya* and *Miotsukushi;* done in color on gold leaf; now owned by the Seikadō Bunko, Tōkyō), and the superb pair of screens representing dances of the Heian court, *Bugaku Dancers* (done in color on gold leaf; owned by the Sambōin priory of the Shingon sect temple Daigoji in Kyōto). In *Bugaku Dancers* the figures are abstracted from classical or medieval prototypes, but their arrangement on an expansive field of gold is uniquely Sōtatsu's.

Among the other works in the mode of *yamato-e* that are attributed to Sōtatsu is an album of *shikishi* illustrating the *Ise monogatari* (the 46 extant paintings are now owned by the Yamato Bunkakan in Nara and a private collection in Chiba Prefecture), which was probably done in the main by members of his atelier. *The Narrow Ivy Road (Tsuta no hosomichi;* done in green pigment over gold leaf, ca 1615–20; private collection, Hyōgo Prefecture), a pair of screens alluding to a passage in the *Ise monogatari* and inscribed by Karasumaru Mitsuhiro with seven of his *waka,* is a *yamato-e* composition that has been called "unequalled in Japanese art" for its "brilliant simplicity of effect," but its attribution to Sōtatsu is questioned by some authorities. Sōtatsu is, however, by no means celebrated only for colorful works in the *yamato-e* tradition. That he was also expert at ink painting in the Chinese manner and thoroughly familiar with the styles of the masters of the Song (Sung; 960–1279) and Yuan (Yüan; 1279–1368) periods, such as Muqi, but without surrendering his originality to their precedent, is evident from such of his works as the hanging scroll *Waterfowl on Lotus Pond* (*Renchi suikin;* Kyōto National Museum) and the screen *(tsuitate)* painting *Wild Ducks in Reeds* (*Ashikamo;* Sampōin, Kyōto). Sōtatsu's multiple accomplishment crowns the art history of the Azuchi-Momoyama period. The traditions of the decorative school established by him and Kōetsu at the period's end and later known as the Rimpa were taken up and fostered by artists such as Ogata KŌRIN (1658–1716), and continued to exert a strong force in Japanese art throughout the Edo period.

In Azuchi-Momoyama art, we observe a contiguity of opulence and elegance, a fusion of Chinese and Japanese artistic tastes, themes, and techniques, and a simultaneous display of innovative concepts in design and of nostalgia for a golden age of the past. The newly powerful and rich were the most important patrons, and secular themes were most in demand among them; their castles having been destroyed, however, the religious institutions which they favored remain to the present day some of the most important repositories of the masterpieces of Azuchi-Momoyama. In reflecting on what is commonly described as the thoroughly secular nature of the period's art, it is therefore worth remembering that—according to art historians—the period began with Kanō Eitoku's work at Jukōin, a Zen priory founded in 1566 by Miyoshi Yoshitsugu (d 1573) in memory of his adoptive father, the warlord Miyoshi Nagayoshi (also known as Miyoshi Chōkei; 1522–64), and ended with Hon'ami Kōetsu's and Tawaraya Sōtatsu's activities at Takagamine, a village of artisans and craftsmen that was also a community of the Nichirenist faith. Rich *machishū* participated in the period's artistic creativity, but this does not mean that the art of Azuchi-Momoyama was somehow the product of the common classes. Rather, it was still elite-centered, Kyōto-centered, and, in the case of Kōetsu's circle, even imperial-court-centered.

Literature —— In the history of literature, the Azuchi-Momoyama period is not nearly as monumental an epoch as it is in the history of art. The most important classical and medieval literary genres continued through the period, but their vital force was expiring, while new traditions were barely beginning. Proficiency at the composition of WAKA (31-syllable poems in Japanese) remained, as it had been since the Heian period, an indispensable accomplishment at court and among those who aspired to be courtly. Hence *waka* in large numbers were produced during the Azuchi–Momoyama period by imperial aristocrats *(kuge),* cultivated members of the old military aristocracy *(buke),* such as HOSOKAWA YŪSAI (1534–1610), and by parvenus who sought to legitimize themselves by the application of cultural cosmetics, most notably Toyotomi Hideyoshi. Among them, however, there were no great poets. Serious *renga* (linked verse), the chief poetic art of the Muromachi period, died toward the Azuchi-Momoyama period's end with the last of its masters, SATOMURA JŌHA (1524–1602), a true professional who in his checkered career had matched wits and capped verses with practically all of the era's high and mighty, from Miyoshi Nagayoshi through Oda Nobunaga and Akechi Mitsuhide to Toyotomi Hidetsugu and Hideyoshi. Comic linked verse *(haikai no renga;* see RENGA AND HAIKAI) continued to be composed, but it was not until the early Edo period that this literary genre would lead, under the transforming influence of Jōha's and Yūsai's sometime disciple MATSUNAGA TEITOKU (1571–1653) and other poets, to the development of an independent form of poetry, the HAIKU (17-syllable poem). NŌ drama, considered an elegant aristocratic pastime since the end of the 14th century, had a great vogue in the last decade of the 16th century when Hideyoshi seized upon it as a vehicle of propaganda. Not content with being a patron of Nō, Hideyoshi sought glory as an actor before noble audiences, and the plays he particularly favored included heroic spectacles he commissioned to be written about his military exploits and the other grand occasions in his life (for example, *Akechi uchi* or The Conquest of Akechi, and *Yoshino mōde* or The Pilgrimage to Yoshino; both 1594). The author of these plays, as well as of several chronicles dealing with Hideyoshi's career, was Ōmura Yūko (d 1596); whether these works are to be termed literature or mere panegyrics is open to question.

Some of the most interesting literary works to appear during the Azuchi-Momoyama period were produced for the Christian mission and printed by the Jesuit mission press. Western literature was introduced to Japan through splendid translations of such masterpieces of the Christian devotional tradition as the perennially popular *Imitation of Christ* (*De imitatione Christi;* published in Japanese under the title *Contemptvs mundi* in 1596 and again in 1610) by Thomas á Kempis (1379?–1471), and Luis de Granada's (1504–88) *Guide for Sinners* (*Guía de pecadores;* published in Japanese under the title

Gvia do pecador in 1599), a spiritual classic which in its own time was an extraordinary success not only in Catholic but also in Protestant Europe, being issued and reissued in dozens of editions during the 16th and 17th centuries. Among the other European works published by the Jesuit mission press was a translation of *Aesop's Fables* (*Esopo no fabvlas,* 1593); and the press also published adaptations of Japanese literature, including a version of the great 13th-century military romance *Heike monogatari* (*Feiqe no Monogatari,* 1592), compiled in romanization—"for the sake of those desirous of learning the language and history of Japan"—by the Japanese Jesuit Fucan FABIAN (1565?–after 1620).

It is highly doubtful, however, that these books reached a substantial audience before the outbreak of the general persecution of Christianity in 1614, which put a stop to the activities of the mission press and thereby ended a cosmopolitan trend in Japanese literature before it had really had a chance to start. In any event, Aesop was the only writer introduced by the Jesuits to survive in the Edo period, becoming naturalized in Japan through the *kana-zōshi* storybook *Isoho monogatari,* which by the period's end had been published in at least 11 editions. To be sure, Fucan Fabian survived as well, but not in a manner that his Jesuit mentors could have wanted. Having in 1605 authored the Christian apologetical treatise *Myōtei mondō* (The Myōtei Dialogue), a work which attacks the principal East Asian systems of thought and belief, Fabian had by 1620 recanted his Christianity, reverted to Buddhism, and published the stinging invective *Ha Daiusu* (Deus Destroyed), which became the foundation of the Edo period's vehement anti-Christian polemics. Although the Neo-Confucian ideologue HAYASHI RAZAN (1583–1657) depreciated *Myōtei mondō* as a book "patched together in the most plebeian Japanese," Fabian's mastery of a colorful rhetoric, amply demonstrated in both of his polemical works and even in his adaptation of the *Heike monogatari,* makes him one of the very few noteworthy Japanese prose writers of the Azuchi-Momoyama period.

Save for a few groups of believers who were driven underground, Christianity was eradicated by the Edo period's inquisition (see SHŪMON ARATAME), and the Christian mission of the Azuchi-Momoyama period left no appreciable effect on Japanese culture. In their works dealing with Japanese language and customs of that era, however, the missionaries left behind a cultural monument of colossal importance to modern-day students of Azuchi-Momoyama. For example, the Japanese-Portuguese dictionary compiled by the Jesuits, *Vocabvlario da lingoa de Iapam com adeclaração em Portugues,* which was published in Nagasaki in 1603 (a *Svpplemento deste vocabulario* followed in 1604), forms the indispensable base for our understanding of Japanese as it was spoken in the 16th and 17th centuries; and the two linguistic works by the Jesuit Padre João Rodrigues Tçuzzu (1561?–1633; see RODRIGUES, JOÃO), *Arte da lingoa de Iapam* (Nagasaki, 1604–08) and *Arte breve da lingoa iapoa* (Macao, 1620) form a comprehensive—if sometimes vexatiously rambling—superstructure for our appreciation of that language. Rodrigues Tçuzzu's *História da Igreja do Japão* (written between 1620 and 1633, and partially translated as *This Island of Japon* in 1973), an elaborate description of the Japanese cultural scene by an extraordinarily perceptive observer who spent the 33 years between 1577 and 1610 in the country, may be the most important single work about the culture of Azuchi-Momoyama by a contemporary author, Japanese or European. It remains to the present day the most sensitive representation of that period's culture drawn by the pen of a Westerner.

Popular Culture —— To be sure, even Rodrigues Tçuzzu, a man of many parts, concentrated almost exclusively on the culture of the elite. The Azuchi-Momoyama period was, however, the seedbed of rich developments in popular culture as well. In the countryside, farmers developed a cycle of songs to accompany rice transplanting, called *Taue-zōshi,* in which the symbol of a burgeoning capital city was used to invoke a bountiful harvest. In the cities—if the evidence of the period's genre paintings *(fūzokuga)* can be believed—Azuchi-Momoyama was an age of robust popular pleasures, festivals, and entertainments. The most contagious of these merriments was the *furyū,* defined by the Jesuit *Vocabvlario* as a "dance with varied steps and farcical postures," performed in fancy dress and with a lively spirit. At mid-century, the Muromachi shogunate had prohibited *furyū* in Kyōto, but failed to arrest its development into a popular craze. By 1571, *furyū* was in high vogue indeed, with Crown Prince Sanehito (1552–86) and the shōgun Ashikaga Yoshiaki watching a grand dance competition among townsman groups. The fad carried over into the first years of the 17th century.

Fittingly enough, the last great mass spectacle of the Azuchi-Momoyama period was a popular pageant performed in 1604 at the Hōkoku Festival, which was held in Kyōto to commemorate the deified Hideyoshi in the seventh year after his death. It involved hundreds of *furyū* dancers from among the *machishū* of Kyōto. A magnificent pair of *kimpeki* screen paintings, *The Hōkoku Festival* (*Hōkoku sairei;* owned by the Hōkoku Shrine, Kyōto), commissioned by Hideyoshi's former lieutenant KATAGIRI KATSUMOTO (1556–1615) and executed in 1606 by Kanō Naizen (1570–1616), brilliantly captures the frenetic spirit of the occasion. The *furyū* performances were repeated a few days later before the new shōgun, Tokugawa Ieyasu, at Fushimi Castle. For all that, this spectacle was undoubtedly an outpouring of the Kyōto townsmen's sympathy for Hideyoshi's heir Toyotomi Hideyori, who was increasingly isolated in his fortress at Ōsaka, and a fervent manifestation of their reverence for the dead hegemon, who had done much to revivify their city. Some historians call this the last great outburst of popular energy before the stiffening authority of the Tokugawa regime made further demonstrations of that type impossible.

Another magnificent pair of screens, *Activities In and Around the Capital* (*Rakuchū Rakugai;* now owned by the Tōkyō National Museum but formerly in the collection of the Funaki family, and therefore known as the "Funaki Screen"), painted by an anonymous artist ca 1615–17, shows us how lively the city of Kyōto was at the end of the Azuchi-Momoyama period and reminds us that some of the most important performing arts of Japan were born in that period. In particular, the "Funaki Screen" shows commercial theaters on the Shijō Riverbed (Shijō-Gawara) where kabuki and puppet plays are being performed before enthusiastic audiences. Both of these theatrical arts were the products of interreaction between the capital city and provincial regions.

The history of the early puppet theatre or *ko jōruri* (old JŌRURI) has been traced back to contacts between puppeteers from Awaji or Nishinomiya (both places in what is now Hyōgo Prefecture) and performers on a pear-shaped lute called the *biwa*, who came from the area of Kyōto. The name *jōruri* derives from a popular oral narrative (*katari-mono*) called *Jōruri Hime* (Princess Jōruri), which originated in the area of Yahagi in Mikawa Province (now part of Aichi Prefecture) and was being recited by blind itinerant priests in a wider region along the eastern seacoast as early as 1531. In the Azuchi-Momoyama period, this tale was adopted by puppet performers and became their most familiar story. It is clear that, by the beginning of the 17th century, puppeteers were putting on plays with fairly complicated plots: in 1614, written sources mention the performance of *Amida no munewari* (The Chest-Splitting of Amida), a rather gruesome tale of sacrifice, which is also one of the *jōruri* plays illustrated in the "Funaki Screen." At some time during the century's first decades, the *biwa* was replaced as the principal instrument used to accompany the *jōruri* recitative by the *shamisen*, a three-stringed plucked lute which had been imported from the Ryūkyū Islands at about the beginning of the Azuchi-Momoyama period, that is, in the 1560s. The introduction of this instrument completed the combination of the three main ingredients—puppeteer, reciter, and *shamisen* accompanist—that went into the development of BUNRAKU, one of the Edo period's two most popular and most enduring performing arts.

KABUKI, the Edo period's other major theatrical form, also has its roots in the Azuchi-Momoyama period. The principal figure associated with its origins, OKUNI, emerged from the anonymity of a group of wandering entertainers into history as a 10-year-old girl who performed a dance in 1582—just before Oda Nobunaga's violent death—in Nara, where the superior of an important Buddhist temple singled her out for mention in his diary, *Tamon'in nikki*. Her next appearance in historical sources occurred in 1600, on the eve of the Battle of Sekigahara, when she was mentioned in a Kyōto aristocrat's diary as one of the performers of a "yayako dance from Izumo Province." What exactly the *yayako* dance was is unclear, although it is known that entertainers calling themselves priestesses (*onna miko*) of the Izumo Shrine performed dances to Shintō litanies (*kagura*) and to "short songs" (*kouta*), the most popular song genre of the 16th century, in Kyōto during the Azuchi-Momoyama period. In any event, the mention of Okuni's "yayako dance" recurred in a primary source in 1603, the year Tokugawa Ieyasu assumed the title of shōgun, but that term was replaced after that by the name "kabuki dance."

We are told in the chronicle *Tōdaiki* (A Record of Our Times; compiled after 1615) that in the kabuki dance "the priestess of the Izumo Shrine who called herself Kuni" was dressed as a man in an odd and extravagant costume and "performed wonderfully the part of a man engaged in amorous dalliance with a teahouse girl." In short, she played the role of a *kabuki-mono*, an "outlandish person" or, if one translates the word *kabuki* literally (one of the definitions in the Jesuits' *Vocabvlario* is *desmandarse,* to swerve away from the norm) but gives it a modern twist, a "swinger." Extravagance and eroticism are elements on which kabuki would capitalize in its later development. What did it mean, however, to be extravagantly modish in Azuchi-Momoyama? One of the most fascinating illustrations of Okuni performing her seductive dance, the *Kabuki sōshi* scroll in the Tokugawa Reimeikai Collection, Tōkyō, portrays her costumed after the Portuguese fashion, wearing a rosary with a large cross around her neck. That was the *dernier cri* of the period's stylish attire and the essence of its extravagance. In our contemplation of kabuki, the giddiest flower to burst into bloom during the cultural efflorescence of Azuchi-Momoyama, we are therefore drawn once again to observe the exotic cosmopolitanism which is one of the period's definitional features.

The International Dimension of the Period —— The pronounced international flavor of Azuchi-Momoyama was brought about largely by the novel presence of European traders and Catholic missionaries, whose activities introduced Japan to a far wider stage of world history than its place on the periphery of East Asia had previously afforded. For the first time, Japan came directly in contact with European civilization, and Europe, through the widely published reports of Jesuit missionaries, was made familiar with events in Japan in great and dramatic detail.

To be sure, the period's international history is not circumscribed solely by the compass of the Portuguese merchants and the Jesuit priests who came to Japan. It will, for instance, be remembered that Toyotomi Hideyoshi's INVASIONS OF KOREA IN 1592 AND 1597 are inexpungible parts of that history. Its most distinctive element, however, was contributed by the commercial and religious activities of the Europeans and the growth of a substantial body of Japanese believers in CHRISTIANITY. Chronologically, the Azuchi-Momoyama period forms the core of the so-called "Christian Century of Japan" (which is variously dated 1549–1650 and 1549–1639 by historians), and conceptually there is also a large overlap between the two epochs. That is to say, from the standpoint of international history it is possible to maintain that the Azuchi-Momoyama period did not end conclusively, or at least that the period's afterglow was not extinguished, until the Tokugawa shogunate eliminated the missionaries, expelled the Portuguese, and eradicated the Catholic Church of Japan under the policy of Sakoku (NATIONAL SECLUSION).

The international dimension of Azuchi-Momoyama history is framed by two sets of dates. The distant and more comprehensive view (which takes in portions of the Sengoku and Edo periods) spans the years from 1543, when the first recorded Portuguese traders arrived in Japan, to 1639, when the Tokugawa shogunate's final Sakoku directive put an end to the Portuguese trade and proscribed all Japanese traffic with Catholic lands. The closer but narrower view (which covers little outside the area contained within the commonly accepted perimeters of Azuchi-Momoyama history) extends from 1563, the year when the Kyūshū baron ŌMURA SUMITADA (1533–87) in order to cement his ties with the Portuguese traders accepted baptism from the Jesuit missionaries and became the first of the CHRISTIAN DAIMYŌ, to 1597, when the TWENTY-SIX MARTYRS of Japan were crucified on Hideyoshi's orders in the first bloody persecution of Christianity. The high point of this second view comes at the middle of its set of dates, in 1580, when Ōmura Sumitada ceded to the Jesuits judicial sovereignty over the city and the environs of Nagasaki, the terminus of the Portuguese trading vessels, and the Society of Jesus thereby assumed the domainal lordship over a portion of Japanese soil.

Between 1543 and 1639, the history of official Japanese initiatives toward foreign lands described a full circle, from strictly defined and limited contacts to booming expansiveness, and back again to rigidly limited contacts. The tributary relationship with Ming China, established in the form of the tally ship trade (*kangō bōeki;* see TALLY TRADE) in the first years of the 15th century, continued until the return of the last official mission in 1549, coincidentally the year when the first Christian missionary, Francis XAVIER (1506–52), landed in Japan. Although pirates (WAKŌ) and illicit traders remained active even after that date, maintaining a flow of contraband between Japan and China, and although some commercial intercourse continued with the Ryūkyū Islands and with Korea, in the 1550s Portuguese traders became the most important source of goods from the mainland, and they maintained that role throughout the Azuchi-Momoyama period, taking silver from Japan and in return bringing "silks and damasks, crapes and golden brocades, . . . as well as all the famous products that there are in China and India." The end of the 16th century, however, saw the beginning of an extraordinary burst of Japanese activities directed toward mainland East Asia and the littoral of the South China Sea. The 1590s witnessed Hideyoshi's abortive military adventure of aggression in Korea, which began with bombastic plans to conquer and divide up not only that country but also Ming China, and ended, after much of Korea was devastated, with the ignominious withdrawal of the stalemated Japanese troops upon Hideyoshi's death. Japanese ambitions for overseas ventures were thereupon redirected into a more peaceful channel with the systematization of the VERMILION SEAL SHIP TRADE (shuinsen bōeki) under Tokugawa Ieyasu in the first years of the 17th century.

As the Azuchi-Momoyama period blended with the Edo period, Spanish, Dutch, and English merchants had joined the Portuguese in Japan, and Japanese traders were ranging as far as Indochina, Siam, and the Spice Islands in search of profits. In the 1620s and 1630s, however, the Tokugawa shogunate applied ever stricter controls both on foreigners resident in Japan and on Japanese voyaging abroad (see HŌSHOSEN and KAIGAI TOKŌ KINSHI REI). Under the aegis of the Tokugawa regime, which was intent on demonstrating its supremacy over Japan's foreign and economic affairs, the country had by 1639 returned to a policy of highly restricted commercial and diplomatic relations with a few foreign countries, namely China, Korea, and the Netherlands. The English factory in Hirado had gone bankrupt in 1623, and the British were not permitted back when they sought to reestablish relations half a century later. Merchants of Catholic countries were excluded under the laws of Sakoku. To demonstrate that it meant what it said in its decrees, the shogunate in 1640 executed 61 members of an embassy sent by the Portuguese of Macao to appeal against that exclusion.

The receptivity to contacts with Europeans and the encouragement of Christian missions that had been characteristic of Japan through the first half of the Azuchi-Momoyama period had been replaced at the Edo period's beginning by the execration of everything Christian and by suspiciousness toward Europeans as the potential bearers of the Christian contagion. In retrospect, it appears clear that the great initial successes of Christianity in Japan were a heritage of the Sengoku epoch. They were made possible by political disunity, the general condition of that epoch, which had permitted individual daimyō to Christianize their domains without the fear of sanctions from a higher authority, even if they used coercion. That condition was eliminated by the Shokuhō regime of Oda Nobunaga and Toyotomi Hideyoshi, although it prevailed in Kyūshū, where the Christian mission was able to make its deepest inroads, until Hideyoshi invaded and pacified that turbulent island in 1587. The missionaries' successes could not be sustained in the newly unified Japanese realm because the unifiers mistrusted Christians not only as the adherents of an alien ideology but also as the representatives of a force contrary to their new order—organized religion. Nobunaga, Hideyoshi, and Ieyasu had exerted themselves to the utmost in eliminating the power of the Buddhist church, and had in particular been tested severely by the fanaticism of the armed confederations of the Honganji. That the Christian church might pose a similar challenge was a view clearly expressed by Hideyoshi in 1587; and Ieyasu, too, by 1614 had concluded that Christianity was a "pernicious doctrine" (jahō) which was socially subversive and therefore had to be suppressed.

In short, as the task of Japan's unification progressed, the Japanese power-holders grew concerned lest Christianity cause a fresh disruption of loyalties in their reintegrated society and state. This indictment was repeated again and again in their ANTI-CHRISTIAN EDICTS and in the polemical literature produced by the exponents of orthodoxy in their employ. Once such a definition of the Christian peril was reached, the doors that had been open to the outside were closed. Azuchi-Momoyama, an extraverted period of history, was followed by a long era of introversion.

▄▄——Araki Yoshio, Azuchi-Momoyama jidai bungaku shi (1969). Asao Naohiro, "Toyotomi seiken ron," in Kinsei 1: vol 9 of Iwanami kōza: Nihon rekishi (Iwanami Shoten, 1963). Michael Cooper SJ, ed, The Southern Barbarians: The First Europeans in Japan (1971). Doi Tsugiyoshi, Momoyama no shōhekiga (1964), tr Edna B. Crawford as Momoyama Decorative Painting (1977). George Elison, Deus Destroyed: The Image of Christianity in Early Modern Japan (1973). George Elison and Bardwell L. Smith, ed, Warlords, Artists, & Commoners: Japan in the Sixteenth Century (1981), including Bardwell L. Smith, "Japanese Society and Culture in the Momoyama Era: A Bibliographic Essay." Fujiki Hisashi, Oda-Toyotomi seiken, vol 15 of Nihon no rekishi (Shōgakukan, 1975). Fujiki Hisashi and Kitajima Manji, ed, Shokuhō seiken, vol 6 of Ronshū Nihon rekishi (Yūseidō, 1974). Haga Kōshirō, Azuchi-Momoyama jidai no bunka (1964). John Whitney Hall, Nagahara Keiji, and Kozo Yamamura, ed, Japan Before Tokugawa: Political Consolidation and Economic Growth, 1500 to 1650 (1981). Hasumi Shigeyasu, "Momoyama bunka," in Kinsei 1: vol 9 of Iwanami kōza: Nihon rekishi (Iwanami Shoten, 1963). Hayashiya Tatsusaburō, Tenka ittō, vol 12 of Nihon no rekishi (Chūō Kōron Sha, 1971). Hayashiya Tatsusaburō, ed, Momoyama jidai, vol 5 of Nihon bunka shi (Chikuma Shobō, 1965). Imaizumi Yoshio, Azuchi-Momoyama bunka (1979). Itō Teiji, Shiro to sono machi (1963). Kawai Masatomo and Wakisaka Atsushi, Momoyama no shōheiga: Eitoku, Tōhaku, Yūshō, vol 17 of Nihon bijutsu zenshū (Gakken, 1978). John B. Kirby Jr, From Castle to Teahouse: Japanese Architecture of the Momoyama Period (1962). Kobayashi Seiji and Ōishi Naomasa, ed, Chūsei Ōu no sekai (1978). Kyōto Shi, ed, Momoyama no kaika, vol 4 of Kyōto no rekishi (1969). Miki Seiichirō, Teppō to sono jidai (1981). Mizuo Hiroshi, Shōhekiga shi (1978). Momoyama: Japanese Art in the Age of Grandeur, An Exhibition at the Metropolitan Museum of Art (1975). Nagahara Keiji, Sengoku no dōran, vol 14 of Nihon no rekishi (Shōgakukan, 1975). Naitō Akira, Mizuno Kōji, and Yuasa Kōzō, Shiro no nihonshi, NHK Bukkusu Karāhan C7 (1979). Sasaki Junnosuke, ed, Tenka ittō to minshū, vol 3 of Nihon minshū no rekishi (Sanseidō, 1974). João Rodrigues Tçuzzu SJ, História da Igreja do Japão, 2 vols (1954–55); abridged English trans. by Michael Cooper SJ, This Island of Japon (1973); complete Japanese trans. by Doi Tadao et al, Nihon kyōkai shi, 2 vols (1967–70). Wakita Osamu, Shokuhō seiken no bunseki, 2 vols (1975–77). William Watson, ed, The Great Japan Exhibition: Art of the Edo Period, 1600–1868 (1981). Yamane Yūzō, Momoyama no fūzokuga (1967), tr John M. Shields as Momoyama Genre Painting (1973).

George ELISON

EDO HISTORY (1600–1868)

The Edo period, also referred to as the Tokugawa period, is customarily dated from either 1600 (when TOKUGAWA IEYASU gained national military hegemony) or 1603 (when Ieyasu became shōgun) to either 1867 (when the last shōgun submitted his resignation) or 1868 (the year of the Meiji Restoration). One of the major epochs of Japanese history, the Edo period is distinguished by its length of over two and a half centuries and, in addition, by the fact that for more than two of these centuries (from 1638 to 1864) Japan enjoyed freedom from warfare at home and abroad. The condition of domestic tranquillity has been explained by some as a consequence of the harsh, authoritarian administration enforced by the military aristocracy, or samurai. Likewise, avoidance of foreign wars is in part accounted for by the Tokugawa policy of NATIONAL SECLUSION adopted in 1639. Despite this and other restrictive measures, however, Japan experienced many significant changes in political organization, social structure, economic capacity, and cultural style under Tokugawa rule.

The Edo period witnessed the highest point in the evolution of the system of local rule by military lords (DAIMYŌ) under strong shogunal authority, vested in this case in the Tokugawa family. It was in the 16th century that the samurai became a separate and self-conscious ruling class able to monopolize all functions of government above the level of village and town self-administration. Under samurai rule, Edo law defined separate classes of commoners, the farmer (hyakushō) and the townsman (chōnin) being the most important. Since almost the entire samurai class left the agrarian countryside to take up residence in the castle towns of their daimyō lords, they stimulated a rapid and widespread growth of cities. Urbanization affected the way of life of both samurai and townspeople. In their castle cities the samurai became a sedentary administrative officialdom, heavily reliant on the services of merchants and other townspeople. Thus, although the samurai managed to keep alive a legacy of "noble arts" inherited from a more aristocratic past, the newly affluent townspeople developed a vigorous popular culture of their own. All of these developments were to have a profound influence on the manner in which the Japanese people were to move into the modern world.

Tokugawa Ieyasu and the Establishment of the Tokugawa Hegemony

The rise of the Tokugawa family to military hegemony over all Japan was achieved by Tokugawa Ieyasu. Ieyasu's family, surnamed Matsudaira in the generations before him, had achieved the status of minor daimyō in the province of Mikawa (now part of Aichi Prefecture) by the 1550s. At that time it still acknowledged the overlordship of the IMAGAWA FAMILY, daimyō of neighboring Suruga and Tōtōmi provinces (both now part of Shizuoka Prefecture). In 1560 Imagawa Yoshimoto was destroyed by ODA NOBUNAGA. Ieyasu, by then head of his house, allied himself with Nobunaga. By the time of Nobunaga's death in 1582, Ieyasu had fought his way into possession of all or parts of the five provinces of Mikawa, Suruga, Tōtōmi, Kai, and Shinano (the latter two now Yamanashi and Nagano prefectures).

Following Nobunaga's death, Ieyasu was obliged to accept the command of TOYOTOMI HIDEYOSHI. In 1590 Tokugawa forces played a prominent role in Hideyoshi's victory over the Go-Hōjō (or Later Hōjō) family at Odawara (see ODAWARA CAMPAIGN). As a reward, and also as a means of moving the Tokugawa farther from the political and economic center of Japan, Hideyoshi transferred Ieyasu from his ancestral lands centering on Mikawa into the Kantō provinces vacated by the Go-Hōjō. Tokugawa Ieyasu thereby became the greatest of Hideyoshi's vassal daimyō, with a domain assessed at over 2.5 million koku (see KOKUDAKA), larger in fact than Hideyoshi's own holdings. Choosing as his headquarters the small castle town of Edo (now Tōkyō), he set to work to build a great citadel from which to rule his new possessions.

As Hideyoshi neared the end of his life and realized that he was destined to leave behind a child successor, he assigned the task of safeguarding Toyotomi rule to a Board of Regents (Gotairō) consisting of the country's five most powerful daimyō: Tokugawa Ieyasu, MAEDA TOSHIIE, Mōri Terumoto (1553–1625), Kobayakawa Takakage (1533–97; replaced after his death by UESUGI KAGEKATSU), and UKITA HIDEIE. This arrangement was inherently unstable, and shortly after Hideyoshi's death in 1598, the daimyō began to maneuver for advantage. Two factions emerged. One, based in Ōsaka Castle and led by lesser daimyō loyal to Hideyoshi's heir, enlisted most of the major daimyō of western Japan, such as the Ukita family and MŌRI FAMILY of western Honshū, the SHIMAZU FAMILY of southern Kyūshū, and the CHŌSOKABE FAMILY of Shikoku. The other was led by Ieyasu and included many daimyō of central and eastern Honshū. The armies of these two groups met in 1600 in the climactic Battle of SEKIGAHARA. The eastern faction won the day, and Ieyasu thereby gained military supremacy over all the daimyō of Japan.

Following Sekigahara, Ieyasu received the title of SHŌGUN from the emperor in 1603, thereby legitimizing his status as military hegemon. But the Toyotomi cause was still alive. Hideyoshi's heir, TOYOTOMI HIDEYORI, though a minor and reduced to the status of daimyō, retained Ōsaka Castle and the potential of challenging Ieyasu for the loyalty of those daimyō who had once served under his father. Ōsaka Castle became the rallying point for many warriors who had been dispossessed at Sekigahara. Ieyasu's final eradication of the Toyotomi remnants came in 1615 when, after two costly assaults and the use of trickery, the Tokugawa forces managed to take Ōsaka Castle and kill its defenders (see ŌSAKA CASTLE, SIEGES OF). Ieyasu died in 1616, having begun the construction of a political system that was to endure for more than 250 years. All that remained to be done was to institutionalize the shogunal control system and to codify its basic policies. These tasks were effectively carried out by Ieyasu's immediate successors TOKUGAWA HIDETADA (r 1605–23) and TOKUGAWA IEMITSU (r 1623–51).

The Tokugawa Power Structure

The political system created by Ieyasu is now generally referred to as the BAKUHAN SYSTEM. As this term implies, government during the Edo period functioned through two political mechanisms: the bakufu or SHOGUNATE and the HAN or daimyō domain. Ieyasu began his rise as a daimyō and remained such until the Battle of Sekigahara, after which he claimed supremacy over all military houses (buke no tōryō) by virtue of his victory. But Ieyasu had achieved his hegemony as the head of a coalition of vassals and allied daimyō, all of whom expected to share in the fruits of military victory. Thus, although at Sekigahara Ieyasu had acquired territories valued at some 5 million koku by confiscation, he was obliged to give out as rewards for loyal service close to 7 million koku. Ieyasu's rise to power did not lead him to eliminate the daimyō. Instead he used the daimyō system, seeking only to establish a favorable balance of power under his authority.

When Ieyasu entered the Kantō Plain in 1590, the Tokugawa band of retainers consisted of at least 38 men whose fiefs were assessed at daimyō size, that is, 10,000 koku or more. After Sekigahara, these and other retainers were set out across the land as daimyō in their own right. Daimyō so created were classed as FUDAI (hereditary vassals), a group that eventually numbered 145 houses. Another special category of daimyō were the SHIMPAN (collateral or cadet daimyō), of which 23 eventually survived. Balanced against these two groups were daimyō who had been created by Nobunaga or Hideyoshi and who had either survived Sekigahara by joining the Tokugawa side before the battle or, having been on the losing side, had been spared extinction by Ieyasu for various reasons. These daimyō, given the status of TOZAMA (outside lords), numbered some 98 at the end of the 17th century. The Tokugawa house itself, of course, constituted a major power bloc, for the shōgun directly held granary lands (known as TENRYŌ) assessed at some 4 million koku, while another 3 million koku were held by the shōgun's enfeoffed HATAMOTO (bannermen), each of whose holdings was less than 10,000 koku.

The balance of power achieved by the Tokugawa shogunate is measurable first in terms of the comparative magnitude and location of the various categories of landholdings. At the end of the first century of Tokugawa rule, total landholdings in Japan had stabilized at about 26.4 million koku, distributed as follows (in 1,000-koku units):

Shōgun's granary lands *(tenryō)*	4,200
Shōgun's bannermen *(hatamoto)*	2,600
Shōgun's hereditary vassals *(fudai)* and collateral *(shimpan)* daimyō	9,300
Outside lords *(tozama)*	9,800
Imperial and court families	140
Temples and shrines	320

As these figures demonstrate, the balance was comfortably weighted in favor of the Tokugawa interests.

The Tokugawa hegemony centered in Edo and stretched out along the irregular pattern of its direct holdings. Although heavily concentrated in the region east of Ōsaka, the tenryō included the most important cities: Ōsaka, Kyōto, Nagasaki, and Edo. As a result of continual dispossession and relocation of daimyō, the Tokugawa achieved a strategic balance in placement of the various categories of daimyō that favored the shogunate. The GOSANKE (Three Successor Houses) or houses directly descended from Ieyasu were strategically placed: in Mito (now part of Ibaraki Prefecture), north of Edo; in Owari (now part of Aichi Prefecture), between Edo and Kyōto; and in Kii (now Wakayama Prefecture), south of Ōsaka. The main tozama houses remained on the fringes of the islands, while the fudai were clustered in the Kantō and central Japan.

Legitimation of the Tokugawa Regime: The Authority Structure

Tokugawa Ieyasu used the office of shōgun as his prime means of legitimation. As shōgun he claimed recognition as chief (tōryō) of the military estate and, by virtue of precedent based on previous shogunal regimes, most of the rights of national governance. In theory the shōgun was the delegate of the emperor, and Ieyasu fully exploited the symbolism of imperial appointment to enhance his own prestige. Thus the Tokugawa made sure that the imperial court had the resources to maintain its traditional rituals and style of life. At the same time, they made every effort to limit the emperor's political influence. The court nobility (kuge) were physically confined to the palace enclosure (gyoen) in Kyōto, watched over by the shōgun's deputy (KYŌTO SHOSHIDAI) and his garrison at Nijō Castle, and placed under the restraints of a set of regulations known as the KINCHŪ NARABI NI KUGE SHOHATTO (Laws Governing the Imperial Court and Nobility). This document, which was drawn up in 1615 after Ieyasu's victory at Ōsaka, excluded the emperor from participation in the affairs of state and made his awarding of court honors to the military aristocracy subject to shogunal approval.

As the emperor's delegate and chief of the military estate, the Tokugawa shōgun exercised broad national authority, regulating affairs among the daimyō and among religious bodies, and setting national military and fiscal policy. In foreign affairs too, the shōgun assumed the right to negotiate with foreign nations, to stamp out Christianity, to control foreign trade, and to restrict the movement of Japanese in and out of Japan. Of all the shōgun's powers the most important was that of ultimate proprietorship of the country's land.

Over the daimyō the shōgun held full rights of suzerainty. All daimyō were his sworn vassals who held their domains as grants from him. The right to grant and withdraw land was used vigorously by the first three shōguns. Under them some 200 daimyō houses were dispossessed, and in another 250 cases daimyō were moved from one location to another (see KAIEKI).

As supreme overlord, the shōgun possessed the right to regulate the daimyō. Basic policy was set down in the BUKE SHOHATTO (Regulations for the Military Houses), drawn up in 1615 after the destruction of Ōsaka Castle. This code specified that marriages and succession arrangements required prior shogunal approval and that military establishments must be kept within prescribed limits. Prohibitions against Christianity and the construction of ocean-going ships were added to the code at a later date. So also was the single most effective control device, the SANKIN KŌTAI, or alternate attendance, requirement. This elaboration of the customary practice of taking hostages to ensure loyalty of vassals obliged all daimyō and their families to establish residences in the environs of Edo Castle from which to pay regular homage to the shōgun. Daimyō were permitted to return to their home territories in alternate years (or, for some, in alternate half-years), leaving their wives, children, and ranking officials in Edo as hostages. The sankin kōtai system continually affirmed the political centrality of Edo.

Although the shōgun's authority over the daimyō was absolute in theory, in practice the daimyō were given considerable freedom in the administration of their domains. And it must be remembered that daimyō were permitted, in fact expected, to maintain their own armed forces, though under shogunate-imposed limitations. Daimyō differed in size of domain, in relationship to the shōgun, and in manner of local administration. The greatest of the daimyō, the MAEDA FAMILY, had a domain covering the three provinces of Kaga, Noto, and Etchū (now Ishikawa and Toyama prefectures) and was assessed at over 1 million koku. Its inhabitants probably numbered over 1 million. Another 22 "great daimyō" had domains comprising one or two provinces with populations numbering from 250,000 to 800,000 persons. But the great majority of daimyō domains were of minimum size, containing only 10,000 to 20,000 inhabitants.

The shōgun did not interfere directly in the internal affairs of the domains, but he did insist upon strict conformity to certain basic policies and regulations. This was made clear in the Buke Shohatto, as amended in 1635, which stated that "throughout the country all matters are to be carried out in accordance with the laws of Edo." The shōgun did not regularly tax the daimyō, but the daimyō were obliged to keep their domains in order, provide military support in times of crisis, and contribute funds and manpower for the building and rebuilding of shogunal castles and residences, imperial palaces, and various public works projects. Moreover, domains were regularly subject to shogunal inspection. Hanging over all daimyō, especially up through the time of Iemitsu, was the threat of dispossession for even a minor infraction of shogunate regulations.

The shōgun exercised the right to regulate religious bodies as well. Up to the emergence of the great military consolidators, Buddhist communities had played a large role in the political and economic life of the country. Monasteries held proprietary rights to extensive territories, and sectarian congregations built castles and resisted the efforts of daimyō to absorb them into their domains. Nobunaga and Hideyoshi succeeded in destroying the political and military power of these religious groups. Under the Tokugawa regime, the religious bodies were reduced in landholdings and the priesthood strictly regulated under the provisions of the Shoshū Jiin Hatto (Regulations for Sects and Temples). Nonetheless, the Buddhist establishment prospered during the Edo period because of the service it performed for the shogunate in the eradication of Christianity (see SHŪMON ARATAME). Under the TERAUKE, or temple guarantee system, Buddhist temples were charged with scrutinizing the religious beliefs of all Japanese.

The Bakuhan System: Central and Local Administration

The administrative map of Japan during the Edo period was extremely complex. To start with, the tenryō was distributed unevenly throughout Japan. Then there were some 270 daimyō jurisdictions, added to which were the holdings of the 5,000 bannermen, the imperial court, and the great temples and shrines. Yet all of this was somehow pulled together under the shōgun's overlordship.

The organs of shogunal administration emerged from the house government that had served Ieyasu when he was still a daimyō in the Kantō. The most significant consequence of this was that, even though Tokugawa authority extended over the entire country, the shōgun's administration (bakufu) was entrusted only to the hereditary-vassal (fudai) class of daimyō, bannermen (hatamoto), and direct retainers (GOKENIN). Shogunate administrative machinery developed pragmatically as the Tokugawa house expanded its responsibilities and as military organization was adapted to civil administrative functions.

As chief of state and supreme overlord, the shōgun worked through two boards of retainers. A group of five or six senior councillors (RŌJŪ) made up a high administrative council with authority over matters of nationwide scope. These included supervision of the imperial court, the daimyō, the religious bodies, foreign affairs, military affairs, currency, taxation, and the distribution of lands and honors. Senior councillors were appointed from among high-ranking fudai daimyō. A second board consisting of three to five junior councillors (WAKADOSHIYORI) had charge of the internal affairs of the shogunate. Appointed from among fudai daimyō of lesser rank, it had jurisdiction over the shōgun's retainers and bannermen, the standing military and guard units, and the shōgun's military establishment.

It was under the senior councillors that the most important functional officers of the shogunate were placed. These included the commissioners of major cities (MACHI BUGYŌ), the commissioners of finance (KANJŌ BUGYŌ), the commissioners of temples and shrines (JISHA BUGYŌ), the keepers (JŌDAI) of Ōsaka and Sumpu castles, the Kyōto deputies (Kyōto shoshidai), the inspectors general (ŌMETSUKE), and a host of lesser officers. All were either fudai daimyō or hatamoto. Symbolic of the shōgun's status as national overlord was the establishment of the shōgun's Judicial Council (Hyōjōsho), staffed by designated senior councillors and other high shogunate officials.

In both the shogunal and daimyō domains government above the level of local headmen was monopolized by the samurai class. Within the shogunate, responsibility for rural affairs started in the office of the commissioners of finance and, for urban affairs, in the office of the city commissioners. Under the commissioners of finance, local intendants (DAIKAN or GUNDAI) were placed over large subdivisions of the tenryō. These officers, numbering between 40 and 50 at any given time, were chosen from among middle- and lower-status bannermen. The intendants divided their time between Edo and the regional offices (daikansho) from which they superintended the collection of taxes and the enforcement of shogunate regulations. Daimyō likewise administered their rural areas in two steps, from central finance office to rural intendant. Below the level of centrally attached samurai officialdom, the common inhabitants lived in self-governing units: villages (mura), or urban wards (machi).

Villages functioned as basic units of rural control and taxation. They were composed of taxpaying farmers (HYAKUSHŌ) and their tenants and dependent workers. It was left to the hyakushō to maintain village self-management. Each village had its headman (nanushi or SHŌYA), assistant headman (kumigashira), and hyakushō representative (hyakushōdai). Village families were obliged to form into neighborhood groups (GONINGUMI), which promoted mutual assistance but also served as units of mutual responsibility to assure payment of taxes and compliance with regulations. Although samurai officialdom normally left the villagers to themselves except for periodic inspection visits, regulations and orders from above did penetrate to the villages. Farmers were forbidden to leave their cultivated land and were restricted in buying or selling land. They could leave the village on trips only for certain purposes and only by permission. They were prohibited from changing their profession and were restricted in many other ways. Most of these prohibitions could be taken care of by the village headman, who served the dual purpose of enforcement and of mediation between village and superior authority. See also MURA YAKUNIN.

The Bakuhan System: Social Structure and Class Policy

The early Tokugawa shōguns inherited a society that had already begun to differentiate into separate functional classes. During the last half of the 16th century Japan had undergone a profound social revolution, the main feature of which was the sharply defined separation of the warrior elite from the farming class—a phenomenon referred to as heinō bunri. The process of separation had been going on for some time.

At the start of the 16th century the lower levels of the samurai class still lived within the agricultural communities that they held as fiefs, exercising proprietary, judicial, and military powers over the farmers; but cultivators began to organize to resist direct samurai control. Village communities eventually won a considerable degree of autonomy in their internal affairs, most often by negotiation with superior daimyō authority at the expense of the local samurai. The trend toward village autonomy placed the rural samurai (often called JIZAMURAI) in an increasingly precarious position. At the same time, daimyō were finding it necessary to concentrate more and more of their military manpower in their castle headquarters for military purposes. These developments became mutually reinforcing after the middle of the 16th century. Jizamurai began moving off the land to reside in the daimyō's castle towns, leaving the villages to self-government under daimyō administration. This movement was institutionalized under Hideyoshi by his nationwide program of land surveys, the so-called Taikō kenchi (see KENCHI).

What the kenchi aimed to do was to measure every piece of cultivated land in Japan, determine its area, assess its productive capacity, and record its cultivator. Productive capacity was determined on the basis of yield per unit measured in KOKU of rice. Cadastral registers (kenchichō) were prepared village by village. The sum total of the yield figures for all fields of a village was known as the kokudaka. These kokudaka figures could be used in a variety of ways. For the villages they became the assessment base upon which the village tax was calculated. For the military authorities they became the means of assigning fiefs and of calculating the total worth of daimyō domains.

Thus the Taikō kenchi became the foundation upon which the legal status of both the samurai and farmer classes rested for the next two and three-quarter centuries. Quite literally, samurai were defined as persons enrolled on the daimyō or shogunal retainer rosters, while hyakushō were those listed on the kenchichō. Use of the kokudaka system also meant that samurai were not only detached from the land but could be paid from the lord's storehouse without reference to any specific fief.

Hideyoshi's domestic measures thus brought into being a new samurai class, urban in residence and bureaucratic in function; most remarkable of all, it was a class that neither owned agricultural land nor had the legal right to acquire land by purchase. The daimyō had the right to tax their domains, but they held their domains not as private owners but as delegates of the shōgun. Their powers were political, not proprietary. By the same token, the hyakushō, by being recorded in the cadastral register, were made more secure in their possession or occupancy of the lands on which they paid taxes.

Class separation took another step forward under Hideyoshi. The SWORD HUNT order of 1588 aimed at disarming the rural populace, thereby giving to the samurai a monopoly in arms-bearing. Thereafter the samurai assumed as a badge of class distinction the wearing of two swords, long and short. Hideyoshi's edict of 1591 prohibiting changes in status from samurai to farmer or merchant, and from farmer to merchant, though hard to enforce, began the process of legal codification of the social class structure.

Tokugawa legislation further refined the class structure of society by adopting for official purposes the four-class concept that had originated in China (see SHI-NŌ-KŌ-SHŌ). These classes, in order of importance, were: warrior elite (samurai), farmers (nōmin), artisans (kōnin), and merchants (shōnin). In actual practice, since artisans and merchants tended to congregate in the cities, they were generally lumped together under the term CHŌNIN (townspeople). Functionally, therefore, Edo society is more correctly conceived of as having had three main classes. In addition, Tokugawa law recognized a number of other social groups, such as the court aristocracy (kuge), priests and nuns (sō and ni), and outcastes (eta—later called BURAKUMIN—and HININ). Each class or group was given a separate identity under law and was treated differently with respect to land rights, tax burden, criminal procedure, and political authority.

The legal separation of the main classes, or estates, gave rise to quite different expectations and styles of life for each segment of society. Samurai lived in towns, within the walled and moated enclosures surrounding their lords' castles. They were restricted to military and civil-bureaucratic service. Chōnin were confined to certain sections, or wards (machi), in towns and cities, where they were expected to provide services for the samurai while maintaining a posture befitting their low status. Farmers by definition lived in village units where they were admonished to work hard and live frugally. Much Tokugawa law dealt with externals, the regulation of housing, clothing, food, and conduct appropriate to each class or group.

Samurai government, by origin an extension of daimyō military organization, was authoritarian and rigorous in enforcement. But it was not necessarily arbitrary. The samurai bureaucrats of the Edo

period gave evidence of reliance on something akin to a concept of "natural law" premised on the existence of a natural social order. Assuming that society by nature was a hierarchy of classes, the legal system first defined the fundamental social divisions and then issued rules of conduct appropriate to each. In Edo society, the individual was born to, and bound to, a particular status. It was his destiny to remain in that status, but within that status he was treated equally under law. To this extent public law had taken the place of custom privately enforced.

Tokugawa law relied heavily on the social concepts of Confucianism. At the start of the Edo period, shōgun and daimyō faced acute problems of social engineering, in legitimizing their rule and in institutionalizing their social controls. Confucianism, with its heavy emphasis on ethical principles and social harmony, proved relevant to their needs. In rationalizing the shift from military to civil rule and from patriarchal society to one of broadly defined classes, samurai government spontaneously turned to Confucianism. The official reliance on Confucianism was symbolized by the employment of HAYASHI RAZAN as Confucian adviser to the shōgun in 1607. Razan and his successors played important roles in drafting shogunate laws and in developing historical justification for the Tokugawa regime. The basic moral concepts advocated by Confucianism—LOYALTY (chū) and FILIAL PIETY (kō)—were conservative and supportive of the existing social and political order.

Although Confucianism supported authoritarian government, it contained a reciprocal feature that should not be minimized. It set before samurai government the ultimate principle that the object of government was the general welfare. Hence it required that samurai government provide "benevolent rule" (jinsei) for the people. The samurai's right to rule was presumed to rest on his ability to set a public example of ethical conduct and to show a sense of social responsibility.

The Retreat to Seclusion——The basic rationale of the bakuhan system did not lead necessarily to the adoption of a policy of National Seclusion. But that policy, once adopted, had a profound effect on life in Edo Japan, on Japan's conception of itself, and on the world's conception of Japan. Neither Hideyoshi nor the early Tokugawa shōguns were fundamentally opposed to foreign contact and trade. Ieyasu had tried to develop Edo as a port for trade with the Dutch and English. The failure of this effort, together with a growing suspicion that Christianity was politically dangerous to his regime, prompted him to issue his first anti-Christian prohibition in 1612. But it was his two immediate successors who pursued this policy to its ultimate conclusion. The SHIMABARA UPRISING of 1637–38 was the event that pushed the shogunate to its most extreme anti-Christian measures. The presumption that the Shimabara rebels were led by masterless Christian samurai made extermination of the foreign religion an absolute necessity. Christians, when found, were executed. From the 1630s the shogunate introduced the terauke (temple register) and shūmon aratame (religious investigation) requirements. All Japanese families of whatever class were obliged to register at a local temple (dannadera) and to give evidence annually that they were not contaminated by Christianity.

Meanwhile, regulation of foreign trade moved in parallel. Efforts were made to convert the trade with Korea into a tributary relationship, using the SŌ FAMILY (daimyō of Tsushima) as intermediaries. The same was attempted with respect to the Ryūkyūs, using the SHIMAZU FAMILY (daimyō of Satsuma). At Nagasaki, which served as the official Tokugawa door to the outside world, elaborate restrictions were placed on trade and foreign contact. In 1635 Japanese nationals were forbidden to travel abroad or to return home from abroad (see KAIGAI TOKŌ KINSHI REI). In 1639 Portuguese ships were excluded from Japanese ports, and only the Dutch and Chinese were allowed a strictly regulated trade at Nagasaki. Thus Japan entered its period of National Seclusion of more than two centuries, during which no warfare either domestic or foreign disturbed the "Great Peace" under the bakuhan regime.

Evolution of the Bakuhan State——The pattern of Japanese society and culture resulting from the perfection of the bakuhan system and the accompanying "Great Peace" retained its general contours until the middle of the 19th century. But isolation and domestic tranquillity did not bring social and political change to a standstill. To observe this, one has only to look at the changes that took place in the structure of Tokugawa rule.

The first three shōguns brought the Tokugawa regime to its full development. Under them the control mechanisms and the administrative machinery were perfected and strenuous efforts were made to increase the balance of power in favor of the shogunate. All three exercised "personal rule" to the fullest, using their power to disenfeoff or transfer daimyō in the shōgun's interests. It was under Tokugawa Iemitsu that the *sankin kōtai* system, the National Seclusion policy, and the anti-Christian *terauke* regulations were first enforced.

Iemitsu was succeeded in 1651 by his son TOKUGAWA IETSUNA (r 1651–80), a fragile youth of 10. There resulted a style of shogunal rule that reflected the interests of the *fudai* daimyō more than the central interests of the shōgun. Policy was largely made by the senior councillors. Certain control measures were reversed or allowed to lapse. For instance, deathbed adoption of heirs by daimyō was made legal, thus eliminating the problem of "failure to produce an heir," one of the main pretexts for confiscation of daimyō domains used by the first three shōguns. Since the country was isolated and at peace, a relaxation of control from the center was welcome. In fact, a virtue was made of the move toward a more humane approach to government, toward what the Confucianists called *bunji seiji*, or rule by scholar-officials.

The fifth shōgun, TOKUGAWA TSUNAYOSHI (r 1680–1709), was both colorful and controversial. A mature man when he became shōgun, he put his personal imprint on shogunate policy from the start. It was under him that yet another pattern of shogunal rule emerged, one in which the shōgun relied heavily on his private, or "inner-chamber," officials to circumvent the senior councillors, or "outer-office" officials. Tsunayoshi's reliance on his favorite, YANAGISAWA YOSHIYASU, set an example of rule through the grand chamberlain (SOBAYŌNIN).

Tsunayoshi vigorously promoted Confucian scholarship, Buddhist observances, cultural activities like the NŌ drama, and shogunate ceremonials. But he gained a poor reputation for his personal life (he openly engaged in homosexual activities) and for his public policy (he ran the shogunate into bankruptcy and resorted to debasement of the coinage). His intemperate edicts against taking animal life, especially of dogs, earned him the nickname "the dog shōgun." Tsunayoshi's two successors, TOKUGAWA IENOBU (r 1709–12), and Tokugawa Ietsugu (r 1713–16), between them stayed for only seven years in office. Although neither put his personal stamp upon shogunal affairs, their years were marked by the influence of one of the most remarkable of Tokugawa officials. ARAI HAKUSEKI, Confucian scholar and personal adviser to both shōguns, exemplified in his life and in the policies he recommended the ideal of the scholar-official.

In 1716 the main (Hidetada) line of the Tokugawa house failed, so that the eighth shōgun had to be found in one of the Three Successor Houses. The choice fell on TOKUGAWA YOSHIMUNE (r 1716–45), daimyō of Kii. Already a mature and experienced man, Yoshimune embarked on a strenuous program of bureaucratic and financial reforms upon taking office. His effort, known as the KYŌHŌ REFORMS, was the first of three major reform attempts made during the period. The main ingredients of these reforms were agrarianism, hard money, fiscal retrenchment, protection of indebted samurai, sumptuary regulation, and control of the commercial economy. The effectiveness of these policies is still in question, but at the time, Yoshimune was lauded for his "back to Ieyasu" policies. Contemporaries assumed these policies to be in the country's interest, ideologically, but 20th-century historians have suggested that they treated only the symptoms and not the causes of the country's problems.

Yoshimune's son and grandson, the shōguns TOKUGAWA IESHIGE (r 1745–60) and Ieharu (r 1760–86), were not men of personal strength. Traditional historiography has judged them harshly. It is claimed that both were manipulated by favorites: Ieshige by Ōoka Tadamitsu (1709–60) and Ieharu by TANUMA OKITSUGU. Both of these officials rose to power from low status by the "inner" route; Tanuma in particular has gone down in history as an extreme example of the corrupt favorite. Although there may have been corruption, Tanuma's bad name resulted mainly from the unorthodox policies he advocated, paticularly in the effort to build up the shōgun's finances. Under Ieharu the shogunate's finance office openly attempted to profit from the commercial sector of the economy. To expand the currency in circulation, silver coins were minted for the first time. Shogunate monopolies were created in products such as copper, silver, brass, cotton, Chinese silk, and lamp oil, and commercial monopolies were licensed (for a fee) in other commodities. Attempts were made to expand foreign trade at Nagasaki and to colonize EZO (now Hokkaidō). Various schemes were devised to create a national pool of capital, contributed by merchants and guaranteed by the shogunate, to provide low-interest loans for financially distressed daimyō and samurai. Whether these measures could have succeeded cannot be known, for they were never fully implemented. So much opposition had grown up around Tanuma that, when his patron Ieharu died in 1786, he was driven from office and his policies reversed.

Admittedly the country at large faced many critical domestic problems by the 1780s. Many samurai were in debt, and the shogunate and most daimyō were in financial trouble. Between 1782 and 1787 crop failures caused famine conditions in several parts of Japan (see TEMMEI FAMINE). Edo was shaken by urban riots, the largest lasting for three days in 1787. A general restlessness gripped Japan, and Tanuma was an easy scapegoat. Upon Ieharu's death, reaction took over the shogunate. The new shōgun, TOKUGAWA IENARI (r 1787–1837), being a minor, was placed under the guidance of a new chief shogunate officer, MATSUDAIRA SADANOBU, who immediately moved to eliminate Tanuma's influence in government. Sadanobu is credited with carrying out the second of the conservative reform programs, the KANSEI REFORMS. His slogan "back to Yoshimune" is indicative of the general thrust of his policies. The results were no more positive or long-lasting than those of the Kyōhō era.

By 1817 Ienari had become master of his own policies (Sadanobu had retired in 1793), and reform was not his concern. Relying upon his personal favorite, Mizuno Tadaakira (1762–1834), he led a turn toward relaxation of controls and uninhibited expenditures backed by currency debasement.

Up to this point the shogunate's problems had been mainly domestic and socioeconomic, but by the beginning of the 19th century, with the appearance of Russian and British ships in Japanese waters, Japan faced an external threat as well. Although the extent of this threat was at first not known, shogunate officials soon realized that the military and economic resources at their disposal were totally inadequate for purposes of defense. By the 1830s and 1840s the shogunate was caught in a double crisis, domestic and foreign. In 1836 the regime experienced one of its worst agrarian uprisings, in the province of Kai. The following year the attempted rebellion in Ōsaka led by ŌSHIO HEIHACHIRŌ (a minor Tokugawa official) shook shogunate officialdom. In 1841, upon the death of Ienari, MIZUNO TADAKUNI, chief of the senior councillors, intiated the last and most drastic of the three reforms, the TEMPŌ REFORMS. Mizuno's program was intended to improve both the economic and the political position of the shogunate. Two of his most controversial policies were his abolition of all merchant monopolies and guilds (see KABUNAKAMA; TOIYA) in order, he thought, to lower commodity prices; and his AGECHIREI, an order transferring all daimyō holdings out of the immediate environs of Edo and Ōsaka castles. Both orders caused consternation among those affected, particularly the 15 daimyō whose lands were jeopardized by the transfer order. Mizuno was soon forced to resign, and his successor as head of the senior councillors, ABE MASAHIRO, rescinded most of his initiatives.

It was Abe, however, who had to face the crisis created by Commodore Matthew PERRY in 1853. Finding himself in an impossible situation, Abe did two things that signaled the end of Tokugawa power. By soliciting all daimyō, including TOZAMA, for opinions on how to handle the American request for the opening of Japanese ports, he abandoned the shogunal prerogative of determining foreign policy unilaterally. By encouraging daimyō to build up their own coastal defenses, he weakened the shōgun's power to control their military strength. Meanwhile, local Tempō Reforms had proved successful in many of the larger domains. Among these were the Satsuma (now Kagoshima Prefecture) and Chōshū (now Yamaguchi Prefecture) domains, traditional enemies of the Tokugawa. The Tokugawa now paid the price for not having increased the centralizing powers achieved by the early shōguns. Edo government relied upon a balance of power between shogunate and domains, a balance that was stable as long as Japan remained isolated and as long as military technology remained unchanged. Neither of these conditions was met after 1853. A last-minute effort by the shogunate to assert its national authority failed, and with that failure the Tokugawa regime came to an end.

Economic and Cultural Developments —— The Japan that was "opened" by Perry was a vastly different country from the one that had closed its doors in 1639. The greatest achievement of the Tokugawa shogunate was surely the long period of peace and stability it gave to Japan. As a result, within the admittedly narrow structural limitations imposed by the *bakuhan* system and the National Seclusion policy, the country prospered both economically and culturally.

One can cite many indices of growth. Most basic was the increase in agricultural production. Total taxable cereal production has been estimated at roughly 18.5 million *koku* at the start of the Edo period. By 1700 this figure had grown to over 26 million *koku*, and by 1873 to 32 million. These increases had come through land reclamation, better technology, and improved plant varieties. In addition to cereals, Edo-period farmers produced ever-larger amounts of cash crops such as cotton, tea, sugar, silk, and rice.

Population increased along with economic growth, but apparently not to the point that it outstripped the economy. There is no reliable evidence on what the total population may have been in 1600. The shogunate ordered a nationwide census for the first time only in 1721. In that census, if we adjust for various unreported groups, the samurai among them, a figure of just under 30 million persons seems reasonable. This figure is assumed to be roughly twice the size of the population in 1600. More important, the 1721 figure, when compared with the more trustworthy figure 33.1 million for 1872, shows that the population did not rise significantly during the last 150 years of the Edo period. The reasons for such a slow growth are still unclear. Famine did indeed periodically take its toll of the rural population. But there is evidence that Japanese families were consciously controlling family size to safeguard a desirable standard of living. The coexistence of a growing economy and a relatively stable population should lead to a general improvement in quality of life. And indeed there is much evidence of a general improvement in housing, food, clothing, and education over most of the Edo period.

The most dramatic change to affect Edo society was without question the spread of city life. With the appearance in the mid-16th century of the unified daimyō domains and the movement of the samurai off the land, regional CASTLE TOWNS sprang up rapidly throughout Japan. Each daimyō built at the center of his domain a castle headquarters in which he housed his samurai retainers. This necessitated the assembling of service groups, merchants, carpenters, artisans, and the like to meet the needs of the assembled samurai. Before long the castle became a castle town (*jōka machi*). Half a century before, only a few commercial cities such as Kyōto, Nara, Hakata, and SAKAI existed in Japan. The *bakuhan* system brought into being a new kind of city, built around the castle, of which a large percentage of the inhabitants were samurai. The prior existence of commerce was incidental to these castle towns. Their layout and size depended not on proximity to already developed centers of economic activity but rather on the size and the strategic needs of the domain. By the end of the 18th century Edo, the greatest of the castle towns, was approaching 1 million in population, while Ōsaka and Kyōto each had in the neighborhood of 300,000 inhabitants. But equally impressive was the fact that cities on the fringe, like Sendai, Kagoshima, and Kanazawa, became communities of 50,000 to 100,000 inhabitants. The samurai, who by tradition considered themselves rural aristocrats, adopted an urban lifestyle. As they made the transition from military duty to civil-bureaucratic service, the samurai became literate, cultured, and urbanized.

Edo society was sharply divided between samurai and commoners in style of life as well as in legal status. Each major stratum of society was given its own cultural norm appropriate to its position on the social scale. To the samurai belonged the martial arts and the aristrocratic cultural tradition inherited from the Muromachi period (1333–1568). It is noteworthy that the Buke Shohatto urged the samurai to divide their time between learning and military training. Given the lack of military action, military training consisted of formalized arts such as archery, swordsmanship, and riding rather than combat readiness. Remarkably, once the Tokugawa "Great Peace" settled upon the samurai class, the real weapons that had won the peace (musket and cannon) were almost totally ignored. Instead, continuous stress was placed on spiritual training, the enforcement of discipline, and the cultivation of BUSHIDŌ, or the Way of the samurai.

As the dominant aristrocratic class, the samurai patronized the traditionally prestigious arts and letters. Their public architecture—castles, palaces, and temples—tended toward the ornate and grandiose. (Ieyasu's mausoleum at Nikkō is an example.) One type of structure, the castle, must stand as a unique and aesthetically pleasing creation of the warrior aristocracy. In the decorative arts they favored the grand style of Chinese painting perfected by the KANŌ SCHOOL. They lavished attention on the Nō theater and became avid consumers of Chinese-style porcelain, lacquer, and ironware.

It was in the field of secular scholarship that the samurai of the Edo period made their truly original contribution. The main body of

such scholarship was rooted in the Confucian tradition. The turn toward Neo-Confucianism and the concurrent rejection of Buddhism began quite soon after the establishment of the Tokugawa shogunate. The precedent set by the Tokugawa shōguns in adding the office of Confucian adviser *(jusha)* to the official bureaucracy and in funding schools, such as the SHŌHEIKŌ (established by Hayashi Razan in 1630), was quickly followed by the daimyō. Soon samurai and former samurai Confucian-trained scholars were at work throughout Japan serving as official advisers, staffing domainal schools, or setting up private academies. The outcome was a highly literate samurai class, the producers and consumers of a great flood of writings on philosophy, history, law, political economy, and literature.

In the early years, Confucian-based scholarship tended to be derivative, as scholars like Hayashi Razan sought to assimilate the Confucian tradition to conditions in Japan (see SHUSHIGAKU). One product of this effort was the formulation of the principles of Bushidō as pioneered by YAMAGA SOKŌ. By the end of the 17th century, Japanese scholars were producing highly original works directed to problems and issues specific to Japan. Arai Hakuseki applied what he believed to be Confucian principles to questions of shogunal law, foreign trade, and international diplomacy. OGYŪ SORAI went to original Confucian sources for his critique of the Edo political system. Both the shōgun and the daimyō patronized the writing of history, as illustrated in the Hayashi school's *Honchō tsugan* (1670, Comprehensive Mirror of Japan) and the MITO SCHOOL's DAI NIHON SHI (History of Great Japan; begun in 1657). By the end of the Edo period, scholars were at work in most domains compiling domainal histories and making collections of laws and precedents. The shogunate had begun to systemize and codify its penal regulations under the eighth shōgun, Tokugawa Yoshimune. Edo-period scholars were instrumental in developing new fields of inquiry such as antiquarianism, philology, and literary criticism. They pioneered in the recovery of ancient Japanese texts such as the KOJIKI, MAN'-YŌSHŪ, and TALE OF GENJI.

It should be noted that schooling and scholarship were not limited to the samurai class. Many commoners were able to educate themselves at domainal or private academies. A modicum of basic literacy was essential for merchants and village headmen, simply for bookkeeping purposes, and to that end small neighborhood "village schools" (TERAKOYA) were available. Also many commoners made their way into high academic and literary circles by means of scholarly ability. The great Tokugawa bibliographer HANAWA HOKIICHI was born a farmer, as was INŌ TADATAKA, the famed shogunate surveyor. ISHIDA BAIGAN, the founder of SHINGAKU, an eclectic school of moral philosophy, began his career as a merchant. Naturally much of the outpouring of scholarship during the Edo period was rigidly scholastic and hardly relevant even in its time. But it was important if for no other reason than that it produced a repertory of political, social, and moral concepts applicable to the growing problems of state and society once Japan was reopened to the outside world.

The maturation of urbanized samurai life was accompanied by the rise of an urbanized commercial and service class, the *chōnin*. Confucian theory and Tokugawa law did not serve this class well. For while the *chōnin* were absolutely essential to the samurai in their urban environment, and though many became wealthy by serving the samurai, government policy operated on the premise that in the natural order of things merchants were at the bottom of the social scale. The merchant class was arbitrarily denied access to foreign markets and subjected to all manner of domestic controls. The small amount of trade permitted at Nagasaki was handled as a shogunal monopoly, and most daimyō used domainal monopoly organizations (HAN'EI SEMBAI) to handle the sale of special local products. Merchants were protected as merchants, to be sure, particularly after 1721 when merchant guilds and monopoly associations *(kabunakama)* were permitted. And it is true as well that the commercial class was not fully or systematically taxed because of the failure of Tokugawa authorities to appreciate commercial economics. But *chōnin* remained vulnerable to arbitrary debt cancellations, confiscation, and unexpected demands for forced contributions. Above all, merchants had no voice in samurai government.

There were some advantages to the situation in which the merchants found themselves. For, being denied political influence, they were generally left alone in their own sphere of activity, where they were free to accumulate wealth and develop their own way of life. And in fact they acquired a sort of political power by virtue of their control of certain aspects of the national economy. Despite its scorn of merchant status, samurai government became increasingly dependent on, and indebted to, the merchant class. Merchants as commodity handlers and financial agents became essential to the tax collection process, especially in the conversion of tax rice to cash or consumer goods. As wholesalers and carriers, they were essential to the effort of samurai authorities to create government monopolies. Ōsaka and Edo grew into major centers of a national market economy served by exchange houses, shipping facilities, and commodity markets. The Ōsaka rice exchange (DŌJIMA RICE MARKET) dealt in futures and could influence the price of rice nationally.

Commercial wealth and a growing chōnin population gave rise to a bourgeois society with its own cultural style. The chōnin had their merchant princes in the great shogunal cities of Edo, Ōsaka, and Kyōto, and to a lesser degree in the provincial castle towns. The greatest of the merchant houses, the MITSUI, SUMITOMO, and Kōnoike (see KŌNOIKE FAMILY), were to continue into modern times. These and others were deeply involved in samurai finances. Some acquired low samurai status, but they remained outside samurai society. From time to time individuals from merchant families might be adopted into samurai families, but the House of Mitsui itself (as an example) remained forever chōnin in status. Thus the chōnin developed their own culture, based on the commercial way of life and its values.

Bourgeois culture (chōnin bunka) had its antecedents in the merchant quarters of Muromachi-period (1333–1568) Kyōto, but it flourished most conspicuously during the Edo period. From the merchant quarters emerged the arts and pastimes of the ukiyo, the "floating world" of theaters and entertainment quarters. The main elements of chōnin culture were brought to their first flowering in Ōsaka during the GENROKU ERA (1688–1704). Such were the JŌRURI (puppet) and KABUKI plays of CHIKAMATSU MONZAEMON, the popular short stories of Ihara SAIKAKU, the woodblock prints of Hishikawa MORONOBU, and the poetic essays and haiku of Matsuo BASHŌ. These genres were further developed and popularized, coming to another high point in Edo during the BUNKA AND BUNSEI ERAS (1804–30). This final burst of creativity was best exemplified by the woodblock arts of Katsushika HOKUSAI and Andō HIROSHIGE, and the didactic historical novels of Takizawa BAKIN.

It is interesting that both Chikamatsu and Bashō were samurai by birth but had become RŌNIN (masterless samurai) and were able to make their way as artists catering mainly to chōnin audiences. This is evidence that culturally the lines between the classes were not strictly enforced. In the great cities, samurai and chōnin life drew together in certain areas. Samurai took off their swords to "pass" in the chōnin theater districts. Conversely, wealthy chōnin engaged in the aristocratic TEA CEREMONY or patronized the Nō theater.

The special cultural life of the cities did not extend directly to rural areas. Yet village life did not remain unchanged during the Edo period. From the beginning of this period, agriculture received the special attention of samurai government. The emphasis was at first on increased production of rice, but eventually commercial crops like cotton, silk, tobacco, tea, and sugar were stressed. Commercial economy affected village life in a variety of ways. As wealth was accumulated, the village elite—mostly headmen's families—sought to acquire education and partake of the culture of the cities.

Commercialization of the rural economy exerted more fundamental though less visible influences on village social structure. In the early Edo period village life was generally dominated by large hyakushō families whose extended kinship organization included hereditarily subservient, or servant, households. These dependent family members did much of the work on the main family's large landholdings. More and more, however, large families broke up into smaller units in which the smaller independent families cultivated their own fields while also working portions of other holdings as tenants. The basis of intravillage relations shifted from kinship to economic ties. The more affluent rural families were able to develop commercially profitable businesses, producing sake, soy sauce, cotton, silk, and like items. Whereas city-based wholesalers had dominated the distribution system for rural products, village entrepreneurs (ZAIGŌ SHŌNIN) eventually developed their own capacity to sell for profit in the cities. By the end of the 18th century the countryside had begun to compete with the city.

Intellectual Ferment and the Sense of Crisis —— By the late Edo period a perceptible sense of unease characterized the national mood, the result of a growing realization that the country faced deep social and economic problems as well as new challenges from abroad. Unease did not translate into a feeling of crisis until well into the 19th century, but it did stimulate social and intellectual

movements, all of which responded in one way or another to these new problems.

The main line of Confucian influence on education and political-economic thought remained largely scholastic and conservative. But Confucian studies nurtured a secular and rational mind and encouraged the application of reason to practical problems. By the beginning of the 18th century, so-called Confucianists in Japan had begun to abandon their reliance on Neo-Confucian orthodoxy, particularly when confronting day-to-day problems of government or economy. Men like DAZAI SHUNDAI struggled with questions of government efficiency and how to select officials for merit in a system based on heredity. Later writers like MIURA BAIEN, KAIHŌ SEIRYŌ, HONDA TOSHIAKI, and SATŌ NOBUHIRO discussed principles of political economy, agricultural technology, mining engineering, military science, and many other subjects as they related to the problems of improving shogunate or domainal finances or military defense. In much of this writing one can see indirect evidence of an awareness of Western science and world geography.

Despite the National Seclusion policy, knowledge of Western scholarship and scientific inquiry managed to filter into Japan, particularly after 1720 when the shōgun Yoshimune lifted the ban on the import of foreign books at Nagasaki and made it possible for persons other than official interpreters to learn Dutch. By the beginning of the 19th century, Dutch studies (Rangaku) or Western studies (Yōgaku) had become fairly widespread and their utility sufficiently recognized so that many daimyō were induced to train specialists in Western medicine and other practical sciences (see WESTERN LEARNING). The shogunate, recognizing the importance of keeping abreast of developments in the West, established in 1811 a center for the translation of Western books.

The spread of Dutch studies occurred at first without the stimulus of a threat from outside Japan. But in the early 19th century, Japanese intellectuals and shogunate officials realized that the world around them had begun to change. The appearance of a new foreign menace eventually revived debate on the issue of National Seclusion and forced a rethinking of the Japanese world view. By the 19th century, Japanese intellectuals, whether they realized it or not, were being influenced by knowledge from abroad and were aware of the possibility of Western encroachment. The orthodox response was intellectual rejection and military defiance. But there were Confucianists who tried to reconcile Confucian concepts with Western scientific discoveries. YAMAGATA BANTŌ, for instance, tried to integrate Western heliocentric theory with Confucian cosmology; and a very few scholars took the risk of advocating abandonment of the National Seclusion policy. But on the whole, specialists in Western studies in Japan did not become a political force agitating for the eventual reopening of their country to foreign intercourse.

The Japanese response to the 19th-century national crisis was not confined to a choice between Confucian orthodoxy and pro-Western radicalism. One important current of thought sought to discover a national identity strong enough to confront both the internal loss of confidence in the "Japanese system" and the threat from without. A considerable nationalistic undercurrent had run through the works of Edo-period Confucianists from the start. Among the early generation of Confucian scholars, Yamaga Sokō had emphasized the principles of bushidō and had claimed for the Japanese warrior class the qualities of the Chinese scholar-bureaucrat. YAMAZAKI ANSAI had found the mythological rulers of Japan's antiquity equal to the Chinese "sage kings." Thus Edo scholars began to find new meaning in early Japanese writings like the Kojiki, the Man'yōshū, and various Shintō rituals. Before long a school of National Learning (KOKUGAKU), devoted to Japanese studies in conscious opposition to Chinese studies (Kangaku), had come into existence. MOTOORI NORINAGA gave prominence to this intellectual movement. Having devoted his life to the study of the Kojiki, he claimed to find in it the secret of the true Japanese way of life. He rejected both Buddhism and Confucianism as foreign and as having corrupted the natural goodness of the Japanese people.

After 1800 many Japanese of all walks of life were attracted to Kokugaku. There was a tendency for this interest to take on both nationalistic and religious dimensions. Members of the Mito school of scholars, like HIRATA ATSUTANE, called for a return to Shintō tradition, asserting Japan's innate superiority to China for having retained an "unbroken line of deified sovereigns." AIZAWA SEISHISAI went even further in his rejection of "foreign beliefs" and in his insistence upon Japan's superiority as a "land of the gods (kami)." Revival of the ideological features of Shintō provided many Japanese with a sense of cultural security in their moment of crisis. It laid the basis for the powerful conservative reaction to the foreign threat under the slogan "Revere the Emperor, Expel the Barbarians" (SONNŌ JŌI).

The search for intellectual or spiritual comfort in a troubled world was not confined to educated intellectuals. Rural areas in Japan were reacting with equal vigor to other problems, primarily domestic but no less troublesome. A persistent phenomenon in rural areas after the middle of the 18th century was mass confrontations and riots gainst the ruling authorities. Rural uprisings (HYAKUSHŌ IKKI) were particularly severe during Tanuma's ascendancy and the Tempō era. No unified political movement resulted from these outbursts, but they gave clear evidence of a mood of restlessness and anger in the rural areas. Two features of the late Edo period directly or indirectly related to such rural restiveness were the spread of millenarian beliefs and the appearance of new popular religious sects. The former manifested itself on numerous occasions when masses of villagers demonstrated a hope for improvement of their lives through the powers of yonaoshi (world-renewal) spirits (see YONAOSHI REBELLIONS). Such occasions were usually spontaneous and ephemeral. The latter phenomenon manifested itself in such sects as TENRIKYŌ, KONKŌKYŌ, and KUROZUMI-KYŌ which established themselves as religious communities. These sects combined elements of Shintō and Buddhism but relied most heavily on founding leaders who claimed special spiritual powers to bring health and well-being to believers. Both types of movement exemplified the efforts of mass society to find security through the reinforcement of communal cohesion.

Bakumatsu: The End of the Tokugawa Regime——It is only by hindsight that one can see that the Tokugawa hegemony and the *bakuhan* system upon which it rested were doomed institutions already at the time of Perry's arrival in Edo Bay in 1853. Yet the American pressure on Japan quickly exposed the weakness of the decentralized balance of power that had kept the peace in Japan for two and a half centuries. It also exposed the fact that the shōgun's claim to the status of head of state had been weakened through lack of explicit legal statement.

Perry's arrival set in motion a chain reaction of disastrous consequences. Abe Masahiro, the chief senior councillor, realized that the shogunate had neither the legitimacy nor the resources to take a stand against the foreign powers unaided. His solicitation of daimyō opinion on how to deal with Perry was an effort to gain a legitimizing mandate, but it failed. And with that failure, shogunal absolutism came to an end. The demise of the shogunate came quickly and in clearly marked stages from 1853 to 1868.

Between 1853 and 1860, the shogunate, unable to resist foreign pressure, abandoned its own National Seclusion policy and opened a number of ports to foreign ships. In 1858, by signing trade agreements (ANSEI COMMERCIAL TREATIES) with the foreign powers without imperial approval, it took a strong stand in favor of free foreign intercourse. But the country was not ready to go along. The assassination in 1860 of II NAOSUKE, the shogunate's strongman, brought this phase to an end. There followed an effort by the shogunate to create a coalition government in which the shōgun and other Tokugawa daimyō would work together with *tozama* daimyō and court nobles under the emperor, who would serve as the symbol of national unity. The shogunate made conciliatory gestures, such as abandoning the *sankin kōtai* requirement in 1862. It also tried to show its strength by ordering a punitive expedition against the Mōri house of Chōshū (see CHŌSHŪ EXPEDITIONS). As the ultimate concession, the last shōgun, TOKUGAWA YOSHINOBU, offered to resign in the fall of 1867 to make way for a coalition government (see TAISEI HŌKAN).

Already, however, an anti-Tokugawa movement had been gathering momentum. The two large *tozama* domains of Satsuma and Chōshū were drawn into alliance by young activist samurai and allied with key figures at the imperial court. In January 1868 this group captured the emperor and declared in his name a restoration of imperial rule (ŌSEI FUKKO). The shōgun had been outmaneuvered. Tokugawa forces made a feeble effort to resist this turn of events. But troops gathered from Satsuma, Chōshū, and Tosa (now Kōchi Prefecture), proclaiming themselves an imperial army, routed the Tokugawa guards in the Kyōto area. The former shōgun was declared a rebel and his lands confiscated. Within a year the new government and the emperor had moved into Edo, where in quick succession the main pillars of the *bakuhan* system were pulled down. In 1871 the daimyō domain system was converted into a centralized prefectural system. In 1872, with the declaration of class equality, the samurai class was abolished. In 1873 the *kokudaka*

system of land registration and taxation was converted to a modern property tax system. Between 1853 and 1873 a revolution had taken place. See MEIJI RESTORATION.

━━━━Robert Bellah, *Tokugawa Religion: The Values of Pre-Industrial Japan* (1957). Harold Bolitho, *Treasures among Men: The Fudai Daimyo in Tokugawa Japan* (1974). Hugh Borton, *Peasant Uprisings in the Tokugawa Period* (1938, repr 1969). Charles Boxer, *The Christian Century in Japan* (1964). Ronald P. Dore, *Education in Tokugawa Japan* (1964). George Elison, *Deus Destroyed: The Image of Christianity in Early Modern Japan* (1973). Grant Goodman, *The Dutch Impact on Japan, 1640–1853* (1967). John W. Hall, *Tanuma Okitsugu: Forerunner of Modern Japan* (1955). John W. Hall and Marius B. Jansen, ed, *Studies in the Institutional History of Early Modern Japan* (1970). Susan B. Hanley and Kozo Yamamura, *Economic and Demographic Change in Preindustrial Japan, 1600–1868* (1977). William B. Hauser, *Economic Institutional Change in Tokugawa Japan* (1974). Dan Fenno Henderson, *Village "Contracts" in Tokugawa Japan* (1975). Kodama Kōta, ed, *Kinseishi handobukku* (1972). Maruyama Masao, *Studies in the Intellectual History of Tokugawa Japan*, tr Mikiso Hane (1974). E. Herbert Norman, *Ando Shōeki and the Anatomy of Japanese Feudalism* (1949). Hermann Ooms, *Charismatic Bureaucrat: A Political Biography of Matsudaira Sadanobu, 1758–1829* (1975). George B. Sansom, *A History of Japan, 1615–1867* (1963). George B. Sansom, *The Western World and Japan* (1949). Charles D. Sheldon, *The Rise of the Merchant Class in Tokugawa Japan, 1600–1868* (1958). Thomas C. Smith, *The Agrarian Origins of Modern Japan* (1955). Conrad Totman, *Politics in the Tokugawa Bakufu, 1600–1843* (1967). Toshio G. Tsukahira, *Feudal Control in Tokugawa Japan: The Sankin Kōtai System* (1970). Herschel Webb, *The Japanese Imperial Institution in the Tokugawa Period* (1967). Kozo Yamamura, *A Study of Samurai Income and Entrepreneurship* (1974).   John W. HALL

MEIJI HISTORY (1868–1912)

The period designated as Meiji extended from 1868 to 1912. The name was selected by lot by the 16-year-old Mutsuhito in October 1868 and extended retroactively to cover the court's declaration of restoration in January of that year; it ended with the emperor's death on 30 July 1912. Its inception coincided with the fall of the TOKUGAWA SHOGUNATE and the MEIJI RESTORATION, and it was followed by the TAISHŌ PERIOD (1912–26). A decree in October 1868 announced that all era-names (*nengō*) would henceforth be coterminous with reigns, and consequently the 45-year reign of Mutsuhito (called Emperor MEIJI or the Meiji emperor since his death) became inseparably associated with the half-century of centralization and modernization that marked Japan's emergence as a modern state.

Meiji in Historical Imagination——The overtones of "Meiji," usually translated as "Enlightened Rule," are those of renewal. The term itself was drawn from the ancient Chinese *Book of Changes* (*Yi jing* or *I ching*). While return of rule to the sovereign had been the goal of the movement to overthrow the Tokugawa and "return to antiquity" (*fukko*), the principal thrust of the Meiji period was one of construction, and within a short number of years phrases like "great undertaking" (*taigyō*) became paired with "restoration" (*ishin*) to indicate the association of Meiji with reform.

The Meiji government emphasized the emperor's role as a symbol of unification and legitimacy by sending him on journeys to all parts of the land, issuing rescripts in his name, and making his birthdate a national holiday and his photograph a near-icon in public schools. The young emperor mirrored in his personal experience and attitude the ambivalence of most of his subjects; while calls to modernization were issued in his name, he was lectured by his Confucian tutor MOTODA NAGAZANE on traditional virtues. In his maturity he was a genuine participant in a decision process dominated by the small oligarchy that had utilized his increasingly numinous aura to validate its actions.

The newly dominant monarchy issued the canons of the modern state: the CHARTER OATH of 1868 (Gokajō no Goseimon), the IMPERIAL RESCRIPT TO SOLDIERS AND SAILORS of 1882, the CONSTITUTION of 1889, and the IMPERIAL RESCRIPT ON EDUCATION of 1890. Each of these documents was the product of debate and compromise among the leaders of the government; each was more "modern" than some would have wished and less so than others would have hoped, but each became sacrosanct with time and gradually restricted and confined the modern spirit. The emperor's success in "leading" his people to equality in international society and regional hegemony through victories over China in 1895 and Russia in 1905, and the annexation of Korea in 1910, together with his own image as a conservative and crusty paterfamilias, combined to make him the symbol of a half-century of rapid and sweeping change.

The First Decade: The Abolition of Feudalism —— The Meiji regime began as an alliance between Satsuma (now Kagoshima Prefecture) and Chōshū (now Yamaguchi Prefecture), the two domains that had led in the overthrow of the Tokugawa shogunate, supported by Tosa (now Kōchi Prefecture) and Hizen (now Saga Prefecture) and legitimized by the presence of the sovereign. There was strong distrust of the Satsuma–Chōshū alliance in other parts of Japan, and for months there was expectation of a further contest for power. The Tosa domain took the lead in organizing a regional league in Shikoku against such a contingency, and northeastern *daimyō* organized themselves into a similar group. Fighting broke out in late January 1868 in the Toba–Fushimi area near Kyōto between Tokugawa forces and Chōshū–Satsuma units. Early in March Prince ARISUGAWA NO MIYA TARUHITO was named commander of new "imperial" forces that advanced north by coastal and inland routes. The Tokugawa seat of Edo was surrendered without bloodshed in early April, renamed Tōkyō, and designated as the national capital six months later. Sharp fighting took place in the northeast, and final pacification of the north was completed only with the surrender of ENOMOTO TAKEAKI in Hokkaidō on 27 June 1869. See BOSHIN CIVIL WAR.

The new government had the double task of maintaining order while trying to reassure daimyō that the new order would be one of justice and opportunity. The first need was met by public notices (GOBŌ NO KEIJI) issued on 7 April 1868 ordering commoners to observe the five principles of Confucianism, to remain in their villages, and to eschew Christianity as before. The second need was met by the Charter Oath, issued the previous day. The Charter Oath had five clauses that promised that deliberative assemblies would be established and all matters decided by public discussion; called on "high and low" to unite; promised that commoners as well as civil and military officials would be able to "pursue their own calling"; pledged to abandon "evil customs" of the past; and pledged to "seek knowledge throughout the world in order to strengthen the foundations of imperial rule." These were sweeping commitments, expressed in terms sufficiently broad for them to be invoked once more by Emperor Hirohito after World War II in an effort to establish for democracy a continuity with Japan's past.

The Charter Oath implied a commitment to abolish feudalism, the "evil custom of the past" that had made it impossible for all men to "pursue their calling" and for "high and low" to unite. Japan's crises in the 1850s and 1860s had shown the need for a single center of administrative decision, and the task of nation-building could not be carried out unless the new government controlled more than the Tokugawa domains that it had acquired. An effort to replace the old administrative structures with new devices for establishing political consensus suggested the wisdom of "assemblies" and "public discussion." To this end a division of labor between administrative, judicial, and legislative functions was attempted by establishing offices (SANSHOKU) staffed by high-ranking daimyō and court officials in January 1868. In June the Constitution of 1868 (SEITAISHO) set forth a clearer allocation of power and responsibility in line with the promises of the Charter Oath and in fact professed to implement that document. Before long, the regime drew back to a more authoritarian structure in which the powers of the executive, in the Grand Council of State (DAJŌKAN), far outweighed those of its competitors. Thereafter reform and innovation proceeded from the initiative of key members of the Restoration leadership from Satsuma, Chōshū, Tosa, and Saga, younger *samurai* who gradually replaced the higher-ranking lords and nobles who had filled the offices at first.

In March 1869 the daimyō of the four Restoration domains were persuaded to petition the court to accept the return of their domain registers (*hanseki hōkan*) and urged that "all the regulations, from the ordering of laws, institutions, and military affairs, even to the fashioning of uniforms and instruments, issue from the Imperial Government, [and that the] conduct of all the affairs of the realm, whether great or small, be placed under unified control. Then only, name and reality complementing each other, the Empire can stand beside the foreign powers." Other daimyō followed suit. The court accepted this and appointed the daimyō governors of their former realms. The next step came in August 1871, when the daimyō-governors were called to Tōkyō and dismissed; their domains were rearranged into larger and more rationally structured prefectures (see PREFECTURAL SYSTEM, ESTABLISHMENT OF).

Shortly after this a large part of the leadership group, a party of over 100 with attendants, left for a tour of the Western world under the leadership of the court noble IWAKURA TOMOMI (see IWAKURA MISSION). Another part of the Charter Oath, the pledge to seek "wisdom throughout the world," was being implemented. The leaders who remained in Tōkyō promised not to undertake major decisions in the absence of their fellows. Nevertheless deep fissures within the Meiji leadership followed when members of the mission changed their priorities after their trip abroad. Their first-hand experience of the modern world was pivotal for these changes. Their associates in Tōkyō meanwhile continued to implement changes that had been agreed upon in advance but also exceeded them in some particulars (such as the substitution of the Western for the Japanese calendar effective January 1873) and finally made decisions of critical importance in foreign policy whose implementation, however, awaited the return of the mission.

Major changes that were implemented involved freedom from feudal restrictions, a loss of status for the privileged, and opportunity for commoners to participate in the new society. In 1869 the regime combined former daimyō and court nobles into a new category of aristocracy (*kazoku;* see PEERAGE); *samurai* were divided into broad categories of gentry (SHIZOKU) and soldiers (*sotsu);* and in 1872 the lower and more marginal classifications of the *sotsu* were abandoned, thus merging the lower ranks of the old ruling class with the commoners (HEIMIN). Commoners' privileges correspondingly improved, freedom to assume family names (October 1870), to mount horses (June 1871), to move, to crop as desired, to buy and sell land, and to intermarry with their betters (October 1871). In 1871 a further reform abolished the outcaste category of HININ and *eta* (see BURAKUMIN) and subsumed them under commoners.

The abolition of feudal domains and feudal dues brought with it the requirement for a new and uniform system of taxation (*chiso kaisei*). In 1873 land surveys were undertaken to make possible a national land tax. Average productivity in previous years was capitalized to produce an estimated market value of land, and the new tax was set at 3 percent of this assessment, with certificates of ownership for the peasants, who had now become owner-farmers. The tax, payable in money and no longer in kind, brought farmers into the market economy, thus completing the commercialization of agriculture that had begun in Tokugawa times. These sweeping changes, many of which were poorly understood and brusquely implemented, aroused much resistance in the countryside. The several hundred recorded instances of opposition range from riots to large-scale resistance. But the countryside was still unarmed, and the authorities prevailed (see LAND TAX REFORM OF 1873–1881).

The central government, as it was becoming, now had to shoulder full responsibility for education and defense, matters previously left to the individual domains under the shogunate. The two were closely linked in the leaders' minds, for popular participation was essential for effective national unity and strength. The samurai no longer provided an acceptable form of military strength: the social base that had supported them was changing; their attachments were too often local rather than national; and their punctilious adherence to a complex system of social gradations suited them poorly for the large-scale formations of modern war. The participation of commoner militia units (see KIHEITAI) in the Restoration war, combined with direct observation of Western patterns by Japanese who went abroad during a decade of warfare that included the American Civil War and the German wars of unification, convinced the government leaders of the importance of a mass commoner army.

The language of the edicts that emerged combined the notes of individual opportunity and national priority that had been sounded in the Charter Oath. The EDUCATION ORDER OF 1872 pointed out that "education is the key to success in life, and no one can afford to neglect it." It set as its goal universal literacy ("in a village there shall be no house without learning, and in a house no individual without learning") and divided the country into higher-school districts, each with its supporting network of middle and lower schools. In this too the experience and example of the West were vital. Continuities with the Edo period were also visible in the transformation of the Kaiseijo, the Tokugawa school for Western studies, into Daigaku Nankō (the future Tōkyō University), at the apex of higher education.

On 28 December 1872 the Dajōkan announced a system of military conscription. The architect of the new system was YAMAGATA ARITOMO, a Chōshū veteran of the Restoration wars who had visited Europe in 1869. Early in 1873 the government issued detailed regulations: these called for three years of active service and four years in the reserves. There were liberal exceptions and provision for a longer term in the reserves for those who did not have to serve. The country was again divided into regions, with local regiments bridging the gap between national patriotism and provincial loyalty. See CONSCRIPTION ORDINANCE OF 1873.

It was the samurai who bore the main cost of this, for while the reforms equalized conditions within the samurai class to some extent, they also deprived it of its reason for being. Indeed, many of the reform edicts included harsh criticism of the Tokugawa social system for the way it had restricted education, privilege, and military service to the samurai. The government soon addressed itself to the high cost of maintaining the former ruling class. Most domains had already reduced samurai stipends very considerably; at the highest level they usually became one-tenth of their former amount; at lower levels it was not possible to achieve so great a reduction, but the effect of even modest reductions was frequently drastic.

The government was, however, committed to the promotion of "men of talent," a frequent cliché of late Tokugawa agitation and the logical thrust of the Charter Oath. A large number of key figures in the government were themselves of relatively modest samurai birth. Moreover, finance officials pointed to the stipend payments as a burden that would interfere with the program to develop national strength. To maintain them temporarily the government had recourse to a foreign loan in 1873. With the return of the Iwakura Mission from abroad it became possible to win over a majority of the leaders to a program of taxing samurai stipends and ending them eventually (CHITSUROKU SHOBUN). In December 1873 a sliding scale of taxation was announced, progressive in that it bore more heavily on larger stipends. Optional commutation for lump-sum payments had been held out earlier to some; in November 1874 this was extended to all grades, and in August 1876 commutation for interest-bearing government bonds became compulsory. Commutation payments were made to 310,000 family heads under these arrangements. Government obligations were met in years of inflation by printed money, and the samurai class was clearly the loser.

Prior to these developments some had sought an outlet for samurai restlessness in overseas adventures. Korea had repulsed early efforts of the Meiji government to establish modern international relations, and there was widespread sentiment for a punitive expedition. The Tōkyō government had in fact reached a firm decision on this matter, but its implementation had to await the return of the Iwakura Mission. When it returned in 1873, an acrimonious debate saw the decision reversed, with the resulting resignation of SAIGŌ TAKAMORI and other advocates of war (see SEIKANRON). A stopgap measure, the TAIWAN EXPEDITION OF 1874 to strengthen Japan's claim to the Ryūkyū Islands by punishing Taiwanese aborigines who had slain Okinawan fishermen, mollified few of the malcontents.

These political differences resonated with the disappointment of samurai from the Restoration domains, where expectations had been highest. The result was a series of samurai revolts that tested and, ultimately, established the stability of the Meiji government. The revolts were in opposition to the decision on Korea (the SAGA REBELLION, led by ETŌ SHIMPEI in February 1874), against the pattern of modernization (the JIMPŪREN REBELLION in Kumamoto, October 1876), or both (the AKIZUKI REBELLION in Fukuoka and the HAGI REBELLION led by MAEBARA ISSEI, both October 1876). By far the hardest test came in Satsuma, where the widely admired Saigō Takamori led a samurai revolt (January to September 1877) that strained the capacities of the new government to its utmost in every sense (see SATSUMA REBELLION).

With that victory the new government could be considered firmly established. Of its three initial giants, Saigō was dead; he had been preceded by KIDO TAKAYOSHI, who died of illness in May 1877, and he was followed by ŌKUBO TOSHIMICHI, assassinated in May 1878. The Tosa leaders had left the government in 1874 and would not again be central to it, while the Saga group, already weakened by the loss of Etō Shimpei, would leave the center after the expulsion of ŌKUMA SHIGENOBU in the POLITICAL CRISIS OF 1881. Henceforth leadership would come from a younger group of Chōshū men (ITŌ HIROBUMI and Yamagata Aritomo), the Satsuma finance expert MATSUKATA MASAYOSHI, and the court nobles Iwakura Tomomi and SAIONJI KIMMOCHI. These, together with their allies and protégés, dominated government at its highest levels. The Meiji government made good use of "outsiders" in important, though not pivotal, positions; Tokugawa veterans like KATSU KAISHŪ and Enomoto Takeaki provided much bureaucratic experience, and allies from other domains became increasingly prominent in diplomatic, military, and administrative posts. The senior statesmen (GENRŌ), however, were from Satsuma and Chōshū.

The Second Decade: Institution Building———The fall of Saigō showed that the government was not likely to be toppled by internal dissidents. Yet as the first decade ended, the Meiji government found itself in a precarious position. It was faced with runaway inflation that had been incurred by printing money to cover the costs of samurai pensions and bonds, to assume the debts of the old domains, and to absorb the costs of the military campaigns of the previous year. Financial retrenchment and consolidation seemed the order of the day.

Economy: the Matsukata era. The measures that followed are inextricably linked with the name of Matsukata Masayoshi, who was in charge of finances for the Meiji government for a total of 16 years and five months. The new land tax, the campaign for industrialization (SHOKUSAN KŌGYŌ), management of the currency, the establishment of the BANK OF JAPAN, and adherence to the gold standard were all carried out under his direction. These measures combined to create the institutional infrastructure for the economic growth that began by the end of the 1880s.

As an advocate of orthodox finance Matsukata made it his first task to put an end to inflation. In the 1870s the government had sponsored many pilot industrial plants in addition to developing radio, rail, and steamship communications (see GOVERNMENT OPERATED FACTORIES, MEIJI PERIOD). Matsukata abandoned those that were not of strategic importance and sold them to private bidders (see KAN'EI JIGYŌ HARAISAGE). Those who bid and bought were close to government leaders, shared their goals, and emerged as the future ZAIBATSU, sharing multiple markets in a pattern of oligopoly. Matsukata's policy of deflation was, however, particularly hard on the agrarian sector, which saw crop and land values decline in a widespread depression that often led to forced sale and tenancy and doomed a large number of inadequately financed measures.

In 1884 Matsukata sponsored a study on manufactures (KŌGYŌ IKEN) that set forth a plan for increasing exports and production by intensified effort in selected markets and commodities and advocated quality control and concentration in areas of comparative advantage. Japan was still shackled by the tariff provisions of the ANSEI COMMERCIAL TREATIES signed in the 1850s (the so-called Unequal Treaties), but the cautious and prudent policies designed by Matsukata and his associates began to bear fruit by the middle years of the Meiji. The rural consequences of some of these measures, however, caused a quickening pace of protests, which contributed to the radicalization of political dissent and the intensification of political repression. See also MATSUKATA FISCAL POLICY.

Military: Yamagata Aritomo. The institutionalization of military authority was preeminently the work of Yamagata Aritomo. Yamagata introduced the measures that separated the command function (TŌSUIKEN) from routine administration, thereby strengthening the military's independent access to the throne it was to serve and protect. The General Staff system was mapped out for Yamagata by his protégé KATSURA TARŌ, who had spent six years in Germany.

Loyalty was of first importance. During and after the Satsuma Rebellion the new conscript army had shown signs of disaffection that was both samurai and political in its origin, and the TAKEHASHI INSURRECTION in 1878 had provided evidence of dangers to be avoided. Thereafter every effort was made to make of the military a loyal and dependable instrument of imperial and governmental will. Samurai virtues of loyalty and unquestioning obedience were stressed in a campaign that culminated in the Imperial Rescript to Soldiers and Sailors, which was personally presented by the emperor in 1882. Military police (kempei) were established in 1881 to monitor political activity. The rising movement for political participation was countered by measures prohibiting military men from engaging in political activities and was crowned in 1900 by regulations that the army and navy ministers were to be a general and an admiral on the active list (see GUMBU DAIJIN GEN'EKI BUKAN SEI).

At the same time that civilian control of the military was undermined in the name of a nonpolitical military, military figures, as loyal and presumably nonpartisan servants, were considered eligible for nonmilitary office. Yamagata himself served as home minister from 1888 to 1890, during which time the organization of local government under central control was consummated along ostensibly Western, especially German, lines. Prefectural elective assemblies, established as early as 1878, were given a modest advisory role in an effort to assimilate and to some degree bureaucratize local leaders. The essential power of appointment of governors and mayors was reserved to the next higher level, ultimately the Home Ministry, however, and the police network was similarly structured. See LOCAL GOVERNMENT.

Yamagata also thought it necessary to mobilize the population in the national interest. To this end, in addition to the conscription system, Yamagata oversaw the development of a system of rural reserve units (IMPERIAL MILITARY RESERVISTS' ASSOCIATION) that would integrate former soldiers, rural elite, and rural governance, into a single network of loyalty and patriotism.

Constitutional government: Itō Hirobumi. The Constitution of 1889 was in great measure the work of Itō Hirobumi of Chōshū, a man who had secretly gone abroad for education as early as 1863 and then accompanied the Iwakura Mission a decade later. The Charter Oath had spoken of public councils, and the Iwakura Mission had returned convinced of the importance of formal constitutional structures in the modern countries of the West. In 1875 a kind of senate (the GENRŌIN) was established as an experimental deliberative body with the charge of working out new administrative principles but without the authority to implement them. When its recommendations seemed likely to lead to a parliament with excessive powers, the government called for constitutional suggestions from its principal leaders. These too were sidetracked in 1881, when the emperor, in response to the political crisis precipitated by Ōkuma Shigenobu, made public promise of a constitution to be complete in 1889 and adjured his people to await its appearance.

In preparation for drafting the constitution Itō traveled once more to Europe, where he was strongly influenced by German constitutional theorists who argued that continuity and stability required that the monarch be given broad powers and that party cabinets were necessarily divisive. Rudolf GNEIST and Albert MOSSE felt that Japan needed the hand of a strong monarchy, that the larger national good made it important to limit the powers of a parliament that would be likely to represent special interests, and that the electorate should be limited along economic lines to maximize the participation of responsible sectors of society. Itō agreed with this. He saw the imperial house as the only possible fulcrum for the new system. Japan was secular, and nothing else could play the role of moderation that was served by religion in Western countries.

Itō's draft was completed in 1888. Four years earlier he had created a new peerage whose members would form an upper house that would balance whatever radicalism the lower house might develop. The peerage was made up of former court nobles, daimyō, and government leaders, and it was augmented by life peerages granted to meritorious citizens and leading taxpayers. Thus the old elite, the new plutocracy, and the new meritocracy were enlisted in support of the new order. To review the constitution, and to guard it in the future, a PRIVY COUNCIL was set up. The emperor presided over sessions in which the new document was discussed clause by clause. Upon its promulgation in 1889 an Imperial Oath claimed lineage for the document from the "Grand Design" of the sun goddess (AMATERASU ŌMIKAMI) and emphasized that the new code was "merely a reiteration in Our own day of the grand precepts of government that have been handed down by the Imperial Founder of Our House and by Our other Imperial Ancestors to their descendants." Innovation was thus cloaked as continuity.

Itō and his associates shared a conviction that there were currents of radicalism in Japan that, if not quickly checked by a carefully weighted charter, would rule out a peaceful solution. Yet they also regarded the bulk of their countrymen as backward and unenlightened, ill prepared for the full exercise of political discretion. The explanation for this is to be found in the contradictions of the FREEDOM AND PEOPLE'S RIGHTS MOVEMENT.

At the time of the decision against mounting a punitive expedition against Korea in 1874, most of the Tosa and several of the Saga representatives in the Meiji leadership group had withdrawn from office and prepared a petition to the emperor calling for an elective assembly. ITAGAKI TAISUKE, GOTŌ SHŌJIRŌ, and Etō Shimpei, the principal spokesmen of this group, pointed out that the government's decisions were being made in an arbitrary and capricious manner and that the majority of the people had little awareness of this. True national strength required greater participation, and such participation would quickly school Japanese in matters of the national interest. Etō Shimpei was lost to the Saga Rebellion, and although Itagaki was persuaded to return to government service briefly, he soon withdrew again and made Tosa a center of agitation for democratic rights. Leaders of the RISSHISHA, a Tosa samurai organization, were instrumental in forming the more broadly based AIKOKUSHA. The latter eventually became the JIYŪTŌ, Japan's first national political party (in 1881). The expulsion of Ōkuma from the government that same year resulted in the founding of a similar political organization, the RIKKEN KAISHINTŌ, in 1882. For a country in which voluntary organizations for political purpose had long been presumed rebellious, these were startling developments.

The government leaders were inclined to see these groups as self-willed and irresponsible, but they could not ignore their rising popularity. The early 1880s saw a nationwide surge of interest in political discussion. Hundreds of political discussion groups sprang up throughout the countryside, and many prepared draft constitutions that gave evidence of the deep interest and considerable discernment of the rural leaders who constituted their membership. Not a few of these documents were considerably more liberal than the draft the government leaders produced. Moreover, in the countryside agitation for political rights coincided with economic distress growing out of Matsukata's deflationary policies. Farmers faced with the loss of their newly gained lands under the pressures of a market economy were full of doubts about the justice of the new order and anxious to protect their interests.

In the mid-1880s several rural outbreaks (CHICHIBU INCIDENT; IIDA INCIDENT; KABASAN INCIDENT) related to the party movements, though unsuccessful, sufficed to alarm the government leaders and to embarrass the leaders of the movement. By the middle of the decade the parties were temporarily disbanded and their leadership in disarray. The government restrained their activities with press and meeting laws, at one point banishing their leaders from Tōkyō, and persuaded Itagaki and Gotō to travel in Europe and Ōkuma to accept the post of foreign minister. And it hoped that the constitution would co-opt the dissidents permanently by granting them limited participation through membership in the lower house of the new IMPERIAL DIET.

Constitutional Government —— The Meiji Constitution of 1889 marked the final institutionalization of imperial rule, and its provisions regulated political life up to the time of its replacement in 1947. Its interpretation and understanding varied over time, but its inviolability also set the limits within which change could take place.

The Meiji Constitution. The Meiji Constitution was promulgated as a gift from a sovereign who was granting his subjects a modern statement of the principles by which his ancestors had ruled. It invested the emperor with full sovereignty, declaring him "sacred and inviolable"; he commanded the armed forces, made peace and declared war, and dissolved the lower house to call elections. Effective power thus lay with the executive, which held it in his name. But that executive power was also poorly defined lest it seem to interfere with the imperial prerogative. The armed forces, in consequence of the imperial right of command, had direct and independent access to the throne. The prime minister was more a first among equals than the head of government.

Yet the constitution also marked a genuine step forward in the direction of popular participation. It recognized private property as inviolate and made provision for a large number of other basic rights "within the limits of the law." However limited by law, such freedoms were still recognition of the gains ordinary Japanese had won since the abolition of feudalism less than two decades earlier. The lower house of the Diet, elected by the approximately half-million voters who met the tax qualifications, could initiate legislation. Moreover, its approval was required to pass the budget. Should approval be denied, the previous year's budget could be used, but since the government's needs grew constantly, the Diet's budgetary control was genuine.

In effect, however, most legislation was prepared by the bureaucracy, a strong and able group trained in the IMPERIAL UNIVERSITIES. The emperor's power of appointment made the Imperial Household Ministry (see IMPERIAL HOUSEHOLD AGENCY) and lord keeper of the privy seal (NAIDAIJIN) important bastions of institutionalized power. The emperor himself reigned rather than ruled; the provisions the German constitutional advisers had made for an active ruler were to a large degree replaced by traditional Japanese methods of indirect decision making by groups that worked in his name.

The constitutional structure was further buttressed by the Imperial Rescript on Education, issued in 1890 to coincide with the institutional maturation of the Meiji state. This provided the ideological capstone for public education and morality, pointing to loyalty and filial piety as "the glory of Our Education." Future generations of schoolchildren would be drilled in the values stressed by this modern formulation of ancient values. Confucian ethics and samurai virtues were thus held up as the model for the masses.

Cabinet government. A cabinet system had replaced the Grand Council of State (Dajōkan) in 1885, but the government that took power under Yamagata Aritomo after the first elections in 1890 was the first to experience the realities of constitutional government. From the very first the lower house, dominated by representatives of the reorganized political parties, many of whom had served earlier in prefectural assemblies, proved troublesome. Its members took offense at the high-handed tone of government statements and retaliated by refusing to approve the government's budget. Soon the Meiji leaders, whose presence in each other's cabinets underscored the collegial nature of the cabinet structure, saw themselves as an embattled elite besieged by office-hungry malcontents. Yet they were also determined to make the new institutions succeed. Japan's was the first constitution to be adopted in the non-Western world, and national pride, foreign approval, and political stability alike depended upon successful implementation of the new organs of government.

The first cabinets, chaired by Yamagata, Matsukata, and Itō, used cajolery and, probably, bribery (Yamagata), coercion at election time (Matsukata), and imperial rescripts (Itō) to try to bring the lower house into line. Elections were generally called after the installation of a new cabinet, so that they operated more as referenda than as a means of selecting governments. Frustration and disappointment with the process dispelled the euphoria with which many had greeted the new order.

Sino-Japanese War, 1894–1895. From this morass in domestic politics Meiji Japan was suddenly called to the higher ground of national unity through war with China. Difficulties in Korean policy had seen "pro-Japanese" Korean modernizers bested several times by Korean conservatives who looked to China for protection against Japanese domination. In 1885 Japan and China had reached agreement on fair play in military involvement on the peninsula (see TIANJIN [TIENTSIN] CONVENTION), and when the Chinese seemed to have gone too far in their response to Korean requests for help with rebels, Japan insisted on sending troops as well. The Chinese and Japanese confrontation in Korea provided the occasion for Japanese proposals for sweeping reform in Korea, and when they were rejected, the Japanese seized the Korean king and forced him to "request" assistance. On the eve of warfare the Japanese government finally secured agreement from the Western powers for abolition of the Unequal Treaties (see UNEQUAL TREATIES, REVISION OF), and the war could for a time be portrayed as an altruistic action against a "backward" China on behalf of a Korea in need of "modernization." Even liberal Christians like UCHIMURA KANZŌ hailed the war as justified violence in a righteous cause.

The Japanese armies were everywhere successful. The battle of P'yŏngyang destroyed Chinese military capability in Korea. Japanese forces seized the Liaodong (Liaotung) Peninsula in southern Manchuria, where modern fortifications had just been completed at PORT ARTHUR. The Japanese navy's seamanship and tactics proved superior to those of the Chinese, whose Beiyang (Pei-yang) fleet suffered serious setbacks at the Naval Battle of YALU RIVER before taking refuge in the port of Weihaiwei in Shandong (Shantung) Province, where it was shelled and sunk by Japanese units that took the heights to the rear of the anchorage. At the peace conference in Shimonoseki in 1895 Itō Hirobumi, as chief Japanese representative, demanded the island of Taiwan, a large indemnity of 200 million taels, and the Liaodong Peninsula. When Germany, Russia, and France forced the retrocession of Liaodong (see TRIPARTITE INTERVENTION) "for the sake of the peace of Asia," the indemnity was augmented by an additional 30 million taels. By the terms of the Treaty of SHIMONOSEKI Japan also became heir to all the privileges the Western powers had extracted from China under the most-favored-nation clause and gained additional rights (to manufacture in treaty ports) for itself and for them. See also SINO-JAPANESE WAR OF 1894–1895.

In Japan, as elsewhere, success in war made for success in politics. The Meiji government, including the Imperial Diet, convened in Hiroshima to be closer to the expeditionary forces. Special war budgets were voted with record speed. The government's only difficulty came when it failed to heed the most chauvinistic of demands for territorial expansion on the Chinese mainland; and when it found it necessary to yield to the Tripartite Intervention, it invited tremendous public indignation that was only partly counteracted by a special imperial rescript urging patience and calm. A liberal like Uchimura, who had approved the war as "righteous," now withdrew that approval because it had become "piratical." But many more

became convinced that, since Japan had been proven still weak and unequal, they would have to work and save for greater national strength.

The growing unanimity now made it possible for the Meiji leaders to enlist prominent party politicians into their cabinets in a search for new and more viable parliamentary tactics. Itō worked with Itagaki, Matsukata with Ōkuma. In 1898 the two party men were even invited to form their own cabinet during a short-lived union of their parties (see ŌKUMA CABINET). When this failed because of squabbling over the division of posts between the two constituent parts of the newly formed KENSEITŌ party, Itō decided to form his own political party.

The RIKKEN SEIYŪKAI (Friends of Constitutional Government Party) that he formed in 1900 resulted from the realization of Itō, the author of the Meiji Constitution, that the political parties could not be excluded from the central executive process. The politicians sacrificed their autonomy as Itō did his; the members of the old Jiyūtō who entered the Seiyūkai encountered a self-willed and autocratic leader who was more interested in their votes than in their opinions. Itō's oligarchic colleagues, especially Yamagata, nevertheless deplored his "surrender" to political self-interest and soon managed to remove Itō from the fray by having him appointed head of the Privy Council, an imperial post that was theoretically above politics. Seiyūkai leadership then devolved upon the court noble Saionji Kimmochi, a man of liberal leanings, and from 1901 to the end of the Meiji period in 1912, the prime minister's office alternated between Saionji and General Katsura Tarō, Yamagata's principal follower.

Effective leadership within the Seiyūkai, however, resided with the party's chief secretary, HARA TAKASHI. A former foreign office official and journalist, Hara was unusually qualified by experience and ability to intercede between the areas of public and private, government and business, and oligarchy and politician that had now formed. The Meiji Constitution thus relied for its implementation on politicians like Hara who were essentially behind the scenes, bureaucratic, and private in their approach.

The Russo-Japanese War and Rise to Great Power Status

Japan had chafed under the restrictions imposed by the Unequal Treaties since the 1850s, and throughout most of the Meiji period the leaders were aware that forceful policies in Korea or China would have to wait until Japan had regained its full sovereignty and equality. The Aoki–Kimberley treaty of 1894 with Great Britain provided for an end to extraterritoriality and the most-favored-nation clause by 1899 and for Japan's right to set its own tariffs by 1911. Similar treaties with other powers soon followed. At the same time the acquisition of Taiwan and the assumption of treaty-power rights in China after the Sino-Japanese War gave Japan partial membership in the circle of Western imperialists. Almost immediately, however, the loss of Liaodong as a result of the Tripartite Intervention showed the limits of that membership.

The years that followed the Sino-Japanese War contained further reminders of Japan's second-class status. In the general round of European concession grabbing in China in 1897–98, Russia appropriated the Liaodong Peninsula that it had forced Japan to relinquish, while France and Germany secured ports in the south and in Shandong respectively. During the BOXER REBELLION of 1900 Japanese troops played an important role in the allied expedition to save the Beijing (Peking) legations, but Russia took advantage of the conflict to occupy all of Manchuria. Worst of all, Korea, where Japan seemed to have gained ascendancy in 1895, soon sought Russian protection as counterpoise to its insistent island neighbor. Thus Japan's victory seemed to result in the replacement of China by a much more dangerous rival there. With the Trans-Siberian Railway nearing completion, permanent Russian control of southern Manchuria and northern Korea seemed likely. Small wonder that a noisy sector of Japanese public opinion, encouraged by elements of the elite, clamored for vigorous action (see SHICHIHAKASE JIKEN; KONOE ATSUMARO).

England's search for an ally in the Far East coincided with Japan's need to offset Russian power and to prevent a second Tripartite Intervention. The ANGLO-JAPANESE ALLIANCE of 1902 provided that each contracting power would maintain neutrality if the other were at war, but that it would join the fight if the other should be attacked by two powers. This alliance, which was renewed in 1905 and 1911, thus gave Japan the protection of the British fleet. Secured against a double attack, Prime Minister Katsura's government now entered on a course of hard bargaining and eventual collision with the Russians. The Japanese fleet began hostilities with an attack on the Russian Pacific squadron at Port Arthur (Ch: Lüshun; now part of Lüda) in February 1904. As in 1894, Japan fastened its hold on Korea in the first days of the conflict.

The war was immensely costly to Japan in men and money, but Japan's proximity to the fronts and the indecision of Russian commanders brought victories in the carnage at Port Arthur, which fell in January 1905, in the drawn-out Battle of MUKDEN (now Shenyang) in March, and in the total destruction of the Russian Baltic fleet late in May in the Battle of TSUSHIMA. A peace conference was convened at Portsmouth, New Hampshire, through the mediation of President Theodore Roosevelt. Japan gained recognition of its paramount interests in Korea, took back the south Manchurian leases and rights it had been denied 10 years earlier, and gained the southern half of Sakhalin (Karafuto). The Japanese people, however, had expected more, in particular a large indemnity like the one paid by China, and the Treaty of PORTSMOUTH was greeted with dissatisfaction and public disorder (see also RUSSO-JAPANESE WAR). The new security interests that followed the war also required extensive additional spending for new divisions and new battleships. Korea now entered the Japanese orbit. Itō Hirobumi went as resident-general in 1906, devoting several years to attempts to guide Meiji-style reforms there. He resigned in 1909 and was assassinated by a Korean patriot shortly afterward. His death served as prelude to formal Japanese annexation of Korea in 1910. See KOREA, ANNEXATION OF.

The last decade of the Meiji period was thus to a large extent dominated by Japan's efforts to assume a major role in the imperialist policies of the time. The FRANCO-JAPANESE AGREEMENT OF 1907, the Russo-Japanese agreements of 1907 and 1912 (see RUSSO-JAPANESE AGREEMENTS OF 1907–1916), and the TAKAHIRA-ROOT AGREEMENT with the United States in 1908 brought implied or explicit recognition of Japan's sphere of hegemony in northeast Asia. Domestic politics meanwhile saw the once troublesome political party movement drawn into the orbit of the political establishment. During cabinets headed by Katsura (1901–05 and 1908–11) the Seiyūkai provided parliamentary support in return for patronage, while under Saionji (1906–08 and 1911–12), Hara, as home minister, developed a strong party base through programs of public works and benefits. Japan's economy also grew rapidly. By 1900 agriculture provided less than half the national product as the share of manufacturing, especially textiles, grew steadily. The needs of the Russo-Japanese War in particular greatly stimulated the development of heavy industry.

Industrialization brought with it concentrations of urban labor and fears of urban discontent. In the last years of the Meiji period the Satsuma–Chōshū leaders and government officials became increasingly worried about possible inroads of Western liberal and radical thought and concerned themselves with maintaining the health of Japan's traditional institutions and ideology.

The Meiji emperor, now associated with success in foreign wars and always the symbol of the larger program of modernization, was raised to new heights of reverence. Textbooks in the compulsory course of ethics (SHŪSHIN) in public schools increasingly emphasized national and military heroes. The family system formally established by the 1898 supplement to the CIVIL CODE, took the samurai family as the norm for the entire nation. It was now glorified as the polity in microcosm, and the larger commonwealth was described as a "family state" in which political and familial loyalties reinforced each other instead of competing for priority as they did in other lands. Tōkyō University philosophers led in expounding the virtues of this unique order, and the worshipful attention given the imperial portrait and imperial rescript in the schools brought the lesson home to children.

To combat fears of Western liberal and radical thought the Home Ministry undertook a program of rural reform designed to place the native cult of Shintō at the service of the imperial state, and Shintō shrines were established within the administrative units (see STATE SHINTŌ). Veterans' associations were encouraged in the countryside to maintain a respect for martial loyalty among the people. Fears of subversion strengthened surveillance and resulted in the arrest and execution of a group of anarchists who had allegedly plotted against the emperor's life (see HIGH TREASON INCIDENT OF 1910). The execution of the prominent intellectual KŌTOKU SHŪSUI in this plot later came to symbolize the price of Japan's rapid modernization.

Interpretations —— The 45 years of the Meiji period provide abundant material for interpretation and debate for those concerned with comparative modernization or Japanese tradition. For many

years official historiography, fostered through the subsidy of massive historiographical projects, focused on the emperor and his statesmen and cast Meiji history as an account of wise and loyal leaders. Upon the emperor's death in 1912, General NOGI MARESUKE, the commander at the siege of Port Arthur, committed ritual suicide to accompany his lord (JUNSHI) and to call his countrymen back to a sense of duty. His wife followed him in suicide. Thus legend could be rooted in fact, and the textbooks gained another hero.

At the other extreme, Marxist historiography of the 1930s and post-World War II years saw the Meiji period as the product of an incomplete revolution, with the energy of restive masses unleashed to overthrow the Tokugawa shogunate only to be shackled once more by the creation of a police state. More recently a group of historians discontent with the shibboleths of the old orthodoxy have directed their attention to the countryside and representatives of local figures. They emphasize the sophistication of rural political discussion groups, which they argue, could have produced a system less oppressive, less fearful of its people, and less encumbered by the emperor symbol created by the Meiji statesmen. The Meiji period is the era of history through which modern Japanese must examine and understand their contemporary society.

—— George Akita, *Foundations of Constitutional Government in Modern Japan* (1967). W. G. Beasley, *The Modern History of Japan* (1963). George M. Beckmann, *The Making of the Meiji Constitution* (1957). Ronald P. Dore, *Land Reform in Japan* (1959). Johannes Hirschmeier, *The Origins of Entrepreneurship in Meiji Japan* (1964). Irokawa Daikichi, *Meiji no bunka* (1970). *Iwanami kōza: Nihon rekishi,* vols 14–17 (Iwanami Shoten, 1962). Marius B. Jansen, ed, *Changing Japanese Attitudes toward Modernization* (1965). Morinosuke Kajima, *The Diplomacy of Japan, 1894–1922,* 2 vols (1976–78). William W. Lockwood, *The Economic Development of Japan* (1954). William W. Lockwood, ed, *The State and Economic Enterprise in Japan* (1965). Byron K. Marshall, *Capitalism and Nationalism in Prewar Japan* (1967). W. W. McLaren, "Japanese Government Documents," *Transactions of the Asiatic Society of Japan* 42.1 (1914). Ian H. Nish, *The Anglo-Japanese Alliance* (1966). E. Herbert Norman, *Japan's Emergence as a Modern State* (1940). Shumpei Okamoto, *The Japanese Oligarchy and the Russo-Japanese War* (1970). Joseph Pittau, *Political Thought in Early Meiji Japan* (1967). Kenneth B. Pyle, *The New Generation in Meiji Japan* (1969). Robert A. Scalapino, *Democracy and the Party Movement in Prewar Japan* (1953). Thomas C. Smith, *The Agrarian Origins of Modern Japan* (1959). Thomas C. Smith, *Political Change and Industrial Development in Japan* (1955). David Anson Titus, *Palace and Politics in Prewar Japan* (1974). Robert A. Wilson, *Genesis of the Meiji Government in Japan* (1957).　　　　　Marius B. JANSEN

TAISHŌ AND EARLY SHŌWA HISTORY (1912–1945)

During the 33 years between the accession of Emperor Taishō in 1912 and the announcement of surrender by Emperor Hirohito in 1945 the Japanese people began to experience both the benefits and the problems of an economically advanced nation. Japan's material wealth grew remarkably. According to the estimates of the economists Kazushi Ohkawa and Henry Rosovsky, the gross national product nearly tripled between 1911 and 1940, from ¥7.9 million to ¥22.9 million. But with this economic surge came rapid population growth, new social movements, a deepening cultural and economic gap between country and city, and increased economic dependence on the outside world. To these socioeconomic problems were added domestic conflicts over political leadership and international conflicts over the maintenance of an empire in East Asia. The convergence of these historical trends produced an era of both lively progress and severe stress, punctuated by periodic crises that eventually culminated in the disasters of World War II. See also MODERNIZATION; MILITARISM.

The Change in National Leadership —— From the turn of the century, the Meiji oligarchs withdrew from the top positions of political leadership. As GENRŌ (elder statesmen) they continued to consult with government leaders on matters of national policy, especially foreign affairs, but they no longer held cabinet posts. Instead they advised the emperor on the appointment of cabinet ministers; in practice, this meant that they selected them. For both practical and ideological reasons, the *genrō* wished to continue the tradition of suprapartisan government established during the Meiji period (1868–1912). They opposed the idea of responsible cabinets or parliamentary rule. From 1901 until 1912 the majority of all ministerial posts, including the prime minister, were occupied by former bureaucrats. See "TRANSCENDENTAL" CABINETS.

Continued *genrō* interference in politics produced discontent. Government leaders such as KATSURA TARŌ, a protégé of YAMAGATA ARITOMO, resented having to listen to *genrō* advice, and the political parties resented their exclusion from power. During the last decade of Meiji, however, political parties had gained considerable political leverage in the Diet. Their ability to stall the national budget or other important legislation made it essential for cabinets to secure their cooperation. From the time of the RUSSO-JAPANESE WAR (1904–05) the RIKKEN SEIYŪKAI, the largest of the parties, followed the tactics of compromise with the government. The party supported not only the cabinets of SAIONJI KIMMOCHI, its nominal leader, but also those of Katsura, who had no formal party affiliation.

The politics of compromise were interrupted by the TAISHŌ POLITICAL CRISIS of 1912–13, which crystallized public resentment over continued *genrō* domination of politics. In the winter of 1912 behind-the-scenes maneuvering by the army and the *genrō* caused the downfall of the second Saionji cabinet. Katsura, who was nominated as his successor, announced he would no longer rely on Seiyūkai support but would form a political party of his own. In response to these events a coalition of Diet politicians organized a national MOVEMENT TO PROTECT CONSTITUTIONAL GOVERNMENT. Its stated goals were to end *genrō* interference in politics and to establish responsible parliamentary cabinets. While the movement achieved neither, it did bring an end to Katsura's cabinet and taught the *genrō* a lesson about the power of the parties and popular movements.

For the next four years the *genrō* continued to nominate prestigious nonparty leaders to head the government: Admiral YAMAMOTO GONNOHYŌE, a key naval leader (prime minister, 1913–14); ŌKUMA SHIGENOBU, a liberal elder statesman (1914–16); and General TERAUCHI MASATAKE, an army leader (1916–18). In reality, all three cabinets found it necessary to rely on political party support in the Diet to carry on their programs, so that, an embryonic two-party system was developing. Political influence shifted between the Seiyūkai, which supported Yamamoto and Terauchi, and the RIKKEN DŌSHIKAI, (later reorganized as the KENSEIKAI), which supported Ōkuma. The two parties had firm control over the still limited electorate, and sporadic attempts to organize new political parties invariably ended in failure.

While their tactics differed, the leaders of both major parties were fully committed to the eventual establishment of party cabinets. KATŌ TAKAAKI, a former diplomat who headed the Kenseikai, was an orthodox and rigid believer in English-style parliamentarism. His rival, HARA TAKASHI, president of the Seiyūkai, was more sensitive to the peculiarities of Japan's political environment. By a canny mixture of tactical compromise and personal persuasion Hara worked his way into the good graces of the *genrō*, particularly Yamagata. When the Terauchi cabinet fell in 1918, Hara was recommended by the *genrō* as prime minister. For the next three years he presided over what can be seen as Japan's first party cabinet.

The assassination of Hara in 1921 temporarily halted the shift of national leadership to the political parties. The *genrō* had appointed Hara as an expedient or experiment but not out of acceptance of responsible party cabinets. The Seiyūkai was badly split by a leadership struggle after Hara's death, and the Kenseikai remained a minority party, so the *genrō* reverted to the practice of nominating nonparty ministers: Admiral KATŌ TOMOSABURŌ (1922–23), Admiral Yamamoto again (1923–24), and Viscount KIYOURA KEIGO (1924).

The establishment of an "aristocratic cabinet" under Kiyoura prompted the political parties to set aside their rivalries and mount a second movement for constitutional government, a party coalition aimed at restoring party cabinets. The coalition did not arouse the popular enthusiasm that the earlier movement had, but it did enable the three coalition parties (Seiyūkai, Kenseikai, and KAKUSHIN KURABU) to win a majority in the election of 1924. Saionji, left as the only remaining *genrō* by the deaths of Yamagata in 1922 and MATSUKATA MASAYOSHI in 1924, had little choice but to nominate a coalition party cabinet headed by Katō Takaaki (see GOKEN SAMPA NAIKAKU). Though Saionji continued to toy with the idea of appointing a nonparty prime minister, in practice he did not, preferring to move with the trend of the times.

Katō's two successive cabinets (1924–26) marked the beginning of the era of "normal constitutional government" (*kensei no jōdō*), which lasted until 1932. To be sure, the political parties constantly

had to strike bargains, and to some degree share power, with the civil and military bureaucracies, but they continued to dominate national political leadership. The parties enjoyed the financial backing of the business community, including the ZAIBATSU (financial combines); they commanded the support of voters by catering to local economic interests and buying votes; and increasingly they were able to influence administrative decisions within the civil bureaucracy. It was a sign of their importance that General TANAKA GIICHI, a ranking army leader, agreed to succeed Hara as president of the Seiyūkai and that a large number of businessmen and former bureaucrats became party members. See also TAISHŌ DEMOCRACY.

The political parties, together with their business and bureaucratic allies, came under increasing criticism in the 1920s, however. The end of World War I saw the emergence of a new political left wing. This movement began mildly enough with a demand for increased democratization of Diet politics. Intellectuals, students, and workers joined in a UNIVERSAL MANHOOD SUFFRAGE MOVEMENT to break the hold of the "privileged classes" on national politics. In 1919 demonstrators took to the streets to call for an end to the tax qualification on the right to vote. These peaceful and well-organized demonstrations impressed moderate politicians but alarmed the more conservative. Although the Kenseikai and other opposition parties came out for the measure, a universal suffrage bill was defeated by Seiyūkai votes in the 1920 Diet.

Partly in frustration at this failure but also in admiration for the new "socialist experiment" in Soviet Russia, popular movements took a radical turn in the early 1920s. The focus of debate shifted from political reform to demands for major structural changes in the capitalist socioeconomic system (see YŪAIKAI; SHINJINKAI; MODERN PHILOSOPHY; ANARCHISM). The labor movement, dominated by the Japan Federation of Labor (SŌDŌMEI) organized in 1921, came under the influence of leaders committed to anarcho-syndicalism, democratic socialism, and Marxism. Student and worker activists took to the countryside to organize tenant unions and rent strikes against landlord oppression (see TENANT FARMER DISPUTES). "Marx boys" and "Engels girls" were found with increasing frequency among middle-class students. Campaigns for WOMEN'S SUFFRAGE and related rights emerged. To confirm the worst fears of the political establishment, the JAPAN COMMUNIST PARTY was organized in 1922; it was outlawed from the beginning.

Such inescapable evidence of popular unrest prompted the Diet to pass moderate social reform legislation such as a labor exchange bill, a health insurance law, tenancy dispute arbitration law, and a minimum wage law. More important, in 1925 the Diet finally passed a universal manhood suffrage law. Thus, moderate left-wing elements were prompted to turn again to parliamentary tactics. Beginning in 1926 a number of small "proletarian parties," such as the RŌDŌ NŌMINTŌ and NIHON RŌNŌTŌ, were organized to represent the interests of the common man and to attract the votes of the newly expanded electorate. While these parties were unable to challenge the dominant position of the existing political parties, they managed to gain in strength steadily during the late 1920s and early 1930s, with some of the moderate elements consolidating into one party called the SHAKAI TAISHŪTŌ.

Conservative and right-wing anxieties over the new left wing led to strict countermeasures. Legislative efforts were made to strengthen the power of the police and the judiciary to control the spread of "dangerous thoughts." The PEACE PRESERVATION LAW OF 1925, passed in the same Diet session as the universal suffrage law, made it illegal to criticize the KOKUTAI (national polity) or the private property system. The penalties for such activities were made heavier under the Tanaka cabinet, and in the MARCH 15TH INCIDENT of 1928 there was a nationwide roundup of communists and other "subversive elements." The police and the judiciary charged with the suppression of left-wing extremism continued to grow in size. By the early 1930s the extreme left had been almost completely suppressed.

The effectiveness of the police was not the only reason for the weakness of the left. The main social division in the 1920s was not between capital and labor so much as between the countryside and the city. The educated urban middle classes continued their relentless passion for Western culture that had begun in the Meiji period. They avidly read the latest translations of Western books and provided the audience for new experiments in literature, drama, music, painting, and sculpture. New kinds of mass media—large circulation newspapers, general monthly magazines like CHŪŌ KŌRON and KAIZŌ, imported and domestically produced films, and radio broadcasts—added to the richness and confusion of cultural life in the cities. On the other hand, the rural population, though highly literate as the result of compulsory education, were more closely tied to traditional ways. Farmers with only a primary education regarded the lively urban culture as frivolous, and they felt threatened by faddish middle-class ideas of reform such as the need to improve the status of women (see WOMEN IN JAPAN, HISTORY OF) or to encourage love matches in marriage. Ideas of revolution and social conflict were more horrifying. Even had the police allowed the extreme left a longer leash, it is unlikely that their ideas would have made much headway among the conservative rural population.

World War I and Postwar Foreign Policy —— The establishment of Japan as a major imperialist power through victory in the Russo-Japanese War (1904–05) thrust the country increasingly into world politics. In addition to the colonies of Taiwan and Korea, Japan had substantial interests in China, where it had both territorial concessions and growing economic involvement. See COLONIALISM.

Although WORLD WAR I had its origins in European power politics, the Ōkuma cabinet decided to side with Great Britain, Japan's formal ally since the ANGLO-JAPANESE ALLIANCE of 1902.

The main diplomatic significance of the war was that it offered Japan the opportunity to further its own interests in East Asia while the European imperialist powers were occupied with their problems at home. In January 1915, partly to settle a number of pending diplomatic issues and partly to expand Japan's influence in postrevolutionary China, the Ōkuma cabinet presented the government of President YUAN SHIKAI (Yüan Shih-k'ai) with a wide-ranging set of proposals, ultimately known as the TWENTY-ONE DEMANDS. Their main thrust was to secure new economic advantages for Japan in China, to ensure a long-term basis for Japan's territorial concessions in the Shandong (Shantung) and Guandong (Kwantung) peninsulas, to prevent territorial concessions on the China coast opposite Taiwan to other powers, and to introduce Japanese advisers into the Chinese governmental system. The Yuan government, hoping for foreign intervention, made the proposals public but in May ultimately acceded to most of the Japanese demands.

The Japanese initiative left a troublesome legacy for future relations with China. The Twenty-One Demands provoked strong anti-Japanese sentiments among the younger generation of Chinese intellectual and political leaders who were to guide the forces of Chinese nationalism in the decades to come. The episode gave the impression that Japan was bent on taking advantage of its helpless neighbor whenever the occasion presented itself. These suspicions were heightened by the so-called NISHIHARA LOANS, a massive credit of ¥145 million advanced in 1917 to Yuan's successor, DUAN QIRUI (Tuan Ch'i-jui). Ostensibly the loans were for economic development, but in reality they were used to stabilize Duan's warlord regime. The loans were followed in 1918 by a Sino-Japanese military agreement giving Japan the right to garrison troops in China. Close ties between the Japanese and the Chinese warlords intensified anti-Japanese feelings, which finally exploded in China's MAY FOURTH MOVEMENT of 1919. Japan's pressure on China also aroused the distrust of the United States, but ill feelings were patched over in 1917 by the LANSING–ISHII AGREEMENT, which reaffirmed the OPEN DOOR POLICY.

With the end of World War I Japan returned to a policy of cooperation with the Western powers. In 1918 the allies requested that Japan contribute military forces to the SIBERIAN INTERVENTION. As one of the major powers Japan participated in the negotiation of the Treaty of VERSAILLES in 1919. While the main focus of the conference was the settlement of European problems, the Japanese delegation was concerned with the status of the Japanese-occupied German concession on the Shandong Peninsula, the disposition of German island possessions in the Pacific, and the inclusion of a racial equality clause in the peace treaty. The Japanese failed to secure the last, but they did retain economic privileges in Shantung (see SHANDONG [SHANTUNG] QUESTION) and eventually were given mandate over the German island colonies in the Pacific Ocean north of the equator.

The most important long-term goal of the conference, especially of the American delegation, was to establish a new international system to prevent another major world conflict. As one of the five major victorious powers, Japan was given a seat on the council of the newly organized League of Nations (see LEAGUE OF NATIONS AND JAPAN). More important, in the postwar years Japanese foreign policy adhered to the principles of international cooperation and collective security.

In 1921, as the result of American initiative, the WASHINGTON CONFERENCE was convened to discuss the naval arms question and

to devise collective security arrangements in East Asia. The naval treaty finally agreed upon a 10:10:6 ratio for the capital ship tonnage of the British, American, and Japanese fleets. The Japanese also signed the NINE-POWER TREATY and the Five-Power Treaty, which reaffirmed the Open Door policy and recognized the territorial status quo in East Asia and the western Pacific. The arrangements devised at Washington were intended to replace the system of bilateral agreements that had characterized prewar diplomacy in East Asia. Under the guidance of SHIDEHARA KIJŪRŌ, who served as foreign minister from 1924 to 1927, the Japanese government attempted to maintain the "spirit of the Washington conference." This became increasingly difficult as nationalism gathered force in China. The newly reorganized Guomindang (Kuomintang; Nationalist Party) was militant in its determination to end the special privileges of the imperialist powers in China. This development was especially threatening to the Japanese, who, more than the other powers, steadily expanded trade and investments on the China mainland during and after the war. While Shidehara continued to argue against intervention in Chinese domestic affairs, elements in Japan's army and political parties began to call for a more "positive" policy in China.

Wartime Boom and Postwar Depression —— The economic impact of World War I was perhaps as important as the diplomatic. Japan's industrialization process had already reached the point of self-sustaining growth well before the war (see ECONOMIC HISTORY: early modern economy). Although the government continued to promote the expansion of the industrial sector through direct subsidies, extension of easy credit, preferential tariff policies, low taxes, and the expansion of communications networks, the main spur to growth was private business initiative and private business investment. Oligopolistic trends were also evident in most modern industries, and a number of large conglomerate business firms such as the MITSUI and MITSUBISHI zaibatsu were beginning to emerge as leaders in the business community.

The withdrawal of European, especially British, business interests from East Asian markets after the outbreak of the war provided an unexpected boost for the modern sector of the economy. The rupture of trade with Germany stimulated the chemical, dye, and drug industries, which had earlier been dependent on German imports; military orders prompted the expansion of the iron, steel, and machine tool industries; cotton textile exports flooded Asian markets to meet demands that could not be satisfied by the British mills; the shipping fleet expanded precipitously to handle the new foreign trade; and the hydroelectric power industry grew in response to the new demands of industrial growth.

The World War I boom added to Japan's general prosperity, but it created serious social dislocations. The shape of the labor force was altered significantly. It not only doubled in size, but with the growth of heavy industry there was an increase in the number of male workers in the factory labor force, which had been dominated by female textile workers. The sudden surge in wartime demand also resulted in rapid price inflation, which outran the rise in wages. Labor disputes, especially those over wages, rose from 50 in 1914 to 417 in 1918. More dramatic, however, were the RICE RIOTS OF 1918. These massive popular demonstrations against exorbitant rice prices spread from provincial villages and towns to major cities like Tōkyō, Ōsaka, and Kyōto. Crowds milled through the streets attacking and looting the shops of rice brokers, moneylenders, and other merchants.

With the end of the war, the boom came to an end. Although the economy continued to grow, it did so at a much slower rate. The boom created economic imbalances that complicated the postwar adjustment. As overseas markets for Japanese goods collapsed in the postwar years, the economy suffered a recession. In 1920 came falling prices, worker layoffs, import surpluses, and tumbling stock prices. Many firms founded during the prosperous war years found themselves saddled with debt and unable to raise new capital for expansion. To make matters worse, the Hara cabinet, fearful of damaging relations with the business community, refused to implement a thoroughgoing deflation policy to weed out unsound firms and bring prices down to levels more competitive in the world market. The financial community was also reluctant to take drastic action.

The TŌKYŌ EARTHQUAKE OF 1923 caused widespread destruction in the Tōkyō–Yokohama area, one of the country's major economic centers. A moratorium was declared on the collection of loans, and the government advanced credits to firms affected by the disaster. The "reconstruction boom" that resulted in 1924–25 provided a temporary respite from the chronic problems of the economy, but a major collapse occurred in 1927 (see FINANCIAL CRISIS OF 1927). A chance remark by the finance minister during a Diet interpellation precipitated the failure of a small Tōkyō city bank. Dozens of others soon followed, including the Bank of Taiwan (TAIWAN GINKŌ). Many unsound trading and manufacturing firms went down with them or were taken over by new interests, often by the *zaibatsu*. During the 18 months after the panic, the number of ordinary banks shrank from 1359 to 1031, and the assets of the *zaibatsu* grew correspondingly. While this drastic deflation apparently benefited the overall economy, it was a severe shock to public confidence.

Economic conditions were also deteriorating in the countryside. As the result of government efforts to promote the import of cheap rice from Taiwan and Korea after the rice riots of 1918, the price of domestic rice stagnated. Land values also dropped, and farming became relatively unprofitable even for landlords, many of whom began to invest in company stocks instead. At the same time, the price of raw silk, the second most important agricultural product, began to decline after 1925 as the result of overproduction and a shift to the use of artificial fiber in the United States. As farm income dropped, the burden of rent, debt, and taxes became heavier for most of the nation's farm families.

A final shock to the economy came with the onset of the world depression in 1929. Given Japan's dependence on foreign trade for the margin of prosperity, the slump hit Japan as well. The deflationary financial policies of the government under HAMAGUCHI OSACHI (1929–30)—the adoption of a balanced budget and a return to the gold standard—intensified its effects. Prices dropped sharply, bankruptcies ensued, and the number of unemployed rose to nearly 1 million.

Years of Crisis——The post-1927 depression coincided with a time of growing tension in Japan's foreign relations. Shidehara's former policies of nonintervention in China and cooperation with the Anglo-American powers came under severe attack. The apparently successful efforts of CHIANG KAI-SHEK to reunify China politically and militarily posed a threat to Japan's territorial rights and political influence there, especially in Manchuria. Strikes by workers in Japanese-owned textile mills in China and popular boycotts of Japanese goods also threatened its economic stake. Anxiety that the country was rapidly outgrowing its domestic food and industrial resources, and resentment over anti-Japanese racist discrimination in the United States and the British Commonwealth, when added to the situation in China, prompted a call for a more "positive" foreign policy.

The cabinet of Tanaka Giichi (1927–29), while maintaining friendly relations with the Chiang regime, attempted to encourage the separatism of ZHANG ZUOLIN (Chang Tso-lin), the local warlord controlling Manchuria. This kind of "positive policy" did not go far enough for activist elements in the GUANDONG (KWANTUNG) ARMY, the Japanese field army stationed in Manchuria; in June 1928 a few of its young officers assassinated Zhang in hopes of provoking a Japanese military occupation of the area. The Tōkyō government failed to do so, but the plotters went unpunished and continued to intrigue. They enjoyed both tacit and covert support from sympathetic elements in the army headquarters in Tōkyō who resented the retrenchment of arms and personnel under the civilian-dominated cabinets of the mid-1920s.

Army advocates of expansionism were gripped by a sense of greater urgency after the formation of the Hamaguchi cabinet in 1929. Its economic policies were disastrous, but it briefly restored the cooperative foreign policy of Shidehara Kijūrō. A major constitutional crisis ensued in 1930, when the Hamaguchi government signed the London Naval Treaty, a new naval arms limitation agreement, over the strong objections of powerful factions in the naval high command (see LONDON NAVAL CONFERENCES). Critics in the navy, the army, and even the Diet opposition accused the cabinet of violating the navy's "right of direct access" to the emperor on matters of military security policy (see TŌSUIKEN). In November 1930 a right-wing radical fatally wounded Hamaguchi. Middle-echelon officers, inspired by the writings of men like KITA IKKI, began a plot for a military coup to overthrow civilian rule and bring about a "SHŌWA RESTORATION." A plan for such a coup was abandoned only when incumbent Army Minister UGAKI KAZUSHIGE refused to cooperate (see MARCH INCIDENT).

It proved easier for discontented army officers to reverse national foreign policy than to overthrow civilian government. On 18 September 1931 the Guandong Army, with tacit approval from elements in the Tōkyō high command, began a long-planned occupation of southern Manchuria (see MANCHURIAN INCIDENT). The public popularity of this action, coupled with a lack of military response by the Chiang government or intervention by the Western powers, made the civilian government unwilling or unable to contain the military action. By early 1932 the region was under Japanese military control, and in March the "independent" state of MANCHUKUO was established under the nominal leadership of PUYI (P'u-i), the last Manchu emperor. A year later, in March 1933, Japan announced its withdrawal from the League of Nations to protest the report of the LYTTON COMMISSION, which condemned the Japanese actions. This marked an end to the cooperative foreign policy of the 1920s and the beginning of a new policy of self-assertion in international politics.

The Return of a Bureaucratic Government——The Manchurian Incident prompted an upsurge in right-wing domestic patriotism. Small nationalist political groups, patriotic religious sects, national socialist organizations, and extremist study groups sprang up, spouting a virulent anti-Westernism. The RIGHT WING also attacked the civilian-dominated party cabinets and their *zaibatsu* connections and expressed a profound revulsion against the spread of "dangerous" liberal and left-wing thought. Their vague ideals were the virtues of Japan's "imperial way," the uniqueness of the Japanese "national polity," and Japan's special "mission" in East Asia. Similar themes appeared in a series of pamphlets published by the Army Ministry (see NATIONALISM; PAN-ASIANISM).

The Manchurian takeover also prompted a new wave of political terrorism by radical officers and civilian right-wing activists. In May 1932 the assassination of Prime Minister INUKAI TSUYOSHI, leader of the Seiyūkai, brought an end to party rule (see MAY 15TH INCIDENT). Prince Saionji, feeling it imprudent to continue the experiment in a time of major domestic and foreign crisis, recommended the appointment of a "national unity" cabinet under Admiral SAITŌ MAKOTO (1932–34). During the remainder of the decade, he relied on the advice of the JŪSHIN (senior statesmen), an informal group made up of the imperial household minister, the president of the PRIVY COUNCIL, and former prime ministers. They consistently favored coalition cabinets with members drawn from all the major elites—the civil bureaucracy, the military and naval leadership, the political parties, and the financial community.

Although some senior army leaders sympathized with the radical officers, many of the older generals did not approve of political activism by army personnel. The army leadership was torn by a factional struggle between the Imperial Way faction (KŌDŌHA), led by General ARAKI SADAO, and its opponents (TŌSEIHA; see also GUMBATSU). After Araki was eased out of power, the Imperial Way radicals used violence against his opponents. The assassination of General NAGATA TETSUZAN by a member of the Imperial Way faction in 1935 indicated the deep divisiveness of the struggle. In February 1936 radical company-rank officers in the First Division, hoping to sweep away the entrenched national leadership, including conservative army leaders, used their troops to occupy the center of Tōkyō. Intended to bring about a military takeover, the coup ended in failure within three days, but it did generate an atmosphere of shock and uncertainty. See FEBRUARY 26TH INCIDENT.

From 1936 onward the army leadership gained an increasing role in national policy making. As part of an attempt to restore discipline within the army, the HIROTA KŌKI cabinet in May 1936 reinstituted a requirement that the war minister be a general officer on active duty (see GUMBU DAIJIN GEN'EKI BUKAN SEI). Since the army leadership could order a general officer not to serve, in effect this gave the army leadership a veto over the formation of cabinets. After 1936 no cabinet was formed without the tacit or explicit support of the army leaders. Party politicians continued to hold ministerial posts, but their number dwindled, giving way to an increasing number of bureaucrats, generals, and admirals. The need to resolve the future direction of Japanese foreign policy also added to the importance of the army's views, since the army had the major military responsibility for consolidating or making new advances on the Chinese mainland.

Since the army was not in full control of the government, its leaders constantly bargained and parleyed with the other elites, especially the navy and the political parties. In an attempt to reconcile the continuing domestic infighting, the *jūshin* recommended Prince KONOE FUMIMARO for the premiership. Konoe, member of an ancient aristocratic family, was well connected in all political circles, but he proved no more adept at providing political stability than his predecessors. Between 1937 and 1940 there was rapid turnover in cabinets and constant shifts in national policy, especially foreign policy.

Economic Recovery —— Despite the unsettled political situation, the decade following the Manchurian Incident saw steady economic recovery. Between 1931 and 1937 the average annual growth rate was 5.7 percent, or more than twice what it had been in the preceding decade. The shift of population to large cities quickened, as did the growth of the male factory labor force. Both trends reflected recovery from the effects of the depression. The main stimuli behind this recovery were the devaluation of the yen, the adoption of deficit spending, and increased demand for the production of arms and other military equipment.

In 1931 Finance Minister TAKAHASHI KOREKIYO effected a de facto devaluation of the yen by placing an embargo on the shipment of gold specie abroad. The result was a sharp fall in the value of the yen relative to other national currencies. This made Japanese goods inexpensive in the world market and in turn led to a new export boom, especially in light industry goods. By 1936, for example, Japan had become the world's chief exporter of cotton piece goods, surpassing even the British. Significantly the new trade advances were made principally in Asian markets, including areas under direct Japanese political control such as Taiwan, Korea, and Manchukuo. But there were also gains in Europe, South America, and Africa. The flood of inexpensive Japanese goods in the world market at a time when other industrial nations were deep in economic slump provoked outcries abroad against "unfair competition." These protests, reflected in rising tariffs in the United States and European colonial areas, added to the Japanese sense of isolation.

Under the leadership of Takahashi the government also pursued a policy of reflation at home. The government initiated public works construction projects, borrowed heavily to finance government expenditures, and lowered interest rates on business loans. The policy of the 1920s based on balanced budgets was abandoned, and no attempt was made to avoid government deficits. The government increased expenditures to pay for the country's new expansionist foreign policy. Funds were needed to finance military operations and to build up the economy of Manchukuo, which was to be developed as a supplier of resources and manufactured goods for Japan. Between 1931 and 1935 national defense expenditures nearly doubled, and by 1939 the military budget amounted to nearly one-fifth of the gross national product (GNP). The metal, machine goods, and chemical industries benefited most conspicuously from the military boom, as did new industries such as automobiles and aircraft.

The agricultural sector lagged behind the recovery of the industrial sector, however. Farm prices did not return to normal levels until 1935. The government attempted to alleviate rural distress by subsidies to support rice and silk prices, by policies to reduce farm family indebtedness, and by keeping down the cost of artificial fertilizer. But expansion of the manufacturing sector was probably more important in helping the farm population. Between 1930 and 1936 the factory labor force swelled by nearly a million new workers, most of them from the countryside. While this meant an increased work burden for farm women, it meant that farm families had to support fewer able-bodied young men. It also brought farm families new income from wages sent home by family members who had migrated to the city.

The expansion of the modern sector was accompanied by the emergence of new *zaibatsu*, most of them engaged in heavy industry. These *zaibatsu* rarely controlled banks or financing institutions of their own and were heavily dependent on military orders. This fostered close ties with the army and the bureaucracy. But the entire business community was feeling increased political pressure. The crisis in foreign policy brought demands for increased bureaucratic control over the economy. Army planners wished to make the economy more responsive to the military needs of the country, and younger economic bureaucrats urged economic planning to minimize the irrationalities and irregularities of a free market economy. Both hoped to make more efficient use of the nation's resources and productive capacity. With the outbreak of war with China came their opportunity to shift the country toward a controlled economy.

The China War —— The Japanese army continued to probe for new opportunities on the continent after the takeover of Manchuria. In 1932 clashes between Japanese and Chinese forces in Shanghai were settled amicably (see SHANGHAI INCIDENT), but in 1932–33 Japan's Guandong Army moved into Rehe (Jehol) Province and in 1935 made arrangements with local Chinese military commanders to exclude Guomindang influence from the North China provinces of Hebei (Hopeh) and Chahar (see HE–UMEZU [HO–UMEZU] AGREEMENT; DOIHARA–QIN [DOIHARA–CH'IN] AGREEMENT). The goal was to build a buffer zone along the southern borders of Manchukuo

and to keep China divided and weak. The government of Chiang Kai-shek was under increasing pressure from students, intellectuals, and others to resist Japanese aggression instead of continuing its military operations against enclaves controlled by the Chinese Communist Party (see DECEMBER NINTH MOVEMENT). In December 1936 Chiang, while forcibly detained at Xi'an by ZHANG XUELIANG (Chang Hsüeh-liang), finally agreed to cooperate with the Chinese communists against the Japanese (see XI'AN [SIAN] INCIDENT).

On 7 July 1937 occurred the MARCO POLO BRIDGE INCIDENT, a minor skirmish between Chinese and Japanese troops on the outskirts of Beijing (Peking), which marked the real start of the SINO-JAPANESE WAR OF 1937–1945. The Chiang government dispatched new troops to the area, and the Japanese responded in kind. Within a month an undeclared war was in full swing. Initially the Konoe government had not intended to expand the war. The army leadership was divided on the advisability of continuing the fighting and had neither clear war goals nor any strategic plans for fighting. But Japanese field armies in China continued to press the attack against Chinese forces in expectation of a quick victory. A war begun by accident gathered momentum as the Japanese won a rapid series of victories culminating in the fall of the Guomindang capital at Nanjing (Nanking) in December 1937, where Japanese atrocities aroused bitter international criticism (see NANJING [NANKING] INCIDENT). The puppet PROVISIONAL GOVERNMENT OF THE REPUBLIC OF CHINA was established in the north to divide and weaken China further. Peace negotiations, carried out through German mediation, failed to produce a settlement, and so early in 1938 the Konoe government announced that it would no longer deal with Chiang. This effectively foreclosed the possibility of a negotiated peace.

A major Japanese offensive in late 1938 brought the capture of the Wuhan and Guangzhou (Canton) areas, but it failed to break Chinese resistance. The Guomindang government retreated to the interior of China at Chongqing (Chungking), beyond the reach of Japanese military forces. The Japanese were in control of the major coastal cities and their hinterlands, as well as the major railroad lines, but they had little effective control of the rest of the country. Both the Guomindang and the communists began guerrilla warfare against the Japanese even in areas ostensibly under their control.

Despite the unpromising military situation, the Konoe government announced its intention to create a "New Order in East Asia" (TŌA SHINCHITSUJO) resting on neighborly friendship, anticommunism, and economic cooperation among China, Japan, and Manchukuo. The goal was not the territorial absorption of China, but a regional political and economic bloc under the hegemony of Japan. Few Chinese were attracted by the slogan, but in March 1940 a pro-Japanese puppet government (the REORGANIZED NATIONAL GOVERNMENT OF THE REPUBLIC OF CHINA) was established at Nanjing under the formal leadership of WANG JINGWEI (Wang Ching-wei), a former Guomindang leader and rival of Chiang who had defected to the Japanese.

The military stalemate in China troubled many army leaders who felt that Japan's main enemy was the Soviet Union. These sentiments were heightened by clashes between Japanese and Soviet troops on the Manchukuo–Soviet border in July 1938, and at Nomonhan on the Manchukuo–Mongolia border in May 1939 (see NOMONHAN INCIDENT). The latter was particularly troubling, since the Japanese forces suffered a clear defeat at the hands of the Russians. If Japanese manpower and resources were tied down in China, effective military action against the Soviet Union was simply not possible, yet there seemed no acceptable way out of the China quagmire.

Enthusiasm for the China War continued to run high on the home front. In an emergency session in late summer 1937 the Diet quickly approved war appropriations and other war-related legislation. In October 1937 the NATIONAL SPIRITUAL MOBILIZATION MOVEMENT was launched to promote popular support for the war and to combat domestic dissent, especially on the left. A number of left-wing activists were rounded up (see POPULAR FRONT INCIDENT), and several prominent professors with liberal or left-wing views were hounded out of their university posts.

The only significant sign of political opposition came with mild Diet resistance to the NATIONAL MOBILIZATION LAW in 1938. Increased economic control was popular with neither the business community nor its political allies in the Diet. But the law was passed, and economic controls were placed on production, the distribution of raw materials, foreign exchange transactions, imports and exports, and wages and hours. Civilian rationing also began, and the quality and availability of consumer goods began to decline as the war continued. But most Japanese were willing to make the personal sacrifices required of the war effort.

The Wartime Political Structure —— The prolongation of the war, coupled with the instability of cabinets after 1937, prompted many politicians, bureaucrats, and military officers to call for the establishment of a "new political order." Certain elements in the army and the civilian right wing wanted to follow the Nazi model of a one-party system; moderate left-wing politicians wanted a new mass political party committed to socio-economic reform; and some party politicians hoped to form a unified Diet party able to transcend partisan interests and to return the Diet to the center of national politics.

With the formation of a new Konoe cabinet in July 1940, the plans for a new political order took concrete shape. In preparation for the reorganization of the domestic political structure, all the Diet parties (including the "proletarian parties") formally dissolved themselves. In October the IMPERIAL RULE ASSISTANCE ASSOCIATION (IRAA) was established, with Konoe at its head (see also NEW ORDER MOVEMENT).

Under pressure from the bureaucracy and the army, the new organization rather quickly became an agency for transmitting government regulations to the public and promoting wartime homefront mobilization. The president ex officio of the IRAA was the prime minister, and prefectural governors served as local branch chiefs. The lowest units of the organization were the TONARIGUMI (neighbor groups), which all households were required to join. The main functions of the *tonarigumi* were to distribute ration cards, collect scrap metal, conduct air raid drills, sell government bonds, recruit labor for public service, and report antiwar activities. Professional organizations were also established to organize factory workers, young people, women, farmers, writers, and others in support of the war effort. Complex in structure, controlled by the bureaucracy, and unwieldy in size, the IRAA was a far cry from the Nazi one-party state in Germany.

The Pacific War —— The outbreak of war in Europe in September 1939 prompted a new turn in Japanese foreign policy. Since its withdrawal from the League of Nations in 1933, Japan had been left without formal allies abroad or any place in international collective security arrangements. In December 1934 the OKADA KEISUKE government announced its intention to abrogate the Washington Naval Treaty, and a new naval conference convened at London failed to produce an agreement to replace it. The breach with the Anglo-American powers widened. Within the army and the diplomatic corps, many urged that Japan form closer ties with Fascist Italy and Nazi Germany. They felt that Japan, like these other powers, was a "have-not" nation whose interest lay in overthrowing an international order dominated by the Anglo-American powers.

In November 1936 Japan signed the ANTI-COMINTERN PACT with Germany, and Italy joined it the following year. Certain Japanese army leaders and right-wing activists wanted to expand the pact into a formal military alliance. Navy leaders, the *jūshin*, and some Diet politicians opposed the idea for fear of antagonizing the Americans and the British. The issue was hotly debated between 1936 and 1940 and was in large degree responsible for the short duration of the cabinets of the period. But the rapid series of German victories in 1939–40 made it seem likely that the Axis powers would emerge victorious in the European conflict. In September 1940 the TRIPARTITE PACT was signed by Japan, Germany, and Italy.

The signing of the pact was in part intended to promote the advance of Japanese military power into Southeast Asia. The army wished for a base in the former French colony of Indochina to stage a new offensive against China from the south, and the navy supported a "move southward" in hopes of gaining access to the rich petroleum and mineral resources in Southeast Asia (see SOUTHERN EXPANSION DOCTRINE). The area had been made vulnerable to Japanese penetration by the collapse of Holland and France. Almost simultaneously with the signing of the Tripartite Pact the Japanese government secured permission from the Nazi-dominated Vichy regime in France to station troops in northern Indochina.

Despite these new diplomatic initiatives, the Konoe government still wished to maintain friendly relations with both the United States and Great Britain. The United States, however, was anxious to prevent further Japanese inroads into China and wished to maintain free access to Southeast Asian resources, especially for Great Britain, in order to continue the fight against the Nazis in Europe. The United States demonstrated its hostility to the Japanese move southward as well as to the Japanese aggression in China by escalating economic actions against Japan. In an effort to improve relations

with the United States the Konoe government began talks with the Roosevelt administration. Since the Americans insisted on the withdrawal of Japanese troops from China and Manchukuo as a basic condition for an East Asian settlement, the parleys could make little progress.

A new turn of events in the early summer of 1941 brought Japan closer to a military clash with the United States. The German attack on the Soviet Union in June substantially reduced the likelihood of conflict with the Russians, and so the army and the navy proposed a new move to the south. In late July Japanese troops moved into southern Indochina, and Japan concluded a neutrality pact with the government of Thailand. The immediate consequence was disastrous. The United States froze Japanese assets in the United States and imposed an embargo on petroleum exports to Japan. The independent government of the Dutch East Indies and the British Commonwealth soon followed suit. In effect, the Japanese were denied access to critically important supplies of oil needed to support its military and naval operations. The Konoe government was faced with the alternatives of withdrawing from Indochina, China, and Manchukuo, or invading the former colonial areas in Southeast Asia before Japan's oil reserves ran out. The latter course meant fighting the United States as well.

At an imperial conference (GOZEN KAIGI) on 6 September 1941 it was finally decided to go to war with the United States if further negotiations were unsuccessful. In October, when it was clear that attempts at a diplomatic solution had failed, the Konoe government resigned. It was succeeded by the cabinet of TŌJŌ HIDEKI, an army leader who had long supported expansionism. On 8 December 1941 (Tōkyō time) a Japanese naval task force launched a brilliantly successful surprise air attack on the United States naval base at PEARL HARBOR in the Hawaiian Islands. The following day the US Congress formally declared war on Japan.

At first the war went in Japan's favor. A rapid series of Japanese victories in Southwest Asia and the central and southwest Pacific left Japan in control of a defense perimeter that stretched from the Aleutian Islands to Burma. But Japanese fortunes took a turn for the worse after a major naval defeat at MIDWAY in June 1942. The conflict then became a war of attrition. The odds were strongly against Japan, which lacked the overwhelming manpower, economic, and technological resources of the United States. American submarine warfare cut off the Japanese home islands from the economic wealth of Southeast Asia, and an American island-hopping campaign across the Pacific brought the Japanese home islands within striking distance of American long-range bombers. The surrender of Italy in September 1943 and the fall of the Nazi regime in May 1945 left Japan fighting alone. In July 1945 Great Britain, the United States, and the Soviet Union issued the POTSDAM DECLARATION calling for Japan's unconditional surrender.

The war came to an end on 15 August 1945 (14 August in the Western Hemisphere). ATOMIC BOMB attacks on Hiroshima (6 August) and Nagasaki (9 August), coupled with the formal entry of the Soviet Union into the war against Japan on 9 August, had made it clear that further resistance was futile. The country's cities were devastated, and the population was suffering from severe shortages of food, clothing, and housing. There was nothing to be gained by holding out until a final Allied invasion. The decision to surrender was humiliating, but it brought to an end 14 years of conflict that had cost Japan 2,880,000 military casualties and 800,000 civilian casualties. See also WORLD WAR II.

◾ —— Gordon Mark Berger, *Parties Out of Power in Japan, 1931–1941* (1977). Dorothy Borg and Shumpei Okamoto, ed, *Pearl Harbor as History: Japanese-American Relations, 1931–1941* (1973). John H. Boyle, *China and Japan at War, 1937–1945: The Politics of Collaboration* (1972). James B. Crowley, *Japan's Quest for Autonomy: National Security and Foreign Policy, 1930–1938* (1966). Peter Duus, *Party Rivalry and Political Change in Taishō Japan* (1968). Hayashi Shigeru, *Taiheiyō sensō* (1967). Imai Seiichi, *Taishō demo-kurashii* (1966). Akira Iriye, *After Imperialism: The Search for a New Order in East Asia* (1965). Itō Takashi, *Jūgonen sensō* (1976). *Iwanami kōza: Nihon rekishi*, vols 18–21 (Iwanami Shoten, 1976–77). Masao Maruyama, *Thought and Behavior in Modern Japanese Politics* (1963). James W. Morley, ed, *Dilemmas of Growth in Prewar Japan* (1971). Tetsuo Najita, *Hara Kei in the Politics of Compromise, 1905–1915* (1967). Nezu Masashi, *Nihon gendai shi*, 7 vols (1966–70). Nihon Kokusai Seiji Gakkai, ed, *Taiheiyō sensō e no michi*, 8 vols (1963). Sadako N. Ogata, *Defiance in Manchuria: The Making of Japanese Foreign Policy, 1931–1932* (1964). Kazushi Ohkawa and Henry Rosovsky, *Japanese Economic Growth: Trend*

Acceleration in the Twentieth Century (1973). Ōuchi Tsutomu, *Fuashizumu e no michi* (1967). Bernard S. Silberman and Harry D. Harootunian, ed, *Japan in Crisis: Essays on Taishō Democracy* (1974). Tanaka Sōgorō, *Nihon fuashizumu shi* (1960). John Toland, *The Rising Sun: The Decline and Fall of the Japanese Empire, 1936–1945* (1970).   Peter Duus

POSTWAR HISTORY (FROM 1945)

Postwar Japan's transformation from a war shattered nation to one of the world's three largest economic powers not unexpectedly generated considerable controversy. Some regarded the growth as a natural result of a highly intelligent and quite disciplined society whose many good features ought to be studied by the rest of the capitalist world. Others claimed that modernization had only been achieved through the brutal exploitation of the natural environment and of the less fortunate members of the society. Still others believed that the rapid growth was due to a series of factors which were unique to the 1960s and 1970s, and hence predicted that Japan would shortly face the problems confronting other post-industrial societies. Whichever view one accepted, it was clear by the 1980s that the very rapid transformation of postwar Japan made that country unusually dependent upon relations with the wider world. Japanese thus worried not only about their own society, but also about their image in the rest of the world community.

Economic Growth —— Few observers would have predicted such rapid growth at war's end. Although the government was able to surrender in time to avoid both a Russian zone of occupation and the abdication of the emperor, Japan had lost all of her empire, suffered over 2 million war deaths, and had most of her cities and factories destroyed. From September 1945 to April 1952, the government was officially responsible to an American-dominated OCCUPATION initially headed by the flamboyant General Douglas MACARTHUR. In its earlier years, the Occupation insisted upon the demilitarization of Japan, WAR CRIMES TRIALS, the purge of individuals held responsible for Japan's allegedly aggressive war (see OCCUPATION PURGE), a new CONSTITUTION, an American-style school system, and extensive reforms in Japan's LABOR UNIONS and the ZAIBATSU or traditional industrial structures. These reforms were on the whole welcomed by a nation that had been truly shocked by its defeat, but they did not do much for Japan's shattered economy until the Occupation outlawed a general strike proposed for 1 February 1947, outlawed the right of public employees to strike, drew back from ambitious plans for ZAIBATSU DISSOLUTION or trust-busting, forced the implementation of the conservative DODGE LINE fiscal policies, and, most important of all, made heavy war purchase orders after the outbreak of the Korean War in June 1950.

Japan's gross national product (GNP) began to grow after the early 1950s. Averaging over 8.6 percent between 1951 and 1955, GNP growth increased by over 9.1 percent between 1955 and 1960, over 9.7 percent between 1960 and 1965, and over 13.1 percent between 1965 and 1970. More recently, it has slowed to about 7 percent. By the early 1970s Japan was the world's largest producer of ships, radios, and televisions, the second largest manufacturer of cars and rubber products, the third largest producer of cement and iron, and had the third largest GNP in the world. By 1981 it had become the largest manufacturer of cars. As Japanese cars and transistor units became known throughout the world, commentators began to talk about the "economic miracle" in Japan.

There were many reasons for Japan's postwar economic growth. First, its population had grown rapidly from 72,147,000 in 1945 to 107,589,000 in 1972, enough to make Japan the seventh most populous country in the world. But unlike other developing countries with a rapidly expanding population base, Japan was able to stabilize its birth rate as early as 1956. Consequently, an extraordinarily high proportion (60 percent) of Japan's population was within the productive labor ages of 15 to 55. Many of these workers were hired for life and paid on a SENIORITY SYSTEM. Lifetime employment increased worker loyalty to the firm and made it easier for management to shift workers from one segment of the firm to another. The seniority system also helped to cut down costs in dynamic and expanding industries by permitting them to hire a relatively large percentage of inexpensive young workers each year. A first set of reasons, then, for Japan's extraordinary postwar growth was its human resources.

A second reason was the nature of Japanese investment patterns. Military expenditures stayed below 1 percent of the GNP, since most of Japan's defense requirements were met by the United States under the mutual security treaty. Investment in the relatively nonpro-

ductive "social overhead" areas of schools, housing, roads, and welfare also remained low. Thus, total government expenditures were kept lower than an estimated 16 percent of the GNP, as opposed to perhaps 30 percent in the United States. The traditionally frugal Japanese were thereby encouraged to save up to 20 percent of their annual income and so provide the capital for investment in modern industrial technology. Japan's capital investment was in fact estimated at 30 percent of its GNP in 1969. Largely because of the increased capital/labor ratio, industrial worker productivity rose, using 1970 as a base of 100, from 36.5 in 1960 to 139.0 in 1973. Real wages rose from 46.5 in 1955 to 56.7 in 1960 and 130.3 in 1973.

A third set of reasons had to do with the special relationship between government and industry in Japan. The popular Western conception of JAPAN INCORPORATED—that every Japanese businessman loyally obeys what growth-conscious bureaucrats decree, and that government and industry function nearly as one—is far too simplistic. What is true is that Japan's conservative governments have sought to create a business environment in which industry could thrive. Low rates of corporate and personal taxation, import restrictions (now largely abolished), and extensive loans by the BANK OF JAPAN, Japan's central bank, have greatly helped industrial expansion. Measures adopted by the MINISTRY OF INTERNATIONAL TRADE AND INDUSTRY (MITI) and other ministries to avoid excessive competition between native industries have also had a positive impact on the economy.

Finally, growth occurred in the 1950s and 1960s because international conditions were favorable. Japan had ready access to cheap raw materials and to Western technology and markets. Japan's growth rate from 1870 to 1936 was 2.3 percent per year, an impressive achievement but not that much lower than its rate from 1945 to 1980. Japan's striking economic growth in the postwar period was thus not so much a "miracle" as it was the story of a skilled people reaching its natural potential after the ravages of World War II.

Social Changes —— Urbanization was the most fundamental social change resulting from industrialization. By the early 1960s the number of rural families stabilized at 5 million, with many of the men commuting to seasonal or full-time jobs in the cities, while wives and grandparents continued to till the traditionally scattered plots of paddy land. Meanwhile, many young men and women flocked into the cities in search of better-paying jobs. Although there was some talk in the 1970s of the "J-turn phenomenon" (moving into the city and then to suburbs or small towns), urban living had undoubtedly arrived in Japan to stay. The percentage of Japanese who lived in cities thus increased from less than 50 percent in 1945 to 64 percent in 1960, 72 percent in 1970, and 76 percent in 1980.

Meanwhile, family life gradually changed from the two or three generational family to the nuclear family. At times this led to a sad neglect of many older people who now had neither family nor state support. There was also some talk of "latchkey children" (children of working parents who had to let themselves into their homes after school) and a rising number of teenage runaways, yet crime and suicide rates on the whole remained very low.

The religious situation also changed dramatically during this period. There had been only 13 Shintō, 28 Buddhist, and 2 Christian groups permitted by the wartime Japanese government, but in the postwar period these figures rose quickly. One hundred and forty-six Shintō-based religions claimed 96 million followers, 13 major Buddhist sects 88 million believers, 44 Christian sects 973,340 believers, and 29 other religious groups 16 million adherents. Since the sects claimed believers numbering 1.7 times the population of Japan, they doubtless exaggerated the number of their faithful, but many Japanese assumed more than one religious affiliation to find emotional stability in a period of rapid change. The so-called NEW RELIGIONS such as the SŌKA GAKKAI, TENRIKYŌ, and PL KYŌDAN also rapidly gained in popularity after the war. Their youth groups, neighborhood meetings, and vigorous conversion techniques were especially effective with new urban residents.

Marxism provided yet another means of group identification. Communists were admired for their courage during the war, their organizational abilities, and their trenchant analysis of Western capitalism. By the 1970s there was a tendency for some Japanese to seek a more flexible theoretical vocabulary, but Marxism remained a common language for most Japanese intellectuals.

On the positive side then, the Japanese family structure proved flexible enough to accommodate rapid social changes. Traditional values of hard work, loyalty, and self-control remained strong. Westerners could look with envy at Japan's full employment, safe urban neighborhoods, and happy family ways. On the negative side, however, many Japanese argued that Japan was still a repressive society in which strong social pressures demanded conformity. They also pointed to the problem of prejudice against the BURAKU-MIN ("outcasts"), pockets of poverty, negligible social welfare programs, urban congestion, and pollution. Most Japanese recognized that their country had been able to rebuild itself after the war with a minimum amount of social disruption, but they wondered if future economic problems might not bring with them a decline in social cohesion.

Educational System —— A strong educational system also contributed to Japan's postwar economic growth. General MacArthur purged right-wing militarists from schools, guaranteed academic freedom, and tried to shift responsibility for educational decisions from the central government to the local school boards. Compulsory education was extended from 6 to 9 years, and the prewar 6-5-3-3 educational system was changed to an American-style 6-3-3-4 system (6 years of elementary, 3 years each for junior and senior high schools, 4 for college).

Despite Occupation attempts at decentralization, the role of the MINISTRY OF EDUCATION remained strong. The replacement of elective school boards by more conservative appointees in 1956, the revamping of the curriculum in 1958, and the tightening of textbook controls despite opposition from academics all led to a sense that the Ministry of Education was becoming not only stronger, but also more conservative. Opposition from the leftist Japan Teacher's Union (NIKKYŌSO) has slowed but not reversed this tendency.

The very nature of the education system also drew criticism from many quarters. In general terms the percentage of the relevant age group graduating from high school increased from 48 percent in 1960 to 59 percent in 1965 and 84 percent in 1976, while the percentage attending universities increased from 10.3 percent in 1960 to 17 percent in 1965 and 36.6 percent in 1976. Two vexing problems sprang from these great changes. First, there was tremendous pressure to gain admission to the most prestigious universities, which were generally agreed to number eight or nine at most. This led to the appearance of expensive CRAM SCHOOLS to prepare high school graduates for the all-decisive ENTRANCE EXAMINATIONS. The phenomenon known as *shiken jigoku,* or "examination hell," has led to severe stress on child and parents alike. The second problem was that, once admitted, students were often bitterly disappointed with the education they received. Classes were European-style lectures given once a week by professors who were often late to class and rarely able to test or relate to their students adequately. Few universities had dormitories, and student life was fragmented. During the late 1960s the tensions inherent in this sort of life exploded in a series of student upheavals (see UNIVERSITY UPHEAVALS OF 1968–1969). The government eventually passed a moderate reform bill designed to restore order in the universities, and student protest declined.

The effectiveness of Japan's educational system was thus a source of some dispute throughout the postwar period. Critics of the system complained that the massive amount of rote memorization required by the examination system all but destroyed genuine intellectual interest. Many critics, some not necessarily conservative, also lamented the lack of moral training in the schools, the overtly political activities of the teachers, and the lack of a warmer relationship between teacher and student. Supporters of the system argued that the examination system was extremely democratic in that it rewarded ability rather than birth or connections. They pointed to the high scholastic achievements of Japanese elementary and secondary school children and to Japan's rapid economic growth; whatever its faults, so they said, the educational system had at least provided the personnel needed to build a new Japan.

The Political System —— Postwar changes in the political system also had considerable impact upon Japan's economic growth. From his arrival General Douglas MacArthur made it clear that he believed a new constitution was imperative. In the face of initial Japanese resistance to anything more than a minor revision of the Meiji Constitution, the Americans presented a draft of a new constitution to the Japanese government on 10 February 1946. The government accepted the draft with only minor amendments and had the new constitution promulgated on 3 November 1946.

The new document was technically an amendment to the Meiji Constitution, but it was in fact a completely new set of basic legal principles. It effectively excluded the emperor from politics by declaring that he was merely "the symbol of the state and the unity of the people . . . with whom resides sovereign power." Individual rights of free speech, assembly, and a decent standard of living were

clearly stated. Article 9 of the constitution renounced war as "a sovereign right of the nation" and declared that Japan would not maintain land, sea, or air forces (see RENUNCIATION OF WAR). Other sections of the constitution required the prime minister and his cabinet to be civilians and generally set up safeguards to prevent the kind of militaristic takeover that seemed to have occurred in the 1930s. See CONSTITUTION.

The actual political system prescribed by the constitution was more in keeping with Japan's tradition of British-style parliamentary democracy than the American system of checks and balances. An independent judiciary was established with the right of judicial review, but the role of the courts was generally not as strong as it was in the United States. The executive branch was also weaker, for the government system consisted of a prime minister and his cabinet, a majority of whom had to be members of the Diet, Japan's bicameral legislative assembly. Generally speaking, the new constitution tried to avoid the prewar problem of rule by militaristic elites by locating almost all political power in the popularly elected House of Representatives. Voters chose these representatives at least once every four years from multimember electoral districts. This voting system tended to be weighted in favor of the rural districts. The multimember system also minimized the practical effects of slight swings in the popular vote, thereby aiming to make the new government of Japan more responsible to the public, yet also less likely to be captured by the popular emotions of the moment.

Political power during nearly all the first 30 years of the new constitution, except for a short-lived socialist government in 1947–48, has been held by a group of conservatives that after 1955 was known as the LIBERAL DEMOCRATIC PARTY (LDP). The party was actually a group of five or six factions that put up candidates in the multimember electoral districts. The political stance of individual members varied somewhat, but there was a general consensus on the importance of the capitalist economic system, the need for close ties with the United States, and the advisability of using most available government funds to encourage high economic growth. The party was heavily influenced by Japan's elite national bureaucracy, as witnessed by the fact that prime ministers YOSHIDA SHIGERU, KISHI NOBUSUKE, IKEDA HAYATO, SATŌ EISAKU, FUKUDA TAKEO, and ŌHIRA MASAYOSHI had all been prominent government officials. It also had strong ties with the business world, farmers, and those who were relatively satisfied with the progress of the nation. A rising group of urban dwellers concerned about pollution and a lack of social services gradually cut into the percentage of popular vote that the LDP received, and the party's strength declined from 66.1 percent of the vote and two-thirds of the House of Representatives seats in 1952 to 47 percent of the vote and 55 percent of the seats in 1972. This downward trend continued into the mid-1970s; however, the party began to recover in the late 1970s, and in 1980 it held 47.9 percent of the vote and 55.6 percent of the seats.

The most powerful opposition party during much of this period was the JAPAN SOCIALIST PARTY (JSP). Emerging after the war as a mildly Christian and Marxist party, the Socialists elected KATAYAMA TETSU as prime minister to head a coalition government with other parties. It ruled from 24 May 1947 to 10 March 1948, when it fell victim to factional squabbles and the economic difficulties of the Occupation period. The party split in 1951 over the ratification of the SAN FRANCISCO PEACE TREATY and the first of the UNITED STATES–JAPAN SECURITY TREATIES, reunited in 1955, and then split again in 1960 into the more leftist Japan Socialist Party and the more centrist DEMOCRATIC SOCIALIST PARTY. Even then, the JSP continued to be divided between men such as SAKISAKA ITSURŌ and NARITA TOMOMI, who wished it to be a proletarian party with a neutralist or even anti-American stance in the cold war, and men such as EDA SABURŌ, whose "Eda Vision" mixed British parliamentarianism, American living standards, and Japanese antimilitarism with Soviet levels of welfare. The party was particularly dependent for money and votes upon the SŌHYŌ labor union, and hence, workers in government-owned enterprises, intellectuals, and those who felt alienated from conservative rule. The party captured 33 percent of the vote and 36 percent of the Diet seats in 1958 but declined to 22 percent of the vote and 24 percent of the seats in 1972, and 19.3 percent of the vote and 20.9 percent of the seats in 1980. The Democratic Socialist Party had 7 percent of the vote and 4 percent of the seats in 1972, and 6.6 percent of the vote and 6.3 percent of the seats in 1980.

The JAPAN COMMUNIST PARTY (JCP) was also active in this period. Emerging from the war as one of the few groups whose members were imprisoned for outspoken opposition to militarism, it initially adopted a program of moderation. The party won 10 percent of the vote and 7.5 percent of the seats in the 1949 election, a time when the failures of the Socialist government of Katayama made the JSP vulnerable. General MacArthur's ban of strikes by public employees and the "RED PURGE" of the post-1949 period, cut into JCP activities, and public support was eroded by their turn to more violent tactics; in the election of 1952 it lost all of its Diet seats. After a brief period of underground activity, the party rebuilt painfully through the chaos caused by the Sino-Soviet split, and in 1972 it won 11 percent of the vote and 8 percent of the seats. In 1980 it won 9.8 percent of the vote and 5.7 percent of the seats. Even then the party was in a difficult position, distrusted by many Japanese who equated communism with the Soviet Union or scorned by "real" radicals who preached a mixture of Maoism, anarchism, and terrorism.

The middle ground between these Marxist parties and the conservative Liberal Democrats was occupied by a wide variety of organizations, the most important of which was the KŌMEITŌ (Clean Government Party). The Kōmeitō was created by the Sōka Gakkai, a "new religion" sect whose often fierce devotion to the NICHIREN SECT of Buddhism won it large numbers of both adherents and enemies. Officially recognized as a party in 1964, the Kōmeitō won 11 percent of the vote and 10 percent of the seats in the 1969 election for the lower house of the Diet. The Sōka Gakkai's attempt to repress a book critical of its practices aroused public antipathy, and the party declared itself independent of the Sōka Gakkai in 1970, partly to broaden its appeal and partly to meet constitutional requirements that church be separated from state. In 1972 it won 9 percent of the votes but only 6 percent of the seats. In the 1980 election it won 9.0 percent of the vote and 6.5 percent of the seats. The party's fortunes were restored, but the Kōmeitō never became in this period the "middle way" between the older and more sharply divided parties.

Critics of this party system have thus had ample grounds for their complaints. They have charged that the conservatives were too often dominated by an unholy alliance of bureaucrats and capitalists tainted by their wartime activities. The conservatives' electoral successes were ascribed to "money politics" rather than ability and wide appeal. The opposition parties were criticized by the public for their seemingly endless bickering over ideological issues and for their inability to do more than slowly whittle away at the LDP's huge majorities. Japan, it was charged, was not a democracy, but rather a "one-and-one-half-party" system in which conservatives ruled while socialists protested in vain (see POLITICAL PARTIES).

Supporters of the system, on the other hand, point to much that is stable. The 1947 constitution, once criticized for being imposed upon the Japanese by the Americans, appears to be fully accepted and effective. Voting rates are consistently high; in 1980 they were an impressive 75 percent (overall national average). A well-educated public is generally informed on at least domestic issues. Furthermore, there has been a change from the confrontational politics of the early postwar period to a greater accommodation and cooperation among the political parties.

Economic Development —— By 1947, in part because of the exigencies of the cold war, both Americans and Japanese began to turn toward measures to revitalize the economy. The ZAIBATSU or financial combines had suffered when their holding companies were disbanded and their stocks placed for sale upon the open market. Further attempts to fragment their economic power were gradually abandoned after 1947. LABOR UNIONS, newly enfranchised by Occupation law, began a series of disruptive strikes but were soon limited by an Occupation order of 31 January 1947 that outlawed a general strike and by later legislation that limited the right of public employees to express any form of dissent. Occupation-sponsored reforms of agriculture raised productivity by encouraging investment in the land, and other, more technical fiscal policies worked to control high inflation. Perhaps most important of all, heavy American war purchase orders made after the outbreak of the Korean War in June 1950 provided Japanese industry with the stimulus it needed for substantial economic growth. By 1952 production was back to its 1936 level.

Foreign Affairs —— As long as Japan was under the Occupation, foreign affairs posed no real problems, but after independence was regained in 1952, such questions as what measures Japan should take to protect its safety and how it would confront a world divided into two hostile camps had to be solved. Even before the end of the Occupation, the American government had begun to press the Japanese to rearm. Some conservatives, such as Prime Minister HATOYAMA ICHIRŌ, wanted the clause renouncing war (known as article 9) taken out of the constitution so that Japan could in fact have an army. Others, including socialist leaders, saw no place for the military, since the prewar power vacuum in East Asia had been filled by a newly unified China and the nuclear superpowers, the United States and the USSR. After bitter debate, Prime Minister Yoshida Shigeru started a NATIONAL POLICE RESERVE in 1950 to replace American Occupation troops that had been sent from Japan to Korea; this evolved into the SELF DEFENSE FORCES in 1954.

The question of American military bases, meanwhile, remained controversial. The United States and its allies agreed to restore sovereignty to Japan in the San Francisco Peace Treaty of 8 September 1951 only after Prime Minister Yoshida formally promised to settle certain outstanding fishery issues, to deal only with the Chinese Nationalist goverment on Taiwan, and to sign, also on 8 September 1951, a Mutual Security Pact permitting US troops to stay on their bases in Japan. Subsequent battles between protesters and police protecting the base at Sunagawa in 1954 led to a decision by a lower court in 1956 that the bases violated article 9 of the constitution, but this decision was overturned by a Supreme Court ruling that sidestepped the question of judicial review (see SUNAGAWA CASE). Other incidents, such as an American sentry's shooting of a woman gathering scrap metal (see GIRARD CASE) led to a new security pact in 1960 giving Japan more authority over the stationing of American troops and permitting either side to withdraw from the pact after a year's notice. Publication of the 1960 pact led to the most massive political protest in Japanese history (see PEACE MOVEMENT), but it was generally agreed that the protest was as much against Prime Minister Kishi Nobusuke, a former member of TŌJŌ HIDEKI's wartime cabinet, as it was against the United States. There was almost no opposition to the renewal of the security treaty in 1970, especially since President Nixon had promised in 1969 to return Okinawa to Japan in 1972.

As Japan moved into the 1960s, trade problems came rapidly to the fore. Using reparations payments in ways that strengthened trade ties, the Japanese government moved from an almost total lack of foreign trade to a situation where some 10 percent of the GNP was absorbed in foreign trade. (This figure was about twice that of the United States but roughly equal to that of some European nations.) It presented the world with a major new set of export products such as automobiles, ships, transistors, and cameras. High-precision products replaced the cheap goods that had dominated Japanese exports prior to the war. Some foreign competitors charged that these exports were being made by cheap labor and that they were being exported by a government that refused to allow foreigners to import to Japan. These charges were largely false; Japan exported well because its products were of good quality.

Japanese relations with the Soviet Union have been strained throughout the postwar period. Diplomatic relations were normalized only in 1956, and as of 1980 the 1951 San Francisco Peace Treaty was still under negotiation. The main problem has been Japanese claims to certain northern territories. In 1945 the Russians seized the entire Kuril chain of islands from Japan. Although the Japanese have requested the return of the two southernmost islands, Kunashiri and Etorofu, as a precondition for a peace treaty, the USSR has refused to discuss the problem at all (the USSR had already agreed to hand over the island of Shikotan and the Habomai Islands upon the signing of a treaty; see SOVIET-JAPANESE JOINT DECLARATION).

Trade with mainland China, meanwhile, grew slowly from 1952 to 1957. After a temporary slump during China's cultural revolution it began to revive, and by the late 1960s Japan was the leading trading partner of the People's Republic of China (PRC). Formal relations with the PRC were established in September 1972 during a visit to China by Prime Minister TANAKA KAKUEI. Hitherto Japan had been reluctant to take this step out of fear that recognition of the PRC might anger the United States and threaten Japan's alignment with it, but President Nixon's surprise announcement in 1971 that he would visit the PRC in early 1972 (see NIXON SHOCKS) removed this restraint. Formal relations were broken with Taiwan, but informal ties and a steadily growing trade relationship were retained. In fact, Japan's trade with Taiwan was about as large as trade with the PRC.

The End of an Era? —— Shortly after the Nixon shocks revealed the fragile nature of the all-important American relationship, the OIL CRISIS OF 1973 reminded Japanese of how fragile their relations were with countries holding vital stocks of raw materials. Although the government was able to recover fairly quickly by adopting a more positive pro-Arab policy, growth dropped to only 5–6 percent, the percentage of unemployed rose to about 2 percent of the work force, and the government experienced record budget deficits. As Europe and the United States started putting pressure on Japan to reduce its embarrassingly high trade surpluses with these areas of the world, the Japanese were forced to undertake some restrictive measures while pointing out that their overall trade accounts were not as favorable as those of the West. To put this another way, the Japanese argued that they needed a healthy trade surplus with the West to pay for their huge trade deficits ($23 billion in 1979) with the OPEC (Organization of Petroleum Exporting Countries) nations. It was unclear how long this explanation would satisfy Western nations faced with their own political problems.

Meanwhile there was also a series of dramatic shocks on the domestic front. Just when LDP support was already quite weak, a major scandal over airplane purchases (the LOCKHEED SCANDAL) revealed an unsavory combination of right-wing machinations and political corruption that led to the indictment of former Prime Minister Tanaka Kakuei. Votes for the LDP actually increased slightly after Prime Minister Ōhira died in the midst of the 1980 election campaign, but it was also clear that voters felt caught between a conservative party too long in power and a fragmented opposition that was often too radical to be appealing. In a decade in which the literary giants MISHIMA YUKIO and KAWABATA YASUNARI committed suicide, radical students fought bitter battles over Tōkyō's huge Narita international airport, and other intellectuals such as ŌE KENZABURŌ spoke bitterly of present-day absurdities, many people naturally wondered if the best years of the postwar period had passed.

The answer to this question depended in large part on the perspective of the viewer. Certainly much of Japan's traditional beauty appeared to have been sacrificed to a rather tawdry materialism. Male workers were extraordinarily productive and well-rewarded, but women were largely relegated to roles that Western feminists would find unsatisfactory. The streets were safe from violent crime, but organized crime maintained a shadowy world of gambling, prostitution, and loan sharking. If most Westerners rejoiced in an honest and gracious society whose growth rate was only "5–6 percent," many Japanese wondered what their future identity would be. Diverse, hard-working, troubled, delightful, postwar Japan was clearly a complex and fascinating nation of intelligent people dedicated to avoiding the mistakes of the past while maintaining the best of their culture.

■ ——James C. Abegglen, *Management and Worker: The Japanese Solution* (1973). William Cummings, *Education and Equality in Japan* (1980). I. M. Destler, Hideo Sato, and Priscilla Clapp, ed, *Managing an Alliance: The Politics of US–Japanese Relations* (1976). George DeVos and Hiroshi Wagatsuma, *Japan's Invisible Race* (1967). Haruhiro Fukui, *Party in Power: The Japanese Liberal-Democrats and Policy-Making* (1970). Frank Gibney, *Japan: The Fragile Superpower* (1975). Kazuo Kawai, *Japan's American Interlude* (1960). Joyce Lebra, Joy Paulson, and Elizabeth Powers, ed, *Women in Changing Japan* (1976). Nakane Chie, *Japanese Society* (1970). George R. Packard, *Protest in Tokyo: The Security Treaty Crisis of 1960* (1966). Hugh Patrick and Henry Rosovsky, ed, *Asia's New Giant: How the Japanese Economy Works* (1976). T. J. Pempel, *Policy Making in Contemporary Japan* (1977). Edwin O. Reischauer, *Japan: The Story of a Nation* (3rd ed, 1981). Robert A. Scalapino, ed, *The Foreign Policy of Modern Japan* (1977). J. A. A. Stockwin, *Divided Politics in a Growth Economy* (1975). Nathaniel P. Thayer, *How the Conservatives Rule Japan* (1969). Ezra Vogel, *Japan's New Middle Class* (1971). Arthur Taylor von Mehren, ed, *Law in Japan* (1963). Robert C. Ward, *Japan's Political System* (1978). Martin E. Weinstein, *Japan's Postwar Defense Policy* (1971). Kozo Yamamura, *Economic Policy in Postwar Japan* (1967).　　　Peter FROST

Hita

City in northwestern Ōita Prefecture, Kyūshū, on the river Chikugogawa. A prosperous castle town during the Edo period (1600–1868), Hita was noted for its merchants. Its chief industry is lumbering and the manufacture of *geta* (wooden clogs), and other wood products. Sightseeing spots are Tsukikuma Park and the remains of Kangien, a school built in 1817 by the scholar HIROSE TANSŌ. Special local products of the city are ONTA WARE pottery and Hita lacquer ware. Pop: 65,356.

Hita Basin

(Hita Bonchi). In western Ōita Prefecture, Kyūshū. Consisting of the flood plain of the river Mikumagawa (the upper reaches of the Chikugogawa), this small basin is surrounded by andesite mountains with flattish summits. Orchards are located on the uplands and rice is grown in the lowlands, while Japanese cedar grows on the surrounding mountains. The remains of ancient ornamented tombs have been discovered in the area. Hita is the major city. Length: 6 km (3.7 mi); width: 8 km (5.0 mi).

Hitachi

City in northeastern Ibaraki Prefecture, central Honshū, on the Pacific Ocean coast. A POST-STATION TOWN surrounded by farming villages during the Edo period (1600–1868), with the wide-scale exploitation of the Hitachi Mines (the forerunner of the NIPPON MINING CO, LTD) in 1905 and the establishment of HITACHI, LTD, in 1909, it developed rapidly into a mining and manufacturing city. It was almost completely destroyed during World War II but recovered after the war; a number of its factories are engaged in the smelting of copper and the production of electric machinery and appliances, electric wire and cable, and cement. The port of Hitachi, opened in 1960, is used for importing industrial raw material and exporting finished products. Fishing is another important industry. Pop: 204,612.

Hitachi Cable, Ltd

(Hitachi Densen). Manufacturer of a wide variety of wire products, including power cables, communication cables, insulated wire, and wire coil, as well as rolled copper and industrial rubber products. Third largest in the electric wire industry, the company was founded in 1956 when the electric wire division of HITACHI, LTD, was made an independent firm. The company's chief export product is power cable; its export ratio was 23 percent in 1980. It has overseas offices in the United Kingdom, Australia, and the Philippines, three production plants in Southeast Asia, and a sales company in the United States. The firm is also pursuing the development of new products such as superconductive wire and optical fiber communication cable. Sales for the fiscal year ending March 1982 totaled ¥203 billion (US $843.3 million), of which cable accounted for 36 percent, other types of electric wire 42 percent, rolled copper products 17 percent, and industrial rubber goods 5 percent. In the same year capitalization was ¥14 billion (US $58.2 million). The head office is in Tōkyō.

Hitachi Chemical Co, Ltd

(Hitachi Kasei Kōgyō). Comprehensive processor of resins. Founded in 1962 when the chemical products division of HITACHI, LTD, became an independent firm. With a broad technological capacity in both organic and inorganic chemistry, the company produces a wide variety of products. The company's four major products consist of electrical equipment, synthetic resins, housing equipment, and construction and environmental products. Many of its products in the areas of electrical insulation materials and electronic components enjoy the largest shares in the market. The company is also working actively to develop products with a high value added such as fine chemicals and organic-inorganic composite products. Copper-clad laminated sheets for printed circuits and electric insulating varnish are exported throughout the world. Overseas operations have developed apace, and the firm controls subsidiary corporations in the United States, West Germany, Taiwan, Singapore, and Hong Kong. Sales for the fiscal year ending March 1982 totaled ¥167.5 billion (US $695.8 million) and capitalization was ¥7.5 billion (US $31.2 million). Corporate headquarters are in Tōkyō.

Hitachi, Ltd

(Hitachi Seisakusho). Major electric machinery manufacturer producing heavy electrical equipment, consumer products, communications and electronic equipment, and transportation equipment. It is the largest electric machinery maker in Japan and the leading member of the Hitachi group, composed of 540 companies. It was established under its present name in 1910 in the town of Hitachi (Ibaraki Prefecture) as an electric machinery repair plant for Kuhara Kōgyōsho, a company founded by ODAIRA NAMIHEI, and it became one of the most important enterprises of the pre–World War II Nissan *zaibatsu*. Developing its own technology, Hitachi Seisakusho initiated production of generators, transformers, various types of industrial machinery, and electric locomotives. It also set up plants for the production of copper wire and components for cast iron products as part of its program to establish the domestic production of heavy electric machinery. It became independent of Kuhara Kōgyōsho in 1920, and in the 1930s solidified its position as a comprehensive producer of electric machinery with a vertically integrated system for producing various types of products from raw materials. In 1941 Hitachi Seiki Co, Ltd, became independent of the parent company, followed by the HITACHI ZŌSEN CORPORATION in 1947. After World War II, with the reconstruction of the electric power industry and the resultant large demand for generators and transmission equipment, Hitachi experienced a recovery and started production of radio and television sets and other household appliances. With the great increase in demand for household electrical appliances stimulated by the rapid growth of the Japanese economy from 1955 on, Hitachi continued to expand. In 1959 it entered the field of electronic computers and later the area of integrated circuits and other advanced electronic products. It also established over 30 subsidiary and affiliated firms in Southeast Asia, the United States, and Europe, and initiated overseas production and sales. Because of its continued research and development, Hitachi's technology is now at the highest levels internationally. Sales for the fiscal year ending March 1982 totaled ¥2.1 trillion (US $8.7 billion), of which heavy electrical machinery accounted for 30 percent, household electrical appliances 21 percent, communications and electronics equipment 26 percent, industrial machinery 12 percent, and transportation equipment 11 percent. In the same year the export ratio was 29 percent and the company was capitalized at ¥138.2 billion (US $574.1 million). Corporate headquarters are located in Tōkyō.

Hitachi Metals, Ltd

(Hitachi Kinzoku). Manufacturer of high-grade special steels (under the brand name YSS), pipe fittings, malleable castings, and magnets. Founded in 1956 as a member of the Hitachi group, the company was a pioneer in the fields of casting and special steels. The company maintains a 23 percent export ratio stemming from its active efforts to expand overseas markets. It has also formed a system of international division of labor by coordinating the production schedules of its domestic plants, four subsidiary firms in the United States, one in Europe, and two in Southeast Asia. The future goal of the company is to develop new raw materials and products with a high value added. Sales for the fiscal year ending March 1982 totaled ¥249 billion (US $1 billion) and capitalization stood at ¥13.7 billion (US $56.9 million). The head office is in Tōkyō.

Hitachi Ōta

City in northern Ibaraki Prefecture, central Honshū. During the Sengoku period (1467–1568), it flourished as a castle town of the SATAKE FAMILY. In the Edo period (1600–1868) it became a part of the Mito domain ruled by a branch of the TOKUGAWA FAMILY and prospered as a distribution center for the area. Traditional products are Japanese paper (washi) and tobacco. Agricultural produce includes rice, konnyaku (a popular ingredient in Japanese cooking), and other fruits and vegetables. Many residents commute to the cities of Mito and Hitachi. Of historic interest are Seizansō, where TOKUGAWA MITSUKUNI retired, and Zuiryūzan, the family grave of the Mito daimyō and some of their retainers. Pop: 35,980.

Hitachi Plant Engineering & Construction Co, Ltd

(Hitachi Puranto Kensetsu). Comprehensive engineering and construction firm specializing in the construction of power plants, industrial plants, buildings, and pollution-control facilities. Established in 1929, the company joined the Hitachi group in 1940 and assumed its present name in 1968. It has enjoyed steady growth because of its efforts in quality control, strict job-site safety measures, and development of advanced construction techniques. It completed 128 projects in 43 countries in the two decades after 1957. Future plans emphasize the construction of utility plants and optimally efficient pollution-control facilities. Sales for the fiscal year ending March 1982 totaled ¥117 billion (US $486 million), distributed as follows: power plants 37.5 percent, building facilities 20.6 percent, pollution-control facilities 20.6 percent, and industrial machinery 21.3 percent. Capitalization stood at ¥5 billion (US $20.7 million) in the same year. Corporate headquarters are in Tōkyō.

Hitachi, Prince (1935–)

(Hitachi no Miya Masahito). Title of the second son of Emperor HIROHITO. As a youth he was known as Yoshi no Miya. In 1958 he graduated from the engineering department of Gakushūin University and continued his studies at Tōkyō University, where he did research in biology. In 1964 he married Tsugaru Hanako and established the princely house of Hitachi (Hitachi no Miya ke). He is director of the Japan Council for Crippled Children, the Society of Inventors, and the Japan Association for the Protection of Wild Birds.

Hitachi Sales Corporation

(Hitachi Kaden Hambai). General wholesale agent of electrical household appliances produced by HITACHI, LTD. The firm was founded in 1955 when it was separated from Hitachi, Ltd, and set up as an independent firm. Since initiating export operations in 1967, numerous sales companies have been established in such countries as the United States, Canada, and England. Sales for the fiscal year ending March 1982 totaled ¥581.8 billion (US $2.4 billion), of which 36 percent came from export sales. In the same year capitalization stood at ¥6.1 billion (US $25.3 million). Corporate headquarters are located in Tōkyō.

Hitachi Zōsen Corporation

(Hitachi Zōsen). Company engaged in shipbuilding and the manufacture and sale of various types of machinery and plants. Hitachi Zōsen's forerunner was Ōsaka Iron Works, established by a British trader in Ōsaka in 1881. It is one of the three largest shipbuilders in Japan, along with ISHIKAWAJIMA–HARIMA HEAVY INDUSTRIES CO, LTD, and MITSUBISHI HEAVY INDUSTRIES, LTD. Ships constructed by Hitachi in the peak year of 1975 totaled 1,418,588 gross tons, which comprised 10 percent of all ships built in Japan that year and 5 percent of the world's tonnage. The company has technical tie-up contracts with Westinghouse Electric Co in the United States and other companies in Denmark, Switzerland, and West Germany. It established a trading company in Panama in 1976 to sell ships, ocean development equipment, and land machinery, and in the same year, a company to build industrial plants in Brazil. Sales for the fiscal year ending March 1982 totaled ¥484 billion (US $2 billion), of which exports constituted 61 percent. The company was capitalized at ¥42.4 billion (US $176.1 million) in the same year. Corporate headquarters are in Ōsaka.

hitobashira

(literally, "human pillar"). A legendary type of human sacrifice. Many Japanese legends claim that during the construction of bridges, dikes, and castles in ancient times a human being was buried alive to ensure the durability of the structure. The earliest mention of such a sacrifice appears in the chronicle Nihon shoki (720) in the section on the reign of Emperor NINTOKU. The legend concerning the building of the Nagara Bridge at Tarumi (in present-day Hyōgo Prefecture) is particularly well known; in it, a villager unintentionally designates himself as the victim. Many of the victims in the legends are women. Human sacrifice legends are believed to have been spread by female shamans (MIKO) who participated in rituals to placate water deities (SUIJIN).   SUCHI Tokuhei

hitodama

The spirit that is supposed to depart from the human body at the time of death and afterwards; commonly believed to take the form of a bluish white ball of fire with a tail. Seeing hitodama was traditionally regarded as a premonition of one's own death, although various ways of exorcising them are mentioned in medieval literature. Even today one hears of people who claim to have seen hitodama hovering over rooftops or in graveyards at night. Shooting stars, phosphorescence, and other natural phenomena are sometimes taken for hitodama.   INOKUCHI Shōji

hitogaeshi

(literally, "returning the people"). Policies designed in 1790 and 1843 to encourage peasants in urban areas to return to the countryside. Attracted by the growing wealth of the cities and despairing of increasingly burdensome taxes, many peasants left the villages during the Edo period (1600–1868), a trend that became particularly pronounced after 1700. In 1790 the chief senior councillor *(rōjū shuseki)* MATSUDAIRA SADANOBU, as part of his KANSEI REFORMS, encouraged peasants in Edo to return to their villages by supplying the necessary transportation money, but this attempt was basically unsuccessful. Later, in 1843, in carrying out the TEMPŌ REFORMS, the chief senior councillor MIZUNO TADAKUNI issued an order (the Hitogaeshi no Hō) requiring peasants in Edo to return to the countryside, which had been ravaged by the famines of 1833 and 1836. He also forbade peasants to move to Edo and limited the length of time they could work as servants in the city. The order was temporarily successful, but since wages in the city far exceeded those in the countryside, it had little effect in the long run.

hitojichi

A hostage or the practice of offering a hostage as guarantee of good faith in political agreements such as alliance and surrender. The practice was most common during the Sengoku (Warring States) period (1467–1568). The hostage, usually a relative or retainer, was kept as a prisoner, concubine, or adopted child and was killed in case of a breach of contract. Perhaps the most famous example of a child *hitojichi* is TOKUGAWA IEYASU, who was once held hostage for 12 years. The policy of the Tokugawa shogunate (1603–1867) requiring *daimyō* to leave their families in Edo (now Tōkyō) may be seen as an institutionalized form of the practice (see SANKIN KŌTAI). A debtor might offer a relative or servant to a creditor as a guarantee, a practice that remained common until the end of the Edo period in 1868.

Hitomi Kinue (1907–1931)

The first Japanese woman athlete of international stature. Born in Okayama Prefecture; graduated from Nihon Joshi Taiiku Semmon Gakkō (now Tōkyō Women's College of Physical Education). In 1926 at the 2nd Women's World Athletic Championship in Sweden, Hitomi set a new world record in the long jump (5.5 m; 18 ft) and became the first Japanese woman athlete to win an international championship. She was singled out as the most valuable athlete at the competition for single-handedly placing Japan fifth overall among participating nations with 15 points (won in various events). In the 1928 Olympics held in Amsterdam, she placed second after Linda Radke of Germany in the 800-meter run, becoming the first Japanese woman to win an Olympic medal. A versatile athlete, she set world records 10 times in seven different events from 1926 to 1929. She died of tuberculosis in 1931. *TAKEDA Fumio*

Hito no Michi → PL Kyōdan

hitorishizuka

Chloranthus japonicus. A perennial herb of the family Chloranthaceae that grows wild in thinly forested mountains and in shady thickets in the hill areas throughout Japan. It stands about 10–20 centimeters (4–8 in) in height. Its single stalk stands erect and has 3 or 4 nodes; from the lower nodes grow little scaly leaves and from the top node grow two pairs of elliptical leaves, opposite each other. The leaves have serrated edges and are dark green in color. In early spring a flower stalk grows at the top of the stem and produces numerous blossoms in a spike, each consisting of a pistil and three prominent white stamens. Another variety with two or more stalks, known as the *futarishizuka (C. serratus)*, blooms in May. The family includes a small evergreen tree *senryō (C. glaber)* which, with its clusters of red round fruits, is a favorite cut flower for the New Year holidays. *MATSUDA Osamu*

Hitotsubashi University

(Hitotsubashi Daigaku). A national university located in the city of Kunitachi, Tōkyō Prefecture. Its predecessor was the Shōhō Kōshūjo (School for Commercial Law), which was established by MORI ARINORI in 1875. It became a government institution in 1884, changing its name to Tōkyō Shōgyō Gakkō (Tōkyō School of Commerce). There were a number of subsequent name changes: Kōtō Shōgyō Gakkō (Higher School of Commerce) in 1887, Tōkyō Kōtō Shōgyō Gakkō (Tōkyō Higher School of Commerce) in 1902, Tōkyō

Shōka Daigaku (Tōkyō University of Commerce) in 1920, and finally Hitotsubashi Daigaku in 1949. It maintains faculties of economics, law, social science, and commerce, and the Institute of Economic Research.

hitotsume kozō

Goblin with a single eye in the middle of the forehead; one of the fantastic and grotesque creatures (see BAKEMONO) that appear in Japanese folktales. It generally takes the form of a novice monk *(kozō)* but is sometimes associated with the Shintō gods of mountain or field (YAMA NO KAMI; TA NO KAMI). In the Kantō and Tōhoku regions it was believed to appear on the night of *kotoyōka,* a taboo day falling on the eighth day of the 2nd and 12th lunar months, and was warded off by attaching an open mesh basket upside-down to a pole set up before a house. The many mesh "eyes" of the openwork basket were believed to shame and intimidate the one-eyed creature. *INOKUCHI Shōji*

hitoyogiri

A vertical bamboo flute with a notched mouthpiece and five finger holes, closely related to the SHAKUHACHI but shorter and thinner in size with only one node along its length *(hitoyogiri:* "one node cut"). Although the name *hitoyogiri* is often used to designate those vertical flutes which appeared in Japan during the 14th and 15th centuries, and especially those played by mendicant *komusō* (straw-hat priests) in the 16th century, it was not until the beginning of the 17th century that the distinction between the standard *hitoyogiri* (one node along its length) and the standard *shakuhachi* (three, and later, seven nodes along its length) became clear. The instrument reached its zenith in the late 17th century when, in addition to maintaining its own repertoire of short solo pieces, it was used in a variety of popular musical genres. Unable to adapt to the evolving musical style of the period, it declined rapidly in the 18th century; an attempt at revival in the early 19th century was unsuccessful. *Ralph SAMUELSON*

Hitoyoshi

City in southern Kumamoto Prefecture, Kyūshū, on the river Kumagawa. During the Kamakura period (1185–1333), Hitoyoshi was a prosperous castle town of the Sagara family. Its proximity to abundant forests has made lumbering its principal industry. The alkali waters of the Hitoyoshi Hot Spring and boat excursions down the Kumagawa are popular with tourists. Pop: 42,236.

Hitoyoshi Basin

(Hitoyoshi Bonchi). In southern Kumamoto Prefecture, Kyūshū. Surrounded by the Kyūshū Mountains, this basin consists of the flood plain of the river Kumagawa's upper reaches and alluvial fans below the fault scarp. Rice is grown on the fans, in fields irrigated by canals, and tobacco growing, dairy farming, and sericulture are also practiced. The major city is Hitoyoshi. Area: approximately 72 sq km (28 sq mi).

Hiuchigadake

Also known as Hiuchidake. Conical volcano in southwest Fukushima Prefecture, northern Honshū; the highest peak in the Tōhoku region. Lava flowing from it dammed the river Tadamigawa to form the swampy regions of OZE. It is part of Nikkō National Park. Height: 2,346 m (7,695 ft).

Hoan Jōrei → Peace Preservation Law of 1887

Hoantai → National Safety Forces

Hoashi Banri (1778–1852)

Scholar and educator of the latter part of the Edo period (1600–1868) whose studies combined Confucianism, Buddhism, and Western science. He was the son of a councillor *(karō)* in the service of the *daimyō* of the Hiji domain in Bungo Province (now Ōita Prefecture). From age 14 he studied under Waki Guzan (1764–1814), an adherent of the Confucian scholar MIURA BAIEN's dogma that the world should be studied objectively without blind recourse to tradition. Banri continued his studies in Ōsaka under Nakai Chikuzan, (1730–1804), Minakawa Kien (1734–1807), and Kamei Nammei (1743–1814). In 1804 he became an instructor at the Hiji domainal school and also opened a private school, where he had hundreds of students. He taught himself Dutch in order to read Western works on natural science. Beginning in 1832, he served for three years as a councillor to his domain lord and worked for domainal reform. He then resigned and returned to teaching. Banri's growing concern over the effects of Japan's NATIONAL SECLUSION from the outside world since the 1630s led him to write many works that combined WESTERN LEARNING with Confucian and Buddhist philosophy and his own speculation. His 1836 work Kyūritsu (Mastery of Truth) discussed such subjects as planets, constellations, the earth, and gravity; his other books included Tōsempu ron (Treatise by an Eastern Recluse), on political economy, and Igaku keimō (Instruction in Medicine), on Western medicine. He emphasized the practical uses of learning and was especially concerned with administration and public welfare.

Hōchi shimbun

A large sports and recreation tabloid published daily in Tōkyō and Ōsaka. Originally known as the YŪBIN HŌCHI SHIMBUN, it began publishing in Tōkyō in 1872 and established itself as a leading Meiji-period (1868–1912) newspaper. In 1894 the name was changed to Hōchi shimbun, and under the management of Miki Zempachi, the Hōchi became a leader among large commercial newspapers. With the advent of the 1920s the Hōchi faced strong competition from other large dailies like the ASAHI SHIMBUN and the YOMIURI SHIMBUN, with which it briefly merged in 1942. In 1946 it came back as an evening paper, and then in 1950 changed over to a sports and recreation newspaper and was distributed mornings. It is a very popular paper because of its comprehensive sports coverage and feature items on recreation. Circulation: 684,000 in Tōkyō and 187,000 in Ōsaka (1980).

Hodosan

Mountain in western Saitama Prefecture, central Honshū; near Chichibu–Tama National Park; it is famous for its views of the NAGATORO gorge, the Chichibu Mountains, and the Kantō Plain. Hodosan Shrine is at the foot of the mountain. Height: 497 m (1,630 ft).

Hoffmann, Johann Joseph (1805–1878)

German scholar of the Japanese and Chinese languages. He worked in Amsterdam as an assistant to Philipp Franz von SIEBOLD, a German physician and early scholar of Japanese culture who lived in Nagasaki during the 1820s. Hoffmann later served as the first professor of Japanese at Leyden University and laid the foundation for Japanese studies in Europe. He died in The Hague, never having set foot in Japan. He published several research works on Japan, including Japanische Spraakleer (1867), a grammar of the Japanese language. SHIMADA Masahiko

Hōfu

City in central Yamaguchi Prefecture, western Honshū, on the Inland Sea coast. Hōfu was a provincial capital in ancient and medieval times and a POST-STATION TOWN on the San'yōdō highway during the Edo period (1600–1868). The port of Mitajiri to the south was a base for ships belonging to the ruling Mōri family. It also shipped salt to various parts of the country. At present, the city is a major rice producer. Two gigantic textile and chemical plants are located in the coastal industrial zone. Historical sites include Hōfu Temmangū Shrine and the remains of an 8th-century provincial temple (KOKUBUNJI). Pop: 111,471.

Hōgen Disturbance

(Hōgen no Ran). Military conflict arising from rivalries within the imperial family, the FUJIWARA FAMILY, the MINAMOTO FAMILY, and the TAIRA FAMILY following the death of the retired emperor TOBA in 1156 (Hōgen 1). The reigning emperor, GO-SHIRAKAWA,

had the support of the regent Fujiwara no Tadamichi (1097–1164), but Tadamichi's ambitious younger brother Yorinaga (1120–56) sided with the retired emperor SUTOKU. Sutoku had the military backing of the Seiwa Genji leader Minamoto no Tameyoshi (1096–1156), while Tameyoshi's son MINAMOTO NO YOSHITOMO joined TAIRA NO KIYOMORI in support of Go-Shirakawa. Sutoku's faction attempted to seize power by force but was soon crushed by Yoshitomo and Kiyomori. Yorinaga was killed in the fighting, Tameyoshi was executed, and Sutoku was exiled. Although Go-Shirakawa thus won control of the imperial house, real political power had passed to the warrior Taira and Minamoto families, who immediately began their contest for supremacy (see HEIJI DISTURBANCE). G. Cameron HURST III

Hōgen monogatari

A war tale (GUNKI MONOGATARI) of the early part of the Kamakura period (1185–1333). It is an account of the power struggle for the imperial succession in the HŌGEN DISTURBANCE of 1156, the first such struggle in centuries to be settled by force, using members of the rising warrior class. It is often paired with HEIJI MONOGATARI, a tale of rebellion to gain control of the imperial court in 1160. Both tales are about the same length, similarly structured in three volumes, and have variant versions. In the early middle ages Hōgen was chanted by itinerant "lute priests" (BIWA HŌSHI), but was overshadowed in popularity by the HEIKE MONOGATARI, a narrative account of the TAIRA-MINAMOTO WAR, which was also chanted. Later versions of Hōgen monogatari seem intended to be read.

Volume 1 gives the background for the conflict: disposition of the throne by the retired emperor TOBA to successors unsatisfactory to his son, the retired emperor SUTOKU. This occasions a struggle in which the factions involved split both the highest court officials (members of the FUJIWARA FAMILY) and the MINAMOTO and TAIRA families, their military supporters.

This section also develops the disposition of the armies and portents of coming events. Volume 2 describes the attack by TAIRA NO KIYOMORI on Sutoku's citadel at the Shirakawa Palace. Despite MINAMOTO NO TAMETOMO's heroism, Sutoku's forces are defeated. Fujiwara no Yorinaga (1120–56) is mortally wounded, and chief military figures, both Minamoto and Taira, are executed. Volume 3 concerns the aftermath. The wounds of war are exacerbated, Sutoku is exiled, and the ill will engendered eventually leads to the HEIJI DISTURBANCE of 1160. The tale proper comes to an end with the sentimental visit by the poet-priest SAIGYŌ to Sutoku's grave at Shiramine (Kagawa Prefecture), although the latest popular version ends with Tametomo's exile and death on the island of Ōshima.

The major theme of the tale is the tragic consequences of violations of the natural order, which requires propriety and harmony in human relationships. In the disturbances, members of both the Fujiwara family and the imperial family are pitted against one another. Taira family members fight each other, and the Minamoto, too, turn against members of their own family. Throughout the tale, the focus is on the figure of Tametomo as a valiant samurai and tragic hero.

Thirty-eight distinctive texts of the Hōgen monogatari are organized into three "families": the nakaraibon, kotohirabon, and rufubon. The first includes a 1318 text, the earliest datable, and has the simplest, least elegant style. Kotohirabon texts are highest in literary quality, and unlike the other two, they are not structured chronologically. Rufubon—the texts circulated in printed form in the Edo period (1600–1868)—are chronological like nakaraibon, but in contrast to the emotional cast of kotohirabon, are moralistic. Only the rufubon have prologues, in KAMBUN, contributing to the didactic tone of the tale in these versions.

Unlike other war tales, themes from this gunki monogatari are not generally found in dramatic works, perhaps because of its unique premise, a conflict between members of the imperial line. Only two NŌ plays, no longer performed, are related to it: one about a magical sword mentioned in later versions, and one about Saigyō's Shiramine visit. Tametomo has a role in one KYŌGEN, but otherwise appears only much later in popular literature, woodblock prints, and as folk hero, particularly in the region of his exile. The Edo-period writer BAKIN used Tametomo as a hero in his historical fiction, Chinsetsu yumiharizuki.

━━━━ Nagazumi Yasuaki and Shimada Isao, ed, Hōgen monogatari; Heiji monogatari, in Nihon koten bungaku taikei, 31 (Iwanami Shoten, 1961). William R. Wilson, Hōgen monogatari: Tale of the Rebellion in Hōgen (1971). William R. WILSON

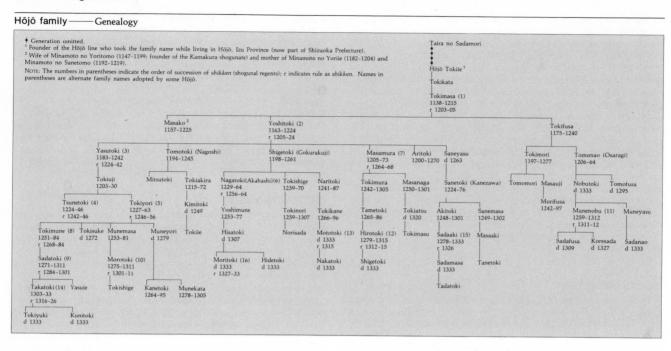

Hōjō family —— Genealogy

♦ Generation omitted.
[1] Founder of the Hōjō line who took the family name while living in Hōjō, Izu Province (now part of Shizuoka Prefecture).
[2] Wife of Minamoto no Yoritomo (1147–1199; founder of the Kamakura shogunate) and mother of Minamoto no Yoriie (1182–1204) and Minamoto no Sanetomo (1192–1219).
NOTE: The numbers in parentheses indicate the order of succession of *shikken* (shogunal regents); r indicates rule as *shikken*. Names in parentheses are alternate family names adopted by some Hōjō.

Hōgen no Ran → Hōgen Disturbance

hōgo → goroku

hōhei kōshō

(arsenals). In 1868 at Tōkyō and in 1870 at Ōsaka the new Meiji government established army arsenals with munitions facilities that it had confiscated from the Tokugawa shogunate (1603–1867) and *daimyō* domains. They received the name *hōhei kōshō* with the issuance of the Arsenal Ordinance (Hōhei Kōshō Jōrei) in November 1879, the culmination of a series of reorganizations in the 1870s. By the early 1890s their production of arms and ammunition fully met government demand. Existing facilities were enlarged and several new branch arsenals created during the Sino-Japanese (1894–95) and Russo-Japanese (1904–05) wars. From 1923 to 1945 the two main facilities were called the Tōkyō Kōshō and Ōsaka Kōshō and were supervised by the Army Arsenal (Rikugun Zōheishō). See also GOVERNMENT-OPERATED FACTORIES, MEIJI PERIOD.

Hohnen Oil Co, Ltd

(Hōnen Seiyu). Manufacturer of vegetable oils and oilseed meals, animal feeds, cornstarch, and synthetic resins. Since its founding in 1922 the company has directed its efforts toward the improvement of production technology and the development of new products chiefly centering on soybean oil and meal. The company leads the industry in the production of soybean oil and is second in the production of vegetable oils. It is dependent on overseas sources for all of its raw materials, including soybeans, rapeseed, and corn. In 1981 total sales were ¥103.3 billion (US $471.8 million) and capitalization was ¥2.8 billion (US $12.8 million). The company's headquarters are located in Tōkyō.

Hōitsu → Sakai Hōitsu

Hōji Conflict

(Hōji Kassen). A battle in 1247 (Hōji 1) in which the HŌJŌ FAMILY destroyed the MIURA FAMILY and thereby firmly established its sole authority as regents *(shikken)* of the Kamakura shogunate (1192–1333). A year after becoming shogunal regent, HŌJŌ TOKIYORI deliberately provoked into battle the powerful and flourishing family of Miura Yasumura, who was married to a daughter of the third Kamakura regent, HŌJŌ YASUTOKI, and a member of the

Council of State (Hyōjōshū). With the aid of his maternal grandfather, ADACHI KAGEMORI, Tokiyori destroyed the Miura family, forcing over 500 of its members and retainers to commit suicide. Thereafter, the actual power of the shogunate government was monopolized by the Hōjō family, although distant kinsmen of the MINAMOTO FAMILY still officially held the title of shōgun.

hōjin

(juristic person). An entity other than a natural person possessing a personality under law. *Hōjin* may be used of a public corporation, private corporation, foundation, stock company, or nonprofit corporation. Private schools, religious organizations, labor unions, professional societies, and sports organizations are examples of juristic persons. Chapter II of the CIVIL CODE, consisting of 51 articles, deals with juristic persons. The code provides that no juristic person can come into existence except under provisions set forth in the code or other laws. The code recognizes two general categories of juristic person: those relating to the public interest, in such fields as religion, charity, science, the arts, etc, which do not have gain or profit as their motive, and those relating to private interest.

Juristic persons have rights and duties, subject to the provisions of laws and ordinances and within the limits of their objectives as set forth in their articles of incorporation. In addition, they are responsible for any damage done to others by their directors or other representatives in the execution of their duties. Juristic persons may be created by different methods: special law enacted by the Diet; permit or license granted by an appropriate government agency; the satisfaction of requirements for organization as determined by law; and government order. In all cases articles of incorporation must cover such matters as the objectives of the organization, financial provisions, appointment and dismissal of officers, and qualification for membership. Dissolution must be carried out according to detailed provisions set forth in the Civil Code. See also GAIKOKU HŌJIN (foreign juristic person). *John M.* MAKI

Hōjō

City in northern Ehime Prefecture, Shikoku, on the Inland Sea. Main industries are textiles, ceramics, and agriculture (mandarin oranges, poultry, and onions). The main tourist attraction is the scenic island of Kashima, a part of the Inland Sea National Park. Pop: 30,409.

Hōjō Dansui (1663–1711)

HAIKU poet and writer of UKIYO-ZŌSHI, a genre of popular fiction of the Edo period (1600–1868). A disciple of SAIKAKU, he edited and published his master's manuscripts after his death. His own *ukiyo-zōshi* resemble in style and subject matter those of Saikaku. A representative work is *Chūya yōjin ki* (1707, An Account of Unrelenting Vigilance).

Hōjō family

1. Warrior family of the Kamakura period (1185–1333); as hereditary regents (SHIKKEN) of the KAMAKURA SHOGUNATE, the Hōjō ruled Japan for more than a century until they were destroyed in the KEMMU RESTORATION. The family was founded by a certain Taira no Tokiie, a descendant of the Kammu Heishi branch of the TAIRA FAMILY, who took the name Hōjō from a local area when he was named governor of Izu Province (now part of Shizuoka Prefecture). His grandson HŌJŌ TOKIMASA (1138–1215) befriended the boy MINAMOTO NO YORITOMO, who was exiled to Izu after his father was killed in an unsuccessful revolt against Taira dictatorship in Kyōto in 1160. Yoritomo married Tokimasa's daughter HŌJŌ MASAKO, and when he set up his military government at Kamakura in 1185 he was ably assisted by his father-in-law. Yoritomo died in 1199, leaving two incompetent sons, and Tokimasa, with the help of Masako, took effective control of the shogunate, becoming regent in 1203. He was succeeded in 1205 by his son HŌJŌ YOSHITOKI (r 1205–24), who further consolidated family rule by eliminating potential rivals and crushing a conspiracy (the JŌKYŪ DISTURBANCE) led by a retired emperor. He also laid the foundations of the TOKUSŌ system to ensure patrimonial succession to the family headship. His son HŌJŌ YASUTOKI (r 1224–42) created the post of cosigner (RENSHO) and the Council of State (HYŌJŌSHŪ) to assure political stability and ordered the compilation of the GOSEIBAI SHIKIMOKU, the legal code of the shogunate. The fifth regent, HŌJŌ TOKIYORI (r 1246–56), established the High Court (HIKITSUKE). Under the leadership of HŌJŌ TOKIMUNE (r 1268–84), the shogunate successfully defended Japan against the MONGOL INVASIONS of 1274 and 1281. The last Hōjō regent of importance was HŌJŌ TAKATOKI (r 1316–26), who remained in control of the shogunate after his retirement and twice frustrated the attempts of Emperor GO-DAIGO to overthrow it. In 1333, however, his principal commanders, ASHIKAGA TAKAUJI and NITTA YOSHISADA, turned against him and joined Go-Daigo's imperial restoration movement. With Kamakura under military attack, Takatoki and his family committed suicide. (See also HISTORY OF JAPAN: Kamakura history.)

2. Another Hōjō family, of the end of the Muromachi period (1333–1568) and the Azuchi-Momoyama period (1568–1600), were regional lords (SENGOKU DAIMYŌ) based in Odawara (in what is now Kanagawa Prefecture). They were unrelated to the earlier Hōjō and are sometimes called the Go-Hōjō (Later Hōjō). Founded by HŌJŌ SŌUN (1432–1519), the family was destroyed by TOYOTOMI HIDEYOSHI in the ODAWARA CAMPAIGN of 1590. Their five generations of power are described in the chronicle HŌJŌ GODAI KI.

Kimura Shigemitsu

Hōjō godai ki

(Chronicle of the Hōjō Family through Five Generations). A chronologically arranged collection of military episodes and anecdotes belonging to the genre GUNKI MONOGATARI (war tales); compiled early in the Edo period (1600–1868). It recounts the rise and fall of the Later Hōjō family (Go-Hōjō, see HŌJŌ FAMILY), a warrior house that dominated the Kantō region from its founding by HŌJŌ SŌUN (1432–1519) until the defeat of Hōjō Ujinao (1562–91) by the national unifier TOYOTOMI HIDEYOSHI. It is composed of selections from the *Keichō kembunshū* (Collection of Things Seen and Heard during the Keichō Era [1596–1615]), written by Miura Jōshin (1565–1644), who had served the family as a retainer until its downfall. The name of the compiler and the date of compilation are not known.

Hōjō Hideji (1902–1977)

Playwright. Born in Ōsaka; real name Iino Hideji. A graduate of Kansai University, he studied writing with the dramatists OKAMOTO KIDŌ and HASEGAWA SHIN. In the mid-1930s he became part of the SHIMPA (New School) modern drama movement and eventually became a troupe playwright for the SHINKOKUGEKI (New National Theater) acting company. He devoted himself to creating drama for the general populace and is recognized as one of the representative playwrights of Japan's commercial theater. Among his many plays is the masterpiece *Ōshō* (1947, Chess Master).

Hōjōki → Kamo no Chōmei

Hōjō Masako (1157–1225)

Eldest daughter of HŌJŌ TOKIMASA; wife of MINAMOTO NO YORITOMO, the founder of the Kamakura shogunate (1192–1333), and mother of his sons and successors MINAMOTO NO YORIIE and MINAMOTO NO SANETOMO. Going against her father's wishes, she married Yoritomo in 1177, during his exile in Izu Province (now part of Shizuoka Prefecture). Although Masako took Buddhist vows after Yoritomo's death in 1199, she gradually became involved in shogunate politics. She and her father removed the politically incompetent Yoriie from the office of shōgun, replacing him with Sanetomo. Thereafter with her father and her brother HŌJŌ YOSHITOKI Masako dominated the shogunate; but when her father plotted with his second wife (Omaki no Kata) to install their son-in-law Hiraga Tomomasa (d 1205) as shōgun, she did not hesitate to exile him. As the "nun shōgun" *(ama shōgun)* she continued to control the shogunate and in 1219 traveled to Kyōto to invite Kujō Yoritsune (1218–56), the infant scion of an illustrious court family, as shōgun-designate to succeed the childless Sanetomo. At the outbreak of the JŌKYŪ DISTURBANCE (1221), a court-inspired insurrection against the shogunate, she induced the shogunate vassals to reaffirm their loyalty, reminding them of their immense debt to Yoritomo. Masako remained powerful in shogunate councils until her death.

G. Cameron Hurst III

Hōjō Sanetoki → Kanazawa Bunko

Hōjō Sōun (1432–1519)

Military and political leader of the Sengoku (Warring States) period (1467–1568). He first went by the name of Ise Shinkurō Nagauji, later adopted the surname Hōjō, and used the religious name Sōun after becoming a Buddhist monk. To distinguish his surname from that of the HŌJŌ FAMILY regents of the Kamakura shogunate (1192–1333), he and his descendants are often called the Go-Hōjō or Later Hōjō. Little is known of his background, but it is said that he was born in Ise (now part of Mie Prefecture) and that he became a retainer of Imagawa Yoshitada (1442–76), the military governor *(shugo)* of Suruga (now part of Shizuoka Prefecture), around 1475. Sōun's rise to power began in 1476, when he helped to suppress a revolt in Suruga in which Yoshitada was killed; Yoshitada's son, Imagawa Ujichika, rewarded Sōun with Kōkokuji Castle. In 1491 Sōun seized control of Izu Province (now part of Shizuoka Prefecture) and in 1495 took over Odawara Castle. By 1516 he also held Musashi and Sagami provinces (now Saitama, Tōkyō, and Kanagawa prefectures). His descendants controlled the Kantō region until their defeat by TOYOTOMI HIDEYOSHI in 1590.

Hōjō Takatoki (1303–1333)

The 14th shogunal regent (SHIKKEN) of the Kamakura shogunate (1192–1333); son of the ninth regent, Hōjō Sadatoki (1271–1311). He became regent in 1316, but because of his youth, the powers of his office were exercised by his maternal grandfather, Adachi Tokiaki, and the minister Nagasaki Takasuke (d 1333), who encouraged Takatoki in a life of dissipation. The shogunate was in decline, and the SHŌCHŪ CONSPIRACY of 1324, Emperor GO-DAIGO's first attempt to overthrow the regime, weakened it further. Falling ill in 1326, Takatoki resigned the regency and became a monk. Go-Daigo struck again in the GENKŌ INCIDENT of 1331, and warriors throughout the country rose up in his support. When the forces of NITTA YOSHISADA attacked Kamakura in 1333, Takatoki, with virtually all the members of his family, committed suicide.

G. Cameron Hurst III

Hōjō Tamio (1914–1937)

Novelist. Born in Seoul, Korea. Real name undisclosed. Stricken with leprosy and admitted to a leper asylum at the age of 20, he sent the manuscript of "Maki rōjin" (1935, Old Man Maki), a story based on his own experience, to KAWABATA YASUNARI, who helped him publish it in the magazine BUNGAKUKAI and encouraged him to continue writing. This and his other stories, insightful and sometimes humorous in their depictions of life within a leper asylum, are affirmations of the value of life in the face of suffering. His works include the short stories "Inochi no shoya" (1936, The First Day of Life) and "Raiin jutai" (1936, A Pregnancy in the Leper Asylum).

Hōjō Tokimasa (1138–1215)

First regent (SHIKKEN) of the Kamakura shogunate (1192–1333). A government official in Izu Province (now part of Shizuoka Prefecture), he gave shelter to the young MINAMOTO NO YORITOMO, who had been exiled to the area by the dictator TAIRA NO KIYOMORI in 1160. His daughter HŌJŌ MASAKO married Yoritomo, much to his displeasure, but when Yoritomo decided to raise troops against Taira rule, Tokimasa came to his son-in-law's aid. He went to Kyōto in 1185 on the pretext of apprehending MINAMOTO NO YOSHITSUNE, Yoritomo's estranged brother; there, he persuaded the court in 1185 to grant Yoritomo the power to appoint JITŌ (estate stewards) and SHUGO (military governors) throughout the country. Tokimasa continued to help Yoritomo to consolidate his rule after the Kamakura shogunate was formed in 1192, but after Yoritomo's death, together with Masako, he stripped the ineffectual shōgun MINAMOTO NO YORIIE of all political power and instituted a system of collegial rule, creating the office of regent for himself in 1203. He then had Yoriie murdered (1204) and installed MINAMOTO NO SANETOMO as shōgun. As regent he eliminated potential rivals (the Hiki, the Kajiwara, and others) and ruled as de facto head of the shogunate. In 1205 he plotted with his second wife, Omaki no Kata, to replace Sanetomo with Omaki no Kata's son-in-law, Hiraga Tomomasa (d 1205). This time he was foiled by Masako and his son HŌJŌ YOSHITOKI, who forced him out of office. He retired to Izu and took holy orders.

Hōjō Tokimune (1251–1284)

The eighth shogunal regent (SHIKKEN) of the Kamakura shogunate (1192–1333); son of HŌJŌ TOKIYORI and of a daughter of Hōjō Shigetoki (1198–1261). He became cosigner (RENSHO) in 1264 and regent in 1268. Throughout his regency, during the latter half of which he dispensed with a rensho, Tokimune faced the threat of the MONGOL INVASIONS. Refusing to accept the Mongols' terms for submission, Tokimune strengthened the defenses of southwestern Japan and mobilized Kyūshū warriors to repel the first invasion in 1274. He then had a long stone wall constructed along Hakata Bay against another attack, which came in 1281; again he organized the shogunate's successful defense of Japan. Tokimune was an ardent follower of Zen Buddhism who invited the priest Wuxue (Wu-hsüeh; J: Mugaku) from Song (Sung) China and built the temple ENGAKUJI in 1282. He died on the day he took holy orders.

G. Cameron HURST III

Hōjō Tokiyori (1227–1263)

The fifth shogunal regent (SHIKKEN) of the Kamakura shogunate (1192–1333); son of Hōjō Tokiuji (1203–30). He became regent in 1246 on the death of his brother Tsunetoki (1224–46). That same year he crushed a plot, led by the former figurehead shōgun Kujō (Fujiwara) Yoritsune (1218–56) and some of his own kinsmen, to overthrow him. The next year he was able to destroy the powerful vassal MIURA FAMILY in the HŌJI CONFLICT. Tokiyori established the High Court (HIKITSUKE) in 1249 to adjudicate the increasing number of lawsuits involving shogunal vassals. Although he took holy orders and relinquished the regency to Hōjō Nagatoki (1229–64) in 1256, he continued to rule in fact. Tokiyori was concerned with just rule of the people, and it is said that he traveled incognito throughout the country to observe conditions at first hand.

G. Cameron HURST III

Hōjō Yasutoki (1183–1242)

The third and perhaps most celebrated of the shogunal regents (SHIKKEN) of the Kamakura shogunate (1192–1333). Eldest son of HŌJŌ YOSHITOKI, Yasutoki led the shogunal forces against those of the imperial court in the JŌKYŪ DISTURBANCE of 1221. After his victory, he remained in Kyōto as the first ROKUHARA TANDAI (Rokuhara deputy) to oversee the court, and on his father's death in 1224 he became regent. Appointing his uncle Hōjō Tokifusa (1175–1240) as RENSHO (cosigner), Yasutoki began to systematize shogunal rule. He established the Council of State (HYŌJŌSHŪ) in 1226, and in 1232 he promulgated the GOSEIBAI SHIKIMOKU, the first

codification of warrior house law (BUKEHŌ). Indeed Yasutoki deserves as much credit as MINAMOTO NO YORITOMO for laying the foundations of WARRIOR GOVERNMENT in medieval Japan.

G. Cameron HURST III

Hōjō Yoshitoki (1163–1224)

The second shogunal regent (SHIKKEN) of the Kamakura shogunate (1192–1333). Yoshitoki followed his father, HŌJŌ TOKIMASA, in the TAIRA–MINAMOTO WAR as a supporter of MINAMOTO NO YORITOMO, who was married to his sister HŌJŌ MASAKO. Together with Masako he ousted his father from the regency in 1205 and took over the post. Having destroyed the Wada family in 1213, he also took the headship of the Board of Retainers (SAMURAI-DOKORO), which WADA YOSHIMORI had held. After the assassination of the shōgun MINAMOTO NO SANETOMO in 1219, Yoshitoki and Masako gained complete control of the shogunate and consolidated the power of their family by confiscating many of their enemies' extensive estates and reassigning them to their own followers. In the JŌKYŪ DISTURBANCE of 1221, the retired emperor GO-TOBA and supporters of the imperial court attempted to overthrow the Hōjō; Yoshitoki crushed the uprising and thereby extended the rule of the shogunate over the entire country.

G. Cameron HURST III

hōka

1. A type of street performance popular during the Muromachi (1333–1568) to the Edo (1600–1868) periods, featuring juggling, acrobatics, and distinctive singing accompanied by striking two short bamboo sticks together. The performers were called *hōka, hōkashi,* or *hōkasō;* the last term alludes to the fact that many were dressed as priests.

2. A present-day folk performance of central Japan (especially Aichi Prefecture), featuring a vigorous dance accompanied by flutes and drums. The dancers carry giant fans on their backs.

MISUMI Haruo

Hōkaiji

Shingon sect Buddhist temple located in the Fushimi district of the city of Kyōto. Originally a Tendai sect monastery, Hōkaiji became affiliated with Shingon in the Edo period (1600–1868). According to legend, Hōkaiji was founded in the 9th century when a courtier, Hino Ienobu (d 877), received a small image of the Buddha Yakushi Nyorai made by the monk SAICHŌ and built a family temple on his own land to enshrine the image. Later Hino Sukenari (d 1070) built a Yakushi hall, an Amida hall, and a Kannon hall. Of these, only the Amida hall (1051), partially rebuilt during the latter part of the Heian period (794–1185), survives. About 9 meters square (730 sq ft), it houses a wooden image of the Buddha Amida in the style of the sculptor JŌCHŌ (d 1057). The image of the Buddha Yakushi in the present Yakushi hall dates from the late Heian period.

Nancy SHATZMAN STEINHARDT

Hokekyō → Lotus Sutra

Hokkaidō

The northernmost and second largest of Japan's four main islands. It is separated from Honshū to the south by the Tsugaru Strait and bounded by the Sea of Japan on the west, the Sea of Okhotsk on the northeast, and the Pacific Ocean on the south and east. Several mountain ranges cross Hokkaidō, and those belonging to the EZO MOUNTAINS run from north to south across the center of the island, separated into two strands by a series of basin areas. To the west of these mountains lies the broad ISHIKARI PLAIN. To the southwest of the plain is a long peninsula, which is the area closest to Honshū and the first part of the island to be inhabited by the Japanese. The climate is unlike that of the rest of Japan, being notably colder and drier.

The prehistoric culture of Hokkaidō seems to have shared many of the characteristics of the early culture of Honshū, except that it lacked a YAYOI CULTURE. Hokkaidō, or EZO, as it was known, was inhabited by the AINU and not included in Japan proper. In the Edo period (1600–1868) the Matsumae domain was established in the extreme southwestern corner of the island. After the Meiji Restoration of 1868, the new government placed great emphasis on Hokkaidō's economic development, setting up a colonial office (KAI-TAKUSHI) and encouraging settlers to come from other parts of Ja-

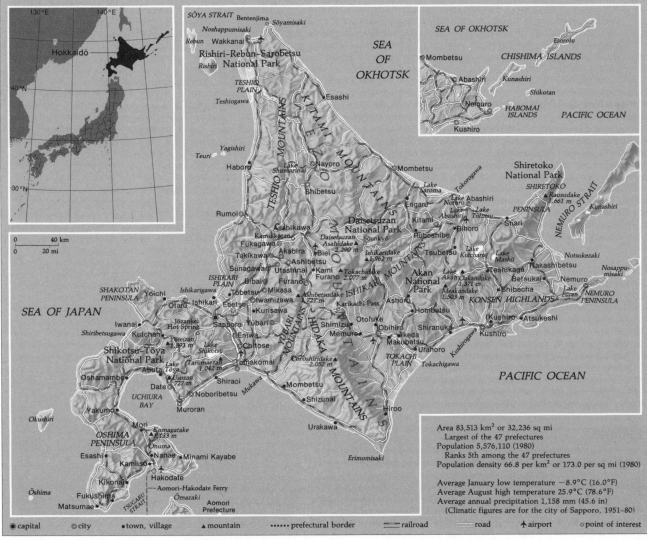

Hokkaidō

Area 83,513 km² or 32,236 sq mi
Largest of the 47 prefectures
Population 5,576,110 (1980)
Ranks 5th among the 47 prefectures
Population density 66.8 per km² or 173.0 per sq mi (1980)

Average January low temperature −8.9°C (16.0°F)
Average August high temperature 25.9°C (78.6°F)
Average annual precipitation 1,158 mm (45.6 in)
(Climatic figures are for the city of Sapporo, 1951–80)

● capital   ◎ city   •town, village   ▲ mountain   •••••• prefectural border   railroad   road   ✈ airport   ○ point of interest

pan. The name of the island was changed to Hokkaidō (literally, "Northern Sea Circuit") in 1869 on MATSUURA TAKESHIRŌ's suggestion. Hokkaidō was divided into three prefectures from 1882 to 1886. These were abolished and the present prefectural form of administration established in 1886. (Within Japan's prefectural system, Hokkaidō alone is called a *dō* [circuit] rather than a *ken* [prefecture]; however, it is the equivalent of a prefecture.)

The main agricultural crop is rice; grain and vegetable farming as well as dairy farming are active. Fishing, forestry, and mining have long been an important part of Hokkaidō's economy, forming a sizable percentage of Japan's total production. They also form the basis for much of Hokkaidō's industrial activity, including food processing, woodworking, pulp, and paper industries. There is an emerging steel industry.

Hokkaidō is noted for its dramatic and unspoiled scenery, which includes active volcanos, large lakes, and vast virgin forests. Major tourist attractions are Shikotsu-Tōya, Akan, Daisetsuzan, Shiretoko, and Rishiri-Rebun-Sarobetsu national parks. The Ainu still live in Hokkaidō, but their language and culture are rapidly disappearing. Area: 83,513 sq km (32,236 sq mi); pop: 5,576,110; capital: SAPPORO. Other major cities include HAKODATE, ASAHIKAWA, OTARU, MURORAN, TOMAKOMAI, OBIHIRO, and KUSHIRO.

Hokkaidō Colonization Office Scandal of 1881

(Kaitakushi Kan'yūbutsu Haraisage Jiken). Political scandal in 1881 centering on the government's proposed sale of the assets of its Hokkaidō Colonization Office (KAITAKUSHI). Recognizing the economic potential and strategic importance of the island of Hokkaidō, the new Meiji government established this office in 1869. From 1872

to 1881 it annually allotted the bureau ¥1 million, an enormous sum at the time. This investment, however, proved unprofitable, and in 1881, one year after the government had decided to sell off many of its enterprises to private entrepreneurs (see KAN'EI JIGYŌ HARAISAGE), KURODA KIYOTAKA, the director of the Colonization Office, proposed the sale of all its Hokkaidō assets. He won the tacit consent of ITŌ HIROBUMI and other government leaders to sell the office's coal mines, railways, food processing factories, and other property in Hokkaidō to the Kansai Bōeki Shōkai, a trading consortium led by his old colleague from the former Satsuma domain, GODAI TOMOATSU. The cost was nominal, about ¥380,000 to be paid over 30 years at no interest. When the terms of the sale leaked out, members of the FREEDOM AND PEOPLE'S RIGHTS MOVEMENT, as well as opposition leaders in the government, expressed outrage. In particular, ŌKUMA SHIGENOBU, at the prompting of the entrepreneur IWASAKI YATARŌ, denounced the "collusion between government and business." Public meetings were held in Ōsaka and Tōkyō, adding impetus to the growing demand to establish a representative assembly. Thus Itō and other government leaders were forced to cancel the sale and issue an imperial rescript promising a national assembly by 1890. In retaliation, however, they dismissed Ōkuma from office on the pretext that he and FUKUZAWA YUKICHI had plotted to end the Satsuma-Chōshū clique's control of the government (see HAMBATSU). See also POLITICAL CRISIS OF 1881.

Hokkaidō Development Agency

(Hokkaidō Kaihatsu Chō). Agency of the Japanese government established under the 1950 Hokkaidō Development Law (Hokkaidō Kaihatsu Hō), charged with implementing the central government's plans for the development of Hokkaidō. It is responsible for the formulation and implementation of plans for the construction of roads, ports and harbors, transportation and communications facilities, and irrigation projects. It is also involved in planning for the improvement and development of housing, cities, and industry, and it supervises the Hokkaidō and Tōhoku development corporations. The agency is attached to the Prime Minister's Office and is headed by a director-general appointed by the prime minister.

Hokkaidō Electric Power Co, Inc

(Hokkaidō Denryoku). Supplier of electricity to the island of Hokkaidō. Founded in 1951 as a result of the reorganization of the electric power industry following World War II. A third of the company's power is generated from coal mined in Hokkaidō. In the future, however, the company plans to use imported coal. The company has a capacity to produce 4.2 million kilowatts from its 59 hydroelectric and 15 thermoelectric plants. It annually sells 16.4 billion kilowatt-hours of electric power. In the fiscal year ending March 1982 income totaled ¥381.2 billion (US $1.6 billion) and capitalization stood at ¥76.5 billion (US $317.8 million). The company's headquarters are located in Sapporo, Hokkaidō.

Hokkaidō shimbun

A leading Hokkaidō daily newspaper. The *Hokkaidō shimbun* was formed through the wartime merger in 1942 of 11 different Hokkaidō dailies under one banner. Its progressive editorials and news stories on Hokkaidō affairs have contributed to the paper's solid reputation and popularity with island residents. The main publishing office is located in Sapporo, with branch offices in Hakodate, Asahikawa, and Kushiro which make use of facsimile transmission in putting out local editions. The *Hokkaidō shimbun* maintains 19 overseas news-gathering bureaus and has agreements with the Associated Press and Tass news wire services. Circulation: 994,000 (1980).

Hokkaidō Takushoku Bank, Ltd

(Hokkaidō Takushoku Ginkō). City bank controlling a national network of branches, with headquarters in Sapporo, Hokkaidō. Among the 13 city-based Japanese banks it ranks last in total capital. Founded in 1900 as a specialized financial institution to supply long-term capital loans for the development of Hokkaidō, it also provided general depositary services. In 1950 it was reclassified as a regular commercial bank, a class of depositary banks which includes city banks. Subsequently it entered the foreign exchange market and expanded operations by establishing branch banks on Honshū, the main island of Japan. In 1982 the bank had 113 branches in Hokkaidō, 41 in Tōkyō, and 25 in other parts of Japan. In 1970 it initiated overseas operations, and now has branches in New York, Los Angeles, Seattle, and London, incorporated banks in Hong Kong and Brussels, and 7 foreign business offices. Long-range plans call for continued overseas expansion. As of March 1982, the bank's total assets were ¥5.3 trillion (US $22 billion), deposits ¥3.8 trillion (US $15.8 billion), and capitalization ¥30 billion (US $124.6 million). The bank's operating profit was ¥11.2 billion (US $46.5 million) in 1981.

Hokkaidō University

(Hokkaidō Daigaku). National university located in Sapporo, Hokkaidō. Its predecessor was the Sapporo Agricultural College, which was established in 1876 as Japan's first agricultural institute of higher learning. In 1907 it became the College of Agriculture of Tōhoku Imperial University, and in 1918 an independent institution. A year later a faculty of medicine was created and it was made a comprehensive university under the name Hokkaidō Imperial University. It was renamed Hokkaidō University in 1947. In 1949 it absorbed the Hakodate Fishery School and other institutions. It maintains faculties of letters, education, law, economics, science, medicine, pharmaceutical sciences, engineering, dentistry, agriculture, veterinary medicine, and fisheries. There are research institutes for low temperature science, applied electricity, catalysis, and immunological science. Enrollment was 9,754 in 1980.

Hokkeji

Convent-temple of the Shingon-Ritsu sect of Buddhism, located in the suburbs of Nara. Also known as Himuro Gosho. Hokkeji was originally a mansion belonging to FUJIWARA NO FUHITO, the father of the empress KŌMYŌ. In 747 Kōmyō, who was the consort of the emperor SHŌMU (r 724–749), converted her father's residence into a nunnery in keeping with Shōmu's edict of 741 calling for the establishment of temples (monasteries and convents) in each province (see KOKUBUNJI). Traditionally regarded as the headquarters for all provincial nunneries (which were all called Hokkeji), the Hokkeji had close connections with the KONOE FAMILY. It became a temple of the Shingon Ritsu sect (see EIZON) in the middle of 13th century. After centuries of decline and disrepair, the temple was refurbished by TOYOTOMI HIDEYORI and his mother in 1601. Its chief icon is a wooden statue of the Eleven-headed Kannon (Jūichimen Kannon), a National Treasure that dates from the 9th century.

Lucie R. WEINSTEIN

Hōkō Fishing Co, Ltd

(Hōkō Suisan). Fishing company established in 1946. The company grew rapidly after 1955 when it expanded its operations to the Okhotsk area. Its fishing fleet covers a wide area, including the Aleutians and Bering Sea and seas off the coasts of West Africa and Indonesia. The company has affiliated firms in Indonesia, Morocco, and the Maldive Islands in the Indian Ocean. Through these overseas affiliates, the company imports marine products and provides training in fishing technique to these countries. Hōkō Suisan is also affiliated with NIPPON REIZŌ, a refrigeration firm. Sales for the fiscal year ending January 1982 totaled ¥89.7 billion (US $399.4 million) and capitalization was ¥3 billion (US $13.4 million). The company's headquarters are located in Tōkyō.

Hokuetsu Paper Mills, Ltd

(Hokuetsu Seishi). Paper manufacturing company founded in Niigata Prefecture in 1907. Its main products include printing paper and coated board. With the establishment of an integrated production process, from raw wood to finished paper, it has grown into a major paper manufacturing firm. After World War II the company concentrated on the production of coated board and various types of special high-quality paper. In the late 1970s the company moved into the production of paper cups and other paper products. In the fiscal year ending April 1982 sales totaled ¥77.6 billion (US $316.9 million), of which 89 percent came from printing paper and coated board, 4 percent from lumber, and 7 percent from other products. In the same year the firm was capitalized at ¥4.1 billion (US $16.7 million). Corporate headquarters are located in the city of Nagaoka, Niigata Prefecture.

Hokuetsu seppu

("Annals of Snow in the Hokuetsu Region"). Collection of essays by the Edo-period (1600–1868) writer Suzuki Bokushi (1770–1842), who was a native of Shiozawa in Echigo Province (now Niigata Prefecture). His work was stimulated by close association with such contemporary literary figures as ŌTA NAMPO and BAKIN. *Hokuetsu seppu*, his foremost work, was published with the help of Bakin and is a detailed record of life and customs in the snow country of northwestern Honshū. Part one (1836) consists of three volumes; part two (1842) consists of four volumes. The work was edited extensively by Santō Kyōzan and illustrations were done by the author and Santō Kyōsui. Suzuki describes in detail winter life in the snow country. His illustrated descriptions of snow crystals—which he observed under a microscope—are notable for their accuracy. He also recorded local products, customs and manners, and annual observances, making his work a valuable source for studying the folk customs of the Echigo area. The essays were edited anew by Okada Takematsu and republished as a part of the Iwanami Bunko series in 1936.

ŌTŌ Tokihiko

hokumen no bushi

A type of warrior-official in the service of the retired emperors of the 12th century (see INSEI); also called *in no hokumen*. *Hokumen no bushi* literally means "warriors of the northern quarter," the name deriving from the area of the palace in which they met. They were first appointed by Emperor SHIRAKAWA, soon after his abdication in 1087, and thereafter they became permanent fixtures. They provided the military power for former sovereigns, serving as guards at the palaces and as troops in the event of a serious disturbance. They

Hokusai

A woodblock print from the series *Fugaku sanjūrokkei*. 25 × 37 cm. Ca 1831. Tōkyō National Museum.

were later divided into upper and lower divisions, 4th-rank officials being appointed to the former, and 5th- and 6th-rank officials to the latter. There was never any formal hierarchy, and it is not certain how many there were at any one time. — *G. Cameron HURST III*

Hokuriku Electric Power Co, Inc

(Hokuriku Denryoku). Supplier of electric power, chiefly to the three Hokuriku prefectures, Toyama, Ishikawa, and Fukui. It was founded in 1951 as a result of the reorganization of the electric power industry following World War II. Of the nine Japanese producers of electricity Hokuriku is the most heavily dependent on hydroelectric power. The firm actively advocates the development of nuclear energy. In 1980 the company operated 114 hydroelectric and four thermoelectric plants and sold 15.9 billion kilowatt-hours of electric power. In the fiscal year ending March 1982 its income totaled ¥336.1 billion (US $1.4 billion) and capitalization stood at ¥78.5 million (US $326.1 million). Corporate headquarters are located in Toyama, Toyama Prefecture.

Hokusai (1760–1849)

UKIYO-E painter, draftsman, illustrator, print designer, and author; one of the great masters of Japanese pictorial art. The artist was born, it is said, on the 23rd day of the ninth month of 1760 to unknown parents in the Warigesui section of the Honjo district of Edo (now Tōkyō) on the east side of the Sumida River (Sumidagawa). His given name was Tokitarō. Around the age of three he was adopted into the family of Nakajima Ise, a highly ranked craftsman who was an official mirror maker for the Tokugawa shogunate. By the age of five, Tokitarō had already shown an interest in pictures and a talent for drawing. At the age of nine his given name was changed to Tetsuzō and he moved to Yokoamichō in the Honjo district. Around the age of 13 he was apprenticed to an engraver of woodblocks, and two years later is known to have engraved the last six pages of the text of *Gakujo kōshi* (1775), a humorous novelette. At 14 he is said to have worked as a clerk in a lending library and to have taught himself the art of book illustration by studying the pictures in the books. At the age of 18 he entered the studio of the actor portraitist and *ukiyo-e* painter KATSUKAWA SHUNSHŌ, and in the summer of 1779 he emerged from obscurity with a series of capably designed actor portraits signed Katsukawa Shunrō. In the next decade little is known of Hokusai's circumstances. He eked out a living as a minor book illustrator, an occasional author, and a designer of inexpensive commercial prints. It may have been during this period that he left the Nakajima family, although he never formally relinquished their name.

In 1791 Shunrō was invited to design a few woodblock prints for the publisher Tsutaya Jūzaburō, which were printed in full color, but for some reason he was not invited to continue and briefly returned to the coarse commercial prints and illustrations with which he had supported himself until then. The death of his teacher Shunshō in 1792 seems to have precipitated a crisis in his life and in the KATSUKAWA SCHOOL, in which Shunrō was passed over in favor of his contemporary, the highly successful actor portraitist KATSUKAWA

SHUN'EI. Reacting to this with indignation, Hokusai seems to have cut his ties with the Katsukawa school, adopted the self-styled name Kusamura, and lapsed into defiant, possibly deliberate, obscurity. His last securely dated actor portrait was published in 1792. In 1793 he designed one unimportant calendar print and one illustrated novelette. In 1794 he designed another minor calendar print and seems to have signed an illustration in a poetry anthology. There are other unsigned works during these years that can plausibly be attributed to Shunrō—there is no doubt that the impoverished artist needed to support himself somehow—but he seems to have been at pains to deny his association with the Katsukawa school.

The vacant years of 1793 and 1794 were crucial in Hokusai's career because they marked the end of his attempts to accommodate his vision to the trite prevailing styles of *ukiyo-e*. Sometime during this period he began experimenting with other styles of painting, studying briefly, it is said, with the academic artist Kanō Yūsen, and perhaps with Tsutsumi Tōrin, with whom he collaborated in illustrating poetry albums a few years later.

He was introduced to the Tawaraya family, a clan of RIMPA style painters, and in 1795 designed an illustration for *Kyōka Edo murasaki*, a verse anthology, which he signed with a new name: Sōri. The refined world of amateur poets was as congenial and kind to Sōri as it had been to Harunobu before him, and at the age of 36, for the first time in his life, the artist was given an opportunity to design pictures that rose from his own vision rather than from the conventions of the market or the stage. Between 1796 and 1799 Sōri designed many single-sheet prints and album illustrations, all for private distribution, and began exploring a newly found talent for painting. His SURIMONO, as these private prints were called, were immediately successful and were imitated by many other artists.

The artist was a devout follower of the Nichiren sect of Buddhism and was particularly devoted to the bodhisattva Myōken, an incarnation of the north star. In 1796 he began using the secondary name Hokusai, by which he is best known. Hokusai means "north studio" and is one of a series of names the artist adopted, including Tatsumasa, Taito, and Raishin, derived from worship of the seven polar stars.

In the winter of 1798, at the height of his new popularity, the artist bestowed the name Sōri on a pupil, keeping the name Hokusai for himself. During the next few years he used a roster of names concurrently: Hokusai for prints and paintings, Tatsumasa for certain privately published illustrations, Tokitarō for commercial fiction, and Kakō (or Sorobeku) for other commercial prints and books. In 1799 he briefly used the secondary name Fusenkyo, and in 1800, at the age of 41, he began to call himself Gakyōjin Hokusai, the "man mad about painting." At an age and date when many of his contemporaries had either declined, retired, or lapsed into obscurity, his prodigious career began in earnest.

From the early 1800s, Hokusai became a celebrity in the art world, and as he designed more book illustrations his fame spread and pupils and imitators appeared throughout Japan. Although he lived as a recluse much of the time, he enjoyed a certain amount of public notoriety and gave public demonstrations of his skills. In 1804 he painted, within the precincts of an Edo temple, a half-length picture of the Zen patriarch Bodhidharma that measured 240 square meters (2,583 sq ft). In 1817 he repeated this feat at a temple in Nagoya.

In 1810 the figures Hokusai painted for a billboard at the Ichimura *kabuki* theater were criticized for being lean and ugly. Perhaps in response to the criticism, the artist gave the name Hokusai to an insignificant pupil the following spring and adopted another astronomically derived name, Taito. The following year, on a journey to the Kyōto–Ōsaka area, the artist stopped in Nagoya, met the artist Bokusen (1775–1824), and began the lifelong friendship that resulted in the publication of *Hokusai manga* (Sketches by Hokusai), a series of picture books that were published in Nagoya between 1814 and 1834.

The Japanese calendar divides time into 60-year cycles, and Hokusai commemorated the beginning of his second cycle in 1820 by adopting the name Iitsu (literally, "one year old again"). During this decade he designed his last *surimono* sets and continued illustrating books with imagination and industry. In 1827 he suffered an attack of palsy but was able to heal himself with medication.

Prussian blue was introduced into Japan in 1829 and used in prints, notably by KEISAI EISEN, the following year. An advertisement in an illustrated novel published in 1831 indicates that Hokusai's celebrated series of landscape prints *Fugaku sanjūrokkei* (Thirty-Six Views of Mt. Fuji) had begun to appear by that year. In the early 1830s Hokusai was over 70 years old, but he worked tirelessly during this period, finished the views of Fuji, and designed the woodblock prints of waterfalls, bridges, birds, and ghosts, for which he is now best known. Late in 1834, just before the publication of *Fugaku hyakkei* (100 Views of Mt. Fuji), his masterpiece of book illustration, he left Edo and lived for over a year in a rural district near Uraga on the Miura Peninsula south of Edo. The reasons for this visit are unknown, but he continued working, sending manuscripts for books to his publishers with long letters of advice about engraving and printing, good-natured descriptions of his circumstances, and statements of account. During his absence, the last important series of woodblock prints began to appear, *Hyakunin isshu uba ga etoki* (Illustrations of the 100 Poems), an anthology of classical verse. Hokusai returned to Edo in the middle of 1836 to find the city ravaged by famine. He managed to support himself by selling sketches and exchanging pictures for measures of rice. Other artists and publishers were not so fortunate; the series of 100 poems was interrupted after 27 pictures were published and was never resumed, although the artist continued designing additional subjects for the set through the summer of 1838.

Around 1839, Hokusai's lodgings burned, and all his study sketches and painting materials were destroyed. Whether demoralized by this event, or for other reasons, Hokusai seems to have produced relatively few paintings, and practically no prints and book illustrations during the last decade of his life. At the age of 82 he began drawing a lion every morning as a talisman to drive off evil and continued this practice for two years. In 1845, he visited a friend in Shinano Province (now Nagano Prefecture) and executed some paintings for a temple there. He died on the 18th day of the fourth month of 1849 and was buried at the temple Seikyōji in the Asakusa district of Edo. Most of his many pupils and imitators took names beginning with the syllables *"hoku."* Perhaps the most outstanding of these was the illustrator and *surimono* designer TOTOYA HOKKEI (1780–1850). Another pupil, Katsushika Taito II (active 1820s to early 1850s), designed prints that have often been mistaken for his master's.

Roger KEYES

holding companies

(*mochikabu kaisha*). Business organizations which control many corporations in a wide range of industries through possession of their stocks and which are thus able to coordinate the activities of all the corporations. Holding companies may be divided into two types: "pure" holding companies, which exist only to hold the stock of other companies (typified in Japan by some of the holding companies of the pre–World War II ZAIBATSU, or financial and industrial combines), and others which engage in a variety of business activities in addition to holding stocks (many of the *zaibatsu* trading companies, for example, also engaged in stockholding).

In the prewar period, *zaibatsu* formed powerful monopolistic systems of enterprises, structured like pyramids, with holding companies at the top. After the end of the war, OCCUPATION authorities decided to dismantle the holding companies because the *zaibatsu* were regarded as one of the pillars of Japan's prewar military-industrial system. In August 1946 the Holding Company Liquidation Commission was established with the aim of dissolving the holding companies through the purchase, sale, and redistribution of their assets and securities. It cited 5 holding companies for dissolution, including those of the Big Four: the MITSUI, MITSUBISHI, SUMITOMO, and YASUDA *zaibatsu*. This first wave of designations was followed by three others; 83 holding companies became targets for dissolution, of which 30 were dissolved and the remainder allowed to reorganize after divestiture of their stocks (see ZAIBATSU DISSOLUTION).

In November 1945 the Supreme Commander for the Allied Powers (SCAP) issued a "Memorandum for Dissolution of Holding Companies" and sought legal enforcement of its antimonopoly policies. This memorandum became the basis for the ANTIMONOPOLY LAW, which was enacted in 1947. Article 9 of this law placed a complete ban on the formation of holding companies, but it defined them as companies whose main purpose is to control other companies through possession of their stocks. The law, however, did not rule out entirely the possession of the stock of other companies.

Thus, holding companies per se do not exist in postwar Japan. The function of coordinating the policies and activities of a group of enterprises has been carried out by a variety of other means, including interlocking directorships, intercorporate exchanges of stock, and informal ties. Though much looser in organization, postwar

ENTERPRISE GROUPS are somewhat analogous to the *zaibatsu*; the GENERAL TRADING COMPANIES and group banks perform some of the coordinating functions of the holding company, although the degree of their control is much diminished. See also KEIRETSU.

KATŌ Masashi

holidays

(*kyūjitsu*). Holidays for working people in Japan include the legal national holidays, Sundays, and usually Saturday afternoons, except for workers in those stores and factories with their own special holiday schedules. In addition, the 2nd and 3rd of January are generally holidays celebrated as part of the NEW YEAR. Government offices close from 27 December; schools generally close from 25 December until 7 January, and also from 25 July to 31 August. The custom of a set summer vacation in private industry is becoming popular; an increasing number of companies have a few days of vacation centered around 15 August (the approximate date of the BON FESTIVAL in the old lunar calendar).

Paid vacations for workers are determined by the Labor Standards Law (see LABOR LAWS). After one year of continuous service a worker gets six days. After two years of continuous service, a day's paid vacation is added for each year after the first year, with a limit of 20 days. Since these paid vacation days must be requested, there are many cases in which workers do not fully exercise their rights.

The five-day workweek is gradually spreading in Japan. In 1977 the majority of workers (71 percent) worked a five-day week at least once a month. In 1976, 5 percent of all companies had a five-day workweek; these companies employed 24 percent of the work force. This is extremely low compared with the US figure of 84 percent (1974) or the British figure of 85 percent (1968). Moreover, there are conspicuous differences according to the size of the firm. In contrast to the 43 percent of workers in companies with over 1,000 employees having a five-day workweek, only 14 percent of those in companies of 100 to 999 employees and a scant 3 percent in businesses with 9 to 30 employees are on the five-day schedule. *KURITA Ken*

holidays, national → festivals

Holy Orthodox Church

The history of the Orthodox Church in Japan began in 1861 with the arrival of the Russian priest NIKOLAI (1836–1912; he later became archbishop and then Saint Nikolai) at Hakodate, Hokkaidō. Nikolai aspired to build an indigenous church and took most of his clergy from among the Japanese. He built a mission society which maintained close relations with the mother church in Moscow, and introduced many aspects of Russian culture into Japan. Church membership did not increase during the later part of the Meiji period (1868–1912) partly because of ideological currents which developed during the Russo-Japanese War (1904–05) and the Russian Revolution (1917). In 1919 the church became independent of the Russian Orthodox Church and was renamed the Nippon Harisutosu Kyōkai (Japan Orthodox Church). After World War II, it received for a time bishops from the American Orthodox Church. In 1965 it normalized relations with the Russian Orthodox Church, becoming in 1970 an autocephalous church. It now has three dioceses: the archdiocese of Tōkyō and the dioceses of Sendai and Kyōto; the archbishop of Tōkyō holds the position of Metropolitan for all Japan. There are approximately 10,700 members (1979). Its Byzantine-style Cathedral of the Holy Resurrection, popularly known as Nikolaidō, is a famous landmark in Tōkyō. *ŌNAMI Yūji*

Holy Spirit Association for the Unification of World Christianity

(Sekai Kirisutokyō Tōitsu Shinrei Kyōkai). Commonly known as the Unification Church. The church was founded by Sun Myong Moon (b 1920) in Seoul, Korea, in 1954, and its first Japanese branch was established in Tōkyō in 1959. The sect teaches Christianity as interpreted by Moon, especially in his book *The Divine Principle* (1977). Emphasis is on perfecting the self, family, and society through belief in the coming of the Messiah in the present day. The church's spirited proselytizing activities (known in Japan by the name *genri undō* or "ultimate principle movement") have recently attracted considerable numbers of young adults. The church claimed some 276,000 members in Japan in 1980.

Kenneth J. DALE

hombyakushō

(literally, "basic" peasants or farmers). Members of the peasant class during the Edo period (1600–1868) who, in contrast to the landless MIZUNOMI-BYAKUSHŌ, owned land and paid taxes in kind (NENGU) to the domainal governments. Early in the period the term was restricted to wealthier peasants who owned land and houses and were liable for labor taxes (BUYAKU). The *hombyakushō* were basically independent cultivators engaged in small-scale but labor- and fertilizer-intensive farming. In time they diversified into commercial ventures, producing cash crops such as raw cotton and silk cocoons; and many of them also developed cottage industries such as weaving and clothing manufacture. As organs of village self-government developed, *hombyakushō* served as headmen (see OSABYAKUSHŌ; SHŌYA). They were restricted by shogunal authorities in conduct, consumption, and various other ways (see KEIAN NO OFUREGAKI), and were even forbidden to buy and sell land (see TAHATA EITAI BAIBAI KINSHI REI). In protest against the crushing burden of taxes, the *hombyakushō*, who were collectively responsible for meeting their village quotas, often rose in rebellion (see HYAKUSHŌ IKKI). With the development of the money economy, stratification of the *hombyakushō* became more pronounced. The wealthier *hombyakushō* managed to acquire more land, while the poorer lost theirs and were reduced to tenancy and wage labor.

MINEGISHI Kentarō

Home Ministry

(Naimushō). Government ministry that supervised matters such as regional administration, police, public works, and elections, from its inception in November 1873 until December 1947, when its functions were variously taken over by the MINISTRY OF HOME AFFAIRS, MINISTRY OF CONSTRUCTION, and MINISTRY OF LABOR.

This specialized organ for internal administration was initially one of the seven agencies *(jimuka)* newly created in 1868 under the SANSHOKU (Three Offices) administrative system adopted by the government immediately following the MEIJI RESTORATION. As the Meiji government modified its administrative structure, some of the original functions of the agency were taken over by other agencies. In August 1871, along with the establishment of the PREFECTURAL SYSTEM, a centralized governmental system was established and proposals were made for setting up a home ministry that would have responsibility for supervising internal affairs. In view of the social unrest, especially among dispossessed *samurai* (SHIZOKU), following the defeat of those advocating an invasion of Korea (see SEIKAN-RON), the creation of such a ministry was considered urgent. Accordingly, a ministry was established in November 1873, with ŌKUBO TOSHIMICHI as its first head. In January 1874 operations began. The original administrative structure had six bureaus in charge of domestic industry, public security, population registration, postal service, public works, and topographical survey. Of these, the bureaus handling domestic industry and public security were most important. In time some of the duties of the ministry were altered, as in 1881, when the development of local industry was entrusted to the newly established Ministry of Agriculture and Commerce (NŌ-SHŌMUSHŌ). After YAMAGATA ARITOMO was put in charge of the Home Ministry in 1883, it was reorganized into nine bureaus for general administration, local government, police, public works, public health, topographical survey, census, religious institutions, and budget. This structure was retained for many years. The bureau of local government was regarded as the most important.

In December 1885 the Dajōkan system of government was replaced by the cabinet system. Yamagata, already head of the ministry, was given the new title of *naimu daijin*. (Under the Dajōkan system his title had been *naimu kyō*; both translate as home minister.) During Yamagata's tenure the ministry strengthened its control over free speech, the right to organize and assemble, and other civil rights. It tightened police surveillance of political activity and increasingly became a strong arm of the central government in local administration. In 1890 the ministry extended its jurisdiction to cover supervision of elections to the House of Representatives, as well as railways (placed under the supervision of the Ministry of Posts two years later). After World War I, in recognition of the need for a government policy on social problems, the Social and Labor

Affairs Bureau was established. The offices of the Home Ministry were destroyed by fire in the great TŌKYŌ EARTHQUAKE OF 1923, and all of the important records and documents collected by the ministry since its inception were lost.

In 1938 the Ministry of Health and Welfare (Kōseishō) was set up, and in 1940 the ministry's Bureau of Religious Institutions was expanded into the extra-ministerial Agency of Shintō Worship (Jingiin). To meet the needs of the wartime situation, in 1941 the Home Air Defense Bureau and Public Works Bureau were established.

After Japan's defeat in World War II, the activities of the Home Ministry were drastically reduced following a directive issued by OCCUPATION authorities in October 1945. All those connected with the SPECIAL HIGHER POLICE, which had functioned under the Home Ministry, were dismissed, and the PEACE PRESERVATION LAW OF 1925 and other repressive laws were suspended. Finally in December 1947 the Home Ministry was abolished.

As an organ specifically created to ensure domestic peace, the ministry bore responsibility for maintaining public order, directing police administration, and supervising elections. It was usually headed by powerful men like Ōkubo and Yamagata. The ministry also played a key role in strengthening local self-government, encouraging local industry, and enlarging the electorate. At the same time, however, the bureaucrats in the Home Ministry had a virtual monopoly over appointments in local government. Moreover, through its use of the Special Higher Police and the Peace Preservation Law, the ministry was able to suppress labor movements and antigovernment activity, meddle with elections (see SENKYO KAN-SHŌ), enforce ideological conformity, and otherwise interfere in the lives of common citizens.

MIKAMI Terumi

Hommonji

One of the four ranking temples of the NICHIREN SECT of Buddhism, located in Ikegami, Ōta Ward, Tōkyō. The Hommonji is built on the site where NICHIREN died in 1282. The land, which was owned by Ikegami Munenaka, a lay supporter of Nichiren, was turned over to Nichiren's disciples after the death of their teacher. The main hall of the temple was completed in 1317 under the supervision of Nichirō (1243–1320), one of Nichiren's six leading disciples. TOKUGAWA IEYASU (1543–1616), the founder of the Tokugawa shogunate, and KATŌ KIYOMASA (1562–1611), a famous warrior, were among the patrons of the Hommonji. After being destroyed in a fire in 1710, the Hommonji was rebuilt by the eighth Tokugawa shōgun, TOKUGAWA YOSHIMUNE (1684–1751). Much of the temple was burnt down in an air raid in 1945, but it has now been restored. Fortunately, the five-story pagoda, built in 1608, escaped damage. A popular ceremony (known as Oeshiki) commemorating the anniversary of Nichiren's death is held 12–13 October.

Stanley WEINSTEIN

homosexuality

(dōseiai). Male homosexuality has a long and well-documented history in Japan. Female homosexuality unfortunately does not share this distinction. Part of the reason for the almost total lack of information about female homosexuality is that sexuality was traditionally expressed from the male perspective in the Japanese language. Thus, male heterosexual love was called *joshoku* (love of women) and male homosexual love was called *nanshoku* (love of men). They were not considered mutually exclusive categories, so it was possible for a man to have both homosexual and heterosexual relations without stigma. Since there were no equivalent terms for female sexual relations, no discussions of female homosexuality exist to shed light on the phenomenon.

Prior to the introduction of Western moral concepts to Japan after the Meiji Restoration of 1868, attitudes toward homosexuality were quite relaxed. During the Edo period (1600–1868), a homosexual subculture flourished along with the erotic world of the pleasure quarters in urban areas such as Kyōto, Ōsaka, and Edo (now Tōkyō). The era could be called the "golden age" of homosexuality in Japan since homosexuality was practiced with an aplomb and attention to beauty rarely seen since. This period spawned a substantial corpus of literature that dealt fictionally with homoerotic themes, called *shudō bungaku* (homosexual literature). The greatest work in this category was Ihara SAIKAKU's *Nanshoku ōkagami* (1687, The Great Mirror of Manly Love), which detailed the homosexual adventures of warriors, actors, and priests. An anthology of classical poetry and prose celebrating male homosexual love, *Iwatsutsuji* (1676, Cliff Azaleas) was compiled by KITAMURA KIGIN and is the first such work in the history of world literature.

The "golden age" of Japanese homosexuality in the Edo period followed a long history of evolution and development. The practice of homosexuality in Japan is traditionally said to date from the early part of the Heian period (794–1185) when Buddhist monks introduced it upon their return from Tang (T'ang) China in 806. Homosexuality surely existed in Japan before then, but the traditional account of its origins helps explain why homosexuality became a preferred form of sexual expression among the Buddhist priesthood, for whom sexual relations with women were forbidden. The priest GENSHIN's famous treatise on Buddhist doctrine, ŌJŌYŌSHŪ (985, Essentials of Pure Land Rebirth), includes an account of the fiery punishments awaiting homosexuals in purgatory. Genshin's terrifyingly vivid descriptions may or may not have deterred homosexual activity, but the fact that such warnings were necessary perhaps indicates how widespread homosexuality had become.

By the end of the Heian period, homosexuality had become popular among the Kyōto aristocracy, perhaps because of the increased contact with the Buddhist clergy. During the reigns of the tonsured emperors SHIRAKAWA (r 1073–87) and TOBA (r 1107–23), attractive young boys were routinely engaged in court service as entertainers and sexual partners. This practice was adopted by the military elite and continued throughout the Kamakura (1185–1333) and Muromachi (1333–1568) periods. By the advent of Tokugawa rule in the 17th century, homosexuality was an integral part of the social fiber of the military and religious elites. When the Jesuit priest Francis XAVIER arrived to proselytize among the Japanese in the 16th century, he was astonished at how openly homosexuality was practiced and dubbed it the "Japanese vice." He was otherwise impressed with the moral standards of the Japanese.

A link between homosexuality and entertainment, especially theater, developed early. The shōgun ASHIKAGA YOSHIMITSU's patronage of the young actor ZEAMI during the latter part of the 14th century stemmed from homosexual attraction and resulted in the establishment of NŌ as the official theater of the military elite. Youthful male physical beauty and the attraction it excited were integral to early Nō and later became an important element in the popularity of KABUKI during the Edo period. Actors of female roles, ONNAGATA, brought to the kabuki theater an electrifying homoerotic element. These actors often began as male prostitutes before achieving the popularity or acting skills necessary to appear on stage.

The legal history of homosexuality in Japan after 1868 closely parallels that of other modern nations. As part of the Meiji government's attempt to achieve social parity with the West, male homosexuality was outlawed with the adoption of a penal code modeled on Prussian law. This new code included sodomy as a crime *(keikanzai)*; this was later subsumed under the crime of obscenity *(waisetsuzai)*, under which homosexuals could be arrested and imprisoned for homosexual activity. Since World War II, there have been no specific provisions dealing with homosexuality in the legal codes. The present legal status of homosexuals is similar to that in many Western countries, where unofficial toleration is not backed by legal protection. Female homosexuality has never received attention in the legal codes.

Homosexuality in modern Japan is a complex phenomenon. Bars where homosexuals can meet abound in all major cities and in many smaller ones, not unlike gay bars in much of the rest of the world. Many Japanese homosexuals feel a definite lack of freedom to express their homosexuality openly and without fear, especially at their work places. As a result, much homosexual activity remains hidden. In general, however, the expression of affection for the same sex is tolerated and even encouraged in most levels of society. Since the stigma attached to homosexuality is not as great as that in the West, the international gay rights movement has had little effect in creating a separate homosexual consciousness for Japanese men and women.

——Iwata Jun'ichi, *Honchō nanshoku kō* (1974). Iwata Jun'ichi, *Nanshoku bunken shoshi* (1973), bibliography. Mishima Yukio, *Kinjiki* (1951), tr Alfred H. Marks as *Forbidden Colors* (1968). Mishima Yukio, *Kamen no kokuhaku* (1949), tr Meredith Weatherby as *Confessions of a Mask* (1958). Both these novels deal with homosexuality. Mutsuo Takahashi, *Poems of a Penisist,* tr Hiroaki Sato (1975).   NOGUCHI Takenori and Paul SCHALOW

Hon'ami Kōetsu

Raku ware teabowl by Kōetsu. The thick white glaze mottled during firing, resulting in the dark bands of ash gray for which this piece is noted. Height 8.5 cm. Early 17th century. Private collection. National Treasure.

Hōmushō → Ministry of Justice

Hon'ami Kōetsu (1558–1637)

Artist widely admired for his calligraphy, pottery, and lacquer and metal designs, and for inspiring the revival of classical court traditions that led to what was later called the RIMPA style.

Kōetsu was born into a family of sword experts who served such military leaders as ODA NOBUNAGA and TOKUGAWA IEYASU as well as members of the imperial court. Little is known of him prior to the death of his father in 1603, though soon thereafter he was a significant artistic force. In 1615 he retired to Takagamine (northwest of Kyōto), to a tract of land granted him by Ieyasu. Often interpreted as a gesture of goodwill, the grant is now believed to have been an order of exile. Kōetsu was joined at Takagamine by a number of Kyōto craftsmen, and he organized a small community. Although the colony at Takagamine became famous for the works of art it produced, it appears that the original focus of the group was religious rather than artistic; for generations the Hon'ami family had been devotees of the NICHIREN SECT of Buddhism. It was at Takagamine that the Rimpa style of painting and design came into being.

In his first important work, beginning in 1604, Kōetsu collaborated with the wealthy businessman and scholar Suminokura Soan (1571–1632) in designing and publishing a set of decorative books called *sagabon,* which included NŌ plays and selections from classical literature.

Although Kōetsu had been trained in his ancestors' profession as a swords craftsman and connoisseur, he also showed great interest in the TEA CEREMONY from his early days and was regarded as one of the outstanding pupils of FURUTA ORIBE. He became extremely accomplished in the design of lacquer ware and ceramics. The latter he studied with the Raku family, whose rustic style of pottery was greatly admired for its suitability in the tea ceremony (see RAKU WARE).

Kōetsu excelled most notably in CALLIGRAPHY. Like many of the calligraphers of his day, he was inspired by the classical traditions of the Heian period (794–1185). In this he may have been influenced by his family's association with court nobles. The style associated with Kōetsu can be seen in his numerous surviving *shikishi* (cardboard-backed paper used in painting and calligraphy), WAKA scrolls, sutra copies, and letters. This style is characterized by a smooth, graceful line that alternates dramatically in width: sometimes delicate, sometimes bold, but always soft, full, and sensuous, reminiscent of the sumptuous works of the Heian period. Kōetsu's calligraphy was so much admired that he became known as one of the Kan'ei no Sampitsu (Three Brushes of the Kan'ei Era), sharing the honor with his friend KONOE NOBUTADA and the monk SHŌKADŌ SHŌJŌ.

Kōetsu often worked in collaboration with the brilliant designer of screens and fans, Tawaraya SŌTATSU, who is reputed to have been his kinsman by marriage. Although it is uncertain how close their relationship was, Sōtatsu is believed to have decorated the papers for many of Kōetsu's calligraphic works.

■——Hayashiya Seizō, *Kōetsu,* no. 101 of *Nihon no bijutsu* (October 1974). *Pat FISTER*

Honchō monzui

Heian-period (794–1185) anthology of poetry and prose in classical Chinese; compiled around 1060 by FUJIWARA NO AKIHIRA. In its division into categories, 39 in this case, it is patterned after the 6th-century Chinese anthology *Wen xuan* (*Wen hsüan;* J: *Monzen*). The collection consists of 427 selections by some 70 contributors and includes the best work in Chinese by Japanese authors from the previous two centuries, the years from the reign of Emperor Saga to that of Emperor Go-Ichijō. A highly regarded anthology at the time, it is often quoted or alluded to in diaries, NŌ plays, and war tales (GUNKI MONOGATARI) of the late Heian and Kamakura (1185–1333) periods.

Honchō seiki

(Chronicle of the Reigns of the Imperial Court; also called *Shikanki* and *Geki nikki*). An official history *(seishi)* of Japan, in annalistic form, compiled in the mid-12th century by FUJIWARA NO MICHI-NORI at the command of the retired emperor TOBA. Intended as a continuation of the Six National Histories (RIKKOKUSHI), it was planned in 30 or 46 chapters, presumably beginning with the reign of Emperor UDA (r 887–897). The work was never completed, but 20 chapters survive, many in fragmentary form, covering the years 935–1153. *Honchō seiki* is an important historical source for the latter half of the Heian period (794–1185). *G. Cameron HURST III*

Honchō shojaku mokuroku

(Catalog of Japanese Books). A one-volume catalog of books, presumably compiled sometime between 1278 and 1292 and believed to be the oldest work of its kind. Also known by other names, such as *Ninnaji shojaku mokuroku* and *Omuro shojaku mokuroku.* The catalog is divided into some 20 categories, such as Shintō gods and ceremonies, imperial affairs, and so forth. There are some 493 entries, including books that were no longer extant, with author, title, number of volumes or chapters, and other pertinent information. *G. Cameron HURST III*

Honda Kōtarō (1870–1954)

Physicist known for his developmental research in materials science, particularly in metallurgy. Born in what is now Aichi Prefecture, he graduated from Tōkyō University in 1897. He studied in Germany from 1907 to 1911 and then returned to become professor at Tōhoku University. He helped to establish the Research Institute for Iron, Steel, and Other Metals in 1922 and served as its first director. Honda developed a number of high-performance magnetic alloys, including KS Magnetic Steel in 1917 and New KS Magnetic Steel (with Masumoto Hakaru) in 1934. His laboratory later became a major center for metallurgical research. He served as president of Tōhoku University from 1931 to 1940 and received the Order of Culture in 1937.

Honda Motor Co, Ltd

(Honda Giken Kōgyō). Manufacturer of motorcycles, four-wheel vehicles, and industrial engines. It is the leading maker of motorcycles in the world, and the fifth leading domestic producer of passenger vehicles. Founded in 1946 by HONDA SŌICHIRŌ as Honda Gijutsu Kenkyūjo, it was reorganized two years later as a corporation, taking on its present name. Honda met initial success when it developed a motorbike by attaching a small engine to a bicycle, and followed this in 1949 with the production of a motorcycle, unique to Japan, which was powered by a small engine of under 100 cubic centimeters. By 1952 Honda controlled 70 percent of the domestic market for this product, and the next year, though capitalized at only ¥15 million (US $41,666), its sales exceeded ¥7 billion (US $19.4 million). Subsequently, with an eye on the international market, it began to produce motorcycles powered by large-capacity engines. In 1961 a Honda motorcycle won a race on the Isle of Man in the United Kingdom; the victory gained the firm a reputation as one of the leading manufacturers in the world. In 1963 Honda produced its first four-wheeled vehicles, and such innovations as the low-pollution Compound Vortex Controlled Combustion (CVCC) engine, which, with the Tōyō Kōgyō rotary engine, was the first to meet the United States Environmental Protection Agency's 1975 standards. Honda also developed its own industrial engine in 1952.

The company, whose motto is "Adopt a World Perspective," was swift to move into foreign markets; after it established American Honda Motor Co, Inc, in 1959, 10 overseas sales companies, fully capitalized by the parent firm, were set up. Overseas production plants, including joint ventures and technology exchange agreements, now number 44 and are based in 29 countries. Among Japanese auto manufacturers Honda was the first to declare its intention to produce passenger cars in the United States by 1982. Sales for the fiscal year ending February 1982 totaled ¥1.5 trillion (US $6.4 billion), of which export sales accounted for 71 percent. In the same fiscal year, 30 percent of total sales was earned by motorcycles, 57 percent by four-wheeled vehicles, and 13 percent by industrial engines and other products. In 1982 capitalization stood at ¥36.7 billion (US $156.1 million). Corporate headquarters are in Tōkyō.

Honda Seiroku (1866–1952)

Dendrologist. Born in what is now Saitama Prefecture. Graduate of Tōkyō Agricultural and Forestry School (now part of Tōkyō University). He studied forestry and economics at Munich University in Germany and served as assistant professor and professor at Tōkyō University from 1893. Pioneer of modern dendrology and the first recipient of a doctorate in forestry in Japan, he became chairman of the Imperial Society of Dendrology late in life. Well-versed in the art and science of landscape gardening, he made a lasting contribution to the beautification and preservation of the natural environment, including the design of the inner and outer gardens of the Meiji Shrine and the establishment of a number of national parks. He is the author of *Zōringaku kakuron* (1927). *KATŌ Shunjirō*

Honda Shūgo (1908–)

Literary critic. Born in Aichi Prefecture. Graduated from Tōkyō University. He participated in the PROLETARIAN LITERATURE MOVEMENT of the early 1930s, gaining some recognition as a critic. After World War II, he joined the progressive literary magazine KINDAI BUNGAKU (1946–64), and established himself as a leading critic with his book *Tenkō bungaku ron* (1957, The Literature of Ideological Conversion; see TENKŌ), an assessment of the historical role of the proletarian literature movement. A humanist who was significantly influenced by Tolstoy's thought, Honda expressed his persistent search for human liberation from political ideology in his reviews of major contemporary and other modern writers. His principal works include *Shirakaba ha no bungaku* (1954), a survey of the humanist writers of the SHIRAKABA SCHOOL, and *Monogatari sengo bungaku shi* (1958–63), a historical digest of post–World War II Japanese literature, which won the 1965 Mainichi Book Award.

Honda Sōichirō (1906–)

Founder of HONDA MOTOR CO, LTD. Born in Shizuoka Prefecture. Studied at Hamamatsu Technical Higher School (now Shizuoka University). A highly innovative engineer, Honda organized Honda Motor in 1948 and revolutionized the motorcycle industry by successfully developing a series of powerful new models, which were exported throughout the world. He later made highly efficient four-wheeled vehicles and led the way in the production of low-pollution cars and automatic transmissions. Aggressive in overseas development, he created motorcycle plants in various parts of the world, including the United States and Europe. *YAMADA Makiko*

Honda Toshiaki (1744–1821)

Mathematician, astronomer, ship captain, and political economist of the late Edo period. Born in Echigo Province (now Niigata Prefecture), he went to Edo (now Tōkyō) at the age of 18 to study mathematics and astronomy. Within six years he opened his own school and was learning Dutch so as to gain access to the latest developments in Western science. He traveled extensively around Japan investigating regional conditions and customs. An accomplished navigator, he maintained close relations with the shogunate's northern explorers such as MOGAMI TOKUNAI and MAMIYA RINZŌ, and in

1801 he captained a vessel which surveyed Ezo (now Hokkaidō). Acutely aware of peasant and warrior impoverishment, Honda became convinced that Japan's economic problems could be overcome by emulating European models, particularly England. He accordingly advanced a number of bold formulas for wealth and power. In *Keisei hisaku* (1798, A Secret Plan for Governing the Country), Honda identified Japan's four top priorities as gunpowder, metals, shipping, and the colonization of Ezo. In SAIIKI MONOGATARI (Tales of the West), which appeared in the same year, he proposed that the capital be moved from Edo to Kamchatka so as to share the same latitude with London. A believer in strong state leadership, he urged that the shogunate not forfeit economic enterprises to merchant capital but energetically involve itself in investment, construction, and commerce. Moreover, he advised that Japan abandon its self-imposed isolation (see NATIONAL SECLUSION) from the rest of the world in favor of state-managed foreign trade and overseas colonization. Honda has been called an early spokesman for absolutism and imperialism, but during his own lifetime he remained essentially an independent and original thinker who, except for brief employment by the *daimyō* of the Kaga domain (now Ishikawa and Toyama prefectures), served no lord.

📖 ——Donald Keene, *The Japanese Discovery of Europe, 1720–1830* (rev ed, 1969).   John J. STEPHAN

Hondo

City on Shimoshima, one of the Amakusa Islands; administratively a part of Kumamoto Prefecture. The principal city of the Amakusa Islands, it is connected to the mainland by several bridges. There are several sites connected with the SHIMABARA UPRISING and early Christians of 17th-century Japan. Pop: 42,460.

Hōnen (1133–1212)

Buddhist priest and founder of the JŌDO SECT who spearheaded the Kamakura Buddhist "reformation." Real name Genku. Born in Mimasaka Province (now part of Okayama Prefecture) as the son of a *samurai*, Hōnen entered the Buddhist order at age eight after the death of his father. He studied at the temple ENRYAKUJI on Mt. Hiei (Hieizan) and became a monk of the TENDAI SECT at age 15. Disenchanted with the secular politics at Hiei, he decided to become a mountain ascetic (HIJIRI) and retired to Kurotani, a monastery in another part of Mt. Hiei, in 1150. He mastered the Tendai doctrines and the scholarship of the Nara sects, but he still felt spiritually unfulfilled. Hōnen finally came to the realization that NEMBUTSU, the recitation of AMIDA Buddha's name, was the only way to achieve *ōjō*, rebirth in Amida's Pure Land (Jōdo). In 1175, Hōnen began to preach the path of *nembutsu* in the city of Kyōto and founded the Jōdo sect. Urged by his patron-disciple KUJŌ KANEZANE, he wrote the *Senchaku hongan nembutsushū* (The Selection of the Nembutsu of the Original Vow; see SENCHAKUSHŪ) and effectively severed his ideological ties with the Tendai sect.

In 1204 the Buddhist establishment launched a campaign against Hōnen's movement, leading to the execution of four of his disciples in 1206. Hōnen himself was laicized and exiled to Sanuki Province (now Kagawa Prefecture) on the island of Shikoku in 1207. The Pure Land faith spread, nevertheless, and Hōnen was finally allowed to return to Kyōto in 1211, just a few months before his death.

Political instability and social upheaval late in the Heian period (794–1185) nurtured religious zeal and the spread of the Buddhist concept of *mappō*, which saw the world as entering an age in which the dharma (law) declined. KŪYA (903–972) had already introduced the practice of *nembutsu* to the common people, and GENSHIN (942–1017) had instilled in them the fear of hell and a longing for rebirth in the Pure Land. Hōnen availed himself of this tradition, but in his single-minded desire for the pure realm beyond death, he broke with the Tendai tradition, which affirmed the immanence of Buddhahood in the world (see HONGAKU). By making salvation a matter of faith rather than meditation, Hōnen gave traditional Buddhist practice a legitimate and confident expression. He also undermined the long tradition of the Buddhist sanctification of political affairs, urging believers to tend rather to the interior life. That his sect won recognition despite the initial ban and the charge of a private and unauthorized origin meant that the gate was open to further schisms within the onetime "mother church" of Tendai.

Devotion to Amida had always been an element in Tendai worship. Heian nobles were known to chant the LOTUS SUTRA in the morning and the *nembutsu* in the evening, but Hōnen gave a new

Hōnen

Portrait of Hōnen painted a century after his death. He is shown preaching in Settsu Province on his way to exile in Shikoku. Detail from the 34th of the 48 scrolls of the *Hōnen Shōnin eden*. Colors on paper. Height of scroll 35.1 cm. Ca 1317. Chion'in, Kyōto. National Treasure.

meaning to the practice. From Genshin's ŌJŌYŌSHŪ (Essentials for Pure Land Rebirth), Hōnen adopted the idea of reciting the *nembutsu* as the most effective means of birth in the Pure Land. "Of all actions leading to *ōjō*, priority belongs to *nembutsu*," he quoted Genshin in his *Senchakushū*. However, whereas Genshin considered *nembutsu* and *ōjō* as one path and one goal in a larger hierarchy of paths and goals, Hōnen designated them the only path and the only goal. He followed the Chinese Pure Land master Dōshaku (Ch: Daochuo or Tao-ch'o; 562–645) in ruling out the more difficult Sage Path (Shōdōmon) of meditation, saying that, in the age of *mappō*, mankind had become too degenerate to pursue this path. He relied especially on the teaching of Daochuo's successor Zendō (Ch: Shandao or Shan-tao; 613–681) and believed vocal *nembutsu* to be a superior path to the Pure Land freely offered by the gracious Amida. The title of his major work, *Senchaku hongan nembutsushū*, captures his meaning well. By *senchaku* is meant Hōnen's choice of *nembutsu* recitation as the sole means of rebirth in the Pure Land, as well as the choice or design so intended by Amida. By *hongan* is meant especially the 18th of the 48 vows of the bodhisattva Dharma-ākara (J: Hōzō Bosatsu), who, having fulfilled his vows, became Amida Buddha. In this vow the Buddha-to-be promised birth in the Pure Land to those who have perfect faith in him and who have repeated the name of Amida even as few as 10 times. In Hōnen's emphasis on the power of Amida, the traditional aspiration for enlightenment (Skt: *bodhicitta*; J: *bodashin*) was deemed no longer necessary for salvation. In preaching a path accessible to all people, Hōnen emphasized more than ever before the element of faith in PURE LAND BUDDHISM.

📖 ——Havelock Coates and Ryūgaku Ishizuka, *Hōnen, the Buddhist Saint: His Life and Thought* (1925). Ishii Kyōdō, ed, *Hōnen shōnin zenshū* (1955, 1974). Katsuki Jōkō, ed, *Jōdoshū kaisōki no kenkyū* (1970). Tamura Enchō, *Hōnen shōnin-den no kenkyū* (1956, rev ed 1972).   Whalen LAI

Honest John Incident

(Onesuto Jon Jiken). Incident surrounding the announcement of the United States Department of Defense on 28 July 1955 that it planned to send "Honest John" rocket launchers to Japan. The announcement did not specify the kind of warheads to be used, but it was known that the Honest John was a battlefield weapon capable of using conventional or atomic warheads. Senior Japanese officials, to whom the plan had been previously communicated in general terms, took the public position that Japan's consent would be required before atomic weapons could be brought into Japan, but they conceded privately to United States officials that no provision in existing agreements required Japanese consent for the introduction of nuclear weapons. A period of strong public interest followed the introduction of the Honest Johns in August 1955 but gradually died down when it became known that no atomic warheads were involved. The incident reflected the strong sensitivity of the Japanese public regarding the nuclear issue. The new security agreements concluded in 1960 by Japan and the United States (see UNITED STATES–JAPAN SECURITY TREATIES) provided for consultation in cases of this kind.

Richard B. FINN

honeysuckle, Japanese

(nindō). Lonicera japonica. Also known as suikazura. An evergreen shrub of the Caprifoliaceae family native to hill and mountain areas throughout Japan. Its oblong leaves do not wither even in the winter, hence the name nindō, which means "endures winter." In early summer fragrant five-lobed flowers bloom in pairs in the axils. The flower is white or pink, later changing to yellow. In Japan nindō leaves are put into bath water or dried and made into tea to be used as a diuretic.

Matsuda Osamu

hongaku

A priori, original, or primordial enlightenment, in contradistinction to shigaku, "incipient enlightenment," which refers to the gradual process of attaining enlightenment. Hongaku (Ch: benjue or penchüeh) first appeared as a concept in the Daijō kishinron (Treatise on the Awakening of Faith in the Mahāyāna; Ch: Dacheng qixin lun, Ta-cheng ch'i-hsin lun), a work of controversial origin for which no Sanskrit version is extant. The Daijō kishinron postulates a symmetry between the mind of sentient beings and the Buddhist absolute or Suchness (tathatā), thanks to which the essence of enlightenment of hongaku is already present within one's deepest consciousness. The concept of hongaku, basic to Mahāyāna Buddhism, permeated Buddhist philosophy in the Heian period (794–1185), encouraging an optimistic perception of enlightenment or Buddhahood, as immanent in all things-as-they-are. In the late Heian period, HŌNEN, founder of the JŌDO SECT of PURE LAND BUDDHISM, initiated a critique of hongaku philosophy by drawing attention to the sinfulness of men and the impurity of this world. While Hōnen encouraged a shigaku orientation, hongaku tendencies reemerged in later Buddhist thinkers.

Whalen LAI

Honganji

Major temple of the Buddhist True Pure Land sect (Jōdo Shinshū; see JŌDO SHIN SECT) over which its abbots claimed primacy from the early 14th century onward. During the Sengoku period (1467–1568), the Honganji surpassed its rivals within the sect, developing an extensive ecclesiastical organization that bound its adherents (monto) with firm religious and secular ties, mobilized armed leagues (IKKŌ IKKI), and ruled entire provinces. The secular power of this religious monarchy was, however, destroyed by the hegemon ODA NOBUNAGA (1534–82) in a bitterly fought 10 years' war (1570–80). At the beginning of the 17th century, a schism split the Honganji into two rival branches, headquartered at NISHI HONGANJI and HIGASHI HONGANJI in Kyōto, which remain to the present day vast religious establishments, each claiming more than 6 million members.

The Honganji originated in a small memorial chapel (Goeidō, Portrait Hall) enshrining an image of SHINRAN (1173–1263), the True Pure Land sect's patriarch, which was built in 1272 by Shinran's daughter Kakushin Ni (1224–83?). This hall was located at Yoshimizu in the Ōtani district at the foot of the Higashiyama hills in Kyōto (on grounds now part of the Jōdo sect's great temple Chion'in and occupied by its subtemple Sūtaiin), and Shinran's remains were reinterred on the site; hence the foundation became known as the Ōtani Byōdō (Ōtani Mausoleum). In 1282 Kakushin Ni deeded this property to the Shinshū community of faith on condition that her descendants retain the mausoleum's custodial rights (rusushiki). Her grandson Kakunyo Sōshō (1270–1351) sought to increase his standing by obtaining the status of a temple for the mausoleum, and it was redesignated Honganji (Temple of the Original Vow) by 1321, the first time the name appears in extant historical sources.

Kakunyo asserted the Honganji's pre-eminence by claiming direct descent from Shinran, not only by blood through Kakushin Ni but also by a special spiritual transmission through the patriarch's grandson Nyoshin (1235–1300); Shinran, Nyoshin, and Kakunyo therefore are the first three names listed in the Honganji's pontifical lineage. Kakunyo's efforts were unsuccessful, because the powerful monto groups of the Kantō (eastern Honshū) region, the sect's original base, refused to recognize the Honganji's pretensions. In the Kansai (western Honshū) region and in Kyōto itself, the Honganji was eclipsed by the Bukkōji, a Shinshū temple built by Ryōgen Ku-

shō (1285–1336) at Shirutani in Higashiyama in 1329, which remained immensely popular well into the 15th century.

The Honganji's fourth to seventh abbots—Zennyo Shungen (1333–89), Shakunyo Jigei (1350–93), Gyōnyo Genkō (1376–1440), and Zonnyo Enken (1396–1457)—continued to press their temple's claims, but progress was slow. By the 1440s the Honganji managed to make inroads into the Hokuriku (northern Honshū) region by taking advantage of succession disputes and factional splits among its Shinshū rivals, securing the affiliation of several of their temples and founding its own branch temples in the provinces of Echizen (now part of Fukui Prefecture) and Etchū (now Toyama Prefecture) as well as Kaga and Noto (now constituting Ishikawa Prefecture). This advance into the provinces was, however, for another few decades contained by the networks of the Honganji's rivals: the Bukkōji; the Kinshokuji of Kibe in Ōmi Province (now Chūzu Chō, Shiga Prefecture); the San-Monto faction of Echizen (the most radical and, from the Honganji's standpoint, "heretical" of the Shinshū groups); and especially the SENJUJI of the Takada district in Shimotsuke Province (now Ninomiya Machi, Tochigi Prefecture). Although an Amida hall was built alongside the Goeidō about 1438, the Ōtani Honganji itself remained an unprepossessing, minor Kyōto temple.

It was under the leadership of RENNYO Kenju (1415–99), who became its eighth abbot in 1457, that the Honganji emerged to preeminence in the True Pure Land sect. Rennyo strove for doctrinal and organizational unity among the Shinshū believers. He preached a return to Shinran's original doctrine of salvation through faith in the grace of Amida Buddha. His novel technique of instructing the populace through pastoral letters (gobunshō; also called ofumi) written in simple language won the Honganji many adherents. Initially, Rennyo's mission activities concentrated on the provinces of Ōmi (now Shiga Prefecture), Mikawa (now part of Aichi Prefecture), and Settsu (now divided between Ōsaka and Hyōgo prefectures), where he drew many defectors from the Bukkōji and Senjuji factions. In 1465, the Senjuji's abbot Shin'e (1434–1512) responded to this threat by moving his temple from Takada to the more centrally located Ishinden in Ise Province (now the city of Tsu, Mie Prefecture). That same year, the great Tendai sect monastery ENRYAKUJI on Mt. Hiei (Hieizan) northeast of Kyōto likewise reacted to Rennyo's incursion into Ōmi, where it held many proprietary interests, by causing the Ōtani Honganji to be ransacked and torn down.

After the destruction of the Ōtani Honganji, Rennyo moved first to Ōmi and then in 1471 to Yoshizaki in Echizen (now Kanazu Chō, Fukui Prefecture). Yoshizaki Gobō, the temple he founded there, attracted many pilgrims and developed into a prototype jinaimachi (town formed within temple precincts, in which the sense of a shared religious identity reinforced residential solidarity); it became the center of the Honganji's elaborate network of affiliated temples in the Hokuriku region. Some of the most important of those temples were run by members of Rennyo's immediate family (ikkeshū; he had 27 children). Typically, they had their own satellite organizations containing branch temples and their subordinate chapels (dōjō), religious confraternities (kō), and secular groups (kumi) of monto.

Through this network, the adherents of the Honganji could be mobilized to defend their sect's interests militarily. The ŌNIN WAR (1467–77) provided the context for the emergence of their armed leagues (the Ikkō ikki) as a powerful force in Japanese politics. In 1474, the monto of the Honganji intervened in a regional by-product of that great war, the struggle between two factions of the Togashi family, the shugo (military governor) house of Kaga; by the end of that year, they had helped Togashi Masachika destroy his brother Kōchiyo, who was backed by the Senjuji's adherents; the next spring, they turned on Masachika, refusing to heed Rennyo's appeals that they go back to farming. Rennyo thereupon left Yoshizaki and returned to the Kansai.

The Hokuriku monto, however, continued their bellicose activities. In 1488 they destroyed Togashi Masachika and took control of the province of Kaga, which they would not relinquish until 1580. In 1506 they were incited by the Honganji's ninth abbot, Jitsunyo Kōken (1458–1525), to champion the cause of Hosokawa Masamoto (1466–1507), the kanrei (chief executive officer) of the Muromachi shogunate, against a large coalition of the region's shugo and shugodai (deputy military governors) supported by the Senjuji and San-Monto factions. Ikkō ikki detachments from as far away as Settsu invaded Echizen, but were defeated by the daimyō Asakura Sadakage (1473–1512); the Honganji's adherents succeeded, however, in consolidating their position in Etchū, where they routed an invasion force from Echigo (now Niigata Prefecture), killing its commander, the *shugodai* Nagao Yoshikage. The Ikkō *ikki* had gained the initiative in a vast area on the coast of the Sea of Japan.

At Yamashina immediately to the east of Kyōto there had in the meantime arisen the first truly impressive Honganji, a great new temple headquarters built by Rennyo between 1479 and 1483. The Yamashina Honganji was a mature *jinaimachi*, consisting of three enclosures surrounded with moats and earthen ramparts: the temple proper, including the two characteristic main halls of prayer of the True Pure Land sect, Goeidō and Amidadō, as well as a residence built in the aristocratic *shinden* style; the "inner *jinai*," containing residences for the *ikkeshū* and the abbot's other principal deputies and prominent adherents; and the "outer *jinai*," composed of eight wards *(machi)* of artisan and merchant townsmen *(machishū)* and governed by a "confraternity of commoners" *(jigeshū kō)*. Here Rennyo had by 1482 received the submission of Kyōgō (thereafter called Renkyō; 1451–92), the abbot of the Honganji's great rival Bukkōji. In 1493 Shōe of the Kinshokuji likewise adhered to the Honganji. They drew many of their followers with them, and their former factions were thrown in disarray. There were also important defections from the Senjuji, which was torn by a succession struggle at Shin'e's death. As the 16th century began, the Honganji established itself as the major branch of the Jōdo Shin sect.

The Honganji fully evolved into a religious monarchy under Shōnyo Kōkyō (1516–54), who became its tenth abbot in 1525. The young Shōnyo was under the influence of his maternal relatives and his majordomo Shimotsuma Raishū (d 1538), who involved the Honganji in ambitious military enterprises. In 1531 Raishū led an army of *monto* from Ōmi and Mikawa into the Hokuriku region, where they scattered local opposition and put Kaga under the Honganji's direct control, eliminating the intermediate *ikkeshū* level. The next year, the Honganji took direct action in daimyō politics of the Home (Kinai) Provinces centering on Kyōto; Ikkō *ikki* occupied the great entrepôt city of Sakai and ravaged Nara, but the Yamashina Honganji itself was burnt by forces of the daimyō Rokkaku Sadayori (1495–1552) of Ōmi and the Lotus Confederation (Hokke *ikki*) of Kyōto's Nichirenist townsmen. Shōnyo moved to Ōsaka, where in 1533 he formally established the ISHIYAMA HONGANJI as his new headquarters. Here the historical process of the abbot's transformation from the custodian *(rusushiki)* of the Honganji into a pontiff *(hossu)* was completed. Shōnyo figured as a "vicar of Amida" *(Mida no daikan)* who held the power to guarantee or withhold the right to rebirth in paradise *(goshō gomen)*; not content with excommunication, he passed the death sentence on "heretics," "rebels," and malcontents such as Shimotsuma Raishū. He was a secular ruler who from his Ōsaka temple fortress could call upon the loyalties of great numbers of *monto* throughout central Japan and who exercised power over his regional domain of Kaga through a special headquarters, the Kanazawa Gobō, established by 1546 in that province. In 1549 the imperial court appointed Shōnyo provisional high priest of Buddhism *(gon no sōjō)*; his son Kennyo Kōsa (1543–92), the eleventh *hossu*, in January 1560 (Eiroku 2.12.15) obtained the status of an imperial abbacy *(monzeki)* for the Honganji. In short, the *hossu* of the Honganji was priest, daimyō, and imperial noble at once.

As the power of the Honganji's *hossu*, the geographical extent of its influence, and the scale of its mobilization of *monto* increased during the latter part of the Sengoku period, so did the vehemence of its confrontations with daimyō. In Echizen, Ikkō *ikki* fought recurrent campaigns against the Asakura, until a tenuous peace was achieved in 1556. In Mikawa, a great rising of the Honganji's adherents between 1562 and 1564 was the first grave test in the career of the young TOKUGAWA IEYASU as a daimyō. Above all, the Honganji was the major obstacle in the career of Oda Nobunaga as a national unifier: its major areas of strength coincided precisely with his primary sphere of interest in central Japan, making a clash between the two uncompromising parties inevitable. Ikkō *ikki* mobilized by Kennyo Kōsa fought Nobunaga from 1570 to 1580 on fronts ranging from Nagashima in Ise (now part of Mie Prefecture) to Saiga in Kii (now Wakayama Prefecture), Aga in Harima (now part of Hyōgo Prefecture), and the Honganji's domains in the Hokuriku area. For a year in the course of this war, the Honganji dominated Echizen Province, but its hold there was eliminated by Nobunaga in 1575 amid scenes of terrible carnage. Characteristically, the Senjuji's adherents supported Nobunaga in this campaign.

In the spring of 1580 Kennyo finally made peace with Nobunaga, agreeing to surrender the Ishiyama Honganji and leaving the temple fortress for Saginomori in Kii. Kennyo's son and designated successor Kyōnyo Kōju (1558–1614), however, refused to honor the agreement. Kennyo therefore disowned Kyōnyo in favor of a younger

son, Junnyo Kōshō (1577–1631), thus laying the ground for a schism in the Honganji. Although Kennyo and Kyōnyo were reconciled immediately after Nobunaga's death in 1582, both Junnyo and Kyōnyo later claimed the succession to their father and the title of the 12th *hossu*, Junnyo becoming the head of the Nishi (western) Honganji faction and Kyōnyo the founding abbot of the Higashi (eastern) Honganji.

The Ishiyama Honganji burned on the day of its surrender to intermediaries sent by the imperial court, Tenshō 8.8.2 (10 September 1580). The Honganji's 10 years' war with Nobunaga ended in the 11th month of that year (December 1580), when Nobunaga's general SHIBATA KATSUIE (1522?–83) reported the conquest of its Kaga stronghold. Kennyo moved the Honganji's headquarters to Kaizuka in Izumi Province (now part of Ōsaka Prefecture) in 1583. In 1584 the national unifier TOYOTOMI HIDEYOSHI (1537–98) moved into Ōsaka Castle, the great fortress he built on the site of the Ishiyama Honganji; the following year, he endowed Kennyo with land at Temma in his new castle town, reestablishing the Honganji in Ōsaka. In 1591, however, Hideyoshi again ordered Kennyo to move his head temple, and it was relocated on the present site of the Nishi Honganji in Kyōto. In 1603 Kyōnyo left the retirement quarters assigned him by his brother Junnyo at the Nishi Honganji and established the Higashi Honganji a few city blocks to the east.

In contrast to the turbulence of their common historical background, both the Nishi Honganji and the Higashi Honganji were pillars of respectability throughout the Edo period (1600–1868), preaching the virtues of submissiveness to the authorities through pontifical directives and collections of edifying tales such as *Myōkōnin den* (1842; Biographies of Wondrously Good People). In reaction to this establishmentarian religion, there arose among True Pure Land believers a private devotional movement, *Kakure Nembutsu* (secret devotion to Amida), which was proscribed by both the Honganji and the Tokugawa regime.

■ ——*Honganji-shi*, 3 vols (1961–69). Inoue Toshio, *Honganji* (1966). Inoue Tashio, *Ikkō ikki no kenkyū* (1968). Kasahara Kazuo, *Kinsei ōjōden no sekai: Seiji kenryoku to shūkyō to minshū* (1978). Kasahara Kazuo, *Rennyo* (1963). Mori Ryūkichi, *Honganji* (1959). Mori Ryūkichi, *Rennyo* (1979). *Shinshū nempyō* (1973). *Shinshū shiryō shūsei*, 13 vols (1975–). Michael Solomon, "Kinship and the Transmission of Religious Charisma: The Case of Honganji," *Journal of Asian Studies*, 33.3 (May 1974). Stanley Weinstein, "Rennyo and the Shinshū Revival," in John Whitney Hall and Toyoda Takeshi, ed, *Japan in the Muromachi Age* (1977).   George ELISON

Hon'imbō

Title of the grand master of the game GO. The name Hon'imbō originally referred to a residence for monks in Jakkōji, a temple of the Nichiren sect of Buddhism in Kyōto. One of the monks of this temple, Nikkai (1558–1623), won renown for his mastery of *go* under the name Hon'imbō Sansa and was chosen to instruct the warlords ODA NOBUNAGA, TOYOTOMI HIDEYOSHI, and TOKUGAWA IEYASU in the game. *Go* masters continued to receive the title Hon'imbō after Sansa. At the beginning of the Edo period (1600–1868), the Tokugawa shogunate patronized *go* by establishing stipends for masters and by formally recognizing several hereditary lines of masters (IEMOTO), including the Hon'imbō line. In the Meiji period (1868–1912), the Hon'imbō school shared prominence with a newly organized group, the Hōensha. A national *go* association, the NIHON KIIN, was established in 1924 with a Hon'imbō master as its head. In 1939 Hon'imbō Shūsai (1874–1940) ended the custom of hereditary succession to the Hon'imbō title. Since that time the Nihon Kiin has decided the successor to the title by a yearly professional championship, which is sponsored by the newspaper *Mainichi shimbun*.

HAYASHI Yutaka

honjibutsu

The original Buddhist prototype of a native Japanese deity. According to the religious syncretism that prevailed in Japan after the 9th and 10th centuries, Shintō deities (KAMI) were believed to be indigenous Japanese incarnations or manifestations of universalistic Buddhist divinities. Thus AMATERASU ŌMIKAMI (the divine imperial ancestress identified with the sun) was regarded as the Japanese manifestation of Dainichi Nyorai (Mahāvairocana Buddha, whose name literally means "Great Sun Buddha"), the Shintō deity ŌKUNI-NUSHI NO MIKOTO was viewed as the manifestation of Yakushi Nyorai (Bhaiṣajyaguru Buddha), and so on. It should be noted, however, that the identifications between specific Buddhist and Shintō deities were not the same at all times. In this system of syncretism, the Buddhist divinity was termed *honjibutsu* (a Buddha who is the original source), whereas his incarnation in Japan as an indigenous Shintō deity *(kami)* was designated *gongen* ("expedient manifestation"). See also HONJI SUIJAKU. *Stanley* WEINSTEIN

honjin

Special inns established for *daimyō,* nobles, shogunal officials, and other important personages at post stations along the main highways during the Edo period (1600–1868). Used during the journeys to and from Edo (now Tōkyō) under the SANKIN KŌTAI system that required daimyō to live at the shogunal capital every other year, *honjin* were operated by local officials. The name dates from 1363, when the shōgun Ashikaga Yoshiakira named his lodgings en route to Kyōto the *honjin,* or "principal headquarters." In addition to *honjin,* there were other subsidiary inns, such as the *wakihonjin* and the *karihonjin. Honjin* were abolished two years after the Meiji Restoration of 1868.

honji suijaku

The theory that the native Shintō deities (KAMI) are Japanese incarnations or manifestations *(suijaku)* of Indian Buddhist divinities who are their original and eternal prototypes *(honji).* As the Buddhist religion gained a foothold in Japan in the 7th century, local Shintō deities came to be viewed as protectors of Buddhism and, particularly, of Buddhist temples. To ward off natural disasters shrines housing the spirits of local deities were often erected on temple grounds.

From around the 10th century on, the *honji suijaku* theory became popular and Shintō deities were seen no longer simply as guardians of temples, but rather as Japanese incarnations of Buddhas and bodhisattvas who had manifested themselves in Japan in the form of Shintō deities in order to deliver the Japanese people from their suffering and ignorance. A Shintō *kami* performing this function was popularly termed *gongen* (an expedient manifestation; see AVATAR) whereas its Buddhist counterpart was known as HONJIBUTSU (the Buddha who is the original source). By the 13th century the deities of most major shrines were identified with specific Buddhist divinities, e.g., AMATERASU ŌMIKAMI (the so-called divine imperial ancestress and sun goddess) of the ISE SHRINE with the Buddha DAINICHI, the deity of the Kumano Hongū Shrine (see KUMANO SANZAN SHRINES) with the Buddha AMIDA, the deity of the Kashima Shrine with the bodhisattva KANNON, and so on.

Shintō theorists like YOSHIDA KANETOMO (1435–1511) tried to refute the concept of *honji suijaku* by asserting that it was rather the Shintō deities who were the true and eternal prototypes, whereas the Buddhas and bodhisattvas were merely Indian manifestations of them. Despite strong opposition from Shintō scholars throughout the Edo period (1600–1868), the *honji suijaku* concept continued to be almost universally accepted among the Japanese people until the government issued a ban in 1868 forbidding Buddhist-Shintō syncretic practices at shrines, as a consequence of which all shrines termed *gongen* were redesignated *jinja,* Buddhist paraphernalia were removed, and the popular Buddhistic names of native deities were changed to Shintō ones. See also SHINTŌ AND BUDDHISM, SEPARATION OF. *Stanley* WEINSTEIN

Honjō

City in southwestern Akita Prefecture, northern Honshū, on the Sea of Japan. A castle town during the Edo period (1600–1868), Honjō is the political, economic, and cultural center of the district. *Honjōmai* rice is produced here; dairy farming and horticulture are also important. Pop: 42,962.

Honjō

City in northwestern Saitama Prefecture, central Honshū. Honjō developed as a POST-STATION TOWN on the Nakasendō highway in the Edo period (1600–1868). Its silk industry, begun in the Meiji period (1868–1912), has been replaced by chemical, electrical appliance, and foodstuff industries since World War II. Pop: 53,462.

Honjō Mutsuo (1905–1939)

Novelist. Born in Hokkaidō. Graduate of Aoyama Normal School. He started to write children's stories and critical articles on education while working as an elementary school teacher and participating in the PROLETARIAN LITERATURE MOVEMENT in the 1920s. Though his active involvement in leftist political activities cost him his job, he continued to write fiction for the proletarian cause. Many of his works express his humanistic protest against social injustice. He is best known for his historical novel *Ishikarigawa* (1938–39), which describes the hardships endured by a band of former *samurai* who settled primeval forestland beside the river Ishikarigawa in Hokkaidō during the early years of the Meiji period (1868–1912). Other works include the short story "Shiroi kabe" (1934).

Honjō Shigeru (1876–1945)

Commander-in-chief of the Guandong (Kwantung) Army, the Japanese field army that overran Manchuria during 1931–32 (see MANCHURIAN INCIDENT). Born in Hyōgo Prefecture into a farming family, Honjō graduated from the Army Academy in 1897 and served in numerous army posts in Japan and on the continent. During 1920–24 he acted as military adviser to ZHANG ZUOLIN (Chang Tso-lin), the Manchurian warlord. In August 1931 he was made head of the Guandong Army. Honjō returned to Japan in July 1932, served briefly on the Supreme Military Council, and on 6 April 1933 was appointed chief aide-de-camp to the emperor. He was regarded as a partisan of the extremist KŌDŌHA (Imperial Way faction) of the army, but he served the emperor faithfully and selflessly. During his tenure as chief aide, Honjō kept a detailed and frank diary about his dealings with the emperor. The diary, published after his death, is an invaluable source of information on the emperor's thoughts and actions during these critical years. Honjō resigned from his post following the attempted coup d'etat by Kōdōha officers in the FEBRUARY 26TH INCIDENT (1936) because his son-in-law was implicated in the affair. He later served as head of the Disabled Veterans Administration (Shōhei Hogo In) and briefly as a member of the Privy Council (Sūmitsuin). Because of his role in this affair, he was charged as a war criminal by the Allied Powers after World War II. He committed *harakiri* in true *samurai* fashion just before his arrest. Honjō's complicity in the plot devised by his staff officers to trigger the Manchurian Incident has not been proven, but to the end he insisted that the Guandong Army's actions were taken in response to provocative acts by Chinese troops.
🔲——Hayashi Masaharu, *Rikugun taishō Honjō Shigeru* (1967). Honjō Shigeru, *Honjō nikki* (1967). *Mikiso* HANE

honkadori

(literally, "taking from an original poem"). The technique in WAKA of echoing a phrase or image from a well-known poem or using it verbatim in a different context in the creation of a new one, thus, by association, giving an added depth to the new poem. Although the device can be seen even in the 8th-century anthology MAN'YŌSHŪ, it was with FUJIWARA NO TOSHINARI (Fujiwara no Shunzei) and other leading poets of the anthology SHIN KOKINSHŪ (1205) that it came to be used consciously as a poetic technique. These poets exploited its potential to create effects of allusive depth and suggestiveness in a poetic form otherwise restricted by its brevity. Toshinari's son FUJIWARA NO SADAIE (Fujiwara no Teika), in critical works such as *Maigetsushō* (ca 1219), and the ex-emperor Juntoku (1197–1242), in YAKUMO MISHŌ, set guidelines governing the usage of *honkadori.* For example, only two lines might be taken from an earlier poem, which should be from one of the first three imperial anthologies, and variation should be effected by changing the season or theme of the original poem to a different one in the new poem. The technique comported well with the characteristic symbolism of the *Shin kokinshū.* The device was also employed in prose works such as the TALE OF GENJI and in the linked verse *(renga)* which emerged midway in the Kamakura period (1185–1333).

honke and bunke

Terms used to describe the relationship between the main household *(honke)* and branch households *(bunke)* of extended families. Also used to describe certain fictive kinship relationships in Japanese society. The head of a household and his successor reside in the *honke,* and married younger sons usually build new homes apart, creating *bunke*. Even when the establishment of the *bunke* occurred long ago and actual kinship is unclear, as long as both parties recognize a relationship, the *honke-bunke* relation continues. A *honke* and the *bunke* associated with it are referred to in sociological literature as *dōzoku*, a corporate group of kin composed of a number of families, usually residing in the same town.

The *honke-bunke* relationship may be based on other than blood ties. This occurs when a servant of the *honke* creates a new household or a new shop (in this case called *norenwake*) or when impoverished peasants or migrants to the area settle as *bunke* of a wealthy or influential *honke*, thus receiving economic protection. In general, *honke* maintain greater social and economic responsibilities for community festivities and ANCESTOR WORSHIP. The status of members of a *honke* and *bunke* is not based on age, but on their position in the overall structure of the *dōzoku*. Even today *honke* maintain great authority and perform substantial functions in rural areas. The pattern of *honke-bunke* is one of the paradigms of Japanese society, seen also in the underworld and in the relationship between companies and their subsidiaries. See also KINSHIP; IE.

NOGUCHI Takenori

honke and ryōke

Terms referring to persons or institutions in a proprietary capacity on a landed estate (SHŌEN). Although the hierarchy of tenure differed according to the size and circumstances of the individual *shōen*, by the end of the 10th century the rights of proprietorship were separated in a threefold division. The RYŌSHU was the original or local proprietor who managed the cultivators (*shōmin*), but in many cases, in order to prevent interference from government officials, the *ryōshu* commended his land to a more powerful proprietor, called a *ryōke* (often translated as central proprietor), who had more influence in the capital. In return for his patronage, the *ryōke* was entitled to a certain share (*ryōke shiki*) of the fruits of the land. In order to secure absolute guarantee of title to the *shōen* as well as certain immunities (see FUYU AND FUNYŪ), however, the *ryōke* often commended the estate to an even more exalted personage or religious institution, called *honke* (often translated as titular proprietor), who in turn received a share (*honke shiki*) of the revenues. The actual business of the *shōen* was conducted in the *honjo* (administrative office), which was either located on the estate itself or in the capital.

G. Cameron HURST III

Honnōji Incident

(Honnōji no Hen). The assassination of the hegemon ODA NOBUNAGA by his vassal AKECHI MITSUHIDE in the early hours of 21 June 1582 (Tenshō 10.6.2). Nobunaga had arrived in Kyōto two days previously, taking up his habitual quarters at the Honnōji, a temple of the Nichiren sect; on the eve on the incident he entertained court nobles there at a tea ceremony. Only a few attendants were with him, the armed retinue of his son Nobutada (b 1557 and also destined to die this day) was quartered elsewhere in the city, and none of his principal captains was in the vicinity. His armies were either assembled about Ōsaka and Sakai, the staging area of a planned invasion of Shikoku; deployed against UESUGI KAGEKATSU in the Hokuriku region on the coast of the Sea of Japan; or engaging Mōri Terumoto (1553–1625) in the struggle for control of the Chūgoku area in western Honshū. Mitsuhide, the *daimyō* of Kameyama in Tamba Province (immediately west of Kyōto), had orders to march his army of 10,000 to Chūgoku, but instead seized the opportunity for a surprise attack on his lord, who had for once let down his guard. Nobunaga met his end in the burning temple, but Mitsuhide did not succeed to the hegemony. It passed instead to TOYOTOMI HIDEYOSHI, who hurried back from the Chūgoku front and defeated Mitsuhide in the Battle of YAMAZAKI a scant 11 days after the Honnōji Incident.

George ELISON

hōnoki

Magnolia obovata. Deciduous tree of the magnolia family (Magnoliaceae) which grows wild in mountain areas of Japan and is often cultivated. It grows to 3 meters (10 ft) in height, and its diameter reaches 1 meter (3 ft). The *hōnoki* has very large alternate leaves that grow in clusters at the tips of branches. The leaves measure 20–45 centimeters (8–18 in) in length and have a long oval shape. The back of the leaf is white and has thin narrow hairs. Around May and June the plant produces fragrant white flowers about 15 centimeters (6 in) in diameter at the tops of young branches. Its

conical fruits are also 15 centimeters in length and ripen in the fall.

The *hōnoki* has been known since ancient times. The large leaves were used as plates, and an extract of *hōnoki* bark was used as a remedy for stomachache and worms and also as a diuretic and expectorant. *Hōnoki* wood is highly valued for making furniture, drafting boards, lacquerware, rulers, boxes, pencils, sword sheaths, and wooden sandals, since its fine, soft grain is easily worked and rarely warps or cracks. Charcoal made of *hōnoki* wood was used in polishing gold and silver. The *hōnoki* was first exported to Europe in 1790 and was introduced to the United States in 1865.

MATSUDA Osamu

honor

(*meiyo*; literally, "glory of the name"). A fundamental concept which has regulated Japanese society in various ways since ancient times. The Japanese traditionally attached overwhelming importance to one's "name," even to the point where it regulated one's actions. The earliest reference to the Japanese concern with name is found in the idea of *imina* (posthumous name) mentioned in the KOJIKI (712) and NIHON SHOKI (720), Japan's oldest chronicles. Although the use of *imina* was probably imported from China, the taboo associated with the utterance of a dead person's name is a characteristic common to many primitive peoples, and as such reflects the attitude of the early Japanese. In the 8th-century poetic anthology MAN'YŌSHŪ, ŌTOMO NO YAKAMOCHI frequently alluded to "pure names" (*kiyoki sono na*) and "brilliant names" (*akirakeki na*). However, the name he referred to was the name of an *uji* (clan or family), and not of an individual. The ancient *ritsuryō* state was essentially a pyramidal hierarchy of various *uji* families with the imperial family at its apex, and Yakamochi's concern for name was a reflection of the authority accorded to the head of a powerful *uji* within the *ritsuryō* hierarchy (see RITSURYŌ SYSTEM).

With the rise of the warrior class in the 12th century, the idea of "valuing one's name" (*na o oshimu*) came to occupy a central place in the psychological makeup of the Japanese. It is highly significant that the constant references to "name" (*na*) and "shame" (*haji*) in the warrior tales written during the Kamakura (1185–1333) and Muromachi (1333–1568) periods are not limited to that of one particular individual but encompass that of one's family and ancestors. Thus, shame to oneself is at the same time loss of honor to one's ancestors as well as descendants. In the Edo period (1600–1868), the merchant class (CHŌNIN) appropriated the idea of honor from the warrior class and expressed it in such phrases as *"bun ga tatanu"* (I will lose my honor) or *"otoko ga tatanu"* (I will lose honor as a man). This new consciousness of one's name was not, strictly speaking, respect for individual honor; nevertheless, it was closely related to the development of an idea of the self. Thus, throughout the medieval and premodern periods, what one may term the culture of honor and shame was shaped by the values of a feudal society.

In the Meiji period (1868–1912) government leaders fostered an ideology in which the state was modeled on the patriarchal family. The historic lord-vassal relationship was also held up as the model for social relationships and a renewed emphasis was given to the importance of honor. Soldiers in particular were taught not to defile the family honor in battle. It was only with defeat in World War II that the Japanese began to reconsider honor as a matter of self-respect.

SAITŌ Shōji

honorific language

(*keigo*). Often referred to in English as "polite speech" or "honorifics." The Japanese language has an extensive system of honorific language to show respect by the speaker to the addressee. *Keigo* in the broad sense refers to the entire system of speech levels, and in its narrow sense means "terms of respect" and refers to honorific words and expressions. The question "Did X go to Tōkyō yesterday?" for instance, can be said in more than two dozen ways depending on who is saying it to whom in what kind of setting and who X is (e.g., *X-san wa kinō Tōkyō e irasshaimashita ka? X-sensei wa kinō Tōkyō e oide ni narare mashita ka? X-kun wa kinō Tōkyō e itta ka? X-san wa kinō Tōkyō e irasshatta no?*). In speaking, a choice is made as to the degree of politeness to be expressed, and *keigo* is used appropriately to the situation.

There are two distinct levels of speech identifiable by the final verb phrase of the sentence: the plain form (*da-tai*) and the polite style (*desu-masu-tai*). The plain style is characterized by the final verb phrase in the plain form, e.g., *da* (is, are), *kuru* (come), *kita* (came); the polite style is characterized by the final verb phrase in the polite form, e.g., *desu* (is, are), *kimasu* (come), *kimashita* (came). The latter can further be subdivided into two categories: the polite and the ultrapolite. The ultrapolite style frequently has *de gozaimasu* (is, are), *de gozaimashita* (was, were) as the final verb phrase of the sentence. Within each style, however, the degree of politeness can be varied by the use of other honorifics.

Choice of speech style. The speech style adopted in any two-person interaction is basically determined by the status of the speaker and the addressee and the degree of intimacy between them. The general rule is that when the addressee is of higher status than the speaker, or when the two are not very intimate, the polite style *(desu-masu-tai)* is to be used. Relative status is determined by a combination of factors, such as age, sex, rank, or social status and favors done or owed. Observance of the status hierarchy is particularly strict within an in-group situation. Hence a member of the junior class of a school is a *sempai* (senior) to a sophomore in the same school as is a company employee to his colleague who entered a year later. Being members of the same club or working in the same section of the company results in greater intimacy than otherwise. In general, however, status superiority supersedes intimacy in the above cases, and the junior ranking person normally is expected to use the polite style of speech in addressing friends or colleagues of a slightly higher status. In the reverse case, where the speaker is of higher status in an in-group situation, the speaker has a choice of plain or polite style. The choice depends partly on how great the status difference is and partly on the personal preference of the person of higher status. When two individuals who do not belong to the same group meet for the first time, both individuals will use the polite style unless there are some obvious differences in age or social status as reflected in dress, manner, or occupation.

The speech style chosen by women is often a step politer than that selected by men. Women are not as likely to speak in the plain style to a junior ranking adult as men are. They tend to use the polite style much more widely and indiscriminately, restricting the use of the plain style to immediate family members, close friends, and children. While the ultrapolite style is used mainly in formal speeches by men, it is used rather regularly in place of the polite style by women identified with the upper social strata.

The customary style of speech used in addressing a particular individual may be broken in special settings depending on the degree of formality appropriate to the occasion. The daughter, who has been using the plain style of speech with her parents, will use the polite style to thank her parents for the care they took in bringing her up as she leaves the family on her wedding day. The company employee may use the plain style of speech as he teases his boss at a drinking party. The professor will give his lecture in the polite style in the classroom, although he may address individual students in the plain style. It can thus be seen that the setting is an additional determinant of the speech style, superseding the two major factors of status and intimacy.

In summary, the polite style is used in addressing a person of higher status or one who is not intimate, except on occasions where the setting is the major determinant of speech style. When the two factors of status and intimacy are at work, the tendency is to err by being overpolite rather than the reverse. Thus many wives speak to their husbands in the polite *desu-masu* style. A senior professional, despite his high status, is likely to use the polite style in speaking to a junior colleague if they are not graduates of the same university or if there was never a professor-student relationship. The polite style, in other words, is the most neutral and standard style of speech in Japanese.

Types of honorific. The final verb phrase of the sentence that differentiates the speech styles is only one aspect of *keigo*. There are innumerable other honorifics to be found in various parts of speech, including nouns, pronouns, verbs, adjectives, adverbs, and conjunctions. These honorifics, also referred to as *keigo*, are normally classified into three groups: *sonkeigo* (exalted terms), *kenjōgo* (humble terms), and *teineigo* (polite terms). Exalted terms are used to refer to the addressee and anything directly associated with the addressee, such as kin, house, possessions, whereas humble terms are used to refer to the speaker and anything associated with the speaker. By elevating the addressee through exalted terms and lowering the speaker through humble terms, a greater distance is created between the two, thereby expressing deeper respect for the addressee. Exalted terms are also used to refer to a third person of higher status if he is not a member of the speaker's in-group. *Teineigo* or polite terms are used without reference to the addressee or speaker and are found in increasing numbers as the speech level goes up.

Most exalted and humble words are derived from neutral words by grammatical rules, but there are also a number of underived independent words that show no resemblance to their neutral equivalents. Verbs are rich in both types of honorifics. Examples of underived independent exalted and humble words are: "to say": *yū* (neutral), *ossharu* (exalted), *mōsu* (humble); "to look at": *miru* (neutral), *goran ni naru* (exalted), *haiken suru* (humble); "to go": *yuku* (neutral), *irassharu* (exalted), *mairu* (humble); "to do": *suru* (neutral), *nasaru* (exalted), *itasu* (humble). For verbs that do not have independent exalted equivalents, the rule *o* + verb + *ni naru* is applied to derive the exalted verb. Thus *kaku* (to write) becomes *okaki ni naru* as an exalted term. Another device is to attach the honorific auxiliary *-rare* or *-are* to the verb. This grammatical device can be applied also to some of the independent exalted verbs to increase the degree of exaltation, such as *irassharare masu*. There is also a device to create humble verbs with the meaning "to do something for the addressee or for someone to whom respect is shown." It takes the form *o* + verb + *suru*. These grammatical rules for deriving exalted or humble terms do not necessarily apply to every verb, and not every exalted verb has a humble verb counterpart. The same holds true for honorific nouns; see below.

There is a group of verbs, namely the give-receive verbs, that play an important role in the *keigo* system. These verbs are used as main verbs in describing the giving and receiving of gifts and as auxiliary verbs in compound verb phrases to express the giving and receiving of actions done as a favor. The group of seven basic give-receive verbs can be divided into three sets: (1) *sashiageru, ageru,* and *yaru* (the speaker or his in-group member gives something to *X*); (2) *itadaku* and *morau* (the speaker or his in-group member receives something from *X*); and (3) *kudasaru* and *kureru* (*X* gives something to the speaker or his in-group member). The first verb of each set is an exalted term to be used when *X* has or is treated as having higher status than the speaker, and the last verb in each set is generally used when *X* is an in-group member of the speaker or has lower status than the speaker. Only the first set has the extra term *ageru* that is relatively neutral. *Ageru, yaru,* and *morau* may be used in give-receive actions between two individuals both of whom are unrelated to the speaker. The rules in using the give-receive verbs are complex and group membership becomes an important factor. Every sentence with one of these verbs carries much more information than the surface meaning may denote, e.g., *John wa sensei ni hon o itadaita* means "Our John received a book from the teacher."

In comparison with verbs, honorific nouns are relatively simple. There are underived exalted and humble nouns, but the majority of these are used in writing. Most exalted nouns are created through grammatical rules. In general, the prefix *o-* is attached to the neutral noun of Japanese origin, such as *oniwa* (garden), *otegami* (letter), and the prefix *go-* for Chinese compounds, such as *gobyōki* (illness), *goiken* (opinion). In the case of nouns referring to people, *-san* is suffixed in addition to the prefix *o-*, such as *otetsudaisan* (maid), *oishasan* (doctor). Many of the kinship terms in the exalted form take *-san* with or without the *o-* prefix. The neutral form of kinship terms is seldom used as neutral in conversation. It usually functions as the humble term and is thus used to refer only to the kin of the speaker. Hence *chichi* or *haha* usually means "my father" or "my mother."

The *o-* prefix used for nouns can also be attached to some adjectives and adverbs to create polite terms *(teineigo)*, such as *oshizuka* (quiet), *osamui* (cold), *ohayaku* (quickly).

In the case of pronouns, there are no grammatical means to derive an honorific pronoun, whether exalted or humble, from a neutral one. In fact, there are hardly any first- and second-person pronouns that can be considered truly neutral. Most students of Japanese tend to equate *watakushi* with "I" and *anata* with "you," and use these terms with great frequency. In Japanese, however, the grammatical subject as well as object can be omitted, and there is a tendency to avoid particularly the use of "I" and "you" in polite speech. Since the humble verb phrase provides the context, the use of "I" is redundant unless it is there for the purpose of emphasis. In the case of "you" also, the exalted verb phrase provides the context for the missing subject or object "you." The pronoun *anata* is not considered an exalted term today. It can be used only to intimate equals or to those lower in status. It is likely to be taken as an insult when *anata* is used in speaking to a person who is higher in status or who is a nonintimate equal. Customarily the second-person pronoun is replaced by the title or the title plus *-san* in speaking to a person of higher status. For example, one must say *Sensei wa iras-shaimasu ka?* to ask a teacher "Are *you* going?" For nonintimate equals, last name plus *-san* or the pronoun *otaku* or *otakusama* is used.

There are many other second-person pronouns, but they belong to the group of words called *keihigo* (scornful terms). *Keihigo* is considered part of the *keigo* system. Like exalted terms *(sonkeigo)*, there are independent, underived scornful terms as well as those derived grammatically from neutral nouns, verbs, and adjectives, which are used to express scorn of the second or third person or his actions in plain-style speech. The speech of *yakuza* (gangsters) is characterized by many such terms.

The use of keigo in referring to a third person. When reference is made to a third person, exalted or humble terms may have to be used for him depending on his group membership. If the third person is a member of the addressee's group, he must be treated exactly in the same way as the addressee would be treated by the use of exalted terms. The most clear-cut example might be one concerning family members. In referring to a little child of the addressee, the same exalted terms are used as in referring to the addressee, such as *otaku no botchan ni itadaita hon* ("the book I, or a member of my family, received from your son"). Although obviously younger than the speaker in this case, the relative status of the third person is ignored. On the other hand, when the third person is a member of the speaker's in-group, he is referred to with the same humble terms as the speaker would use to refer to himself, even though the third person may be of higher status than the speaker. Thus, an employee of a company, dealing with customers or outsiders in his official capacity, will refer to his boss, an in-group member in this situation, not with exalted terms but with humble terms. Within the company, however, the same employee will address his boss with exalted terms and will refer to him in such terms when speaking to coworkers.

To summarize, within an in-group situation, where the status hierarchy is strictly observed, exalted terms are used to varying degrees in speaking to or of individuals of higher status. In speaking to an out-group member, however, the status of every member of one's own in-group is reduced to the low level at which one treats oneself, whereas the status of everyone in the addressee's group is raised to a high level. In other words, status is ignored in in-group/out-group interaction; all out-group members are treated as higher status persons, and all in-group members are treated as lower status persons. In referring to a third person who does not belong to either the addressee's or speaker's group, the speaker may use exalted or neutral terms depending on the social status of the third person, and on how the addressee and the speaker feel toward that person.

Keigo in world perspective. Japanese is not alone in having honorific expressions. Because of the structure of human society, it is only natural that in different settings different behavior, including speech behavior, would be expected anywhere. Special expressions to show deference in addressing a member of the royalty or a high status person are found in most languages. Many European languages have two second-person pronouns, the formal and the intimate (e.g., *vous/tu* in French, *Sie/du* in German). The choice between the two depends mainly on the status difference and the degree of intimacy between the speaker and the addressee, like the choice between the plain *da-tai* style and the polite *desu-masu-tai* style in Japanese. Honorifics of various other types are found in numerous other languages. The characteristics of the Japanese honorifics are that they are all-pervasive in speech; that group membership is a major determinant in addition to status and intimacy; and that they allow for fine gradations in the level of politeness within each speech style. Thus, the utterance *Oimōtosan wa Tōkyō e okaeri ni natta no?* (Has your younger sister returned to Tōkyō?) in the plain style addressed to a fairly close friend shows respect for the addressee by the use of exalted terms in reference to the addressee's in-group member. There are co-occurrence restrictions, and therefore consistency in the use of exalted and humble terms is required. However, the availability of a large number of verb phrases with the same meaning but different shades of politeness allows for respect in informal situations as well as a subtle disrespect in formal situations.

■──Bunkachō, ed, *Taigū hyōgen* (1971). Bernice Z. Goldstein and Kyoko Tamura, *Japan and America: A Comparative Study in Language and Culture* (1975). Kokuritsu Kokugo Kenkyūjo, ed, *Keigo to keigo ishiki* (1957). Samuel E. Martin, *Reference Grammar of Japanese* (1975). Roy Andrew Miller, *The Japanese Language* (1967). Agnes M. NIYEKAWA

honryō ando → ando

Honsaroku

A 17th-century treatise on statecraft. The title constitutes an attribution of authorship to Honda Sado no Kami Masanobu (1538–1616), combining *hon* and *sa*, the first syllables of his family name (Honda) and his title (Sado no Kami), with the word for "account," *roku*. Honda was one of the most influential men of the early years of the Tokugawa shogunate (1603–1867), and is said to have written the work for the guidance of the second shōgun, TOKUGAWA HIDETADA (r 1605–23). The treatise circulated under several other titles, including *Tenka kokka no yōroku* (How to Rule the Realm) and *Chiyō shichijō* (The Seven Essentials of Government), and was attributed also to FUJIWARA SEIKA (1561–1619), the first purveyor of Neo-Confucian ideology to the Tokugawa; in fact, neither the author nor the date of composition is known. Although dressed with a veneer of Neo-Confucian parlance, the work is unburdened by heavy intellectual content. It instructs the ruler to "know *tentō* (the Way of Heaven, which governs the affairs of the universe)," to be proper in his behavior, to choose good subordinates and advisers, and to keep the population, especially the farmers, content. Drawing examples from Chinese and Japanese history, it guarantees success to a lord who "maintains the principle of *tentō* and unselfishly exerts himself for the realm." George ELISON

Honshū

The largest of Japan's four major islands. The majority of the country's population and industries is concentrated on this island. Its terrain is predominantly mountainous, with few plains and little arable land. The climate is temperate, and the annual precipitation exceeds 1,000 mm (39 in) in almost all districts. Districts on the coast of the Sea of Japan have long winters and heavy snowfall. The coastal districts of the Pacific Ocean and the Inland Sea extending from southern Kantō to Yamaguchi Prefecture are the most industrialized and urbanized regions in Japan; the largest cities of the country (for example, Tōkyō, Ōsaka, and Kyōto), principal industries, and universities and other cultural institutions are concentrated here. Together with northern Kyūshū, these districts are called the Pacific Coast Corridor (Taiheiyō Beruto Chitai). The economy of districts along the Sea of Japan centers on agriculture, dairy farming, and fishery. Area (including offshore islands): 230,897 sq km (89,126 sq mi); pop: 93,246,786 (including the population of surrounding islands).

Honshū Paper Co, Ltd

(Honshū Seishi). Manufacturer of paper, pulp, and related products. Founded in 1949 when former ŌJI PAPER CO, LTD, was divided into three companies. It produces a wide variety of products, such as paper, paperboard, processed paper products, plastic film, and chemicals, and has been particularly successful in the manufacture of wrapping paper. Strongly technology-oriented, the company has exported its technique for manufacturing biaxially oriented polypropylene and for recycling newspapers to industrially advanced nations in the Americas and in Europe. Honshū Paper's overseas joint venture operations include a pulp plant in Canada, a chip plant in New Guinea, and a cardboard plant in Taiwan. The firm is also active in providing technological guidance to developing nations. Sales for the fiscal year ending March 1982 totaled ¥239.4 billion (US $994.5 million) and capitalization stood at ¥7.1 billion (US $29.5 million). Corporate headquarters are in Tōkyō.

honto mononari

(annual land tax). The major tax levied on peasants during the Edo period (1600–1868). Also called *honto, mononari, shomu, narika, torika,* or *hommen.* Calculation of the annual land tax was based on several factors: the *assessed* value of all agricultural and residential land in a village (expressed as the putative rice yield of the land or KOKUDAKA); estimates of the *actual* yield of the village's arable land; and, in some cases, the overall economic condition of the village. Prior to TOYOTOMI HIDEYOSHI's land survey (KENCHI) in 1582, similar taxes had been levied in cash on rice paddies (see KANDAKA). Thereafter, the tax base was expanded to include dry fields and residential lands. In principle, the tax was to be paid in rice, but in fact a portion of the land tax was frequently commuted to a cash payment.

The value of arable and residential land was generally calculated by assigning each grade of land an official estimated yield (*todai* or *kokumori*), measuring the area of a plot, and multiplying the area by the official yield value. In some domains, such as Kaga (now Ishikawa and Toyama prefectures), a single value was used for all grades of land in each district *(gun)*. Grasslands, forests, etc within the village, which the peasants used as sources of firewood, fertilizer, etc, were not included in the area of land measured; taxes on these lands were assessed separately (see KOMONONARI).

The official tax rate *(men)* was expressed as a percentage of the total assessed value of the arable and residential land of the village. The most common methods of determining the tax involved either inspection of the actual crop yield and annual reassessment of the tax (see KEMI) or averaging the crop yields for several years and establishing a tax rate to be effective for a period of 5 years, 10 years, or an indefinite time (see JŌMEN). In both cases sample harvesting (*tsubogari* or *bugari*) often formed the basis for the estimate of the actual crop yield. The yield in the sample would be multiplied by a tax rate of 40 percent or 50 percent and the product would be converted to a percentage of the village's *kokudaka*. This was the official tax rate for the village.

Honto mononari formed the bulk of taxes paid to the shogunal and domainal governments during the Edo period. After the Meiji Restoration (1868) it was replaced by a system of taxation based on the market value of the land rather than its estimated yield (see LAND TAX REFORM OF 1873–1881). *Philip BROWN*

hōō

Abbreviation of *dajō hōō* (priestly retired sovereign), a formal title given to retired emperors who became Buddhist priests. Emperor UDA (r 887–897) was the first to receive the title, in 899, when he took holy orders and moved to the temple NINNAJI after his abdication. Most retired sovereigns eventually took the tonsure, but neither abdication nor Buddhist vows prevented them from remaining politically active. This was especially true in the last century of the Heian period (794–1185), when the former emperors SHIRAKAWA, TOBA, and GO-SHIRAKAWA in turn ruled the country from retirement (see INSEI). Emperor Reigen (r 1663–87) was the last to receive the title. *G. Cameron HURST III*

Hōōzan

Mountain in the northern part of the Akaishi Mountains, northwestern Yamanashi Prefecture, central Honshū. It is the most popular mountain for climbing in the Southern Alps (the Akaishi Mountains) and a prominent part of Southern Alps National Park. Height: 2,841 m (9,318 ft).

Hopeh-Chahar Political Council → Ji-Cha
(Chi-Ch'a) Autonomous Political Council

horagai

A horn formed by attaching a simple mouthpiece to the end of a conch shell. Of Indian origin, the instrument diffused along with Buddhism throughout Southeast Asia and East Asia, entering Japan via Korea in the Nara period (710–794). It was employed in Buddhist ceremonies and as one of the religious accoutrements of the ascetic SHUGENDŌ practitioners. The *horagai* was also used to sound the signal for advance and retreat in premodern warfare. *MISUMI Haruo*

Hōraijisan

Mountain in eastern Aichi Prefecture, central Honshū. It is noted for Hōraiji, an ancient Buddhist temple of the Shingon sect, and for its screech owls. Birds, animals, and rare rocks abound. It has a natural science museum. Nearby are hot springs, such as Hōraikyō and Yuya, and camping grounds. Height: 684 m (2,244 ft).

Hōreki Incident

(Hōreki Jiken). The censure by the Tokugawa shogunate of TAKENOUCHI SHIKIBU and several antishogunate nobles in 1758 (Hōreki 8). Shikibu, a Shintō scholar in the employ of the house of Toku-

daiji, had been lecturing on Shintō, Confucianism, and military arts from a pro-imperial viewpoint to Tokudaiji Kimmura and other nobles at the court of Emperor Momozono (1741–62; r 1747–62). Many of these nobles resented the autocratic behavior of the shogunate and conveyed some of Shikibu's ideas to the emperor himself. When rumors circulated that the nobles were practicing military arts, the imperial regent, worried lest their action exacerbate court-shogunate relations, decided to report them to the shogunal deputies (*shoshidai*) in Kyōto. The nobles continued lecturing to the emperor on Shintō, and in 1758, Tokudaiji and several other nobles were dismissed by the *shoshidai* from their positions at the court and ordered into domiciliary confinement. The following year Shikibu himself was banished from Kyōto. The incident, along with the MEIWA INCIDENT, is seen as an early instance of shogunate repression of the nascent movement to restore the emperor to full power.

Horie Ken'ichi (1938–)

Yachtsman; international racer. Born in Ōsaka. He became interested in yachting as a high school student and saved enough money to build a small yacht, the *Mermaid I*, 5.8 meters (19 ft) long and 2 meters (6.5 ft) wide. In 1962 he became the first Japanese to make a solo crossing of the Pacific Ocean, from Nishinomiya (Hyōgo Prefecture) to San Francisco, in 94 days. He sailed around the world in 275 days (August 1973–May 1974) in the *Mermaid II* and set a world record for sailing alone nonstop. In 1975 he crossed the Pacific in 40 days, and later the same year he participated in the Singlehanded Trans-Pacific Yacht Race in the *Mermaid IV*. Horie continues to be active in the yachting world. *TAKEDA Fumio*

Horie Shigeo (1903–)

Banker. Born in Tokushima Prefecture. Graduate of Tōkyō University. A long-time employee of the Yokohama Shōkin Ginkō (YOKOHAMA SPECIE BANK), Horie played a leading role in reorganizing it as the BANK OF TŌKYŌ, LTD, after World War II. He became the bank's president in 1957 and chairman in 1965. Horie played an international role as an expert in businesses involved in foreign exchange in the post–World War II period. *TATSUKI Mariko*

Horiguchi Daigaku (1892–1981)

Poet. Born in Tōkyō. Studied at Keiō University. In his collection of translated poems, *Gekka no ichigun* (1925), he introduced the works of 66 modern French poets, including Jean Cocteau, Raymond Radiguet, and Guillaume Apollinaire. This collection greatly influenced poetry circles in the mid-1920s and early 1930s. His translation of *Ouvert la nuit* (1924) by Paul Morand influenced the style of writers of the SHINKANKAKU SCHOOL. Besides being a highly skilled, prolific translator, he also wrote over 20 books of original poems, including *Gekkō to piero* (1919) and *Ningen no uta* (1947). *ASAI Kiyoshi*

Horiguchi Sutemi (1895–)

Architect and architectural historian. Born in Gifu Prefecture. In 1920, prior to graduation from Tōkyō University, he helped organize the aggressively modern Secessionist group, modeled after the Viennese *Sezession* and German expressionism. He visited Europe in 1923–24 and on his return to Japan published an introduction to modern Dutch architecture. Horiguchi's interest in traditional Japanese culture grew, however, leading to research on the tea ceremony and the small, detached tearoom or *sukiya* (see SUKIYA-ZUKURI). His buildings include the European-influenced villa Shiensō (1926), Wakasa House (1939), and the *sukiya*-style Miyuki no Ma, a room at the inn Hasshōkan (1950). He also taught at several major universities and wrote books, including *Rikyū no cha* (1941), a study of the teamaster SEN NO RIKYŪ, and *Katsura rikyū* (1952), on the internationally famous KATSURA DETACHED PALACE. *WATANABE Hiroshi*

Hori Hidemasa (1553–1590)

Warrior of the Azuchi–Momoyama period (1568–1600). Born in Mino (now part of Gifu Prefecture). He helped ODA NOBUNAGA in the suppression of the Jōdo Shin sect rebellions (IKKŌ IKKI) and other military campaigns. After Nobunaga's death, he served under TOYOTOMI HIDEYOSHI in the Battle of YAMAZAKI, the KOMAKI NAGAKUTE CAMPAIGN, and the Kyūshū campaign, winning Hideyoshi's esteem for his strategic brilliance. He died in the ODAWARA CAM-PAIGN.

Horikoshi Jirō (1903–1982)

Aeronautical engineer. Designer of the famous Japanese ZERO FIGHTER of World War II. Born in Gumma Prefecture, he graduated from Tōkyō University in 1927. He joined what later became MITSUBISHI HEAVY INDUSTRIES, LTD, and was sent to study in Germany and the United States from 1929 to 1930. After his return to Japan, he directed the design of such fighter aircraft as the Zero, the Raiden, and the Reppū. He remained with Mitsubishi after the war until his retirement in 1967.

Horikoshi Kubō (1435–1491)

(Lord of Horikoshi). Popular name of Ashikaga Masatomo, younger brother of ASHIKAGA YOSHIMASA, eighth shōgun of the Muromachi shogunate. In 1457 Masatomo was sent to Kamakura to regain shogunal control of the Kantō region, where Ashikaga Shigeuji (1434–97), the son of the last Kamakura kubō (governor-general of the Kantō), was defying the shogunate from his base at Koga in Shimōsa Province (now Ibaraki Prefecture) and presuming to call himself KOGA KUBŌ. Unable to advance as far as Kamakura, Masatomo established a base at Horikoshi in Izu Province (now part of Shizuoka Prefecture) and took the name Horikoshi Kubō. Masatomo had little power, however, and Shigeuji on his own made peace with the shogunate in 1482. Masatomo was given the province of Izu, but soon after his death, it was taken over by HŌJŌ SŌUN.

Hori Kyūsaku (1900–1974)

Businessman and director of the NIKKATSU CORPORATION, a major movie company. Born in Tōkyō and graduated from Ōkura Commercial Higher School (now Tōkyō University of Economics). After serving as secretary to Matsukata Otohiko, a well-known businessman, Hori became director of Nikkatsu in 1935. He played an early role in the production of "talkies" and expanded his own network of movie houses. He was the head of Nikkatsu during the years when the company first achieved prosperity. *MORI Masumi*

Hori Ryūjo (1897–)

Dollmaker. Born in Tōkyō, real name Yamada Matsue. In her youth she joined a handicraft group led by the painter and illustrator TAKEHISA YUMEJI and began making dolls and other art objects out of cloth. Drawing upon traditional doll-making techniques, she later developed her own style of *kimekomi ningyō*, wooden dolls dressed in *kimono*. In 1936 her work appeared for the first time in the Imperial Academy Exhibition, a prestigious annual government-sponsored art exhibition for which she later served as judge. In 1955 she became the first woman honored as a Bearer of an Important Intangible Cultural Asset (Jūyō Mukei Bunkazai Hojisha; see LIVING NATIONAL TREASURES). *YAMADA Tokubei*

Hori Tatsuo (1904–1953)

Novelist, poet. Born in Tōkyō; graduate of Tōkyō University. While still a student he participated in a literary coterie sponsored by the poet MUROO SAISEI, and contributed to its magazine *(Roba)* translations of such modern French poets as Jean Cocteau and Guillaume Apollinaire. His own poems and novelettes, characterized by the atmosphere of mountain resort sanatoriums and a thematic preoccupation with death, reflect his long battle with tuberculosis which eventually took his life. Impressionistic and often plotless, Hori's writings describe a fragile world of love and beauty. Among his works are the short story "Seikazoku" (1930; tr "The Holy Family," 1976) and the novelettes *Kaze tachinu* (1936–38, The Wind Has Risen) and *Naoko* (1941).

hōritsu

(law; statute). Term commonly used to denote laws in general, but technically referring to that form of law that has been enacted by the Diet according to its procedure for enacting laws.

Hōritsu (as statutes enacted by the Diet) rank below the constitution and above other forms of laws such as cabinet orders *(seirei)* and ordinances *(jōrei)* in binding force. As a general rule, hōritsu

must be passed by both the House of Representatives and the House of Councillors, but the constitution recognizes some exceptions. First, when the House of Representatives, thought to be more representative of the will of people, passes a bill and the House of Councillors passes a modified version of the same bill, the resolution of the House of Representatives alone will become law if passed again in the House of Representatives by two-thirds of those members present. The second exception covers interim actions passed by the House of Councillors in emergency session. Third, a hōritsu that is to affect only certain local public bodies requires for enactment not only passage by the Diet, but also majority approval by the local residents in a referendum. Upon passage of a bill, the minister responsible for the bill signs it, the prime minister countersigns it, and the emperor promulgates it. As a general rule, hōritsu become effective 20 days after promulgation. *ITŌ Masami*

Horiuchi Masakazu (1911–)

Modern sculptor. Born in Kyōto. He studied sculpture briefly in 1928 and 1929 at the Tōkyō Kōtō Kōgei Gakkō (Tōkyō Higher School of Arts and Crafts) before joining the artists' group Nikakai. He was influenced by the sculptor Fujikawa Yūzō (1882–1935). In the 1930s Horiuchi produced his first abstract works, but during the war years he temporarily abandoned sculpture and studied French and classical languages. After the war, when the Nikakai was reorganized, Horiuchi resumed his artistic activity and began experimenting with a variety of new media. Since 1954 he has worked primarily in metal, using iron wire and sheet metal to create geometric forms on a monumental scale. From 1950 to 1974 he taught sculpture at what is now called the Kyōto City University of Arts. He received the sixth TAKAMURA KŌTARŌ Prize in 1963, and the grand prize at the first International Exhibition of Contemporary Sculpture held at Hakone in 1969.

hōroku

A flat, lidded cooking vessel; used especially for roasting sesame seeds, beans, rice, salt, tea leaves, medicinal herbs, and the like over flame or live coals. Once a standard utensil used in preparation of traditional Japanese food, it has in modern times been supplanted by metal cookware. The *hōroku* lent its name to a cooking method broadly known as *hōroku-yaki,* or "*hōroku*-grilling." A more specific cooking technique utilizing the earthenware *hōroku* was *mushi-yaki,* or "steam-grilling," in which fish, mushrooms, or other ingredients were steamed on a layer of salt inside the covered *hōroku.* According to an old Japanese belief, throwing a *hōroku* from a high place and breaking it protects one from evil. *MIYAMOTO Mizuo*

horsecars

(*tetsudō basha* or *basha tetsudō*). Horse-drawn streetcars on rails, generally using two horses and carrying 20 to 30 passengers. The first horsecar line in Japan was opened between Shimbashi and Nihombashi in Tōkyō in 1882, 50 years after such vehicles came into use for public transportation in New York. The young students who accompanied the IWAKURA MISSION of 1871–73 first encountered horsecars in San Francisco. After their introduction into Japan, horsecars quickly supplanted RICKSHAWS in the major cities, and rickshawmen organized to protest the loss of their livelihood (see SHAKAITŌ). With the appearance of electric streetcars in Japan in 1895, horsecars soon fell into disuse, although they could be found in some smaller cities as late as the 1920s. See also TRANSPORTATION. *TANAKA Akira*

horse chestnut, Japanese

(*tochinoki*). Aesculus turbinata. A deciduous tree of the family Hippocastanaceae which grows wild in mountain areas throughout Japan and is sometimes cultivated. In mountain areas, many trees reach a height of 30 meters (98 ft) and a circumference of 2 meters (7 ft). The leaves are palmate and compound, made up of 5 to 7 obovate leaflets which are 20 to 30 centimeters (8–12 in) long, with sharp pointed tips and blunt serrated edges. The backs of the leaflets have soft reddish brown hairs on the veins. The tree flowers about May with numerous 4-petaled white flowers, 1.5 centimeters (0.5 in) in diameter, growing in large erect clusters about 20 centimeters (8 in) long. The fruit is funnel-shaped and splits into three when it ripens, releasing reddish brown seeds.

In northern Honshū mountain villages, starch taken from these seeds is used to make *tochimochi*, a food resembling rice cake (*mochi*). In addition, the wood is used for floorboards, decorative shelves, ceilings, alcove pillars, and Western-style furniture.

The common horse chestnut (French: *marronier*, *A. hippocastanum*), which is called *seiyō tochinoki* (Western *tochinoki*), is often planted along streets in Tōkyō. This tree is similar to the Japanese species but distinguished by the thornlike projections of the fruit.

MATSUDA Osamu

horsemanship

(*bajutsu*). An entirely indigenous style of horsemanship can be traced in Japan to the reign of Emperor TENJI in the latter half of the 7th century. Toward the end of the 12th century, with the ascendancy of the warrior class, activities such as horseback riding and archery became very popular. Gradually, different schools of *bajutsu* were formed, among them Ogasawara, Ōtsubo, and Hachijō, then later, Sasaki, Araki, and Ueda. At its peak, between the years 1650 and 1850, there were some 20 schools. Although the Meiji period (1868–1912) marked the end of traditional horsemanship, there are still several traditional events performed today at certain festivals, including YABUSAME, shooting arrows from galloping horses, and *dakyū*, a kind of polo.

Modern equestrianism was given a boost in 1872 when the Japanese army invited a Frenchman named Descharmes to give instruction in the French sport. Around the same time imported Western horses virtually replaced the stocky native animal, moving the sport even further toward Western horsemanship. In 1889 an equestrian association was established in Tōkyō, and by 1921 Japan was participating in the International Equestrian Federation. Japanese equestrians were sent for the first time to the Olympics in Amsterdam in 1928, and in 1932 NISHI TAKEICHI won Japan's first gold medal in the equestrian field at the 10th Olympics, in Los Angeles. After World War II horsemanship lost its main support and went into a decline when the military was virtually abolished. But the Japan Equestrian Federation, formed in 1946, sent representatives to the International Equestrian Federation in 1951, and since the 18th Olympics in Tōkyō in 1964, horsemanship has once again become a popular sport in Japan.

TOMIKI Kenji

horse-rider theory

(*kiba minzoku setsu*). A theory that seeks to explain the process by which the first unified Japanese state was established and in a larger sense frames a hypothesis on the formation and constitution of the Japanese people themselves. It generally holds that the unified state was founded by a group of horse-riding warriors who entered or invaded the Japanese islands, conquered the native rulers, and established themselves as Japan's ruling class. The original Asiatic home of the supposed intruders, their ethnic identity, their relationship to Koreans and to Korean history, the circumstances and time of their arrival in Japan, and the process by which they might have come to dominate Japanese society are all matters on which various proponents of this theory differ. Although there is thus no single horse-rider theory, most Japanese historians recognize as standard the version of Egami Namio (b 1906), long a professor of Asian history at Tōkyō University. Egami dramatically proposed the theory during a symposium held in 1948 and refined the idea in several later articles and in a book, *Kiba minzoku kokka* (1967, The Horse-Rider State). While from the very beginning the theory attracted the interest of both scholars and the public at large, so did it generate an atmosphere of controversy that has never abated.

The controversy arises in part from the fact that most Japanese have been accustomed to seeing their history as more or less self-generated and self-contained. This was as true of the writers of the earliest historical works as it is of mainstream Japanese historians today. Modern scholars of course long ago abandoned literal belief in the legends of Japan's origin in the classical works KOJIKI (712) and NIHON SHOKI (720), according to which the first emperor, JIMMU, was descended directly from the gods, who themselves had physically created the Japanese islands. But aside from the conclusion, evident from linguistics, comparative mythology, and anthropology, that the earliest Japanese may have had some vague connections with early Asiatic and Oceanic peoples, no link had been proposed with any specific people or group of peoples and no specific historical process had been hypothesized to explain how these alien peoples and cultures might have entered Japan. Japanese

historians tended to conclude that the developmental process from the oldest archaeologically known preagricultural communities to the states of the early centuries of the Christian era was largely an indigenous one. Undoubtedly there were cultural influences from Oceania, Southeast Asia, China, Korea, and Northeast Asia, and possibly immigrants from some or all of these sources, but these elements would have been added to a dominant Japanese core that was already established on its own self-set course of development. Such was the general view of Japanese scholars when Egami launched his horse-rider concept in 1948.

The 1948 Symposium on Japanese Origins —— For about a decade prior to the end of the Pacific War in 1945, discussion of Japanese origins beyond the legendary accounts had been generally discouraged; in a showcase trial in 1942, the historian TSUDA SŌKICHI had been convicted of insulting the dignity of the imperial family by questioning the historicity of the first nine emperors of the classical books. After 1945 there was an enthusiastic return to genuine historical research and a greater interest in the earliest periods by anthropologists, ethnologists, and linguists. The 1948 "Symposium on the Origins of the Japanese People and Culture and the Formation of the Japanese State" was organized by the cultural anthropologist ISHIDA EIICHIRŌ and included, in addition to Egami Namio, the ethnologist Oka Masao (1898–1982) and the archaeologist Yawata Ichirō (b 1902).

Although the symposium became famous for the launching of Egami's theory, it was really an integrated approach to the problem of Japan's origins by the group as a whole. The basic inspiration came from Oka Masao, who had studied in Vienna and absorbed the ideas of historical ethnology elaborated by Wilhelm Schmidt (1868–1954) and others. This school sought to find in a given culture the cultural strata left historically by constituent earlier cultures, and by means of systematic analysis and comparison to clarify the relationships between the strata and between them and other cultures either historically known or reconstructable. Oka's doctoral thesis, "Kulturschichten in Alt-Japan" (Cultural Strata in Ancient Japan), presented in Vienna in 1933, had applied this methodology to Japan. However, it was never translated into Japanese or even published in German, and it was not until the 1948 symposium that its conclusions were introduced to other Japanese scholars.

Oka believed that four cultural strata could be identified in the Japanese ethnological record. Oldest was a matriarchal, potato-cultivating culture that had possibly entered Japan in the middle of the JŌMON PERIOD (Oka gave no dates, but modern archaeologists would place this in the third millennium BC). Second was a matriarchal rice-cultivating society, possibly of Austroasiatic linguistic affiliation, which would have arrived around the Final (Latest) Jōmon period (ca 1000 BC–ca 300 BC). These two cultures would have been of southern Chinese or Southeast Asian origin. Third was a patriarchal, age-graded, fishing and rice-growing society, possibly of Austronesian linguistic affiliation, which would have played the dominant role in the YAYOI PERIOD (ca 300 BC–ca AD 300). This would have been of Oceanic or Southeast Asian origin. Finally, there was a patriarchal society organized in patrilineages and characterized by a broad social and military organization into five tribal groups. An agricultural society sprung from herding origins, it had a slave system and a "regnal" or "baronial" (*ōkōteki*) pattern of dynastic rule and dominance. Oka called it the "imperial race" (*tennō zoku*) and identified it as the dominant force of the Tomb or KOFUN PERIOD (ca 300–710). He linked it with societies historically known in Korea and Manchuria and associated it linguistically with the Altaic peoples. In later revisions, Oka divided this stratum into two strata in order to account for some developmental details but retained the Altaic and Northeast Asian origin for both.

Of these four strata it was the last, the "imperial race," that came to be associated with the horse riders of Egami. Oka believed that this group had originated in eastern Manchuria as a mixed herding and farming people, and that around the 2nd or 3rd century AD they moved through the Korean peninsula and into the Japanese archipelago. They would have conquered the peoples of the earlier cultural strata, in the process absorbing many of their traits and beliefs. Oka did not specifically identify this conquering people, but he suggested that they were in close relationship, culturally and ethnically, with the ancient Puyŏ and KOGURYŎ states. The Koguryŏ (J: Kōkuri), whose state included southern Manchuria and most of Korea and lasted from its traditional founding in 37 BC to AD 668, were one of the major constituents of the Korean people. The Puyŏ (J: Fuyo) state in Manchuria lasted from the 1st through the 3rd centuries; after its destruction in 286, its people continued to play an important role in Manchuria, and one of its branches founded the southern Korean state of PAEKCHE during the 4th century.

The Horse Riders in Historical Perspective —— Oka was mainly concerned with identifying cultural strata in Japan and suggesting possible affinities with mainland cultures. It was Egami who developed the historical implications of these proposed ethnic relationships. He was a specialist in Asian history, particularly in the great nomadic confederacies (Scythians, Xiongnu [Hsiung-nu], Turks, Mongols, and others) that had periodically risen to dominate Asian events on a continental scale.

Egami's starting point was the nature of the Tomb age associated by Oka with the "imperial race." Egami argued, as had his symposium colleague Yawata Ichirō, that the Tomb age was not a consistent whole but should rather be divided into two contrasting periods that he called Early and Late (in the more standard three-part division, Early corresponded to Tomb I, Late, to Tomb II and III). The Early Tomb burials (generally 4th century) differed from those of Late Tomb (5th and 6th centuries) both in tomb structure and in the character of the burial objects interred with the deceased. Early assemblages included BRONZE MIRRORS, ritual knives, comma-shaped beads known as *magatama,* and other items that Egami characterized as "magical, religious, agricultural, and Southeast Asian." Late assemblages included weapons, armor, horse trappings, and ceramic figurines (HANIWA) of houses and of warriors and other persons, all of which Egami characterized as "realistic, warlike, baronial, horse rider, and North Asian."

The image of the horse rider, in the context of East Asian history, evoked the mixed "Chinese-barbarian" culture that had evolved on the frontiers of China in the early centuries AD. This was a mounted-warfare culture accustomed to nearly permanent military activity, ruthless domination of men and wealth and the celebration of luxury and power, and with a pronounced fondness for the horse. Although much in this horse-rider culture derived from nomads, its typical representative societies were more often conglomerates of semiagricultural, semivenatic frontiersmen of non-Chinese origin. Such societies conquered northern China in the 4th century and dominated Manchuria and Korea from the 3rd or 4th to the 7th centuries. Following Oka, Egami cited the Puyŏ and Koguryŏ peoples as characteristic horse riders and said they had a "special relationship" to the ruling class of Japan in the Late Tomb period.

Egami enunciated the general case for his theory in seven statements: (1) the Early and Late Tomb periods were fundamentally different; (2) the transition from one to the other was not evolutionary but sudden and dramatic; (3) agricultural societies such as that of Yayoi Japan did not aggressively borrow foreign culture or reform their own; thus horse-rider culture had not been peacefully imported into Japan, but rather both southern Korea and Japan had been conquered by horse-riding people; (4) Japan's adoption of horse-rider culture was not partial but total, and was "completely in common" with horse-rider culture on the mainland; (5) the horses did not come to Japan by themselves, but with their riders; (6) the Late Tomb culture was baronial in character and was spread over Japan by force; (7) horse-riding peoples did not stop when they reached the sea, but, like the Vandals, Mongols, and others, got into boats and continued their conquests.

Egami attempted to specify historically the Korean connections with the conquerors. He believed that a southern Korean hegemon king, called the "Chin king" in a 3rd-century Chinese source, was of horse-rider origin and had some connection with the Puyŏ or Koguryŏ, and that he ruled much of southern Korea through a dynasty of conquest. Toward the end of the 3rd century, he or one of his descendants, pressed by a changing strategic situation on the peninsula, would have migrated with his followers to Japan. Egami thought that SUJIN, the 10th Japanese emperor listed in the classical books and the earliest to be considered a historical figure by most historians, was linked to or identical with the Chin king line. Sujin's name, Mimaki ("Sujin" being a much later posthumous designation), seemed to evoke the place name Mimana, thought by Japanese (but not by Korean) historians to have been a Japanese enclave in southern Korea. The *Kojiki* dubbed Sujin "the first emperor to rule the land." Egami postulated that Sujin, once in Japan, would have taken over the area of Himuka or Hyūga in western Kyūshū (now Miyazaki Prefecture), from which the classical books claim that Japan's first emperor launched the eastward movement that led to the establishment of the state of Yamato in the Kinai (Kyōto–Ōsaka–Nara) region. The *Nihon shoki* says that the legendary Jimmu was "the first emperor to rule the land," but Egami, having chosen to follow the testimony of *Kojiki* that Sujin filled this role, assigns the

leadership of the decisive eastward campaign to Sujin's descendant Homuda (posthumously Emperor Ōjin). Thus the movement leading to the establishment of Yamato would have been a two-stage process, one a migration or invasion from Korea to Himuka under the Chin king, alias Sujin, the other a movement eastward led by Emperor Ōjin.

Egami adduced a number of comparative features in the ruling practices, the social structure, and the material culture of both the continental and Japanese horse-rider regimes. Although much of this evidence is circumstantial in character, it is structurally interesting and supportive of his basic thesis.

Criticism and Revisions of the Horse-Rider Theory —— Although many scholars found Egami's concept dramatic and stimulating, most considered his imaginative leap too long, and some even found it offensive. For instance, YANAGITA KUNIO, the great folklorist and promoter of Japan's traditional arts, considered it "unthinkable" that an alien conquest of Japan "could even be considered." Linguists, who believed Altaic elements in Japanese to have been already documented in the Chinese WEI ZHI (*Wei chih;* see also YAMATAI) for a period prior to Egami's proposed conquest, could not accept such a late Altaic intrusion. If Japanese was Altaic at all, the Altaic immigration must have been much earlier. Some historians believed that Japan was already a unified state in the 3rd century and that, far from being conquered, it had itself conquered part of southern Korea. The presence of horse-rider elements hardly implied the coming of the horse riders themselves. Others thought that Egami ignored evolutionary forces in Japan itself, that Japan was too "complex" to be easily conquered, that the Korean archaeological record was in fact quite different from that of Japan, and that any horse-rider influence would have been either much earlier, perhaps around the 1st century AD or BC, or much later, in the 5th and 6th centuries, when many Korean immigrants supposedly arrived in Japan. An archaeologist argued that horse trappings did not occur in burials until late in the 5th century, ruling out earlier horse riders.

Some of these arguments were substantial, some perhaps less so. To all of them Egami could and did reply, with a certain measure of effectiveness, but few minds were changed. Many ethnologists remained impressed by Oka's hypothesis but put some distance between themselves and Egami's ideas. A symposium to review the "Oka theory" in 1970 mentioned Egami exactly once. A few writers, notably the Waseda University historian Mizuno Yū (b 1918), accepted the theory of a horse-rider invasion, but believed that it occurred in the 1st century AD and that the conquerors, who had no known connection with Korean history, remained in southern Kyūshū for more than 300 years before launching the eastward conquest to the Kyōto–Ōsaka–Nara region.

Few Western writers have examined the idea seriously, and most Western historians of Japan follow their Japanese colleagues in remaining skeptical. The present writer believes Egami's basic concept valid but has rejected the connection with the Chin king and proposed instead that Japan's horse riders invaded subsequent to the Puyŏ establishment of Paekche, which he dates in the mid-4th century. He also believes, developing a proposal of Mizuno, that the dynasty founded by the horse riders came to an end around the beginning of the 6th century, being replaced by a native ruling group. Thus horse riders, even if they once ruled Japan, would have had no connection with the later imperial family.

Egami's arguments have an impressive overall structure and are in accord with general East Asian history. But problems with specific details, the lack of direct historical sources, the equivocal character of the sources we have, and the as yet incomplete archaeological work all leave room for honest doubt. Whether accepted or rejected, Egami's theory has done much to stimulate new research.

——John H. Douglas, "The Horsemen of Yamato," *Science News* (3 June 1978). Namio Egami, "The Formation of the People and the Origin of the State in Japan," *Memoirs of the Tōyō Bunko* 23 (1964). Egami Namio, *Kiba minzoku kokka: Nihon kodaishi e no apurōchi* (1967). Gamō Masao, ed, "Shimpojiumu: Oka setsu to Nihon minzoku bunka no keitō kigenron no gen dankai," in Oka Masao Kyōju Koki Kinen Rombun Shū Kankō Iinkai, ed, *Minzoku-gaku kara mita Nihon: Oka Masao kyōju koki kinen rombun shū* (1970). Ishida Eiichirō, ed, "Taidan to tōron: Nihon minzoku bunka no genryū to Nihon kokka no keisei," *Minzokugaku kenkyū* 13.3 (1949), repr with additional material as *Nihon minzoku no kigen* (1958). Gari Ledyard, "Galloping along with the Horseriders: Looking for the Founders of Japan," *Journal of Japanese Studies* 1.2

(1975). Mizuno Yū, *Nihon kodai no kokka keisei* (1967). Yū Mizuno, "Understanding Japan: Origins of the Japanese People," *Bulletin of the International Society for Educational Information* 22 (1968). Oka Masao, *Nihon minzokugaku taikei* (1958).

Gari LEDYARD

horses

(uma). Judging from skeletons and teeth unearthed from archaeological sites such as SHELL MOUNDS, horses may have been introduced to Japan from the Asian continent as early as the middle of the Jōmon period (ca 10,000 BC–ca 300 BC). There were two types of horse, small and medium, at the time of introduction. The former had a shoulder height of about 110–120 centimeters (43–47 in) and is thought to be the same as the *tokara uma,* which inhabited the Ryūkyū Islands until recently. The larger horse was about 130–150 centimeters (51–59 in) high and is thought to be the same as the *misaki uma* and *kiso uma,* raised extensively until the Meiji period (1868–1912). Both are thought to be derived from the Mongolian horse, which in turn was descended from the Central Asian Przewalski's horse, with a possible mixture of Tarpan. There are some records of the introduction of a few large breeds such as Arab in the middle ages, but systematic breeding was not tried, and there is no trace of any genetic influence on the Japanese horse.

Horses were primarily used as draft animals and for war. After the Meiji period the government bred larger horses for military purposes. Many of these were of the Arab, Anglo-Norman, and Percheron breeds. Since World War II, horses have been bred mainly for racing purposes, the chief areas being Hokkaidō and the Tōhoku district in northern Japan.

IMAIZUMI Yoshiharu

Horses are mentioned in the chronicles *Kojiki* (712) and *Nihon shoki* (720). The religious custom of dedicating horses to Shintō gods dates back to ancient times. Even today horses are kept by Shintō shrines as divine horses *(shimme)* and paraded on festival days. In medieval times a fine horse was indispensable to a warrior; the horse figures frequently in military chronicles. Military arts using bow and arrow on horseback, such as YABUSAME and KASA-GAKE, developed in the Kamakura period (1185–1333).

Even in times of peace like the Edo period (1600–1868), *daimyō* were enthusiastic in breeding horses. Horses bred in the Nambu domain (now Iwate Prefecture) were particularly sought after. Horse racing is believed to have been introduced in 1861 by Western residents in Yokohama, although horse races *(kurabe uma)* of a ceremonial nature have been performed at the KAMO SHRINES in Kyōto from medieval times.

▄——Egami Namio, *Kiba minzoku kokka* (1967). Ikata Teiryō, *Nihon kodai kachiku shi* (1945). Kamo Giichi, *Kachiku bunka shi* (1973). Saitō Shōji, *Nihonjin to shokubutsu, dōbutsu* (1975).

SANEYOSHI Tatsuo

horseshoe crab

(kabutogani). Tachypleus tridentatus. A marine arthropod with a black helmetlike shell and a long swordlike tail. Its distribution ranges from western Japan to Southeast Asia, with two species of this genus and one species of another genus found in the tropics and one species of the genus *Limulus* found in North America. Known as a "living fossil," it lives on relatively deep sea bottoms, but in summer it appears on shallow sandy bottoms near the shore. The female lays its eggs on sandy beaches at high tide at night between 10 July and 10 August, always accompanied by a male. The egg is globular, 3 millimeters (0.1 in) across and hatches in about six weeks. The horseshoe crab sheds its shell several times in the first year, once a year thereafter; it seems to live over five years.

NAKANE Takehiko

horse trappings, ancient

(bagu). Horse trappings used as funerary objects have been recovered from 5th-century mounded tombs (KOFUN), attesting to the fact that horse riding had become widespread among the elite in Japan by the middle of the Kofun period (ca 300–710). They include iron bits, ring stirrups, nose guards, gilt bronze fittings, small bronze horse bells, bell ornaments, and gold openwork decorations. Horse trappings are also clearly depicted on funerary HANIWA horse sculptures of the same period.

In the Nara period (710–794) a Chinese style of saddlery was adopted. Known as *karakura,* the accoutrements became increasingly elaborate during the Heian period (794–1185) and were used on state occasions. The *karakura* were subsequently modified to suit native tastes and needs; some of these later trappings, known as *yamatogura,* are finely wrought works of art, combining metal, wood, and leather craftsmanship with gold ornamentation (MAKI-E), ivory or mother-of-pearl inlay, and lacquerwork. See also ARMS AND ARMOR.

KITAMURA Bunji

horticulture

The Japanese have only comparatively recently set themselves to the full-scale development of home gardening as it is known in Western countries. Although Japan has a large number of native tree species, it has few species of annual flowering plants, and the traditional Japanese garden is composed of such elements as stones, trees, and water, all arranged to give the impression of natural scenery (see GARDENS).

Japan was isolated from other countries for over 200 years during the Edo period (1600–1868), and thus cut off from developments in horticulture abroad. Such developments as did occur within Japan were confined to the hobbyist cultivation of certain traditional plants, e.g., IRISES, PRIMROSES, MORNING GLORIES, CHRYSANTHE-MUMS, CAMELLIAS, OMOTO *(Rhodea japonica),* YABUKŌJI *(Ardisia japonica),* and BONSAI (dwarf trees). In particular, flowers such as the chrysanthemum and the morning glory, not native but long naturalized, were hybridized to an extent unprecedented elsewhere.

Modern and Contemporary Horticulture—— Early in the Meiji period (1868–1912), both government and private individuals began introducing new fruit trees and flowering plants to Japan. Plants now common in Japanese horticulture such as the cyclamen, rose, carnation, kaffir lily *(Clivia miniata),* western orchid, cactus, saintpaulia, and various foliage plants were introduced at this time. However, these plants were grown only in botanical gardens or as a hobby of the upper classes, not in the gardens of ordinary homes.

The Taishō period (1912–1926) saw the first commercial cultivation of the rose, carnation, sweet pea, and dahlia, as well as the creation of markets to sell them. Appreciation for the new varieties grew, and home gardening became widespread in the Shōwa period (1926–), reaching a pre–World War II peak in 1935–39. The horticultural industry revived after the war, first as a result of the demand for decorative flowers by the Occupation forces and then, from around 1955, because of the increased economic prosperity of the ordinary household.

At present, horticulture is enjoyed as an avocation by roughly 10 million Japanese. The extremely limited space available in homes has led to the cultivation of potted plants. Even vegetables are grown in this fashion but with the exception of *bonsai,* home cultivation of fruit trees is still limited by lack of space.

To cite only a few examples in the field of commercial horticulture, approximately 3.4 billion cut flowers are grown on about 10,000 hectares (25,000 acres). In addition, about 100 million potted plants, about 500 million flower bulbs such as tulips, and about 1 billion flowering trees such as AZALEAS are produced annually. See also AGRICULTURE: farming techniques.

EJIRI Kōichi

Hōryūji

A monastery temple, also known as Ikarugadera, located in the town of Ikaruga, some distance north of the Asuka region, Nara Prefecture. Originally it was a modest temple built between 601 and 607 by the order of Prince SHŌTOKU, the prince regent, whose palace, Ikaruga no Miya, was being erected nearby. In time Hōryūji was enlarged into a monastery famous for Buddhist studies, especially the doctrines of the HOSSŌ SECT. Always associated with the life of Shōtoku, who was popularly regarded as the patron saint of Japanese Buddhism, Hōryūji became the focus of a widespread Shōtoku cult. After World War II, Hōryūji was designated head temple of the newly created Shōtoku sect. Although the original temple has vanished, works of art dating from the time of its construction have survived. Hōryūji, which owns one of the finest collections of Buddhist art in Japan, is unsurpassed in masterpieces from the Asuka period (latter part of the 6th century to 710; see ASUKA CULTURE; HAKUHŌ CULTURE). The buildings extant today are arranged for the most part around a major compound known as the Western Precinct (Saiin) to which a subtemple compound, the Eastern Precinct (Tōin), was added during the 8th century. The nucleus of the Western Precinct, erected primarily during the 4th quarter of the 7th century, constitutes the oldest temple compound extant in Japan.

The founding of Hōryūji is controversial. Poorly documented, it has been the subject of scholarly debates since the Meiji period (1868–1912). According to an inscription dated 607 on a bronze image of Yakushi (Skt: Bhaiṣajyaguru), the Buddha of Healing, now in the *kondō* (main hall), Emperor Yōmei (r 585–587) had intended to erect an image of Yakushi and a temple to contain it shortly before his death in 587. The emperor's wish was carried out by his son, Prince Shōtoku, in cooperation with his aunt, Empress SUIKO. The project was completed 20 years later. Excavations in 1939, southeast of the Western Precinct, disclosed the main buildings of the original Hōryūji. The foundations of a pagoda and a *kondō* were uncovered on an axis, one behind the other, in a traditional arrangement known as the SHITENNŌJI style, which had been transmitted from Korea. The compound was destroyed by a conflagration in 670 according to the NIHON SHOKI (720; Chronicles of Japan).

After this disaster, at a time when the memory of Shōtoku was worshiped, Hōryūji was rebuilt on a larger scale, northwest of the original site, within the compound later designated as the Western Precinct. Construction began in the 670s. Now the architects broke with the traditional axial plan and placed the five-storied pagoda and the two-storied *kondō* side by side within the corridors, boldly balancing height with width in a manner not found in continental temple layouts.

Although the Hōryūji layout was inventive, the buildings were conservatively constructed, reflecting architectural practices employed in China more than 100 years earlier. Remarkable are the supports on the second-story railing of the *kondō*, which consist of alternating brackets and inverted V-shaped braces commonly called *kaerumata*, or "frogs legs." The eaves are supported by vigorously curved corbels carved with cloud motifs (*kumogata*). The wooden colonnades have curved shafts like those of Doric columns, a style that may have been transmitted to Japan via Gandhara on the silk routes to China. The pagoda, *kondō*, inner gate (*chūmon*), and part of the surrounding corridors are extant to this day. They are the oldest wooden buildings in the world.

Upon entering the dimly lit *kondō*, the worshiper steps into the world of the Buddhas. Most of the floor space is occupied by a rectangular altar platform (*shumidan*), which symbolizes Mt. Sumeru, the center of the universe in Buddhist cosmology. It is surrounded by an ambulatory used for circumambulation when the *kondō* was completed. The images on the altar originally faced the four directions so that they could be invoked during the ritual of circumambulation. When looking at the walls of the *kondō*, the worshiper was confronted with magnificent paintings of the Buddhas in their respective Pure Lands: Shaka Nyorai to the east, AMIDA to the west, and Yakushi and MIROKU to the north. On the narrow walls were depictions of the great bodhisattvas: three manifestations of KANNON, as well as Nikkō, Gakkō, Monju, and Fugen. Flying celestials were painted on the small sections above the divinities. The deities of the *kondō*, whether in sculptured form on the altar or painted on the walls, were united beneath a great canopy represented by the coffered ceiling decorated with lotus motifs.

During the course of the centuries some of the images on the altar were removed, others were added, depending upon changing religious needs. The three major icons now face south. Central is the triad of the Buddha Shaka with two attending bodhisattvas made by the celebrated sculptor KURATSUKURI NO TORI in 623 to commemorate the death of Prince Shōtoku. The Yakushi, dated 607, which traditionally had been regarded as the main icon of the original Hōryūji, is now placed to the east of Shaka. To the west an image of Amida dated 1232 was made by the sculptor Kōshō to balance with the Yakushi. Each image, cast in bronze, is seated on a high rectangular pedestal beneath a canopy carved as though it were carried by phoenixes to the accompaniment of heavenly music played by celestials. On the corners of the altar platform stand the Shitennō (see TEMBU), the Four Heavenly Kings, dressed in military garb, who watch over the Buddhist realm. Unlike later guardian figures they stand motionless with faces expressive of earnest devotion in keeping with the dignified ambiance of the sanctuary. The guardian kings were made around 650 by the sculptor YAMAGUCHI NO ATAI ŌGUCHI.

Unlike the conservative architectural features of the buildings, the murals, completed in the early 690s, were executed in a style current at that time in great metropolitan temples of China. They were painted in vivid colors, exotically shaded within outlines so

Hōryūji

The main hall (*kondō*) and five-storied pagoda in the Western Precinct. Believed to date from the 7th century, these are among the oldest wooden buildings in the world. Main hall 18.4 × 15.2 m. Pagoda height 32.55 m. National Treasures.

powerful and precise that they were known as "iron wire lines." Long regarded as masterpieces of Buddhist painting, the wall paintings of the *kondō* were ravaged by an electrical fire in 1949. It was one of the greatest losses suffered by world art in modern times.

The Western Precinct of Hōryūji was completed in 711 when the two dynamic guardians, Niō, were installed in the inner gate. In the same year four tableaux representing scenes from the life of the Buddha were placed on the ground floor of the pagoda. Made of unbaked clay, they were executed in a realistic manner, new to Japan at that time.

The lecture hall, sutra repository, and belfry, originally located north of the Western Precinct, were joined to the corridors during the tenth century. Outside the enclosure, to the east and west, monks' quarters (the Higashimuro and Nishimuro) were built, which contained the Shōryōin and Sangyōin chapels. The present Shōryōin chapel was erected in 1284. It contains a portrait statue of Prince Shōtoku lecturing on the *Shōmangyō* (Skt: Śrīmālā-sūtra).

On the slope northwest of the main compound is the octagonal chapel, the Saiendō, first built during the Nara period but reconstructed in 1250. It houses a late 8th-century monumental drylacquer image of Yakushi, nicknamed Mine no Yakushi or "Yakushi on the Hill." Another great Yakushi statue of 10th-century date serves as the main deity in the lecture hall. Made of gilded wood, the image is seated on a lotus pedestal in front of a mandorla carved in openwork, in a manner that foreshadowed the Fujiwara style.

During the early 8th century when Buddhist temples began to flourish in Nara, Hōryūji at Ikaruga village, about 7 miles (11 km) southwest of the capital, became neglected. The adjacent Ikaruga palace, once the residence of Prince Shōtoku, had been left in ruins owing to a fire in 643. The Hossō scholar-priest Gyōshin (d 750), who resided at Hōryūji, was devoted to the memory of Prince Shōtoku. He persuaded members of the imperial family to contribute to the monastery. Through Gyōshin's efforts the devastated site of Ikaruga Palace was converted by 739 into the Eastern Precinct which centers around the well-preserved, octagonal chapel, the Yumedono or "Dream Hall." According to a legend Gyōshin had this graceful building erected over the ruins of Shōtoku's chapel, where he is said to have struggled with difficult passages in Buddhist scripture. When he fell asleep, the story goes, a golden image would appear to instruct him. Today a gilded camphorwood image of Guze Kannon made around 650 is enshrined in the Yumedono as the principal icon. Tradition has it that the Kannon is of Shōtoku's height. Locked into a tabernacle for over a thousand years, the image is in excellent condition. It is on public view only twice a year, a splendid golden image in the Tori Busshi style. The Yumedono also contains a dry-lacquer portrait of its founder, Gyōshin, made shortly after his death, and a clay statue of the priest Dōsen (d 876), who restored the chapel in the 9th century.

In 1941, commemorating the 1,350th anniversary of the death of Prince Shōtoku, a museum called the Daihōzōden was built to the east of the Western Precinct. In it are exhibited numerous works of Buddhist art assembled from other Hōryūji buildings. Outstanding

Treasures of Hōryūji

This group of gilt-bronze figurines shows the miraculous birth of the historic Buddha from the sleeve of Queen Māyā (center). Celestial attendants appear at left and right. Height 12.4 cm (left), 16.7 cm (center), 10.3 cm (right). Early 7th century. Shijūhattai Butsu ("48 Buddhas") collection, Hōryūji Treasure House, Tōkyō National Museum.

Treasures of Hōryūji

One of the six sections of the *Kanchōban*, a gilt-bronze openwork banner used during Buddhist ordination rites. Flying celestials and palmette motifs form the main components of the filigree design. Each section 83 × 33 cm. Late 7th century. Hōryūji Treasure House, Tōkyō National Museum. National Treasure.

is the Kudara Kannon, a slender, tall image with gently curving scarves, carved during the Asuka period. The Roku Kannon (six statues of Kannon) with expressions of childlike purity are characteristic of Buddhist sculpture of the Hakuhō era style. The Yumetagai Kannon or "Dream-changing Kannon," who has power to change bad dreams into good ones, was made late in the 7th century when such T'ang influences as a fleshy body, clinging drapery and better proportions became apparent.

Two magnificent miniature shrines were also placed in the Daihōzōden: the Tamamushi Shrine and the Shrine of Lady Tachibana. The Tamamushi Shrine was erected during the middle of the 7th century and represented a miniature sanctuary on a high pedestal with architectural features resembling those of the Hōryūji. Originally iridescent wings of a beetle called the *tamamushi* were placed beneath the filigree openings along the borders of the shrine. The outer panels are covered with oil paintings on lacquered wood. The

Shrine of Lady Tachibana (d 733), the mother of the empress KŌ-MYŌ, is boxlike in appearance. It stands on a high pedestal and is topped by a canopy made to resemble that over the Shaka triad in the *kondō*. In it is enshrined the Buddha Amida flanked by the bodhisattvas Kannon and Seishi emerging from a lotus pond. Exquisitely crafted and delicately executed, the triad is a masterpiece of Hakuhō Buddhist art.

The Hōryūji complex with its many works of art represents living proof of the great variety of artistic traditions that were transmitted to Japan from Korea and China during the 7th century. They were copied, absorbed, and gradually transformed in accordance with Japanese aesthetic preferences. See also BUDDHIST ARCHITECTURE.

——Seiichi Mizuno, *Asuka Buddhist Art: Hōryūji* (1974).
Lucie R. WEINSTEIN

Hōryūji Great Treasure House

(Hōryūji Daihōzōden). Located at the temple HŌRYŪJI, in Ikaruga, Nara Prefecture. One of the older (it was opened in 1939) and more important Buddhist temple treasure houses, it is particularly famous for its Buddhist sculptures, which date from the Asuka period (latter part of the 6th century–710) through the Kamakura period (1185–1333). Among the objects are the Kudara Kannon, the Tamamushi Shrine (Tamamushi Zushi), and the Shrine of the Lady Tachibana (Tachibana Fujin Zushi) with its AMIDA triad in bronze. There are also bronze figurines of the Asuka period, a Yumetagai Kannon of the Nara period (710–794), a number of Fujiwara statues, and a collection of *bugaku* (see GAGAKU) masks. The Hōryūji Treasure House (Hōryūji Hōmotsukan), a separate building at the TŌKYŌ NATIONAL MUSEUM in Ueno Park, Tōkyō, houses many other items from the temple. See HŌRYŪJI, TREASURES OF.

Laurance ROBERTS

Hōryūji, treasures of

(Hōryūji Kennō Hōmotsu; literally, "Treasures Donated by Hōryūji"). A collection of precious objects preserved in the Hōryūji Treasure House (Hōryūji Hōmotsukan), located on the grounds of the TŌKYŌ NATIONAL MUSEUM in Ueno Park, Tōkyō. The collection includes sculpture, painting, metal and lacquer articles, Buddhist and secular documents, GIGAKU masks, and musical instruments. The objects were made over a period of nearly 1,300 years, beginning with the founding of the temple HŌRYŪJI in Nara in 607. Though far less in number than the objects in the 8th-century SHŌSŌIN art repository, the Hōryūji treasures rival those of the Shōsōin in quality and surpass them in antiquity. Whereas the Shōsōin contains primarily articles associated with the reign of Emperor SHŌMU, donated to the temple TŌDAIJI in 756, the Hōryūji collection focuses on the life and subsequent veneration of Prince SHŌTOKU, the founder of Hōryūji.

The buildings of Hōryūji housed the treasures, many of which had been objects of worship over the centuries. But after the Meiji Restoration of 1868, Buddhist temples suffered great economic hardship because the government forced them to surrender much of the landholdings from which they derived their revenues (see HAIBUTSU KISHAKU). As a result Hōryūji became impoverished; its dilapidated buildings were unable to provide adequate shelter for its many treasures. Therefore, in 1878, the temple authorities donated these treasures to the Imperial Household in exchange for a grant of ¥10,000, which was sorely needed for the restoration of temple buildings. Before the decision had been reached to donate the precious objects to the government, Hōryūji selected about half of them to be exhibited at the Nara Exposition in 1875 held at the Daibutsuden of Tōdaiji. After the close of the exposition, the objects were stored temporarily in the Shōsōin.

When the museum in Ueno Park was completed in 1882, the collection was shipped to Tōkyō, where the objects were copied, photographed, and catalogued. Four years later, the museum was officially named the Imperial Museum (Teishitsu Hakubutsukan) and the Hōryūji objects were given the formal designation Hōryūji Kennō Gyobutsu (Imperial Treasures Donated by the Hōryūji). After World War II, when the museum became the Tōkyō National Museum, the Hōryūji collection, remaining in its custody, was renamed the Hōryūji Kennō Hōmotsu. A special gallery to house it, long under consideration, was finally completed in 1964.

Among the most remarkable objects in the collection are a group of gilt-bronze devotional images. The Japanese call them the SHIJŪ-

HATTAI BUTSU, "The 48 Buddhas," even though there are more than 50 pieces in the collection. They constitute the largest group of small-scale images extant in Japan. Averaging around 30 centimeters (1 ft) high, these statuettes include the earliest known Japanese Buddhist images. They were probably made for aristocratic worshipers who had them enshrined for private devotion. Many are beautifully finished. Since they comprise a wide variety of styles, one assumes they were made in various ateliers. Some may be of Korean or Chinese origin. A number of the images are in the style originated by KURATSUKURI NO TORI in the early 7th century; others have the youthful faces of the style associated with HAKUHŌ CULTURE (latter part of the 7th century); still others show the Indian manner of shifting the hip to one side, which was a fashionable style in Tang (T'ang; 618–907) China and made its appearance first with the small-scale images in Japan. The Shijūhattai Butsu consist of 21 KANNON, 12 Buddhas, 10 MIROKU, one AMIDA triad, one Seishi Bosatsu, four unidentified bodhisattvas, and a unique group of figurines centering around Queen Māyā giving birth miraculously to the Buddha. The numbers of the deities are indicative of their popularity as devotional images during Japan's first flowering of Buddhism, the bodhisattva Kannon being worshiped more than any of the others.

There are 38 nimbuses in the collection, widely varied in magnificence of design. Some were originally attached to the statuettes, others belonged to images now lost. A boat-shaped body-halo of a lost triad resembles the mandorla of the Shaka trinity in the Hōryūji kondō, or main hall, which was originally surrounded by flying celestials resembling those of the miniature mandorla. This type of mandorla had been employed in China during the Northern Wei dynasty (386–534).

More up to date stylistically are the 11 reliefs hammered out of copper in repoussé, reflecting the Tang (T'ang) manner. The largest represents an Amida group that resembles the murals of the kondō made around 690.

During the 6th and 7th centuries the styles of Buddhist art were many and the workmanship was often exquisite. The gilt-bronze banner, 5 meters (17 ft) high, suspended from a canopy, known as Kanchōban, is a masterpiece. Its filigree design, with flying celestials and palmette motifs, is unsurpassed. Made in the latter half of the 7th century, the Kanchōban was used during ordination rites. Although no others exist today, gilt-bronze banners, as well as brocades and embroidered silk banners, were hung from pillars and canopies during Buddhist services. Remnants of silk banners, magnificently woven and embroidered, are included in the collection.

Prince Shōtoku is the subject of several important paintings among the Hōryūji objects. One is the oldest extant portrait of him, made after his death, probably in the 8th century, when Chinese influence reached Japan directly rather than by way of Korea. Dressed in a Chinese garment, Shōtoku, with a princeling on each side, is portrayed in the Tang (T'ang) manner. The composition is reminiscent of the painter Yan Liben (Yen Li-pen; d 673), who depicted 13 emperors flanked by attendants in a similar way. Yet there is a difference in perception here. Shōtoku, appearing less ornate than the emperors, is shown stark and iconic. Like the central deity of a Buddhist triad he towers high above his attendants, whose garments do not overlap with his. It is a portrait intended for worship.

Reverence for Shōtoku is also apparent in the paintings on five two-fold screens, known as Shōtoku taishi eden, which deal with scenes from the prince's life. They were painted in 1069 by Hata no Chitei on silk sliding doors for the edono (picture hall), located in the Eastern Precinct of Hōryūji. Later they were transferred onto the screens. Although these paintings are in delicate condition, they show Japanese landscapes, people, and buildings executed in a self-reliant manner that developed during the Heian period (794–1185), when official contact with China had ceased. The screens are among the harbingers of the YAMATO-E school of painting.

During the Kamakura period (1185–1333), Shōtoku was widely worshipped as a saint. The demand for biographical depictions of Shōtoku led to the production of screens, handscrolls, and hanging scrolls. The collection includes a set of four hanging scrolls dealing with his life, painted in 1305.

The written documents in the collection are extensive. They comprise manuscripts of every period in Japanese history beginning with the Asuka period (latter part of the 6th century to 710) and ending with the Edo period (1600–1868). Of foreign derivation is a Sanskrit text (the Prajñapāramitā-hyṛdaya-sūtra; known in Japanese as the Hannya shingyō) which was written in India during the Gupta dynasty on tala leaves. The Hokke gisho, which is one of the earliest Japanese documents, is a manuscript commentary on the LOTUS SUTRA attributed to Prince Shōtoku. Whether or not Shōtoku was its author, the hand that wrote it was a cultured one, trained in the Chinese Six Dynasties (280–589) style that was employed in Japan during the early part of the 7th century. Another important manuscript is the Kokon mokuroku shō, compiled by the priest Kenshin between 1230 and 1253, which, in addition to being a major biography of Shōtoku, is also an invaluable sourcebook for information on the architecture, images, and other works of art at Hōryūji.

A sense of humor pervades the 32 gigaku masks, which show a wide range of expressions. They were worn during gigaku performances accompanied by music played on such instruments as drums and flutes included in the collection. The performances often accompanied Buddhist services. Sixteen of the masks carved in camphorwood date from the 7th century; the rest were made in the 8th century when paulownia was preferred.

Among the textiles there are embroideries, brocades, and fabrics dyed by various means. A number of them were imported from Korea and China during the 7th and 8th centuries. The collection also contains robes, shoes, writing equipment, an incense burner, bows and arrows, and much more that, according to tradition, belonged to Prince Shōtoku. The objects bear witness to the deep devotion lavished on the saintly prince over the centuries. See also HŌRYŪJI GREAT TREASURE HOUSE; BUDDHIST ART.

🔖 ——Tōkyō Kokuritsu Hakubutsukan, *Illustrated Catalogue, Former Imperial Treasures from Hōryūji* (1975).

Lucie R. WEINSTEIN

Hōsa Bunko

(Hōsa Library). Collection of books originally owned by the Owari branch of the TOKUGAWA FAMILY. The majority of the 65,000 volumes in the library are old Chinese and Japanese editions. Especially valuable are those from the collection of TOKUGAWA IEYASU at Sumpu (now the city of Shizuoka) that were transferred to the Hōsa Bunko after his death in 1616. Many other works were assembled at the time of the Meiji Restoration (1868), and the whole constitutes perhaps the finest library of any of the Tokugawa branch families. The collection was removed from Nagoya to Mejiro, Tōkyō, in 1932 and opened to scholars in a newly built facility there. In 1950 financial circumstances necessitated the return of the library to Nagoya, where it became the property of the municipality. The library is richly endowed with such treasures as 15th- and 16th-century Korean printed books, a few KANAZAWA BUNKO books, woodblock editions of the Song (Sung) dynasty (960–1279) of China, and manuscripts from the Kamakura period (1185–1333).

Theodore F. WELCH

Hōseidō Kisanji (1735–1813)

Mid-Edo-period writer of the light fictional genres KIBYŌSHI and SHAREBON, and KYŌKA ("mad verse") poet. He was born in Edo (now Tōkyō). Adopted by the *samurai* Hirasawa family of the Akita domain (now part of Akita Prefecture), he served that domain as a liaison officer in Edo. His real name was Hirasawa Tsunetomi, but he is better known by several literary aliases, including Hōseidō Kisanji, Hirasawa Heikaku, Tegara no Okamochi, and Kisanjin. A friend and literary collaborator of KOIKAWA HARUMACHI, his style is noted for its lighthearted satire, urbane wit, and keen perception of the fashions and foibles of his day. The Tokugawa shogunate banned his most famous *kibyōshi*, *Bumbu nidō mangoku-dōshi* (1788, Sifting for Practitioners of the Dual Paths of Literary and Martial Learning), which satirized the general degeneracy of the samurai class and the KANSEI REFORMS instituted by the regime of MATSUDAIRA SADANOBU. His domain ordered him to stop writing fiction, and he turned exclusively to the writing of *kyōka*, which he continued well into his later years. See also GESAKU.

Hōsei University

(Hōsei Daigaku). A private university located in Chiyoda Ward, Tōkyō. Its predecessor was the Tōkyō Hōgaku Sha, which was established in 1880 as the first private law school in Japan. In 1889 it merged with the Tōkyō Futsu Gakkō (Tōkyō School of French Law) and took the name of Wafutsu Hōritsu Gakkō (School of French and Japanese Law). It was renamed Hōsei University in 1903 and became an officially accredited university in 1920. In 1952 it absorbed the Chūō Rōdō Gakuen Daigaku, a school specializing in the study of labor relations. It maintains faculties of law, arts and sciences, engineering, and business administration. Hōsei University is known for the following institutes: the Institute of Okinawan Culture, the Nogami Memorial Noh-Play Research Center, the Boissonade Institute of Modern Law, and the Ohara Institute for Social Research. Enrollment was 21,719 in 1980.

Hoshina Masayuki (1611–1672)

Daimyō of the early Edo period. A son of the second Tokugawa shōgun, TOKUGAWA HIDETADA, and half-brother of the third shōgun, TOKUGAWA IEMITSU. As a child he was given in adoption to the Hoshina family, succeeding to the lordship of the Takatō domain (in what is now Nagano Prefecture) in 1631. He was transferred to a larger domain in Dewa Province (now Yamagata Prefecture) and then in 1643 was made daimyō of the Aizu domain (now part of Fukushima Prefecture) assessed at 230,000 *koku* (see KOKUDAKA). There he distinguished himself as a capable ruler, reorganizing the system and building granaries for emergency purposes. In 1651, in accordance with Iemitsu's last wishes, Hoshina became official guardian *(hosa)* of the infant shōgun TOKUGAWA IETSUNA. During 10 years of service he was responsible for the construction of the Tamagawa Canal and the Ryōgoku Bridge in Edo (now Tōkyō), and it was he who proposed the banning of the practices of JUNSHI (suicide as an act of loyalty following the death of one's lord) and HITOJICHI (the holding of hostages)—policies that were adopted in 1665, after his retirement. As a serious student of the Zhu Xi (Chu Hsi) school of Confucianism (SHUSHIGAKU), Hoshina could be narrowly moralistic, but he is generally remembered for his benevolent leadership.

Hoshino site

Archaeological site located in Hoshino, in the city of Tochigi, Tochigi Prefecture. Scientific excavations beginning in 1965 by Serizawa Chōsuke (b 1919) of Tōhoku University have yielded thousands of STONE TOOLS from the paleolithic period (before 10,000 BC). A group of chert implements from the lower eight layers underlying a volcanic pumice, dated by radiocarbon and fission track to about 40,000 years ago, supports interpretations for an early occupation of Japan. See also HISTORY OF JAPAN: prehistory; PALEOLITHIC CULTURE.

■ ———Serizawa Chōsuke, *Tochigi Shi Hoshino iseki: Daisanji hakkutsu chōsa hōkoku* (1969).   *Fumiko IKAWA-SMITH*

Hoshi Shin'ichi (1926–)

Author; chiefly known for his science fiction. Born in Tōkyō. Graduate of Tōkyō University, where he majored in agricultural engineering. He published his first science fiction work, "Sekisutora" in 1957, and with such later works as "Jinzō bijin" (1961, Man-made Beauty) and "Bokko chan" (1971) he established the science fiction "short short story" form in Japan. His short stories are cleverly interwoven with humor and irony. Hoshi's other works include *Sofu Koganei Yoshikiyo no ki* (1974), a biography of his grandfather KOGANEI YOSHIKIYO, a pioneering anthropologist.

Hoshi Tōru (1850–1901)

Politician. Born in Edo (now Tōkyō), he studied law in England from 1874 to 1877. Under the patronage of MUTSU MUNEMITSU he entered the government, working as lawyer for the Ministry of Justice. He joined the JIYŪTŌ (Liberal Party) at the time of its formation in 1881. A frequent writer for the party newspaper, he criticized the domination of politics by *han* cliques (HAMBATSU) and was twice jailed for his antigovernment activities. In 1892 he was elected to the House of Representatives and was named chairman, but he was soon ousted from his post by the anti-Hoshi faction in the Jiyūtō on grounds of having received bribes in connection with the establishment of the National Stock Exchange. He was appointed minister to the United States in 1896, again through Mutsu's intercession, but in 1898, hearing of the formation of a coalition cabinet under ŌKUMA SHIGENOBU and ITAGAKI TAISUKE, he rushed back to Japan without permission. Hoshi later helped ITŌ HIROBUMI to form the RIKKEN SEIYŪKAI party and was rewarded with the post of communications minister in the fourth Itō cabinet (1900). He was forced to resign after two months in office, when he was implicated in a financial scandal. Hoshi, nonetheless, continued to wield political influence and was named head of the Tōkyō municipal assembly. He was assassinated in 1901 by Iba Sōtarō (1851–1903), a master swordsman who blamed Hoshi and his cohorts for corruption in the Tōkyō city government.

Hōshō school

(Hōshōryū). One of the five major *shite kata* (principal player) schools (or troupes) of professional NŌ theater actors. Also known as the Kamigakari Hōshō school. The school claims direct descent from the Tobiza (Tobi troupe), one of the original four Yamato SARUGAKU Nō troupes. Although its exact origin is unclear, it was led by the elder brother of the early Nō master KAN'AMI of the KANZE SCHOOL and is thus considered to be older than the Kanze school. During the Edo period (1600–1868) it was patronized by the Tokugawa shogunate. After the MEIJI RESTORATION of 1868 the 16th troupe head *(tayū)*, Hōshō Kurō (1837–1917), attempted to revive Nō, which was suffering a decline, along with the fortunes of the school. His successor also made great efforts to preserve the characteristically severe acting style of the school. The present 18th hereditary head is the son of the 17th head. Other famous actors who were members of the school include Noguchi Kanesuke (1879–1953) and Kondō Kenzō (b 1890).

Hōshō is also the name of a leading *waki* (secondary player) school of Nō actors whose outstanding members include Matsumoto Kenzō (b 1899) and Hōshō Yaichi (b 1908).   *KIKKAWA Shūhei*

hōshosen

Vessels *(sen)* licensed to trade overseas by administrative directives *(hōsho)* issued for the Tokugawa shogunate by its senior councillors (RŌJŪ) and addressed to its Nagasaki commissioners (BUGYŌ). After 1631 such endorsement was required, in addition to the traditional "vermilion seal" credentials (SHUINJŌ), for all foreign voyages; this practice made the control of the shogunate's central administration over traffic with foreign lands tighter than had been the case with the VERMILION SEAL SHIP TRADE licensing system, which had been circumvented or abused by some merchants and *daimyō*. In 1633 Japanese travel overseas was restricted to *hōshosen*; in 1635 even this was terminated (see KAIGAI TOKŌ KINSHI REI), in accord with the policy of NATIONAL SECLUSION.   *George ELISON*

Hosoda Eishi (1756–1829)

UKIYO-E artist. Real name Hosoda Tokitomi. Ranked with UTAMARO and TORII KIYONAGA as one of the three great masters of *bijinga*, or pictures of beautiful women. Born to a *samurai* family in Edo (now Tōkyō), he first studied painting with Kanō Eisen'in (1753–1811). For three years he served as attendant to the 10th Tokugawa shōgun, Ieharu, before leaving his post at the shogunate to become a professional *ukiyo-e* artist. He is said to have been a pupil of the *ukiyo-e* artist Torii Bunryūsai, and his use of the professional name "Chōbunsai" on his earlier works emphasizes his connection to the TORII SCHOOL. Later, he increasingly used his KANŌ SCHOOL name, Eishi, which it is said was bestowed on him by Ieharu. In his pictures of beautiful women Eishi developed an elegant, elongated figure style that became his hallmark. He is credited with introducing the use of pale yellow backgrounds *(kitsubushi)* in his prints and with developing *murasaki-e* (purple pictures), a style that employs the color purple rather than red, producing a more subtle effect. From around 1800 Eishi abandoned printmaking and devoted himself entirely to *ukiyo-e* painting (*nikuhitsuga* or *nikuhitsu ukiyo-e*), a medium in which he excelled. Of his numerous disciples, CHŌKYŌSAI EIRI is best known.   *Aya Louisa McDONALD*

Hōsōhō → Broadcasting Law

Hosoi Heishū (1728–1801)

Confucian scholar of the Edo period (1600–1868). Born in the Owari domain (now part of Aichi Prefecture), he studied in Nagoya with Nakanishi Tan'en (1709–52), a scholar associated with the SETCHŪGAKUHA, or eclectic school of Confucianism. After further study in Kyōto and Nagasaki, he went to Edo (now Tōkyō), where he opened a school. In 1772 Heishū was invited by UESUGI HARUNORI, the *daimyō* of the Yonezawa domain (now part of Yamagata Prefecture), to assist in educational reform and to teach in the domainal school. In 1780 he was invited back to Owari as lecturer to the daimyō, and three years later he was named head of the Meirindō, the domainal school. A scholar with a practical rather than a theoretical turn of mind, Heishū stressed the importance of benevolent rule and the education of all people.

Hosoi Kōtaku (1658–1735)

Chinese-style calligrapher. Also known as Hosoi Kōkin, Gyokusen, or Kishōdō. He was born in Kyōto, the son of a physician to the Kakegawa family in Tōtōmi Province (now part of Shizuoka Prefecture). As a young man Kōtaku went to Edo (now Tōkyō) to study Confucian philosophy with Sakai Zenken and calligraphy with Kitajima Setsuzan (1636–97). Kōtaku then accepted a post as personal retainer and adviser on firearms to shogunate councilor YANAGISAWA YOSHIYASU. Widely talented, Kōtaku excelled in seal carving, astronomy, mathematics, painting, and poetry, but he eventually resigned his official position and devoted himself to calligraphy.

The calligraphic style that Kōtaku learned from Setsuzan was based on classical Chinese models, especially that of the Ming dynasty literatus Wen Zhengming (Wen Cheng-ming). The new interest in Chinese calligraphy in his day led to widespread recognition of his talents. Kōtaku published several woodblock books on calligraphy, the most influential being the *Shibi jiyō* (1724), in which he explained the eight basic strokes in the character for "eternal" that are the fundamental brushstrokes in calligraphy. Kōtaku's friend, the great sinophile OGYŪ SORAI, contributed an introduction, stating that it was now the best time for literature, a new golden age for calligraphy, and that no one but Kōtaku could teach the correct method.

Kōtaku's calligraphy survives in both scroll and screen formats. His writing is bold and strong, resembling that of Wen Zhengming but with a more blunt and massive quality. His standard script *(kaisho)* emphasizes the verticality of characters, while his running script *(gyōsho)* displays a confident balancing of varied character shapes. Kōtaku also mastered seal *(tensho)*, clerical *(reisho)*, and grass or cursive *(sōsho)* scripts. In seal carving, Kōtaku followed the lead of the Chinese immigrant monks Ōbaku Dokuryū and Tōkō Shin'etsu (1639–95).

■ ——Addiss and Li, ed, *Catalogue of the Oriental Collection, Spencer Museum* (1979). *Stephen* ADDISS

Hosokawa family

Warlords and shogunal deputies of the Muromachi period (1333–1568); subsequently *daimyō* in the Edo period (1600–1868). A branch of the Ashikaga family, the Hosokawa took their name from their estate in Hosokawa, Mikawa Province (now part of Aichi Prefecture). In the 1330s Hosokawa Akiuji (d 1352) helped ASHIKAGA TAKAUJI to found the Muromachi shogunate. In consequence the Hosokawa were made military governors (SHUGO) of seven provinces scattered in Shikoku and central Honshū, and, with the SHIBA FAMILY and the HATAKEYAMA FAMILY, traditionally held the extremely important administrative post of shogunal deputy (KANREI). They reached the peak of their power under the leadership of HOSOKAWA KATSUMOTO (1430–73), but their resources were exhausted in the ŌNIN WAR (1467–77), after which they remained in control of the shogunate but shared in its decline. HOSOKAWA YŪSAI, a *waka* poet and scholar, restored the family to prominence through service with the national unifiers ODA NOBUNAGA and TOYOTOMI HIDEYOSHI. His son HOSOKAWA TADAOKI fought under TOKUGAWA IEYASU at the Battle of SEKIGAHARA (1600); as lords of the Higo domain (now Kumamoto Prefecture), assessed at 540,000 *koku* (see KOKUDAKA), the Hosokawa were by 1632 among the most important of the TOZAMA (outer) daimyō.

Hosokawa Gracia (1563–1600)

(Japanese name: Hosokawa Tama). Christian convert of the 16th century, often held up as a model of the virtuous and valiant *samurai* wife. Hosokawa Tama was the third daughter of AKECHI MITSUHIDE. In 1578 she was married to HOSOKAWA TADAOKI (1563–1646), eldest son of HOSOKAWA YŪSAI, *daimyō* of western Yamashiro Province (now part of Kyōto Prefecture). She bore him six children. When Akechi rose up against ODA NOBUNAGA and tried unsuccessfully to seize power in the HONNŌJI INCIDENT of 1582, Tadaoki refused to assist his father-in-law, and Tama was obliged to retire to Mitono in the mountainous Okutango Peninsula. Two years later the new ruler, TOYOTOMI HIDEYOSHI, allowed her

to return and take up residence in Ōsaka. In 1587 Tama became a Christian, receiving the baptismal name Gracia. She showed herself a fervent convert and is often mentioned in contemporary Jesuit correspondence. On the death of Hideyoshi in 1598, Tadaoki sided with TOKUGAWA IEYASU in the ensuing struggle for power. Before leaving Ōsaka to fight for Ieyasu's cause, Tadaoki instructed his retainers to put his wife to death rather than allow her to fall into the hands of his enemies. When ISHIDA MITSUNARI, Ieyasu's chief rival, attempted to seize Gracia as a hostage on 25 August 1600 (Keichō 5.7.17), Ogasawara Shōsai, the senior retainer of the family, executed her in accordance with Tadaoki's orders and then committed suicide himself. Some Hosokawa records, edited more than a century after the event, maintain that Gracia committed suicide, but contemporary Jesuit reports agree that she allowed herself to be killed without offering any resistance. In view of the Christian injunction against suicide and Gracia's fervent religious faith, the latter version of her death appears more probable. *Michael* COOPER

Hosokawa Karoku (1888–1962)

Journalist and politician. Born in Toyama Prefecture; graduate of Tōkyō University. From 1921 he was a member of the ŌHARA INSTITUTE FOR SOCIAL RESEARCH, where he studied international, colonial, and labor problems. He also wrote for various journals, consistently taking a critical view of Japan's expansionist policies. In 1942 he was arrested by the police for writing an article with alleged communist tendencies (see YOKOHAMA INCIDENT) and spent the rest of World War II in prison. He was released in September 1945 and was elected to the House of Councillors in 1947 as a member of the Communist Party. He was reelected in 1950 but was forced to resign in 1951 during the so-called RED PURGE and devoted the rest of his life to projects promoting peace, especially reconciliation with China.

Hosokawa Katsumoto (1430–1473)

General of the Muromachi period (1333–1568); son of Hosokawa Mochiyuki (1400–1442). He succeeded his father as military governor (SHUGO) of Settsu (now part of Ōsaka and Hyōgo prefectures), Tamba (now part of Hyōgo and Kyōto prefectures), Sanuki (now Kagawa Prefecture), and Tosa (now Kōchi Prefecture). The HOSOKAWA FAMILY, with the SHIBA FAMILY and the HATAKEYAMA FAMILY, had taken turns holding the important post of shogunal deputy (KANREI) in the Muromachi shogunate, and Katsumoto himself occupied the office for three terms (1445–49, 1452–64, 1468–73). He and the warrior YAMANA SŌZEN were the de facto leaders of the shogunate, but they came into conflict when succession disputes broke out in the shogunal ASHIKAGA FAMILY and in the Hatakeyama and Shiba families. Katsumoto and Sōzen supported different candidates for the shogunal office and rival claimants to the headship of the two *kanrei* families. This confrontation was one of the chief causes of the ŌNIN WAR (1467–77), in which the armies of Katsumoto and Sōzen between them devastated the city of Kyōto. Katsumoto died of illness before the struggle was resolved. A devout adherent of Zen Buddhism, Katsumoto built the temple RYŌANJI in Kyōto.

Hosokawa Tadaoki (1563–1646)

Also known as Hosokawa Sansai. *Daimyō* and amateur of the arts. Son of the literary daimyō HOSOKAWA YŪSAI and husband of HOSOKAWA GRACIA. Tadaoki's bravery in the campaign that destroyed Matsunaga Hisahide (1510–77) in 1577 drew the personal praise of ODA NOBUNAGA; he participated in several of that hegemon's subsequent campaigns, including the conquest of the TAKEDA FAMILY in 1582. When Nobunaga was killed by AKECHI MITSUHIDE later that year, Tadaoki refused his father-in-law Mitsuhide's request for assistance, joining instead the national unifier TOYOTOMI HIDEYOSHI to destroy Mitsuhide. Tadaoki succeeded his father as daimyō of Tango Province (now part of Kyōto Prefecture) in 1582; he rose to positions of high responsibility and courtly rank in Hideyoshi's service, which included participation in the KOMAKI NAGAKUTE CAMPAIGN in 1584, the conquest of Kyūshū in 1587 and of the Later Hōjō in the ODAWARA CAMPAIGN in 1590, and the invasion of Korea in 1592 (see INVASIONS OF KOREA IN 1592 AND 1597). In the climactic Battle of SEKIGAHARA in 1600, Tadaoki fought on the side of the future shōgun TOKUGAWA IEYASU, and after the victory he was rewarded with a domain assessed at 399,000 *koku* (see KOKU-

DAKA) including Buzen Province and two districts in Bungo Province (now parts of Fukuoka and Ōita prefectures); his initial residence here was at Nakatsu, but he moved to Kokura in 1602. Tadaoki retired early in 1621, passing on this domain to his son Tadatoshi (1586–1641). When Tadatoshi was transferred to a 540,000-*koku* fief at Kumamoto in Higo (now Kumamoto Prefecture) in 1632, Tadaoki took up residence at Yatsushiro Castle in that province, where he died. A highly accomplished man, Tadaoki was a poet, painter, and expert on etiquette and ceremonial matters (YŪSOKU KOJITSU); he ranked as one of the great tea master SEN NO RIKYŪ's "Seven Great Disciples" (Rikyū Shittetsu) and was the author of works on the art of tea.

George ELISON

Hosokawa Yūsai (1534–1610)

Also known as Hosokawa Fujitaka. *Daimyō* and poet of the Azuchi-Momoyama period (1568–1600). The son of Mitsubuchi Harukazu (d 1570), an intimate of several Ashikaga shōguns, Yūsai was adopted by Hosokawa Mototsune (d 1553), the *shugo* (military governor) of Izumi Province (now part of Ōsaka Prefecture), and himself became an important shogunal vassal. Yūsai was a key intermediary between ASHIKAGA YOSHIAKI and the hegemon ODA NOBUNAGA, who installed Yoshiaki as shōgun in 1568. In 1573, when Nobunaga expelled Yoshiaki from Kyōto, Yūsai broke with the shōgun and sided with the hegemon, being rewarded by Nobunaga with "all the area west of the river Katsuragawa in Yamashiro Province" (now part of Kyōto Prefecture) and assuming the family name Nagaoka from the location of his castle, Shōryūji, on the site of the 8th-century capital NAGAOKAKYŌ. Yūsai served Nobunaga with distinction in various military campaigns, and was in 1580 made daimyō of Tango Province (now part of Kyōto Prefecture). Upon Nobunaga's assassination by AKECHI MITSUHIDE in 1582 he refused a request for assistance made by Mitsuhide, his former close associate, and retired from affairs, passing on his domain to his son HOSOKAWA TADAOKI and assuming the priestly style Yūsai. Thereafter he devoted himself to cultural pursuits, becoming known as the outstanding authority on WAKA (classical Japanese poetry): he instructed the national unifier TOYOTOMI HIDEYOSHI (1537–98) in that art and initiated Prince Hachijō Toshihito (1579–1629) into the secret traditions of the 10th-century KOKINSHŪ anthology (see KOKIN DENJU). In the great conflict of 1600, Yūsai supported the Tokugawa side, and his residence, Tanabe Castle (now the city of Maizuru), was besieged by troops loyal to ISHIDA MITSUNARI. Yūsai, however, was conveyed to safety through the intercession of Prince Toshihito and his brother, Emperor Go-Yōzei (1572–1617; r 1586–1611), who were concerned lest an irreplaceable cultural resource be lost. Yūsai is described in *Taionki*, the memoirs of the litterateur MATSUNAGA TEITOKU (1571–1653), as a man for all seasons who "attained mastery in all the arts he set his mind to, from military accomplishments, *waka*, and *renga* (linked verse; see RENGA AND HAIKAI) to courtly football (*mari*), carving (*hōchō*), and percussion music (*uchihayashi*)." Among his notable literary works are the poetry collection *Shūmyōshū* (Collection of Many Marvels) and the commentary *Hyakunin isshu shō* (Notes on One Poem Each by One Hundred Authors).

George ELISON

Hossō sect

(Hossōshū; Ch: Faxiang Zong; Fa-hsiang Tsung). One of the six sects of NARA BUDDHISM. The sect draws on the doctrine of the Indian Buddhist school Vijñānavāda ("mind-only" school; J: Yuishikishū). This school, which is also known as the Yogācāra ("practice of yoga") school, is represented by Vasubandhu (4th century) and Asaṅga (4th century), who emphasized the workings of consciousness (Skt: *vijñāna*) in its interrelation with environment. This doctrine was expounded in China by Kuiji (K'uei-chi; 632–682), Xuanzang (Hsüan-tsang; 600–664), and others. The basic scriptures for this school include the work known in Japanese as *Jōyuishiki ron* (Skt: Vijñaptimātratāsiddhi-śāstra), which was originally a collection of commentaries on one of Vasubandhu's works but was modified when translated into Chinese so as to center on the interpretation of the 6th-century Indian commentator Dharmapāla; the *Yuga shiji ron* (Skt: Yogācārabhūmi-śāstra); and the *Gejin mikkyō* (Skt: Saṃdhinirmocana-sūtra). Like other Buddhist schools that flourished mainly during the Nara period (710–794), the Chinese school was transplanted into Japan by monks such as DŌSHŌ and GEMBŌ over the period 653–735. The school has been located at KŌFUKUJI, HŌRYŪJI,

and YAKUSHIJI, the three institutions that served as representative centers of Buddhist studies during the medieval period (13th–16th centuries). GYŌGI, Gomyō (750–834), and Jōkei (1155–1213) were famous monks from this sect. In 1950 Hōryūji seceded from the sect, which now has two main temples, Kōfukuji and Yakushiji, and some 35 other temples.

TSUCHIDA Tomoaki

Hotakadake

Mountain on the border of Nagano and Gifu prefectures, central Honshū. It comprises the four peaks of Kita Hotakadake (3,100 m; 10,168 ft), Oku Hotakadake (3,190 m; 10,463 ft), Mae Hotakadake (3,090 m; 10,135 ft), and Nishi Hotakadake (2,909 m; 9,542 ft). It is Japan's third highest mountain and the highest mountain of the HIDA MOUNTAINS. Ice-scoured areas, including the Karasawa Cirque, are on the eastern side of the mountain. Mae Hotakadake was first climbed by Walter WESTON, a British missionary and mountaineer, in 1893. One of the two most popular rock-climbing areas in the JAPANESE ALPS, the other being Tsurugidake. It forms a principal part of Chūbu Sangaku National Park.

Hotakayama

Stratovolcano in northeastern Gumma Prefecture, central Honshū. The summit is divided into several peaks. On the northwest side are located a wide plateau, Hotaka Shrine, and several hot spring spas. Height: 2,158 m (7,078 ft).

hotarugari → firefly viewing

hotoke → Buddha

Hototogisu

A leading HAIKU magazine that was launched in 1897 in conjunction with the haiku reform movement of MASAOKA SHIKI; by 1920 it had become one of the most influential organs in haiku circles.

Hototogisu was first published in the city of Matsuyama (Ehime Prefecture) in January 1897. Yanagihara Kyokudō (1867–1957) was the publisher and Masaoka Shiki the editor. In 1898 Shiki's disciple TAKAHAMA KYOSHI took over as editor and publisher, and the magazine moved to Tōkyō. By 1906 Kyoshi had become more interested in prose and *shaseibun* (sketch pieces), and *Hototogisu* was changed from a poetry magazine to a general literary arts magazine. For example, it carried the serialization of NATSUME SŌSEKI's popular novel *Wagahai wa neko de aru* (1905–06; tr *I Am a Cat*, 1961). In 1912 *Hototogisu* turned back to haiku in an attempt to counter the movement for unconventional haiku launched by the poet KAWAHIGASHI HEKIGOTŌ, a rival of Kyoshi's; Kyoshi took up the cause of preserving the traditional style, which emphasized objective reflection of the natural world. From 1915 to 1925 *Hototogisu* was at the height of its influence, and regular contributors included the four leading poets who became known as the "Four S's": MIZUHARA SHŪOSHI, AWANO SEIHO, YAMAGUCHI SEISHI, and TAKANO SUJŪ. In the early 1980s, the magazine was still being published by Kyoshi's son, Takahama Toshi.

hototogisu

(toad lily). *Tricyrtis hirta*. Perennial herb of the lily family (Liliaceae) which grows wild in mountain areas of the southern part of central Japan; it is also planted in gardens. The stem stands straight or at a slant, reaching a height of about 60 centimeters (24 in), and has coarse hairs. The alternate leaves are elliptical and pointed at the tip. In fall, it produces lilylike flowers with six lobes, which grow upward from the leaf axils. The three petals and three sepals are alike, white on the outside with deep purplish spots inside. Similar species native to Japan include the *yamajino hototogisu* (*T. affinis*) and species with yellow flowers with purple spots such as the Tamagawa *hototogisu* (*T. latifolia*), the *kibana hototogisu* (*T. flava*), the *chabo hototogisu* (*T. nana*), and others.

MATSUDA Osamu

hototogisu → cuckoos

hot springs

(onsen). Hot springs are numerous in Japan, and for many centuries the Japanese people have enjoyed hot spring bathing. Visits to hot spring resorts were hailed not only as a means of relaxation but also for the beneficial medicinal properties attributed to thermal spring water. Hot springs are still one of the major tourist resources for vacationing Japanese, and many have been modernized and developed into large-scale resort complexes. The use of very high temperature hot springs as an energy source for geothermal electrical production is a noteworthy example of their modern-day utilization.

Definition —— A hot spring is defined by the Hot Spring Law (Onsen Hō) of 1948 as "hot water, mineral water, water vapor and other gases (except natural gas containing hydrocarbons as the main element) that issue from the ground with a temperature in excess of 25°C (77°F) or that contain more than a prescribed amount of designated substances." Thus a cool mineral spring under 25°C but containing more than a prescribed amount of said designated substances may be called a hot spring; even volcanic gas or volcanic vapor may be called a hot spring, creating cases which do not agree with the general concept of hot spring water. The required temperature for hot springs is 20°C (68°F) in most Western European countries.

World Distribution —— The 1965 report of the US Geological Survey gives the number of hot springs and mineral springs in the United States as 1,003, in Iceland as 516, in Italy as 149, and in France as 124. In addition to these, other hot springs and mineral springs are found all over the world. According to the summary of Japanese hot springs and mineral springs compiled by the Geological Survey of Japan in 1975, there are a total of 2,237 hot springs in Japan, of which hot springs with high temperatures, especially those capable of generating geothermal electricity, form only a small number.

High temperature geothermal zones are distributed along the rim of plates in the earth's crust where there is volcanic or seismic activity. For example, geothermal zones that border expanding plates are found in Iceland and in the East African trough zone. An example of a geothermal zone bordering on slipping plates is the fault zone in southern California. Two more kinds of geothermal zones include those bordering on contracting plates such as in the island arc system and those located along squeezing plate borders; the geothermal zones of Japan, the Philippines, Indonesia, and New Zealand belong to the former, while those of Italy and Turkey belong to the latter. The areas of terrestrial heat found in Yellowstone National Park and Hawaii are called geothermal hot spots.

Distribution of Hot Springs in Japan —— Hot springs are found in many places in Japan. After World War II the popularization of tourism brought about a rapid development of the tourist industry and hot springs became one of the leading attractions. Additional sources of thermal water were sought by drilling, in some cases as deep as 1,000 meters (3,280 ft), in order to tap subterranean hot water. As a result, the number of hot spring resorts increased from 863 in 1931 to 2,237 in 1975. Of these, hot spring resorts where hot water over 60°C (140°F) is found number about 300, and hot spring resorts where hot water over 90°C (194°F) is found number about 110. The distribution of hot springs with high temperature water is very closely related to that of Quaternary VOLCANOES.

Water Volume and Heat Radiation —— The volume of thermal water that issued from hot springs in Japan in 1969 totaled 6.99×10^6 m³/year, 70 percent of which was over 42°C (107°F). The amount of heat radiated from hot springs reaches 1.5×10^{24} ergs a year, which is approximately equivalent to 2.5 times the amount of energy released by an earthquake with a magnitude of 8 on the Japanese scale. A comparison of the amount of energy released by a volcanic eruption with the energy released by Japan's hot springs reveals that the energy released by the hot springs during the course of a year comes close to the value of the energy released by a small-scale volcanic eruption.

The Japanese and Hot Springs —— The Japanese take special pleasure in mineral and hot-spring bathing. Hot springs have been recognized to be medically effective since ancient times in treating both degenerative and chronic diseases. How hot springs were utilized in ancient Japan is described in the regional chronicles called FUDOKI. The *Izumo fudoki* reports that Tamatsukuri Hot Spring was continually thronged with visitors and says that by "bathing

once, the visitor was made fair of face and figure; bathing twice, all diseases were healed: its effectiveness has been obvious since of old." As described in the *Izumo fudoki* and *Iyo fudoki*, hot springs have been utilized mainly for bathing since ancient times. According to Japanese folklore, ŌKUNINUSHI NO MIKOTO and Sukunahikona no Mikoto (two Japanese gods of medicine) made hot springs gush forth in various places in Japan and used them for medical treatment. This is why Ōkuninushi no Mikoto and Sukunahikona no Mikoto are enshrined in hot-spring shrines found throughout the country. There are also numerous hot-spring centers said to have been opened by such distinguished Buddhist monks as GYŌKI and KŪKAI.

In the Edo period (1600–1868) UDAGAWA YŌAN, who is said to be the originator of Japanese analytical chemistry, wrote *Seimi kaisō*, a book in which he describes the methods of analysis and classification of hot springs. KAIBARA EKIKEN, a physician of the Chinese school of medicine (kampō), advocated bathing in hot springs and explained in detail the method of bathing to be observed for proper treatment. Perhaps because many hot springs in Japan are of the volcanic type and contain arsenic, he warned against drinking the water.

Utilization of Hot Springs —— Hot springs are used mainly for bathing in Japan. However, in some places the heat released by hot springs is utilized for other purposes. For example, in addition to heating rooms and cooking food, it is used as a source of heat in hothouses where tropical plants and young nursling plants are cultivated. It is also used for brewing *sake* and making *miso* (bean paste), and to heat brooders used for raising chickens and fish. Pipelines for the supply of hot spring water have been laid in urban areas in Kami Suwa, Nagano Prefecture (see KAMI SUWA HOT SPRING) and KUSATSU, Gumma Prefecture, and the spring water is utilized like running water. Recently, centralized control systems have been introduced in many hot springs, where sources are integrated and the spring water distributed by pipelines. The heat of hot springs was formerly used for salt manufacture in Obama, Nagasaki Prefecture, Shimo Kamo, Shizuoka Prefecture, and Shikabe, Hokkaidō. Pipelines carrying thermal spring water run under the roads to melt snow and prevent freezing at JŌZANKEI HOT SPRING.

Geothermal Electrical Generation —— In 1904 the first geothermal generation of electricity in the world was carried out at Larderello, Italy. P. Ginori Conti ran a 3/4 horsepower generator using gushing natural steam. In Italy full-scale geothermal generation of electricity has been carried on since 1932, and output had reached 300,000 kilowatts in 1960.

The first geothermal generation of electricity in Japan was successfully carried out by Tachikawa Heiji in BEPPU, Ōita Prefecture, in 1925, the amount of electricity generated being 1 kilowatt. During the period when electric power was in short supply after World War II, geothermal generation of electricity was attempted at a number of hot spring resort areas including Beppu, ATAGAWA HOT SPRING in Shizuoka Prefecture, Narugo in Miyagi Prefecture, and HAKONE in Kanagawa Prefecture. They succeeded in generating electric power in the 10 to 30 kilowatt range, which was used for lighting and as a source of power for sawmills. The Tone Boring Co, Ltd, succeeded in generating 3 to 8 kilowatts of electricity at their Atagawa laboratory in 1946. Generation of 30 kilowatts of geothermal electricity was carried out at the Kowakien Hotel in Hakone, Kanagawa Prefecture, from about 1955 until 1962. However, as the supply of inexpensive electricity from other sources increased, geothermal generation, which operated on a small scale and involved high costs and difficulties of maintenance, was stopped about 1960.

The natural steam available at Larderello, Italy, was dry steam which made the operation of electric generators easy, but in Japan the steam gushed out together with large quantities of hot water. Because it was wet, it could not be used efficiently to operate an electric generator. In the 1950s, however, a technique was developed to utilize jetting steam containing large quantities of hot water for the geothermal generation of electric power at Wairakei, New Zealand, and this prompted a return to active geothermal electric power generation in Japan.

In 1966 the generation of 22 megawatts of electricity was successfully achieved by the Japan Metals & Chemicals Co, Ltd, at Matsukawa, Iwate Prefecture, and in 1967 the generation of 13 megawatts was achieved by the Kyūshū Electric Power Co, Inc, at Ōtake, Ōita Prefecture. These successes were followed by the completion of a 10-megawatt power station by Mitsubishi Metal Corporation at Ōnuma, north of Matsukawa, in 1973. In 1975 the Electric Power

Development Co, Ltd, started operation of a 25-megawatt power plant at Onikōbe, Miyagi Prefecture, and a 50-megawatt plant at Hatchōbaru, Kyūshū; and in 1977 Tōhoku Electric Power Co, Inc, completed a 50-megawatt geothermal power generating plant at Takinoue, Iwate Prefecture. Spurred by the oil crisis of 1973, the development of geothermal energy has become a national project of high priority.

Geothermal power production in Japan, a land of volcanoes, is small in scale despite its long history. The output of geothermally generated electricity in 1978 was only about 170 megawatts. There are more than 100 areas in Japan that have hot springs with temperatures of over 90°C (194°F), but they are all utilized by hot spring enterprises, deterring the establishment of new geothermal power stations in these areas. Geothermal power generation in established hot springs involves the following problems: thermal generation rapidly absorbs great volumes of terrestrial heat, lowering the temperature of hot springs and causing hot springs to dry up and disappear very quickly; it spoils the tourist value; it destroys the natural environment; control over terrestrial heat is taken away from hot-spring enterprises and is given to electric power companies.　　Ōki Yasue

Balneotherapy in Japan —— *History.* The Japanese love of bathing is mentioned in early accounts of Japan by foreigners, and hot springs have been used for therapeutic bathing in Japan since ancient times. DŌGO HOT SPRING in Iyo Province (now Ehime Prefecture), reputedly the oldest hot spring in Japan, was the site, according to tradition, of theraputic bathing by several legendary or early historical emperors. Distinguished Buddhist monks such as Gyōgi, En no Gyōja, and Kūkai are said to have traveled extensively throughout Japan, developing hot springs for medical purposes. Hot springs were also used for religious purification. Bathing was regarded as an integral part of Buddhist purification ritual. Farmers and fishermen visited hot springs at various times during the course of a year and engaged in such ritualistic baths as the "New Year's bath," "mid-winter bath," "spring bath cure," "Bon Festival bath," "preharvest bath," "postharvest bath," "autumn bath cure," and "winter bath cure." Hot springs were thus used for bathing throughout the year not only for medicinal purposes, but for rest and recreation.

GOTŌ KONZAN (1659–1733), a doctor in Edo (now Tōkyō), noticed the effectiveness of hot-spring bathing as a remedial cure for certain disorders and in 1709 initiated the first medical study of hot springs. He advocated the therapeutic use of baths as a treatment for various ailments and outlined the proper method of bathing, the correct method for drinking mineral water, the principal cures and inadvisable treatments and procedures. His disciple KAGAWA SHŪTOKU enlarged upon Gotō's study of balneotherapy. He expounded on the so-called bath-cure-reaction and set down in detail the optimum frequency of bath-taking, the optimum period of submersion time in the bath, and the aftercare treatment. According to Kagawa, a hot spring was maximally effective only when used at its source. The therapeutic effect was greatly reduced if the spring water was conveyed over a long distance. He further maintained that the effect of a bath cure could be enhanced by a combination of general medical treatments and dietetics. Influenced by developments in the field of balneotherapy in Europe, the Japanese government undertook the chemical analysis of mineral springs in 1874. In 1886 the *Nippon kōsen shi* (Japanese Mineral Spring Magazine) appeared, and analytical and medical studies of hot springs gradually expanded. At the time of the Sino-Japanese War of 1894–95 and the Russo-Japanese War of 1904–05, temporary hot-spring sanatoriums were set up for post-treatment of the war-wounded.

Present conditions. After the founding of the Balneotherapy Institute at Beppu Hot Spring by Kyūshū University in 1931 the medical study of hot springs began to be systematized. It was followed by the founding of research facilities by Hokkaidō University at Noboribetsu Hot Spring in 1936, by Kagoshima University at Kirishima Hot Spring in 1939, by Okayama University at Misasa Hot Spring in Tottori Prefecture in 1939, by Tōhoku University at Narugo Hot Spring in Miyagi Prefecture in 1944, and by Gumma University at Kusatsu Hot Spring in 1952. During World War II, nursing homes were built at a number of hot-spring resorts for the purpose of treating the war-wounded. After the war they were maintained as national hot-spring hospitals, making hot springs for medical treatment available around the country. Hot springs are utilized in the treatment of chronic rheumatism, neuralgia, chronic diseases of the stomach, intestines, liver, and gall bladder, hypertension, hemiplegia, glucosuria, and gout. In addition to these, they are used for treating external injuries and for postoperative treatment and rehabilitation.

The time-bath at Kusatsu Hot Spring (a representative acid spring, peculiar to Japan, containing isolated mineral acid) is a center for high-temperature balneotherapy. This therapeutic method consisting of a three-minute immersion in water at 48°C (118°F) repeated four times a day was perfected by Nojima Kohachirō in 1878. It was introduced in Europe by Erwin von BÄLZ in 1896 and continues to be applied in cases of chronic rheumatism and chronic dermatitis.

The Hot Spring Law was enacted in 1948 for the purpose of protecting and rationalizing the development and utilization of Japan's abundant resources of hot springs, and the Ministry of Health and Welfare has, since 1954, designated 64 hot-spring resorts with environment and climatic elements suitable for medical treatment as national health and recreational hot-spring areas. Since 1976 the Japanese Association of Physical Medicine, Balneology and Climatology has issued certificates to so-called hot-spring physicians at various health and recreational hot-spring resorts.

　　　　　　　　　　　MORINAGA Hiroshi

🐟 —— Fujinami Gōichi, *Onsen chishiki* (1938). Nihon Onsen Kagaku Kai, ed, *Nihon onsen bunken mokuroku 1921–1970*, (1973). Nishikawa Yoshikata, *Onsen suchi* (1937). Ōshima Yoshio and Yano Ryōichi, *Onsen ryōyō no tebiki* (1975).

Hotta Masatoshi (1634–1684)

Great elder *(tairō)* of the Tokugawa shogunate. The third son of the senior councillor *(rōjū)* Hotta Masamori (1608–51). On orders from the shōgun TOKUGAWA IEMITSU he was adopted by KASUGA NO TSUBONE, Iemitsu's nurse. After serving as personal attendant to the fourth shōgun, TOKUGAWA IETSUNA, he was promoted to junior councillor *(wakadoshiyori)* in 1670 and to senior councillor in 1679. When Ietsuna died without an heir in 1680, Masatoshi successfully supported Ietsuna's brother TOKUGAWA TSUNAYOSHI, in opposition to Great Elder SAKAI TADAKIYO's candidate (an imperial prince) for the succession. Tsunayoshi appointed him great elder in 1681 and assigned him domains with an assessment of 130,000 *koku* (see KOKUDAKA). Masatoshi strove to bring discipline and order to the shogunate, but he was increasingly shunned by other officials and eventually by the shōgun himself, and was assassinated in 1684 by the junior councillor Inaba Masayasu (1640–84).

Hotta Masayoshi (1810–1864)

Daimyō of the Sakura domain (now part of Chiba Prefecture) and senior councillor *(rōjū)* of the Tokugawa shogunate. As a daimyō Hotta was known for his progressive views and encouragement of the study of Western medicine and military science. In the fall of 1855 he replaced ABE MASAHIRO as chief senior councillor and immediately faced pressure from Western powers to conclude agreements similar to the one (KANAGAWA TREATY) signed with the United States the previous year. He signed an agreement with the Dutch in 1856, and in 1858 he negotiated with the American representative Townsend HARRIS a full commercial treaty. Hotta then went personally to Kyōto to gain Emperor KŌMEI's approval, but failed. The controversy over the treaty was further complicated by a shogunal succession dispute in which Hotta supported TOKUGAWA YOSHINOBU. When the candidate favored by II NAOSUKE became shogunal successor and Ii was appointed great elder *(tairō)*, Hotta was forced to resign. Ii eventually signed the HARRIS TREATY (the treaty that Hotta had negotiated) as well as other commercial agreements (ANSEI COMMERCIAL TREATIES) without imperial sanction.

Hotta Shōzō (1899–)

Banker. Born in Aichi Prefecture. After graduating from Kyōto University, Hotta joined SUMITOMO BANK, LTD, becoming president in 1952 and chairman in 1970. Under the banner of stabilized and rationalized management, he successfully turned Sumitomo Bank into the third largest bank in Japan (in deposits). Using his bank's financial resources, he played a key role in the postwar regrouping of the Sumitomo corporations.　　ASAJIMA Shōichi

Hotta Yoshie (1918–)

Novelist. Born in Toyama Prefecture. Graduate of Keiō University. Serving as a Japanese army propagandist in Shanghai, China, during

World War II, he later wrote of his experiences at the end of the war in *Sokoku sōshitsu* (1950, Loss of the Motherland) and in other novels. Hotta received the 26th Akutagawa Prize for his *Hiroba no kodoku* (1951, Alone in the Marketplace), in which he described the psychological impact of the outbreak of the Korean War on a Japanese intellectual. His works, which often have as background international political events, deal with the dilemmas faced by the modern intellectual in critical situations. Other works by Hotta include the novels *Jikan* (1953, Time) and *Uminari no soko kara* (1960–61, From Beneath the Sea Roar), a historical novel which deals with the conflict of native and foreign ways of thinking during the Christian SHIMABARA UPRISING, and *Ransei no bungakusha* (1958), a collection of essays.

Ho-Umezu Agreement → He-Umezu (Ho-Umezu) Agreement

house codes → kakun

House, Edward Howard (1836–1901)

American journalist who played an important role in shaping 19th-century American opinion about Japan and the Japanese. Born in Boston. House pursued a variety of careers—musician, theatrical manager, Civil War correspondent, and music and drama critic—before arriving in Japan in 1871 to take a teaching position at the Kaisei Gakkō, one of the predecessors of Tōkyō University. His pro-Japanese views made him very popular with the Japanese government, especially with the oligarch ŌKUMA SHIGENOBU. In 1873 he resigned his teaching post to accompany the Japanese army on the Formosa Expedition (see TAIWAN EXPEDITION OF 1874) as a war correspondent. In 1877, with the aid of a generous government subsidy, House founded an English-language newspaper, the *Tōkyō Times,* which he edited until 1880. During these years he championed the Japanese positions on various issues, including extraterritoriality, treaty revision, and foreign policy. In 1880 House returned to the United States and early in 1881 moved to London, where he took a position in theatrical management. After he suffered a disabling stroke in 1883, he was awarded a lifetime pension by the Japanese government and was decorated with the Order of the Sacred Treasure (Zuihōshō) in recognition of his services. House returned to Japan and spent his remaining days fostering an appreciation of Western music. *Edward R.* BEAUCHAMP

House Food Industrial Co, Ltd

(Hausu Shokuhin Kōgyō). Manufacturer, processor, and vendor of spicy foods such as curry, as well as dry foods, wheat products, and instant foods. Established in 1947, the company has developed techniques to produce a wide variety of processed foods ranging from curry and spices to snack foods and instant noodles. The company depends largely on imports from the United States, Canada, India, and China for such raw materials as spices, wheat flour, and potato flakes. Sales for the fiscal year ending November 1981 totaled ¥123.8 billion (US $553.3 million) and capitalization was ¥3.4 billion (US $15.2 million). The head office is in Ōsaka.

household registers

(koseki). Official documents that record important information about a household, which in Japan is defined as consisting of a married couple, a married couple and their unmarried children (natural or adopted) of the same surname, an individual with unmarried children (natural or adopted) of the same surname, or an individual. Every Japanese national is listed in a *koseki,* which constitutes legal proof of his or her status. In the *koseki* is recorded such information as the members' names, dates of birth and death, reasons for entry into the *koseki* (e.g., marriage or birth), and the names of the natural (or foster) mother and father of each member listed. The first member listed in the *koseki* is called the *hittōsha.* The *hittōsha* is the spouse whose surname the couple has taken; after the *hittōsha* are listed the other spouse and the children in order of birth. The *hittōsha,* however, does not have the special privileges accorded to the *koshu* (family head) under the pre-1947 Civil Code (see PRIMOGENITURE). A child enters the *koseki* of the parent whose surname he or she has taken. The location of the permanent domicile listed in the

koseki is called the *honseki.* This has no necessary relation to where a person is actually living and can be anywhere in Japan, or can be transferred at any time. The *koseki* is compiled in the city, town, or village that is the person's *honsekichi* (place of permanent domicile). *Koseki* are arranged in the order of lot numbers and bound together in what are called *kosekibo* (household register books). The original *kosekibo* is kept at the local municipal office and a duplicate is deposited with the regional bureau of the Ministry of Justice. When a person enters another *koseki* (e.g., in the case of marriage), his or her name is stricken from the former *koseki* (a line is drawn through his or her name). In the event all persons listed in *koseki* are stricken from it, the *koseki* is removed from the *kosekibo* and placed in another register, the *josekibo* (removal register).

A new *koseki* is compiled for a couple when they report their marriage (see MARRIAGE LAW), except when the husband or wife was a *hittōsha* in his or her former *koseki* and the couple takes on the name of that spouse, in which case the other's name is entered in the *hittōsha's koseki.* If a person in the *koseki* other than the *hittōsha* or the spouse has or adopts a child, another *koseki* is compiled for that person and the child. This happens, for example, when a daughter gives birth to an illegitimate child. It is thus impossible for two couples or three generations (parents, children, and grandchildren) to be listed in one *koseki.* Returning to one's former *koseki* is permitted in several cases: when a person reverts to a former surname because of divorce or dissolution of adoption; when a person whose spouse has died reverts to his or her former surname; or when a child whose parents have different family names changes his or her surname from that of one parent to the other's and then reverts to the name of the first parent. A new *koseki* may be made if the *koseki* to which the person hoped to return has been removed to the *josekibo.* When a person reaches adulthood (20 years of age), as long as he or she is not the *hittōsha* or the spouse of the latter, he or she can leave the *koseki* and have a new *koseki* compiled upon application.

When a Japanese woman marries a non-Japanese, her surname and place of permanent domicile *(honsekichi)* legally remain the same and the fact of marriage is entered into her *koseki.* If a Japanese man marries a non-Japanese, his wife's name is entered in his *koseki.* A child born to a Japanese woman married to a non-Japanese is not entered in her *koseki* and as a result cannot be considered a Japanese national. However, if the child is illegitimate, he or she may be entered in the woman's *koseki* and thus be considered a Japanese citizen. A child born to a Japanese man married to a non-Japanese is entered in his *koseki* and is accorded the privileges of citizenship.

Any change in the status of a person is supposed to be recorded in the *koseki* through notification by the person or his relatives. Notification can be made to an office located in a place other than the person's *honsekichi.* In this event, notification is first sent to the office in the *honsekichi,* and then the change in status is registered. There are two types of change. The first type involves matters that change a person's legal status, such as birth, death, and court decisions regarding divorce or annulment, and notification must be made within a prescribed period of time or a fine may be imposed. The second type involves matters that do not have to be reported but remain legally invalid unless reported, such as marriage, divorce by agreement, adoption, and annulment by agreement.

A reproduction of the entire *koseki* is called a *koseki tōhon.* An abstract or copy of part of the register is called a *koseki shōhon.* Anyone can apply to obtain a *koseki tōhon* or *koseki shōhon* of anybody's *koseki* or a certificate concerning items in the *koseki* upon payment of a fee. *Koseki tōhon* and *koseki shōhon* are used on many occasions, such as when registering real estate, applying for a passport, seeking employment, entering school, investigating another person's status, and getting married. The *koseki* is used not only to clarify a person's status but also to provide demographic and other information for the government. See also FOREIGNERS IN JAPAN; MINORITIES. *ONO Kōji*

History —— *Koseki* were apparently compiled as early as the 6th century at imperial granaries *(miyake)* for the purpose of levying a rice tax. Under the RITSURYŌ SYSTEM of government that developed in the late 7th century, *koseki* came to be institutionalized as a means of facilitating government control and land distribution (see KŌGONEN-JAKU; HANDEN SHŪJU SYSTEM). *Koseki* were to be compiled every six years, corresponding to the six-year cycle of the land distribution system, with information such as the name of the head of the household *(ko),* the number of household members (including slaves), their relations, positions, ranking, ages, sex, and even physical characteristics. The household head *(koshu)* presented three copies of the *koseki* to the village headmen, who forwarded one copy to the provincial seat and the other two to the central government (DAJŌKAN) in the capital. The oldest surviving examples of *koseki* are fragments of the 702 compilation kept in the SHŌSŌIN.

With the decline of the *ritsuryō* system and the development of private landed estates (SHŌEN) in the Heian period (794–1185) compilation of *koseki* virtually ceased until early in the Edo period (1600–1868), when the shogunate became concerned over the activities of Christians in the wake of the SHIMABARA UPRISING of 1638. The shogunate ordered the domains to compile household registers, known as the *shūmon aratame nimbetsu chō* (see SHŪMON ARATAME), which listed temple affiliation in addition to general information about the household. These registers were compiled throughout the Edo period and became the basis for the *koseki* compiled under the Meiji government, which in 1871 enacted the Koseki Hō (Household Register Law), resulting in the JINSHIN KOSEKI of 1872, the first nationwide compilation of family records. In 1898, with the enactment of the CIVIL CODE establishing the IE (household) system, a register was compiled for each family unit listing all members of the household. One person was designated the family head *(koshu)* and was responsible for the welfare of the entire family. After World War II, with the promulgation of the new constitution in 1947, the *ie* system as a legal entity was abolished and the Koseki Hō was amended to place an emphasis on the individual.

Barbara Bowles SWANN

House of Councillors → Diet

House of Peers

(Kizokuin). One of two legislative chambers of the IMPERIAL DIET that existed until 1947 under the 1889 CONSTITUTION. In contrast to the Shūgiin (House of Representatives), whose members were popularly elected, membership in the House of Peers was by appointment. It was composed of adult males of the imperial family, heads of the hereditary PEERAGE, and other imperial nominees that included certain of the nation's biggest taxpayers and a few illustrious scholars. The minimum age was 30. Princes, marquis, and some imperial nominees were granted lifetime membership, while the rest were appointed to seven-year terms. The house thus represented the ruling class, and, as intended by ITŌ HIROBUMI, the chief architect of the constitution, it functioned as a conservative check on the lower house. Several attempts were made to reform the house (see MOVEMENT TO PROTECT CONSTITUTIONAL GOVERNMENT), but most measures were superficial. The House of Peers was superseded by the House of Councillors under the 1947 constitution.

House of Representatives → Diet

housewives

Being a housewife is still the most widely expected and most socially approved role for Japanese women; it is generally seen as a respected job requiring the skill, training, and devotion of a full-time professional. Modernization since the Meiji Restoration of 1868 and democratization following World War II have brought many changes to the lives of Japanese women, but the importance of the housewife as mother, as nurturing caretaker of the family, has not changed. Other roles are available to Japanese women today, but the housewife-mother role is still the only one carrying full social approval.

However, traditional Confucian-inspired rules requiring a woman to be subservient to some man (her father, her husband, or her son) have now been replaced by the post–World War II constitution that proclaims legal equality of the sexes. The small nuclear family has become common, so daughters-in-law have generally been freed from bondage to their mothers-in-law. Modern technology allows housewives to spend less time on household chores; time is now available for Japanese women to pursue either traditional hobbies like tea ceremony and flower arranging or newer activities like tennis or participation in the CONSUMER MOVEMENT. Because of widespread FAMILY PLANNING, one or two children per couple is now modal. Extensive Western influence since World War II, coupled with a higher educational level for women as well as men, has led Japanese women to expect more romance and companionship in their marriages and to consider careers outside marriage.

Despite these changes in outlook, the essential nature of the housewife's role remains the same. The division of labor by sex continues to be strong: men are expected to devote themselves to their jobs, while women take care of all family needs. A large majority of women keep to the basic traditional ideal of "the good wife and wise mother" *(ryōsai kembo)*. Their maternal responsibilities tend to be so heavy and so extensive that they need to be available at home most of the time. The Japanese still call a wife *okusan* (referring to someone else's wife) or *kanai* (referring to one's own wife), both terms meaning the one inside the house.

Nature of the Housewife's Job—— The Japanese housewife's tasks focus on mothering, on nurturing family needs, more so than in most other societies. In contrast to the American housewife's, for instance, her life does not include a range of other possible roles within the family, such as hostess, conversationalist, entertainer, wage-earner, dispenser of worldly wisdom, or even sex object or lover, unless some of these tasks are clearly a necessary part of her mothering job.

Her children, therefore, are the central core of a housewife's life. Yet her nurturing task also includes her husband and other relatives, when necessary. She cares for her husband so that he will remain healthy and free of worry, able to devote himself to his work. Her responsibility is to create a home environment where all family members can gain strength and prosper.

Yet it must be noted that over half of all married women are also employed in some other way as well (see WOMEN IN THE LABOR FORCE). Some wives work in family enterprises such as shops or farms, others work for necessary income, and a few work for their own interest. These latter are liable to criticism for not devoting themselves to their primary duty in the home, but those clearly working for the good of the whole family are sanctioned. The preferred model for most Japanese women is still that of the full-time housewife who does not have to work outside the home and who is available to her family at all times, at least while her children are young.

Despite the smaller number of children and the convenience of many household appliances, family needs can keep Japanese wives busier than their American counterparts. Grocery shopping and housecleaning are done on a daily basis. Most middle-class Japanese mothers (and most Japanese are now middle-class in income and self-definition) spend a large part of their time on their children's education in order to promote their success in the all-important school examination system. They sit with their children while they study, bring them pencils or snacks, take the child to tutoring lessons after school, frequently attend meetings of PTAs, cultivate good relations with teachers, and learn about the best study methods. At each educational level they research and plan for which school the child should take the entrance examination. Even after the children are safely in college or employed, the Japanese mother's nest tends to be less empty than a comparable American mother's. Her children are likely to live with her until they marry, they will need her to find suitable spouses for them, and she will usually continue to be close to her children and grandchildren in a mutual helping relationship. See CHILDHOOD AND CHILD REARING.

Becoming a Housewife—— Virtually all Japanese women expect to marry and virtually all do. Preparation for their housewife careers begins early with their sex role socialization during childhood. Since marriage is a woman's expected lifetime employment, her training for this career consists of collecting the credentials for making a prestigious match, much as any man looking for a job needs a good curriculum vitae. It is important for a woman today to pass difficult entrance examinations in order to graduate from a good school (preferably in a field considered suitable for women, such as literature), and to demonstrate competence in something like piano, calligraphy, tennis, or tea ceremony, as well as to have an agreeable personality and housekeeping skills. It is considered good for a girl not to marry right out of high school or college, but to add to her credentials by working for a few years, typically in an office job that does not lead up any promotion ladder but is designed with the expectation that she will work for a few years before her real career, marriage, begins.

It is estimated that about one-third to one-half of middle-class marriages are still arranged through the traditional system of introducing the man and woman only after each family has thoroughly investigated and approved the other side. If the young couple then date for a few months before marriage, they may refer to their union as a "love match," since this is considered more fashionable. An institution as permanent as marriage is not usually left to the whims of romance. Yet under the law no young person can be forced to marry against his or her wishes. In any case, couples do not marry whenever a romantic urge overtakes them, but when the proper age of responsibility arrives, usually between 23–26 for women and 25–30 for men.

Relations with Husbands——Although most young people these days express a wish for romantic and companionable marriages, after marriage most couples tend to fall into the previous pattern of separate social worlds for men and women, with a minimal emphasis on sexual compatibility or shared activities.

While men spend longer and longer hours at work, their wives' lives are taken up with children, female relatives, old school friends, neighbors, and school activities. The wife's emotional attachments are primarily to her children first, and next, to her mother, sisters, or mother-in-law, whereas a man's ties are to his work group. These allegiances do not usually create marital problems, since the parental roles, which are considered most important, continue undisturbed.

The husband is the nominal head of the household, but the sexual division of labor gives the housewife autonomy in her own sphere. She is effectively in charge of family finances as well as housekeeping, child rearing, and educational planning. The husband typically turns his paycheck over to his wife, who then does the shopping, budgeting, and even gives her husband his spending allowance.

Since, as has been stated, the main job of the Japanese housewife is mothering, she often mothers her husband. He turns to her for comfort, but she generally does not rely on him except for financial support. Japanese housewives are strong and independent, often having no one to lean on, except perhaps their children or their own mothers. They are taught to take care of their husbands, supporting the men's self-esteem and deferring to them in public. Yet they do not seem to need to have a man in love with them, as many Western women do.

Today some Japanese housewives are pushing for shared household chores, more companionship with their husbands, and more equality in employment opportunities, but most housewives still prefer to protect their autonomy and control over their homes. They value the lifetime security of a stable family system with little threat of divorce and take pride in their central role in the family. See also FAMILY; DIVORCE; KINSHIP; MARRIAGE; WOMEN, RURAL.

■——Michael Berger, "Japanese Women—Old Images and New Realities," *The Japan Interpreter* (Spring 1976). Daigaku Fujin Kyōkai, *Nihon ni okeru fujin no chii to fukushi* (1976). Susan Pharr, "The Japanese Woman: Evolving Views of Life and Role," in Lewis Austin, ed, *Japan: The Paradox of Progress* (1976). Carmi Schooler and Karen C. Smith, "'. . . and a Japanese Wife.' Social Structural Antecedents of Women's Role Values in Japan," *Sex Roles* (1978). Suzanne H. Vogel, "Professional Housewife, the Career of Urban Middle Class Japanese Women," *The Japan Interpreter* (Winter 1978). *Suzanne H. VOGEL*

Housing and Urban Development Corporation

(Jūtaku Toshi Seibi Kōdan). A special corporation whose purpose is to accelerate the supply of housing and residential land and urban development. Established in October 1981. Housing construction had previously been carried out by the Japan Housing Corporation and the acquisition, development, and sale of land by the New Town Development Public Corporation, but in response to strong popular demand for a more comprehensive housing program the two bodies were amalgamated into the Housing and Urban Development Corporation. The Japan Housing Corporation was established in 1955 to provide inexpensive apartment complexes for workers in districts lacking adequate housing. With the sharp rise in land prices accompanying the ill-advised government proposal in 1972 to "remodel the Japanese archipelago" (see NIHON RETTŌ KAIZŌ RON) and the oil crisis of 1973, however, the corporation was forced to shift its housing sites to areas far from places of work. Furthermore, rents rose and housing became more constricted. The corporation subsequently started constructing larger and better housing from around 1978. As of July 1981 the corporation had supplied a total of 1,110,-000 housing units. It manages about 640,000 rented units and owns 26,294 hectares of land. The New Town Development Public Corporation was established in September 1975 to take over the Japan

History of housing

Zashiki of a traditional-style contemporary house with *tatami*-covered floors. The *fusuma* can be extended to divide the area into two rooms. Two layers of sliding panels—*shōji* on the inside, glass doors on the outside—close the exterior door. The *tokonoma* is visible at the right of the frosted-glass window.

Housing Corporation's business of land development for housing projects. The Housing and Urban Development Corporation was capitalized at ¥99,300 million ($451 million) as of 1981.

housing developers

Individuals or corporations engaged in urban development, including construction of "new towns" and urban renewal projects. A majority of developers work through such public organizations as the HOUSING AND URBAN DEVELOPMENT CORPORATION (Jūtaku Toshi Seibi Kōdan) and local governments, since their activities require close coordination with public works projects. Recently, however, private corporations in railway transportation, real estate, and construction have rapidly emerged as full-fledged developers. Developers have become more active as a result of the rapid population concentrations and the serious housing shortages in big city areas in the late 1950s and the early 1960s. These conditions led to a sharp increase in demand for housing as incomes subsequently rose. As a result, there was a phenomenal growth in housing construction in the late 1960s and early 1970s. Taking advantage of this development, suppliers of residential lots and ready-built houses, usually referred to as "home builders," rapidly expanded the scope of their activities from convenient but expensive areas close to big cities to less expensive far-off districts with insufficient infrastructures and facilities to support new housing. The "sprawling" activities of home builders have stimulated the rise of developers who are capable of carrying out large-scale integrated development projects that encompass transportation, educational, and medical facilities; water supply and sewage systems; shopping centers; and so forth. Since the mid-1970s, however, the developers' profits have declined considerably because of a decrease in housing demand, tighter controls by central and local governments on housing development projects, an increased share of developers' investment in the total construction costs of infrastructures, and a slower rate of increase in land prices. Although developers are expected to be involved in urban renewal, it will be long time before such projects are tackled seriously, since such immense projects require much coordination between government and private sectors. See also LAND PROBLEM. *Suyama Kazuyuki*

housing, history of

The history of housing in Japan reflects two primary influences, the indigenous influence of climate, land formation, and natural occurrences (such as earthquakes and typhoons), and the external influence of encounters with the architecture and construction methods of foreign cultures. The character of Japanese dwellings began to emerge in prehistoric times and was well established before regular contact with foreign cultures began around the 5th century AD. China, Korea, and India were the primary sources of foreign influence, which was transmitted largely through religious institutions and thoroughly assimilated into traditional housing styles.

History of housing

A contemporary house with a traditional-style tiled roof in a southern
Ibaraki Prefecture farm community. The various sliding glass doors and
windows provide ventilation, light, and a closeness with the out-of-doors.
A walkway leads to the main entrance; the sliding doors open into an
entryway where shoes are removed.

Prehistoric Dwellings —— The first known Japanese dwellings
were the PIT HOUSES (tateana), which were inhabited by the Jōmon
people in prehistoric times. According to archaeological evidence,
the Jōmon people were essentially hunting tribes and used bone,
shell, and stone implements to hunt wild animals, gather shellfish,
and catch fish. Their dwellings were often located on hillside ridges
near the shore or on other sites which were easily defensible and
close to food sources. Excavations of the pit houses show that they
were constructed in rather large groups, indicating the existence of
communities. The dwellings were constructed over a shallow rectangular pit, from which slanting rafters rose directly to support
lintel beams. The rafters themselves formed both the frame of the
house and roof. The appearance was of an elongated tent shape
with a peaked roof. The roof was covered with bark and grass, and
open ridges allowed smoke to escape. See also JŌMON CULTURE.

Around 300 BC the Yayoi people appeared. Although recent anthropological research has indicated that the Jōmon and the Yayoi
people were the same, it was long believed that the two were completely different tribes because of their seemingly different cultural
patterns. The Yayoi people engaged in agriculture and had an organized architectural system. Settlements were sited in the lower mid-
lands where crop irrigation, particularly for the cultivation of rice,
was possible. Archaeological evidence shows that the Yayoi people
created an elevated-floor (takayuka) structure which was originally
used as a granary, probably because the elevated floor served to
protect crops from humidity and from animals. In this stable society, a noble class evolved, and they may have gradually taken to
using the granaries as dwellings (see STOREHOUSES, TRADITIONAL).
Cooking was still done on the ground level because of the necessity
of constructing a hearth. Around the 5th century AD, the takayuka
dwelling with a balcony appeared. The elevated floor became a fundamental element of the Japanese house and has remained unchanged apart from refinement in detail. Pit houses may still have
been built as dwellings for commoners after the takayuka dwelling
evolved because of practical advantages of the former. See also YA-
YOI CULTURE.

Clay house models excavated from the mounded tombs (KOFUN)
of noble chieftains of the Yamato period (ca 300–710) show the existence of katsuogi, or wooden logs attached to the roof ridge of noble
dwellings. This architectural symbol of distinction was later restricted to imperial architecture and Shintō shrines. Large windows
found in some of the excavated clay models might have been developed originally for taking in light for inside work and for emitting
smoke from an inside hearth. The invention of windows definitely
brought the outside world closer to the inside and may have inspired
the Japanese to cultivate the surrounding landscape into GARDENS.

Ancient Religious Influence —— Japanese identification with nature was reinforced by the spread of the Shintō belief that Japanese
deities created nature first and then created humans as a part of
nature. Shintō beliefs were already widespread when written history began late in the Yamato period with the introduction of writing
from China. Shintō shrines were considered the residences of the

deities and were always located in natural surroundings. Rocks of
certain shapes were also believed by the Japanese to have the divine
spirit (kami) inside. Thus, the close relationship between the deities
and nature was emphasized. Shintō buildings such as the ISE
SHRINE are constructed of hinoki (Japanese cypress), which is utilized for posts, beams, framing, and boards. The wood is planed
smooth and left unpainted, relying for its effect upon the absolute
purity of the material. Strips of hinoki bark are used for roofing.
The preference for natural surfaces remains one of the main characteristics of residential buildings in modern times. See also SHINTŌ
ARCHITECTURE.

Traditional Japanese architecture is essentially architecture of
wood, probably because timber is the most abundant natural building material in Japan. In addition, the skeleton wood frame proved
remarkably resistant to earthquakes and also made quick reconstruction possible. This style of construction also provided sufficient
ventilation and protection from frequent rains and humidity. The
deep projecting roof, which is a chief feature of traditional Japanese
houses, was developed to protect against the rains.

Buddhism was introduced to Japan from China around the 6th
century. Buddhist temples were imported, bringing new styles of
grandeur which, though they might have seemed rather arrogant to
the Japanese, were adopted without modification. But the original
meanings of the forms were gradually disassociated from the architecture, which was then more easily adapted and transmuted into
forms that could satisfy the physical and conceptual requirements of
the Japanese. During the Nara period (710–794), Buddhist influences
spread to Shintō buildings. For example, decorative brass ornaments were added to the balustrade and the steps of the Shōden (the
main sanctuary) at the Ise Shrine.

A large number of architectural monuments of the Nara period
survive, including the Hokkedō of TŌDAIJI (733), the Yumedono of
HŌRYŪJI (739), and the SHŌSŌIN (756), all of which were built in
Nara. Newly imported Buddhism became the state religion, usher-
ing in the golden age of Buddhism in Japan. The city of Nara was
laid out according to the first Japanese civil code (see RITSURYŌ
SYSTEM), which was copied from the Chinese code and contained
volumes on city planning and on systems of measurement and notes
on individual urban dwellings. See BUDDHIST ARCHITECTURE.

Emergence of Residential Styles —— During the Heian period
(794–1185) new Buddhist sects prevailed, and the cultural connection
with China was temporarily severed when the Japanese embassy was
withdrawn from China in 894. During this period of cultural isolation, the Japanese were forced to use their own imagination to meet
the high level of aesthetic quality demanded by the aristocrats in the
capital city, Heiankyō (now Kyōto). This resulted in the emergence
of the first Japanese style of residential dwelling—SHINDEN-ZUKURI.
In this style the house was laid asymmetrically in a garden. At the
end of the period the court life of the aristocracy reached a peak of
luxury and refinement, and elaborate gardens were constructed,
since gardens were an essential element in shinden-zukuri. The
main feature of the style is the placement of individual halls around
a central main hall (moya) with interconnecting corridors. The style
reflects a clear Chinese influence with its majestic appearance.

The refinement and elegance of court life was succeeded by
strong military government in the Kamakura period (1185–1333).
This samurai regime reestablished cultural ties with China, which
brought the introduction of Zen Buddhism. Zen was particularly
attractive to the samurai because its disciplined doctrines were quite
in accord with the austere samurai style of life. Shinden-zukuri was
still predominant as a residential style for the nobility though some
modifications were made, in part as a result of Zen's influence on the
Japanese concept of nature. Before the introduction of Zen, the concept of nature had been rather intuitive. Zen doctrines held that
discipline and simplicity were required in order to exist harmoni-
ously with nature, a belief that yielded a domestic architecture which
is aesthetically simple and organic. The formative elements of Zen
Buddhist residences were gradually adapted in secular residences of
the nobility and the warrior class.

The gradual transformation of the shinden-zukuri continued into
the Muromachi period (1333–1568), when Kyōto again became the
political center of Japan under a samurai regime. A new residential
style, called SHOIN-ZUKURI, manifested itself around this time. The
distinctive features of the style include the tokonoma (a picture alcove, with tana or shelves) and the shoin (study-alcove). The study-
alcove was adopted from Zen Buddhist residences that had been
built from Chinese plans. Chinese architectural features such as the
raked roof, roof tiles, and portable screens were also adopted. In the

course of development, modification and refinement of the features was carried out. The portable screen of Chinese origin, for instance, was transformed into Japanese opaque sliding panels (fusuma).

The residential style of the lower-ranking nobility and the samurai class was a modified version of the shoin-zukuri, which integrated architectural features of the residences of the farmer, the priest, and the nobility. This style is sometimes called the shuden or hiroma style. During the Muromachi period, the tea ceremony developed, and the teahouse (chashitsu) became its distinctive architectural expression. The chashitsu is a small thatch-roofed structure, using plain materials with no decoration. Only the natural color and texture of the building materials are used to give the structure character. The chashitsu reflects the austerity of Zen Buddhism.

The Elements of Japanese Architecture —— By the 16th century, the main elements of Japanese architecture, such as the structural system, floor plan, and building materials, had been fully established to meet religious, philosophical, aesthetic, and practical requirements of the Japanese. The same use of structure, materials, and principles of plan persists today. Structurally, a joined skeleton frame of post-and-beam construction with an elaborate joinery system is the main feature of a Japanese house. The floor is raised above the ground, and its posts rest on foundation stone, not only to prevent moisture from rotting the posts, but also to allow the entire structure to bounce in case of earthquakes.

Procedural conventions regarding measure, construction, orientation, and ceremony to be observed were originally copied from the scripts of Chinese Buddhist architecture brought to Japan in the 7th and 8th centuries. These imported rules were modified, combined with existing techniques, and finally developed into a Japanese code in the Azuchi-Momoyama period (1568–1600). The Japanese modular system, based on a method of column spacing, allows for versatile use of interior space and an unconstrained selection of exterior openings. The Chinese originally used a modular system for aesthetic proportions. The most elaborate modular system, kiwari (allotment of timber), was mentioned for the first time in a carpenters' manual called Shōmei, which was written in 1608 in the form of five paper scrolls. The kiwari module was consistently used thereafter in Japan, though with some deviations and differences in ratio.

Protruding eaves protect the structure from frequent rains and also allow winter sun to penetrate into the interior while blocking the strong summer sun. Shōji or shōji-do (sliding doors; made of thin wood covered with translucent paper) allow diffuse daylight to illuminate the interior and maintain a sense of closeness with the out-of-doors. Interior space is partitioned by shōji-do or fusuma, and sometimes by folding screens. TATAMI (straw mats) cover the floors; futon (sleeping quilts; see BEDDING) are stored in an oshiire (closet) during the day. Without any large or specialized furniture, room functions are totally interchangeable. The tokonoma (picture alcove) with a raised floorboard is the focal point of the zashiki (sitting room) and is reserved for the display of a scroll painting, flower arrangement, or a ceramic object.

Only certain classes of people in medieval Japan lived in houses, such as court scholars, the nobility, samurai chieftains, and priests, and the most elaborate architecture was limited to large palaces and institutional buildings. Commoners such as farmers and merchants lived in primitive huts with straw-thatch, reed-thatch, or wooden-board roofs. Most of the huts had earthen floors (doma) with partially raised wooden platforms. However, a vernacular tradition of farmhouse construction developed from early times. Because of its simplicity and humble appearance, the farmhouse was sometimes used as a model for teahouses.

In the Edo period (1600–1868) social and economic conditions stabilized, and wealthy citizens adopted the features of the houses of the nobility. Kawarabuki yane (tiled roofs) were extensively utilized in domestic architecture (see MINKA), especially after the development of a new tiling technique in the latter half of the 17th century which made less expensive tiling possible (see ROOF TILES). In the major urban centers such as Edo (now Tōkyō) and Kyōto, the machiya (townhouse) style developed. However, the main features of the Japanese house remained largely in the form developed by the Momoyama period.

Modern Housing —— Japan was completely cut off from the West under the Tokugawa shogunate. With the reestablishment of Western contact during the Meiji period (1868–1912), new institutional buildings in the Western style (yōkan) began to be built in Japan. Houses in the Western style were built by some upper-class Japanese, some of whom had traveled to Europe or America. However, the majority of the Japanese continued to live in traditional houses.

Modern housing

Housing project (danchi) at Senri New Town, a residential community north of Ōsaka built during the 1960s.

Thorough modernization of Japanese housing occurred mainly after the end of World War II. In 1945 the shortage of houses in Japan was extreme because of destruction caused by air raids during the war. Individual, single-family houses were mass-produced, and the concentration of population in the urban centers spurred the construction of apartments. Multi-story apartments of concrete have been constructed at an unprecedented pace. However, most new houses, including apartment buildings, have retained vestiges of traditional Japanese architecture. At the same time, new designs and housing schemes have been developed by aspiring young architects. See also ARCHITECTURE, TRADITIONAL DOMESTIC; BATH; FURNITURE, TRADITIONAL; GATES. — KOZAWA Tadahiro

Housing Loan Corporation

(Jūtaku Kin'yū Kōko). Government agency capitalized entirely by national funds; provides long-term, low-interest loans for the construction of houses. Established in 1950. Some 7.17 million houses were constructed with corporation loans between 1950 and December 1981; the loans totaled ¥20.7 trillion (US $93.8 billion). Loans are supplied for the construction of personal homes, the purchase of condominiums and houses, and additions to houses already standing. The loans in 1981 ranged from ¥5.5 million (US $24,900) to ¥10.5 million (US $47,600) at an annual interest rate of 5.5 percent and for terms of 25 to 35 years. The corporation also makes loans to building contractors for construction of housing developments and company housing, redevelopment of urban areas, preparation of housing lots, and construction of roads, sewage systems, schools, and other public facilities. Over 50 percent of the Japanese building private homes have utilized the corporation's loans, an indication of the large role it plays in the housing market. In 1981 the corporation budgeted a total of ¥3.3 trillion (US $15 billion) in loans for the construction of 510,000 houses. See HOUSING PROBLEMS. — HIRATA Masami

housing, modern

Housing in Japan has changed dramatically in the past century as a result of rapid urbanization, population pressures, changes in family and social relationships, and the influence of Western architecture. Especially in large cities, multiunit dwellings have become the norm, although the majority of people still aspire to own their own home.

In 1978 there were 32,188,700 housing units in Japan, with an average of 3.6 persons per unit. Of this total, 65 percent were single-family dwellings and 35 percent multiple-unit dwellings. Of the single-family units 85.7 percent were owned and 11.8 percent rented; of the multiple-unit dwellings 11.9 percent were owned and 73.3 percent were rented. The percentages of owned and rental units, as well as the percentages of single-family as opposed to multiple-unit dwellings, had changed little by the early 1980s.

Changes in Housing Design —— A fundamental departure of modern housing (both single- and multiple-unit dwellings) from traditional models is in spatial organization. In the traditional house, ceremonial occasions (hare) took place in a special reception room (zashiki), while everyday activities (ke) took place in the kitchen and

Modern housing

A typical area of developer-built houses in the suburbs of a large city.

work space. Though seldom used, the reception area constituted the symbolic center of the dwelling. From the time of the Taishō period (1912–26), the living room *(ima)* replaced the reception room as the center of the home, especially in urban middle-class houses, and formal functions were moved out of the house to public halls and restaurants. This change, however, was more the result of a desire to assume the trappings of modernity than a genuine acceptance of a new style of life. The Western-style living room has yet to be fully assimilated into Japanese life, and without a true alternative center the modern house lacks the clear hierarchical order of traditional dwellings. It remains, instead, a simple collection of rooms of the same importance.

The elimination of the ceremonial space was also due in part to the shrinking of the middle-class house, from an average total floor space of 165 square meters (1,776 sq ft) at the turn of the century to 100 square meters (1,076 sq ft) by the beginning of the Shōwa period (1926–). This reflected the rising cost of land, which made free-standing houses within the city high-priced and drove many would-be homeowners into the suburbs and into the market for *tateuri jūtaku* (ready-built developers' houses).

Another modern innovation in Japanese houses was the introduction of the corridor. Circulation in traditional houses was from room to room; the rooms were separated by sliding screens *(shōji* and *fusuma),* which allowed for flexible, multipurpose use of the rooms. With the introduction of the corridor, rooms have become more permanently compartmentalized and private, and their functions have become fixed.

Multiunit Dwellings—— The *nagaya,* a traditional style of wood-frame, one-story rowhouse, is still common. Traditionally there was an *omote* (front) *nagaya* facing a public road, and a poorer *ura* (back) *nagaya* facing a private back alley. Residents of the back part shared kitchen and bathroom facilities in the back alley. Somewhat comparable in its involuntary communality is the *mokuchin apāto* (short for *mokuzō chintai apāto,* or wood construction rental apartments). These are wood-frame, two-story units of generally low quality, with shared kitchens and toilets.

The first American-style apartment house *(apāto)* in Japan may have been the Bunka Apartment (1925) in the Ochanomizu section of Tōkyō. The apartments built by the Dōjunkai (Mutual Benefit Association), formed after the Tōkyō Earthquake of 1923 to provide housing for the homeless, made Western-style accommodations widely available to the middle class. A typical unit had two rooms with a small kitchen and an average total floor space of 33 square meters (355 sq ft). Apartment houses became increasingly popular in the 1930s, because they symbolized progress and offered convenience, better sanitation and maintenance, and greater protection from fire, earthquakes, and burglaries. Many early apartments were of wood construction; reinforced concrete apartment buildings only came into their own after World War II.

In 1955, the Japan Housing Corporation (JHC; see HOUSING AND URBAN DEVELOPMENT CORPORATION) was established, and apartment buildings and housing projects *(danchi)* became familiar phenomena. The JHC standardized apartment layouts, introducing the concept of the dining-kitchen area (DK), a space of about eight square meters (86 sq ft) which is used for both cooking and dining.

This soon became a popular feature, thus further blurring the distinction between everyday space and what remained of the ceremonial space in the home.

The most common unit in the early JHC housing was the 2DK, or two rooms and the dining-kitchen area; in an apartment like this, one of the rooms would serve as a living room during the day. An enlarged DK is called an LDK, or living room-dining-kitchen area. The emphasis in recent JHC housing has been on 3DK and 3LDK units.

Generally, apartment buildings called *manshon* ("mansions") are private, middle-to-high rise buildings with individual units for sale (similar to the condominium in the United States). They became popular in the 1960s and are now widespread. And townhouses—basically connected rows of single-unit dwellings—are an increasingly popular alternative to apartment dwelling.

Most of these modern trends are to be observed in urban areas, while rural homes often retain the multiple function rooms of the old style. Rural homes tend to be larger, and many ceremonial functions still take place at home.

While the national ideal remains fixed on a wooden, two-story Japanese-style house with a tile roof, the small supply of wood available domestically makes this style affordable only to the very wealthy. Cement is one resource which Japan has in abundance, and the large majority of modern dwellings are thus built from concrete. See also HOUSING PROBLEMS; HOUSING, HISTORY OF; ARCHITECTURE, MODERN; ARCHITECTURE, TRADITIONAL DOMESTIC.

——Nishiyama Uzō, *Nihon no sumai* (1975). Onobayashi Hiroki, "A History of Modern Japanese Houses," *Japan Architect* (June 1965). HAYAKAWA Kunihiko and WATANABE Hiroshi

housing problems

A problem of particular importance in Japan because of the high concentration of people in urban areas. The availability of housing has not been consonant with the great economic and industrial development of recent years. The housing census of 1978 shows that the average number of persons per room was 0.8 and the average number of rooms per dwelling was 4.5. Although these figures represent a small improvement over the corresponding figures of 1.0 and 3.8 in 1968, they are still indicative of the prevailing low housing standards relative to other industrial countries. The corresponding figures for the United States in 1970 were 0.6 and 5.1 respectively according to the United Nations Statistical Yearbook (1978).

Urban housing problems in Japan arose as the country entered into the stage of industrialization and urbanization around the turn of the century. Before the end of World War II, however, housing was generally considered a concern of the private sector of the economy and no public measures were taken except for emergency housing after the Tōkyō Earthquake of 1923 and wartime housing for military procurement.

The shortage of houses at the end of World War II was estimated at 4.2 million dwelling units. Several emergency measures were taken to cope with this desperate shortage, including restriction on migration to big cities, rent control, and subsidy from the central government to local authorities for the construction of public housing units.

In the 1950s, three major pieces of legislation on housing were enacted which constituted a general framework for Japanese housing policy. The first was the establishment of the Japan HOUSING LOAN CORPORATION (Jūtaku Kin'yū Kōko) in 1950 as a means of channeling public funds for low-interest, long-term loans for owner-occupied housing. The Public Housing Law (Kōei Jūtaku Hō) of 1951 was the second piece of legislation. Under the law local authorities were empowered to build public housing for rental to low-income households with subsidies from the central government. Finally, the Japan Housing Corporation (Nihon Jūtaku Kōdan; see HOUSING AND URBAN DEVELOPMENT CORPORATION) was founded in 1955 as a public nonprofit developer to supply housing units in large cities for urban dwellers. The corporation is authorized to build housing units both for rental and for sale as condominiums and also to develop large tracts for housing purposes. Since the corporation set its rentals on a long-term full-recovery basis, urban middle-class families have become its main beneficiaries.

In spite of the high rate of economic growth in the years 1955–65, housing conditions did not show much improvement. Priority was placed on investment for industrial expansion. According to the 1963 Housing Census, 4.3 million households, or 20.4 percent of all households, were reported to have housing problems, including 3.6 million households in substandard housing, 600,000 dual family

Housing problems

Housing Quality Indicators and Costs, Selected Years

	1963	1968	1973	1978 [1]		
				Overall	Rural	Densely populated areas
Total dwellings (millions)	21.09	25.59	31.06	35.45	7.44	21.43
Vacancy rate (%) [2]	2.5	4.0	5.5	7.6	6.1	8.4
Facilities (%)						
Piped water	67.9	80.1	86.9	92.7	84.5	97.8
Flush toilet	9.2	17.1	31.4	45.9	15.7	62.0
Bath	59.1	65.6	73.3	82.8	92.8	74.9
Average size						
No. of rooms	3.82	3.84	4.15	4.52	5.52	3.92
Total area (sq m)	72.52	73.86	77.14	80.28	105.59	66.28
Persons per room	1.16	1.03	0.87	0.77	0.70	0.81
Area per person (sq m)	8.1	9.2	10.9	12.8	14.7	11.6
Average cost						
Monthly rent per sq m ($)	0.4	0.7	1.7	3.5	1.7	3.9
Cost of owner-constructed house w/o land ($1,000)	—	—	—	47.9	44.5	52.6
Cost of owner-constructed house including land ($1,000)	—	—	22.3	84.3	—	106.4
Cost of ready-made house including land ($1,000)	—	—	26.1	92.6	66.6	95.2

[1] For data other than the cost of buying or constructing a house, rural = all towns and villages; densely populated areas = areas with a population density of 4,000 per sq km or more. For house purchase costs, densely populated areas = 14 prefectures including Tōkyō, Ōsaka, and Kyōto; rural = all 33 other prefectures.

[2] Total number of vacant dwellings (not including those under construction or occupied temporarily) divided by the total number of dwellings.

SOURCE: Ministry of Construction, unpublished data. Prime Minister's Office, Statistics Bureau, *Japan Statistical Yearbook* (annual): 1982.

households and over 100,000 households living in quarters built for nonresidential purposes.

In 1966 the Housing Construction Planning Law (Jūtaku Kensetsu Keikaku Hō) was enacted to coordinate public policy measures for housing. The act gives mandate to the central government to formulate five-year comprehensive housing construction plans at five-year intervals starting in 1966. The first Five-Year Housing Construction Plan aimed at achieving "one housing unit for one household" in five years by constructing a total of 6.7 million housing units.

In the projected five-year period, 2.57 million housing units were built with public assistance and 4.18 million housing units by entirely private funds, exceeding the stated target in numerical terms. However, the housing census of 1968 reported that 3.6 million households, or 14.6 percent of the total households, still had housing problems, including 300,000 dual family households.

The second Housing Construction Plan was initiated in 1971, aiming at achieving "one room for one member of the household." Although the original plan was to construct 9.6 million housing units in five years, only 8.26 million units were actually built, including 3.12 million housing units with public assistance and 5.14 million by entirely private funds.

The housing census of 1973 reported that there were a total of 31,059,000 housing units in Japan as compared to a total of 29,103,000 households, giving a net surplus of about 2 million. The vacancy ratio which was 2.5 percent in 1963 increased to 5.5 percent in 1973. Households with housing problems declined to 2.5 million, or 8.5 percent of the total. These statistics prompted the Ministry of Construction to state that the housing problem had been solved at least in quantity, if not in quality.

The third Housing Construction Plan, approved in 1976, thus stated explicitly that the main priority of housing policy should be transferred from the emphasis on quantity to the improvement of quality. The plan defined minimum and average standards for housing quality in terms of floor area, number of rooms, plumbing and utilities, as well as environmental factors, such as noise and sunlight. The plan aimed at cutting subminimum standard housing in half by building 8.6 million new housing units, of which 90 percent (7.7 million units) were actually built. However, according to a 1978 survey, 40 percent of all households (more than 55 percent of those in rental units) living in large cities complained about housing conditions, giving overcrowded, dilapidated, or inadequate facilities as major causes for dissatisfaction. The purpose of the fourth Housing Construction Plan, which began in 1981, is to continue to improve housing quality, especially in urban areas. By 1985, 7.7 million housing units are expected to be built, including 3.5 million units with public assistance funds.

A stable element of Japanese postwar housing policy has been the encouragement of owner-occupancy. In terms of 1978 occupied dwellings (not including dwellings additionally used for nonresidential purposes), some 60 percent of the total were owner-occupied. Publicly assisted rental units constituted only 8 percent of the occupied dwellings, while the remaining 32 percent were private rental units, including housing provided for employees by public employers. See also HOUSING DEVELOPERS; POPULATION REDISTRIBUTION; STANDARD OF LIVING; HOUSING, MODERN.   MERA Kōichi

Hōya

City in western Tōkyō Prefecture, contiguous with Nerima Ward. It was formerly known for its radishes *(daikon)*. With the construction of many housing projects, Hōya has become a dormitory suburb for nearby Tōkyō. Pop: 91,251.

Ho Ying-ch'in → He Yingqin (Ho Ying-ch'in)

Hozugawa

River in Kyōto Prefecture, central Honshū. A section of a longer river that originates in the Tamba Mountains and flows into the river YODOGAWA in the Kyōto Basin. The Hozugawa is that part of the river between Kameoka and Arashiyama. The upper reaches, above Kameoka, are called the Ōigawa, and the lower reaches, from Arashiyama, are called the KATSURAGAWA. There is boating in the scenic gorge of Hozukyō. Length: 16 km (10 mi).

hōzuki

1. The ground cherry or Chinese lantern plant *(Physalis alkekengi)* of the potato family (Solanaceae). 2. A noisemaking toy improvised from the fruit of the Chinese lantern plant. The noisemaker (traditionally a toy for girls) is made by taking the cherrylike fruit from its lantern-shaped pod and kneading it carefully until soft. The pulp and seeds are removed through a small hole, emptying the skin, which is then pressed between the tongue and the roof of the mouth to make a squeaking noise. Imitations of this toy were made from the egg pouches of shellfish (the so-called *umi hōzuki*), and manufactured versions have been made of rubber or other substances. The *hōzuki* plant is also used for folk medicine and as a decoration. For the latter, see HŌZUKI ICHI.

hōzuki ichi

Fair at which HŌZUKI (Chinese lantern plants) are sold; held at the Asakusa Kannon temple in Tōkyō on 10 July. This fair is also known as Shimanrokusennichi ("46,000 days") because one visit to the temple on this particular day is said to be as meritorious as 46,000 ordinary visits. During the Edo period (1600–1868) the fair drew throngs of men and women who came to pray and to purchase not only *hōzuki,* but also ears of corn used to ward off thunder and lightning; the cosmetic used by women to blacken their teeth; and bamboo tea whisks. The potted plants are placed inside bamboo baskets to which WIND-BELLS *(fūrin)* are attached. *Hōzuki* are also used for their medicinal properties, for making toy whistles, and for adorning the altars used for the Buddhist BON FESTIVAL.

INOKUCHI Shōji

Hozumi Nobushige (1856–1926)

Scholar of legal history and drafter of the CIVIL CODE. Born in what is now Ehime Prefecture. Hozumi studied at Kaisei Gakkō (now Tōkyō University) and from 1876 to 1881 in England and Germany. As a professor at Tōkyō University from 1881 onward, he actively promoted the study of German law. In 1888 he became Japan's first Doctor of Laws (Hōgaku Hakushi). Especially interested in the anthropological aspects of legal history, Hozumi studied the legal implications of Japanese ancestor worship. With UME KENJIRŌ and TOMII MASAAKI he drafted the Civil Code of 1898. He was appointed to the House of Peers in 1890 and to the Privy Council in 1916, becoming president of the latter body in 1925. Under the influence of such jurists as Henry Maine (1822–88), he applied evolutionary theory to the study of law; in this respect he contrasted sharply with the narrow, conservative nationalism of his younger brother, the constitutional scholar HOZUMI YATSUKA. Hozumi Nobushige's writings include *Goningumi seido ron* (1921, On the Goningumi System) and *Hōritsu shinka ron* (1924–27, Theory of the Evolution of Law). He was the father of the legal scholar HOZUMI SHIGETŌ.

NAGAO Ryūichi

Hozumi Shigetō (1883–1951)

Legal scholar; born in Tōkyō, the son of HOZUMI NOBUSHIGE and nephew of HOZUMI YATSUKA, both distinguished scholars of law. He was graduated from Tōkyō University in 1908 and taught there until his retirement as dean of the law faculty in 1943. He specialized primarily in the family-law provisions of the CIVIL CODE. His academic works include *Rikon seido no kenkyū* (1924, Studies on Divorce Law), *Shinzokuhō* (1933, Family Law), and *Sōzokuhō* (1946, Inheritance Law). Hozumi also wrote popular books on the law, such as *Hyakumannin no hōritsugaku* (1950, Law for the Millions). He was appointed to the Supreme Court in 1949 and came to public notice for his dissenting opinion that the law punishing murder of a lineal ascendant (see PARENTICIDE) more severely than other murders was unconstitutional.

BAI Kōichi

Hozumi Yatsuka (1860–1912)

Scholar of constitutional law. Born in what is now Ehime Prefecture, he was graduated from Tōkyō University in 1883 and studied at the University of Strassburg under Paul Laband (1838–1918) from 1884 to 1888. As a professor at Tōkyō University he lectured on constitutional law from 1889 to 1912 and served as chairman of the Faculty of Law from 1897 to 1911. Hozumi's theories on the constitution supported and strengthened imperial sovereignty. An enemy of parliamentary government, he opposed giving political parties power over both legislation and administration. A defender of Japan's traditional virtues, he criticized the original draft (1890) of the Civil Code, based on the French model, saying that its enactment would mean "the death of loyalty and filial piety" (see CIVIL CODE CONTROVERSY). In the 1920s, the years of the so-called TAISHŌ DEMOCRACY, Hozumi's constitutional theories were gradually supplanted by the more liberal views of MINOBE TATSUKICHI and others. With the rise of ULTRANATIONALISM in the 1930s, however, his views— promoted by his successor UESUGI SHINKICHI—gained renewed popularity. His writings include *Kempō taii* (1896, The Essence of the Constitution) and *Kempō teiyō* (1910, Outline of the Constitution). He was the younger brother of the legal scholar HOZUMI NOBUSHIGE.

■──Richard H. Minear, *Japanese Tradition and Western Law: Emperor, State, and Law in the Thought of Hozumi Yatsuka* (1970).

SATŌ Kōji

Hsin-min Hui → Xinmin Hui (Hsin-min Hui)

Huang Xing (Huang Hsing) (1874–1916)

(J: Kō Kō). Cofounder, along with SUN YAT-SEN, of the revolutionary United League (Tongmeng Hui or T'ung-meng Hui) and leader of the revolutionary activities that led up to the overthrow of the Qing (Ch'ing) dynasty in 1911. While a student at the Kōbun Institute in Tōkyō from 1902 to 1903, Huang met a number of anti-Manchu students. Returning to Hunan, he founded the Huaxing Hui (Hua-hsing Hui; Society for the Revival of China). After a failed uprising, he went again to Tōkyō, where he met Sun Yat-sen through MIYAZAKI TŌTEN, Sun's close friend and a sympathizer of the Chinese revolutionary cause. In 1905 they founded the Tongmeng Hui. In 1908 many Chinese revolutionaries in Tōkyō, critical of Sun's tactics and handling of funds, moved to replace him with Huang. Huang refused to split the United League, and, after the 1911 revolution, he also declined to become provisional president of the new Chinese republic. In 1913 Huang and Sun led an unsuccessful revolt against the increasingly authoritarian president YUAN SHIKAI (Yüan Shih-k'ai). Forced to flee to Japan, Huang broke with Sun over the latter's insistence on an oath of personal loyalty from all members of his newly organized (July 1914) Chinese Revolutionary Party.

The SHINJINKAI, a study group organized by leftist law students at Tōkyō University, was founded in a house that Huang had entrusted to Miyazaki.

■──Chün-tu Hsüeh, *Huang Hsing and the Chinese Revolution* (1961).

Huang Zunxian (Huang Tsun-hsien) (1848–1905)

(J: Kō Junken). A Chinese diplomat, reformer, and poet, Huang Zunxian was the author of a book about Japan which was the chief source of information on Meiji reforms for the Chinese reformers of the 1890s. In 1877 Huang was appointed counselor to the Chinese legation in Tōkyō. (Modern diplomatic relations between Qing [Ch'ing; 1644–1912] China and Japan were established in 1871.) Huang remained in Japan until 1882 and produced two books on Japan, the *Riben Zashi Shi* (Jih-pen tsa-shih shih; 1879, Miscellaneous Poems on Japan), and the *Riben guozhi* (Jih-pen kuo-chih; 1890, Japan's National Aspiration), a political history of Japan from the Meiji Restoration (1868) to 1882. The book praised Japan's selective adoption of Western institutions and the FREEDOM AND PEOPLE'S RIGHTS MOVEMENT of the 1880s. Huang's history of Japan had a great impact on late-Qing-period Chinese who strove to reform the imperial system. Huang himself was an active reformer in China during the 1890s. Associated with such famous reformers as KANG YOUWEI (K'ang Yu-wei) and LIANG QICHAO (Liang Ch'i-ch'ao), he organized study societies and edited newspapers.

Hukbalahap

The wartime Hukbo ng Bayan Laban sa Hapon (Tagalog for People's Anti-Japanese Army), or its postwar successor, HMB, Hukbong Mapagpalaya ng Bayan (People's Liberation Army). Commonly called "the Huks." It was first organized on 29 March 1942 as the Army of the Communist Party of the Philippines to fight the Japanese. Under the leadership of Luis Taruc, the Huks fought 1,200 engagements with Japanese forces in central Luzon. After World War II HMB attracted many peasants by emphasizing land reform and appealing to resentment against the government. The HMB's activities declined after a peak in 1949–51, and Taruc surrendered to government forces in 1954. The organization became inactive in the mid-1960s. Throughout its history its major power base was in central Luzon.

YOSHIKAWA Yōko

Hull, Cordell (1871–1955)

American political leader and secretary of state. Born in Tennessee. Received a law degree from Cumberland University in 1891. Hull belonged to the Democratic Party, representing his district in the US House of Representatives for 22 years (1907–21; 1923–31) and in the Senate (1931–33) until he was appointed secretary of state by President Franklin D. Roosevelt in 1933. He played an important role in promoting reciprocal trade programs and in improving US relations with Latin America by implementing the "Good Neighbor Policy." Before the outbreak of the Pacific War in 1941, Hull handled the delicate negotiations with Japan. In the so-called Hull Note, he strongly supported the territorial integrity of China and urged Japan to abandon its military conquests on the Asian mainland and in French Indo-China. The uncompromising tone of his note led directly to Japan's decision to attack Pearl Harbor. During the war, Hull made efforts toward organizing the United Nations. He resigned as secretary of state in November of 1944 because of failing health. In 1945 he was awarded the Nobel Peace Prize.

Hundred Regiment Offensive

(Hyakudan Taisen). A large-scale offensive by the Chinese communist Eighth Route Army and Shanxi (Shansi) New Army against Japanese forces in five northern provinces of China. Launched on 20 August 1940, the Hundred Regiment Offensive was the sole instance during the SINO-JAPANESE WAR OF 1937–1945 of a conventional offensive by the Chinese communists, who otherwise relied on guerrilla tactics against the Japanese. One of its major aims was to prove to the CHONGQING (CHUNGKING) GOVERNMENT the Chinese communists' ability to resist Japan in North China and thereby to dissuade Chongqing from negotiating a compromise peace with Japan.

In the surprise attack on 20 August, 400,000 communist troops disrupted railways, communication lines, and coal mines and overran outlying Japanese posts, crushing several Japanese battalions. Although the well-fortified, fixed positions of the Japanese were not much damaged and communist casualties were high, it was not until October that the Japanese regained the initiative. The Japanese responded to the offensive with harsh policies of punishment and destruction in North China that lasted through early 1943.

hunting

Archaeological findings show that the early inhabitants of Japan lived by hunting and gathering. Nuts, fruits, wild boar, and deer were their staple food. During the Jōmon period (ca 10,000 BC–ca 300 BC) hunting and fishing were the main source of livelihood. Bows, arrows, and spears of wood, bamboo, and stone were frequently used, as well as dogs. With the introduction of agricultural techniques in the Yayoi period (ca 300 BC–ca AD 300), hunting became less important. Later, when an agricultural economy was firmly established, hunting remained a livelihood only for those special small groups scattered in the mountains (see MATAGI). It otherwise served principally for obtaining additional protein, animal organs for making medicine, and materials for clothing, as well as for eliminating harmful birds and animals. Hunting was also considered a method of martial training. Some feudal lords used hunting as a pretext for maintaining a watch on the boundaries of their domains or investigating the conditions of the populace. Throughout the Edo period (1600–1868) there was no marked decrease in the total game population. This was because land was mostly uncultivated, hunting was forbidden to the majority of the population, and Buddhism forbade the killing of animals.

Hunting Policy —— In modern times the number of birds and animals has diminished despite regulatory laws and administrative guidance. To solve this problem, the Meiji government promulgated the Wildlife Hunting Law in 1873 and further established the Hunting Law in 1895. These regulations, however, proved powerless against the tide of modernization. Hunting tools developed, and national income rapidly increased, as did the amount of land needed for residences, business, and industries, which spurred reclamation of seashores and lakes, as well as cultivation of wild fields. Uncultivated areas also decreased because of lumbering in the mountains, the spread of agricultural chemicals, and development of transportation systems. To counteract these tendencies, the Law regarding Wildlife Protection and Hunting was enacted in 1963. Hunting in Japan is regulated by this law, which now requires a hunting license and limits hunting weapons, seasons, and areas. There are also limits on the variety and numbers of birds and beasts that may be hunted.

Of the approximately 490 types of wild bird in Japan, 30 varieties may be hunted, including pheasant and wild duck. The total number of birds hunted (including harmful birds) was about 12 million in 1975. The total number of beasts hunted (including harmful beasts) was about 1 million in 1975, mainly bears, wild boars, stag, and hares.

The maximum possible hunting season fixed by law is from 15 October (15 September in Hokkaidō) to 15 April, but this may be changed from year to year. Since 1975, the season has been from 15

Hyakunin isshu

Selection of playing cards used in the traditional game called *uta karuta*, which tests players' knowledge of the *Hyakunin isshu*. In the set of cards shown here, the earliest such cards extant, the "reading" card also bears the likeness of the poet.

November (1 October in Hokkaidō) to 15 February (31 January in Hokkaidō). The season for *anaguma* (badger), weasel, fox, stag, *tanuki* (raccoon dog), marten, *musasabi* (flying squirrel), and squirrel is from 1 December to 31 January (15 November to 15 January in Hokkaidō). The number of important birds and beasts that can be hunted during each season is fixed.

Hunting is prohibited in the following areas: areas intended for wildlife preservation (2,435 areas nationwide); temporary no-hunting areas (2,169 areas nationwide); no-hunting areas (areas prohibiting hunting of designated kinds of wildlife); areas prohibiting small-weapon hunting (1,276 areas nationwide); public roads; parks; precincts of temples and shrines; graveyards.

Permissible hunting equipment includes small arms, nets, and snares. Devices absolutely forbidden are explosives, powerful medicines, poisons, larger firearms, dangerous snares and traps, and so forth. *Kasumiami* ("fog net," made of very thin thread), *oshi* ("weight trap"), fishhooks, bird lime, and such equipment are permitted for eliminating harmful birds and beasts and may also be used in scholarly research.

A hunting license is necessary for all hunters. The requirements are a hunting course, a license for possessing firearms, and payment of hunting taxes. No license is necessary for hunting permissible wildlife with "free hunting tools," such as falcons, bare hands, or bows and arrows, during the hunting season and in designated hunting areas.   SHIRAI Kunihiko

Hyakunin isshu

(Single Poems by 100 Poets). Also known as the *Ogura hyakunin isshu*. A collection of 100 TANKA (31-syllable poems), each by a different poet, organized in rough chronological order beginning with Emperor Tenji (626–671) and ending with retired emperor Juntoku (1197–1242). FUJIWARA NO SADAIE (also called Teika) probably compiled the collection, though it may have been revised by someone else, perhaps his son FUJIWARA NO TAMEIE. The entry for 14 June 1235 in Teika's journal MEIGETSUKI (1180–1235, Bright Moon Diary) tells how Utsunomiya no Yoritsuna prevailed on Teika to write out single poems by 100 poets to decorate the sliding doors of his retreat near the mountain Ogurayama. If these poems became the *Hyakunin isshu*, the collection must date from 1235 to 1241. The *Hyakunin shūka* (Superior Poems by 100 Poets), compiled by Teika at about the same time, may have been its forerunner; the two works share, though in different order, 97 poems. The preponderance of autumn and love poems and the style of intense passion and sensual beauty that permeate the *Hyakunin isshu* reflect Teika's later poetic predilections. The work inspired a flurry of study, the first extant commentary appearing early in the Muromachi period (1333–1568); many collections, such as the *Buke hyakunin isshu* (Single Poems by 100 Samurai Poets) from the latter part of the Edo period (1600–1868) and the *Aikoku hyakunin isshu* (Patriotic Collection of Single Poems by 100 Poets) in 1942, were modeled after the work. As the basis for the popular card game *uta karuta* (see PLAYING

Hyakushō ikki

Peasant Uprisings, 1590-1867				
	Number of uprisings	Yearly average	Number of uprisings	Yearly average
1590–1600	34	3.1	1731–40	86	8.6
1601–10	35	3.5	1741–50	130	13.0
1611–20	60	6.0	1751–60	116	11.6
1621–30	45	4.5	1761–70	108	10.8
1631–40	38	3.8	1771–80	78	7.8
1641–50	30	3.0	1781–90	229	22.9
1651–60	36	3.6	1791–1800	122	12.2
1661–70	42	4.2	1801–10	98	9.8
1671–80	44	4.4	1811–20	166	16.6
1681–90	46	4.6	1821–30	133	13.3
1691–1700	40	4.0	1831–40	279	27.9
1701–10	55	5.5	1841–50	129	12.9
1711–20	73	7.3	1851–60	170	17.0
1721–30	70	7.0	1861–67	194	27.8
			Total	2,586	9.3

Source: Aoki Kōji, *Hyakushō ikki no nenjiteki kenkyū* (1966).

CARDS), the poems of the original *Hyakunin isshu* have been memorized since the Edo period. The game is still widely played today. To distinguish it from later imitations, the collection is more correctly called *Ogura hyakunin isshu*. Other names are *Ogura sansō shikishi waka* (Japanese Poems on Poem Cards for a Mountain Retreat at Ogura) and *Ogura hyakushu* (100 Poems from Ogura).

Susan Downing VIDEEN

Hyakurenshō

Historical work compiled sometime late in the 13th century; author unknown. The work, written in classical Chinese *(kambun)*, covered the period from 968 through 1259 in a chronological arrangement, but the first 3 of the original 17 volumes are now missing. It is an especially valuable source for information about events in Kyōto during the first part of the Kamakura period.

G. Cameron HURST III

hyakushō

Term for peasants or farmers, particularly in reference to their social status. In ancient times this term was pronounced *hyakusei* or *ōmitakara;* it originally meant "people with family names" (it is written with Chinese characters that mean literally "the hundred names") and referred to those who worked in imperial ricefields *(miyake)*. It did not include *bemin* (those who belonged to BE, special service groups owned by wealthy chieftains) or slaves (NUHI). With the institution of the RITSURYŌ SYSTEM of government and the designation of all rice land as public domain in the TAIKA REFORM of 645, *hyakushō* came to mean subjects of the sovereign *(kōmin)*, including newly freed *bemin*, who were given plots of land under the land allotment system (see HANDEN SHŪJU SYSTEM) and paid the SO, YŌ, AND CHŌ taxes.

With the breakdown of the *ritsuryō* system and the rise of private estates (SHŌEN) in the middle of the Heian period (794–1185), those who worked the land came to be known variously as *heimin, domin,* JIGENIN, *bonge,* and *heimin-byakushō*. The term *hyakushō* was generally reserved for free cultivators who worked on *shōen* or on public lands *(kōryō* or *kokugaryō)* and paid land taxes (NENGU) and other levies (KUJI). The term *hyakushō* connoted a social status to be distinguished from the governing classes, such as court nobles and warriors, and from those below, such as bondsmen (GENIN or *shojū),* landless peasants *(mōdo),* and vagrants *(furōnin).* (As taxpayers, blacksmiths, metal casters, woodsmen, and fishermen were also classed as *hyakushō*.) From the mid-11th through the 16th centuries, more powerful owner-cultivators known as MYŌSHU tended to become landlords or warriors, making other cultivators their tenants.

Although members of the ruling class referred contemptuously to cultivators as *domin* (people of the soil) or *jigenin* (people below the ground), to be a *hyakushō* was theoretically a respectable calling and the term was often given an honorific prefix *(ohyakushō)*. As long as they remained identified with a particular village and paid their taxes, *hyakushō* had certain recognized rights and freedoms. They were even allowed to appeal to the imperial court or the shogunate, a privilege denied to those of lower status. Around the 14th century, with the decline of the *shōen* system, many landholding cultivators formed self-governing groups called sō.

During the turmoil of the Sengoku period (1467–1568), some of the wealthier landholders acquired arms and became vassals of *daimyō* or of lesser warriors. In the Azuchi-Momoyama period (1568–1600), however, the military unifiers ODA NOBUNAGA and TOYOTOMI HIDEYOSHI adopted a policy of disarming local landholders. Hideyoshi in particular, in his SWORD HUNT of 1588, confiscated all weapons from those classified as peasants and forbade them to move or to change their occupation.

Under the shōgun-daimyō system (BAKUHAN SYSTEM) established by the Tokugawa shogunate (1603–1867), the people were classified as warriors, farmers, artisans, or merchants (SHI-NŌ-KŌ-SHŌ), and *hyakushō* became synonymous with farmer or peasant. Among the *hyakushō*, there were finer distinctions, such as OSABYA-KUSHŌ, *hirabyakushō,* and *kobyakushō*. Those who were listed as landholders in the cadastral registers *(kenchichō;* see KENCHI) and considered eligible for certain village offices were called HOMBYA-KUSHŌ; those in semibondage to them were called *hikan* or *hikan-byakushō* or NAGO; and those without land, and thus exempt from taxes, were called MIZUNOMI-BYAKUSHŌ (water-drinking peasants). Villages were organized and administered according to the GŌSON SYSTEM. The burden of taxes fell heavily on the *hyakushō* during the Edo period (1600–1868), and more than 2,500 uprisings (HYAKU-SHŌ IKKI) are recorded.

Since the Meiji Restoration (1868) and the abolition of the class system, the term *hyakushō* has been used for peasants or farmers in general. Today, however, *nōka* is the preferred term. See also LAND TAX REFORM OF 1873–1881.

MINEGISHI Sumio

hyakushō ikki

Popular uprisings and other forms of peasant defiance against government authorities during the Edo period (1600–1868). The most recent and reliable statistics reveal that there were more than 2,500 recorded instances of *hyakushō ikki* and that they took place in every part of the country and in all forms during the 267 years of Tokugawa rule. The statistics also indicate that uprisings occurred more frequently during the latter half of the Edo period; the three peak periods occurred in the 1780s, the 1830s, and the 1860s, roughly corresponding to periods of famine and political uncertainty (see table).

It is difficult to generalize about the nature of the peasant uprisings that occurred during the Edo period. One can say, however, that the *hyakushō ikki* of the early phase of Tokugawa rule usually took the form of mild resistance. Peasants would desert the land to avoid tax responsibilities or make direct or indirect appeals to protest against high land taxes, forced labor, and other forms of economic burden imposed on them by the feudal authorities. More important, the peasant protests of the early period were initiated by influential members of the village, such as the village head, whose prestigious position enabled them to incite the peasant masses to rise against the authorities.

The *ikki* that involved more than 200 villages in the Sakura domain (now part of Chiba Prefecture) in the 1640s is a classic example of peasant protest during the formative period of Tokugawa rule. This *ikki*, led by a legendary village head, SAKURA SŌGORŌ, originated in the mistreatment of peasants by the *daimyō* of Sakura, who imposed high land taxes and forced labor. It culminated in the JI-KISO (direct appeal) submitted by Sakura Sōgorō on behalf of the peasants to the shōgun in Edo (now Tōkyō). His daring appeal for justice to the shogunal authorities—an act punishable by death under the law of the time—succeeded, since the shōgun himself accepted Sōgorō's formal plea and ordered a thorough investigation of the situation in the Sakura domain. The authorities, however, executed Sōgorō and his entire family for this act.

The *hyakushō ikki* that occurred after 1750 took on more complex features. First, the *ikki*, which often became violent, were larger, involving thousands of peasants from village communities under the jurisdiction of several domainal governments and the shogunate. Second, the *ikki* of this period were well organized and hence more effective in putting up resistance against the authorities. Third, and most important, peasants planned and executed these *ikki* themselves, thus taking the initiative away from the village officials. Finally, the rebellious peasants of this period not only attacked the government authorities but also set upon merchants and other privileged segments of rural communities for rent-gouging, loansharking, and other exploitive practices.

The peasant revolt in the Sasayama domain in Tamba Province (now part of Kyōto and Hyōgo prefectures) in 1771 typifies the *hyakushō ikki* of this period. This revolt initially broke out in the economically advanced western part of the domain, but it soon spread to other parts of Sasayama. The main cause of this uprising was the domain's attempt to establish a monopoly over the distribution of cash crops in the market. More than 5,000 peasants from all parts of the domain actively protested this action: they not only attacked many government offices but also destroyed several merchant establishments. It took several months and military reinforcements from neighboring domains to put down the rebellion.

Development of Political Ikki—— Peasant uprisings that occurred during the post–1830 period assumed a more political tone. Peasants more often than not started the *ikki* to bring about political reforms within the village organization, although economic motivations were still important. For example, the *ikki* that occurred in the Chōshū domain (now Yamaguchi Prefecture) in the 1830s took the form of a *murakata sōdō* (disturbance within the village), and featured a fierce internal political campaign that called for the dismissal of the incumbent village head and the introduction of a more democratic procedure that would permit the election of village officials. There were other *ikki* in which peasants campaigned for the dismissal and punishment of local intendants (*daikan*) who were adjudged to be corrupt and unscrupulous, while in other cases rebels openly challenged village authorities by burning the land registers and other tax-related documents.

Both the shogunate and domainal governments quickly perceived the changed nature of these uprisings and tried to deal with them by adopting stronger measures. For example, in 1769 the shogunate issued a directive to local officials specifying ways to suppress *ikki* within its own domain (TENRYŌ). This directive stated in part, "We hear that the peasant actions in recent years have been excessively contemptuous of the authorities, taking advantage of appeasement measures adopted in the past. From now on, however, we urge you to take more forceful measures, including the use of the military forces of neighboring domains, to suppress such acts of insolence." In another directive issued in 1770, the shogunate reiterated the point by stressing the need to coordinate the military forces of various domains in the event of large-scale uprisings transcending their respective boundaries. This directive stated in part, "If those peasants in the Kamigata [Kyōto–Ōsaka area] gather together to form groups against the government, we urge you to suppress them, using our [shogunate] military forces, but in case they get out of control, arrange the matter in such a way that various neighboring domains can cooperate in dealing with the problem."

The growing anxieties expressed in the shogunal directives that were issued repeatedly in the latter half of the Edo period indicated that, more than anything else, the peasants' resistance had become a formidable threat. Therefore, the shogunal and domainal governments were obliged to reassess traditional tactics and to adopt a series of unprecedented measures, such as the use of combined military forces, to quell the rebellions.

Pioneering studies on the *hyakushō ikki* were conducted before World War II mainly by Marxist scholars such as Kokushō Iwao (1895–1949), Ono Takeo (1883–1949), Tsuchiya Takao (b 1896), and HANI GORŌ. In his "Bakumatsu ni okeru shakai keizai jōtai: Kaikyū kankei oyobi kaikyū tōsō" (Social and Economic Conditions during the Late Tokugawa Period: Class and Class Struggle), Hani ascertained among other things that the peasant uprisings of the Edo period, especially those that took place during the last years of shogunal rule, represented a revolutionary force that not only destroyed the feudal order in Japan but also defended the country from the menace of Western imperialism.

Studies since 1945 have been marked by differences in interpretation between Marxist and non-Marxist scholars. Marxist scholars readily accepted Hani's basic premise that the peasant uprisings constituted a revolutionary force, and went on to expand the scope of the study of peasant movements. For example, Kitajima Masamoto,

the author of "Hyakushō ikki ron," studied the relationship between the frequency and nature of peasant uprisings and existing economic conditions. He noticed that uprisings in the Edo period took place more frequently in economically backward, purely agricultural areas. Other scholars such as Okamoto Ryōichi and Tsuda Hideo challenged his view, claiming that a different form of peasant protest movement, usually taking the form of lawsuits and characterized as the *settsu-gata ikki,* occurred in the advanced regions.

Marxist interpretations have also stressed that the nature of peasant uprisings changed in the course of the Edo period. Hayashi Motoi, for example, has suggested in his work that the *ikki* of the early Edo period contained no revolutionary character and usually took the form of mild protest. The *ikki* that took place during the latter half of the Edo period, however, became a form of "class struggle," often developing into open insurrection. Horie Hideichi was more explicit; he divided the nature of the uprisings into three distinct categories: *daihyō osso* (appeals by representatives), *sō byakushō ikki* (popular peasant uprisings), and *yonaoshi ikki* (millenarian uprisings; see YONAOSHI REBELLIONS). It was the last category of *ikki* that shook the foundation of Tokugawa feudalism.

Non-Marxist scholars assert that peasant uprisings in the Edo period never exhibited a revolutionary character and that they merely represented a way of expressing complaints against feudal injustices. They reject the Marxist contention on two specific grounds: that peasants who took part in *ikki* were not consciously revolutionaries, and that those peasant rebels lacked the skills and experience to organize a systematic rebellion. This general notion is succinctly expressed by Hugh Borton, who states that peasant uprisings were largely "disconnected, having little concern for the overthrow of feudalism as such, but caring more for a rectification of those minor injustices which were inherent in the feudal society of the times." He thus totally rejects the Marxist notion that the average peasant was conscious or desirous of taking part in a social revolutionary movement. Several Japanese historians, including the authors of *Hōken shakai no seijuku* (1951, *Kyōdai nihonshi* series, vol 4), have also rejected the Marxist view on the ground that the peasants had no interest in overthrowing the government. To substantiate their point, they stress the fact that most uprisings ended promptly when the peasants' demands were met.

These conflicting claims are perhaps prompted more by an interest in presenting a partisan view than in objective scholarship. The debate, nevertheless, has brought attention to the complex nature of the *hyakushō ikki* and the role of peasants in the social changes that took place during the Edo period.

📖——Aoki Kōji, *Hyakushō ikki no nenjiteki kenkyū* (1966). Hugh Borton, *Peasant Uprisings in Japan of the Tokugawa Period* (1938, rev ed 1968). Hani Gorō, "Bakumatsu ni okeru shakai keizai jōtai: Kaikyū kankei oyobi kaikyū tōsō," in *Nihon shihon shugi hattatsu shi kōza* (Iwanami Shoten, 1932, repr 1982). Hayashi Motoi, "Shoki hyakushō ikki kenkyū nōto," *Rekishi hyōron* 3.4 (1948). Hayashi Motoi, *Kinsei ni okeru kaikyū tōsō no shokeitai,* in *Shakai kōseishi taikei,* vol 7 (Nihon Hyōronsha, 1949). Horie Hideichi, *Bakumatsu ishin no nōgyō kōzō* (1963). *Iwanami kōza: Nihon rekishi,* vols 9–13 (Iwanami Shoten, 1963–64). Kitajima Masamoto, "Hyakushō ikki ron," in *Shin nihonshi kōza,* vol 5 (Chūō Kōron Sha, 1947). Shōji Kichinosuke, *Yonaoshi ikki no kenkyū* (1951).

Isao SORANAKA

hyakushōuke

(peasant tax contracts; also called *jigeuke*). A form of tax farming developed in the 14th century in which the whole populace of a village or its representatives, such as MYŌSHU (local landholders) and JIZAMURAI (farmer-*samurai*), took joint responsibility for delivering annual taxes to the proprietor. The spread of such contracts through the 16th century is often regarded as an indication of increased village autonomy (see SŌ). While this may have been true when contracts were made with an entire village, it was less clearly the case when proprietors successfully evaded villagers' demands by contracting only with the wealthy and more influential of the villagers. This latter form of contract seems to have been common. Contracts with *myōshu* reinforced the existing village social structure by adding to *myōshu* prestige and authority while at the same time providing a secure tax income for the proprietor. Similar tax arrangements were sometimes made with townsmen (see EGŌSHŪ).

Philip BROWN

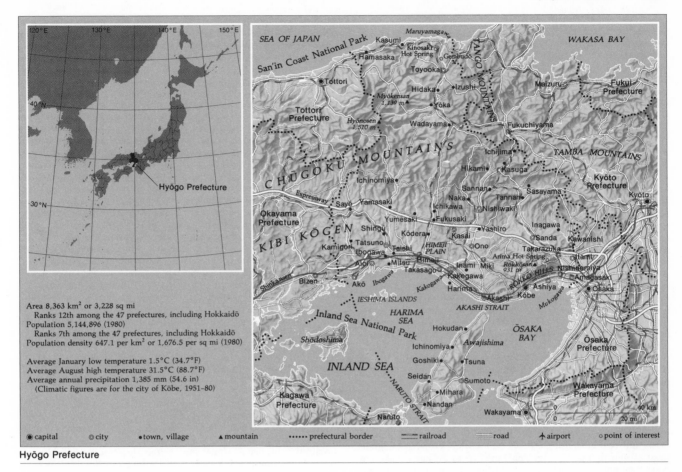

| ● capital | ◎ city | ● town, village | ▲ mountain | ⋯⋯ prefectural border | ══ railroad | ══ road | ✈ airport | ○ point of interest |

Hyōgo Prefecture

Area 8,363 km² or 3,228 sq mi
  Ranks 12th among the 47 prefectures, including Hokkaidō
Population 5,144,896 (1980)
  Ranks 7th among the 47 prefectures, including Hokkaidō
Population density 647.1 per km² or 1,676.5 per sq mi (1980)

Average January low temperature 1.5°C (34.7°F)
Average August high temperature 31.5°C (88.7°F)
Average annual precipitation 1,385 mm (54.6 in)
  (Climatic figures are for the city of Kōbe, 1951–80)

hydrangea, Japanese

(ajisai). *Hydrangea macrophylla* var. *otaksa*. A deciduous shrub of
the family Saxifragaceae or Hydrangeaceae, developed in Japan as a
horticultural variety from the wild *gakuajisai* (*H. macrophylla*) and
cultivated widely as a decorative plant. Its stems grow in clusters to
1.5 meters (5 ft) high; the leaves are opposite, ovate to broadly ovate,
thick, and dark green, with serrated margins. In summer numerous
small flowers appear in ball-shaped clusters (corymbs). The cluster
is composed mostly of sterile flowers, each with 4–5 large, petallike
sepals with a light bluish to deeper purple color. Formerly the *ajisai*
was thought to be native to China, but MAKINO TOMITARŌ
(1862–1957) asserted that it was native to Japan and introduced to
China long ago; this theory is now widely accepted.

Japan is particularly rich in hydrangea varieties, with over 20
species belonging to the genus. The name *ajisai* is often applied
generically to other species in addition to the *Hydrangea macrophylla*. References to *ajisai* in Japanese literature appear as far back
as the *Man'yōshū*, an anthology of poetry completed in the 8th century. Mention of *ajisai* usually alludes to the spring rainy season.
The temple Meigetsuin, popularly called Ajisaidera, in Kamakura, is
renowned for hydrangea.

In 1790 specimens from China were taken to England to be
grown in the Royal Botanic Gardens at Kew, near London; this is
said to be the first introduction of the plant to Europe. But it was
P. F. von SIEBOLD (1796–1866), a German, who really popularized
the Japanese hydrangea in Europe. It is thought that *otaksa*, which
he added to the plant's botanical name in his book *Flora Japonica*,
comes from the name of Otaki san, a Japanese woman he loved.

The Japanese hydrangea, or varieties developed from it, is now
the most common hydrangea grown in gardens throughout the
world. New varieties with bright colors developed in Europe were
reimported to Japan and now are being cultivated there. The acidity
of the soil changes the color of the plant's flowers; acid soils produce
more bluish blossoms and alkaline more pink. Varieties developed
in Europe often feature reddish flowers.

▬——Uehara Keiji, *Jumoku dai zusetsu* (1961).

Matsuda Osamu

Hyōgo Prefecture

(Hyōgo Ken). Located in western Honshū, bordered by the Sea of
Japan to the north, Kyōto and Ōsaka prefectures to the east, Ōsaka
Bay and the Inland Sea to the south, and Okayama and Tottori
prefectures to the west. It is the only prefecture in central Japan with
coasts on both the Inland Sea and the Sea of Japan. The middle
portion is occupied by a ridge of mountains and highlands; the area
to the south of these mountains contains some broad coastal plains
watered by rivers. Most of Hyōgo's population is concentrated in
this area, where the climate is temperate and comparatively dry.
The area to the north is hillier and more humid, with snowy winters
typical of the Sea of Japan coast. The island of AWAJISHIMA in the
Inland Sea is one of the largest of Japan's offshore islands.

The Hyōgo area was inhabited early on, and remains of primitive
man were found there near the city of AKASHI (see JAPANESE PEO-
PLE, ORIGIN OF). Under the ancient system of provinces (KOKUGUN
SYSTEM), the area was designated as the three provinces of Harima,
Tajima, and Awaji, and part of Settsu and Tamba provinces. From
the 8th to 12th centuries the port of Hyōgo (now KŌBE) was a base
for trade with the Asian continent. Hyōgo's position between the
Nara–Kyōto capital regions and western Japan added to its importance, and it was the site of numerous battles between contending
warlords, including the TAIRA–MINAMOTO WAR. During the Edo
period (1600–1868) it was divided into many small domains; these
were combined into the present single prefecture in 1876.

Formerly a flourishing agricultural and fishing area, the prefecture is now dominated by industry, especially along the Inland Sea
coast. Products include ships, steel, transportation equipment, ceramics, and textiles. Kōbe developed into one of Japan's major port
cities in the late 19th century.

Most of its tourist attractions are located within the Inland Sea
and SAN'IN COAST NATIONAL PARK. ROKKŌSAN, a mountain located behind the city of Kōbe, is a favorite summer resort. HIMEJI
CASTLE is known as one of Japan's most distinctive historical structures. Awajishima is the home of a folk puppet theater with a long
tradition, and its beaches attract vacationers from the Ōsaka–Kōbe
area. Area: 8,363 sq km (3,228 sq mi); pop: 5,144,896; capital: Kōbe.
Other major cities include NISHINOMIYA, AMAGASAKI, and HIMEJI.

Hyōgo Shipyards

(Hyōgo Zōsensho). Predecessor of Kawasaki Shipyards, now part of KAWASAKI HEAVY INDUSTRIES, LTD; located in the Hyōgo district of the city of Kōbe. Originally built by the Kanazawa domain (now part of Ishikawa Prefecture) in 1870, it was taken over by the central government in 1872. In 1887, as part of the government's program of selling state enterprises to private interests (see KAN'EI JIGYŌ HARAISAGE), the shipyard was sold to the entrepreneur Kawasaki Shōzō (1837–1912), who, combining it with shipyards he had established in Tōkyō and Kōbe, renamed it the Kawasaki Shipyards (Kawasaki Zōsensho).

Hyōjōshū

(Council of State). The highest office of the Kamakura (1192–1333) and Muromachi (1338–1573) shogunates, where administrative matters and legal disputes were discussed in council. The Hyōjōshū was established by the shogunal regent HŌJŌ YASUTOKI in 1226. Originally there were 11 members (later there were around 15), including heads of other important shogunate offices, Hōjō kinsmen, legal specialists and scholars from such families as the Ōe and Kiyohara, and warriors from the Sasaki, Chiba, MIURA, and other powerful eastern vassal houses. Meetings were presided over by the shogunal regent (SHIKKEN) and cosigner (RENSHO), and decisions were reached by majority vote. Although the Hyōjōshū was originally set up to allow broader participation in government affairs, by the mid-14th century it was dominated by members of the Hōjō family. The Hyōjōshū was retained by the Muromachi shogunate, but it gradually lost its administrative powers and was finally abolished during the Sengoku period (1467–1568).   G. Cameron HURST III

Hyō, Lake

(Hyōko). Irrigation pond in the town of Suibara, central Niigata Prefecture, central Honshū. Known for the white swans that migrate from Siberia (in numbers ranging from 100 to 200) and make the pond their habitat from January to March every year. Also known for the mute swans that were presented to the town by the Soviet Union. Area: 0.1 sq km (0.04 sq mi).

hyōrōmai

(commissariat rice). A rice tax levied by the Kamakura (1192–1333) and Muromachi (1338–1573) shogunates to pay for military provisions in times of war. First imposed in 1180 by TAIRA NO KIYOMORI during the TAIRA–MINAMOTO WAR, it was formalized in 1185 by MINAMOTO NO YORITOMO, who was empowered by the court to appoint land stewards (JITŌ) in public lands (kōryō) and private estates (SHŌEN) and to collect five shō (1 shō = about 1.6 qt or 1.8 liters) of rice from each tan (1 tan = about 0.3 acre, or 0.12 hectare), or about 2 percent of the average yield. Discontinued in the following year, the tax was later reinstated as need arose; the government tried to prevent stewards from demanding it regularly for their own profit. Early in the Muromachi period ASHIKAGA TAKAUJI assigned certain shōen lands (hyōrō ryōsho) to his military supporters; the hyōrōmai that they levied often amounted to one-half of the income of the shōen (see HANZEI). Military governors (SHUGO) and shōen proprietors also collected hyōrōmai to maintain their armies. During the period of the NORTHERN AND SOUTHERN COURTS (1336–92), the Southern Court relied on this tax for its support.

hypothec

(teitōken). In Japanese law, a right created to secure an obligation to a creditor even though there is no actual prior transfer of possession of immovable property owned by the debtor (or a third party); the creditor has the right to receive payment prior to other creditors from the immovable property if the obligor does not fulfill his obligatory duty (Civil Code, art. 369). As a general rule, a hypothec is created in immovable property, but it may also be created in superficies and perpetual land leases. There are also special laws, such as the Automobile Hypothec Law, which allow a hypothec in certain movable property. A hypothec is most commonly used to secure financial loan obligatory duties and is usually recorded. Until the commencement of the debt repayment period, the owner of the hypothecated property (the debtor or a third party) may use the property, but if, after the repayment period, the debtor has not fulfilled his obligation, the creditor may request a court to auction the hypothecated property in accordance with the auction procedures defined in the Civil Execution Law. The hypothec right holder will then receive payment of the debt from the proceeds of the auction.

In transactions between banks and companies and trading company dealings, unlike the common hypothec, fixed collateral (ne-teitō) is used to secure unspecified debts which fluctuate in amount within limits set by the parties. The secured creditor can obtain payment from immovable property fixed collateral prior to other creditors for the amount of the debt within the limits of the maximum amount.

Other concepts similar to hypothec include provisionally registered security and assignments of security. Provisionally registered security is used to secure a monetary obligation. A creditor enters into a contract with either the debtor or a third party who owns immovable property. Under the contract, the creditor will acquire rights to the immovable property of the debtor or the third party if the debtor fails to pay the debt. The creditor therefore provisionally registers the ownership rights, which he may acquire in the future. If the creditor actually acquires ownership of the property, he must pay the debtor or the third party the amount by which the value of the immovable property, upon liquidation, exceeds the amount of the debt. Assignment of security is also used to secure an obligation. Ownership rights to property of the debtor or a third party are transferred to the creditor with the recognition that if the debtor fulfills the obligation, the ownership rights will revert to the obligor or the third party.   KAWAI Takeshi

Hyūga

City in northeastern Miyazaki Prefecture, Kyūshū, on the Hyūga Sea. Sugar refining, chemical, and textile factories, as well as oil-storage and lumbering facilities, have been constructed within the last 15 years. Hyūga is noted for its white GO stones, made from clamshells. Ferry boats depart from its industrial port of Hososhima for the cities of Kawasaki, Ōsaka, Kōbe, and Hiroshima. Pop: 58,347.

I

iai

A technique of swordsmanship that includes the skill of cutting one's adversary on the draw, usually at the temple or at eye level, or, if the initial attack fails, following by a vertical cut through the head. When attacked, *iai* involves drawing, parrying, and riposte with a lethal blow through the shoulder and spine. When the blade is freed, it is swung to shake off the blood and then wiped clean before being returned to the scabbard. In practice the wiping of the blade is omitted. *Iai* was an essential part of *kenjutsu* (fencing) during the Edo period (1600–1868). The *samurai* trained himself to attack or parry a blow and riposte against a single opponent or several opponents while seated, standing, or walking. In recent years the term *iaidō* (the Way of *iai*) has come into common usage.

Hayashizaki Jinsuke Shigenobu (b 1542) is believed to be the founder of *iai*. The basic technique evolved with the practice of carrying the sword thrust into the sash with the cutting edge up. Prior to the 16th century, swords had been suspended with the cutting edge down. Many schools of *iai* evolved during the Edo period. Some were integral to *kenjutsu* schools, others were components of multiweapon schools, and some were devoted solely to *iai*. The All-Japan Kendō Federation has created an eclectic *iai* form derived from several historical schools. See also KENDŌ.

Benjamin H. HAZARD

Ibara

City in southwestern Okayama Prefecture, western Honshū. Known for its textiles for over 300 years, Ibara now mainly produces work clothes and blue jeans. There are also emerging automotive, electronics, machinery, and metal industries. Farm products are tobacco and grapes. Pop: 37,374.

Ibaraki

City in northeastern Ōsaka Prefecture, about 16 km (10 mi) northeast of the city of Ōsaka. A castle town from the late 16th century through the beginning of the 17th century, the city now manufactures electrical equipment and metals and processes food. Large-scale land development during the 1950s resulted in a tremendous increase in population, making it a satellite city of Ōsaka. A cluster of mounded tombs (the Shikinzan KOFUN) and an inn (the Kōriyama Honjin) once used by traveling *daimyō* are of interest. Pop: 234,059.

Ibaraki Prefecture

(Ibaraki Ken). Located in central Honshū and bounded by Fukushima Prefecture to the north, the Pacific Ocean to the east, Chiba Prefecture to the south, and Tochigi and Saitama prefectures to the west. The northern part is occupied by mountains of the Abukuma and Yamizo ranges, and the larger southern section is an extension of the Kantō Plain. The prefecture contains several large lakes and lagoons. The climate is relatively mild.

It was known as Hitachi Province under the ancient provincial system (KOKUGUN SYSTEM). The city of MITO was the seat of an important branch (see GOSANKE) of the TOKUGAWA FAMILY in the Edo period (1600–1868) and became a center of scholarship. The present prefectural name and boundaries were established in 1875 after the Meiji Restoration.

Relative abundance of level land and proximity to the great market of Tōkyō help to make Ibaraki a leading agricultural prefecture. Rice, other grains, and a wide variety of fruits and vegetables are produced in great quantity. Fishing and mining have long been important. More recently, Ibaraki's proximity to the Tōkyō–Yokohama industrial area has led to the development of electrical

equipment, food processing, steel, and petrochemical industries. Recent large-scale projects include the Kashima Coastal Industrial Region and TSUKUBA ACADEMIC NEW TOWN.

Tourist attractions include the KAIRAKUEN in Mito, one of Japan's most famous gardens, and lakes, lagoons, and sandy beaches. One of Japan's larger waterfalls is located near the hot spring resort of Fukuroda (see FUKURODA FALLS). Area: 6,090 sq km (2,351 sq mi); pop: 2,557,903; capital: Mito. Other major cities include HITACHI, TSUCHIURA, and KOGA. See map on following page.

Iba site

Archaeological site in the city of Hamamatsu, Shizuoka Prefecture. The principal features are wooden artifacts and PIT HOUSES from the Yayoi (ca 300 BC–ca AD 300) and Kofun (ca 300–710) periods, building remains that are believed to have been a provincial seat during the Nara period (710–794), and a large ditch 13 meters (43 ft) wide. More than 100 inscribed wooden tablets (MOKKAN) have been recovered from the site. In 1973, despite scholarly objections, a large part of the site was covered by a car barn constructed by the Japanese National Railways; the remainder is preserved as a park.

■——Hamamatsu Shi Kyōiku Iinkai, ed, *Iba iseki hakkutsu chōsa hōkoku,* vol 1 (1976). *KITAMURA Bunji*

Ibigawa

River in Gifu Prefecture, central Honshū, originating in the Ryōhaku Mountains at the border between Fukui and Gifu prefectures and emptying into Ise Bay. It is one of the three great rivers of the Nōbi Plain together with the Kisogawa and the Nagaragawa. Farming settlements surrounded by protective embankments, known as WAJŪ, are found on the delta of its lower reaches. A dam on the upper reaches is used by electric power plants. Length: 114 km (71 mi); area of drainage basin: 3,880 sq km (1,498 sq mi).

IBM Japan, Ltd

(Nihon IBM). Japanese subsidiary of the International Business Machines Corporation (IBM). It was established by IBM in 1937 as the Watson Business Machines Co of Japan to sell IBM's punch card system; in 1949 the company reincorporated under the name IBM Japan, Ltd. With the Japanese government's adoption of IBM's punch card system for compiling the 1950 national census, the company increased its sales tremendously. In 1958 the Japan ATOMIC ENERGY RESEARCH INSTITUTE purchased the country's first IBM computers. In 1960 the company commenced production of computers in Japan and since then has controlled the largest share of the nation's computer market. Since 1961 IBM Japan has exported its computers, and Japan remains one of the most important production bases for the corporation. With its distinctive rental arrangement and the leasing of its software programs, the company is a pioneer in the development and spread of computers in Japan. It has also contributed to the foreign currency holdings of the country through the export of its products. The company's market share of small-sized computers is diminishing, but that of its large and super-large systems continues to increase. The prestige of its brand name, coupled with its marketing strategies, has resulted in an exceptional profit ratio for the company. Annual sales in 1982 totaled ￥428.9 billion (US $2 billion); capitalization, wholly controlled by the IBM World Trade Co, stood at ￥75 billion (US $342.6 million). Corporate headquarters are located in Tōkyō.

IBRD

(abbreviation of International Bank for Reconstruction and Development). Commonly known as the World Bank. Japan has been a

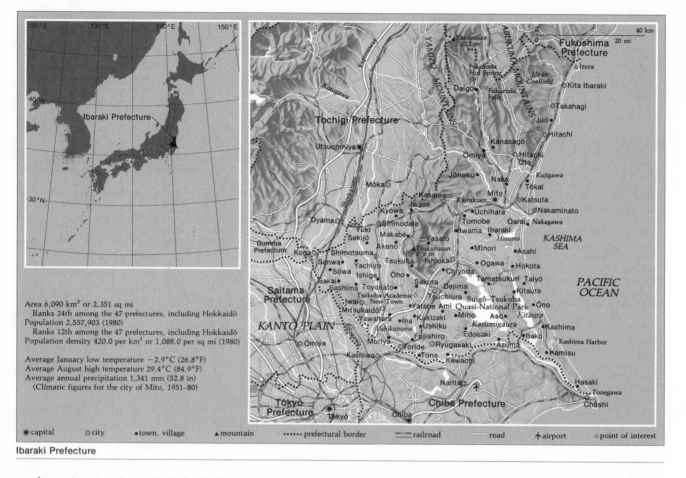

Ibaraki Prefecture

Area 6,090 km² or 2,351 sq mi
  Ranks 24th among the 47 prefectures, including Hokkaidō
Population 2,557,903 (1980)
  Ranks 12th among the 47 prefectures, including Hokkaidō
Population density 420.0 per km² or 1,088.0 per sq mi (1980)

Average January low temperature −2.9°C (26.8°F)
Average August high temperature 29.4°C (84.9°F)
Average annual precipitation 1,341 mm (52.8 in)
  (Climatic figures for the city of Mito, 1951–80)

◉ capital   ○ city   • town, village   ▲ mountain   ⋯⋯ prefectural border   ┅┅ railroad   ═══ road   ✈ airport   ○ point of interest

member nation since August 1952. In 1953 Japan obtained its first loan from the IBRD of approximately 40 million US dollars. This loan was granted to the Japan Development Bank to be used by three electric companies—Kansai, Kyūshū, and Chūbu—to purchase coal-fired power plant equipment. This was the first long-term loan given to the Japanese government since World War II. From that year until 1966, Japan received IBRD loans almost every year for a grand total of $860 million. After 1960, however, Japan became a supplier of funds to the IBRD, and the Bank of Japan has been underwriting IBRD bonds and providing yen credit loans ever since.

SUZUKI Kōichi

Ibuka Masaru (1908–)

Entrepreneur and founder of the SONY CORPORATION. Born in Tochigi Prefecture. Graduated from Waseda University. He established the Tōkyō Tsūshin Kōgyō (a forerunner of Sony) in 1946 with MORITA AKIO and others, and developed and marketed tape recorders for the first time in Japan in 1950, thereby laying the groundwork for his company's spectacular success. Ibuka's company succeeded in developing transistor radios in 1954, many of which were exported to the United States. This success led to the debut of a powerful semiconductor industry in Japan. Ibuka made Sony products world famous by placing extra emphasis on research and development and making exports strictly under the company's own brand name. He became the company's president in 1950 and served as chairman from 1971 to 1976.

KOBAYAKAWA Yōichi

Ibuse Masuji (1898–)

Novelist, short story writer, essayist, and poet. He was born on 15 February 1898 in Kamo in Hiroshima Prefecture. Using the rich resources of his literary tradition, Ibuse has carefully experimented with a number of styles. In his books, the stale conventions of the I-NOVEL (watakushi shōsetsu) are enlivened, the ancient stock of romantic nature-lyricism acquires a robust, epic quality, and into the often too serious or, conversely, too sentimental art of modern Japanese prose writing, he introduces his own brand of dry humor.

Ibuse was born into a family of independent farmers. He moved to Tōkyō in 1917 to study literature at Waseda University, and painting at the Nihon Bijutsu Gakkō. French literature was his major, but Russian literature, especially Tolstoy and Chekhov, also engaged his attention. In 1923, Ibuse's first successful story, "Yūhei," appeared in a student magazine. This gentle satire on intellectual pretense is better known by its later title, "Sanshōuo" (1929; tr "Salamander," 1971). Another story, "Yofuke to ume no hana" (1925; tr "Plum Blossom at Night," 1971), casts his self-mockery in a dream-like, symbolic mode. The allegorical or symbolist overtones in these early works suggest the influence of Western literature, but in "Koi" (1926; tr "Carp," 1971), Ibuse uses a more traditional technique. In typical Japanese I-novel mode, he blends fiction and reality. But in contrast to the self-absorption of other I-novelists, Ibuse controls his personal emotions to better portray the depth of his relationship with a dead friend.

During the following years, Ibuse's interest shifted from Tōkyō to the rural areas of southern Japan where he was born. A painstaking craftsman from the very beginning, he always spent more time revising and polishing his stories than taking sides in ideological polemics. When his literary friends joined the popular PROLETARIAN LITERATURE MOVEMENT in the late 1920s, Ibuse found himself an outsider in the field.

His native countryside was the setting of some of his best stories, for example, "Tange shi tei" (1931; tr "Life at Mr. Tange's," 1971) and "Kawa" (1931–32, The River). Skillful use of dialect, subtle contrast in dialogue, delicate nuances of mood, wry humor, and spare characterization through gesture and speech mannerisms are the main qualities of his mature style.

During the rise of fascism and the approach of war, Ibuse worked steadily on the most remarkable of his works on historical themes, a long novella called Sazanami gunki (1930–38). The action is set against the decline and annihilation of the Taira family in the late 12th century and shows the initiation of a sensitive young Taira samurai into a brutal world. In 1937, a period of increasing xenophobia, Ibuse published another important historical novella, Jon Manjirō hyōryūki (1937; tr John Manjirō, the Cast-away: His Life and Adventure, 1940), which dealt with the actual experiences of a Japanese fisherman who was taken all the way to America and back when contacts outside Japan were strictly forbidden. His last major prewar work, "Tajinko Mura" (1939; tr "Tajinko Village," 1971), took an affectionate farewell of a gentler way of life that is now almost extinct. Ibuse wrote little during the war and his unwilling induction into the army as a war correspondent probably inspired a biting satire on army drill in "Yōhai taichō" (1950; tr "Lieutenant Lookeast," 1971).

His longest and most important novel is *Kuroi ame* (1965; tr *Black Rain*, 1969) which deals with the atomic ordeal of Hiroshima. This unhistrionic elegy for a city and its people stands out from the many sentimental or political accounts of the bombing as a significant work of art. Rather than trying to deal with the disaster in its totality, Ibuse chose to bring out the beauty of the southern landscape, and the manners and colorful foibles of its people against the absurd brutality of the holocaust. All his earlier techniques and thematic interests served him in good stead here: his feeling for details of people's everyday lives, his intimate knowledge of popular lore, and the calm, detached tone he had learned in his earlier historical tales. Great skill was needed to synthesize a documentary montage from the mass of original material. *Kuroi ame* has little plot except for the efforts of the elderly Shigematsu to prove his niece Yasuko is untouched by radiation sickness and is eligible for marriage. Although there is little hope for Yasuko, Shigematsu succeeds in recording his own and other survivors' will to live and to preserve vital memories. Shigematsu is probably the most memorable of Ibuse's gallery of earthy and wise old men.

Ibuse is a recipient of numerous awards, including the Naoki Prize, the Noma Prize, and The Order of Culture, and in 1960 was nominated to the Japan Art Academy. He is also an expert amateur fisherman, and has written many essays on the subject.

■——Works by Ibuse Masuji: *Ibuse Masuji zenshū*, 14 vols (Chikuma Shobō, 1974–75). *Jon Manjirō hyōryūki* (1937), tr Hisakazu Kaneko as *John Manjirō, the Cast-away: His Life and Adventure* (1940). *Kuroi ame* (1965), tr John Bester as *Black Rain* (1971). "Yōhai taichō" (1950), tr John Bester as "Lieutenant Lookeast," in *Lieutenant Lookeast and Other Stories* (1971). Works about Ibuse: Arthur Kimball, "After the Bomb," *Crises in Identity and Contemporary Japanese Novels* (1973). Kumagai Takashi, *Ibuse Masuji: kōen to taidan* (1978). Robert J. Lifton, "Black Rain," in *Death in Life* (1967). Anthony V. Liman, "Ibuse's *Black Rain*," in Kinya Tsuruta and Thomas E. Swann, ed, *Approaches to the Modern Japanese Novel* (1976). Anthony V. Liman, "The Old Man and the Bomb," in Reiko Tsukimura, ed, *Life, Death, and Age in Modern Japanese Fiction* (1978). Matsumoto Tsuruo, *Ibuse Masuji ron* (1978). Nihon Bungaku Kenkyū Shiryō Kankōkai, ed, *Ibuse Masuji, Fukazawa Shichirō* (1977).   Anthony V. LIMAN

Ibusuki

City in Kagoshima Prefecture, Kyūshū, on the southeastern tip of Satsuma Peninsula. Ibusuki is noted for its hot springs, especially its sand baths. The Experimental Station for Tropical Plants of Kagoshima University is located here. Pop: 32,859.

ichiba machi → market towns

ichien chigyō

(sole or exclusive proprietorship). Also known as *ichien ryōchi*. A type of landownership in the Kamakura (1185–1333) and Muromachi (1333–1568) periods whereby an area of land was owned and administered completely and exclusively by a single authority. *Ichien* means whole or entirety; CHIGYŌ means management or proprietorship.

As the government land-allotment system (see HANDEN SHŪJU SYSTEM), instituted under the RITSURYŌ SYSTEM of administration in the late 7th century, gradually collapsed early in the Heian period (794–1185), the private ownership of landed estates (SHŌEN) developed. The spread of private rights to land occurred at many levels, however, and it was unusual for a shōen to be held under a single, exclusive authority. Various "proprietors" in the hierarchy of ownership, such as HONKE AND RYŌKE (titular proprietors or guarantors in the capital and central proprietors, respectively), JITŌ (military land stewards), and SHŌKAN (local estate agents), each possessed certain rights and obligations, called *shiki*, which in turn gave them specific claims on the fruits of the land. The relation between land rights and income was extremely complicated, the right to collect land rent (see NENGU) belonging to one proprietor, the right to corvée labor (see KUJI) to another, and so forth. This kind of multiple management was known as *kakubetsu chigyō* (separate or divided proprietorship).

When one person or authority assumed complete administrative and fiscal rights, he was said to hold *ichien chigyō*. The elimination of competing rights and claims became particularly pronounced from the Kamakura period onward, as conflicts between the *ryōke* and the increasingly powerful *jitō* were resolved (in favor of the latter) by adopting such procedures as SHITAJI CHŪBUN or *ukesho*. Under *shitaji chūbun* a shōen estate was physically divided into halves, each half being placed under the exclusive control of a single proprietor. *Ukesho* was a practice whereby *jitō* were empowered to manage the entire shōen in exchange for paying a stipulated amount of land rent each year to the estate proprietors. Through these means the complex system of overlapping *shiki* was greatly simplified, and the authority of the original proprietors, mostly court nobles and religious institutions, steadily weakened. By the late 14th century, shōen estates had come almost completely under the control of the warrior class, that is, the *jitō* and the SHUGO, the provincial military governors appointed by the shogunate. Proprietary rights to land were completely clarified and redefined under the nationwide cadastral survey (KENCHI) carried out after 1582.

KOYANAGI Shun'ichirō

Ichihara

City on Tōkyō Bay in central Chiba Prefecture, central Honshū. Once a POST-STATION TOWN on the highway Kisarazu Kaidō, it is now a part of the Keihin Industrial Zone. Its industries (oil and shipbuilding) are built largely on reclaimed land. The eastern section of the city remains a residential and agricultural district. Pop: 216,395.

ichii

(Japanese yew). *Taxus cuspidata*. An evergreen of the family Taxaceae which grows wild in the mountainous regions of Hokkaidō, northern and central Honshū, and Shikoku. It is also planted in home gardens and as hedges. Some trees grow to 20 meters (66 ft). The trunk is straight and the bark is reddish brown with shallow fissures. The needles are slender and grow in pinnate lines. It has separate male and female flowers; the female flowers appear in the leaf axils and develop into succulent red fruits, the fleshy seed coverings (arils) of which are sweet and edible. The sapwood is white and the heartwood is reddish brown, hard, fine-grained, flexible, and glossy and finds many uses as material for carvings, tools, and furniture.

The *kyaraboku* (*T. cuspidata* var. *umbraculifera*), a variety of *ichii*, grows aslant to a height of about 1–2 meters (3–7 ft) and is planted as an ornamental tree in gardens. The *ichii* is also known abroad, having been introduced to England in 1855 and to the United States in 1862, and many horticultural varieties have been developed.   MATSUDA Osamu

Ichijitsu shintō ki

A theoretical work by the Tendai monk Jihon (1795–1869) setting forth the history and doctrines of SANNŌ ICHIJITSU SHINTŌ, a syncretic school that held that Ōyamakui no Kami, the Shintō deity who presides over Mt. Hiei (HIEIZAN) where the main temple of the TENDAI SECT is situated, was essentially an embodiment of the highest truth of the Tendai school of Buddhism. Written in 1831, the *Ichijitsu shintō ki* (Record of Ichijitsu Shintō) consists of 31 chapters that deal with such subjects as the Shintō creation myths, the founding of ENRYAKUJI (the name of the Tendai temple complex on Mt. Hiei) and its relation to the HIE SHRINE, and biographies of prominent monks connected with Mt. Hiei. In addition it includes many medieval documents that would otherwise have been lost and which are important in tracing the doctrinal development of Sannō Ichijitsu thought.   Stanley WEINSTEIN

Ichijō, Emperor (980–1011)

The 66th sovereign (*tennō*) in the traditional count (which includes several nonhistorical emperors); reigned 986–1011. Son of Emperor En'yū (r 969–984) and of Senshi (better known as Higashi Sanjō'in, 961–1001), a daughter of the imperial regent FUJIWARA NO KANEIE.

It was in Ichijō's reign that Kaneie's son FUJIWARA NO MICHINAGA, aided by his sister's relationship to the emperor, brought the Fujiwara family to the height of its political influence. To balance the two principal factions of that family, Ichijō was obliged to maintain two nearly equal-ranking empresses (see CHŪGŪ): FUJIWARA NO TEISHI, a daughter of Fujiwara no Michitaka (953–995), and Fujiwara no Shōshi (JŌTŌ MON'IN), the eldest daughter of Michinaga. Much of the greatest feminine literature of the Heian period (794–1185) was produced in the courts of these two consorts, where SEI SHŌNAGON, MURASAKI SHIKIBU, and AKAZOME EMON were ladies-in-waiting.

G. Cameron HURST III

Ichijō family → Gosekke

Ichijō Kaneyoshi (1402–1481)

Also known as Ichijō Kanera. Courtier, scholar, classical (WAKA) poet, and critic. Grandson of the regent NIJŌ YOSHIMOTO, a famous poet and scholar of *renga* (linked verse; see RENGA AND HAIKAI), and son of the regent Tsunetsugu, Kaneyoshi was a member of the noblest branch of the Fujiwara family and the heir to a rich family tradition of participation in and patronage of the arts. By virtue of his exalted birth, he rose rapidly in rank and office, becoming grand minister of state (*dajō daijin*) in 1446 and regent (KAMPAKU) and head of the Fujiwara family in 1447. However, the times were chaotic, the court politically powerless and in economic and cultural decline. Constant warfare between rival feudal barons, whom the weak Ashikaga shōguns were unable to control, resulted in the devastation of the imperial capital of Kyōto, particularly during the decade and more of fighting known as the ŌNIN WAR. In 1467 Kaneyoshi's mansion and extensive library of precious manuscripts were burnt down, and he was reduced to virtual penury. The following year, he moved to the safer environment of Nara, where he spent some ten years, resigning the regency in 1470 and taking holy orders in 1473. When he returned to Kyōto in 1477, he was looked after chiefly by HINO TOMIKO (1440–96), wife of the eighth shōgun, ASHIKAGA YOSHIMASA. Kaneyoshi also instructed and advised the ninth shōgun, Yoshihisa (1465–89), and eked out a living by expounding upon classical poetry and literature for members of the court and military aristocracy. He was conducting a course of lectures on court ceremonial and rites for the benefit of Emperor Go-Tsuchimikado (1442–1500) at the time of his death.

Kaneyoshi was the foremost scholar of the Muromachi period (1333–1568). Unusually intelligent, energetic, and purposeful, he became well versed in practically every branch of learning recognized by his age—history, traditional rites and practices, government, Chinese and Japanese literature, Shintō, Confucianism, and Buddhism. As the most important conservator of the court tradition of literature and learning during Japan's "Dark Ages," Kaneyoshi was instrumental in ensuring the survival and perpetuation of traditional culture. He was especially active in teaching and scholarship during his years of residence at Nara. An original and careful scholar, he compiled works of permanent value. These include: on traditional customs and practices, *Kuji kongen* (ca 1422, Origins of Court Ritual), *Gōshidai shō* (Notes on Ōe Masafusa's Writings on Court Ceremonial), and *Nenchū gyōji taigai* (Outline of Annual Rites and Observances); on the classic court romance, *Kachō yojō* (1472, Atmosphere of Blossoms and Birds) and *Gengo hiketsu* (1477, Secret Wisdom on *The Tale of Genji*); on government, *Sayo no nezame* (ca 1477–78, Wakeful Thoughts in the Small Hours) and BUMMEI ITTŌKI (ca 1478, On the Unity of Learning and Culture).

As a religious thinker, Kaneyoshi was eclectic and syncretic, advocating the amalgamation of Shintō, Buddhist, and Confucian thought and belief. His most important religious writings are: on Shintō, *Nihon shoki sanso* (Notes and Fragments on the *Nihongi*); on Confucian studies, *Shisho dōjikun* (A Child's Primer of the Four Classics); on Buddhism, *Kanshū nembutsu ki* (A Call to Recite the Invocation of Amida's Name).

Primarily a scholar, Kaneyoshi was also a poet and critic of importance, although the age was one of serious decline for the classical poetic tradition. The last of the 21 imperial anthologies, *Shin zoku kokinshū* (1439, New Collection of Ancient and Modern Times, Continued), for which he wrote the Japanese preface, contains nine of his poems, and he was a patron and participant in many poetry contests and events. Among his treatises on classical poetry and song are *Karin ryōzai shū* (Good Timber from the Forest of Verse), an introduction to poetic practice; *Kokin dōmōshō* (1476,

Primer of the Kokinshū); and *Ryōjin guanshō* (My Foolish Ideas on the Ryōjin Collection), a set of notes and comments on the traditional song forms KAGURA UTA and SAIBARA. His works on *renga* include *Renju gappeki shū* (ca 1476, Gems of Linked Verse); and with the *renga* master Sōzei, he produced an expanded and updated edition of the official rules of linked verse composition, *Renga shinshiki* (New Rules of Linked Verse). In TŌKA ZUIYŌ (Leaves from the Peach Blossom [Manse]) he recorded the traditions of his family concerning court etiquette, costume, ceremonial, and the like.

Robert H. BROWER

Ichijō Norifusa (1423–1480)

Court noble of the Muromachi period (1333–1568). The eldest son of the scholar and statesman ICHIJŌ KANEYOSHI, he became imperial regent (KAMPAKU) in 1458. In 1467, when the ŌNIN WAR broke out, he resigned from that office and moved to Nara with his father to escape the fighting. The following year Norifusa moved to Tosa Province (now Kōchi Prefecture), where his family owned some land. With the support of the CHŌSOKABE FAMILY, he established his base in the town of Nakamura and made it into a cultural center.

Ichijō Sanetsune (1223–1284)

Court noble of the Kamakura period (1185–1333); third son of Kujō Michiie (1193–1252) and founder of the Ichijō family (see GOSEKKE). After serving briefly as KAMPAKU (regent) for Emperor GO-SAGA, he became SESSHŌ (regent for a minor) for Emperor GO-FUKAKUSA in 1246. He returned in 1263 to his former post as minister of the left (*sadaijin*), and two years later he became *kampaku* for Emperor KAMEYAMA.

Ichijō Tsunetsugu (1358–1418)

Court noble of the early part of the Muromachi period (1333–1568). A son of the court official and *renga* (linked verse) poet NIJŌ YOSHIMOTO, he was adopted by another courtier, Ichijō Fusatsune. In 1388 he was named inner minister (*naidaijin*) and in 1391 achieved the junior first rank in the imperial court. Three years later he became minister of the left (*sadaijin*) as well as regent (KAMPAKU) for the first of three terms under Emperor GO-KOMATSU. Respected for his broad learning, Tsunetsugu was considered the nobleman *par excellence* of his time.

Ichikawa

City in northwest Chiba Prefecture, central Honshū, on the river Edogawa. Mainly a residential district for commuters to Tōkyō, it is also a part of the Keihin Industrial Zone, with many heavy industry and chemical plants built on reclaimed land. Pears and vegetables are still grown in the northern district. The remains of an 8th-century provincial temple (KOKUBUNJI) may be seen. Jōmon-period (ca 10,000 BC–ca 300 BC) shell mounds have been discovered within the city. Pop: 364,244.

Ichikawa Beian (1779–1858)

Calligrapher of the Edo period (1600–1868). Also known as Ichikawa Sangai, Kōyō, or Rakusai. He was the eldest son of the poet and Confucian scholar Ichikawa Kansai (1749–1820), from whom he received his early education, studying along with HAYASHI JUSSAI and SHIBANO RITSUZAN. As a young man Beian devoted himself to calligraphy, particularly following the style of Mi Fu of Song (Sung) dynasty (960–1279) China. At age 22 Beian published a book on the Mi style in calligraphy. Two years later he journeyed to Nagasaki to meet Chinese scholars. He became sick and received medical attention from Hu Zhaosin (Hu Chao-hsin), a Chinese physician who was an accomplished calligrapher; the two had ample opportunity to discuss brushwork and the more recent stylistic developments in China.

When his father died, Beian accepted employment from the *daimyō* of Kanazawa. His calligraphy was much admired; it is estimated that by his death he had taught more than 5,000 pupils including monks and women. He resigned his position in 1850. His published works include *Beika shoketsu* (Mi-Style Calligraphy), *Beian bokudan* (Beian's Discussions of Ink), and a number of books on calligraphy, writing materials, and his own poetry. Beian's calligraphic style followed late Tang (T'ang) models as interpreted by Mi Fu, and also shows traces of influence from Ming and early Qing

(Ch'ing) calligraphers. His brushwork is relaxed, strong but not rigid, and often rather thick in line. See also CALLIGRAPHY.

——Kanda Kiichirō and Tanaka Shimmi, ed, *Shodō zenshū,* Vol 23: Nihon 10—Edo II (Heibonsha, 1958). *Stephen ADDISS*

Ichikawa Danjūrō

The most illustrious of the major acting family lines in the KABUKI tradition that were identified with the Edo (now Tōkyō) region. Danjūrō I (1660–1704) created the *aragoto* (rough business) style of acting which was used particularly in the portrayal of heroes with superhuman powers. He starred in the earliest versions of four of the most celebrated works which later entered the KABUKI JŪHACHI-BAN, 18 favorite plays of the Ichikawa family. These were *Sayaate* (later known as *Fuwa*), *Narukami Fudō kitayama-zakura* (Narukami and the God Fudō), *Shibaraku* (Wait a Moment), and *Kanjinchō* (The Subscription List). Danjūrō I also wrote plays under the pen name Mimasuya Hyōgo. His son Danjūrō II (1688–1758) established the prestige of the Ichikawa name on a firm basis. He premiered a majority of the *kabuki jūhachiban,* including *Sukeroku,* and also adapted JŌRURI puppet plays for the kabuki stage.

The lineage of Danjūrō IV (1711–78) still remains uncertain. He was a versatile performer who carried on the *aragoto* tradition with distinction and excelled as an ONNAGATA (female impersonator). His son Danjūrō V (1741–1806) also acted with consummate skill in both male and female roles.

Danjūrō VII (1791–1859) is best remembered as the compiler of the *kabuki jūhachiban,* which he formally established as the special repertory of the Ichikawa family. As a performer, he had extraordinary range and flexibility. Among his various accomplishments, Danjūrō VII's version of *Kanjinchō* (1840) is regarded as a masterpiece.

Taking after his father Danjūrō VII, Danjūrō IX (1838–1903) displayed similar virtuosity as a kabuki actor. He continued to promote the long-standing kabuki tradition but also reflected the influences of the Meiji period (1868–1912) when Japan was emerging from feudalism into the modern era. With the aid of scholars and intellectuals, Danjūrō IX promoted the *katsureki-mono* ("living history" plays), which stressed greater factual accuracy and pictorial realism. Through his association with influential elements among the Meiji elite he helped to elevate the status of kabuki to a theater of respectability attended by aristocrats, foreign dignitaries, and even members of the imperial family. Both he and Morita Kan'ya XII (see MORITA KAN'YA), the prominent theater manager, shared this strong aspiration to upgrade the kabuki theater. During the last half of the 19th century, Danjūrō IX and Onoe Kikugorō V (see ONOE KIKUGORŌ) contributed enormously to the stability of the kabuki theater as it underwent an uncertain period of sweeping social and cultural changes.

Danjūrō XI (1909–65), the son of Matsumoto Kōshirō VII (1870–1949), belonged to a group of actors whose prominent careers started in the postwar period. He performed both heroic and romantic roles in the traditional repertory with great distinction but was also popular in kabuki plays based on works by contemporary novelists. His superb performance in an adaptation of *Genji monogatari* (TALE OF GENJI) in the lead role of Prince Genji with the noted *onnagata* Onoe Baikō VII (b 1915) as costar, remains an unforgettable chapter in the history of postwar kabuki theater.

——James R. Brandon, *Kabuki: Five Classic Plays* (1975). Ihara Toshirō, *Ichikawa Danjūrō no daidai* (1917). *Kabuki,* special issue: *Bessatsu daiichigō: Sōke Ichikawa Danjūrō* (1969).

Ted T. TAKAYA

Ichikawa Fusae (1893–1981)

Feminist and politician; leader of the prewar WOMEN'S SUFFRAGE movement who, after World War II, was elected five times to the House of Councillors on the basis of her campaigns for social equality and against government corruption. Born into a farm family in Aichi Prefecture, Ichikawa later claimed that she became determined to improve women's lot when she saw her father's cruelty to her mother. Completing her teacher training education in Nagoya, Ichikawa taught in an elementary school, then became the first woman reporter for the liberal newspaper *Nagoya shimbun.*

She went to Tōkyō in 1918, where YAMADA WAKA introduced her to HIRATSUKA RAICHŌ, founder of the feminist group SEITŌSHA (1911–16, Bluestocking Society); the next summer, Ichikawa guided Hiratsuka in Nagoya on tours to observe the harsh conditions for women factory workers. Concerned with both labor and feminist issues, Ichikawa in late 1919 and early 1920 joined Hiratsuka and OKU MUMEO in establishing the SHIN FUJIN KYŌKAI (New Woman's Association). In July 1921 Ichikawa left for two and a half years in the United States, where she was especially inspired by contact with Alice Paul and the National Women's Party.

Ichikawa returned to Japan in early 1924, determined to work for women's rights at home. In December 1924 she helped found the FUSEN KAKUTOKU DŌMEI (Women's Suffrage League), and for the next 16 years she tried to persuade liberal politicians to support legislation in the Diet that would grant women political rights. She also encouraged housewives to take a more active interest in local community affairs. The Fusen Kakutoku Dōmei dissolved in 1940 as all liberal trends became submerged in the national commitment to war.

During World War II Ichikawa still attempted to promote women's interests by mobilizing women to confront the problems associated with war (scarcity of food, absence of male household heads), but because she was a member of the government-sponsored Dai Nihon Genron Hōkokukai (Great Japan Patriotic Speech Association) during the war, she was briefly barred from any political activity under the US Occupation purge.

Ichikawa first ran for political office in April 1953, seven years after women were given the right to vote in Japan. Five of her six bids for a seat in the House of Councillors were successful. She was unique in asserting her independence, neither belonging to any of the major political parties nor siding consistently with the conservative ruling party, as independents usually do. She was also able to solicit mass support without recourse to financial backing from politicians or big business. In both the 1975 and 1980 elections she won by one of the highest numbers of votes ever received by a single candidate in Japan. In addition to her activities as a Diet member, she devoted much of her time to the League of Women Voters (Nihon Fujin Yūkensha Dōmei), which she founded in 1945, and to the Women's Suffrage Hall (Fusen Kaikan), a research institute designed to increase women's political consciousness.

——Ichikawa Fusae, *Ichikawa Fusae jiden* (1974).

Kathleen MOLONY

Ichikawa Kon (1915–   )

One of Japan's finest contemporary film directors. Ichikawa was born in 1915 in Ise, Mie Prefecture. Leaving school, he became a cartoonist and a designer before entering films. He has said that he thinks of himself as a craftsman rather than an artist, that he takes what the studio gives him and then does his best with it. This would account for the widely varying quality of his pictures. Even his less successful productions display fine craftsmanship, such as his series of popular melodramas made between 1976 and 1978 and based on the mystery novels of YOKOMIZO SEISHI which are splendidly photographed, rigorously edited, and well acted.

When Ichikawa is given (or fights for) a vehicle which excites his interest, however, the result is usually an outstanding film. This is particularly true of those written with the help of his wife, Wada Natto. These include the early comedies *Pūsan* (1953, Mr. Pu) and *Okuman chōja* (1954, A Billionaire), as well as the finest of the later films: *Biruma no tategoto* (1956, The Harp of Burma), which first brought him to international attention; *Enjō* (1958, Conflagration), based on the MISHIMA YUKIO novel *Kinkakuji; Kagi* (1959, The Key; shown abroad as Odd Obsession), based on the TANIZAKI JUN'ICHIRŌ novel; *Bonchi* (1960, The Sin); and *Hakai* (1961, The Broken Commandment; shown abroad as The Outcast), based on the SHIMAZAKI TŌSON novel.

Though like most directors Ichikawa usually makes adaptations, he brings to them his own distinguished style. This is a highly visual style, and the spare and handsome outlines of his compositions are often enough to identify any of his pictures. One particularly remembers the asymmetrically balanced scene of *Kagi*, the bold, blocked outlines of *Enjō*, and the visual magnificence of *Yukinojō henge* (1963, The Revenge of Yukinojō; also known as An Actor's Revenge)—a much-filmed melodrama, turned by Ichikawa into a film of great visual splendor.

Another element of the Ichikawa style is an unusually incisive, even brusque, editing. This, coupled with his ability to get fine performances from even inferior actors, results in a richness of texture which is perhaps best illustrated in *Tōkyō Orimpikku* (1965, Tōkyō Olympiad), that extraordinary documentary of the games of 1964.

Here Ichikawa will often cut from the main events to show the athletes (and the spectators) being themselves. The humanity of the assembled throngs is as important to him as are the sports events. In the excellent if little known *Seishun* (1968, Youth) he emphasizes the joys and sorrows of high-school baseball more than he does the concluding game.

In Ichikawa's best pictures, the aspirations (or pretensions) of people are contrasted with their essentially aimless humanity. The result, as in the excellent *Matatabi* (1973, The Wanderers), is sometimes funny, and nearly always moving. The vagaries of the human condition are contrasted with typically human pretensions and presented with a kind of incisiveness rare in cinema. *Donald* RICHIE

Ichikawa Shōichi (1892–1945)

One of the leading figures of the JAPAN COMMUNIST PARTY (JCP) before World War II. Born in Yamaguchi Prefecture. A graduate of Waseda University, he worked as a newspaperman and later started a socialist magazine, *Musan kaikyū* (Proletariat), with AONO SUEKICHI and others. In January 1923 he joined the JCP and became an editor of the party organ *Sekki* (later renamed *Akahata*; both names mean "Red Flag"). He escaped arrest in the MARCH 15TH INCIDENT of 1928, in which over a thousand leftists were arrested, and attended the sixth Comintern meeting, held that year in Russia, as a representative of the JCP. Ichikawa was arrested the following year in another mass arrest of communists (see APRIL 16TH INCIDENT). His testimony during the subsequent public trial was published posthumously as *Nihon kyōsantō tōsō shōshi* (A Short History of the Struggle of the Japan Communist Party). Given a life sentence, Ichikawa steadfastly refused to recant and died of malnutrition two months before the end of World War II.

Ichikawa Utaemon (1907–)

Period-film motion-picture actor whose career began in silent movies and who is especially remembered for the movie series *Hatamoto taikutsu otoko* (1950–63). He was born in Kagawa Prefecture. Formerly a KABUKI actor, Ichikawa entered the motion picture world in 1925, making his film debut in *Kurokami jigoku* (1925). He appeared in more than 20 pictures following his first hit series and went on to become a popular box-office star. He specialized mainly in period dramas, appearing in films with a modern-day setting only rarely. One such film was *Jiruba no tetsu* (1950), whose scenario was written by the well-known director-screenwriter KUROSAWA AKIRA. Since the mid-1960s Ichikawa has appeared in films only occasionally. SHIRAI *Yoshio*

Ichimura Kiyoshi (1900–1968)

Businessman. Born in Saga Prefecture. Studied at Chūō University. With a recommendation from ŌKŌCHI MASATOSHI, director of the Institute of Physical and Chemical Research (Rikagaku Kenkyūjo), Ichimura was invited to join Rikagaku Kōgyō Co, one of the companies related to Rikagaku Kenkyūjo, in 1933. He established a company to make photosensitive paper, Riken Kankōshi (now RICOH CO, LTD), in 1936 and later founded other new companies, including Nihon Kōkū Heiki, San-Ai, San-Ai Oil, and Ricoh Watch. He also formed the Ricoh–San-Ai business group. YAMADA *Makiko*

Ichimura Sanjirō (1864–1947)

Scholar of Asian history. Born in what is now Ibaraki Prefecture; graduate of Tōkyō University, where he majored in Chinese classics. In 1905 he became a professor at Tōkyō University and, with SHIRATORI KURAKICHI, was a leading figure in East Asian studies in Japan. His most famous work is *Tōyōshi tō*, 4 vols (1939–50, Comprehensive History of East Asia).

Ichinomiya

City in northern Aichi Prefecture, central Honshū, 17 km (10 mi) northwest of Nagoya. Ichinomiya developed in the Edo period (1600–1868) as a shrine town around the Masumida Shrine, and as a market town. Its principal industry is textiles, particularly wool. Pop: 253,138.

Ichinoseki

City in southern Iwate Prefecture, northern Honshū. Ichinoseki developed as a castle town in the Edo period (1600–1868). Rice, dairy goods, and apples are its principal products. In recent years many electronics and precision instrument companies have built factories here. GEMBIKEI, a gorge on the river Iwaigawa, and Sukawa Hot Spring, a part of the Kurikoma Quasi-National Park, draw visitors. Pop: 60,217.

ichirinsō

Anemone nikoensis. A perennial herb of the family Ranunculaceae which grows in mountain woods and on grassy foothills in Honshū, Kyūshū, and Shikoku. Its stem grows straight and reaches a height of 18–25 centimeters (7–10 in). The compound leaves are composed of three pinnate leaflets. Each plant produces a single flower about 4 centimeters (1.6 in) across, which opens around April with five white sepals that resemble petals and are often tinged with pink. *Ichirinsō* (literally, "one-flower plant") is related to *nirinsō (A. flaccida)*, which has two flowers. MATSUDA *Osamu*

ichirizuka

(milestone mounds). Markers to indicate distances in *ri* (approximately 2.44 mi or 3.9 km), placed in pairs along major highways in the Edo period (1600–1868), one on each side of the road. Each *ichirizuka* consisted of a 30-foot-square mound, 10 feet high, planted with nettle or pine trees. Distances were measured from Nihombashi, a bridge regarded as the center of Edo (now Tōkyō) and the place where all the major highways (GOKAIDŌ) converged.

ichō → ginkgo

Idemitsu Art Gallery

(Idemitsu Bijutsukan). Located in Tōkyō. A large private collection, founded by IDEMITSU SAZŌ of the Idemitsu Kōsan Co, Ltd, and opened in 1966, it includes Japanese paintings, Chinese and Japanese calligraphy and ceramics, Chinese bronzes, and Southeast Asian and Near Eastern objects. The representation of UKIYO-E and BUNJINGA painters is extensive; particularly notable is the group of paintings and calligraphy by SENGAI GIBON. The Chinese ceramic section is one of the largest in Japan. An equally large collection of shards from kiln sites in Japan, China, Korea, and the Middle East offers individuals an unusual opportunity to study ceramics firsthand. There is a nine-volume catalog of the collection, and each major exhibit is accompanied by a special catalog. *Laurance* ROBERTS

Idemitsu Kōsan Co, Ltd

Company engaged in petroleum refining; petrochemical production; the development and extraction of petroleum and other mineral resources; marine transportation; ship chartering; and import, export, sales, storage, and other business operations related to these products. Founded originally as Idemitsu Shōkai by IDEMITSU SAZŌ in 1911, it was reorganized and took its present name in 1940.

The company operates refineries with a total daily capacity of 860,000 barrels (137,000 kl) in Hokkaidō, Yamaguchi, Chiba, Hyōgo, and Aichi prefectures. The first company in the world to establish a direct desulphurization facility for crude oil, it has taken the initiative in other environmental protection systems. To ensure a stable supply of oil, Idemitsu operates a tanker fleet of 2.1 million tons, owned by Idemitsu Tanker Co, Ltd, including the *Idemitsu maru* (210,000 tons), the world's first supertanker. In response to the sharp increase in demand for oil, the company is also engaged in exploration activities on the continental shelf of the Sea of Japan and in other areas of the world. Idemitsu Oil Development Co, Ltd, was incorporated in 1976 to promote further development. Idemitsu recently entered the field of alternative energy sources (coal, uranium, and geothermal) in an effort to head toward becoming an all-around energy enterprise.

The company has some 8,600 filling stations across the nation and a sales network of 49 branch offices, with corporate headquarters in Tōkyō. It also maintains branch offices in New York, Los Angeles, Denver, London, Kuwait, Teheran, Riyadh, Abu Dhabi, Singapore, Sydney, and Rio de Janeiro. Total sales amounted to

¥3.1 trillion (US $12.8 billion) at the end of March 1982; stocks are not publicly offered.

Idemitsu Sazō (1885–1981)

Entrepreneur. Born in Fukuoka Prefecture; graduate of Kōbe Commercial Higher School (now Kōbe University). Idemitsu established Idemitsu Shōkai (forerunner of IDEMITSU KŌSAN CO, LTD), an oil products dealership, in 1911. He rapidly expanded his business into a broad retail enterprise and turned the company into a major oil corporation financed by Japanese capital. Idemitsu had a 130,000 ton tanker constructed as early as 1951, and started importing high-octane gasoline from the United States as well as crude oil from Iran. He also made inroads into the oil refining business from 1955. He was well known for his large collection of Asian art, which is housed in the IDEMITSU ART GALLERY.   TOGAI Yoshio

ideographs → kanji

ideological "conversion" → tenkō

Idojiri Archaeological Hall

(Idojiri Kōkokan). Located in the town of Fujimi, Nagano Prefecture; the hall houses Jōmon potteries (see JŌMON POTTERY), STONE TOOLS, and other artifacts excavated from several of the more than 50 sites, mainly of the Middle Jōmon period (ca 3500 BC–ca 2000 BC), in the Idojiri area at the southeastern foot of the mountain Yatsugatake. Established in 1959, the museum moved to new facilities in 1974. See also TOGARIISHI SITE.

■——Fujimori Eiichi, ed, *Idojiri* (1965).   *Laurance* ROBERTS

ie

(household). The *ie* is the primary unit of social organization in Japan. *Ie* is often translated as "family," but the English term "household" comes closer to conveying the Japanese concept of *ie*. In Japanese there are no specific terms for "family" as distinct from "household," although the Chinese-derived *kazoku* does mean family. Etymologically *ie* is a term which signifies "hearth." *Ie* is the residential domestic group which is often symbolically expressed in phrases such as "under the same roof," or "the relationship in which one shares the meals cooked in the same pot." The house building is also called *ie*.

A household *(ie)* is normally formed by, or around an elementary family as a nucleus, and the residential household may include relatives and nonrelatives other than these immediate family members. Household composition may vary according to specific situations, such as the stage in the cycle of the domestic family and the economic situation of the household. However, the sociological importance of the *ie* is such that regardless of its composition it is regarded as one distinct unit in society, represented externally by its head and internally organized under his leadership. Once established, a household is expected to persist in spite of the succession of one generation by another. The house building itself with the house site is considered an indivisible spatial unit. The property is considered to be attached to the household rather than to its individual members, though the household head assumes the de facto right of ownership, property being, since the Meiji Civil Code, registered in the name of the household head.

The concept of *ie* thus involves complex elements, and the *ie* is the basic social unit in a community. An individual must be a member of a household. There has been a widespread custom for well-established households to have their own house-name. Such a house-name is different from a surname, as it applies to only one household. In a village community the house-name is more frequently used than the surname (it is often the case that several households in a village have the same surname). The organization of a community in Japan is built only on the basis of the household, not on individuals nor on larger descent groups. Therefore, the *ie* is seen as not simply a contemporary household, but as existing in a time continuum from the past to the future, embracing not only the current living members but also their deceased predecessors, with some projection toward future members yet unborn. For the Japanese, their ancestors include those who were once members of their household, not merely remote figures linked with the individual through genealogies. The *ie* is always conceived of as persisting in

time through the succession of the members. Hence succession to the headship is of great functional importance, and the line of succession is the axis of the structure of *ie*.

The Principle of Succession——There are two important rules of succession to the headship common throughout Japan. One is that the head should be succeeded by a "son," not by any other kind of kinsman. However, the successor is not necessarily the real son; any male (whether he be related to the head or not) can be the "son" provided the necessary legal procedure has taken place. This involves his becoming a member of the household through the relationship commonly expressed as "adopted son" *(yōshi)* or "adopted son-in-law" *(muko yōshi)*.

A "son" is adopted, for example, when the head has no son but only a daughter. When the daughter's husband becomes the successor of his father-in-law, as well as the inheritor of the father-in-law's household property, he is called an adopted son-in-law. When the head has no children he may adopt a daughter first and later by her marriage obtain an adopted son-in-law, or he may adopt a young married couple. Even when he has a son, if he considers him unfit to be his successor he may adopt another. Such cases are occasionally found among those *ie* that have businesses. An adopted son may be taken from among the kinsmen of the head, such as his nephew, cousin, or more remote relatives including his wife's. But it is equally possible for a man who has no kinship relation at all to the head to be adopted into the family, such as a servant or a collaborator of the head. Normally the ADOPTION takes place between households of fairly equal status, as in the case of a marriage arrangement.

This type of adoption has been very common among the Japanese. An adopted son or adopted son-in-law has the same rights in succession and inheritance as the real son. This is closely related to the rule that rights of succession and inheritance in the *ie* only go along the line of "father" to "son" and not through any relationship. Through this "father-son" relationship (whether by initial kinship or by adoption) inescapable economic and moral ties are established: the son, being given the economic advantage, has an obligation to take care of his predecessor in his old age, with his household members. Among the agricultural population the household is thus a distinctive enterprise offering insurance for old members, and not simply the residence of a family. Thereby it displays a strong desire to ensure continuity: to get a successor is an overriding concern for the household head.

The other important rule of succession to headship of the household is that it should be by one son only; never by two or more sons jointly. Hence in Japan theoretically there has been no joint family structure like that of the Chinese or the Hindus. If a household is occupied by two brothers with their wives and children, there is a sharp functional and status distinction between the successor and the nonsuccessor. The family of the nonsuccessor is considered as comprising "extra members," not "full members" of the household. In fact it is very rare for two married brothers to reside in the same household for a long time. Nonsuccessors are supposed to leave the father's household on marriage, whether or not they receive a share of the property. Once they have established their own independent households, each forms a distinctive property holding unit, in which again the same principle operates. (See also HONKE AND BUNKE.)

In actual practice, inheritance tends to be subsumed by the principle of succession; the successor always gets the father's house and tends to receive the lion's share of the father's property. It is interesting that today, although the 1947 Civil Code gives equal inheritance rights in the father's property to all sons and daughters, among agriculturists nonsuccessors hardly ever demand this right. It is still very common for them to sign over their rights and leave the house and land intact for their brother who succeeds and takes the responsibility for the parents.

As the result of this system, there are two kinds of household in Japan, viewed in sociological terms: one is that of a successor, and the other is that of a nonsuccessor. The former includes the successor's elementary family and his parents (or parents-in-law) with their unmarried sons and daughters, while the latter is formed normally by one elementary family. However, in the next generation this small household also will grow into a larger one and may again produce new households by its extra sons. The genealogical relationship between the individual members of the various households has by itself no sociological importance, as it has in the case of a clan or lineage, for example, unless a set of such households is involved in a common economic and political relationship.

This is also in accordance with the weak relationship between siblings, as compared with the strong functional relationship of father and successor son. Social organization in rural Japan is structured by this outstanding principle, in which the vertical line is regarded as of supreme importance over the collateral link. The well-known Japanese proverb, "The sibling is the beginning of the stranger," reflects this structural process.

Functional Meaning of Ie and Its Decline —— The concept of *ie*, the distinctive unit in the Japanese community, has penetrated every nook and cranny of Japanese society. The ideal manifestation of it was particularly strong among well-established households in rural as well as urban areas, as the continuity of the household was greatly valued among those with property and active management. It was also the basic unit of the *samurai* community in the Edo period (1600–1868). The status of samurai was assigned to the household *(ie)*, so that the head of the household alone could enjoy its privileges, and it was transmitted to his successor alone, as "one man for one household" was the rule of the *ie* system. Indeed, the old civil code concerning the family took its patterns from the samurai code, so that the family institution under the *ie* system with its overtones of feudal moral precepts was further prescribed legally for the entire population, regardless of social strata. It was only in the new post–World War II Civil Code that the *ie* institution was abolished.

However, the real decline of the *ie* institution took two or three decades after the legal change was instituted. The major force for the decline was the change in the total economic structure of the society. There was a rapid increase of population in urban centers—people who live on their income from salaries rather than the management of household property. Since the functional importance of the continuity of the *ie* lies in the succession from father to son, if the son is not engaged in the same activity as his father, and further if the household has no significant property, there would be little point in making elaborate arrangements for the continuity of the household. The vast increase of this urban salaried population, accompanied by the drastic drain of the younger population from rural areas, has resulted in the current decline of the *ie* system. This tendency has also been encouraged by women of the younger generation who openly resist living with their husbands' parents, in particular with their mothers-in-law. Under the *ie* institution, women had been assigned a low status, in particular the successor's wife, who often had a hard life under the authority of her mother-in-law. Today, however, the institution is found mostly among farmers and men of particular occupations such as traditional arts and crafts, techniques which have to be handed down to the next generation, or professions with fairly fixed clientele, such as a medical practice or the position of temple priest. These professions, however, account for a rather small percentage of the total population. The majority of contemporary Japanese households are of the elementary family type. Older parents may live by themselves or with their married daughters, not necessarily with their eldest sons' families. Thus as a family or household institution, the *ie* has greatly declined, so much so that the younger generation in urban areas is not familiar with the traditional *ie* institution. There is a general consensus among the citizenry that the *ie* institution is disappearing from Japanese society.

The Concept of Ie in Group Consciousness —— Despite the decline of the *ie* system as a family institution, the basic concept as a form of group consciousness has in fact survived. The concept of *ie* is well maintained in a modern guise as a structural basis for contemporary Japanese groups. If viewed in terms of group structure, the characteristic *ie* institution is found in the corporate residential group, and as a managing body, as manifested in the case of farmers, manufacturers, and merchants.

The *ie* comprises household members (usually the family members of the household head, but others may be included), who thus make up a distinct social group. In other words, the *ie* is a social group constructed on the basis of an established frame of residence and often of a management organization. The human relationships within this household group are thought of as more important than all other human relationships. Thus the wife and daughter-in-law who have come from outside have incomparably greater importance than one's own sisters and daughters, who have married and joined other households. A brother, when he has established a separate house, is thought of as belonging to another social group; on the other hand, a son-in-law, who was once a complete outsider, takes a position as a household member and becomes more important than the brother living in a separate household. This principle contributes to the weakening of kinship ties. Kinship, which is normally regarded as the primary and basic human attachment, seems to be compensated for in Japan by a personalized relation to a corporate group based on work, in which the major aspects of social and economic life are involved. This is the basic principle on which Japanese society is built.

Among groups larger than the household are those described by the medieval concept, *ichizoku rōtō* (one family group and its retainers). The idea of group structure as revealed in this expression is indeed the concept of one household, in which family members and retainers are not separate but form an integrated corporate group. The equivalent in modern society of the *ie* and the *ichizoku rōtō* is a group such as "the National Railway family" (Kokutetsu *ikka*), which signifies those associated with the Japanese National Railways. In any Japanese enterprise "management-labor harmony" is highly appreciated by both workers and management. A company is conceived of as an *ie*, all its employees qualifying as members of the household, with the employer at its head. When speaking to outsiders, they call their own work organization, *uchi*, which is the same colloquial term used for household *(ie)*. A large household, a company, envelops the employee's personal family; it "engages" him "totally" *(marugakae)*. The employer readily takes social or economic responsibility for his employee's family, which in turn, considers the company its primary concern. In this modern context, the employee's family, which is normally composed of the employee himself, his wife, and children, is a unit that can no longer be conceived as an *ie*, but simply a family. The unit is comparable to the family of a servant or clerk who worked in the master's *ie*, the managing body of the premodern enterprise. The role of the *ie* institution as the distinguishing unit in society in premodern times is now played by the company, or any unit of work organization.

This social group consciousness, symbolized in the concept of the *ie*, of being one distinctive unit, has been promoted by slogans and justified by traditional morality. In this manner, the concept of the traditional *ie* institution still persists in group identity, as the basis of Japanese social structure.

▬ —— Nakane Chie, *Kinship and Economic Organization in Rural Japan* (1967). Nakane Chie, *Japanese Society* (1970).

NAKANE Chie

Iejima

Island west of the Motobu Peninsula of the main island of Okinawa. Iejima is generally flat but a 172 m (564 ft) rock mountain, Gusuku-san (also called Ie Tatchū), is located in the eastern part. Iejima was the site of fierce fighting between Japanese and American forces during World War II. Area: 23 sq km (8.9 sq mi).

iemoto

A term used in the world of traditional Japanese arts such as music, dance, flower arrangement, Nō, and *kabuki* to refer to either the founder of a school or the current head of the school, usually a direct descendant of the founder.

The *iemoto* of each school inherits the secret traditions and prized art objects of the school from the previous *iemoto*. He (or more rarely she) is the final arbiter regarding the orthodox practices of the school and has the authority to pass them on by hereditary means. He also has the sole right to award certificates of achievement, to publish the school's secret techniques, and to expel members of the school in order to maintain doctrinal orthodoxy. *Iemoto* are expected to take an active role in the personal lives of their disciples, and it is not unusual for them to serve in such roles as marriage go-between.

Each *iemoto* is followed by disciples who are recognized by him as accredited teachers *(natori)*, who in turn are masters of their own disciples. Many of the *iemoto*-led schools are hierarchical organizations of considerable magnitude: two of the largest flower arrangement schools, for example, consist of 1.5 million members each, with local chapters throughout Japan and in certain cities abroad.

The *iemoto* is one of many manifestations in Japanese society of the hierarchical pattern of relationships modeled on the *ie* or household and *dōzoku* or extended kin group. This pattern (present also in a slightly different form in business, industry, and education) is marked by all-inclusive and nearly unbreakable command-allegiance, succoring-dependence relationships between senior and junior, or superior and subordinate. From this point of view each *iemoto*-led school is a giant kinshiplike establishment, with the same kind of closeness and inclusiveness in its interpersonal links but without the kinship limitations on its size.

Francis L. K. HSU

Ienaga textbook review case

(*kyōkasho saiban,* also known as Ienaga *saiban*). A case challenging the constitutionality and legality of Japan's educational textbook review system. The textbooks used in primary and secondary education are subject to official approval by the Ministry of Education under provisions of the School Education Law, without distinction as to whether the texts are used in public or private schools. In 1965 Ienaga Saburō, a professor at Tōkyō University of Education, filed suit seeking recovery of royalties lost due to the 1963 rejection of an application for official approval of the fifth edition of his high school textbook *Shin nihonshi* (New History of Japan); he also asked for compensation for mental distress caused by ministry demands for 300 alterations before approval of the text was granted in 1964. In 1967 Ienaga filed a second suit seeking the reversal of the ministry's 1966 rejection of a new application for approval of the unrevised version of the text.

The Tōkyō District Court, presided over by Chief Judge Sugimoto Ryōkichi, ruled on the second suit in 1970. The court held that article 26 of the constitution, which guarantees the right to education, does not imply the state's right to educate and control educational content; textbook review is constitutional when limited to technical design and objective accuracy, but such review constitutes censorship when ideological and philosophical considerations arise in the approval process. The court found the Ienaga case to be an examination of the substance of the ideas of the writer of the textbook, constituting unconstitutional censorship and unjust control of education in violation of the Basic Law on Education (17 July 1970, *Hanrei jihō,* 604).

In 1974 the same district court, under Chief Judge Takatsu Tamaki, dismissed Ienaga's first suit, holding that only the state could bear direct responsibility toward the citizenry as a whole concerning public education and that official approval of textbooks did not constitute censorship. Even if freedom of the press were limited, the court ruled, to the extent that the official approval was rational, it should be accepted as a restriction intended to serve the public welfare (16 July 1974, *Hanrei jihō,* 751). In December 1975 the Tōkyō High Court dismissed the Ministry of Education's appeal of the second suit. The Supreme Court, however, overturned this judgment and referred the case back for further review (8 April 1982; *Hanrei jihō,* 1040). SHIMIZU Hideo

Ie no hikari

(The Light of the Home). Monthly magazine designed especially for rural readers. Founded in 1925 by the Sangyō Kumiai Chūōkai, forerunner of Nōkyō (see AGRICULTURAL COOPERATIVE ASSOCIATIONS), for the purpose of popularizing the agricultural cooperative movement. Although in 1928 its circulation was only 20,000, the depression led to increased efforts to expand the agricultural cooperative movement throughout the country. As the movement expanded, so did the circulation of *Ie no hikari,* reaching 1 million in 1935. After World War II, a more popular format was introduced, aimed more toward the rural housewife and offering reading entertainment for the rural population in general. It now claims a larger circulation than any other Japanese magazine (1,250,000 in 1980). KAKEGAWA Tomiko

ienoko and rōtō

(warriors' vassals). The subordinate members of a warrior band (BUSHIDAN) in the middle part of the Heian period and the Kamakura period (i.e., 10th–14th centuries). *Ienoko,* literally "children of the house," were, as the name implies, blood kinsmen of the chief of the warrior band. Although the term was used before the Heian period (794–1185), it was only with the sudden rise of military houses at the end of the period that the close bonding of branch families to the main family became an important and widespread means of strengthening a family's position. *Ienoko* held their own estates *(honryō)* and managed their family affairs independently of the lineage chief *(sōryō),* but their actions were under his supervision. Family members without landed inheritance were called *kenin,* but in the Kamakura period (1185–1333) direct retainers of the shōgun were called GOKENIN, and their branch-family members were called *ienoko.*

Rōtō originally signified warriors with no blood ties to the band they joined, and compared to *ienoko* they came from relatively low-ranking *samurai* families. They held no land of their own but received their income from those who possessed estates or from other *rōtō.* Later the term was applied to all nonlineage members of a warrior band, even those who held land. Under the Kamakura shogunate the *rōtō* of the *gokenin* were considered the shōgun's vassals at one remove (BAISHIN) but not as members of the samurai class. Except during wartime they resided in rural areas.

With the rise in power of the main lineage chief and the decline of the practice of dividing estates among potential heirs, those kinsmen without inheritance were relegated to a subordinate position similar to that of *rōtō.* The distinctions between the two classes became blurred, and the two terms were eventually combined into one, *ienoko rōtō,* to designate all of a warrior's retainers. See also SŌRYŌ SYSTEM. *Philip* BROWN

Iesu no Mitama Kyōkai Kyōdan → Spirit of Jesus Church

Igakujo

A school of Western medicine initially founded in 1858 in the Kanda district of Edo (now Tōkyō) as a smallpox vaccination clinic by ITŌ GEMBOKU and other scholars of WESTERN LEARNING. The clinic was placed under the supervision of the Tokugawa shogunate in 1860, and after a reorganization of its activities under OGATA KŌAN, it was named the Igakujo (Medical School) in 1863. By 1865 the school's curriculum included chemistry, anatomy, physiology, pathology, pharmacology, internal medicine, and surgery. Taken over by the Meiji government in 1868, the Igakujo later became the medical school of Tōkyō University.

Igarashi Chikara (1874–1947)

Scholar of Japanese literature. Born in Yamagata Prefecture. Graduate of Tōkyō Semmon Gakkō (now Waseda University). Igarashi taught for many years at Waseda University, giving lectures on Japanese literature in the Heian period (794–1185) and on war chronicles (GUNKI MONOGATARI). He became one of the few pioneers in the study of rhetoric in Japan with *Bunshō kōwa* (1905) and subsequent works. *Asai* Kiyoshi

Iga ware

(*iga-yaki*). Ceramics made in Iga Province (now Mie Prefecture; near the city of Iga Ueno). Iga ware was most highly prized for TEA CEREMONY use, the height of production being in the later part of the Azuchi–Momoyama (1568–1600) and early part of the Edo (1600–1868) periods; the finest pieces were made between 1585 and 1608, and 1624 and 1643, with the best being produced between 1635 and 1638.

Up to the late 16th century, Iga ware had been crude and rustic, primarily for local domestic use; production then became associated with the tea master FURUTA ORIBE and was intended mainly for tea-ceremony use. The noted tea master KOBORI ENSHŪ recognized the merits of Iga ware and, under the authorization of the local rulers, Kyōto potters were invited in 1635 to participate in production at the Iga kilns. The pieces they produced are almost exclusively for tea-ceremony use, flower vases being considered the most excellent of their products. In the late 17th century production slowed down because of local political involvements, and by the late 18th century production stopped altogether. In 1937 Kikuyama Taneo resumed production, which continues today.

Iga ware is made from a mixture of two types of clay. The mixture is screened and fine stones are added. The finest pieces require up to 13 firings at temperatures of 1500°C (2732°F), with each firing requiring up to 30 hours to reach that temperature. The repeated firings bring the stones to the surface, one of the characteristics of the ware. The pine wood used to fire the kiln provides a natural ash glaze. Each piece is carefully placed in the kiln to produce the desired subtle color and to allow the proper amount of ash to settle on the surface for a rich glaze coating. In a kiln load of 300 pieces, only 5 to 10 might be considered perfect.

Iga ware shares many characteristics with SHIGARAKI WARE. In general, Iga pieces have fewer and smaller stones than Shigaraki, and the glazing is more transparent. Cracks or splits on the surface are desired, and the primitive appearance, with twisted and rugged shapes, more closely resembles a product of nature than of man. *Ellen F.* CARY

Igaya Chiharu (1931–)

Skier; the first Japanese to win a Winter Olympics medal. Born on one of the Kuril Islands. From the age of three he began receiving ski instruction from his father, an expert skier who moved his family several times to ensure the best training for his son. When Igaya was eleven he won the All-Japan Championship in the slalom. With the help of industrialist Cornelius Vander Starr he transferred from Rikkyō University to Dartmouth College in America, to take advantage of its skiing instruction. In the 1956 Winter Olympics held in Italy, Igaya won second place in the slalom behind Austria's Anton Sailer. *Takeda Fumio*

igo → go

Iha Fuyū (1876–1947)

Also known as Iba Fuyū. Linguist, ethnologist, and folklorist; founder of modern linguistic study of the Okinawan language. Also a pioneer in the study of Okinawan folklore and literature. Iha was born and raised in Naha, Okinawa. His interest in the linguistic study of Okinawan culture developed while he was attending the Third Higher School in Kyōto (1900–1903) and the linguistics department of Tōkyō University (1903–06). Upon his graduation, he returned to Okinawa, taught at the Okinawa Prefectural Normal College, and launched upon a career of frequent lectures and other research activities on Okinawa's cultural heritage. He also became known for his activities as a devoted Christian, prohibitionist, Esperantist, and advocate of the rights of the Okinawan people.

Upon the founding of the Okinawa Prefectural Library in 1909, he was appointed the first director and enthusiastically contributed to the establishment of a collection of more than 5,000 sources on Okinawan culture. In 1924 he resigned from the library directorship and moved to Tōkyō to devote the rest of his life to various research projects, including the textual study of *Omoro sōshi*, an anthology of poems (1531–1623?) of the Okinawan kingdom, the compilation of a dictionary of the Okinawan language, the collection of Okinawan folklore and drama, and a study of the vowel system of ancient Okinawan. His publications and lectures covered a wide range of archaeological, historical, linguistic, philosophical, ethnological, and literary topics concerning the Okinawan heritage. His significant works are collected in the 11-volume *Iha Fuyū zenshū* (Heibonsha, 1974–76). *Susumu Nagara*

Ihara Saikaku → Saikaku

Iha shell mound

Prehistoric site in Iha, in the city of Ishikawa, Okinawa Prefecture; contemporary with the Late Jōmon period (ca 2000 BC–ca 1000 BC) culture in Japan proper. A shell stratum about 60 centimeters (24 in) thick extends over an area of 150 square meters (1,614 sq ft) on a limestone fault slope. Excavated in 1920, it is one of the few Okinawan SHELL MOUNDS to have been investigated. The site yielded STONE TOOLS, shell and BONE ARTICLES, and deep, flat-bottomed pots with rim punctuate design. Although the pottery is related to the Late JŌMON POTTERY of Kyūshū, it exhibits a regional character of its own. See also OGIDŌ SHELL MOUND.

📖——Ōyama Kashiwa, *Ryūkyū Iha kaizuka hakkutsu hōkoku* (1922). *Abe Gihei*

Iida

City in southern Nagano Prefecture, central Honshū. Iida developed as a castle town in the Edo period (1600–1868). Mulberry trees are grown on the terraced slopes of the river Tenryūgawa for silkworm cultivation. Other products are pears, apples, kōri-dōfu (dried bean curd), and MIZUHIKI (paper strings used for decorations). In recent years an electronics and precision instruments industry has been set up. Tourist attractions include the flowering apple trees on the main street and boating on the Tenryūgawa. Pop: 78,515.

Iida Dakotsu (1885–1962)

HAIKU poet. Real name Iida Takeharu, also known as Sanro. Born in Yamanashi Prefecture. Graduate of Waseda University. Influ- enced by the naturalist literary movement (see NATURALISM) and one of the foremost disciples of TAKAHAMA KYOSHI, the leader of the Hototogisu school of traditional haiku, he contributed to HOTO- TOGISU magazine and became a member of the group in 1914. His haiku are characterized by forceful descriptions of nature. Collections of his works include *Sanroshū* (1932) and *Kodamashū* (1940, Echoes).

Iida Incident

(Iida Jiken). An unsuccessful plot by activists of the FREEDOM AND PEOPLE'S RIGHTS MOVEMENT to overthrow the government in 1884. In April 1884, members of Kōdō Kyōkai (Justice Society), a political society based in Nagoya, began to act in liaison with members of the Aikoku Seirisha (Patriotic Truth Society), a political society in Iida, Nagano Prefecture. Their avowed purpose was to awaken people to the necessity of parliamentary constitutional government, first through underground publications, and later, if necessary, by force. Muramatsu Aizō of the Kōdō Kyōkai engineered the conspiracy. He was a student of Russian and had made a careful study of the tactics employed by the Russian revolutionaries in the assassination of Alexander II. Muramatsu hoped to organize the peasant unrest caused by the deflationary policy of Finance Minister MATSUKATA MASAYOSHI into a general uprising against the central government. One member of the Kōdō Kyōkai even attempted to infiltrate the Imperial Army. In August the conspirators met in Tōkyō and sought the cooperation of the JIYŪTŌ, the political party headed by ITAGAKI TAISUKE, and asked UEKI EMORI to compose a manifesto outlining the crimes of the central government. Although the Jiyūtō refused to give its support, Muramatsu continued to plot the overthrow of the government by force. He secretly canvassed the rural areas for funds and supplies, smuggled in gunpowder and weapons, and organized local militia. Careful plans were made to burn the town of Iida, go on to Nagoya and destroy the army camp there, and then, gathering peasant support, to march on to Ōsaka. With these two cities under the control of the revolutionary forces, Muramatsu reasoned that peasants from throughout Japan would join their cause. In early November news of the CHICHIBU INCIDENT, a large-scale peasant revolt in Saitama Prefecture, also led by people's rights activists, convinced the conspirators that the time for action had arrived. Ueki's manifesto was secretly published, and the following slogans were appended: Reduce Taxes! Abolish the Conscription Law! Abolish the Revenue Stamp Law! Help the Poor! Detailed army regulations were also drawn up, but the plot was discovered by the police before it could get underway. The Revolution for Freedom (jiyū kakumei), as one of the rebel banners proclaimed it, had failed. In early December the leaders of the conspiracy were tracked down and imprisoned. *M. William Steele*

Iimoriyama

Hill in the northeastern part of the city of Aizu Wakamatsu, Fukushima Prefecture, northern Honshū. Famous as the burial place of the BYAKKOTAI (White Tiger Brigade), a group of youths who committed suicide after failing to defend Wakamatsu Castle against imperial troops in 1868 in the BOSHIN CIVIL WAR accompanying the Meiji Restoration. Their tombstones, 19 in all, stand on the hillside beside a monument erected in their memory. Height: 380 m (1,246 ft).

Ii Naomasa (1561–1602)

Warrior of the Azuchi–Momoyama period (1568–1600) and one of the chief vassals of TOKUGAWA IEYASU. Although the Ii family of Tōtōmi (now part of Shizuoka Prefecture) had served the IMAGAWA FAMILY for generations, Naomasa's father, Naochika, was killed in 1562 on suspicion of disloyalty, and the family's domain was confiscated. Naomasa, who escaped death at that time, came to serve Ieyasu in 1575. When Ieyasu was given extensive territory in the Kantō region by TOYOTOMI HIDEYOSHI in 1590, Naomasa was appointed lord of Minowa Castle in Kōzuke (now Gumma Prefecture), receiving a domain assessed at 120,000 koku (see KOKUDAKA). As a reward for his role in the Battle of SEKIGAHARA in 1600, he was also given a fief in Ōmi (now Shiga Prefecture) with an additional 60,000 koku, and this remained the seat of the Ii family until the end of the Edo period (1600–1868).

Ii Naosuke (1815–1860)

Fourteenth *daimyō* of the Hikone domain (assessed at 350,000 *koku;* see KOKUDAKA) who, as TAIRŌ (great elder) of the Tokugawa shogunate, was effectively the dictator of Japan for 23 months in 1858–60. During his rule Ii stemmed temporarily the erosion of shogunal primacy in Japan. However, he failed to initiate any vigorous policies that could protect the shogunate against Western encroachment from without and dissension within.

Youth —— Naosuke, the 14th son of the retired daimyō Naonaka, was born in Hikone (now part of Shiga Prefecture). Because he had so many elder brothers, his career prospects seemed bleak. Living on a modest stipend, he busied himself with the study of WAKA poetry, tea ceremony, painting, and Buddhism. He also attended to his *samurai* training duties, discussing military and civil matters with his retainers. In the course of his studies, he met the poet-scholar Nagano Shuzen (1815–62), who became a confidant, retainer, and close adviser in later years.

Before Naosuke's birth his eldest brother, Naooki (1796–1850), had succeeded their father, and as years passed his other elder brothers died or were adopted into other families. By 1846 it was apparent that Naooki would have no children of his own, and by then Naosuke was the only eligible brother left at Hikone. Consequently he was designated Naooki's heir and succeeded him four years later.

Emergence —— Initially Naosuke governed Hikone vigorously and constructively, but the arrival of Commodore PERRY's ships in 1853 diverted his attention from Hikone to national affairs. This was because the Hikone daimyō were traditionally expected to play a prominent, although passive, role in the shogunate during periods of difficulty with the sinecure title of *tairō,* which several of Naosuke's ancestors had held for short periods in the past.

Naosuke was not a passive man by nature, however, and he soon became embroiled in the heated discussions surrounding Perry's demands for a treaty. Naosuke argued that defiance would be suicidal and that a treaty must therefore be granted. In the course of the debate and the signing of the KANAGAWA TREATY in 1854, he and TOKUGAWA NARIAKI of the Mito domain (now part of Ibaraki Prefecture) clashed sharply and became bitter personal enemies. That bitterness was exacerbated in succeeding years, especially by the difficulties of 1857–58.

Two new issues—negotiation of a commercial treaty with the American consul Townsend HARRIS and selection of a successor for the ill and heirless shōgun Iesada (1824–58)—emerged simultaneously. Because the former issue was of immense importance not only to the shogunate but also to the nation as a whole, the daimyō were anxious to ensure a satisfactory outcome. The succession issue assumed great importance because the choice of shogunal successor was the key to shaping all future shogunate policy. The situation prompted several important daimyō, notably Nariaki of Mito, MATSUDAIRA YOSHINAGA of the Echizen or Fukui domain (now part of Fukui Prefecture), and SHIMAZU NARIAKIRA of the Satsuma domain (now Kagoshima Prefecture), to thrust themselves into national affairs in unprecedented ways. Their apparent attempt to seize control of the shogunate by having Nariaki's son TOKUGAWA YOSHINOBU designated heir to Iesada and their disruption of the regular procedures and principles of shogunal succession and governance dismayed many within the shogunate. Encouraged by Ii, these latter men gave their support to a rival candidate, TOKUGAWA IEMOCHI, the youthful daimyō of Wakayama and a grandson of the former shōgun Ienari. When early in 1858 the chief senior councillor *(rōjū shuseki)* HOTTA MASAYOSHI failed to secure either imperial approval of the draft treaty or imperial support for Iemochi, some shogunal officials and members of the shogunal household arranged Naosuke's appointment as *tairō* on 4 June 1858 (Ansei 5.4.23).

Naosuke as Tairō —— As *tairō,* Ii moved promptly to secure his control of the shogunate, shunting aside uncooperative officials and warning others to obey his instructions. He hoped at this point to secure daimyō support and subsequently imperial sanction for the treaty, which he would then have the shōgun formally approve. With that matter settled, he would then arrange to have Iemochi designated heir to Iesada.

Unfortunately for Ii's strategy, Harris, who was ignorant of the shogunate's situation, grew impatient with Edo's delays and threatened that a British armada would soon arrive and extort a more punitive treaty if his own draft were not accepted as a model for later negotiations. Reports of naval movements lent weight to Harris's warning, and Naosuke concluded that he must sign the treaty even without imperial approval. On 29 July 1858 (Ansei 5.6.19) his delegates signed the HARRIS TREATY.

A new burst of concerted opposition from the great daimyō and concurrent agitation involving politicized samurai only reinforced Ii's determination to settle the succession issue as well, and six days later he had Iemochi designated heir.

The immediate issues were thus settled, but Naosuke correctly saw the unprecedented political activism by the court, great daimyō, and samurai as a threat to the political order, and he resolved to stop it. During the rest of 1858 and well into 1859 he took decisive measures to discipline Nariaki, whom he and Nagano Shuzen incorrectly saw as the leader of the opposition. He also punished Yoshinobu, Yoshinaga, Nariakira, a few other daimyō, certain of their advisers, fractious members of the court, and a number of activist samurai. This policy of repression, known to history as the ANSEI PURGE, was to be brought to a decisive end by Ii's assassination in March 1860.

By the autumn of 1859, however, most signs of political disruption had subsided, and Naosuke felt encouraged to move to a policy of gradual reconciliation. He now planned to arrange a marriage between the new shōgun, Iemochi, and Princess KAZU, a sister of Emperor KŌMEI. During the winter negotiations progressed, and as spring approached it appeared that a new and more harmonious political period was dawning. (See also MOVEMENT FOR UNION OF COURT AND SHOGUNATE.)

In other matters of governance, Ii took the administrative steps necessary to implement the new commercial treaties, establishing new trade and port authorities and dispatching a mission to the United States on the ship KANRIN MARU to exchange ratifications of the Harris treaty. He showed little awareness, however, of the fundamental implications of the new foreign relationships to which he had committed Japan. He did not pursue policies of military reform or naval strengthening, nor did he attempt to modify the overall pattern of decentralization that had characterized the Tokugawa political system (see BAKUHAN SYSTEM).

The one area of domestic political difficulty that persistently clouded Naosuke's policy of reconciliation was Edo's relationship to Mito. His conviction that Nariaki was the source of his difficulties led him to pursue a policy of exceptional harshness toward that domain, punishing not only Nariaki but also many of his most ardent supporters in Mito. As a result, factional tension that had plagued Mito for over two decades reached unprecedented levels. Within days of Nariaki's incarceration in July 1858, large numbers of Mito retainers began to maneuver and agitate against Ii, against the shogunate, and against one another. As bitterness, fear, and overt military activity grew in Mito during 1859, Naosuke responded by increasing the pressure, at one critical juncture advocating the use of armed force to crush the Mito dissidents. An open collision was avoided, but finally a group of Mito men, supported by a few activists from elsewhere, determined to resolve the crisis by killing Ii. On the snowy morning of 24 March 1860 (Man'en 1.3.3) a band of men intercepted Ii on his way to Edo Castle and murdered him (see SAKURADAMONGAI INCIDENT).

After Ii's death, ANDŌ NOBUMASA assumed leadership of the shogunate in cooperation with KUZE HIROCHIKA. He continued the general policy of reconciliation and gradually extended it to embrace Mito. Andō, however, lacked Ii's resolve, and in succeeding months the shogunate lost the commitment to hegemonial leadership, however uncreative and inadequate, that Ii briefly had given it.

—— Edwin Lee, *The Political Career of Ii Naosuke* (1960). Yoshida Tsunekichi, *Ii Naosuke* (1963).　　　*Conrad* TOTMAN

Iinuma Yokusai (1782–1865)

Botanist and doctor of medicine who introduced modern European botany into *honzōgaku* (traditional pharmacognosy) studies in Japan. Born in Ise (now Mie Prefecture), he studied medicine and practiced in Mino (now Gifu Prefecture). He engaged in Dutch studies (Rangaku) under UDAGAWA YŌAN in Edo (now Tōkyō) and studied honzōgaku under ONO RANZAN and Mizutani Toyobumi. His *Sōmoku zusetsu* (1856, Plant Atlas) is in 20 volumes and contains 1,215 species of herbs arranged in the Linnaean system of plant classification rather than in the traditional system.　　　*Suzuki* Zenji

Iiyama

City in northeastern Nagano Prefecture, central Honshū, on the river Chikumagawa. A castle town since the construction of a castle by

UESUGI KENSHIN in 1564, Iiyama has long been the commercial center of northern Nagano. Local products are rice, skis, Buddhist altars, and Japanese paper *(washi)*. There is a fast-growing electronics industry. Heavy snows make it a popular skiing area. SHIMAZAKI TŌSON's novel *Hakai* (1906; tr *The Broken Commandment*, 1974) was set in Iiyama. Pop: 30,073.

Ii Yōhō (1871–1932)

Actor. Born in Tōkyō; real name Ii Shinzaburō. His father was a photographer known as Kitaniwa Tsukuba. At one time Ii worked at a bank, but after developing an interest in drama, he joined in 1891 the KAWAKAMI OTOJIRŌ troupe, popular for its social satire plays. Ii soon tired of Kawakami's arrogance, calling him a "politician's parasite," and decided to concern himself wholly with the creation of art-for-art's sake realistic drama. In 1895 he founded the Isami Engeki drama troupe, whose wide repertoire ranged from CHIKAMATSU MONZAEMON to Shakespeare. He created stage productions of such works as *Futari Urashima* by MORI ŌGAI, *Hakai* by SHIMAZAKI TŌSON, and *Wagahai wa neko de aru* by NATSUME SŌSEKI. Around 1915, Ii, KITAMURA ROKURŌ, and Kawai Takeo, who had joined forces some 10 years earlier, came to be called "the SHIMPA (new school) three." He also starred in MAKINO SHŌZŌ's film *Jitsuroku chūshingura* (1928). *ITASAKA Tsuyoshi*

Iizaka Hot Spring

(Iizaka Onsen). Located in the city of Fukushima, northern Fukushima Prefecture, northern Honshū. A simple thermal spring; water temperature 40–70°C (104–158°F). Situated along the river Surikamigawa, it is one of the most famous spas in the Tōhoku region. A popular tourist area, there are approximately 120 inns in the vicinity.

Iizawa Tadasu (1909–)

Playwright. Born Izawa Tadasu in Wakayama Prefecture. Son of Izawa Takio (1869–1949), a prominent bureaucrat-politician, and nephew of the educator IZAWA SHŪJI. Following graduation from Bunka Gakuin in 1933, he worked as an editor for the *Asahi shimbun*. Until leaving the newspaper in 1954, he served as editor-in-chief of such magazines as *Fujin asahi* and *Asahi gurafu*. Iizawa began writing plays in the 1930s, and was recognized early on for his humorous works that drew heavily on the comic KYŌGEN tradition. During World War II he wrote several plays that criticized government repression and expressed his pacifist sentiments. He received the first Kishida Prize for Drama in 1950 with *Nigō* (Number Two) and continued to produce plays in which he displayed his keen wit and penchant for satire. Throughout the 1960s his radio and television dramas for children were extremely popular. His best-known stage play is *Mō hitori no hito* (1970, The Other Person), a satire on Japanese leadership during the war.

Iizuka

City in central Fukuoka Prefecture, Kyūshū, on the river Ongagawa. The city developed as a POST-STATION TOWN along the highway Nagasaki Kaidō during the Edo period (1600–1868). It was a prosperous coal-mining center from 1882, but recent closure of many mines has resulted in a population decrease. Several machinery, food-processing, and electrical appliance plants have been established. There is a Self Defense Force base here. Pop: 80,288.

Iizuka Kōji (1906–1970)

Geographer and critic. Born in Tōkyō, Iizuka graduated in 1930 from Tōkyō University, where he majored in economics. He also studied geography at the Sorbonne from 1932 to 1934. He later translated Paul Vidal de La Blache's *Principes de la géographie humaine* (Principles of Human Geography) into Japanese (1940). His own works, which exerted considerable influence in geographical circles in Japan, include *Chirigaku no hihan* (1947, Criticism of Geography) and *Sekai to Nihon* (1955, The World and Japan). Iizuka taught at Rikkyō University in Tōkyō and served as head of the INSTITUTE OF ORIENTAL CULTURE at Tōkyō University. He was known for his theories on the comparative study of cultures, his criticism of histories that centered on the West, and his advocacy of the historical significance of the Third World. *NISHIKAWA Osamu*

Ijūin family

Provincial leaders in southern Kyūshū from the 13th century. The family was descended from Shimazu Tadatsune, who renamed his branch of the SHIMAZU FAMILY after the Ijūin estate in Satsuma Province (now part of Kagoshima Prefecture) of which he was appointed land steward (JITŌ). In the 1340s the Ijūin opposed the main line of the Shimazu family by siding with Prince KANENAGA in the skirmishes that followed the KEMMU RESTORATION. From the 16th century through the Edo period (1600–1868), the Ijūin served as retainers of the Shimazu. Ruins of the family's Uji Castle can still be found west of the present-day city of Ijūin.

ika → squid and cuttlefish

Ikaho

Town in central Gumma Prefecture, central Honshū. Situated on the eastern slope of Mt. Haruna (Harunasan), Ikaho is chiefly known as a health resort, with hot springs. The fields of wildflowers on Harunasan from June through September and nearby Lake Haruna also attract tourists. Pop: 5,016.

ikai → court ranks

Ikaruga

Town in northern Nara Prefecture, central Honshū. Its principal products are textiles, metal goods, rice, and fruits. It is the site of Ikaruga no Miya, the residence of Prince SHŌTOKU, political and cultural leader of the 7th century, and numerous temples associated with the prince, such as HŌRYŪJI, CHŪGŪJI, Hokkiji, and Hōrinji. Pop: 25,751.

Ikaruga no Miya

Palace at IKARUGA built by Prince SHŌTOKU in 601, according to the chronicle NIHON SHOKI. Remains of what has been identified as the palace were found in 1934, when buildings in the east precinct of the temple HŌRYŪJI in Nara Prefecture were undergoing reconstruction. After Shōtoku's death the palace was passed on to his son, Prince YAMASHIRO NO ŌE. The destruction of the palace in 643 by SOGA NO IRUKA and the suicide of Yamashiro no Ōe at the time signaled the end of the princely family. In 739 the priest Gyōshin (d 750) built on the site of the palace what is now the Eastern Precinct of the temple HŌRYŪJI. *KITAMURA Bunji*

ikebana → flower arrangement

Ikebe Sanzan (1864–1912)

Meiji-period journalist. Real name Ikebe Kichitarō. Born in the city of Kumamoto in Kyūshū, he studied at Keiō Gijuku (now Keiō University) in Tōkyō. In 1890 he worked as a guest journalist for the *Nihon*, one of the representative newspapers of the day. In 1892 he went to Paris, where he wrote for the newspaper a series of articles on the political situation in Europe entitled *Pari tsūshin* (News from Paris), under the pen name Tekkonron. Returning to Japan, he served in 1896 as editor of the newspaper *Ōsaka asahi shimbun*; the following year he became the chief editor of the *Tōkyō asahi shimbun* (see ASAHI SHIMBUN). Until his retirement in 1911, Ikebe steered the *Asahi* on an even course and contributed greatly to its growth as a first-class forum of public opinion. It was Ikebe who introduced the serialized newspaper novel (SHIMBUN SHŌSETSU) to the *Asahi*, providing such well-known writers as FUTABATEI SHIMEI and NATSUME SŌSEKI with a publishing outlet. He also did much to expand the paper's coverage of cultural events. Notable among his own publications is *Meiji ishin sandai seijika* (1912). *KŌUCHI Saburō*

Ikeda

City in northwestern Ōsaka Prefecture, central Honshū, 18 km (11 mi) northwest of Ōsaka. It is said that the art of weaving was first introduced to Japan by Chinese immigrants (KIKAJIN) who settled here in the 4th century. The city prospered as a market town for charcoal in premodern times; its *sake* brewing still flourishes. Ikeda is known for its plants and flower nurseries, but because of its proximity to Ōsaka, much of its farmland is being converted into residential land. Several automobile and photographic equipment plants are located here. Ōsaka International Airport occupies the southern fringe of the city. Pop: 101,116.

Ikeda

Town in northwestern Tokushima Prefecture, Shikoku, on the river Yoshinogawa. Ikeda is the focal point of routes leading to all four prefectures on the island. Its climate is particularly suited to tobacco, and the Japan Tobacco and Salt Public Corporation has a plant here. Many people come to see the nearby gorges IYADANI and ŌBOKE. Pop: 21,291.

Ikeda Daisaku (1928–)

Religious leader. Third president of the SŌKA GAKKAI, one of the NEW RELIGIONS. He contributed to bringing the Sōka Gakkai into the national political arena by creating a Sōka Gakkai-related political party, the KŌMEITŌ, in 1964. (In the 1967 general election 25 Kōmeitō candidates were elected to the Diet.) In 1970 he adopted a policy of separation of politics and religion, and then turned his attention to scholarship, international communications, and world peace. Ikeda was elected president of Sōka Gakkai International in 1975 and retired as president of Sōka Gakkai in 1979.

Ikeda Hayato (1899–1965)

Prime minister from July 1960 to November 1964, Ikeda presided over a rapidly expanding economy, marked by his plan to double national income in 10 years and by the staging of the 18th Olympiad in Tōkyō (1964).

Ikeda was born in 1899 in Hiroshima Prefecture. Upon graduation from Kyōto University in 1925, he joined the Finance Ministry and served in a number of prefectural tax offices. In 1932 he contracted a skin disease that interrupted his career for five years. However, by missing promotion, he did not rise high enough to be among those purged by the Allied OCCUPATION after World War II.

In 1947 he was named vice-minister of finance by Prime Minister YOSHIDA SHIGERU. In January 1949 he was elected to the House of Representatives as a member of the Democratic Liberal Party (Minshu Jiyūtō) and a month later was appointed minister of finance in the third Yoshida cabinet. In October 1952 he was named minister of international trade and industry in Yoshida's fourth cabinet. A month later he was forced to resign after being censured for saying, during a speech on antiinflationary measures, that the government was not at fault if small businessmen went bankrupt and committed suicide. Ikeda visited Washington in October 1953 as Yoshida's representative. In his talks with Walter S. Robertson, assistant secretary of state, Ikeda recognized the necessity of increasing Japan's Self Defense Forces in order to protect Japan from possible aggression and to reduce the US burden related to the defense of Japan (see also IKEDA-ROBERTSON TALKS). Ikeda returned to the international trade and industry portfolio in KISHI NOBUSUKE's second cabinet (1959). On Kishi's resignation Ikeda became his successor.

As prime minister, Ikeda set the tone for Japan's growth-oriented economy of the 1960s. His policies called for expansion of public expenditures, reduction of taxes, and a low rate of interest, all of which were geared to maximize Japan's potential for growth. He actively sought reduction of trade barriers against Japanese products overseas but in other matters assumed a low posture in domestic and foreign policies. During Ikeda's tenure in office, Japan became a member of the Organization for Economic Cooperation and Development (1964). In 1964 Ikeda fell ill with terminal cancer and named SATŌ EISAKU as his successor.　　　　　　　　　　*David J. Lu*

Ikeda–Kennedy Agreements

Three agreements for cooperation between the United States and Japan reached by Prime Minister IKEDA HAYATO and President John F. Kennedy during their Washington meetings and announced on 22 June 1961. The two leaders also reviewed the international situation and bilateral relations between the two countries. Separate agreements established three bilateral committees: a United States–Japan Joint Committee of Trade and Economic Affairs, consisting of five cabinet officers from each government; a committee to expand edu-

cational and cultural cooperation; and a United States–Japan Joint Scientific Committee to increase scientific cooperation. The Committee of Trade and Economic Affairs held nine meetings in which senior officials consulted on key economic issues; other forms of economic consultation proved more effective, however, and the committee has not met since 1973. The committee on educational and cultural cooperation, known as CULCON, and the committee on scientific matters have both proved extremely active and effective, involving many persons and meetings each year, including a number of subcommittees and affiliated groups.

■——US, Department of State, *Bulletin,* 10 July 1961.

　　　　　　　　　　Richard B. Finn

Ikeda Kikunae (1864–1936)

Chemist prominent in the development of physical chemistry in Japan in the early 1900s. He also extracted monosodium glutamate (MSG) from *kombu* (kelp); MSG was later developed into a commercial seasoning product known as *ajinomoto* (see AJINOMOTO CO, INC). Ikeda proposed a set of theories on liquid solvent and osmotic pressure. Born in Kyōto, he graduated from Tōkyō University, where he became a full professor in 1901 and professor emeritus in 1923. He played a major role in the establishment of the INSTITUTE OF PHYSICAL AND CHEMICAL RESEARCH and became the first director of its chemistry department.

Ikeda, Lake

(Ikedako). Caldera lake in the southwestern Satsuma Peninsula, southwestern Kagoshima Prefecture, Kyūshū. The largest freshwater lake in Kyūshū, it is also a popular tourist attraction. Its water is used for irrigation and for drinking. Area: 11 sq km (4 sq mi); circumference: 15 km (9 mi); depth: 233 m (764 ft).

Ikeda Mitsumasa (1609–1682)

Daimyō of the early part of the Edo period (1600–1868) renowned for his authoritarian but enlightened rule. Mitsumasa inherited a domain assessed at 420,000 *koku* (see KOKUDAKA) at Himeji in Harima Province (now part of Hyōgo Prefecture) upon the death of his father, Toshitaka (1584–1616), but the next year he was transferred by the Tokugawa shogunate to a 320,000-*koku* domain covering most of Hōki and Inaba provinces (now Tottori Prefecture). In 1632 he was again transferred to Okayama, a 315,000-*koku* domain comprising Bizen and a portion of Bitchū (now parts of Okayama Prefecture), where he became known as a model administrator. Mitsumasa's policies were marked by the effort to institute centralized bureaucratic controls over his vassals and populace; his reputation rests on his use of Confucian principles as a rationale for government and his employ of Confucian scholars, such as KUMAZAWA BANZAN, as political advisers. A convinced Confucian, Mitsumasa repressed Buddhism, closing 54 percent of that religion's temples and purging 43 percent of its priests in his domain; instead of compelling people to register at Buddhist temples (see TERAUKE), a device commonly used to stamp out Christianity, he instituted in 1666 the novel system of registration in Shintō shrines (*shinshoku-uke*). A more positive reflection of Mitsumasa's active Confucianism was his extensive educational enterprise. In 1641 he founded the Hanabatake Kyōjō, often called the first domain school (*hankō*) in Japan, which was in 1666 replaced by a new college for *samurai*, Karigakkan, that drew students also from other regions; in 1668 he embarked on an elaborate scheme to establish 123 elementary schools (*tenaraijo*) "for peasant youths" throughout his domain. Upon Mitsumasa's retirement in 1672, this progressive but costly scheme was abandoned by his successor, Tsunamasa (1638–1714); only one of the domain-sponsored institutions of popular education planned by Mitsumasa, the famous Shizutani Gakkō, survived throughout the Edo period.　　　　　　　*George Elison*

Ikeda Nagaoki (1837–1879)

Retainer of the Tokugawa shogunate (1603–1867); also known as Ikeda Chōhatsu and Ikeda Naganobu. Born in Edo (now Tōkyō), Ikeda rose swiftly in the bureaucratic ranks and in 1863 was appointed city commissioner (*machi bugyō*) of Kyōto. Later the same year he was selected to head a shogunate mission to France to negotiate the closing of the port of Yokohama (the port had been opened in place of nearby Kanagawa in 1859 under the provisions of the

ANSEI COMMERCIAL TREATIES of 1858); the mission was unsuccessful (see SHOGUNATE MISSIONS TO THE WEST). Upon his return to Japan, he made a recommendation to the shogunate to hasten the opening of the country; for this view he was dismissed from his position as commissioner of foreign affairs (gaikoku bugyō). In 1867 he was reinstated as a naval commissioner (gunkan bugyō), but he soon retired to Okayama, pleading illness.

Ikeda-Robertson Talks

Discussions between the United States and Japan in October 1953 regarding US military assistance and increase of Japan's defense forces. A joint statement was issued 30 October 1953 by IKEDA HAYATO, personal representative of Prime Minister YOSHIDA SHIGERU of Japan, and Walter S. Robertson, assistant secretary of state for Far Eastern affairs, who had been meeting in Washington for several weeks. Their statement reported agreement that Japan should increase its self-defense forces, although the statement noted Japan's constitutional and financial limitations, and that the United States should assist Japan by supplying major items of military equipment. The United States agreed to supply Japan with agricultural commodities worth $50 million under the US Mutual Security Act, and Japan agreed to use the proceeds from the sale of these commodities to promote the development of its defense production and industrial potential. It was also agreed that Japan's contribution to the support of US forces in Japan might be reduced from time to time and that the US forces would be reduced as Japan's forces increased their capability. These discussions led to the conclusion of the UNITED STATES–JAPAN MUTUAL DEFENSE ASSISTANCE AGREEMENT on 8 March 1954.

■——US, Department of State, Bulletin, 9 November 1953.

Richard B. FINN

Ikeda Shigeaki (1867–1950)

Businessman and politician; also called Ikeda Seihin. Born into a samurai family of the Yonezawa domain (now part of Yamagata Prefecture). A graduate of Keiō Gijuku (now Keiō University), Ikeda went to the United States to study at Harvard College, from which he received a BA degree in 1895. Upon returning to Japan, he entered the MITSUI BANK, LTD. His talents were soon recognized by the head of the bank, NAKAMIGAWA HIKOJIRŌ, whose daughter he later married. By 1909 Ikeda had become managing director, a position he held until 1933. In that year he succeeded DAN TAKUMA, who had been assassinated by an ultranationalist the previous year, as managing director of the Mitsui holding company, the Mitsui Gōmei Kaisha. As the top Mitsui executive, Ikeda set out to rationalize the combine and to improve its public image, removing Mitsui family members from managerial positions, introducing compulsory retirement for executives, making donations to charitable works, and putting Mitsui-owned stock on sale to the public. He retired from Mitsui in 1936. The following year, as part of the military's effort to secure business cooperation in implementing its plans for economic development, Ikeda was appointed governor of the Bank of Japan. As finance minister and minister of commerce and industry in the first KONOE FUMIMARO cabinet (1937–39), he exerted great influence on policy and worked to restrain the military and to limit economic controls placed on the business community. He was appointed to the Privy Council in 1941. After World War II Ikeda was barred from public office under the OCCUPATION PURGE.

Ikeda Terumasa (1564–1613)

Daimyō of the Azuchi–Momoyama period (1568–1600). With his father, Terumasa served ODA NOBUNAGA and TOYOTOMI HIDEYOSHI. When his father and brother died in the KOMAKI NAGAKUTE CAMPAIGN (1584), Terumasa became the lord of Ōgaki Castle in Mino (now part of Gifu Prefecture). In 1590 he was moved to Yoshida Castle in Mikawa (now part of Aichi Prefecture) with a domain assessed at 152,000 koku (see KOKUDAKA) for his distinguished service to Hideyoshi. He supported TOKUGAWA IEYASU in the Battle of SEKIGAHARA in 1600 and was given the domain of Harima (now part of Hyōgo Prefecture), assessed at 520,000 koku. He extensively renovated HIMEJI CASTLE, which still stands.

Ikedaya Incident

(Ikedaya Jiken). Armed encounter in July 1864 between antishogunate proimperial samurai and a special police force of the shogun-

ate, the SHINSENGUMI, at the Ikedaya Inn, located in the outskirts of Kyōto. After the COUP D'ETAT OF 30 SEPTEMBER 1863, in which extremists from the Chōshū domain (now Yamaguchi Prefecture) were expelled from Kyōto, moderate forces from the Satsuma (now Kagoshima Prefecture) and Aizu (now part of Fukushima Prefecture) domains who advocated reconciliation between the court and the shogunate dominated Kyōto politics. A number of pro-Chōshū loyalists sought to regain control of Kyōto and plotted the assassinations of Tokugawa leaders and proshogunate court nobles. On the night of 8 July (Genji 1.6.5) the Shinsengumi, led by KONDŌ ISAMI, attacked a gathering of these activists at the Ikedaya Inn. Eight were killed and 4 seriously wounded. Over 20 antishogunate activists were arrested, many of them from Chōshū. News of this encounter was an important factor in Chōshū's decision to attempt to retake Kyōto by military force (see HAMAGURI GOMON INCIDENT). See also MEIJI RESTORATION.

Ikegai Shōtarō (1869–1934)

Inventor and industrial pioneer. Born in Tōkyō. After working as an apprentice in a machine tool shop, in 1889 he established Ikegai Tekkōsho, the first facility in Japan to manufacture industrial lathes. His designs for the Ikegai-type semidiesel engine and numerous other inventions contributed to the modernization of numerous Japanese industries.

Ikejima Shimpei (1909–1973)

Editor and president of BUNGEI SHUNJŪ, LTD, one of Japan's major publishing houses. Born in Tōkyō. He entered the company after graduating from Tōkyō University in 1933 and quickly proved himself a skilled interviewer in informal discussions. Appointed chief editor of Bungei shunjū, the firm's leading magazine in 1956, he increased its circulation to 1 million. He was president of the firm from 1966 until his death in 1973. A mild conservative, to the end he remained a constructive critic of political extremes.

ARASE Yutaka

Ikenishi Gonsui (1650–1722)

Haikai (prototype of HAIKU) poet. Born in Nara. He lived in Edo (now Tōkyō) for seven or eight years and traveled extensively in the country before settling in Kyōto in 1684. Like BASHŌ, he turned away from the use of haikai as mere rhetorical wordplay and sought to raise the poetic form into a serious mode of artistic expression. Noted for the sensuous grace of his haikai, his main collections are Edo shimmichi (1678, New Streets in Edo) and Miyakoburi (1690, Tunes from the Capital).

Ike no Gyokuran (1728?–1784)

Also known as Tokuyama Gyokuran. Real name Ike no Machi. BUNJINGA (literati painting) artist and WAKA poet. Her grandmother, Kaji, and her mother, Yuri, were well-known waka poets who operated a teahouse, which Gyokuran inherited, in the Gion district of Kyōto. Gyokuran grew up in the Kyōto demimonde society, and contemporary accounts credit her with a highly individual and somewhat eccentric character. She studied under the literati painter YANAGISAWA KIEN and married the literati master IKE NO TAIGA. The couple led a rather unconventional life. Her painting style closely resembles that of her husband. Her fan paintings are her finest works, and some of them achieve an excellence rivaling that of Taiga.

■——Matsushita Hidemaro, Ike no Taiga (1967).

Melinda TAKEUCHI

Ikeno Seiichirō (1866–1943)

Botanist. Born in Edo (now Tōkyō). A graduate of Tōkyō University, he later taught there. He proved the presence of motile spermatozoa in some gymnosperms while working with HIRASE SAKUGORŌ in 1896. Ikeno used the Japanese sago palm (sotetsu; Cycas revoluta) in making the discovery and Hirase used the gingko (ichō). This discovery greatly influenced botanical studies. Ikeno later became interested in genetics, analyzing the genes of rice and other plants. He wrote Zikken idengaku (Jikken idengaku; 1913) in Japanese, using the Roman alphabet.

SUZUKI Zenji

Ike no Taiga

A detail from one panel of *Chinese Gentlemen in a Mountain Retreat*. Covering four panels of a sliding door, this Chinese-inspired landscape is one of several Taiga painted for the temple Henjōkōin. Colors on paper. Each panel 167.2 × 91.8 cm. Ca 1760. Henjōkōin, Wakayama Prefecture. National Treasure.

Ike no Taiga (1723–1776)

Artist and calligrapher in the BUNJINGA (literati painting) tradition. He was born in the Kyōto area, where his father worked in the silver mint. From an early age Taiga showed extraordinary talent; at six he was taken to the Ōbaku Zen temple MAMPUKUJI in Uji, an important repository of Chinese art and culture, where he gave a calligraphy demonstration that won him praise and prizes. This marked the beginning of Taiga's lifelong friendships with various Mampukuji monks. Around 1738 Taiga met YANAGISAWA KIEN, one of the pioneers of Japanese *bunjin* painting, who became his teacher and benefactor. It is from Kien that Taiga learned the technique of painting with fingernails in lieu of a brush, and it was through him that in 1751 Taiga met GION NANKAI, also prominent in the early *bunjinga* movement, from whom he received a Chinese woodblock-print style manual. Under the tutelage of these men Taiga deepened his understanding of Chinese literati painting. He was also influenced by the techniques of SŌTATSU and KŌRIN, by Zen painting (ZENGA), and by Western painting. His understanding of Chinese literati and nonliterati painting was further advanced by contact with the paintings of Yi Fujiu (I Fu-chiu; J: I Fukyū; early 18th century), a merchant and amateur artist who came several times to Nagasaki with trade missions.

Inscriptions on Taiga's paintings point to connections with a host of important Confucian scholars. Foremost among them were Kō Fuyō (1722–84), a renowned seal engraver, and Kan Tenju (1727–95), a dedicated student of Chinese calligraphy, both of whom accompanied Taiga in 1760 on a journey through Japanese mountain regions. His close observation of nature is apparent in his landscapes. Taiga was noted for his eccentric behavior, of which anecdotes abound in contemporary records. Taiga's wife, IKE NO GYOKURAN, became a creditable *bunjinga* painter in her own right.

In all, some 2,000 existing paintings have been attributed to Taiga. The majority are landscapes, although he also painted figures of the "four gentlemen" (SHIKUNSHI: orchid, bamboo, plum, and chrysanthemum). His most noteworthy landscapes are those with Chinese themes, as well as views of Japanese scenes, a genre inspired by his extensive travels and which developed into a popular subject for later Edo period (1600–1868) painters. His painting techniques varied greatly, from monochrome ink applied with a few informal brushstrokes to elaborate compositions with vivid colors and fine detail, some utilizing vigorous, short brushstrokes that pro-

duced a rich, scintillating surface texture. In addition to the usual hanging scroll format, he also executed a large number of folding screens and small albums and fans.

Taiga's reputation as a calligrapher is predicated on the same mastery of the brush and originality that characterize his painting. He was one of the earlier Edo-period calligraphers to make extensive use of archaic Chinese script styles, which are employed in the two earliest of his surviving paintings. At one extreme is his standard script, marked by elongated, elegant characters; short, neat lines; and much open space within and around the characters; at the other is his powerful, cursive script.

Taiga fell ill and died on 30 May 1776 at the age of 53, leaving a large number of pupils and followers who continued the artistic tradition he had developed. It was Taiga's accomplishment to establish a uniquely Japanese *bunjinga* style, influenced by, but distinct from, Chinese *bunjinga*.

———James Cahill, *Scholar-Painters of Japan: The Nanga School* (1972). *Ike no Taiga sakuhin shū*, 2 vols (1960). Suzuki Susumu, "Ike Taiga: Painter of Nanga," *Japan Quarterly* (July–September 1959). Yonezawa Yoshiho and Yoshizawa Chū, *Japanese Painting in the Literati Style* (1974).   Melinda TAKEUCHI

Ike no Zenni (fl mid-12th century)

Wife of the warrior TAIRA NO TADAMORI and stepmother of TAIRA NO KIYOMORI, leader of the Taira family at the height of its power. After the HEIJI DISTURBANCE of 1160, Kiyomori ordered the execution of MINAMOTO NO YORITOMO, 13-year-old son and heir of his defeated rival MINAMOTO NO YOSHITOMO, but Ike no Zenni persuaded Kiyomori to commute the sentence to exile. Twenty years later Yoritomo rallied the Minamoto against the Taira in the TAIRA–MINAMOTO WAR (1180–85), which ended with the downfall of the Taira family and Yoritomo's rise to supreme power. The 13th-to 14th-century chronicle AZUMA KAGAMI states that Yoritomo restored 34 confiscated estates to Ike no Zenni's son Taira no Yorimori (1131–86) out of gratitude for her intercession.   Barbara L. ARNN

Iki

Island in the Genkai Sea, 20 km (12 mi) northwest of Saga Prefecture, northwestern Kyūshū. It is administratively a part of Nagasaki Prefecture. Composed principally of basalt; the highest point is the volcano Dakenotsuji (213 m; 699 ft). It was a vital point in transportation between Japan and the Asian continent in ancient times. Farming is the chief activity; crops are sweet potatoes, soybeans, and tobacco. Other activities include cattle raising, offshore fishing, and pearl culture. Part of the Iki–Tsushima Quasi-National Park. Area: 134 sq km (51.7 sq mi).

iki and sui

Aesthetic and moral ideals of urban commoners in the Edo period (1600–1868). The concept of *sui* was cultivated initially in the Ōsaka area during the late 17th century, while *iki* prevailed mostly in Edo (now Tōkyō) during the early 19th century. Aesthetically both pointed toward an urbane, chic, bourgeois type of beauty with undertones of sensuality. Morally they envisioned the tasteful life of a person who was wealthy but not attached to money, who enjoyed sensual pleasure but was never carried away by carnal desires, and who knew all the intricacies of earthly life but was capable of disengaging himself from them. In their insistence on sympathetic understanding of human feelings, *sui* and *iki* resembled the Heian courtiers' ideal of *aware* (see MONO NO AWARE), yet they differed from it in their inclusion of the more plebeian aspects of life. They are well reflected in the popular literature of the period.

Sui——The origin of the word *sui* is not clear. In modern Japanese it is usually written with a Chinese character meaning "pure essence" (Ch: *cui* or *ts'ui*), but other characters, like "sour" (*suan*), "to infer" (*tui* or *t'ui*), "water" (*shui*), and "leader" (*shuai*), were also used for transcribing the word. *Sui* comprised all these meanings: it described the language and deportment of a person who fully knew the sour taste of this life, was able to infer other people's suffering, adapt himself to various human situations with the shapelessness of water, and become a leader in taste and fashion for his contemporaries. Typically he was a person of the merchant class in Ōsaka or Kyōto, over 40, and financially well off. He had spent his prime years in pursuit of wealth; having attained it, he now sought out all the pleasures on this earth, especially in the licensed pleasure quarters. An expert in two of the greatest human passions (wealth and sexual gratification), he represented the "pure essence" of the man of the world. *Sui* is frequently manifest in the characters of the genre of fiction called UKIYO-ZŌSHI, particularly in those of Ihara SAIKAKU (1642–93). His masterpiece, *Kōshoku ichidai otoko* (1682; tr *The Life of an Amorous Man*, 1964), can be read as a novel describing a man's progress from ignorance to knowledge in terms of *sui*.

Iki——*Iki* originally denoted "spirit" or "heart." Later it came to mean "high spirit" or "high heart" and referred also to the way in which a high-spirited person talked, behaved, or dressed. As it became expressive of the Edo commoners' ideal, its connotations were affected by the Ōsaka concept of *sui* and moved closer to the latter. Indeed, *iki* was sometimes used as an equivalent of *sui*. Yet normally it carried a slightly different shade of meaning. As an aesthetic concept, *iki* leaned toward a beauty somewhat less colorful than *sui*. Many men of *iki* liked such colors as gray, dark brown, and navy blue, showing a distaste for bright colors and multicolored designs. Also, *iki* seems to have had a slightly more sensual and coquettish connotation than *sui*. It was often applied to the description of a woman, especially a professional entertainer who knew exactly how much display of eroticism was desirable by the highest standard of taste. Compared with a woman of *sui*, a lady with plenty of *iki* in her heart seems to have been more high-spirited—almost manly—in her conduct, always willing to make sacrifices for the man she loved. On the other hand, her behavior sometimes indicated resignation, and consequently a sense of sadness and loneliness emerged. *Iki* had its best literary expression in works of the NINJŌBON genre. *Shunshoku umegoyomi* by TAMENAGA SHUNSUI (b 1789) presents especially fine examples of people who conduct themselves in accordance with the ideal of *iki*. Some of the types of popular song of the late Edo period, such as *hauta*, KIYOMOTO-BUSHI, and *shinnai*, are also permeated with *iki*. In drama, *kabuki* plays by MOKUAMI (1816–93) often include characters embodying this ideal.

📖——Hisamatsu Sen'ichi, *The Vocabulary of Japanese Literary Aesthetics* (1963). Kuki Shūzō, *"Iki" no kōzō* (1930).

Makoto UEDA

ikigai

(that for which life is worth living; from *iki*, "living" and *kai*, "value, effectiveness, meaning"). A popular phrase often used in discussions of individual life goals and a frequent subject of public opinion surveys in Japan. A Japanese mother will often say that her children are her only *ikigai*, or a man will find his *ikigai* in his job. Individuals may commit suicide when they no longer have an *ikigai*. Since the early 1960s this word has become a focal point for public concern. With Japan's defeat in World War II, many old values and beliefs were smashed. The economy was completely destroyed, but as Japan recovered and became more affluent, the Japanese people began to question their purpose in life. Many people found their *ikigai* in material comforts and a happy family life, no doubt in reaction to the traditional stress upon frugality, hard work, and selfless dedication to collective causes. The phrase *mai hōmu shugi* ("my home-ism") became popular in the 1960s. A number of opinion surveys on *ikigai* seem to confirm this new attitude; among men and women a happy home and children consistently rank the highest, while service to society ranks very low, if not lowest. This is particularly notable among women, while men tend to be divided between work and home. Cross-generational research has shown that work (or study) ranks highest as *ikigai* for men until they reach their 40s, when they split into two groups: for one group, work continues to be the most important, while for another, the home becomes more important than work.

📖——Mita Munesuke, *Gendai no ikigai: Kawaru nihonjin no jinseikan* (1970). Nihon Chiiki Kaihatsu Sentā, ed, *Nihonjin no kachikan* (1971).

Hiroshi WAGATSUMA

ikigami

(living human deity). Individuals revered as a deity (KAMI) while still living. Representing this class of deity were the emperors, who were called *akitsukami* or *arahitogami* (living deity) until 1946, when the status, which had been supported by the STATE SHINTŌ (Kokka Shintō) system, was renounced by the emperor himself. Generally the Japanese would deify individuals with extraordinary charisma

after their death until the Edo period (1600–1868), when the concept was applied to the living too. Some recent charismatic leaders of religious movements, such as Nakayama Miki and Kitamura Sayo, were declared to be *ikigami*. The Buddhist counterpart of this concept is *ikibotoke*, i.e., living Buddha.

Stuart D. B. PICKEN

Iki no Muraji Hakatoko no fumi

Journal kept by Iki no Hakatoko, a diplomat who was a member of a mission to Tang (T'ang) China in 659 led by Sakaibe no Iwashiki. Although the journal is no longer extant, passages are quoted in four different places in the 8th-century chronicle *Nihon shoki*. Its descriptions of the hardships endured by the many monks and students who accompanied the numerous missions sent to China and the attitude of the Chinese officials toward Japanese diplomats, are valuable for studying relations between the two countries (see SUI AND TANG [T'ANG] CHINA, EMBASSIES TO). Most scholars seem to agree that the journal was presented to the court of Empress JITŌ by Hakatoko in order to advance his own career.

KITAMURA Bunji

Ikiru

KUROSAWA AKIRA's 1952 film about a civil servant dying of cancer who comes to question his life and attempts at the end to redeem it. This moving story is presented in an incisive, controlled, and completely unsentimental manner. The film, most rigorously photographed and edited, breaks naturally into two parts. In the first the civil servant, Watanabe Kanji (played by SHIMURA TAKASHI), attempts in various ways to escape his fate, or hide from himself his knowledge of it. Pleasure, companionship, family solace, devotion to another person—all these means are attempted and all fail. In the second half of the picture Watanabe has died, and we, attending his wake, learn from workers in his office that he had ended by devoting himself to his work, but now in a truly meaningful way. In the face of bureaucratic lack of interest and laziness (of which he himself had before been an outstanding example), he pushes through the project of a small children's park. Through flashbacks we see his fight and witness his determination. During the wake and its successive revelations it becomes clear that Watanabe has found his vindication through action. He has finally discovered himself through doing.

Kurosawa makes the moral meaning of his picture quite clear. Perhaps without even grasping the profound truth he was acting out, Watanabe behaves as though he believed that it is action alone that matters; that a man is not his thoughts, nor his wishes, nor his intentions, but that he is simply what he does. Watanabe discovers a way to be responsible for others, he finds a way to vindicate his death and, more important, his life. He finds out what it means to live. And this phrase, "to live," is what this extraordinary film is finally about—and what the title plainly indicates. *Ikiru* is the intransitive verb meaning "to live."

Donald RICHIE

ikki

A term which originally meant to do something in agreement, but which came to denote both a league formed for military purposes and an uprising by local warriors and peasants in the Muromachi period (1333–1568). By the Edo period (1600–1868), it was used to refer to any kind of peasant revolt. The most common forms of uprisings were the TSUCHI IKKI and KUNI IKKI of the Muromachi period, and the HYAKUSHŌ IKKI of the Edo period.

The earliest *ikki* were an outgrowth of the struggle to establish Ashikaga rule in the first half of the 14th century. Leagues of local warriors united in an effort to thwart the attempts by SHUGO (military governors) to control the provinces. In the beginning, many of these leagues, such as the Shirahata and Taira, were united by blood ties, but soon land became the common unifying factor. The new leagues operated on pledges of mutual loyalty, instead of along vassalage lines, to protect their independence. This latter form of *ikki* evolved into what would later be known as the *kuni ikki*.

At about the same time, the peasants of central Japan were also forming leagues, called *tsuchi ikki* (or *doikki*), directed against SHŌEN (estate) proprietors. The early *tsuchi ikki* of the second half of the 14th century were generally concerned with the reduction of taxes and corvée or the removal of unpopular estate officials. The Ōmi Uprising in 1354 is an example of this early type of *tsuchi ikki*.

By the 15th century, when the number of *tsuchi ikki* was at its peak, the general motivation for revolting had changed to inducing the shogunate to proclaim a cancellation of debts (TOKUSEI). Starting with the Shōchō Uprising of 1428, more than 100 *tsuchi ikki* followed before the end of the century. Although most were local rebellions, the Kakitsu Uprising of 1441 expanded to include tens of thousands of peasants before winning its demand for debt cancellation. Also falling under this general classification of uprisings are the *bashaku* (teamster) and *tokusei* (debt cancellation) *ikki,* which basically had the same concerns and objectives as the *tsuchi ikki.*

By the end of the 15th century, the *tsuchi ikki* began to die out, as the peasant leaders *(dogō)* became small landowners and made peace with the local military leader *(kokujin).* When the *sengoku daimyō* (territorial warlords) came upon the scene, they used the *dogō* to control the peasants and their *ikki.*

Although local warrior groups had formed leagues in the 14th century, it was not until the 15th century that provincial uprisings, known as *kuni ikki,* came to play an important role. The uprisings were led by local landowners and warriors *(kokujin)* against the military governors *(shugo),* and they differed from the *tsuchi ikki* in their large scale and political goals. The first important *kuni ikki* was in Harima Province (now Hyōgo Prefecture) in 1429, while the largest and best known was the YAMASHIRO NO KUNI IKKI of 1486. The *kuni ikki* helped the *kokujin* gain power at the expense of the centrally appointed *shugo,* and it was not until some of these *kokujin* had emerged as autonomous territorial lords (Sengoku daimyō) that anyone had enough military strength to permanently destroy this form of *ikki.*

The large-scale uprisings by the followers of the Jōdo Shin sect of Buddhism in the late 15th and 16th centuries (referred to as IKKŌ IKKI), were a special type of provincial uprising, but, nonetheless, they still belong to the *kuni ikki* classification. Beginning in the 1470s, and including the Kaga Ikkō *ikki* of 1486 in which the military governor was expelled, the uprisings continued until 1580, when the Sengoku daimyō ODA NOBUNAGA (1534–82) finally destroyed their military power. In the early years the main purpose of the Ikkō *ikki* was the defense of *kokujin* against the *shugo,* and later it was to stop the centralization efforts of the Sengoku daimyō. They succeeded in the former and failed in the latter, much as other *kuni ikki* had done. Therefore, even though Jōdo Shin doctrine and organization are important in explaining their broad appeal, they still must be viewed primarily as *kuni ikki.*

Uprisings, such as the TEMMON HOKKE REBELLION of 1536 and various smaller *tsuchi* and *kuni ikki,* continued to occur until late in the 16th century, but by the time of the national unifier TOYOTOMI HIDEYOSHI (1537–98) most organized local opposition had ended. By the 17th century the term *ikki* had lost its earlier meaning, and during the Edo period it came to refer to any kind of peasant revolt *(hyakushō ikki).*

Recent research has estimated that during the Edo period there were more than 2,500 peasant uprisings. There were three general phases of these *hyakushō ikki* under Tokugawa rule. In the early phase (1600–1750), the uprisings took the form of mild resistance against economic burdens imposed by authorities. These protests were usually organized by village heads. The *hyakushō ikki* of the middle phase (1750–1830) were larger and more violent. They were also better organized and were planned and executed by the peasants themselves. The peasants attacked not only government authorities, but merchants and privileged rural groups who tried to exploit them. The peasant uprisings of the final phase (1830–68) usually tried to bring about political reforms within the village organization, although economic motivations were still important.

By the latter half of the Edo period, the peasant uprisings offered such a formidable threat to Tokugawa rule that they had to be put down by large military forces. Besides the *hyakushō ikki,* there also occurred in the late Edo period and the early part of the Meiji period (1868–1912) YONAOSHI REBELLIONS ("world renewal" rebellions) protesting a precipitous rise in prices. These uprisings show that the peasants in Tokugawa Japan played an important and active role in the social changes that occurred in the period.

From the beginning of the Muromachi period to the end of the Edo period, the *ikki* served as the major vehicle for organizing local warriors and peasants to challenge the rule of government authorities. How these authorities reacted to the *ikki* helped determine both the form and strength of government rule in Japan for more than 500 years.

■■——Aoki Kōji, *Hyakushō ikki no nenjiteki kenkyū* (1966). David L. Davis, "Ikki in Late Medieval Japan," in John W. Hall and Jeffrey P. Mass, ed, *Medieval Japan* (1974). Hayashi Motoi, *Hyakushō ikki no dentō* (1976). Inoue Toshio, *Ikkō ikki no kenkyū* (1968).

Kasahara Kazuo, *Ikkō ikki no kenkyū* (1962). Nakamura Kichiji, *Doikki kenkyū* (1974). Nakamura Kichiji, *Tokusei to doikki* (1959).

Lane R. EARNS

Ikkō ikki

Large-scale uprisings in the late 15th and 16th centuries by adherents of the JŌDO SHIN SECT of Buddhism. Ikkō (single-minded) is another name for the sect; IKKI (league or uprising) is a term for lawless activity of an organized kind. Militant acts by Ikkō sectarians began in the 1470s, when the abbot RENNYO, fleeing religious persecution, established his base in the Hokuriku region. By 1488 the Ikkō *ikki* had killed the military governor *(shugo)* of Kaga Province (now part of Ishikawa Prefecture) and taken control of the province, which they retained for nearly a century. Uprisings spread to the neighboring provinces and eventually to the central provinces and beyond. In 1563 TOKUGAWA IEYASU suppressed a serious Ikkō uprising in his native Mikawa Province (now part of Aichi Prefecture), but it was not until their defeat in 1580 by the national unifier ODA NOBUNAGA that the military power of the Ikkō *ikki* was finally crushed.

The tenets of the Jōdo Shin sect encouraged peasant solidarity and millenarian goals, but the local lords (KOKUJIN) who led the early Ikkō *ikki* were motivated by more worldly ambitions. Rennyo disapproved of insurrection, and after his death the temple HONGANJI in Kyōto, the center of the sect, was reluctant to assume leadership. It was not until the mortal confrontation with Nobunaga that the Ikkō *ikki* became a nationally unified force. Although the circumstances and results of the Ikkō *ikki* were extremely diverse, scholars agree that in their early phase they strongly resembled the contemporary provincial uprisings (KUNI IKKI) in their leadership and political goals. Nonetheless, the growth of Ikkō *ikki* into a coordinated national force can be explained only in terms of Jōdo Shin doctrine and organization.

■■——Akamatsu Toshihide and Kasahara Kazuo, ed, *Shinshū shi gaisetsu* (1966). David L. Davis, "Ikki in Late Medieval Japan," in John W. Hall and Jeffrey P. Mass, ed, *Medieval Japan* (1974). Inoue Toshio, *Ikkō ikki no kenkyū* (1968). Kasahara Kazuo, *Ikkō ikki no kenkyū* (1962). Kasahara Kazuo and Inoue Toshio, ed, *Rennyo Ikkō ikki* (1972).

Michael SOLOMON

Ikkoku Ichijō Rei

(literally, "Law of One Castle per Province"). Order by TOKUGAWA IEYASU designed to trim *daimyō* power by reducing the number of castles under their control. A few weeks after Ōsaka Castle fell to Tokugawa forces in 1615 (see ŌSAKA CASTLE, SIEGES OF), Ieyasu issued a regulation ordering daimyō to demolish all castles in their domains except those in which they were living. In following years some 400 castles, mostly perimeter defense forts, were torn down. Most of these were in the western part of Japan, where TOYOTOMI HIDEYOSHI's earlier orders for castle reduction had not been applied. See also BUKE SHOHATTO.

Conrad TOTMAN

Ikkyū (1394–1481)

(Ikkyū Sōjun). Zen monk and eccentric who played a major role in the rebuilding and revitalization of Kyōto's temple DAITOKUJI after the ŌNIN WAR (1467–77). He was a noted poet and calligrapher and an important contributor to the infusion of Japanese art and literature with Zen attitudes and ideals. Popular writers of the Edo period (1600–1868) so capitalized upon the unconventional side of Ikkyū's personality that he is known to most modern Japanese primarily as a comic Zen character.

It is generally held that Ikkyū was the son of Emperor GO-KOMATSU (1377–1433; r 1382–1412) and a court noblewoman, but that because of her low rank or inappropriate political connections, Ikkyū's mother was obliged to give birth to her son away from court. Ikkyū was placed in the temple Ankokuji in Kyōto as an acolyte at the age of five. There he was schooled in the Buddhist scriptures and given a solid foundation in the classical literature of China—his gift for the composition of Chinese verse becoming evident as early as his 12th year. In 1410 Ikkyū left the sophisticated confines of Ankokuji to become the disciple of Ken'ō Sōi (d 1415), under whose tutelage he undertook a strict program of meditation and study.

After Ken'ō's death in 1415, Ikkyū left Kyōto to join the demanding master Kasō Sōdon (also known as Kesō Shūdon; 1352–1428) at a small hermitage in Katata, a commercial town on the shores of Lake Biwa. Kasō was a monk of the Daitokuji line, but he had grown disgusted with the cultural, political, and commercial connections of Kyōto Zen and left the mother temple to establish a small, highly disciplined center of Zen practice away from the corrupting influences of the capital. Ikkyū responded positively to Kasō's harsh methods of training and experienced spiritual insight (SATORI) in 1420 when the unexpected cry of a crow pierced his nighttime meditation in a small boat on Lake Biwa.

By the late 1420s, Ikkyū settled in the port town of SAKAI, where he began to express himself in the unconventional style of "mad Zen." He spent more time in brothels and wineshops than in temples and hermitages, going out of his way to amaze and offend the citizenry of Sakai. On one occasion he waved a wooden sword at passersby to illustrate the difference between his own "keen-as-steel" Zen and the "wooden Zen" of the orthodox Five Temples (GOZAN) of Kyōto. One New Year's Day, Ikkyū paraded the streets of Sakai waving a human skull at the startled holiday crowds, in a graphic display of the Buddhist doctrine of impermanence.

In Sakai Ikkyū developed close connections with the nouveau riche merchant class. During a subsequent period of protracted wanderings, he began to attract the interest of a number of literary and artistic figures, including the Nō playwright KOMPARU ZENCHIKU (1405–70?), the linked-verse (renga) masters SōGI (1421–1502) and SōCHō (1448–1532), and several painters of the emerging SOGA SCHOOL. Foremost among Ikkyū's disciples and confidants was the painter Bokusai (also known as Motsurin Shōtō; d 1496), who is credited with the first biography of Ikkyū and a masterful life-sketch portrait of him.

In 1455 Ikkyū circulated a collection of poems called the Jikaishū (The Self-Admonition Anthology) in which he shifted his attack on the "inauthentic" Zen of the Gozan temples to excesses that he felt were destroying the Zen of Daitokuji. In particular, Ikkyū heaped abuse upon an elder disciple of Kasō, Yōsō Sōi (1376–1458), whom he charged with fostering a Zen dedicated to fame, rank, and profit. In spite of his dissatisfaction with the state of Zen at Daitokuji in the 1450s and 1460s, in 1474 Ikkyū accepted an appointment as the temple's 47th abbot. Ikkyū's seeming return to a more conventional religious life was motivated by his desires to physically rebuild the temple, which had been destroyed in the Ōnin War, and to bring an end to the divisive factionalism that had marked the internal policies of Daitokuji during the preceding two or three decades. Though his tenure as abbot was brief, Ikkyū did manage to marshal financial support from the Sakai merchants and to heal at least some of the internal political divisions. That Ikkyū's return to conventionality was more apparent than real, however, can be seen in his famous love affair late in life with the blind singer Mori, whom he knew in the 1470s. Ikkyū's final years were spent mostly in retreat at his Shūon'an hermitage in Takigi, a village halfway between Kyōto and Sakai, where he died in 1481 at the age of 87.

Ikkyū is best known for his writings in the difficult idiom of classical Chinese poetry, but he also wrote poems and several prose works in Japanese. His chief poetic work is the Kyōunshū (The Crazy-Cloud Anthology), a collection of over one thousand Chinese poems. Some of the Kyōunshū poems are conventional pieces that recall the massive poetic output of the Gozan school (see GOZAN LITERATURE), but many are quite irregular either in content or structure. Of special interest are a number of explicitly erotic love poems.

Eight prose pieces are attributed to Ikkyū. Most of these are simple sermons intended for a popular audience, but at least three are of sufficient literary quality to note by title: "Gaikotsu" (1457, Skeletons; tr "Ikkyū's Skeletons," 1973), a rather elegant prose-poem on the vanity of life; "Bukkigun" (tr "The Buddha's Great War against Hell," 1980), a philosophic transposition of the medieval genre of the war tale (GUNKI MONOGATARI); and the Maka-hannya-haramita shingyō ge (Explication of the Mahā-prajñāpāramitā-hṛdaya-sūtra), a highly poetic commentary on the Heart Sutra.

Extant examples of Ikkyū's calligraphy range in style and format from fluid lines to harsh, dry brushwork and from single phrases to long texts, but virtually all are characterized by a powerful dynamism that is both attractive and unsettling and which recalls the rough unconventionality of Ikkyū's best poems.

■ ——Ikkyū Sōjun, "Gaikotsu" (1457), tr R. H. Blyth as "Ikkyū's Skeletons," in Eastern Buddhist 6.1 (1973). Sonja Arntzen, Ikkyū Sōjun: A Zen Monk and His Poetry (1973). Furuta Shōkin, Ikkyū (1946). Hirano Sōjō, Kyōunshū zenshaku, vol 1 (1976). Hirano Sōjō, Ikkyū oshō nempu no kenkyū (1977). Ichikawa Hakugen,

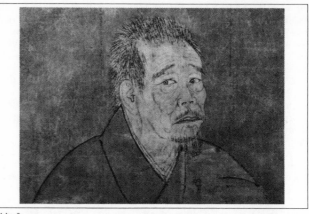

Ikkyū

Detail of a portrait of Ikkyū by his disciple Bokusai. Ink and colors on paper. 43.8 × 26.3 cm. Late 15th century. Tōkyō National Museum.

Ikkyū," in Donald Keene, Landscapes and Portraits: Appreciations of Japanese Culture (1971). Minakami Tsutomu, Ikkyū (1975). James H. Sanford, "Mandalas of the Heart: Two Prose Works by Ikkyū Sōjun," Monumenta Nipponica 36.3 (1980). Yamato Bunka-kan, ed, Yamato bunka 41: Ikkyū tokushū (1964).

James H. SANFORD

Ikoku nikki

(Register of Foreign Affairs). A register of Japan's relations with foreign countries, compiled in the 17th century by SŪDEN, a Zen priest active in affairs of state under the first three Tokugawa shōguns, and Saigaku Genryō (d 1657), Sūden's successor as superior of the Konchiin priory and abbot of the Nanzenji monastery in Kyōto. Part one contains accounts of the conduct of foreign affairs and external trade, as well as copies of diplomatic correspondence (much of it drafted by Sūden), from the years between 1608 and 1639. Part two includes information on the Korean embassies (CHŌSEN TSŪSHINSHI) of 1636, 1643, and 1655; further copies of diplomatic correspondence with lands from Luzon to Siam; and examples of letters drafted by Zen monks dating back to the 13th century.

George ELISON

Ikokusen Uchiharai Rei → Gaikokusen Uchiharai Rei

Ikoma

City in northwestern Nara Prefecture, central Honshū, 17 km (11 mi) east of Ōsaka. Formerly a farming village, with the opening of a railway line in the Taishō period (1912–26) and the construction of a cable car line to the temple Hōzanji on the slope of Ikomayama, the city has flourished. Many of its residents commute to Ōsaka. A special local product is chasen, bamboo whisks used in the tea ceremony. The grave of the Buddhist monk GYŌGI (668–749) is at the temple Chikurinji. Pop: 70,456.

Ikomayama

Mountain on the border between Nara and Ōsaka prefectures, central Honshū; tallest peak in the Ikoma Mountains. Made up of diorite. A Buddhist temple, Hōzanji, is located on the eastern slopes. It is a developed recreational center with cable cars and roads. On the summit are located a playground and an observatory of Kyōto University. Height: 642 m (2,106 ft).

Ikukunitama Shrine

(Ikukunitama Jinja; popularly known as Ikutama Jinja). Shintō shrine in Tennōji Ward in the city of Ōsaka, dedicated to the deities Ikushima no Kami and Tarushima no Kami, who are believed to be protectors of the Japanese islands. Although the origin of the shrine is not known, it was ranked by the Engi Shiki (927; tr Procedures of the Engi Era, 1970–72) as an eminent shrine (myōjin taisha) of the empire. During the period between 850 and the early 13th century, an imperial envoy was dispatched to this shrine following the enthronement of each emperor (with several exceptions) to participate in the Yasoshima Matsuri (Festival of the Eighty Islands, i.e., Japan), a solemn ritual held only once during the reign of an emperor, in which prayers for the well-being of the nation were offered. The shrine has been located at its present site since around 1583. Its annual festival is observed on 9 September.   *Stanley WEINSTEIN*

Ikuno Disturbance

(Ikuno no Hen). Armed uprising in November 1863 by lower-ranking *samurai* and peasants in Ikuno, a silver-mining town under direct shogunate rule in the Tajima domain (now part of Hyōgo Prefecture). Having learned of the uprising of the antishogunate Tenchūgumi (see TENCHŪGUMI REBELLION) in the Nara area two months earlier, HIRANO KUNIOMI and other proimperial samurai under the figurehead leadership of SAWA NOBUYOSHI organized about 2,000 peasants, among them landlords and wealthy farmers, in the Ikuno area. Joined by like-minded samurai from the KIHEITAI, the mixed militia that had recently been organized in Chōshū (now Yamaguchi Prefecture), they attacked the shogunal deputy's office. The shogunate immediately ordered neighboring domains to subdue the rebels; the samurai became divided among themselves, the peasants deserted, and within three days the uprising was crushed. Although the uprising was ostensibly a protest against the expulsion of Chōshū samurai from Kyōto (see COUP D'ETAT OF 30 SEPTEMBER 1863) and to give the emperor "peace of mind," it is clear that many of the peasants were lured in by the promise to reduce the land rent by 50 percent if they joined. Still, the confluence of such disparate elements in this early instance of armed rebellion against the Tokugawa shogunate is distinctive.   *TANAKA Akira*

Ikuno Silver Mine

(Ikuno Ginzan). Located in Ikuno, Hyōgo Prefecture; discovered as early as 807 and developed intensively in the 16th century by the local *daimyō*, Yamana Suketoyo (d 1580). Toward the end of that century the mine came under direct control of the hegemons ODA NOBUNAGA and TOYOTOMI HIDEYOSHI, and ownership later passed to the Tokugawa shogunate. It was the most productive silver mine in the country during much of the Edo period (1600–1868), its greatest annual yield being 3,836.25 kilograms in 1704. The Meiji government, which modernized the mine with French techniques, controlled it until the Mitsubishi company bought it in 1896. Its silver exhausted, the mine, with the largest tin refinery in Japan, produced mainly copper and zinc until it was closed in 1973.

Ikuta Chōkō (1882–1936)

Literary critic. Real name Ikuta Kōji. Born in Tottori Prefecture; graduate of Tōkyō University. A free thinker influenced by Nietzsche, Ikuta was an active literary and social critic and a supporter of the women's movement. Among his works are translations of Nietzsche's *Thus Spake Zarathustra*, D'Annunzio's *The Triumph of Death*, Dante's *The Divine Comedy*, and a commentary on contemporary authors, *Saikin no shōsetsuka* (1912).   *ASAI Kiyoshi*

Ikuta Shungetsu (1892–1930)

Poet. Real name Ikuta Seihei. Born in Tottori Prefecture. Although his early poetry expresses a Christian humanism, from about 1917 his writing reflects an increasing tendency toward nihilism and anarchism. Among his works are collections of poetry, *Reikon no aki* (1917, Autumn of the Soul) and *Shōchō no ika* (1930, The Cuttlefish Symbol); a collection of translations of Heinrich Heine's poetry; and an autobiographical novel in three volumes, *Aiyoru tamashii* (1921–24, Spirits That Gather).   *ASAI Kiyoshi*

Ikuta Yorozu, Rebellion of

(Ikuta Yorozu no Ran). An uprising in Echigo (now Niigata Prefecture) staged by Ikuta Yorozu (1801–37) and a small band of his students and local farmers in July 1837. As a youth Ikuta had studied in Edo (now Tōkyō) under the KOKUGAKU (National Learning) scholar HIRATA ATSUTANE. He returned to his home domain of Tatebayashi (now part of Gumma Prefecture) but was expelled for presenting a memorial critical of the domain administration. After several years in Edo, in 1836 he moved to Kashiwazaki in Echigo,

where he opened a school and soon won the respect of his students and of the poor farmers in the area. Like most of the country Echigo was then suffering from a severe famine (see TEMPŌ FAMINE); domain officials and rice brokers had bought up all the available rice, causing rice prices to rise even higher. Yorozu appealed repeatedly to domain officials for relief for the starving farmers but was turned away each time. Finally, in desperation, he and seven followers attacked the local deputy's stronghold at Kashiwazaki. The rebellion was quickly quelled, and Yorozu committed suicide. This uprising is often mentioned in conjunction with the rebellion in Ōsaka led by ŌSHIO HEIHACHIRŌ earlier in the same year.

Imabari

City in northern Ehime Prefecture, Shikoku, on the Hiuchi Sea. Imabari developed as a castle town after the construction of Imabari Castle by TŌDŌ TAKATORA in 1600. A cotton textile industry grew thereafter, and even today Imabari is the largest producer of cotton towels in Japan. Pop: 123,237.

Imagawa family

Warrior family of the Muromachi period (1333–1568). The family was descended from Ashikaga Kuniuji, who inherited an estate at Imagawa in Mikawa Province (now part of Aichi Prefecture). His grandson Norikuni (1304?–84) served with distinction under ASHIKAGA TAKAUJI, founder of the Muromachi shogunate, and the Imagawa were made hereditary military governors *(shugo)* of Suruga and Tōtōmi provinces (now parts of Shizuoka Prefecture). The most famous member of the family was the poet and general IMAGAWA SADAYO (Imagawa Ryōshun; b 1326), but the family reached the peak of its power in the Sengoku period (1467–1568) under the leadership of Imagawa Ujichika (1473?–1526) and his son IMAGAWA YOSHIMOTO (1519–60), who were overlords of Suruga, Tōtōmi, and Mikawa provinces. Yoshimoto aspired to control the whole country, and in 1560 he marched on Kyōto, but he was intercepted and killed by ODA NOBUNAGA in the Battle of OKEHAZAMA. TAKEDA SHINGEN and TOKUGAWA IEYASU thereupon seized the Imagawa domain. The descendants of the Imagawa family served the Tokugawa shogunate (1603–1867) as masters of court ceremony (KŌKE). The family's domainal code, the IMAGAWA KANA MOKUROKU, was drawn up by Ujichika and Yoshimoto.

Imagawa Kana Mokuroku

(The Kana List of Articles of the Imagawa). A domainal law code (BUNKOKUHŌ) of the Sengoku period (1467–1568), enacted by Imagawa Ujichika (1473?–1526), lord of Suruga and Tōtōmi provinces (now parts of Shizuoka Prefecture), on 25 May 1526 (Taiei 6.4.14); contains 33 articles (31 in an alternate version). Ujichika had been appointed SHUGO (military governor) of the two provinces by the MUROMACHI SHOGUNATE, but this code testifies to his transformation into a SENGOKU DAIMYŌ, the independent ruler of a regional domain. The code reiterates the supremacy of the daimyō and his officers in that domain and proscribes the "willful" *(jiyū)* pursuit of private interests in matters such as the alienation of land (art. 13); the daimyō not only regulates the amount of interest to be charged on loans (arts. 18–19) but also intrudes into the affairs of religious institutions (arts. 28–29) and prohibits marriages between his people and those of other provinces (art. 30). As could be expected of a Sengoku *daimyō*, the medieval privilege of immunity from entry (see FUYU AND FUNYŪ) by *shugo* officials into private landholdings is abridged if not totally abrogated (arts. 22–23). The 21-article supplement *(tsuika)* to the Kana Mokuroku issued by Ujichika's son IMAGAWA YOSHIMOTO on 8 April 1553 (Tembun 22.2.26) further curtails recourse to that privilege and consigns it to the dustbin of a time past when the shogunate's orders and appointments were still honored throughout the land, Yoshimoto stressing that he now passes laws for his domain "in my own capacity" (supp. 20); other supplementary items reinforce or complement the articles of the original list. A 13-article set of regulations *(sadame)* governing lawsuit procedures, undated but assumed to be Yoshimoto's provision, is commonly attached to the other two documents. The Imagawa Kana Mokuroku was one of the earliest *bunkokuhō* and substantially influenced the contents of subsequent domainal codes, such as the Kōshū Hatto no Shidai (first enacted 1547; see SHINGEN KAHŌ) of the TAKEDA FAMILY.   *George ELISON*

Imagawa Sadayo (1326–?)

Warrior and general, classical (WAKA) poet, and poet of linked verse *(renga)*; commonly known as Imagawa Ryōshun, Ryōshun being the name he took on entering the priesthood in 1367.

Military Career—— Born in Kyōto to a *samurai* family, Sadayo distinguished himself in the service of the Ashikaga shōguns Yoshiakira (1330–67) and Yoshimitsu (1358–1408). He succeeded his father Norikuni (1304?–84) as military governor *(shugo)* of the province of Tōtōmi (now part of Shizuoka Prefecture), and was later assigned a position in the shogunal courts of law. In 1371 Sadayo, now Ryōshun, was dispatched as shogunal deputy *(tandai)* to Kyūshū, where for nearly 25 years he fought to establish the shōgun's authority, especially over the powerful KIKUCHI FAMILY. His efforts were undercut by jealous rivals and by local chieftains opposed to any increase of shogunal power in Kyūshū. Summoned back to Kyōto in 1395 by the shōgun ASHIKAGA YOSHIMITSU, whose suspicions had been aroused against him by the slander of the powerful warrior-general Ōuchi Yoshihiro (1356–1400), Ryōshun was shunted off as *shugo* of the province of Suruga (now part of Shizuoka Prefecture). When Yoshihiro finally revolted against the shōgun in 1398, Ryōshun was suspected of complicity, but he escaped a force sent againt him. Later he was pardoned and returned to Kyōto, but he retired from active life and devoted himself to religious pursuits, to poetry, and to the study of old ceremonial lore and precedents. He appears to have spent his last years in Tōtōmi. The year of his death is uncertain, but he almost certainly died before 1418, perhaps as early as 1414.

Poetic Activities—— Ryōshun began his study of classical poetry at an early age, first with his grandmother, then under Tamemoto, adopted son of KYŌGOKU TAMEKANE (1254–1332), leader of the Kyōgoku poetic faction. However, in his early twenties he became the disciple of Reizei Tamehide (d 1372). An energetic man with a warrior's decisive and combative nature, Ryōshun threw himself enthusiastically into the battle between the conservative Nijō and the innovating Kyōgoku–Reizei poetic factions. He vigorously espoused the Reizei cause, defending it in treatise and apologia. Because a total of only 98 of his own poems survive, none of them of exceptional quality, his literary importance rests far more on his narrative and polemical writings, ranging from a travel diary to rebuttals and manifestos against the conservative Nijō school. A number of these works are extremely valuable, providing a straightforward, practical approach to problems of versification and a poetic ideal calling for a return to the basic styles and teachings of the great master and progenitor of all three poetic houses, the great FUJIWARA NO SADAIE (Fujiwara no Teika; 1162–1241). Among Ryōshun's disciples was SHŌTETSU (1381–1459), himself an important Reizei adherent and apologist and a major critic.

Only five of Ryōshun's poems were included in imperial anthologies, but this may well have been because he was *persona non grata* with the Nijō poets, who all but monopolized compilation of the imperial collections from the late 1200s on. A list of Ryōshun's most important writings follows.

Wakadokoro e fushin jōjō (A List of Questions Submitted to the Bureau of Poetry), completed 1403. A treatise concerned largely with distinctions between elegant (poetic) and vulgar language as interpreted by conservative and innovative poetic arbiters, and the consequent disagreements concerning what is and what is not acceptable poetic diction. According to the Nijō school, the only correct poetic language was that employed in the first three imperial anthologies, the KOKINSHŪ (ca 905), GOSEN WAKASHŪ (ca 955–966), and SHŪI WAKASHŪ (ca 996–1007). Opposed to this rigidly conservative viewpoint, Ryōshun argues for the admission of new diction, provided that it is graceful and pleasing to the ear. He bolsters his argument by quoting some 59 older poems by such innovators-become-classics as MINAMOTO NO TOSHIYORI and SAIGYŌ. Ryōshun then turns to criticism of poems by TON'A, the principal Nijō apologist and critic; attacks his rejection of the poetry of REIZEI TAMESUKE (1263–1328), founder of the Reizei school; and protests vigorously against blanket condemnation of Reizei poetic practice by the Nijō school. Although addressed to the Bureau of Poetry, the treatise is thought to have been written for the benefit of the current Reizei leader, Tamemasa (1361–1417).

Gonjinshū (Collection of Verbal Trash), 1406. A handbook in the traditional mold, giving a brief account of changes in poetic style through the ages; the state of contemporary poetry; and notes on exemplary poems, diction, correct treatment of poetic topics, and so forth.

Shisetsu jikenshū (The Master's Teachings and My Personal Opinions), about 1408. Handbook primarily on diction, but with additional information of a traditional sort for beginners. Examples of the use of important images, with illustrative poems. Reports the teachings of Reizei Tamehide, with added comments by Ryōshun.

Ryōshun isshi den (Ryōshun's Testament to His Heir); also called *Ben'yōshō* (Notes on the Fundamentals of Poetry), 1409. An introductory treatise, written for Ryōshun's son Hikogorō. It stresses constant discipline and practice and the need for efforts to achieve harmony and balance between poetic materials and personal feelings. Practical and instructive, it is typical of Ryōshun's approach.

Rakusho roken (The Anonymous Document Revealed), about 1412. Primarily a refutation of Nijō attacks against the Reizei leader Tamemasa. Originally circulated anonymously, its authorship was soon discovered, and Ryōshun gave it its present title. Although largely taken up with circumstantial argument against Nijō criticism of Tamemasa's poetry, the work also discusses the ideals and practice of *renga*, or linked verse (see RENGA AND HAIKAI). As an adherent of the *renga* master NIJŌ YOSHIMOTO (1320–88), Ryōshun deplores the current decline of the art into frivolity and inconsequence and urges a return to Yoshimoto's ideals and artistic standards. He also questions the genuineness of certain poetic documents upon which the Nijō classical poets based their claim to poetic infallibility.

Michiyukiburi (Along the Road), 1370. A poem-studded travel account of Ryōshun's journey from Kyōto to take up his duties as shogunal deputy in Kyūshū; contains many poems on famous places along the way.

Rokuon'in Den Itsukushima mōde no ki, 1389. Record of a pilgrimage to the Itsukushima Shrine at Miyajima by the shōgun Yoshimitsu.

Nan Taiheiki (Errors in the *Taiheiki*), 1402. An attack on the historical work TAIHEIKI for being biased in favor of the court and for failing to include the valorous deeds and achievements of Ryōshun's forebears. An inquiry into the historicity of the work and an attempt to correct the record.

In addition to the above, Ryōshun left several works on court ceremonial, ritual implements and their uses, and the like.

▟——Araki Hisashi, *Imagawa Ryōshun no kenkyū* (1977). Robert H. Brower and Earl Miner, *Japanese Court Poetry* (1961). Kawazoe Shōji, *Imagawa Ryōshun* (1964). Koyama Keiichi, *Imagawa Ryōshun* (1944). Earl Miner, *An Introduction to Japanese Court Poetry* (1968).　　　　　　　　　　　　　　Robert H. BROWER

Imagawa Yoshimoto (1519–1560)

Prominent *daimyō* of the Sengoku period (1467–1568); third son of Ujichika (1473?–1526), the *shugo* (military governor) of Suruga and Tōtōmi provinces (now parts of Shizuoka Prefecture). Sent to a monastery at an early age, Yoshimoto renounced the priesthood at his brother Ujiteru's death in 1536 and successfully contested the family headship with another brother. Having established ties by marriage with the TAKEDA FAMILY of Kai Province (now Yamanashi Prefecture), he fought intermittently with the third of the major eastern daimyō houses, the Later Hōjō family (see HŌJŌ FAMILY) of Odawara, until the formation of their tripartite alliance in 1554. Expanding westward, he had by 1548 gained control of most of Mikawa Province (now part of Aichi Prefecture). Yoshimoto thereby became the eastern seaboard's greatest daimyō, but his westward advance had as early as 1540 brought him in conflict with the ODA FAMILY of Owari Province (now part of Aichi Prefecture). When he mounted an invasion of that province in 1560, he was surprised in his encampment by the vastly inferior force of ODA NOBUNAGA and lost his life in the Battle of OKEHAZAMA, the emergent hegemon's first major strategic victory. Yoshimoto is also known for his attempts to consolidate daimyō power in his domains through land surveys (KENCHI) and the rigorous control of his vassals; to that end he issued in 1553 a set of 21 supplements to the IMAGAWA KANA MOKUROKU, a domainal law code (BUNKOKUHŌ) originally formulated by his father in 1526.　　　　　　　　　　　　George ELISON

Imaichi

City in west central Tochigi Prefecture, central Honshū. During the Edo period (1600–1868) Imaichi flourished as a market and POST-STATION TOWN on the highway Nikkō Kaidō leading to the mausoleum of TOKUGAWA IEYASU. Formerly a major producer of lumber, furniture, and *senkō* (incense sticks), it is now the site of several electrical appliance and ceramic factories. It is the gateway to the Nikkō National Park; the grave of NINOMIYA SONTOKU is at the Hōtoku Ninomiya Shrine. Pop: 50,423.

Imai Sōkyū (1520–1593)

Merchant and tea connoisseur of the Sengoku (1467–1568) and Azuchi–Momoyama (1568–1600) periods. Sōkyū was an influential citizen of the strategic entrepôt city SAKAI, where he was engaged in warehousing and the medicine and arms trades; accordingly, he came into contact with some of the era's most eminent personages, whose acquaintance he cultivated through the medium of the cult of tea. In 1568 he presented two priceless tea ceremony utensils to ODA NOBUNAGA, thereby ingratiating himself with the emergent hegemon. Upon obtaining Sakai's submission the next year, apparently in part through Sōkyū's efforts, Nobunaga installed him as intendant (daikan) in the northern part of the city and granted him a variety of privileges. Thereafter Sōkyū served Nobunaga in the dual capacity of master of the tea ceremony and purveyor of munitions. These qualifications also brought him to the attention of Nobunaga's general TOYOTOMI HIDEYOSHI, the future national unifier, with whom he had established contact by 1570. After Nobunaga's death, Sōkyū for a time enjoyed high favor under Hideyoshi, being ranked as one of his premier tea masters (sadō) alongside TSUDA SŌGYŪ and SEN NO RIKYŪ, but from 1584 he was eclipsed by the other two. According to one account, his decline in Hideyoshi's esteem was caused by a slip of the hand during a tea ceremony.

George ELISON

Imai Tadashi (1912–   )

Film director. Born in Tōkyō; Imai's father was until World War II chief priest of the Reisen'in at the temple Shōunji. He entered the literature department of Tōkyō University but left before graduating. Imai's reaction to his conservative background was expressed by participation in radical activities in college as a member of the communist youth league, for which he was arrested. In 1935 he joined J. O. Studios as an assistant director, moving to TŌHŌ CO, LTD, when J. O. merged with Tōhō in 1937. He joined the Japan Communist Party after the war, and during the "red purge" following the 1948 strike at Tōhō, Imai was blacklisted and was able to begin making films again only in the early 1950s.

Imai's filmmaking style might be referred to as "nakanai realism," or "realism without tears." He was particularly influenced by Italian neorealists such as Vittorio De Sica, as evidenced in Dokkoi ikiteiru (1951, And Yet We Live), the first Japanese movie made without institutional financing. An earlier film, Mata au hi made (1950, Until the Day We Meet Again), is set in wartime and ends with the hero dying at the front after the heroine has been killed in an air raid. Imai's Himeyuri no tō (1953, The Tower of Lilies), treats the death of a group of Okinawan schoolgirl-nurses during the American invasion. Each of these films does at times border on the sentimental, achieving its effects through traditional catharsis, dissolving the audience in tears.

Imai's finest work includes Nigorie (1953, Muddy Waters), MAHIRU NO ANKOKU (1956, Darkness at Noon), about a group of young men falsely charged with murder, and Yoru no tsuzumi (1958, Night Drum). Nigorie and Yoru no tsuzumi are compassionate explorations of the condition of women in feudal Japan. Nigorie, a three-part film based upon stories by the well-known woman writer HIGUCHI ICHIYŌ, is an assault upon the persistence of feudal ethics during the Meiji period (1868–1912), and in particular, their circumscription of the freedom of women. Yoru no tsuzumi, based upon a play by the master 17th-century dramatist CHIKAMATSU MONZAEMON, unfolds the multifarious abuse of women during feudalism in its depiction of the wife of a samurai retainer forced by the shōgun to reside in Edo (now Tōkyō) under the SANKIN KŌTAI system. In her husband's absence she commits adultery and, by Tokugawa law, must die for it. The film describes the psychic destruction wreaked upon all, men as well as women, by pervasive injustice.

Imai differs from other masters of the Japanese film in the informality with which he works. He has said that he never plans elaborate continuity in advance, but rather decides exactly how a scene will be shot when he comes to it. At his best, Imai displays a richness of social perception and an ongoing critique of injustice which render his films evocative studies of the workings of Japanese society.

■ ——Joan Mellen, Voices from the Japanese Cinema (1975). Joan Mellen, The Waves at Genji's Door: Japan Through Its Cinema (1976). Joan MELLEN

Imakagami

("Mirror of the Present"). Historical tale of the latter part of the Heian period (794–1185). Author unknown, although Fujiwara no Tametsune has been mentioned as a possibility. Compiled in 1170, it recounts the events at court during the 150 years from the reign of Emperor Go-Ichijō (r 1016–36) to that of Emperor Takakura (r 1168–80). It is written in the form of recollections by a fictional narrator, who claims to have served the noted author MURASAKI SHIKIBU at one time, and who presents herself, interestingly enough, as the granddaughter of the ŌKAGAMI's narrator Ōyake no Yotsugi. Clearly modeled on the Ōkagami and continuing the historical narrative from 1025 where the older work left off, it resembles the Genji monogatari (TALE OF GENJI) and the EIGA MONOGATARI in its nostalgic treatment of Heian aristocratic life at a time when the power of the court nobility was rapidly declining. Following the tradition of historical tales established by the Eiga, Imakagami focuses on the daily pageantry of court life and the private affairs of high-ranking nobility, provides useful information on poetry and the performing arts of its day, and recounts only sketchily political and military upheavals—the larger public events of the late Heian period.

Imamura Arao (1887–1967)

Internist. Born in Nara Prefecture; graduate of Tōkyō University. The author of a series of studies on BCG, a tuberculosis vaccine, he was an indefatigable pioneer in the use of BCG inoculation in Japan. He also stressed the importance of examinations to detect tuberculosis. He was professor at and president of Ōsaka University, and a member of the Japan Academy from 1951. ACHIWA Gorō

Imamura Shikō (1880–1916)

Painter instrumental in the modernization of Japanese-style painting (NIHONGA). Born in Yokohama, Shikō went to Tōkyō in 1897 to study under Matsumoto Fūko (1840–1923). In 1901, along with YASUDA YUKIHIKO and others, he organized and became the leader of the Kōjikai artists' group. In 1907 he met OKAKURA KAKUZŌ at the Nihon Bijutsuin (JAPAN FINE ARTS ACADEMY). Through his contact with Okakura, Shikō became increasingly influenced by the RIMPA-school style and the work of his contemporary HISHIDA SHUNSŌ. In 1911 Shikō moved to Odawara with Yasuda and other artists and experimented with new styles under the patronage of the influential businessman-art collector Hara Tomitarō. When the Kōjikai disbanded in 1913, Shikō returned to Tōkyō and joined Hayami Gyoshū (1894–1935), Ushida Keison (1890–1976), and other painters in a loosely aligned group known as the Meguro school. In 1914 he traveled extensively in India, China, and Korea. When he returned to Japan he exhibited his masterpiece, Nekkoku no maki (The Tropics), a two-volume set of handscrolls in an idiosyncratic style, which caused great excitement in the Tōkyō art world. His style was innovative and his works were among the first to combine BUNJINGA style with elements of northern European realism.

Imamura Shōhei (1926–   )

Film director of the postwar period. Imamura's work reveals his fascination with the superstitious and irrational elements which he feels form the basis of the Japanese character. His most compelling protagonists are lower-class provincial women who, for Imamura, embody the intuition, superstition, and surviving primitivism of the Japanese, which cannot be dispelled by the influx of industry, material affluence, and Western values. Imamura has avoided depicting the self-sacrificing heroines favored by a previous generation of Japanese filmmakers; in his own personal experience, he claims, no such women exist.

Born and raised in Tōkyō, Imamura is the son of a physician. He attended all the elite schools that should have set him on a course toward Tōkyō University and a comfortable government or business career. However, Imamura felt uncomfortable in such an atmosphere, and instead developed a strong interest in theater. To avoid being drafted into the army, he entered technical school in Tōkyō, where he remained until the end of World War II. After the war, he entered Waseda University to study Western history. While he was enrolled at Waseda, Imamura wrote plays and appeared on stage with many of the actors who would later appear in his films; among them were Ozawa Shōichi (b 1929), Kitamura Kazuo (b 1927), and Katō Takeshi (b 1929). While these actors later entered the modern theater, Imamura joined Shōchiku Motion Picture Company (see SHŌCHIKU CO, LTD) as assistant director in 1951. His aversion to the directorial method of OZU YASUJIRŌ, whom he assisted at Shōchiku, was one of the reasons he moved to Nikkatsu (see NIKKATSU CORPORATION), Japan's oldest motion picture studio, in 1954.

In contrast to the rigidity of an Ozu film, the need to produce a film as close to reality as possible, along with a continued interest in the experimental aspects of modern theater, are reflected in Imamura's works. He does all of his filming on location, with sync-sound, to "do away with the accepted convenience of sets and post-synchronized sound," as he puts it. Many of his films, which are often made in obscure corners of Japan, such as the red-light district of the American naval base town of Yokosuka, and the Ryūkyū Islands, abound in local dialect and provincial attitudes and sensibilities. His interest in the improvisational aspects of modern theater is reflected particularly in his later works. Imamura planned *Ningen jōhatsu* (1967, A Man Vanishes) by selecting one woman who filed a missing-persons police report and then helping her try to find her fiancé under the watchful eye of the camera. For his *Nippon sengo shi: Madamu Omboro no seikatsu* (1970, History of Postwar Japan as Told by a Bar Hostess) he selected a middle-aged woman who operated a bar for the American military men near Yokosuka. The film is a profile of the woman in her words. The bar hostess fits into the pattern of other Imamura heroines: practical, with an earthy sense of humor, and determined above all to give herself and her daughter some stable means of financial and material comfort.

Imamura's recent films employ a favorite theme of his approach to drama: chance. *Fukushū suru wa ware ni ari* (1979, Vengeance Is Mine), his first feature in nearly a decade, treats a murder case in which no motive can be found. The 1980 *Eejanaika* (Eijanaika) is his first period film. Prior to these theatrical films, Imamura made several television documentaries in Southeast Asia, where he found many expatriate Japanese who had never returned home after the Pacific War. *Karayuki san* (1973, Karayuki San: The Making of a Prostitute) was subsequently released as a feature. KARAYUKI SAN were young women from Kyūshū, often sold by their impoverished families into service as prostitutes in Southeast Asian cities. The stories these women tell, many of them still in great poverty, along with their feelings toward the Japan of past and present, are a remarkable record of undefeated, surviving women. Imamura has also absorbed himself since 1975 with the television and film school (Yokohama Hōsō Eiga Semmon Gakkō) he founded in Yokohama, where he presides and teaches.

📖———Audie Bock, *Japanese Film Directors* (1978).

Audie BOCK

Imanishi Kinji (1902–)

Biologist and anthropologist. Born in Kyōto. A graduate of Kyōto University, he began his research career by studying the ecology of the mayfly. Based on these studies, he developed the biological theory of "habitat segregation," according to which different species inhabiting a single area maintain spatially and temporally different living habits. After he joined the Kyōto University faculty, Imanishi's interest in mountain climbing and exploration led him to carry out various research expeditions in Inner Mongolia (1938–39, 1944–46), Ponape Island (1941), the Himalayan Mountains in Nepal (1952), and many other places. After World War II he became a member of the KYŌTO UNIVERSITY RESEARCH INSTITUTE FOR HUMANISTIC STUDIES, where he initiated behavioral studies on primates; his studies of the Japanese monkey (*Macaca fuscata*) have attracted considerable attention from scientists outside of Japan.

Imanishi received the Order of Culture in 1979. His best-known publications are: *Seibutsu no sekai* (1941, The World of Living Things); *Seibutsu shakai no ronri* (1949, Logic of the World of Living Things); and *Imanishi Kinji zenshū* (1974–75, Collected Works of Imanishi Kinji). *SUZUKI Zenji*

Imari

City in western Saga Prefecture, Kyūshū, on Imari Bay. The city developed in the Edo period (1600–1868) as a shipping port for Imari ware (see ARITA WARE). After World War II it flourished temporarily as a coal-mining town, but today its principal industries are plywood and shipbuilding. Special local products are Ōkawachi ware, with a history of 300 years, *kamaboko* (boiled fish paste), and pears. Pop: 61,248.

Imari ware → Arita ware

Imbanuma

Marsh in northern Chiba Prefecture, central Honshū, located west of the city of Narita. It was created by deposits of the river Tonegawa damming a valley in the plateau of Shimōsa. It is currently divided into two ponds, north and east, because of the completion of a land reclamation project initiated by the government in 1963. (During the Edo period [1600–1868] the shogunate had made repeated efforts to drain the marsh.) A 13.9 sq km (5.4 sq mi) area of land has been reclaimed from the marsh. The water of the two ponds is utilized for irrigation, industry, and drinking. The area of the marsh before land reclamation was 21.3 sq km (8.2 sq mi).

Imbe family

Family that, together with the Nakatomi family, was in charge of religious affairs at the ancient YAMATO COURT (ca 4th century–ca mid-7th century). Originally of rather inconsequential status at the court, the family gradually grew in influence as the imperial institution came to be invested with secular and sacerdotal powers. After the 7th century the Imbe were eclipsed by the newly emergent FUJIWARA FAMILY in a power struggle. In 807, in a vain attempt to give due credit to the family's past achievements and to revive its fortunes, Imbe no Hironari wrote the KOGO SHŪI. *KITAMURA Bunji*

IMF

(International Monetary Fund). The IMF was established by the Bretton Woods Agreement in 1944 and began functioning in 1947. Its goals are the promotion of international monetary cooperation, the stabilization of exchange rates, and the expansion of the international liquidity of currencies.

Japan became a member of the IMF in 1952. This was the nation's first affiliation with an international organization after World War II, and it marked a watershed in the postwar reconstruction. Because Japan's economic recovery was not yet complete and the nation faced a deficit in its international BALANCE OF PAYMENTS, it was exempted from article 8 of the IMF's articles of agreement, which requires the elimination of all restrictions on foreign exchange. Japan was operating at the time under a strict system of FOREIGN EXCHANGE CONTROL and trade restriction, which was intended to preserve the nation's scarce reserves of foreign currency.

Once the postwar economic recovery was complete and Japan was experiencing consistent economic growth, trade restrictions were progressively eliminated. In the early 1960s, some 40 percent of Japan's trade had been liberalized; the percentage rose to 90 by 1964. During this same period, many foreign exchange restrictions were also lifted: nonresident YEN deposit accounts were established, a yen exchange system was developed, and the exchange rate band was broadened. On the basis of these preparations, Japan assumed the status of an article-8 nation in 1964.

In the late 1960s, Japan's international balance of payments turned from a deficit to a surplus. As a result of the strength of the Japanese currency, the yen was officially revalued at the 1971 Smithsonian talks from 360 to 308 per US dollar. In February 1973 a floating exchange rate system was adopted. Following the OIL CRISIS OF 1973 the yen's value decreased, but it then recovered and in October 1978 reached a high-water mark of 176 yen to the dollar. By the end of 1980 the rate had slipped back to 203 yen to the dollar.

At the beginning of 1970, the IMF implemented a system of special drawing rights (SDRs), which standardized the holdings of the fund from which member nations with balance of payments deficits may borrow to cover their shortfall. Japan's quota for investment in the fund was 12 billion SDRs in the 1979 figures. Japan has become one of the five largest investment countries in the IMF, making the transition from borrower to lender. *TSUCHIYA Rokurō*

IMF–JC

(abbreviation of the International Metalworkers' Federation–Japan Council). Also known as Zen Nihon Kinzoku Sangyō Rōdō Kumiai

Kyōgikai. IMF-JC was founded in 1964 to help individual unions join the IMF, which in turn is a member of the International Confederation of Free Trade Unions (ICFTU). At first it was a loose organization, but after 1967 it became actively involved in collective bargaining. It has emerged as a new national labor federation similar to SŌHYŌ (General Council of Trade Unions of Japan), DŌMEI (Japanese Confederation of Labor), and CHŪRITSU RŌREN (Federation of Independent Unions). It has acted in unison with Dōmei in pursuing an anticommunist policy and in seeking harmony between workers and employers. In recent years, IMF-JC has been more vocal in expressing its differences with Sōhyō—in particular with the Council of Public Corporation and National Enterprise Workers' Unions (KŌRŌKYŌ), a major Sōhyō affiliate. IMF-JC's membership includes seven industrial unions and six nationwide federations of unions, among which are the Japanese Federation of Iron and Steel Workers' Unions (Tekkō Rōren) and the Confederation of Japan Automobile Workers' Unions (JIDŌSHA SŌREN). It had a total membership of 1,876,000 in 1978.

Kurita Ken

imikotoba → taboo expressions

Imo Mutiny

(J: Jingo Jihen). A revolt of traditionalist Korean troops in 1882 (*imo* in the sexagenary system of year designations as pronounced in Korean; *jingo* in Japanese). The previous year, a Japanese military assistance group had arrived in Korea to initiate the modernization of the Korean army. A newly organized select unit was given benefits that aroused the anger of the traditional units whose troops had gone without pay for over a year. In mid-1882 these troops mutinied, killed prominent Korean government officials and Japanese officers, and attempted unsuccessfully to assassinate Queen MIN. Both China and Japan dispatched troops to Korea, and the Chinese seized the TAEWŌN'GUN, the king's father who was believed to have incited and directed the mutiny, and held him in exile in Tianjin (Tientsin). The mutiny set the stage for growing rivalry between China and Japan over Korea, which culminated in the SINO-JAPANESE WAR OF 1894–1895. See also KOREA AND JAPAN: early modern relations.

C. Kenneth Quinones

imori

Triturus pyrrhogaster. A small newt of the family Salamandridae commonly found throughout Japan except Hokkaidō. Body 8–12 centimeters (3.1–4.7 in) long. It has a unique combination of beautiful colors, black or blackish brown above and bright red below. It usually lives in wetland areas, and large numbers gather in the fresh water of swamps, ponds, paddy fields, and streams to spawn from spring through summer. The larva, a tadpole with three pairs of external gills, metamorphoses after three to five months. In autumn it leaves the water and hibernates, usually under a stone or fallen leaves. It is prized as a pet because of its attractive coloring, and is kept in Europe and the United States as well as in Japan.

Imaizumi Yoshiharu

The name *imori* is said to be derived from *i mori* meaning one who lives in an old well and protects it. The unusual appearance of its red belly is thought to have created superstitious fears that the *imori* is poisonous or would never release anything it bites. It is also said that when a male and a female are put in a bamboo tube separated by a node, they eat open the node and copulate. According to another superstition, a man who sprinkled the powder of charred *imori* on the object of his love, or let her drink *sake* with the powder, would gain her heart. For this reason charred *imori* was sold as a purported love-philter by apothecaries in the Edo period (1600–1868).

Saneyoshi Tatsuo

impeachment

(*dangai*). The system for the removal from office for cause of JUDGES and commissioners of the NATIONAL PERSONNEL AUTHORITY. Japanese law does not provide for impeachment of the prime minister or other high government officials. The 1947 CONSTITUTION provides that judges shall not be removed except by impeachment (art. 78) and that the Diet shall establish an impeachment court for the trial of judges against whom removal proceedings have been

instituted (art. 64). The Law for the Impeachment of Judges (Saibankan Dangai Hō) enacted in 1947 establishes a Committee for the Prosecution of Judges (Saibankan Sotsui Iinkai) consisting of 20 members, 10 each from the House of Representatives and the House of Councillors. Any person may request a charge of impeachment from the committee. Grounds for impeachment are conspicuous failure to discharge responsibilities, extreme neglect of duties, or misconduct in or out of court that causes a conspicuous loss of dignity as a judge. The committee may discharge the complaint, defer action, or find cause for impeachment.

If the committee finds grounds for impeachment, it transmits a letter of impeachment to the Court for the Impeachment of Judges (Saibankan Dangai Saibansho), which consists of 14 members, 7 each from the House of Representatives and the House of Councillors. The members are elected by their respective houses and are independent in the exercise of their duties. Trials and the pronouncement of the verdict must be public, but the court's deliberations are private. Verdicts are decided by a majority vote of those participating, but a verdict to dismiss must be approved by a two-thirds majority of those participating. A member of the three-person National Personnel Authority may also be impeached. In such cases the Diet brings charges and the Supreme Court hears the case and renders the verdict.

John M. Maki

imperial anthologies

(*chokusenshū*). Anthologies of Japanese court poetry (WAKA) compiled at the direct command of an emperor or retired emperor. Altogether 21 were compiled, the first in 905 and the last in 1439. Inclusion of a poem in one of these prestigious anthologies was the highest accolade and an honor eagerly sought by every poet, while the even greater honor of being appointed a compiler was yet more avidly coveted by the leading poets and was a source of bitter rivalry. The command by Emperor Daigo for the compilation of the first imperial anthology, the KOKINSHŪ (Collection of Ancient and Modern Times; 905), marks the rise of *waka* to full literary and social acceptance after more than a century of obscurity, and was a conscious attempt to establish its status and produce an equivalent in Japanese of the three imperial anthologies of Chinese poetry (*chokusen shishū*), which had been ordered in the mid-9th century. The *Kokinshū*, divided into 20 books and with its poems arranged not by poet but in carefully regulated order of topic, became the model for all subsequent imperial anthologies. The development of *waka* can be traced through the first 8 anthologies: the *Kokinshū*, *Gosenshū* (GOSEN WAKASHŪ; Later Collection; ca 955–966), *Shūishū* (SHŪI WAKASHU; Collection of Gleanings; ca 996–1007), *Go shūishū* (Later Collection of Gleanings; 1086), *Kin'yōshū* (KIN'YŌ WAKASHŪ; Collection of Golden Leaves; 1124–27), *Shikashū* (SHIKA WAKASHŪ; Collection of Verbal Flowers; 1152–53), *Senzaishū* (SENZAI WAKASHŪ; Collection of a Thousand Years; ca 1187–1188), and SHIN KOKINSHŪ (New Collection of Ancient and Modern Times; ca 1205), collectively known as the *hachidaishū* (collections of eight generations); but most critical and scholarly attention is focused on the *Kokinshū* and the *Shin kokinshū*. Of the 13 anthologies following the *Shin kokinshū*, only three, the *Shin chokusenshū* (New Imperial Collection; 1232), *Gyokuyōshū* (GYOKUYŌ WAKASHŪ; Collection of Jeweled Leaves; 1312–14) and *Fūgashū* (*Fūga wakashū;* Collection of Elegance; 1344–49), are worthy of note, with the others, and particularly the last four, showing a sad state of stagnation and then decline.

Phillip T. Harries

imperial conferences → gozen kaigi

Imperial Diet

(Teikoku Gikai). Bicameral national assembly established by the Meiji CONSTITUTION of 1889. It was first convoked on 25 November 1890 and dissolved in 1947 after World War II.

The government leaders of the early part of the Meiji period (1868–1912) sought to contain the political demands of the FREEDOM AND PEOPLE'S RIGHTS MOVEMENT. Although they saw the wisdom of making some concessions to popular demands for a parliamentary assembly, they firmly believed that sovereignty should reside in the emperor and that popular participation in the political process should be kept at a minimum. It was on these principles that the Meiji Constitution was framed. Under the provisions of the constitution, the emperor combined in his person the rights of sovereignty, exercising all legislative, administrative, and judicial powers. The

Imperial Diet was an organ designed to "assist and approve" *(kyō-san)* the emperor's exercise of these rights. The emperor convoked, opened, closed, and prorogued the Imperial Diet; he could also dissolve the lower house, the House of Representatives. Since in actuality the emperor exercised his rights with the advice and consent of his governmental ministers, government dominance of the Diet was ensured by the constitution. Apart from these sovereign rights, the emperor was empowered to issue IMPERIAL ORDINANCES *(chokurei)* and special imperial ordinances *(kinkyū chokurei)* for emergencies, determine the organization of different branches of the administration, and appoint and dismiss all civil and military officials. The emperor had supreme command over the army and navy, determined the organization and size of the military, declared martial law and war, made peace, and concluded treaties. Thus, the Imperial Diet from its inception was severely limited in its powers.

The Diet's primary power was to initiate legislation. Both it and the government were authorized to introduce bills, and the emperor as a matter of course sanctioned all laws passed by the Diet. Thus, the Diet exercised legislative powers, but only to a limited extent, since the emperor's sovereign rights were exempted from parliamentary debate and laws concerning the Diet's structure and its members' election and tenure of office had to be first reviewed by the PRIVY COUNCIL (Sūmitsuin). The Diet also held the power to determine the annual budget, but appropriations fixed by the emperor's exercise of his sovereign rights (e.g., imperial household and military expenses) could neither be reduced nor rejected by the Diet without the concurrence of the government. Moreover, if the Diet rejected the government's proposed budget, the government could reinstate the budget of the previous year. These provisions, then, curtailed the Diet's budgetary powers. Apart from these rights, the Diet was authorized to present memorials to the emperor, make representations to the government concerning laws or any other subject, and receive petitions from the people.

Organization——The Diet consisted of two houses, the HOUSE OF PEERS (Kizokuin) and the House of Representatives (Shūgiin). The House of Peers was composed mainly of members of the imperial family, the nobles *(kazoku; see* PEERAGE), and other eminent members of society. Members of the imperial family, princes, and marquises were appointed for life. Nobles of lower rank (counts, viscounts, and barons) were elected by their peers to seven-year terms. Members of the House of Peers who had been nominated by the government for imperial appointment *(chokusen giin)* were generally eminent scholars and men who had distinguished themselves in various other fields. They too received life appointments. Persons who paid high taxes, nominated by the government, and certain members of the JAPAN ACADEMY (Nihon Gakushiin), chosen by fellow academicians, were appointed to seven-year terms.

In contrast, members of the House of Representatives were elected to four-year terms by popular vote. The electorate was initially limited to about 1.25 percent of the population, however, since the first election law stipulated that only males over 25 years of age who paid ¥15 or more in national tax could vote. A movement to extend the franchise arose from about 1897, and in 1925 universal manhood suffrage (see UNIVERSAL MANHOOD SUFFRAGE MOVEMENT) was enacted.

ITŌ HIROBUMI and other government leaders who drafted the constitution explicitly stated that the House of Peers would be an assembly of "representatives of the upper classes" that would "maintain an equilibrium in the government and restrain political parties from running to extremes." The power of the two houses was theoretically equal, but the upper house could not be dissolved, and the lower house was not allowed to participate in any amendment of the ordinance defining the structure and organization of the House of Peers. Consequently, the House of Representatives, which theoretically reflected the will of the people, could act only within the limits permitted by the House of Peers.

Operation——There were three kinds of Diet session: ordinary sessions convoked once a year, extraordinary sessions in case of emergency, and special sessions convoked within five months of the dissolution of the House of Representatives. The duration of an ordinary session was limited to three months. Although Diet activity in principle centered on this session, for matters of special consideration there were three committees: a Diet committee (initially attended by all Diet members but not convened after the 13th session), a standing committee (composed of three subcommittees in charge of appropriations, discipline, and petitions, to which were added an audit subcommittee from the 6th session onward; the House of Peers had also a committee to screen qualifications for

membership), and a special committee to debate specific issues. There was also a bicameral conference that acted as a mediator when differences arose between the two houses.

As a rule, deliberations in the Diet were held in public. Upon demand of the government or by a resolution of the House (introduced by the speaker or by more than 10 members), deliberations could be held in camera. Thus, whenever it chose, the government could conceal its debates from the public. Again, because a session could not be prolonged, Diet failure to pass a bill within the brief term of a session amounted to its rejection.

History: Meiji Period (1868–1912)——The first session was convoked by Emperor MEIJI on 25 November 1890 and opened four days later. The first six sessions, up to 1894, were dominated by the heirs to the people's rights movement, the opposition JIYŪTŌ (Liberal Party) and RIKKEN KAISHINTŌ (Constitutional Reform Party), which held more than half of the seats in the lower house. When the government refused to cooperate with the political parties, it met vigorous opposition from the lower house on questions of treaty revision (see UNEQUAL TREATIES, REVISION OF) and expansion of the military budget. Consequently, it resorted to the issuance of imperial rescripts in order to push through its programs. With the outbreak of the SINO-JAPANESE WAR OF 1894–1895 and the emergence of a spirit of "national unity," the so-called popular parties (MINTŌ) decided to compromise with the government to participate, however feebly, in political decision making.

In September 1900 Itō, now a GENRŌ (elder statesman), formed the RIKKEN SEIYŪKAI (Friends of Constitutional Government Party) as a progovernment party and succeeded in enlisting Diet members formerly affiliated with the Jiyūtō. For the first time, the government could count on a firm base of support in the lower house. In the following decades, the Seiyūkai regularly if not always maintained its position as the party in power and expanded its influence in opposition to the KENSEI HONTŌ (True Constitutional Party), founded in 1898 by former Kaishintō elements.

The various factions in the House of Peers, in contrast, never attained the cohesive force of a political party. They remained loose groupings of men bound together by personality, regional or other extra-Diet clique affiliation, and level of aristocratic rank. During the Meiji period, the House of Peers on the whole vigorously opposed party politics. Those who had received imperial appointment tended to be more politically active. The Kenkyūkai (Study Association), formed in 1891, represented the largest faction. Although the factions sometimes opposed the government, in the main they supported government policies. During the RUSSO-JAPANESE WAR (1904–05), the Seiyūkai courted several factions, particularly the Kenkyūkai, and caused some disunity in its ranks.

Taishō Period (1912–1926)——With the development of capitalism, political parties also gained in power. During the TAISHŌ POLITICAL CRISIS of 1912–13 the Seiyūkai, RIKKEN KOKUMINTŌ (successor to the Kensei Hontō), and nonparty intellectuals organized the MOVEMENT TO PROTECT CONSTITUTIONAL GOVERNMENT (Kensei Yōgo Undō) and succeeded in toppling the KATSURA TARŌ cabinet. Later, in the wake of the RICE RIOTS OF 1918 and the resignation of the TERAUCHI MASATAKE cabinet, the politician HARA TAKASHI formed Japan's first genuine party cabinet, composed mainly of Seiyūkai members. The Hara ministry was able to consolidate its political power by securing the cooperation of the Kenkyūkai. Hara was assassinated in 1921, however, and the Seiyūkai found itself racked with dissension. Moreover, in the House of Peers, those identified with the arch-conservative YAMAGATA ARITOMO faction gained the upper hand. As a result, the three cabinets from 1922 to 1924 were made up of military men and bureaucrats whose main support came from the House of Peers.

In the face of these undemocratic tendencies, the popular call for a return to party government—the so-called TAISHŌ DEMOCRACY—and for reform in the House of Peers grew stronger. In 1924 the KENSEIKAI (Constitutional Association), Seiyūkai, and KAKUSHIN KURABU (Reform Club) organized a second movement to protect constitutional government. They gained an overwhelming majority in the May elections, and in June KATŌ TAKAAKI formed a coalition cabinet. Party government was once again firmly established; the prestige of political parties and the Diet within the framework of an imperial monarchy reached new heights, while that of the House of Peers sank to its lowest ebb.

Shōwa Period (1926–)——Party politics during the early Shōwa period revolved around the struggle between the two largest conservative parties, the Seiyūkai and the RIKKEN MINSEITŌ (Constitutional Democratic Party), formed in 1927 as successor to the

Imperial household —— Imperial family as of 1983

Emperor Hirohito 1901– r 1926–	Empress Nagako 1903–	Prince Chichibu (Chichibu no Miya Yasuhito) 1902–53	Princess Chichibu (Chichibu no Miya Setsuko) 1909–	Prince Takamatsu (Takamatsu no Miya Nobuhito) 1905–	Princess Takamatsu (Takamatsu no Miya Kikuko) 1911–	Prince Mikasa (Mikasa no Miya Takahito) 1915–	Princess Mikasa (Mikasa no Miya Yuriko) 1923–
Crown Prince Akihito 1933–	Crown Princess Michiko 1934–	Prince Hitachi (Hitachi no Miya Masahito) 1935–	Princess Hitachi (Hitachi no Miya Hanako) 1940–	Prince Mikasa (Mikasa no Miya Tomohito) 1946–	Princess Mikasa (Mikasa no Miya Nobuko) 1955–	Prince Mikasa (Mikasa no Miya Yoshihito) 1948–	Princess Mikasa (Mikasa no Miya Masako) 1951–

Prince Hiro (Hiro no Miya Naruhito) 1960– Prince Aya (Aya no Miya Fumihito) 1965– Princess Nori (Nori no Miya Sayako) 1969–

Princess Mikasa (Mikasa no Miya Ayako) 1981–

Prince Mikasa (Mikasa no Miya Norihito) 1954–

NOTE: Japanese names of princes and princesses consist of a title and personal name, e.g., in the case of Takamatsu no Miya Nobuhito, Takamatsu no Miya (Prince Takamatsu) is the title and Nobuhito the personal name. Members of the imperial family do not have surnames. Children of princes other than the crown prince take the titles of their father. Former princesses Higashikuni Shigeko, Takatsukasa Kazuko, Ikeda Atsuko, Shimazu Takako (daughters of Emperor Hirohito), and Konoe Yasuko (daughter of Mikasa no Miya Takahito) have become commoners through marriage, taking the surnames of their husbands.

Imperial household

The imperial family on New Year's Day 1982. Shown are (from left) Prince Hiro, Princess Nori, Crown Princess Michiko, Crown Prince Akihito, Emperor Hirohito, Empress Nagako, Prince Aya, Prince Hitachi, and Princess Hitachi.

Kenseikai. After the MAY 15TH INCIDENT, an attempted coup d'etat by naval officers in 1932, parliamentary democracy was to suffer a series of setbacks. Although the political parties repeatedly tried to act in concert to regain political power, they ultimately failed. The passage of the NATIONAL MOBILIZATION LAW in the year following the outbreak of the SINO-JAPANESE WAR OF 1937–1945 struck a fatal blow: the government arrogated political powers on a wide scale, and the Diet was reduced to being an "imperial assistance Diet" (yokusan gikai) that rubber-stamped all government policies.

Political parties reestablished themselves immediately after World War II. The OCCUPATION PURGE carried out by the Allied Powers and the extension of the franchise to women in 1946 drastically changed the complexion of Diet membership. With the approval of the new constitution in the 90th session of 1946, and the closing of the 92nd session on 31 March 1947, the Imperial Diet was formally dissolved after 56 years and four months. See also DIET.
▬ —— Shūgiin and Sangiin, ed, Gikai seido shichijūnen shi, 12 vols (1960–63). KISAKA Jun'ichirō

imperial edict

(shōsho). Form of document used to relay imperial orders. Under the RITSURYŌ SYSTEM of government developed in the late 7th century, the kind of imperial order called mikotonori (also pronounced shō) was used for extraordinary matters and the kind called choku for routine matters. Shōsho refers to the document that embodies a mikotonori or shō. From the Heian period (794–1185), shōsho were written exclusively in kambun, or classical Chinese, and differentiated from SEMMYŌ, which were written in pure Japanese (using Chinese characters). Under the Meiji Constitution (1889), imperial edicts were divided into two categories: kammu shōsho, relating to the imperial family, and seimu shōsho, relating to the declaration of war and the convocation of the IMPERIAL DIET. Under the present constitution (1947), imperial edicts are issued only for matters in-

volving the emperor as head of state, such as convoking the Diet and dissolving the House of Representatives. Cabinet approval is required, and the prime minister signs in addition to the emperor. See also DIPLOMATICS.

Imperial Hotel

(Teikoku Hoteru). Internationally known hotel famous especially for its former building, which was designed by Frank Lloyd WRIGHT. Completed in 1922 after six years of construction, the structure faced Hibiya Park in Tōkyō. It consisted of reinforced concrete with roof trusses of wood. Wright made extensive use of a native stone known as ōyaishi, which had rarely been used before as a building material. The foundation and walls were specially designed to withstand earthquakes. The hotel survived the TŌKYŌ EARTHQUAKE OF 1923, although according to some, the short piling foundation system in fact caused most of the damage to the hotel's concrete structure. With its deep eaves, decorative elements, and interpenetrating spaces, it was representative of Wright's organic architectural style. Once familiar to many foreign visitors in Tōkyō, it has since been demolished and replaced by a newer building; the lobby, however, was preserved and moved to the open-air museum at MEIJI MURA in 1976. WATANABE Hiroshi

imperial household

(kōshitsu). General term applied to the emperor and the imperial family. The imperial family consists of the empress (kōgō), the grand empress dowager (tai kōtaigō), the empress dowager (kōtaigō), imperial princes (shinnō) and their wives (shinnōhi), imperial princesses (naishinnō), princes (ō) and their wives (ōhi), and princesses (jōō). The grand empress dowager is the emperor's grandmother and the empress dowager his mother. Imperial princes and imperial princesses are the legitimate sons and daughters of the emperor or his eldest son; princes and princesses are his legitimate grandsons and granddaughters.

Only males can succeed to the imperial throne. The order of succession as established by law is as follows: the eldest son, the eldest son's eldest son, other sons and grandsons of the eldest son, the second eldest son and his sons and grandsons, other imperial sons and grandsons, imperial brothers and their sons and grandsons, and imperial uncles and their sons and grandsons. The crown prince (kōtaishi) is the eldest son of the emperor.

Imperial princes (except for the crown prince and the imperial grandson), imperial princesses, princes and princesses may renounce their status as members of the imperial family. The Imperial Household Council (Kōshitsu Kaigi) consists of two members of the imperial family, the speakers and vice-speakers of the House of Representatives and the House of Councillors, the prime minister, the chief justice and one other justice of the Supreme Court, and the head of the IMPERIAL HOUSEHOLD AGENCY. The council deliberates on important matters relating to the imperial household, such as renunciation of status and the establishment of regency. The affairs of the imperial household are governed by the IMPERIAL HOUSEHOLD LAW, enacted by the National Diet in 1947. John M. MAKI

Imperial Household Agency

(Kunaichō). Government agency responsible for the personal, ceremonial, and official affairs of the emperor and his family. Formed in

1947 to replace the former Imperial Household Ministry (Kunaishō), it takes charge of the affairs concerning the emperor's acts in matters of state, and takes custody of the imperial seal (gyoji) and the seal of state (kokuji). It is responsible for maintaining imperial records and documents and caring for imperial tombs and any state property used by the imperial family.

Administratively attached to the Prime Minister's Office, the agency is headed by a grand steward (Kunaichō chōkan) who is appointed by the prime minister but is not a cabinet member. It contains the Grand Steward's Secretariat, the Board of Chamberlains, the Office of the Crown Prince's Household, the Board of Ceremonies, the ARCHIVES AND MAUSOLEA DEPARTMENT, and the Maintenance and Works Department.

Imperial Household Law

(Kōshitsu Tempan). The law concerning matters relating to the IMPERIAL HOUSEHOLD, such as succession to the throne, membership in the imperial family, titles of family members, regency, and the establishment of the advisory Imperial Household Council. There have been two such laws, one under the Meiji CONSTITUTION (1889) and the other under the present constitution (1947). The former was promulgated simultaneously with the Meiji Constitution, and both were regarded as having been bestowed on the nation by the emperor. No amendments were ever made. The present law was enacted by the National Diet in January 1947, after the constitution was enacted but before it was promulgated. The law is treated as ordinary legislation and therefore can be amended by the Diet. Reflecting the change in the constitutional status of the emperor, the 1947 law contains provisions relating to withdrawal from imperial family status.   John M. MAKI

Imperial Japanese Army

(Dai Nippon Teikoku Rikugun). Official name of the Japanese army established under the direct command of the emperor Meiji in 1868 and disbanded in 1945 following Japan's surrender in WORLD WAR II. It fought three major wars: the SINO–JAPANESE WAR OF 1894–1895, the RUSSO–JAPANESE WAR of 1904–05, the Pacific phase of World War II (1941–45), and several other major military actions. During World War II, the army expanded to a peak strength of 6,400,000, organized into at least 172 infantry divisions, four armored divisions, and 13 air units. The central organization consisted of the ARMY MINISTRY, charged with military administration, and the ARMY GENERAL STAFF OFFICE, charged with the military command. The Imperial Japanese Army gained world renown for its exceptional spirit and Spartan devotion to duty. See also ARMED FORCES, IMPERIAL JAPANESE.   KONDŌ Shinji

Imperial Japanese Navy

(Dai Nippon Teikoku Kaigun). Founded in 1868 following the Meiji Restoration, Japan's prewar naval force rose to world rank after its victories in the SINO–JAPANESE WAR OF 1894–1895, RUSSO–JAPANESE WAR (1904–05), and WORLD WAR I. It was virtually annihilated in the Pacific War and formally dissolved on 30 November 1945 (see WORLD WAR II). The central structure consisted of the NAVY MINISTRY, charged with military administration, and the NAVAL GENERAL STAFF OFFICE, charged with military command. These supervised a regional network of naval stations, minor naval posts, and the first-line units of the Combined Fleet. See also ARMED FORCES, IMPERIAL JAPANESE.   ICHIKI Toshio

Imperial Military Reservists' Association

(Teikoku Zaigō Gunjinkai). Also translated as Imperial Veterans' Association. Pre-World War II organization of men who had completed military service or who had passed the physical examination and were eligible for military service. Founded in 1910 under the leadership of Army Minister TERAUCHI MASATAKE and TANAKA GIICHI, then at the Military Affairs Bureau, with the aim of promoting patriotism and military ideals. Branches were established on the city, town, and village level. The association became increasingly politicized in the 1930s, taking an active part, for example, in the rightist movement to discredit the emperor-as-organ theory (TENNŌ KIKAN SETSU) of Minobe Tatsukichi (see KOKUTAI DEBATE). In 1936 it was put under the direct jurisdiction of the war ministries, and was used to facilitate the wartime mobilization of the civilian populace. It was dissolved in August 1945.

Imperial New Year's Poetry Reading

(Utakai Hajime). Poetry (WAKA) reading held at the Imperial Palace to celebrate the New Year. It was held irregularly in the Heian period (794–1185) and was rarely observed during the Muromachi (1333–1568) and Edo (1600–1868) periods. However, since 1869, the year following the Meiji Restoration, it has been held annually on or about 10 January. Initially only the imperial family and guests offered poems, but since 1879 contributions have been solicited from the public. Poems are written on a subject chosen by the emperor, usually a natural theme such as spring mist or cherry blossoms, and must be submitted before 10 November. Poems selected by a committee of judges are read along with those of the imperial family and their guests.   INAGAKI Shisei

imperial ordinance

(chokurei). A type of law issued by the emperor under the Meiji CONSTITUTION (1889). Because the administration in practice could enact such imperial orders without approval of the Imperial Diet, these orders played an important role in maintaining the superior position of the executive branch under the Meiji Constitution. In addition to orders enacted with specific statutory authority, imperial orders included so-called "independent orders" (dokuritsu meirei), intended to preserve public peace and order or to advance the welfare of the citizens (art. 9), and so-called "emergency imperial orders" (kinkyū chokurei), which were to be issued in crisis situations (art. 8). Imperial orders generally ranked below statutes (HŌRITSU) and could not alter their provisions, but emergency orders were accorded the same effect as statutes.

Under the 1947 Constitution of Japan, there is no provision for the imperial orders as a form of law. When the 1947 constitution was enacted, existing imperial orders covering matters that were to be prescribed by statute became void after a certain period. Those covering other matters, however, continued in effect, having the same force as cabinet orders (seirei).

During the period of the Allied Occupation (1945–52), a series of executive orders was promulgated by the Japanese government to implement the instructions and orders of the Supreme Commander for the Allied Powers (SCAP). Of these government orders, generally known as "Potsdam government orders," those issued in the form of emergency imperial orders prior to the enactment of the 1947 Constitution are referred to as "Potsdam emergency imperial orders." The latter included such important political measures as the OCCUPATION PURGE of former militarists and other unwanted personnel from public offices.   ITŌ Masami

imperial regalia

The three sacred objects, collectively known as sanshu no jingi, sanshu no shingi, or sanshu no shimpō, which are the symbols of the legitimacy and authority of the emperor. The regalia consist of the curved jewels (yasakani no magatama) that, according to Japanese mythology, were presented by the deities of heaven to AMATERASU ŌMIKAMI, the sun goddess and so-called imperial ancestress, when she reappeared after secluding herself in a cave; the sacred mirror (yata no kagami) that was used to entice Amaterasu from the cave and then presented to her; and the sacred sword (Ame no Murakumo no Tsurugi) removed from the tail of the serpent YAMATA NO OROCHI in Izumo by Amaterasu's brother, SUSANOO NO MIKOTO, and presented to her as a sign of his submission. The three regalia were handed by Amaterasu to her grandson, NINIGI NO MIKOTO, as a symbol of her authority when he was about to begin his descent to the Japanese islands.

The regalia are said to have been passed from one emperor to the next and to have been housed in the Imperial Palace until the time of the legendary 10th emperor, Sujin, when the sacred mirror and sword in the emperor's possession were replaced by replicas. The originals were, according to legend, removed in accordance with the instructions revealed in an oracle to prevent pollution from human contact and were eventually, in 4 BC, enshrined at Ise. The sacred sword is said to have been subsequently lent to the legendary prince YAMATOTAKERU by the priestess of the Ise Shrine, which he visited while on a campaign to bring eastern Japan under imperial rule. After saving the life of Yamatotakeru, the sacred sword was renamed Kusanagi no Tsurugi ("the sword that cut the [burning] grass"), and it is supposed to be enshrined in the ATSUTA SHRINE at Nagoya.

The original curved jewels are purportedly kept in the Imperial Palace along with the replicas of the mirror and sword. The replica sword reputed to have been made at the time of Emperor Sujin was lost in the Battle of DANNOURA in 1185 and was replaced shortly thereafter by a sword from Ise. The replica mirror is enshrined in the Kashikodokoro ("Place of Awe"), one of the three palace shrines. The supposed original curved jewels and the replica sword are stored in a special room of the palace known as the Kenji no Ma ("Room of the Sword and Seal"). The accession of a new emperor *(senso)* is accomplished when he receives the transfer of the replica sword and "original" jewels, a solemn ritual known as the Kenji Togyo no Gi. See also DAIJŌSAI. *Stanley WEINSTEIN*

Imperial Rescript on Education

(Kyōiku Chokugo). Rescript issued in the name of Emperor MEIJI on 30 October 1890 articulating the guiding principles of education in Japan. Vested with absolute authority, the rescript remained in effect until the end of World War II.

Two major tasks faced the government after the MEIJI RESTORATION (1868). One was the legitimation of political rule by strengthening the imperial institution; the other was rapid Westernization to ensure national independence. Given these conflicting goals, it is not surprising that the educational policies of the Meiji government in the 1870s and 1880s should have gone through a series of changes. The EDUCATION ORDER OF 1872, which established compulsory education, emphasized the needs of the individual. A conservative reaction set in during the late 1870s. Its spokesman was MOTODA NAGAZANE, Confucian scholar and tutor to the emperor, who called for a revival of Confucian thought and morality. ITŌ HIROBUMI defended the government position, although he conceded that henceforth emphasis should be on the scientific and technological aspects of Westernization. A compromise was reached, and it was decided that a more Confucian ideology would be incorporated into public education, at least on the elementary level. Behind this decision was doubtless the government's hope that the Confucian emphasis on duty and order would curb the FREEDOM AND PEOPLE'S RIGHTS MOVEMENT, then at its height.

The change in educational policy met criticism from several quarters: FUKUZAWA YUKICHI decried the revival of Confucianism, and MORI ARINORI asserted that education should inculcate a social ethic that was based on the Rousseauian notion of a social contract. Indeed, when Mori became head of the newly established Ministry of Education in 1885, he set about creating a Western-style educational system aimed at training responsible citizens of a modern nation-state, although by this time he had converted to a more German political philosophy. He reduced the classroom time devoted to SHŪSHIN ("moral" education) and forbade the use of any text materials suggestive of Confucianism. Mori was assassinated in 1889.

It was against this background that Prime Minister YAMAGATA ARITOMO in 1890 ordered the Ministry of Education to draw up a statement defining the basic aims of education. The ministry's draft, written by NAKAMURA MASANAO, was criticized as having too strong a religious and philosophical bent, and INOUE KOWASHI, then director general of the Cabinet Legislation Bureau and the drafter of several legal documents, wrote a new draft. Motoda Nagazane also drafted a statement. The final text was the cooperative effort of Inoue, Motoda, and several other educators and government leaders.

The 315-word rescript begins with the statement that Japan's unique national polity (KOKUTAI) is based on the historical relation between its benevolent rulers and their loyal subjects and that the fundamental principles of education in Japan are based upon this polity. The rescript then lists some 14 virtues, the most important of which are loyalty *(chū)* and filial piety *(kō)*. Finally it exhorts all subjects to cultivate these virtues for the greater glory of the imperial house. It is significant that the rescript upholds not only traditional Confucian virtues but also those necessary for a modern state, such as respect for the constitution and working for the public good. At the same time, by presenting the principles of education as eternal truths, it pretends to be an apolitical document.

The Ministry of Education distributed certified copies to every school in Japan; school principals were instructed to read the rescript to the student body and display the imperial portraits on appropriate occasions (national holidays, graduation ceremonies, etc). Commentaries on the text—which was couched in obscure and archaic language—were also distributed. Students were required to study the text for moral education classes and to commit it to memory. Thus the rescript served as a powerful instrument of political indoctrination for over half a century. After World War II, the formal reading of the Imperial Rescript was forbidden by OCCUPATION authorities.

◾ ——Inada Masatsugu, *Kyōiku chokugo seiritsu katei no kenkyū* (1971). Kaigo Tokiomi, *Kyōiku chokugo seiritsu no kenkyū* (1965). Kokumin Seishin Bunka Kenkyūjo, ed, *Kyōiku chokugo kampatsu kankei shiryōshū*, 3 vols (1939). *SATŌ Hideo*

Imperial Rescript to Soldiers and Sailors

(Gunjin Chokuyu). Rescript issued by Emperor MEIJI on 4 January 1882. The most important document in the development of the modern Japanese armed forces, aside from the CONSCRIPTION ORDINANCE OF 1873. Intended as the official code of ethics for all soldiers and sailors, it is often cited, along with the IMPERIAL RESCRIPT ON EDUCATION (1890), as having provided the moral underpinning for the prewar national ideology that defined service to the state in terms of absolute loyalty to the emperor.

Unlike all previous Meiji rescripts, which were issued through the head of the Grand Council of State (Dajōkan), the Rescript to Soldiers and Sailors had the distinction of being presented directly to the army minister by the emperor at a special ceremony at the palace. This unprecedented act was meant to symbolize the personal bond between the emperor and the military services, as if he were giving private instructions to his personal army, and elevated the observance of these precepts to a sacred obligation to the throne. A second distinguishing feature of the rescript was that, unlike previous imperial rescripts, it was published in classical Japanese rather than in classical Chinese (kambun) to make it more readily understandable to rank-and-file servicemen. But more important than its style of language or mode of presentation was its content.

The 2,500-word rescript began with an official version of imperial history, from Emperor JIMMU onward, that stressed the emperor's continuous command of the armed forces. This authority, it was admitted, had been delegated for a time to the warrior class, but it had been returned at the time of the MEIJI RESTORATION to the emperor, who now as commander-in-chief relied upon the faithful support of soldiers and sailors to protect the state and guard the empire. The rest of the rescript identified the five key principles that should guide the conduct of servicemen: loyalty, propriety, valor, righteousness, and simplicity.

The proper fulfillment of each of these precepts was then elaborated. Loyalty, for example, called for absolute obedience to the emperor and eschewal of political activities. Propriety demanded strict discipline, the acceptance of the authority of one's superiors, and considerate treatment of one's inferiors. Valor required the courage never to despise an inferior nor fear a superior enemy, but at all times to fulfill one's duty. Righteousness meant honesty and faithfulness in personal relations and in carrying out one's duty. Finally, simplicity enjoined soldiers and sailors to avoid luxury and to cultivate frugality as a means of reinforcing loyalty and bravery. The rescript's final paragraph declared that these precepts must be put into practice in a spirit of sincerity. In many respects these injunctions, stressing the moral and spiritual basis of proper conduct, evolved rationally from the need to foster a strong military establishment. On the other hand, unlike previous instructions issued to define norms of conduct for servicemen, the rescript embodied military virtues in a sacrosanct doctrine that gave these precepts the status of sacred obligations. It is this feature of Japan's modern armed forces, with their inculcation of absolute loyalty to the emperor as supreme commander and the stress on spiritual training and values, that has attracted the attention of foreign observers.

Many of the principles set forth in regulations and pronouncements to guide the conduct of the military in the early Meiji years anticipated the contents of the 1882 rescript. From the beginnings of the organization of the new Meiji military forces, there had been serious concern about maintaining discipline and loyalty. Universal conscription, adopted as the basis of the modern military, was a radical reform that shattered the military monopoly of the *samurai* class, and it was an enormously difficult task to develop a cohesive, unified, modern force. To that end, a series of regulations were issued by the military. In 1871, for example, the so-called Rules to Be Read (Dokuhō) were issued in a handbook to each soldier in the army. The rules were revised occasionally, but they usually included eight articles that instructed soldiers to be loyal, respectful of superiors, obedient, courageous, and honorable; the rules reminded them that "the army is established for the purpose of executing the will of the emperor, to strengthen the foundations of the nation, and to protect the country."

In August 1878, a more important set of instructions was issued by Army Minister YAMAGATA ARITOMO to warn all soldiers on their conduct and discipline. Known as the "Admonition to Soldiers"

(Gunjin Kunkai), it was intended to enhance the morale and ensure the loyalty of the imperial army following the unsuccessful challenge to central authority by rebellious Satsuma forces (see SATSUMA REBELLION). It was also issued to counter the collapse of discipline in the ranks of the imperial guard that had led to a serious mutiny earlier that month (TAKEHASHI INSURRECTION). The admonition enjoined soldiers to build up the inner spirit of the army by cultivating the three ideals of loyalty, bravery, and obedience. Seventeen rules were spelled out as ways of achieving these ideals, among them reverence for the emperor, respect for and cooperation with civil authorities, courtesy toward commoners, and close friendship with comrades-in-arms. Another admonition was that members of the armed forces must abstain from political activities. "Such behavior as questioning imperial policies," read the ninth rule, "or expressing private opinions on the constitution, or criticizing government announcements and regulations, runs counter to the duty of the soldier."

It is well known that the principal author of many of the rules and regulations issued by the military in the first 15 years of the Meiji period was NISHI AMANE. A scholar of Western philosophy and an advocate of enlightened reform, he served as a senior bureaucrat in the Army Ministry between 1870 and 1886, drafting regulations at the behest of the army minister. These laws and regulations reflected his belief in the need for a strong military organization and his conviction, reinforced by his acquaintance with Western examples, that an effective military establishment required discipline, obedience, loyalty, and a clear distinction between civil and military society. His ideas were given full expression in the admonition of 1878. Nishi also prepared a draft for the Rescript to Soldiers and Sailors, but it is clear from the numerous revisions made by others before its promulgation in 1882 that there was a significant shift in emphasis from his original draft. The final form of the rescript must be seen against the political circumstances of the time, in particular the POLITICAL CRISIS OF 1881, which had been precipitated by demands for a constitution and resolved by the government's promise of a constitutional system by 1890. INOUE KOWASHI, a key figure in the drafting of the CONSTITUTION of 1889, was almost certainly the crucial person in shaping the final version of the document. The rescript reiterated the duties and obligations of the military found in earlier pronouncements, expanding to five the three cardinal virtues of the military man identified in the 1878 admonition. More important, the term used for the concept of "loyalty," a recurrent injunction in all instructions to the military, was changed; in place of the word used in Nishi's draft for loyalty (chūjitsu), with its primary stress on obedience to the military order, was substituted the word chūsetsu, meaning absolute loyalty to the emperor. The rescript included earlier warnings to the military not to be led astray by current opinions and to avoid politics, but it excluded Nishi's ideas about respecting civil authority, implying the special privileges of the military above politics. As the capstone of a series of documents setting forth the ideals and proper conduct of the military man in the early Meiji period, the rescript transformed an official military code into a code of ethics and converted it into a canon of sacred obligations of absolute loyalty to the emperor as supreme commander.

The rescript was widely disseminated soon after its promulgation and solemnly read to all army and navy units on designated occasions. Memorized by officers and absorbed by the rank and file, it served as the moral basis of military training. In time, the values embodied in the rescript were transmitted by servicemen returning to their home villages. In this way, the Imperial Rescript to Soldiers and Sailors fostered loyalty and duty to the emperor and became an integral part of the national ideology of prewar Japan.

Roger F. HACKETT

Imperial Rule Assistance Association

(Taisei Yokusankai). Association established on 12 October 1940 as the chief institution to promote the goals of the NEW ORDER MOVEMENT. Originally conceived as the nucleus of a mass-based "reformist" political party, the IRAA instead became an instrument for governmental control of popular morale and resources during World War II and included every Japanese subject as a member. It is remembered as a symbol of both the failure of the reformist impulses of the New Order Movement and the wartime government's success in imposing reformist impulses, ideological conformity, and economic restrictions on its subjects.

During the summer of 1940, Prime Minister KONOE FUMIMARO launched plans for a totalitarian political system that would absorb all existing political parties. Because the 37 members he appointed to his Preparatory Commission for Establishing a New Political Order (Shin Taisei Jumbi Kai) represented a broad political spectrum, they had great difficulty agreeing about the suggested reforms. Konoe's proposals sought the establishment of a totalitarian mass political party, with administrative headquarters and deliberative councils at both the national and local levels. The party was to assign members to branches according to their occupation or cultural group; by challenging the allocation of political power among Japan's elite groups, it was intended to provide the masses with otherwise unavailable channels for spontaneous political participation (i.e., "assisting the imperial rule," or *taisei yokusan*).

They intended the new party structure to parallel—and dominate—the administrative and legislative organs of the state. The most ardent supporters of this viewpoint included army officers who hoped to enlist mass political support to override conservative business, bureaucratic, and parliamentary opposition to their plans for a controlled economy; antimainstream political party members who sought to break the Rikken Seiyūkai and Rikken Minseitō parties' domination of the House of Representatives; other party leaders anxious to regain political power from the bureaucracy and military; labor and farmers' groups opposed to local political and economic domination by traditional elite groups and big business; and intellectuals inspired by European models of mass totalitarian political action to overcome elite political and economic controls and to bring the masses further into the political process.

"Japanist" *(kannen uyoku)* commission members objected that a totalitarian party would usurp the power of the emperor's government, as successive shogunates had done before the Meiji Restoration (1868). Many criticized the new party proposal as an unJapanese emulation of Nazi and Communist Party models, declaring that the "sacred" bonds and channels of expression between the emperor and his subjects were already strong enough for the people to "assist the imperial rule." Other critics, primarily career bureaucrats in the Home Ministry, maintained that the proposed network of local party units would overwhelm local administration at a time when the nation needed to use its administrative resources to mobilize support for its foreign policies. Indeed, these commission members wanted the IRAA to reinforce the Home Ministry's power to control the energies and resources of local populaces.

Konoe's enthusiasm for creating a new party gradually waned during the autumn of 1940. The permanent directors and advisers he selected to guide the IRAA represented all political viewpoints, thereby preventing the IRAA from becoming highly partisan even at the outset. Also, local IRAA branches were established as the Home Ministry supporters proposed, according to existing territorial administrative units—the prefecture, city, town, and village—not according to vocation or cultural group. The initial threat of a parallel but independent system of units was further diminished by the preparatory commission agreement to have the existing local governmental leaders at each level automatically head their local IRAA branches.

After the IRAA's formal inauguration in October, its leaders set about staffing administrative branches throughout Japan. In the national headquarters, five bureaus (general affairs, organization, Diet affairs, policy, and planning) and 23 divisions were created, and the national deliberative council first convened in Tōkyō in mid-December. "Reformist" influence was particularly strong in the General Affairs Bureau, under ARIMA YORIYASU, and the Organization Bureau under GOTŌ RYŪNOSUKE (b 1889), since these men appointed their supporters to key positions in local IRAA branches. The army's attempt to fill the branches with members of the IMPERIAL MILITARY RESERVISTS' ASSOCIATION was frustrated by the Home Ministry's establishment of branch control by local government officials but a new effort to create a pro-Army support group was subsequently launched under the aegis of the IRAA East Asia Division.

In the end, Konoe decided after late November 1940 to weaken the reformist character of the IRAA. In December he replaced cabinet ministers Kazami Akira (1886–1961) and Yasui Eiji (1890–1982), the former a strong supporter of the IRAA, with retired Lieutenant General Yanagawa Heisuke (1879–1945) and HIRANUMA KIICHIRŌ, two prominent "Japanists" seeking to limit the scope of IRAA activity. Early in 1941, he undermined the position of the antimainstream Diet members in the IRAA by striking several compromises with Diet leaders that thwarted IRAA interference in the House of Representatives. Finally, at the end of March, he replaced most of the IRAA reformist leaders, including Arima and Gotō, with officials more sympathetic to Home Ministry views.

These decisions guaranteed that the IRAA remained under the control of the existing alignment of political elites. Admittedly, the army attempted later in 1941 and in early 1942 to establish local support groups through the Yokusan Sōnendan (Imperial Rule Assistance Men's Associations), and General TŌJŌ HIDEKI's government tried to eradicate the influence of Diet leaders through an officially sponsored election-nomination commission in March 1942. Moreover, following the 1942 general elections, virtually all Diet members were obliged to join a single party, the Yokusan Seijikai (Imperial Rule Assistance Political Association). But neither the activities of the Yokusan Sōnendan nor the nomination system led to the creation of a mass totalitarian party, and the old Diet leadership retained control of the Yokusan Seijikai.

Instead, the Home Ministry used the IRAA to extend its local administration to every city, town, village, and hamlet, where citizens were organized into small neighborhood associations called *tonarigumi* or *rinpohan*. Traditional community pressures reinforced compliance with the government. Until its dissolution on 13 June 1945 the IRAA focused largely on enlisting popular support and work for the wars in China and the Pacific. Many of its campaigns, for example, encouraged higher industrial and agricultural productivity, increased savings and less consumption by civilians, and popular awareness of and preparedness for civil defense.

OCCUPATION authorities believed that the IRAA had played a political role analogous to that of the Nazi Party in Germany, and so they purged thousands of officials and community leaders from public life for their IRAA works. Many postwar Japanese historians have taken an even harsher view of the IRAA. To be certain, IRAA national leaders had worked energetically to stifle dissent and resistance to the war, and to evoke ever-greater sacrifices from the Japanese people for the state. But just as the wartime Japanese government lacked many attributes of the fascist dictatorships in Europe, the IRAA never served as an instrument of terror or lawlessness as the Nazi Party had in Germany. Moreover, unlike the Nazi Party, the IRAA never became a major policy-making body and never acquired totalitarian control over the people or the state. Local IRAA officials could argue with some reason that since membership had been compulsory, and since as local community leaders they had been automatically designated as local IRAA leaders, their IRAA service did not necessarily signify total support of the IRAA.

The legacy of the IRAA remains to be studied fully, but it will probably be judged a mixed one. Although the IRAA reinforced traditions of national and local elite authority over the people, it also minimized the disruptive social effects of the war sufficiently to facilitate postwar reconstruction. Similarly, the failure of IRAA planners to create a vehicle for true popular participation in national politics perpetuated popular apathy toward national political issues. On the other hand, the large-scale IRAA popular mobilization campaigns—particularly those related to increasing productivity and personal savings and reducing consumption—familiarized Japanese with the very type of activity required in the postwar era for Japan's economic recovery.

📖——Gordon Mark Berger, *Parties Out of Power in Japan, 1931–1941* (1977). Edward J. Drea, *1942 Japanese General Elections: Political Mobilization in Wartime* (1980). Ishida Takeshi, *Heiwa to hakyoku* (1968). Kisaka Jun'ichirō, "Taisei yokusankai no seiritsu," in *Iwanami kōza: Nihon rekishi*, vol 20 (Iwanami Shoten, 1976). Tanaka Sōgorō, "Taisei yokusankai: Nihonteki fuashizumu no shōchō to shite," *Rekishigaku kenkyū* 212 (October 1957). Yabe Teiji, *Konoe Fumimaro*, vol 2 (1952). Yokusan Undō Shi Kankōkai, ed, *Yokusan kokumin undō shi* (1954).　　Gordon M. BERGER

imperial universities

(*teikoku daigaku*). National universities established by the Imperial University Order of 1886 and maintained until the reform of the education system in 1947. They were founded with the aim of training capable Japanese scholars and bureaucrats. The first such university was Tōkyō Imperial University, established in 1886 through the reorganization of the former Tōkyō University; this was followed by Kyōto (1897), Tōhoku (1907), Kyūshū (1910), Hokkaidō (1918), Ōsaka (1931), and Nagoya (1939) imperial universities. The universities in Tōkyō and Kyōto had graduate schools and five colleges (*bunka daigaku*): law, medicine, engineering, art, and natural sciences. Colleges of agriculture and economics were added later. The other universities had four or fewer colleges. These colleges were transformed into university departments (*gakubu*) by the University Order of 1918.

The smallest unit for education at the imperial university was the *kōza* (lecture group); *kōza* were grouped together into subject areas (*gakka* and *gakubu*). Professors were high-ranking members of the government bureaucracy and enjoyed academic freedom as long as they did not criticize official state ideology. The faculty assembly was given self-governing rights that included the selection of the university president.

The period of study at the imperial universities was three to four years, but this presupposed three years of preparatory education at a HIGHER SCHOOL (*kōtō gakkō*). Students at the imperial universities enjoyed many special privileges, including deferment of military service and exemption from the state license examinations for medicine, law, and middle-school teaching. Imperial university graduates occupied the most important positions in the state bureaucracy and private corporations.

Although the imperial university system was abolished after World War II, even now, the national universities which succeeded them continue to dominate the higher education system in Japan. See also UNIVERSITIES AND COLLEGES.　　*AMANO Ikuo*

Imperial Way faction → Kōdōha

Imphal Campaign

(Impāru Sakusen). Aborted military operation undertaken by the Japanese army to seize Imphal in northeastern India during the final stages of WORLD WAR II. The campaign is remembered as a poignant example of the failure to take into account the problems of logistics and topography. The original purpose of the campaign was to eliminate the Anglo-Indian forces controlling the Imphal Basin, a strategic point in the northern Arakan mountains on the Indian-Burmese border. Three Japanese divisions under Lieutenant General Mutaguchi Ren'ya started to advance from the Burma front in March 1944. Because of the unanticipated difficulties in maintaining supply routes through the mountainous area, however, the Japanese exhausted their food and munitions. A powerful Allied counteroffensive extended the planned campaign period into the monsoon season, destroying the already fragile system of communications and transportation. After suffering heavy losses because of battle action, disease, and starvation, the Japanese army gave up the campaign on 9 July 1944. The retreat was even more disastrous as the army dissolved. It is estimated that the total number of Japanese casualties in the campaign approached 73,000.　　*KONDŌ Shinji*

Important Cultural Properties → National Treasures

Important Intangible Cultural Assets → Living National Treasures

in → seals

Ina

City in southern Nagano Prefecture, central Honshū, on the river Tenryūgawa. In the Edo period (1600–1868) it developed as a POST-STATION TOWN on the highway Ina Kaidō and as a river port. The main agricultural products are rice, pears, and tomatoes; dairy farming also flourishes. There is an emerging electronics and precision instruments industry. Ina Park is noted for its cherry blossoms. Ina serves as a base camp for excursions into the Central Japanese Alps. Pop: 56,087.

Ina Basin

(Ina Bonchi). In southern Nagano Prefecture, central Honshū. Flanked by the Kiso and Akaishi mountains, this long fault basin consists of piedmont alluvial fans below the fault scarp in the west, river terraces along the river Tenryūgawa's upper reaches, and a flood plain on its lower reaches. Orchards and mulberry fields are found on the uplands, and rice is grown on the lowlands. The major cities are Ina, Komagane, and Iida. Length: 70 km (43 mi); width: 5 km (3 mi).

Inada Ryōkichi (1874–1950)

Also known as Inada Ryūkichi. Internist. Born in Aichi Prefecture. A graduate of Tōkyō University, where he studied under AOYAMA TANEMICHI, Inada pursued further studies in Germany. He became a professor at the Fukuoka Ika Daigaku (now the Medical Department of Kyūshū University). In 1915, with Ido Yutaka, he discovered the pathogen *Leptospira icterohaemorrhagiae*, which causes Weil's disease. After moving to Tōkyō University in 1918, he studied influenza and internal medicine. He was director of Kōraku Hospital, attached to the Japan Foundation for Cancer Research, and during World War II served concurrently as president of the Japan Medical Association and of the newly organized Japan Medical Care Group. He received the Imperial Prize of the Japan Academy in 1916 and the Order of Culture in 1944. *NAGATOYA Yōji*

Inagaki Hiroshi (1905–1980)

Film director. Specialist in period films. Inagaki began his career as an actor before becoming a director in 1928. After World War II he remade most of his more important films. He is chiefly known outside Japan for his three-part *Miyamoto Musashi* (1954–56, Samurai) and *Muhō Matsu no isshō* (1958, Rickshaw Man), each of which he had made previously in the 1940s. Although the earlier versions are considered superior, portions of them have been lost.

Inagaki was one of several directors who flourished in the 1930s making serious period films that bore some allegorical message for modern man. Many of his films were versions of popular historical legends grounded in fact and centered on actual figures from Japanese history. However, rather than merely presenting the adventures of these characters, he imbued them with special purpose. His *Musashi*, for example, after a spiritual awakening seeks the ideals of truth and justice through his skill as a swordsman. Inagaki himself said that the true period film died with the 1930s, being subsumed into such categories as historical romances and literary adaptations. *David OWENS*

Inagaki Taruho (1900–1977)

Author; poet. Born in the Semba district of Ōsaka in 1900, Inagaki graduated from the Kansei Gakuin Middle School. He then went to Tōkyō intending to become an airplane pilot. His interests, however, soon shifted to painting, and he contributed a work titled "Moon Prose Poem" to the First Futurist Exhibition held in Tōkyō in 1921. Around this time he became acquainted with the novelist and poet SATŌ HARUO and turned to literature, publishing his first work, *Issen ichibyō monogatari* (1923, The Tale of 1001 Seconds), untranslated, as are all of Inagaki's full-length works. He soon established himself as a writer opposed to conventional realism and deeply interested in modernism in all its forms. He also came under the influence of the mystery-fantasy writer EDOGAWA RAMPO (whose name is a punning reference to the 19th-century American author Edgar Allen Poe), and became increasingly interested in the subject of homosexuality. In 1931 he returned to the Kansai region of his birth to recover from the effects of alcoholism and general physical debility. He returned to Tōkyō in 1936, but his level of literary activity, which had declined since his illness in 1931, continued to be low due to personal problems.

After World War II, Inagaki resumed his literary activities with the novels *Miroku* (1946, Maitreya) and *Karera* (1946–47, Them), the latter of which dealt with pederasty, a topic of continuing interest to Inagaki. A collection of his works was published in 1948 under the rather curious title *Wita makinikarisu* (Vita Mechanicalis [?]: perhaps a mistake for Vita Mechanica or Vita Machinalis], a title that echoes MORI ŌGAI's early novel *Wita sekusuarisu* (Vita Sexualis). After his marriage and move to Kyōto in 1950, Inagaki began contributing regularly to a literary coterie magazine called *Sakka*, in which he published the short essay "Tosotsu jōshō" (1950, Rebirth in the Tuṣita Heaven). In 1954 he wrote an essay entitled "A kankaku to V kankaku" (The A Sensibility and the V Sensibility) in the nationally known literary journal *Gunzō*. Here he returned to one of his favorite themes with new boldness and vigor, arguing that the "anal sensibility" (i.e., pederasty) is superior to the "vaginal sensibility" (i.e., heterosexuality) in respect to creative imaginative power.

In the mid-1960s he wrote a number of works dealing with his move back from Tōkyō to the Kansai region and the cultural differences he observed—a topic reminiscent of TANIZAKI JUN'ICHIRŌ, though dealt with from Inagaki's own highly individual point of view. Returning once again to a favorite and familiar theme, he

Inari

A stone fox of the kind commonly found within the precincts of Inari shrines. The drawing shows one of the red bibs often put on the statues in gratitude for prayers answered.

published *Shōnen'ai no bigaku* (The Aesthetics of Pederasty) which won for him in 1969 the Japan Literary Prize, sponsored by the Shinchōsha publishing house. Critics see the 1960s as marking the beginning of a "Taruho boom," and the aged author continued to produce stories and essays dealing with the topics that had occupied him throughout his career, as exemplified by such works as *Hikōki yarōtachi* (1969, The Fly Boys), *Vuanira to Manira* (1969, Vanilla/Manila), *Raito kyōdai ni hajimaru* (1970, Beginning with the Wright Brothers), and *Kinshoku no anus* (1972, The Violet Anus).

Having won a considerable degree of both critical and popular acclaim in his last years (ranging from highly laudatory essays by such major figures as Mishima Yukio to articles in the weekly magazines, complete with photos of "Taruho in the bath" and "Taruho with motorcycle enthusiasts"), Inagaki Taruho died in Kyōto in November 1977. *Paul McCARTHY*

Inagi

City in southern Tōkyō Prefecture, on the river Tamagawa, contiguous with the city of Kawasaki, Kanagawa Prefecture. Formerly a farming area, Inagi's urbanization began in 1961. The area is still noted for its pears. Several electrical appliance manufacturers are also located here. Pop: 48,154.

Inamura Sampaku (1758–1811)

Scholar of Dutch studies (Rangaku; see WESTERN LEARNING) and compiler of the HARUMA WAGE (1796), the first reliable Dutch-Japanese dictionary. Born in the Tottori domain (now part of Tottori Prefecture) and adopted by a family who were hereditary doctors to the *daimyō*, Sampaku studied under the Rangaku scholar ŌTSUKI GENTAKU. Because of the Tokugawa shogunate's NATIONAL SECLUSION policy limiting Japan's contact with the Western world to Dutch traders in Nagasaki, Dutch was the principal medium of Western knowledge at the time. Sampaku saw the need for a Dutch-Japanese dictionary, and in 1796, with the help of Udagawa Genzui (1755–97) and others, he completed a dictionary based on a Dutch-French dictionary, *Woordenboek der Nederduitsche en Fransche Taalen* (1708), by François Halma (1653–1722). The dictionary, popularly known as the *Haruma wage*, contained over 80,000 entries, and, though only 30 copies were made, it made a significant contribution to Western Learning. Sampaku's dictionary was also known as the "Edo Haruma," to distinguish it from the later "Nagasaki Haruma" by the Dutch trade commissioner in Nagasaki, Hendrick DOEFF. Sampaku spent his later years teaching Rangaku in Kyōto.

Inari

Originally one of the names of the deity of cereals. Popularly called Inari Daimyōjin. Inari has been the deity most widely worshiped by Japanese people because of a close association with the nation's rice-centered agriculture. With the development of manufacturing in medieval times (roughly 13th to 16th centuries) the deity was worshiped as a guardian of foundries (blacksmiths) and commerce.

Later popular among the warrior class, Inari has in modern times been installed as a guardian deity in households (yashikigami) of all social classes.

In medieval times, belief in the sacredness of the fox, especially the white fox, was common. Eventually the fox came to be associated with Inari and regarded as the deity's messenger. Thus, the fox as a symbol has often been referred to as inari, and a piece of fried soybean curd which is offered to an Inari shrine in the belief that it was the fox's favorite food has also been called inari. Throughout Japan, there are innumerable mounds and forests where foxes were reputed to have lived and worked wonders, and either a full-scale Inari shrine or a miniature shrine is often found at those sites.

The FUSHIMI INARI SHRINE of Kyōto is among the more eminent Inari shrines, along with the Takekoma Inari Shrine in Miyagi Prefecture, the Kasama Inari Shrine in Ibaraki Prefecture, the Toyokawa Inari (formally, a Buddhist temple, Myōgonji) in Aichi Prefecture, and the Yūtoku Inari Shrine in Saga Prefecture. Apart from the enormous numbers of small Inari shrines and private household Inari shrines, there are now about 40,000 Inari shrines that are officially accredited as legally incorporated religious institutions.

Based on the myths in such works as the KOJIKI and NIHON SHOKI, Shintō theology identifies the deity Inari as Uka no Mitama (or Uganomitama) no Kami, also variously called Toyoukehime or Toyuke Hime no Kami (the deity at the Outer Shrine of the ISE SHRINE), Wakauka no Me no Kami, Ukemochi no Kami, Ōgetsuhime no Kami, or Miketsu Kami. (In these names the elements uka, uke, ke, and ge all mean food; kami or gami means deity.) All these are names of the deity of cereals, the Japanese version of the Great Earth Mother. There are several hypotheses concerning the etymology of the name Inari, but none is certain. According to one theory, the name is an abbreviation of ine-nari (ripening of rice).

Shrine histories, however, trace the origins of the deity Inari back to the Fushimi Inari Shrine, where the tutelary deity of the HATA FAMILY, an ancient clan in the area, was enshrined by Hata no Kimi Irogu. According to tradition, Irogu had become so conceited about his abundant stock of harvested rice that he used a rice cake as a target in archery. When he shot an arrow at this target, however, it changed into a swan and flew away to a nearby mountain and there became a rice plant; hence ina-nari ("rice-becoming"), which became the word inari and the name of the mountain (Inariyama). The descendants of Irogu made amends for his arrogance: they brought a tree from Mt. Inari (Inariyama) to their home, planted it in their yard, worshiped it as god, and thus instituted the Inari shrine. This legend seems to indicate that Inari was originally the god of fields (TA NO KAMI), who was at the same time the clan deity (UJIGAMI) of the Hata family (see also YAMA NO KAMI). As the same tradition holds that this enshrinement took place on the first "Horse Day" (HATSUUMA) in the second month of AD 711, it is still the custom to hold the festival of Inari on this day each year all over the country.

From the end of the 8th century, when the capital of Kyōto was built, Fushimi gradually became an important suburb. As the Hata family augmented their political and economic influence in the area, the Inari shrine gained in popularity. Later the monk KŪKAI, founder of the Shingon sect of Buddhism, adopted Inari as the guardian deity of the temple TŌJI in Kyōto. This resulted in the synthesis of the Inari deity with the Buddhist guardian deity Ḍākinī (J: Dakiniten) and added further prestige to Inari (Myōgonji, mentioned above, is a good example of this synthesis). In the Kyōto area, sorcerers known as ommyōji (see OMMYŌDŌ) sometimes practiced magic using foxes as mediums.

There has been a popular belief that the spirits of animals may possess a man, drive him insane, or gain control of the fate of his family's fortunes. Among such spirits, that of the fox is best known, so that this deity, who supposedly used the spirit of the fox as a messenger, was believed to be most receptive to prayers for good fortune. In the Edo period (1600–1868), not only merchants and craftsmen who desired business prosperity but also many warriors who wished for success erected Inari shrines in their homes to worship the so-called shusse Inari (Inari of success). Thus the Inari shrine became the most popular of all shrines.　SONODA Minoru

Inariyama tomb

An early-6th-century mounded tomb (KOFUN), one of a cluster of 10 tombs (generally known as Sakitama Tomb Cluster) located in the city of Gyōda, Saitama Prefecture. It was originally keyhole-shaped, measuring about 120 meters (394 ft) in length, but in 1938 the front

part was destroyed, leaving only the round section intact. Excavations in 1968 revealed fragments of HANIWA funerary sculptures and two coffin enclosures, one of which yielded horse trappings (see HORSE TRAPPINGS, ANCIENT), small bells, BRONZE MIRRORS, curved magatama (see BEADS, ANCIENT), belt fittings, and iron weapons and armor. In 1978 one of the swords sent out for repair was discovered to bear a 115-character inscription; it was ascertained that several of the characters referred to a ruler of the YAMATO COURT known posthumously as Emperor Yūryaku (latter half of the 5th century). Together with a sword from the ETA FUNAYAMA TOMB in Kyūshū with a similar inscription, it is considered as evidence of the far-ranging authority of the Yamato court in the 5th century.

KITAMURA Bunji

Ina Tadatsugu (1550–1610)

Civil administrator of the Azuchi-Momoyama (1568–1600) and Edo (1600–1868) periods. Born in Mikawa Province (now part of Aichi Prefecture), Ina served as a personal attendant to TOKUGAWA IEYASU before the latter's rise to power and distinguished himself in the ODAWARA CAMPAIGN (1590) by his brilliant handling of provisions, supplies, and other logistical operations. He was subsequently appointed intendant of the eight Kantō provinces (Kantō GUNDAI) after Ieyasu's assignment there by the hegemon TOYOTOMI HIDEYOSHI. As intendant, Ina was in charge of flood control, irrigation of rice fields, and cultivation of wastelands; it was said that under his administration agricultural production in the Kantō region more than doubled. Later he conducted land surveys for the Tokugawa shogunate in several provinces. The cadastral and tax-assessment methods he devised were adopted as models by the shogunate. Ina's descendants inherited his position as intendant until the end of the 18th century.

Inatomi Naoie (1552?–1611)

Also known as Inatomi Ichimu. Authority on gunnery and founder of the Inatomi school of gunnery. Born in Tango Province (now part of Kyōto Prefecture), he studied gunnery with his grandfather. He entered the service of Hosokawa Tadaoki (1563–1645), the daimyō of Tango, but incurred his wrath for not having sufficiently guarded Tadaoki's wife HOSOKAWA GRACIA against ISHIDA MITSUNARI, Tadaoki's enemy. He escaped punishment through the intervention of TOKUGAWA IEYASU and subsequently served Ieyasu and his successor TOKUGAWA HIDETADA in Edo (now Tōkyō).

Inawashiro Kensai (1452–1510)

Renga, or linked verse poet (see RENGA AND HAIKAI). Along with SŌGI, he compiled and edited the second honorary imperial renga anthology SHINSEN TSUKUBASHŪ. Born into an old samurai family in Aizu, Iwashiro Province (now part of Fukushima Prefecture), he became a disciple of SHINKEI in 1470 at the age of 19 during the master's sojourn in Aizu. Following Shinkei's death in 1475, he moved to Kyōto, where in 1489 he was appointed to succeed Sōgi as master of the Kitano Shrine renga office, the highest honor for a renga poet in those days. He was a well-known figure among the feudal lords both in the capital and in the provinces. He wrote a renga handbook (Renga entoku shō) for the daimyō Ōuchi Masahiro (d 1495), whom he visited in 1490. One of his last works was a 100-verse sequence composed in 1505 as a prayer to reconcile a warring father and son of the Ashina family in Aizu. His verses written during the period 1469–1508 are collected in the anthology Sono no chiri; they have a sharply delineated, realistic quality that is often contrasted with Shinkei's spirituality. Among his works on renga theory are Shinkei sōzu teikin (1488), a record of Shinkei's teachings on the proper training for a renga poet, and Renga honshiki and Yōjinshō, both of which deal with the rules and practices of the art.

Inawashiro, Lake

(Inawashiroko). In central Fukushima Prefecture, central Honshū. Located on the southern slopes of the mountain Bandaisan within Bandai-Asahi National Park. Water source of the ASAKA CANAL. The house in which the scientist NOGUCHI HIDEYO was born (now the Noguchi Memorial Museum) is located on the northern bank. Area: 104 sq km (40 sq mi); circumference: 49 km (30 mi); depth: 94 m (308 ft).

Income distribution——Table 1

Prewar Income Differentials

Household consumption ratios (owner-farmer/tenant farmer)

1890	1,83	1912	1.78
1899	1.70	1920	1.90
1908	1.60		

SOURCE: Akira Ono and Tsunehiko Watanabe, "Changes in Income Inequality in the Japanese Economy," in Hugh Patrick, ed, *Japanese Industrialization and Its Social Consequences* (1976).

Wage ratios for males (industrial/agricultural)

1885	1.47
1909	1.49
1934	2.38

SOURCE: Koji Taira, *Economic Development and the Labor Market in Japan* (1970).

Wage differentials among manufacturers

Daily wage indices (establishments with over 1,000 workers = 100)

Number of workers

	500–999	100–499	50–99	30–49	10–29	5–9
1909	94	97	94	94	97	100
1914	91	84	84	81	86	91

Annual wage index (establishments with assets of over ¥500,000 = 100)

Value of assets in ¥1,000 units

	100–500	50–100	10–50	5–10
1932–33	84	78	68	54

SOURCE: Yasukichi Yasuba, "The Evolution of Dualistic Wage Structure," in Hugh Patrick, ed, *Japanese Industrialization and Its Social Consequences* (1976).

Household consumption ratios (nonfarmer/farmer)

1887	1.38	1919	1.39
1897	1.55	1930	2.06
1904	1.35	1938	1.65
1913	1.34		

SOURCE: Kazushi Ohkawa, "Personal Consumption in Dualistic Growth," in Kazushi Ohkawa and Yujiro Hayami, ed, *Economic Growth: The Japanese Experience since the Meiji Era* (1973).

Inayama Yoshihiro (1904–)

Business leader. Born in Tōkyō, he graduated from Tōkyō University in 1927 and entered the Ministry of Commerce (forerunner of the modern Ministry of International Trade and Industry), where he was assigned to the government-operated YAWATA IRON AND STEEL WORKS. A 1934 merger in which this firm became a central participant gave birth to the Nippon Steel Co. Inayama, however, remained at Yawata Steel, a private-sector concern. In 1950 the merged companies in the Yawata and Fuji steel corporations split, and Inayama became executive director of the Yawata firm, rising to vice-president in 1961 and president the following year. In 1970 he joined with NAGANO SHIGEO, president of Fuji Steel, to effect a merger of the two firms in order to avoid competition for production facilities and to secure a stable supply of steel. This was the start of the NIPPON STEEL CORPORATION. Inayama became president and, in 1973, chairman of the board. He has argued that cartels produce price stability and has campaigned for a more flexible application of the antitrust laws. Inayama traveled to China as leader of the representatives of the steel companies in Japan, and since then has labored to expand trade between the two nations. In 1968, he became vice-chairman of KEIDANREN (Federation of Economic Organizations), becoming its fifth chairman in 1980.　　*Kobayakawa Yōichi*

Inazawa

City in western Aichi Prefecture, central Honshū, 13 km (8 mi) northwest of Nagoya. Inazawa is noted for its tree nurseries. It is fast becoming a satellite city of Nagoya. The Kōnomiya Festival at the Owari Ōkunitama Shrine is a major tourist attraction. Pop: 90,892.

incense ceremony

(kōdō). An aesthetic pursuit in which participants appreciate the fragrance emitted by the burning of scented wood or combinations of wood and other substances. The art of *kōdō* was brought to Japan in the 6th century with the introduction of Buddhism, and in the late 17th century, it reached the height of its popularity as a highly refined secular accomplishment.

History——Incense was originally burnt as an offering to Buddhist images in temples. By the 8th century, however, the burning of incense in order to scent rooms and clothing had become a popular custom among the upper classes. For the Heian court lady, in particular, the lingering fragrance of incense on her robes was an indispensable part of her toilette. Many descriptions of incense used for this purpose may be found in the TALE OF GENJI and other literature of the Heian period (794–1185). During this period incense competitions at court were also popular pastimes. Guests would bring their own incense (mixtures of pulverized scented wood and animal scents, kneaded with honey and other substances) and decide which was the best. From the latter half of the 15th century, wood from aromatic trees began to be used as well.

Eventually this aristocratic entertainment was adopted by the common people, and recognizing the need for rules, literary figures such as SANJŌNISHI SANETAKA, Shino Munenobu (d 1480), SŌGI, SHŌHAKU, and others helped to create a format for the burning of incense. The Sanjōnishi and Shino schools, which have since become the core of the incense tradition, continue to the present day. The incense ceremony reached its height during the Genroku era (1688–1704), when it was considered equal in importance to the tea ceremony and flower arrangement. At present, in contrast to the two other arts, *kōdō* attracts few adherents.

Various Ceremonies——*Single scent:* the burning of a single variety of aromatic wood may be enjoyed in a solitary or social setting.

Incense competition: participants try to guess the name of an incense; this is difficult since there are as many as 2,500 kinds of incense.

Matching incense: a participant burns one kind of incense, and someone else burns another that will combine pleasantly with the first.

Combined fragrances: using two or more kinds of incense, the participant tries to create the atmosphere of a particular literary

Income distribution———Table 2

	Gini Coefficients for Employee Households Total Incomes in Postwar Period	
	Large cities	Whole country
1953	0.287	
1954	0.294	
1955	0.299	
1956	0.293	
1957	0.305	
1958	0.304	
1959	0.300	
1960	0.307	
1961	0.315	
1962	0.301	
1963	0.303	0.276
1964	0.298	0.264
1965		0.256
1966		0.260
1967		0.254
1968		0.241
1969		0.232
1970		0.229
1971		0.232
1972		0.235

NOTE: The Gini coefficient measures the difference between a completely equal distribution, in which each household receives the same income, and the actual distribution; the smaller its value, the closer is the distribution to perfect equality.
SOURCE: Ross Mouer, "Income Distribution in Japan: An Examination of the FIES Data," *Keio Economic Studies* 10.1 (1973) and 11.1 (1974).

Income distribution———Table 3

	Wage Differentials Annual wage indices (establishments with over 500 regular employees = 100)			
	Number of regular employees			
	100–499	30–99	5–29	1–4
1959–60	80.7	69.3	51.9	33.8
1964–65	85.9	77.9	65.0	50.0
1969–70	85.9	76.5	65.0	48.5
1974–75	87.2	80.5	65.6	48.9

SOURCE: Ministry of Labor, *Yearbook of Labor Statistics* (annual): various issues.

work, for example, a combination that will call to mind the poems of the KOKINSHŪ. There are about 700 such combinations, each having its own literary association.

Before participating in an incense ceremony, special precautions are necessary. Incense may not be used in one's hair or clothes, and it is also necessary to refrain from eating any strong-smelling food the day before the gathering. A special set of utensils is set aside for the ceremony. Each step demands the use of a specific utensil. The extravagant gold and silver lacquerwork applied to many older utensils attests to the taste and wealth of past devotees.

Sanjōnishi Sanetaka chose as his favorite 10 kinds of scents: Hōryūji, Tōdaiji, Shōyō, Miyoshino, Kōjin, Kareki, Nakagawa, Hokekyō, Hanatachibana, and Yatsuhashi. The basic ingredient for these is aloeswood, a product of Southeast Asia, especially the East Indies. Since the aloeswood tree grows in such a wide area, the participants are often asked to guess the country of origin, thus posing an additional challenge. *YUKAWA Osamu*

income distribution

The way in which the total income generated in a country over a given period of time is distributed to individuals or families, to particular regions, or to factors of production (such as labor and capital). The following discussion considers the distribution of income among Japanese households, focusing on the degree of inequality. The main features of household income distribution in Japan have been a trend toward greater inequality in the prewar period; a sharp narrowing of differentials immediately after World War II, only partly reversed in the early postwar years; increasing equality in the years of rapid growth through the 1960s; and relative stability in the 1970s. From an international point of view, Japan appears to be one of the more equal market economies, comparable with some of the northwestern European countries.

Prewar and Postwar Patterns of Distribution——Income distribution data on prewar Japan are scanty and incomplete. The statistics normally used to determine distribution to households—including figures on income (or consumption), differentials between urban and rural areas, various kinds of wage differentials, tax returns, and the share of national income accruing to labor—suggest three observations (Table 1). (1) In the agricultural sector, income distribution remained relatively stable throughout the prewar period. (2) In the industrial sector, a period of relative stability (or even narrowing differentials) from the late 1880s to the early 1920s was followed by a sharp increase in inequalities. (3) Urban/rural differentials followed a similar pattern: relative stability until perhaps 1915–20, and much larger inequalities in the following 20 years.

The main reason for the sudden increase in inequality in the 1920s was the rapid growth of capital-intensive and technologically advanced industries during World War I (see CORPORATE HISTORY). The need of these industries for skilled workers caused sharp wage differentiation in a labor market where skills were in short supply. Other reasons for inequality were a slowing of overall economic growth, which widened wage differentials, and a lower demand for workers from the agricultural sector, which diminished the growth of productivity on the farms and depressed rural income more than urban ones.

A sharp narrowing of differentials appeared in the postwar period. Though the data are not strictly comparable, the evidence shows that Japan became a much more equal society than it had been under the militarists in the 1930s or in the Meiji (1868–1912) and Taishō (1912–1926) periods. The main reason for this change is to be found in the postwar reforms. Both the LAND REFORMS OF 1946 and the dissolution of the ZAIBATSU helped to correct the very uneven distribution of wealth that had characterized Japan in prewar days. Large-scale physical destruction during the war and runaway inflation in 1945–48 made the population much poorer, but also much more equal, than before.

Reconstruction brought a return to some inequality, but this trend was halted in the mid-1950s. Developments since then (for which the data are much more abundant and accurate) suggest that from the late 1950s to the early 1970s there was a steady reduction of income differentials, followed by some stabilization thereafter. This can be seen in Table 2, which shows trends in a widely used (though far from perfect) overall measure of income inequality—the Gini coefficient—for the period 1953–72.

The narrowing of income differentials resulted from the spread of middle and higher education, which increased the supply of skilled personnel, and from the gradual disappearance of what has been called dualism, the division of the economy into two sectors—a developed, high-productivity, high-wage industrial sector and a less-developed, low-income, largely agricultural sector. The disappearance of dualism, in turn, resulted from rapid economic growth, which permitted the absorption of surplus labor from the countryside and from low-wage service occupations. By the late 1970s, the gap between urban and rural incomes had virtually disappeared. In 1975 the average income of farming households was some 15 percent above that of nonfarming households, but within the latter category incomes were somewhat lower in rural and small-city areas than in the more urbanized regions (by 7.5 percent in 1970). Wage differentials between high- and low-productivity sectors, or by size of firm, also diminished considerably from what they had been at the outset of the rapid-growth period (Table 3).

International Comparisons——International comparisons of income distribution are fraught with statistical difficulties, since the coverage of data and the definitions of income vary widely across countries. The Organization for Economic Cooperation and Development (OECD) has recently examined the available statistics for a large number of developed market economies and selected those (almost exclusively based on household surveys) that were felt to be reasonably comparable across countries. According to the findings reported in the first column of Table 4, Japan's income distribution is one of the most "equal" in the sample, and, when measured by the Gini coefficient, similar to that of Australia and the United Kingdom.

This result is surprisingly favorable, in view of the following negative considerations, all of which might be expected to make Japan appear less equal than the other countries in the sample. First, the data are on a posttax, posttransfer basis and therefore take into account the redistributive roles of governments. Yet Japan's tax system is not very progressive by international standards, and transfer payments to households—one of the main instruments of income redistribution—are in Japan lower (as a share of gross domestic product) than in all the other countries shown in Table 4. Second, in comparison with other developed countries, Japan shows larger wage differentials by size of firm, differentials that should make the overall distribution of income less equal. Third, Japan also shows greater wage differentials by age than other comparable market economies (see WAGE SYSTEM; EMPLOYMENT SYSTEM, MODERN). Japanese regional income differentials, too, are greater than those of several of the geographically smaller and/or more compact countries shown in Table 4. The above considerations are offset, however, by several positive factors that account for Japan's favorable showing. They are of four kinds.

Statistical factors. Japan's figures are based on the *National Survey of Family Income and Expenditure,* which omits agricultural households and most forms of nonmonetary compensation. The latter are probably more important in Japan than elsewhere, in view of the widespread use of EXPENSE ACCOUNTS and the existence of company-subsidized housing, medical insurance, leisure activities, and so forth (see COMPANY WELFARE SYSTEM). Because these benefits are usually a direct function of company size, they probably increase, rather than diminish, income inequalities. Expense accounts alone seem insufficient to increase inequality very greatly, but the inclusion in the survey of all other benefits, if it were possible, would lower Japan's apparent degree of equality. The exclusion from the survey of the rural sector might also bias Japan's income distribution toward equality if distribution inequalities in the countryside were much greater than in urban areas and/or if there were pronounced urban/rural income differentials. But the absence of a seniority wage system in the rural sector and the relatively equal pattern of landholding suggest that, if anything, agricultural incomes are more equally distributed than nonagricultural ones, while the abovementioned figures on average incomes in the economy show that farmers are slightly better off than nonfarmers.

Economic factors. Among economic factors explaining Japan's relative equality are the almost continuous full employment during the postwar period and the very high female labor participation rate. Of the countries in the sample, only West Germany had lower average unemployment in the 1960s and early 1970s, and only Sweden recorded a higher employment rate among women. Very low unemployment and very high female participation in the labor force, particularly in poorer households, go a long way to offset some of the negative factors mentioned earlier (see UNEMPLOYMENT; WOMEN IN THE LABOR FORCE).

Historical factors. The postwar land reform and the dissolution of the *zaibatsu,* already mentioned in connection with the sharp changes in income distribution between the prewar and postwar periods, also help to explain Japan's favorable international position. In their effect on the concentration of wealth (and therefore also on income distribution), they went well beyond most of the social-democratic reforms introduced after World War II in Western Europe. A further historical reason for Japan's relative equality is to be found in the cultural and social homogeneity of the population, resulting from the virtual absence of some of those groups (e.g., racial minorities and immigrants) that form the bulk of the poor in Western countries. This is best shown by the figures for the lowest (or poorest) deciles in the overall distribution. While Japan's top (or richest) 10 percent of households received some 27 percent of total household income in 1969—a figure above the 26-percent average for all the countries in the sample—Japan's bottom 20 percent received nearly 8 percent of total income, well above not only the overall average (6 percent) but also the figures for such high-welfare countries as the Netherlands and Sweden. It is the relative absence of real poverty at the bottom of the scale, rather than the absence of

Income distribution —— Table 4

Gini Coefficients for Posttax Incomes: An International Comparison

	Actual distribution	Standardized household-size distribution[1]
Japan (1969)	0.316[2]	0.336
Australia (1966–67)	0.312	0.354
Canada (1969)	0.354	0.348[3]
France (1970)	0.414	0.417
Italy (1969)	0.398	—
Netherlands (1967)	0.354	0.264
Norway (1970)	0.307	0.301
Spain (1973–74)	0.355	0.397[4]
Sweden (1972)	0.302	0.271
United Kingdom (1973)	0.318	0.327
United States (1972)	0.381	0.369
West Germany (1973)	0.383	0.386

[1] See explanation in text under International Comparisons.
[2] Not comparable with figure in Table 2 because of different coverage.
[3] 1972.
[4] 1971.
SOURCE: Malcolm Sawyer, "Income Distribution in OECD Countries," *OECD Economic Outlook: Occasional Studies* (July 1976).

Income distribution —— Table 5

Income Ratio for 1972 (Old-Age Pensions/Average Income): An International Comparison

Japan[1]	0.118	Sweden	0.296
Australia[2]	0.194	United Kingdom	0.218
Canada	0.185	United States	0.180
France	0.442	West Germany[1]	0.511
Italy	0.225		
Netherlands[1]	0.259		
Norway	0.247		

[1] 1973.
[2] 1971–72.
SOURCE: Organization for Economic Cooperation and Development, *Public Expenditure on Income Maintenance Programmes* (1976).

great riches at the top, that makes Japan a more equal society than many.

Social factors. The last point above is somewhat tempered by the fact that a large group of the potentially poor—the elderly (see OLD AGE AND RETIREMENT)—hardly appear in the data. This is due not to statistical omissions, but to social customs on the one hand, and economic necessity on the other. The tradition of the extended family has meant that the old, even after RETIREMENT, tend to remain within the family structure, while the insufficiency of pension arrangements has, in any case, precluded their financial independence. (As a percentage of average earnings, pensions in Japan are much lower than in other developed market economies [Table 5]; see SOCIAL WELFARE.) Thus the figures here shown are not really comparable, because in Western Europe and North America, owing to different traditions and better welfare provisions, old people frequently form independent one- or two-person households, often clustered at the bottom of the income scale. Some allowance for this factor has been made in column 2 of Table 4, which presents Gini coefficients for a hypothetical income distribution calculated on the assumption that all countries had identical household size distribution. For Japan this results in increasing the weight of (relatively poor) one-person households from 9.5 percent of all households to 23 percent, the average for all the countries in the sample. In the picture that now emerges, Japan still ranks among the more equal countries in the table, but is well below the northwestern European group.

The above considerations to some extent prevent precise comparison of income distribution patterns between countries with differing social standards and traditions. But while this qualifies the earlier findings, it does not invalidate them. Not only is Japan's actual, rather than hypothetical, distribution relatively equal, but this state of affairs is enhanced by some of the country's traditional customs. First, to many, particularly to the old, the extended family may seem preferable to the smaller "nuclear" family common in Western industrial society; hence not only does the system reduce apparent income inequalities, it may also increase well-being. Second, given Japan's preference for a system of seniority wages in the urban sector, much of the country's apparent income inequality represents life-cycle differences that are presumably more acceptable to the population at large than differences arising solely from status, wealth, or skills.

While these final comments may suggest that Japanese society is even more equal than those of the West, they suggest also that this state of affairs, which has prevailed only in the postwar period, may be temporary. The progressive aging of the population, increasing urbanization, and changes in family structure are swelling the numbers of old people living alone. A slowing of the economy's overall growth rate (widely expected over the remainder of this century) will, at the same time, preclude significant improvement of the grossly inadequate pension system. Given that slow growth over the long term may also increase the levels of open and hidden unemployment, widen wage differentials by size of firm, and cause modifications of the seniority wage system, it is likely that Japan's household income structure will become less equal in the foreseeable future.

■ ——Personal Distribution: Ross Mouer, "Income Distribution in Japan: An Examination of the FIES Data, 1963–1971," *Keiō Economic Studies* 10.1 (1973); 11.1–2 (1974). Hiroshi Niida, "The Redistributional Effects of the Inflationary Process in Japan, 1955–75," *Review of Income and Wealth* (June 1978). Akira Ono and Tsunehiko Watanabe, "Changes in Income Inequality in the Japanese Economy," in Hugh Patrick, ed, *Japanese Industrialization and Its Social Consequences* (1976). Malcolm Sawyer, "Income Distribution in OECD Countries," *OECD Economic Outlook: Occasional Studies* (July 1976). Kōji Taira, *Economic Development and the Labor Market in Japan* (1970). Chōtarō Takahashi, *Dynamic Changes of Income and Its Distribution in Japan* (1959). Richard O. Wada, "Impact of Economic Growth on the Size Distribution of Income: The Postwar Experience of Japan," *ILO Working Paper* WEP 2–23/ WP 37 (1975).

Functional Distribution: Andrea Boltho, *Japan: An Economic Survey* (1975). Kazushi Ohkawa, "Changes in National Income Distribution by Factor Shares in Japan," in Jean Marchal and Bernard Ducros, ed, *The Distribution of National Income* (1968). Kazushi Ohkawa and Henry Rosovsky, *Japanese Economic Growth* (1973). Kōtarō Tsujimura, "The Employment Structure and Labor Shares," in Ryūtarō Komiya, ed, *Postwar Economic Growth in Japan* (1966).

Andrea BOLTHO

Income-Doubling Plan

(Shotoku Baizō Keikaku). An economic plan during the period of rapid growth of the Japanese economy. Developed by the ECONOMIC PLANNING AGENCY under Prime Minister IKEDA HAYATO in 1960, the plan was designed to bring about the doubling of the real national income during the decade from 1961 to 1970.

The plan was prepared by the Economic Council (Keizai Shingikai), a MINISTERIAL DELIBERATIVE COUNCIL attached to the Economic Planning Agency. The key elements of the plan called for an increase in social capital, revision of the industrial structure to make it suited for rapid growth, development of trade and international economic cooperation, investment in science and technology, and maintenance of social stability. Through a combination of public investment and favorable monetary and fiscal policies with the initiative of private enterprise, the plan aimed to achieve an annual growth rate of at least 7.2 percent, the minimum necessary to bring about the doubling of the national income in a decade.

In actuality, the economy grew at a much faster pace, averaging about 10.8 percent during the decade. However, rapid growth was accompanied by a rise in the cost of living, and criticism of the plan's focus on growth at the expense of social welfare became widespread. As a result, the plan was dropped in 1965 by the cabinet of SATŌ EISAKU, and subsequent long-term plans included a new emphasis on social development. The goal of a doubled national income was reached sometime in 1967 or 1968.

incomes policy

(shotoku seisaku). Guidelines drawn up by the government to promote stabilization of the price of goods by restraining both prices and incomes. However, in Japan competition among big business is relatively intense, and there is less price fixing among oligopolies than in some Western industrial nations.

Labor unions are company unions, so when corporate profits drop, wage demands tend to go down. Therefore it cannot be necessarily said that wage hikes cause inflation in Japan. Since business has no need to carry out price increases in order to secure profits, government has little need to keep wage increases systematically under control. Incomes policy guidelines are not regarded in Japan as necessary and have never in practice been instituted.

In 1968 and 1972 the government set up committees to study thoroughly the possible need for wage and price guidelines. On both occasions the groups concluded that such guidelines were unnecessary. They maintained that the best solution was a policy encouraging competition between producers by such means as promoting labor mobility and making partial changes in the government's price support systems.

As far as control over wage hikes is concerned, guidelines are effectively used by employer's organizations such as NIKKEIREN (Japan Federation of Employers' Associations) rather than by the government. The stabilization of labor-management relations in large enterprises makes that possible. However, with the lowering of the economic growth rate, the productivity increase rate has declined. As a result, since there is an indication that the wage increase rate will exceed the productivity increase rate, some believe that the adoption of wage and price guidelines by the government may become necessary in the future.

KURITA Ken

Increase Production and Promote Industry → shokusan kōgyō

Independence Club

(Kor: Tongnip Hyŏphoe). A political coalition advocating Korean independence from all foreign control. It was founded in 1896 by Sŏ Chae-p'il (1866–1951), a former member of the KAEHWAP'A (Enlightenment Faction) who fled to the United States in 1884 after the group's unsuccessful KAPSIN POLITICAL COUP. He became a US citizen and took the American name Philip Jaisohn. During the KABO REFORM (1894–95), he returned to Korea and began its first mass newspaper, the *Tongnip sinmun* (The Independent), which gave birth to the Independence Club. The club initially rallied support from anti-Japanese, anti-Westernization, anti-Russian, and Christian leaders including Syngman RHEE (Yi Sŭng-man), Yu Kilchun (1856–1914; a former Kaehwap'a member and the first Korean student in the United States), and Yun Ch'i-ho (1865–1946). The group encouraged the Korean king to declare the nation the TAEHAN EMPIRE in 1897, with himself as emperor of a realm equal to all of the other empires of the world. As the club's influence grew, its activities were seen by some to be threatening to the established political order and even to the throne itself. In the spring of 1898, Sŏ was persuaded to return to the United States, and a few months later the king ordered the club disbanded and its leaders arrested. Yun fled to Japan, but Rhee was imprisoned. The king thereafter pursued a policy that intensified rivalry between Russia and Japan and culminated in the RUSSO-JAPANESE WAR in 1904. See also KOREA AND JAPAN: early modern relations.

C. Kenneth QUINONES

independent movie productions

Motion-picture production firms established by directors, actors, or actresses who are not under contract with the giant movie companies. The first independent movie productions in the history of Japanese cinema were those formed by such stars of the 1920s and 1930s as KATAOKA CHIEZŌ and ARASHI KANJURŌ. After World War II, people in the Japanese motion picture industry who were driven from their companies by the RED PURGE formed independent production companies and began to produce motion pictures. At present there are a number of independent film production companies, mostly established by movie stars, as well as production ventures that are like subcontractors for the large movie companies.

SHIRAI Yoshio

India and Japan

Despite Japan's early interest in some elements of Indian culture, especially BUDDHISM, there was little contact between the two countries until relatively recently. Those contacts that did take place were generally indirect, with China and Korea serving as intermediaries. In the modern era, the nature of Indian-Japanese relations has largely been shaped by the two countries' differing experiences with and reactions to encroachments of the Western powers and has been marked by alternating moods of admiration and resentment. India continually had to strive for Japan's support and respect. Today, cultural and trade agreements exist between the two nations, and relations continue to improve.

Early Buddhist Influence —— The introduction of Buddhism in the 6th century via China and Korea made Japan aware of the existence of India, but India was completely ignorant of Japan. Buddhist monks like Bodhisena (704–760), who visited Japan from China, did not return to India to report, and there were no travelers to India from Japan. Along with Buddhism, the worship of various Hindu deities was introduced into Japan as part of the Buddhist rituals. The study of Sanskrit provided inspiration for the development of the KANA syllabary in Japan, and Indian legends found a place in Japanese literature through Buddhist scriptures. Customs and manners of Indian origin were adopted, and Indian influences survive to this day in Japanese cremation customs and ancestor veneration practices. Japanese art forms such as fresco painting can be traced to the wall paintings of the cave temples of Ajanta in India. Japan's traditional court dance and music still preserve some of the forms introduced into Japan by Bodhisena.

Japanese engaged in the study of Sanskrit and Buddhism idealized India and felt reverence and admiration as well as a sense of longing for the country they could not visit. By the Kamakura period (1185–1333), however, these sentiments had weakened considerably, and the Buddhist priest NICHIREN talked in terms of the special role Japan had to play in the propagation of Buddhism.

Early Attitudes toward India —— With the arrival of Christian missionaries and traders from Europe in the 16th century, the geographical position of India in the world was correctly understood and knowledge about India trickled into Japan. This did not, however, encourage Japanese merchants to visit Indian ports during their trips to Southeast Asia. Even the four young Christians who became the first Japanese to step on Indian soil in Goa in 1583 during their journey to Rome (see MISSION TO EUROPE OF 1582) did not evince particular interest in India. It is noteworthy, though, that India was included in TOYOTOMI HIDEYOSHI's plans for conquest of the world in 1591 and that Hideyoshi considered India to be under the control of the Portuguese.

In the Edo period (1600–1868), criticism of Buddhism and Buddhist monasteries aroused feelings of antagonism toward India because of its identification with that religion. Some scholars such as ARAI HAKUSEKI, however, tried to approach India from another framework. Arai's *Seiyō kibun* (1715) contains accounts of Mughal rule in India and life in Indian ports such as Goa, Cochin, and Nagapatnam, gleaned from European merchants. In the early 19th century, when it was feared that Japan would become a target of European imperialism, efforts were made to learn about methods of subjugation employed by the British in India so that Japan could evolve effective means to counter them.

Japan and British India —— After the opening of Japan to the world in the mid-19th century, contacts with India were governed by Japan's relations with Great Britain, as India was a British colony. Japan accepted Britain's right to consider India its own sphere of influence and even agreed to protect British interests there under the revised ANGLO-JAPANESE ALLIANCE of 1905. For the people of India, Japan became an example to be emulated, as it had been successful in modernizing and preserving its independence. As early as 1892 Swami Vivekananda (1863–1902), who visited Japan on his way to the World Congress of Religions held in Chicago in 1893, declared that Indians could learn a great deal from Japan and urged Indian youth to go and study in Japan. OKAKURA KAKUZŌ in Japan and Rabindranath TAGORE in India played a positive role in ex-

changes of students and scholars between Japan and India. While the tradition of Indian studies based on Buddhism, philosophy, and Sanskrit was revived and encouraged, a beginning was also made in the field of modern Indian studies, including Indian languages. Tagore was enthusiastically welcomed in Japan in 1916 as the first Asian to receive the Nobel Prize in literature, but his idealism did not strike a responsive chord among Japanese intellectuals, who were critical of India's inability to throw off the British yoke and modernize. Tagore had his own disappointments over the contempt shown by the Japanese toward the Chinese and Koreans and over Japan's aggression on the Asian continent.

Japan's victory in the RUSSO-JAPANESE WAR in 1905 was a source of inspiration to Indians engaged in the struggle for freedom from British imperialism and kindled hope that Japan would assist in the Asian resistance against the West. Indian students in Japan formed a base for Indian revolutionaries who looked to Japan as a refuge. Britain, on the other hand, expected the Japanese government to assist in curbing the activities of these revolutionaries and in deporting them. The Japanese government was not very successful in this, as Indian leaders such as Rash Behari BOSE and Lala Lajpat Rai were actively encouraged and assisted by influential Japanese nationalists, including TŌYAMA MITSURU, who dreamed of putting an end to Anglo-Saxon dominance in Asia.

The attitude of the Japan government changed following the outbreak of the Pacific War, when the strategic advantages of befriending the large Indian populations in Southeast Asian nations were perceived. Japan helped in the creation of the INDIAN NATIONAL ARMY (INA) under the leadership of Subhas Chandra BOSE. Taking as its mission the liberation of India from the British, the INA set up its own independent command and refused to be employed in the suppression of rebellions against the Japanese in occupied Southeast Asian nations. Japan's military occupation of India was restricted to the sparsely populated Andaman and Nicobar islands. Japan was also defeated in the IMPHAL CAMPAIGN and proved unable to help the INA in liberating India. Yet, the wartime experience promoted a close relationship between Indians and Japanese without leaving a legacy of hatred, as it did in other Asian nations. At the same time, the majority of Indian nationalists condemned Japanese aggression in China and doubted the wisdom of accepting Japanese assistance, suspecting that Japan would substitute its own domination for that of the British.

Prewar economic relations between Japan and India were principally promoted by cotton. The importance of cotton to the industrialization program of Japan led to the stationing of representatives of Japanese trading companies in India, resulting in contacts in the commercial sector of Indian society. There was also collaboration with Indian entrepreneurs whose ships carried the cotton to Japan. The British allowed Japan to exploit the Indian cotton market and even watched the Indians losing out to the Japanese in the Chinese cotton market, but once Japanese textiles became competitive with Lancashire goods, heavy tariffs were levied in 1932. Japan also had to accept quotas both in imports of cotton and exports of textile products. Japan invested very little capital in India, probably in deference to Britain and also because of heavy commitments in China.

Postwar Political Relations —— Japan's relations with India in the postwar period have been cordial. India, however, still remains low in the foreign policy priorities of Japan. As a member of the FAR EASTERN COMMISSION, India participated in the formulation of policies for the postwar Allied Occupation of Japan. An Indian army unit participated in the Occupation but was withdrawn once India became independent. Justice Radha Binode Pal, a judge of the International Military Tribunal for the Far East, assuaged the feelings of the Japanese through his dissenting judgments; while not justifying Japanese aggression, he questioned the right of the victorious nations to pass judgment on the vanquished (see WAR CRIMES TRIALS). There were other friendly gestures by India, including the gift of a baby elephant to the Ueno Zoo in Tōkyō and an invitation to Japan to participate in the Asian Games held in New Delhi in 1951.

India terminated its state of war with Japan on 28 April 1952, although it was not a signatory to the SAN FRANCISCO PEACE TREATY. The Indian government objected to the exclusion of the People's Republic of China and argued that the security treaty with the United States should be negotiated after Japan regained independence. The bilateral peace treaty concluded on 9 June 1952 was the first treaty Japan signed on terms of equality after regaining its sovereignty. With its provision for restoration of Japanese assets in India and the renunciation of reparation claims, it was a treaty of friendship and goodwill.

Japan's policy of alignment with the United States on the basis of a security treaty that was clearly aimed at defending the world against communist expansion could not lead to close political ties with India, which maintained a policy of nonalignment and advocated relations with all nations. Neither could Japan look to support from India in its claims against the Soviet Union regarding the Northern Territory issue (see TERRITORY OF JAPAN). However, the two nations mutually respected their different approaches. India welcomed Japan's participation in the Bandung Conference in 1955 (see AFRO-ASIAN CONFERENCES) and advocated Japan's early entry into the United Nations. In the 1950s Japan was preoccupied with the problem of normalization of relations with Southeast Asian nations and opening diplomatic relations with the Soviet Union, and its interest in India was generally confined to resumption of economic relations. However, it seemed that the people of Japan had high expectations that India would carve out a new path for the Asian nations under the leadership of Prime Minister Jawaharlal Nehru. The visit of Japanese Prime Minister Kishi Nobusuke to India in May 1957 and the warm welcome given to Nehru on his visit to Japan in October 1957 heralded a new stage in the relationship, and Japan began giving development aid to India. This period also marked the beginning of a change in the Japanese people's assessment of India. India's inability to solve basic problems, including poverty and social inequality, reduced its prestige. A further shock was administered when India and China resorted to armed conflict over their border dispute, tarnishing India's image as an upholder of peace, nonviolence, and nonalignment. The Japanese government did not respond to the Indian appeal for support in the dispute. During the wars between India and Pakistan in 1965 and 1971 Japan followed the United States in stopping all aid and asking both parties to stop hostilities. The treaty signed by India with the Soviet Union in 1971 raised some apprehensions in Japan that India had joined the Soviet Union in its policy of containment of China.

The normalization of relations between Japan and China in September 1972 and the growth of Sino-Japanese economic and cultural relations, culminating in the Peace Treaty of August 1978, did not present new problems in Japanese-Indian relations, as there was also gradual improvement of relations between India and China. In Japanese diplomacy, "Asia" has generally signified Southeast Asia, and India falls on the periphery. India has only started taking more interest in relations with Japan since 1977, China previously having demanded more of its attention.

Postwar Economic Relations —— Iron ore has gradually replaced cotton as the main commodity of import from India. However, India's share in Japan's total trade has declined to less than 2 percent in the postwar era, far below the prewar average of 12 percent. The emergence of China as a major economic partner for Japan might make the Japanese market less accessible to the light manufactured products of India. The volume of Japanese investments in India is less than 1 percent of Japan's total overseas investments; Indian policies, including the restriction of avenues for foreign investment, are said to be a deterrent.

Japan plays a significant role as a supplier of financial and technical aid to India in both the industrial and agricultural sectors; India receives nearly 16 percent of the total yen credits granted by Japan to developing nations. Japan has applied its "develop-and-import" policy in the field of iron ore production. Japanese collaboration has made possible the production of a wide range of consumer goods. Indians are participating in various Japanese technical training programs, both in the private sector and in those sponsored by the government. In recent years, the possibility of cooperation in setting up plants and undertaking construction projects in third countries has been explored: India could supply skilled and semiskilled labor, while Japan would provide the necessary capital and technology.

Postwar Cultural Relations —— The cultural agreement signed between Japan and India in 1956 provides for exchanges in various fields, such as education, science, sports, theater, and visual arts. This has led to a growing familiarity with Japanese art and literature in India and vice versa. Greater interest is being shown by Japanese scholars in the study of medieval, modern, and contemporary India, including regional histories and cultures. Centers for teaching Indian languages are also being developed. In India it has only been since independence that academic studies on the modernization of Japan were initiated along with the study of the Japanese language. The two main centers for Japanese studies are at the Jawaharlal Nehru University in Delhi and Delhi University; Japan has been assisting in the development of both centers. In the field of science and engineering, there is scope for greater cooperation and ex-

change. The establishment of a leprosy treatment center at Agra in 1965 by the Japan Leprosy Mission for Asia (JALMA) is highly appreciated by Indians.

There are a growing number of opportunities for direct communication between Indian and Japanese scholars in various fields, facilitating better appreciation of each other's problems. Japanese Buddhist organizations have built temples and a peace pagoda in India. A large number of correspondents of major Japanese newspapers are stationed in India, and Japanese of all age groups and from various walks of life are visiting India in increasing numbers.

■ ——English language: W. G. Beasley, *Great Britain and the Opening of Japan, 1834–1858* (1951). Arun Coomer Bose, *Indian Revolutionaries Abroad* (1971). The Embassy of Japan, New Delhi, *The Lotus and the Chrysanthemum: India and Japan* (1977). Stephen N. Hay, *Asian Ideas of East and West* (1970). The Indo-Japan Committee for Studies on Economic Development in India and Japan, comp, *India and Japan: A Bibliography of Books Published in India and Japan 1945–1975* (1976). Hajime Nakamura, *Parallel Developments* (1975). P. A. Narasimhamurthy, "India and the Peace Settlement with Japan," in M. S. Rajan, ed, *Studies in World Politics* (1971). Savitri Vishwanathan, *Japan* (1976).

Japanese language: Gaimushō Keizai Kyōryoku Kyoku, ed, *Namboku mondai to kaihatsu enjo* (1978). Nakamura Hajime, *Nihon ni okeru Indo bunka no hakken* (1958). Ōgata Kōhei, ed, *Nihon to Indo* (1978).

Savitri VISHWANATHAN

Indian National Army

(INA). The Indian National Army, organized in 1942 with the support of Japan, consisted of Indian officers and soldiers taken prisoner during the fall of Singapore. A plan for a military action in India was developed in 1943 under the influence of Subhas Chandra BOSE. This Indian force was to return home to fight for the liberation of India from the British, realizing the dreams of Indian nationalists as well as the desires of Japanese military leaders, who also wished to see the British influence removed from the subcontinent. The army failed on the battlefield in 1944.

On the eve of the Pacific War, Japan did not intend to include India in its GREATER EAST ASIA COPROSPERITY SPHERE. Its main interests in India were strategic. The Allies' air supply route to Chongqing (Chungking) in China originated in India, and as a British stronghold, India posed a threat to Burma, an area essential to the sphere. Thus in January 1942 the Liaison Conference of the Japanese cabinet and the Imperial Headquarters (Daihon'ei) decided on a policy of separating India from Britain, for which it approved two measures: anti-British propaganda and assistance to anti-British activities of Indians.

Major Fujiwara Iwaichi, an officer of the Imperial Headquarters who headed the intelligence group, called FUJIWARA KIKAN, or Efu (F) Kikan, was assigned the task of winning over the support of Indian soldiers in the Malayan campaign. He suggested to Captain Mohan SINGH, a surrendered Indian officer, the formation of an Indian volunteer force to support the Japanese army. Singh concurred, and sought Fujiwara's help in raising an independent army from among Indian POWs. Most of the 40,000 officers and soldiers who joined the INA in 1942 were influenced either by concern for the safety of Indians living in Southeast Asia or by patriotism. Soon, however, Singh fell out with another Indian leader, Rash Behari BOSE, as well as the Japanese liaison officer, Colonel Iwakuro Hideo, and disbanded the INA. Ironically, this was the only time during the war when India's military unpreparedness offered the INA the chance to enter India.

Japan's policy toward India and the INA underwent a dramatic change after the Indian nationalist leader Subhas Chandra Bose arrived in Tōkyō in May 1943 and won Japanese recognition for his Provisional Government of Free India. The INA had been revived earlier that year, but it was Subhas Bose who turned it into a fighting force striving to free India from British rule. Bose expanded the INA and persuaded the Japanese to approve military action in India. He believed that an attack on his home province of Bengal, where his influence was strong, was sure to succeed. But, as Japan's military interests lay in the defense of Burma and disruption of the supply link with Chongqing, the Imperial Headquarters preferred an attack on Imphal, capital of the Indian border state Manipur, further north. Japan's decision to attack Imphal in 1944 with inadequate forces and supplies was ill conceived (see IMPHAL CAMPAIGN), and the campaign itself was mismanaged. Bose had moved to Rangoon his advance headquarters, and under Japanese command joined his troops to the Japanese battalions marching to the north from Rangoon. They fought at Hakka-Falam and Temu, entered India at Manipur, engaging British Indian forces at Palel and Kohima and advancing to the edge of Imphal by May.

The total strength of the INA-Japanese forces which appeared on the front at different times was 95,000 (83,000 Japanese troops, 8,000 INA, and 4,000 reinforcements), according to an American source, and 96,000 (84,000 Japanese troops, 8,000 INA, and 4,000 reinforcements), according to a British source. The British with their 155,000 combatants held them off until the monsoons arrived to make further battles impossible in that jungle terrain for the duration of the three-month rainy season. By then, the British had time to call in reinforcements, and the Japanese and the INA surrendered at Rangoon in May 1945.

After the war the court-martial of some INA officers in India sparked anti-British agitation in 1945–46, which transcended the long-standing communal divisions among Indians, created uncertainty over the loyalty of a large section of the Indian officer corps, and led the British cabinet to send a cabinet mission with a definite proposal of transfer of power to India.

■——Fujiwara Iwaichi, *Efu kikan chō no shuki* (1959). Fujiwara Iwaichi, *Efu kikan* (1966), tr Yoji Akashi as *F Kikan* (1980). Kalyan Kumar Ghosh, *The Indian National Army: Second Front of the Indian Independence Movement* (1969). Kalyan Kumar Ghosh, "The Indian National Army: Motives, Problems, and Significance," *Asian Studies* (April 1969). Joyce C. Lebra, *Jungle Alliance: Japan and the Indian National Army* (1971).　　　*Kalyan Kumar* GHOSH

indigo

(ai). A blue dye obtained from the indigo plant. There are some 50 varieties of indigo found throughout much of the world. It has been used as a dye since ancient times; cloth fragments dyed in indigo, dating from about 2500 BC, have been found in Egypt. The variety most used in Japan is *tadeai (Polygonum tinctorium Lour),* native to the Indochina peninsula. The earliest example of Japanese indigo-dyed fabric is in the Nara temple HŌRYŪJI and dates from about AD 620. Records mentioning the cultivation of *tadeai* and dye methods of craftsmen include the legal code Buyakuryō and records preserved in the SHŌSŌIN art repository (8th century) and the ENGI SHIKI (927). Indigo-dyed material was only for the aristocracy through the Nara period (710–794), but with the advent of vat dyeing, it became accessible to the common people.

The indigo plant contains indikan, a water-soluble substance which, when acted upon by fermentation, forms indigo. Reduced in an alkaline solution to form indigo white, it is fixed to the fiber by oxygenation. Indigo is an extremely fast dye, particularly to light and water. With repeated dipping and oxygenating, deep shades of blue are possible.

The earliest known dye method in Japan (*namahazome;* raw-leaf dyeing) involved the use of fresh *tadeai* leaves cut just before blooming. Crushed with water and strained, the indikan-filled juice combines with the fiber. Only a pale blue is possible.

The vat-dye method *(tatezome),* thought to date from the Nara period, allowed for a long dyeing season, greater quantities to be dyed at once, and more shades of blue. There are various recipes, but the most common involves the preparation of the form of indigo dye known as *sukumo.* The indigo leaves are dried, then sprinkled with water and left to ferment before being pounded to a paste called *aidama.* The *aidama* is mixed with lime to control fermentation, nourishment (*fusuma;* wheat bran paste, or any starch) to feed the bacteria, and water. Wood-ash liquor is added and the mixture heated to approximately body temperature. *Fusuma* and lime are added several times, the entire process taking about one week. Temperature and the quantity of alkali are crucial.

Tokushima Prefecture in Shikoku has traditionally produced the most indigo, peaking in 1900 when 17,760 tons of *sukumo* were produced. The introduction of synthetic indigo in the 20th century crushed the industry. Some 148 traditional dye houses remain active, but a great many mix *sukumo* with synthetic and India indigo. See also DYES AND DYE COLORS.

■——Gotō Shōichi, "Awa ai kobanashi," in *Aruku miru kiku* (October 1976). Maeda Ujō, "Nihon kodai no ai," in *Senshoku to seikatsu* (Autumn 1975). Stuart Robinson, *A History of Dyed Textiles* (1969). Yoshioka Tsuneo, *Tennen senryō no kenkyū* (1974).
　　　Diane Wright ARIMOTO

Indochina, Japanese occupation of

The Japanese takeover of France's colonies in Indochina in the early stages of World War II. Taking advantage of the fall of France to Germany in 1940, Japan negotiated in September of the same year with the Vichy government to allow the stationing of Japanese forces in northern French Indochina (now Vietnam). In July 1941, with tensions between Japan and the United States mounting, Japan decided to station troops in southern French Indochina as well, and negotiated a new "joint defense" agreement that left the Vichy government with only nominal authority. The United States responded by placing a total embargo on exports to Japan and freezing Japanese assets in the United States. The quickly deteriorating relations between the two countries led directly to the outbreak of the Pacific War.

Indonesia and Japan

The earliest known contacts between Indonesia and Japan date from the late 16th century, when Japanese settled in a number of Indonesian towns. After a hiatus of almost two and a half centuries caused by Japan's NATIONAL SECLUSION policy, trade and Japanese settlement resumed in the Meiji period (1868–1912). The Japanese occupation during World War II proved to be a significant stage in the Indonesian independence struggle, but its harshness bred widespread resentment. In recent years, relations have been marked by the rapid growth of economic ties in the form of Japanese exports of manufactured goods and investments in Indonesia and Indonesian exports of petroleum and other raw materials to Japan, developments which have brought new tensions.

The first Indonesian place name known to the Japanese was probably Sumatra, a certain incense being named *"sumotara"* by the nobles of the Heian period (794–1185). The Portuguese began visiting Japan in 1543 and took some Japanese to Southeast Asian countries, including Indonesia. Japanese traders also began to visit Indonesian ports, and some settled there; European colonial authorities as well as local Asian rulers welcomed the Japanese as mercenaries, merchants, and craftsmen. Unlike in other major cities in Southeast Asia where they formed an exclusive quarter (NIHOMMACHI), the Japanese immigrants in Indonesia during the 17th century lived together with the local people. They lived in Djakarta, which they called "Jagatara," Bantam in Java, Jambi in Sumatra, and several other places throughout the archipelago; a Dutch census of Djakarta numbered 108 Japanese residents out of the city's total population of 8,058 as of November 1632.

The policy of National Seclusion enacted by the Tokugawa shogunate prohibited Japanese abroad from returning home, and the Japanese in Indonesia were gradually assimilated into the local society. Even during the seclusion period, however, Indonesia was slightly more familiar to Japan than the rest of Southeast Asia, as the Dutch, then the only European nation allowed to maintain contact with Japan, regularly arrived via Indonesia, which they were gradually taking over as the Netherlands East Indies.

Following the rescinding of the National Seclusion policy and the overthrow of the shogunate in 1868, Japanese again began to arrive in Southeast Asia. For a few decades the majority were women known as KARAYUKI SAN who were transported, often illegally, and settled in port towns as prostitutes. They were soon followed by men of various professions such as barbers, photographers, and dentists. Most popular were grocers whose shops, called *toko jepang* (Japanese shops) by the Indonesians, competed successfully with Chinese merchants. Understandably, the social prestige of these earlier immigrants was low. However, in 1899, as Japan rapidly modernized, Japanese immigrants were granted a civil status equal to that of Europeans, i.e. above the Chinese and the natives, much to the resentment of the latter. The increase in imports of cheap Japanese textiles and other light industrial products often caused economic conflicts. As of 1 October 1938 Japanese residents in the Netherlands East Indies numbered 6,469, of whom 2,190 were reportedly engaged in commerce.

Desperately in need of war materials, Japan unsuccessfully tried to negotiate for petroleum from the Netherlands East Indies until a few months before the outbreak of the Pacific War. Initial Japanese military successes in Southeast Asia gave some Indonesian nationalists the hope of terminating Dutch rule with Japan's assistance; after Japanese forces occupied all of the archipelago early in 1942, SUKARNO, Mohammad HATTA, and a few other political prisoners were released and used by the Japanese occupation authorities as collaborators. The military administration divided Indonesia into two districts: Sumatra, Java, and Madura came under the army and the rest under the navy. The Indonesians' hopes for self-rule soon faded into frustration as the Japanese imposed strict controls on speech and assembly, forced deliveries of foodstuffs, and drafted manpower for public works and military training.

While the navy intended the permanent occupation of the territory within its jurisdiction, the army became more sympathetic to the cause of Indonesian independence, especially after the Greater East Asia Conference (see GREATER EAST ASIA COPROSPERITY SPHERE) of November 1943, in which Burma and the Philippines were treated as independent nations. In September 1944 Prime Minister KOISO KUNIAKI stated that Japan would grant independence to the East Indies in the near future. As the war situation worsened, the Japanese gave military training to Indonesian youths (see PETA ARMY). Although Japan surrendered to the Allies before carrying out its plans to sponsor Indonesian independence, the Republic of Indonesia declared its own independence under Sukarno on 17 August 1945. Their wartime experience provided the Indonesians with valuable lessons for their subsequent struggle with the Dutch, which ended with transfer of sovereignty in 1949.

The Indonesian government signed but did not ratify the SAN FRANCISCO PEACE TREATY of 8 September 1951 because its conditions of war reparations remained ambiguous. Prolonged bilateral talks between the two governments resulted in the 20 January 1958 Agreement on Reparations stipulating that Japan would pay $223 million in services and goods over a 12-year period. From 1959 to 1965 President Sukarno held dictatorial powers under the system he called "guided democracy," but his favoritism and secret maneuvers, as in the case of the Japanese "reparation lobbies," invited corruption. After Sukarno's fall in 1967, his successor, President Suharto, adopted a more pro-Western policy, asking noncommunist countries for economic aid. Among the Inter-Governmental Group on Indonesia (IGGI), Japan is the greatest investor. With the completion of the Japanese reparations payments in 1970, the political and economic ties between the two governments grew still closer, but the Indonesian economy remained stagnant. In recent years, the highly visible Japanese economic presence in Indonesia has led to the buildup of anti-Japanese sentiments which erupted into violent protests during Prime Minister TANAKA KAKUEI's visit to Djakarta in 1974.

▬——Benedict R. O'Gorman Anderson, *Java in a Time of Revolution: Occupation and Resistance* (1972). Masashi Nishihara, *The Japanese and Sukarno's Indonesia: Tokyo-Jakarta Relations, 1951–1966* (1976). Bernard H. M. Vlekke, *Nusantara: A History of Indonesia* (1959).   NAGAZUMI Akira

Industrial Bank of Japan, Ltd

(Nihon Kōgyō Ginkō). Private bank specializing in long-term credit to industrial enterprises. Established in 1902, the bank is the largest of the three such credit banks in Japan, the other two being the LONG-TERM CREDIT BANK OF JAPAN, LTD, and the NIPPON CREDIT BANK, LTD. Before World War II the bank played a major role in the attraction of foreign capital to Japan, underwriting corporate debentures and municipal bonds, as well as acting as a consignee for the overseas issuance of these debentures and bonds. It also made financial investments in development projects in Korea and China. After the war the bank switched temporarily to the status of an ordinary bank, but in 1952, following the inception of the Long-Term Credit Bank Law, it once again became a long-term credit bank. See BANKING SYSTEM.

During the period of high economic growth in the 1960s, the bank loaned funds to large enterprises in the heavy and chemical industries for investment in fixed capital. It also assisted such enterprises in obtaining foreign funds by underwriting foreign loans and bonds. In these large-scale financial transactions, as well as in the procurement of international funds, the bank has helped to promote cooperation between the government and private financial institutions and enterprises. With the increase in Japan's foreign currency reserves in the 1970s, the bank began issuing yen-based bonds through the Asian Development Bank and the World Bank. It also underwrote bonds issued by various governments and enterprises around the world, playing an increasingly important role in the international financial market. Beginning with subsidiary banks in West Germany (Industrie-Bank von Japan) and Hong Kong (I.B.J. Finance Co), the bank has increased its international network of operations. Now there are subsidiaries in Luxembourg, New York,

London, and Saudi Arabia, among others. The bank has also been quite active in loaning funds for the development of natural resources overseas as well as in giving loans to developing countries. At the end of March 1982, the total assets were ¥15.8 trillion (US $65.6 billion), total debentures and deposits were ¥11.5 trillion (US $47.8 billion), 70 percent of which was obtained through the issuance of debentures. The bank was capitalized at ¥103.7 billion (US $430.8 million). The head office is in Tōkyō.

industrial complexes

(kombināto). Groups of closely interrelated and integrated factories based around one or more large-scale core factories. These complexes are designed so that the products of one factory can be easily and efficiently used by the others. Most of the complexes produce chemical and petrochemical products, and typically include a petroleum refinery; a few specialize in iron, steel, and other products.

The complexes were developed in Japan after World War II by major industrial concerns, sometimes as cooperative efforts by competing companies, and were promoted by the Japanese government as a way to avoid duplication of facilities. These complexes are located in or near major industrial cities along the Pacific coast ranging from Kita Kyūshū in northern Kyūshū to Muroran in Hokkaidō. The coastal locations allow for easy access to raw materials imported via the Pacific Ocean and Japan's major areas of consumption. Such complexes often cause severe pollution problems, and the high cost of pollution abatement has resulted in a trend toward locating new complexes in areas far from population centers such as Tomakomai in Hokkaidō and Mutsu Ogawara in northern Honshū, as well as sites abroad.   NISHIDA Shunji

industrial design → design

industrial funds

(sangyō shikin). Capital supplied to industry, normally for long-term capital investment. The term has special significance in Japan because a number of nonmarket mechanisms were set up to ensure that the government's industrial priorities were observed in the allocation of funds to industry during the pre-1973 period of rapid industrial expansion.

The chief sources of industrial funds, in the sense of long-term investment funds, were the long-term credit banks and trust banks. Both types of bank were set up with this mission in mind. The long-term credit banks were permitted to issue savings certificates with long maturities and to pay higher interest rates on these certificates. Thus, the long-term and trust banks established a strong long-term funding base and attracted long-term deposits from both the household and corporate sectors.

The bank's choice of borrowers was constrained by varying degrees of legal and informal guidance. For example, specific legal regulations on the trust banks during the 1950s and 1960s indicated industries where long-term loans could be made and forbade loans to consumers and certain low-priority borrowers. Supervision of lending was carried out through periodic, detailed reviews of the loan portfolios. Because of a decline in loan demand for housing construction, these regulations were subsequently changed. But most trust and long-term credit banking institutions still find it more desirable to lend in large amounts to large companies where loan demand is strong enough to permit a profitable spread between costs of raising funds and return from lending them.

The direct cost of industrial funds was often controlled rather than left entirely to the market. Deposit rates on long-term savings certificates were set above rates on other types of savings. The long-term lending rate was set at a comfortable margin above the deposit rate to permit a reasonable profit to long-term lending institutions. Lending rates in Japan during the pre-1973 period were generally higher than those in major capital markets abroad, because of strong domestic demand for funds.

Authorities defended control of interest rates on grounds that control lowered both level of costs and variance of costs below what would have happened had interest rates been left to market forces. But a side effect was that credit generally had to be rationed. With interest rates below the market equilibrium level, industrial funds were scarce for low-priority borrowers.

The system of priority lending of long-term funds helped Japan allocate the huge shares of investable capital to basic industries, such as steel, petrochemicals, shipbuilding, and automobiles. The result was high international competitiveness for these key industries.

C. Tait RATCLIFFE

industrial injuries

(*rōdō saigai*). Injuries sustained by workers as a result of work-related accidents. Because of the growing number of factory laborers in Japan after the Meiji Restoration (1868), laws pertaining to industrial safety and sanitation were instituted early on and continue to be implemented up to the present day.

In 1877 the Ōsaka Prefecture Manufacturing Site Control Ordinance (Ōsaka Fu Seizōjō Torishimari Kisoku) was enacted, and shortly thereafter similar control measures were passed in various prefectures. Factory regulations were implemented uniformly in Japan with the FACTORY LAW OF 1911 (Kōjō Hō), and special regulations were established separately for hazardous types of industry. In 1929 an ordinance to prevent industrial injury as well as a sanitation ordinance was enacted. In shipping and mining, safety standards were regulated by separate laws established in 1899 and 1905, respectively. In 1948, two years after the end of World War II, the Labor Standards Law (Rōdō Kijun Hō) was enacted. Minimum safety standards applicable to all industries and enterprises were clearly delineated, and regulations were consolidated to guarantee safe, sanitary conditions for workers. Along with the Labor Standards Law, which aimed at accident prevention, various legislative measures, including the Workers' Compensation Law (Rōdōsha Saigai Hoshō Hoken Hō), were also enacted to cover work-related accidents. The Labor Safety and Sanitation Law (Rōdō Anzen Eisei Hō) was passed in 1972 to deal with an increase in factory accidents because of the rapid growth, as well as the changing nature, of the Japanese economy since the late 1950s. Included in this law were provisions covering the responsibilities of the parent company and of the government in providing technical advice and financial aid to subcontracted workers. Because of these measures, the frequency of industrial accidents in Japan has been greatly reduced and is now comparable to that of the United States and Europe. See also LABOR LAWS.

KURITA Ken

industrial organization

The concentration of power within the industrial structure, including such factors as the degree of monopolistic or oligopolistic control of markets and the ownership of capital. Although for the most part Japan's antimonopoly program has been weak, economic concentration during the post–World War II period has been checked by economic growth. More recently the antimonopoly program has been strengthened. While international comparisons are difficult to make, the degree of market control exercised by large firms in the modern Japanese economy does not appear unusual. However, the existence of "enterprise groups" and cartels must be considered in gauging the extent to which markets are controlled.

Historical Background —— To understand the industrial organization of the Japanese economy, it is first necessary to consider several major aspects of the economic development of Japan. Let us begin by viewing the economy in the decade preceding World War II, when Japan was an industrializing country in mid-passage. From the time of the Meiji Restoration (1868) its economic growth had been substantial (with the annual rate of increase in gross national product at various times exceeding 6 percent), and marked changes had been wrought in its industrial structure. Adoption of Western technology had spawned many large-scale industries—textiles, iron and steel, engineering, electrical products, and chemicals among others. Nonetheless, before the special industrial adjustments associated with the armament program of the 1930s, almost 50 percent of Japan's occupied labor force was still employed in the primary areas of agriculture, forestry, and fishing; manufacturing accounted for no more than 16 percent of total employment. Within the field of manufacturing itself a "dual structure" had developed. On the one hand there was the modern sector employing capital-intensive methods of production. Encouraged by the state (through direct subsidies, easy credit, low tax rates on profits, and tariff protection), this sector had been growing since the middle of the first decade of the century. On the other hand a substantial proportion of output was produced in a plethora of small enterprises using little capital and much labor. Enterprises of this nature—often located in the homes of workers whose labor force was drawn wholly from the family—catered to the traditional tastes of the Japanese, produced a wide

array of light industry products (inexpensive bicycles, footwear, textiles, and toys), and, on a subcontracting basis, served the needs of heavy industry in the most advanced sector of the economy. As late as 1930, 60 percent of the manufacturing labor force was to be found in establishments with fewer than 10 workers. See ECONOMIC HISTORY: early modern economy.

Although Japan emerged from defeat in World War II with much of its industrial plant a shambles and its foreign resources entirely gone, this proved to be the prelude to a performance of extraordinary dimensions. Within a short span of time, Japan's economic growth rate soared to levels without precedent in its own experience and exceeding the postwar expansion of any other large industrial nation. With gross national product growing at an average of about 10 percent annually for most of the postwar period, Japan became the third most productive nation of the world. Its share of total exports of manufactured products, which was about 5 percent in the early 1950s, has since expanded to 15 percent. As assimilation of Western technology progressed, changes in industrial structure proliferated. Older large-scale industries developed at an accelerated rate, industries producing new commodities appeared, the modern sector of the economy burgeoned, and the relative importance of the traditional and small-scale sector rapidly shrank. Between 1930 and 1971 the proportion of net national product accounted for by agriculture, forestry, and fishing declined from 17 to 7 percent, while the proportion originating in manufacturing grew from 21 to 30 percent. By 1975 the proportion of the manufacturing labor force in establishments with less than 10 workers had dropped from the 1930 level of 60 percent to 19 percent, and 44 percent was in establishments employing 100 or more workers. Vestiges of the traditional past, with the extensive reliance on small-scale operation, however, remain a prominent feature of the Japanese economy to the present day. Although the rise in wage rates accompanying Japan's postwar growth has progressively intensified the need for modernization in these highly labor-intensive and low productivity areas, the small plant still bulks anomalously large in a country so highly industrialized. In the United States, by contrast, the proportion of the manufacturing labor force employed in establishments with less than 10 workers is slightly under 3 percent, or about one-sixth the proportion in Japan. See ECONOMIC HISTORY: contemporary economy.

History of Economic Concentration —— Japan's ascent to the ranks of the world's industrial leaders heightens interest in the extent of economic concentration in its industrial structure. This is a question with many facets, and before considering it in detail it is well to recall the relevant Japanese experience up to the end of World War II.

Throughout this period Japan had no antimonopoly policy. During the transition from the feudalism of the Edo period (1600–1868) to the modernization that followed the Meiji Restoration nothing comparable to the Western ideology of individualism emerged; in view of the rapidity of the transition, this is scarcely surprising. Consequently, in the years preceding the end of World War II there is nothing to suggest that the Japanese government saw any virtue in competition. In the interests of promoting economic growth, the large and powerful firm, bringing with it heavy investment in new areas of industry, was not only welcomed but also received governmental support, as mentioned above.

As in all countries undergoing industrialization, the technological change introduced into Japan would in itself have led to a growth in the scale of enterprise. But emerging virtually on the heels of feudalism and developing in an environment congenial to an open-ended expansion, the largest enterprises soon established hierarchical, clan-like organizations of their own—the ZAIBATSU (literally, "financial cliques"), as they came to be known. The *zaibatsu*, exemplified by the Big Three—MITSUI, MITSUBISHI, and SUMITOMO—were groups of firms that were controlled (through full ownership or through strategically distributed security holdings) by family-dominated holding companies. Although a single *zaibatsu* might have more than one affiliate in the same industry, generally its holdings were spread over a wide array of industries. The Big Three thus had interests in manufacturing, mining, finance (each of the groups owning its own bank), transportation, and, through their trading companies, in foreign commerce. Oligopoly in the advanced sector of the economy was common, and typically the affiliates of the Big Three were among the leading firms in their industries. Often they and other *zaibatsu* had interests in the same industry and together accounted for a very substantial, if not a dominating, portion of the the total industry output. Notwithstanding this, there is disagreement concerning the extent to which the *zaibatsu* collaborated for

Industrial organization——Table 1

Market Concentration in Japan, 1956 and 1970

Sector	Proportion of sector income produced under "high concentration" conditions		Proportion of sector income to national income	
	1956	1970	1956	1970
Manufacturing	34.6	37.5	24.8	29.9
Mining	22.0	100.0	2.1	0.6
Transportation	47.3	41.0	5.4	5.4
Communications and public utilities	100.0	100.0	3.6	2.6
Agriculture, forestry, and fishing	0.0	0.0	19.6	7.5
Construction	0.0	0.0	4.5	7.5
Trade	0.0	0.0	16.1	18.1
Finance and real estate	10.0	20.0	7.3	11.3
Services	0.0	0.0	11.9	13.3
Government	—	—	4.5	3.9
Income from overseas	—	—	0.2	−0.1
Total	16.0	18.6	100.0	100.0

NOTE: High concentration conditions are defined as existing when the four largest firms in an industry account for 50 percent or more of the income of that particular industry. Thus in 1956, 34.6 percent of the income of all manufacturing industries was produced under these conditions. For both 1956 and 1970, when there were no published data on concentration ratios or on the size of sector components, estimates from the Fair Trade Commission and other government agencies were used in preparing this table. Government communications and national railways were classified among the high concentration industries and were not included in the unclassifiable "government" portion of the national income.

SOURCE: Eugene Rotwein, "Economic Concentration and Monopoly in Japan—A Second View," *Journal of Asian Studies* (November 1976).

purposes of controlling industry output and price. Some observers contend that such collaboration was extensive, while others have argued that group loyalties led to intense rivalry among the *zaibatsu*.

It is clear, in any event, that these groups had the power to perpetuate their growth relative to independent enterprises. *Zaibatsu* affiliates could secure equity capital from group resources, and they had preferential access to credit from the group bank. Since Japan's security markets were but little developed and the *zaibatsu* banks controlled a substantial proportion of bank assets, the financial advantages of group affiliation were of strategic significance. Group affiliates, further, could share important technological information, join managerial forces in launching new enterprises, and provide markets for each other's products at home while the group trading company promoted the sale of their products abroad. Beyond this, the *zaibatsu* gained from their special role in serving various economic needs of the government, with which they developed intimate ties. It is estimated that at the end of World War II the Big Three controlled 23 percent of the total paid-in capital of Japanese corporations, while 35 percent of this total was controlled by the 10 largest *zaibatsu*.

The government was not only receptive to the growth of large and conglomerate business organizations. It also sought actively to promote collaboration between independent enterprises. In the 1920s trade associations *(kumiai)* received substantial government encouragement in a number of industries with firms of widely varying size. The objectives were several, but they did not exclude cartel arrangements in the marketing of industry products. With the onset of the depression of the 1930s support for cartels grew. The Major Industries Control Law (Jūyō Sangyō Tōsei Hō, 1931) empowered the government to order cartelization in a variety of industries and to impose penalties for noncompliance. The penalties were not invoked, but official policy contributed directly to the spread of collusive arrangements. The collaboration between firms continued during the war, when it served as a vehicle for implementing the war production program.

Such was the legacy that Japan brought to its postwar industrial organization. The American OCCUPATION saw it as a pattern of institutional arrangements that sanctioned the enrichment of a powerful economic oligarchy at the expense of the community, inhibited a salutary growth of competition in the modern sector of the economy and, by severely limiting economic opportunities for the individual, precluded the emergence of a broad-based, independent, and vigorous middle class. More generally viewed—and especially in light of the close relations that had prevailed between major business interests and government—the legacy was seen as a barrier to the growth of an open and democratic society. Along with other measures designed to promote economic democracy (land reform and the encouragement of trade unionism), the Occupation accordingly sought to revamp the organization of Japanese industry. It dissolved the *zaibatsu* holding companies and removed designated business executives from their positions (see ZAIBATSU DISSOLUTION). It instituted a program to dismember large individual firms (although the original program was subsequently truncated owing to the fear, with the advent of the Cold War, that continued dismemberment would weaken Japan as an ally against the spread of communism). And with longer range policy in view, it introduced an ANTIMONOPOLY LAW similar to, and in some respects more stringent than, the American statutes, and established a Fair Trade Commission to administer the law. Not long after its passage the Japanese substantially weakened the statute through amendment. But Japan has remained formally committed to an antimonopoly policy throughout the postwar period, and recently the law was re-strengthened.

Capital Concentration—— With this background in view, let us return to our central question. How extensive is economic concentration in Japanese industry? A very general indication of this is found in the pattern of control of corporate paid-in capital by the largest corporations. Judged by this standard, concentration in Japan is considerable. The most recent year for which data are available is 1963, at which time the largest 100 nonfinancial corporations (directly and through their affiliates) controlled 53 percent of the paid-in capital of all Japanese corporations. It is estimated that in 1960 the largest 100 nonfinancial corporations in the United States controlled 31 percent of all American corporate assets, although in drawing a comparison between the two countries it should be borne in mind that the distribution of assets may differ from the distribution of paid-in capital and, in considering the economy as a whole, that the importance of unincorporated business in the two countries

Industrial organization —— Table 2

Comparisons of Movements in Average Concentration Ratios in Selected Japanese Manufacturing Industries
(in percentages)

	Average concentration ratios		Change	Average concentration ratios		Change	Average concentration ratios		Change	Average concentration ratios		Change	Average concentration ratios		Change
	1937	1950		1950	1956		1956	1966		1966	1970		1970	1974	
Top firm	36	31 (34)	−5	33	27 (53)	−6	26	26 (90)	0	26	26 (47)	0	—	—	—
Top 3	61	57 (37)	−4	56	52 (57)	−4	52	51 (90)	−1	54	55 (168)	+1	55	55 (219)	0
Top 5	73	69 (37)	−4	67	63 (57)	−3	66	64 (90)	−2	68	69 (168)	+1	69	69 (219)	0
Top 10	83	83 (34)	0	79	78 (53)	−1	80	80 (90)	0	82	83 (168)	+1	83	84 (219)	+1

NOTE: The concentration ratio is the percentage of the total output of an industry produced by the largest firm or firms in that industry; ratios given here are averages for the industries in each sample. Numbers in parentheses indicate the number of industries in the samples for each pair of years being compared (for example, data for the top firms in each industry in 1937 and 1950 were for the same 34 industries in both years). Sample sizes vary according to the availability of data. The reader should not, therefore, compare average concentration ratios for any single year with those for single years in other pairs, but rather the degree of change represented in one pair of years with that in others. The comparison for the top firm appearing under the 1966–70 heading is for 1966–69, since here 1970 data were not available.

SOURCE: For 1937–50: Eugene Rotwein, "Economic Concentration and Monopoly in Japan—A Second View," *Journal of Asian Studies* (November 1976). For 1970 and 1974: Kōsei Torihiki Iinkai (Fair Trade Commission), *Kōsei torihiki iinkai nenji hōkoku* (annual): 1975.

may likewise differ. General measures such as these provide rough indications of the limitations on the opportunities for the small business enterprise in the economy at large and, as financial power is related to political influence, these measures have political implications. They do not, however, afford an indication of the power of firms to control their own markets, since this depends ultimately not on the firm's absolute size but on its share of the total industry output and its relations to other firms in the industry.

Turning then to market control, let us consider three major questions: What is the extent to which Japanese industry output is concentrated in the hands of large firms? What is the influence of Japanese business "groups"? How significant are legal cartels in Japan?

Market Concentration —— For purposes of gauging the general importance of market concentration in Japan, we may classify industries into "low concentration" and "high concentration" categories, with the lower limit of the "high concentration" class set at the point where the largest four firms in the industry produce 50 percent of the industry's output. If we aggregate the income originating in all "low concentration" and "high concentration" areas respectively, the totals indicate the relative importance of each in the Japanese economy as a whole. The results for two different years are given in Table 1 (which also indicates the wide variation in concentration in different sectors of the economy). This shows that in the most recent year—1970—approximately 19 percent of the Japanese national income was produced under "high concentration" conditions. It would be inappropriate simply to identify "low concentration" with competition and "high concentration" with oligopoly, for while the degree of concentration has a fundamental impact on the market, there is no single level of concentration that enables us to separate competitive from oligopolistic industries. Making allowance for this, however, the findings would indicate that the bulk of the Japanese national income is not produced under effective oligopoly conditions. The overall level of concentration in Japan, moreover, is not unusual. It appears to be roughly comparable to that of the United States. Further, concentration levels in individual manufacturing industries in both countries show a high degree of correlation.

As already noted, the composition as well as the level of total Japanese output has changed substantially in the postwar period. Despite this, it is evident from Table 1 that between 1956 and 1970 overall market concentration changed only to a small degree—rising by about 2 to 3 percent. This reflects the importance of elements of stability in the Japanese economy notwithstanding the unusually high growth rate. It also reflects the importance of mutually offsetting concentration movements during the period. For example, the comparatively highly concentrated manufacturing sector grew rela-

tive to the low concentration area of agriculture, forestry, and fishing; but the relative importance of several high concentration areas—mining, transportation, and utilities—declined. Mutually offsetting movements are also found within the important manufacturing sector itself, where—as might be expected—changes were most numerous. The resulting moderate 3 percent growth in concentration here, moreover, is partially illusory, since manufacturing industry classifications in 1970 were narrower than those in 1956 and this alone would produce a purely statistical increase in concentration. It is probable then that in the 1956–70 period the true increase in manufacturing concentration—attributable both to the changing importance of various industries in this sector and to shifts in concentration within manufacturing industries—was negligible.

In view of its significance, let us consider the area of manufacturing in somewhat more detail. Table 2 shows the movements in manufacturing concentration for various periods from 1937 to 1974. This lends support to the view that in 1970 concentration in this area was approximately the same as in 1956. An overall decline in concentration from 1956 to 1966 was roughly offset by an overall increase from 1966 to 1970. It should be noted further that in the preceding two periods—1937–50 and 1950–56—concentration declined. In 1970 the level of concentration was thus below that of the early postwar years and, it would appear, though the sample is small, below the level for the immediate prewar period as well.

As also indicated by Table 2, in the most recent period—1970–74—manufacturing concentration remained substantially unchanged. Projections cannot be based on such short term experience. It seems improbable, however, that there will be a resumption of anything approximating the decline in concentration of the earlier portion of the postwar period, for it appears that this decline was due primarily to an unusual combination of factors—the economic disorganization caused by the war and the rapid economic growth rate. The economic disorganization unsettled the positions of leading firms (as seems to be apparent in the decline in concentration between 1937 and 1950), and it may be presumed that their markets grew more vulnerable to invasion at the same time that the rapid economic growth opened new opportunities for expansion by other firms. That this condition was beginning to vanish, however, became evident in the recurrence of episodes of serious overinvestment that first appeared toward the end of the 1950s. As seems clear from this, despite continuing rapid growth, the profitability of competitive plant expansion was beginning to wane as established firms consolidated their positions (through growing experience with new technology and new products, the development of low-cost sources of inputs, and the cultivation of "goodwill" through extensive advertising). Opportunities to invade their markets consequently shrank.

This is also reflected in the conspicuously higher levels of merger activity that have prevailed since 1959; that is, the decline in the profitability of competitive plant expansion enhanced the relative attractiveness of expansion through the absorption of existing plant (a development which, though not extensively involving mergers between dominant firms, contributed to the increase of concentration in the more recent period). With the economic disorganization of the war now in the distant past, a resumption of the earlier declining concentration movements seems especially unlikely in view of the apparent improbability that Japan will be able to reattain the high growth rates of this earlier period.

The Importance of Groups ——— The *zaibatsu* phenomenon of prewar Japan sprang from a disposition toward "group" operation that is quite pronounced in Japan generally. In the postwar period several types of business groups or alleged groups (KEIRETSU; see also ENTERPRISE GROUPS) have drawn attention, and the question of their influence is important since the market concentration material we have examined treats each firm as an independent entity.

Let us return first to the *zaibatsu* and consider specifically the major cases of Mitsui, Mitsubishi, and Sumitomo. The dissolution of the *zaibatsu* holding companies did not destroy all equity relations between affiliates. With the holding company gone, interaffiliate stockholding developed. Beyond this, relations between the principal affiliates of each of the Big Three were maintained through weekly meetings of their presidents. It was commonly contended, moreover, that the group banks in particular were increasingly assuming the unifying function the holding companies had previously performed. To many it began to appear that a "*zaibatsu* revival" was in the making. But if the dissolution of the holding companies did not result in the full disintegration of the older groups, their postwar descendants are substantially different from the prewar organizations. The intercorporate stockholding among group affiliates, which varies widely within each group, is often quite moderate or small—usually far smaller than the holding company interests in the subsidiaries of the prewar *zaibatsu*. These holdings are generally shared by many affiliates, so that in any case stockholdings would not afford a basis for the domination of the group by a small number of companies. The present-day availability of various sources of credit, moreover, limits the capacity of the group bank to exercise control of affiliates through its lending power. There is further no evidence indicating domination of any group by "outside" (i.e., non-group) stockholding interests. These "outside" holdings are typically fragmented. It appears clear that group affiliates generally are under the direction of their own managements.

The power of these groups may also be questioned on the basis of the market positions of their affiliates. As in the prewar period, the affiliates of the present-day Big Three are often among the leading firms in their markets. A study made for the year 1955, for example, indicated that, among a group of 64 major industries, firms commonly regarded as Big Three affiliates occupied the top rank in 15 industries, the second rank in 16, and the third rank in 14. However, while there were cases where affiliates had very large shares of the market, on the whole their market shares were far from overwhelming. Frequently the market occupancies of individual affiliates among the top 10 firms in the industry did not exceed 10 percent. The study showed that in many instances a group had more than one high-ranking affiliate in the same industry. But even on the assumption that it fully coordinated the policies of these affiliates (an assumption that is dubious in light of the internal structure of these organizations), the group typically would not have attained a commanding market position; and to a substantial extent, there would have been no domination of the market on the (still more dubious) supposition that all three groups collaborated in the industries in which they operated in common.

Whatever the influence of the former Big Three *zaibatsu*, their postwar descendants—their internal structures relatively loose and the market positions of their affiliates frequently quite limited—can scarcely be regarded as monoliths sitting astride a substantial portion of the Japanese economy. Nonetheless, they cannot be written off as organizations of only nominal significance. The degree of intercorporate stockholding among affiliates, if often small, is not negligible among the major or "core" companies of each group—standing at 15 percent for Mitsui, 20 percent for Mitsubishi, and 33 percent for Sumitomo. While sources of credit have grown more numerous, these "core" companies, moreover, still secure a substantial portion of their credit from their respective group banks. Further, the affiliates of each group show a preference for the products of others in the same organization (although it should be noted that there is much purchasing from outside the group). And it is difficult to dismiss the weekly meetings of the presidents within each group as entirely empty rituals.

Taken as a whole, the evidence would suggest therefore that these groups enjoy special advantages, but their advantages are substantially more limited than those of their *zaibatsu* predecessors. Further indication of their limited advantages is found in the growth records of long-standing affiliates of the Big Three. Between 1959 and 1968 the "core" companies of these groups, which were among industry leaders, increased their market shares by a very impressive 35 percent (although their average market share in 1968 was less than 13 percent). Over the same period second-line affiliates also expanded their occupancies, but by a much smaller 8 percent. It would thus seem that "core" affiliates in particular gained from group membership (perhaps through greater access to equity capital, credit, technological information, and the markets of their affiliates, or joint participation in new ventures). Nonetheless, during approximately the same period (1957–70) the proportion of all nonfinancial corporate assets controlled by both these major and second line affiliates rose only slightly (from 11.3 percent to 11.8 percent). While it appears that group membership was of value, it therefore only enabled long-standing affiliates roughly to hold their own in the expanding economy of postwar Japan. The record would indicate that, faced with the rapid growth of other enterprises, group resources were strained to the point where they could provide major assistance primarily to their most important members.

As noted, it has been alleged that various other types of business groups have developed in postwar Japan. However, only one of these clearly has the attributes of a distinct "group." This is the *shihon keiretsu* (capital grouping)—a type which bears a resemblance to the old *zaibatsu*. Here, through equity interests, a single operating-holding company controls a large number of subsidiaries. By 1971, the largest 100 of such operating-holding companies had 7,612 subsidiaries in which their interest exceeded 10 percent, 5,881 in which their interest exceeded 25 percent, and 2,818 in which it exceeded 50 percent. There are plainly grounds for concern over this development. By acquiring a number of subsidiaries in the same industry, these groups may increase market concentration; by providing special assistance to subsidiaries they may promote the growth of large firms with market power; and to the extent that different *shihon keiretsu* develop leading positions in the same markets, collusion between them would be facilitated. There is little indication to date, however, that these consequences have materialized. A study of the patterns of the holdings of these groups shows that generally they have not concentrated their acquisitions on particular markets but have spread them widely and that in the vast majority of cases, in any event, the subsidiaries acquired thus far have been distinctly minor firms.

The Place of Legal Cartels ——— It has been observed that cartels received governmental encouragement in prewar Japan. After the war cartel activity was prohibited by the Occupation-sponsored Antimonopoly Law. In amendments to the statute, however, the Japanese subsequently legalized a variety of cartels. The number of cartels approved under this law was 53 as of March 1978 (see CARTELS). In addition, from 1958 to 1967 the MINISTRY OF INTERNATIONAL TRADE AND INDUSTRY (MITI) informally established ADMINISTRATIVE GUIDANCE cartels in key industries under the Small and Medium Enterprise Group Organization Law (Chūshō Kigyō Dantai no Soshiki ni Kansuru Hōritsu) when these were deemed to be suffering from depression. The number of legal cartels under this law reached a peak in 1965, when it totaled 1,079. In this total each regional arrangement in the same industry is counted as a separate cartel, and the total number of different products covered by the cartels was therefore considerably smaller. Nonetheless in 1968, 19 percent of the value of manufacturing shipments was subject to control by legal cartels regulating price, quantity, or equipment. More recently, legal cartel activity has been declining sharply, principally because of a drop in the number of cartels sanctioned under the Small and Medium Enterprise Group Organization Law. In 1976, however, there were still 528 such cartels in Japan.

Although the numbers are imposing, ideally one would like to be able to assess directly the restrictive effects of these arrangements. Owing to the inaccessibility of much of the necessary information, however, no such general assessment can be made. But here several considerations are of relevance. About 18 percent of the present-day legal cartels are designed to deal with foreign markets. They administer quotas on exports, seek to prevent dumping, or attempt to secure favorable import prices for groups of producers. These may well facilitate collusive activity within Japanese domestic markets, but here the impact is indirect and problematic. Further, and of greater importance, about 80 percent of all legal cartels are in small-scale industries where, owing to the generally competitive relationships in such areas, a coordinated price-output policy is not easy to maintain. About 50 percent of the small-scale industry cartels were established under the Small and Medium Enterprise Group Organization Law for purposes of checking "excessive competition." Some of these are classified as "voluntary" and, among those that are subject to direct government control, it appears that sanctions to enforce compliance have rarely if ever been imposed. Under these circumstances it is questionable whether these cartels have a highly restrictive effect.

In appraising cartel effectiveness, two other types of cartels warrant special consideration because of the nature of the evidence available on their performance. These are the "depression cartels" administered by the Fair Trade Commission (FTC) and the previously mentioned cartels organized by MITI. Here there is published information on production adjustment targets, and these may be compared with the actual production adjustments that took place under the cartel. With regard to the MITI cartels, in 60 percent of the cases the actual industry production adjustment was at least two-thirds of the magnitude of the production adjustment target, but in the remainder the production adjustment was less than 30 percent of the target (and in most of these cases production actually rose). With respect to the FTC depression cartels, the actual production adjustment was at least two-thirds of the production adjustment target in 25 percent of the cases, less than 30 percent of the target in 44 percent of the cases, and between 33 percent and 50 percent in the remainder. A majority of the MITI cartels and a conspicuously smaller proportion of the FTC cartels appear, on this showing, to have been substantially successful. The industries covered by these cartels, however, are largely oligopolistic, and in cases such as these a marked degree of success might have been expected. In view of this, the quite mixed character of the findings, and particularly the very spotty record of the FTC cartels, are especially noteworthy, and they reinforce doubts concerning the effectiveness of the large number of Japanese cartels in small-scale and more competitive industries.

Contemporary Industrial Organization in Summary——Considered in broad terms, it may be said that the contemporary pattern of industrial organization in Japan reflects the continuing interplay between Japanese tradition on the one hand and the effects of economic growth on the other. The persistence of older tradition in shaping this pattern is evident in much postwar government policy. During most of the postwar period the government was antagonistic to the antimonopoly program it had inherited from the American Occupation. Many in policy-making positions regarded the program simply as a barrier to economic growth, and this resulted in emasculating amendments to the Antimonopoly Law (most of which were adopted in 1953). These not only legitimized large numbers of cartels (thereby probably also encouraging illegal collusion); they also eliminated a broad restriction on intercorporate stockholding—thus reopening an avenue to the strengthening of group relations—and facilitated a permissive and at times explicitly supportive policy with respect to mergers, including mergers between giant enterprises. Authority to take action to break up large and powerful firms, which had originally been delegated to the FTC, was itself removed from the Antimonopoly Law.

However, the impact of Japan's postwar economic growth has run counter to the thrust of these policy measures. For growth rapidly expanded economic opportunity, and this has had widespread effects favorable to competition. The absence of any distinct trend toward market concentration over the postwar period as a whole—despite the increasing numbers of mergers and the government's supportive attitude toward big business generally—owes much to the competitive forces generated by economic growth. Similarly, it may be presumed that Japan's growth rate, by improving the prospects for independent competitive business, reduced the attractiveness and hence the effectiveness of cartels. The stimulus to competition flowing from the postwar expansion clearly also helps explain why Japanese business groups, despite any growth they may have experienced over the period, have not generally attained dominating positions in the markets of their affiliates.

Japan's economic growth, moreover, has intensified the drive for a more effective antimonopoly program. Rising incomes have enlarged consumer horizons and expectations, while expanded economic opportunities have lent force to the consumer's insistence

(which has grown more pronounced during the recent inflation) that producers should meet the tests of a competitive market. These developments have already borne fruit. As mentioned earlier, MITI terminated its administrative guidance cartel program in 1967 and the number of cartels approved by MITI under the Small and Medium Group Organization Law has fallen off substantially. MITI has taken the position that the modernization of small-scale industry, which the government has assisted, has reduced the need for cartels in this area. The FTC—badly weakened during the 1950s—has been setting more stringent standards in reviewing industry requests for depression cartels and has expanded its investigations of illegal cartel activity. Most importantly, the Antimonopoly Law has recently been strengthened. The FTC has again been given authority to institute legal action to dismember large firms when they threaten competition. The limit on corporate stockholding by banks, contained in the original statute, has been restored. A general restriction on intercorporate stockholding has been reintroduced into the law. And civil penalties may now be imposed on firms found guilty of illegal cartel activity.

Since the mounting effectiveness of the antimonopoly program over the past decade owes much to the rate of Japanese economic growth, it may be presumed that the course of the program will be shaped largely by Japan's future growth experience. Frequently recurring depression and slow growth rates provide fertile ground for the resurgence of traditional Japanese perspectives, particularly in the willingness to accept cartels. Should future growth rates prove at least reasonably satisfactory, however, the concern to protect and promote competition may well become more deeply rooted and over the long run lead to an enduring and fundamental modification in Japanese tradition itself.

■ ——George C. Allen, *A Short Economic History of Modern Japan 1867–1937* (1972). George C. Allen, "Japanese Industry: Its Organization and Development to 1937," in Elizabeth B. Schumpeter, ed, *Industrialization of Japan and Manchukuo* (1940). T. A. Bisson, *Zaibatsu Dissolution in Japan* (1954). Richard E. Caves and Masu Uekusa, *Industrial Organization in Japan* (1976). Economic and Scientific Section, GHQ, SCAP, *Mission and Accomplishments of the Occupation in Economic and Scientific Fields* (1949). Eleanor M. Hadley, *Antitrust in Japan* (1970). Kōsei Torihiki Iinkai, *Kōsei torihiki iinkai, Dokusen kinshi seisaku sanjūnen shi* (1977). William W. Lockwood, *The Economic Development of Japan* (1954). Misonou Hitoshi, "Kabushiki shoyū no keitai to kigyō shihai—Nihon biggu bijinesu ron nōto," *Kōsei torihiki* (April 1959). Eugene Rotwein, "Economic Concentration and Monopoly in Japan," *Journal of Political Economy* (June 1964). Eugene Rotwein, "Economic Concentration and Monopoly in Japan: A Second View," *Journal of Asian Studies* (November 1976). US Department of State, *Report of the Mission on Japanese Combines* (1946). Kozo Yamamura, *Economic Policy in Postwar Japan* (1967).   Eugene ROTWEIN

industrial policy

(*sangyō seisaku*). Policies concerning industrial structure, development, and organization developed and implemented by government agencies and ministries in conjunction with business interests.

Unlike the terms "economic policy," "fiscal policy," and "monetary policy," which were introduced to the Japanese language along with Western economics, industrial policy is an original Japanese term and does not have a clearly defined academic meaning. Rather, the concept was custom-made to fit the specific social and historical situation of post–World War II Japan. Industries under the jurisdiction and policy guidance of the MINISTRY OF INTERNATIONAL TRADE AND INDUSTRY (MITI) experienced rapid development in the early postwar period, resulting in a strong association of industrial policy with that ministry. However, other ministries with jurisdiction over industry and business (such as the MINISTRY OF AGRICULTURE, FORESTRY, AND FISHERIES and the MINISTRY OF FINANCE) also engage in industrial policy making. Since 1970, the term has also been used in reports of the Organization for Economic Cooperation and Development, indicating that it is gradually acquiring international recognition.

Industrial policy generally falls into three areas: INDUSTRIAL ORGANIZATION (antimonopoly policy and other measures to maintain order in the market); INDUSTRIAL STRUCTURE (policies aimed at the promotion of certain industries and the accelerated decline of others); and industrial development (those areas of fiscal and monetary policy, INCOMES POLICY, and foreign trade policy that influence industrial activities). The emphasis of industrial policy in the United

States and Europe is on industrial organization, and industrial structure policies are carried out piecemeal.

The focus of postwar Japanese industrial policy has been on industrial structure. This policy was based on the recognition that the mechanisms of the free market will not independently produce the most efficient and appropriate distribution of resources. Faced with the task of achieving rapid recovery and economic growth in the context of a free economy, the government pursued policies that would elevate the country's industrial structure through the expansion of industries with high elasticity of demand and high productivity growth rates. Many of the industries which satisfied both of these requirements were in the heavy and chemical industrial categories, and it was through the promotion of these industries that Japan attained rapid growth and an increase in international competitive ability.

The primary means for implementing industrial policy have been import restrictions and FOREIGN EXCHANGE CONTROL; ADMINISTRATIVE GUIDANCE; monetary and tax measures; and the enactment of industrial promotion legislation. Restrictions on the allocation of foreign exchange for imports, first practiced in the early 1950s, was a particularly effective means for protecting the heavy and chemical industries at a time when the international competitiveness of Japan was weak. By the time trade was liberalized in the early 1960s, Japanese-made iron and steel products and electrical goods were competitive in international markets, but restrictions remained in place on such strategic commodities as automobiles. Controls were retained on computers and semiconductors into the 1980s. See FOREIGN TRADE, GOVERNMENT POLICY ON.

Administrative guidance, a unique Japanese practice of semiofficial government direction of industry, has been utilized to maintain order in the domestic market. The steel and petrochemical industries are typical of those subjected to administrative guidance over such matters as the curtailment of equipment investments, the reduction of operations during periods of recession, and the formation of depression cartels. Monetary policy has been utilized to assist developing industries. Government financial institutions have provided long-term, low-interest loans to priority areas: basic industries in the early 1950s, heavy and chemical industries in the late 1950s, and regional development since the 1960s. Tax measures have also assisted corporations in such areas as the depreciation of new capital investments. Specific legislation to promote the development of strategic industries includes laws targeting the machinery industry (1956) and the electronics industry (1957).

Industrial development based on the heavy and chemical industries resulted in the emergence of a number of serious problems in the 1970s, including heavy industrial pollution and increasing dependence on imported raw materials. As a result, emphasis shifted to the promotion of such knowledge-intensive industries as the computer industry in the late 1970s. HARADA Yukihiro

industrial property

(kōgyō shoyūken). A legal concept first formally used in Japan in the 1894 trade and navigation treaty between Japan and England, when Japan agreed to the Paris Convention for the protection of industrial property. Thus, the meaning of the concept is to be understood in the terms of that convention. Article 1 states, "The protection of industrial property has as its object patents, utility models, designs, trademarks, trade names, indications of source on goods or appellations of origin and the prevention of unfair competition." The convention also provides that "industrial property taken in its broadest sense extends not only to industry and commerce but also to fields such as agriculture and the harvesting industry."

In Japan, the term "industrial property" is not used in its broad sense but commonly refers only to four rights: patent, utility-model, design, and trademark rights. These four rights are regulated by very similar legal provisions, and their administration is handled by the Patent Office, a special bureau of the Ministry of International Trade and Industry. Thus it is necessary to distinguish between industrial property in the narrow sense (see PATENT LAW; UTILITY-MODEL PATENT LAW; DESIGN LAW; and TRADEMARK LAW), and industrial property in the broad sense, which, along with copyrights, is considered to lie within the domain of incorporeal property.

Industrial property is divided into two classes. The first, industrial production activities, includes inventions, devices, and designs. All of these, whether or not the objects themselves are actually used, have a fixed value and contribute to industrial development by being open to the public. The second class, markings for the maintenance

of industrial order, includes trademarks, trade names, service marks, indications of source on goods, appellations of origin, product containers, wrappings, shape, etc. These markings in and of themselves have no common value. However, in their actual use, they function to distinguish between one product or business and another. They acquire consumer trust and come to have a definite value.

The protection of industrial property functions in two ways. First, patents, registered designs, trademarks, and trade names involve a property right by which one can exercise complete control and exclude competitive use by others. Because the objects of these rights are always incorporeal, their establishment, change, and extinction are clarified by means of a registration or recording system. The registration system ensures a competitive and profitable position through the monopoly use of the object of the right and also benefits the right holder by enabling him or her to convey or license the right to others. If another person makes unauthorized use of the registered object, the right holder may seek an injunction or compensation for damages. However, because inventions, devices, and designs are of such a nature that their general use must be permitted, these rights are subject to stringent limitations, such as a limited time period for monopoly rights.

Second, product markings other than trademarks and trade names initially carry no monopoly use rights. Once these markings have become commonly known through wide usage, they receive exclusive monopoly protection under the Unfair Competition Prevention Law (Fusei Kyōsō Bōshi Hō). The user of a recognized marking then has the right to seek injunctive or compensatory relief against activity which confuses a product or business with that of another by employing the same or a similar marking. Service marks are markings used by service traders in such businesses as financing or broadcasting. In the United States, the same registration and protection system is used for service marks and trademarks, but in Japan there is no registration system for service marks. Product containers, product shape, etc, are essentially not markings, but, through usage, they acquire the same distinguishing function as markings.

Because the objects of industrial property have no international boundaries, there is a strong need for their international protection. Beginning with the Paris Convention, various international treaties have been concluded on the matter. In 1978 the Patent Cooperation Treaty became effective, and the Japanese Patent Office is an important international searching and preliminary examining authority. SENGEN Ryūichirō

industrial relocation policy

(kōgyō saihaichi seisaku). Moving factories out of large urban areas into areas where the concentration of industries is low, and encouraging new industrial construction outside metropolitan areas in order to realize relocation of industry on a national scale. The current design, based on the Industrial Relocation Promotion Law of 1972, was announced through the Ministry of International Trade and Industry in 1977. The plan consists of seven sections: (1) setting goals for industrial relocation by type of industry and area of relocation; (2) encouraging city-based industries to move to less concentrated areas; (3) encouraging the establishment of new industrial zones in regions wishing to attract industry; (4) considering environmental and safety problems when encouraging industrial relocation; (5) promoting movement of the labor force (especially of younger workers) into new areas; (6) creating the necessary buildings, water supply, energy, and transportation networks for new industrial areas; and (7) enacting appropriate government policies to ensure the achievement of industrial relocation.

The plan for the relocation of industries has set the following goals for the period 1974–85: that the total area occupied by factories in congested urban areas be reduced by 30 percent, and that 70 percent of the total land area allocated for new industrial building during this period be located in new industrial zones outside the urban areas.

Industrial relocation encounters many difficulties because of its close connection with investment plans in industry and because of the problems involved in moving a labor force. The current plan is not proceeding smoothly. In the long run, however, it may prove effective in improving efficiency of land use when coordinated with other policies. See also NIHON RETTŌ KAIZŌ RON. MOMOSE Hiroto

industrial reorganization

The efforts of leading corporations within an industry to realign affiliations and investments in order to rationalize production and stabilize business operations. Industrial reorganization in Japan went hand in hand with heavy capital investment during the high-growth period of the 1960s. As major industries expanded production capacity and modernized equipment, enterprise groupings were also created. Key corporations in such strategic areas as the IRON AND STEEL INDUSTRY, the ELECTRONICS industry, and the AUTOMOTIVE INDUSTRY established direct subsidiaries through heavy financial investment and entered into production, technology, and sales affiliations with smaller firms (see ENTERPRISE GROUPS).

As economic growth slowed in the second half of the 1970s, however, industrial reorganization took on a defensive character. Primary actions included scrapping of unprofitable sectors, rationalization of production, establishment of business tie-ups, and outright mergers. Depressed industries, such as the TEXTILE INDUSTRY and the structurally depressed aluminum industry, were prime targets of industrial reorganization. MASUDA Yūji

industrial revolution in Japan

The precise meaning of the term "industrial revolution" is controversial. Since its coinage by Arnold Toynbee (1852–83), it has taken on a wide variety of meanings. Generally, however, it refers to the classic case of English industrial development from the mid-18th to the mid-19th centuries. Some see "industrial revolution" in terms of the growth of particular industries (such as steel), and others in terms of the rapid expansion of production in several industrial sectors; still others equate it with the growth of technological innovation in general. Yet these views only blur the essential characteristics of the industrial revolution as an epochal phase in history.

The English industrial revolution was internally generated, as the steady and cumulative development of the cotton, tool, and steel industries, in succession, laid the basis of English capitalism. In Japan, by contrast, the industrial revolution was a piecemeal and discontinuous process that was bound to create economic distortions. Beginning in the late 1880s, after the deflationary MATSUKATA FISCAL POLICY had achieved a "primitive accumulation" of capital, it lasted until about 1910. Because during much of this time Japan suffered political and economic encroachment by Britain and other Western powers (see UNEQUAL TREATIES, REVISION OF), its industrialization, unlike England's, had to be rushed and directed from above, largely by government fiat.

In accord with its policy of promoting trade and industry (SHOKUSAN KŌGYŌ), the Meiji government in the early 1870s had purchased foreign machinery for the domestic textile industry. Such aid, however, was not always effective. By contrast, the privately owned ŌSAKA SPINNING MILL independently imported the latest steam-powered machinery from England and raw cotton from China, India, and the United States. Soon after its opening, double work shifts were required to meet the demand for its products. The Ōsaka mill set an example for the rest of the cotton textile industry, which subsequently expanded at a rapid pace.

To pay for the foreign raw materials and textile machinery, the government encouraged the domestic production of raw silk as an export commodity. As with the cotton industry, the government-owned filatures, despite their reliance on French and Italian technicians, did not fare as well as their privately operated counterparts, located in the Suwa area of Nagano Prefecture. These factories employed both traditional and Western techniques as well as cooperative rereeling and cooperative marketing; they also relied heavily on the labor of peasant girls forced by growing LANDLORDISM to leave their villages and work in factories for subsistence wages.

The heavy industries in Japan developed quite differently from such light industries as cotton and silk. Their modern development began in the late 1880s with the implementation of the government's decision in 1880 to sell many of its industrial enterprises, most of them unprofitable, to private entrepreneurs (see KAN'EI JIGYŌ HARAISAGE). In 1887 the NAGASAKI SHIPYARDS were sold to MITSUBISHI, and two years later the MIIKE COAL MINES were sold to MITSUI. These transactions not only signaled the beginnings of the shipping and coal industries, which were to play a central role in the formation and development of Japanese capitalism, but also stimulated the growth of these private companies into enormous business combines (ZAIBATSU).

Although the government relied heavily on economically advanced countries for textile machinery, it established its own steel mill at Yawata, in Kyūshū, after the Sino-Japanese War of 1894–95. Importing technology from Germany, which had recently survived a severe depression and bid fair to surpass Britain as the foremost industrial power, the government sought through the YAWATA IRON AND STEEL WORKS to ensure a steady supply of steel for the domestic machinery and shipbuilding industries. The army and navy arsenals were tied in with the Yawata mill and became the center of a burgeoning armaments industry. Later, after the Russo-Japanese War of 1904–05, the government established the Anshan Steel Works in Manchuria. In this manner, the state took the lead over private concerns in a critical sector of modern industry.

In sum, the Japanese industrial revolution differed from the classic English model in that the Japanese state took a more active role in fostering industrialization; it maintained close ties with, and actively encouraged, leading industrial concerns in the private sector. Thus Japan was able to pass with relative rapidity through the critical take-off stage into sustained industrial growth. KATŌ Kōzaburō

industrial robots

(sangyōyō robotto). Flexible and versatile manufacturing devices that perform functions similar to those of human hands and arms; some robots are capable of sensory perception and even something resembling cognition.

In 1980 Japan had more industrial robots in operation than any other country. The Japan Industrial Robot Association (Nihon Sangyōyō Robotto Kōgyōkai) has estimated there were 14,000 advanced industrial robots in operation in Japan at the end of that year, or about 60 percent of the advanced robots in the world. In addition, Japan had some 62,000 simpler robots such as manual manipulators and fixed sequence robots.

The spreading use of robots has brought a number of social and economic benefits. Among these are the improvement of productivity and product quality, increased return on investment, the prevention of industrial accidents, and the freeing of workers from dangerous and unpleasant work. Robots have made the automation of small-batch production possible and changed industrial production from a man-machine system to a man-robot-machine system.

Growth of the Robot Industry —— The first advanced robot was imported to Japan from the United States in 1967 during a decade of rapid growth and labor shortage in Japan and it therefore created a great impact. Research into the development and utilization of robots began the following year. The 1970s were a decade of development and application, while 1980 is considered to be the beginning of a period of wide diffusion of robots in Japanese manufacturing. Rapid growth in the robotization of industry is expected in the future, as is the application of robots to fields other than manufacturing, which now accounts for about 98 percent of all the robots in use.

The development and production of robots in Japan came first in response to a severe shortage of skilled labor (estimated at 1.8 million workers in 1965). Early development efforts were interrupted by the recession of the early 1970s and by the oil crisis of 1973. These economic crises, however, ultimately ushered in a period of moderate growth, in which Japanese industry turned increasingly to new technology as a source of increased productivity and lowered costs. The production of industrial robots increased rapidly in the late 1970s: total production was ¥21.6 billion (US $80 million) in 1977; by 1979 it had increased to ¥42.4 billion ($193 million); and in 1980 production grew by 85 percent to ¥78.4 billion ($346 million). In 1980, some 150 companies were involved in the production of robots.

Future demand for robots is expected to be strong, as enterprises continue their efforts to increase productivity. The continuing shortage of skilled labor will also be a contributing factor. The Japan Industrial Robot Association forecasts that demand for robots for manufacturing will reach ¥290 billion ($1.4 billion) by 1985 and ¥520 billion ($2.2 billion) by 1990. Nonmanufacturing demand for robots, which accounted for only 1 percent of total demand in 1980, could add as much as ¥60 billion ($270 million) to total production by 1990. Industrial robots are thus expected to follow a growth curve similar to those followed by numerical control machine tools and computers.

Exports of industrial robots accounted for only 3 percent of output in 1980, but exports are expected to reach 16 percent of output by 1985 and 17 percent by 1990. The lag in export growth is due to the fact that the utilization of industrial robots requires sophisticated system engineering at the production site prior to installation, and maintenance service after installation. For exports to grow, Japanese makers will have to team up with overseas engineering firms, a process that was beginning to take place in the early 1980s.

Types and Primary Uses of Industrial Robots —— Industrial robots are classified in Japan by mode of operation and programming into the following types. A manual manipulator, the simplest type, is an armlike mechanism (manipulator) that is operated by a human being. A fixed sequence robot has a manipulator that is programmed to follow a sequence of movements from an established position under predetermined conditions; its program cannot be easily modified. A variable sequence robot likewise operates according to one set of instructions, but its program can be changed. A playback robot is capable of remembering and repeating a sequence of operations that are first performed manually. The operations of a numerical control robot are controlled by instructions encoded on punched tapes, cards, or digital switches. The most sophisticated robot, called an intelligent robot, is capable of recognizing objects and positions and performing required operations in response. Robots are also classified according to the movements of their manipulators as follows: cylindrical-coordinate robot, polar-coordinate robot, cartesian (right angle) coordinate robot, and articulated robot.

The highest concentrations of robot use by industry in Japan are in electronic machinery manufacturing (36 percent), automobile manufacturing (30 percent), plastic molding (10 percent), metal working (5 percent), and the manufacturing of metalworking machinery (4 percent). The primary functions of robots in these industries are assembly, welding, machining, press operation, plastic molding, die casting, and painting. The electronic products industry experienced especially rapid growth in the utilization of robots in 1980; these were primarily numerical control robots used for the insertion of condensers, resistors, and integrated circuits in printed circuit boards. With the further development of sensors and computers, it is expected that robots with artificial intelligence will increasingly be utilized for complex assembly and inspection of finished products.

Robots with sensors capable of high speed visual discrimination are essential for the automation of multiple-type, small-volume production. The development of sensors capable of recognizing objects by shape and position had been largely completed by 1980; those capable of recognizing color and posture were expected to be perfected and widely adopted by the mid-1980s. Machine tool robots were expected to be developed by the early 1980s and were expected to reach the diffusion stage by the end of the decade. Robots for deburring small cast iron and steel pieces (less than 20 kg) were expected to be in wide use by the mid-1980s, while those for finishing medium and large castings (more than 300 kg) were expected to be in use by the end of the decade. Robots for painting automobiles were developed rapidly in the late 1970s and were to be widely deployed by the early 1980s. The diffusion of automation technology for the assembly of small metal parts of a medium range of types and medium volume was expected in the mid-1980s, while multiple-type, small-volume production technology will be widespread by the end of the decade. The production of medium-size metal products, such as motorcycles, was expected to be automated by the end of the 1980s, but numerous problems stand in the way of the automation of the production of large items such as railway cars, and it is difficult to predict when this will be achieved.

In the early 1980s, industrial robots were almost exclusively used for manufacturing, but their application to other fields is anticipated in the future. Among those fields are nuclear energy, where robots may be used for the maintenance and repair of equipment that emits radiation; health and social welfare, where robots may be used for the assistance of the physically disabled, fire fighting, emergency assistance, and garbage collection; ocean development, where robots may be used for undersea construction and exploration; agriculture and forestry, where robots may be used for harvesting, spreading fertilizer and agricultural chemicals, pruning and felling trees, and other purposes; and construction and transportation.

The Economic and Social Role of Robots —— The first role of robots is to improve industrial productivity. The capacity of robots to move with versatility enables the automation of small-batch production. Some 80 percent of total production of machinery in Japan is small-batch production, the automation of which can and will contribute to a remarkable improvement in productivity. Secondly, robots contribute to the improvement of product quality, since the stability and accuracy of their functions results in uniform production. Third, industrial robots contribute to the humanization of work life in some cases by releasing human beings from heavy, dangerous, and monotonous work. Production thus changes from a man-machine system to a man-robot-machine system, which results in the upgrading of the quality of work life, job satisfaction, and the stability of employment (since workers are less likely to leave jobs because of unfavorable work conditions).

A fourth role of robots is in the development of new industries, such as ocean development and nuclear energy. These offer new employment opportunities and the possibility of new industrial operations. Another role is contribution to the saving of resources and energy: flexible movement enables robots to be easily fitted to design and model changes, thus saving the expense of remodeling unipurpose automatic machinery when such changes are made. The durability of robots allows the extension of the work day to two or three shifts and thus results in savings in investment. Finally, robots contribute to the solution of the shortage of skilled labor that has been a serious problem in postwar Japan.

Government Programs to Foster the Use of Robots —— The Japanese government has four programs that promote the diffusion of robots. The first is a robot leasing operation run by the Japan Robot Leasing Corporation (JAROL), supported by special financing from the Japan Development Bank. JAROL was established in April 1980 by 24 robot producers and 10 insurance companies to purchase robots and make them available for lease, especially to smaller enterprises that could not otherwise afford to undertake automation. A second measure allows enterprises to take a special depreciation on investment in high performance industrial robots provided with computer control. A third program provides financing for smaller enterprise investment in industrial safety, which comes into play when an enterprise automates jobs involving dangerous or strenuous labor. A final program, operated by prefectural governments, provides financing to smaller enterprises for the purpose of modernizing or rationalizing their production facilities. This program also includes the rental of robots to the enterprise. *YONEMOTO Kanji*

industrial structure

The structure of an economy by industry, typically measured by the percentage distribution of economic activities (in terms of output, capital, and labor) by major sectors and industries. National economies are conventionally divided into three sectors—PRIMARY INDUSTRIES (agriculture, forestry, and fisheries), SECONDARY INDUSTRIES (mining, manufacturing, construction, transport, and communications), and TERTIARY INDUSTRIES (retail and wholesale trade, banking, finance and real estate, business services, personal services, and public administration). In general, national economies in the early stages of development are dominated by primary production related to land (often including mining). As the economy develops and income rises, the primary sector shares of output, capital, and labor tend to fall, and those of the secondary sector tend to rise. In late stages of development, the primary sector accounts for only a small fraction of total economic activities, the secondary sector begins to decline in relative terms, and the tertiary sector comes to the fore.

Japan's Historical Experience —— Japan's economic development since the Meiji Restoration (1868) is an excellent illustration of these patterns. Table 1 shows how shares of the labor force by sector have changed over the past century. In the distribution of the labor force between agriculture (including forestry) and nonagriculture, changes were relatively slow until the first decade of the 20th century, considerably accelerated from then up to World War II, temporarily reversed in direction after the war, and were very rapid during the last three decades.

The relative contraction of Japanese agriculture was accompanied by a continuous outflow of labor from agriculture to industry. Table 1 shows that the labor force in agriculture remained virtually stationary before World War II, except for the decade beginning in 1910. This statistic implies that labor migration out of agriculture was about equal to the net natural increase of the agricultural labor force. Before World War II, those who migrated from farms were farmers' children, excluding the first sons and their spouses, who inherited land. Boys in their mid-teens left home after a primary education of six to eight years to get apprentice training in urban jobs and became independent industrial workers upon reaching maturity. These per-

Industrial structure —— Table 1

	Total labor force (millions)	Agriculture and forestry (millions)	Agriculture and forestry (percent)	Nonagriculture (percent)								
				Total	Fishing	Mining	Manufacturing	Construction	Facilitating industries[2]	Commerce[3]	Services[4]	Public administration[5]
1872	21.4	15.7	73.5	26.5	—	—	—	—	—	—	—	—
1880	21.9	15.9	72.5	27.5	—	—	—	—	—	—	—	—
1890	23.0	15.9	69.0	31.0	—	—	—	—	—	—	—	2.4
1900	24.4	16.1	66.1	33.9	—	—	—	—	—	—	—	2.9
1910	25.5	16.1	63.0	37.0	2.2	0.8	11.5	2.5	2.9	10.2	6.9	3.4
1920	27.3	14.2	52.0	48.0	2.0	1.6	16.9	2.9	4.3	12.4	8.0	4.1
1930	29.6	14.1	47.7	52.3	1.9	1.1	16.1	3.4	4.4	16.6	8.9	4.2
1940	34.2	13.8	40.5	59.5	1.6	1.7	20.3	2.9	4.5	14.3	14.1	5.4
1950	36.2	17.4	48.1	51.9	1.9	1.4	17.2	3.3	4.7	10.3	11.2	2.9
1960	45.1	13.9	30.8	69.2	1.3	1.1	21.1	5.2	5.4	18.8	16.1	3.2
1970	51.5	8.4	16.3	83.7	0.9	0.4	26.7	7.6	6.9	22.2	17.9	3.2
1979	55.8	6.3	11.3	88.7	0.8	0.2	24.5	9.7	6.8	25.5	21.0	3.5

Labor Force Composition by Industry[1]

[1] For 1872–1940: gainful workers.
[2] Transportation, communication, electricity, gas, and water.
[3] Wholesale and retail trade, finances and insurance, and real estate.
[4] Including public administration. For 1890 and 1900, only public administration figures available.
[5] For 1890–1940: based on Kazushi Ohkawa et al, *National Income* (1974.) For 1950–79: Prime Minister's Office, *Labor Force Survey*.
NOTE: Data is from a different source than, and differs slightly from, that in Table 1 at LABOR MARKET.
SOURCE: For 1872–1970: Kazushi Ohkawa and Miyohei Shinohara, ed, *Patterns of Japanese Economic Development* (1979). For 1979: Prime Minister's Office, Statistics Bureau, *Annual Report on the Labor Force Survey* (annual): 1980.

Industrial structure —— Table 2

Composition of Manufacturing Production
(in percentages)

	Light manufacturing								Heavy manufacturing					
	Total	Food processing	Textiles and apparel			Wood and lumber	Printing and publishing	Miscellaneous	Total	Chemicals	Stone and clay products	Iron and steel	Nonferrous metals	Machinery
			Total	Cotton	Silk									
1874–79	84.5	59.1	9.4	2.8	3.8	6.8	0.2	9.0	15.4	11.0	2.2	0.3	1.0	0.9
1880–89	85.0	55.4	15.0	5.1	3.7	5.2	0.4	9.0	15.0	10.3	1.4	0.4	1.3	1.6
1890–99	86.7	47.2	26.7	12.5	5.3	3.6	0.6	8.6	13.3	8.4	1.5	0.4	1.2	1.8
1900–09	81.8	44.5	24.3	8.0	6.0	3.9	1.6	7.5	18.2	9.7	1.8	0.7	1.3	4.7
1910–19	72.4	33.7	27.5	13.4	6.8	2.8	2.6	5.8	27.5	9.3	2.2	1.9	3.7	10.4
1920–29	68.8	30.4	29.4	13.4	7.4	2.4	3.0	3.6	31.9	9.8	2.6	4.7	3.7	11.1
1930–39	55.7	18.2	28.9	10.6	7.4	2.8	2.5	3.3	44.3	14.7	2.6	9.1	3 5	14.4
1950–59	42.8	18.9	14.3	—	—	3.1	3.6	2.9	57.3	19.6	3.9	10.1	4.2	19.5
1960–69	31.5	13.2	9.7	—	—	2.0	2.0	4.6	68.5	19.7	3.6	10.5	4.0	30.7
1970–78	22.4	9.2	5.8	—	—	1.2	1.1	5.1	77.5	21.4	3.2	10.2	3.6	39.1

NOTE: Percentages of total manufacturing production for each year. Based on value of production in 1934–36 prices.
SOURCE: For 1874–1939: Miyohei Shinohara, *Mining and Manufacturing* (1972). For 1950–69: Kazushi Ohkawa and Miyohei Shinohara, *Patterns of Japanese Economic Development* (1979). For 1970–78: extrapolated by the author from the Ministry of International Trade and Industry production indexes.

manent migrants from farms accounted for two-thirds of the increases in the nonagricultural labor force in the prewar period.

Agriculture's share of the labor force fell below 50 percent in the 1920s. However, toward the end of World War II, many urban residents were evacuated to rural areas, and after the war millions of repatriates from overseas returned to their old rural families. Thus, agriculture's share of the labor force temporarily surpassed the 50 percent mark again. As the economy recovered from the war's devastation by the early 1950s, demand for industrial labor increased and a steady pattern of rural-urban labor migration was resumed. During the 1950s, migration was mostly limited to teenage school graduates as before. By 1960, however, the increase in the urban demand for labor started to outstrip the supply of farm youths, and older farmers were recruited for urban employment. The agricultural labor force began to contract in absolute terms, and even those who remained on farms worked only part-time as farmers.

In the secondary sector, Table 1 shows a continued relative expansion in employment and production until the mid-1970s, except for a temporary reversal in World War II. The tertiary sector maintained a relatively stable share in net domestic product before World War II, although its share of employment expanded. After World War II its share of employment continued to increase, while its share of net domestic product remained stable until the early 1960s when it, too, started to rise. See also LABOR MARKET.

Changes in Manufacturing —— A broad comparison of light and heavy manufacturing reveals that light manufacturing accounted for as much as 85 percent of total production until 1900. From then on, the share steadily declined, and reached 22 percent in the 1970s (see Table 2). Thus, after 100 years, the relative positions of light and heavy manufacturing were completely reversed. Among light manufacturing industries, the FOOD PROCESSING INDUSTRY was the most important in the early part of the Meiji period (1868–1912),

Industrial structure———Table 3

Economically Active Population, by Industry
(in percentages)

	Japan (1970)	United States (1970)	United Kingdom[1] (1970)	France (1968)
Agriculture, forestry, and fisheries	19.3	3.5	2.7	15.7
Mining and quarrying	0.4	0.8	1.6	1.2
Manufacturing	26.2	24.2	34.1	27.6
Electricity, gas, and water	0.5	—	1.5	0.9
Construction	7.5	5.6	7.1	10.2
Wholesale and retail trade, restaurants and hotels	19.3	20.1	15.7	15.3
Transportation and communications	6.2	4.8 ·	6.6	6.0
Finance, insurance, real estate, and business services	4.3	6.3	5.8 }	23.0
Community, social, and personal services	16.2	30.7	24.0 }	
Activities not adequately defined	0.1	4.3	0.8	0.1

[1] England, Wales, and Scotland.
SOURCE: United Nations, *Demographic Yearbook* (annual): 1972.

Industrial structure———Table 4

Gross Domestic Product, by Industry, 1977
(in percentages of total GDP)

	Japan	United States	United Kingdom	France
Agriculture, forestry, and fisheries	5.7	3.3	3.4	5.9
Mining and quarrying	0.6	3.2	3.5	1.0
Manufacturing	32.3	29.0	34.4	43.8
Electricity, gas, and water	2.7	3.0	4.2	2.2
Construction	9.3	5.4	7.9	9.5
Wholesale and retail trade, restaurants and hotels	18.0*	21.4	12.3*	16.1
Transportation and communications	7.4	7.7	10.0	6.6
Finance, insurance, real estate, and business services	16.3**	20.6	16.5**	19.3
Community, social, and personal services	12.7	7.1	12.5	9.0
Less: imputed bank service charges	−5.0	−2.5	−4.7	−4.4
Statistical discrepancy	—	1.7	—	—
Per capita GDP (in US dollars)	$6,098	$8,666	$5,860	$7,172

*Restaurants and hotels included in community, social, and personal services.
**Business services included in community, social, and personal services.
SOURCE: Organization for Economic Cooperation and Development, *National Accounts of OECD Countries, 1960–1977*, vol 2 (1979).

accounting for 60 percent of total production, but its share shrank steadily over the next 100 years. The TEXTILE INDUSTRY behaved differently. Textile output was less than 10 percent of the total in the 1870s but jumped above 25 percent in the 1890s and stayed close to 30 percent for the next half century until World War II. The early surge of textile production, particularly in cotton spinning and weaving and silk reeling, was the dynamic element in Japan's industrialization. It was in this industry that the factory system was first introduced. Of particular importance was the fact that workers in textile mills were mostly women, farmers' daughters in their late teens or early twenties who left their homes to work in mills for two to three years before going back home. Thus, the continued expansion of these mills through the prewar period provided significant employment opportunities for surplus female labor in agriculture. This feature of DEKASEGI, or temporary migration, was a salient feature of prewar labor mobility. As is well known, much of Japan's textile production was directed toward the export market, supplying foreign exchange sorely needed to finance imports of raw materials and capital goods essential to industrial expansion. After World War II, the textile industry began to decline because of the development of synthetic fibers and competition from emerging producers in less developed countries.

In heavy manufacturing, basic metals (see IRON AND STEEL INDUSTRY and NONFERROUS METALS INDUSTRY) initially accounted for a very small fraction of total output. The industry began to expand in the decade beginning in 1910, but government protection was necessary to shield it from international competition, and in fact the largest steel mill, YAWATA IRON AND STEEL WORKS, was run by the government until 1934. After World War II, basic metals maintained a stable share of manufacturing output. On the other hand, the MACHINE TOOL INDUSTRY (metal products, electrical machinery, transport equipment, and precision instruments) began its ascent in the 1900s. With the rising demand for munitions, the machine industry's output rose in the 1930s. But despite this relative expansion, it remained in its infancy before World War II, lagging far behind the Western nations in technology and scale of operations. The three decades following World War II witnessed a spectacular expansion of the machinery industry, which accounted for less than 20 percent of manufacturing output in 1950 but exceeded 40 percent by 1972. Japan is now one of the world's leading exporters of machinery. The CHEMICAL INDUSTRY (chemicals, petroleum and coal products, petroleum refining, paper and pulp, plastics, and rubber products) maintained a relatively stable 10 percent share before World War II, and rose to 20 percent after the war.

Relationship to the Foreign Trade Structure——The composition of a nation's exports and imports closely reflects its stage of industrialization. Japan's main exports were tea and raw silk when the country opened its doors to foreign powers in the 1860s, and raw silk remained the most important export item until 1929, thanks to the rapidly growing demand for silk goods in the United States.

Cotton textiles followed raw silk. Cotton exports were initially in cotton yarns and then shifted to cotton fabrics. In the 1930s, cotton replaced raw silk as the most important category of Japan's exports. In the early postwar period, more than half of Japan's exports were in light manufacturing, but with the expansion of heavy industries Japanese exports continued to shift to heavy manufactured goods, which came to account for more than 80 percent of the total value of exports by the late 1970s.

Japan's imports consisted almost entirely of manufactured products in the early years of the Meiji period. Industrialization in the subsequent decades enabled Japan to carry on import substitution of consumer goods and to increase imports of crude materials. Thus, in the 1930s, Japan's imports consisted of light manufactures (12 percent), heavy manufactures (30 percent), foodstuffs (18 percent), raw materials (33 percent), and fuels (7 percent). Comparable figures in 1975–78 were 7, 15, 15, 20, and 43 percent, respectively. See also FOREIGN TRADE.

Conclusion —— By the 1970s, Japan had become a leading industrial power. Its per capita income and industrial structure are now comparable to those of other leading nations. Tables 3 and 4 show that Japan is most like France in production structures. As regards employment, Japan lags behind other developed countries in terms of significance of heavy manufacturing employment. Similarities are far stronger in the distribution of value added, reflecting the fact that value added productivity per worker is larger in heavy than in light manufacturing in Japan. (The productivity differential can be attributed to the dual structure prevalent in manufacturing.)

The most recent stage in the development of national economies has been called postindustrialism, which is marked by a decrease in the employment share of the secondary sector, a shift from production of goods to services, and the growing importance of knowledge as a factor in production. This "service revolution" brings the continuing growth of tertiary industries.

In the United States, this point was reached around 1950. The tertiary sector's share of employment exceeded the 50 percent mark in the mid-1950s, the first such case in any country. Recently, other leading nations have followed this pattern. The service revolution seems to have begun in Japan in the mid-1970s, when manufacturing employment started to decline. Though tertiary sector employment is still a little short of the 50 percent mark, this level will be passed soon. The event will mark a new era for a country that has long placed paramount emphasis upon expansion of material production.

——Kazushi Ohkawa and Henry Rosovsky, *Japanese Economic Growth* (1973). Kazushi Ohkawa et al, *National Income* (1974). Kazushi Ohkawa and Miyohei Shinohara, ed, *Patterns of Japanese Economic Development* (1979). Miyohei Shinohara, *Mining and Manufacturing* (1972). *Kazuo* SATŌ

Industrial Structure Council

(Sangyō Kōzō Shingikai; also known as Sankōshin). An advisory council sponsored and controlled by the MINISTRY OF INTERNATIONAL TRADE AND INDUSTRY (MITI), whose purpose is to study and make recommendations on questions posed by the minister concerning the industrial structure of the national economy.

The council is one of the best-known and most influential of the approximately 250 advisory councils and commissions attached to various government ministries and agencies. It was created in 1964 by combining the Industrial Structure Study Commission (Sangyō Kōzō Chōsakai) and the Industrial Rationalization Council (Sangyō Gōrika Shingikai). The council analyzes the long-term prospects of the development pattern of the national economy, thereby providing a broad policy vision to MITI. Also, its various committees study and make recommendations on specific issues and for specific industries.

Organization and Membership —— The council has a maximum authorized membership of 130 "persons of learning and experience," who are appointed by the minister for a renewable two-year term. The regular membership list of September 1978 included 28 officials of industrial and trade associations, 20 heads of private corporations, 9 university professors, 3 officers of consumer organizations, 2 officers of private research institutes, 2 labor union leaders, 1 newspaper editor, 1 head of a private bank, 1 director of the Bank of Japan, and the president of the National Mayors' Conference. (Only 2—both consumer group representatives—were women.) The producer orientation of the council's membership is suggested by the fact that nearly three-quarters of the 68 regular members of the council were representatives of commerce and industry. The chairperson of the council is elected from among its regular members. The council consists of a plenary session (sōkai), a general committee (sōgō bukai), and specialized committees (bumonbetsu bukai). The council chairperson may appoint temporary and specialist members to committees, subcommittees, and research groups.

Functions and Council Reports —— The general committee serves as the executive committee for the council. It determines the rules and operating procedures for the council activities, establishes specialized committees, and coordinates the work of the committees. Meeting once or twice a year, it deliberates upon, and gives acknowledgment to, the key industrial policies of MITI. The ministry's Industrial Structure Section serves as secretariat for the council in general and for the general committee in particular, providing clerical, statistical, and research work. Other committees are similarly tied to various sections within the ministry. The close working relationships established between MITI's bureaus and Sankōshin's various committees provide a convenient forum for the former in carrying out ADMINISTRATIVE GUIDANCE. The reports of the council also thus reflect to a considerable extent the views and opinions of MITI officials.

Between the inception of the council in 1964 and the summer of 1978, 47 questions were posed by the minister to the council. During the same time period, 103 reports, including interim reports, were prepared by various committees and submitted to the minister. The most important and influential reports have been prepared by the general committee. In May 1971, for example, the general committee submitted an interim report entitled "Commercial and Industrial Policy for the 1970s." The report stated that Japan's future industrial development must center upon the so-called knowledge-intensive industries—computers, electronics, aircraft, and the like. This suggested new direction was hailed as a fresh departure from the "heavy and chemical industrialization" (jūkagaku kōgyōka) policy of the 1950s and 1960s. The final report, entitled "The Direction of Japan's Industrial Structure" (Wagakuni sangyō kōzō no hōkō), was published in September 1974. It provided a target industrial structure for 1985, and stressed the importance of satisfying more fully the various needs of consumers and reducing dependency on imported energy resources. *Kanji* HAITANI

industrial waste

The industrial waste emitted by manufacturing and mining industries and power plants in Japan in 1976 totaled approximately 230 million metric tons (254 million short tons), about seven times the volume of garbage (about 32 million tons metric or 35 million short tons) discharged that year. The iron and steel industry accounted for 43.3 percent of the total volume of industrial waste, the chemical industry 13 percent, the textile industry 8.1 percent, and nonferrous metals industry 6.3 percent. Major industrial wastes consisted of slag (28.4 percent), spent acid (32.1 percent), and sludge (14.9 percent).

In the summer of 1975, it was discovered that a highly toxic chemical, hexavalent chromium, had been contaminating the area surrounding a chemical waste dump in the Kōtō Ward in Tōkyō. Following this discovery, the problem of industrial waste attracted considerable attention. The Law concerning the Treatment and Cleaning of Discharge (Haikibutsu no Shori oyobi Seisō ni Kansuru Hōritsu), enacted in 1970, had established a system for the treatment of industrial waste; in 1976 some of the standards prescribed in the law were tightened. The number of disposal facilities for industrial waste increased each year after the law came into effect, and by 1977 there were 5,343 government and private facilities.

Proper disposal of the wastes is the responsibility of the private enterprises which discharge them; however, in the case of small- and medium-sized companies, local governments sometimes dispose of the discharge together with other wastes. In some areas, public corporations have been established to dispose of the discharge. The overall rate of resource recovery from industrial waste is still low, although in some categories high recycling rates have been achieved—for example, metal slag (96.4 percent), animal and plant residue (91.7 percent), and varieties of industrial dust (78.4 percent). As the discharge of industrial waste increases in the future, both the government and corporations will have to work harder toward the acquisition of appropriate land for more disposal facilities, development of more efficient and safer disposal technology, and the acceleration of recycling processes. See also ENVIRONMENTAL QUALITY. *ODA* Yukio

industrial zones

(kōgyō chitai). Industrial zones were first created in Japan during the middle of the Meiji period (1868–1912) when modern industries were introduced in Japan's industrial revolution. Most of Japan's principal industrial regions have developed around ports and river mouths along the sea coast, chiefly because Japanese industry depends heavily on imported raw materials such as petroleum, cotton, iron ores and other metals, and coking coal. Moreover, Japanese coalfields lie in the two extremities of Japan, Hokkaidō and Kyūshū, thus underscoring the importance until very recently of sea routes for carrying coal to industrial centers. Another reason for the creation of these industrial zones is the fact that a large proportion of manufactured goods is shipped to foreign markets. The major industrial zones are: Keihin (Tōkyō–Yokohama), Hanshin (Ōsaka–Kōbe), Chūkyō (Nagoya), Kita Kyūshū (Northern Kyūshū), Tōkai (between Nagoya and Tōkyō), and Setouchi (Inland Sea).

inflation and price stability

While achieving rapid growth, the Japanese economy since the end of World War II has experienced a sustained rise in the general level of prices. This is seen clearly in several price indices, including the wholesale price index put out by the BANK OF JAPAN, the consumer price index from the PRIME MINISTER'S OFFICE, and the gross national product deflator from the ECONOMIC PLANNING AGENCY. The first index covers a wide variety of commodities, the second covers the commodities and services purchased by the household sector, and the third covers all goods and services. The second and third indicators have moved fairly closely together.

There was a sustained rise in prices in the period from 1915 to 1920 associated with World War I, and a gradual decline from the late 1920s to the mid-1930s related to the Depression. The price level rose sharply during and immediately following World War II. Between 1935 and 1951, the wholesale price index rose 343 times, and the consumer price index 256 times. Many of these rises were due to the postwar inflation associated with the Allied Occupation and the government's effort to promote reconstruction through inflationary devices such as the RECONSTRUCTION FINANCE BANK loans and the price differential subsidies (kakaku chōsei hokyūkin), when the war-devastated economy lacked raw materials from overseas (see PRIORITY PRODUCTION PROGRAM).

In the succeeding quarter century (1951–75), the wholesale price index rose 83 percent and the consumer price index 287 percent. This period can be divided into three subperiods. First is the 1950s, when both the wholesale price index and the consumer price index were fairly stable, the annual rate of increase being 0.3 percent for the former and 2.8 percent for the latter. Second is the 1960s, when a different trend set in: the wholesale prices remained fairly stable, but consumer prices began rising at a faster pace. The annual rate of increase was 1.3 percent for the wholesale price index and 5.8 percent for the consumer price index. One important factor contributing to the relative stability of the wholesale prices was rising labor productivity in heavy industries resulting from the fast pace of investment in new plants and technologically advanced equipment. The major factor accelerating consumer price inflation was the rising price of services. This reflected the rise in wages stemming from the labor shortage caused by the rapid economic growth beginning in the 1950s. The third subperiod is the 1970s, when wholesale prices as well as consumer prices rose sharply. The annual rate of increase for 1970–75 was 9.4 percent for wholesale prices and 11.3 percent for consumer prices. This phase coincided with the worldwide inflation culminating in the oil price hikes of 1973 and after, and the commodity price explosion.

The postwar Japanese economy has experienced a number of new types of inflation described by such terms as demand-pull inflation, cost-push inflation, administered-price inflation, imported inflation, demand-shift inflation, and differential productivity growth inflation, all of which are common to mixed economies. But the inflationary forces can be divided into two groups, domestic and international. Like other market economies, Japan pursued full employment and economic growth through monetary and fiscal policy derived from Keynesian economic theory. While this policy prevented depressions, it also produced the domestic tendency toward inflation. For most of the postwar period, Japan, like other market economies of the world, has been part of an international financial system in which most countries are engaged in inflationary policy and in which inflation is transmissible throughout the system.

◾ ——Sōrifu Tōkeikyoku, Nihon tōkei nenkan (annual since 1949). KOGIKU Kiichirō

inga

(cause and effect; Skt: hetu and phala). An important concept of Buddhism. In the Buddhist tradition the term in refers to an inner and direct cause, while en (Skt: pratyaya) is an external and indirect cause. The two combine to produce effect (J: ka or ga). In conjunction with the Buddhist conception of karmic retribution (inga ōhō), it is held that a good karmic cause will invariably produce a good karmic result and a bad karmic cause will produce a bad karmic result. In human terms, this means that depending on one's good or bad actions, one will obtain pleasurable or painful karmic retribution. The karmic realm of cause and effect, with its perpetual cycle of death and rebirth, is called rinne (Skt: saṃsāra). The goal of Buddhist devotion is to achieve deliverance from karmic retribution, which is the cause of suffering, and enter nirvāna.

Robert RHODES

Ingen (1592–1673)

Also known as Ingen Ryūki (Ch: Yinyuan Longji or Yin-yüan Lung-chi). Chinese Zen monk and the founder of the ŌBAKU SECT of Zen Buddhism in Japan; he and his followers, Mokuan and Sokuhi, were known as the "Three Brushes of Ōbaku." The son of a poor family in Fuqin (Fu-ch'in) in Fujian (Fukien) Province, China, Ingen became a Zen monk of the Rinzai sect at the age of 29, and by the time he left China for Japan, he had gained great respect as the abbot of Wanfusi (Wan-fu-ssu) temple of Mt. Huangbo (Huang-po) in Fujian Province. At the third request of ITSUNEN and other Chinese Zen monks and laymen in Nagasaki, Ingen at the age of 63 left China during the political confusion that followed the fall of the Ming dynasty. In 1654 he arrived in Nagasaki accompanied by 20 monks and 10 artisans.

Through contact with the government rulers and imperial family, Ingen was given an audience with the fourth shōgun TOKUGAWA IETSUNA. In 1659 he was granted a large tract of land in Uji, near Kyōto, where he built a major temple of his sect. This temple was named MAMPUKUJI (Japanese name for Wanfusi), and his sect was called Ōbaku (Ch: Huangbo). Because of his high reputation as a Zen monk and man of learning, and also because of the artisans he brought with him, Mampukuji became the center of exotic Chinese culture. Ingen's powerful and fresh calligraphy, which is characterized by strong curves and smoothly rounded, thick brush strokes, was highly regarded, and was important in making the Ōbaku style of calligraphy popular. Pat FISTER

ingo

(secret language; argot). A general term for the specialized vocabulary and idioms employed by a particular group in order to exclude outsiders or to reinforce in-group feelings. Within Japanese there are many varieties of such special language. Ingo particularly appears among certain professional groups, in the restaurant and entertainment business, and among thieves, gamblers, vagrants, and others on the fringe of society. Many ingo words result from abbreviation, as in yaji from oyaji (father); inversion, as in doya from yado (lodgings); association, as in uji (from Uji, a city famous for its tea) for cha (tea); or extension of meaning, as in morau (receive, take) for nusumu (steal). Some are references to the way a word is written, as in sanzui for sake (rice wine, liquor), sanzui being the name of one of the two elements that make up the Chinese character for sake.

Ingo words from the criminal subculture include satsu for police (from keisatsu, police), shoba for place or territory (from basho, place), and deka (derived, rather complicatedly, from kakusode, the old-style policeman's cape) for detective. Conversely, the police have their own vocabulary: hoshi (star) for suspect, tataki (beating) for armed robbery, and so on. Juvenile delinquents and hoodlums have slang words for members of their own group, who are called dachi (from tomodachi, friend), and the group leader, banchō (from hanchō, squad leader).

Japanese students, like their counterparts elsewhere, are verbally inventive; for example, a dull-witted person is called piiman (green pepper) as they are both hollow inside. A party is kompa (from company) and part-time employment is baito (from arubaito, which in turn is from the German Arbeit meaning work). Hawkers at street fairs have a special way of counting: yari (one), furi (two), kachi (three), and so on. For brokers, yari (from yaru, give away) means sell and tombi (from tobi, kite, hawk), a broker's fee. Much of the ingo of the restaurant and entertainment world has found its way into the common vocabulary: murasaki (purple) for soy sauce, *agari* (to finish; the last item) for tea, and *oaiso* (from *aiso*, pleasant treatment) for the bill. Also frequently heard are *hanagusuri* (snuff) for bribe money, *okama* (from *kama*, hips) for homosexual, and *daikon* (large white radish) for a good-looking but untalented actor. See also FEMININE LANGUAGE; MASCULINE LANGUAGE; NYŌBŌ KOTOBA.

YAMAZAKI Yukio

inheritance law

(sōzoku hō). The inheritance system played an important role in the functioning of Japanese society in premodern times, for it was concerned with succession to the headship of the family line. The traditional system was abolished after World War II, and freedom in the disposition of one's assets became the central legal principle.

History of the Inheritance System —— The nature of the inheritance system in ancient Japan is not absolutely clear, but it does appear that there was division between inheritance of a lineage (UJI) chieftain's position and title, and the inheritance of his assets. This division was codified under the RITSURYŌ SYSTEM of law that was developed in the 7th century; inheritance of position involved a determination of who would succeed to the rank *(ikai)* of the decedent. Later in the YŌRŌ CODE (effective 757), inheritance of rank came to mean succession to ritual offices held by the various classes, and this formed the basis of the IE (family or household) inheritance system. Inheritance of assets involved division of the estate among descendants (divided inheritance). However, with the emergence of the feudal system and the practice of designating the first-born legitimate son as family head (see SŌRYŌ SYSTEM), alienation of landholdings was prohibited in order to prevent fragmentation into numerous smaller tracts. The eldest son, as representative of all the children, became de facto heir to the land (except in some special cases). During and after the Muromachi period (1333–1568), as this variant type of single inheritance became firmly established, the *katoku* or patrimonial system, in which previously the head of the extended lineage had represented the rights of other members, lost its original meaning. *Katoku* came to mean the headship of a single household, succession to which became one and the same as succession to the family estate. The primogeniture inheritance system became a basic principle of the *bukehō*, the legal codes drawn up by warrior houses.

During the Edo period (1600–1868) private ownership of land by *samurai* was in principle not permitted. Thus, with respect to inheritance of fiefs *(hōchi)* received from the Tokugawa shogunate, succession took the form of petitioning the shogunate and being enfeoffed anew. Under this practice, variously known as *hōroku*, *katoku*, or *atome sōzoku*, there was no question of disposition of assets or family trade in a will. In the case of commoners, where fields and residences were concerned, there evolved a trend to single inheritance, and in imitation of the samurai, succession was known as *katoku sōzoku*. As for merchants, since assets usually consisted of money, a shop, and its name or trademark, inheritance was known as *kamei* ("house name") *sōzoku*. Merchant families, however, often set up branch establishments (see HONKE AND BUNKE). For both warrior and commoner families, *inkyo* (retirement from active life and the transfer of responsibilities to an heir) instead of death could precipitate succession.

During the Meiji period (1868–1912), all inheritance systems were unified in the CIVIL CODE based on the inheritance laws for warriors. The code had provisions for family headship succession and for property inheritance, both based on male primogeniture. Farm families, however, were allowed to choose youngest-child or elder-sister inheritance. Under the present Civil Code, adopted after World War II, the traditional household *(ie)* system was abolished and, accordingly, the legal concept of succession to the family headship was also abolished. This left only inheritance of the estate, which is initiated only by death. The single person inheritance system was also changed to that of joint inheritance.

Summary of the Inheritance Law —— The basic principle in the Japanese Civil Code is freedom to dispose of one's assets as one wishes (although legally secured portions may not be infringed upon). In fact, inheritance without a will (statutory inheritance) is overwhelmingly the most frequent case. Of 690,074 deaths in 1977, the number of cases in which a will was probated in family court was 2,139. In the same year the number of estates that paid inheritance taxes was 17,853.

The scope of assets from which the inheritance will come is all rights and obligations accrued by the decedent while he was living. This includes a wide variety of rights, such as claims for compensatory damages and claims on a leased house, as well as every kind of

obligation in addition to money obligations. Life insurance proceeds, however, are generally the property of the designated beneficiary. According to custom, the family genealogy, the equipment used in funerals, and the family grave are inherited by those who are responsible for these functions.

In regard to heirs *(sōzokunin)*, the order of inheritance is as follows: (1) the children and spouse; (2) if there are no children, then the lineal ascendants and spouse; (3) if there are no lineal ascendants, then the siblings and the spouse; (4) if there are no siblings, then the spouse; (5) if there is also no spouse, procedures to prove the nonexistence of an heir are initiated. If it is confirmed that there is no heir and, if some assets still remain after the debts and obligations related to the succession are settled, they escheat to the state, except where a family court recognizes the partial or total acquisition of the property by parties such as the wife in a *naien* (common-law) marriage, a de facto adopted child who lived with the decedent, or parties who had had some kind of special relationship with the decedent, such as those who cared for the deceased during medical treatment. An unborn child can be an heir. Children are treated without distinctions between natural and adopted children and between legitimate and illegitimate children. Issue of children and children of siblings of the decedents have rights of representation. Where a potential heir predeceases the decedent, or is excluded or loses his qualifications as an heir, then his issue by order of generation (except in the case of siblings) shall be the heirs by representation.

Disqualification from inheritance. Parties punished for murder or attempted murder of the decedent or of parties with superior or equal inheritance rights and parties who forge, destroy, or conceal a will fall within provisions of the Civil Code that disqualify such parties from inheriting.

Disinheritance. During his life or by his will, an individual, via a request to the family court, may with good reason disinherit heirs in the first order (parties in a position such that they would become heirs directly upon the death of the decedent) with the exception of siblings, who do not have secured portions in the estate. Reasons for disinheritance are ill treatment of or serious insults to the decedent or exceptionally reprehensible activities on the part of the potential heir. An individual may request at any time during his life the cancellation of the disinheritance.

Acceptance and renunciation. The heir is free to decide whether or not to inherit. An heir's manifestation of intent to consent to inheritance is called acceptance of inheritance *(sōzoku no shōnin),* and his manifestation of intent to refuse inheritance is called renunciation of inheritance *(sōzoku hōki).* Among the former type of manifestations are acceptance without reservation, called absolute acceptance *(tanjun shōnin),* and qualified acceptance *(gentei shōnin),* in which the heir limits his or her acceptance of the obligations of the decedent (the decedent's debts and bequests) to the extent of the positive assets he receives in the inheritance. Qualified acceptance or renunciation of inheritance are accomplished by the heir making a statement to that effect to the family court within three months of the date he or she becomes aware of the initiation of succession proceedings. If this time period is exceeded, the heir is regarded as having made an absolute acceptance.

Renunciation of inheritance was intended for use in situations where the obligations of the estate exceed the assets. However, there are many cases where it is used to leave the assets to one child. Today a de facto renunciation of inheritance can be made by using a so-called advancement certificate *(tokubetsu jueki shōmeisho),* which states that nothing remains to be inherited since property in excess of one's inheritance portion has already been received, during the life of the decedent, by the person filing the certificate. This procedure, resulting in an increase in the amount of inheritance received by one of the children, is more commonly used than the other renunciation procedures. After World War II, in order to prevent the division of farmlands into small tracts, an agricultural assets inheritance bill was proposed to provide for one-child succession, but because of the use in practice of the advancement certificate technique, it was never enacted.

Shares. The shares of heirs are determined by the order of the heirs: (1) Where there are children and the surviving spouse as heirs, the surviving spouse receives half and the other half is divided among the children. (2) Where there are a surviving spouse and lineal ascendants, a surviving spouse receives two-thirds and lineal ascendants one-third. (3) Where there are a surviving spouse and siblings, a surviving spouse receives three-fourths and the siblings one-fourth. (4) Where there is only a surviving spouse, the surviving spouse takes the entire estate. (5) Where there is no surviving

Ink painting——Kaō Ninga

Detail of a painting by Kaō of the legendary Chinese Zen eccentric Hanshan (J: Kanzan). Hanshan, a popular subject for Zen painters, is often paired with his companion Shide (Shih-te; J: Jittoku). Hanging scroll. Ink on paper. Entire scroll 98.5 × 33.3 cm. Early 14th century. Private collection. National Treasure.

spouse, the other heirs take the entire estate. (6) Where there is more than one child or parties on the same level in the inheritance order, each receives an equal share. But illegitimate children receive one-half that of legitimate children, while siblings born of different parents (half-blood siblings) receive one-half that of whole-blood siblings. (7) Where there are heirs who received gifts from the decedent at the time of a wedding, adoption, coming-of-age ceremony, and the like (for example, a gift of capital), the amount given will be added to the total value of the estate. Each heir's share is then decided by multiplying the total amount by the percentage of his share, less the amount he has already received. When this calculation yields a negative number, it is not necessary to repay the minus amount. Furthermore, where the decedent is a father who was running a farm or a business and where an heir, who is one of the children, has contributed or cooperated in that enterprise, such an heir takes his normal share plus an amount in keeping with his contribution.

Administration of estates. In principle, the administration of an estate is done jointly by the heirs, but where the division of the estate has been requested of a family court, where procedures for disinheriting an heir are in progress, where there is a qualified acceptance to inheritance or a renunciation of inheritance, or where procedures to prove the nonexistence of an heir have been initiated, an administrator of the estate appointed by the family court shall manage the estate.

Partition of estates. When succession is recognized, the estate is divided in accord with the share to which each heir is entitled. The procedure is as the decedent directs in his will, but if he dies intestate, it is based on the agreement of the heirs. If no agreement is possible upon petition of the heirs, the family court will mediate or make a judgment *(shimpan)*. In determining how to divide the estate, consideration is given to the nature of those properties and rights belonging to the estate; age, occupation, mental and physical state, and living conditions of the heirs; and any other relevant factors. For example, heirs of farming families receive most of their inheritance in farmland. As a method of partition, besides dividing the property, converting the estate into cash and dividing that is also permissible. Acquisition of the property by one or more of the common heirs and the assumption by the acquirer of debts to the other common heirs for their portions is also permissible. When the partition of the estate is completed, the property that the common heirs inherited shall be regarded as inherited at the time of death.

Secured portions. Since family members who have come to depend on the assets of the deceased in order to live expect to inherit part of the estate, the law requires that a fixed portion of the estate be reserved for such heirs, with the exception of siblings. This portion is called the secured portion *(iryūbun).* If a will provides for the disposal of the portion of the estate that is secured, parties entitled to secured portions can claim an amount against the estate up to the equivalent of their secured portions. The secured portion is one-half of the estate where the entitled parties are lineal descendants or a spouse; otherwise it is one-third of the estate. Each secured party's share is calculated by dividing the secured amount by that party's inheritance share. The amount of the secured portion is calculated by (1) totaling the value of assets of the estate, the value of any gifts given within one year preceding the initiation of succession, any amounts given more than one year before such proceedings that both parties to the gift knew infringed upon the secured portions, and any amounts given to common heirs, (2) subtracting from that total any inheritance obligations, and (3) dividing the remainder by each secured heir's share. See also WILLS; PARENT AND CHILD, LEGAL DEFINITION OF.   ISHIKAWA Minoru

injiuchi

Also called *inji* or *ishigassen.* A game once traditionally played on Boy's Day (5 May); a mock battle, in which boys divided themselves into two groups and threw pebbles at each other. With the rise of the warrior class in the latter part of the Heian period (794–1185), it became a game for men, first popular in Kyōto and then throughout the country. However, it became increasingly violent, often resulting in injury or even death, and the practice was for a time forbidden in the Edo period (1600–1868).   INAGAKI Shisei

ink painting

(suibokuga; literally, "water-ink painting"; Ch: *shuimohua.* In Japanese also called *sumi-e* or "ink pictures"). A Chinese style of painting adopted by Japanese painters in the 14th century. Gradually adapted to Japanese aesthetics and assimilated into the cultural matrix, *suibokuga* emerged by the end of the 15th century as the mainstream of Japanese painting. Expanded by its absorption of elements from YAMATO-E, the indigenous mode of painting, *suibokuga* in turn enriched the native tradition first as the medium out of which the Sino-Japanese synthesis of the KANŌ SCHOOL emerged, and in later centuries as the source of other schools of painting, even for such mutually exclusive styles as Rimpa and literati painting.

Technique——In its purest form, *suibokuga* is monochrome ink painting *(bokuga)* characterized by the use of black ink *(sumi),* a charcoal or soot-based solid Chinese ink, diluted with water and executed with a brush on plain silk or paper. The medium offers a potentially infinite range of ink values, recognized long ago by Chinese painters as "the colors of ink." When color is present it is usually applied in subtle, transparent washes that remain subordinate to the descriptive and expressive role of the ink. Quality lies in the inherent strength of the line, whose supportive bone-like structure depends entirely on the artist's control of the brush. In the shared dependence on economy of brush and ink and on the mastery of their expressive potential, the basic principles of CALLIGRAPHY and ink painting coincide. As a result of this intimate relationship, ink-painting styles were sometimes associated with calligraphic styles, especially *kai* (regular), *gyō* (running), and *sō* (cursive). *Hatsuboku* or "splashed ink," the most abbreviated and expressive style of *suibokuga,* was, for instance, regarded as the counterpart of the cursive script.

Hatsuboku and HABOKU were ink-painting techniques used by Chinese painters of the Tang (T'ang) dynasty (618–907). Both words are pronounced in Chinese as *po mo (p'o mo),* but are written with different characters. *Haboku* is traditionally regarded as a technical innovation associated with Wang Wei (ca 699–ca 759), who dispensed with color and painted entirely in monochrome. Although the meaning of *haboku* remains elusive, it seems to describe an ink technique used to suggest the volume, mass, and even the texture of objects through an interplay of washes. *Hatsuboku* literally describes the untrammeled, expressive style first associated with such unorthodox Chinese painters of the 8th century as Wang Mo, who applied his ink with such wild abandon that he seldom needed to use a brush. The most well-known example of this style is SESSHŪ TŌYŌ's *Haboku Landscape* (1495; Tōkyō National Museum).

Subjects —— A corpus of traditional themes associated with *suibokuga* evolved through the centuries. These fall roughly into two main categories, landscapes (SANSUIGA) and figures *(jimbutsuga)*, the latter including animals, plants, fruits, and vegetables. The role that landscape painting played in China as a metaphorical vehicle of Taoist and Confucian thought had no direct counterpart in Japan; landscape, nevertheless, became a popular ink-painting theme, especially when it focused on the scholar and his retreat from the vulgar world and into poetry, painting, music and calligraphy, the four gentlemanly accomplishments (see KINKI SHOGA). Zen monks, who spent long hours in the study of Chinese classics, strongly identified with this way of life and *shosaizu* or "pictures of the scholar's study" are among the earliest Japanese ink paintings to appear. *Shosaizu* depicted idealized places that existed only in the minds of the Zen monks for whom they were often painted as farewell gifts given in recognition of mutual spiritual goals. These paintings, which were often inscribed with poems, belong to the larger classification of *shigajiku* or "poem-painting scrolls," exemplified by MINCHŌ's *Cottage by a Stream* (1413; Nanzenji, Kyōto).

Aside from rare exceptions like Sesshū's *Amanohashidate* (ca 1501; Kyōto National Museum), the landscapes in Japanese ink paintings were not usually directly inspired by nature but by other paintings. This accounts for the popularity of certain Chinese landscape themes, such as the *Eight Views of the Xiao (Hsiao) and Xiang (Hsiang) Rivers* (SHŌSHŌ HAKKEI), painted by Japanese artists who never left their native country; the majority of Japanese ink landscapes are composed of stock elements ultimately derived from Chinese landscape painting: towering peaks, pines silhouetted against the mist, bamboo forests, waterfalls, gorges, mountain temples, rustic hermits, travelers, and lonely fishermen.

Before the establishment of the Kanō-school repertoire of *kanga*, or subjects from the Chinese literary tradition, ink figure painting was almost entirely Zen in content. It included figures of Zen patriarchs and the enigmatic personalities of KANZAN AND JITTOKU, as well as versions of traditional Buddhist deities, such as KANNON and Bodhidharma (J: Daruma). To this group also belong illustrations of KŌAN or Zen puzzles, of which JOSETSU's *Catching a Catfish with a Gourd* (ca 1413; Myōshinji, Kyōto) is perhaps the best-known example, and a broad range of anecdotal and narrative themes known collectively as *zenkiga* or "Zen activities."

Birds and flowers (see BIRD-AND-FLOWER PAINTING), fruits, and vegetables all became important painting subjects. The leaves and stems of orchid and bamboo lent themselves quite naturally to ink painting. Moreover, orchid and bamboo, along with plum blossoms, chrysanthemum, and pine, symbolize Confucian virtues and were among the favorite themes of Chinese literati painters of the 13th and 14th centuries. Particularly, the *lan* (J: *ran*), the rarest of fragrant orchids, was emblematic of the morally superior Confucian gentleman often overlooked by the less worthy. The bamboo, whose strong but supple stalks are hollow, suggests the Taoist state known as "empty of desire," a spirit close to the self-denying philosophy of Zen. The most famous Japanese masters of orchid and bamboo, TESSHŪ TOKUSAI and GYOKUEN BOMPŌ, lived in close harmony with the ideals of the Chinese literati.

History —— Paintings from the 8th century preserved in the SHŌSŌIN imperial art repository reveal that Japanese artists of the Nara period (710–794) were familiar with the fundamental techniques of Chinese painting and the calligraphically fluid, expressive lines associated with the style of the great Tang master Wu Dao (Wu Taotzu). However, despite the early mastery of ink-painting techniques revealed in extant Japanese painting from the 8th to the 13th century, the overwhelming interest in *suibokuga* is a phenomenon that belongs to the latter part of the Kamakura (1185–1333) and early part of the Muromachi (1333–1568) periods.

The phenomenal rise of ink painting in Japan is inextricably bound to the growing importance of Zen Buddhism and the cultural transformations emerging under its influence. A combination of factors stemming from the free exchange between Zen monks of China and Japan, which was accelerated at the end of the 13th century by the Mongol conquest of China and the emigration of many Chinese priests to Japan, accounts for the prominence of imported Chinese cultural elements along with Zen, including Chinese literature, especially poetry, and more significantly, the Confucian-based value system associated with the literati class.

In the middle of the 14th century the older Zen center of Kamakura gave way to Kyōto, the seat of the Ashikaga shōguns. In Kyōto, on the model of Kamakura, a second GOZAN temple complex was established and soon filled with collections of Chinese books, paint-

Ink painting —— Sesshū Tōyō

Detail from Sesshū's long handscroll *Landscape of the Four Seasons*. In this segment of the spring section of the scroll, small human figures can be seen walking among rocks and pines. Ink and pale colors on paper. Entire scroll 40 × 1,586 cm. Signed and dated 1486. Mōri Museum, Hōfu, Yamaguchi Prefecture. National Treasure.

ing and porcelain. The temples NANZENJI and SHŌKOKUJI in Kyōto contained representative examples of Chinese literature, painting, and porcelain of the Song (Sung; 960–1279), Yuan (Yüan; 1279–1368), and Ming (1368–1644) dynasties, all brought to Japan by monks who had studied in China. The Gozan temples in Kyōto became important centers of Chinese culture and Zen monks called themselves *bunjinsō*, "literati monks."

It was in such a milieu that the first Zen monks began to paint *suibokuga*. MOKUAN REIEN and KAŌ NINGA belong to this group. The legendary skills of Mokuan, who went to China and never returned to Japan, were taken as evidence that he was a reincarnation of the great Muqi (Mu-ch'i; J: MOKKEI), whose painting style he emulated. It is somehow fitting that the early Japanese *suibokuga* painters should have begun with the styles of the early Chinese Chan (Ch'an; J: Zen) painters. In adopting monochrome painting as the special prerogative of Chan, Muqi and his followers transformed it into spiritual discovery. They transcended the existing boundaries of religious iconography and reached deep into the realm of art as the medium of personal or individual expression first defined by the Chinese literati painter. For the Zen painter, then, the painting itself, above and beyond its content or subject matter, became a material symbol of nonmaterial values, a paradox that by its very nature strikes close to the central dilemma of Zen.

With the appearance of the artist Josetsu, the painting academy established at the temple Shōkokuji and patronized by the shōgun Ashikaga Yoshimochi (1386–1428) and his successors began to take on importance. The most famous of the Shōkokuji painters was Josetsu's pupil, SHŪBUN, whose contribution to the evolution of Japanese ink painting lay largely in his personal interpretation of the Southern Song academic style of Ma Yuan (Ma Yüan) and Xia Gui (Hsia Kuei). Shūbun was familiar with their asymmetrical "one-corner" compositions and "axe-cut" brush strokes from the paintings in the shōgun's collection as well as from versions of their styles filtered through their Yuan and Ming, and even Korean, followers. Paintings attributed to Shūbun reveal landscapes rich in pictorial interest replete with angular pines, crystalline peaks, ribbon-thin waterfalls, and elegant buildings of architectural complexity, and with all features, textures, and spatial relationships clearly articulated.

In many ways, it is Shūbun's successor, Sesshū Tōyō, who represents the culmination of the first generation of Zen monk ink painters; after Sesshū the direction of *suibokuga* was determined by several rival schools: the AMI SCHOOL, the SOGA SCHOOL, and finally the KANŌ SCHOOL. Sesshū, who is traditionally considered a disciple of Shūbun, left the Shōkokuji to set up an independent atelier, the Unkokuan, in Suō Province (now part of Yamaguchi Prefecture). In 1468 he visited China and became the first major Zen painter to see firsthand the landscapes of China and the paintings of the Ming academy. After his return, he continued to study and copy Chinese originals in the shōgun's collection and evolved several different styles, revealing alternately the study of Muqi and the Ma Xia (Ma-Hsia) school, the articulate phrasing of Shūbun, and the free, expres-

Ink painting ——— Hasegawa Tōhaku

Detail of an ink painting of monkeys on a tree. Entire work 155 × 115 cm. Late 16th century. Ryūsen'an, Myōshinji, Kyōto.

sive, splashed ink manner of the Chinese painter Yujian (Yü-chien). Sesshū left behind an important legacy that would be the object of rival claims by the 16th-century artists HASEGAWA TŌHAKU and UNKOKU TŌGAN.

After Sesshū, the acculturation of *suibokuga* was completed by the artists of the Ami school, NŌAMI, GEIAMI, and SŌAMI, in whose hands the aesthetic appeal of the *suibokuga* became more purely Japanese. The painters of the Ami school, unlike these *suibokuga* artists of the first generation, were not Zen monks but professional artists attached to the court of the shogunate. Belonging to a particular class of shogunal attendants called *dōbōshū*, the Ami painters were responsible not only for painting commissions but for curatorial duties as well, cataloging and arranging the shōgun's collection, and giving aesthetic advice on artistic matters from NŌ drama to the TEA CEREMONY and *renga* or linked verse (see RENGA AND HAIKAI). The paintings of Nōami, Geiami, and Sōami reveal a close study not only of Shūbun and Sesshū, but of the Chinese artists represented in the shōgun's collection. Sōami, especially, was strongly influenced by the watery landscapes of Mi Youren (Mi Yu-jen) and Gao Kegong (Kao K'o-kung), whose atmospheric effects and characteristic manner of wet brush strokes, called the "Mi dot," were put to work in his own broad horizontal compositions, paraphrasing the rounded hills of the Southern Chinese style in a way reminiscent of *yamato-e*.

Except for the independent paintings of artists such as SESSON SHŪKEI, 16th-century *suibokuga* is dominated by the large, decorative compositions of the Kanō school, and gradually the links between Zen and ink painting were replaced by nonreligious, purely aesthetic concerns involving design and the disposition of large space. Through the inventive genius of KANŌ MASANOBU and his son KANŌ MOTONOBU, the foundations of the Kanō-school synthesis were established: *suibokuga* techniques and the brilliant sense of color harmony of the *yamato-e* tradition were brought together in a gorgeous decorative style executed on gold ground.

No school of the Edo period (1600–1868) was unaffected by *suibokuga*. Even Tawaraya SŌTATSU and KŌRIN and their RIMPA school followers owe a debt to ink painting, which is acknowledged in the fluid calligraphic handling of their brush. Japanese literati artists like IKE NO TAIGA, AOKI MOKUBEI, Yosa BUSON, and URAGAMI GYOKUDŌ returned directly to Chinese painting for inspiration (see BUNJINGA). In the modern period, *suibokuga* was brought into the broad range of Japanese-style painting (see NIHONGA), by artists like YOKOYAMA TAIKAN, HISHIDA SHUNSŌ, SHIMOMURA KANZAN, and many others who turned to *suibokuga* to reaffirm their heritage.

■ ——— Mainichi Shimbunsha, ed, *Suibokuga*, 3 vols (Mainichi Shimbunsha, 1971–73). Matsushita Takaaki, Tanaka Ichimatsu, Yo-nezawa Yoshiho, et al, ed, *Suiboku bijutsu taikei*, 17 vols (Kōdansha, 1973–77). Matsushita Takaaki, *Muromachi suibokuga*, vol 1 (Ōtsuka Kōgeisha, 1960). Matsushita Takaaki, *Suibokuga*, no. 13 of *Nihon no bijutsu* (May, 1967), translated and adapted by Martin Collcutt as *Ink Painting* (1974). Yoshiaki Shimizu and Carolyn Wheelwright, ed, *Japanese Ink Paintings from American Collections: The Muromachi Period: An Exhibition in Honor of Shujiro Shimada* (1976). Ichimatsu Tanaka, *Japanese Ink Painting: Shubun to Sesshu*, tr Bruce Darling (1972). Tanaka Ichimatsu and Yonezawa Yoshiho, *Suibokuga*, in *Genshoku Nihon no bijutsu*, vol 11 (Shōgakukan, 1970). *Aya Louisa MᶜDONALD*

inkyo

Traditional Japanese practice of retirement of the household head. In colloquial speech *inkyo* (literally, "seclusion") indicates retirement in general, a retired person, or an old person. A household head need not become old or incapacitated before relinquishing his role, nor need he cut back on other activities when doing so. The position of head of household has had no legal standing since 1947, but it remains important in everyday thought and conduct.

Forms of household retirement have varied by era, area, and social class through Japan's long history. Many think the form specified in the 1898 CIVIL CODE was typical in Japan prior to the Meiji Restoration (1868), but the family section of the 1898 code was in fact taken from customs of the Edo-period (1600–1868) *samurai* elite. Whether the majority of the population followed similar practices is far from certain.

A samurai household had to subsist on the stipend a samurai received from his lord. At retirement he lost that stipend (though a few domains provided pensions) and had to be supported out of the stipend given to his successor. Among the common majority (peasants, artisans and merchants), however, each household was a unit of economic activity. It could draw upon the labor power of all its members. Retirement was a flexible process. It could be adjusted in response to factors such as occupation, wealth, family size, or the availability of unexploited resources. Thus, an array of forms of household retirement evolved in different sectors of society, and some remain in practice today.

Forms of retirement can be viewed as ways of reconciling practical needs with the ideals of family living. Three ideals are pertinent and have had wide support in Japan in recent centuries.

The first is that the incumbent head should be a person of vigor and competence in order to maintain the household descent line intact generation after generation. This has tended to favor early retirement, with the head yielding the position once an able successor (most often the eldest son) was ready for it. Since people usually married by about age 20 in premodern Japan, the retiring head might well be yet in the prime of life.

The second ideal is that the retired head and spouse, and the succeeding head and spouse, remain members of a single household unit (IE), but in order to avoid intergenerational discord they should set up housekeeping separately. If possible the retiring head would move to a separate house, or at least to separate quarters within the main house.

The third ideal is that when retired members grow old, juniors in the household should provide for their care. The 1898 Civil Code held the incumbent head responsible for providing such care and granted him full control of household property. The present code holds all offspring responsible for the welfare of aged parents and allows all of them a share of the inheritance.

We know the distribution of different types of household retirement in the 20th century but not how frequently such types are actually practiced. The national census does not distinguish among types of household retirement, and ethnographic research offers data only for a few communities. A 1957 study of a village in Mie Prefecture found that half of the 264 households had a separate *inkyo* residence; 16 of them had two such residences, one for each of two generations of retirees.

Neither do we have adequate information on the roles of women as partners in the retirement process or as interim heads of households. The position of *shufu* (wife of the household head) in a household long has had popular recognition though no legal standing. Retirement from this position is described in folk imagery as a handing over of the rice ladle *(shamoji)* to one's successor.

Retirement from household leadership probably takes place later in life today than a century ago because of factors such as later marriage age, decrease of family enterprises and rise in paid employment, and improved health and longevity. See also OLD AGE AND RETIREMENT; LIFE CYCLE; ANCESTOR WORSHIP; CONFUCIANISM.

——Chie Nakane, *Kinship and Economic Organization in Rural Japan* (1968). Takeuchi Toshimi, "Inkyo," *Nihon shakai minzoku jiten,* vol 1 (Seibundō Shinkōsha, 1952).   David W. PLATH

Inland Sea

(Seto Naikai). Bounded by Honshū on the north and east, Shikoku on the south, and Kyūshū on the west. Encompasses Ōsaka Bay and the Harima, Bingo, Hiuchi, Iyo, and Suō seas. Dotted with over 1,000 islands and islets, the largest of which is Awajishima. Connected to outer seas by the Kitan Strait and NARUTO STRAIT to the east, Hōyo Strait to the southwest, and KAMMON STRAIT to the west.

The Inland Sea and its coasts have played an important role since ancient times in transportation from the early capitals of Nara and Kyōto to Kyūshū, and in trading with Korea and China. The relatively flat terrain around the sea has led to the rapid industrialization and growth in population of the region in recent decades. Since the end of World War II the Inland Sea Industrial Region has become one of the major industrial regions of Japan.

The Inland Sea is famous for its natural beauty. A spectacular coastline, mountains in the background in all areas, and the many islands and thousands of islets covered with pines make it a major tourist attraction. It forms the Inland Sea National Park. In recent years the great beauty of this region has been marred by the effects of industrialization, and the increase in pollution is resulting in a rapid decline of the once prosperous fishing industry. Area: 9,500 sq km (3,667 sq mi); average depth: 44 m (144 ft).

Inland Sea Industrial Region

(Setouchi Kōgyō Chitai). Consists of a long row of industrial cities along the Inland Sea coasts on Honshū and Shikoku and is located between the two great industrial zones of Hanshin and Kita Kyūshū. Excellent marine and land transportation is available to this region. Prominent cities in this zone are Tokuyama (oil refinery), Iwakuni and Kurashiki (steel and petrochemicals), Matsuyama (oil refinery and petrochemicals), Kudamatsu and Fukuyama (steel), Niihama (chemicals and metals), Hiroshima (automobiles), and Sakaide, Kure, Innoshima, and Tamano (shipbuilding). In recent years industrial complexes have been constructed at Iwakuni, Tokuyama, Kurashiki, Harima, and Niihama.

Inland Sea National Park

(Seto Naikai Kokuritsu Kōen). National park covering the entire expanse of the INLAND SEA, which is bordered by western Honshū, Kyūshū, and Shikoku, as well as coastal regions of the prefectures of Wakayama, Ōsaka, Hyōgo, Okayama, Hiroshima, and Yamaguchi on Honshū, Fukuoka and Ōita on Kyūshū, and Ehime, Kagawa, and Tokushima on Shikoku. The park extends some 400 km (248 mi) east to west and has a maximum width of 60–70 km (37–43 mi). It is characterized by the irregular shoreline of the Inland Sea and the over 1,000 islands in it, some no larger than a rock, on which grow red pines *(akamatsu)* or bamboos.

AWAJISHIMA, the largest of the islands, is located between the Kii Peninsula of central Honshū and northeastern Shikoku, and is separated from the latter by the NARUTO STRAIT, known for its violent whirlpools. To the island's west lies SHŌDOSHIMA, the second largest island, noted for the scenic beauty of the gorge KANKAKEI. Another island, SENSUIJIMA, has a fine view of the Inland Sea, as does the hill WASHIUZAN (133 m or 436 ft) in Okayama Prefecture.

As evidence of its close links with Japan's religious history, the Inland Sea has a number of ancient shrines, such as KOTOHIRA SHRINE (also called Kompira Shrine) in northeastern Shikoku; Ōyamazumi Shrine on ŌMISHIMA; and the ITSUKUSHIMA SHRINE south of the city of Hiroshima. The famous historical sea battles of Yashima and Dannoura, between the Taira and Minamoto families, were also fought in the area.

Near the resort of Beppu Hot Spring in Kyūshū is TAKASAKIYAMA (628 m or 2,060 ft) with its Natural Zoological Park that contains a monkey sanctuary. Total area: 9,500 sq km (3,667 sq mi); land area: 631.2 sq km (243.6 sq mi).

Inland Sea National Park

The noted view of the Inland Sea from the hill Washiuzan near Kurashiki in southern Okayama Prefecture.

inner minister → naidaijin

Innoshima

City in southeastern Hiroshima Prefecture, western Honshū. The city incorporates the entire island of Innoshima and a part of the island of Ikuchishima in the Inland Sea. Formerly a farming and fishing village, it has expanded rapidly since the introduction of the shipbuilding industry in 1911. Local products include mandarin oranges, olives, peaches, and chrysanthemums. Pop: 38,579.

Innoshima

Island in the central Inland Sea, Hiroshima Prefecture. One of the GEIYO ISLANDS. A base of operations of the Murakami pirates during the Muromachi period (1333–1568), the island is scheduled to become one link in a proposed series of bridges connecting Honshū and Shikoku (expected completion date: 1987). It is known for its shipbuilding industry. Area: 34 sq km (13 sq mi).

inns

(ryokan). Lodging facilities, generally with Japanese-style architecture, accommodations, and service, in contrast to Western-style hotels. The primary difference between an inn and a hotel is that at an inn guest rooms have TATAMI mat floors and Japanese BEDDING *(futon)* instead of beds. The food served at inns is almost always Japanese, whereas hotels serve mainly Western food.

Many Japanese inns actually do have Western-style rooms for the convenience of foreigners. There are some 80,000 inns nationwide. Among this number are inns that specialize in accommodating foreign guests, known as International Travel Inns (Kokusai Kankō Ryokan). There are about 2,000 of these, and each carries a special mark to aid the visitor in identifying it.

In recent years the number of purely Japanese-style inns has been decreasing. Inns operate on the basis of one night's lodging with two meals included in the rate. Reservations at inns can be made in person, but they are usually handled by Japanese travel agents.   *Naitō Kinju*

Inō Jakusui (1655–1715)

Specialist in *honzōgaku* (traditional pharmacognosy) and an early scholar of Japanese natural history during the Edo period (1600–1868). Born in Edo (now Tōkyō), he studied medicine, pharmacognosy, and Confucianism and started a private school in Kyōto. MATSUOKA JOAN and NORO GENJŌ were among his students. The work for which he is known is *Shobutsu ruisan,* a 1,000-volume herbal originally compiled from Chinese texts on medicinal herbs and later used as a reference for the study of natural history. He began the work in 1699 and completed 362 volumes before his death. The series was continued after his death by his students, with the cooperation of shōgun Tokugawa Yoshimune.   *Suzuki Zenji*

Inokuchi Ariya (1856–1923)

Scientist. A leading figure in the early development of mechanical engineering in Japan, Inokuchi is known for his work on the centrifugal pump. Born in the Kanazawa domain (now part of Ishikawa Prefecture), he graduated from what is now the Department of Mechanical Engineering at Tōkyō University. He taught there and at the Naval War College.

Inomata Tsunao (1889–1942)

Marxist economist and political commentator. Born in Niigata Prefecture, Inomata graduated from Waseda University. From 1915 to 1921 he studied in the United States and became a Marxist under the influence of the American economist R. T. Ely and visiting Japanese labor leader KATAYAMA SEN. Upon his return to Japan, Inomata joined the Waseda faculty and in 1922 participated in the formation of the JAPAN COMMUNIST PARTY (JCP). He was arrested the following year and dismissed from the university. Together with YAMAKAWA HITOSHI and ARAHATA KANSON, he founded the periodical *Rōnō* in 1927 and served as a spokesman for the group of Marxist theorists known as the RŌNŌHA in their debates with the rival KŌZAHA over the nature of capitalism and revolution in Japan (see NIHON SHIHON SHUGI RONSŌ). In 1929 he left *Rōnō* and devoted himself to writing educational books. He was arrested again in the 1937 POPULAR FRONT INCIDENT, and died of illness in 1942. Inomata's works include *Kin'yū shihon ron* (1925, Theory of Financial Capital), *Kin no keizaigaku* (1932, Economics of Gold), and *Nōson mondai nyūmon* (1937, Introduction to Agricultural Problems).

SUGIHARA Shirō

Inō Tadataka (1745–1818)

Also known as Inō Chūkei. Geographical surveyor of the late Edo period. Tadataka was the first to use Western scientific methods in his surveys of the entire country. His magnum opus was a collection of maps covering all of Japan based on an actual coastal survey. His maps, popularly referred to as "the Inō maps," served as the basis for Japanese mapmaking during the Meiji period (1868–1912) and later.

Tadataka was born on the coast of Kujūkuri, Kazusa Province (now part of Chiba Prefecture). At age 17 he was adopted as the heir to the Inō family in the city of Sawara, and brought to prosperity the family's brewing and rice-dealing business. He studied calendar making and astronomy on his own while attending to his trade. Having renounced the headship of his family at age 49, he went to Edo (now Tōkyō) the following year (1795) and became a pupil of TAKAHASHI YOSHITOKI, a young astronomer of the Tokugawa shogunate. Yoshitoki was a scholar well versed in Chinese texts on European astronomy. (Tadataka used these in his study of Western astronomy and mathematics, and it was from them that he learned the technique of using astronomical observations in order to make scientific surveys on a large scale.)

Yoshitoki had been ordered by the shogunate to revise the calendar. The production of an accurate calendar required knowledge of the actual distance of one degree latitude, which in turn required a knowledge of the actual size of the earth. For this a north-south survey over a long distance was necessary. Yoshitoki convinced the shogunate of the necessity of surveying and producing maps of Ezo (now Hokkaidō). In 1800 Tadataka and several other students of Yoshitoki commenced a 180-day survey of Ezo. After they had submitted their completed maps to the shogunate, the government ordered Tadataka to survey the coasts of Honshū. This survey resulted in the completion of a set of maps of the coast of the eastern half of Japan in 1804. The excellence of these maps led to Tadataka's appointment as an official in the shogunate. Thereafter, Tadataka's party of surveyors was engaged in an official survey of western Japan. The number of days he had spent surveying throughout Japan by the age of 70 totaled 3,737 and he had covered over 43,700 kilometers (27,160 mi), a distance exceeding the circumference of the earth.

Generally speaking, Tadataka's surveying methods were an extremely meticulous application of techniques already known by that time in Japan. His chief innovation was the use of various kinds of precision instruments for his astronomical observations. Valuable assistance in this was provided by Hazama Shigetomi (1756–1816), a merchant of Ōsaka and one of Yoshitoki's close friends, who had a knowledge of Western astronomy and made various surveying instruments based on astronomical texts in Chinese. Utilizing these instruments, Tadataka calculated latitudes by measuring the altitudes of fixed stars at various points. He attempted the calculation of longitude by observing solar and lunar eclipses, but did not obtain satisfactory results. Therefore, on the Inō maps, the meridian that passes through Kyōto was fixed as the zero degree, and other longitudes were added later on the basis of his calculation of the size of the earth.

Tadataka died at age 73 before completing his maps. His friends and pupils completed them and in 1821 compiled the *Dai Nihon enkai jissoku zenzu* (214 sheets of maps on a large scale, 1:36,000; 8 sheets of maps on a middle scale, 1:216,000; 3 sheets of maps on a small scale, 1:432,000), and the *Dai Nihon enkai jissokuroku*, 14 vols (Records of an Actual Survey of the Japanese Coast). The outstanding features of the Inō maps are that the distances between points along coastlines and along surveyed roads are accurate, that latitude and longitude are indicated (one degree apart), and that areas other than those actually surveyed are left blank rather than being supplied from maps or materials made or collected by others. The maps also have an artistic value, as coasts and mountains are drawn by hand in harmonious colors and mountainous or hilly areas are drawn in a birds'-eye view.

Although the maps were kept under the custody of the shogunate, Phillip Franz von SIEBOLD, the Dutch physician in Nagasaki, secretly obtained copies of some of the maps and sent them to Europe, where they were published. In 1861, when Commander J. Ward of the British survey fleet arrived in Yokohama for a coastal survey of Japan, he saw some of the Inō maps and was impressed by their accuracy. Ward abandoned his own survey and returned to England with copies he had received from the shogunate. Some maps of Japan published by the British Navy were based on Inō's maps. Early in the Meiji period the government undertook a mapping project using triangulation, but it had to be abandoned, and in 1884 the land survey section of the army general staff compiled maps based on Inō's medium-scale maps. Some of these were used until 1924.

A large number of Tadataka's books, his own works, diaries, maps, and instruments are preserved as Important Cultural Properties at the Inō Tadataka Memorial Hall in the city of Sawara, Chiba Prefecture. See also MAPS.

——Hoyanagi Mutsumi, *Inō Tadataka no kagakuteki gyōseki* (1974). Ōtani Ryōkichi, *Inō Tadataka* (1917), tr Kazue Sugimura as *Tadataka Ino: The Japanese Land-Surveyor* (1932).

HOYANAGI Mutsumi

Inoue Enryō (1858–1919)

Buddhist thinker and educator whose life-long endeavor was the popularization of philosophy. Born in Niigata of a family belonging to the JŌDO SHIN SECT of Buddhism, he graduated from Tōkyō University in 1885 and was the founder in 1887 of the institute of philosophy known as the Tetsugakukan, the forerunner of Tōyō University. He attempted a synthesis of the thought of Gautama Buddha, Confucius, Socrates, and Kant; especially unique was his interpretation of Buddhism in the light of Western philosophy. He wrote over 120 books and is known for his study of spirit phenomena, *Yōkaigaku kōgi* (1895, Lectures on Ghosts).

Inoue Hisashi (1934–)

Playwright, novelist. Real name Uchiyama Hisashi. Born in Yamagata Prefecture. Graduate of Jōchi Daigaku (Sophia University). Before gaining recognition as a comic playwright for such plays as *Omoteura Gennai kaeru gassen* (1971) and *Chin'yaku seisho* (1973), he wrote scripts for animation series. His writings are imbued with a lively wit and are in the tradition of the satirical humor of the GESAKU writers of the Edo period (1600–1868). He won the 1972 Naoki Prize for his novel *Tegusari shinjū* (1972, Double Suicide Handcuffed). Other works include the play *Dōgen no bōken* (1971, Dōgen's Adventure).

Inoue Junnosuke (1869–1932)

Politician and banker. Born in what is now Ōita Prefecture, he graduated from Tōkyō University in 1896. Entering the BANK OF JAPAN, he became head of the YOKOHAMA SPECIE BANK (now Bank of Tōkyō, Ltd) in 1913 and governor of the Bank of Japan in 1919. In 1923 he was named finance minister in the YAMAMOTO GONNO-

HYŌE cabinet and worked to remedy the financial disorder resulting from the TŌKYŌ EARTHQUAKE OF 1923. After the cabinet resigned at the end of that year, he was appointed to the House of Peers. In 1927 he again became governor of the Bank of Japan and helped to overcome the FINANCIAL CRISIS OF 1927. In 1929 he was named finance minister in the HAMAGUCHI OSACHI cabinet and joined the RIKKEN MINSEITŌ political party. To stabilize exchange rates and prices, he returned Japan to the gold standard and put into effect a retrenchment program. After the assassination of Hamaguchi, Inoue remained in office in the succeeding WAKATSUKI REIJIRŌ cabinet and sought to continue his financial policy. The worldwide economic depression, however, intensified the deflationary impact of his program, and Japan sank into the SHŌWA DEPRESSION. Incurring the hostility of the army over its opposition to military expenditure and losing popular support as the economy deteriorated, the cabinet resigned in 1931 in the crisis resulting from the military's takeover of Manchuria (see MANCHURIAN INCIDENT). While serving as a senior manager of the Rikken Minseitō in the 1932 Diet election, Inoue was assassinated by Onuma Shō (b 1911), a member of the ultranationalist terrorist group Ketsumeidan (see LEAGUE OF BLOOD INCIDENT). Inoue's orthodox financial policy of 1929–1931 was reversed by his successor as finance minister, TAKAHASHI KOREKIYO, who took Japan off the gold standard and implemented a program of increased government spending through deficit financing.

Inoue Kaoru (1836–1915)

Politician of the Meiji period (1868–1912). He served as minister of public works, foreign affairs, agriculture and commerce, home affairs, and finance in the Meiji government. His illustrious political career and close ties to financial circles enabled him eventually to attain great influence as one of the elder statesmen (GENRŌ).

Born into a *samurai* family of the Chōshū domain (now Yamaguchi Prefecture), he participated in the SONNŌ JŌI (Revere the Emperor, Expel the Barbarians) movement that began in the late 1850s, and in January 1863 he joined TAKASUGI SHINSAKU and other nationalists in an attack on the British legation in Edo (now Tōkyō).

Inoue was not a simple-minded xenophobe. In his youth he had studied WESTERN LEARNING, and later, on orders from his domain, he had conducted research on the British navy. Recognizing Japan's need to learn further from the West, he set forth in June 1863 on a British trading ship to study in England. During the voyage he had the good fortune to initiate a close, lifelong friendship with two shipmates destined to become Meiji oligarchs, ITŌ HIROBUMI and Yamao Yōzō (1837–1917). After a half year in England Inoue and Itō learned from newspaper accounts that Chōshū guns had fired on Western ships passing through the Shimonoseki Strait. They quickly returned to Chōshū and led the negotiations for a cease-fire agreement following a joint Western retaliatory attack on Chōshū (see SHIMONOSEKI BOMBARDMENT). Later Inoue played a key role in the formation of the SATSUMA–CHŌSHŪ ALLIANCE against the Tokugawa shogunate; he purchased arms from England and personally led troops in battle against the Tokugawa forces.

After the establishment of the Meiji government, Inoue served successively as junior councillor (san'yo), minister of foreign affairs, and a staff member first to the governor-general for the pacification of Kyūshū and then to the Nagasaki law courts. In September 1871 he was appointed vice-minister of finance. During the absence of the cabinet ministers dispatched to Europe and America on the IWAKURA MISSION (1871–73), he forcefully strove to implement such radical policies as the LAND TAX REFORM OF 1873–1881, the termination of samurai and aristocratic stipends (see CHITSUROKU SHOBUN), and the promotion of industrial enterprises. These policies enraged the more conservative elements of the government, who eventually forced Inoue and his assistant SHIBUSAWA EIICHI to resign from office in May 1873.

Inoue then began to develop the close ties with Japanese business circles, especially the MITSUI group, for which he later became famous. It was his handling of the bankruptcy of the ONO-GUMI company in 1874 that rescued the Daiichi Kokuritsu Ginkō (now DAI-ICHI KANGYŌ BANK, LTD) and the Mitsui organization from serious financial difficulty. He also helped establish the Senshū Kaisha trading company, one of the two companies later merged to form what is now MITSUI & CO, LTD.

After acting as mediator at the ŌSAKA CONFERENCE OF 1875, Inoue returned to the government, eventually becoming minister of public works in July 1878 and minister of foreign affairs in September 1879. Upon taking office as foreign minister, Inoue set about

preparing for negotiations to recover some of the legal and tariff rights Japan had earlier ceded to the Western powers (see UNEQUAL TREATIES, REVISION OF). He had the ministries of foreign affairs and justice engage highly knowledgeable and experienced foreigners, notably the Frenchman Gustave Emile BOISSONADE DE FONTARABIE and the American Henry W. DENISON, to draft treaties providing for the recovery of these rights.

Handed the completed documents in July 1880, the foreign powers' representatives immediately rejected them. The British envoy proposed that drafts to serve as the basis for negotiations should be drawn up not by the Japanese but by the foreign representatives at a preliminary conference. Consequently, from 25 January 1882 Inoue chaired a series of 21 meetings with the representatives and other Westerners during which he proposed several treaty revisions, including the complete termination of extraterritoriality upon the opening of the entire country to foreigners and the appointment of foreign judges to each level of the Japanese court system to hear cases involving foreigners (see NAICHI ZAKKYO). Inoue's proposals, however, met with strong opposition not only from foreigners skeptical of the justice administered in Japanese courts, but also from Japanese serving within the government. And so, on 27 July, the treaty revision conferences were adjourned with the issues unresolved.

In May 1886 negotiations on treaty revision were reopened at the Ministry of Foreign Affairs with Inoue again serving as chairman. Nearly a year later, on 22 April 1887, agreement was reached on a protocol for court jurisdiction stipulating that foreign judges be used in Japanese courts and that a foreign country's consent be obtained before its citizens could be treated according to Japanese law.

The terms of this agreement aroused unprecedented domestic criticism of the government. Public sentiment, recently aroused against the British by the NORMANTON INCIDENT, strongly opposed consular jurisdiction. Members of the FREEDOM AND PEOPLE'S RIGHTS MOVEMENT contended that the treaty negotiations constituted diplomatic humiliations for Japan and so expanded their general opposition to the government's policies. The ultranationalists, for their part, incensed by Inoue's recent efforts to hasten treaty revision through rapid Westernization of Japanese customs, added their denunciation to the storm of protest against the government. Confronted with such fierce resistance from numerous interest groups, the government was forced to notify foreign representatives in Japan of the indefinite postponement of the treaty revision conference. Seven weeks later, on 16 September 1887, Inoue resigned from his post as minister of foreign affairs.

Inoue subsequently served as adviser to the imperial household, minister of agriculture and commerce, and minister of home affairs. On 15 October 1894, after the outbreak of the SINO-JAPANESE WAR OF 1894–1895, he was dispatched as ambassador extraordinary and plenipotentiary to Korea. His mission ended in failure when the Korean government rejected his proposals for political reform, which, if implemented, would have replaced its close ties to China and Russia with greater dependence on Japan.

From 1901 Inoue served as an elder statesman (GENRŌ) and considered himself the government's foremost adviser on financial matters. His close relations with the financial world—which in the 1870s had prompted the popular Meiji politician SAIGŌ TAKAMORI to give him the unendearing sobriquet "The Chief Manager of Mitsui"—helped him perform effectively as a genrō.

📖——Inoue Kaoru Kō Denki Hensankai, ed, *Seigai Inoue Kō den*, 5 vols (1933–34, repr 1968). Nakahara Kunihei, ed, *Inoue Haku den*, 9 vols (1907). Sawada Akira, ed, *Seigai Kō jireki ishin zaisei dan*, 3 vols (1921). Tsuzuki Seiroku, *An Episode from the Life of Count Inoue* (1912). Inō Tentarō

Inoue Kiyonao (1809–1867)

Official of the Tokugawa shogunate; younger brother of KAWAJI TOSHIAKIRA. Born in Edo (now Tōkyō). In 1855, soon after the signing of the KANAGAWA TREATY with the United States, Inoue was appointed by the chief senior councillor (rōjū shuseki) ABE MASAHIRO as commissioner (bugyō) of the newly opened port of Shimoda. In this capacity he entered into negotiations with the American representative Townsend HARRIS and in 1857 signed supplementary agreements to the Kanagawa Treaty. In July 1858, following preliminary negotiations by Inoue, HOTTA MASAYOSHI, and IWASE TADANARI, Inoue and Iwase were given full powers by Great Elder (tairō) II NAOSUKE to conclude the HARRIS TREATY, the first of the so-called ANSEI COMMERCIAL TREATIES. Thereafter Inoue held numerous offices, including commissioner of foreign affairs *(gaikoku bugyō)* again in 1862, and commissioner of finance *(kanjō bugyō)*.

Inoue Kowashi (1844–1895)

Bureaucrat. Born in Higo Province (now Kumamoto Prefecture). He fought on the imperial side in the BOSHIN CIVIL WAR. After the Meiji Restoration of 1868 Inoue joined the Ministry of Justice and was sent to study in France and Germany in 1872–73. He became a protégé of the oligarch ŌKUBO TOSHIMICHI and accompanied him to Beijing (Peking) to assist in negotiations following the TAIWAN EXPEDITION OF 1874. After Ōkubo's death Inoue became closely associated with the statesmen ITŌ HIROBUMI and IWAKURA TOMOMI. Soon after the POLITICAL CRISIS OF 1881 he was appointed to the House of Councillors and ordered to draw up a memorial on constitutional government. Under the supervision of Itō Hirobumi (who was appointed chairman of a bureau for the drafting of a constitution) and working closely with K. F. Hermann ROESLER, the German adviser to the government, he prepared drafts that became the base for the Meiji CONSTITUTION and the Imperial Household Laws. He was also responsible, with MOTODA NAGAZANE, for the IMPERIAL RESCRIPT ON EDUCATION and had a hand in drawing up numerous other edicts and laws. He was appointed to the Privy Council in 1890 and in 1893 became minister of education in the second Itō cabinet.

Inoue Mitsuharu (1926–)

Novelist. Born in Manchuria, where his father worked as an itinerant potter. The family returned to Japan when Inoue was four years old. He obtained a middle-school education by correspondence while working in the coal mines of Kyūshū. After World War II, he joined the Japan Communist Party and began to write for the Marxist literary magazine *Shin Nihon bungaku,* which was founded in 1945. In 1950 he was expelled from the Communist Party for his short story "Kakarezaru isshō," which deals with the frustrations of a party member forced to follow the party's impractical bureaucratic orders, divorced from the realities of local life. He continued to criticize the deteriorating party leadership in "Yameru bubun" (1951), establishing his name as an independent Marxist writer. After that he refused to rejoin the Communist Party. In 1956 he founded the magazine *Gendai hihyō,* which serialized his *Kyokō no kurēn* (published in 1960), a novel about the mental anguish of a youth beset with self-doubts about his participation in World War II. He is known for his exploration of controversial topics, including Japan's actions in World War II, the role of the emperor, the position of the Communist Party, and discrimination against minorities. Recalling his early, dark years as a coal miner and as a soldier, his writings are somewhat reminiscent of William Faulkner, somber in tone and richly descriptive in style.

Inoue Nisshō (1886–1967)

Rightist ideologue of the 1930s. Born Inoue Akira, in Gumma Prefecture. He left school at an early age to go to China and Manchuria, where he gathered information for the Japanese military. Upon returning to Japan in 1921, he converted to the Nichiren sect, a particularly militant and nationalistic branch of Buddhism, and took the name Nisshō. In 1928 he founded a school, the Risshō Gokoku Dō, in Ibaraki Prefecture to propagate his ideas on agrarian nationalism (NŌHON SHUGI) and social reform among farm youth. He also became gradually convinced of the efficacy of force as a means of national reform, and he established contacts with young military officers. After the aborted coup d'etat by rightist officers and civilians in the OCTOBER INCIDENT (1931), he formed his own terrorist group, the Ketsumeidan (League of Blood), and directed the assassinations of DAN TAKUMA, chairman of the MITSUI company, and INOUE JUNNOSUKE, the politician and former finance minister (see LEAGUE OF BLOOD INCIDENT). He turned himself in and was sentenced to life imprisonment in 1934 but was released in the general amnesty of 1940. After World War II he continued his rightist activities but had very little influence.

Inoue Tetsujirō (1855–1944)

Philosopher and educator. Born in what is now Fukuoka Prefecture, he graduated from Tōkyō University in 1880 and went to Germany for further study. He spent his entire academic career teaching philosophy at Tōkyō University. Inoue is credited with having introduced German idealism to the Japanese academic world. Interested also in Buddhism and Confucianism, he sought to synthesize Eastern and Western thought. He was an ardent nationalist, criticizing Christianity as being inimical to Japan's unique national polity (KOKUTAI), and stressed the primacy of loyalty to emperor and country. His works are collected in *Inoue Hakase kōronshū* (2 vols, 1894–95) and *Sonken rombunshū* (2 vols, 1899–1901).　　TANIKAWA Atsushi

Inoue Yasushi (1907–)

Novelist. Born in Asahikawa, Hokkaidō, where his father, an army medical officer, was temporarily stationed. Separated frequently from his parents, who moved often in compliance with military orders, he spent most of his childhood living with his grandmother on the Izu Peninsula, not far from Mt. Fuji (Fujisan). After devoting his early adult years to independent literary studies in Tōkyō, he resumed his formal education and graduated at the age of 28 from Kyōto University with a degree in art history.

Although Inoue had already received professional recognition as a writer of fiction, he chose to become a newspaperman and wrote for the MAINICHI SHIMBUN for the next dozen years, except for a half year in 1937 spent as a soldier in Northern China.

In the chaotic postwar society of Japan, Inoue found the subject for his novel *Tōgyū* (1949, The Bullfight), which depicts the frenzied activities of an enterprising newspaper executive promoting a bullfight, the success or failure of which will determine the fate of his firm. This work earned him the coveted Akutagawa Prize in 1950. A simultaneous success was *Ryōjū* (1949; tr *The Hunting Gun,* 1961), on the theme of loneliness and world-weariness in modern society. In 1950 Inoue relinquished the opportunity to rise up the executive ladder and entered upon a new career as a professional writer, a fledgling author at the age of 43.

Inoue has become one of Japan's most prolific and respected authors, writing in various genres and for all levels of readers. His *Kuroi ushio* (1950, The Black Tide), a dramatization of the mysterious murder of a prominent public figure, encouraged the vogue for novelistic treatment of contemporary social and political events. *Hyōheki* (1956, Wall of Ice), about a love triangle culminating in sudden death as the antagonists scale an alpine slope, was published serially in a daily newspaper; though addressed to readers of popular fiction, its high level of artistry led to recognition in the form of the Japan Art Academy Award (Geijutsuin Shō), which the author received in 1959.

Inoue's most important works are historical and autobiographical narratives, often only thinly disguised as fiction. His Japanese readers especially admire *Tempyō no iraka* (1957; tr *The Roof Tile of Tempyō,* 1975), for which the author received the Ministry of Education Prize. No ordinary historical novel, it is an artistic reconstruction of the drama of Japanese and Chinese monks in the 8th century who dedicated their lives to transmitting Buddhist ideals from Tang (T'ang; 618–907) China to Japan, which was just then beginning to develop as a civilization. Other historical novels which exhibit the same preference for authenticity and a straightforward, sparse style, are *Fūtō* (1963, Wind and Waves), a poignant portrayal of the struggles of Korean monarchs to keep their nation independent despite the predatory Mongol invaders, and *Go-Shirakawa In* (1972), a portrait of a medieval Japanese monarch based on diaries kept by close attendants. In *Saiiki monogatari* (1969; tr *Journey Beyond Samarkand,* 1971), Inoue writes primarily as a historian and traveler depicting the past and present of ancient cities in central Asia and the caravan route that had once connected them. *Waga haha no ki* (1975, Records of My Mother) is an excellent example of autobiographical writing that is invested heavily with the characteristics of the traditional Japanese poetic diary as well as the classical ZUIHITSU, a highly personal mode of recorded experiences and observations.

Inoue has received every major literary prize in Japan; furthermore, in 1964 he was elected a member of the Japan Art Academy and, in 1976, received the Order of Culture (Bunka Kunshō), the highest decoration awarded by the Japanese government to individuals for contributing to the advancement of the arts and sciences. Because Inoue's approach to fiction is remarkably and intensely Japanese, the historical works that exemplify this approach and that the Japanese consider to be his best writings might not easily lend themselves to appreciation among Western readers, whereas stories on contemporary themes, such as *Aru gisakka no shōgai* (1951; tr *The Counterfeiter and Other Stories,* 1965), surely do.

James T. ARAKI

I-novel

(*watakushi shōsetsu* or *shishōsetsu*). Type of modern Japanese fiction that centers on "self-directed" narration usually with the author as the central character. Analogous to such European forms as the German *Ich Roman* and the French *roman personnel*, the I-novel is best described as autobiographical or personal fiction. It is typically devoid of such structural elements as plot, characterization, and dramatic tension and may range in length from four- or five-page short stories to full-length novels of 500 or more pages. The narration may be in the first or third person.

The evolution of the I-novel dates from the latter part of the Meiji period (1868–1912). It was a product of the naturalist literary movement (see NATURALISM), which dominated the Japanese literary establishment from the early 1900s to about the mid-1920s, when the PROLETARIAN LITERATURE MOVEMENT came to the fore. The origin of the I-novel is attributed to the novel *Futon* (1907) of TAYAMA KATAI. An embarrassingly honest account of the feelings of its central character, a writer, toward a young female pupil who comes to live with his family, it shocked readers, since it was obvious that the feelings and experiences were those of the author. This novel opened up new territory for the Japanese novelist: the realistic depiction of the course of events (often mere trivialities) in his or her own daily life. Novels with a similar approach were written by naturalist authors such as SHIMAZAKI TŌSON, TOKUDA SHŪSEI, and KASAI ZENZŌ. Many took to writing only about their own experiences and in some cases appeared to be vying with one another to see who could confess to the most unusual or sordid conduct. There was a tendency to focus solely on the act of confession with no attempt to take responsibility for the conflicts engendered. This type is often referred to as the confession form of I-novel.

The other type of I-novel is the *shinkyō shōsetsu*, or the novel of mental states. A shorter form, in general, than the confession form, it is an essay-like sketch focusing on the mental, emotional, or spiritual state of the author. There is much about it that is suggestive of the traditional genre of the ZUIHITSU (essays or random jottings). The best examples of this subgenre of Japanese fiction are the masterful sketches of SHIGA NAOYA (such as "Kinosaki nite"). The short prose of Kasai Zenzō is also illustrative of the writing that was achieved in this form. The *shinkyō shōsetsu* can be seen as a purified form of I-novel. In some respects, particularly in its compact use of language, it closely approaches the prose poem. It is not a confession but rather an inward look at the self in search of the meaning of life. As in the confession form, there is a sense of crisis, but here the author seeks to resolve it by transcending it or moving to a higher plane of existence. The confession form is an attempt to find salvation in art, that is to say, writing becomes an act of catharsis. The *shinkyō shōsetsu*, on the other hand, is an attempt to use art as a way of attaining a higher consciousness of life. Writing is viewed as a means to an end, not as the end itself, as in the case of the confession form.

The I-novel emerged as the main current of modern Japanese fiction and dominated Japanese literature during the Taishō period (1912–26). Other writers who made extensive use of the form are MUSHANOKŌJI SANEATSU, UNO KŌJI, and MUROO SAISEI. With the emergence in the mid-1920s of a new approach to literary realism engendered by the proletarian literature movement, the I-novel temporarily lost much of its appeal. In the mid-1930s, however, proletarian literature writers were jailed or forced to make ideological conversions (see TENKŌ). As a result, many turned to the traditional I-novel form as a means of expression. Important postwar writers of I-novels include DAN KAZUO, KAWASAKI CHŌTARŌ, and DAZAI OSAMU. MISHIMA YUKIO also employed the confession form in his novel, *Kamen no kokuhaku* (1949; tr *Confessions of a Mask*, 1958).

The words *watakushi shōsetsu* and *shishōsetsu* were coined by literary critics around 1920 as a disparaging reference to many of the works of the naturalist school, and criticism of the I-novel has thus been closely tied with the evaluation of naturalism. In the 1920s the I-novel was also referred to as *jumbungaku* (pure literature), a critical term that came into use at the time as a means of differentiating "serious literature" from POPULAR FICTION (*taishū bungaku*). In postwar criticism, the I-novel has received both praise and blame. Many critics believed that its lack of plot and narrow perspective had a stunting effect on the growth of the modern novel in Japan. None could deny its longlasting popularity; no single form has had the dominance in 20th-century Japanese fiction of the I-novel. The popularity of the genre has been affirmed by the number of works that have appeared since the 1960s by a new breed of I-novelists, which include SHIMAO TOSHIO, SHŌNO JUNZŌ, YASUOKA SHŌTARŌ, YOSHIYUKI JUNNOSUKE, ABE AKIRA, and Tomioka Taeko (b 1935).

■——Hirano Ken, *Geijutsu to jisseikatsu* (1974). Itō Sei, *Shōsetsu no hōhō* (1956). Kobayashi Hideo, "Watakushi shōsetsu ron," *Kobayashi Hideo zenshū*, vol 3 (Shinchōsha, 1968). Kume Masao, "Watakushi shōsetsu to shinkyō shōsetsu," *Bungei kōza* (January and February 1926). Noriko Mizuta Lippit, *Reality and Fiction in Modern Japanese Literature* (1980). Janet A. Walker, *The Japanese Novel in the Meiji Period and the Ideal of Individualism* (1979).

Dennis M. SPACKMAN

input-output analysis

(*sangyō renkan*). A perspective on economic activity that emphasizes the web of interdependence among industries. Three factors dictate how strongly one industry influences another. The first is production technology, i.e., the physical input-output relations between raw materials and finished products. The second is the sector by sector balance of value of supply and demand, namely, whether the value of products supplied within an economy corresponds product by product to the value demanded. Imbalances of supply and demand are relieved by foreign trade. The third is the balance between value of outputs and value of inputs, i.e., how the price of output fluctuates relative to input costs such as wages, salaries, and profits.

As supply adjusts to demand and sales to expenditure on factors, short-run changes accumulate into a long-run input-output structure—with technology developing in the interim.

The "Skyline" of Japanese Industry—— A convenient method for comparing the industrial structures of countries is to imagine a city skyline, with each building representing an industry. The breadth of a building represents the industry's share of value in the nation's industrial activity. The height represents the export-import balance of the industry. A common, horizontal line can represent self-sufficiency (i.e., domestic supply equaling domestic demand) for all industries; if actual domestic supply exceeds domestic demand, the building's roof is above the horizontal line—i.e., the industry exports. If the roof is below the line, this means domestic consumption exceeds supply, and the difference must be imported. Thus, the shape of the industrial skyline represents both the internal importance and the trade intensity of a country's industrial structure.

The industrial skyline of the United States is the least jagged of the advanced industrial countries, showing considerable self-sufficiency. But the skyline of the Japanese industry is highly uneven. Skylines based on Japanese input-output tables show deep troughs for agriculture, forestry, and mining. On the other hand, most Japanese manufacturing industries—including iron and steel, metal products, machinery, and chemicals—form high peaks. These industries produce far more than necessary for domestic use and thus export. (But there are some exceptions, e.g., foodstuffs and petroleum-coal products, which are import intensive.)

The skylines of both Japan and West Germany are considerably more jagged than that of the United States. But there are also marked differences between the Japanese and the West German skylines. Among Japanese manufacturing industries, export intensity is more prevalent than import substitution. In West Germany, on the other hand, import substitution is just as vigorous as export production. Thus, West Germany exhibits a high degree of horizontal division of labor, i.e., intraindustry specialization, while Japan exhibits vertical division of labor, i.e., interindustry specialization.

But the Japanese industrial skyline will change in days to come. Import dependence in agriculture, forestry, and mining will deepen. Moreover, the share of imports will rise in all fields of manufacturing, including foodstuffs. Import expansion will be particularly brisk in spinning and other light industry, and in such fields as paper and pulp. In machinery and chemicals, both imports and exports will grow considerably. All these developments suggest gradual progress for Japan in horizontal, intraindustry specialization.

Relative Price Changes and Input-Output Analysis—— An important impetus to this transformation is changes in relative prices of industrial products and in factors of production. The Japanese economy exhausted its surplus of labor in the 1960s, and the wage and salary levels in Japan are now among the highest in the world. Moreover, Japan overcame its chronic balance of payments deficits in the 1960s and even ran huge surpluses. And since 1973, when the nation unpegged the exchange rate, the yen has risen sharply. On the other hand, oil price increases by OPEC dealt a serious blow to

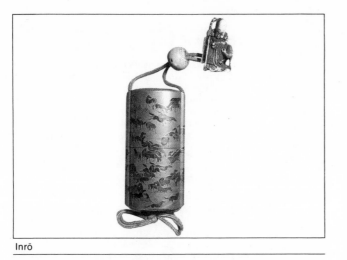

Inrō

An *inrō* with seven compartments, a cord, bead, and ivory *netsuke* or toggle depicting Jurōjin, god of longevity. Lacquered wood, with *maki-e* design of frolicking horses on a gold background by Yamada Jōka. 10.0 × 4.9 cm. Late 17th century. Tōkyō National Museum.

Japanese industry, which depends overwhelmingly on crude oil for energy. Industry also suffers considerably from mounting costs for pollution control.

Thus, yen fluctuation and rising costs of labor, crude oil, imported raw materials, and pollution control have generated heavy cost-push pressure on the prices of basic goods. This, in turn, has generated transmission effects to all industries according to how intensively each uses basic goods as inputs. The result has been a change in relative prices. In addition to general inflation, relative prices are higher for oil products, electric power, and gas, all of which are directly affected by the price of crude oil. Relative prices have also increased for foodstuffs, spinning, sundries, fisheries, housing, and in some areas of the service industries, all of which are labor intensive. Japan's various industries, once sharply divided into sectors with comparative advantages and those without, were affected very differently by the shocks of the 1970s. Thus, the Japanese industrial skyline is now undergoing a major change. The final picture will be dictated by how well each industry can raise productivity and thus offset mounting cost-push pressure.

Commodities Industries and Services Industries —— Service sectors and information sectors are becoming increasingly important in input-output analysis in Japan. According to computations based on input-output tables, inflation transmission effects are greater in Japan than in the United States or West Germany, because Japan imports fewer manufactured goods than other countries. From now on, however, the strength of transmission effects in Japan will approach those of Western countries, as horizontal division of labor progresses across countries.

On the other hand, inflation transmission from services industries tends to be stronger in more advanced countries, such as the United States. The same is true of indirect transmission effects flowing from basic goods industries to service industries, as shown by time series data of input-output coefficients. In other words, information and services are new—and along with energy, indispensable—inputs for almost all industries. Nonphysical activities that use high-grade equipment, such as in the computer and communications fields, have introduced a new feature into the usual physical input-output relations of the Japanese economy and add a new aspect to input-output analysis in Japan.

■ ——A. Carter and A. Brody, ed, *Applications of Input-Output Analysis* (1970). Government of Japan, *1975 Input-Output Tables: Explanatory Report* (1979). K. Miyazawa, *Input-Output Analysis and the Structure of Income Distribution* (1976).

Mɪʏᴀᴢᴀᴡᴀ Ken'ichi

inrō

(literally, "seal basket"). Small containers, usually of ʟᴀᴄǫᴜᴇʀ ᴡᴀʀᴇ and made up of snugly fitted compartments worn suspended by a cord and toggle from the ᴏʙɪ, the sash used to secure the ᴋɪᴍᴏɴᴏ. *Inrō* were used to carry medicines, although the name suggests an earlier association with the seals and seal-paste stamped on documents as marks of personal identity. *Inrō* apparently came into use during the 17th century and became an important personal accessory for Japanese men of the middle to late years of the Edo period (1600–1868). Their decoration encompasses in miniature virtually the entire range of lacquering styles and techniques current during this period. The rich variety of themes and styles among *inrō* reflects their importance as an emblem of the taste, status, and wealth of the owner.

Inrō may have one or more compartments surmounted by a lid. The usual shape has a rectangular face and a flattened, elliptical cross-section, which hangs conveniently close to the body when suspended from the *obi*. Cord-channels run vertically through all the sections of an *inrō*, so that the sections are held in place by a silk cord threaded through all the sections. The ends of the cord are passed through a bead, then secured to a toggle, usually a miniature carving, known as ɴᴇᴛsᴜᴋᴇ. One *netsuke* was often used to hold both the *inrō* and a pouch. The ensembles were selected to harmonize in mood and theme and to reflect the owner's personal taste. The *ojime*, a sliding bead, was used to secure the sections of the *inrō* or to control the opening of one section at a time.

Inrō bodies were very difficult and laborious to construct and fit, requiring many applications of priming materials and lacquer, each followed by smoothing and fitting. They were usually constructed by lacquerers specializing in making *inrō*. The *inrō* were then decorated by ᴍᴀᴋɪ-ᴇ artists, some of whom belonged to families that worked almost exclusively on this one type of lacquer ware. *Inrō* decoration shows great inventiveness. In many the design is carried over all surfaces, often continuously. Aesthetically, the decoration ranges from lavish *maki-e* designs utilizing much gold to subdued, almost colorless designs imitating monochromatic ink painting.

Although the use of *inrō* declined during the Meiji period (1868–1912) as Western clothing became more popular, *inrō* continued to be manufactured to fulfill the demand among European and American collectors, who were intrigued by their skillfully executed miniature designs and their unique form. *Ann* Yᴏɴᴇᴍᴜʀᴀ

In school

(Impa). A Kyōto school of Buddhist sculptors who worked in the style of ᴊōᴄʜō (d 1057); active from the late years of the Heian period (794–1185) through the early part of the Kamakura period (1185–1333). There were two In school workshops (ʙᴜssʜᴏ) in Kyōto: the Shichijō-Ōmiya *bussho*, established by Injo (d 1108), a grandson of Jōchō, and the Rokujō Madenokōji *bussho*, set up by Inchō (fl mid-12th century). The sculptors from these two workshops came to be known as the In school because most of·them included in their names the Chinese character for "*in*," to demonstrate their common artistic lineage. The In school was in competition with the ᴇɴ sᴄʜᴏᴏʟ, another Kyōto school of sculpture descended from Jōchō, during the time of Inkaku (fl 1114–41) and ɪɴsᴏɴ (1120–98), but, from the middle to the end of the 12th century, the In school flourished and temporarily dominated the field. Increasing mannerism, however, and a gradual hardening of the delicate style of Jōchō favored by the Fujiwara nobility, coupled with the rise of a warrior class that preferred the dynamic sculptural realism of ᴜɴᴋᴇɪ and his followers, contributed to the eventual decline of the In school.

inscriptions

(kinsekibun). Literally, "metal and stone writings." A generic term for all manner of inscriptions recorded on diverse objects made of a variety of materials, including metal, stone, clay, and wood. The types and techniques of *kinsekibun* were inspired by continental practice. Their appearance in Japan probably coincided with the introduction of the Chinese language and script, and their number and variety grew with the spread of writing. Methods used to inscribe objects included carving, casting, making impressions, brush writing, and inlay.

Some of the objects on which inscriptions have been discovered were made to be seen, for example, Buddhist images, bells, mirrors, swords, and stone monuments—others were buried in the ground immediately after manufacture. The latter include tiles, stones, and other objects inscribed with passages from Buddhist scripture. These were often buried in sᴜᴛʀᴀ ᴍᴏᴜɴᴅs, which were built to ensure the survival of Buddhist doctrine through the period of decay (*mappō*) prophesied in numerous sutras.

The earliest *kinsekibun* recovered to date are of continental origin and include inscriptions on metal mirrors and swords and a gold seal (KAN NO WA NO NA NO KOKUŌ NO IN) thought to have been presented to the ruler of Nakoku (Na state) by the founding emperor of the Later Han dynasty (25–220) of China. The oldest extant native Japanese inscriptions occur on swords excavated from the ETA FUNAYAMA TOMB and the INARIYAMA TOMB, thought to date from the mid-5th and early 6th century, respectively, and on a bronze mirror (see BRONZE MIRRORS) in the possession of the Suda Hachiman Shrine in Wakayama Prefecture, probably from the early 6th century.

With the exception of many recently excavated wooden tallies (MOKKAN), only about 60 *kinsekibun* can be accurately dated from before 794. Most numerous are stone memorials (see KŌZUKE MONUMENTS), metal statues, and burial tablets. The tablets, all discovered by chance, account for about a fifth of the total; they are made of metal, usually copper, and record the career of the person buried. Other early *kinsekibun* are known only through mention in historical records.

Approximately 550 inscriptions can be dated from the Heian period (794–1185); for later periods their numbers increase tremendously. Sutra containers and tiles excavated from sutra mounds are especially numerous since the late Heian period witnessed a growing conviction that the age of decay had come; accompanying Buddhist images were made of wood rather than of metal as in earlier images, and inscriptions were written on them in black ink.

Kinsekibun are extremely valuable as a source of historical information; those that can be dated to the Nara period (710–794) and earlier are especially useful to researchers, for there are few other early written sources extant. *Kinsekibun* have revealed inaccuracies in historical records and have enabled historians to interpret more correctly events described in diaries and other writings. Certain inscriptions on religious objects have provided valuable information about folk Buddhist practices of the late Heian period. Because *kinsekibun* faithfully recorded the language of their age, the older ones, including the famous BUSSOKUSEKI ("Buddha's footprint stones") at the temple Yakushiji in Nara, are an important source of information about the Japanese language during the Nara and pre-Nara periods. The study of inscriptions has also contributed to knowledge in the fields of Japanese archaeology and art history. The extent of the information that can be gleaned from *kinsekibun* is limited, however, since in most cases the inscription concerns only a particular event or the life of a single individual.

Kinsekibun aroused interest early—one of Japan's earliest chronicles, the *Nihon shoki* (720), mentions several—but they were not systematically collected and studied until the 17th century. The pioneer in this field was TOKUGAWA MITSUKUNI, *daimyō* of the Mito domain (now part of Ibaraki Prefecture) and an enthusiastic patron of historical studies. After Mitsukuni's time, many scholars and collectors continued his work. Most famous of these was MATSUDAIRA SADANOBU, whose monumental *Shūko jisshu* (1800? Collection of Ancient Objects Classified in Ten Categories) represents the peak of the first stage in the study of inscriptions, when collecting and recording were the overriding concerns. From that time on, *kinsekibun* became the object of serious study. Of later scholars, Kariya Ekisai (1775–1835) deserves special mention for his *Kokyō ibun* (1818? Literary Remains from Ancient Capitals), an analytic study of all known inscriptions dating from before 900, which laid the foundation for modern scholarship and is still frequently consulted. The major modern work in the field is the *Dai Nihon kinseki shi* (1921) by Kizaki Aikichi (1865–1944), a collection of all major extant *kinsekibun* through the beginning of the 17th century.

Research on inscriptions has grown more and more specialized, and they are now studied according to the type of object or geographical area. A recent development that will help to determine the course of future study is the recovery since 1961 of thousands of inscribed *mokkan* during excavation of the early palace sites of ASUKA KIYOMIHARA NO MIYA, FUJIWARAKYŌ, and HEIJŌKYŌ. Heijōkyō alone has yielded more than 20,000 tablets, and some scholars have called for the establishment of an independent discipline devoted to the study of *mokkan*.

🔳——Fukuyama Toshio, "Nihon kodai no kinsekibun," *Sho no Nihon shi* 1 (1975). Ōba Iwao, "Kinsekibun," in Nihon Rekishi Gakkai, ed, *Nihon kōkogaku no genjō to kadai* (1974). Okazaki Takashi and Hirano Kunio, "Nihon no kodai kinsekibun," in Takeuchi Rizō et al, ed, *Kodai no Nihon*, vol 9 (Kadokawa Shoten, 1971).

Noboru HIRAGA

Insei

Reigning and Retired Emperors under the Insei System

Reigning emperor	Reign dates	Senior retired emperor	Junior retired emperor
Go-Sanjō	1068–1073	—	—
Shirakawa	1073–1087	—	—
Horikawa	1087–1107	Shirakawa	—
Toba	1107–1123	Shirakawa	—
Sutoku	1123–1129	Shirakawa	Toba
Sutoku	1129–1142	Toba	—
Konoe	1142–1155	Toba	Sutoku
Go-Shirakawa	1155–1156	Toba	Sutoku
Go-Shirakawa	1156–1158	—	—
Nijō	1158–1165	Go-Shirakawa	—
Rokujō	1165–1168	Go-Shirakawa	—
Takakura	1168–1180	Go-Shirakawa	Rokujō (to 1176)
Antoku	1180–1185	Go-Shirakawa	Takakura (to 1181)
Go-Toba	1183–1192	Go-Shirakawa	—
Go-Toba	1192–1198	—	—

SOURCE: Adapted from George Sansom, *A History of Japan to 1334* (1958).

insects → animals

insei

(literally, "cloister government"). The system of government that prevailed between the abdication of Emperor Shirakawa in 1087 and the establishment of WARRIOR GOVERNMENT in 1192. Political control was restored to the imperial house from the Fujiwara regents but was exercised by retired emperors rather than by the titular rulers. *In* refers to the buildings, often a cloister or monastery, where a former emperor resided; *sei* is an abbreviation of *seiji*, politics or government. It is usual to describe the political structure during this period as having two centers: the reigning emperor, presiding over the traditional court and bureaucracy, and a retired emperor (the reigning emperor's father or grandfather), with his personal retinue and administration. The latter was clearly dominant.

Reassertion of Imperial Rule——For much of the Heian period (794–1185)—intermittently from 857 and continuously from 967—the imperial house had been controlled and its powers exercised by the northern branch of the FUJIWARA FAMILY, which had established a REGENCY GOVERNMENT based on close marital ties with the imperial line. Successive emperors were born of Fujiwara mothers, were married to Fujiwara wives, and were dominated throughout their lives by their Fujiwara uncles and grandfathers. The imperial house lacked all cohesion.

In 1068, however, there was an unusual dearth of imperial princes who were direct Fujiwara descendants. In the absence of more suitable candidates, Emperor GO-SANJŌ (r 1068–73) was allowed to ascend the throne. Because of his weak Fujiwara connection, he could, and did incline to, assert himself much more forcefully than any of his recent predecessors, and his accession marked the decline of the Fujiwara regency.

Go-Sanjō's abdication in 1073 brought to the throne his son Emperor SHIRAKAWA (r 1073–87), whose Fujiwara connection was also weak. Moreover, Go-Sanjō established a line of succession that would perpetuate the newly won independence of the imperial house: the next two emperors were to be his sons by a consort from the MINAMOTO FAMILY. Japanese historians have traditionally seen Go-Sanjō's actions following his abdication as a deliberate attempt to establish what is now known as cloister government.

Shirakawa and the Establishment of Insei——Although Go-Sanjō died shortly after his retirement, his plans were ultimately realized. Shirakawa also enjoyed considerable freedom of action and became a more powerful ruler than his father had been. While he diverted the succession from Go-Sanjō's sons to his own Fujiwara-descended sons, he nevertheless prevented the Fujiwara regents from regaining control of the throne. Shirakawa too abdicated, in 1087, but kept close watch over his son Emperor Horikawa (1079–1107; r 1087–1107), continuing to govern the country from retirement for more than 40 years.

It was during Shirakawa's retirement that cloister government became fully institutionalized. Earlier Heian emperors had often retired to Buddhist monasteries, sometimes entering holy orders.

An office, located in the monastery *(in)* and called the Cloister Office (In no Chō), had long existed to serve the needs of former emperors. During Shirakawa's retirement the functions of this office expanded in proportion to his power; the lands under its control and the personnel in its service grew apace. By the time of Shirakawa's death in 1129, the imperial house was a stronger entity than it had been for 300 years; and within the house, the retired emperor was supreme.

Insei after Shirakawa —— During the 12th century the power and wealth of the retired emperors increased tremendously; the Cloister Office came to employ dozens of directors, clerks, scribes, and other functionaries who administered vast landholdings throughout the country. Retired emperors were not the only beneficiaries of the political and economic resurgence of the imperial house. The reigning emperors as well as their consorts and children all shared in the bounty. For example, high-ranking imperial ladies, too, often retired to palaces or convents, established cloister offices, and accumulated clients and estates of their own.

As the frequency of abdication increased because of factional strife over the imperial succession and the rewards of high office, there was often more than one retired emperor at a given time (see table). Only one of them, however, exercised real power as senior cloistered emperor *(hon'in),* a position held by only three men in this period: Shirakawa (cloistered 1087–1129) for 43 years; his grandson TOBA (1129–56) for 27 years, and Toba's son GO-SHIRAKAWA (1158–92) for 34 years. Although the other, junior, retired emperors were effectively excluded from power, they were frequently a cause of political unrest. The HŌGEN DISTURBANCE of 1156, for example, resulted largely from the frustrations and machinations of the junior retired emperor SUTOKU, who sought by force of arms the power that had been denied him.

Interpretations of Insei —— Japanese historians traditionally held that Go-Sanjō and Shirakawa deliberately established the cloister system as a new form of government to free the imperial house from domination by the Fujiwara regents. But because they and their successor cloistered emperors ruled in an equally extralegal manner, bypassing the institution of the throne, historians have discussed them in similarly negative terms.

Recent scholars, however, placing *insei* in the broader perspective of Heian political practice, have denied that it was a new form of government. They argue that the Cloister Office was not a separate "court," but rather a family administrative office. The Fujiwara, Minamoto, and other great courtier families had long maintained such offices (MANDOKORO) to govern and increase their estates and clients and otherwise to maintain and enhance family power. The establishment of the Cloister Office under the leadership of successive retired emperors was simply a reorganization of the imperial house along similar lines in order to compete more effectively for economic and political resources and power within the existing political system.

The difference between the new and traditional interpretations of cloister government may simply be one of emphasis, one view stressing its origins and the other its subsequent functions. In any case, it is a fact that Emperor Go-Sanjō restored political power to the imperial line and that the pattern of rule he established, whereby emperors relinquished the throne but continued to govern, continued until the warrior class wrested hegemony from the Heian nobility.

■ —— John W. Hall, *Government and Local Power in Japan, 500–1700* (1966). Hashimoto Yoshihiko, "Insei seiken no ichikōsatsu," *Shoryōbu kiyō* (Kunaichō) 4 (March 1955). G. Cameron Hurst III, *Insei: Abdicated Sovereigns in the Politics of Late Heian Japan* (1976). Ishimoda Shō, *Kodai makki seiji shi josetsu* (1964). Takeuchi Rizō, "Insei no seiritsu," in *Iwanami kōza: Nihon rekishi,* vol 4 (Iwanami Shoten, 1962). Herschel Webb, *The Japanese Imperial Institution in the Tokugawa Period* (1968). Yoshimura Shigeki, *Insei* (1958).   *G. Cameron* HURST III

Inson (1120–1198)

Buddhist sculptor of the latter part of the Heian period (794–1185) and early part of the Kamakura period (1185–1333); lived and worked in Heiankyō (now Kyōto). The leading representative of the IN SCHOOL and a member of the Shichijō-Ōmiya workshop, Inson received many important commissions, including the main restoration work at the Nara temples Tōdaiji and Kōfukuji, destroyed by fire in the Taira–Minamoto War (1180–85). Inson was honored with two Buddhist clerical titles—*hokkyō* in 1154 and *hōin* in 1183. His chief rivals were MYŌEN and Seichō (fl 1180–94). After Inson's

death the quality and fortunes of the In school gradually declined. No sculpture that can be definitely attributed to Inson has survived to the present day.

Installment Sales Law

(Kappu Hambai Hō). A law enacted in 1961 to ensure fairness in installment sales transactions and to protect the interests of purchasers. Amended in 1968 and 1972 to strengthen its consumer protection aspects, the current law comprises 6 chapters and 55 articles.

Under this law, an installment sale means the sale of certain designated products under terms calling for payment of the purchase price by the purchaser over a period of two months or longer in three or more payments. Cabinet Orders designate certain durable products as appropriate objects for the law's application.

The general thrust of the Installment Sales Law's provisions are as follows. (1) Merchants who sell the designated products by the installment sale method must disclose to purchasers the cash price, the installment sale price, the number and periods for payments, the annual rate for charges, and for layaway installment sales in which the purchase price is paid before delivery of the goods, the time of delivery, all according to regulations of the Ministry of International Trade and Industry. (2) The merchant must provide the purchaser with a written contract stating the terms of the transaction. (3) Installment sale contracts that result from door-to-door sales are subject to a four-day "cooling off" period. (4) A merchant may not cancel an installment sale contract for late payment of an installment without giving 20 days' written notice. (5) The law limits the amount of compensation for damages in the event of cancellation of the contract.

To prevent damage to consumers in the event of bankruptcy of a person in the business of making layaway installment sales—defined as collecting all or part of the purchase price from the purchaser in two or more payments before delivery of the designated goods—such merchants are required to obtain a license from the minister of international trade and industry and to make arrangements with a bank or other financial institution to preserve for the purchasers 50 percent of the amount of prepayments received. In addition, the law deals with loan-sale transactions, special prepayment transactions (in which the purchaser pays a membership fee in installments and receives services such as wedding and funeral services) and installment purchase agencies. See also DOOR-TO-DOOR SALES LAW.
                                                                      TAKEUCHI Akio

instant foods

The earliest example of "instant food" in Japan is *hoshi-ii;* or dried boiled rice, which was an essential provision for travelers and warriors in ancient times. In the 1920s, instant *shiruko* (a thick sweet soup made of adzuki beans) and instant curry sauce were introduced on the market. During World War II powdered *misoshiru* (bean-paste soup) and dried vegetables were used by the army. It has only been since the mid-1950s, however, with the appearance of instant *rāmen* (Chinese noodles), that instant foods have become familiar to the Japanese public. Besides instant noodles and coffee, a wide variety of frozen, freeze-dried, and vacuum-packed foods is available.
                                                                      ŌTSUKA Shigeru

Institute of Oriental Culture, Tōkyō University

(Tōkyō Daigaku Tōyō Bunka Kenkyūjo). Established in 1941, the institute consists of the Asian Studies Documents Center and 12 research departments specializing in Asian humanities, social sciences, law, and economics. In addition to teaching duties at Tōkyō University, the academic staff of some 118 persons conducts individual research projects; sponsors fieldwork projects, often overseas; and participates in international exchanges of scholars. Journals published: *Tōyō bunka kenkyūjo kiyō, Tōyō bunka.* Library resources: 309,332 volumes.
                                                                      Gina Lee BARNES

Institute of Pacific Relations

(Taiheiyō Mondai Chōsakai; IPR). Research institute founded in Honolulu in 1925 by private citizens from a number of Pacific countries, including the United States and Japan, to "study the conditions of the Pacific peoples with a view to the improvement of their mutual relations." Privately organized and financed, the institute consisted of councils and groups in each participating country and a

Pacific Council, consisting of one representative from each national council, which was to meet every two or three years. A conference to complete the organization, including designation of staff members, was held in Honolulu in 1927. Thirteen Council meetings were held, including one at Kyōto in 1929; the last meeting was in Lahore in 1957. Prominent members of the various member organizations of the IPR included Ray Lyman Wilbur (1875–1949), Philip C. Jessup (b 1897), Henry R. Luce (1898–1967), INOUE JUNNOSUKE, SHIBU-SAWA EIICHI, NITOBE INAZŌ, Takagi Yasaka (b 1889), George SAN-SOM, Arnold Toynbee (1889–1975), and Hu Shi (Hu Shih; 1891–1962). The councils that orignally formed the IPR represented Australia, Canada, China, Japan, New Zealand, and the United States; seven additional councils took part at various times, including the United Kingdom, France, the Philippines, India, and the Soviet Union. The subjects discussed at the Pacific Council meetings, in the IPR magazine, *Pacific Affairs,* and in the several hundred books and pamphlets it published covered a broad range of political, economic, and social issues like United States immigration legislation, Japan's policy in China, and the Chinese civil war. Japan's IPR council played an important role in Japanese-American relations until it merged with the League of Nations Association in 1935, and it resumed active participation after World War II. The American council of the IPR, the largest and most active of the national councils, came under political attack after the war because of the alleged pro-communist sympathies of leading members like Owen Lattimore (b 1900), who had been editor of *Pacific Affairs* from 1933 to 1941. Hearings by two congressional committees, led by Senator Joseph McCarthy (1908–57), greatly damaged the American council, which voted to dissolve itself in 1961. That same year the Japanese council was also dissolved. The magazine *Pacific Affairs* was continued under the sponsorship of the University of British Columbia in Canada.
📖——John N. Thomas, *The Institute of Pacific Relations* (1974).

Richard B. FINN

Institute of Physical and Chemical Research

(Rikagaku Kenkyūjo). Laboratory established in 1917 to advance and improve Japanese science and technology. Located in the city of Wakō, Saitama Prefecture. It has many achievements to its credit in the fields of basic and applied physics and chemistry and has produced many excellent scientists and technologists.

The demand for the establishment of a national scientific laboratory by the chemist TAKAMINE JŌKICHI in 1913 led to the creation of the Institute of Physical and Chemical Research with an imperial grant, a government subsidy, and private contributions. One of the institute's founders was ŌKŌCHI MASATOSHI. It was initially headed by KIKUCHI DAIROKU. Researchers have included chemists such as IKEDA KIKUNAE, SUZUKI UMETARŌ, and MAJIMA TOSHIYUKI. Outstanding physicists have included NAGAOKA HANTARŌ, TERADA TORAHIKO, HONDA KŌTARŌ, and NISHINA YOSHIO. It is the main center in Japan for the study of science and technology. After World War II the institute was briefly a private enterprise under the name Institute for Scientific Research (Kagaku Kenkyūjo). It was made a public corporation under its present name in 1958. Riken Industries (founded in 1927) is a commercial offshoot of the institute. Publications include the *Scientific Papers of the Institute of Physical and Chemical Research.*

insurance, miscellaneous

In Japan, all insurance other than life insurance is called *songai hoken* (nonlife or casualty insurance). Marine insurance and fire insurance were inaugurated in 1879 and 1888, respectively. Thereafter, various types of *songai hoken* have made their debut in the country.

Insurance handled by private insurance companies includes coverage for fire and automobile accidents, as well as compensation insurance, aimed chiefly at guaranteeing a minimum income. Additional types utilized principally by enterprises and businesses cover offices and stores, machinery, construction, as well as aircraft, cargoes, and hulls. The government insures nonprofitable risk that private insurance companies will not handle. Among these are forest insurance, shipowners' mutual insurance, and export credit insurance. In addition to practically every type of nonlife insurance found in Western countries, Japan also has special types such as a long-term comprehensive insurance that includes a savings plan and earthquake insurance.

As of 1981, there were 22 Japanese insurance companies and 40 foreign companies in the field of nonlife insurance in Japan. Premiums paid to these firms in 1980 totaled approximately ¥3.6 trillion

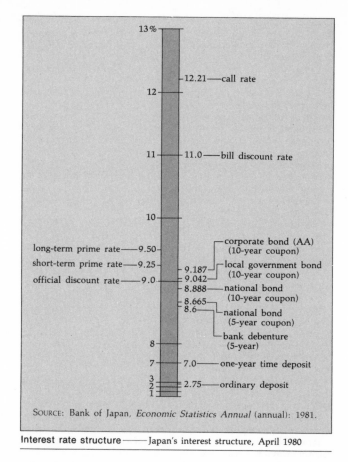

SOURCE: Bank of Japan, *Economic Statistics Annual* (annual): 1981.

Interest rate structure——Japan's interest structure, April 1980

(about US $15.8 billion). Japan ranks after the United States, West Germany, and France as an insurance market. See also INSURANCE SYSTEM.

Nagao Masakazu

insurance system

Since the introduction of European and American insurance systems in the latter part of the 19th century, insurance has developed along with the Japanese economy as a whole. It is now one of the most widespread insurance systems in the world. The 1980 earnings of Japanese miscellaneous (property and casualty) insurance companies ranked fourth in the world after the United States, West Germany, and France; life insurance ranked second after the United States in both policies sold and earnings.

History——In premodern Japan MUJIN (mutual financing associations) resembled the insurance systems of the West. Modern insurance systems made their appearance in the mid-19th century when the seclusion policies of the Tokugawa shogunate came to an end. Beginning in 1859 in port cities such as Yokohama and Nagasaki, foreign insurance firms opened up business to deal with foreign trading companies. The Tōkyō Marine Insurance Co (present-day TOKIO MARINE & FIRE INSURANCE CO, LTD) opened in 1879 as Japan's first marine insurance company. In 1881, Japan's first life insurance firm, the MEIJI MUTUAL LIFE INSURANCE CO, began business and was followed in 1888 by the Tōkyō Fire Insurance Co (present-day YASUDA FIRE & MARINE INSURANCE CO, LTD). Maritime insurance saw rapid growth before World War II due to the development of the maritime industry. The government began a simple national life insurance system in 1916 which received widespread use. As a means of effecting economic and social policies, the Japanese government established several forms of social insurance, beginning with health insurance in 1927. Japanese insurance systems received a severe blow with the outbreak of World War II. In postwar years, however, together with rapid recovery and economic growth, the insurance systems have developed into some of the world's best.

Private Insurance Companies——Japan has established an extremely strict regulatory system for its insurance enterprises. Detailed statutes control the opening of insurance firms and how business is to be conducted. The MINISTRY OF FINANCE acts as the

Interest rate structure

Japan's Official Discount Rate, 1945–1980

Year	Rate	Year	Rate
1945	3.29	1963	5.84
1946	3.65	1964	6.57
1947	3.65	1965	5.48
1948	5.11	1966	5.48
1949	5.11	1967	5.84
1950	5.11	1968	5.84
1951	5.84	1969	6.25
1952	5.84	1970	6.00
1953	5.84	1971	4.75
1954	5.84	1972	4.25
1955	7.30	1973	9.00
1956	7.30	1974	9.00
1957	8.40	1975	6.50
1958	7.30	1976	6.50
1959	7.30	1977	4.25
1960	6.94	1978	3.50
1961	7.30	1979	6.25
1962	6.57	1980	7.25

NOTE: Figures as of end of calendar years.
SOURCE: Nippon Ginkō (Bank of Japan), *Gaikoku keizai tōkei nempō* (annual): various issues.

regulatory agent, and insurance firms must obtain a license from this ministry in order to do business.

Insurance for private firms is divided into the two categories of property and casualty insurance (see INSURANCE, MISCELLANEOUS) and LIFE INSURANCE. Companies are not allowed to deal in both areas at the same time. As of 1981 there were 22 domestic firms and 40 foreign firms dealing in miscellaneous insurance, and 21 domestic and 2 foreign firms dealing in life insurance.

Insurance firms are divided into incorporated companies and mutual enterprises. Japan does not allow individuals to deal in insurance. Domestic miscellaneous insurance firms tend to be incorporated while mutual enterprises comprise the vast majority of the life insurance field. Miscellaneous insurance firms conduct sales through a network of some 260,000 agents. Life insurance firms employ some 300,000 sales representatives, the majority of whom are women. Insurance brokerage, which enjoys popularity in other countries, is not permitted in Japan.

Government Insurance Systems —— The government is involved in social insurance and industrial insurance systems. Social insurance is operated as one of the national SOCIAL SECURITY PROGRAMS, along with social welfare and public assistance. These programs cover expenses in cases of sickness, injury, maternity, death, old age, unemployment, and industrial accident. Social insurance systems for employed persons include health insurance, employee pensions, unemployment insurance, and workers' accident compensation insurance (see WORKERS' COMPENSATION). NATIONAL HEALTH INSURANCE and national PENSIONS are provided for the public at large.

Industrial insurance has been established to protect and promote selected industries. At present this includes woodlands, agricultural, and fishery insurance, as well as insurance programs to protect fishing vessels, housing loans, medium and small enterprises, and exports. The government acts as the insurer or reinsurer for these programs. See also MEDICAL AND HEALTH INSURANCE.

■■ ——Life Insurance Association of Japan, *Life Insurance Business in Japan* (Annual). Marine and Fire Insurance Association of Japan, *Non-life Insurance Facts in Japan* (Annual). Ministry of Finance, *Hoken nenkan* (Annual). KIMURA Eiichi

intangible property rights

(mutai zaisan ken). Exclusive rights in various types of intellectual creations such as literary and artistic works, inventions, devices, designs, trademarks, and trade names. These rights are broadly divided into copyright and industrial property. Since the estab-

lishment of the World Intellectual Property Organization by a 1967 convention in Stockholm, the expression *chiteki shoyū ken* (intellectual property rights) is more frequently used of various exclusive rights that fall under copyright and industrial property. See also KNOW-HOW. DOI Teruo

Interest Limitation Law

(Risoku Seigen Hō). A law that imposes maximum limits on interest for the purpose of limiting high rates of interest. The current law was promulgated in 1954, completely revising the old Interest Limitation Law proclaimed in 1877 by the Dajōkan (Great Council of State).

The maximum rate of interest is 20 percent in the case of a loan involving principal under ¥100,000 ($454 at $1 = ¥220), 18 percent in the case of principal in the amount of ¥100,000 or over but below ¥1 million ($4,545), and 15 percent in the case of principal in the amount of ¥1 million or over. If interest exceeds this limit, the interest in excess of the allowable amount will be deemed void (art. 1, sec. 1). If the obligor has already voluntarily paid this excess amount, he should, properly speaking, be able to demand its return, but the statute contains a special provision precluding such a claim (art. 1, sec. 2). Nevertheless, the Supreme Court has dulled the effect of the special provision by holding that the amount in excess of the allowable interest is to be applied to the principal, and that any amount remaining after the principal has been thus extinguished is unjust enrichment, the return of which may be demanded by the borrower.

The Interest Limitation Law is not strictly observed in Japan. There is a regulatory law applicable to persons in the business of lending which imposes a fine in the case of interest in excess of 109.5 percent per annum (0.3 percent per day), but by the same token, the charging of interest up to that amount, even if violative of the Interest Limitation Law, is in practice acknowledged.

The harshness of the high rates of interest charged by commercial lenders is considered to be a serious financial problem especially for consumers, and in the early 1980s proposals for lowering interest rates, as well as for revising the Interest Limitation Law, were being discussed. KATŌ Ichirō

interest rate structure

Japan's two key interest rates are the official discount rate of the BANK OF JAPAN, which is the rate at which the central bank discounts prime commercial notes presented to it by banks, and the long-term prime lending rate.

The official discount rate is decided by a committee of the Bank of Japan, after giving due consideration to economic and financial conditions. The official discount rate acts as a reference point for setting other short-term rates in the interest rate structure. For example, by agreement among banks, the short-term prime lending rate, or lowest rates at which banks will offer loans to their customers for a period of less than one year, is set 0.25 percent above the official discount rate. The average lending rates of banks are set with reference to the official discount rate, the short-term prime, and levels of deposit interest rates.

Deposit rates are controlled by the Bank of Japan acting together with the MINISTRY OF FINANCE. These deposit rates, along with the costs of funds from the Bank of Japan and money obtained from the interbank money markets, are the principal determinants of the funds costs of the banks. Rates in the interbank markets, the call and bill discount markets, in the past have been closely supervised and regulated by the Bank of Japan. But in recent years there has been a movement toward allowing increased freedom of movement of these rates in line with market demand and supply conditions.

The long-term prime rate is essentially a negotiated rate, set through discussions with a range of interest groups, including the Bank of Japan, the Ministry of Finance, long-term credit banks, trust banks, and securities companies. This type of rate exists in Japan, but not elsewhere, because long-term lending, at least in principle, is the province of specialized long-term credit banks and trust banks. In practice, the distinction between long-term credit banks and trust and ordinary commercial banks is not clear-cut, but a sufficiently large percentage of the lending of long-term and trust banks is still long-term, that is, loans of maturity of one year or more, to justify a long-term prime lending rate. The long-term prime is set with reference to the long-term government bond rate and the rates paid on savings certificates issued by long-term credit banks. The upper limits on the latter are set by the monetary authorities.

Although all rates are influenced in some degree by economic and financial conditions, rates on government bonds, and long-term prime and the Bank of Japan's official discount rate are determined by the monetary authorities. The same is true of various deposit rates, as noted above. Rates on bank lending, interbank money market rates, and rates on certificates of deposit at present are generally permitted to fluctuate in response to market forces. See also BANKING SYSTEM.

C. Tait RATCLIFFE

internal organization of Japanese companies

The internal organization of Japanese companies has played a part in Japan's post–World War II economic performance at the same time that it has been influenced by the latter, and the two are thus interdependent. Characteristics of Japanese firms such as career-long employment, the seniority system, enterprise unions, and especially group identity have contributed in major ways to Japan's industrial development. These features, coupled with the work ethic, have not remained static but have changed with the rapid growth and restructuring of the postwar economy. The most important issues affecting the internal organization of large Japanese firms are technological progress, aging of the work force, corporate diversification, and personnel motivation.

Impact of Technological Progress——"Bottom-up" decision making has played a central role in promoting technological imports, which were crucial to Japan's industrial development. Individual experts in the operations departments of Japanese companies had engaged in research and feasibility studies for new technologies largely without instruction from central planning departments. The latter's function was to provide financial and personnel support. As the technological gap between the advanced Western countries and Japan narrowed, however, Japanese companies have had to invest increasingly larger sums on research and development.

The central planning department, recognizing the need to allocate management resources optimally, has thus taken on more of a strategic function. Recently, central planning has begun to institute more "top-down" decision making for better long-range planning and to make more thorough evaluations of the costs and benefits. In contrast to the phase of large-scale technology imports during the 1950s and 1960s, when the trial-and-error experiences of foreign firms were absorbed by lower-ranking experts, more emphasis is now being placed on higher decision making concerning technological innovation.

Impact of Changing Demographic Structure——The increase in average lifespan will continue to affect the employment system significantly, despite the fact that in Japan only one-third of the labor force is covered by the "lifetime" employment system. These workers are assured of their jobs until they reach 55 years of age, or a few years later, depending on the firm. Such guarantees began as a practice in the 1930s, when average longevity was just beyond 55. Currently, the average Japanese lives to 75 or 80 years of age, and many workers consider the 55 mandatory retirement age of most large companies to be too young.

Because of a decline in the economic growth rate there is a decrease in the number of positions for senior executives. During periods of rapid economic expansion personal conflicts could be resolved by promoting senior staff. In most cases this is no longer possible. In most companies, the proportion of older employees to young workers is growing, making transfer of senior staff more difficult.

Large companies are dealing with the aging work force in part by adopting the merit system for middle-age employees while providing more attractive retirement benefits. Many companies have begun offering older staff improved early retirement packages in order to allow middle-age employees to move up in corporate ranks. There is also a movement to raise the retirement age beyond 55 years.

Impact of Corporate Diversification——Japanese companies have fewer affiliates than their Western counterparts, stemming largely from the use of personal contacts rather than financial control to solidify ties between firms. Yet many Japanese companies have been forced to diversify as markets became saturated and consumers demanded more product diversity. Corporate diversification has often taken the form of vertical integration, resulting in a new importance for "top-down" management and for study of American and European managerial techniques. Companies have started to conduct detailed analyses to establish information systems.

Changing Motivation of Personnel——High motivation among workers and a strong work ethic have contributed greatly to the dynamism of Japanese companies. It is often stated that Japanese internal corporate organization is based on labor and American corporate organization relies on capital. Improved living standards, however, have resulted in a relaxed work ethic and increased demands from Japanese employees. The younger generation emphasizes leisure as well as work. The job turnover ratio is also growing. Within three years, approximately 75 percent of workers with a junior high school degree change jobs; among high school graduates the figure is 50 percent; and among college graduates, 20 percent. Raising motivation, especially among noncollege graduates, has been an important issue for Japanese managers.

To enhance worker motivation, Japanese management is taking four approaches: raising incomes, paying more attention to the wishes and complaints of individual employees, adopting proposals made by workers, and valuing individualism more highly. The Japanese believe the Western assumption that higher salaries tend to increase motivation. Giving greater attention to individual employees has become the task of personnel departments and middle-level managers. Taking workers' suggestions uses information acquired by employees and increases their sense of participation.

Japanese management, wishing to achieve corporate objectives and to adapt to socioeconomic changes, has found broader studies of internal organization essential, whereas previously firms relied more heavily on personal contact and human relations. In the coming decade it is likely that Japanese management will lean toward an increasingly "scientific" system of management, resembling that promulgated in Europe and the United States since the late 19th century. See EMPLOYMENT SYSTEM, MODERN; WAGE SYSTEM; LABOR UNIONS.

📖——Rodney Clark, *The Japanese Company* (1979). Robert E. Cole, *Work, Mobility, and Participation* (1979). J. Victor Koschmann, ed, *Authority and the Individual in Japan* (1978). Richard Tanner Pascale and Anthony G. Athos, *The Art of Japanese Management* (1981).

INOUE Munemichi

International Christian University

(Kokusai Kirisutokyō Daigaku). A private, coeducational university located in the city of Mitaka, Tōkyō Prefecture. It was established in 1953 by a foundation composed of 15 different Protestant denominations in the United States and a group of Japanese Christians, for the purpose of providing higher education based on Christian values through bilingual instruction (Japanese and English). YUASA HACHIRŌ was the first president of the university. The administrative and educational system resembles an American college of liberal arts, with courses in humanities, social science, natural science, languages, and education. It is known for its Institute of Educational Research and Services, Social Science Research Institute, Institute for the Study of Christianity and Culture, and Institute of Asian Studies. Enrollment stood at 1,803 in 1980.

international communications

The principal means and sources of Japanese communications with the rest of the world community are news agencies, both foreign and domestic, news correspondents, communications satellites, business networks, and international telegraph and telephone.

Japanese News Agencies——The major Japanese news agencies are the KYŌDO NEWS SERVICE and JIJI PRESS. Kyōdo and Jiji, as well as NHK (Japan Broadcasting Corporation) and leading newspapers, each have from 20 to 30 branch offices in foreign countries where they station correspondents. Of the 50 or 60 news articles that Kyōdo distributes daily to newspapers and broadcasting stations, telegrams from their own correspondents account for approximately one-half, the other half being supplied by foreign news agencies.

The Kyōdo News Service transmits news in English to newspapers and news agencies around the world by means of private cable or teletype; to branches of overseas newspapers and news agencies, and foreign embassies and legations in Tōkyō; and to Japanese-language newspapers in foreign countries by facsimile transmission in Japanese. It also mails weekly English newsletters to approximately 40 countries. Jiji Press transmits news abroad in English, Chinese, and Spanish; its foreign bureaus issue reports of news from home in Japanese for resident Japanese overseas. However, the communication of Japanese news to the world at large is still chiefly handled by world news agencies.

Foreign News Agencies —— Japanese newspapers and broadcasting stations mainly use for their sources of international news and events the news agencies of the capitalist countries, such as Associated Press, United Press International, Reuters, and Agence France-Presse. It is quite rare that news from the news agencies of socialist countries, such as Tass and Xinhua She (Hsin-hua She) is heard or read by the ordinary citizen. This is because the evaluation of the news is different or the news arrives too late to be newsworthy. In addition to contracting directly with foreign news agencies, leading Japanese newspapers and broadcasting stations contract with the Kyōdō News Service and Jiji Press, which themselves contract with 47 and 14 foreign news agencies, respectively. In 1979 the Japanese news media paid over ¥1 billion (over US $4 million) to foreign news agencies in total yearly fees under contract, which made Japan a major market for foreign news agencies. The volume of news flowing into the Kyōdō News Service reaches one million words per day, but dwindles to roughly 3,000 words when translated and distributed to newspapers and broadcasting stations.

Business Communications —— The news media are not the only organizations that engage in international communication. General trading companies and large businesses actively handle a much greater volume of news than the agencies. For example, MITSUI & CO, LTD, has a network connecting 136 overseas points with 1,035 overseas representatives (as of January 1978) and over 2,000 local employees. The main branch in Japan receives an average of 20,000 pieces of information daily. Altogether, the number of overseas representatives of the nine major trading firms reaches nearly 6,000, many times the number of foreign correspondents of the news media. This information network has greatly contributed to the high growth of the Japanese economy.

Television Relay —— Television picture and sound was relayed to and from Japan by satellite for the first time on 23 November 1963, when NHK received and relayed news of the assassination of President John F. Kennedy. In 1964 the Tōkyō Olympic Games were transmitted worldwide by satellite. Japanese television networks make hundreds of international relays each year.

International Telephone and Telegraph —— In 1978 there were 4 million international telegraphic messages dispatched to and from Japan, and 27 million messages sent via subscribed international telegraph (telex). Over 15 million international telephone calls were made the same year.   *ARAI Naoyuki*

international crimes

Crimes involving offenses or persons in more than one country. The criminality of an offense is determined in each nation according to its own criminal law, and infringements upon the laws of each country become subject to punishment. As international travel and transactions involving several countries have become more common, international crime has increased. The International Criminal Police Organization was initiated in an effort to curtail such crime. Under Japanese criminal law, certain serious crimes committed by Japanese abroad, such as sedition, murder, and arson, are still punishable in Japan as "overseas crimes" (kokugaihan).

Acts such as piracy, buying or selling of slaves, and illicit drug dealing are considered international crimes, which each nation punishes in its domestic courts according to its own criminal law. Recently nations have occasionally begun to take joint action against such crimes, considering them as "common enemies of humanity" or matters affecting the common good of all civilized nations.

In international law, war and other exercises of military force have come to be prohibited as offenses against international society as a whole. The Nuremburg Trials and the WAR CRIMES TRIALS in Tōkyō after World War II led to the first instances of punishment for this type of international crime.   *HIGASHI Jutarō*

international cultural exchange

Between the OPENING OF JAPAN to foreign contact in the late 19th century and World War I, cultural exchange in Japan stressed the importation of Western culture rather than the introduction abroad of its own culture. Behind this effort was the intention of creating a modern state based on the Western model. Foreign experts were hired (see FOREIGN EMPLOYEES OF THE MEIJI PERIOD) and students and government officials were sent abroad for study. Following World War I, the importance of promoting international understanding of Japan through cultural exchange was recognized, and in 1934 the Kokusai Bunka Shinkōkai (Japan Cultural Society; KBS) was established to further overseas cultural activities. In the period

of recovery following World War II, there was virtually no Japanese involvement in international cultural exchange. Rapid economic growth in the 1960s, however, accompanied by increased visibility in the international community, prompted greater interest in Japanese culture. With the aim of conducting Japan's international cultural relations more systematically, the Japanese government reorganized the Kokusai Bunka Shinkōkai, naming the new organization the JAPAN FOUNDATION (1972).

Among the programs that are implemented by the government or its agencies are: (1) educational exchange, including the exchange of students and scholars; (2) academic exchange, including support of Japanese studies and promotion of Japanese language teaching abroad; (3) artistic exchange, including sponsoring of performing and visual art programs on Japan; (4) cultural materials exchange, including production and distribution of books, films, and television programs on Japanese culture; and (5) multilateral cultural exchange, including cooperation with UNESCO, SEAMEO (Southeast Asian Ministers of Education Organization), ASEAN Fund, and other international organizations.

The government agencies involved in international cultural exchange are primarily the Ministry of Foreign Affairs and the Ministry of Education. At the Ministry of Foreign Affairs, it is the Public Information and Cultural Affairs Bureau which directly handles the business of cultural exchange. It negotiates cultural agreements, convenes conferences on international cultural exchange, collaborates with other cultural exchange organizations, and sponsors cultural events at Japanese diplomatic missions overseas. The office in charge of academic exchange at the Ministry of Education is the Science and International Affairs Bureau. Its activities include, among other things, development of programs for international education, administration of study abroad programs, support of international collaborative research, and cooperation with international cultural and educational organizations. The Prime Minister's Office and the Science and Technology Agency also sponsor cultural exchange programs.

The Japan Foundation and the JAPAN SOCIETY FOR THE PROMOTION OF SCIENCE are two major public corporations established by the government explicitly for the purpose of promoting international cultural and academic exchanges. The activities of the JAPAN INTERNATIONAL COOPERATION AGENCY include some programs that are related to cultural exchange. There are also some 175 private foundations and cultural organizations whose activities relate in a substantial measure to the promotion of international cultural exchange. They include such organizations as the Hōsō Bunka Foundation, the International House of Japan, the Japan Association of International Education, the Japan Center for International Exchange, the Toyota Foundation, and the Yoshida International Education Foundation. In addition, a large number of educational institutions, civic organizations, and municipalities are involved in a wide range of international cultural and educational activities.

SUGIYAMA Yasushi

international friendship organizations

The Japanese government has been active in the postwar period in encouraging cultural exchange with various nations throughout the world, particularly with Asian and other Third World nations. Various private organizations also play a role in international exchange.

The Institute of Asian Economic Affairs (since 1969, the Institute of Developing Economies) was established in 1958 to carry out research into the economies, societies, politics, and legal systems of the developing nations in Asia and to draw up plans for economic cooperation and exchange. It is also active in the training of economic specialists in the developing countries and in joint research projects with such scholars. In recent years its sphere of activities has been extended to include Africa as well.

In 1961 the OVERSEAS ECONOMIC COOPERATION FUND was founded to provide funds for assisting the development of nations in Asia, Africa, and Central and Latin America; it is a special status corporation funded by the Japanese government. Nine years later, in 1970, the Asia Trade Development Association was established for the promotion of industry in the developing countries and of imports to Japan of primary products from those nations; this organization is now known as the Japan Overseas Development Corporation.

Then in 1974 the JAPAN INTERNATIONAL COOPERATION AGENCY was formed by combining the Overseas Technical Cooperation Agency, the Japan Emigration Service, and the Overseas Agricultural Development Foundation; this is also a special service corporation funded by the Japanese government. It is responsible for aid to Japanese emigrants abroad and for the dispatch of technical information and resources to developing nations; the JAPAN OVERSEAS COOPERATION VOLUNTEERS, the Japanese equivalent of the American Peace Corps, is also under its jurisdiction.

Through the Japan International Cooperation Agency, centers have been established for the propagation of technical skills in Burma, Malaysia, the Philippines, Thailand, Egypt, Peru, and other countries. Japan has provided equipment and trained personnel, and the host countries have been responsible for the necessary land, buildings, native staff, and operating funds; upon the expiration of the agreed term of joint cooperation, the entire facilities become the property of the host country. The training carried out at these centers includes instruction in such fields as agriculture, fishing, medicine, and telecommunications.

Branches of such international organizations as the LIONS CLUB, ROTARY CLUB, and KIWANIS CLUB have been founded in Japan, but their role tends to be limited to socializing on the local level. In addition, in 1974 the JAPAN CHAMBER OF COMMERCE AND INDUSTRY, aided by government funds, established the Asian Club for Promoting Economic Cultural Communication, now known as the Asian Club. The Japanese economic advance into Asia in the 1960s and 1970s had aroused much opposition and criticism there, and this organization was aimed at improving relations with these countries. Composed primarily of businessmen, with scholars, journalists, and government officials also participating, it tries to develop concrete policies for promoting economic ties between Japan and the other Asian nations.

Friendship societies between Japan and individual nations also are active; these play a particularly important role in the case of countries without normal diplomatic relations with Japan. For example, before the normalization of relations with the Soviet Union, the Japan–Soviet Society and the Japan–Soviet Friendship Society were instrumental in economic and technological as well as cultural exchange. Similarly, the Japan–China Friendship Association and the Japan–China Association for Economy and Trade played an important role in the resumption of diplomatic relations and the conclusion of a peace treaty between these two nations. Other such organizations include the America–Japan Society, the Japan-US Friendship Commission, and the Japan–Korea Friendship Association. The Shimoda Conference (Japanese American Assembly) aiming at the bettering of Japanese-American relations is held frequently, and in 1970 a Japanese branch of Amnesty International was established. The latter helped organize an Amnesty International Pacific Regional Meeting in Japan in 1976. See also INTERNATIONAL CULTURAL EXCHANGE; JAPAN FOUNDATION; JAPAN P.E.N. CLUB. HOMMA Yasuhei

International Monetary Fund → IMF

international relations

Japan's relations with foreign nations, following abandonment of the shogunal policy of NATIONAL SECLUSION in 1853–54, can be divided into the periods before and after the end of World War II. The first period witnessed the entrance of Japan into the community of nations, its participation as an equal in international affairs, and the development and collapse of the GREATER EAST ASIA COPROSPERITY SPHERE. The second period includes the Allied OCCUPATION (1945–52), the SAN FRANCISCO PEACE TREATY (1951), admission to the United Nations (1956), and the gradual rebuilding of an independent diplomatic policy.

The Opening of Japan —— After the arrival in Japan of Commodore Matthew PERRY and his "black ships" (see KUROFUNE) in 1853, the Tokugawa shogunate was forced to agree to the OPENING OF JAPAN in the KANAGAWA TREATY of 1854. Formal diplomatic relations were soon established with the United Kingdom, Russia, the Netherlands, and other Western countries. Japan had essentially been forcibly incorporated into an international system developed by the Western powers, and the various treaties of friendship and commerce it concluded with Western nations contained broad grants of extraterritoriality and restrictions of Japan's right to levy customs duties. When the new Meiji government was formed in 1868, it set as a goal the establishment of Japan as a modern state, and it thus denounced the prejudicial terms of the treaties with the West. The effort to revise these unequal treaties, however, was not successful for decades afterwards (see UNEQUAL TREATIES, REVISION OF).

Territorial Issues and Treaty Revision —— As with many premodern states, Japan's national borders were not clearly established, and territorial disputes thus became a central concern of Japan's early international relations. The Kuril Islands, a chain between Kamchatka and Hokkaidō, had been divided between Russia and Japan by the Russo-Japanese Treaty of Amity (1855), but disposition of the island of SAKHALIN remained undecided. Sakhalin was inhabited by both Japanese and Russians even after the establishment of the Meiji government. Negotiations between Japan and Russia to resolve the dispute over Sakhalin resulted, in May 1875, in the signing of the Treaty of ST. PETERSBURG (Sakhalin-Kuril Islands Exchange Treaty) according to which all of the Kuril Islands came into the possession of Japan and Sakhalin went to Russia.

Japan placed the OGASAWARA ISLANDS in the Pacific Ocean southeast of Japan under the jurisdiction of its Home Ministry in 1876, thus consolidating its territorial title. The United States, Britain, and other countries were notified of Japan's unilateral action. The RYŪKYŪ ISLANDS in the South China Sea, long a tributary kingdom of China, had come under the control of the Satsuma domain in 1609. The Ryūkyū kingdom maintained a tributary relationship with China, however, and when the Meiji government took initial administrative steps to establish full sovereignty over the islands, a dispute with China developed. Japan's claim to the islands was formalized as a direct result of its victory in the SINO-JAPANESE WAR OF 1894–1895.

The revision of the "Unequal Treaties" was a subject of negotiation when the IWAKURA MISSION toured the United States and Europe between 1871 and 1873. Succeeding foreign ministers also sought the resolution of this problem, but Western powers were reluctant to relinquish vested rights, and negotiations proceeded slowly. It was not until the signing of the ANGLO-JAPANESE COMMERCIAL TREATY OF 1894 that the extraterritorial rights of a foreign power were first abolished. Japan did not recover fully autonomous customs rights or attain equal status in diplomatic relations with the Western nations until 1911.

Expansion on the Asian Mainland —— Another issue confronting the Meiji government was the threat to Japan's security posed by the unstable political situation on the Korean peninsula. Toward the end of the 19th century, growing internal strife in Korea provided foreign powers with an opportunity to intervene. China based its involvement on the tributary relationship Korea had maintained for several centuries, but the Chinese military and political presence on the peninsula caused friction to develop with Japan. Following numerous political crises, including the IMO MUTINY of July 1882, the KAPSIN POLITICAL COUP of December 1884, and the TONGHAK REBELLION of 1894, war broke out between Japan and China. Japan's defeat of China, which had been considered the dominant nation in East Asia, brought Japan recognition as an important power in the region. In the agreement ending the hostilities, China ceded Taiwan and the Pescadores, giving Japan its first colonies and providing it with a springboard to expand its influence to the south (see SHIMONOSEKI, TREATY OF). Reparation money received from China played a significant role in the industrialization of Japan, while the opening of numerous Chinese ports and cities to Japanese industry and commerce established a legal base for future economic expansion in the Chinese domestic market.

Japan's overwhelming victory in its first large-scale modern war increased Japanese pride vis-à-vis foreign countries and implanted in the minds of some the idea that war was an effective means of territorial expansion. Consequently, there was a strong popular reaction when the TRIPARTITE INTERVENTION by Russia, Germany, and France forced Japan to give up the Liaodong (Liaotung) Peninsula, which it had obtained from China after the war. This development had a great impact on the political leaders of Japan and convinced them that the isolation of Japan from the international community must be avoided.

Japan as a Major Power —— Although the Japanese victory eliminated Chinese influence in Korea, Japan did not gain control over the peninsula. Russia took China's place as Japan's rival, and a growing atmosphere of confrontation emerged.

China's weakness was made fully apparent by the Sino-Japanese war, and in the aftermath the Western powers vied with one another to obtain leased territories and expand influence on the continent. Japan had emerged as a power in Asia and was ready to enter the struggle among the imperialist nations. The confrontation between Japan and Russia spread to Manchuria. During the BOXER REBELLION in 1900, Japan, Russia, and other nations sent troops to China to quell the insurgents; Russia maintained troops in Manchuria after the rebellion and aroused the suspicion of some Japanese, who perceived a grave threat. Under these circumstances, Japanese leaders came to believe that war with Russia was inevitable.

A military alliance concluded between Japan and Britain in January 1902 also played an important role in preparing the way for the RUSSO-JAPANESE WAR of 1904–05. The ANGLO-JAPANESE ALLIANCE, the first military treaty ever concluded by Japan with a foreign country, was renewed in 1905 and 1911 and remained for 20 years the strongest pillar of Japan's foreign policy. The pro-British sentiment of the Japanese people—particularly among upper class Japanese—nurtured during this period was an important factor in the development of Japan's international relations prior to World War II. See UNITED KINGDOM AND JAPAN.

Japan's victory over Russia—the first victory by a modern Asian power in a war with a Western nation—increased the self-confidence of the Japanese people and accelerated the nation's movement down the road to MILITARISM. As spoils of war, Japan obtained the southern half of Sakhalin and the Russian lease concessions in China, including the Liaodong Peninsula; the latter provided a foothold for eventual Japanese political domination of southern Manchuria. Japan, now the unrivaled power on the Korean peninsula, finally annexed Korea in 1910 and controlled the country for the following 35 years. See KOREA AND JAPAN: Japanese colonial control of Korea.

Japanese foreign policy began to show an increasing inclination toward imperialist expansionism. In a series of agreements with Russia in 1907, 1910, and 1912, Japan established a sphere of influence in south Manchuria and the eastern part of Inner Mongolia (see RUSSO-JAPANESE AGREEMENTS OF 1907–1916). With the SOUTH MANCHURIA RAILWAY as a lever, Japan began to strengthen its position in the two areas with the ultimate aim of monopolizing their markets and natural resources. This effort, however, stood in direct opposition to the American OPEN DOOR POLICY, which was based on equal access to Chinese markets. A dispute developed between Japan and the United States around the issue of railway rights and interests in Manchuria, and this was compounded by the problem of restrictions on Japanese immigration to the United States (see JAPANESE AMERICANS) and the threat each country posed to the other as the strongest naval powers in the Pacific.

World War I and Its Aftermath —— World War I resulted in the further elevation of Japan's international status and provided the country with an opportunity to fulfill its ambition of expanding influence on the Chinese continent. With the attention of the Western powers centered on Europe, Japan intensified efforts to strengthen its position in south Manchuria and eastern Inner Mongolia. Japan sought formal recognition of its occupation of the German holdings on the Shandong (Shantung) Peninsula, the extension of the terms of its leases, and a general increase of its influence over the Chinese in the TWENTY-ONE DEMANDS presented to the government of the Republic of China in January 1915.

Japan was included as one of the five victorious nations at the peace conference at Versailles (see VERSAILLES, TREATY OF) and was thus formally recognized as a power of the first order. At the same time, the League of Nations extended to Japan the mandate for the Pacific islands formerly held by Germany. Japan was able to expand its control of the Shandong Peninsula and was well on its way to becoming one of the dominant powers in Asia and the Pacific. However, Japan's strong pressure in China sparked antagonism among the Chinese, and tension and confrontation between Japan and China increased.

After Versailles, the stage was once again set for power politics involving Japan and the Western powers in East Asia. The emergence of Russian communism and Chinese nationalism complicated the political situation, and it became necessary for Japan to adjust its relations with the United States and Britain to prevent the new influences from changing the status quo in East Asia. It was also necessary for Japan to keep in political step with the United States and Britain, because Japan had developed heavy commercial and financial dependence upon them.

The WASHINGTON CONFERENCE of 1921–22 formulated a system of international cooperation called the "Washington System"; during the 1920s, Japan acted as a country interested in maintaining political equilibrium in Asia, while it also worked to maintain its established interests. When the Nationalist Party (Guomindang or Kuomintang) of China extended its sphere of activity to include Manchuria and Inner Mongolia, which were under Japanese influence, Japan responded with extreme measures, such as the Shandong (Shantung) Expeditions (see SHANDONG [SHANTUNG]

QUESTION) and the assassination of ZHANG ZUOLIN (Chang Tso-lin), which offended the United States.

Incursions in Manchuria and China —— The MANCHURIAN INCIDENT of September 1931 and the establishment of the Japanese puppet state MANCHUKUO in 1932 brought the Japan–US confrontation in Asia close to the point of explosion. Japan ignored the NINE-POWER TREATY and other legal restrictions, and used military force to protect its interests in Manchuria, indicating openly its intention to place Manchuria under Japanese political control. The United States responded with the Stimson Doctrine (see NONRECOGNITION POLICY) opposing all of Japan's activities in Manchuria.

Japan's challenge to the "Washington System" was denounced by a large majority of the members of the League of Nations, which supported the basic lines of the 1932 LYTTON COMMISSION recommendation of an accommodation between Japan and China. In response, Japan left the League of Nations in March 1933 (see LEAGUE OF NATIONS AND JAPAN). As the confrontation grew increasingly bitter, Japan increased its imperialist penetration of mainland Asia in order to compensate for the economic loss resulting from estrangement from the United States and Britain. From Manchuria, Japan extended its influence into northern China.

Meanwhile, the military dominance of Japan over the entire area of Manchuria created tension in Japan-Soviet relations, further isolating Japan from the world and giving rise to the possibility of an alliance with Nazi Germany, which was then calling for a revision of the European political order established at Versailles. Cooperation between Japan and Germany was established by the November 1936 ANTI-COMINTERN PACT, which linked Japan with the Berlin-Rome Axis and formed the basis for the tripartite military alliance created in 1940. See also GERMANY AND JAPAN; ITALY AND JAPAN.

Japan's expansion into northern China escalated into general armed conflict, triggered by the MARCO POLO BRIDGE INCIDENT in July 1937. The scope of Japanese military activities in China gradually increased, and the United States reacted by enforcing an embargo against Japan. (See SINO-JAPANESE WAR OF 1937–1945.)

World War II and the Greater East Asia Coprosperity Sphere
The scope of Japanese ambitions continued to expand. The 1938 declaration of a TŌA SHINCHITSUJO (New Order in East Asia), followed in 1940 by the announcement of the Greater East Asia Coprosperity Sphere, which included Southeast Asia, clearly stated Japan's desire for a new political order throughout Asia. The outbreak of WORLD WAR II in Europe in September 1939 had a decisive influence on Japanese foreign policy. Impressed by the sweeping victories of the German forces in Western Europe, Japan had negotiated the TRIPARTITE PACT of September 1940 with Germany and Italy. In the same month, Japan invaded the northern part of French Indochina in order to gain access to strategic raw materials and further its Asian strategy (see INDOCHINA, JAPANESE OCCUPATION OF). Already in the spring of 1940, Japan had set up a Chinese puppet government led by WANG JINGWEI (Wang Ching-wei).

The complete collapse of Japan-U.S. relations seemed imminent. Negotiations were held in Washington, but they proved fruitless. Japan attempted to shore up its position with the Soviet-Japanese Neutrality Pact in April 1941, but this too proved ineffective. Japan then advanced into the southern part of French Indochina, and in retaliation the United States froze Japanese assets in the United States and banned oil exports to Japan. The stage was set for a decisive showdown. The Japanese government, faced with the choice between bowing to the United States or resorting to military force, upon receiving the Hull Note made its final decision—to go to war.

With the start of the Pacific War in December 1941, Japan came into armed conflict with all the major countries with territories bordering the Pacific, except the Soviet Union: the United States, Britain, France, the Netherlands, China, and Australia. Overwhelming victories in the initial stages of the war opened the way for Japanese occupation and military administration of French Indochina, the Philippines, the Dutch East Indies, Malaya, and Burma. The Greater East Asia Conference, held in Tōkyō in November 1943, was attended by the chief executives of the Japanese-backed governments of Occupied China, Thailand, Manchukuo, the Philippines, and Burma. The conference adopted a Greater East Asia Declaration affirming the coexistence and coprosperity of the nations of Asia, and it seemed as if Japan's dream of a united Asia was about to be realized. However, the declaration was empty of substance, and the conference itself a sham. Imperial Japan, at the height of its power, was on the verge of collapse.

International relations

Selected Indicators of Japan's Foreign Relations						
Country[1]	Type of diplomatic mission in Japan (1 January 1983)	Type of Japanese diplomatic mission (1 January 1983)	Exports to Japan in thousands of US dollars (1982)	Imports from Japan in thousands of US dollars (1982)	Foreign nationals residing in Japan[2] (31 December 1982)	Japanese nationals residing abroad[3] (1 October 1981)
Asia						
Democratic Republic of Afghanistan[4]	E	E	620	96,626	93	14
People's Republic of Bangladesh	E	E	56,221	210,668	266	355
Kingdom of Bhutan	—	—	12	2,047	7	1
Socialist Republic of the Union of Burma	E	E	48,978	230,812	213	370
People's Republic of China	E*	E*	5,352,417	3,510,825	59,122	6,601
Republic of India	E*	E*	1,122,105	1,408,298	2,232	912
Republic of Indonesia	E*	E°	12,004,985	4,260,554	1,494	6,792
Democratic Kampuchea	E[5]	E°	573	5,316	358	—
Republic of Korea	E*	E*	3,253,813	4,881,133	} 669,854	2,836
Democratic People's Republic of Korea	—	—	152,026	313,162		—
Lao People's Democratic Republic	E	E	1,158	9,786	500	40
Malaysia	E	E*	3,009,574	2,502,017	970	3,539
Republic of Maldives	—	E°	3,121	2,298	1	16
Mongolian People's Republic	E	E	8,000	1,786	18	31
Kingdom of Nepal	E	E	1,411	54,112	138	214
Islamic Republic of Pakistan	E	E*	236,133	765,343	497	375
Republic of the Philippines	E*	E*	1,576,210	1,802,969	6,563	4,365
Republic of Singapore	E*	E	1,826,119	4,373,218	706	9,078
Democratic Socialist Republic of Sri Lanka	E	E	70,890	226,293	364	307
Kingdom of Thailand	E	E	1,040,695	1,907,094	1,974	6,768
Socialist Republic of Vietnam	E	E	36,018	92,339	3,132	60
(Taiwan)	—	—	4,717,792	2,443,115	—	5,100
(Hong Kong)	—	CG	622,268	4,717,792	—	7,802
Middle East						
State of Bahrain	—	E°	277,842	227,452	6	198
Islamic Republic of Iran	E	E*	2,566,883	934,904	319	595
Republic of Iraq	E	E	779,534	2,755,179	138	4,425
State of Israel	E	E	186,291	202,245	175	128
Hashemite Kingdom of Jordan	E	E	17,734	249,038	33	345
State of Kuwait	E	E	1,626,571	1,789,937	15	1,205
Republic of Lebanon	E	E	115	159,683	42	34
Sultanate of Oman	E	E°	1,702,408	460,544	0	51
State of Qatar	E	E	1,783,775	347,360	2	276
Kingdom of Saudi Arabia	E	E	20,527,593	6,621,316	82	3,172
Syrian Arab Republic	E	E	1,553	167,943	70	101
United Arab Emirates	E	E	7,982,868	1,492,530	0	1,339
Yemen Arab Republic	E	E°	1,533	190,928	1	138
People's Democratic Republic of Yemen	E	E°	18,443	89,394	5	109
Oceania						
Australia	E*	E*	6,961,157	4,580,588	1,419	5,793
Fiji	E	E	5,747	53,561	20	110
Republic of Kiribati	E°	E°	925	4,059	0	2
Republic of Nauru	C	E°	2,248	2,149	1	2
New Zealand	E	E*	857,473	928,570	424	693
Papua New Guinea	E	E*	286,369	127,415	17	334
Solomon Islands	—	E	42,953	8,322	3	47
Kingdom of Tonga	—	E°	28	1,552	25	22
Tuvalu	E°	E°	—	1,542	0	0
Republic of Vanuatu	—	E°	288	5,231	0	31
Western Samoa	—	E°	3,961	4,480	29	56
Africa						
Democratic and People's Republic of Algeria	E	E	525,080	677,204	129	1,242
People's Republic of Angola	—	E°	1,511	52,042	2	65
People's Republic of Benin	—	E°	3,125	27,213	0	2
Republic of Botswana	—	E°	377	1,057	0	1
Republic of Burundi	E°	E°	2,382	12,722	0	1
United Republic of Cameroon	—	E°	38,214	71,483	3	16
Republic of Cape Verde	—	E°	2	292	0	0
Central African Republic	E	E	6,969	5,161	1	9
Republic of Chad	E°	E°	650	5	1	0
Federal and Islamic Republic of the Comoros	—	E°	107	118	0	0
People's Republic of the Congo	—	E°	11,429	22,973	2	6
Republic of Djibouti	—	E°	1	25,011	0	0
Arab Republic of Egypt	E	E	166,569	661,093	222	1,100
Republic of Equatorial Guinea	E°	E°	37	62	0	0
Ethiopia	E	E	31,700	56,819	31	49
Gabonese Republic	E	E	10,786	45,634	35	24
Republic of the Gambia	—	E°	—	5,860	0	0
Republic of Ghana	E	E	77,095	22,723	42	110
People's Revolutionary Republic of Guinea	E	E	109	4,126	2	11
Republic of Guinea-Bissau	—	E°	—	995	0	0
Republic of Ivory Coast	E	E	49,030	74,039	4	145
Republic of Kenya	E	E	9,347	112,762	61	671
Kingdom of Lesotho	—	E°	15	77	1	2
Republic of Liberia	E	E	165,866	1,008,538	3	26
Socialist People's Libyan Arab Jamahiriya	E	E	46,120	284,960	75	682
Democratic Republic of Madagascar	E	E	40,549	22,889	6	86
Republic of Malawi	—	E°	12,267	13,503	3	196
Republic of Mali	E°	E°	4,132	5,322	2	51
Islamic Republic of Mauritania	—	E°	56,920	9,438	1	14
Mauritius	—	E°	118	15,783	12	36
Kingdom of Morocco	E	E	107,048	80,834	20	105
People's Republic of Mozambique	—	E°	22,226	17,788	1	67
Republic of Niger	E°	E°	1,143	15,877	0	21
Federal Republic of Nigeria	E	E	8,002	1,209,057	93	906
Republic of Rwanda	E	E°	2,496	22,617	1	1
Democratic Republic of São Tomé and Príncipe	—	E°	—	890	0	0
Republic of Senegal	E	E	14,169	14,569	7	52
Republic of Seychelles	—	E°	772	4,429	6	1
Republic of Sierra Leone	E°	E°	811	20,792	0	6
Somali Democratic Republic	E	E°	—	3,174	0	5
Republic of South Africa	CG	CG	1,840,164	1,654,731	105	639
Democratic Republic of the Sudan	E	E	45,699	77,136	24	76
Kingdom of Swaziland	—	E°	8,633	4,362	0	20
United Republic of Tanzania	E	E	18,023	90,599	46	288
Republic of Togo	—	E°	2,476	26,279	2	1

International relations (continued)

Selected Indicators of Japan's Foreign Relations

Country[1]	Type of diplomatic mission in Japan (1 January 1983)	Type of Japanese diplomatic mission (1 January 1983)	Exports to Japan in thousands of US-dollars (1982)	Imports from Japan in thousands of US dollars (1982)	Foreign nationals residing in Japan[2] (31 December 1982)	Japanese nationals residing abroad[3] (1 October 1981)
Africa (continued)						
Republic of Tunisia	E	E	950	66,594	32	288
Republic of Uganda	E	E°	24,414	7,675	7	12
Republic of Upper Volta	—	E°	11,276	8,780	1	5
Republic of Zaire	E	E	60,239	51,500	17	288
Republic of Zambia	E	E	227,155	51,412	7	124
Republic of Zimbabwe	E	E	45,139	54,510	6	60
Western Europe						
Republic of Austria	E	E	149,990	338,466	243	1,184
Kingdom of Belgium	E*	E	337,671	1,154,807	280	2,829
Republic of Cyprus	E°	E°	799	149,170	15	2
Kingdom of Denmark	E	E	266,650	441,882	435	561
Republic of Finland	E	E	169,751	407,603	329	211
French Republic	E*	E*	1,214,699	2,318,099	2,026	7,591
Federal Republic of Germany	E*	E*	2,354,808	5,018,221	2,960	13,942
Hellenic Republic (Greece)	E*	E	37,807	585,498	179	1,005
Republic of Iceland	E°	E°	25,438	28,101	5	9
Ireland	E	E	184,444	202,376	206	239
Republic of Italy	E	E*	941,941	863,713	759	3,161
Principality of Liechtenstein[6]	—	—	—	—	3	7
Grand Duchy of Luxembourg[7]	—	E°	963	5,516	14	90
Republic of Malta	—	E°	971	23,832	1	22
Principality of Monaco	—	—	830	586	0	2
Kingdom of the Netherlands	E*	E	347,251	1,660,940	470	2,127
Kingdom of Norway	E	E	176,903	828,246	618	337
Republic of Portugal	E	E	49,039	261,086	256	217
Republic of San Marino[8]	—	—	—	—	0	0
Spain	E	E	368,056	643,816	712	2,767
Kingdom of Sweden	E	E	351,961	745,645	580	1,029
Swiss Confederation	E*	E*	1,233,323	1,016,949	762	2,132
Republic of Turkey	E	E*	40,356	215,683	142	247
United Kingdom of Great Britain and Northern Ireland	E*	E*	1,874,196	4,813,019	5,642	11,724
State of the Vatican City[8]	E	E	—	—	0	84
Eastern Europe						
People's Socialist Republic of Albania	—	E°	3,817	10,296	0	0
People's Republic of Bulgaria	E	E	19,641	86,547	41	81
Czechoslovak Socialist Republic	E	E	45,064	69,138	91	145
German Democratic Republic	E	E	36,703	192,539	73	197
Hungarian People's Republic	E	E	21,711	73,152	66	168
Polish People's Republic	E	E	38,935	60,835	216	214
Socialist Republic of Romania	E	E	34,107	91,357	22	178
Union of Soviet Socialist Republics	E*	E*	1,682,017	3,898,841	342	784
Socialist Federal Republic of Yugoslavia	E	E	22,003	48,761	81	234
North America						
Antigua and Barbuda	—	—	22	4,151	0	—
Commonwealth of the Bahamas	—	E°	25,156	62,973	0	3
Barbados	—	E°	165	13,054	0	3
Belize	—	—	102	2,424	0	—
Canada	E	E*	4,440,533	2,860,653	1,847	13,508
Republic of Costa Rica	E	E	10,582	26,522	28	341
Republic of Cuba	E	E	114,831	125,693	44	277
Commonwealth of Dominica	—	E°	23	1,673	7	0
Dominican Republic	E*	E	11,489	77,352	8	590
Republic of El Salvador	E	E	22,744	24,161	52	23
State of Grenada	—	E°	14	1,658	0	3
Republic of Guatemala	E	E	78,980	46,863	35	149
Republic of Haiti	E*	E°	3,047	25,460	1	15
Republic of Honduras	E	E	48,270	35,697	32	123
Jamaica	—	E°	8,847	47,635	8	31
United Mexican States	E*	E	1,522,146	975,941	504	3,570
Republic of Nicaragua	E*	E	48,744	9,057	17	13
Republic of Panama	E*	E	107,079	2,924,828	26	767
State of Saint Lucia	—	E°	19	2,880	0	0
St. Vincent and the Grenadines	—	E°	28	1,887	0	0
Republic of Trinidad and Tobago	E°	E°	9,437	213,325	5	179
United States of America	E*	E*	24,179,206	36,329,876	24,825	125,432
South America						
Argentine Republic	E*	E	413,121	267,450	314	15,984
Republic of Bolivia	E	E	12,820	42,082	89	3,798
Federal Republic of Brazil	E*	E*	1,602,744	1,042,761	1,643	131,363
Republic of Chile	E*	E	579,044	231,053	177	489
Republic of Colombia	E	E	141,216	595,893	196	903
Republic of Ecuador	E*	E	24,067	219,172	42	320
Cooperative Republic of Guyana	E°	E°	18,575	3,188	10	22
Republic of Paraguay	E*	E*	19,421	31,544	90	4,925
Republic of Peru	E	E*	541,180	323,340	399	8,408
Republic of Surinam	—	E°	19,297	33,032	0	38
Oriental Republic of Uruguay	E	E	21,061	21,739	18	348
Republic of Venezuela	E	E	723,344	1,178,507	72	1,418

E: Embassy.
E*: Embassy plus consulate(s) general and/or consulates.
E°: Nonresident legations.
CG: Consulate general.
C: Consulate.
[1] Includes 164 countries recognized by Japan as of 1 January 1983 as well as Taiwan, the Democratic People's Republic of Korea (not yet recognized), and the British colony of Hong Kong.
[2] Aliens registered with the Japanese government, having been resident in Japan for over 90 days; includes approximately 650,000 Korean and 55,000 Chinese permanent residents. US figures do not include military personnel.
[3] Japanese citizens residing more than three months in a foreign country. Figures include Japanese with dual nationality and approximately 124,000 permanent residents in Brazil and 66,000 in the United States. Dash indicates number unknown.
[4] No exchange of ambassadors as of June 1983.
[5] Embassy closed.
[6] Liechtenstein's foreign affairs are handled by Switzerland and its trade statistics are listed with those of Switzerland.
[7] Belgium and the Netherlands administer Luxembourg's foreign affairs.
[8] Import and export statistics are included with those of Italy.
SOURCE: Gaimushō (Ministry of Foreign Affairs), *Sekai no kuni ichiranhyō* (annual): 1983. Nihon Kanzei Kyōkai (Japan Tariff Association), *Gaikoku bōeki gaikyō* (February 1983). Hōmushō (Ministry of Justice), *Dainijūni shutsunyūgoku kanri tōkei nempō* (annual): 1983. Gaimushō, *Kaigai zairyū hōjin sū chōsa tōkei* (annual): 1982.

Japan conceded defeat on 15 August 1945. Defeat brought an end to the period of expansion that had begun in the Meiji period with the attempt to establish a colonial system and to gain acceptance as an equal among world powers, and culminated in the first 15 years of the Shōwa period (1926–) in defiant militarism.

The Occupation Period —— Japan formally surrendered to the Allied Powers on 2 September 1945 and was occupied by their military forces (see SURRENDER, INSTRUMENT OF). The Japanese right to rule the country was made subject to the authority of the Supreme Commander for the Allied Powers (SCAP). As SCAP, Douglas MAC-ARTHUR, who had played a leading role in Japan's defeat, presided over the General Headquarters (GHQ) and set about implementing plans for the demilitarization and democratization of Japan. With the loss of Japan's colonial territories of Korea, Taiwan, South Sakhalin, and the Pacific Islands, the disbanding of its army and navy, and the wartime destruction of its industrial plants, the country's power and wealth were greatly diminished. During the Occupation, Japan was not allowed to engage in diplomatic activities, and external affairs were restricted principally to negotiations with SCAP; Japan was allowed only restricted trade with foreign countries.

In September 1951, Japan and the Allied Powers (excluding the Soviet Union, China, India, and Burma) signed the San Francisco Peace Treaty, which became effective in April of the following year. This enabled Japan to reenter the international community as an independent nation. Prohibited from possessing land, sea, and air forces and other war potential by its new CONSTITUTION (1947), Japan was now confronted with the problem of safeguarding its security. This issue was partially resolved when, at the time of the signing of the peace treaty, Japan concluded the first of the UNITED STATES–JAPAN SECURITY TREATIES. Thereafter, the country came under the protective umbrella of American military strength, and the military bases used by the army of Occupation remained in the hands of US forces under the provisions of the security treaty and the UNITED STATES–JAPAN ADMINISTRATIVE AGREEMENT (1952).

Japan in the Cold War —— The postwar period saw the development of the cold war between the United States and the Soviet Union, which intensified and split the world into opposed blocs centered on the two superpowers. Japan formally joined the American camp with the conclusion of the Security Treaty and thus came into confrontation with the Soviet Union and Mainland China. When the San Francisco Peace Treaty went into effect, Japan also signed the Japan–China Peace Treaty with the Nationalist government on Taiwan, which it recognized as the official government of China. Normal diplomatic relations between Japan and the People's Republic of China were not established for approximately 20 years. During this period, Japan maintained contact with Mainland China on a nongovernmental basis and trade was resumed by private firms. Although intercourse between the two countries gradually increased, Japan–China relations until the 1970s were dominated by mutual distrust (see CHINA AND JAPAN: China and Japan after 1912).

The cold war began to thaw in the latter part of the 1950s, and the Soviet Union initiated negotiations on the restoration of normal diplomatic relations in 1955. The talks were suspended in a dispute over the Northern Territory issue in mid-1956. Two months later, during a visit to Moscow by Prime Minister HATOYAMA ICHIRŌ, it was decided to enter into an interim agreement terminating the state of war between the two countries, while continuing negotiations on a peace treaty. A SOVIET–JAPANESE JOINT DECLARATION to this effect was signed in October 1956, and diplomatic relations were resumed after a ten-year lapse. Since then, trade and cultural exchanges between the countries have progressed and various administrative agreements concerning commerce, aviation, and consular service have been concluded. Moreover, joint economic projects were inaugurated for the development of timber resources and natural gas in Siberia (see SOVIET–JAPANESE DEVELOPMENT OF SIBERIA). However, there has been little overall progress in the development of friendship and cooperation between the two countries. As of 1980, a peace treaty had still not been concluded. The biggest obstacle to improving relations is the Northern Territory issue, centering on the islands Kunashir (J: Kunashiri) and Iturup (Etorofu) of the southern Kurils and the islands of Shikotan and the Habomai chain. The Japanese have demanded the return of these islands as a precondition to signing a peace treaty, while the Soviets have repeatedly stated that the territorial issue is not subject to negotiation (see TERRITORY OF JAPAN).

Another factor obstructing friendly relations between Japan and the Soviet Union is anti-Soviet sentiment among the Japanese people as a whole. Japan's historic distrust of tsarist Russia has been sustained by the territorial dispute and further aggravated by the increasing Soviet military presence in East Asia. Soviet restrictions on Japanese fishermen trawling for salmon in the Sea of Okhotsk, once a traditional Japanese fishing area, have also contributed to distrust. See RUSSIA AND JAPAN.

Following the independence of Korea from Japan at the end of World War II and Japan's acknowledgment of its independence in the 1951 peace treaty, negotiations to normalize diplomatic relations were begun in October 1951. However, the anti-Japanese policies of Korean President Syngman RHEE (Yi Sŭng-man), indemnity claims, and the 1952 establishment of the so-called RHEE LINE restricting Japanese maritime activity proved to be difficult obstacles, and negotiations between the two countries failed to make progress. With the overthrow of the Rhee government in March 1960, the assumption of power by the Pak Chŏng-hŭi regime, and pressure from the United States, negotiations were intensified. They finally resulted in the signing of the KOREA–JAPAN TREATY OF 1965 and the establishment of normal diplomatic relations. Since then the two countries have grown closer, particularly in economic relations. Financial and technological assistance provided to the Republic of Korea greatly accelerated the modernization of its basic industries. The volume of trade between the two countries also expanded considerably. Ties between political and business leaders developed to the point that the term *nikkan yuchaku* ("Japan–South Korea collusion") came into vogue. On the other hand, relations with the Democratic People's Republic of Korea have not been close; since Japan recognizes the ROK as the only lawful government on the peninsula, relations with the north are largely unofficial. See KOREA AND JAPAN: relations with the Republic of Korea; relations with the Democratic People's Republic of Korea.

Japan's postwar relations with Southeast Asia began with the problem of war reparations. The first country with which Japan reached agreement on reparations was Burma, followed by the Philippines, Indonesia, and South Vietnam, all in 1954. With Thailand there was no reparations problem, but the Thai government demanded the repayment of a special yen account debt accumulated during the wartime. Agreement was reached on the settlement of this account, and assistance grants were given to Cambodia and Laos, thus resolving the reparations issue. In the 1960s, Japan made considerable economic inroads into this region and was only partially successful at assuaging anti-Japanese sentiment. Japan's foreign policy was based on a recognition of its place as a member of the Asian community of nations, and particular emphasis in foreign aid was placed on Southeast Asia. See SOUTHEAST ASIA, THE PACIFIC ISLANDS, AND JAPAN.

Toward a More Independent Diplomacy —— In 1967 Thailand, Malaysia, Singapore, Indonesia, and the Philippines organized the Association of Southeast Asian Nations (ASEAN). This regional cooperative organization became particularly active during the 1970s with the decline of American military power in Asia. To fill the power vacuum, member countries of ASEAN worked to increase economic cooperation, particularly in trade and industry. Capital funding and technology were provided by Japan, which helped to accelerate regional industrial development and promote cultural exchange. See ASEAN AND JAPAN.

Australia, Canada, New Zealand, and Mexico have become increasingly important to Japanese industry as providers of required raw materials. The growing economic interdependence between Japan and these countries lent itself to the idea of a "Pacific Basin Economic Sphere," the emergence of which will provide a backdrop to Japanese diplomacy in the 1980s. See AUSTRALIA AND JAPAN; CANADA AND JAPAN; MEXICO AND JAPAN; NEW ZEALAND AND JAPAN.

Ever since the OIL CRISIS OF 1973, mounting interest has been focused on nations of the Middle East, such as Saudi Arabia, Iran, Kuwait, and the United Arab Emirates, from which Japan obtains the greater part of its oil supplies. Japan has established strong economic relations with these countries, not only in regard to the importing of oil but also the exporting of manufacturing and refining plants and other industrial goods. (See MIDDLE EAST AND JAPAN.) Political upheavals in the Middle East such as the Iranian revolution in 1979 directly affect Japan's economic well-being to an extent not experienced by oil-producing nations.

The Japanese government achieved a significant diplomatic breakthrough in September 1972 with its joint communiqué establishing formal diplomatic relations with the People's Republic of China. In August 1978 the CHINA–JAPAN PEACE AND FRIENDSHIP

TREATY was concluded and Japan, which had previously maintained a position of neutrality in regard to China and the Soviet Union, showed itself leaning toward the Chinese. The improvement of relations between Japan and China will certainly influence the political situation in Asia. Until recently, Japan has been careful to avoid entanglement in geopolitical maneuverings, but with the improvement of relations with China, involvement appears inevitable.

At present Japan is in the process of dramatically expanding trade and technological cooperation as well as the exchange of technicians with China, and economic relations between the two countries have shown extraordinary progress. During Prime Minister Ōhira Masayoshi's visit to Beijing (Peking) in December 1979, Japan agreed to provide loans to China for the construction of ports and harbors, hydroelectric plants, railways, and other projects.

Evolving Relations with the United States —— During the immediate postwar years, Japan's foreign policy was based on the principle that its security was guaranteed by the shield of American military power, and hence Japan's relationship to the United States in the 1950s can be compared to that of a protectorate. It was in part due to generous assistance provided by the United States that Japan, devastated by the war, was able to achieve complete economic rehabilitation. With American backing, Japan was accepted as a member of the General Agreement on Tariff and Trade (GATT) in 1955, and of the United Nations in 1956 (see UNITED NATIONS AND JAPAN).

At the end of the 1950s, Japan announced "three principles" of foreign policy, stressing its position as a member of the Asian community, diplomacy centered on the United Nations, and maintenance of Japan's position in the free world. Japan's international relations, which were based on its special relationship with the United States, did not change during the 1960s. Nevertheless, there was considerable domestic turmoil in 1960 at the time of the revision of the United States–Japan Security Treaty, and further public criticism of the United States–Japan military alliance following the outbreak of the Vietnam War. Despite these issues, the fundamental pattern of Japan's foreign policy continued to be characterized by a dependence on American military power for its national security, a reticence to speak out on international political issues, and a gradual shift of concern from economic recovery to development and then to overseas expansion.

During the latter part of the 1960s, however, Japan's economic power (industrial output, foreign trade volume, and technical know-how) became competitive with the United States and the European Community (EC). Coupled with the deterioration of US leadership in international politics as a partial consequence of the Vietnam War, economic growth created friction over trade issues between the two countries. This new phase in Japan–United States relations is best exemplified by the textile dispute between the two countries from 1969 to 1971. Signs of friction in the economic area and disunity in the sphere of foreign policy became more apparent in the 1970s. A discordant note was sounded by the so-called NIXON SHOCKS of July 1971, when, without previous consultation with Japan, President Richard Nixon announced he would visit Beijing in an attempt to normalize diplomatic relations with China. The failure to consult about a diplomatic development of great significance to Japan was construed as a snub in retaliation for Prime Minister SATŌ EISAKU's stance in the Japan–United States textile dispute. Other "shocks," relating to economic policies and trade, followed in the same year.

However, the improvement of relations between the United States and China resulted in stimulating relations between China and Japan and creating a new political order in East Asia. Postwar cooperation between Japan and the United States and their concerted opposition to the Soviet Union and China changed to a pattern of Japan, the United States, and China loosely aligned against the Soviet Union.

Economic Issues —— Japan's chief trade partner continued to be the United States. However, friction between the two countries again grew heated during the latter half of the 1970s: the trade balance between the two countries was overwhelmingly in favor of Japan; increasing Japanese exports of steel and electronic products to the United States created problems; and the United States sharply criticized Japan for its closed markets against such American exports as oranges, beef, and high-technology products. See UNITED STATES AND JAPAN; UNITED STATES, ECONOMIC RELATIONS WITH, 1945–1973.

A similar trade dispute developed between Japan and the countries of Western Europe. An imbalance in trade, the enormous export volumes of Japanese steel, electronic products, ships, automobiles, and ball bearings, and Japan's closed markets, caused trade frictions. The intensification of trade rivalry between Japan and these industrialized countries is now stimulating the formation of a new protectionism and new economic blocs, problems which are expected to confront Japan in the 1980s. See EUROPEAN COMMUNITY AND JAPAN.

During the 1970s, Third World countries emerged as forces in international politics. Utilizing their abundance of natural resources as a diplomatic weapon, they are beginning to demand the formation of a new international economic order. Japan has frequently stated its intention to act as a bridge to help resolve the problem of inequality between nations of the northern and southern hemispheres; but practically speaking, it has been able to do little to alleviate poverty, oppression, and inequality among people of less developed nations. In relation to its gross national product, the amount of economic assistance provided by Japan to such countries (particularly direct government assistance) is conspicuously less than that extended by other economically developed countries. Japanese private investments in developing countries are gradually increasing, and the scope of Japanese technological cooperation with such countries is also expanding. However, financial and technical assistance is still far below what the less developed countries require, necessitating increased Japanese diplomatic activity. See FOREIGN AID POLICY.

Future Prospects —— In the 1970s Japan has been called a "great economic power" and its leaders have attended summit conferences with the other developed countries and other important international economic meetings. Japan's international status has risen considerably, and its voice in international affairs has grown stronger. Nevertheless its military forces remain small compared to those of other great powers, and miniscule in comparison to those of the United States and the Soviet Union (see SELF DEFENSE FORCES). Japan has been cautious about assuming an active role in the community of nations. The chief question of the 1980s is whether Japan will maintain this relative diplomatic passivity or take a more aggressive role among the nations of the world. See also AUSTRIA AND JAPAN; FRANCE AND JAPAN; INDIA AND JAPAN; NETHERLANDS AND JAPAN; PORTUGAL AND JAPAN; SPAIN AND JAPAN; AFRICA AND JAPAN; EASTERN EUROPEAN NATIONS AND JAPAN; LATIN AMERICA AND JAPAN.

◾ —— Dorothy Borg and Shumpei Okamoto, ed, *Pearl Harbor as History* (1973). I. M. Destler, Hideo Sato, and Priscilla Clapp, ed, *Managing an Alliance: The Politics of US-Japanese Relations* (1976). Gaimushō Gaikō Shiryōkan Nihon Gaikō Jiten Hensan Iinkai, ed, *Nihon gaikō shi jiten* (1979). Kajima Heiwa Kenkyūjō, ed, *Nihon gaikō shi*, 34 vols, 4 supp vols (1970–74). James W. Morley, *Japan's Foreign Policy, 1868-1941: A Research Guide* (1974). Nagano Nobutoshi, *Nihon gaikō handobukku* (1981). Ian Nish, *Japanese Foreign Policy, 1869–1942: Kasumigaseki to Miyakezaka* (1977). Robert A. Scalapino, ed, *The Foreign Policy of Modern Japan* (1977).

HOSOYA Chihiro

international trade → foreign trade

Inubōzaki

Cape on Chōshi Peninsula, northeastern Chiba Prefecture, central Honshū. Location of one of the oldest modern lighthouses in Japan, built in 1874 on a sea cliff. Noted for its beautiful beaches. Part of Suigō–Tsukuba Quasi-National Park.

inu hariko

A papier-mâché dog popular during the Edo period (1600–1868) as a talisman for safe childbirth and the protection of children. During the Heian period (794–1185) a forerunner of *inu hariko*, known as *inubako* (a lidded container in the shape of a dog), was used by the nobility as a talisman against difficult birth. During the Edo period the *inu hariko* became popular among the general populace, particularly in Edo (now Tōkyō). It was included in a bride's trousseau and also displayed at festivals with *hina* dolls (see DOLL FESTIVAL). It became common practice for a newborn infant to be given an *inu hariko* by relatives on its first visit to the family's tutelary shrine. The custom continued to be quite popular into the early part of this century, but today *inu hariko* are used mainly as dolls for children.

YAMADA Tokubei

Inukai Tsuyoshi (1855–1932)

Statesman and prime minister (1931–32). Born at Niwase in what is now Okayama Prefecture. While studying at Keiō Gijuku (now Keiō University) in Tōkyō he became a reporter for the newspaper *Yūbin hōchi shimbun* and covered the SATSUMA REBELLION in 1877. Though he served briefly (1881) in the government's Statistics Office on the recommendation of ŌKUMA SHIGENOBU, he continued his journalistic activities with the newspapers *Tōkai keizai shimpō*, the *Akita nippō*, and the *Chōya shimbun*.

Beginning with his involvement in the formation of a political party called the RIKKEN KAISHINTŌ in 1882, Inukai persistently supported liberal political causes and was invariably critical of the domination of the government by political leaders from the former Chōshū (now Yamaguchi Prefecture) and Satsuma (now Kagoshima Prefecture) domains. He joined GOTŌ SHŌJIRŌ's coalition against the government in 1888 and supported Ōkuma Shigenobu in his efforts to revise the Unequal Treaties with Western powers in 1889 (see UNEQUAL TREATIES, REVISION OF). Elected to the House of Representatives in the first general election in 1890 and thereafter reelected a total of 18 times, he was a leading figure first in the SHIMPOTŌ and then in the KENSEITŌ and was appointed minister of education in the last days of the Ōkuma cabinet (1898).

After the split of the Kenseitō, he remained with the KENSEI HONTŌ until being expelled from that party because of his unwillingness to appease the clique-dominated government (see HAMBATSU). He then organized the RIKKEN KOKUMINTŌ (1910), and when General KATSURA TARŌ, who represented the Chōshū clique, formed his third cabinet in 1912, Inukai, together with OZAKI YUKIO, mounted a national campaign to "protect constitutional democracy" and to "undermine the domination of domain cliques." This movement forced the Katsura cabinet to resign in 1913 (see TAISHŌ POLITICAL CRISIS).

The early implementation of universal suffrage and opposition to an increase in army divisions were the main goals of the Kokumintō, which was later reorganized as the KAKUSHIN KURABU in 1922. After serving as minister of communications in the second YAMAMOTO GONNOHYŌE cabinet in 1923, Inukai and his party joined forces with the KENSEIKAI and RIKKEN SEIYŪKAI in a second campaign to "protect constitutional democracy" when KIYOURA KEIGO formed his nonparty cabinet with the sole support of the House of Peers in 1924. With the dissolution of the Kiyoura cabinet, the KATŌ TAKAAKI cabinet was formed from a coalition of the three parties involved, with Inukai serving as minister of communications (1924).

Although the realization of universal suffrage in 1925 was a triumph for Inukai's liberal principles, he decided to dissolve the gradually weakening Kakushin Kurabu and to allow its merger with the more powerful Seiyūkai. He announced his resignation from the cabinet and his retirement from political activities, but his supporters would not allow him to retire, and he continued to be elected to the House of Representatives as the senior member of the Seiyūkai until his death.

Inukai was concerned with the revolutionary movement in China as early as the 1890s and endeavored to assist the revolutionaries. His assistance to SUN YAT-SEN while the latter was in Japan in 1897 was particularly notable. At the time of the Chinese revolution in 1911, he went to China with TŌYAMA MITSURU in an unsuccessful attempt to mediate between Sun and other Chinese leaders, and he continued to support Sun during his later exile in Japan (1913).

With the death of TANAKA GIICHI, Inukai accepted the presidency of the Seiyūkai in 1929, and, after the fall of the second WAKATSUKI REIJIRŌ cabinet, he was asked to organize a cabinet of his own in 1931. Japan was at that time in serious economic straits as a result of the world depression and Japan's own untimely return to the gold standard under the Wakatsuki cabinet, and Inukai's cabinet, the day it was formed, announced the reembargo on gold. Having won an absolute majority in the lower house in the general election of 1932, the Inukai cabinet, with TAKAHASHI KOREKIYO as minister of finance, set about trying to reflate the Japanese economy.

The Inukai cabinet also had to cope with the settlement of the MANCHURIAN INCIDENT, which had begun in 1931. Faced with the formation of an army-sponsored puppet regime in Manchuria, Inukai attempted through a personal envoy, Kayano Nagatomo, to negotiate a settlement with the Chinese government that would recognize China's sovereignty over Manchuria while allowing local autonomy. Inukai's determination to solve the Manchurian problem by tightly controlling the army, together with his vigorous defense of parliamentary democracy, prompted an uprising of military officers

in what was known as the MAY 15TH INCIDENT (1932), and Inukai was assassinated in his official residence.

An accomplished orator and calligrapher, Inukai was one of the most uncompromising figures in Japanese politics, who unfailingly fought for parliamentary democracy and friendly relations with China. Throughout the war, the postwar years, and even today, his followers have continued to assemble every May 15th to commemorate his tragic death.

🕮 ——Kojima Kazuo, *Ichi rō seijika no kaisō* (1951). Oka Yoshitake, *Kindai Nippon no seijika* (1960). Washio Yoshinao, *Inukai Bokudō den*, 3 vols (1939). OGATA Shijūrō

inuoumono

(literally, "dog chasing"). A sport of the warrior class that involved shooting arrows from horseback at dogs. It originated during the Kamakura period (1185–1333) and was especially popular during the Muromachi period (1333–1568). After a period of decline, it was revived during the Edo period (1600–1868) but never achieved its former popularity and disappeared soon after the Meiji Restoration of 1868. A large circle was roped off in the center of a riding ground about 14.3 meters (47 ft) in diameter. A smaller circle was made inside the larger one and the area was spread with clean sand. Warriors waiting outside the outer rope then shot their arrows from galloping horses at dogs released inside the inner circle. The skill of the archers was determined by where the dogs fell when shot.

INAGAKI Shisei

Inuyama

City in northern Aichi Prefecture, central Honshū, on the river Kisogawa. It is the site of Inuyama Castle, which has one of the oldest donjons in Japan (ca 1599). Because of its proximity to Nagoya, it is fast becoming a satellite city, with emergent machinery and food-processing industries. Tourists are drawn to MEIJI MURA, a complex of Meiji-period (1868–1912) buildings brought from all over the country, the Japan Monkey Center, boating on the Kisogawa (the so-called Japan Rhine), and CORMORANT FISHING *(ukai)*. Pop: 64,614.

invasions of Korea in 1592 and 1597

(Bunroku Keichō no Eki). TOYOTOMI HIDEYOSHI's two invasions of Korea were launched in 1592 (Bunroku 1) and 1597 (Keichō 2). One major cause was Korea's refusal to allow passage of Japanese troops through its territory for Hideyoshi's planned conquest of China. In time, China entered the war and with its land forces dominated the defense effort. After six and a half years of hostilities, Korea was exhausted and devastated, China was weakened and left vulnerable to the Manchu conquest that engulfed it half a century later, and Japan was unable, except in its spectacular initial attacks, to hold more than the southern Korean coastal areas closest to Japan. The final withdrawal was occasioned by Hideyoshi's death in 1598, but by that time the war was already at a stalemate.

In launching the war, Hideyoshi was clearly motivated by a desire to obtain territories with which to reward his restless generals and from which to dominate East Asian trade and commerce. Beyond that there was his own nearly boundless ambition. His postwar plans included the installation of the Japanese emperor (Go-Yōzei, r 1586–1611) in Peking (now Beijing) and the establishment of his own headquarters at the Chinese port of Ningbo (Ningpo), from which he would rule all of Japan, Korea, China, the Ryūkyūs, Taiwan, and the Philippines. But none of this came to pass.

The Bunroku Campaign (1592–1593) —— Hideyoshi's plans, which had been developing in his mind at least since 1577, became concrete soon after his unification of Japan in 1590. He built Nagoya Castle (in northern Kyūshū, not to be confused with the present Nagoya) as his headquarters and assembled an invasion force of nine divisions totaling over 158,000 men. When diplomatic initiatives to secure Korea's voluntary compliance were spurned, he decided to launch the attack.

The Korean court had been clearly informed of Hideyoshi's intentions but was divided on how to interpret them. Some believed that an invasion was coming, others that the threat was only a bluff. Unfortunately for Korea, the latter interpretation prevailed, and when the attack actually began with the invasion of Pusan on 23 May 1592, its regular army forces were woefully ill prepared. As the defenders were rapidly defeated or scattered, the king and his chief officials fled to the north.

Japan's armies moved quickly through the peninsula. The two vanguard divisions under KONISHI YUKINAGA and KATŌ KIYOMASA took separate attack routes but both arrived in Seoul on 11 June. Meanwhile the other divisions moved in to consolidate the Japanese gains. Konishi pushed forward and occupied P'yŏngyang on 23 July; Katō moved to the northeast and by 30 August reached the Tumen River and even crossed briefly into Manchuria.

At this point the Japanese attack began to lose momentum as serious problems developed. On the one hand, Korean naval forces under Admiral YI SUN-SIN had begun to decimate the Japanese supply fleet: during the summer of 1592, approximately 375 Japanese ships were either sunk or captured. Korean naval superiority was able to block Japanese movement into the Yellow Sea, and this in turn prevented any maritime supplies from reaching Konishi's by now overextended armies. On the other hand, Korean irregulars constantly harassed the overland supply lines and kept Japanese forces from consolidating their positions.

Meanwhile, Korea had appealed to the Chinese Ming dynasty (1368–1644) for help. China's Liaodong (Liaotung) defense forces were at that time far away in Ningxia (Ninghsia), pacifying a Mongol rebellion, and only a small force of 5,000 men was available for Korea. This detachment attacked P'yŏngyang in August but was easily defeated by Konishi. At this point, China, playing for time, proposed a 50-day truce, and Konishi, deeply troubled by supply problems, accepted it. The Chinese now completed their Ningxia campaign and force-marched an army of 40,000 men into Korea. Their attack (February 1593) overwhelmed Konishi and forced him to retreat to Seoul. But while a Japanese counterattack north of Seoul severely mauled the Chinese, west of the city the Koreans defeated a sizable Japanese force at Haengju. These battles convinced both sides that the time had arrived for negotiations.

Peace Negotiations (1593–1596) —— During the Bunroku Campaign, Chinese and Japanese generals spent considerable time in the truce tent, trying to achieve there what had proved elusive on the battlefield. Preliminary talks led to the withdrawal of most of the Chinese army and the removal of all Japanese forces to the southeastern coast. Senior Chinese officials went to Nagoya Castle in June 1593 and there heard Hideyoshi's demands, which included a marriage alliance between the Chinese and Japanese imperial families, high-ranking hostages from Korea, the cession of the four southernmost Korean provinces to Japan, and the restoration of the TALLY TRADE previously conducted between the Ming and the Muromachi shogunate (1338–1573). As a gesture, two Korean princes who had been captured by Katō were returned.

In Chinese eyes, formal trade involved a tributary relationship in which the Ming emperor invested the Japanese ruler as "king." This investiture had been accepted by one of the Muromachi shōguns, yet it conflicted with Japanese attitudes of parity with China that had deep historical roots. In spite of this, Chinese negotiators apparently extracted from Konishi a Japanese agreement to accept investiture; with that accomplished, it was hoped, an atmosphere would exist for the resolution of the other items on Hideyoshi's agenda. After many misunderstandings and delays, and much internal debate in China and Korea (Confucian critics argued that one did *not* invest one's invaders as kings), there was a mutual reduction of troops leading to the investment ceremony, which finally took place at Ōsaka Castle on 22 October 1596. But the next day, at a banquet for the envoys, Hideyoshi had the investiture documents read aloud and was infuriated by the condescending tone of the Ming decree and the fact that none of the other conditions involving trade and the Korean issues were even mentioned. The whole affair was then broken off and the Ming envoys ordered out of the country. Hideyoshi now resolved to gain his Korean foothold by another campaign.

The Keichō Campaign (1597–1598) —— Throughout the negotiations Japan had maintained some of its coastal fortresses in Korea, but with the exception of a brutal massacre at Chinju there had been little military activity. Konishi and Katō now raced back to Korea to reopen the war, with the immediate objective of securing the southern provinces. As in 1592, surprise and solid organization secured initial victories. A Japanese intrigue that exploited Korean factional rivalries led to the dismissal of Yi Sun-sin as commander of the Korean fleet, which with less able leadership was now defeated in a major battle on 27 August 1597. The sea secure, Japanese units advanced successfully into Chŏlla Province (southwestern Korea), captured two major towns, and prepared to march on Seoul. The

determined redeployment of Ming forces at Chiksan stopped the Japanese advance, however, and Yi Sun-sin, vindicated and reappointed as naval commander, achieved a dramatic victory over the Japanese fleet at the strategic Myŏngnyang Strait at the southwestern corner of the peninsula, again denying it access to the Yellow Sea (26 October). With this the Japanese thrust lost momentum, and gradually the attacking armies took refuge in the approximately 20 fortresses constructed along the coast. A major Chinese-Korean offensive against the Japanese positions in Ulsan nearly succeeded, but a heroic defense by Katō (February 1598) turned near defeat into a spectacular victory with heavy Chinese losses. Yet by the summer of 1598, a huge Chinese army, including a powerful naval force, had assembled in Korea, and another Japanese march northward became increasingly unlikely. On the other hand, the Japanese coastal fortresses were nearly impregnable. A Chinese division attacking the Sach'ŏn fortress fell into a Japanese trap that resulted in over 10,000 Chinese deaths (31 October 1598).

As this strategic stalemate was developing, it became known to the Japanese commanders that Hideyoshi had died (18 September 1598) and left a deathbed order for the withdrawal of the troops from Korea. Katō and other commanders in the southeast were able to arrange local truces during which they evacuated their men. But Konishi, on the south central coast near Sunch'ŏn, was besieged by a huge army and blockaded by a powerful Chinese-Korean fleet. With the timely aid of SHIMAZU YOSHIHIRO, who had masterminded the dramatic ambush at Sach'ŏn, Konishi and his forces were able to slip through the blockade, but hundreds of Shimazu's ships and thousands of his men were lost in this final action, known as the battle of Noryang (16 December 1598). The Korean hero Yi Sun-sin also lost his life in this action.

Thus ended Hideyoshi's grand attempt to conquer Korea and China. Tactically his armies had operated with great success, winning many victories and causing heavy Chinese and Korean losses. But strategically the odds against the Japanese proved too great to overcome. The chief difficulties were control of the sea, the maintenance of secure supply lines, and successful occupation of territory beyond the fortified bases. In addition, the ability of the Chinese to send large and well-supplied armies from as far away as Sichuan (Szechwan) and Guangdong (Kwangtung) created a military situation that eventually neutralized the Japanese forces. Hideyoshi's death occurred at a time when both sides were in considerable difficulty and thus provided an opportunity for the resolution of a long and inconclusive war. See also KOREA AND JAPAN: premodern relations.

■ —— Ikeuchi Hiroshi, *Bunroku-Keichō no eki (seihen)*, vol 1 (vol 3 of *Minami Manshū tetsudō rekishi chōsa hōkoku*; Minami Manshū Tetsudō Rekishi Chōsabu, 1914). Ikeuchi Hiroshi, *Bunroku-Keichō no eki (beppen)*, vol 1 (vol 25 of *Tōyō bunko ronsō*; Tōyō Bunko, 1936). Ishihara Michihiro, *Bunroku-Keichō no eki* (1963). Nakamura Hidetaka, "Bunroku-Keichō no eki," in *Iwanami kōza: Nihon rekishi*, vol 3 (Iwanami Shoten, 1935). Nakamura Hidetaka, "Bunroku-Keichō no eki," in Takayanagi Mitsutoshi, ed, *Dai Nihon senshi*, vol 3 (1939). George Sansom, *A History of Japan, 1334–1615* (1961). Yi Hyŏngsŏk (Ri Keiseki), *Jinshin senran shi*, 3 vols (1977).
Gari LEDYARD

investment trusts

(*tōshi shintaku*). Investment trusts are companies that gather funds from the general public and invest them in bonds, stocks, and other instruments, including short-term interbank money markets. The profits from investments by the trust are divided among investors by proportion of total funds provided. Dividends are therefore a uniform percentage of paid-in investments, although the rate of dividend may vary from period to period, depending on the performance of the trust's investments. Under the Securities Investment Trust Law, securities companies may set up investment trust companies, but the funds gathered must be entrusted to one of Japan's seven trust banks (or the one city bank engaged in trust management). The trust banks act according to the instructions of managers of the investment trust, buying and selling or moving funds in and out of short-term money markets. The trust banks assume responsibility for supervision of the portfolio, for safekeeping of securities and related records, and for paying dividends and interest accruing to the investment trust. Japan's investment trusts differ from mutual and other types of funds in that no stock in the trust is issued. Investors pay into the fund and assign rights of operation to the investment trust company in return for a pledge of payment of dividends based on the performance of the trust. Investment trusts based on stock ownership do not now exist in Japan. The principal paid into the trust is not guaranteed, as is the case with some other investments.   *C. Tait* RATCLIFFE

inzō

(Skt: *mudrā;* also known in Japanese as *ingei* or *in*). In ESOTERIC BUDDHISM, the concrete manifestation of the contents of a Buddha's or BODHISATTVA's enlightenment through the positioning of the hands and fingers, or through the implements held in the hands. An important part of the practice of esoteric Buddhism is to identify oneself with a particular enlightenment and receive its powers through the imitation of the *inzō*. In Buddhist iconography the *inzō* symbolizes a particular aspect of Buddhism, such as meditation, teaching, wisdom, and so forth.   *Robert* RHODES

Ioffe (Joffe), Adolf Abramovich (1883–1927)

Known also as Victor Krymsky. Soviet diplomat active in negotiations with Japan and China. Although born into a wealthy business family and educated as a physician, Ioffe became a Menshevik (a member of the more moderate faction of the Russian Social Democratic Party) in 1903. Trying to subvert the Tsarist government from abroad, Ioffe worked with Leon Trotsky in Vienna editing *Pravda* (1908–12), the antecedent of the current Soviet Communist Party newspaper. When he returned to Russia in 1912, he was immediately arrested and imprisoned for five years. In August 1917 Ioffe, together with Trotsky, joined the Bolsheviks (the more radical faction of the Russian Social Democratic Party, eventually known as the Communist Party). Following the Bolshevik Revolution, Ioffe was in charge of the peace negotiations with Germany at Brest–Litovsk in 1918 and became the first Soviet ambassador to Germany the same year. He represented Moscow in the peace negotiations with Estonia, Lithuania, Latvia, and Poland (1920 and 1921) and at the Genoa Conference (1922), during which Soviet Russia tried unsuccessfully to rejoin the European diplomatic community from which it had been separated because of the revolution and its refusal to recognize the war debts of the tsarist government. In the fall of 1922 Ioffe conferred unsuccessfully with the Chinese government at Beijing (Peking) about the disposition of the CHINESE EASTERN RAILWAY in Manchuria, Chinese sovereignty over Mongolia, and use of the indemnity due Russia as a result of the Boxer uprising of 1900. SUN YAT-SEN, the leader of the opposition at Shanghai, was more responsive to the Soviet position, and in January 1923 Ioffe and Sun issued a joint manifesto declaring, on the one hand, that there did not exist in China the conditions for the successful establishment of communism or the Soviet system and, on the other hand, that the Russian people sympathized with the Chinese struggle for national unification and full independence and would support it.

Ioffe had interrupted his negotiations in Beijing to hasten to Changchun, where he took an active part in the negotiations between Japan and the Soviet FAR EASTERN REPUBLIC regarding the withdrawal of Japanese troops sent in the SIBERIAN INTERVENTION. In February 1923 Ioffe proceeded from Shanghai to Japan as a guest of the mayor of Tōkyō, GOTŌ SHIMPEI, a fellow physician and formerly minister of foreign affairs, for medical treatment and informal talks about the restoration of diplomatic relations between the two countries. A heart attack aggravated Ioffe's already poor health. Undeterred, he opened informal preliminary negotiations with Foreign Minister Kawakami Toshitsune about Japanese recognition of the USSR. Although Ioffe returned to Moscow without reaching an agreement, he had contributed to a general improvement in Soviet-Japanese relations.

In 1925–27 Ioffe strongly supported Trotsky in the intraparty struggle. When Joseph Stalin gained the upper hand, Ioffe committed suicide. The agony of his protracted illness and prolonged psychiatric treatment may have been factors in his decision to take his life.

■——Xenia Joukoff Eudin and Robert C. North, *Soviet Russia and the East: A Documentary Survey* (1957). George Alexander Lensen, *Japanese Recognition of the U.S.S.R.: Soviet-Japanese Relations, 1921–1930* (1970). C. Martin Wilbur, *Sun Yat-sen: Frustrated Patriot* (1976).   *George Alexander* LENSEN

Iō Islands

(Iō Rettō). Also known as the Iwo Islands; known internationally as the Volcano Islands. Group of volcanic islands in the Pacific Ocean

at latitude 24–25° north. Part of the OGASAWARA ISLANDS. Composed of Kita Iōjima, Naka Iōjima, and Minami Iōjima. Naka Iōjima, the largest island, is usually called Iōjima (also known as Iwojima). It was the scene of fierce fighting between American and Japanese forces in World War II. Under American rule after World War II, these islands came in 1968 under the jurisdiction of the Tōkyō prefectural government. Area: Kita Iōjima, 5.4 sq km (2.1 sq mi); Naka Iōjima, 20.1 sq km (7.76 sq mi); Minami Iōjima, 3.8 sq km (1.5 sq mi).

Iōjima

Volcanic island, approximately 50 km (31 mi) south of the Satsuma Peninsula, Kagoshima Prefecture, southern Kyūshū. Sulfur has been mined since ancient times from the tallest peak, Iōdake (704 m; 2,309 ft); hence the name "sulfur island." The mines were closed in 1964 and now the chief activity is small-scale farming and fishing. Iōjima is believed to be the Kikaigashima to which the priest SHUNKAN was exiled in 1177. Not to be confused with the island of the same name in the IŌ ISLANDS. Area: 8.3 sq km (3.2 sq mi).

Iōjima (Iwojima), Battle of

(Iōjima Sakusen). A fiercely fought battle on the island of Iōjima (also known as Iwojima) during WORLD WAR II. The United States forces were anxious to acquire Iōjima, part of the Iō Islands (also known as the Volcano Islands), as a base for flying escort missions for the B-29 bombing campaign against mainland Japan. They also hoped to use the island to effect a blockade of Japanese sea lanes and to ensure the defense of primary American bomber bases in the Marianas Islands. Landing of the US forces began on 19 February 1945. Japanese forces, commanded by General Kuribayashi Tadamichi, numbered 23,000. In the battle, which lasted almost a month, US casualties totaled 25,000, including almost 7,000 killed, and Japanese losses were 20,000 killed and about 1,000 captured. It was one of the fiercest battles in the Pacific War.   KONDŌ *Shinji*

Ionushi

(The Hermit). Late-10th-century work attributed to the priest Zōki (fl ca 950–1000). It consists of three essentially unrelated sections. The first is a lyrical account containing 30 poems of a pilgrimage to the KUMANO SANZAN SHRINES in the Kii Peninsula, the second section a loosely arranged set of 43 poems on famous pilgrimage centers and scenic spots, interspersed with a few love poems, and the third section ostensibly an account of a journey through the province of Tōtōmi (now part of Shizuoka Prefecture). The prose narrative is quite sketchy, consisting almost entirely of brief headnotes to the 50 poems (some having nothing to do with Tōtōmi) which it contains. Zōki, the supposed author and the "hermit" of the title, is thought to have been a priest of the Tendai monastery ENRYAKUJI on Mt. Hiei, but little is known of him apart from a few anecdotes and references in such sources as the YAMATO MONOGATARI.

The reputation of *Ionushi* rests largely on the first section, which is often referred to independently as *Kumano kikō* (Journey to Kumano). It is frequently compared with the more famous *Tosa nikki* (Tosa Diary) of KI NO TSURAYUKI (872?–945) and is considered only second to it in importance as an example of the genre of *kikō*, or poetic travel account written in the vernacular.   *Robert H.* BROWER

Ippen (1239–1289)

Founder of the JI SECT of PURE LAND BUDDHISM; known as a "wayfaring saint" *(yugyō shōnin)* and a "saint of abandonment" *(sute hijiri),* who emphasized the importance of reciting the name of Amitābha Buddha (J: Amida Butsu; see NEMBUTSU) for salvation. He was the second son in a prominent family in Iyo Province (now Ehime Prefecture) on Shikoku. From his early childhood he received a Buddhist education. He realized the impermanence of life at his mother's death when he was 10 years old, and this experience led him to renounce the world and become a Buddhist monk, taking the name Zuien.

He first studied Tendai Buddhism at the monastery ENRYAKUJI on Mt. Hiei, but, feeling unfulfilled, in 1251 went to Dazaifu in Kyūshū to study under Shōtatsu, a disciple of Shōkū (1177–1247), the founder of the Seizan branch of JŌDO SECT Buddhism. Changing his name to Chishin, he resolved to convert the masses to Pure Land Buddhism. In 1263, upon the death of his father, he returned

Ippen

Ippen (on the veranda at left) preaching the "dancing *nembutsu*". A detail from the fourth of the 12 scrolls of the *Ippen Shōnin eden*. Painted by En'i in 1299. Colors on silk. 37.7 cm. Kangikōji, Kyōto. National Treasure.

to his homeland, where he remained for seven years. Although little is known about this period in his life, it is believed that he resumed a secular life, taking a wife, and yet never renouncing his devotion to the Buddha. He renounced the world once again, however, in 1271, and returned to Shōtatsu in Dazaifu. On Shōtatsu's recommendation, Ippen set out for a pilgrimage to ZENKŌJI, a temple in Shinano Province (now Nagano Prefecture) famed for its image of Amitābha believed to be from India. There he copied a picture of the Chinese monk Shandao's (Shan-tao) parable of the two rivers of blind passion separated by the thin path of aspiration for rebirth in the Pure Land. He then returned to Shikoku to visit a place where Avalokiteśvara (J: KANNON), the bodhisattva of compassion, was said to have revealed herself. The rugged terrain provided an ideal setting for the rigorous ascetic training commonly practiced by the order of Shingon esoteric monks known as "mountain ascetics" (YAMABUSHI).

At this juncture in his life, Ippen made a decision to combine his own practice of total asceticism with extensive travel, preaching the practice of *nembutsu*. He left Shikoku in 1274 and traveled to SHITENNŌJI, a temple founded by Prince SHŌTOKU in Ōsaka and known as a center of Pure Land faith; he also visited the headquarters of Shingon Buddhism on Mt. Kōya, which at the time was also a popular place for Amida worship, and the KUMANO SANZAN SHRINES, sacred to Shintō. At Kumano, Ippen claimed to have seen the deity of this ancient shrine manifest as Amitābha. Considering the traditional folk belief that the Kumano region was the abode of the dead, the vision of Amitābha gave Ippen the assurance that Amitābha had indeed triumphed over death. He discovered that in the utterance of Amitābha's name all dualities dissolved: life and death, this world of desires and the afterworld—Amida's Pure Land of unsurpassed bliss. This conviction gave Ippen a profound sense of mission, and he spent the remainder of his life traveling throughout the country preaching the importance of reciting Amitābha's name. Thus was born the Ji sect, Ippen's unique religion, combining Pure Land Buddhism, Shingon Buddhism, and folk Shintō. The year 1274 is regarded by Ji sectarians as marking the founding of their sect.

Ippen hastened back to Dazaifu to share his experience with Shōtatsu and then journeyed farther south in Kyūshū. In 1276, after much tribulation, he won a lay convert in Ōtomo Yoriyasu (1222–1300), military governor of Bungo Province (now Ōita Prefecture). Yoriyasu later established the first Ji sect temple in Chinzei, a garrison town in Kyūshū from which Ippen's teaching spread. In the same year, Ippen also acquired the faithful disciple Shinkyō (1237–1319), who was to become his successor; he acquired many other disciples during his trips through Shikoku and southern Honshū. After returning to Zenkōji with his followers in 1279, Ippen started preaching the "dancing *nembutsu*" in the manner of the Heian period (794–1185) Pure Land monk KŪYA. His ecstatic dancing and preaching won a great following from the masses of people living in an age of social unrest.

In 1280 Ippen reached the northern part of Honshū. He then headed southwest toward Kamakura, seat of the ruling military gov-

ernment, to Mishima Shrine in Izu, and to Kyōto, the capital city. In Kyōto, his evangelistic activity was met with a formidable resistance from the two centers of the Tendai establishment, Enryakuji on Mt. Hiei and MIIDERA near Lake Biwa. The people, however, gave him an enthusiastic welcome. In spite of his deteriorating health after 16 years of travel, Ippen headed for his native Shikoku. From there he sailed to the island of Awaji and then to Hyōgo (now the city of Kōbe). In 1289 Ippen died in a trance with the parting words, "There shall be no funeral rite; just give my corpse to the wild animals of the field."

In contrast to the teachings of SHINRAN, the founder of the Jōdo Shin sect, which centered around rebirth in the Pure Land and emphasized the believer's faith, Ippen's teaching of the ecstatic incantation of Amitābha's name focused on abandonment, that is, on entrusting oneself totally to the Buddha. Ippen taught that one need only have unswerving trust in Amitābha's grace and to invoke his name. His teaching, therefore, did not question whether or not one had faith. Salvation had already been decided by Amitābha's Primal Vow eons earlier. Illustrations of Ippen's life are found in the scroll *Ippen Shōnin eden* (A Pictorial Biography of Monk Ippen), in the possession of the temple Kangikōji in Kyōto (one section is at the National Museum in Tōkyō).

🔲 ——*Ippen shōnin goroku* (1811), tr Dennis Hirota as "The Record of Ippen," in *The Eastern Buddhist*, 11.1 (1978). Kanai Kiyomitsu, *Ippen to Jishū kyōdan* (1975). Ōhashi Toshio, *Ippen, sono kōdō to shisō* (1971). Sōshun, *Ippen shōnin ekotoba engi* (1659).

T. James KODERA

Ippitsusai Bunchō (fl ca 1768–1790)

UKIYO-E artist active in Edo (now Tōkyō). A contemporary of HARUNOBU, Bunchō was one of the foremost innovators of full-color woodblock printing; he specialized in pictures of beautiful women and courtesans (*bijinga*) and actors (*yakusha-e*), in all of which he displayed great individual portrait realism. His unusual practice of identifying the courtesans by name soon became the standard form. Before turning to *ukiyo-e*, Bunchō studied KANŌ SCHOOL painting and illustrated anthologies of *senryū* comic verse (see ZAPPAI AND SENRYŪ) and HAIKU. In 1770 he collaborated with KATSUKAWA SHUNSHŌ on a popular three-volume edition of fan-shaped actor portraits called *Ehon butai ōgi*.

Iragomisaki

Cape on western Atsumi Peninsula, southern Aichi Prefecture, central Honshū. Noted for its coastal scenery consisting of towering rocks, especially a rock formation known as the Stone Gate of Hii. A National Vacation Village and a flower center are located on the cape, and it is part of Mikawa Bay Quasi-National Park.

Irako Seihaku (1877–1946)

Poet, physician. Real name Irako Teruzō. Born in Tottori Prefecture. Graduate of Kyōto Prefectural Medical School. He had gained some recognition as a WAKA poet by around 1900, publishing poems in Tōkyō literary magazines while practicing medicine. These were thematically modern poems written in the classical language. He published only one collection, *Kujaku-bune* (1906, The Peacock Boat), whose verses display a richly imaginative romanticism. When *Kujaku-bune* was reprinted in 1929, it was highly praised by the poets HINATSU KŌNOSUKE, KITAHARA HAKUSHŪ, and SAIJŌ YASO.

irezumi → tattoos

iriai

(literally, "to enter collectively"). A term referring to the time-honored system of collective landownership of nonarable or "mountain" areas of Japan before the Meiji period (1868–1912). With the collective ownership went an agreement to share that land's natural resources. These so-called mountain areas usually included such marginal lands as mountain forests, marshes, bamboo groves, dried-up riverbeds, and other sites not suitable for growing crops but still indispensable for agricultural activities. These mountain areas, or *yama* as they were called, were open to all rural inhabitants who possessed the necessary entry permits and who observed the rigid regulations for collecting their portion of its resources: grass, foliage, and other vegetation, as well as edible plants, roots, and firewood. The right to enter, called *iriaiken,* was jealously guarded by the collective.

Various types of *iriai* were distinguished according to ownership. In *murajū iriai,* an area was owned and controlled collectively by the population of a single village. *Mura mura iriai,* the collective ownership and use of the available resources by the inhabitants of several neighboring villages, was the most common form of *iriai* in the latter part of the Edo period (1600–1868). In this type of *iriai,* the collectively owned land was designated as an *iriaichi. Tason mochiji iriai* involved entrance into the mountain area by individuals who possessed no real right or privilege to use the said premises but were given special permission to use the site to gather specified materials in return for the payment of fees *(yama yakugin),* either in money or in kind. Other forms of *iriai* holdings in the Edo period included mountain districts that were owned either by the domainal or shogunal government or by private persons. The former was called *han'yūchi iriai* and the latter *shiyūchi (jitsukiyama) iriai.* As in the case of the *tason mochiji iriai,* the use of government or privately owned mountain sites required the payment of fees, known variously as *yama yakugin* or *yama yakuei.* Those inhabitants who entered such mountain areas to gather the agreed products were, of course, supervised closely by those who issued permits.

Before the TAIKA REFORM of 645, collective ownership and utilization of both agricultural land and other types of land resources appears to have constituted the basic mode of ownership. Thus both arable and nonarable land resources were managed collectively by farming communities organized locally in a hierarchical order. This meant that as yet no individual claims had been laid to the exclusive ownership or use of the basic means of livelihood—land.

After the Taika Reform, following the Chinese example, the central government proclaimed public ownership of the entire agricultural, that is, rice-producing, land in the country. It subsequently distributed this land to able-bodied peasants—men, women, and children—in return for taxes, which were customarily paid in the form of *so* (a rice tax), *yō* (corvée labor), and *chō* (miscellaneous taxes). Under this new system, the cultivators never enjoyed exclusive ownership of the land they occupied but instead possessed the exclusive right to use it (see HANDEN SHŪJU SYSTEM).

It is also significant to note that at the time the nonarable sites and the various resources of such marginal areas still remained outside the control of the public authority; local communities were permitted to utilize these marginal land resources freely. Thus the collective use of these resources by local communities began in a relatively early phase of the agricultural development of Japan, although, at this stage, rules and regulations with respect to the use of these resources could not have been clearly formulated or rigidly imposed.

After about the 10th century the central government in the capital city (Kyōto) lost its effective political power over the country, so much so that it could not prevent noble families and powerful religious organizations from appropriating its landholdings illicitly. This absorption of public land by private interests gave rise in turn to the unique landholding method known as the SHŌEN system. This permitted the taking over of rice land by groups of individuals or organizations, such as temples and shrines, which in turn claimed a certain portion of the harvest from these estates as income. The right to receive a portion of the harvest, as enforced by those groups, was called *shiki.*

Under the *shōen* system, the practice of using the resources of undeveloped areas was continued by the local inhabitants, who were now incorporated into *shōen* units, which collectively utilized the mountain resources by adhering to locally established rules and regulations.

During the Edo period Japan witnessed a period of unprecedented economic prosperity. This was largely stimulated by the dynamic development of the agricultural sector. It has been estimated that the land under cultivation increased by more than 60 percent between 1600 and 1700: one conservative estimate states that it increased from 2.12 million *chō* (1 *chō* = 1 hectare or 2.45 acres) in 1600 to 3.5 million *chō* by the 1700s. Although the rate of increase declined after the 1700s, the area under cultivation expanded steadily during the remainder of the Edo period. This is evidenced by the fact that there were approximately 4.6 million *chō* of arable land in the 1870s. This expansion of arable land, especially in the early Edo period, was brought about by a number of factors, such as an increase in population, encouragement of systematic land reclamation, and a series of public and private irrigation projects.

The increase in arable land led to an increase in demand for mountain areas and other marginal sites as a source of much-needed fertilizers. Reliance on mountain-area vegetation as fertilizer remained high during the Edo period, since rice cultivation continued to dominate the agricultural scene. As is well known, rice cultivation became highly intensified over the centuries, and this was largely made possible by the massive use of both natural and composite fertilizers, together with a greater input of labor hours per unit of land. For example, it is estimated that a farmer in the Edo period used 300 to 500 *kan* (1 *kan* = 3.8 kg or 8.3 lb) of dried grass on his rice field, which was usually less than one-fourth of an acre. The function of marginal lands thus remained exceedingly important, although commercial fertilizers such as dry fish *(hoshika), sake* dregs, rice bran *(nuka),* soybean dregs *(mamekasu),* and other types of material gradually reduced the use of natural fertilizer in the 19th century.

The ever-growing need for these mountain resources by farmers also served to increase the number of disputes in the local areas. For instance, a dispute could occur between two villages over an unclear boundary established in the distant past. It could also take the form of a feud among members of the same village over an alleged inequity in the distribution of mountain resources. Finally, an unfriendly encounter could occur over the question of who actually had the outright ownership and control of a certain area. This type of conflict often took the form of a legal battle between influential villagers—those with official standing who claimed the ownership of a disputed area—and the remaining members of the village, who rejected such an outright assertion.

A legal battle that took place in the village of Horado in Mino Province (now part of Gifu Prefecture) in 1655 clearly illustrates the kind of issue involved in such disputes. The dispute started when a village official named Shin'emon demanded payment for the use of a certain area. Shin'emon justified his demand on the grounds that the mountain area in dispute had been the private property *(jitsuki-yama)* of his family for generations and that villagers from time immemorial had paid their dues to his family. The villagers rejected his claim and argued instead that the area in contention was *iriaichi* and reserved for the village. They not only demanded a fair sharing of the resources in the area but also called for the end of any monetary payment to Shin'emon, interpreting past payment as merely a generous monetary donation by the villagers at a time when Shin'emon's ancestors had fallen into bankruptcy.

After a prolonged dispute, the government, assisted by the village officials in the neighboring area, finally settled on a compromise which confirmed that a greater portion of the area was, in fact, *iriaichi,* not private property as claimed by Shin'emon. At the same time, it recognized Shin'emon's rights by granting him absolute ownership of a small portion of the area. Judging from this case and various other lawsuits, one can see that the government did play an important role in the settlement of disputes concerning the ownership and use of vital resources, such as water and other materials already mentioned.

After the Meiji Restoration of 1868 the government established a modern landholding system. In the 1870s, it formally recognized private ownership of land resources and conferred land titles to protect the properties of legitimate title holders. The government also proceeded to establish clear ownership of collective landholdings that had hitherto been owned and controlled by organized entities such as villages. As for resources under collective management, the government usually classified those designated as *iriaichi* during the Edo period as "public" domain and seized them to enrich its coffers. Appropriation of such properties without compensation was made on the premise that legal justification for the ownership of such lands by any individuals or groups could not be presented. In some instances, the government issued land titles to individual claimants of specific holdings.

It is important to note here that when conflicts arose, the Meiji government often neglected the welfare of the actual cultivators by giving preferential treatment to powerful segments of rural communities. For example, it often accepted claims filed by litigants who could provide some form of legal documentation, while it usually rejected claims filed by poor cultivators who could not submit any written documents. It may be argued, then, that the Meiji government's land policy promoted the concentration of landholdings, a

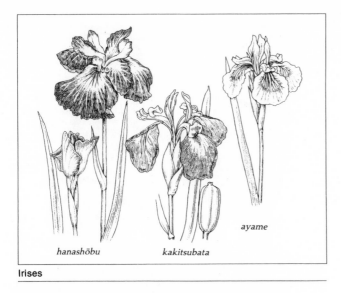

hanashōbu   kakitsubata   ayame

Irises

tendency that was to create serious socioeconomic problems in the late 19th century and the first half of the 20th century.

■——Nakata Kaoru, *Mura oyobi iriai no kenkyū* (1949). Ono Takeo, *Nihon sonraku shi gaisetsu* (1937). Sasaki Junnosuke, *Daimyō to hyakushō* (1966).   *Isao* SORANAKA

Irie Takako (1911–   )

Film actress. Real name Tōbōjō Hideko. Born in Tōkyō, the daughter of a viscount. In the 1930s Irie became a popular star of Nikkatsu (see NIKKATSU CORPORATION) studios, a company otherwise less blessed with beautiful actresses than its rival, Shōchiku (see SHŌCHIKU CO, LTD). Although she starred in several of director MIZOGUCHI KENJI's films, beginning with *Taki no Shiraito* (1933; Taki no Shiraito, the Water Magician), she eventually aroused his dislike, and Mizoguchi removed her from the role of the heroine in his *Yōkihi* (1955, The Princess Yang Kwei-fei). In later years she starred in mysteries such as *Kaidan Sagayashiki* (1953, Ghostly Tales from Saga Mansion) and *Kaibyō Arimagoten* (1954, The Ghostly Cat at Arima Castle) and earned the unflattering nickname of "Cat Lady."
ITASAKA Tsuyoshi

Iriomotejima

Island approximately 450 km (279 mi) southwest of Okinawa. The largest island of the YAEYAMA ISLANDS, hilly, with mountains averaging 400 m (1,312 ft) high. The highest mountain is Komidake (470 m; 1,542 ft). Some 96 percent of the island is covered with subtropical forests, and mangroves flourish at the mouths of the rivers. The island is the habitat of the Iriomote *yamaneko* (*Mayailurus iriomotensis;* see WILDCATS), a wildcat unique to the island. Malaria-carrying mosquitoes were exterminated after World War II, and the island has been developed as a tourist area in recent years. Part of IRIOMOTE NATIONAL PARK. Area: 284 sq km (110 sq mi).

Iriomote National Park

(Iriomote Kokuritsu Kōen). Situated in the YAEYAMA ISLANDS, in the chain of the RYŪKYŪ ISLANDS, 1,000 km (621 mi) southwest of Kyūshū. This maritime park, administered by Okinawa Prefecture, features coral islands, mangrove swamps, subtropical forests, and rare animals. The major part of the park is on the hilly island of IRIOMOTEJIMA, and it includes the small islands of Kobamajima, Kuroshima, and TAKETOMIJIMA, and their surrounding waters to the east of Iriomotejima. The two islands of Kobamajima and Taketomijima are situated in the largest coral reef in Japan, which measures 20 km (12.4 mi) east to west and 15 km (9.3 mi) north to south. The park has dense subtropical forests and vegetation, poisonous snakes, rare butterflies, and mangrove swamps at the mouth of the river Nakamagawa in Iriomotejima. In 1965 a species of wildcat (Iriomote *yamaneko;* see WILDCATS) was discovered on the island. Total area: 445 sq km (172 sq mi); land area: 125 sq km (48 sq mi).

irises

Perennial herbs of the family Iridaceae, genus *Iris,* many of which are indigenous to Japan and frequently cultivated as ornamentals. Among the best-known iris species in Japan is the *ayame* (*Iris nertschinskia* or *I. sibirica* var. *orientalis*), which is common in fields and on mountains from Hokkaidō to Honshū and Kyūshū, as well as in eastern Siberia and northeastern provinces of China. It has long been cultivated in gardens for its beautiful flowers. It grows 30 to 50 centimeters (12–20 in) high. The purple flower, 7 to 8 centimeters (3 in) across, usually opens early in summer at the top of the stem. Cultivated varieties include the white-flowered *shiroayame,* the *kurumaayame* with large inner petals (standards), and the *chaboayame,* a small plant with a purple or white flower. Until the Heian period (794–1185), the name *ayame* was used to refer to the plant now known as SHŌBU or sweet flag (*Acorus calamus* var. *asiaticus*). Shōbu is often translated as "iris," but the plant is not an iris and should not be confused with the *hanashōbu,* another well-known Japanese iris.

The *hanashōbu* (*Iris ensata* var. *hortensis*) averages 60–80 centimeters (24–32 in) in height. It grows in clusters. The flower stalk is green and stands up straight. The leaves are sword-shaped and prominently veined. In early summer, violet, white, and violet-white variegated flowers bloom with a diameter of 8–24 centimeters (3–9 in). The *nohanashōbu* (*I. ensata* f. *spontanea*) is the mother species. At present there are approximately 300 varieties of *hanashōbu.*

By the Edo period (1600–1868) there were already 200 varieties. The center of cultivation was in Edo (now Tōkyō) in what is now the Horikiri flower garden in Katsushika Ward. From some of these, improved varieties were developed later in the Higo area (the Higo *hanashōbu*) and the Ise area (the Ise *hanashōbu*). Horticulturally, *hanashōbu* are now classified into three groups corresponding to the three areas mentioned above: Edo, Higo, and Ise. The distinctive characteristics of the Edo group are their suitability to cultivation in swampy land and the delicate and elegant qualities of their flowers. The Higo group are distinguished by their ability to grow even in hilly areas (since they were developed as potted plants and thus need less water), by the large size of their flowers, and by their broad petals. The Ise group are distinguished by their long drooping flowers and fine wrinkles in their petals.

Hanashōbu were first introduced to the West in 1852 by P. F. von SIEBOLD (1796–1866) and appeared in a full-color print in a Belgian horticulture journal in 1857. Their name first appeared in England in 1874, where they were praised as garden flowers and as a superior variety of the iris. Around the same time, they were introduced into North America and later Germany and Russia. At present they are grown in large numbers in areas along the Atlantic coast of North America, including a large number at the Brooklyn Botanical Gardens.

Another popular iris species, the *kakitsubata* (*I. laevigata*), has long been cultivated, but it also grows wild in moist places and at the water's edge in various parts of Japan. Its distribution extends into Korea, northern China, and eastern Siberia. It reaches a height of 50 to 70 centimeters (20 to 28 in). The leaves are sword-shaped or broad linear with pointed tips but without midribs. Early in summer two to three dark bluish-purple flowers, 12 centimeters (5 in) across, open at the top of the stem. The flowers consist of wide drooping outer petals (falls), yellow at the center bottom, and erect inner petals (standards). This flower was the earliest known of the irises among the Japanese, and in early times its juice was rubbed into clothing as a dye. The *kakitsubata* of Yatsuhashi in Mikawa Province (now Aichi Prefecture) are noted in Japanese literature. Compared to the similar species *hanashōbu,* which has hundreds of varieties, relatively few horticultural varieties of *kakitsubata* have been developed, since the plant was customarily appreciated in its natural habitat; it was only in the Edo period that cultivation was started. Present horticultural varieties include plants with white flowers and purple-streaked flowers.

The *shaga* (*I. japonica*) grows wild in large colonies on moist wooded slopes all over Japan and is also widely cultivated in shady areas of home gardens. The leaves, which develop in two rows from a shallow rhizome, are swordlike, pointy, glossy, and bright green in color. Around May a flower stalk (scape) grows from among the leaves, ramifying in the upper part, and produces light bluish-white flowers 5–6 centimeters (2–2.4 in) across with distinctive yellow spots and a crest-shaped process in the center of the toothed outer petals. The flowers wither after blooming for one day. The *shaga* is also found in China, where it bears fruits and large flowers; the Japanese plants seldom bear seeds and propagate by means of rhizomes.

A miniature species called *himeshaga* (*I. gracilipes*), grows in fields and mountains and is also planted in home gardens and in pots. It has light purple or, more rarely, white flowers.

Among other species, the *ichihatsu* (*I. tectorum*), originally from China, is also widely cultivated in Japan and is occasionally found growing on thatched roofs; the *hiōgiayame* (*I. setosa*) with wide obovate falls and very short standards is found in the northern part of Japan.   MATSUDA Osamu

Iroha jirui shō

A Japanese-language dictionary compiled in the latter part of the Heian period (794–1185) by the courtier Tachibana no Tadakane (fl late 12th century). There exists a two-volume version and a three-volume version. This dictionary classifies the standard vocabulary of the period into 47 divisions according to the traditional *iroha* syllabic alphabet (see IROHA POEM) and then further subdivides the contents according to meaning, supplying the Chinese characters (KANJI) used to write the word and examples of usage. It is a useful document for investigating how Chinese characters were used at the time to write Japanese. Its influence on later dictionaries was considerable. There is another work with the same name dating from the Kamakura period (1185–1333) which amounts to a 10-volume expansion of the former work. See also DICTIONARIES.
                                                    UWANO Zendō

iroha karuta

A simple recognition game based on 47 of the 48 written symbols of the Japanese phonetic syllabary (see KANA), using cards printed with pictures and proverbs. (The omitted symbol is that for syllable-final *n*; some sets have a 48th card using the Chinese character for *kyō* or capital.) The name derives from the first three syllables of an older traditional arrangement of the *kana* syllabary (*i-ro-ha* and so on; see IROHA POEM) and the Japanese transliteration of the Portuguese word for card (*carta*). There are 96 cards divided into two equal sets, one for "reading" and one for "taking." On each card of the reading set is a proverb that begins with a particular syllable, while on each of the taking set is a single syllable written in cursive script (*hiragana*) and a picture illustrating the proverb that begins with that syllable. Thus the proverb card for the syllable "ha," for instance, reads, "*Hana yori dango*" (literally, "Dumplings are better than flowers"). On its companion card are the written symbol for *ha* and a picture of a youth smugly enjoying a stick of dumplings while cherry blossoms fall unnoticed around him.

In the game of *iroha karuta*, the picture cards are spread in front of the players on the *tatami*-matted floor. Proverb cards are held by one person who reads them in random order. The object of the game is to spot and seize the corresponding picture card as the proverb is being read. The player holding the most cards at the end of the game wins.

Iroha karuta in its present form is said to have been invented in Kyōto around 1850, commercialized in Ōsaka, and then popularized in Edo (now Tōkyō). A children's game with educational overtones, *iroha karuta* had the double benefit of teaching the alphabet and traditional wisdom as well. Once so popular that almost every child knew the "*iroha*" proverbs (*iroha tatoe*) by heart, the game now takes a distant back seat to television and the products of the toy industry. See also PLAYING CARDS.   John E. THAYER III

iroha poem

(*iroha uta*). Poem dating from the Heian period (794–1185) made up of 47 characters of the phonetic KANA syllabary, excluding only the 48th (for syllable-final *n*). The author of this poem is unknown, but it has traditionally been ascribed to the Buddhist monk KŪKAI. It first appears in 11th-century documents and, in a Buddhist view of life, likens the transience of human existence to the short-lived beauty of a flower.

In the *iroha* poem the signs are arranged in the following order:

i	ro	ha	ni	ho	he	to	chi	ri	nu
ru	(w)o	wa	ka	yo	ta	re	so	tsu	ne
na	ra	mu	u	(w)i	no	o	ku	ya	ma
ke	fu	ko	e	te	a	sa	ki	yu	me
mi	shi	(w)e	hi	mo	se	su			

Iroha karuta

Shown are the "taking" and "reading" cards for the syllables *i* (top), *ro* (center), and *ha* (bottom). The cards read *Inu mo arukeba bō ni ataru* (Every dog has its day), *Ron yori shōko* (Example is better than precept), and *Hana yori dango* (Dumplings are better than flowers).

The poem is read (with voicing of some consonants) in modern pronunciation as:

Iro wa nioedo chirinuru o
Waga yo tare zo tsune naran
Ui no okuyama kyō koete
Asaki yume miji ei mo sezu

This can be roughly translated as

The colors blossom, scatter, and fall.
In this world of ours, who lasts forever?
Today let us cross over the remote mountains of life's illusions,
And dream no more shallow dreams nor succumb to
    drunkenness.

Much like the Roman alphabet, the *iroha* poem is sometimes used to assign an order to various items in dictionaries and the like, although the order of the chart known as the GOJŪON ZU is more frequently used now.   UWANO Zendō

Irohazaka

Popular name for two toll roads in NIKKŌ NATIONAL PARK, western Tochigi Prefecture, central Honshū. The roads ascend a towering ridge from Umagaeshi near the city of Nikkō to the vicinity of Lake Chūzenji. The name Irohazaka is derived from the fact that the two roads have a total of 48 hairpin curves, the same number as the *iroha* arrangement of the Japanese *kana* syllabary (see IROHA POEM). The first toll road covers a distance of 6.5 kilometers (4 mi) with 28 hairpin curves. The second toll road covers a distance of 9.5 km (5.9 mi) with 20 hairpin curves. It is used for driving up to the lake while the No. 1 road is used for descending the ridge.

iron age

(*tekki jidai*). If Japan had an iron age, it was the Kofun period (ca 300–710). Iron had been imported from the continent during the preceding Yayoi period (ca 300 BC–ca AD 300), but iron tools and weapons were most conspicuously used during the 4th and 5th centuries. Iron-working itself did not become well established in Japan until the 6th century. The major archaeological features of the Kofun period are large mounded tombs (KOFUN), which were erected

Iron and steel industry

One of the four blast furnaces at Nippon Steel's Kimitsu works in Chiba Prefecture.

for the leaders of society. During the Kofun period Japan changed from a land of small, independent polities to a unified state. See also HISTORY OF JAPAN: protohistory.   Peter BLEED

iron and steel

Iron has been known in Japan since ancient times. In about AD 300 various kinds of ironware and an iron-making process were introduced from China, by way of Korea, and iron production began on a very small scale. By the 15th century the tatara process (see TATARA-BUKI) had been perfected and was generally used until the beginning of the Meiji period (1868–1912), when a European iron-making process using a blast furnace was introduced into Japan. In 1896 the modern steel industry was inaugurated with the establishment of the YAWATA IRON AND STEEL WORKS, which began operations in 1901. During the 80–year period since then, Japan has become one of the major manufacturers and exporters of steel in the world.

The Tatara Furnace —— Iron was formerly made from iron sand instead of iron ore. The refining process utilized a kind of furnace known as the tatara furnace. Initially, a hole was dug underground, and a mixture of iron sand and charcoal fuel placed inside. The mixture was heated by means of blasts of air from a set of bellows. The iron sand was reduced to sponge-like solid iron or wrought iron. The sponge iron was then broken into pieces, which were classified by an examination of fracture surfaces.

The first tatara furnace is said to have been built in Izumo Province (now Shimane Prefecture) in the middle of the 13th century. The furnace was later enlarged and the draft technique improved. By the 15th century the tatara process was established as a steel-making process. Iron made by this process was in great demand for the manufacture of arms and agricultural implements. At the end of the 16th century, gourd-shaped iron lumps called nambantetsu were imported, by means of Portuguese ships, and used as material to manufacture arms, especially swords. Apparently, nambantetsu was manufactured in furnaces similar to the tatara type, but it contained more phosphorus and carbon than tatara iron. The tatara process was used for refining iron and making steel until the early part of the Meiji period when modern iron-making technology using the blast furnace was introduced into Japan from Europe.

Swords —— Traditional Japanese swords have excellent metallurgical properties, which testify to their high level of craftsmanship. This is because the iron sand found in Japan was of high quality and well-suited for the tatara process. Iron sand was extracted by alluvial mining at recovery plants called kanna nagashiba, built on mountain slopes near surface deposits of sand and gravel containing iron particles. The heavy iron sand was separated by gravity from a mixture of sand, rock, and water. The separated iron sand was purified and loaded into a tatara furnace, together with charcoal, where it was reduced with the aid of bellows. Since the reducing temperature inside the tatara furnace was low, impurities in the molten iron could not be completely removed. However, by the use of carefully prepared charcoal from selected types of wood, sulfur and phosphorus, which were harmful impurities, were eliminated, with the result that a high quality forgeable iron called tamahagane could be produced.

The traditional Japanese sword was the product of a highly developed craft and exhibited two major properties, that of being very sharp and not easily broken or bent. To produce these incompatible properties, a soft low-carbon steel was wrapped in a medium-carbon steel, which could then be hardened by successive forging and heat treatments. The outer layer (medium-carbon steel) was made from a small amount of tamahagane by repeated heating in a furnace, followed by an intensive process of hammering and folding. The impurities in the steel were thus eliminated and the carbon content controlled. The center part (low-carbon steel) was wrapped in this layer of steel and forged into shape. By following a carefully developed process of heating, cooling, and hammering, Japanese swordsmiths produced blades with extremely hard steel at the edge that were very sharp nevertheless. The layered-application of composite material; the bathing method, using different cooling speeds; and the forging method demonstrate the high technological level of steelmaking achieved by the middle of the Edo period (1600–1868).

Modern Steelmaking and the Steel Industry —— In 1896 a government enterprise, the Yawata Iron and Steel Works, was established to form the foundation of the modern steel industry. By 1912 the private enterprises that are now known as SUMITOMO METAL INDUSTRIES, LTD, KŌBE STEEL, LTD, the KAWASAKI STEEL CORPORATION, and NIPPON KŌKAN, had been organized. In 1934 Nippon Steel was established as a national company. After World War II this company was broken up into Yawata Steel and Fuji Steel. In March 1970 these two companies were again amalgamated as the NIPPON STEEL CORPORATION. In the last decade Japan has aggressively developed its steelmaking industry and leads the world in the amount of exported steel. See also IRON AND STEEL INDUSTRY.

■——Hoshino Yoshirō, ed, Atarashii tekkō gijutsu (1961). Sangyō Zairyō Chōsa Kenkyūjo, ed, Nihon no sangyō zairyō (1971).

MAKINO Noboru

iron and steel industry

Japan's steel industry is the world's second largest and possibly the most efficient. Japan is the world's leading exporter of steel, even though the country is almost completely dependent on foreign supplies of iron ore and coal. The industry played a key role in Japan's post–World War II economic growth and was given high priority by the government. As a result, Japan's steel production has grown much faster than that of any other country in the postwar era.

Origins of the Modern Industry —— Japan's traditional iron-making and steelmaking technology (see TATARA-BUKI) satisfied the country's needs during the Edo period (1600–1868), but with the opening of Japan in the 1850s there was a new demand for iron and steel of quality high enough to produce firearms. In 1858 ŌSHIMA TAKATŌ, an engineer from Morioka, built furnaces based on Western designs at Kamaishi in what is now Iwate Prefecture. Ōshima's furnaces were primitive and small, each producing only a few hundred tons of steel per year, but they were the first in Japan to succeed in the commercial production of iron from iron ore.

After the Meiji Restoration (1868), the new government took over the Kamaishi Iron Mine in 1873 and built a new iron works with two 9,000-metric ton (9,900-short ton) per year blast furnaces imported from England. Efforts to operate the English blast furnaces failed, despite the help of foreign advisers. Ownership of the works passed to Tanaka Chōbei (1858–1924), a Tōkyō businessman, who made iron using Ōshima's type of furnace. Finally, in the 1890s, Tanaka successfully started operating the English furnaces.

The Kamaishi Iron Mine had blast furnaces, but lacked the other facilities of an integrated steel plant. In 1896 the government decided to build Japan's first integrated iron and steel works at Yawata in Kyūshū. The first blast furnace at the new works was blown-in in 1901 with a rated annual capacity of 60,000 metric tons (66,000 short tons)—more than double Japan's total existing iron-making capacity. Modern steelmaking and rolling equipment was also installed. Ger-

Iron and steel industry——Table 1

				West	United
	Japan	US	USSR	Germany	Kingdom
1900	1	10,351	2,214	6,646	4,979
1910	250	26,512	3,444	13,699	6,476
1920	845	42,807	162	8,538	9,212
1930	2,289	41,351	5,761	11,511	7,443
1940	7,528	60,765	19,000	19,141	13,183
1950	4,839	87,848	27,300	12,121	16,553
1955	9,408	108,647	45,271	21,336	20,108
1960	22,138	91,920	65,292	34,100	24,695
1965	41,161	122,490	91,000	36,821	27,439
1970	93,322	119,310	115,886	45,041	28,314
1973	119,322	136,805	131,481	49,521	26,649
1975	102,313	105,818	141,325	40,415	19,782
1980	111,395	101,457	148,000	43,838	11,278

Crude Steel Production by Major Countries (in thousands of metric tons)

NOTE: Pre–World War II figures for Japan include Korea and Manchuria; for West Germany, all of Germany. Pre–1917 figures for USSR are for Russia.
SOURCE: Iida Kaichi, Ōhashi Shūji, and Kuroiwa Toshirō, *Tekkō* (1969). Nihon Tekkō Remmei (Japan Iron and Steel Federation), *Tekkō tōkei yōran* (annual): 1981.

man engineers and workers helped with the start-up, but the operation did not go smoothly and much of the equipment was soon out of operation. Several years passed before Yawata was able to achieve its rated production capacity.

In the first decade of the 20th century many steel-using industries started to develop in Japan, and private capital moved into the production of steel. By 1912 four major private steelmakers had been established: NIPPON KŌKAN, Kawasaki Shipyard Co (now KAWASAKI STEEL CORPORATION), SUMITOMO METAL INDUSTRIES, LTD (then part of the SUMITOMO *zaibatsu*), and KŌBE STEEL, LTD (then a subsidiary of Suzuki Shoten).

World War I brought a boom in the industry. The private firms expanded capacity and many new firms were established. Plants were built in Manchuria and Korea. The end of the war brought an abrupt end to the boom, and the industry suffered further in the FINANCIAL CRISIS OF 1927 and the worldwide depression beginning in 1929.

In the 1930s Japan's leaders sought to strengthen the steel industry. One measure was the 1934 formation of Nippon Steel, a KOKU-SAKU KAISHA (government policy company). Nippon Steel was an amalgamation of the state-owned YAWATA IRON AND STEEL WORKS with five private firms, some of them *zaibatsu*-owned. The strongest private firms, Nippon Kōkan, Kawasaki, Sumitomo, and Kōbe, remained independent, but Nippon Steel had most of Japan's iron-making capacity and more than half of its steelmaking capacity.

Other strategic measures included the building of new blast furnaces to reduce dependence on foreign sources of pig iron and scrap, and the construction of new steelmaking capacity. Annual domestic steel production rose from about 2 million metric tons (2.2 million short tons) in 1930 to a wartime peak of 7.7 million metric tons (8.5 million short tons) in 1943. Production dropped in 1944 because of shortages of raw materials and fell to below 2 million metric tons (2.2 million short tons) again in 1945.

After the end of the war the raw material shortage became even more acute and many plants were forced to close, bringing steel production down to just over half a million metric tons in 1946. Under OCCUPATION policies many top executives in the steel industry were forced to retire, and plans were made for the dissolution of the major steel firms and the removal of plants and equipment for war reparations. Militant labor unions came into existence and there were strikes at many steel plants. After about 1948 the Occupation began to modify its demands for reform and started to encourage the reconstruction of the industry. No plants were seized as reparations, but some equipment was. See also ECONOMIC HISTORY: Occupation-period economy.

Postwar Recovery and Growth——The Occupation reforms were completed by 1950. The most significant change was the breaking up of Nippon Steel into Yawata Steel and Fuji Steel. These two firms were soon engaged in intense competition with each other and with Japan's third major integrated steelmaker, Nippon Kōkan.

Competition was intensified as the three major open-hearth steelmakers, Kawasaki, Sumitomo, and Kōbe, rushed to become integrated steelmakers, each struggling to increase its market share. Many smaller firms went bankrupt or came under the control of these six steelmakers.

The Korean War brought prosperity to the industry, but the inefficiency of Japanese plants and equipment caused steelmaking costs to be far above the international level. A massive effort to modernize the industry was carried out under a series of rationalization programs coordinated with government help. The first program (1951–55) emphasized the reconditioning of existing facilities. The second (1956–60) brought the construction of new integrated steelworks and the large-scale introduction of new technology.

Tremendous progress was made under these programs. The domestic price of steel sheet, for example, was two to three times the US price in 1950 but about the same as the US price in 1960. Japan produced 4.8 million metric tons (5.3 million short tons) of steel in 1950, slightly more than half of France's steel output. By 1960 Japan had more than quadrupled its 1950 production to surpass France's and become the world's fifth largest steel producer. Progress continued under the third rationalization program (1960–65), and was further stimulated by the 1960 INCOME-DOUBLING PLAN (under which per capita income was to be doubled by 1970). All of the major firms built new integrated steel plants incorporating advanced technology.

Japan surpassed Great Britain in 1961 and West Germany in 1964 to become the world's third largest steelmaker. Production doubled again between 1964 and 1969 and reached a peak of 119.3 million metric tons (130.9 million short tons) in 1973—near the level of the United States and the Soviet Union (see Table 1). In 1980 Japan's production of 111 million metric tons (122 million short tons) surpassed the United States (101 million metric tons or 111 million short tons) to become the second largest producer.

The construction of new plants further increased production efficiency, and labor productivity apparently surpassed that of the United States in the mid-1970s. Japan is now widely considered to be the world's lowest-cost producer of steel. Competition among the six major firms continued to be intense, though efforts were made to moderate it during downturns in the economy through the formation of cartels, and in 1970 Yawata and Fuji merged to form a new NIPPON STEEL CORPORATION.

Structure of the Industry——Japan's steel industry includes integrated steelmakers, electric steelmakers, rolling firms, and special steelmakers, but it is dominated by the five large integrated steel firms: Nippon Steel, Nippon Kōkan, Kawasaki, Sumitomo, and Kōbe. Nippon Steel is the world's largest steelmaker and accounts for about one-third of Japanese production. Together the big five firms produced 70.4 percent of Japan's steel in 1980 (see Table 2). In contrast, the five largest steelmakers in the United States accounted for 58.7 percent of total production in 1975. There are also three

Iron and steel industry——Table 2

Crude Steel Production by Leading Japanese Steelmakers

| | 1976 | | 1981 | |
	Production (million metric tons)	Share of total Japanese output (percent)	Production (million metric tons)	Share of total Japanese output (percent)
Nippon Steel	34.0	31.6	30.0	29.5
Nippon Kōkan	14.7	13.6	12.8	12.6
Sumitomo	13.3	12.4	11.5	11.3
Kawasaki	13.3	12.4	11.5	11.3
Kōbe	7.8	7.3	6.8	6.7
Total for five largest firms	83.1	77.3	72.6	71.4
Total for all firms	107.4	100.0	101.7	100.0

SOURCE: For totals for all firms: Nihon Tekkō Remmei (Japan Iron and Steel Federation), *Tekkō tōkei yōran* (annual): 1982. Figures for individual firms: annual reports for respective firms.

smaller integrated steelmakers, two of which are affiliates of Nippon Steel.

At one time a large share of Japan's steel was produced by non-integrated open-hearth and electric steelmakers. The largest of the open-hearth firms, Kawasaki, Sumitomo, and Kōbe, all built integrated plants in the 1950s. By the late 1970s no open-hearth furnaces were in operation, but there were still a large number of electric steelmakers. Many of these firms were being squeezed out of their markets by the integrated producers, and they were merging or curtailing production to survive. Several of the electric steelmakers were affiliates of Nippon Steel and Nippon Kōkan.

Rolling firms purchase ingots from integrated or electric steelmakers and roll them into various products, including pipe, special sheet, and small bars. Some of these have well over a thousand employees, while others are very small. Special steelmakers produce forgings, castings, high-alloy steels, stainless steels, and tool steels. Some of these firms are affiliates of the integrated steelmakers, others are affiliated with major industrial firms such as HITACHI, LTD, and TOYOTA MOTOR CORPORATION, and still others are independent.

Labor and Industrial Relations——Steelworkers, like other industrial workers in Japan, fall into two categories: those who are regular employees of major firms and those who are either temporary employees of major firms or employees of subcontractors. The permanent employees have some assurance of employment until they reach retirement age. Their wages rise steadily with seniority and many benefits are available to them from the company. The other workers enjoy little job security, few benefits, and are often assigned to unpleasant or dangerous work that the permanent employees do not want to do. Since the early 1960s the steel industry has not made much use of temporary employees, but has relied extensively on subcontractors. In 1976 more than 40 percent of the people working at Japan's steel plants were employees of subcontractors; at a few major plants the proportion was as high as 60 percent.

Most of the permanent employees of the major firms belong to Tekkō Rōren (Japanese Federation of Iron and Steel Workers' Unions). Tekkō Rōren is considered a conservative organization, despite its membership in the left-leaning SŌHYŌ (General Council of Trade Unions of Japan). Often Tekkō Rōren is chosen to spearhead the annual spring wage offensive (SHUNTŌ).

Labor-management relations were generally antagonistic through the 1950s, but have been more harmonious in the past two decades. As the industry rushed to modernize in the 1950s and 1960s, steelworkers had to adapt to a very high rate of technological change. Many workers found their skills suddenly made obsolete and changes in workplace management were necessary. The high rate of growth of the industry made it unnecessary, however, for the firms to lay off large numbers of technologically displaced employees—many were simply transferred to new plants.

Raw Material Supply——Japan is poorly endowed with the resources used in steelmaking. In the late 1970s it was importing nearly 99 percent of the iron ore and 88 percent of the coal it used in

steelmaking. Until the late 1950s this import dependence led to high costs and an instability of supply. These problems were overcome through a series of measures: (1) long-term contracts were signed overseas to ensure a stable supply of high-quality iron ore and coal; (2) giant ore and coal carriers were developed, which dramatically cut shipping costs; (3) new tidewater integrated iron and steel plants were built on reclaimed land complete with docking facilities to accommodate the giant carriers; and (4) technologies were developed to reduce the materials needed to make each ton of steel.

In addition to ensuring a steady supply of low-cost raw materials, these measures offered other benefits. Large tonnages of ore and coal with highly uniform characteristics could be brought into plants at one time to facilitate the flow of production. Steel products could be shipped out from the plants on efficient large ships with lower delivery costs.

Facilities and Technology——Eleven of the 21 major integrated steel plants have been built after World War II, 7 of them since 1960. Most are large, well situated for the efficient delivery of raw materials and shipment of products at tidewater sites, and laid out for maximum efficiency. Generally, provisions have been made for further expansion if demand should justify it.

Japan has been a leader in blast furnace technology since the early 1960s and now has many of the world's largest and most productive blast furnaces. The efficient basic oxygen steelmaking process was adopted early and the industry has pioneered many of the advances in this technology. More recently, Japan has led in the use of continuous casting and in the development of new applications for computers.

Sources of Finance——Steelmakers, like other firms in Japan, have relied far more on external funds, particularly bank loans, than their counterparts in the United States or Europe. Typically, two-thirds of the funds used by the industry have been borrowed. In the late 1940s and early 1950s, interest-subsidized loans were received from such government financial institutions as the BANK OF JAPAN, with other funds coming from private Japanese banks and various foreign lenders. In the late 1950s most of the loans came from private Japanese banks. The World Bank and other foreign sources were also very important. Since the mid-1960s Japanese city banks, insurance companies, and trust banks have been the main sources of finance.

The steel firms have made relatively little use of increases in capitalization or the sale of bonds in raising capital. There was some increase in the reliance on these forms of finance between 1955 and 1965, but it has declined since.

Steel Exports——In 1969 Japan replaced West Germany as the world's leading exporter of steel, and in 1976 more than one-fourth of all the steel traded internationally was from Japan. By far the biggest customer was the United States, which took 20.9 percent of Japan's steel exports in 1976. Other important customers included China (8.4 percent), the USSR (8.3 percent), Iran (4.8 percent), and South Korea (4.1 percent).

Steel has been Japan's most important export in most of the years since the mid-1950s, bringing in about $11 billion in 1976, although

Japan also imported over $7 billion worth of iron ore, coal, and other steelmaking materials. The export trade took about one-third of total steel output in 1976. This is far larger than the percentage of production exported by the United States or the Soviet Union, but smaller than the percentages typically exported by West Germany, France, and many other nations.

Problems and Prospects —— In the late 1970s the outlook for the steel industry did not seem promising. The OIL CRISIS OF 1973 caused uneasiness about dependence on foreign iron ore, coal, and fuel; subsequent years saw substantial increases in the prices of these materials. The oil crisis also appeared to usher in an era of slower growth for the economy, which already seemed to have reached a point in its development where further growth would not be matched by growth in demand for steel. Several relatively new blast furnaces were shut down in the mid-1970s, and most plants were operating considerably below capacity.

New emphasis was given to exports, but resistance was met, and restrictions had to be placed on sales to the United States and Europe. A further threat to Japan's export markets appeared as many third-world nations started to build modern steel plants, often with Japanese assistance. These rising manufacturers may well drive Japanese steel out of their home markets, only to compete with it in other countries. The industry was also faced with new environmental control regulations in the 1970s, a problem shared by steelmakers in many other countries. In 1976 the industry spent about 20 percent of its total investment in plant and equipment on pollution control equipment. On the positive side, the Japanese steel plants have been designed for efficient operation and low-cost expansion. These factors could give the industry new prosperity if world steel demand should turn upward.

—— Ichikawa Hirokatsu, *Nihon tekkōgyō no saihensei* (1977). Iida Kaichi, Ōhashi Shūji, and Kuroiwa Toshirō, *Tekkō* (1969). Kiyoshi Kawahito, *The Japanese Steel Industry* (1972). Leonard Lynn, *How Japan Innovates: A Comparison with the U.S. in the Case of Oxygen Steelmaking* (1982). Nippon Steel Corporation, *History of Steel in Japan* (1973). Nihon Tekkō Remmei, *Sengo tekkō shi* (1959). Nihon Tekkō Remmei, *Tekkō jūnen shi* (1969). Nihon Tekkō Remmei, *Tekkō tōkei yōran* (annual). Ōhashi Shūji, *Tekkōgyō* (1975). *Leonard* LYNN

Irōzaki

Cape on southern Izu Peninsula, Shizuoka Prefecture, central Honshū. It ends abruptly with a large sea cliff and a group of fantastically shaped rocks that rise above the surface of the sea. Tourist attractions include a lighthouse, an extensive greenhouse, and Ishimuro Shrine. Irōzaki is part of Fuji–Hakone–Izu National Park.

Iruma

City in southern Saitama Prefecture, central Honshū. A prosperous market and POST-STATION TOWN in the Edo period (1600–1868), Iruma has long been famous for its tea. It is rapidly being urbanized, with textile and brewing industries. The American military base that was established here after World War II is now used by the Self Defense Force. Pop: 104,034.

Irwin, Robert Walker (1844–1925)

American businessman and diplomatic representative of the Kingdom of Hawaii in Japan. Born in Pennsylvania. Irwin went to Japan in 1866 to work for the trading firm of Walsh, Hall and Co; in 1876 he joined the MITSUI company. He was later appointed the first Hawaiian consul general in Japan, and in 1884, having been promoted to special envoy, he negotiated the first formal immigration treaty between Hawaii and Japan. Known as the "father of Japanese immigration to Hawaii," he saw to it that Japanese immigrants were transported safely and given jobs on the sugar plantations of Hawaii. In 1900 he established the Taiwan Seitō Company, a sugar refinery in Taiwan. Irwin became a naturalized Japanese citizen and for his services to Japan was awarded the Order of the Rising Sun and the Order of the Sacred Treasure by the Japanese government.

His eldest daughter, Sophia A. Irwin (1884–1957), also known as Bella Irwin, was born in Tōkyō. She was educated at Columbia University in New York and returned to Japan in 1916. Devoted to the education of the young, she established in Tōkyō in 1917 the Gyokusen School for nursery-school teachers and an adjoining kindergarten. She became a Japanese citizen in 1942. In 1947, with funds inherited from her father, she expanded her school, which continues today as the Irwin School.

Isahaya

City in southern Nagasaki Prefecture, Kyūshū. A former castle town, the city is the terminus of several railways and national highways. Rice is grown on reclaimed land. Commerce and industry, particularly the metal industries, flourish. Tourist attractions include the remains of the castle called Kamenoshiro, the azaleas, and the bridge Meganebashi, all in Isahaya Park. Pop: 83,725.

Isawa

Town in central Yamanashi Prefecture, central Honshū, on the river Fuefukigawa. A castle town of the TAKEDA FAMILY in the medieval period (roughly 13th–16th centuries), in the Edo period (1600–1868), Isawa was a POST-STATION TOWN on the highway Kōshū Kaidō. Products include grapes, peaches, and persimmons. The Isawa Hot Spring is located here. Pop: 17,542.

Ise

Formerly Uji-Yamada. City in southeastern Mie Prefecture, central Honshū. The site of ISE SHRINE, Ise welcomes thousands of pilgrims and tourists each year. It is also a commercial city, with electrical appliance and textile industries and shipyards in the Ōminato district. Numerous educational and cultural facilities as well as shrines affiliated with the Ise Shrine are located here. Ise is part of the Ise–Shima National Park. Pop: 105,621.

Ise (ca 877–940)

Court lady, classical (WAKA) poet. Her real name is unknown, Ise being the name of a province of which her father, Fujiwara no Tsugikage, was governor at one stage of his career, and the sobriquet by which she was called when a lady-in-waiting at court. At least two of her close male relatives had held appointments as rector of the court university, and her father had also been a student there in his youth, so that she was evidently reared in an environment favorable to cultural interests and pursuits. She is thought to have entered the service of Empress Onshi, consort of Emperor Uda (867–931; r 887–97) around 892. After rejecting overtures from several men, she caught the eye of the emperor, to whom she bore a son who died in infancy. She also became a favorite of Uda's fourth son, Prince Atsuyoshi, to whom she bore a daughter after Empress Onshi's death in 907. The child was later known as Lady Nakatsukasa, and became a famous poet in her own right. Ise's later life is obscure, but literary references suggest that she had affairs with at least two other courtiers.

One of the Thirty-Six Poetic Geniuses (SANJŪROKKASEN), Ise ranks with ONO NO KOMACHI as one of the two most accomplished women poets of the late 9th and early 10th centuries. Although Komachi is unquestionably the greater of the two, their poetry shares important characteristics—the wit, ingenuity, and subjectivity typical of the favored styles of the day, and also a vein of passion which gives fire and intensity to their love poems, in particular. The compilers of the first imperial anthology of Japanese classical poetry, the *Kokinshū* (905, Collection from Ancient and Modern Times), included 22 of Ise's poems as against only 18 for Komachi, and 70 of her poems are included in the second imperial anthology, GOSEN WAKASHŪ or *Gosenshū* (ca 960, Later Collection), more than for any other woman poet. Some 90 additional poems are contained in subsequent imperial anthologies. Her personal anthology, *Iseshū*, exists in three principal versions, all of which contain poems by others besides herself. The total number of poems varies from 483 to 518.

—— Robert H. Brower and Earl Miner, *Japanese Court Poetry* (1961). *Robert H.* BROWER

Ise Bay

(Ise Wan). Inlet of the Pacific Ocean, on the coast of Mie and Aichi prefectures, central Honshū. Extends from the Atsumi Peninsula on the east to the Shima Peninsula on the west. In addition to Nagoya to the north, various industrial and fishing ports are located on this bay. In recent years the fishing industry has declined due to expanding industrialization. The bay includes the Ise-Shima National Park and the Mikawa Bay Quasi-National Park. Length: approximately

60 km (37 mi); width: approximately 30 km (19 mi); depth: approximately 35 m (115 ft) in the center, up to 100 m (328 ft) at the mouth.

Isehara

City in central Kanagawa Prefecture, central Honshū. Isehara developed as a shrine town around the Afuri Shrine on the mountain Ōyama. Today it is a satellite city of Tōkyō, with plants producing automobile components and electrical appliances. Pop: 70,052.

Iseki & Co, Ltd

(Iseki Nōki). Manufacturer of machinery and other equipment used chiefly for rice farming but also for dry-field, fruit, and dairy farming. Founded in 1936, the firm set a goal of mechanizing the rice-growing industry; it succeeded in developing a unified system of mechanization for all stages of the process, from the planting of seedlings to their harvesting, a system which resulted in a considerable saving of labor. The firm's chief products are rice-transplanting machines and small- and medium-scale tractors and combines, which it exports to over 50 foreign countries. Sales for the fiscal year ending November 1981 totaled ¥102 billion (US $455.9 million), of which 12 percent came from export sales, and capitalization was ¥7.8 billion (US $34.9 million). Corporate headquarters are in Tōkyō.

Ise monogatari

(Tales of Ise). A mid-10th century collection of some 125 brief lyrical episodes (variant texts range from 110 to 140 or more episodes) combining elements of prose and poetry of anonymous aristocratic authorship. It is the oldest of the *uta monogatari* (collections of short tales built around one or more poems), a hybrid literary genre which marks an important stage in the development of full-fledged prose literature in Heian-period (794–1185) Japan. Familiarity with the *Ise monogatari*, together with the KOKINSHŪ (ca 905, Collection from Ancient and Modern Times), the first imperially commissioned anthology of WAKA poetry with which it shares a number of common poems, was indispensable for well-bred courtiers and court ladies of the latter part of the Heian period. This collection is probably based upon the *Narihira kashū* (Narihira Collection)—a private collection of poems by the famous 9th-century poet ARIWARA NO NARIHIRA to whom authorship of the collection has been traditionally ascribed—to which were added materials from other sources and popular traditions, all woven into an organic whole. The theory that Narihira was the author is no longer accepted, but to some extent the collection gives the impression of being a quasi-biography of this famous poet, emphasizing his love adventures.

There are a large number of old manuscripts of this *monogatari*, the most reliable of which is the *Den Teika hitsu hon,* one of three versions going back to a manuscript written by FUJIWARA NO SADAIE (or Fujiwara no Teika, 1162–1241), who made at least a half dozen handwritten copies of the *Ise monogatari* in the second half of his life. This text contains 125 sections and 209 poems. The title of the book comes from the fact that toward the end of the 10th century there existed a version which began with the story about Narihira's visit to the Ise Shrine (section 69 of the *Den Teika hitsu hon*). Other titles of the collection, now obsolete, are *Zaigo ga monogatari* (Tales of Ariwara of the Fifth Rank) and *Zaigo Chūjō no nikki* (Diary of the Middle Captain Ariwara of the Fifth Rank).

An example of an episode (section 110) is:

"Once a certain man had a woman whom he frequently visited in secret. One day she sent him a message: 'You have appeared in my dreams last night.' Therefore he replied:

> 'My spirit which has wandered away
> Out of excessive love for you
> Will have been at your place . . .
> If, late at night, it comes again,
> Subdue and hold it with a spell!' "

The *Ise monogatari* was already much studied by the end of the Heian period by members of the scholarly Rokujō family. The oldest coherent commentaries, however, are no older than the Kamakura period (1185–1333). The first serious study, *Ise monogatari gukenshō*, was written by ICHIJŌ KANEYOSHI (1402–81). In the Edo period (1600–1868) a large number of commentaries appeared, the most important of which are: *Ise monogatari shūsuishō* by KITAMURA KIGIN (1624–1705), *Seigo okudan* by KEICHŪ (1640–1701), *Ise*

monogatari dōjimon by KADA NO AZUMAMARO (1669–1736), and *Ise monogatari koi* by KAMO NO MABUCHI (1697–1769). For modern studies see the bibliography.

The *Ise monogatari* exerted a tremendous influence upon later Japanese literature, a phenomenon which was greatly facilitated by the fact that each separate section could serve as a source of inspiration for later writers. The first part of the YAMATO MONOGATARI consists of short stories centered around poems in the same manner as in the *Ise monogatari*; several sections of the latter work have served as material for the former. Other important *monogatari* influenced by the *Ise monogatari* are the UTSUBO MONOGATARI, *Genji monogatari* (see TALE OF GENJI) and KONJAKU MONOGATARI. Four NŌ plays have plots inspired by the *Ise monogatari*: Unrin'in, Kakitsubata, Izutsu, and Oshio. In the Edo period the *Ise monogatari* was one of the most widely read classics, and this interest stimulated several authors to write imitations of it. Of these particular mention can be made of the *Nise monogatari* (Imitation Tales), ascribed by some to the poet KARASUMARU MITSUHIRO (1579–1638).

Probably from the middle Heian period there existed picture scrolls *(emakimono)* illustrating various episodes of the *Ise monogatari*. In the Edo period an enormous number of printed editions with illustrations appeared, the first one of which was published as early as 1608. An especially beautiful album of paintings based on *Ise monogatari* was done by the early Edo period artist Tawaraya SŌTATSU. See also MONOGATARI BUNGAKU.

📖 ——Western works: Oscar Benl, *Liebesgeschichten des japanischen Kavaliers Narihira: Aus dem Ise-monogatari* (1957). *Ise monogatari,* tr H. Jay Harris as *The Tales of Ise* (1972). *Ise monogatari,* tr Helen Craig McCullough as *Tales of Ise: Lyrical Episodes from Tenth-Century Japan* (1968). G. Renondeau, *Contes d'Ise (Ise monogatari)* (1969). Frits Vos, *A Study of the Ise-monogatari with the text according to the Den-Teika-hippon and an annotated translation,* 2 vols (1957). Japanese works: Fukui Teisuke, *Ise monogatari seiseiron* (2nd ed, 1968). Ikeda Kikan, *Ise monogatari ni tsukite no kenkyū,* 3 vols (1933–34). Morino Muneaki, *Ise monogatari no sekai* (1978). Ōtsu Yūichi, Fukui Teisuke, and Ban Hisami, *Ise monogatari ni tsukite no kenkyū: Hoi, sakuin, zuroku hen* (repr 1961). Watanabe Minoru, *Ise monogatari,* vol 2 of *Shinchō Nihon koten shūsei* (1976).　　　　　　　　　　　　　　　　　　　　　*Frits Vos*

Ise Plain

(Ise Heiya). Located in Mie Prefecture, central Honshū. Bounded by mountains on three sides and Ise Bay on the east, these alluvial and diluvial plains, where rice, tea, and tobacco are cultivated, have long been a rich agricultural region. The major cities are Yokkaichi, part of the Chūkyō Industrial Zone, Tsu, Matsusaka, and Ise. Length: 80 km (50 mi); width: 15 km (9 mi).

Ise Province

(Ise no Kuni; also called Seishū). One of the 15 provinces of the Tōkaidō (Eastern Sea Circuit) in central Honshū; established under the KOKUGUN SYSTEM in 646, at which time it comprised most of what is now Mie Prefecture. The area was associated from very early times with native Shintō cults, and during the ancient period much of its land was owned by Shintō shrines, the largest and most important of which was the ISE SHRINE in Uji-Yamada (now the city of Ise). Late in the Heian period (794–1185) Ise became the home base of the Ise Heishi branch of the powerful TAIRA FAMILY. After the destruction of the Taira the province was governed by local warlords such as the ŌUCHI and later the KITABATAKE and TOKI families until the end of the Muromachi period (1333–1568), when it came under the control of the hegemon ODA NOBUNAGA. In the Edo period (1600–1868) Ise was divided into seven *daimyō* domains (HAN), with a supervising commissioner *(bugyō)* stationed at Uji-Yamada. Besides rice, its principal products included tea, cotton, and seafood. With the establishment of the PREFECTURAL SYSTEM in 1871, Ise was combined with Iga and Shima provinces to form MIE PREFECTURE.

Ise Rebellion

(Ise Bōdō). Peasant uprising on 18 December 1876 in the Ise district of Mie Prefecture, the largest of several uprisings against the new Meiji government protesting the LAND TAX REFORM OF 1873–1881. Payment of the land tax had previously been assessed as a fixed percentage of crops and other products. In July 1873 the government decided to establish payment in cash, and with a view to regularizing revenues, it substituted the assessed value of taxable land as the basis of taxation. Peasants were angered because in some cases the new land tax represented an increase over the old one. Moreover, in spite of provisions to the contrary, the rate (3 percent), once fixed, remained constant regardless of good or bad harvests. In the Ise district dissatisfied peasants attacked prefectural offices; the branch office of the Mitsui Bank, which acted as tax collector; schools; and post offices. Violence spread to the neighboring prefectures of Aichi and Gifu. The rioting peasants, who numbered more than 50,000, were finally subdued on 23 July. The riots, together with those in Wakayama and Ibaraki prefectures, persuaded the government to reduce the land tax from 3 to 2.5 percent of assessed land value.

Isesaki

City in southeastern Gumma Prefecture, central Honshū. Long known for its silk called Isesaki *meisen*. Isesaki's principal industries are textiles, most notably, woolens for export, machinery, electrical and communications equipment. Pop: 105,728.

Ise–Shima National Park

(Ise–Shima Kokuritsu Kōen). Situated in central Honshū on the SHIMA PENINSULA, Mie Prefecture, this maritime park, encompassing the hilly hinterland of the peninsula and its surrounding coastal waters, is characterized by the rias coastline that features numerous small bays and islets. The two main cities are ISE, famed for the ancient ISE SHRINE, lying at the northern edge of the park, and TOBA, a port to its east, which is the center of the Mikimoto pearl industry, founded by MIKIMOTO KŌKICHI (1858–1954). Between the two cities is FUTAMIGAURA beach, with its "wedded rocks" (*meotoiwa*), which are two sacred rocks linked by ropes. In the south of the peninsula is AGO BAY, a fishing and pearl cultivation center, with the National Pearl Research Institute located on KASHIKOJIMA. The women divers (*ama*), employed by the pearl industry, are a major tourist attraction of the park. Land area: 555.5 sq km (214.4 sq mi).

Ise Shrine

(Ise Jingū). One of the two or three most important Shintō shrines. Located in the city of Ise in Mie Prefecture and comprising the Inner Shrine (Kō Taijingū or Naikū) and the Outer Shrine (Toyouke [also called Toyuke] Daijingū or Gekū), with other affiliated shrines called *betsugū*, *sessha*, and *massha*. Enshrining the ancestral gods of the imperial family, these shrines were not originally open to the public. However, following the outbreak of the ŌNIN WAR in 1467, the power of the imperial family declined, and it became difficult for them to maintain the shrines. Consequently, in line with the growing popularity of pilgrimages to shrines and temples, the Ise Shrine was opened to the public. Since then, strong ties have been formed between this shrine and the Japanese people.

Inner Shrine —— The Inner Shrine is said to date from the 3rd century and to enshrine AMATERASU ŌMIKAMI, the mythical ancestor of the imperial family, who is represented by the sacred mirror (*yata no kagami*), one of the three IMPERIAL REGALIA. According to the legend of the shrine's founding in the NIHON SHOKI (720), this sacred mirror was transferred from the imperial palace to Kasanui no Mura in Yamato (now Nara Prefecture) during the reign of the legendary emperor Sujin. Then, during the reign of the legendary emperor Suinin, the emperor's daughter Princess YAMATOHIME was appointed priestess of the shrine. According to the legend, Yamatohime traveled throughout the country in search of an eternal resting place for the sacred mirror. When she came to Ise, she heard the voice of Amaterasu Ōmikami, saying, "This is a good place and I would like to stay here." The princess thereupon built a shrine on the banks of the river Isuzugawa and enshrined the goddess. According to the legend, it was from this time that the priestess of the shrine was chosen from among the imperial princesses. In historical times the practice continued until the reign of Go-Daigo (1318–39).

The main building of the Inner Shrine is constructed of unpainted Japanese cypress wood. It is designed in a special form of *shimmei-zukuri* architectural style (see SHINTŌ ARCHITECTURE) that is prohibited for other shrines. The shrine is razed and rebuilt at regular intervals in a rite called *shikinen sengū*. This observance began during the reign of Empress JITŌ (r 686–697) and at first took place every 20 years, but since the reign of Emperor Go-Mizunoo (r

Ise Shrine —— Inner Shrine

The main building of the Inner Shrine. Its simple design is believed to derive from that of the granaries and storehouses of prehistoric Japan.

1611–29) it has been carried out once every 21 years. It should be mentioned that at times, as during the civil strife of the 15th and 16th centuries, reconstruction was not carried out regularly. The most recent reconstruction took place in 1973. The most important rite at the shrine is the Kannamesai in October, when the new rice crop is dedicated; other rites include the Toshigoi no Matsuri, to pray for a rich harvest, and Tsukinamisai, which is conducted every month.

Not only the rites, but the preparation of food offered to the deities follows ancient practices. Fire for cooking is made by rubbing sticks of wood. Rice is cultivated in a special paddy, and *sake* (rice wine) is made in the same way as in the ancient past. Salt, vegetables and fruits, and abalone, an essential offering, are all produced at specially designated places. Of the utensils used, earthenware vessels are made in a special shrine kiln and thrown away after being used once. Fabrics are also woven at a special weaving place.

Outer Shrine —— The Outer Shrine is said to date from the late 5th century and to enshrine Toyouke (Toyuke) Daijin, the god of food, clothing, and housing, who is said to have been in charge of Amaterasu Ōmikami's food supply. According to the KOJIKI (712), the shrine was first located within the imperial palace grounds but was transferred to Tamba Province (now part of Kyōto and Hyōgo prefectures) and then to its present site during the reign of Emperor Yūryaku (latter half of the 5th century). Architecturally, the Outer Shrine is much like the Inner Shrine, although there are some differences in detail such as the finials of the rafters on the thatched roof (*chigi*) and the number of cross-pieces on the ridgepole (*katsuogi*). It is also razed and reconstructed at regular intervals.

The Cult of Ise Shrine —— Ise Shrine has long had a special significance for the Japanese. A poem mentioning the shrine is included in the 8th-century anthology MAN'YŌSHŪ, and the poem by the poet-monk SAIGYŌ (1118–90) about his emotional reaction to its ineffable presence is well known. The German architect Bruno TAUT (1880–1938) praised its perfection of form and claimed that it was the fount of Japan's unique culture.

Veneration of Ise Shrine became particularly strong during the 15th century, largely owing to the activities of *oshi*, lower-ranking clerics in the employ of the shrine, who went around the provinces proselytizing and collecting funds. They also preached the benefits of visiting Ise, adding that seven pilgrimages ensured salvation. Ise *kō* (see KŌ), or associations for pilgrimages to the shrine, were formed in various provinces.

Devotion to Ise Shrine was such that even the ruthless warlord ODA NOBUNAGA felt obliged to donate huge sums of money to revive the custom of reconstructing the shrines—an event that had not taken place for the past 120 years. The national unifier TOYOTOMI HIDEYOSHI donated rice to the shrine, and the Tokugawa shogunate (1603–1867) also furnished funds.

The importance of Ise to the Japanese is borne out by the number of pilgrimages recorded during the Edo period (1600–1868). Thus, as many as 2,500 pilgrims a day are said to have visited from March to May in 1650; from April to May in 1705, 3,620,000 visited the shrine; from April to August in 1771, when the total was 2,700,-000; and from the end of March to August in 1830, when the figure was 4,579,000. To be sure, these figures were higher than those for

Ishibutai tomb

A side view of the tomb. The granite boulders, which form the ceiling of the tomb's chamber, rest on smaller rocks. Excavations beginning in 1933 have yielded *sue* and *haji* wares, metalwork, coins, and other artifacts. 7th century. Asuka, Nara Prefecture.

average years, representing visits made during *okagedoshi*, years considered particularly auspicious and occurring roughly at 20-year intervals (see OKAGE MAIRI).

In the more secularized modern period Ise Shrine has become somewhat removed from the minds of the Japanese. During the militaristic 1930s, the cult of Shintō was used for nationalistic purposes, and every household was required to have a talisman (*ofuda*) issued by the shrine. Now Ise is significant more for its literary and historic associations and for its architecture than as a place of worship.

📖——Kenzo Tange and Noboru Kawagoe, *Ise: Prototype of Japanese Architecture* (1965).

NARAMOTO Tatsuya and TODA Yoshio

Isetan Co, Ltd

Leading department store with headquarters in the Shinjuku district of Tōkyō and five retail stores in the Tōkyō metropolitan area, as well as four overseas outlets. Its predecessor, Iseya Tanji Dry Goods, was founded in 1886. A comprehensive department store selling foods, household products, and clothing, Isetan is particularly noted for its marketing strength in the field of high-fashion women's wear. Established in its present form in 1930, Isetan was late to enter the field but achieved success by such means as anticipating the emergence of Shinjuku as an important urban center and developing market research geared toward the age and sex of its customers. Isetan has also been active in introducing to its stores fashion trends and merchandise from overseas. Sales for the fiscal year ending November 1981 totaled ¥241.9 billion (US $1.1 billion), of which the sale of clothing was 49 percent, food products 17 percent, household goods 10 percent, and others 24 percent. In the same year capitalization stood at ¥5.8 billion (US $25.9 million).

Ishibashi Ningetsu (1865–1926)

Literary critic, novelist. Real name Ishibashi Tomokichi. Born in Fukuoka Prefecture. Graduate of Tōkyō University. An amateur literary critic from his student days, he became an important contributor to *Kokumin no tomo*, an influential magazine of the 1890s. His methodical approach to criticism, based on Aristotle's aesthetic criteria, helped to stimulate both the literature and the criticism of the Meiji period (1868–1912) and made him one of the foremost critics of his time. Originally trained in German law, he worked as an attorney in his later years. His son, YAMAMOTO KENKICHI, is a contemporary critic. Ishibashi's criticism is collected in *Ishibashi Ningetsu hyōron shū* (1939).

Ishibashi Shōjirō (1889–1976)

Businessman and founder of BRIDGESTONE TIRE CO, LTD. Born in Fukuoka Prefecture. Ishibashi expanded his family's footwear (see TABI) business by producing inexpensive goods on a mass scale.

After World War I he developed rubber-soled *tabi* for work and later went into the production of rubber boots. He established Bridgestone Tire in 1931 in order to produce automobile tires domestically. His company enjoyed great prosperity during World War II because of mounting demands from the military. He signed a contract for technical cooperation with Goodyear Tire and Rubber Co of the United States in 1950 and greatly improved the quality of domestically manufactured tires. A famous collector of art objects, Ishibashi established the Bridgestone Museum of Art in 1952.

MORI Masumi

Ishibashi Tanzan (1884–1973)

Journalist, Keynesian economist, and politician; held postwar cabinet posts and was briefly (1956) prime minister. Born in Tōkyō, he graduated from Waseda University, where he studied philosophy. He wrote for many magazines and newspapers, including *Waseda bungaku, Tōkyō mainichi shimbun,* and TŌYŌ KEIZAI SHIMPŌ. As an editorial writer and later as president of the *Tōyō keizai shimpō*, he was an outspoken critic of the militarists during the 1930s. After World War II he joined the Liberal Party (Nihon Jiyūtō) and served as finance minister in the first YOSHIDA SHIGERU cabinet (1946). He was barred from office (1947–51) by the OCCUPATION PURGE, after which he served as minister of international trade and industry in the HATOYAMA ICHIRŌ cabinet (1954). He became prime minister in 1956 but had to resign after two months because of illness. After regaining his health he devoted himself to normalizing relations between Japan and the People's Republic of China.

Ishibutai tomb

A 7th-century mounded tomb (KOFUN) believed to be that of SOGA NO UMAKO, a powerful figure at the YAMATO COURT; located in the village of Asuka, Nara Prefecture. The tomb originally consisted of a square earthen platform, ca 50 meters (164 ft) to a side, possibly topped by a round earthen mound and surrounded by a wide moat. Gradual erosion of the mound exposed the ceiling rocks of the corridor-type stone burial chamber embedded within, thus giving the tomb its name, meaning "rock platform." In 1933 the chamber was excavated by HAMADA KŌSAKU and now stands open for tourists to view as one of the largest of its type in Japan. The chamber interior measures 7.7 meters (25.3 ft) long, 3.4 meters (11.2 ft) wide, and 4.8 meters (15.7 ft) high; the larger of the two ceiling rocks weighs 77 metric tons (84.7 short tons).

📖——Hamada Kōsaku, "Yamato Shimanoshō ishibutai no kyoseki kofun," *Kyōto teikoku daigaku bungakubu kōkogaku kenkyū hōkoku* 14 (1937). *Gina Lee BARNES*

Ishida Baigan (1685–1744)

Religious and moral teacher; founder of the SHINGAKU movement. Born in a farming village in Tamba Province (now part of Kyōto Prefecture), he spent his youth working on the family farm. He was apprenticed to a Kyōto merchant at the age of 11, but for reasons unknown, abandoned his apprenticeship a few years later and returned to his native village.

Baigan in his youth became deeply interested in Shintō. He went to Kyōto at the age of 23 for the purpose of preaching Shintō beliefs but found few listeners. To support himself he accepted employment in the merchant house of Kuroyanagi, and before many years had passed, worked his way up to the position of chief clerk.

Baigan's religious interests did not wane, and he spent his leisure time studying Neo-Confucianism, Shintō, and Buddhism. He began studying in his late thirties with an elderly scholar named Oguri Ryōun (1669–1729), who was learned in both Neo-Confucian and Buddhist doctrines. Baigan practiced meditation under his guidance, and within a few years underwent several enlightenment experiences.

At the age of 43 Baigan resigned his duties at the merchant house, and two years later, when Ryōun died, opened his own lecture hall. He lectured daily, even though attendance was at first small. Several of his followers also underwent powerful enlightenment experiences, and from then on Baigan's following increased.

Baigan continued lecturing for many years, and his fame as an inspiring teacher spread. He did not marry, and despite the success of his teachings, he continued to live an extremely frugal life. He died at the age of 60 of a sudden illness, leaving only his books and clothing.

Baigan's doctrines were called Shingaku ("Heart Learning"). He preached in terms of "heart" and "knowing the nature." The purpose of devotion was to overcome one's "selfish heart," thereby discovering one's "true heart." This meant realizing that conventional morality (as epitomized by Confucius' Five Relationships) was completely natural and in accord with the laws of the universe.

Books might help one in this quest, but other methods were also recommended by Baigan, namely meditation leading to enlightenment, asceticism or frugality, and dedication to one's own humble earthly occupation. In short, Baigan used Zen enlightenment techniques to achieve some of the doctrinal ends of Neo-Confucianism. This combination was an appealing one for the townsmen who made up Baigan's following. It allowed them the possibility of achieving enlightenment by doing well what they did anyway and without the arduous years of study expected of the Confucian scholar.

Ishida Baigan's disciples included Saitō Zemmon (1700–1761), Kimura Shigemitsu (1703–56), and TESHIMA TOAN (1718–86). Toan proved to be the most successful of these in propagating his teacher's beliefs and in developing the institutional basis for the Shingaku movement. Baigan's principal writings are *Tohi mondō*, a four-volume catechism based on his lectures, completed in 1739, and *Seikaron* (1744).

📖 ——Robert N. Bellah, *Tokugawa Religion* (1957). Shibata Minoru, *Baigan to sono monryū* (1977). Shibata Minoru, ed, *Ishida Baigan zenshū*, 2 vols (Sekimon Shingaku Kai, 1956–57).

Thomas M. HUBER

Ishida Eiichirō (1903–1968)

Pioneer of cultural anthropological studies in Japan. Born in Ōsaka, Ishida attended Kyōto University (he was forced to leave because of his leftist political activities) and studied ethnology under Wilhelm Schmidt and William Koppers at the University of Vienna. In 1951 he was appointed to the newly founded chair of cultural anthropology at Tōkyō University. Ishida examined what are regarded as certain peculiar features of Japanese culture in light of a wider East Asian cultural context by using the comparative ethnological method known as *Kulturkreislehre*. His comparative study of the KAPPA (mythical creatures that appear in Japanese folklore) legend, *Kappa komahiki kō* (1948), is one of the major products of this research. Later he developed a theory of culture that reflected his idea that a close relationship exists between the materialist-Marxist view of history and society and the anthropological concept of culture as defined by the neo-evolutionist school. He tried to bridge the gap between social thought and anthropology. His collected works in eight volumes are found in *Ishida Eiichirō zenshū* (1970).

📖 ——Ishida Eiichirō, "The *Kappa* Legend," *Folklore Studies* 9 (1950). AOKI Tamotsu

Ishida Hakyō (1913–1969)

HAIKU poet. Real name Ishida Tetsuo. Born in Ehime Prefecture. Studied at Meiji University. As a middle school student, he began writing haiku after the style of the magazine HOTOTOGISU, but he was later inspired by the works of MIZUHARA SHŪŌSHI, who rejected the objective nature descriptions of the Hototogisu group in favor of a more subjective style, and joined Mizuhara's new coterie, writing for its magazine *Ashibi*. In 1936 he published his first collection and became a leading figure in the new-style haiku movement of the 1930s. His collection *Shakumyō* (1950, Desire for Life) is noted for the sharp clarity of its images and the passionate conviction of their expression.

Ishida Mitoku (1587–1669)

KYŌKA and *haiku* poet. Born in Edo (now Tōkyō). He became a disciple of MATSUNAGA TEITOKU and eventually, along with NAKARAI BOKUYŌ, the leading figure in the early development of Edo *kyōka*. His *kyōka* anthology, *Gogin wagashū* (1648–51, the title parodying the early-10th-century anthology *Kokin wakashū*; see KOKINSHŪ), exerted a great influence over later generations of *kyōka* poets.

Ishida Mitsunari (1560–1600)

Warlord of the Azuchi–Momoyama period (1568–1600). Born in Ōmi Province (now Shiga Prefecture). As a youth, Mitsunari became an attendant to TOYOTOMI HIDEYOSHI, who was still one of

many warlords contending for national hegemony. He quickly earned Hideyoshi's trust and accompanied his master on the expeditions to the Chūgoku region (1576–83) and at the battles of YAMAZAKI (1582) and SHIZUGATAKE (1583). When Hideyoshi assumed the highest court title of *kampaku* in 1585, Mitsunari was appointed one of the 12 ministers (*shodayū*). In the following year, while continuing to serve as one of Hideyoshi's generals in the campaigns against the SHIMAZU FAMILY in Kyūshū and the Later Hōjō family (Go-Hōjō; see HŌJŌ FAMILY) in the Kantō region, Mitsunari became increasingly influential in political affairs by virtue of his competence as an administrator. Upon Hideyoshi's unification of the nation with the defeat of the Hōjō, Mitsunari became the most important figure on his administrative staff. He was endowed by Hideyoshi with a large domain at Sawayama in Ōmi, which by 1595 was assessed at about 200,000 *koku* (1 *koku* = about 180 liters or 5 US bushels; see KOKUDAKA). Mitsunari served as a general in the first of Hideyoshi's invasions of Korea in 1592–93 (see INVASIONS OF KOREA IN 1592 AND 1597) and was a major figure in the execution of the nationwide land survey that was known as the Taikō *kenchi* (see KENCHI). After Hideyoshi's death in 1598, in the middle of his second venture in Korea, Mitsunari championed the cause of Hideyoshi's son TOYOTOMI HIDEYORI and organized forces against TOKUGAWA IEYASU, who was rapidly expanding his military influence. He formed a league with several major *daimyō* from western Japan, such as Mōri Terumoto (1553–1625) and UKITA HIDEIE, and confronted Ieyasu and his allies in the Battle of SEKIGAHARA in 1600. He lost the battle and was captured and executed in Kyōto.

Yoshiyuki NAKAI

Ishida Taizō (1888–1979)

Businessman. Born in Aichi Prefecture. After graduation from middle school, he worked on various jobs before joining the Toyoda Spinning & Weaving Co in 1927. He rose through the ranks to become president of TOYODA AUTOMATIC LOOM WORKS, LTD, in 1948. While still in this position, he took over the presidency of TOYOTA MOTOR CORPORATION in 1950. The financially troubled automaker was revived under his leadership. Ishida established an efficient production system to begin the mass manufacture of Toyopet Crown passenger cars, and Toyota began its rise to its current position as one of the world's leading motor vehicle manufacturers. Ishida served on the board of many Toyota group companies and contributed substantially to the group's prosperity.

UDAGAWA Masaru

Ishigaki

City in southwestern Okinawa Prefecture; on Ishigakijima, the principal island of the YAEYAMA ISLANDS. The city is the political, economic, and cultural center of the islands. Pineapple cultivation is the principal industry; sugar cane and bonito fishing are also important. Its subtropical scenery attracts many tourists. Air flights and ship and ferry routes connect the city with Naha, the prefectural capital. Pop: 38,824.

Ishigakijima

Island approximately 400 km (248 mi) southwest of Okinawa. One of the YAEYAMA ISLANDS. The city of Ishigaki covers the entire island. The island is surrounded by coral reefs. Today it is the largest producer of pineapples in Okinawa Prefecture. The highest peak in Okinawa Prefecture, Omotodake (526 m; 1,725 ft), is located here. Area: 221 sq km (85.3 sq mi).

Ishiguro Munemaro (1893–1968)

Ceramist. Best known for the iron glazes known as *temmoku* inspired by Chinese wares of the Song (Sung) dynasty (960–1279). Born to an old family of means in Shimminato, Toyama Prefecture, Ishiguro left school in 1912. In 1917 he tried making RAKU WARE, first using his father's kiln and then in 1922 using a kiln he built in Shirakawa, Fukushima Prefecture. In 1925 he borrowed a kiln in Kanazawa and tried IGA WARE, *mishima*, and *hakeme* (brushed design) pieces. In 1927 he built a kiln in Kyōto and experimented with recreating Southern Song Jun (Chün) ware porcelain, Tang (T'ang) dynasty (618–907) three-color ware, and Korean-style decorated Kōrai (Kor: Koryŏ) pieces. In 1932 he studied KARATSU WARE techniques with Nakazato Tarōemon in Karatsu. In 1935 Ishiguro built a kiln in the Kyōto suburbs. He perfected the first even persimmon *temmoku* glaze in Japan (1939), the first tree-leaf *temmoku* outside China (1940), and versions of partridge-spotted ware and Henan (Honan) *temmoku*. After World War II, he devised new techniques and his designs showed increasing freedom. Because he never held one-man shows and led the life of a retiring literatus, Ishiguro's work failed to reach a wide audience. However, he won top prizes at the Paris International Exposition (1939) and the Ministry of Commerce and Industry Crafts Exhibition (1941). Because of his work in *temmoku* glazes, in 1955 he was designated one of the LIVING NATIONAL TREASURES. He played an important role in the formation of the Japan Handicrafts Association (Nihon Kōgeikai) in 1955. Except for his Jun-ware porcelain pieces, Ishiguro concentrated on pottery; both his free reinterpretations of traditional styles and his nontraditional pieces are marked by powerful potting and bold, simple, and vigorous designs. *Frederick* BAEKELAND

Ishiguro Tadaatsu (1884–1960)

Agricultural administrator. Born in Tōkyō. After graduating from Tōkyō University, he entered the Ministry of Agriculture and Commerce, where he served as bureau director, vice-minister, and twice as minister of agriculture and forestry before the end of World War II. His administrative philosophy, which was based on concepts of agrarian nationalism (NŌHON SHUGI), exercised a great influence on government agricultural policy in the 1920s and 1930s. Although the son of viscount Ishiguro Tadanori (1845–1941), the eminent surgeon-general, he disliked the aristocratic way of life and preferred to socialize with farmers. *Katō* SHUNJIRŌ

Ishihara Shinobu (1879–1963)

Ophthalmologist. Born in Tōkyō. After graduating from Tōkyō University in 1905, he entered the army as a medical doctor. He went to Germany for further study in 1912. Ishihara retired from army service and taught at Tōkyō University from 1936 to 1940. A color-blindness test table he devised is widely used throughout the world. He received the Asahi Cultural Prize (1940) and the Japan Academy Prize (1941) for his work on the causes of idiopathic nyctalopia (1930). *Achiwa* GORŌ

Ishihara Shintarō (1932–)

Novelist and politician. Born in Kōbe; graduated from Hitotsubashi University. Ishihara started writing in 1954, publishing his first work "Hai iro no kyōshitsu" (The Gray Classroom) in *Hitotsubashi bungaku*, a literary magazine. His 1955 work *Taiyō no kisetsu* (Season of the Sun; tr as *Season of Violence*, 1966) won him the Bungaku-kai's newcomer's award and the prestigious Akutagawa Prize. Depicting the life of postwar Japanese youth opposed to all established morals and customs, the novel gave the name *taiyōzoku* ("sun tribe") to a generation of alienated youth. Ishihara wrote numerous other novels, including *Kiretsu* (1956–58, The Crevice), *Kanzen naru yūgi* (1957, Utter Decadence), and *Seinen no ki* (1959, The Tree of Youth). He then turned to politics and was elected to the House of Councillors in 1968 as a Liberal Democratic Party candidate; he received more votes than any other candidate in this election. He was elected to the House of Representatives in 1972, but was defeated by Minobe Ryōkichi when he ran for governor of Tōkyō in 1975. He was reelected to the House of Representatives in 1976. The film and television actor Ishihara Yūjirō is Ishihara's younger brother.

Ishii Kikujirō (1866–1945)

Diplomat of the Meiji (1868–1912) and Taishō (1912–26) periods. Born in Awa Province (now part of Chiba Prefecture). Following his graduation from Tōkyō University, Ishii was successively attaché at the legation in Paris (1890–96); consul in Korea (1896–1900); secretary of the legation in Beijing (Peking) (1900); director of the Commerce Bureau (1904–07); ambassador to France (1912–15); minister of foreign affairs (1915–16); ambassador in charge of a special mission to the United States (1917); ambassador to the United States (1918–19); ambassador to France (1920–27); president of the Council and Assembly of the League of Nations (1923, 1926).

Among Americans, Ishii is best remembered for his efforts during World War I to smooth relations between Japan and other states warring against the Central Powers. While serving as ambassador to France, he was a key figure in negotiations to secure Japan's adherence to an allied declaration foreswearing any separate peace. Later, as foreign minister, and then as head of a special mission to the United States, he addressed problems associated with an increasingly tense American-Japanese rivalry that was rooted in conflicts over China and American treatment of Japanese living in the United States. His approach to these problems reflected the conviction of an increasingly important group of Japanese civil bureaucrats, businessmen, and politicians that an accommodation with the United States was vital to Japan's continuing growth as a power. At the time of his talks in 1917 with the American secretary of state, Robert LANSING, Ishii favored accommodation through a formula that encouraged American-Japanese cooperation by limiting Japan's imperial designs. He theorized that Japan had more to gain by international trade and cooperation than by building an empire. Such views were welcomed by Secretary Lansing, but, once launched into their negotiating sessions, neither Lansing nor Ishii proved to be a free agent. Their governments were unwilling to make the concessions that would have made a compromise possible. Thus the LANSING–ISHII AGREEMENT of 1917 presented the semblance rather than the substance of an agreement. Despite these troubles, Ishii was warmly received in the United States. His government was to send him back to Washington, where, as ambassador, he continued to wrestle with American-Japanese tensions as they were exacerbated by conflicts in Siberia (see SIBERIAN INTERVENTION) and at the Paris Peace Conference. *Burton F.* BEERS

Ishii Mitsujirō (1889–1981)

Politician. A graduate of Tōkyō Higher School of Commerce (now Hitotsubashi University), he was a career journalist and later managing director of the Asahi Shimbun Sha before being elected to the House of Representatives in 1946. He was appointed Minister of Transportation in 1953 and subsequently held numerous cabinet posts, including Minister of International Trade and Industry (MITI) in Ikeda Hayato's first cabinet. He played a major role in the formation of the LIBERAL DEMOCRATIC PARTY (LDP) and became one of its main leaders. He ran for the post of party president in 1960 but lost to Ikeda Hayato. He was elected Speaker of the House of Representatives in 1967 and later became one of the "elder statesmen" of the LDP.

Ishii Ryōsuke (1907–)

Legal historian. Born in Tōkyō, he graduated from Tōkyō University in 1930 and received a Doctor of Laws degree in 1937. In 1942 he succeeded NAKADA KAORU as professor of Japanese legal history at Tōkyō University and became professor emeritus in 1968. Since 1950 he has been a director of the Japan Legal History Society (Nihon Hōseishi Gakkai). His prodigious publications, known for their meticulous analyses of laws and legal practice, are among the major accomplishments of Japanese legal research in the past half-century. They began with a study of medieval immovable-property law and later expanded to broad studies of public and private law in all periods. His works include *Hōseishi ronshū* (Collected Essays on the History of Law), 10 vols (1972–); *Japanese Legislation in the Meiji Era*, tr and adapted by W. T. Chambliss (1958); and *A History of Political Institutions in Japan* (1980). *Koyanagi* SHUN'ICHIRŌ

Ishikari Coalfield

(Ishikari Tanden). Located in the western Yūbari Mountains, central Hokkaidō. Japan's largest and most productive coalfield. During the mid-1970s it averaged an output of about 9 million metric tons (10 million short tons) per annum, almost half of the national total. Famous for its high quality coking coal which can be heated to extremely high temperatures. Length: 90 km (56 mi); width: 30 km (19 mi); estimated volume of deposits: approximately 6.4 billion metric tons (7 billion short tons).

Ishikaridake

Mountain in central Hokkaidō; highest peak of the Ishikari Mountains. It is the source of the rivers Ishikarigawa and Otofukegawa. Primeval forests of Yeddo spruce (*ezomatsu*) and Sakhalin fir (*todomatsu*) cover the mountain. It forms the central part of Daisetsuzan National Park. Height: 1,962 m (6,435 ft).

Ishikarigawa

River in central western Hokkaidō, originating in the mountain ISHI-KARIDAKE in the Daisetsuzan National Park, flowing through the Kamikawa Basin and Ishikari Plain, and emptying into the Sea of Japan. The name is derived from the Ainu word *ishikaribetsu,* meaning a zig-zagging river. Large peat bogs along the lower reaches have been formed by deposits of the Ishikarigawa and its tributary, the Yūbarigawa. Floods were frequent in the past, but dams and embankments have been built. The fertile river basin yields abundant rice crops; coal mines are located along the Yūbarigawa and the Sorachigawa, another tributary. Scenic spots include the gorge SŌUNKYŌ on its upper reaches. Length: 262 km (162.7 mi); area of drainage basin: 14,300 sq km (5,520 sq mi).

Ishikari Mountains

(Ishikari Sammyaku). Mountain range in central Hokkaidō. Part of the EZO MOUNTAINS, it forms the watershed between the Pacific Ocean to the east, the Sea of Japan to the west, and the Sea of Okhotsk to the northeast. The major peaks are ISHIKARIDAKE (1,962 m; 6,435 ft), Otofukeyama, and Mikuniyama. Forming part of Daisetsuzan National Park, the range contains numerous lakes, passes, and a swamp.

Ishikari Plain

(Ishikari Heiya). Alluvial plain in western Hokkaidō. Bordering the Sea of Japan and formed by the meandering river Ishikarigawa, it has numerous oxbow lakes and marshes. The establishment of Sapporo in 1869 and the subsequent arrival of colonist militia (TONDEN-HEI) have made the region one of the most productive farmlands in Hokkaidō. Rice, apples, and onions are grown, and dairy farming and market gardening are also flourishing. The major cities are SAPPORO and IWAMIZAWA. Area: approximately 4,000 sq km (1,544 sq mi).

Ishikawa

City in Okinawa Prefecture, on the main island of Okinawa. A remote village before World War II, Ishikawa was for a while the site of a refugee camp operated by the American Occupation forces. It is still dependent on American military bases for its economy, although efforts are being made to reclaim coastal land and introduce various enterprises. Its principal farming activities are the cultivation of sugarcane and rice. The IHA SHELL MOUND is located here. Pop: 18,532.

Ishikawa Chiyomatsu (1861–1935)

Zoologist who helped spread the theory of evolution in Japan. Born in Edo (now Tōkyō). A graduate of Tōkyō University, he later taught there. He studied in Germany under August Weismann (1834–1914). Ishikawa published notes on the theory of evolution from lectures given in Japan by the American Edward S. MORSE, and wrote *Shinka shinron* (1891) and other books about evolution. He was also active in applied zoology, experimenting with the artificial breeding of AYU (sweetfish).   *Suzuki Zenji*

Ishikawa Ichirō (1885–1970)

Businessman. Born in Tōkyō. After graduating from Tōkyō University in 1909, Ishikawa became assistant professor in the engineering department of his alma mater. He had planned to become a scholar, but in 1915 he left the university and joined Kantō Oxygen (now NISSAN CHEMICAL INDUSTRIES, LTD), then run by his father. Ishikawa was the manager when the company became a successful producer of sulphuric acid and soda. He became managing director of Dai Nippon Jinzō Hiryō Kaisha, the largest chemical fertilizer firm in Japan at the time, and then president of Nissan Chemical Industries in 1941. Although most other business leaders and corporation executives were purged after World War II, Ishikawa reorganized various economic organizations and became president of KEIDANREN (Japan Federation of Economic Organizations) in 1948. He played an important role in the reconstruction of the war-torn Japanese economy until 1956, when ISHIZAKA TAIZŌ took over as chairman of Keidanren.   *Yui Tsunehiko*

Ishikawajima–Harima Heavy Industries Co, Ltd

(Ishikawajima–Harima Jūkōgyō). Major manufacturer of land-based machinery, plants, ships, and jet aircraft engines. Commonly known as IHI, it was established in 1960 through a merger of Ishikawajima Heavy Industries and Harima Zōsenjo. The history of Ishikawajima Heavy Industries dates back to 1853, when the Mito domainal authorities constructed a shipyard on Ishikawajima, an island at the mouth of the Sumidagawa in Edo (now Tōkyō). This facility also manufactured machinery. Harima Zōsenjo, which developed its own technology for the construction of large ships, was established in 1907 in Hyōgo Prefecture and developed as an affiliate of the SUZUKI SHŌTEN. It merged with KŌBE STEEL, LTD, in 1921 but became independent in 1929. The 1960 merger resulted in a diversified heavy industrial enterprise that excels in shipbuilding and machinery production.

IHI has established wholly-owned subsidiaries and joint ventures overseas and is actively involved in technical assistance abroad. In addition to the licensing of patents and the providing of expertise, IHI dispatches technical supervisors and receives trainees from other countries. The company also offers drawings and material package deals, management and administration of shipbuilding and repair work, the rationalization of production control and construction methods, and the computerization of facilities. Sales for the fiscal year ending March 1982 totaled ¥777.7 billion (US $3.2 billion), ranking the company second among heavy manufacturers after MITSUBISHI HEAVY INDUSTRIES, LTD. The export ratio in that year was 50 percent. Of the total sales, land-based machinery and jet engines accounted for 75 percent, with the remainder generated by shipbuilding operations. The company was capitalized at ¥64 billion (US $265.9 million) in 1982. Corporate headquarters are located in Tōkyō.

Ishikawa Jōzan (1583–1672)

Confucian scholar and writer of *kanshi* (poems in Chinese; see POETRY AND PROSE IN CHINESE). After a distinguished military career in the army of TOKUGAWA IEYASU that went unrewarded because of an infraction of the military code, he resigned from service and took Buddhist orders at the temple Myōshinji in Kyōto. He later studied with FUJIWARA SEIKA, founder of Neo-Confucian studies in Japan, gaining fame as a poet and calligrapher. At the age of 58 he retired to a hermitage built at the foot of Mt. Hiei, which he called Shisendō (Hall of the Immortal Poets), and there went into seclusion, devoting the rest of his life to poetry. The Shisendō still stands in the outskirts of Kyōto. Jōzan's poems in Chinese demonstrated his particular interest in the poetic styles of such Tang (T'ang) China poets as Li Bo (Li Po; 701–762) and Du Fu (Tu Fu; 712–770) and received lavish praise from his contemporaries. His principal work of poetry was the *Fushōshū* (1671).

Ishikawa Jun (1899–)

Translator, novelist, and critic. Born in Asakusa, Tōkyō; educated in French literature at Tōkyō School of Foreign Languages. Translated Anatole France's *Le Lys rouge* (1923) and Andre Gide's *L'Immoraliste* (1924) and *Les Caves du Vatican* (1928). Along with schoolmate Yamanouchi Yoshio (1894–1973), who translated *La Porte étroite* (1923), Ishikawa was the first to introduce Gide's novels to Japan. Later, Gide's concept of the *roman pur* as put forth in *Paludes* and *Les Faux-Monnayeurs,* and the thinking of other European modernists, would exert considerable influence upon the formation of Ishikawa's view of the novel.

In 1935, after nearly a decade of artistic vagabondage, he began publishing a series of *récits* commencing with "Kajin" (The Lady) and "Hinkyū mondō" (Dialogue on Poverty) that depict a solitary writer, *watashi* (I), who lives in the city and who is engaged in a desperate struggle to create a Parnassian fiction. From the outset he states that his *watashi* is not to be confused with the first-person protagonist of the *watakushi-shōsetsu* (I-NOVEL) and declares himself an antinaturalist. His first novel, *Fugen* (The Bodhisattva), appeared the following year and reiterated this theme: "The breezes that stir the pages of the novel are a far different wind from the gusts of the mundane world." It was awarded the Akutagawa Prize in 1936, and Ishikawa was looked to as one of the promising young talents of the mid-1930s.

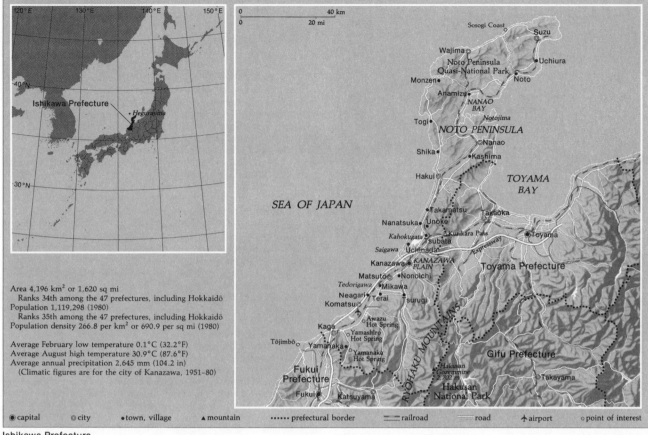

Area 4,196 km² or 1,620 sq mi
Ranks 34th among the 47 prefectures, including Hokkaidō
Population 1,119,298 (1980)
Ranks 35th among the 47 prefectures, including Hokkaidō
Population density 266.8 per km² or 690.9 per sq mi (1980)

Average February low temperature 0.1°C (32.2°F)
Average August high temperature 30.9°C (87.6°F)
Average annual precipitation 2,645 mm (104.2 in)
(Climatic figures are for the city of Kanazawa, 1951–80)

◉ capital ◎ city ● town, village ▲ mountain ⋯⋯ prefectural border ⟢railroad ══road ✈ airport ○ point of interest

Ishikawa Prefecture

In 1938 Ishikawa's "Marusu no uta" (I Hear the War God Singing) was banned by the military. During the war years he produced several important nonfiction works: his famous critique of author-physician MORI ŌGAI (published in 1941 as *Mori Ōgai*), a biography of WATANABE KAZAN (in 1941), and a theory of prose *Bungaku taigai* (1942, All about Literature), in which he enunciated his concepts of automatic living or "movement of the spirit" *(seishin no undō)* and automatic writing or "thinking with the pen" *(pen to tomo ni kangaeru)*. He wrote only one novel during the war years, *Hakubyō* (1939, A Plain Sketch) and, unable to seek refuge abroad as he wished, he sought a retreat in Edo literature, especially the KYŌKA or comic verse of the Temmei era (1781–89). At this time he adopted the pen name Isai, ("the *kyōka* poet at his desk"). The literature of the Temmei era came to represent for Ishikawa the incipience of a "modernist" movement within Japanese letters.

Ishikawa is numbered among the "first wave" of writers of the immediate postwar era. He basked in the limelight showered upon him and his contemporaries DAZAI OSAMU and SAKAGUCHI ANGO. Their lifestyles were characterized by hard drinking and living and a rebellion against traditional values. They are grouped together as members of the "libertine" *(buraiha)* or "new burlesque" *(shingesaku)* school, a loose term for their iconoclastic ways and interest in the burlesque parodies (GESAKU) of Edo fiction. The short stories that Ishikawa wrote from 1946 to 1948, such as "Ōgon densetsu" (1946, Legenda Aurea) and "Yakeato no Iesu" (1946, Christ amidst the Ruins), are his most representative pieces.

As the chaos of the early postwar years subsided, Ishikawa faded from public attention and became the "novelist's novelist" that he is known as today. Since 1950 he has divided his time evenly between creative writing and criticism. In the case of his novels, *watashi* disappears and is replaced by material of a surrealistic and satirical nature, a strain that dates from "Yamazakura" (Wild Cherries), written in 1936. His principal "experimental novels" *(jikken shōsetsu),* as he calls them, are *Taka* (1953, Hawks), *Hakutōgin* (1957, Lays of the White-Haired), *Aratama* (1963, Wild Spirits), and *Shifukusennen* (1965, The Millennium). *Shion monogatari* (1956; tr *Asters,* 1961) was awarded the Prize of the Minister of Education for the outstanding work of literature for 1957. His critical essays, beginning with *Isai hitsudan* (1950–51, Isai's Propos), form an ongoing

"Isai" series. They are conceived in an irreverent and acerbic style and cover a wide range of topics on art and literature. Ishikawa has also pioneered in the revival of the lost art of the *kijinden,* a cycle of sketches concerning unusual personalities from Japanese history, with his *Shokoku kijinden* (1955–57, Eccentrics and Gallants from around the Country), and the creation of short *deformé* tales which he calls *otoshibanashi* ("stories with a clincher").

Today he is anthologized alongside ABE KŌBŌ and ŌE KENZABURŌ, Japan's internationalist writers. They share a love of modern French literature and a desire to wrest the novel from subjects and styles peculiar to Japanese culture. Ishikawa is recognized as not only a superb craftsman but also a thoroughgoing methodologist of the novel, the latter making him an anomaly among Japanese writers. At the same time that he belongs to the modernist tradition within twentieth-century fiction, he can be seen as part of the "literati" *(bunjin)* tradition that originates in the poets and BUNJINGA painters of the Temmei years and that descends through Mori Ōgai and NAGAI KAFŪ. Indeed, Ishikawa is often called Japan's "last belletrist" *(saigo no bunjin)*.

📖———*Ishikawa Jun zenshū,* 14 vols (Chikuma Shobō, 1974–75). Aoyagi Tatsuo, *Ishikawa Jun no bungaku* (1978). Izawa Yoshio, *Ishikawa Jun* (1961). Donald Keene, *Three Modern Japanese Short Novels* (1961). Noguchi Takehiko, *Ishikawa Jun ron* (1969). Sasaki Kiichi, *Ishikawa Jun sakkaron* (1972). William Tyler, "The Agitated Spirit: Life and Works of Ishikawa Jun," PhD dissertation, Harvard University (1981).   William J. TYLER

Ishikawa Masamochi (1753–1830)

KYŌKA poet and KOKUGAKU scholar of the latter part of the Edo period (1600–1868). Son of the *ukiyo-e* artist ISHIKAWA TOYONOBU. Ishikawa was an innkeeper in Edo (now Tōkyō) and his *kyōka* pen name was Yadoya no Meshimori ("Maid at the Inn"). He was a disciple of ŌTA NAMPO and eventually founded his own school of *kyōka*, stressing satire and wit as opposed to the pseudo-classical elegance advocated by SHIKATSUBE MAGAO, his arch rival. He also compiled philological studies of the classics, including *Genchū yoteki* (ca 1818) and the still valuable dictionary of the classical language, *Gagen shūran* (1826–49). His *kyōka* are found in the anthology *Manzai kyōka shū* (1783).

Ishikawa Prefecture

(Ishikawa Ken). Located in central Honshū and bounded by the Sea of Japan on the west and north, Toyama Bay and Toyama and Gifu prefectures on the east, and Fukui Prefecture on the south. It is divided into two main areas, the Kaga region to the south and the NOTO PENINSULA to the north. There are also several islets north of Noto in the Sea of Japan, the largest of which is HEGURAJIMA. The southern portion of the Kaga region is largely mountainous, and the area around the city of KANAZAWA forms the prefecture's largest plain with several small rivers and lakes. The Noto Peninsula is hilly, with an uneven coastline forming many natural harbors. Both areas are warmed by the Tsushima Current, but precipitation is heavy and the weather frequently cloudy.

The area that is now Ishikawa Prefecture was once part of Echizen Province as established under the KOKUGUN SYSTEM in 646. In 718 part of this area was made Noto Province, and in 823 another part was made Kaga Province. In the 15th century, a religious sect overthrew the local ruler of Kaga (see IKKŌ IKKI) and controlled the province for nearly a century. Later, both Kaga and Noto came under the rule of the powerful MAEDA FAMILY, who encouraged scholarship and the arts. Noto and Kaga were combined in 1872 to form the present Ishikawa Prefecture. (The remainder of the original Echizen Province is now part of Fukui Prefecture.)

Agriculture is dominated by the production of rice, which is grown mainly on the KANAZAWA PLAIN. Fishing is a major industry on the Noto Peninsula. Although industry is not highly developed, there are textile and heavy machinery plants. The area is also known for several traditional handicrafts such as *wajima-nuri* lacquer ware and KUTANI WARE.

Tourist attractions include the rugged scenery of both the Kaga and Noto seacoasts and Kanazawa, which was the castle town of the Maeda family. There are many hot spring resorts, the most representative being Yamanaka, Yamashiro, and Awazu. Area: 4,196 sq km (1,620 sq mi); pop: 1,119,298; capital: Kanazawa. Other major cities include KOMATSU, KAGA, and NANAO. See map on previous page.

Ishikawa Sanshirō (1876–1956)

Socialist and later anarchist. Born in Saitama Prefecture, he graduated from Tōkyō Hōgakuin (a predecessor of Chūō University). In 1902 he began to work for the newspaper YOROZU CHŌHŌ but left the following year, together with KŌTOKU SHŪSUI and SAKAI TOSHIHIKO, when the paper decided to support the RUSSO-JAPANESE WAR. He joined the socialist group HEIMINSHA, which Kōtoku and Sakai had formed, and wrote antiwar articles for its newspaper, the *Heimin shimbun*. Ishikawa was also drawn to Christianity (he was baptized by EBINA DANJŌ), and when the Heiminsha disbanded in 1905 he joined ABE ISOO and KINOSHITA NAOE in founding *Shinkigen* (New Era), a Christian-socialist journal. Becoming involved with the socialist-feminist FUKUDA HIDEKO, he helped to edit her journal, SEKAI FUJIN. He also helped to revive the Heiminsha in 1907 and began publishing its newspaper as a daily; but it was soon banned, and Ishikawa was imprisoned for more than a year on charges of violating the press laws.

After the HIGH TREASON INCIDENT OF 1910, in which Kōtoku and other socialists were executed for plotting to assassinate the emperor, Ishikawa went to Europe. During his self-imposed exile (1913–20) he became attracted to anarchism and, returning to Japan, worked actively to promote its cause through his group, the Kyōgakusha (Mutual Study Society), and its journal *Dynamic*. In 1946 he helped to found the Anarchist League of Japan (Nihon Anākisuto Dōmei). In addition to his works on socialism and anarchism, Ishikawa translated Zola and Daudet and wrote on ancient Chinese history. His autobiography was published in two volumes as *Jijoden* (1956).

■——Kitazawa Fumitake, *Ishikawa Sanshirō no shōgai to shisō*, 3 vols (1974–76).

Ishikawa Tairō (1766–1817)

Shogunate official and Western-style illustrator of the Edo period (1600–1868). Born in Edo (now Tōkyō), he served in the Great Guard (Ōban) of the Tokugawa shogunate in Kyōto and Ōsaka. He studied painting with masters of the Kanō school and also cultivated friendships with several scholars of WESTERN LEARNING. These interests led him to experiment with Western-style drawing, in which he showed a singular aptitude for making copies of engravings in Dutch books. He provided illustrations for ŌTSUKI GENTAKU's *Enroku*, a translation of a Dutch medical treatise, and also for a treatise by Sugita Rikkei (1786–1845) on the eye, *Gankyū kaibō zu*, this time working from a cadaver.

Ishikawa Takeyoshi (1887–1961)

Editor and publisher who created the prototype of the Japanese magazine for housewives. Born in Ōita Prefecture, he left middle school, moved to Tōkyō in 1906, and became a live-in apprentice to a magazine publisher. In 1917 he founded *Shufu no tomo* (The Homemaker's Friend), a monthly magazine that reflected his traditional views of women and their domestic role. In just three years, *Shufu no tomo* became the most popular women's magazine in Japan. See WOMEN'S MAGAZINES.   KAKEGAWA Tomiko

Ishikawa Takuboku (1886–1912)

Poet and novelist; especially known for his *tanka*, the traditional Japanese short poem of 31 syllables (see WAKA), to which he brought new life by capturing everyday life and feelings in startlingly fresh language and imagery. Takuboku was born in the village of Hinoto, Iwate Prefecture. His father, a Zen Buddhist priest, was given a post soon afterward in the nearby village of Shibutami, and there Takuboku was raised and had his early education. Recognized as a youth of great promise, he entered Morioka Middle School at the age of 12, developed a strong interest in literature, and began in his early teens to write poetry. Encouraged by the publication of some of his poems in *Myōjō*, one of the leading literary magazines of the day, Takuboku dropped out of school in 1902 and went to pursue connections in Tōkyō with YOSANO TEKKAN, editor of *Myōjō*, and his wife, YOSANO AKIKO, both prominent poets in the Romantic Movement. However, illness and lack of funds forced him to return home the following year.

Takuboku continued to write during his recuperation, and his first volume of poetry, *Akogare* (Longing) was published in 1905. UEDA BIN, the well-known poet and translator from the French, wrote the preface, and Yosano Tekkan added a postface to the book. Written in the free verse manner of the *shintaishi*, or "new-style poetry", after the example of European poetry, *Akogare* attracted immediate public and critical attention for its startling imagery and outspokenness. Upon the merits of this collection, Takuboku attained recognition as a rising young modern poet.

That same year Takuboku married and, after his father lost his post in the local temple, assumed responsibility for support of the entire family. He took a position as a substitute primary school teacher in Shibutami, then moved to Hokkaidō in 1907, working as an editor and reporter for local magazines and newspapers in Hakodate, Sapporo, Otaru, and Kushiro. He returned to Tōkyō in 1908 and found employment for the next year as a proofreader for the ASAHI SHIMBUN, one of Japan's leading national daily newspapers. These years were marked by periodic separations from his wife and child, illness in the family, and unremitting financial difficulties.

Becoming interested in NATURALISM, a movement then current in Japanese literary circles, Takuboku began during this period to write fiction, but met with limited success and later abandoned these efforts. While in Hokkaidō he wrote several new collections of poems in the modern style, but after his arrival in Tōkyō, Takuboku began to turn more and more to the traditional *tanka* form. Takuboku devoted himself almost exclusively at the height of his powers to the writing of *tanka*, and it is on the quality of these short poems, and on his innovations within the form, that his considerable fame as a poet rests.

Takuboku's first collection of *tanka*, *Ichiaku no suna* (tr *A Handful of Sand*, 1934), was published in 1910 and contains about 550 poems written in simple, direct language. Dealing with emotions and experiences taken from his daily life, these poems have a frankness and vitality all but unprecedented in Japanese poetry. During this period Takuboku also published a statement of his poetics in an essay entitled "Kurōbeki shi" (1909, Poems to Eat) in which he challenged the prevalent notion that poets or poetic experiences are in any way exalted, and advocated a poetry that is down-to-earth and based on real life.

Deeply shocked by the arrest of KŌTOKU SHŪSUI and other socialists on the charge of plotting to assassinate the emperor, in the HIGH TREASON INCIDENT OF 1910, Takuboku began to take a serious interest in the socialist movement, reading widely in socialist thought and writing on the subject. Early the following year he fell ill and died on 13 April 1912 at the age of 26. A second *tanka* collection, *Kanashiki gangu* (tr *Sad Toys,* 1977), was published a few months later.

Considered by many to be Japan's finest modern poet, Takuboku exercised a major influence upon the subsequent development of *tanka* written in the modern language, and Takuboku societies have sprung up in many parts of Japan, devoted to the study of his works and the carrying on of his literary ideals. Since the 1920s, Takuboku has attained international stature; his poetry has been translated into most Western European languages, and into Russian and Chinese as well.

■——Works by Takuboku: *Ishikawa Takuboku zenshū,* 8 vols (Chikuma Shobō, 1967–69). *Ichiaku no suna* (1910), tr Shio Sakanishi as *A Handful of Sand* (1934, repr 1977). *Kanashiki gangu* (1912), tr Sanford Goldstein and Seishi Shinoda as *Sad Toys* (1977). *Takuboku: Poems to Eat,* tr Carl Sesar (1966). Works about Takuboku: Yukihito Hijiya, *Ishikawa Takuboku* (1979). Iwaki Korenori, *Ishikawa Takuboku* (1961). Kindaichi Kyōsuke, *Ishikawa Takuboku* (1951). Carl SESAR

Ishikawa Tatsuzō (1905–)

Novelist. Born in Akita Prefecture. Studied at Waseda University. Intending to emigrate to Brazil, he went to São Paulo but returned in two months. He wrote about this experience in a long novel, *Sōbō* (1935–39), the first part of which was awarded the first Akutagawa Prize in 1935. Writing in the journalistic style typical of much of his work, Ishikawa described the life of poor Japanese emigrants to Brazil set against the domestic and international political situation of the 1930s. After World War II, he established his name as a major novelist with such works as *Kaze ni soyogu ashi* (1949–51) and *Ningen no kabe* (1957–59). He has been a central figure in both the Japan Writers Association and the Japan P.E.N. Club.

Ishikawa Toyonobu (1711–1785)

UKIYO-E artist. Specialized in portraits of beautiful women *(bijinga)* and actor prints *(yakusha-e).* Born in Edo (now Tōkyō). As a student of the *ukiyo-e* artist Nishimura Shigenaga (d 1756), he worked under the name Nishimura Shigenobu and produced actor prints in the style of the TORII SCHOOL. When he married the daughter of an innkeeper of the Kodemmachō section of Edo, he inherited the name Nukaya Shichibei, traditionally used by the family head. However, around this time he began signing his work with the name Ishikawa Toyonobu and developed a style of his own, especially in his portraits of warm and elegantly beautiful women. Along with OKUMURA MASANOBU, he experimented in the utilization of wood-grain patterns *(kimezuri)* in the backgrounds of his prints. He influenced both KITAO SHIGEMASA and Suzuki HARUNOBU but, eclipsed by the latter, his artistic activity ceased in the Meiwa era (1764–72). His son ISHIKAWA MASAMOCHI was an important literary figure in the late 18th and early 19th centuries.

Ishinomaki

City in eastern Miyagi Prefecture, northern Honshū, at the mouth of the river Kitakamigawa. Principal activities are fishing and the cultivation of seaweed *(nori)* and oysters; the pulp, shipbuilding, and marine food-processing industries are also active. Construction of a coastal industrial belt is proceeding and an industrial port has been completed. Pop: 120,698.

Ishioka

City in central Ibaraki Prefecture, central Honshū, on Lake Kasumigaura. At one time the site of a provincial capital *(kokufu)* and provincial temple *(kokubunji),* Ishioka developed as a lake port. Today it is a growing residential and industrial city. The area is known for its fine *sake* and soy sauce. Pop: 47,830.

Ishiwara Jun (1881–1947)

Theoretical physicist. Responsible for the introduction and subsequent promotion of relativity and quantum theory in Japan; the immense enthusiasm that he generated for this new approach to PHYSICS contributed to the emergence of many eminent Japanese physicists, including YUKAWA HIDEKI and TOMONAGA SHIN'ICHIRŌ, in the 1920s and 1930s. Born in Tōkyō, he graduated from Tōkyō University in 1906. He went to Germany in 1912 to study with Arnold Sommerfeld (1868–1951) and later studied with Albert Einstein in Switzerland. He returned to Japan in 1914 to become professor at Tōhoku University. In his later years, Ishiwara endeavored to popularize physics for all levels of understanding in Japan. He is also known as a TANKA poet, contributing to the journal ARARAGI. His publications include *Sōtaisei genri* (1921, Principles of Relativity) and *Shizen kagaku gairon* (1929, Outline of Natural Science).

Ishiwara Kanji (1889–1949)

(also called Ishihara Kanji). Army officer and nationalist writer. Born 18 January 1889 in the city of Tsuruoka, Yamagata Prefecture, the second son of a policeman. After military preparatory school training, he graduated from the Army Academy in 1909. Commissioned a lieutenant in the infantry, Ishiwara's first assignments were in regimental garrisons in rural Korea and northern Honshū. He graduated in 1918 from the prestigious Army War College, where he gained a reputation as a brilliant and unorthodox candidate. Now a captain, Ishiwara about this time combined wide reading in the history of war with an intense study of the apocalyptic doctrines of the medieval Buddhist monk NICHIREN, which led him to formulate the beginnings of a theory of the evolution and future of war. He continued to develop the theory during tours of duty for study in Hankou (Hankow) and Berlin, so that when he returned to Japan in 1922 to take up the post of lecturer in military history at the War College from 1925 to 1928, he was prepared to present his ideas centering on a concept of past and future conflict that he believed would culminate in a cataclysmic global collision—"The Final War"—between Japan and the United States. Japan must prepare for this conflict, Ishiwara believed, by harnessing the resources of Asia, particularly Manchuria, and reordering the domestic political, economic, and social order. His ideas gained the enthusiastic interest of a powerful group of middle-echelon activists in central army headquarters. In 1929 with their support, Ishiwara, now a lieutenant colonel, obtained assignment as operations officer of the GUANDONG (KWANTUNG) ARMY in Manchuria.

In Manchuria Ishiwara worked closely with Guandong Army Senior Staff Officer ITAGAKI SEISHIRŌ (1885–1948) to undertake the operational planning basic to Japan's swift and sudden military takeover of Manchuria, launched on the evening of 18 September 1931 in Mukden (now Shenyang). Ishiwara, not the nominal Guandong Army commander HONJŌ SHIGERU, is generally regarded as the driving force behind the subsequent runaway operations over which the civil and military authorities in Japan were rarely in control (see MANCHURIAN INCIDENT). In 1932 Ishiwara, as a full colonel and with a reputation as an officer of uncompromising personality, unorthodox ideas, and nearly insubordinate behavior, returned to Japan, the idol of younger activist officers and the object of some concern by the Japanese military establishment. After two years as regimental commander in Sendai where the economic privations of rural northern Japan contributed to his growing conviction of the need to restructure Japan, Ishiwara was assigned in 1935 as section chief in the Operations Division of the General Staff. In that position, one of the most powerful in the Japanese army at the time, Ishiwara set about drafting plans for the establishment of a "national defense state." This was a vast scheme for economic, industrial, and political mobilization in Japan and Manchuria that was designed to prepare Japan for major hostilities, in particular with the Soviet Union, now seen by the army as Japan's most immediate enemy. In 1936 his attention to this program was distracted by the FEBRUARY 26TH INCIDENT, an uprising by young officers. As chief of operations of the martial law headquarters Ishiwara was instrumental in mobilizing the military force that brought about the rebellion's swift collapse, a triumph that left him with heightened prestige and power in the army.

This influence, however, Ishiwara dissipated in a series of futile backstairs political maneuvers in the winter of 1936–37. In company with an odd assortment of military and civilian sympathizers he managed to derail the formation of a government by premier-designate UGAKI KAZUSHIGE but was frustrated in his efforts to shape the government of the subsequent prime minister, General HAYASHI SENJŪRŌ.

These machinations earned him the distrust and enmity of the army's top echelon and served to undermine his apparent position and prestige when, in March 1937, he was promoted to major general and appointed chief of the entire Operations Division of the General Staff. Added to this, his unorthodox advocacy of a policy of greater accommodation toward China brought him into conflict with the hard-line "old China hands" in central headquarters. His policy of military moderation on the Asian continent was fatally compromised when the SINO-JAPANESE WAR broke out in July of 1937. Striving with diminishing success to prevent escalation of the operations against Chinese forces around Beijing (Peiping; now Beijing or Peking), Ishiwara found his remaining influence completely drained by September, when he was reassigned as vice-chief of the Guandong Army Staff. But his abrasive personality, unorthodox views, and strident criticisms of his superiors soon served to undermine his influence there as well. In August 1938 Ishiwara returned to Japan; the remainder of his military career was blighted. Two backwater assignments from 1938 to 1941, first as garrison commander at Maizuru, then as commander of a reserve division in Kyōto, allowed him leisure time to publicize his "Final War" theories, to which he now added the concept of an "East Asian League" (Tōa Remmei), a union of Japan, Manchukuo (the Japanese puppet state in Manchuria), and China that would mobilize the energies and resources of East Asia to confront the Western imperialist presence there.

In 1941 Ishiwara reached the rank of lieutenant general, but was forced out of the army in March of that year by old enemies in the service, including Army Minister TŌJŌ HIDEKI. After a brief stint on the faculty of Ritsumeikan University in Kyōto, Ishiwara in 1942 returned to Tsuruoka, where for the duration of the Pacific War he and his small agricultural community of devoted followers turned to the study of problems of rural self-sufficiency. The remainder of his life was one of discouragement and infirmity. Japan's defeat shattered much of his theory of war and, despite a brief flurry of postwar popularity as an exponent of a totally reconstructed Japan, he was purged from public life by the Occupation authorities. He did serve as a rather testy defense witness at the Tōkyō War Crimes Trials in 1947, but by then he had succumbed to slowly declining health. His last years were spent in semimystical speculation on the regeneration of his nation.

——Gordon Berger, *Parties Out of Power in Japan, 1931–1941* (1977). John Hunter Boyle, *Japan and China at War, 1937–1945* (1970). Ishiwara Kanji, *Saishū sensō ron* (1972 re-ed). Sadako Ogata, *Defiance in Manchuria: The Making of Japanese Foreign Policy, 1931–1932* (1964). Mark Peattie, *Ishiwara Kanji and Japan's Confrontation with the West* (1975). Ben-Ami Shillony, *Revolt in Japan: The Young Officers and the February 26, 1936 Incident* (1973). Tsunoda Jun, ed, *Ishiwara Kanji shiryō*, 2 vols (1967).

Mark R. PEATTIE

Ishiwara Ken (1882–1976)

Historian of Christianity. Born in Tōkyō. Graduate of Tōkyō University. He studied under H. von Schebert and others at Heidelberg from 1921 to 1923. Ishiwara was named associate professor of Tōkyō University in 1921, and three years later became professor at Tōhoku University. He was president of Tōkyō Women's University from 1940 to 1948, and in 1953 became a member of the Japan Academy. He worked with the entire history of Christian thought (his doctoral dissertation was on Clement of Alexandria), with particular interest in Augustine and Luther. His works include *Kirisutokyō shi* (1934, A History of Christianity), *Kirisutokyō shisō shi* (1949, A History of Christian Thought), and *Chūsei kirisutokyō kenkyū* (1952, Studies on Medieval Christianity).

TOKUZEN Yoshikazu

Ishiyamadera

A ranking temple of the TŌJI branch of the SHINGON SECT of Buddhism, located in the city of Ōtsu, Shiga Prefecture. Ishiyamadera is said to have been founded in 749 by the eminent monk RŌBEN (689–773), who had been requested by Emperor SHŌMU (r 724–749) to pray for the discovery of gold, urgently needed to gild the colossal image of the Buddha Vairocana that was being cast for the temple TŌDAIJI at Nara. Rōben withdrew to Kimbusen, a sacred mountain situated in the southern part of what is now Nara Prefecture and invoked Kongō Zaō, a ferocious divinity of the esoteric tradition, who finally appeared in a dream and instructed Rōben to pray at a place sacred to KANNON at Ishiyama. Rōben followed these instructions and prayed to an image of the bodhisattva Kannon, which the emperor owned. When gold was discovered shortly thereafter in Mutsu Province in northern Honshū, Rōben converted his hermitage into a temple, Ishiyamadera, and installed as the object of worship a newly carved large image of Kannon (Nyoirin Kannon). Rōben placed the earlier image of Kannon within the newly carved larger image and flanked the latter with two other esoteric divinities.

Emperor Shōmu had Ishiyamadera designated a *chokuganji*, i.e., a temple at which prayers were to be regularly offered for the well-being of the imperial family and the tranquillity of the nation. In 754 Emperor Shōmu presented the temple with a set of the Buddhist canon that he himself had copied. Ishiyamadera enjoyed enormous popularity at all levels of Japanese society; its sacred image was reputed to possess the power of working miracles. The image of Kannon is kept in a sealed shrine that is opened to public viewing only once every 33 years. The sectarian affiliation of Ishiyamadera was changed from Tōdaiji to the Shingon sect after the learned Shingon cleric Kanken (853–925) took up residence there. Over the centuries the temple was frequented by emperors and aristocrats. MURASAKI SHIKIBU (fl ca 1000) is said to have written several chapters of her TALE OF GENJI while staying here. Ishiyamadera was completely gutted by fire in 1078, although there is some controversy over whether the original sacred image was lost at that time. The temple was rebuilt some twenty years later. Among its patrons were MINAMOTO NO YORITOMO (1147–1199), who built the Tahōtō—a two-storied pagoda dedicated to Tahō (Prabhūtaratna) Buddha—the oldest such structure in Japan, and Toyotomi Hideyoshi's concubine, YODOGIMI (1567?–1615), who endowed the temple with huge estates and sponsored the construction of several new buildings.

Ishiyamadera is particularly rich in art treasures. The temple is also known for its extremely valuable collection of some 5,000 rolls of Buddhist manuscripts that date from the 8th to the 15th centuries and a famous picture scroll describing the origin of the temple and wonders effected there. Ishiyamadera is the 13th of the 33 holy places of Kannon visited by pilgrims in western Japan.

Stanley WEINSTEIN

Ishiyama Honganji

A temple and town, located on Naniwa Bay in the estuary of the rivers Yodogawa and Yamatogawa, which was from 1533 to 1580 the headquarters of the religious and secular organization of the HONGANJI, the major branch of the Buddhist True Pure Land Sect (Jōdo Shinshū; see JŌDO SHIN SECT); the origin of the modern city of Ōsaka.

The temple was founded as the Ishiyama *dōjō* (chapel) by RENNYO Kenju (1415–99), the eighth *hossu* (pontiff) of the Honganji, in 1496. It came into prominence when Shōnyo Kōkyō (1516–54), the 10th pontiff, moved there in 1532 after the Yamashina Honganji to the east of Kyōto was destroyed by the forces of the *daimyō* Rokkaku Sadayori (1495–1552) of Ōmi Province (now Shiga Prefecture) and the Lotus Confederation (Hokke *ikki*) of the Nichirenist townsmen (MACHISHŪ) of Kyōto. It became the official headquarters of the organization in 1533.

Shōnyo built up the Ishiyama Honganji into an elaborate complex containing great halls of prayer, a residence in the aristocratic *shinden* style, and gardens; the whole was surrounded with moats and walls, becoming an almost impregnable temple fortress. Within these fortified temple precincts (*jinai*) there developed a town (*jinai machi*) which eventually grew to comprise ten wards (*machi*) populated by artisans and merchants; its size may be gauged from the report that a fire in 1562 destroyed 2,000 houses. The Ishiyama Honganji was at the same time a religious center, attracting numerous pilgrims and, accordingly, a great inflow of wealth; a commercial center whose *machishū* engaged in various trades; and a cultural center where such arts as the tea ceremony and the Nō theater flourished. Above all, it was the governing center of the Honganji's vast power structure, fittingly called a religious monarchy, which by the 1570s encompassed entire provinces, including Kaga and Noto (which now constitute Ishikawa Prefecture) as well as Echizen (now part of Fukui Prefecture) on the coast of the Sea of Japan.

In 1570 the religious monarchy of the Honganji came into conflict with ODA NOBUNAGA, becoming embroiled in a 10 years' war with the rising hegemon. The Ishiyama Honganji withstood a siege in 1576, but four years later the 11th *hossu*, Kennyo Kōsa (1543–92), upon the imperial court's intercession agreed to a peace that included the surrender of the temple fortress among its conditions. On Tenshō 8.4.9 (22 May 1580), Kennyo withdrew to Saginomori in Kii Province (now Wakayama Prefecture); but his designated heir Kyōnyo Kōju (1558–1614) defied the agreement and remained at Ishiyama, urging the adherents (*monto*) of the Honganji to continue fighting the "enemy of the Buddhist Law," Nobunaga. Disowned by his father for his truculence, Kyōnyo finally surrendered the Ishiyama Honganji on Tenshō 8.8.2 (10 September 1580); it burned that day, presumably set afire on his orders.

The strategic position of the Ishiyama Honganji was, however, recognized by the national unifier TOYOTOMI HIDEYOSHI, who built Ōsaka Castle on its site. When Hideyoshi moved into that magnificent fortress in 1584, he restored Ōsaka's central place in Japanese affairs and assured its development into a major city.

George ELISON

Ishizaka Kimishige (1925–　)

Immunologist. Born in Tōkyō; graduate of Tōkyō University. In 1948 he became a researcher at the National Institute of Health in Tōkyō, and in 1962 (after a period of study at California Institute of Technology), he was appointed director of research at the Children's Asthma Research Institute in Denver, Colorado. Between 1960 and 1966 he succeeded in isolating immunoglobulin E (IgE), which acts as an antibody and contributes to the occurrence of certain allergic syndromes such as bronchial asthma and pollen reactions. His discovery is regarded as an important contribution to immunology. In 1970, Ishizaka joined the Faculty of Medicine at Johns Hopkins University, and from 1974 to 1980 served concurrently as a professor at Kyōto University. He has received the Passano Award, a medical award for distinguished accomplishment in the field of immunology in the United States. He received the Order of Culture in 1974. His wife, who has long been his coworker, is an assistant professor at Johns Hopkins.

NAGATOYA Yōji

Ishizaka Taizō (1886–1975)

Businessman. Born in Tōkyō. After graduating from Tōkyō University, Ishizaka joined the Communications Ministry (now Ministry of Posts and Telecommunications) but shifted to Daiichi Seimei, an insurance firm, in 1915 at the invitation of YANO TSUNETA. He served as its president from 1938 to 1946. Although purged by the Allied Occupation authorities after World War II, he later returned to public life, and as president of the faltering Tōkyō Shibaura Electric (now TŌSHIBA CORPORATION) in 1949, he supervised the company's reconstruction. He became the second president of KEIDANREN (Japan Federation of Economic Organizations) in 1956, leading the organization during the period of the nation's high economic growth. Ishizaka opposed governmental intervention in economic affairs, particularly in trade and capital liberalization, and led the business-industrial community toward policies conducive to good relations with the United States.

YUI Tsunehiko

Ishizaka Yōjirō (1900–　)

Novelist. Born in Aomori Prefecture. Graduate of Keiō University. While teaching at a girls' high school in his hometown, Hirosaki, he began contributing short stories to literary magazines in Tōkyō. He eventually established his name with his novel *Wakai hito* (1933–37), serialized in the magazine *Mita bungaku*. This novel, about the dilemma of a young male teacher who falls in love with two uninhibited women, one his student and the other his colleague, became the prototype for his *seishun-mono*, novels dealing with teenage life. Characterized by sympathetic and humorous descriptions of the exuberance of youth freed from feudalistic social conventions, many of his works have been made into films. He was one of the most popular writers of the 1950s. Other works include *Mugi shinazu* (1936) and *Aoi sammyaku* (1947).

Ishizuchisan

Mountain on the southwest edge of the city of Saijō, central Ehime Prefecture, Shikoku; chief peak in the Shikoku Mountains, composed of andesite. Rare plants such as *shikokushirabe* (a kind of abies) and *omogozasa* (a kind of bamboo grass) grow there. The Ishizuchi Shrine is located on the summit. Tens of thousands of worshipers yearly go to the mountain for the 1–10 July summer mountain festival. Designated as the Ishizuchi Quasi-National Park. Height: 1,982 m (6,501 ft).

Ishizuka Tatsumaro (1764–1823)

National Learning (KOKUGAKU) scholar; known for his discovery of a special form of ancient KANA orthography. Born in Tōtōmi Province (now Shizuoka Prefecture), he was a student of the much respected classicist and philologist MOTOORI NORINAGA. He conducted an exhaustive study of the literature of the Nara period (710–794), including the KOJIKI (712, Records of Ancient Matters) and NIHON SHOKI (720, Chronicle of Japan), the two oldest extant histories of Japan; the MAN'YŌSHŪ, an 8th-century anthology of Japanese classical verse; and other early texts. As a result of his research, he demonstrated the existence of two special categories of characters within the writing system known as *man'yōgana*, an early Japanese orthography derived from Chinese characters (KANJI). He further demonstrated that the distinction between the two was maintained in writing different words. Among Ishizuka's writings, *Kanazukai oku no yamamichi*, a three-volume orthographic study probably completed before 1798, and *Kogen seidaku kō* (1801) are especially well known.

UWANO Zendō

Ishō nihonden

(Foreign Accounts of Japan). Collection of excerpts from Chinese and Korean documents concerning Japan's contacts with the Asian continent; the first known attempt to compile a history of Japanese diplomatic relations. It was compiled by the Confucian and National Learning (KOKUGAKU) scholar Matsushita Kenrin (1637–1703), who completed it in 1688 after 30 years of work and published it in 1693. It also contains comments and bibliographical notes on the 127 works from which Kenrin drew.

Isoda Kōichi (1931–　)

Literary critic. Born in Yokohama. Graduate of Tōkyō University. A scholar of the English Romantic poets, he began to write literary criticism during the early 1960s. He gained recognition for his *Junkyō no bigaku* (1964), a collection of his early essays. His extremely laudatory critique of MISHIMA YUKIO is philosophically consistent with Isoda's other work; he believes in an indigenous Japanese "mentality" of a traditional character, which he claims transcends political ideology. Other works include a collection of literary essays *Seitō naki itan* (1969).

Isoda Koryūsai (18th century)

UKIYO-E artist. Real name Isoda Masakatsu. The son of a *rōnin* (masterless *samurai*), he is thought to have studied under Nishimura Shigenaga, a master of *bijinga*, and to have been strongly influenced by Suzuki HARUNOBU (1725?–70). His style resembles Harunobu's and his earlier works are often signed Haruhiro or Koryūsai Haruhiro, the name Haruhiro being patterned on Harunobu. However, in contrast to the dreamlike quality of Harunobu's women, Koryūsai's *ukiyo-e* are marked by a sensual directness. Harunobu used soft, middle-range colors; Koryūsai's colors, such as the Indian red that he particularly liked, are more subdued. Koryūsai produced numerous *abuna-e* (mildly erotic *ukiyo-e*), *nishiki-e* (full-color prints), and SHUNGA (erotic pictures). In his later years he produced paintings rather than prints and was granted the title of *hokkyō* (an honorific title, originally Buddhist, given to artists).

Isoho monogatari

A 17th-century Japanese translation of *Aesop's Fables*, it was the first, and remained the only, Western literary work widely read in Japan until the 19th century. Appearing in various editions from early in the century on, the work appealed to educated adults for its wit and charm as well as for its didactic content, and influenced subsequent Japanese fiction considerably. Many of its stories were later used by professional storytellers (see RAKUGO). An earlier translation, *Esopo no fabulas*, published in 1593 by Portuguese missionaries in romanized, colloquial Japanese, remains a valuable source for linguistic research. See JESUIT MISSION PRESS.

Isonokami no Yakatsugu (729–781)

Courtier and poet of the Nara period (710–794). A descendant of the ancient MONONOBE FAMILY, he held a variety of posts in the imperial court during his distinguished public career and was appointed great counselor (*dainagon*) in 780. Yakatsugu was a celebrated poet in his time, and several of his verses in classical Chinese are preserved in the anthology KEIKOKUSHŪ (827). A noted Buddhist scholar and bibliophile, he established the UNTEI library, perhaps the earliest important private collection in Japan.

Isonokami Shrine

(Isonokami Jingū). Shintō shrine in the city of Tenri, Nara Prefecture, dedicated to Futsunomitama no Ōkami, a sacred sword presented to the legendary first emperor, Jimmu, by the deity Takemikazuchi no Kami upon the former's conquest of the Japanese islands. The gift of the sacred sword was made in accordance with the wish of the imperial ancestress, Amaterasu Ōmikami. The MONONOBE FAMILY, who exercised military authority on behalf of the imperial family in the 5th and 6th centuries, regarded the deity of this shrine as their own clan deity (ujigami). The shrine holds many treasures, including the famous seven-pronged sword (shichishitō), which contains one of the earliest inscriptions found in Japan, probably dating from the year 369. The oratory (haiden) of the shrine is one of the oldest examples of haiden architecture and is designated as a National Treasure. The annual festival is held on 15 October.

Stanley WEINSTEIN

Isozaki Arata (1931–   )

Architect. Born in Ōita Prefecture. A student of TANGE KENZŌ, Isozaki graduated from Tōkyō University in 1954 and completed his doctoral studies there in 1961. His first independent work was the Ōita Prefectural Medical Association Hall (1960). Among his early designs are contributions to the futuristic and technologically based proposals then current in Japanese architecture, but more recent designs show a manneristic, allusive quality coupled with a highly inventive play of geometrical forms. His buildings include the Ōita Prefectural Library (1966), the Fukuoka Mutual Bank main office (1971), the Gumma Prefectural Modern Art Museum (1974), and the Kita Kyūshū Municipal Art Museum and Library (1974).

WATANABE Hiroshi

Issa (1763–1827)

Also known as Kobayashi Issa. HAIKU poet of the late Edo period. Real name Kobayashi Nobuyuki. In addition to Issa which means "a cup of tea," he used a number of other pen names. Born as the first son of a middle-class farmer in the village of Kashiwabara in the province of Shinano (now Nagano Prefecture), he was educated by a village teacher, who wrote haiku under the pen name of Shimpo. Issa's mother died when he was three, and five years later, his father married again. This was the beginning of his lifelong family struggle; the stepmother was cold to Issa, and he fell victim to a stepson mentality. In 1777 he went to Edo (now Tōkyō), where he had to do "rough, servile jobs." In 1787 we find him studying haiku under Chikua, a poet of the Katsushika group, which was interested in reviving the sublime style of BASHŌ. Following Chikua's death in 1790, Issa decided to live the life of a poet-priest. He spent the following 10 years or so on a series of wandering journeys. During this period, Issa visited many poets, especially in the Kansai (Kyōto–Ōsaka) area, and gathered his poems in such collections as Kansei kuchō (1794) and Kansei kikō (1795). In 1801 his father died, and he wrote about this experience in Chichi no shūen nikki (1801, Diary of My Father's Death). Carrying out his father's wish, Issa decided to settle in his native village, but negotiations with his half brother prevented his settling until 1813. During this period, he went back and forth between Edo and Kashiwabara and gathered his poems in such collections as Kyōwa kuchō (1803) and Bunka kuchō (1804–08). In 1813 his half brother finally consented to share the family house with Issa. In the following year Issa married a 27-year-old woman named Kiku. Four children were born in quick succession, but none of them lived long. The birth and death of his second child, Sato, inspired Issa to write Oraga haru (1819; tr The Year of My Life, 1972), the best known of all his works. Written in HAIBUN (haiku mixed with prose passages), this work is primarily a biographical account of his most unforgettable year, but Issa succeeded in weaving into his fine fabric thoughts and experiences from other years and areas of his life. Poems he wrote after settling in his native village were gathered in such collections as Shichiban nikki (1810–18), Hachiban nikki (1819–21), Kuban nikki (1822–24), and Bunsei kuchō. The last years of Issa's life were darkened by deaths and other unhappy events. In 1823 Kiku died, and in the following year Issa married and divorced his second wife. In 1827 his house was burned down except the storehouse, which still remains. Issa died in the same year, survived by his third wife and unborn child.

Issa was always ready to acknowledge his indebtedness to Bashō. He advised his disciples not to follow him, but to imitate the style of Bashō. This advice reveals Issa's awareness of the difference between Bashō and himself. His style is characterized by a bold acceptance of down-to-earth daily expressions and animal images, by the use of personification and witty figures of speech, by the presence of a comic spirit which provokes earthy laughter, and by the frequent expression of a stepson mentality and a poverty complex. Issa, however, successfully combined these unconventional elements with the high seriousness he inherited from Bashō, as can be seen in the following poems:

Medetasa mo	Quite auspiciously
chūkurai nari	I find myself half-happy
ora ga haru	On my New Year's Day.
Suzume no ko	My baby sparrows,
soko noke soko noke	Off the road, I say, off the road,
ouma ga tōru	Sir Horse is coming along.
Umasōna	Deliciously soft
yuki ga fūwari	Snow flakes come down upon us
fuwari kana	Dancing and tossing.

📖 ——Kawashima Tsuyu, ed, Issa shū, in Nihon koten bungaku taikei, vol 58 (Iwanami Shoten, 1959). Ozawa Yoshio, ed, Issa zenshū, 9 vols (Shinano Mainichi Shimbun Shuppambu, 1979). Oraga haru, tr Nobuyuki Yuasa as The Year of My Life (1972).

Nobuyuki YUASA

Issan Ichinei (1244–1317)

(Ch: Yishan Yining; I-shan I-ning). Chinese Zen monk who is considered the founder of GOZAN LITERATURE (Chinese learning in medieval Japanese Zen monasteries). Born in Zhejiang (Chekiang) Province. In the wake of the unsuccessful MONGOL INVASIONS OF JAPAN of 1274 and 1281, he was sent to Japan by Khubilai's successor in an attempt at a goodwill gesture. He himself had no interest in politics and, though first met with suspicion, was welcomed to Kamakura by the shogunal regent Hōjō Sadatoki and later installed as abbot of the temple Nanzenji in Kyōto by Emperor GO-UDA. Broadly learned in secular subjects and well acquainted with Song (Sung; 960–1279) historical and philosophical thought, he was a devoted and stimulating teacher of his numerous Japanese disciples, of whom the most distinguished were KOKAN SHIREN and SESSON YŪBAI. Although the secular knowledge he taught was new to Japan, the literary tastes it represented were already somewhat old-fashioned in China; his literary lineage nevertheless continued to flourish even after the introduction from the continent of newer, more fashionable literary styles.

Marian URY

Issumbōshi

(One Inch Boy). Folktale. The equivalent of Tom Thumb in England, it recounts how a couple pray for a child and are finally granted an extraordinarily small boy, whom they fondly call Issumbōshi (literaly, "One-inch Monk"). The boy seeks his fortune in Kyōto and vanquishes demons on an island; thanks to a miraculous mallet that they have left behind, he becomes a tall man and makes a fortunate marriage. The story gained wide circulation when it was printed as an OTOGI-ZŌSHI during the Edo period (1600–1868). Similar legends belonging to the "small-boy" genre are found throughout Japan.

SUCHI Tokuhei

Isuzu Motors, Ltd

(Isuzu Jidōsha). Comprehensive automotive manufacturer producing Isuzu-brand commercial vehicles and passenger cars; especially known worldwide for its diesel engines. One of the oldest automotive manufacturers in Japan, it started operations in 1916, was incorporated in 1937, and assumed its present name in 1949. Isuzu became affiliated with the General Motors Corporation of the United States in 1971. It is the largest truck manufacturer in Japan. Expansion into overseas markets with commercial vehicles came early, and the company's export ratio, including passenger cars, is high (55 percent in 1978). Sales for the fiscal year ending October 1981 totaled ¥727.4 billion (US $3.1 billion), of which commercial vehicles generated 60 percent, passenger cars 16 percent, engines and others 24 percent. Capitalization stood at ¥38 billion (US $164.2 million) in 1981. Corporate headquarters are located in Tōkyō.

Itabashi Ward

(Itabashi Ku). One of the 23 wards of Tōkyō. On the Musashino Plateau and bordered by the river Arakawa. A residential area. In the Edo period (1600–1868), Itabashi was a POST-STATION TOWN on the Nakasendō highway. Before World War II, it was a semiurban area. After the war, many large housing complexes were constructed, and the population grew rapidly. There are many small and medium-sized machinery, pharmaceutical, and chemical industries in the ward. Pop: 498,038.

itadori

(Japanese knotweed). *Polygonum cuspidatum,* a large perennial herb of the buckwheat family *(Polygonaceae),* found in fields and mountains throughout Japan, as well as in Korea and China. The stems grow from rhizomes and are usually thick and strong, reaching 30–150 centimeters (12–59 in) in height; they are hollow and have reddish purple dots when young. The leaves are alternate and ovate or ovately elliptic. The *itadori* has male and female flowers on different plants, and in summer it grows flower stalks at leaf nodes and branch tips bearing numerous small white flowers. The *beniitadori* is a variety with red flowers, and *meigetsusō* is an alpine dwarf variety.

Raw young stems are edible but taste sour. The dried rhizome is used as a laxative and diuretic and is also said to be effective for relieving pain. Reference to the plant as *"tajii"* appears in the KOJIKI (712), the oldest Japanese chronicle. *Matsuda Osamu*

Itagaki Seishirō (1885–1948)

Army general. Born in Iwate Prefecture. Graduate of the Army Academy (1904) and the Army War College (1916). At the time of the MANCHURIAN INCIDENT (1931) he and ISHIWARA KANJI, another officer in the operational planning staff of the Japanese Guandong (Kwantung) Army, worked out details for the military occupation of Manchuria, even engineering the bombing that started the incident. He was named commander of the Fifth Division at the time of the outbreak of the Sino-Japanese War in July 1937, but was recalled to Japan to serve as army minister in the first KONOE FUMIMARO cabinet. In 1939 he became chief of the general staff of the China Expeditionary Army and two years later was promoted to general. After the Japanese defeat in 1945, Itagaki was tried as a war criminal at the Tōkyō WAR CRIMES TRIALS. Charged by the Soviet prosecutor as being the chief instigator of all anti-Soviet aggression on the Asian continent, he was executed in 1948. *Kondō Shinji*

Itagaki Taisuke (1837–1919)

Politician of the Meiji (1868–1912) and Taishō (1912–26) periods. He was a leader of the FREEDOM AND PEOPLE'S RIGHTS MOVEMENT and founder of Japan's first major political party, the JIYŪTŌ. Itagaki was born in Kōchi, castle town of the Tosa domain (now Kōchi Prefecture), into an upper *samurai* family of hereditary retainers to the *daimyō*. At age 18 Itagaki was sent by his daimyō to Edo (now Tōkyō) to study, and there he came into contact with the politically conscious samurai of the Mito domain (now part of Ibaraki Prefecture). When he returned to Tosa later in the year, he was banished to a remote village for four years for insulting Tosa officials. He spent his time studying and hunting. He was called back to Kōchi to study military subjects at the instance of an influential Tosa official, YOSHIDA TŌYŌ, and was soon appointed a domainal official in charge of a group of tax collectors.

In 1861 he was transferred to the Edo residence of the Tosa daimyō to take charge of accounts and military matters. Although Itagaki was of upper samurai background, in 1864 he identified more with the lower samurai, with whom he shared antiforeign and antishogunate sentiments. This faction soon rivaled the upper samurai group in power.

In the final months before the MEIJI RESTORATION of 1868 Itagaki met with SAIGŌ TAKAMORI of the Satsuma domain (now Kagoshima Prefecture) and agreed to help to overthrow the Tokugawa shogunate. Itagaki purchased 300 American-made rifles in Ōsaka and secretly gathered his followers in Tosa to await the signal from Kyōto to lead his men. Itagaki fought against shogunate troops in February 1868 in the BOSHIN CIVIL WAR. By the time of the Restoration Itagaki had become the most powerful leader in Tosa. The bases of his power were his own political organization in Tosa, his

position as a link between upper and lower samurai there, his leadership of the Tosa military forces, and his close bond with Saigō.

In 1869 he entered the new government in Tōkyō and became involved in several key reforms, including the return of the land registers to the emperor, the abolition of the domains, and the creation of prefectures (see PREFECTURAL SYSTEM, ESTABLISHMENT OF).

In 1873 Itagaki became involved in a critical debate in the government over whether a punitive expedition should be sent to Korea (see SEIKANRON). His friend Saigō was one of the more vocal advocates of war, and Itagaki decided to support him. When IWAKURA TOMOMI and ŌKUBO TOSHIMICHI, who had been touring the United States and Europe (see IWAKURA MISSION), returned in 1873, however, they rejected the plan. Itagaki resigned in protest, together with Saigō, GOTŌ SHŌJIRŌ of Tosa, and ETŌ SHIMPEI and SOEJIMA TANEOMI of the Hizen or Saga domain (now Saga Prefecture).

Back in Kōchi, Itagaki met with Gotō and with Etō and Soejima. Together with seven other associates they decided on two goals: to establish a large political association to arouse public opinion and to submit a memorial to the government calling for the establishment of a representative national assembly. The group organized a proto-political party, the AIKOKU KŌTŌ, or Public Party of Patriots in Tōkyō. In January 1874 it submitted to the government the so-called Tosa Memorial. The memorial borrowed ideas from Western liberalism, in particular Mill's *On Liberty*. It also criticized the government for its arbitrary exercise of power and called for the formation of a national assembly. Publication of the document in the press touched off a national debate, even though the memorial was formally rejected by the government. In 1874 Itagaki organized a second society, the RISSHISHA (Self-Help Society). The society included many former samurai of the old antishogunate faction in Tosa. The society derived inspiration from Samuel Smiles's *Self Help,* a book widely read at the time, and reflected a combination of the samurai spirit with the philosophy of the new liberal movement, which stressed equality and freedom. In February 1875 Itagaki extended the scope of his activities and organized (in Ōsaka) a national association, the AIKOKUSHA (Society of Patriots). Establishing its headquarters in Tōkyō, the association began to use the term *minken* (popular rights) in its discourses.

In January 1875 government leaders met at the ŌSAKA CONFERENCE, hoping to entice Itagaki and others back into the government. The conference agreed to create the GENRŌIN, a proto-senatorial body, and the GREAT COURT OF CASSATION, and to convene an ASSEMBLY OF PREFECTURAL GOVERNORS. These concessions persuaded Itagaki to return to the government in March as a *sangi* (councillor). He hoped that the Genrōin would become a genuine legislative body, but it had little power. Itagaki opposed the concentration of power in the DAJŌKAN (Grand Council of State), and in October of the same year he again resigned from government, not returning until 1896.

Itagaki renewed his efforts to realize the popular-rights ideal of establishing a national representative assembly. Through the Risshisha he presented a memorial in 1877 demanding the establishment of a constitutional system. In 1880 the Aikokusha was renamed the Kokkai Kisei Dōmei (LEAGUE FOR ESTABLISHING A NATIONAL ASSEMBLY). Finally, in October 1881 Itagaki and others formed Japan's first genuine political party, the Jiyūtō (Liberal Party). He decided against joining forces with the other major popular-rights group under ŌKUMA SHIGENOBU. Several young liberals of Tosa joined the new party, notably UEKI EMORI, NAKAE CHŌMIN, and BABA TATSUI. The leadership of the Jiyūtō was heavily Tosa based, as was the membership, which included wealthy landowners and brewers. The government immediately sought to suppress the Jiyūtō on the grounds that it had violated the Public Assembly Ordinance (SHŪKAI JŌREI) of 1880 by not receiving police permission before its meeting.

In April 1882, when Itagaki was in Gifu on a speaking tour, a man attempted to kill him with a knife. When the would-be assassin was grabbed by his followers, Itagaki shouted, "Itagaki may die but liberty never!" His wound was not serious, and his cry became an inspiration for the popular rights movement.

In November 1882 the government succeeded in persuading Itagaki to go to Europe, where he hoped to study constitutional government. Although the Jiyūtō opposed the trip on the grounds that it was a plot to get rid of Itagaki, he departed. When Itagaki returned in 1883, he found that the party had deteriorated because of government repression, factional rivalries, and a wave of violent acts perpetrated by party members. In 1884 the party disbanded. Itagaki presented several memorials critical of government policy and voicing the demands of the popular rights movement. By 1890 the party had been revived (as the Rikken Jiyūtō) in time for the first session of the Diet. Itagaki developed some rapport with ITŌ HIROBUMI, and in April 1896 he was persuaded by Itō, who felt he needed the support of Itagaki's party, to enter the second Itō cabinet as home minister.

In 1898 the efforts of followers of Itagaki and Ōkuma Shigenobu to bring about a union of the two major political parties (Itagaki's Jiyūtō and Ōkuma's SHIMPOTŌ [formerly the Rikken Kaishintō]) finally succeeded. In June 1898 Itagaki and Ōkuma agreed to form a joint party, the KENSEITŌ (Constitutional Party). A few days later the new party was ordered to form Japan's first party cabinet (see ŌKUMA CABINET). Itagaki was at first reluctant but finally agreed to serve as home minister. The new cabinet, however, immediately became divided over the allocation of cabinet posts among the two factions. After four months the short-lived cooperation broke down and Itagaki led his faction in forming a party without the Ōkuma faction but using the same party name. Ōkuma responded by forming the KENSEI HONTŌ (True Constitutional Party). Itagaki shortly thereafter retired from politics and spent the rest of his life writing.

■ ——Works by Itagaki Taisuke: Itagaki Taisuke, *Itagaki Taisuke zenshū*, ed, Itagaki Morimasa (Shunjūsha, 1933). Itagaki Taisuke, *Jiyūtō shi*, 2 vols (1910). Itagaki Taisuke, "Itagaki jōsōbun," in Yoshino Sakuzō, ed, *Meiji bunka zenshū*, vol 2 (1928). Itagaki Taisuke and Ōkuma Shigenobu, *Fifty Years of New Japan*, tr and ed Marcus B. Huish, 2 vols (1910). Works about Itagaki Taisuke: Cecil Earl Cody, "A Study of the Career of Itagaki Taisuke, a Leader of the Democratic Movement in Meiji Japan," PhD dissertation, University of Washington (1955). Fukuchi Shigetaka, *Itagaki Taisuke* (1951). Hattori Shisō, *Meiji no seijika tachi*, vol 1 (1950). Itō Chiyū, *Yamagata Aritomo, Itagaki Taisuke*, in *Itō Chiyū zenshū*, vol 24 (Heibonsha, 1931).   Joyce C. LEBRA

itai itai disease → pollution-related diseases

Itako

Town in southeastern Ibaraki Prefecture, central Honshū, southeast of Lake Kasumigaura. An important center of water and land transportation in the Edo period (1600–1868), Itako has declined with the opening of the Jōban railway line. Its principal occupations are rice cultivation and garden farming. A part of the Suigō–Tsukuba Quasi-National Park, the town is known for its Iris Festival held in June. Pop: 22,581.

Itakura Katsukiyo (1823–1889)

Daimyō of the Matsuyama domain (now Matsuyama Prefecture) and twice a senior councillor *(rōjū)* of the Tokugawa shogunate in the 1860s. After losing his post in the ANSEI PURGE (1858–60), he served again from 1862 to 1864 and from 1865 to 1868 as senior councillor and was active in foreign affairs and finance. He became a close adviser of TOKUGAWA YOSHINOBU, the 15th and last Tokugawa shōgun, and staunchly supported his reforms. After the restoration of imperial rule and the defeat of Tokugawa forces in the Battle of TOBA–FUSHIMI in early 1868, Itakura returned with Yoshinobu to Edo (now Tōkyō) to resist an imperial takeover (see BOSHIN CIVIL WAR). Unsuccessful, he fled to Hakodate, where eventually in 1869 he and other Tokugawa diehards, including ENOMOTO TAKEAKI, capitulated to the imperial army. Put under house arrest for life, he was pardoned in 1871.

Itakura Katsushige (1545–1624)

Important administrator of the early Tokugawa regime. A native of Mikawa Province (now part of Aichi Prefecture), Katsushige at an early age was placed in a Buddhist temple, but he returned to the laity to assume the headship of his *samurai* family in 1581, when his brother Sadashige was killed in the service of TOKUGAWA IEYASU. Katsushige served Ieyasu as a city commissioner *(machi bugyō)* of Sumpu (now the city of Shizuoka), the future shōgun's headquarters from 1587; upon Ieyasu's transfer to Edo (now Tōkyō) in 1590, he became an EDO MACHI BUGYŌ. In 1601, a year after Ieyasu's victory at SEKIGAHARA and assumption of hegemony over Japan, Katsushige was made a city commissioner of Kyōto, the imperial capital; he served the Tokugawa shogunate as KYŌTO SHOSHIDAI (the shogunal deputy in Kyōto) from 1603, the year of the shogunate's foundation. The responsibilities of this crucial office included not only the administration of civil affairs and criminal justice in the city and its surrounding countryside but also the supervision of the shogunate's

direct holdings (TENRYŌ) in the Kyōto–Ōsaka region and the surveillance of the *daimyō* of western Japan; the post also had a military function, as for instance in the Ōsaka Campaigns of 1614–15 (see ŌSAKA CASTLE, SIEGES OF), and on occasion involved Katsushige in foreign affairs. His early training as a Buddhist priest made Katsushige particularly well equipped to handle the shogunate's relations with the imperial court and the many religious institutions of the Kyōto area, another of the post's important responsibilities; but the cordial relations he enjoyed with the Kyōto aristocracy may have been the reason for his replacement in 1619, when the shogunate was subjecting the imperial court to severe pressures to bring about the marriage of the shōgun TOKUGAWA HIDETADA's daughter Kazuko (1607–78) to Emperor GO-MIZUNOO. Katsushige's son Shigemune (1586–1656) succeeded him as Kyōto *shoshidai*, serving in the position until 1654; both father and son gained the reputation of wise judges.   George ELISON

Italy and Japan

The first contact between Italy and Japan took place in the 16th century with the arrival of Italian missionaries to Japan. Regular contact was not established until the late 19th century, when the new Meiji government, in an effort to introduce Western culture to Japan, invited Italian teachers of art to Japan. Since then, cultural intercourse, particularly in the fine arts and music, has been quite active. Trade between the two countries increased significantly after World War II, although the volume is still small. There is a good deal of technological interchange.

Catholic missionaries from Italy first arrived in Japan in the late 1500s. On the initiative of Alessandro VALIGNANO, the most intellectual of 16 Italian missionaries who came to Japan, four youths representing the three so-called Christian *daimyō* of Kyūshū (ŌTOMO SŌRIN, ŌMURA SUMITADA, and ARIMA HARUNOBU) were dispatched to the Vatican in 1582. This "Tenshō mission to Europe" (see MISSION TO EUROPE OF 1582) lasted until 1590. In 1613 the daimyō DATE MASAMUNE sent a retainer, HASEKURA TSUNENAGA, on an unsuccessful mission to Rome to negotiate a trade agreement. These contacts were soon halted by the repressive anti-Christian policies of the Tokugawa shogunate (1603–1867). In 1708, even after the enactment of the NATIONAL SECLUSION laws forbidding foreigners from entering Japan, the Jesuit missionary Giovanni Battista SIDOTTI attempted to enter the country; captured, he later died in prison (see also CHRISTIANITY).

Cultural Exchange after 1868 —— Regular intercourse between the two countries began after the Meiji Restoration (1868). In 1870 Count Alessandro Fé became the first Italian minister to Japan, and SANO TSUNETAMI was dispatched by the Japanese government in 1873 as minister to Italy and Austria. The Meiji (1868–1912) and Taishō (1912–26) periods were marked by the introduction to Japan of modern Italian military technology and Italian culture. Two army majors, Pompeo Grillo and Scipione Braccialini, were invited to Japan by the government. Grillo arrived in 1884 to teach the technology of manufacturing arms and ammunition, and the 28-centimeter (11.0-in) cannon that was produced under his supervision played an important role in the RUSSO-JAPANESE WAR of 1904–05. Braccialini, who arrived in 1892, was an authority on ballistics and contributed much to the development of artillery and to Japanese engineering in general. These two men also facilitated the import of Italian arms to Japan. The Italian engraver Edoardo CHIOSSONE, who was employed by the government from 1875 to 1891, designed Japan's first modern paper money.

Italians contributed significantly to the development of Western painting in Japan. When the first art academy, the Kōbu Bijutsu Gakkō, was established in Japan in 1876, a number of Italian artists and art critics were invited to teach at the school: Antonio FONTANESI (theory and techniques of painting), Giovanni Vincenzo Cappelletti (painting techniques and basic theory), and Vincenzo RAGUSA (sculpture and painting). Fontanesi's students included ASAI CHŪ and YAMAMOTO HŌSUI. Their disciples in turn were Ishii Hakutei (1882–1958), UMEHARA RYŪZABURŌ, and YASUI SŌTARŌ, later leading exponents of Western painting. Chiossone painted the portraits of members of the Japanese imperial family, including the emperors Meiji and Taishō, and government officials like SAIGŌ TAKAMORI and ŌKUBO TOSHIMICHI. Since Chiossone made Japan his permanent residence, his contributions to painting in Japan were extensive. Ragusa married a Japanese woman, Kiyohara Tama, and returned to his native Palermo in 1882. There he helped the lacquer artist Kiyohara Einosuke (Tama's brother-in-law) obtain a position as a lecturer at the local art and handicraft academy. Tama Ragusa became a prominent figure in social circles and contributed much to friendship between Italy and Japan.

Italy's contribution to music in Japan took place largely during the Taishō period. Adolfo Sarcoli, who lived in Japan between 1910 and 1928, transmitted knowledge of Western music in general and also contributed much to the development of vocal music. Many famous Japanese singers, including Miura Tamaki (1884–1946) and Fujiwara Yoshie (1893–1976), were either taught personally by Sarcoli or nurtured in his vocal musical traditions. In 1912, Giovanni Vittorio Rossi opened the Royal House in the Akasaka section of Tōkyō and was active in the introduction of dance, operetta, and vocal music. Among his most famous pupils was Hara Nobuko (1893–1979). He was also instrumental in having an Italian opera company come to Japan for the first time in 1929.

In literature, the classics of Dante and Boccaccio and modern works by D'Annunzio and Pirandello were translated into Japanese, chiefly by the painter Arishima Ikuma (1882–1974) and his pupils. Japanese classics such as the TALE OF GENJI and KAMO NO CHŌMEI's Hōjōki, as well as works by modern writers like NATSUME SŌSEKI and YOSANO AKIKO were translated into Italian by Marcello Muccioli of the Instituto Orientale di Napoli, the linguist Pietro Silvio Rivetta, and Shimoi Harukichi, a Japanese residing in Italy.

The War Years——In the 1930s the governments of both countries assumed fascist tendencies. Close political and military relations followed the conclusion of the ANTI-COMINTERN PACT (1937) and the TRIPARTITE PACT (1940), while relations between the people of Japan and Italy were enhanced by the establishment of the Italo-Japanese Society (forerunner of the present Japan–Italy Institute) in 1937 and the Società Amici del Giappone in Italy in 1938. Also in 1938, an agreement was concluded for the exchange of professors and students, maintained only by the Italians after the third year, because of the outbreak of war in Europe.

In 1941 an agreement for the monthly exchange of music and news broadcasts was concluded. The Japanese broadcast news and lectures in Italian once a week. The Italians promoted Japanese culture through performances of jōruri, Nō, kyōgen (produced by Corrado Pavolini), and Japanese music; they also put out a monthly magazine called Yamato (1941). The Japanese on their part did little to promote Italian culture.

Relations after World War II——After World War II and the establishment of democratic forms of government in both countries, there was a significant increase in exchange in economic, political, and social matters. During the immediate postwar years, Japan imported salt and rice from Italy. Later the principal imports from Italy were olive oil, canned tomatoes, cheese, wine, agricultural seeds, fluorite, gypsum, chemical products, industrial machinery, computers, typewriters and other office equipment, musical instruments, leather products, and textiles. Principal Japanese exports to Italy were ships, steel products, metals, electric appliances, motorcycles, ceramic wares, pearls, tea, agar-agar, bamboo material, peppermint, and fresh and frozen marine products.

The volume of trade is relatively small compared with that of other trade partners of the two countries. In 1978 Japan exported a total of $489 million worth of goods to Italy and imported a total of $656 million. Japanese trade with Italy was only about 7 percent of the total trade with the European Community countries. Among the most important Italian and Japanese business affiliations are the tie-ups between Ignanto and TŌRAY INDUSTRIES, INC, for the production of synthetic leather; between Montedison Eslon and SEKISUI CHEMICAL CO, LTD, for the production of polyvinyl pipes; between IAP and HONDA MOTOR CO, LTD, for the production of motorcycles in the 125-cc class, and between Mediterraneo and YOSHIDA KŌGYŌ for the production of zippers. Most of the large Japanese banks and trading firms have branches in Italy. Banca Commerciale Italiana, the largest bank in Italy, and the huge trading firm of Olivetti have branches in Japan, as do most other major financial and trade enterprises. There are no outstanding political problems between the two countries, and major politicians on both sides have made visits in recent years.

A great number of Italian writers, literary critics, and newspaper reporters have traveled to Japan, and their visits have been returned by such Japanese writers as MISHIMA YUKIO. Numerous exhibitions of Italian paintings, sculptures, etchings, and woodblock prints have been held in Japan, the Pompeii exhibition and Leonardo Da Vinci's Mona Lisa being particularly well received. Representative Japanese paintings, watercolors, calligraphy, and the tea ceremony have been exhibited in Italy. Japanese students of music have studied under Italian masters. Hirayama Michiko, for example, has completed an epoch-making study of Gregorian chant. Active exchange also takes place in the fields of medicine, architecture, and design.

━━━━━Nichii Kyōkai, ed, Nichii bunka kōshō shi (1941). Yoshiura Morizumi, Nichii bunkashi kō (1968). YAMAZAKI Isao

Itami

City in southeastern Hyōgo Prefecture, western Honshū, 14 km (9 mi) northwest of Ōsaka. A castle town during medieval times (13th–16th centuries), it developed as a sake-brewing center under the patronage of the KONOE FAMILY. Now a satellite city of Ōsaka, its major industries are food-processing machinery, nonferrous metals, textiles, and chemicals. Produce farming is carried on in the area. It is the location of Ōsaka International Airport. Pop: 178,229.

Itami Mansaku (1900–1946)

Film director and scenarist. Real name Ikeuchi Yoshitoyo. He was born in Ehime Prefecture. After graduating from middle school, Itami aspired to become a painter but on the recommendation of a schoolmate, film director ITŌ DAISUKE, he entered the movie world. He became a director in 1928 with Adauchi ruten. Itami became known for his skillful direction of period films with intellectual and modernistic themes, and is noted for such movies as Kokushi musō (1932) and Akanishi Kakita (1936). Itami is also known for his work as a scenarist beginning with Tenka taiheiki (1928), directed by INAGAKI HIROSHI. Other works include Muhōmatsu no isshō (1943, The Life of Matsu Untamed) and Te o tsunagu kora (1948), also directed by Inagaki. After contracting tuberculosis in 1938, he concentrated mainly on writing scenarios and essays. His writings are collected in Itami Mansaku zenshū (Chikuma Shobō, 1961).

SHIRAI Yoshio

Itaya Hazan (1872–1963)

Porcelain artist best known for his low relief and lightly lustrous mat-glaze polychrome designs. Real name Itaya Kashichi. Born in Shimodate, Ibaraki Prefecture, to a merchant father with literati tastes. Unable to pursue the military career he sought, he attended the Tōkyō Art School (now Tōkyō University of Fine Arts and Music) and graduated from its sculpture department in 1894. From 1896 he taught sculpture and then ceramics at the Ishikawa Prefectural Industrial School; in 1903 he left for Tōkyō to teach at Tōkyō Industrial College and established his own kiln, eventually achieving recognition and financial success. He won a number of gold medals at exhibitions, including the 1928 Teiten. He exhibited yearly at the Teiten, the BUNTEN, and the Nitten. In 1929 he was appointed to the Imperial Fine Arts Academy (Teikoku Bijutsuin); in 1934 he became an imperial court household artist (teishitsu gigeiin); in 1953 he received the Order of Culture.

Hazan's graceful, restrained, and painstakingly executed porcelains (about 1,000 survive) range from celadon, white and cinnabar pieces, and iron glaze temmoku tea wares emulating ancient Chinese models, to the more innovative mat glaze, powdery, pastel polychrome works for which he was famous. His sure relief modeling and his naturalistic but increasingly abstract designs, most often floral and based on direct sketches from life, greatly enhance his exquisite glazes. Frederick BAEKELAND

Itō

City in eastern Shizuoka Prefecture, central Honshū, on the Izu Peninsula. Its mild climate and hot springs have made it a popular resort. Itō is also a base for deep-sea fishing; mandarin oranges and flowers are grown on the surrounding slopes. A part of the FUJI-HAKONE-IZU NATIONAL PARK, the city also has a marine park, a cactus park, and historical sites associated with MINAMOTO NO YORITOMO, NICHIREN, and William ADAMS. Pop: 69,638.

Itō Daisuke (1898–1981)

Film director. Born in Ehime Prefecture. In 1920 he entered the acting school affiliated with Shōchiku Kinema. He joined the scriptwriting department of Shōchiku's Kamata studios, and then its contemporary drama section. His debut as a director came in 1924 with Shuchū nikki, after which he became independent and founded the Itō Eiga Kenkyūjo (Itō Movie Research Center) in 1926. Despite great financial strain, he managed to produce Kyōko to Shizuko

(1926) and *Nichirin* (1926, The Sun) but incurred tremendous debts. His films *Chōkon* (1926) and *Chūji tabi nikki* (1927, Chūji's Travel Diary), starring ŌKŌCHI DENJIRŌ and produced after Itō joined Nikkatsu's Kyōto studios (see NIKKATSU CORPORATION), were, however, great successes. In the early "talkies" era he created such renowned works as *Chikemuri Takatanobaba* (1928), *Tange Sazen* (1933), and *Satsuma hikyaku* (1938). With his historical period works he broke away from the tradition of heroic films by portraying tragic, rebellious protagonists, and gained the sympathy of the antiestablishment proletarian class. In the post-World War II era, he created such great works as *Ōshō* (1948) and *Hangyakuji* (1961).

ITASAKA Tsuyoshi

Itō Einosuke (1903–1959)

Novelist. Born in Akita Prefecture. After graduating from middle school (8th grade), he became involved in the PROLETARIAN LITERATURE MOVEMENT, writing novels and criticism. Around 1931, a time of widespread famine in the Tōhoku region where he was born, Itō started to write novels about its farmers. When the influence of the proletarian literature movement began to decline, he turned to a simple narrative style, akin to the folktale, in which dialogue blended into the underlying narrative, and described the poverty of agrarian life with humor and pathos. After World War II he continued to write in a folkish style with warmth and understanding about life in the destitute villages of the northeast. *Keisatsu nikki* (1952, The Policeman's Diary) a representative collection of his short stories, employs the device of observing the farm people through the eyes of a village policeman.

Itō Gemboku (1800–1871)

Physician. The foremost authority on Western medicine in the latter part of the Edo period (1600–1868). He pioneered the use of the smallpox vaccine in Japan, and the vaccination center he established in 1857 in the Kanda district of Edo (now Tōkyō) eventually evolved into Tōkyō University's School of Medicine. Born in what is now Saga Prefecture, he studied the Dutch language under Inomata Denjiemon and medicine under Philipp Franz von SIEBOLD. In 1826, he established the Shōsendō, a school of Western sciences in Edo from which many prominent physicians and scholars of the late Edo and Meiji (1868–1912) periods graduated. In 1828 he was imprisoned briefly in connection with an alleged exchange of maps with Siebold. In 1844 he was appointed official physician of the Saga domain, and in 1858 physician to the Tokugawa shogunate. His written works include *Iryō seishi*, a 24-volume translation, from the Dutch, of Austrian medical texts.

Itō Ham Provisions Co, Ltd

(Itō Hamu Eiyō Shokuhin). A processed-food manufacturer, specializing in ham, sausage, and processed meats. The largest producer of ham and sausage in Japan, the company was established in 1928 in Ōsaka by Itō Denzō. Vienna sausage wrapped in cellophane and fish-meat sausage were two new products developed by the firm. After World War II it became one of Japan's leading meat packers with such new products as pressed ham. It has joint ventures in the United States and Brazil. Sales for the fiscal year ending February 1982 totaled ¥250.9 billion (US $1 billion); capitalization stood at ¥9.6 billion (US $40.8 million) in the same year. Corporate headquarters are located in Nishinomiya, Hyōgo Prefecture.

Itō Hirobumi (1841–1909)

Preeminent statesman of modern Japan; his long career spanned nearly the entire Meiji period (1868–1912), beginning with his participation in the struggle to overthrow the Tokugawa shogunate. As the chief architect of Japan's first constitution and as prime minister four times, he guided his country in its formative years as a modern nation state.

Youth —— Itō was born in the Chōshū domain (now Yamaguchi Prefecture) the son of a farmer, Hayashi Jūzō. When he was 14, his father was adopted by Itō Naoemon, a low-ranking *samurai* of the Chōshū domain, and the son took the name Itō Shunsuke. The young Itō studied with Kuruhara Ryōzō (1829–62), an important official in Chōshū and brother-in-law of KIDO TAKAYOSHI. In 1857 he entered the Shōka Sonjuku, the school run by YOSHIDA SHŌIN, and came under the influence of Shōin's ardent proimperial views. From

Itō Hirobumi

Itō in the last decade of his life.

there he went to Nagasaki to study Western methods of military drill. In 1862 he accompanied Kido to Edo (now Tōkyō) and Kyōto, where together they established contact with other activists in the SONNŌ JŌI (Revere the Emperor and Expel the Barbarians) movement. In December of that year he joined with fellow Chōshū man TAKASUGI SHINSAKU in burning down the British legation in Edo.

For his achievements Itō was made a samurai in 1863 by his domain, which was then the leader in the movement to overthrow the shogunate. He was then ordered to go abroad with INOUE KAORU and several other Chōshū samurai; they smuggled themselves aboard a ship and managed to get to England. During his stay Itō saw the enormous technical superiority of the West, and, abandoning his anti-Western stance, he came to favor the opening of Japan. Returning home the next year, he and Inoue led the negotiations following the SHIMONOSEKI BOMBARDMENT, a retaliation by Western ships for earlier attacks by Chōshū. Itō thereafter allied himself with the Chōshū reformist clique under Takasugi and worked for domain reform and for an alliance with Satsuma (now Kagoshima Prefecture), the other leading domain in the antishogunate movement (see SATSUMA–CHŌSHŪ ALLIANCE).

Early Career —— With the overthrow of the Tokugawa shogunate and the establishment of a new government in the MEIJI RESTORATION (1868), Itō was appointed san'yo (junior councillor; see SANSHOKU), with responsibility for foreign affairs. He became, in rapid succession, governor of Hyōgo Prefecture and assistant vice-minister of finance and of popular affairs. It was during this period that he changed his name to Hirobumi. On the advice of the British minister Harry PARKES, he set in motion plans to construct a railway between Tōkyō and Yokohama (completed in 1872).

Early in 1870 Itō was sent to the United States to study Western currency systems. When he returned home the following year, he was made director of the Tax Division and National Mint and, soon after, vice-minister of public works. In October of the same year he traveled as a member of the IWAKURA MISSION to Europe and the United States. When the mission returned in 1873, the government became divided over the question of invading Korea (see SEIKANRON). With the resultant departure of SAIGŌ TAKAMORI, ITAGAKI TAISUKE, and other proinvasion leaders from the government, Itō was appointed SANGI (councillor) and, concurrently, minister of public works. In 1874 he presided as chairman of the first Assembly of Prefectural Governors. The resignation of Kido in opposition to the TAIWAN EXPEDITION OF 1874 led to a further thinning in government ranks, and in 1875 Itō, Inoue Kaoru, and ŌKUBO TOSHIMICHI convened the ŌSAKA CONFERENCE and succeeded in wooing both Kido and Itagaki back into the government with promises of greater popular participation in politics. In order to make good these promises, Itō formed a committee to review government organization and subsequently, as head of the Legislation Bureau (Hōseikyoku), worked to reorganize the legal system.

During this period, insurrections of former samurai, who had been stripped of their feudal privileges, occurred throughout Japan. The largest of these was the SATSUMA REBELLION (1877), led by Saigō. Itō labored with other government leaders to quell the disturbance, which ended in Saigō's suicide. Kido's death soon afterward and Ōkubo's assassination in 1878 signaled a change in the leadership; Itō, now home minister, and Finance Minister ŌKUMA SHIGE-NOBU emerged as the most powerful figures in the government. Itō disagreed with Ōkuma, however, on the procedure for establishing a constitutional form of government, favoring a gradualistic approach; and Ōkuma, who urged speedy implementation, was ousted in the POLITICAL CRISIS OF 1881. Thereupon Itō moved into a position of unchallenged power and proceeded with his plan for a Prussian form of constitutional government.

Drafter of the Constitution —— As chairman of a bureau that had been established to draft a constitution, Itō traveled to Europe in 1882 to study various constitutional systems. His meetings with Rudolf von GNEIST and Lorenz von STEIN strengthened his conviction that a constitutional system under an absolute monarch was best suited for Japan. Following his return in 1883, he worked together with INOUE KOWASHI, ITŌ MIYOJI, KANEKO KENTARŌ, and Herman ROESLER in drafting the CONSTITUTION of the Empire of Great Japan. At the same time, Itō legally set aside lands and funds to ensure the economic independence of the ruling family and wrote the draft of the IMPERIAL HOUSEHOLD LAW. In 1884, as a further means of bolstering the prestige of the imperial family, he issued the Peerage Ordinance (Kazokurei).

The year 1885 saw the abolition of the DAJŌKAN system of government and the establishment of a modern cabinet system. Itō became the first prime minister, serving concurrently as imperial household minister and chairman of the Constitutional Commission. He was now at the pinnacle of his career. The new cabinet addressed itself to strengthening the bureaucracy and rectifying the so-called Unequal Treaties imposed on Japan since the 1850s. In an attempt to win equal recognition from the Western powers, the government accelerated its Westernization policies; but Foreign Minister Inoue Kaoru's proposals for treaty revision met with opposition within the government and from the FREEDOM AND PEOPLE'S RIGHTS MOVEMENT and were not realized (see UNEQUAL TREATIES, REVISION OF).

The final draft of the constitution was completed in 1888. Itō established the PRIVY COUNCIL (Sūmitsuin), a supra-cabinet body, to "discuss" and give formal approval to the constitution, resigning as prime minister so that he himself might become its head. The constitution was promulgated on 11 February 1889, and at the end of that year Itō received a special commendation from the emperor.

Party Politics —— With the establishment of the bicameral IMPERIAL DIET in 1890, Itō became head of the upper house, the House of Peers. He again became prime minister in 1892, remaining in that position until 1896. Itō stood at odds with the so-called popular parties (MINTŌ) in the lower house on budgetary matters, particularly on increases in military spending, but he managed to win house approval with the help of an imperial rescript that called for cooperation between the central government and the Diet. Efforts toward treaty revision continued, and in 1894 extraterritoriality was abolished. In the meantime Japan had come into conflict with China over Korea, and in 1894 it initiated hostilities. At the end of the SINO-JAPANESE WAR OF 1894-1895, Itō personally represented his country in negotiating the Treaty of SHIMONOSEKI.

In 1898 Itō became prime minister for the third time. He was opposed by both the JIYŪTŌ (Liberal Party) and the SHIMPOTŌ (Progressive Party) on his proposal for imposition of extra land taxes. He accordingly dissolved the Diet, an action that prompted the two parties to merge into a single party, the KENSEITŌ (Constitutional Party), which won an absolute majority in the Diet in the succeeding election. Itō resigned and had the Kenseitō leaders Ōkuma and Itagaki form the next cabinet. His experiences with obstructionist party men convinced him of the need for a new progovernment political party, and in 1900 he organized the RIKKEN SEIYŪKAI (Friends of Constitutional Government Party). It was made up largely of his supporters in the bureaucracy and several former Jiyūtō members who had defected from the Kenseitō. A month after the new party's founding, Itō formed a fourth cabinet composed mainly of Seiyūkai politicians. The House of Peers, however, was not pleased with Itō's party cabinet and a Diet dominated by political parties. It withheld its approval of the cabinet's proposal for tax increases, but Itō once again prevailed upon the emperor to issue a rescript, and the tax proposal passed unamended.

Last Years —— Weary of politics, Itō resigned in 1901 and journeyed to Russia to establish closer trade relations. Following his return in 1903 and his appointment for the third time as head of the Privy Council, Itō ceded his duties as Seiyūkai president to SAIONJI KIMMOCHI. Even after the war with China, Korea had remained a sensitive issue, and in 1904 Japan went to war with Russia, its new

rival in Northeast Asia. With Japan's victory in the RUSSO-JAPANESE WAR (1904-05), Russia recognized Korea as lying within the Japanese sphere of influence. Itō traveled to Korea to sign the KOREAN-JAPANESE CONVENTION OF 1905, which gave Japan full control of Korea's foreign relations. Returning to that country in 1906 as the first Japanese resident general, Itō initiated programs for economic development and the reorganization of the courts and the police system. In the following year he forced the Korean emperor to abdicate and established a full Japanese protectorate over Korea, thus gaining control of the country's internal affairs and paving the way for eventual annexation (see KOREA, ANNEXATION OF). When he resigned as resident general in 1909 to return to the headship of the Privy Council, Itō was opposed to outright annexation; nevertheless, during a tour of Manchuria later that year, he was assassinated in Harbin by a Korean nationalist, AN CHUNG-GŬN.

In presiding over the government at a time of momentous changes, Itō, more than other government leaders, enjoyed the full confidence of the Meiji emperor. He was a consummate politician, decisive and yet flexible; he was also magnanimous and openhearted and known to be indifferent to money. He had a fondness for reading, a quality rare among politicians, and wrote many Chinese poems under the pen name Shunho (Spring Field). His immediate family included his wife Umeko, his adopted heir Hirokuni, who was Inoue Kaoru's nephew, and a daughter, Ikuko, who became the wife of SUEMATSU KENCHŌ.

▬ ——Itō Hirobumi, *Itō Kō zenshū*, ed Komatsu Midori, 3 vols (Shōwa Shuppansha, 1928). George Akita, *Foundations of Constitutional Government in Modern Japan, 1868-1900* (1967). Nakamura Kikuo, *Itō Hirobumi Kō* (1958). Shunho Kō Tsuishōkai, ed, *Itō Hirobumi den*, 3 vols (1940; repr 1965).   *NASU Hiroshi*

Itoigawa

City in southwestern Niigata Prefecture, central Honshū, on the Sea of Japan. A castle town during the Edo period (1600-1868), Itoigawa has been traditionally known for its hot springs, jade, and ceramic industry. The development of hydroelectric power utilizing the nearby river Himekawa has led to the construction of several factories. Numerous skiing grounds are near the city. Pop: 36,080.

Itō Jakuchū (1716-1800)

Painter known for his meticulously detailed, almost surrealistic, depictions of exotic birds and fowl. Jakuchū was the eldest son of a prosperous Kyōto greengrocer, and following the death of his father, assumed management of the store. By the early 1750s, however, Jakuchū had formed a friendship with Chikujo Taiten (1717-1801), a well-known artist-monk of the temple SHŌKOKUJI, whose *To Keiwa gaki* (Painting Record of Jakuchū) provides the earliest account of the youthful artist. In order to pursue his ambitions as a painter, Jakuchū relinquished the management of the family business to his brother in 1755.

There is scant documentation on Jakuchū's training as a painter. In the *Gajō yōryaku*, which contains much information about early artists, it is recorded that his teacher was Ōoka Shumboku (1680-1763), a Kanō-style artist active in Ōsaka and known for compiling printed painting manuals. The same record mentions Jakuchū's study of Chinese BIRD-AND-FLOWER PAINTING, and it is likely that his friendship with Taiten gave him access to the important holdings of the Shōkokuji. According to some accounts, Jakuchū, rather than relying on conventional painting formulas, kept exotic birds in his garden, which he studied and painted. The pristine detail of Jakuchū's depictions of parrots, roosters, peacocks, and other birds may indeed have stemmed from close personal observation. However, they were also reminiscent of Western botanical and zoological illustrations, which had been introduced to Japan by the Dutch in Nagasaki.

Beginning around 1758 Jakuchū worked on a spectacular set of 30 large hanging scrolls as a votive offering to the Shōkokuji. Conceived as a set of ceremonial paintings for Buddhist ritual, the set consisted of 27 paintings of flowers, birds, and fishes flanking a central triptych of Śākyamuni Buddha and two bodhisattvas, Fugen (Skt: Samantabhadra) and Monju (Skt: Mañjuśrī). The entire set of paintings was presented to the Shōkokuji in 1770; in 1889 all but the central triptych were given by the temple to the imperial family.

In the mid-1770s, Jakuchū retreated to the mountains of Tamba Province (now part of Kyōto Prefecture) and embarked on a project at the temple Sekihōji: to erect an outdoor sculptural series of the eight phases of Śākyamuni's life (Shaka hassō), which included 500 stone images of arhats, or RAKAN. In order to support himself, Jaku-chū exchanged paintings for rice, often signing his paintings Tobeiō (Old Man Bushel of Rice). After the great fire of 1788, which destroyed most of Kyōto, Jakuchū was left destitute, and two years later he contracted an eye disease. Despite illness and misfortune, he returned to Sekihōji to complete his sculptural project, and died shortly thereafter. *Catherine* KAPUTA

Itō Jinsai (1627–1705)

Confucianist philosopher and educator. Founder of the Kogigaku (Study of Ancient Meaning) school. The eldest son of a lumber dealer from the Horikawa district in Kyōto, Jinsai did not join the family business or accept the suggestions, often made to brilliant young men in those days, that he become a physician. Instead he dedicated himself to the study of Confucian teachings. From the age of about 16 he concentrated on Neo-Confucian doctrines, chiefly those derived from the philosophy of Zhu Xi (Chu Hsi; see SHUSHI-GAKU). Confident that he had comprehended the essence of these concepts by the time he was about 27, he developed his own original ideas, which he expounded in his works *Taikyokuron* (A Treatise on the Ultimate), *Seizenron* (On the Goodness of Human Nature), and *Shingaku genron* (Principles in the Study of Mind). He used the pen name Keisai, since *kei* (Ch: *jing* or *ching*, seriousness) was the concept most valued among Zhu Xi school Confucianists.

Later, however, he became skeptical of the Zhu Xi school philosophy and explored the teachings of Wang Yangming (1472–1529; see YŌMEIGAKU) and Zen. He came to believe that the path of the sages should be understood by direct readings in such Confucian classics as the *Analects* or *Mencius*, and he discouraged reliance upon later interpretations. Although sometimes referred to as Hori-kawagaku (School of Horikawa) after the place where he lived, Jinsai's studies are more generally called Kogigaku, since the aim was the clarification of the original meanings of the classics. Kogigaku is considered part of the KOGAKU (Ancient Learning) school.

Jinsai emphasized *jin* (Ch: *ren* or *jen*), the virtue of love or benevolence (from this came his later pen name, Jinsai), while Neo-Confucianists in Song (Sung) China (960–1279) gave emphasis to *li* (J: *ri*; principle) and *jing* (*ching*; J: *kei* or TSUTSUSHIMI, seriousness). Jinsai thought that since *jin* was displayed only when one could embrace others in love and compassion and make them happy, it was too difficult for ordinary people to achieve this virtue. Hence he taught loyalty (*chū*; Ch: *zhong* or *chung*) and faithfulness (*shin*; Ch: *xin* or *hsin*) as the basis of his practical ethics. By loyalty and faithfulness, he meant genuine truthfulness in actions, free of deception and lying. Through loyalty and faithfulness, the virtue of love would be realized.

Jinsai regarded the Confucian *Analects* as the supreme book of the universe and the *Book of Mencius* as an exegesis of the *Analects*. He based his teachings of love, loyalty, and faithfulness on a philological study of Confucius' thought in the *Analects*. In his studies of the other two works included as classics in the Zhu Xi school canon, i.e., *Zhongyong* (*Chung-yung*; The Doctrine of the Mean) and *Daxue* (*Ta-hsüeh*; The Great Learning), Jinsai argued that there were later interpolations in the former and that the latter was not the work of Confucius.

Although Jinsai had friends among aristocrats, wealthy merchants and physicians, he would never serve *daimyō*. Instead, he opened a private school in Kyōto, named Kogidō (The Hall of Ancient Meaning), and committed himself to teaching. His self-imposed distance from the establishment was singular among contemporary Confucianists, who primarily sought posts under *daimyō*. This attitude became a notable tradition of his school, whose successive masters did not serve in the government.

For Jinsai, the influence of education was unlimited and that of politics very limited. He considered Confucius, though of humble origins, to be far superior to the ancient sage kings such as Yao and Shun, who had been regarded as ideals for all later politicians. In its attempts to follow the path of Confucius, Jinsai's philosophy of life demonstrates the self-assertive spirit of the rising townsfolk of the Genroku era (1688–1704).

Jinsai's scholarship inspired OGYŪ SORAI, another important figure in Confucian studies, who gave attention to political and literary concepts. Jinsai remains the most noteworthy figure, however, in the history of Confucian thinking in the Edo period (1600–1868). His stress upon loyalty and faithfulness led to the general emphasis on *makoto* (sincerity) which was characteristic of ethical thought in the Edo period. *SAGARA Tōru*

Itojō

(Ito Castle). Fortress built in the Nara period (710–794) in the western part of Chikuzen Province (now the town of Maebaru, Fukuoka Prefecture). According to the chronicle *Shoku nihongi* (797), construction began in 756 and took 13 years to complete. Located on the western slope of Mt. Takasu, the castle covered an area of 250 hectares (617.8 acres), and its walls were two kilometers (1.2 mi) in length; its design was clearly based on continental models. The project was supervised by KIBI NO MAKIBI, who had strongly recommended it to the imperial court as the base for a proposed invasion of the Korean kingdom of SILLA; the castle was abandoned soon after its completion, when the invasion did not materialize. Excavation of the ruins in 1936 revealed remains of the gate and a watchtower.

Itokawa Hideo (1912–)

Aeronautical engineer and leading figure in the development of the Japanese space program in the 1950s and 1960s. Born in Tōkyō, he graduated from Tōkyō University in 1935. During World War II he helped to design the HAYABUSA and other fighters at Nakajima Airplane Co (now FUJI HEAVY INDUSTRIES, LTD). In 1951 he began his study of high-speed projectiles and rockets at Tōkyō University's Institute of Industrial Science. He also served as professor at Tōkyō University from 1948 to 1967.

Itō Keiichi (1917–)

Novelist. Born in Mie Prefecture. Completed secondary school in Tōkyō. Itō began his writing career as a poet but was soon drafted into the armed forces. He served in Manchuria and China in World War II. Most of his novels are based on his wartime experiences with the Japanese cavalry, and although they are essentially stories about war, they have a lyrical quality that stresses man's intimate connection with the natural world. His best-known novels include *Hotaru no kawa* (1961) and *Rakujitsu no senjō* (1965).

Itō Keisuke (1803–1901)

Specialist in *honzōgaku* (traditional pharmacognosy) and botany who helped modernize the study of pharmacognosy in the Edo period (1600–1868). Born in the city of Nagoya, Aichi Prefecture. He first studied traditional medicine and went into private practice. Later he studied pharmacognosy under Mizutani Toyobumi and botany under Philipp Franz von SIEBOLD in Nagasaki. He wrote *Taisei honzō meiso* (1829) based on Carl Peter THUNBERG's *Flora Japonica* given to him by Siebold. In his book he used the Linnaean plant classification system and the Latin names of plants for the first time in Japan. He was the first doctor of science in Japan. *SUZUKI Zenji*

Itokoku

A dependent state of the ancient Japanese state YAMATAI; mentioned in the WEI ZHI (*Wei chih*), a 3rd-century Chinese history of the Wei dynasty (220–265). It is believed to have been situated in the area of the town of Maebaru in the Itoshima district of Fukuoka Prefecture. The *Wei zhi* records that Itokoku was the site of diplomatic negotiations between Yamatai and envoys from Daifang (Taifang; J: Taihō) Commandery, the Wei colony in Korea. An official representative of HIMIKO, queen of Yamatai, was stationed there. The Maebaru area is now the site of archaeological excavations. The artifacts discovered there, including mirrors and other bronze objects, indicate that Itokoku was the cultural center of western Japan in the Yayoi period (ca 300 BC–ca AD 300). *KITAMURA Bunji*

Itoman

City in Okinawa Prefecture, on the southern tip of the main island of Okinawa. Itoman has long been known for its daring fishermen who sailed on small boats as far away as the Indian Ocean. Fishing is still the principal industry. Sugarcane is also cultivated. The southern part of the city was a battlefield during the last months of World War II; the area, designated as the Okinawa War Memorial Quasi-National Park, has several memorials to those who died there. Pop: 42,239.

Itōman & Co, Ltd

Trading firm handling primarily textile goods. Founded in 1883. Initially the company sold cotton and other textile goods in Japan, Korea, Manchuria, and Taiwan, but following World War II it handled wool imported from Australia and in the 1960s diversified into the fields of steel and food products. Itoman has formed a close relationship with NISSHIN SPINNING CO, LTD, and handles a large quantity of that firm's products. Overseas the company has 23 business offices and 5 incorporated firms. Sales for the fiscal year ending September 1981 totaled ¥381.3 billion (US $1.7 billion) and capitalization was ¥3 billion (US $13 million). Corporate headquarters are in Ōsaka.

Itō, Mancio (ca 1570–1612)

Nominal leader of the MISSION TO EUROPE OF 1582 sent by the CHRISTIAN DAIMYŌ of Kyūshū. Born Itō Sukemasu in Hyūga Province (now Miyazaki Prefecture), he is believed to have been a grandson of the warlord Itō Yoshisuke (1513–85) and a nephew of ŌTOMO SŌRIN, daimyō of Bungo (now Ōita Prefecture). He was baptized Mancio in 1580 and studied at the seminary in Arima. In 1582 he and three other boys left for a tour of southern Europe that culminated in a papal audience in 1585. Returning to Japan in 1590, Itō entered the Society of Jesus in the following year and was ordained in 1608. Little is known of his subsequent activities; he died in Nagasaki.   *Adriana* BOSCARO

Itō Miyoji (1857–1934)

Bureaucrat and politician. Born in what is now Nagasaki Prefecture. Recognized early on by the statesman ITŌ HIROBUMI for his skill in languages, he accompanied Itō to Europe in 1882 and later, with INOUE KOWASHI and KANEKO KENTARŌ, assisted him in drafting the Meiji CONSTITUTION. He served as chief cabinet secretary in the second Itō cabinet (1892) and as minister of commerce and agriculture in the third Itō cabinet (1898). As president of the progovernment newspaper *Tōkyō nichinichi shimbun* (now *Mainichi shimbun*) from 1891 to 1904, he consistently defended the idea of a stable government bureaucracy. In 1899 he was appointed privy councillor, in which capacity he worked to preserve the prerogatives of the emperor system. At the same time, he was not above involvement in party politics, showing favoritism to the RIKKEN SEIYŪKAI. During the FINANCIAL CRISIS OF 1927, he brought about the collapse of the first WAKATSUKI REIJIRŌ cabinet by denying its request to the Privy Council for emergency funds for the Bank of Taiwan. An advocate of hard-line diplomacy, he criticized the administration of HAMAGUCHI OSACHI for infringing on the "prerogative of [the emperor's] supreme command" (see TŌSUIKEN) by accepting the proposals of the LONDON NAVAL CONFERENCES for limitation on the size of the Japanese navy.

Itō Noe (1895–1923)

Feminist and anarchist. Born in Fukuoka Prefecture. After graduating from Ueno Girls' High School, she was forced into an arranged marriage in her native village, but she soon fled back to Tōkyō. There she joined the feminist group SEITŌSHA (Bluestocking Society) and edited its magazine, *Seitō* (Bluestocking) from 1915 to 1916. In the latter year she left her second husband, the writer Tsuji Jun (1884–1944), and began living with the anarchist ŌSUGI SAKAE. Itō worked with him in promoting the anarchist movement, and she helped to found the socialist women's group SEKIRANKAI in 1921. Two years later, shortly after the birth of her seventh child, she and Ōsugi were killed by military police during the chaos following the massive TŌKYŌ EARTHQUAKE OF 1923, when many left-wing activists were arrested or slaughtered. Itō's publications include joint translations of the works of the anarchists Emma Goldman and P. A. Kropotkin, as well as some 80 articles on feminism and anarchism and several autobiographical novels such as *Zatsuon* (1916, Noises) and *Tenki* (1918, Turning Point).

■——Itō Noe, *Itō Noe zenshū*, 2 vols (Gakugei Shorin, 1970).
                                          Nancy ANDREW

Itō Sachio (1864–1913)

WAKA poet, novelist. Real name Itō Kōjirō. Born in Chiba Prefecture. He was obliged to withdraw from school because of eye trou-

ble. In 1900 his interest in poetry spurred him to visit MASAOKA SHIKI, and he became one of his most faithful disciples. After Shiki's death, Itō was instrumental in establishing the poetry magazine *Ashibi* in 1903, serving as its editor until its demise in 1908. The same year, with other members of the Negishi Tanka Kai, a poetry group founded by Shiki, he founded the magazine *Araragi*, in which he published poems, critical works on *waka*, and studies of the MAN'YŌSHŪ. His novels, such as *Nogiku no haka* (1906, Grave amidst Asters), were written in a prose style learned from Shiki which emphasized close attention to detail. SAITŌ MOKICHI and SHIMAKI AKAHIKO are two of the younger poets whom Itō encouraged. *Sachio kashū*, a collection of his poems, was published in 1920.

Itō Sei (1905–1969)

Literary critic, novelist, translator. Real name Itō Hitoshi. His works, both literary criticism and fiction, reveal an abiding interest in the thought and behavior of the Japanese intelligentsia: they reflect the need for self-analysis felt by that generation of Japanese intellectuals who lived through the particularly traumatic years of immediate prewar, wartime, and post-World War II Japan.

The son of a low-ranking military officer, Itō Sei was born and educated in Hokkaidō. His first literary effort was a collection of poems titled *Yukiakari no michi* (1926, Snow-lit Path), a lyrical tribute to his birthplace. In 1927 he enrolled at the Tōkyō Shōka Daigaku (now Hitotsubashi University), but soon abandoned his studies in favor of a professional writing career.

Itō embarked on a literary career at a time when the Japanese literary establishment (see BUNDAN) was shaken by the impact of the Marxist-oriented PROLETARIAN LITERATURE MOVEMENT. He emerged firmly in the antiproletarian camp as the leader of a modernistic movement: the so-called new psychological literature *(shin shinri shugi bungaku)*, which introduced to Japan 20th century European writers like James Joyce, Virginia Woolf, and Marcel Proust. A collection of essays, *Shin shinri shugi bungaku* (1932, New Psychological Literature), and a collection of his early short stories, *Seibutsusai* (1932, Festival of the Living), marked his debut in the literary world. In his two novels *Yūki no machi* (1937, A Ghost Town) and *Yūki no mura* (1938, A Ghost Village) he attempted a reconciliation between the established view of pure literature as it was expressed through the autobiographical genre of the I-NOVEL and the new psychological approach. An endeavor to widen the scope of the I-novel and to overcome its artistic limitations was a constant motif of his work. Between 1940 and 1941 he wrote *Tokunō Gorō no seikatsu to iken* (Life and Opinions of Tokunō Gorō), a psychological I-novel describing the dilemmas faced by the Japanese intelligentsia during the war years.

Finding writing increasingly difficult as the war progressed, he became an employee of a publishing firm, Shinchōsha Company, in 1944 and then withdrew to his native Hokkaidō to await the end of the war. In 1946 he published a sequel to *Tokunō Gorō* entitled *Narumi Senkichi*, which was the first major postwar novel to depict the confusion and uncertainty of intellectual life during the years just after the war.

Between 1947 and 1948 Itō published a series of critical essays which subsequently appeared under the title *Shōsetsu no hōhō* (1948, The Method of the Novel). These essays, together with NAKAMURA MITSUO's *Fūzoku shōsetsu ron* (1950, On the Novel of Manners), constituted an important contribution to postwar criticism of Japanese literature and the I-novel. The strength and originality of his theory, which established him as one of the foremost postwar literary critics, lay in connecting the emergence and the character of the I-novel with the escapist modes of life and thought of the Japanese literary elite. The ideas formulated in *Shōsetsu no hōhō* were subsequently developed in other works: *Shōsetsu no ninshiki* (1955, Consciousness of the Novel), *Geijutsu wa nan no tame ni aru ka* (1957, What is Art For?), and *Kyūdōsha to ninshikisha* (1962, Seekers and Perceivers). In 1952 Itō started serialization of *Nihon bundan shi* (History of the Japanese Literary Establishment), for which he received the Kikuchi Kan Prize in 1963; though not completed it is regarded as his major work.

In 1951 Itō was named, together with publisher Koyama Kyūjirō, as a defendant in the so-called LADY CHATTERLEY'S LOVER CASE on account of his allegedly obscene translation of D. H. Lawrence's novel *Lady Chatterley's Lover*. This highly publicized trial was viewed by writers as a fight for freedom of expression as guaranteed by the postwar constitution of 1947. The litigation continued for eight years until the final verdict of not guilty was handed down by the Supreme Court. The years of trial coincided with a period of spectacular popularity for Itō. He published two works describing his involvement in the trial and wrote three novels in serial form for newspapers. His novel *Josei ni kansuru jūnishō* (1953, Twelve Chapters on Women) made the best-seller list.

In 1958 Itō traveled to Europe and in Asia, and in 1960 spent a year lecturing in the United States at the invitation of Columbia University. He was an officer of the JAPAN P.E.N. CLUB and the Association of Japanese Writers (Nihon Bungeika Kyōkai) and was a cofounder of the MUSEUM OF MODERN JAPANESE LITERATURE (Nihon Kindai Bungakukan).

Itō Sei's stature in modern Japanese literature rests on the originality and penetrating insight of his literary criticism. His later novels *Hanran* (1958, Flood), *Hakkutsu* (1968, Excavation), and *Hen'yō* (1968, Changed Appearance) deal with the preoccupations of old age, sex, and death. He was posthumously awarded a Shinchō Prize in 1970 for his last novel *Hen'yō*. In his creative writing he adopted the position of a mediator between the narrow and subjective approach of the Japanese I-novel and modern European fiction.

■——*Itō Sei zenshū*, 24 vols (Shinchōsha, 1972–74). Itō Sei, *Nihon bundan shi*, 18 vols (1952–73). Kamei Hideo, *Itō Sei no sekai* (1969). Senuma Shigeki, *Itō Sei* (1971).   *Irena* POWELL

Itō Shinsui (1898–1972)

Japanese-style painter and print designer, best known for his *bijinga* (pictures of beautiful women). Born in Tōkyō, he studied under KABURAGI KIYOKATA, a Japanese-style painter who specialized in genre painting and *bijinga*. Itō made his first color print in 1916; it immediately established his reputation. His most famous series, the *Eight Views of Ōmi (Ōmi hakkei)*, produced in 1917, established the close relationship of his work to traditional Japanese prints in both style and subject matter. However, unlike traditional UKIYO-E, his prints were made by craftsmen from finished paintings. The color effects of both his paintings and his prints are exquisite and demonstrate his meticulous technique and skill. *Madman on the Roof*, a woodcut of 1922 and one of his finest works, shows his distinctive use of color. His paintings of beautiful women, such as *Vapor* (1924), are painted in the soft, misty palette of modern Japanese-style painting *(nihonga)* and are generally considered his finest works.

■——Fujikake Shizuya, *Japanese Wood-block Prints* (Tourist Library, Japan Travel Bureau, 1959). Suzuki Susumu, ed, *Nihon kaigakan 10: Taishō* (Kōdansha, 1971).

Elizabeth de Sabato SWINTON

Itō Shizuo (1906–1953)

Poet. Born in Nagasaki Prefecture. Graduate of Kyōto University. He contributed poetry to the magazines *Kogito* and *Nihon rōmanha*, and in 1935 published his first collection of poems, *Waga hito ni atauru aika* (Sad Poems for My Lady). It was highly praised by the symbolist poet HAGIWARA SAKUTARŌ. Itō taught middle school and continued to write poems during World War II, publishing in 1940 his second collection, *Natsubana* (Summer Flowers), which won the Kitamura Tōkoku Prize in 1942, and his third collection, *Haru no isogi* (Spring's Haste), in 1943. Ito's poems, characterized by recurrent death imagery and a lyrical quality reminiscent of the European poet Rainer Maria Rilke, had a profound impact on many young people during the war.

Itō Sukechika (?–1182)

Warrior of the latter part of the Heian period (794–1185). Sukechika's appropriation of his nephew Kudō Suketsune's estate in Izu Province (now part of Shizuoka Prefecture) led Suketsune to instigate the murder of Sukechika's son. In revenge, Sukechika's grandsons, the Soga brothers, murdered Suketsune in 1193 (see SOGA MONOGATARI). Sukechika had charge of the young MINAMOTO NO YORITOMO—who had been exiled to Izu by TAIRA NO KIYOMORI—and hated him for fathering a child of his daughter. In 1180 he fought against Yoritomo and was captured; although he was released in 1182, he committed suicide.   *Douglas E.* MILLS

Itō Tōgai (1670–1738)

Confucian scholar and teacher. Tōgai was the eldest son of ITŌ JINSAI. Refusing public office, he devoted himself to writing and teaching. He carried on the work of his father, who rejected the Zhu Xi (Chu Hsi; see SHUSHIGAKU) and Wang Yangming (YŌMEIGAKU) interpretations and emphasized the study of the Analects and other Confucian classics (KOGAKU). Although he lacked his father's originality of thought, Tōgai was known for his breadth of knowledge. He was proficient in Confucian classics and literature and in Japanese and Chinese institutional history, linguistics, and Korean literature. The noted scholar AOKI KON'YŌ was one of his outstanding disciples. Tōgai wrote a total of 53 works and also revised and published many of Jinsai's posthumous works.   ŌNISHI *Harutaka*

itowappu

A system under which certain merchants were granted a monopoly of the Chinese raw-silk trade during the Edo period (1600–1868); also called *shiraitowappu*. During the last half of the 16th century, all raw silk was imported by Portuguese merchants, who alone had access to trade with China. Because of the great demand for raw silk in Japan, there was fierce competition among Japanese merchants, which resulted in high prices and enormous profits for the Portuguese. In the early 17th century, the Portuguese monopoly was challenged by the Dutch, the British, and the Japanese themselves, the last of whom began their trade with Chinese merchants in Southeast Asian ports. In order to strengthen its control of foreign trade, in 1604 the Tokugawa shogunate established the *itowappu* system, granting a group of merchants from Sakai, Nagasaki, and Kyōto exclusive power to buy, allocate, and negotiate the import price of raw silk. Later, merchants from Ōsaka and Edo (now Tōkyō) were added to the group (see NAGASAKI KAISHO). The system effected a reduction of the import price—the merchants and the shogunate sharing the profit—and a decline of the Portuguese domination of the trade. The *itowappu* system was applied to trade with the Chinese in 1631 and, after the shogunate's enactment of the NATIONAL SECLUSION policy and its expulsion of the Portuguese in 1639, to trade with the Dutch (in 1641). The Chinese and the Dutch were the only foreigners now allowed to enter Japan, and trade was restricted to the port of Nagasaki (see NAGASAKI TRADE; DUTCH TRADE). The system was abolished in 1655 because of strong opposition from Chinese traders. Although it was reimposed in 1685 and endured until the opening of Japan in the 1850s, profits dwindled as demand for Chinese silk flagged with the increase of domestic production.

Itō–Yōkadō Co, Ltd

Chain store chiefly handling retail sale of commercial goods in the areas of clothing, food products, and housing. The firm is also engaged in various business operations related to these fields. It was founded in 1913. In 1981 it was second in total sales and first in profits among businesses in the retail industry. The firm has 106 stores, mainly in the Tōkyō area, which emphasize low-price sales by concentrating on goods with a high rate of turnover. Among its affiliates in the United States are convenience stores operated jointly with Southland, Inc, and suburban restaurants operated in cooperation with Denny's, Inc. Itō–Yōkadō actively raises capital in the overseas market, and was the first Japanese business to issue continental depositary receipts (CDRs) in Europe (1976) and to float unsecured debentures in the United States (1978). Sales for the fiscal year ending February 1982 totaled ¥764.5 billion (US $3.3 billion) and capitalization stood at ¥10.7 billion (US $45 million). Corporate headquarters are located in Tōkyō.

Itsukaichi

Town in southwest Hiroshima Prefecture, western Honshū. It is a suburb of Hiroshima. A branch of the government mint is located here, as well as furniture and food-processing factories. Seaweed *(nori)* and oysters are cultivated on the coast. Pop: 87,326.

Itsuki Hiroyuki (1932–   )

Writer. Born in Fukuoka Prefecture, he lived in Korea, where his father was a teacher, until the end of World War II. Itsuki attended Waseda University, where he studied Russian literature. After working as a copywriter and becoming well known as a song writer and radio disc jockey, he emerged as a promising young writer in 1966 with *Saraba Mosukuwa gurentai* (Farewell to Moscow Misfits), a novel about a Japanese jazz pianist's unsettling encounter in Moscow with an offbeat Russian youth who is looked on as a misfit because he lives on the fringe of Russian society and wants to play

Itsukushima——Itsukushima Shrine

The vermilion *torii* with part of the main shrine complex (left), a view taken from the island looking toward the mainland. Originally erected late 12th century; rebuilt 1241.

the jazz trumpet. The following year Itsuki won the Naoki Prize for *Aozameta uma o miyo* (1966, See the Pale Horse). His great appeal to young people made him one of Japan's best-selling writers of popular fiction in the 1960s and 1970s. The first segments of his ongoing autobiographical novel, *Seishun no mon* (The Gate of Youth), begun in 1971, were made into a movie and serialized on television.

Itsukushima

Also known as Miyajima. Island in Hiroshima Bay, west central Inland Sea, 15 km (9 mi) southwest of the city of Hiroshima, Hiroshima Prefecture. Made up of granite, the entire island is covered with forests with little level ground. Famous for the ITSUKUSHIMA SHRINE on the northern shore, with its vermilion *torii* (gateway) in the bay between the island and Honshū. This forms one of the NIHON SANKEI, the three most beautiful views in Japan. Area: 30.2 sq km (11.7 sq mi).

Itsukushima Shrine

Sometimes called Aki no Miyajima. A Shintō shrine on the island of ITSUKUSHIMA in the Saeki district of Hiroshima Prefecture, dedicated to Ichikishima Hime no Mikoto and two other deities, originally of the MUNAKATA SHRINES, who protect seamen and oversee fishing. According to tradition, the shrine was established in 593 after the three deities appeared at its present site and instructed a local inhabitant to erect a shrine there. TAIRA NO KIYOMORI, after his appointment as protector of Aki, the province in which Itsukushima was located, provided lavish support for the shrine, building a predecessor of the present large TORII gate 160 meters (525 ft) out into Hiroshima Bay. Much of the shrine, including its many corridors connecting various buildings, is constructed over water so that when the tide rises, it appears to be floating. Itsukushima Shrine is rich in national treasures, many of which, like the richly ornamented scrolls of the LOTUS SUTRA, were dedicated to the shrine by the Taira family. From the medieval period (13th century–16th century), under the influence of Shintō Buddhist syncretism (see HONJI SUIJAKU), the Buddhist goddess Benzaiten (Skt: Sarasvatī) sometimes represented the divinity of this shrine and gained wide popularity throughout the country, resulting in some 6,000 subshrines. In addition to the annual festival on 17 June, many observances take place throughout the year. The shrine is well known as one of the most scenic sights in Japan. *Stanley WEINSTEIN*

Itsunen (1601–1668)

(Ch: Yiran or I-jan). Chinese painter and one of the first ŌBAKU SECT Zen monks to come to Japan. He left China in 1644 after the fall of the Ming dynasty (1368–1644) and went to Nagasaki. He was appointed the third abbot of the temple Sōfukuji and subsequently persuaded the Chinese abbot INGEN to come to Nagasaki. Ingen became the first patriarch of the Ōbaku sect in Japan and was granted land in Uji to build a major Ōbaku temple, MAMPUKUJI.

Like many Ōbaku monks, Itsunen was a talented artist. His paintings generally depicted Buddhist subjects and often included inscriptions by Ingen and other Zen masters. Itsunen's paintings created a great deal of interest among the Japanese, and he had a number of pupils in Nagasaki. Before his arrival, the Japanese had little knowledge of late-Ming styles in figure painting. He especially inspired artists of the KANŌ SCHOOL and NAGASAKI SCHOOL, but they were never able to fully capture the strength and spirituality that distinguishes Itsunen's work. See also ZENGA.
——Stephen Addiss, *Obaku: Zen Painting and Calligraphy* (1978). *Pat FISTER*

Itsuō Art Museum

(Itsuō Bijutsukan). Located in Ikeda, Ōsaka Prefecture. A choice collection of Japanese painting, calligraphy, and lacquer; Chinese sculpture; Japanese, Chinese, Korean and Western ceramics; all assembled by the late KOBAYASHI ICHIZŌ and shown in a Western-style house opened in 1957 and in an adjoining gallery added in 1973. Among the paintings are scrolls of the Kamakura (1185–1333) and Muromachi (1333–1568) periods, a large group of works by BUSON and MATSUMURA GOSHUN, and a good representation of many other artists from the Edo period (1600–1868). The calligraphy dates from the Nara (710–794) and Heian (794–1185) periods through the Edo period. Nearly all the well-known ceramic kilns are represented; there are also pieces by CHŌJIRŌ, NIN'AMI DŌHACHI, and HON'AMI KŌETSU. Chinese porcelains date chiefly from the Song (Sung; 960–1279) through the Ming (1368–1644) dynasties.
Laurance ROBERTS

Iwafune no ki

(also known as Iwafune *no saku*). A fortified frontier post (SAKU) established in 648 near what is now the city of Murakami in Niigata Prefecture as part of a military campaign conducted by the YAMATO COURT against the aboriginal EZO tribes of northeastern Honshū. It is likely that the stockade was in operation for about 60 years until rendered unnecessary by the northward advance of the effective frontier. In 1957 remains believed to be those of Iwafune *no ki* were discovered in the vicinity of Iwafune Shrine, north of Murakami. See also NUTARI NO KI.

Iwai

City in southwestern Ibaraki Prefecture, central Honshū, on the river Tonegawa. With the opening of direct routes to Tōkyō in 1958, Iwai has witnessed rapid urbanization and industrialization. Principal products are electrical appliances and corrugated cardboard. There are numerous shrines and historical sites connected with TAIRA NO MASAKADO, a 10th-century warrior. Pop: 40,377.

Iwai Akira (1922–)

Leader of Japan's labor movement. Born in Nagano Prefecture, he served as secretary-general of SŌHYŌ (General Council of Trade Unions of Japan) from 1955 through 1970. Iwai worked for the Japanese National Railways as an engineer from 1937. After World War II he became active in the labor union movement, joining the JAPAN SOCIALIST PARTY. In a major schism within the labor movement which occurred at the time of the Korean War, Iwai allied himself with the left wing of Sōhyō. Appointed secretary-general of Sōhyō in 1955, he remained in the post for 15 years. With his colleague ŌTA KAORU, he played a key role in establishing the annual wage offensive known as SHUNTŌ. Since his retirement in 1970, Iwai has remained influential not only in the labor movement but also in the policy making of the Japan Socialist Party. *KURITA Ken*

Iwai, Rebellion of

Rebellion of the early 6th century, traditionally dated 527–528. Said to have been led by Iwai, governor (KUNI NO MIYATSUKO) of the province of Tsukushi in Kyūshū, it is the first recorded instance of rebellion against the YAMATO COURT. According to the early-8th-century chronicle NIHON SHOKI and other historical sources, Iwai, as provincial governor, had extended his sway throughout the northern half of Kyūshū. Supported by the Korean kingdom of SILLA, he obstructed the attempts of the Yamato court to send a relief force to the Korean region of KAYA (thought by some to have been a Japanese enclave on the Korean peninsula), which was then beleaguered by Silla. Iwai was defeated and killed by court forces under the chieftains of the MONONOBE FAMILY and the ŌTOMO FAMILY, and his son surrendered to them. Although the authenticity of some of the details is questionable, the traditional account is useful for the insights it affords into Korean-Japanese relations, the status of Kaya, and the nature of provincial governorships in the early historical period. Iwai is said to be buried in the so-called YAME TOMB CLUSTER in the city of Yame, Fukuoka Prefecture. The stone figures of men and horses excavated there, as well as the scale of the tomb, attest to the magnitude of his power.　　KITAMURA Bunji

Iwajuku site

The first paleolithic site to be recognized in Japan, discovered in 1946 by AIZAWA TADAHIRO; located in the Iwajuku section of Nitta District, near the city of Kiryū, Gumma Prefecture. Aizawa's recovery of STONE TOOLS from Iwajuku's KANTŌ LOAM strata provided the first convincing evidence that the Japanese islands were occupied by human groups before 10,000 BC (see HISTORY OF JAPAN: prehistory). Excavations by Sugihara Sōsuke (b 1913) of Meiji University in 1949 confirmed the existence of two cultural horizons. The older Iwajuku I stratum is believed to be about 20,000 years old; it contained large oval quartz tools originally described as "hand axes" but with evidence of polishing on the edges. The younger Iwajuku II stratum contained small tools such as points and blades made of obsidian and agate. In 1970 another part of the site was excavated by Aizawa and Serizawa Chōsuke (b 1919) of Tōhoku University; thousands of pieces of chert were recovered from a formation called Iwajuku Zero stratum, more than 40,000 years old. Whether these were products of human work or natural forces still remains controversial. See also PALEOLITHIC CULTURE; HOSHINO SITE; NOGAWA SITE.

▬▬——Serizawa Chōsuke, "Zenki kyūsekki no shomondai," Daiyonki kenkyū 9.3–4 (1970). Serizawa Chōsuke and Aizawa Tadahiro, "Iwajuku iseki no saihakkutsu o megutte: 'Zero bunkasō' hakken no igi," Kagaku asahi 30.7 (1970). Sugihara Sōsuke, "Gumma Ken Iwajuku hakken no sekki bunka," Meiji daigaku bungakubu kenkyū hōkoku: Kōkogaku I (1956).
　　Fumiko IKAWA-SMITH

Iwaki

City in southeastern Fukushima Prefecture, northern Honshū. Iwaki was created in 1966 with the merger of the five cities of Taira, Iwaki, Uchigō, Jōban, and Nakoso with four other towns, and five villages. The complex of cities prospered with the opening of the Jōban Coalfield in 1883; most of the mines are now closed. The city is an industrial center of the Onahama Coastal Industrial Area. The Taira district is the center of government, commerce, transportation, and education. The Onahama district is an industrial district, while Jōban and Uchigō are tourist and residential centers; Nakoso is both industrial and residential. Tourist attractions are the Jōban–Yumoto Hot Spring and the remains of Nakoso no Seki, a medieval barrier station (SEKISHO) celebrated in literature. Pop: 342,076.

Iwakigawa

River in western Aomori Prefecture, northern Honshū, originating near Gammoridake, changing to a northerly course at the city of Hirosaki, passing through Tsugaru Plain, and emptying into Lake Jūsan on the western coast of the Tsugaru Peninsula. It is the largest river in the prefecture. Vast ricefields are located along its lower reaches, and apples are cultivated along its middle reaches. The Meya Dam is located on the upper reaches. Length: 102 km (63 mi); area of drainage basin: 2,544 sq km (982 sq mi).

Iwakisan

Conical composite volcano in the Chōkai Volcanic Zone. In western Aomori Prefecture, northern Honshū. Also called Tsugaru Fuji. Composed of andesite. Iwakisan Shrine is in the foothills. The summit abounds in alpine flora and offers a view of Hokkaidō. Skiing is popular. Iwakisan is part of Tsugaru Quasi-National Park. Height: 1,625 m (5,330 ft).

Iwakuni

City in eastern Yamaguchi Prefecture, western Honshū, on the river Nishikigawa. During the Edo period (1600–1868), Iwakuni was a

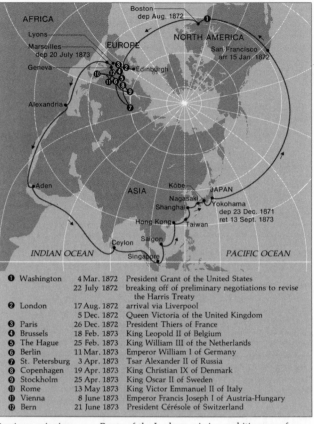

❶ Washington	4 Mar. 1872	President Grant of the United States
	22 July 1872	breaking off of preliminary negotiations to revise the Harris Treaty
❷ London	17 Aug. 1872	arrival via Liverpool
	5 Dec. 1872	Queen Victoria of the United Kingdom
❸ Paris	26 Dec. 1872	President Thiers of France
❹ Brussels	18 Feb. 1873	King Leopold II of Belgium
❺ The Hague	25 Feb. 1873	King William III of the Netherlands
❻ Berlin	11 Mar. 1873	Emperor William I of Germany
❼ St. Petersburg	3 Apr. 1873	Tsar Alexander II of Russia
❽ Copenhagen	19 Apr. 1873	King Christian IX of Denmark
❾ Stockholm	25 Apr. 1873	King Oscar II of Sweden
❿ Rome	13 May 1873	King Victor Emmanuel II of Italy
⓫ Vienna	8 June 1873	Emperor Francis Joseph I of Austria-Hungary
⓬ Bern	21 June 1873	President Cérésole of Switzerland

Iwakura mission——Route of the Iwakura mission and itinerary of audiences with heads of state

castle town of a branch of the MŌRI FAMILY. In the early 20th century, it became an industrial center with the establishment of pulp and spinning industries. After World War II, a giant petrochemical industrial complex and oil storage base were constructed on former military land. The bridge Kintaikyō is a popular tourist attraction. Pop: 112,527.

Iwakura

City in western Aichi Prefecture, central Honshū, some 11 km (7 mi) north of Nagoya. A farming area, it is fast becoming a suburb of Nagoya. Special products are carp streamers (koinobori) for CHILDREN'S DAY and tent cloth. Of historic interest are a Yayoi-period (ca 300 BC–ca AD 300) archaeological site and the ruins of Iwakura Castle. Pop: 42,800.

Iwakura mission

(Iwakura Kengai Shisetsu). Eighteen-month embassy to the United States and Europe in 1871–73 by leading members of the early Meiji government; one of the most remarkable journeys in world history. Commissioned by Emperor MEIJI and reputedly costing a million dollars, the mission was led by the influential senior minister IWAKURA TOMOMI, as chief ambassador, and his close political allies and followers ŌKUBO TOSHIMICHI, KIDO TAKAYOSHI, ITŌ HIROBUMI, and Yamaguchi Naoyoshi (1842–94), as vice-ambassadors. Associated with them as commissioners were several high-ranking officials representing each of the departments of the central bureaucracy, including Sasaki Takayuki (1830–1910), Yamada Akiyoshi (1844–92), and TANAKA FUJIMARO. In all there were about 50 members, ranging from ambassadors and commissioners to secretaries, interpreters, clerks, attendants, and baggage handlers, most of whom had never been outside Japan. The number varied slightly as some of the original appointees were replaced abroad by more knowledgeable recruits. Many students accompanied the mission, including five girls ranging from 6 to 15 years in age (see TSUDA UMEKO), the first Japanese females to go abroad for study, but they were not officially part of the mission.

This impressive group of statesmen and experts, dispatched at a time of great uncertainty, had an ambitious threefold task. First, they were to pay good-will visits on behalf of the emperor to the monarchs and heads of state of the 15 Western countries with which Japan had concluded treaties of friendship and commerce (see ANSEI COMMERCIAL TREATIES). The mission hoped to convince the advanced nations of the Western world that the Japanese, unlike other Asians, were a progressive people and open to new ideas. Second, the ambassadors were to exchange views with the heads of foreign offices on the actual operation of the treaties, which the Japanese had come to regard as demeaning and in violation of their national sovereignty. The Meiji government, however, fearful that it might lose more than it could possibly gain at the bargaining table, had decided after long and searching debate not to seek immediate revision, although the HARRIS TREATY of 1858 had made provision for renegotiation after 12 years, but to postpone it until the mission learned what kinds of reform were required to end extraterritoriality, fixed tariff schedules, and other unequal practices that interfered with Japan's judicial and economic autonomy (see UNEQUAL TREATIES, REVISION OF). The third purpose was to examine Western society closely both for its sources of wealth and power and for the nature and extent of its enlightenment. This was the most dramatic of the many ways in which Japan during the era of bummei kaika (civilization and enlightenment; see MEIJI ENLIGHTENMENT) was systematically acquiring Western learning: translations, overseas study, employment of foreign teachers and advisers, and tours of limited duration by lower-ranking officials to gain specialized information. In this case, prominent leaders had decided to see the Western world for themselves, since they were the ones responsible for basic policies. Neither social theoreticians nor designers of grandiose programs, they were nevertheless discontented with ad hoc decisions and wished to determine priorities and long-range solutions rationally and on the basis of principles. For this, they believed they must have first-hand information and broader perspective. Travel abroad might furthermore bolster the ambassadors' political position by deepening their superficial Western expertise. Unlike their predecessors on the SHOGUNATE MISSIONS TO THE WEST in the 1860s, they chose to dress in Western attire, cut their hair in the Western fashion, and eat Western food. Before departure, the ambassadors and leading members of the caretaker government, such as SAIGŌ TAKAMORI, ITAGAKI TAISUKE, and ŌKUMA SHIGENOBU, signed a pledge to remain in frequent communication, to concentrate for the time being only on those reforms that were crucial to the centralization of power, and to refrain from making new high-level political appointments. Upon the mission's return, there was to be a grand review of foreign and domestic policy, incorporating its findings.

Escorted by the United States minister to Japan, the mission set sail from Yokohama on the Pacific Mail steamship America on 23 December 1871 and arrived in San Francisco in January 1872 for a seven-month stay in the United States, prolonged far beyond the original plan by the unexpected willingness of President Ulysses S. GRANT and Secretary of State Hamilton Fish to negotiate a revised treaty. Their subsequent extremely frustrating experience in Washington confirmed the ambassadors in their original estimate that it was much too soon to expect equal relations, and thereafter in Europe they carefully confined the mission's diplomacy to polite discussions. They remained in Britain for four months (August–December 1872) and traveled on the continent for over seven months (December 1872–July 1873), visiting France, Belgium, the Netherlands, Germany, Russia, Denmark, Sweden, Italy, Austria-Hungary, and Switzerland. Only Hawaii, Spain, and Portugal were omitted from the original itinerary. Their voyage home took them through the recently completed Suez Canal to the Indian Ocean and the East China Sea for brief glimpses of the leading harbors of southern Asia and the treaty ports of southeast China. Ōkubo and Kido, at the urgent request of the caretakers, returned early, in the late spring and summer of 1873, and Iwakura arrived in Tōkyō with the main party in September.

During the long tour, the mission had been received with much pomp and ceremony by presidents and prime ministers, kings and queens, and titled aristocrats. Curious throngs flocked to greet them, and publicity was extensive. The mission went everywhere: government offices, historical monuments, public museums and libraries, art galleries, zoological parks and botanical gardens, factories, shipyards, mines, public and private schools, cathedrals, military academies, law courts, banks, stock exchanges, and chambers of commerce. Out of a sense of duty or for pleasure, they also attended plays, concerts, opera and ballet, and even a circus performance or two, a fox hunt, and a masked ball. While in Vienna, they roamed through the splendid exhibits of the International Exposition. Always, there were banquets and speeches. Fully informed of

events back home by letters and personal messengers, the ambassadors contributed to important reform measures adopted in their absence and assisted education officials in investigating arrangements for Japan's overseas students.

The journey, well documented in public and private correspondence, diaries, memoirs, and official reports, had taken Iwakura and his colleagues to Grant's America, Victoria's England, Bismarck's Germany, Thiers' France, and Alexander II's Russia. Responding to the diversity and complexity of Western life, they came to conceptualize it not as a monolithic culture but rather in terms of levels of power and enlightenment, with the United States, Britain, and France at the top, Germany in the middle, and Russia at the bottom. In political matters, they returned with a firm commitment to the gradual adoption of a constitution as the fundamental law of Japan but remained hesitant to share power broadly or allow an elective legislative assembly. Ōkubo was strengthened in his desire to establish a HOME MINISTRY. Their observation of diplomatic practices and single attempt at negotiations, though unsuccessful, enhanced their sophistication in international power politics and helped them to define a more realistic strategy of treaty revision. The trip was extremely beneficial as a primer in economics. Leaders like Iwakura, Ōkubo, and Kido, essentially politicians with limited knowledge of business, came to understand more clearly the requirements of modern economic life, especially factory production, the application of science to industry and agriculture, mass transportation and communications, rational management, and international trade. Industry and trade were redefined as means to increase productivity and raise levels of consumption by larger numbers of people and not, as Neo-Confucians argued, to produce luxuries. Less convinced by British arguments for free trade than American and German advocacy of protectionism, they resolved that the Meiji government should give greater encouragement to Japanese businessmen in initiating modern enterprises and should itself act more vigorously as an entrepreneur. Classroom visits simply bolstered their previous conviction that elementary education for all classes and both sexes was vital to the training of good citizens and self-supporting adults, but their many excursions to public museums, sources of endless delight and intellectual stimulation, suggested new means to attain popular enlightenment. Their survey of military and naval establishments prompted the comforting conclusion that the Western world, especially Russia, was not as immediately threatening to Japan's security as they had previously imagined. For insurance, Japan would need a larger standing army, but its function in the near future would more likely be to quell civil unrest than to repel foreign invaders. Rejecting Christianity and individualism as the keys to Western progress while recognizing their importance, they instead stressed hard work, long-range planning, and organization and management skills. Although aware of the period from 1800 to 1850 as years of unprecedented change in Europe and America, they took pains to emphasize, as did their British mentors, that the West in fact had taken a long time to reach its present high state of development and in the process had retained respect for history and tradition. Inspired by the trip, the mission's leaders refined their theory and rhetoric of gradualism. Fundamental change was necessary, they conceded, but reform must be orderly, selective, and calculated not to exceed the capacity of the people to understand or accept. Japan must retain its distinctive qualities and avoid shallow, unworkable, or wholesale cultural borrowing. To help in creating a public mood receptive to this version of change, Iwakura supported the publication in 1878 under the auspices of the Grand Council of State (Dajōkan) of a five-volume account of the journey, Tokumei zenken taishi: Beiō kairan jikki (A True Account of the Tour in America and Europe of the Special Embassy), compiled by his private secretary, KUME KUNITAKE.

Instead of a grand policy debate, the mission returned in 1873 to domestic unrest, a power struggle, and a crisis in foreign relations. The main issue, ostensibly whether to send a punitive expedition to Korea (see SEIKANRON), was much broader, encompassing who should be in charge and how far and fast the reforms should go. When the chief councillor of state, SANJŌ SANETOMI, collapsed in late October, Iwakura took his place, counseled the young emperor, and helped to force the resignation of many of the caretakers. Iwakura and his allies, primarily from the former domains of Satsuma (now Kagoshima Prefecture) and Chōshū (now Yamaguchi Prefecture), were more powerful than before and had a clearer vision of the future they wished for Japan. Drawing upon their experiences in the West, they promoted policies of internal reconstruction at home and national rights diplomacy abroad.

■ ——Kume Kunitake, *Tokumei zenken taishi: Beiō kairan jikki*, 5 vols (1878, 2nd ed 1977–82). Charles Lanman, *Leaders of the Meiji Restoration in America* (1931). Marlene J. Mayo, "Rationality in the Restoration: The Iwakura Embassy," in Bernard S. Silberman and Harry D. Harootunian, ed, *Modern Japanese Leadership* (1966). Marlene J. Mayo, "A Catechism of Western Diplomacy: The Japanese and Hamilton Fish, 1872," *Journal of Asian Studies* 26.3 (1967). Marlene J. Mayo, "The Western Education of Kume Kunitake, 1871–76," *Monumenta Nipponica* 27.1 (1973). Nakano Reishirō et al, ed, *Kume Hakase kyūjūnen kaikoroku*, vol 2 (1934). Nihon Shiseki Kyōkai, ed, *Iwakura Tomomi kankei monjo*, vols 5–7 (1931–34). Nihon Shiseki Kyōkai, ed, *Kido Takayoshi monjo*, vols 4–5 (1930). Nihon Shiseki Kyōkai, ed, *Kido Takayoshi nikki*, vol 2 (1933). Ōkubo Toshiaki, ed, *Iwakura shisetsu no kenkyū* (1976). Tanaka Akira, *Iwakura shisetsu dan* (1977).   *Marlene J. MAYO*

Iwakura Tomomi (1825–1883)

Statesman who played an important role in the MEIJI RESTORATION. Born in Kyōto, the second son of Horikawa Yasuchika, a low-ranking courtier, he was adopted into the more prestigious Iwakura family. He became a chamberlain to Emperor KŌMEI in 1854. In 1858, when the shogunate senior councillor *(rōjū)* HOTTA MASA-YOSHI went to Kyōto to seek imperial sanction for the HARRIS TREATY between Japan and the United States, Iwakura, together with other court nobles, persuaded the emperor to withhold his approval. He later became a supporter of the MOVEMENT FOR UNION OF COURT AND SHOGUNATE and helped to arrange the marriage of Princess KAZU to the shōgun TOKUGAWA IEMOCHI. For this he was criticized by the more extremist antishogunate *samurai* then ascendant at the court and was forced to retire to Iwakura village, north of Kyōto. During his confinement he became convinced that the days of the shogunate were numbered, and he secretly communicated with ŌKUBO TOSHIMICHI and SAIGŌ TAKAMORI, leaders of the movement to overthrow the shogunate. He joined them in engineering the seizure of the Imperial Palace on 3 January 1868 that initiated the Restoration (see ŌSEI FUKKO).

With the establishment of the new government, Iwakura was appointed to a series of important posts in which he was largely responsible for the formulation of the CHARTER OATH and the establishment of the PREFECTURAL SYSTEM. Soon after his appointment in 1871 as minister of the right *(udaijin)* in the Grand Council of State (DAJŌKAN), he was ordered to lead a mission abroad to observe political and social institutions in Europe and the United States (see IWAKURA MISSION). Upon his return in 1873 he vigorously opposed the plans made in his absence by Saigō and others in the caretaker government to send a military expedition to Korea (see SEIKANRON), arguing that it was necessary first to strengthen the country internally.

Iwakura believed firmly in a strong imperial institution and opposed the FREEDOM AND PEOPLE'S RIGHTS MOVEMENT. At the same time, he realized the wisdom of adopting a constitutional system, if only to attain parity with Western nations, and accordingly in 1881 he ordered INOUE KOWASHI to draw up guiding principles for a CONSTITUTION. In 1882 he sent ITŌ HIROBUMI (who had been made chairman of a bureau established to draft a constitution) to Europe to study various forms of constitutional government. Iwakura also worked to increase the property holdings of the imperial house and arranged for the establishment of the Fifteenth National Bank (Daijūgo Ginkō) and the Japan Railway Company (Nihon Tetsudō Kaisha) to ensure the prosperity of his fellow nobles. During his final illness he was attended by Erwin von BÄLZ and was honored by a personal visit by Emperor Meiji.

Of the men who shaped the Meiji government in its early years, Iwakura, apart from the less forceful SANJŌ SANETOMI, was the only court noble. Shrewd and wily and with a taste for political intrigue, he was significant as a mediator between the Satsuma and Chōshū factions (see HAMBATSU) and as a strong influence on the emperor.

■ ——Iwakura Kō Kyūseki Hozonkai, ed, *Iwakura Kō jikki*, 3 vols (1927). Ōkubo Toshiaki, *Iwakura Tomomi* (1973).

Iwami Silver Mine

(Iwami Ginzan). A mine in the city of Ōda, Iwami Province (now part of Shimane Prefecture), discovered early in the 14th century; one of the most important sources of silver during the Edo period (1600–1868). During the 15th and 16th centuries a new method of silver recovery imported from Korea made possible the extraction of great quantities of silver from the Iwami mine. This led to armed struggles for its possession among the neighboring warlords and its eventual control by the MŌRI FAMILY. The Tokugawa shogunate assumed control of the mine in the early 17th century, and under the direction of the commissioner ŌKUBO NAGAYASU it produced as much as 14.88 tons of silver annually. By the latter half of the century, however, the mine was exhausted and reverted to private management. Despite the discovery in 1726 of a new high-quality vein that yielded 2.19 tons annually, by 1814 only half that amount could be extracted, and the mine was abandoned. The Fujita-Gumi, a mining company founded by FUJITA DENZABURŌ, briefly reactivated the mine for its copper ore during the Meiji period (1868–1912). During the Edo period "Iwami ginzan" was a popular name for a rat poison made from arsenic, a by-product of silver ore.

Iwamizawa

City in central Hokkaidō, some 40 km (25 mi) northeast of Sapporo. Food-processing, brewing, and ceramics have replaced coal mining as the principal industry. Formerly a rice-producing district, Iwamizawa now produces onions and potatoes. It is becoming a satellite city of Sapporo. Pop: 78,311.

Iwamoto Yoshiharu (1863–1942)

Educator; chief editor and cofounder with Kondō Kenzō (d 1886) of JOGAKU ZASSHI (Magazine of Women's Learning), the first important magazine in Japan aimed at the cultural and social education of women. Born in Hyōgo Prefecture. Under the influence of TSUDA SEN, with whom he studied Western agricultural techniques, he converted to Christianity and briefly edited a Christian newspaper with UKITA KAZUTAMI. Becoming interested in women's rights and education, Iwamoto advocated women's economic independence and the abolition of prostitution. In 1884 he helped found the women's magazine *Jogaku shinshi*, renamed *Jogaku zasshi* the following year. In 1885 he helped Kimura Kumaji (1845–1922) and his wife Tōko to start the Meiji Jogakkō, a Christian-oriented secondary school for women; Iwamoto then headed this school after Kimura Tōko's death in 1886 until it closed in 1908. He was married to the writer and translator WAKAMATSU SHIZUKO.

Iwanaga Yūkichi (1883–1939)

News agency director. Born in Tōkyō. Graduate of Kyōto University. In 1920 he started the Iwanaga News Agency and later became managing director of the Nippon Shimbun Rengōsha (Japan Associated Press). In 1933 he acted as a mediator in a dispute between Reuters and the Associated Press in Japan and went on to establish measures for autonomy among the news agencies of various countries. For many years Iwanaga advocated an amalgamation of the national news agencies to form a state-represented news firm. In 1936 he became director of the DŌMEI TSŪSHINSHA (Dōmei News Agency) which closely followed government policy lines.

ARAI Naoyuki

Iwanami Shigeo (1881–1946)

Founder of IWANAMI SHOTEN PUBLISHERS. Born in Nagano Prefecture; attended classes in the Department of Philosophy, Tōkyō University as an auditor. Iwanami opened a second-hand book store in the Kanda district of Tōkyō in 1913. In 1914 he published NATSUME SŌSEKI's novel *Kokoro*, which proved so successful that Iwanami was encouraged to convert his store to a publishing company. His early publications consisted of literary and philosophical essays by former classmates at the university. These sold well, and Iwanami continued to publish scholarly works in the fields of philosophy, the natural sciences and the social sciences. In 1927, when the inexpensive editions of literary works known as *empon* ("one-yen books") had become popular, Iwanami launched his well-known paperback series of classics, the Iwanami Bunko (Iwanami Library). His company eventually became one of Japan's most distinguished publishing houses and an opinion leader among liberal intellectuals. He received the Order of Culture in 1946. *ARASE Yutaka*

Iwanami Shoten Publishers

Publishing house founded by IWANAMI SHIGEO. Starting in 1913 in the Jimbōchō section of Tōkyō as a dealer in secondhand books, Iwanami published NATSUME SŌSEKI's novel *Kokoro* the following year. With the publication of *Tetsugaku sōsho* (1915), which went into many editions, and the full-length versions of KURATA HYAKU-ZŌ's *Shukke to sono deshi* (1917) and ABE JIRŌ's *Santarō no nikki* (1918)—the latter a best-seller—his company was put on a firm financial footing. In 1917 Iwanami launched a journal of philosophy, *Shichō* (renamed *Shisō* in 1921); it later came to include articles on the humanities and social sciences. This was followed in 1931 by *Kagaku,* a periodical on natural science, and in 1933, by *Bungaku,* a literary journal. For these ventures, Iwanami succeeded in attracting contributors who were leaders in their fields.

It was with the Iwanami Bunko (Iwanami Library) series, begun in 1927, that the firm came to be definitely associated with a serious, elitist, intellectual culture that came to be known as "Iwanami culture." Modeled after the Reclam Universal-Bibliothek published in Germany by Anton Phillip Reclam, these paperbacks—especially translations of Western literature—became familiar to a growing audience. In 1928 the firm started a new series, Iwanami Kōza: Sekai Shichō, general introductions to philosophies of the world by outstanding scholars. The NIHON SHIHON SHUGI HATTATSU SHI KŌZA, a series of articles on Japanese capitalism begun in 1932, became a forum for Marxist scholars before World War II. The Iwanami Zensho series (from 1933) aimed at a wider audience, publishing summaries of achievements in various disciplines. The Iwanami Shinsho series, begun in 1938 and patterned after Pelican Books in England, dealt with what were considered urgent, even controversial, topics. Many of the books in the Iwanami Bunko and Iwanami Shinsho series were subsequently banned. In 1940 both Iwanami Shigeo and the author TSUDA SŌKICHI were arrested on the grounds that the latter's works on ancient Japanese history were disrespectful of the imperial institution. (Found guilty of lese majesty at the first hearing, they were acquitted at the second.)

SEKAI, begun in 1946, became one of the leading journals of opinion in postwar Japan; the editorials of Yoshino Genzaburō (1899–1981), criticizing the American–Japanese security arrangement and Japanese rearmament, carried special weight during the early 1950s.   *ARASE Yutaka*

Iwano Hōmei (1873–1920)

Poet, playwright, critic, and novelist. Born in Sumoto on the island of Awaji in the Inland Sea, he was the oldest son of a *samurai* who became a policeman following the Meiji Restoration. His real name was Yoshie; his pseudonym, Hōmei (literally, "foam and roar"), is an allusion to Awa, the domain to which his family belonged, and to the Naruto Strait.

His early education included Chinese classics, mathematics, and English. The fourteen-year-old Hōmei resolved to become a missionary and was baptized, but he soon turned away from Christianity. While at Meiji Gakuin, a Christian college, his interest in literature was stimulated by such senior students as SHIMAZAKI TŌSON, later an important writer of the Japanese naturalist school.

Hōmei began his career as a poet by publishing his *shintaishi* (new style poetry) in the magazine *Bundan* (Literary World), founded in 1890 by, among others, KUNIKIDA DOPPO and Hōmei himself. Between 1901 and 1915 he published five poetry anthologies. Writing mostly in classical language and fixed meters, Hōmei experimented with various metrical units and word-spacing. His critical works include a detailed study of Japanese metrics, *Shintaishi no sahō* (1907, The Composition of New Style Poetry) and *Shintaishi shi* (1907–08, The History of New Style Poetry). His 1908 turning from fixed-form verse to colloquial prose poems roughly corresponds to his shift from poetry to fiction, foreshadowed by his long narrative poems, poetic dramas, and tragedies.

His first tragedy, *Tama wa mayou getchū no yaiba* (1894, The Wandering Soul and the Moonlit Sword), later retitled *Katsura Gorō,* after the hero's name, reflects Hōmei's indebtedness to the theatrical conventions of KABUKI and to the plots of *Faust* and *Hamlet*. Although not successful as a playwright, he continued to compose plays even after he established himself as a novelist and critic.

In 1906 Hōmei published his first critical book, *Shimpiteki hanjū shugi* (The Principle of the Mystic Demi-Animal). He rejected idealism and used the term "demi-animal" to emphasize the long-suppressed instinctive, nonrational element of man. He later eliminated even the term "mystic." He saw each individual human being as the sole center of the universe, striving to live fully and intensely at every moment and to make his life a symbol of a total reality without dichotomies—either between flesh and soul, subjectivity and objectivity, or god and man. This philosophy, labeled "mo-

mentarism," reveals the influence of such Western writers as Emerson, Swedenborg, Maeterlinck, Nietzsche, and Schopenhauer. Hōmei himself correctly believed this book to be an indispensable introduction to his subsequent criticism and novels.

Hōmei is considered one of the chief representatives of Japanese NATURALISM. He expounded his concept of naturalism in *Shin shizen shugi* (1908, New Naturalism), an attempt to combine what he found in the decadent literature of the West, as represented by Baudelaire, Verlaine, Rimbaud, and others, and the strong instinctive desire for life that Hōmei discovered in the gods of Japanese MYTHOLOGY. Calling this blend "naturalistic symbolism" he distinguished it on the one hand from the symbolism of Europe, and on the other from the naturalism of contemporary Japanese writers. This interpretation of Japanese mythology became the basis of his writings on ancient Shintō and of the magazine *Shin Nihon shugi* (New Japanism), which he founded in 1916.

His rejection of a dualistic view of life was developed in his theory in the form of an insistence that life be presented through the action, mental and physical, of the central character, with whom the author strives to identify. He is best known for his autobiographical works: *Tandeki* (1909; usually translated as "Indulgence," though Hōmei himself preferred "Decadence"), and *Hōmei gobusaku* (1910–19, The Pentalogy of Iwano Hōmei), a series of novels sharing the same hero: *Hatten* (Development), *Dokuyaku o nomu onna* (The Woman Who Drinks Poison), *Hōrō* (Wandering), *Dankyō* (Broken Bridge), and *Tsukimono* (Possession). Together these works exemplify Hōmei's view that literature is action; they employ a powerful, occasionally rough, and often symbolic language to record the period of his life from 1908 to 1909 during which he failed in a crab-canning venture to Sakhalin. Its dynamism and grandeur of scale distinguish this pentalogy from other Japanese naturalist novels, which are characterized by their concentration on personal details.

Hōmei also wrote short stories depicting humorous situations encountered in ordinary life, such as "Noda Shimpei" (1912, Rookie Noda) and "Bonchi" (1914, Young Master). Hōmei's translations ranged from Arthur Symons' *The Symbolist Movement in Literature,* which influenced such critics as Kobayashi Hideo and Kawakami Tetsutarō, to Plutarch's voluminous *Parallel Lives*. *Hitsū no tetsuri* (The Philosophy of Sorrow and Suffering), published a month after his death in May 1920, is a collection of his major critical works, including *Shin shizen shugi* and the retitled *Hanjū shugi*. The titular essay, "Hitsū no tetsuri," was originally published in 1910 as a refutation of criticism of Hōmei's philosophy.

■——*Hōmei zenshū,* 18 vols (Kokumin Tosho, 1921–22). Yoshida Seiichi, ed, *Iwano Hōmei shū,* vol 71 of *Meiji bungaku zenshū,* (Chikuma Shobō, 1965). Funabashi Seiichi, *Iwano Hōmei den* (1971). Ōkubo Tsuneo, *Iwano Hōmei* (1963). Ōkubo Tsuneo, *Iwano Hōmei no jidai* (1973).   *Reiko TSUKIMURA*

Iwanuma

City in southern Miyagi Prefecture, northern Honshū. About 20 km (12 mi) south of Sendai. An important terminus for railway, road, and air transportation, it is rapidly becoming a satellite city of Sendai. Formerly a rice-producing area, pulp and rubber factories have been constructed here in recent years. Garden farming and fruit growing are also popular. Pop: 34,913.

Iwasaki Kan'en (1786–1842)

Specialist in *honzōgaku* (traditional pharmacognosy). Born in Edo (now Tōkyō). He learned pharmacognosy from ONO RANZAN and lectured on the subject. He may have painted Philipp Franz von SIEBOLD's portrait when Siebold came to Edo. His *Honzō zufu* in 92 volumes is highly valued for its color illustrations.   *SUZUKI Zenji*

Iwasaki Koyata (1879–1945)

Businessman and leader of the Mitsubishi *zaibatsu,* a powerful industrial and financial combine before World War II. Born in Tōkyō. Nephew of the famous entrepreneur IWASAKI YATARŌ. Iwasaki Koyata studied at Tōkyō University and Cambridge University. Upon his return to Japan in 1906, Iwasaki became vice-president of Mitsubishi Gōshi and, in 1916, president. He separated various divisions of Mitsubishi Gōshi into independent companies and created Mitsubishi Shipbuilding (now MITSUBISHI HEAVY INDUSTRIES, LTD) in 1917, Mitsubishi Mining (now MITSUBISHI MINING & CEMENT CO, LTD) and MITSUBISHI CORPORATION in 1918, and MITSUBISHI BANK,

LTD, in 1919. Through this reorganization Mitsubishi Gōshi became a holding company. Iwasaki also created Mitsubishi Internal Combustion Machinery Mfg in 1920 and MITSUBISHI ELECTRIC CORPORATION in 1921, both from Mitsubishi Shipbuilding, and laid ground for the heavy industry division of the Mitsubishi *zaibatsu*. He was enthusiastic about overseas expansion and eagerly sought development rights in Asian countries. Also active in ventures with foreign corporations, Iwasaki introduced technology imported from Westinghouse Electric to Mitsubishi Electric and established MITSUBISHI OIL CO, LTD, in a joint venture with an American oil company in 1931.

KOBAYAKAWA Yōichi

Iwasaki Yatarō (1835–1885)

Founder of the MITSUBISHI financial empire. Born in the Tosa domain (now Kōchi Prefecture), the eldest son of a farmer who claimed *samurai* lineage. Though his family was poor, Iwasaki's education included Chinese classics taught by a samurai who recognized the boy's native intelligence. At the age of 20 he bought, as it had become easy to do, the status of GŌSHI (the lowest-ranked rural samurai) with financial aid from his relatives. In this he was motivated by the fact that samurai status, however marginal, was essential to obtain a position in the domain government.

He became an aide to a samurai and a low-ranking assistant at the Kaiseikan (Industry Promotion Office) of Tosa, but he did not remain long in these posts, finding them unsatisfying and even humiliating. In 1867, at the age of 33, Iwasaki was unemployed with no immediate prospects. In ordinary times he might never have proven his abilities, but these were hardly ordinary times. Militant Tosa, one of several domains that would soon openly challenge the Tokugawa shogunate, was buying all the arms it could through the Nagasaki office of the Kaiseikan and accumulating a huge debt. The domain found itself in need of funds and an able person who could manage the debt-ridden office. The position was offered to Iwasaki in 1867 by a former superior who remembered his talents. He readily accepted, although it must be noted that the post would not have come his way had it been at all attractive to anyone of higher rank.

Shortly after assuming the position Iwasaki succeeded in refinancing the huge debt by borrowing 300,000 RYŌ (1 *ryō* could buy 1 KOKU [1 *koku* = about 180 liters or 5 US bushels] of rice at the time) from an American merchant in exchange for exclusive rights to deal in the domain's camphor production. He consummated the difficult negotiations by employing what were to become standard Iwasaki tactics: coaxing, cajoling, hinting about nonexistent rivals, and extensive "wining and dining." Domain officials were quick to recognize his unusual abilities and soon asked him to act as financial agent for the domain. Iwasaki devised a scheme to counterfeit shogunate coins and to print supposedly convertible domain notes (HANSATSU) in order to buy rations for the army of the nearly bankrupt Tosa. For the next few years he continued to manage the Nagasaki office and to act as a troubleshooter for domain finances. In short, Iwasaki's talents were ideally suited to the topsy-turvy world of the late 1860s. When the domains were abolished in 1871, three years after the MEIJI RESTORATION, and the Tosa government withdrew from all commercial activities, Iwasaki was chosen to take over the domainal enterprise. To extricate itself from its large debt of 300,000 *ryō*, the domain is said to have given Iwasaki its fleet of 11 ships, 230,000 *ryō* in cash, and all the assets and privileges connected with its business in camphor, tea, silk, lumber, and coal mining. It is impossible to estimate accurately the worth of the transaction to Iwasaki, for not only was the value of these domain assets unknown, but the value of the former monopoly rights of domain businesses now depended entirely on Iwasaki's ability to manage them skillfully. Perhaps it is fair to say that Iwasaki did not benefit by this transaction per se but was able to gain a strategic position that he could exploit.

Immediately following the acquisition of the former domain enterprises, Iwasaki began to acquire ships of all sizes that were being sold by former domains and foreign merchants. Those who were inexperienced and eager to sell became easy prey for Iwasaki, and even those who were experienced and shrewd often found themselves outwitted. The profits, however, were small compared to what he earned in the conversion of domain notes to government notes. The new national government, assuming responsibility for the depreciated former domain currencies, offered to convert the notes of Tosa at face value into DAJŌKAN SATSU, the new national currency. Iwasaki, who obtained this information before it reached the holders of domain notes, bought up a large quantity and made a considerable fortune.

On the strength of these profits and the successful operation of the former domain businesses, in 1873 Iwasaki founded the Mitsubishi Shōkai trading company, with shipping as its principal business. The shipping business in Japan at this time was entirely coastal and fiercely competitive. Iwasaki's competitors consisted of a large number of small firms, each with a few vessels, that specialized in short-haul transport, and also the Yūbin Jōkisen Kaisha (Steamship Mail Company). The last had been organized by the joint capital of wealthy merchant houses and enjoyed a large subsidy from the government. Iwasaki eliminated most of the small firms by undercutting prices and offering longer and better-integrated shipping routes. Soon his only competitor was the Steamship Mail Company.

To all appearances the remaining rival seemed more than a match for Iwasaki, whose unsubsidized fleet was smaller and older. However, during 1873–74, after a fierce rate war that all but ignored the safety of passengers, Iwasaki bankrupted his rival, largely because the latter operated in the most bureaucratic fashion and could not compete against Iwasaki's aggressive tactics.

The victory, however, was costly to Iwasaki, and his trading firm was faltering when the government launched the TAIWAN EXPEDITION OF 1874, which proved to be a godsend to Iwasaki: for transporting troops and provisions for the government, his company was rewarded handsomely. With this windfall, plus large subsidies obtained from political leaders whom Iwasaki carefully cultivated, the Mitsubishi Trading Company grew rapidly. By the mid-1870s his ships were serving the Shanghai–Japan route, and the stiff challenge mounted by the American Pacific Mail Steamship Company was effectively crushed within a year, owing both to Iwasaki's price-cutting tactics and to government aid in the form of generous subsidies and shipping regulations that favored Iwasaki. By early 1875 the American shipping line had no choice but to sell its fleet to Iwasaki, who bought it with the aid of another government subsidy. In 1876 he employed the same tactics against the English Peninsular and Oriental Navigation Company (P&O), which enjoyed predominance on the Hong Kong–Shanghai and Shanghai–Yokohama routes but was soon forced to withdraw from the latter. Iwasaki's victory over the P&O, again with government backing, was followed by the SATSUMA REBELLION of 1877, which enriched him even more than the Taiwan Expedition had done. By 1877 Iwasaki owned over 80 percent of all ships in Japan and virtually monopolized its coastal trade.

Iwasaki's golden years were from this time until his death in 1885. Although he had still to wage a major battle against a MITSUI-backed challenge to his shipping empire in 1882 and came under extensive public criticism for his close and lucrative associations with high government officials, neither circumstance seriously affected his efforts to expand into mining, banking, insurance, iron foundry, and other fields. His reputation was little damaged by public criticism; his funeral was attended by more than 50,000 people, including all of the important figures in the political and business circles of early Meiji Japan. Within two decades after his death, the ZAIBATSU established by Iwasaki had become one of the undisputed cornerstones of the rapid industrialization of Japan.

■ ——Johannes Hirschmeier, *The Origins of Entrepreneurship in Meiji Japan* (1964). Iwasaki Yatarō–Iwasaki Yanosuke Denki Hensan Kai, ed, *Iwasaki Yatarō den,* 2 vols (1967). Kozo Yamamura, *A Study of Samurai Income and Entrepreneurship* (1974).

Kozo YAMAMURA

Iwasa Matabei (1578–1650)

Also known as Iwasa Katsumochi, Iwasa Shōi, Dōun, Un'ō, and Hekishōkyū. Painter of classical themes in the YAMATO-E style. The son of Araki Murashige, the lord of Settsu (now part of Ōsaka and Hyōgo prefectures), Matabei was raised in the temple Nishi Honganji of Kyōto after his father's unsuccessful revolt against ODA NOBUNAGA. Iwasa was Matabei's mother's maiden name, which Matabei later adopted.

Although raised in Kyōto, Matabei studied painting in Sakai with Tosa Mitsunori (1583–1638). In June, 1650, Matabei painted a set of Thirty-Six Poets (SANJŪROKKASEN) for the shrine Kawagoe Tōshōgū and in them signed himself: "the last of the line of Tosa Mitsunobu" (see TOSA SCHOOL). This statement has led to the identification of Matabei as a Tosa artist, but Matabei also studied painting with Kanō Naizen (see KANŌ SCHOOL). Matabei may have known HASEGAWA TŌHAKU and Tawaraya SŌTATSU as well. Matabei was acquainted with SEN NO RIKYŪ, who taught the tea ceremony to Matabei's father at the temple Nanshūji in Sakai. Matabei also met

Matsudaira Tadanao, the lord of Echizen (now Fukui Prefecture), and in 1617, Matabei became Tadanao's official painter.

Recent discoveries of paintings such as the *Scroll of Professions,* the *Screen of Harvesters,* and the *Screen of Classical Themes* in the Kanaya collection confirm the association of Matabei with the *machishū.* However, since it is known that Matabei moved to Edo (now Tōkyō) in 1637 to serve shōgun TOKUGAWA IEMITSU, Matabei cannot be classified simply as a *machishū.* Matabei's service under the shogunate and a certain element of sensuality in his style associates Matabei with UKIYO-E, the artistic tradition of the Edo commoners. Thus, Matabei is best remembered as both the last of the Tosa and the first of the *ukiyo-e* artists.   *Sandy* KITA

Iwase Tadanari (1818–1861)

Official of the Tokugawa shogunate. In 1854 he was appointed inspector *(metsuke)* by the senior councillor *(rōjū)* ABE MASAHIRO and entrusted with strengthening coastal defenses. In 1857 he was sent to Nagasaki to negotiate supplements to trade agreements that had been signed with the Dutch and the Russians, and in the following year he and INOUE KIYONAO assisted the senior councillor HOTTA MASAYOSHI in negotiating a commercial treaty with Townsend HARRIS, the American consul in Shimoda. He accompanied Hotta to Kyōto to obtain imperial approval of the treaty and used the occasion to try to convince court nobles of the necessity of opening the country to foreign intercourse. The HARRIS TREATY was signed without imperial sanction in July 1858, soon after II NAOSUKE had become Great Elder *(tairō)* and Hotta had been forced to resign. Iwase's position became precarious, however, because of his support of TOKUGAWA YOSHINOBU in the shogunal succession dispute (Ii favored another candidate), and he was eventually dismissed and ordered into permanent retirement.

Iwase "thousand-mound" tomb cluster

(Iwase *senzuka kofungun*). A cluster of 500 to 600 mounded tombs (KOFUN), most of them built in the 6th and 7th centuries; located in the hills south of the river Kinokawa in Iwase, Wakayama Prefecture. This tomb cluster is representative of burial patterns of the latter part of the Kofun period (ca 300–710). It consists mostly of round tumuli ranging from 4 to 30 meters (13 to 98 ft) in diameter, although some are keyhole-shaped or square. The majority of the tombs have corridor-type stone chambers constructed of local green schist, the larger ones being constructed with stone partitions, beams, and drainage facilities. Several of the more important tombs were excavated between 1962 and 1965.

━━━Suenaga Masao, Sonoda Kōyū, and Mori Kōichi, *Iwase senzuka* (1967).   ABE Gihei

iwashi → sardines

Iwashimizu Hachiman Shrine

(Iwashimizu Hachimangū). Also known as Otokoyama Hachimangū. Shintō shrine in the Tsuzuki district of Kyōto Prefecture, dedicated to the spirits of Emperor ŌJIN (late 4th to early 5th century) popularly worshiped as HACHIMAN, and the legendary Empress JINGŪ and to the deity Hime Ōkami (also known as Himegami). The shrine was established in 859 by a Buddhist monk, Gyōkyō, who petitioned the court for authorization to invite the deity of the USA HACHIMAN SHRINE in Kyūshū to take up residence in the region in order to protect the capital. The shrine has been greatly venerated by the court and the imperial family throughout Japanese history. In the 11th and 12th centuries the Minamoto family regarded Hachiman as their clan deity (UJIGAMI) and the first Kamakura shōgun MINAMOTO NO YORITOMO established a branch of this shrine, TSURUGAOKA HACHIMAN SHRINE, in Kamakura. This helped increase the popularity of this deity among warriors and led to the establishment of Hachiman shrines throughout the country. The succeeding Ashikaga and Tokugawa shogunates also gave special patronage to the Iwashimizu Shrine. The annual festival, known as Iwashimizu Hōjōe, which used to be one of the three great imperial festivals along with those of KAMO SHRINES (see AOI FESTIVAL) and KASUGA SHRINE, is held on 15 September.

Stanley WEINSTEIN

Iwashita Sōichi (1889–1940)

Catholic priest, theologian, and philosopher. Born in Tōkyō, he studied philosophy under Raphael Koeber (1848–1923) at Tōkyō University and went on to teach at the Seventh Higher School in Kagoshima Prefecture. He studied in Europe from 1919 to 1925 and was ordained to the priesthood in Rome in 1925. Along with Yoshimitsu Yoshihiko (1904–45), he was one of the pioneers in Japanese research on medieval European philosophy. He worked actively for the propagation of the Christian faith among university students. He also served as director of the leprosarium Fukusei Hospital in Shizuoka Prefecture from 1930 to 1940. His collected works in nine volumes are found in *Iwashita Sōichi zenshū* (1961–64).

Iwata

City in western Shizuoka Prefecture, central Honshū, on the river Tenryūgawa. Formerly a provincial capital *(kokufu),* Iwata developed as a POST-STATION TOWN on the Tōkaidō, the major highway during the Edo period (1600–1868). Principal products are tea, mandarin oranges, and melons; there are several textile, ball bearing, and automobile plants. Several ancient tombs and the ruins of an 8th-century provincial temple *(kokubunji)* may be seen. Pop: 75,810.

Iwatahara

Diluvial upland along the eastern bank of the river Tenryūgawa, Shizuoka Prefecture, central Honshū. Most of it is in the city of Iwata. Vegetables, tea, and tobacco are grown. In the southern part, industrial plants and residences are increasing. Elevation: 10–125 m (33–410 ft); length: approximately 13 km (8.1 m); width: approximately 4 km (2.5 mi).

Iwate Prefecture

(Iwate Ken). Located in northern Honshū and bounded by the Pacific Ocean on the east, Aomori Prefecture on the north, Akita Prefecture on the west, and Miyagi Prefecture on the south. The terrain consists of mountain and plateau areas, with the ŌU MOUNTAINS running through the western section of the prefecture and the KITAKAMI MOUNTAINS rising in the east. Between them lies the basin of the river KITAKAMIGAWA, the prefecture's main level area and population center. The climate is generally cool and dry.

Known as Mutsu Province after the TAIKA REFORM of 645 and inhabited by the ancient indigenous people known as EZO, the area came under the control of the central government only in the Heian period (794–1185). During the 11th and 12th centuries it was ruled independently by the ŌSHŪ FUJIWARA FAMILY, whose capital at HIRAIZUMI became northern Japan's major cultural center. It then came under the control of the Kamakura shogunate. The Nambu family and the DATE FAMILY ruled the area in the 16th century, and in the Edo period (1600–1868) the province was divided into several domains. The present prefectural name and boundaries were established in 1876.

Agriculture is centered on rice production and livestock farming. Both forestry and fishing are important. Although not extensively industrialized, food-processing, lumber, and electrical appliance industries are growing. It is also one of Japan's leading sources of iron and copper ore.

Iwate offers some of Japan's most dramatic coastal scenery, and much of its shoreline is included in RIKUCHŪ COAST NATIONAL PARK. TOWADA–HACHIMANTAI NATIONAL PARK is also a major tourist attraction, and the prefecture has many hot spring resorts such as Hanamaki, Getō, and Tsunagi. Hiraizumi has several historic sites. Iwate is also known for its traditional folk crafts and customs, such as Nambu cast iron ware, KOKESHI dolls, *kembai* (a sword dance), and the *shishi odori* (deer dance). Area: 15,277 sq km (5,897 sq mi); pop: 1,421,969; capital: Morioka. Other major cities include MIYAKO, HANAMAKI, and ICHINOSEKI. See map on following page.

Iwatesan

Conical composite volcano in the Nasu Volcanic Zone, northwestern Iwate Prefecture, northern Honshū. Also called Nambu Fuji (from an old domainal name) and Iwate Fuji. It is composed of two peaks, Higashi Iwatesan and Nishi Iwatesan, and numerous hot springs are found in the vicinity. Japan's first geothermal electric plant, producing 20,000 kilowatts, was constructed in the Matsukawa Hot Spring area on the northwestern slopes of the mountain in 1966. On the mountain's southern skirts is Japan's largest dairy farm, the Koiwai Farm (area 26 sq km or 10 sq mi). Iwatesan is part of the Towada–Hachimantai National Park. Height: 2,041 m (6,694 ft).

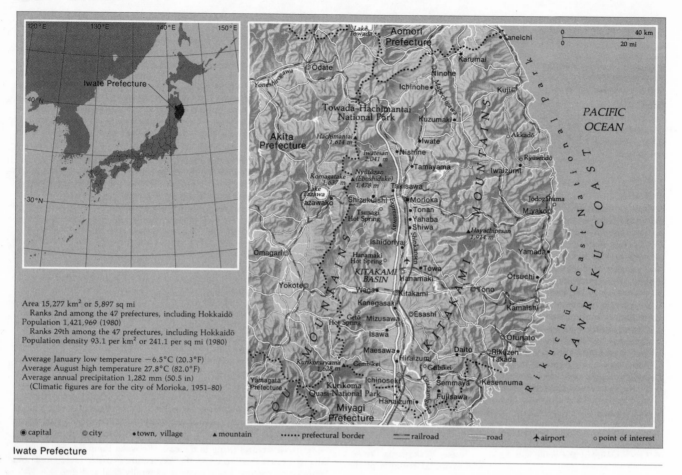

Area 15,277 km² or 5,897 sq mi
    Ranks 2nd among the 47 prefectures, including Hokkaidō
Population 1,421,969 (1980)
    Ranks 29th among the 47 prefectures, including Hokkaidō
Population density 93.1 per km² or 241.1 per sq mi (1980)

Average January low temperature −6.5°C (20.3°F)
Average August high temperature 27.8°C (82.0°F)
Average annual precipitation 1,282 mm (50.5 in)
    (Climatic figures are for the city of Morioka, 1951–80)

⊚ capital   ◎ city   ● town, village   ▲ mountain   ⋯⋯ prefectural border   ══ railroad   ══ road   ✈ airport   ○ point of interest

Iwate Prefecture

Iwatsuki

City in eastern Saitama Prefecture, central Honshū, about 30 km (19 mi) from Tōkyō. A castle town during the 15th century (a castle was built by ŌTA DŌKAN), in the Edo period (1600–1868) it prospered as a POST-STATION TOWN on the highway leading to the mausoleum of TOKUGAWA IEYASU. In recent years there has been an increase in factory construction and residential land development, and an interchange of the Tōhoku Expressway is located here. The city has long been known for its *hina ningyō* (dolls) and HAGOITA (battledores). Pop: 94,695.

Iwaya Sazanami (1870–1933)

Novelist and scholar of juvenile literature. Real name Iwaya Sueo. Born in Tōkyō. A student of the popular writer OZAKI KŌYŌ, his work for children, *Koganemaru* (1891), in which animals represent humans, was a popular success. He edited the 24 volumes of *Nihon mukashibanashi* (1894–96), a collection of Japanese folktales and legends, which formed the basis of modern juvenile literature. In 1900 he taught Japanese language at the University of Berlin.

Asai Kiyoshi

Iwojima → Iōjima

Iyadani

Gorge on the middle reaches of the river Iyagawa (a tributary of the Yoshinogawa) in western Tokushima Prefecture, Shikoku. Located in the foothills of the mountain Tsurugisan. Said to have been the place where the warriors of the Taira family (Heike) hid after their defeat, giving rise to many legends of the Heike which have been passed down to the present day. Famous for its rugged beauty and Kazura Bridge (Kazurabashi; a bridge made of vines). Length: approximately 20 km (12 mi).

Iyo

City in central Ehime Prefecture, Shikoku. Situated on the Iyo Sea, Iyo developed as a fishing port in the Edo period (1600–1868). Man-

darin oranges and loquats are cultivated here; the area is also known for its production of *kezuribushi* (a mixture of shavings of dried mackerel, bonito, Japanese sardine, etc), used for flavoring stock. Pop: 29,726.

Iyo Mishima

City in eastern Ehime Prefecture, Shikoku, on the Hiuchi Sea. Iyo Mishima's paper industry, together with that of the neighboring city of Kawanoe, is second only to the city of Fuji in Shizuoka Prefecture. The city is also known for its MIZUHIKI, paper strings used for ornamentation. Lake Kinsha (Kinshako) is popular with hikers and campers. Pop: 38,475.

Izanagi and Izanami

(full names: Izanagi no Mikoto and Izanami no Mikoto; an alternate pronunciation of Izanagi is Izanaki). Male and female deities appearing in the KOJIKI (712, Records of Ancient Matters) and NIHON SHOKI (720, Chronicle of Japan) as the mythological creators of Japan and its gods. According to the legends, the two stand on the Floating Bridge of Heaven and thrust down the Heavenly Jeweled Spear into the ocean below. The brine that drips from the spear coagulates to become the island of Onokorojima, to which they descend and perform a marriage rite, first with the female Izanami taking the initiative, then again "properly," with the male Izanagi speaking first. Izanami gives birth to the islands of Japan, with their deities of mountains, rivers, trees, and crops. But in giving birth to the fire deity (Kagutsuchi no Kami), Izanami is burned and dies. In his grief Izanagi slays the fire deity and pursues Izanami to the nether world (Yomi no Kuni), where he finds her horribly transformed by the ravages of death. Ashamed and enraged that he has disregarded her entreaty not to look at her, Izanami and the Eighty Ugly Females of Yomi pursue Izanagi, who narrowly escapes by blocking off the exit of Yomi (Yomotsu Hirasaka); thus the worlds of the living and the dead are separated. To rid himself of the impurities of Yomi, Izanagi performs a ceremony of ablution (MISOGI), an act that produces the sun goddess AMATERASU ŌMIKAMI, the moon god Tsukumi no Mikoto, and the important deity SUSANOO NO MIKOTO.

According to some scholars, Izanami and Izanagi may have originally been the regional deities of the fishing population of the Awaji region, and the *Kojiki* and *Nihon shoki* accounts of them may be related to similar Polynesian myths. See also MYTHOLOGY.

KITAMURA Bunji

Izawajō

Fortress built in the Heian period (794–1185) and located in the province of Mutsu (now Iwate Prefecture) near the confluence of the rivers Kitakamigawa and Izawagawa. The fortress was built in 802 by the military leader SAKANOUE NO TAMURAMARO to subjugate the EZO, and in 804 Sakanoue transferred his CHINJUFU (Headquarters for Pacification and Defense) to this fortress. The ruins of the fortress are located in the city of Mizusawa, Iwate Prefecture.

Izawa Shūji (1851–1917)

Educational leader in the Meiji period (1868–1912). Born in the Takatō domain (now part of Nagano Prefecture), he studied at the Daigaku Nankō (now Tōkyō University). In 1875 he went to the United States to study the American educational system. After returning to Japan in 1878, he served as head of the Tōkyō Normal School and chief of the editorial bureau of the Ministry of Education. In 1888 he became the first head of the Tōkyō School of Music (now Tōkyō University of Fine Arts and Music), which he organized with the help of his former teacher, Luther W. MASON. He also edited the first national textbook of the Japanese language and promoted the introduction and spread of Western music. Izawa also served as chief of the educational bureau in the government-general of Taiwan. He actively supported education for the blind and deaf, creating the Japanese braille system and adapting sign language for use in Japan. One of his major works on education is *Kyōikugaku* (1882).

Izayoi nikki → Abutsu Ni

Izu Gold Mine

(Izu Kinzan). Collective name for several gold mines in Izu Province (now part of Shizuoka Prefecture) that were operated by the Tokugawa shogunate during the Edo period (1600–1868). Toi, Yugashima, and Nawaji, the principal mines, were first developed at the end of the 16th century. Production increased under ŌKUBO NAGAYASU, who was commissioner from 1606 to 1613. For a time the annual yield averaged 45 kilograms (99 lb) but declined after water began to flood the mines.

Izu Islands

(Izu Shotō). Group of volcanic islands in the Pacific Ocean, southeast of the Izu Peninsula, including the islands of ŌSHIMA, TOSHIMA, Niijima, Kōzujima, MIYAKEJIMA, Mikurajima, HACHIJŌJIMA, Shikinejima, and Udonejima. Administratively under the jurisdiction of the Tōkyō prefectural government. Extending for approximately 540 km (335 mi) north to south, these islands form part of the Fuji-Hakone-Izu National Park. There are farms on the islands and good fishing grounds surround them.

Izumi

City in central Miyagi Prefecture, northern Honshū, north of Sendai. A POST-STATION TOWN on the Ōshū Kaidō highway during the Edo period (1600–1868), Izumi is now a suburb of Sendai. Pop: 98,015.

Izumi

City in southern Ōsaka Prefecture, central Honshū. Contiguous with Sakai to the north, Izumi is a satellite city of Ōsaka. Its principal industry is textiles; glass products and artificial pearls are also produced. Farm products include flowers and mandarin oranges. As the site of a provincial capital *(kokufu)* in the past, Izumi has several temples and shrines of note. Pop: 124,322.

Izumi

City in northwestern Kagoshima Prefecture, Kyūshū. Local products include rice, mandarin oranges, sweet potatoes, saplings, poultry,

seaweed, and prawns. Izumi also has alcohol, paper, and electric industries. Large numbers of migrating cranes from northeast Asia winter here between October and February. Pop: 39,375.

Izumi Kyōka (1873–1939)

Novelist. Real name Izumi Kyōtarō. Living in an age of change and innovation characterized by an influx and adaptation of Western ideas, Kyōka was noted for his supernatural themes and adherence to the more traditional style of Edo-period (1600–1868) literature.

Kyōka was born in Kanazawa (Ishikawa Prefecture) to an artisan family. His mother introduced him at an early age to the KUSAZŌSHI, a genre of Edo fiction. Because of his family's straitened circumstances, he attended the tuition-free Hokuriku English–Japanese School run by Christian missionaries. Upon graduating, Kyōka took the entrance examination for the Ishikawa Prefecture Kanazawa Specialist School (now Kanazawa University) but failed. He left for Tōkyō in November 1890, hoping to become a writer under the tutelage of the celebrated novelist OZAKI KŌYŌ (1867–1903).

Kyōka was attracted to Kōyō's style, which was essentially an adaptation of Edo fiction techniques. But nearly a year passed before Kyōka could bring himself to seek out Kōyō. Under Kōyō's auspices, Kyōka's first work *Kammuri Yazaemon* (the title is the name of the protagonist) was serialized in a newspaper in 1893, although it was an undistinguished piece written more or less in imitation of a *kusazōshi*.

Two years later Kyōka made his mark as a writer with the publication of *Giketsu kyōketsu* (The Righteous and the Chivalrous). Although he was no longer under the patronage of Kōyō, Kyōka found that Kōyō still exercised a considerable influence on his personal life. Due to Kōyō's objections, Kyōka's marriage to Suzu, a geisha, was delayed until after Kōyō's death.

An eccentric and superstitious man, Kyōka distinguished himself as a writer of the grotesque and fantastic. "Kōya hijiri" (The Itinerant Monk), published in 1900, exemplifies the style for which Kyōka became noted—a mixture of grace, the grotesque, and the supernatural. It is a tale recounting the adventures of a monk as he journeys through mountain recesses, encountering strange and frightening experiences.

Kyōka was particularly fascinated by the supernatural, borrowing and embellishing themes from Edo fiction, NŌ, and folklore. More than two-thirds of his some 300 works incorporate a supernatural element of some kind. AKUTAGAWA RYŪNOSUKE (1892–1927) was said to have especially admired Kyōka's handling of the supernatural and the grotesque. Kyōka depicted the supernatural with a great degree of sophistication and realism, portraying it through the psyche of the protagonist. The ghost in *Shirasagi* (1909, The White Heron) is an example of this technique.

Although Kyōka had a number of admirers among the literati, he did not establish any kind of literary coterie. As a novelist, he is often linked with NAGAI KAFŪ (1879–1959) and TANIZAKI JUN'ICHIRŌ (1886–1965) because he shared their love for Edo culture and their depiction of life in the pleasure quarters. His more notable works along this line are *Onna keizu* (1907, The Genealogy of Women) and *Nihombashi* (1914, named after a famous geisha district in Tōkyō).

Kyōka's style was very much influenced by aspects of Edo culture, especially the *kusazōshi*. His use of a complex and suspenseful plot development was a common technique found in the GŌKAN, a type of *kusazōshi* that flourished at the end of the Edo period. He also incorporated the narrative techniques of RAKUGO (storytelling), a traditional genre, and adapted certain types of dramatic dialogues from KABUKI.

The theme of a beautiful, gentle older woman loving and caring for a young boy or youth can often be seen in Kyōka's works. *Teriha kyōgen*, published in 1896, is an example of this theme, which is supposedly linked to the death of his mother when he was nine. Kyōka is said to have idolized her, transforming her into a kind of an ideal female protagonist.

Kyōka spent the latter part of his life in the idyllic environs of Zushi, a summer resort area not far from Tōkyō. There he wrote some of his better-known works, including *Onna keizu, Shirasagi,* and *Uta andon* (1910). He died of lung cancer at the age of 65.

■ ──Collected Works: *Kyōka Zenshū*, 28 vols (Iwanami Shoten, 1973–76). Jean FUNATSU

Izumi Mountains

(Izumi Sammyaku). Mountain range running east to west, forming a natural boundary between Wakayama and Ōsaka prefectures, central Honshū. It consists of numerous peaks under 1,000 m (3,280 ft), including Iwakiyama (898 m; 2,945 ft), Mikuniyama, and Katsuragi-san. It is known for citrus fruit production.

Izumi Ōtsu

City in southern Ōsaka Prefecture, central Honshū. Located on Ōsaka Bay, it was a provincial capital in ancient times and a prosperous port town during the Edo period (1600-1868). It is now a textile center, producing cotton cloth, braids, and 95 percent of the blankets made in Japan. Pop: 67,474.

Izumi Sano

City in southern Ōsaka Prefecture, central Honshū, on Ōsaka Bay. A market town from the 8th century on, during the Edo period (1600–1868) Izumi Sano was the site of many wholesale houses dealing in fish and cotton. It is now a textile center, producing more than 50 percent of the towels made in Japan. Pop: 90,684.

Izumi school

(Izumiryū). One of the three major schools of KYŌGEN. The founder of the school was Yamawaki Izumi no Kami Motoyoshi (d 1659), who was asked in 1614 by the *daimyō* of the Owari domain (now part of Aichi Prefecture) to be the official *kyōgen* performer of the domain; the school continued to serve the domain throughout the Edo period (1600–1868). The Izumi school was particularly influential in Nagoya and Kyōto (the home of the school), often performing for the imperial court, whereas the other two major *kyōgen* schools, the ŌKURA and Sagi, were patronized by the shogunate in Edo (now Tōkyō). In 1881, after the Meiji Restoration (1868), Motokiyo, the head of the school, unsuccessfully tried to establish the school in Tōkyō, the new capital of Japan. When his son, Mototeru, died at an early age in 1916, the main family line of the school came to an end. Miyake Yasuyuki, the son of Miyake Tōkurō, a leading member of the school, succeeded to the house, taking the name first of Izumi Yasuyuki, and later, in 1979, of Izumi Motohide. Other leading families of the school include those of Nomura Matasaburō and Nomura Manzō.

Izumi Seiichi (1915–1970)

Cultural anthropologist who was instrumental in the establishment of cultural anthropology as an academic discipline in Japan. Born in Tōkyō, Izumi studied social anthropology at Keijō University in Korea (then a Japanese colony), where he was influenced by Malinowskian functionalism. While teaching at Keijō University he conducted anthropological field work in Korea and other areas of northeast Asia. His special interest was the culture of Cheju Island (off the Korean peninsula in the East China Sea). In 1951 Izumi was appointed to the faculty of Tōkyō University. With ISHIDA EIICHIRŌ he was responsible for founding its department of cultural anthropology. In his later years his interest turned to ancient Andean culture. He organized large expeditions to Peru, and his excavation work at the pre-Columbian site of Kotosh near the city of Huánuco in Peru received worldwide recognition. His collected works are found in *Izumi Seiichi chosakushū* (Yomiuri Shimbun Sha, 1971–72).

■——Izumi Seiichi, ed, *Andes: Excavations at Kotosh, Peru* (1960–72). AOKI Tamotsu

Izumi Shikibu (fl ca 1000)

The most interesting and accomplished poet of the middle of the Heian period (794–1185) was a woman, Izumi Shikibu. Izumi's birth and death dates are unknown; probably she was born in the 960s or 970s, and there are traces of her activity into the late 1020s. Along with a collection of over 1,500 WAKA (31-syllable poems), she has left a legacy of great personal fascination. Brought up at court, she was twice married, in both cases to men of the middle stratum of the bureaucracy, from which she herself came. But the parabola of her life carried her to giddier heights, for between her two marriages she was the mistress, successively, of two imperial princes, brothers, both of whom died young in the full tide of their passion. The younger brother, Prince Atsumichi (981–1007), was the great love of

Izumo Plain

A view of the isolated houses or groups of houses for which the plain is known—a settlement pattern called *sanson* ("scattered villages").

her life; she mourned his death in over a hundred poems. Her reputation and hints in her poetry suggest that there were other men in her life besides these four. The career of Izumi Shikibu is thus a better documented version of that of ONO NO KOMACHI (fl mid-9th century), of whom much is guessed but little known. Like Komachi she is famous for her intense love poetry and exploitation of Buddhist themes. In fact, Izumi's poetry shows her possessed of two strongly contrasting sides of character: an amorous tendency, now playful, now serious, and an earnest, even prayerful urge which seeks release from the toils of passion through Buddhist enlightenment and renunciation. Both aspects speak with a conviction that allows us to see her as we can few other poets in the classical tradition. Her poetry itself is exceptionally skilled. She mastered every style and manner current in her day, from simple descriptive nature poetry to the most artful of introspective conceits. She was fond of verbal games, indulging in outrageous repetitions of a single word. Her tone is often arch and deliberately wicked, and multiple meanings are put to superlative use in some of her finest verse. And yet, she could write with the most classic simplicity, creating poems of seemingly effortless transparency. A single such verse, a plea for enlightenment on the "dark path" of mortal love and death, has been preserved in the *Shūishū*, the third imperial *waka* anthology, compiled during her lifetime. Her fame after death was so great that the next anthology, the *Goshūishū* of 1086, contains 67 of her poems, the largest number by any single poet. She was certainly the most gifted poet of her day (to be sure, the time in which she lived was more notable for its prose writers than its poets), but beyond that she belongs to the company of truly outstanding masters of the *waka* of all ages. She is also one of the unforgettable personalities of Japanese literature. Her poems are preserved principally in two collections, the *Seishū* (Main Collection), and the *Zokushū* (Continued Collection).

A fictionalized version of the love story of Izumi Shikibu and Prince Atsumichi exists in the *Izumi Shikibu nikki*. The events related occurred in 1003 and 1004, at the outset of this most intense of Izumi's affairs. Although containing the word *nikki* in its title, the work is not a diary, not even as the term is loosely used to refer to the autobiographical writings which began their vogue in Heian times. The narrative is in the third person. Simultaneous scenes in different locations are described, and dialogue is reported which could not have been overheard by a diarist. Rather, the work is cast in the form of a story, structured on the poem-exchange. The authorship, long ascribed to Izumi Shikibu herself, has recently become a matter of controversy. Although scholarly opinion still favors the traditional attribution, it has been argued persuasively that the work is intended as a kind of paradigm of the classic love affair as seen in the imperial *waka* anthologies. Based as it is on fact, however, its author apparently felt loyalty also to what actually happened, the result being a curious unresolved tension between the schematic and the real. The work lapses entirely into prose, and ends abruptly, after the poetess goes to live with the prince. The wooing is over, and that is where the love story ends.

■——Endō Yoshimoto, ed, *Izumi Shikibu nikki*, in *Nihon koten bungaku taikei*, vol 20 (Iwanami Shoten, 1957). Enchi Fumiko and Suzuki Kazuo, ed, *Zenkō Izumi Shikibu nikki* (1965). Fujioka Tadami, ed, *Izumi Shikibu nikki*, in *Nihon koten bungaku zenshū*

Izumo Shrine——Main building (honden)

The hall's architectural format is ancient, preserving more than 1,500 years of tradition; it was last rebuilt in 1744. National Treasure.

(Shōgakukan, 1971). Saeki Umetomo, Murakami Osamu, and Komatsu Tomi, ed, *Izumi Shikibu shū zenshaku* (1959). Edwin A. Cranston, tr, *The Izumi Shikibu Diary: A Romance of the Heian Court* (1969). Earl Miner, tr, *Japanese Poetic Diaries* (1969). Janet A. Walker, "Poetic Ideal and Fictional Reality in the *Izumi Shikibu nikki*," *Harvard Journal of Asiatic Studies* 37.1 (June 1977).

Edwin A. CRANSTON

Izumo

City in eastern Shimane Prefecture, western Honshū, on Lake Shinji. A market town from the 14th century, with the opening of the National Railway San'in Main Line in 1911, it became a textile center. Tiles, *sake,* and farming implements are also made. It is the gateway to IZUMO SHRINE, one of the most venerable Shintō shrines in Japan. Numerous sites of historic interest are located in this area. Pop: 77,301.

Izumo Plain

(Izumo Heiya). Located in eastern Shimane Prefecture, western Honshū. Bordering the Sea of Japan and Lake Shinji to the east, this plain was formed by the deltas of the Hiikawa and Kandagawa filling up the graben valleys of the Chūgoku Mountains in the south and the Shimane Peninsula in the north. Peculiar to the area are the stands of native pine trees *(tsuiji matsu)* that surround farmhouses to protect them from the strong westerly winds in winter. The major city is IZUMO. Area: approximately 130 sq km (50 sq mi).

Izumo Province

(Izumo no Kuni; also known as Unshū). One of the eight provinces *(kuni)* of the San'indō region along the Sea of Japan in southern Honshū before the establishment of the prefectural system in 1871; it is now the eastern half of SHIMANE PREFECTURE. It is thought that Izumo, associated with many myths and legends recorded in the oldest Japanese histories, *Kojiki* (712) and *Nihon shoki* (720), was once a religious and political center rivaling the YAMATO COURT of the Nara region, which eventually gained hegemony. In the Kamakura period (1185–1333) the province was controlled by the Sasaki family and in the Muromachi period (1333–1568) by the YAMANA, KYŌGOKU, and AMAKO families. In the late 16th century Izumo was seized by Mōri Terumoto (1553–1625), who destroyed the Amako. Early in the Edo period (1600–1868) the Horio family built a castle in MATSUE, but in 1634 it passed to the Kyōgoku, who in turn were supplanted by the Matsudaira family (see TOKUGAWA FAMILY) in 1638. From that time until the Meiji Restoration (1868) the Matsudaira served there as *daimyō,* ruling over the three domains of Matsue, Hirose, and Mōri, into which the province was divided in 1684.

Izumo Shrine

(Izumo Taisha). One of the most important Shintō shrines; located in the town of Taisha (Taishamachi), Shimane Prefecture. Also known as Izumo no Ōyashiro. The chief god of the shrine is ŌKUNI-NUSHI NO MIKOTO, although it is also dedicated to other gods such as Ame no Minakanushi no Kami and Takamimusubi no Kami. The mythic origin of the shrine as described in the 8th-century chronicles KOJIKI and NIHON SHOKI is as follows: Ōkuninushi no Mikoto had first started developing the world of mortal man, but when NINIGI NO MIKOTO, the grandson of the sun goddess AMATERASU ŌMIKAMI, descended to earth from the heavens, Ōkuninushi no Mikoto turned over this land to him. This so pleased Amaterasu Ōmikami that she had a large shrine erected in honor of Ōkuninushi no Mikoto at the present location of the Izumo Shrine and put it under the care of Amenohohi no Mikoto. In actual fact, however, the Izumo Shrine is believed to have developed out of a shrine dedicated to local deities. In ancient times people said to be the descendants of Amenohohi no Mikoto served as the KUNI NO MIYATSUKO or local chieftains of Izumo. They were in charge of Shintō rituals and political affairs of the province of Izumo, but after the TAIKA REFORM of 645, they carried out only the religious rites. In the middle of the 14th century, the Senge and Kitajima families which claimed direct descent, alternated as *gūji,* or chief priest. Since the beginning of the Meiji period (1868–1912), the Senge family has served in this post. In 1882 Senge Takatomi established the Ōyashirokyō (Grand Shrine sect), based on devotion to the Izumo Shrine. This eventually became the Izumo Ōyashirokyō in 1951; it now has branches throughout Japan and approximately 10,000 believers. The yearly number of visitors to the Izumo Shrine is said to number approximately 3 million.

The shrine is built in the so-called *taisha-zukuri* style, considered the oldest of shrine architectural styles in Japan. The present main building *(honden)* was built in 1744, the 25th building since the original structure. Now approximately 24 meters (79 ft) high, it was reportedly once 96 meters (315 ft) high. The structure of the main shrine is built around 9 pillars, including the large central pillar known as the Shin no Mihashira, made of nine smaller pillars put together. The entrance is to the right of the building, with a 15-step stairway. The main building exemplifies the residential architecture of ancient times.

The main festival at Izumo Shrine occurs on 14 May. Another festival, the Kamiari Matsuri (the "gods being present" festival), is held on 11–17 October by the old lunar calendar. It is said that at this time the gods gather from all over Japan and confer with each other about their respective realms. For this reason the ancient name for October (in other parts of Japan) was Kannazuki, or the "Month without Gods." During this period small box-shaped houses are lined up in the shrine precincts to house the gods. The god of Izumo has traditionally been regarded as the god of marriage, good fortune, and agriculture. In folk religion the god has been identified with the Buddhist deity Daikokuten (Mahākāla), one of the seven gods of fortune.

TODA Yoshio

Izu Nagaoka

Town in eastern Shizuoka Prefecture, central Honshū, on Izu Peninsula. Noted for its hot springs since the 12th century, Izu Nagaoka commands a fine view of Mt. Fuji (FUJISAN). Its climate is suited to mandarin oranges and strawberry cultivation. An azalea festival is held in May and an iris festival from late June to early July. Pop: 13,730.

Izu Peninsula

(Izu Hantō). Located in Shizuoka Prefecture, central Honshū, extending southwest into the Pacific Ocean between Suruga Bay and the Sagami Sea. It is mountainous and has a long, indented coastline. A major portion of the Amagi mountains dominates the peninsula. It has a warm, subtropical climate and many beautiful beaches; the peninsula also contains the hot spring spas of Atami, Itō, Shimoda, and Shuzenji, which attract numerous visitors. Earthquakes have occurred here frequently in recent years. Much of the coastline is part of Fuji–Hakone–Izu National Park.

Izura

Coastal area in the city of Kita Ibaraki, northeastern Ibaraki Prefecture, central Honshū. Located on the Pacific Ocean, the coast is noted for its picturesque scenery including white beaches and craggy cliffs. OKAKURA KAKUZŌ transferred the Japan Art Institute (now the JAPAN FINE ARTS ACADEMY) here in 1906, and the building is currently used as the Izura Art Research Institute attached to Ibaraki University.